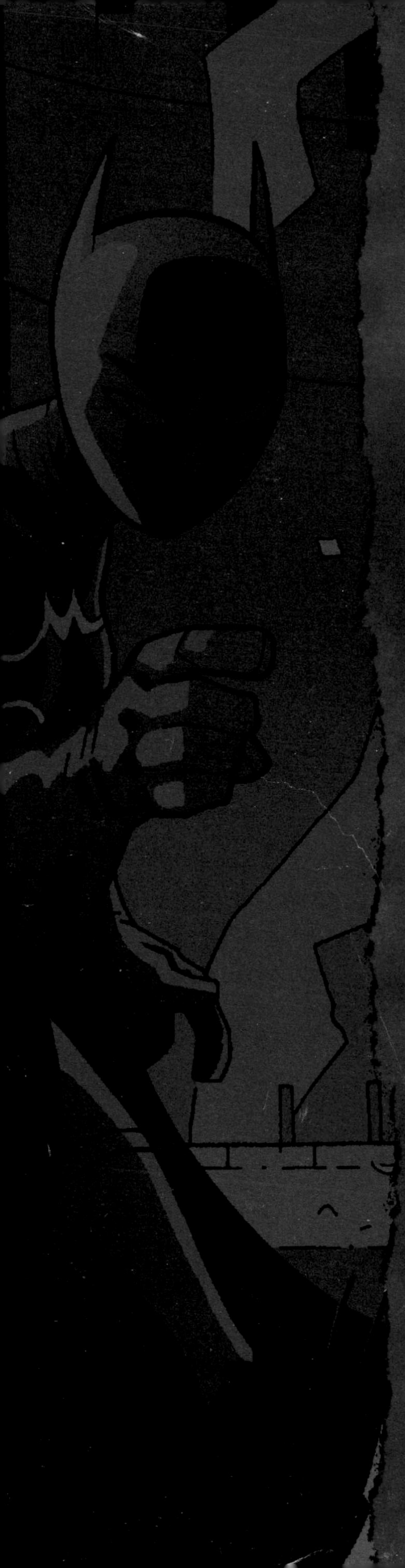

BATMAN
WAR GAMES
BOOK TWO

TABLE C

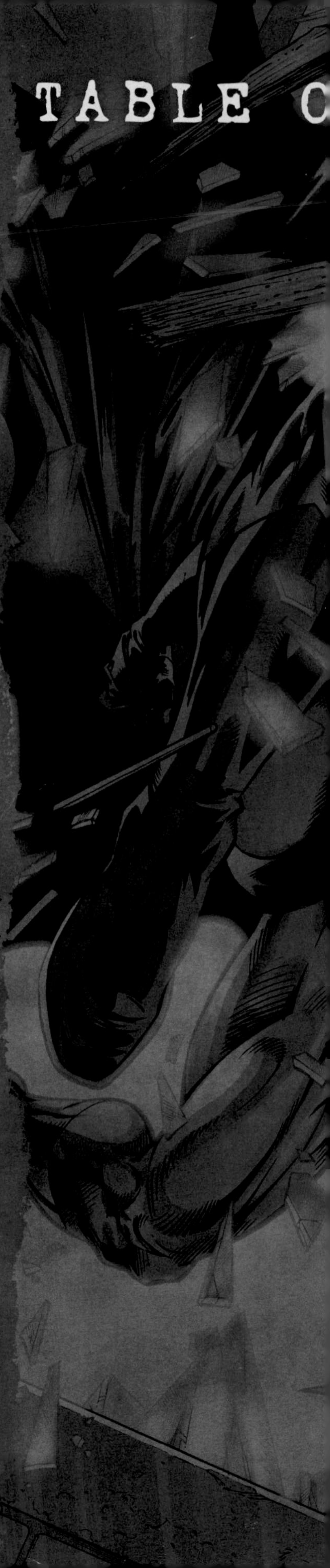

ONTENTS

BATMAN created by BOB KANE with BILL FINGER
Collection Cover by JAE LEE & JUNE CHUNG

BOB SCHRECK MATT IDELSON IVAN COHEN Editors - Original Series
MICHAEL WRIGHT NACHIE CASTRO Associate Editors - Original Series
JEB WOODARD Group Editor - Collected Editions
PAUL SANTOS Editor - Collected Edition
STEVE COOK Design Director - Books
SARABETH KETT Publication Design

BOB HARRAS Senior VP - Editor-in-Chief, DC Comics

DIANE NELSON President
DAN DIDIO and JIM LEE Co-Publishers
GEOFF JOHNS Chief Creative Officer
AMIT DESAI Senior VP - Marketing & Global Franchise Management
NAIRI GARDINER Senior VP - Finance
SAM ADES VP - Digital Marketing
BOBBIE CHASE VP - Talent Development
MARK CHIARELLO Senior VP - Art, Design & Collected Editions
JOHN CUNNINGHAM VP - Content Strategy
ANNE DEPIES VP - Strategy Planning & Reporting
DON FALLETTI VP - Manufacturing Operations
LAWRENCE GANEM VP - Editorial Administration & Talent Relations
ALISON GILL Senior VP - Manufacturing & Operations
HANK KANALZ Senior VP - Editorial Strategy & Administration
JAY KOGAN VP - Legal Affairs
DEREK MADDALENA Senior VP - Sales & Business Development
JACK MAHAN VP - Business Affairs
DAN MIRON VP - Sales Planning & Trade Development
NICK NAPOLITANO VP - Manufacturing Administration
CAROL ROEDER VP - Marketing
EDDIE SCANNELL VP - Mass Account & Digital Sales
COURTNEY SIMMONS Senior VP - Publicity & Communications
JIM (SKI) SOKOLOWSKI VP - Comic Book Specialty & Newsstand Sales
SANDY YI Senior VP - Global Franchise Management

BATMAN: WAR GAMES BOOK TWO

DC Comics, 2900 West Alameda Avenue, Burbank, CA 91505
Printed by RR Donnelley, Salem, VA, USA. 4/15/16. First Printing.
ISBN: 978-1-4012-6070-5

Library of Congress Cataloging-in-Publication Data is Available.

PEFC Certified
Printed on paper from sustainably managed forests and controlled sources
www.pefc.org
PEFC/29-31-75

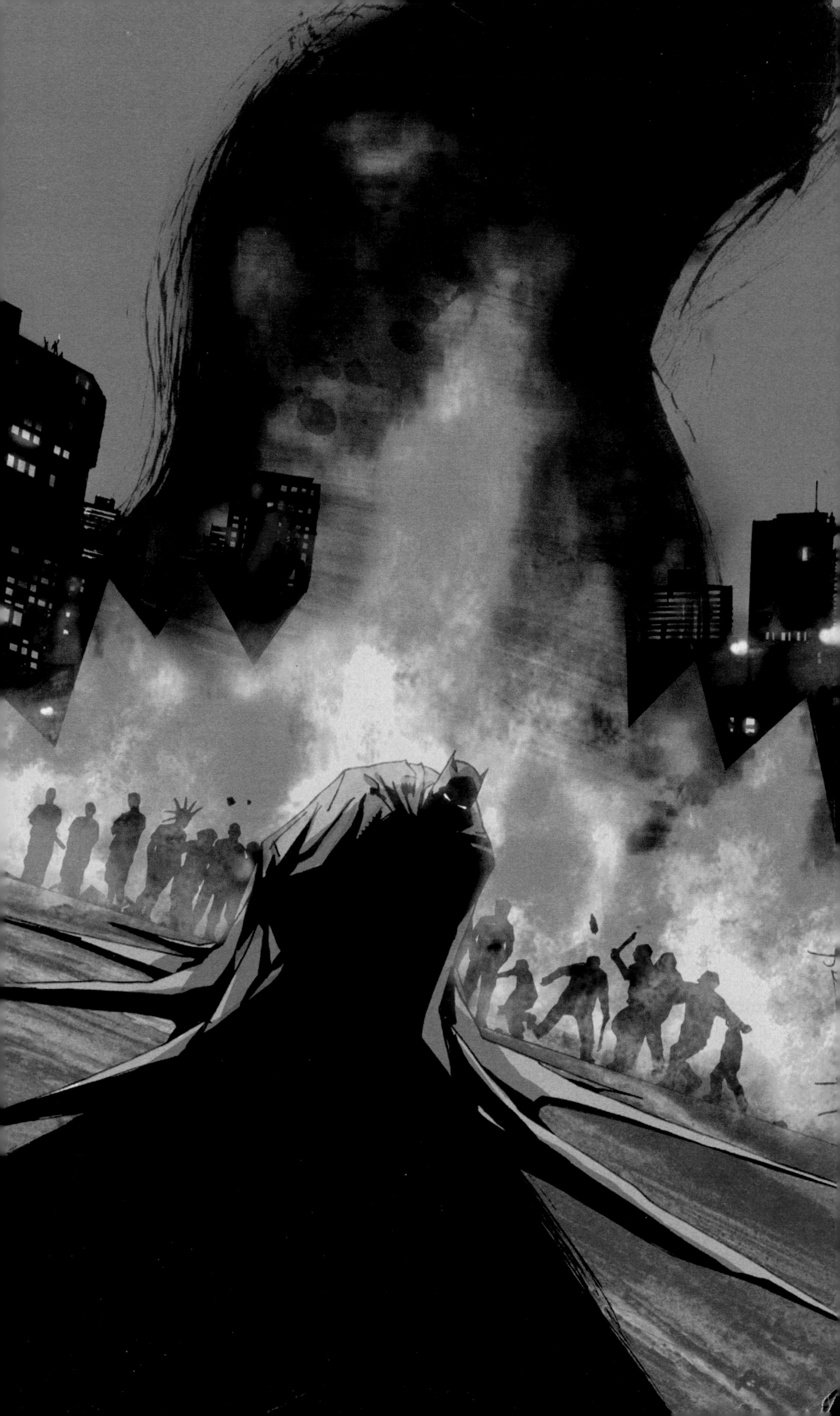

COVER ART BY
JOCK

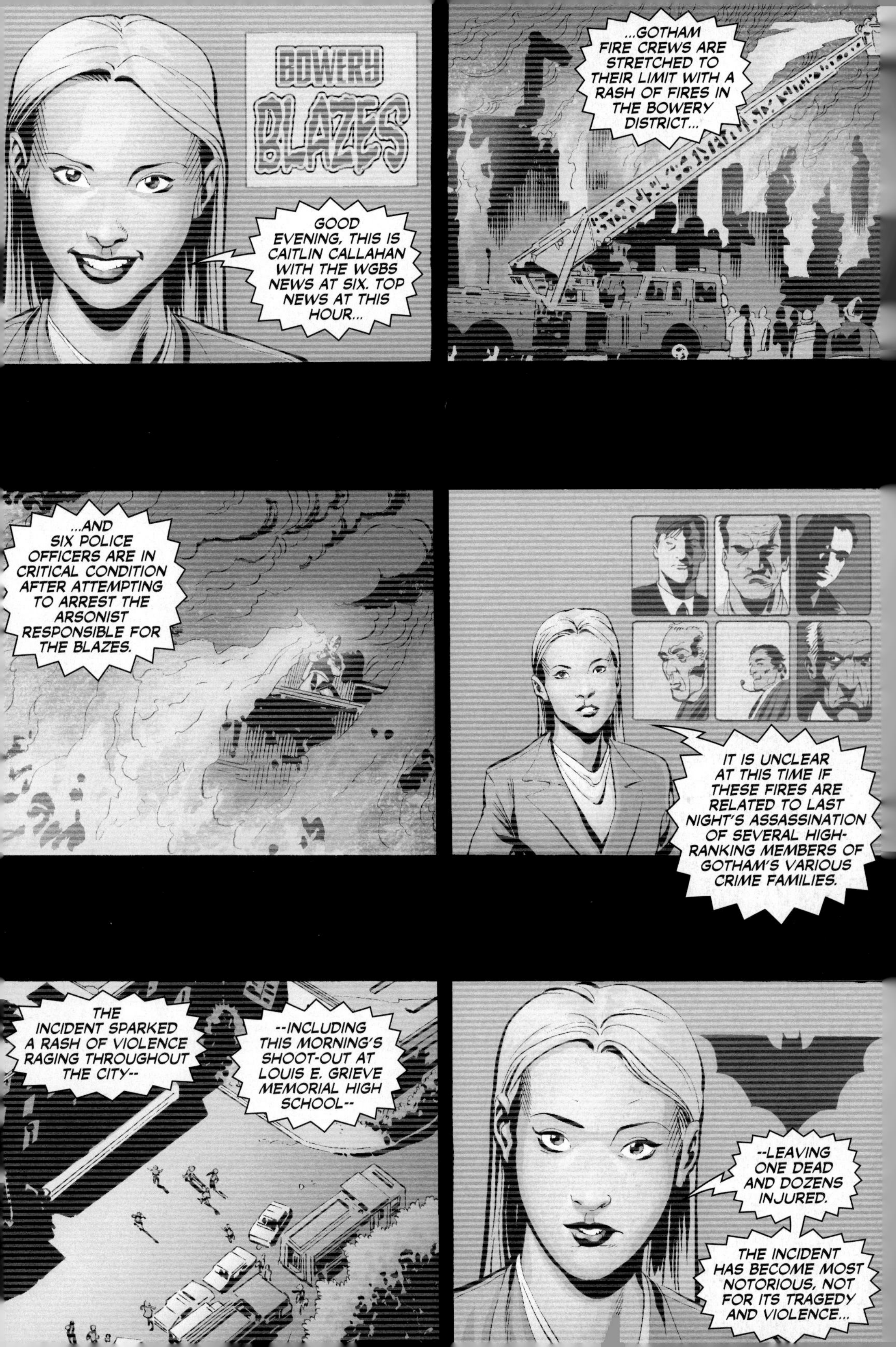
BOWERY
BLAZES
GOOD EVENING, THIS IS CAITLIN CALLAHAN WITH THE WGBS NEWS AT SIX. TOP NEWS AT THIS HOUR...
...GOTHAM FIRE CREWS ARE STRETCHED TO THEIR LIMIT WITH A RASH OF FIRES IN THE BOWERY DISTRICT...
...AND SIX POLICE OFFICERS ARE IN CRITICAL CONDITION AFTER ATTEMPTING TO ARREST THE ARSONIST RESPONSIBLE FOR THE BLAZES.
IT IS UNCLEAR AT THIS TIME IF THESE FIRES ARE RELATED TO LAST NIGHT'S ASSASSINATION OF SEVERAL HIGH-RANKING MEMBERS OF GOTHAM'S VARIOUS CRIME FAMILIES.
THE INCIDENT SPARKED A RASH OF VIOLENCE RAGING THROUGHOUT THE CITY--
--INCLUDING THIS MORNING'S SHOOT-OUT AT LOUIS E. GRIEVE MEMORIAL HIGH SCHOOL--
--LEAVING ONE DEAD AND DOZENS INJURED.
THE INCIDENT HAS BECOME MOST NOTORIOUS, NOT FOR ITS TRAGEDY AND VIOLENCE...

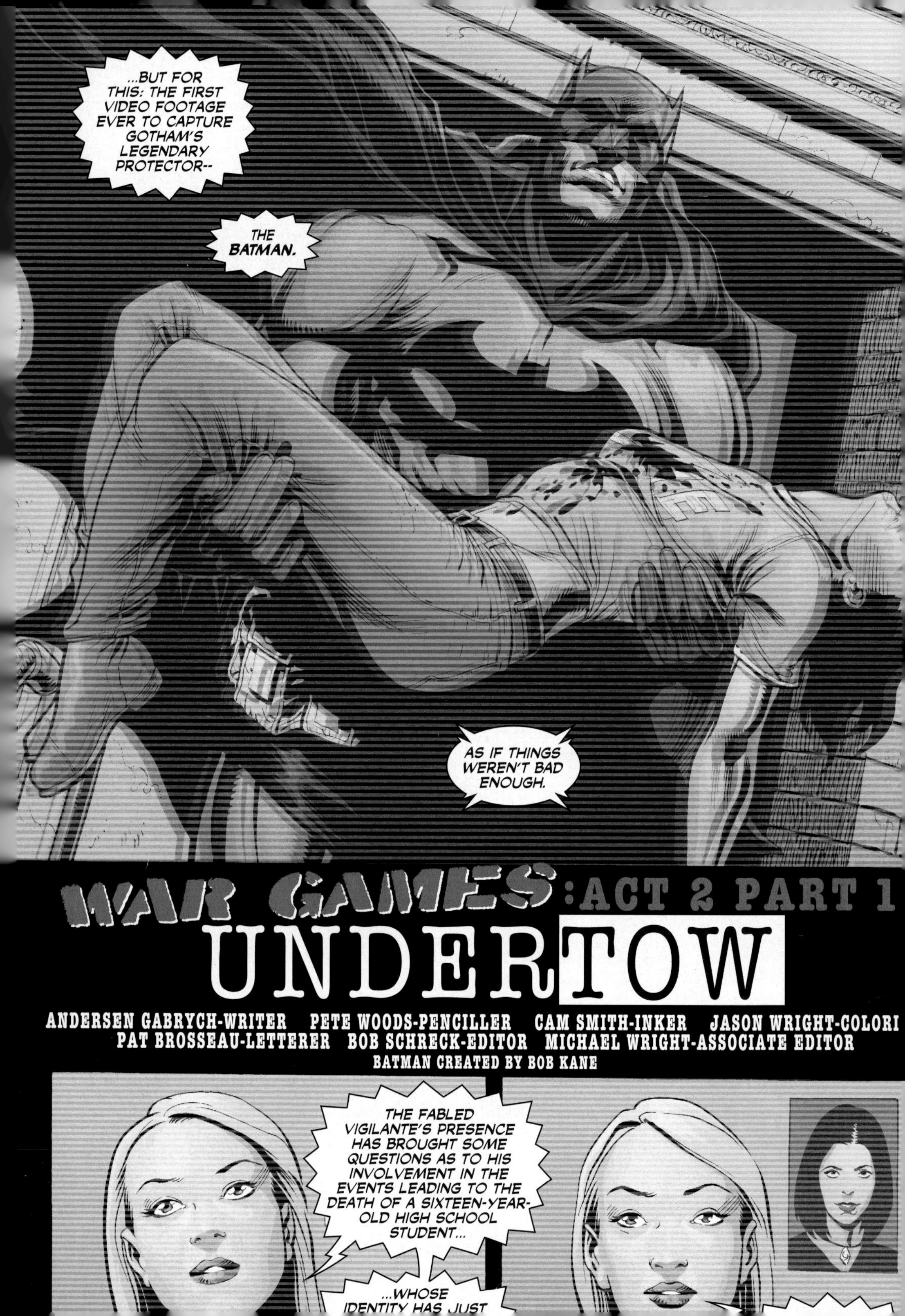
...BUT FOR THIS: THE FIRST VIDEO FOOTAGE EVER TO CAPTURE GOTHAM'S LEGENDARY PROTECTOR--
THE BATMAN.
AS IF THINGS WEREN'T BAD ENOUGH.
WAR GAMES: ACT 2 PART 1
UNDERTOW
ANDERSEN GABRYCH-WRITER PETE WOODS-PENCILLER CAM SMITH-INKER JASON WRIGHT-COLORI
PAT BROSSEAU-LETTERER BOB SCHRECK-EDITOR MICHAEL WRIGHT-ASSOCIATE EDITOR
BATMAN CREATED BY BOB KANE
THE FABLED VIGILANTE'S PRESENCE HAS BROUGHT SOME QUESTIONS AS TO HIS INVOLVEMENT IN THE EVENTS LEADING TO THE DEATH OF A SIXTEEN-YEAR-OLD HIGH SCHOOL STUDENT...
...WHOSE IDENTITY HAS JUST

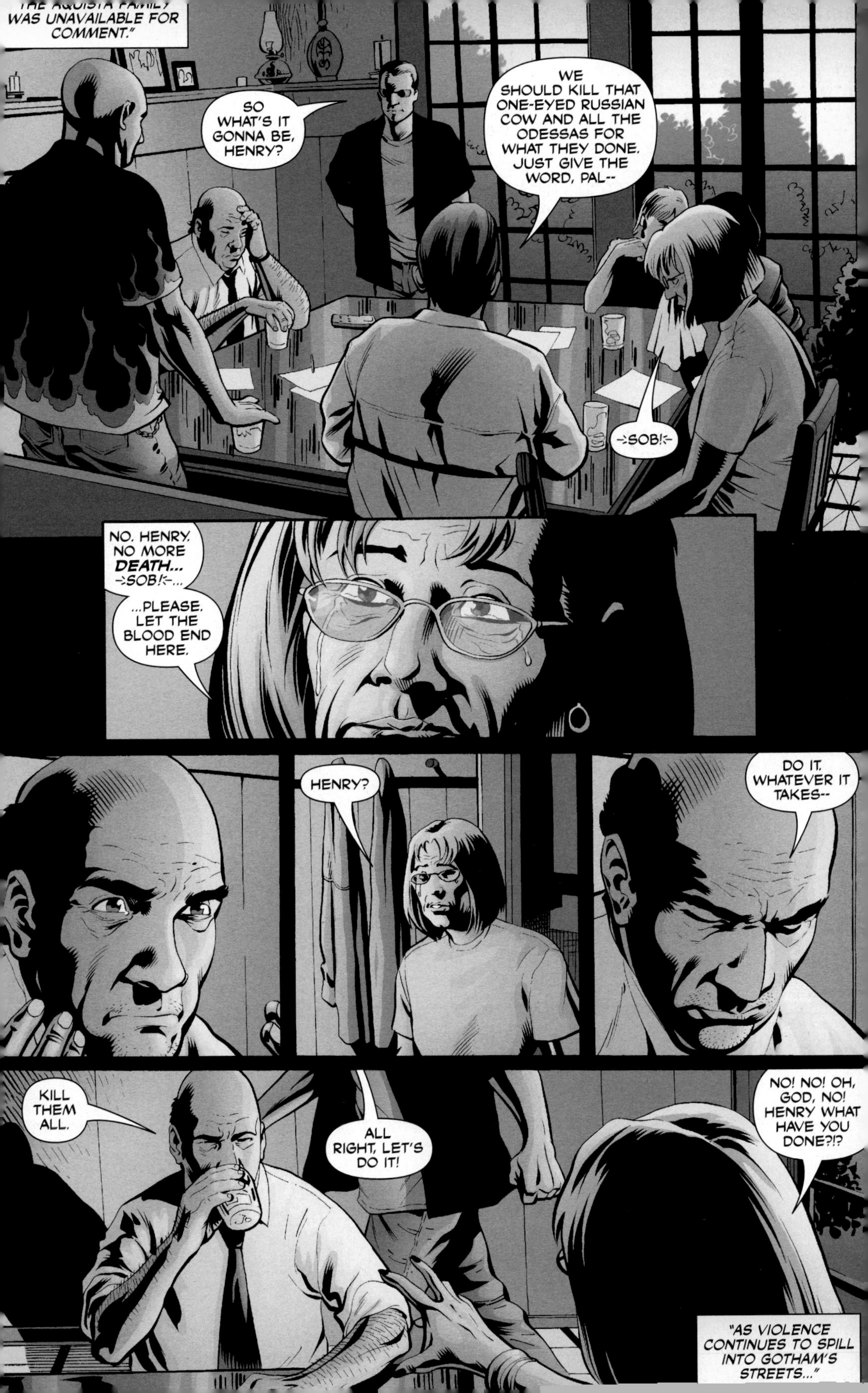

THE AQUISTA FAMILY WAS UNAVAILABLE FOR COMMENT."
SO WHAT'S IT GONNA BE, HENRY?
WE SHOULD KILL THAT ONE-EYED RUSSIAN COW AND ALL THE ODESSAS FOR WHAT THEY DONE. JUST GIVE THE WORD, PAL--
-SOB!-
NO. HENRY. NO MORE DEATH... -SOB!-...
...PLEASE. LET THE BLOOD END HERE.
HENRY?
DO IT. WHATEVER IT TAKES--
KILL THEM ALL.
ALL RIGHT, LET'S DO IT!
NO! NO! OH, GOD, NO! HENRY WHAT HAVE YOU DONE?!?
"AS VIOLENCE CONTINUES TO SPILL INTO GOTHAM'S STREETS..."

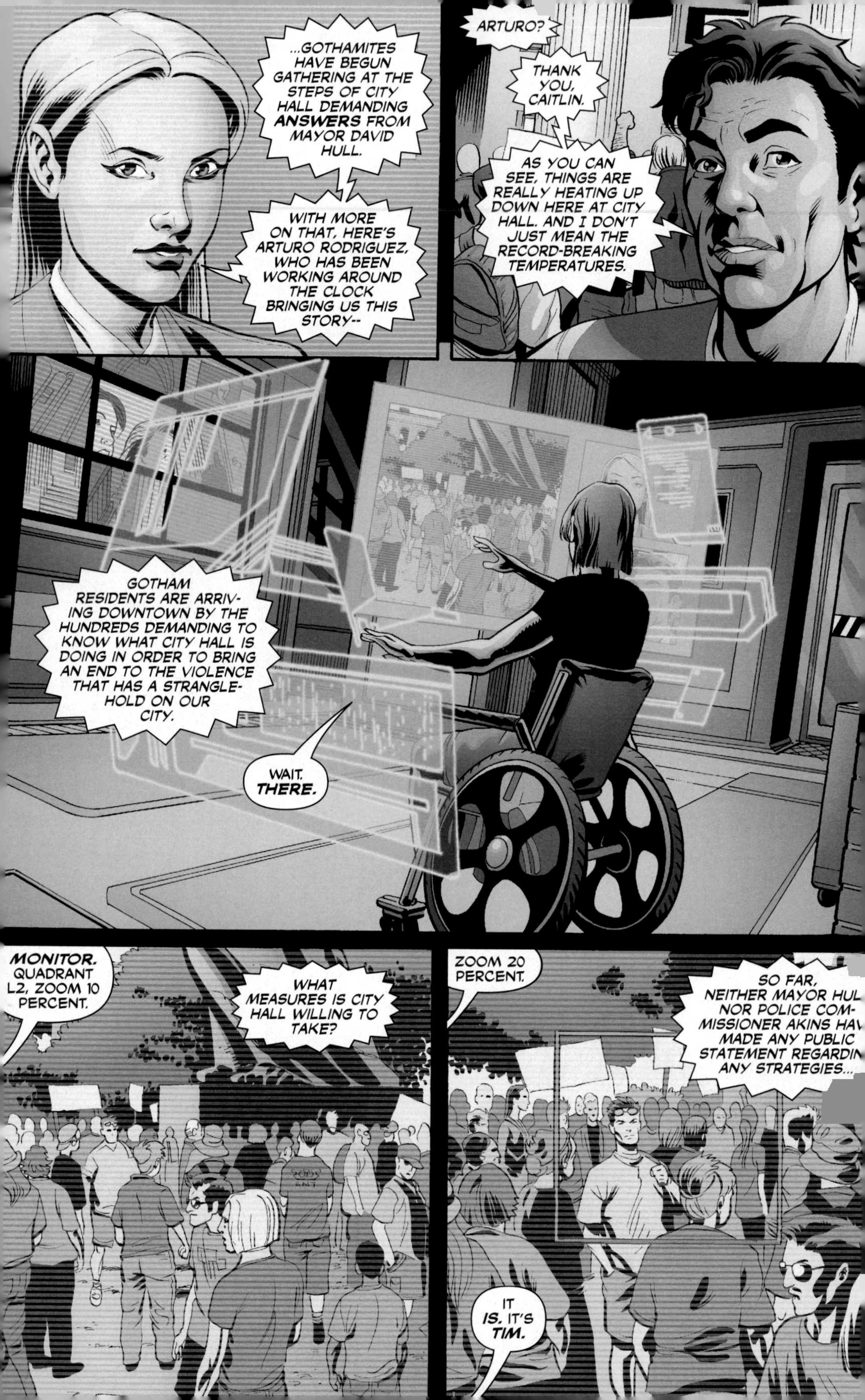
...GOTHAMITES HAVE BEGUN GATHERING AT THE STEPS OF CITY HALL DEMANDING **ANSWERS** FROM MAYOR DAVID HULL.
WITH MORE ON THAT, HERE'S ARTURO RODRIGUEZ, WHO HAS BEEN WORKING AROUND THE CLOCK BRINGING US THIS STORY--
ARTURO?
THANK YOU, CAITLIN.
AS YOU CAN SEE, THINGS ARE REALLY HEATING UP DOWN HERE AT CITY HALL. AND I DON'T JUST MEAN THE RECORD-BREAKING TEMPERATURES.
GOTHAM RESIDENTS ARE ARRIVING DOWNTOWN BY THE HUNDREDS DEMANDING TO KNOW WHAT CITY HALL IS DOING IN ORDER TO BRING AN END TO THE VIOLENCE THAT HAS A STRANGLEHOLD ON OUR CITY.
WAIT. ***THERE.***
MONITOR. QUADRANT L2, ZOOM 10 PERCENT.
WHAT MEASURES IS CITY HALL WILLING TO TAKE?
ZOOM 20 PERCENT.
SO FAR, NEITHER MAYOR HUL NOR POLICE COMMISSIONER AKINS HAV MADE ANY PUBLIC STATEMENT REGARDIN ANY STRATEGIES...
IT ***IS.*** IT'S ***TIM.***

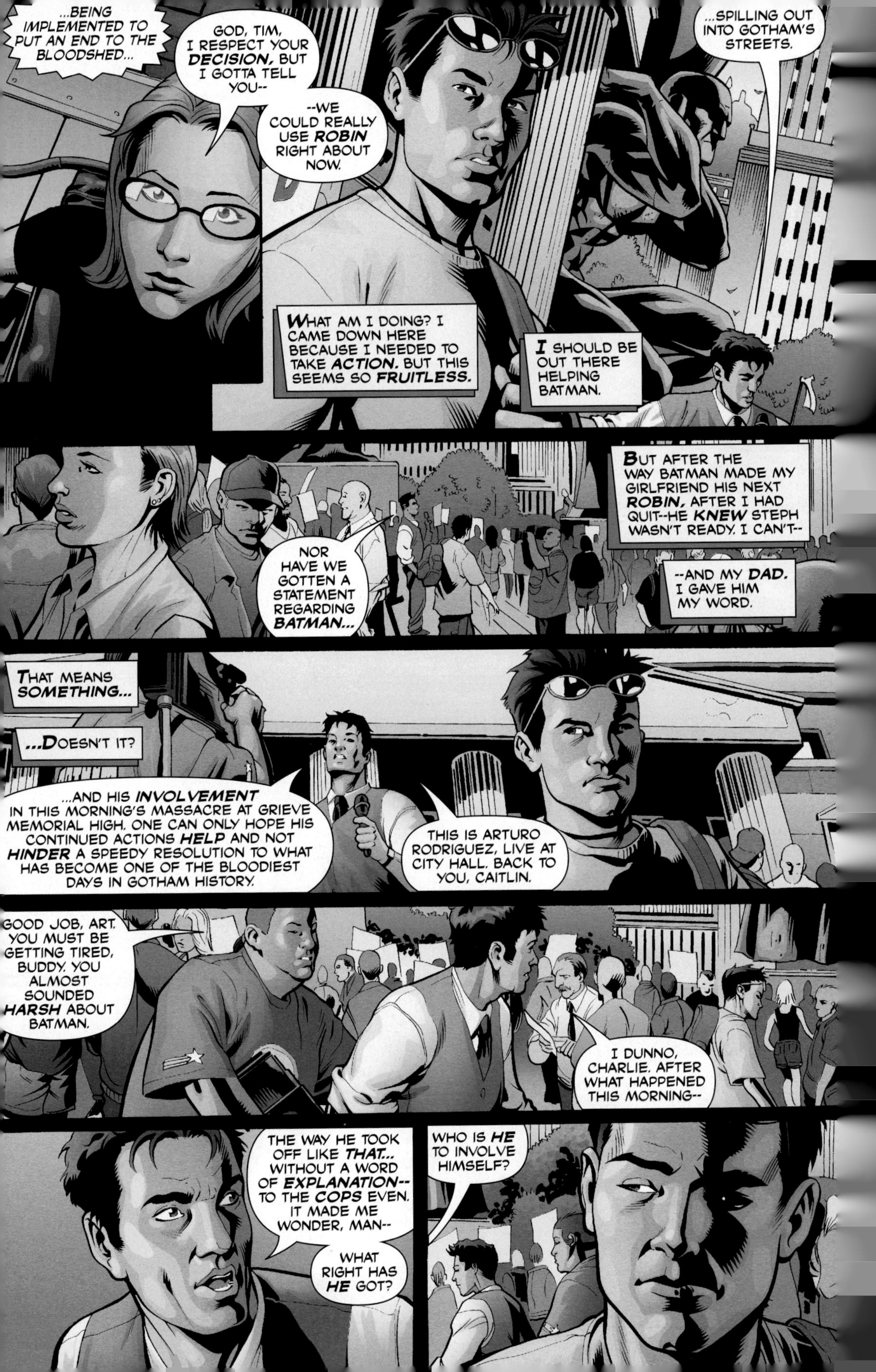
...BEING IMPLEMENTED TO PUT AN END TO THE BLOODSHED...
GOD, TIM, I RESPECT YOUR DECISION, BUT I GOTTA TELL YOU--
--WE COULD REALLY USE ROBIN RIGHT ABOUT NOW.
...SPILLING OUT INTO GOTHAM'S STREETS.
WHAT AM I DOING? I CAME DOWN HERE BECAUSE I NEEDED TO TAKE ACTION. BUT THIS SEEMS SO FRUITLESS.
I SHOULD BE OUT THERE HELPING BATMAN.
NOR HAVE WE GOTTEN A STATEMENT REGARDING BATMAN...
BUT AFTER THE WAY BATMAN MADE MY GIRLFRIEND HIS NEXT ROBIN, AFTER I HAD QUIT--HE KNEW STEPH WASN'T READY. I CAN'T--
--AND MY DAD. I GAVE HIM MY WORD.
THAT MEANS SOMETHING...
...DOESN'T IT?
...AND HIS INVOLVEMENT IN THIS MORNING'S MASSACRE AT GRIEVE MEMORIAL HIGH. ONE CAN ONLY HOPE HIS CONTINUED ACTIONS HELP AND NOT HINDER A SPEEDY RESOLUTION TO WHAT HAS BECOME ONE OF THE BLOODIEST DAYS IN GOTHAM HISTORY.
THIS IS ARTURO RODRIGUEZ, LIVE AT CITY HALL. BACK TO YOU, CAITLIN.
GOOD JOB, ART. YOU MUST BE GETTING TIRED, BUDDY. YOU ALMOST SOUNDED HARSH ABOUT BATMAN.
I DUNNO, CHARLIE. AFTER WHAT HAPPENED THIS MORNING--
THE WAY HE TOOK OFF LIKE THAT... WITHOUT A WORD OF EXPLANATION--TO THE COPS EVEN. IT MADE ME WONDER, MAN--
WHAT RIGHT HAS HE GOT?
WHO IS HE TO INVOLVE HIMSELF?

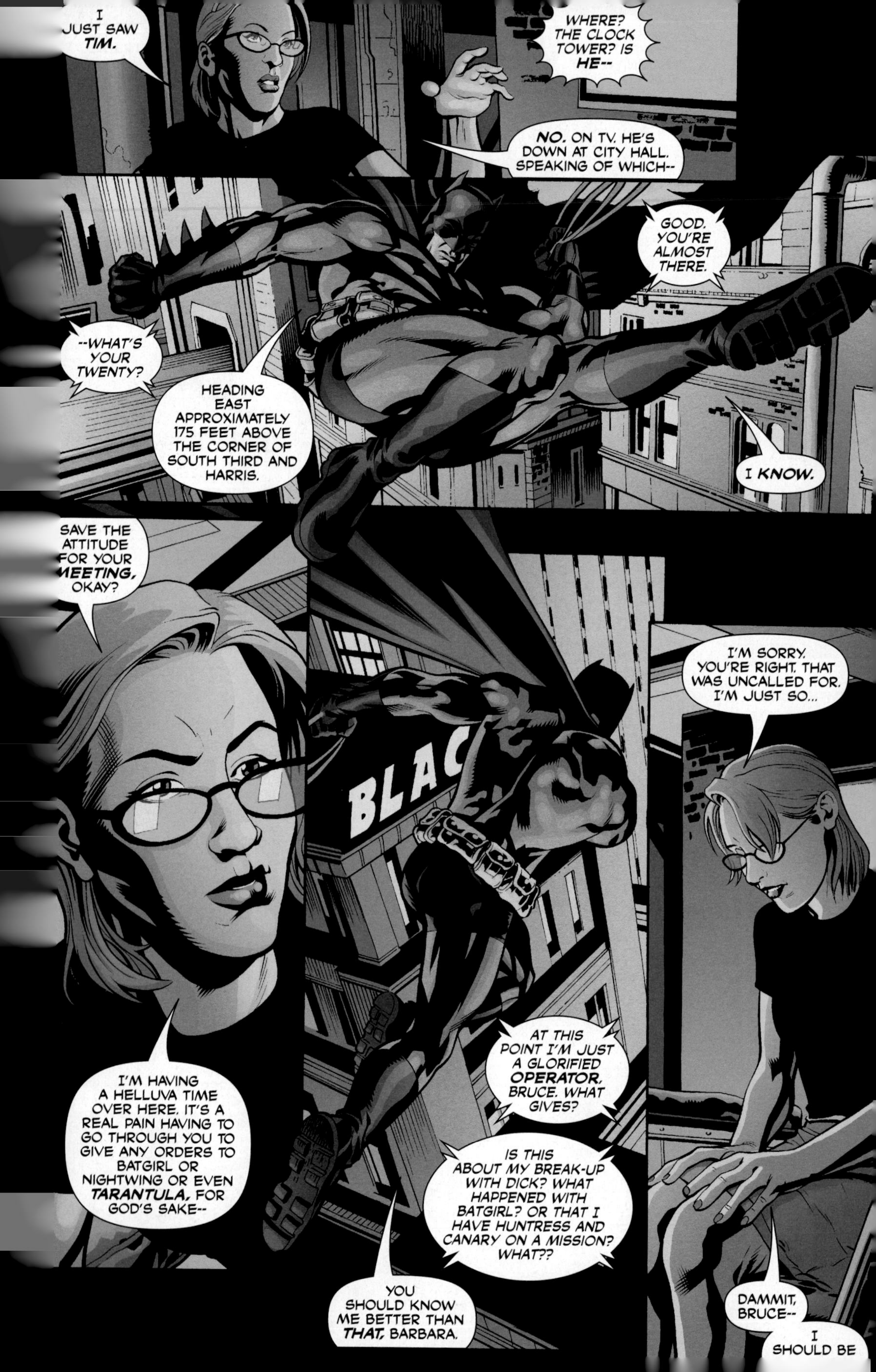
I JUST SAW TIM.
WHERE? THE CLOCK TOWER? IS HE--
NO. ON TV. HE'S DOWN AT CITY HALL. SPEAKING OF WHICH--
--WHAT'S YOUR TWENTY?
HEADING EAST APPROXIMATELY 175 FEET ABOVE THE CORNER OF SOUTH THIRD AND HARRIS.
GOOD. YOU'RE ALMOST THERE.
I KNOW.
SAVE THE ATTITUDE FOR YOUR MEETING, OKAY?
BLAC
I'M SORRY. YOU'RE RIGHT. THAT WAS UNCALLED FOR. I'M JUST SO...
I'M HAVING A HELLUVA TIME OVER HERE. IT'S A REAL PAIN HAVING TO GO THROUGH YOU TO GIVE ANY ORDERS TO BATGIRL OR NIGHTWING OR EVEN TARANTULA, FOR GOD'S SAKE--
AT THIS POINT I'M JUST A GLORIFIED OPERATOR, BRUCE. WHAT GIVES?
IS THIS ABOUT MY BREAK-UP WITH DICK? WHAT HAPPENED WITH BATGIRL? OR THAT I HAVE HUNTRESS AND CANARY ON A MISSION? WHAT??
YOU SHOULD KNOW ME BETTER THAN THAT, BARBARA.
DAMMIT, BRUCE--
I SHOULD BE

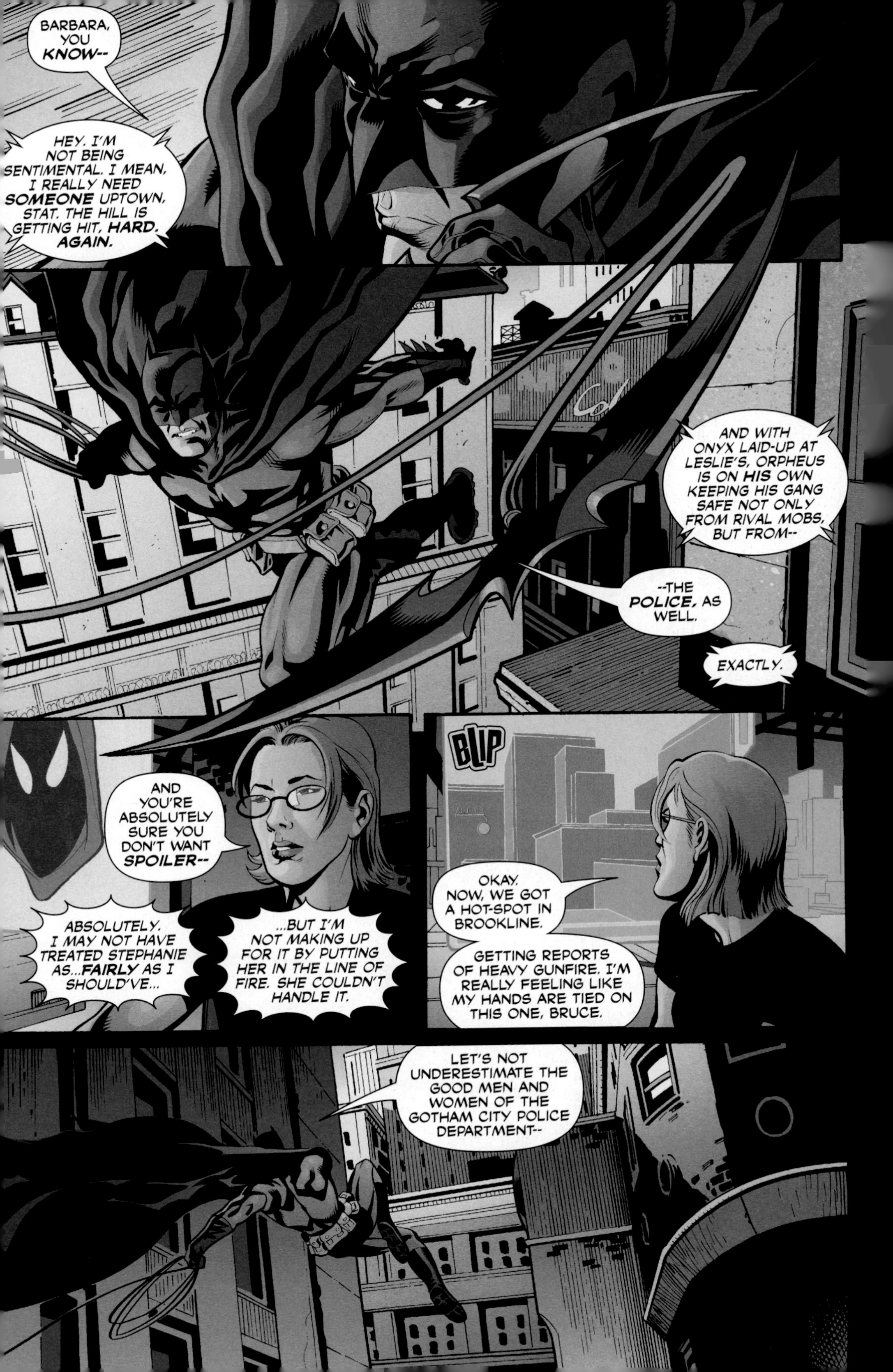
BARBARA, YOU KNOW--
HEY. I'M NOT BEING SENTIMENTAL. I MEAN, I REALLY NEED SOMEONE UPTOWN, STAT. THE HILL IS GETTING HIT, HARD. AGAIN.
AND WITH ONYX LAID-UP AT LESLIE'S, ORPHEUS IS ON HIS OWN KEEPING HIS GANG SAFE NOT ONLY FROM RIVAL MOBS, BUT FROM--
--THE POLICE, AS WELL.
EXACTLY.
AND YOU'RE ABSOLUTELY SURE YOU DON'T WANT SPOILER--
ABSOLUTELY. I MAY NOT HAVE TREATED STEPHANIE AS...FAIRLY AS I SHOULD'VE...
...BUT I'M NOT MAKING UP FOR IT BY PUTTING HER IN THE LINE OF FIRE. SHE COULDN'T HANDLE IT.
BLIP
OKAY. NOW, WE GOT A HOT-SPOT IN BROOKLINE.
GETTING REPORTS OF HEAVY GUNFIRE. I'M REALLY FEELING LIKE MY HANDS ARE TIED ON THIS ONE, BRUCE.
LET'S NOT UNDERESTIMATE THE GOOD MEN AND WOMEN OF THE GOTHAM CITY POLICE DEPARTMENT--

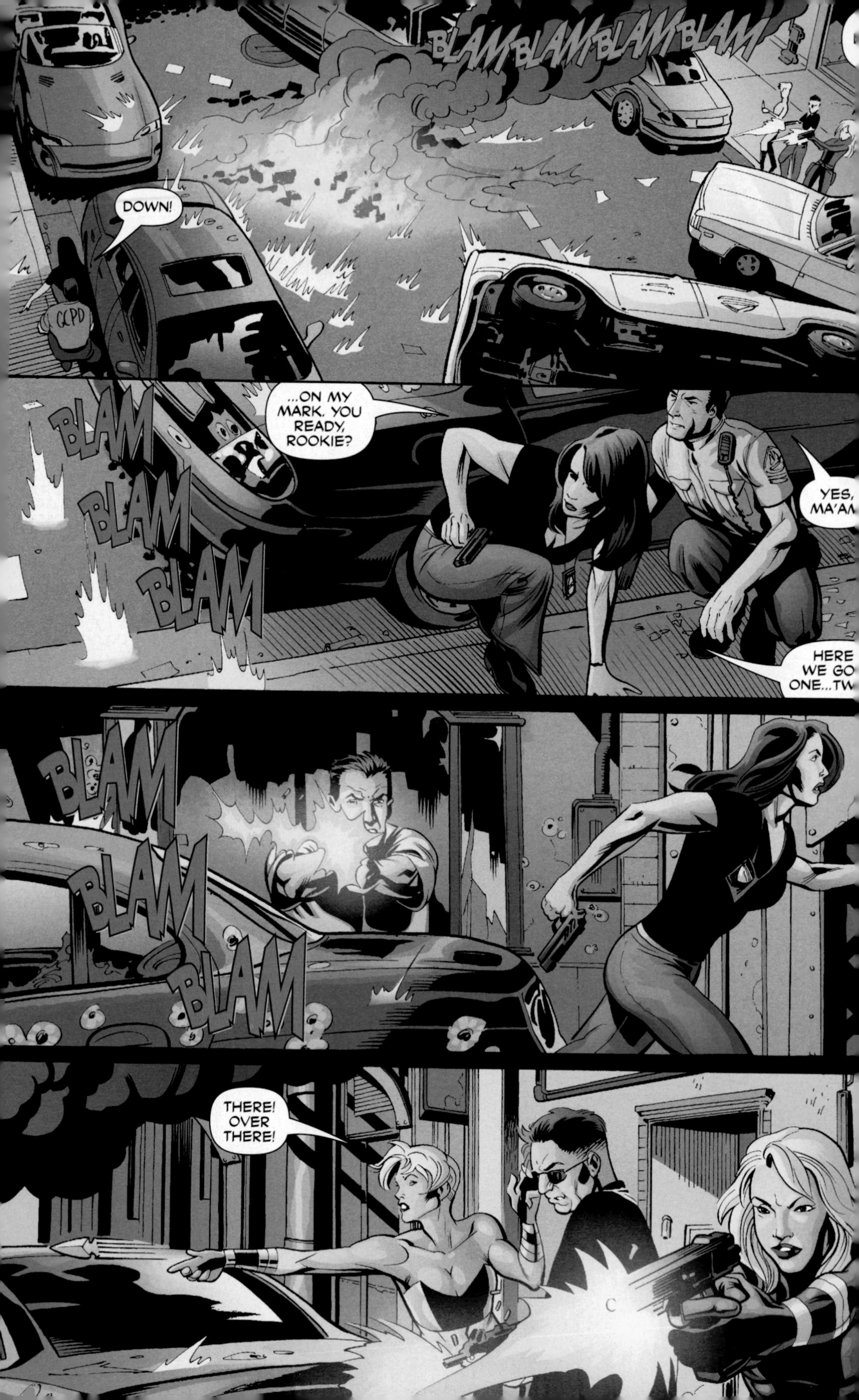

BLAM BLAM BLAM BLAM
DOWN!
GCPD
...ON MY MARK. YOU READY, ROOKIE?
YES, MA'AM
BLAM
BLAM
BLAM
HERE WE GO ONE...TW
BLAM
BLAM
BLAM
THERE! OVER THERE!

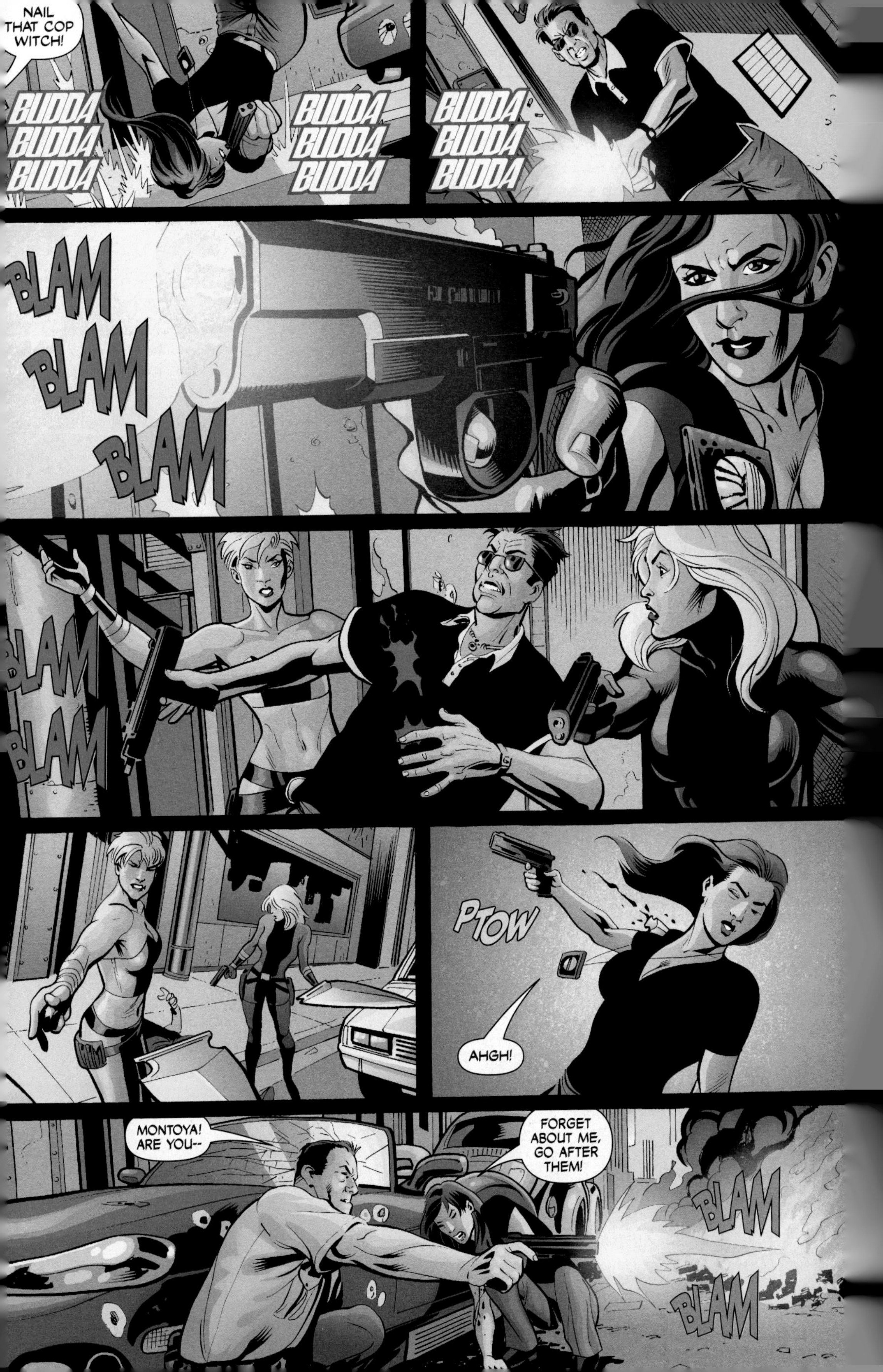
NAIL THAT COP WITCH!
BUDDA BUDDA BUDDA
BUDDA BUDDA BUDDA
BUDDA BUDDA BUDDA
BLAM BLAM BLAM
BLAM BLAM
PTOW
AHGH!
MONTOYA! ARE YOU--
FORGET ABOUT ME, GO AFTER THEM!
BLAM
BLAM

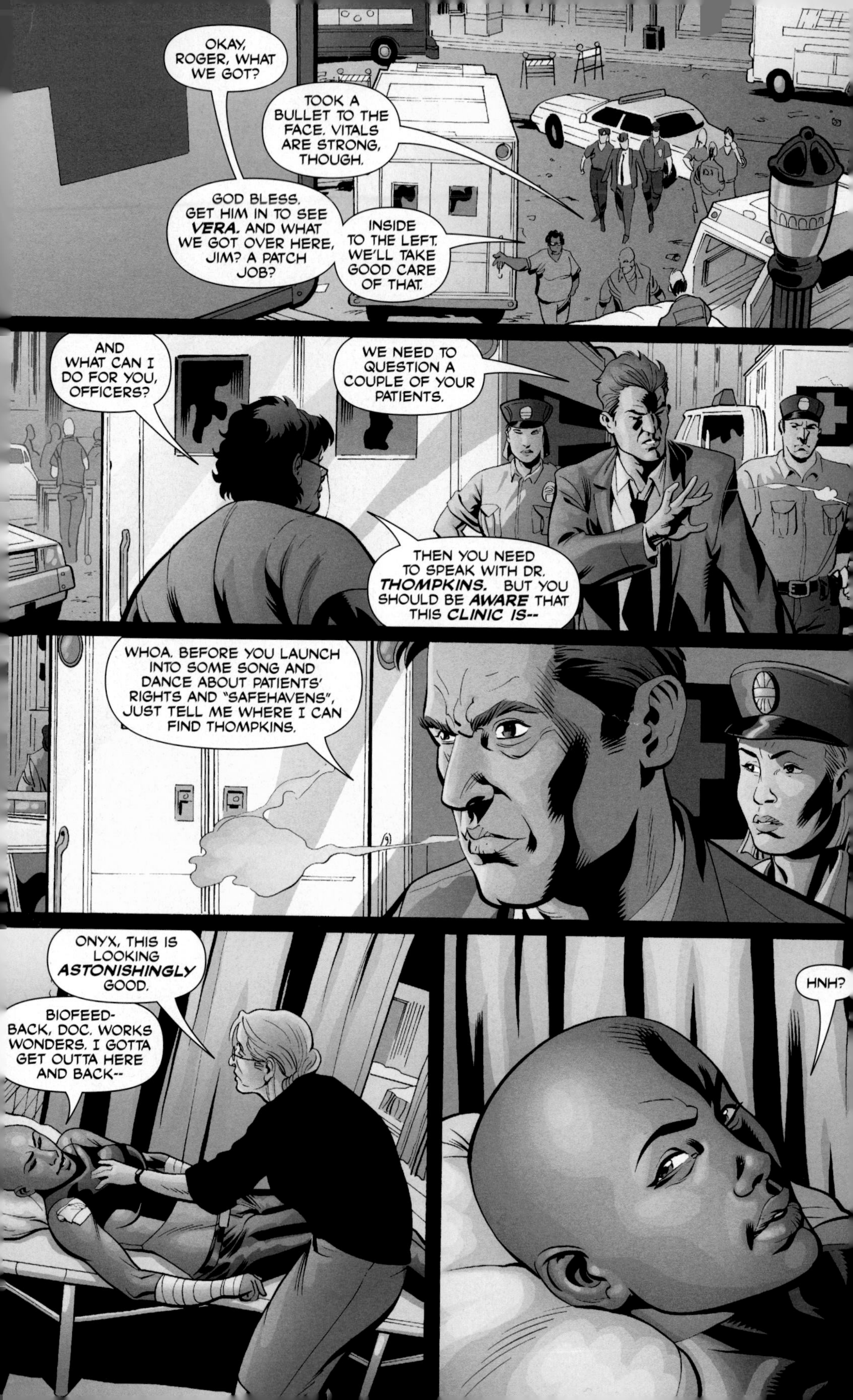
OKAY, ROGER, WHAT WE GOT?
TOOK A BULLET TO THE FACE. VITALS ARE STRONG, THOUGH.
GOD BLESS. GET HIM IN TO SEE VERA. AND WHAT WE GOT OVER HERE, JIM? A PATCH JOB?
INSIDE TO THE LEFT. WE'LL TAKE GOOD CARE OF THAT.
AND WHAT CAN I DO FOR YOU, OFFICERS?
WE NEED TO QUESTION A COUPLE OF YOUR PATIENTS.
THEN YOU NEED TO SPEAK WITH DR. THOMPKINS. BUT YOU SHOULD BE AWARE THAT THIS CLINIC IS--
WHOA. BEFORE YOU LAUNCH INTO SOME SONG AND DANCE ABOUT PATIENTS' RIGHTS AND "SAFEHAVENS", JUST TELL ME WHERE I CAN FIND THOMPKINS.
ONYX, THIS IS LOOKING ASTONISHINGLY GOOD.
BIOFEED-BACK, DOC. WORKS WONDERS. I GOTTA GET OUTTA HERE AND BACK--
HNH?

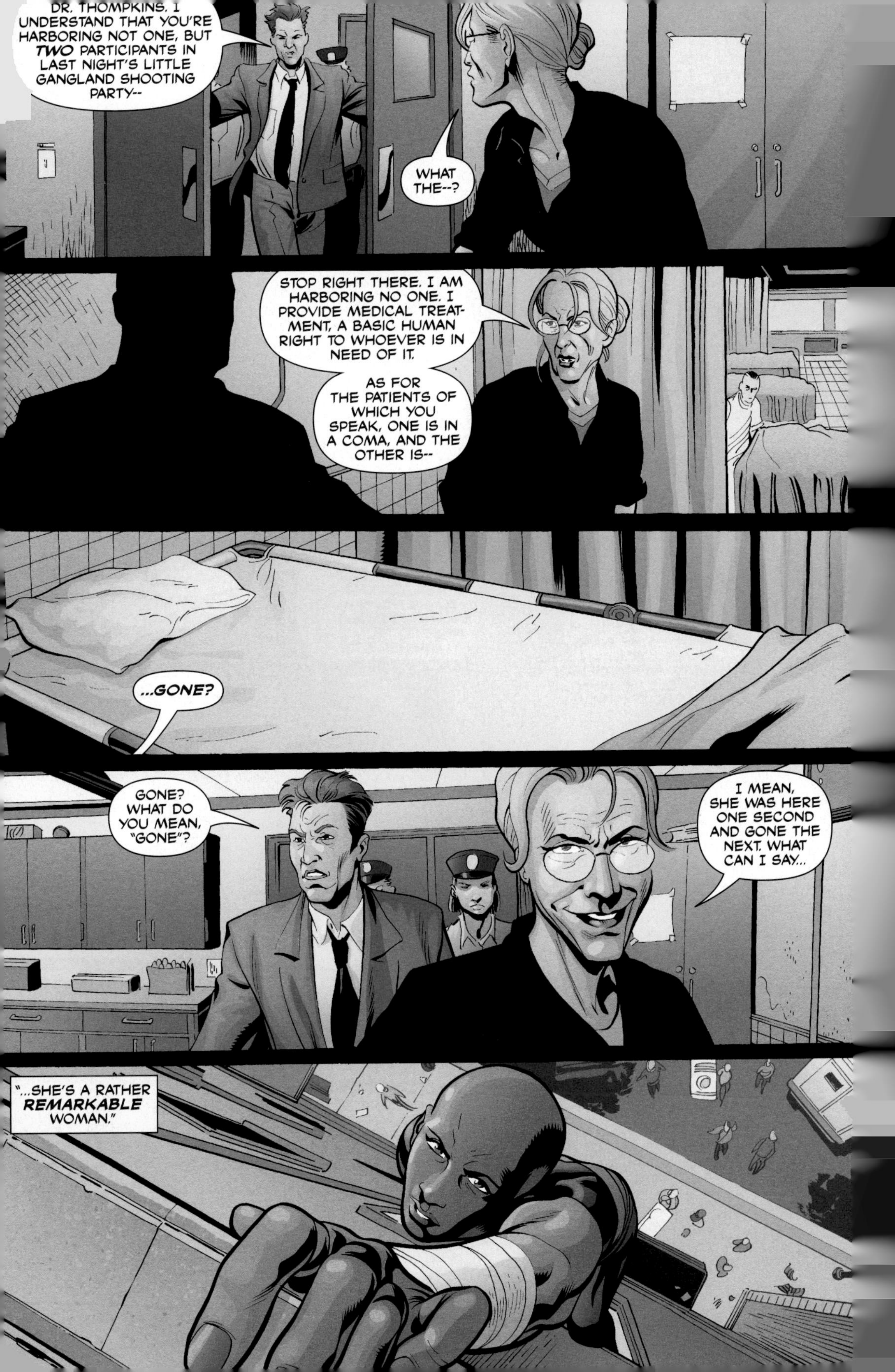
DR. THOMPKINS. I UNDERSTAND THAT YOU'RE HARBORING NOT ONE, BUT *TWO* PARTICIPANTS IN LAST NIGHT'S LITTLE GANGLAND SHOOTING PARTY--
WHAT THE--?
STOP RIGHT THERE. I AM HARBORING NO ONE. I PROVIDE MEDICAL TREATMENT, A BASIC HUMAN RIGHT TO WHOEVER IS IN NEED OF IT.
AS FOR THE PATIENTS OF WHICH YOU SPEAK, ONE IS IN A COMA, AND THE OTHER IS--
...GONE?
GONE? WHAT DO YOU MEAN, "GONE"?
I MEAN, SHE WAS HERE ONE SECOND AND GONE THE NEXT. WHAT CAN I SAY...
"...SHE'S A RATHER *REMARKABLE* WOMAN."

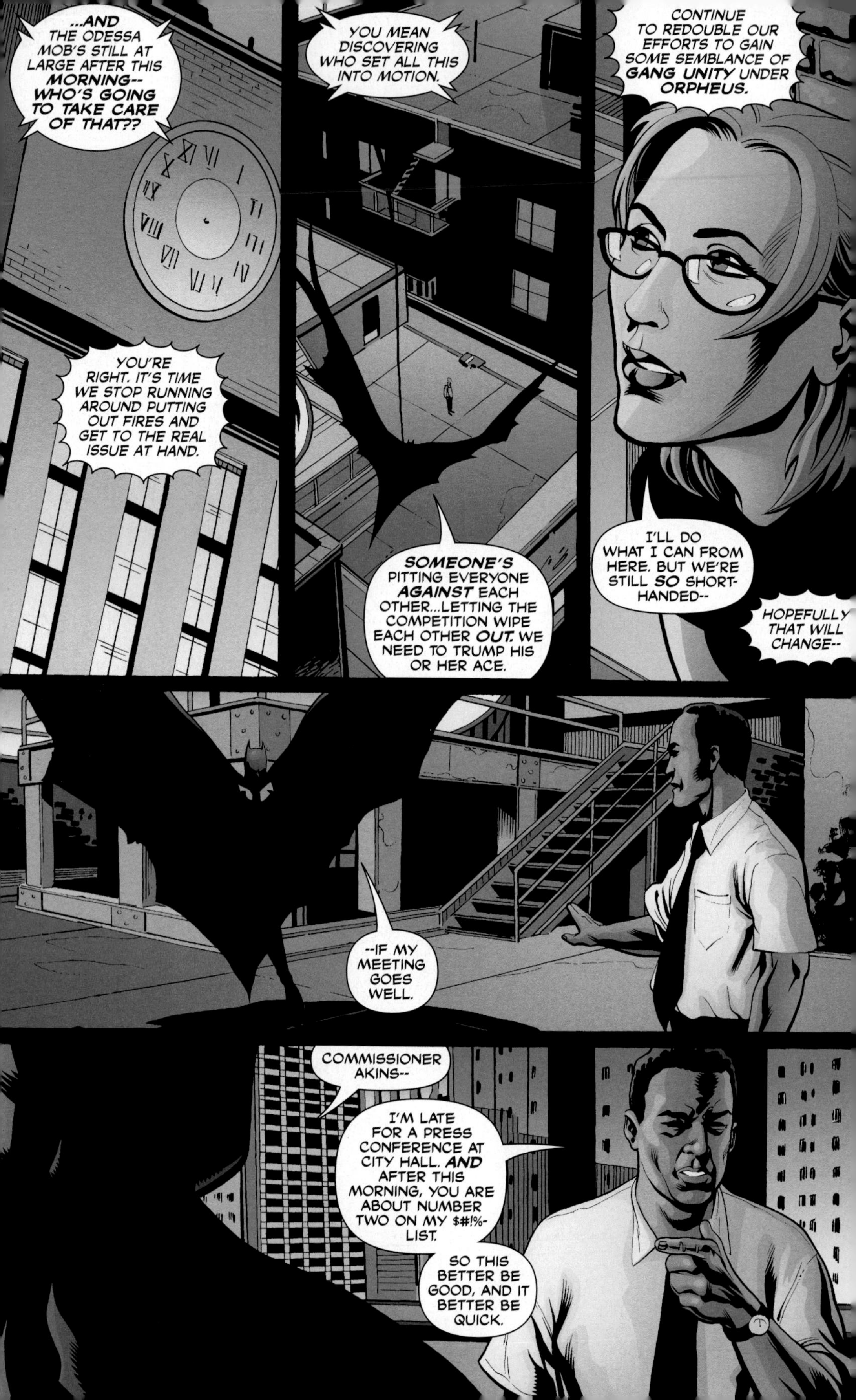

...AND THE ODESSA MOB'S STILL AT LARGE AFTER THIS MORNING-- WHO'S GOING TO TAKE CARE OF THAT??
YOU'RE RIGHT. IT'S TIME WE STOP RUNNING AROUND PUTTING OUT FIRES AND GET TO THE REAL ISSUE AT HAND.
YOU MEAN DISCOVERING WHO SET ALL THIS INTO MOTION.
SOMEONE'S PITTING EVERYONE AGAINST EACH OTHER...LETTING THE COMPETITION WIPE EACH OTHER OUT. WE NEED TO TRUMP HIS OR HER ACE.
CONTINUE TO REDOUBLE OUR EFFORTS TO GAIN SOME SEMBLANCE OF GANG UNITY UNDER ORPHEUS.
I'LL DO WHAT I CAN FROM HERE. BUT WE'RE STILL SO SHORT-HANDED--
HOPEFULLY THAT WILL CHANGE--
--IF MY MEETING GOES WELL.
COMMISSIONER AKINS--
I'M LATE FOR A PRESS CONFERENCE AT CITY HALL. AND AFTER THIS MORNING, YOU ARE ABOUT NUMBER TWO ON MY $#!%- LIST.
SO THIS BETTER BE GOOD, AND IT BETTER BE QUICK.

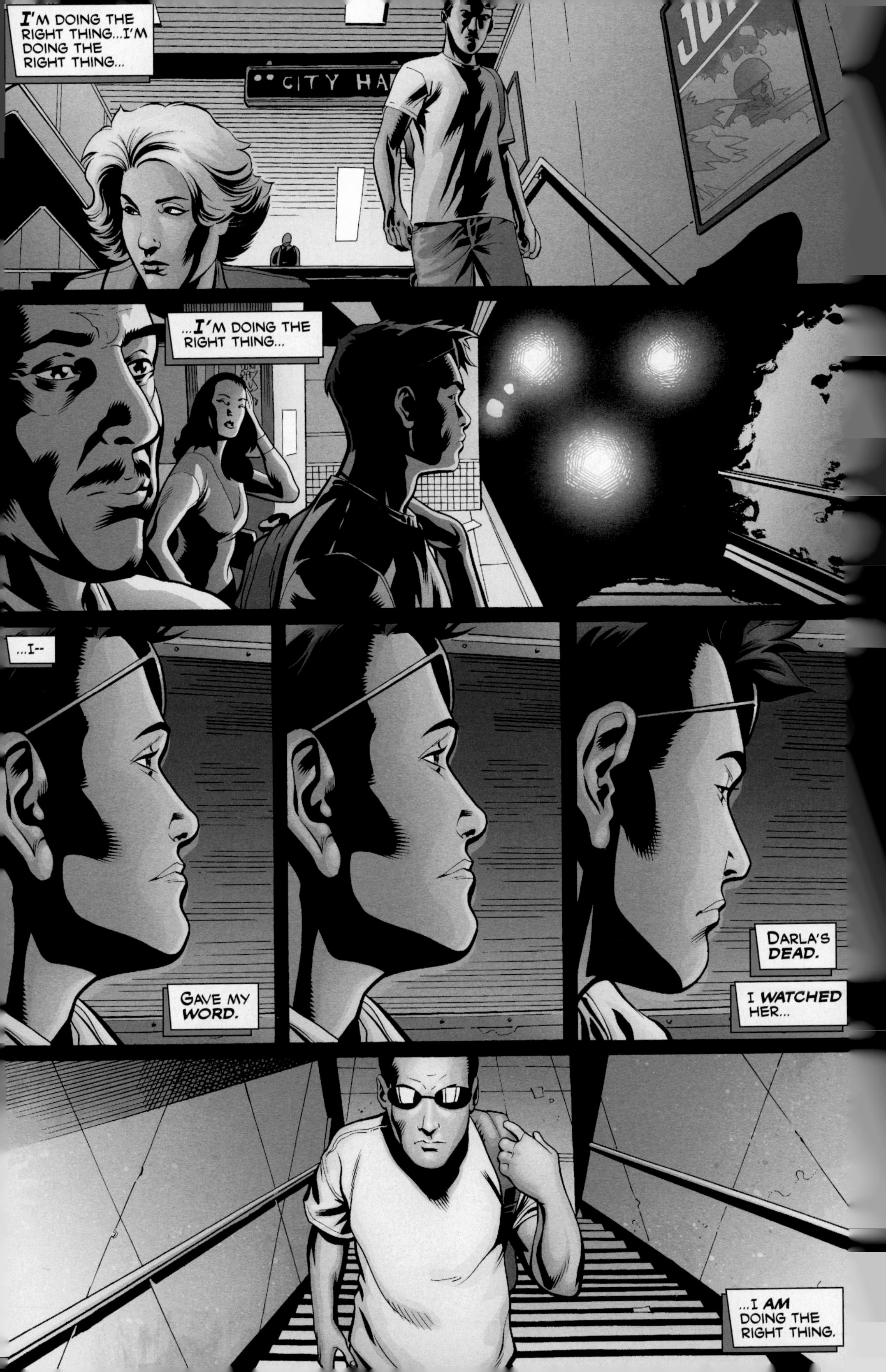
I'M DOING THE RIGHT THING...I'M DOING THE RIGHT THING...
CITY HA
...I'M DOING THE RIGHT THING...
...I--
GAVE MY WORD.
DARLA'S DEAD.
I WATCHED HER...
...I AM DOING THE RIGHT THING.

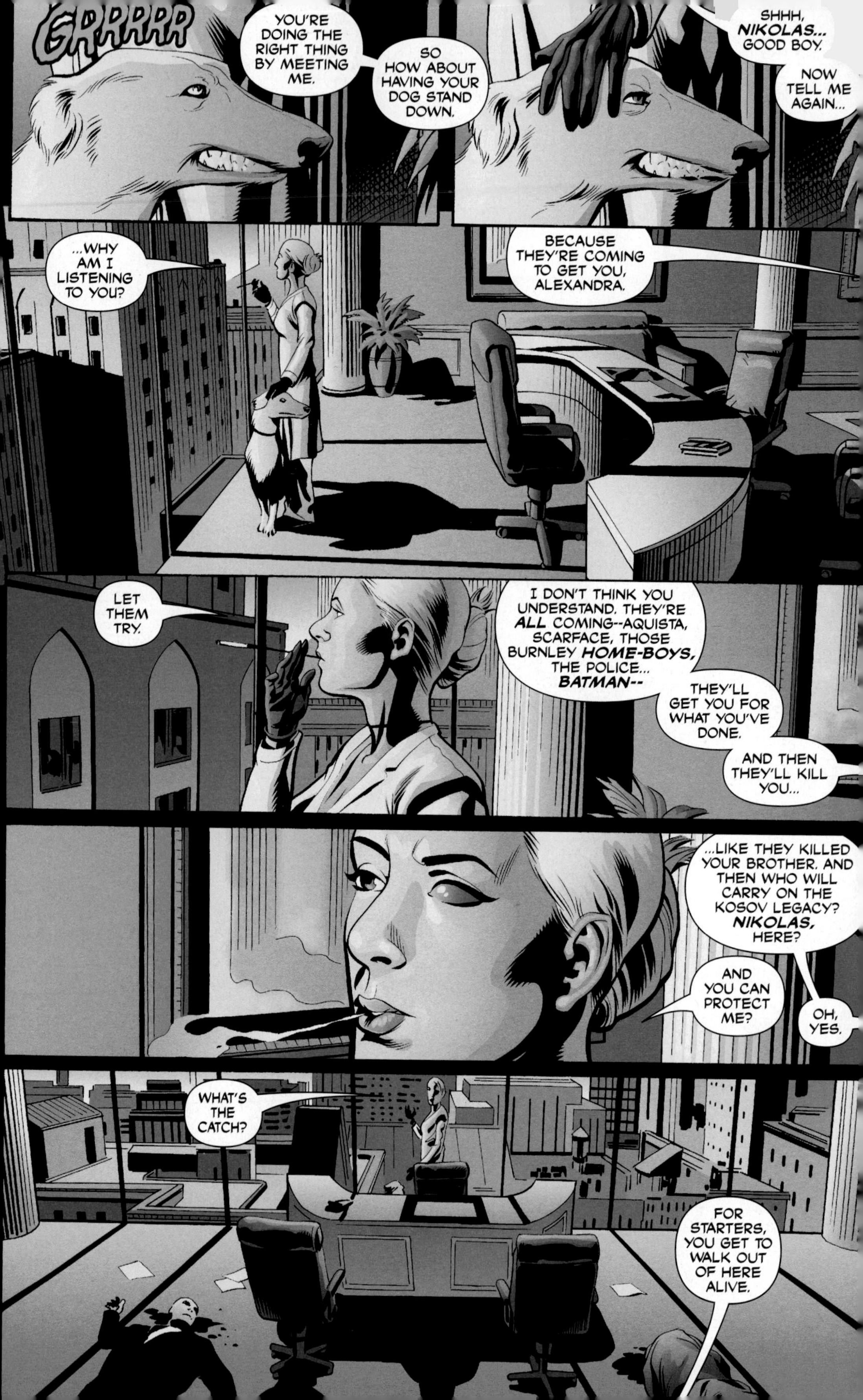
GRRRRR
YOU'RE DOING THE RIGHT THING BY MEETING ME.
SO HOW ABOUT HAVING YOUR DOG STAND DOWN.
SHHH, NIKOLAS... GOOD BOY.
NOW TELL ME AGAIN...
...WHY AM I LISTENING TO YOU?
BECAUSE THEY'RE COMING TO GET YOU, ALEXANDRA.
LET THEM TRY.
I DON'T THINK YOU UNDERSTAND. THEY'RE ALL COMING--AQUISTA, SCARFACE, THOSE BURNLEY HOME-BOYS, THE POLICE... BATMAN--
THEY'LL GET YOU FOR WHAT YOU'VE DONE.
AND THEN THEY'LL KILL YOU...
...LIKE THEY KILLED YOUR BROTHER. AND THEN WHO WILL CARRY ON THE KOSOV LEGACY? NIKOLAS, HERE?
AND YOU CAN PROTECT ME?
OH, YES.
WHAT'S THE CATCH?
FOR STARTERS, YOU GET TO WALK OUT OF HERE ALIVE.

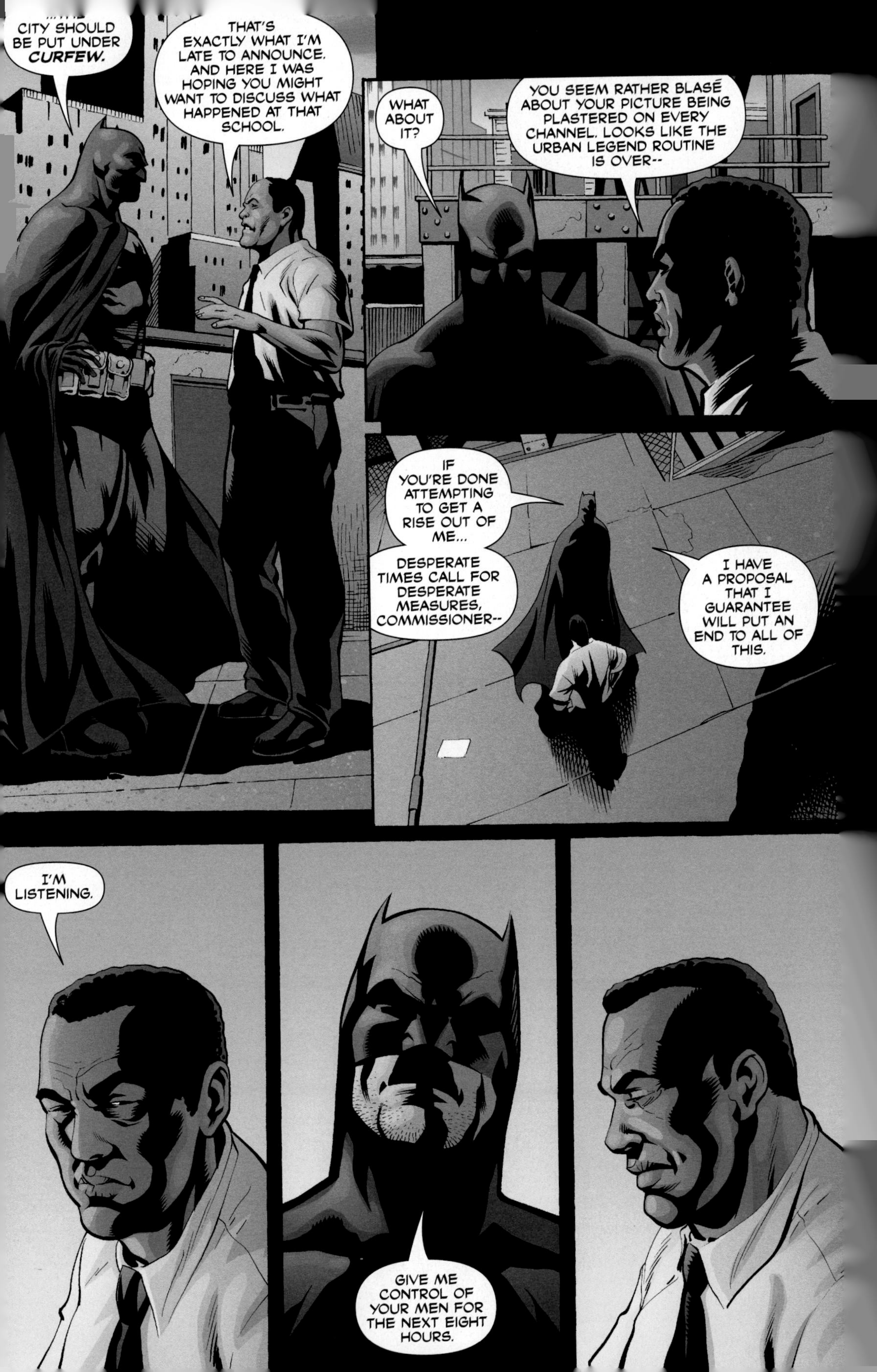
...THE CITY SHOULD BE PUT UNDER CURFEW.
THAT'S EXACTLY WHAT I'M LATE TO ANNOUNCE. AND HERE I WAS HOPING YOU MIGHT WANT TO DISCUSS WHAT HAPPENED AT THAT SCHOOL.
WHAT ABOUT IT?
YOU SEEM RATHER BLASÉ ABOUT YOUR PICTURE BEING PLASTERED ON EVERY CHANNEL. LOOKS LIKE THE URBAN LEGEND ROUTINE IS OVER--
IF YOU'RE DONE ATTEMPTING TO GET A RISE OUT OF ME...
DESPERATE TIMES CALL FOR DESPERATE MEASURES, COMMISSIONER--
I HAVE A PROPOSAL THAT I GUARANTEE WILL PUT AN END TO ALL OF THIS.
I'M LISTENING.
GIVE ME CONTROL OF YOUR MEN FOR THE NEXT EIGHT HOURS.

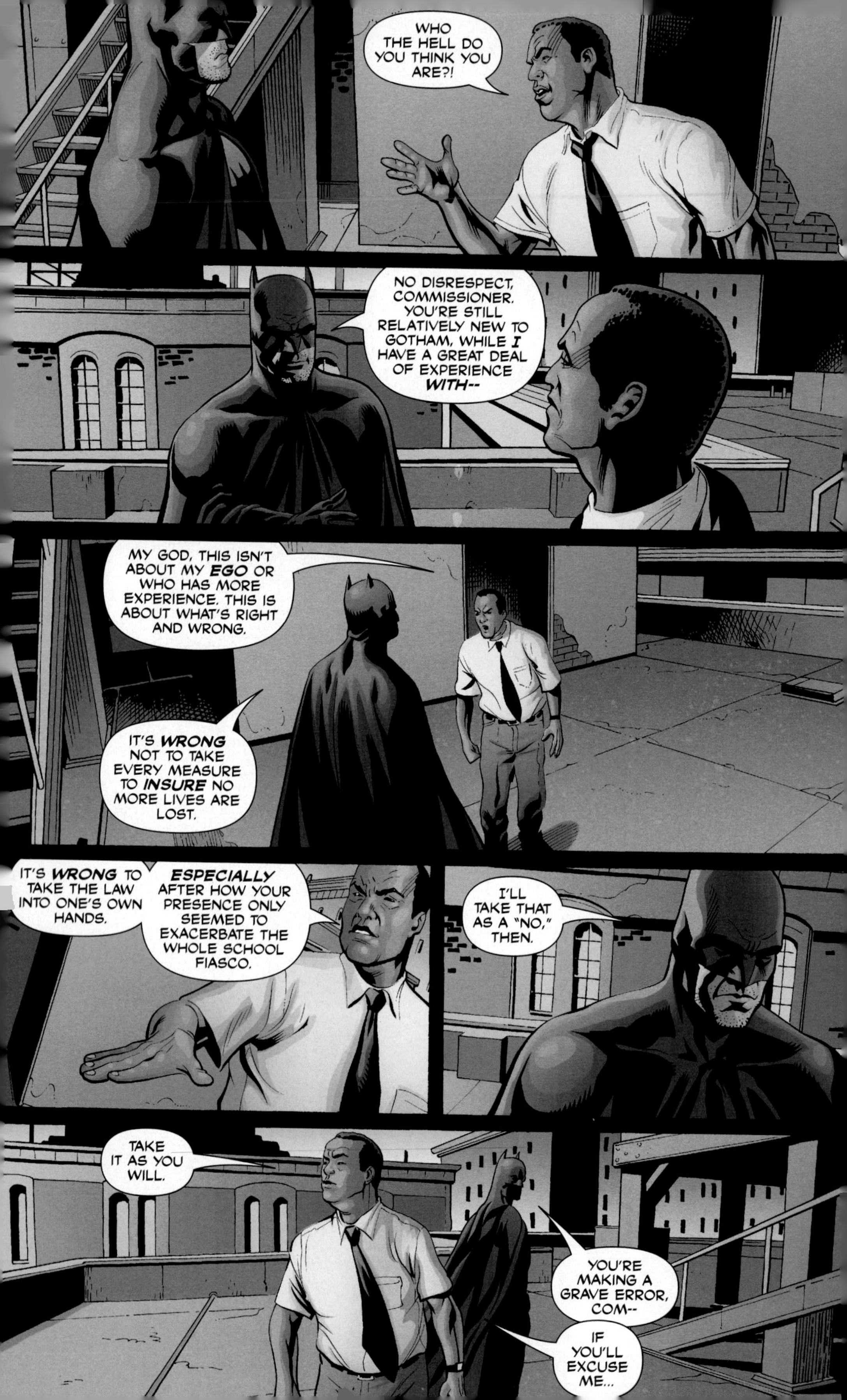
WHO THE HELL DO YOU THINK YOU ARE?!
NO DISRESPECT, COMMISSIONER. YOU'RE STILL RELATIVELY NEW TO GOTHAM, WHILE *I* HAVE A GREAT DEAL OF EXPERIENCE *WITH--*
MY GOD, THIS ISN'T ABOUT MY *EGO* OR WHO HAS MORE EXPERIENCE. THIS IS ABOUT WHAT'S RIGHT AND WRONG.
IT'S *WRONG* NOT TO TAKE EVERY MEASURE TO *INSURE* NO MORE LIVES ARE LOST.
IT'S *WRONG* TO TAKE THE LAW INTO ONE'S OWN HANDS.
ESPECIALLY AFTER HOW YOUR PRESENCE ONLY SEEMED TO EXACERBATE THE WHOLE SCHOOL FIASCO.
I'LL TAKE THAT AS A "NO," THEN.
TAKE IT AS YOU WILL.
YOU'RE MAKING A GRAVE ERROR, COM--
IF YOU'LL EXCUSE ME...

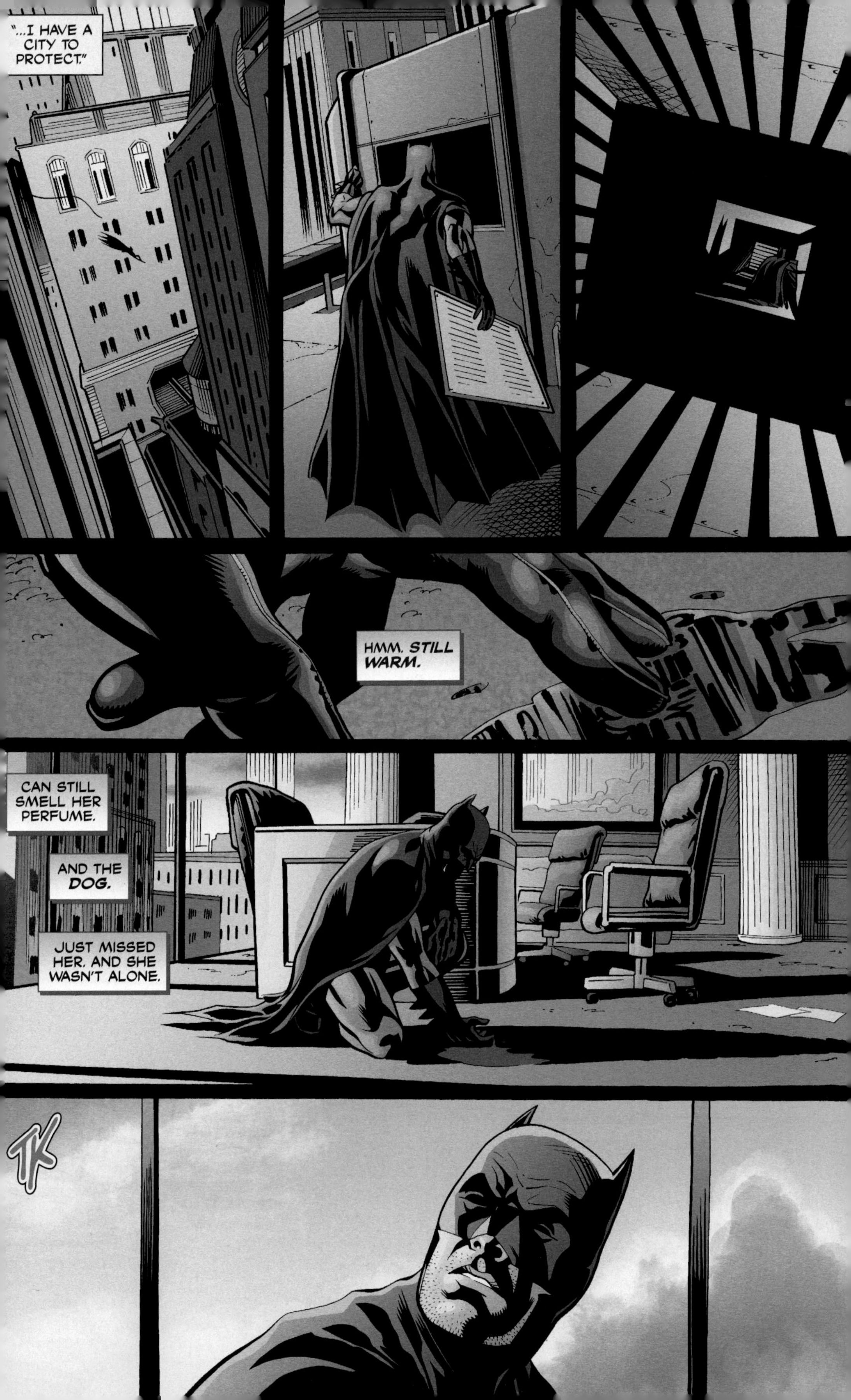
"...I HAVE A CITY TO PROTECT."
HMM. STILL WARM.
CAN STILL SMELL HER PERFUME.
AND THE DOG.
JUST MISSED HER. AND SHE WASN'T ALONE.
TK

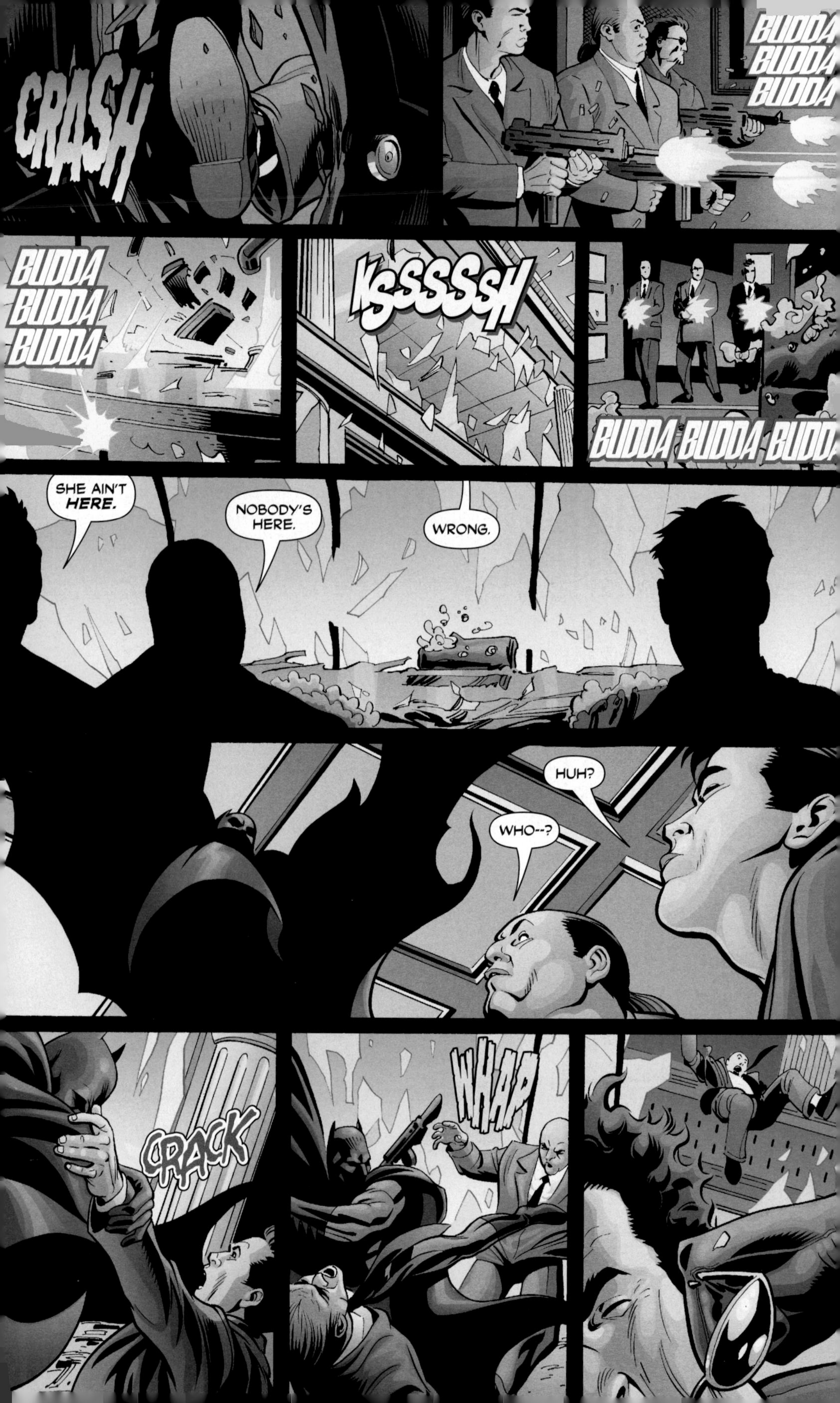
CRASH
BUDDA BUDDA BUDDA
BUDDA BUDDA BUDDA
KSSSSSH
BUDDA BUDDA BUDDA
SHE AIN'T HERE.
NOBODY'S HERE.
WRONG.
HUH?
WHO--?
CRACK
WHAP

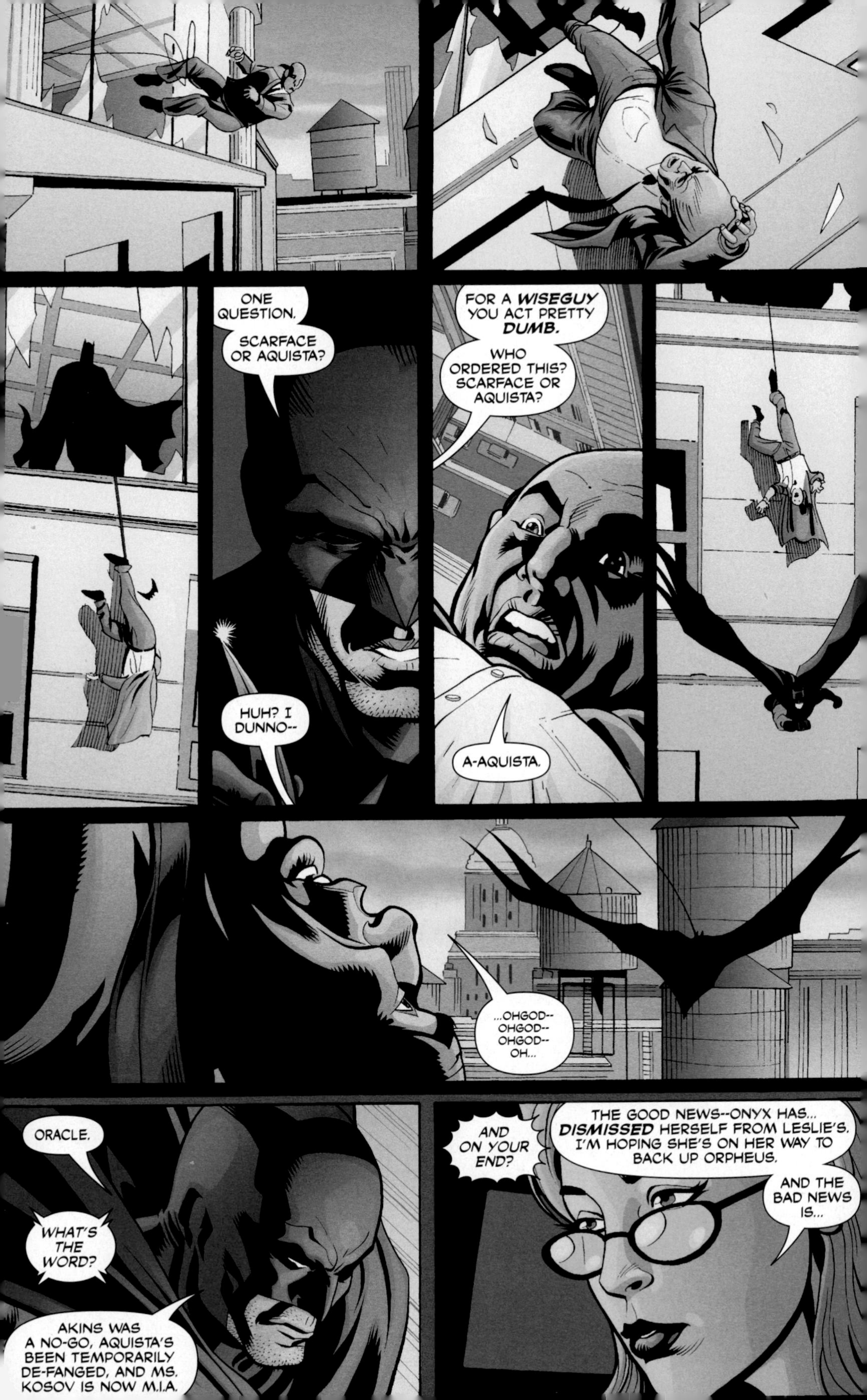
ONE QUESTION.
SCARFACE OR AQUISTA?
HUH? I DUNNO--
FOR A WISEGUY YOU ACT PRETTY DUMB.
WHO ORDERED THIS? SCARFACE OR AQUISTA?
A-AQUISTA.
...OHGOD-- OHGOD-- OHGOD-- OH...
ORACLE.
WHAT'S THE WORD?
AKINS WAS A NO-GO, AQUISTA'S BEEN TEMPORARILY DE-FANGED, AND MS. KOSOV IS NOW M.I.A.
AND ON YOUR END?
THE GOOD NEWS--ONYX HAS... DISMISSED HERSELF FROM LESLIE'S. I'M HOPING SHE'S ON HER WAY TO BACK UP ORPHEUS.
AND THE BAD NEWS IS...

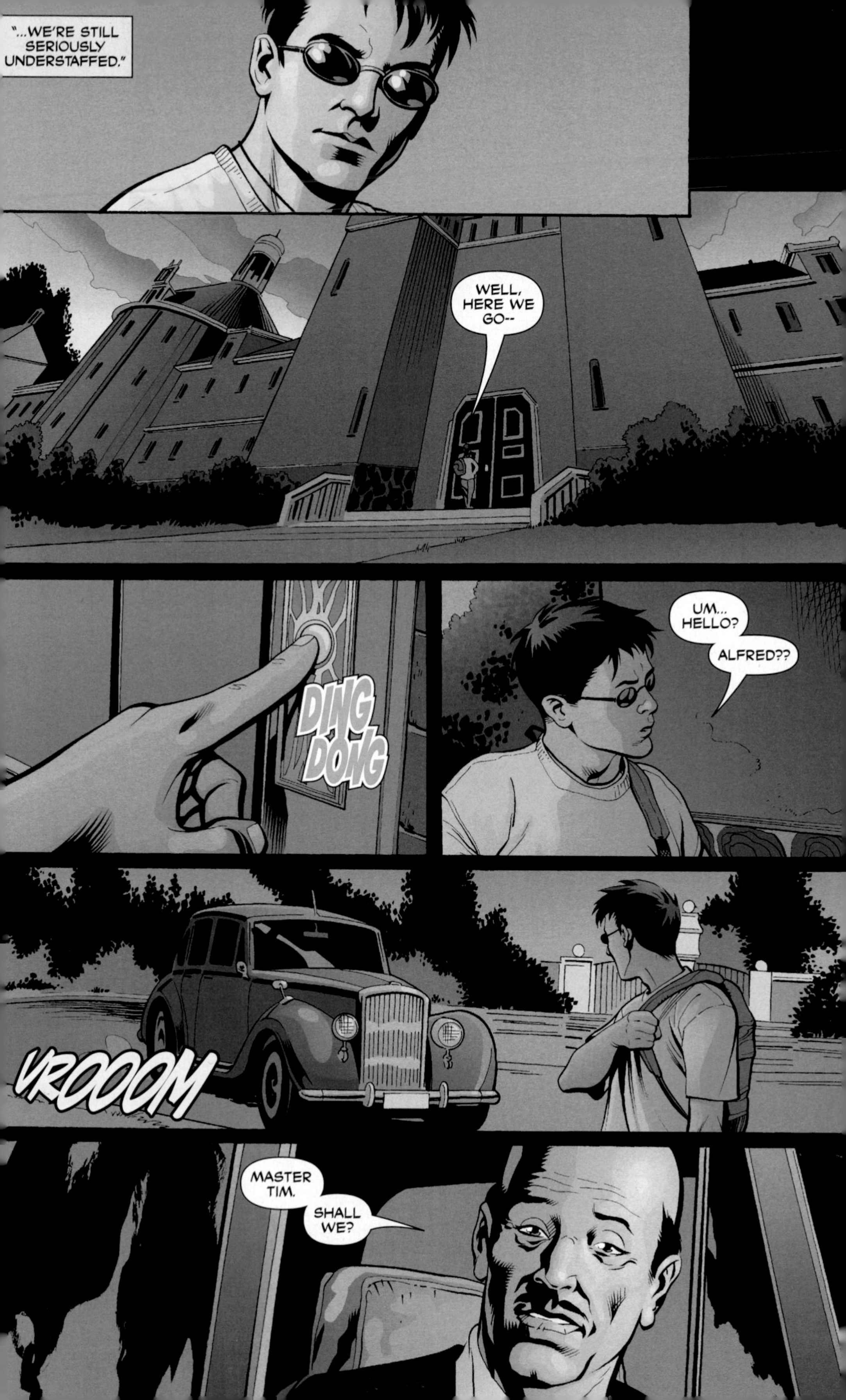
"...WE'RE STILL SERIOUSLY UNDERSTAFFED."
WELL, HERE WE GO--
DING DONG
UM... HELLO?
ALFRED??
VROOOM
MASTER TIM.
SHALL WE?

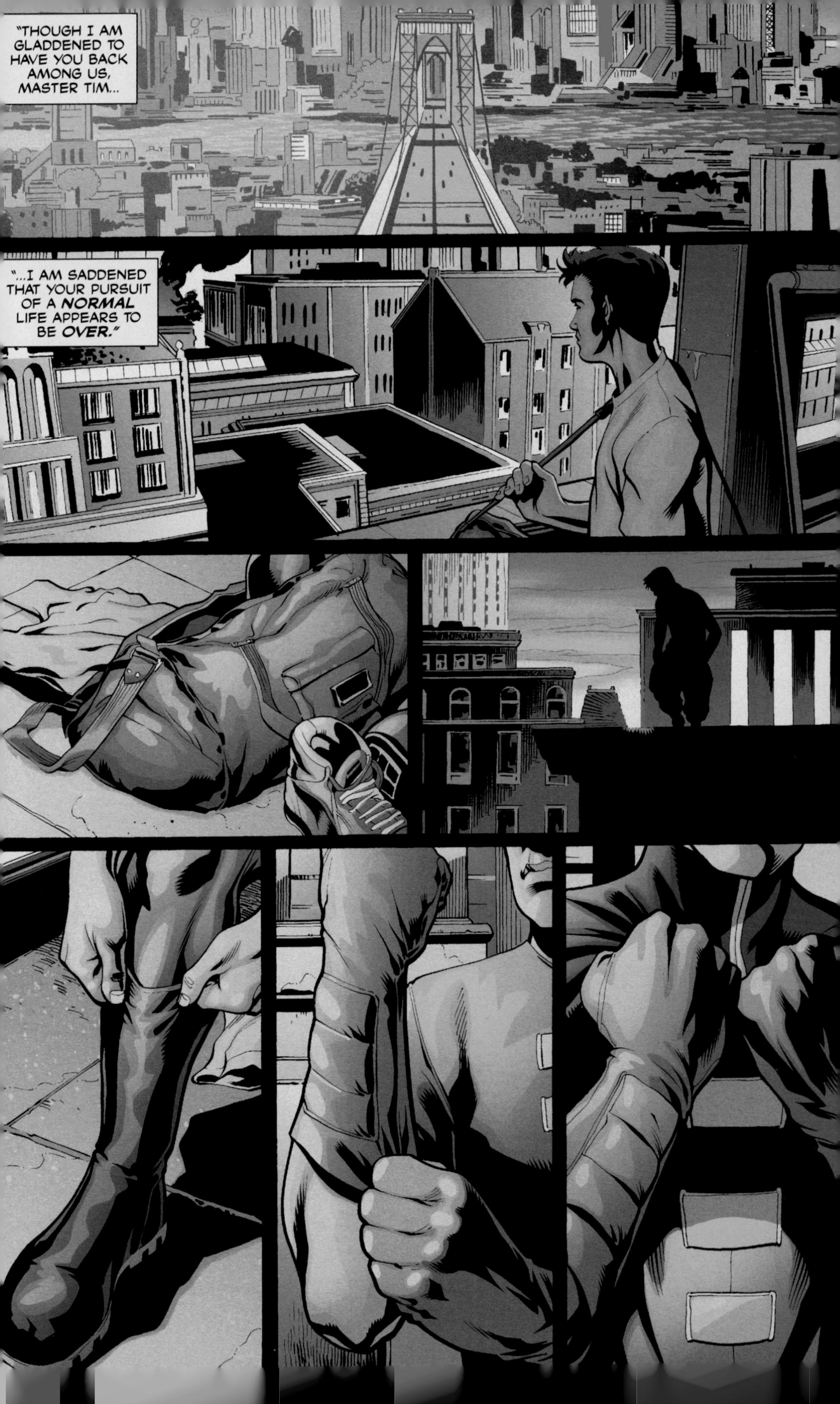
"THOUGH I AM GLADDENED TO HAVE YOU BACK AMONG US, MASTER TIM...
"...I AM SADDENED THAT YOUR PURSUIT OF A NORMAL LIFE APPEARS TO BE OVER."

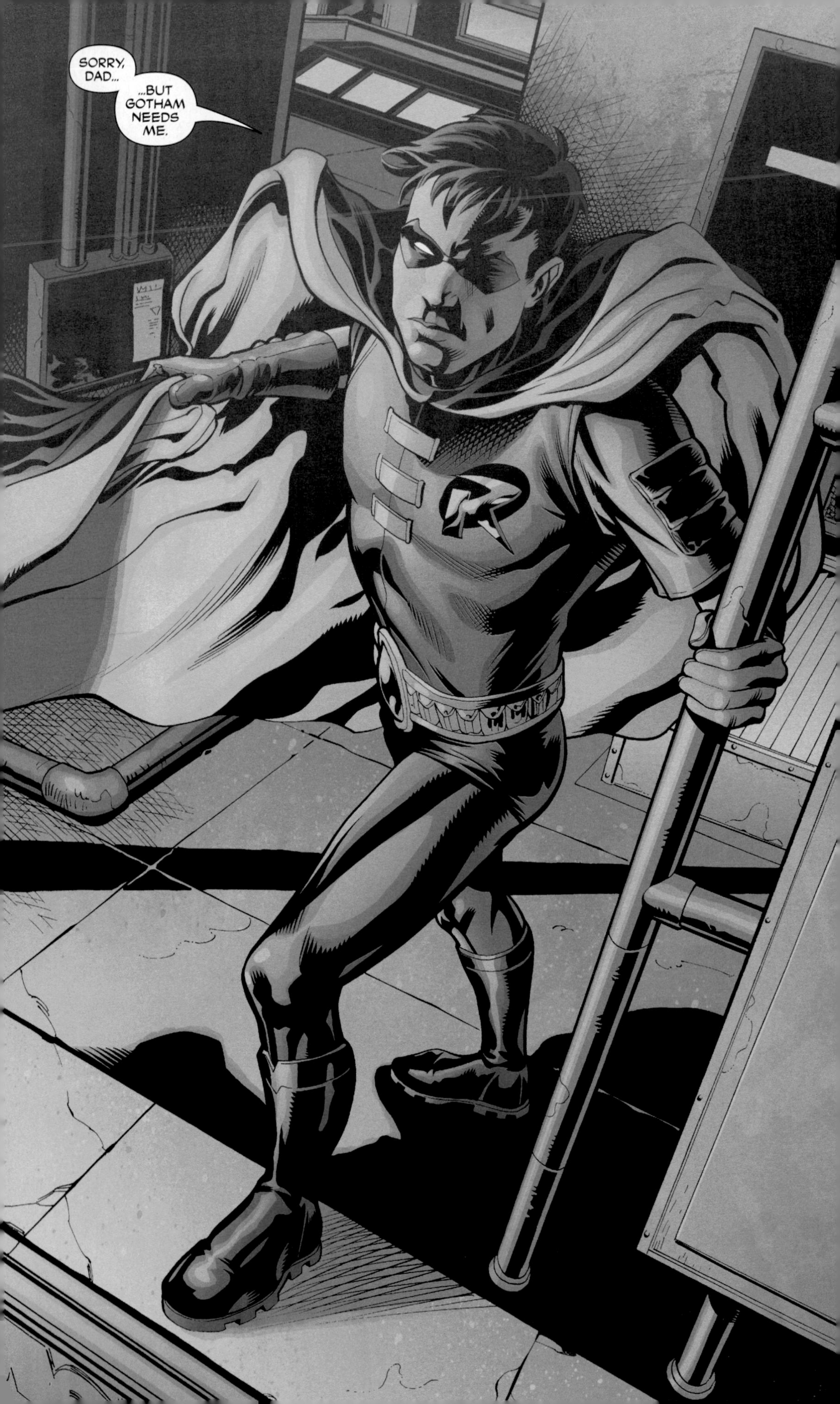
SORRY, DAD...
...BUT GOTHAM NEEDS ME.

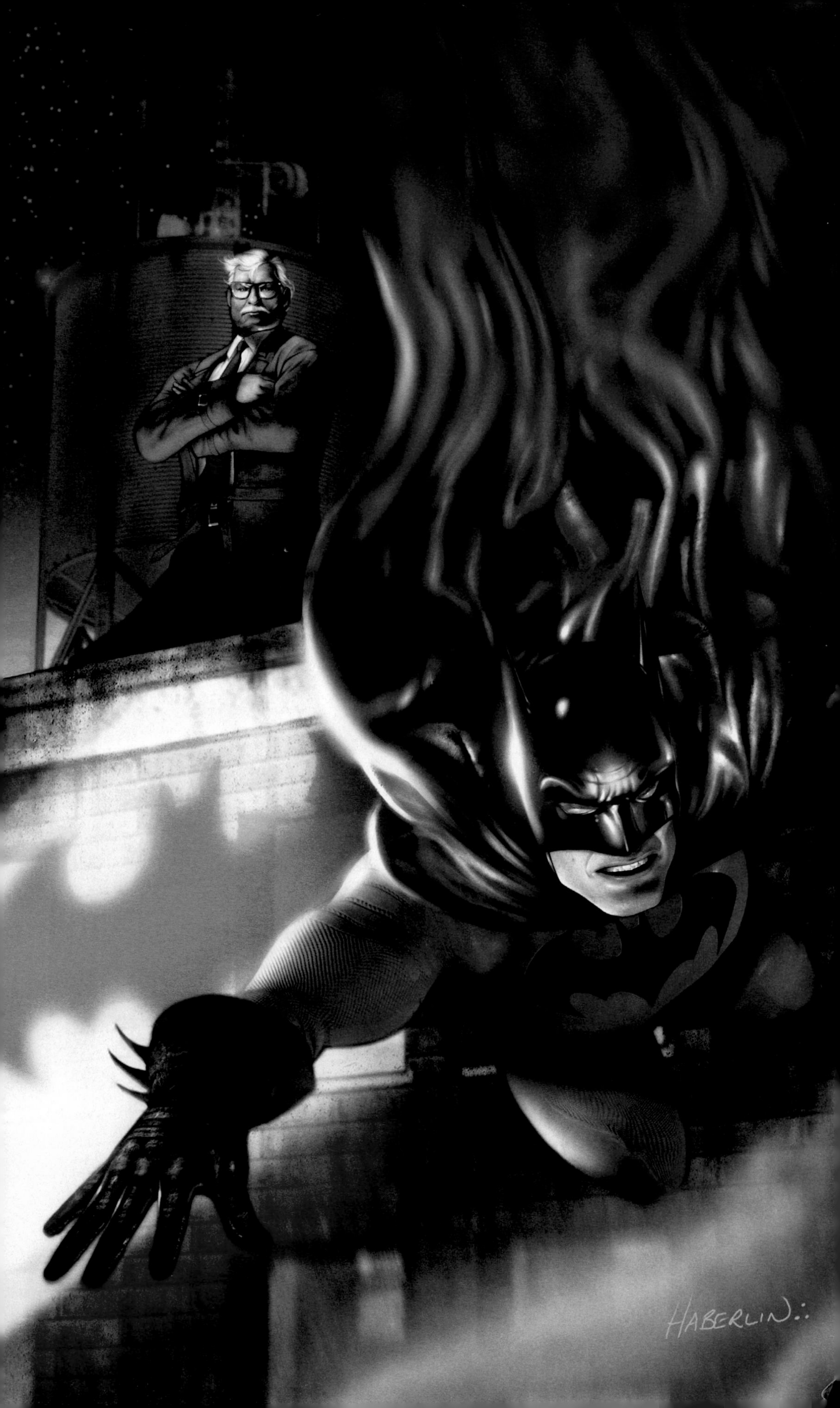
HABERLIN

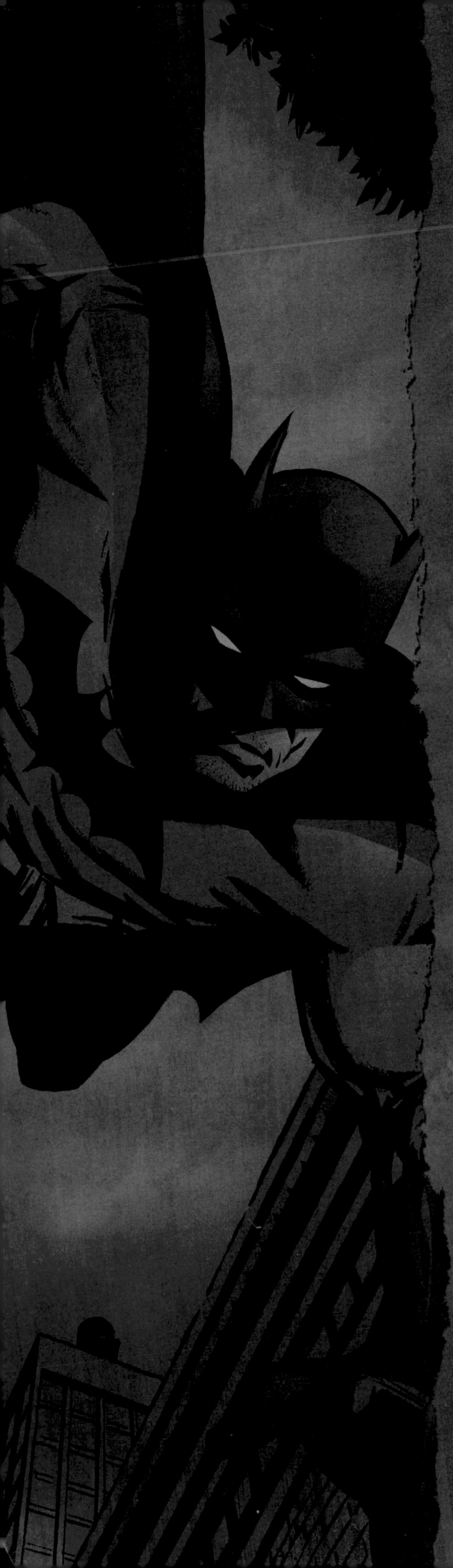

COVER ART BY
BRIAN HABERLIN

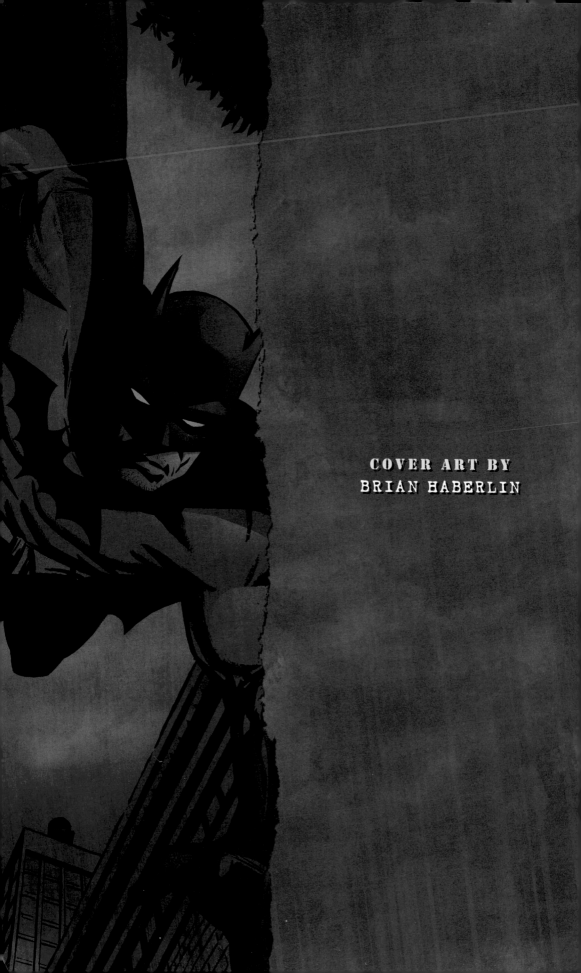

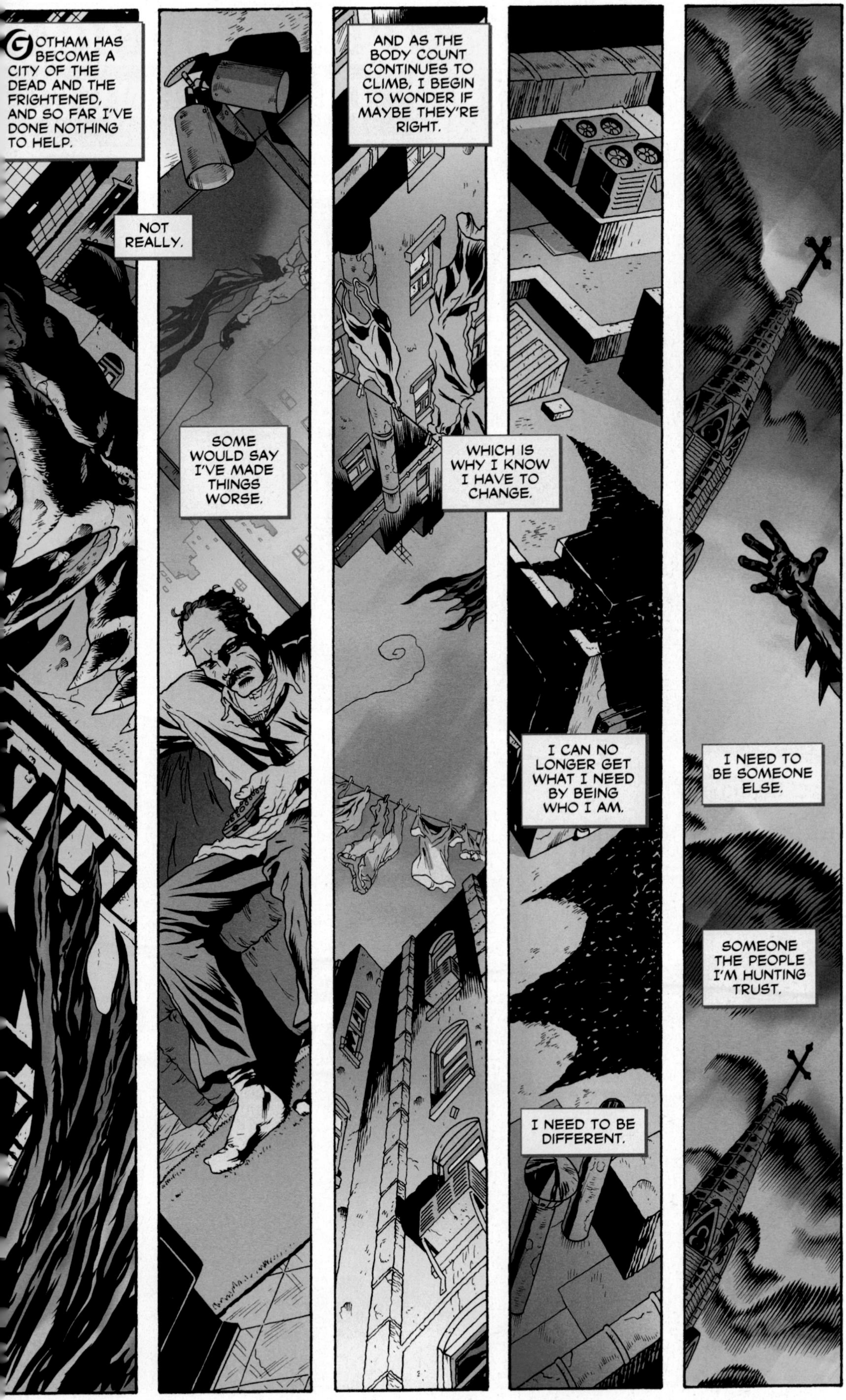
GOTHAM HAS BECOME A CITY OF THE DEAD AND THE FRIGHTENED, AND SO FAR I'VE DONE NOTHING TO HELP.
NOT REALLY.
SOME WOULD SAY I'VE MADE THINGS WORSE.
AND AS THE BODY COUNT CONTINUES TO CLIMB, I BEGIN TO WONDER IF MAYBE THEY'RE RIGHT.
WHICH IS WHY I KNOW I HAVE TO CHANGE.
I CAN NO LONGER GET WHAT I NEED BY BEING WHO I AM.
I NEED TO BE DIFFERENT.
I NEED TO BE SOMEONE ELSE.
SOMEONE THE PEOPLE I'M HUNTING TRUST.

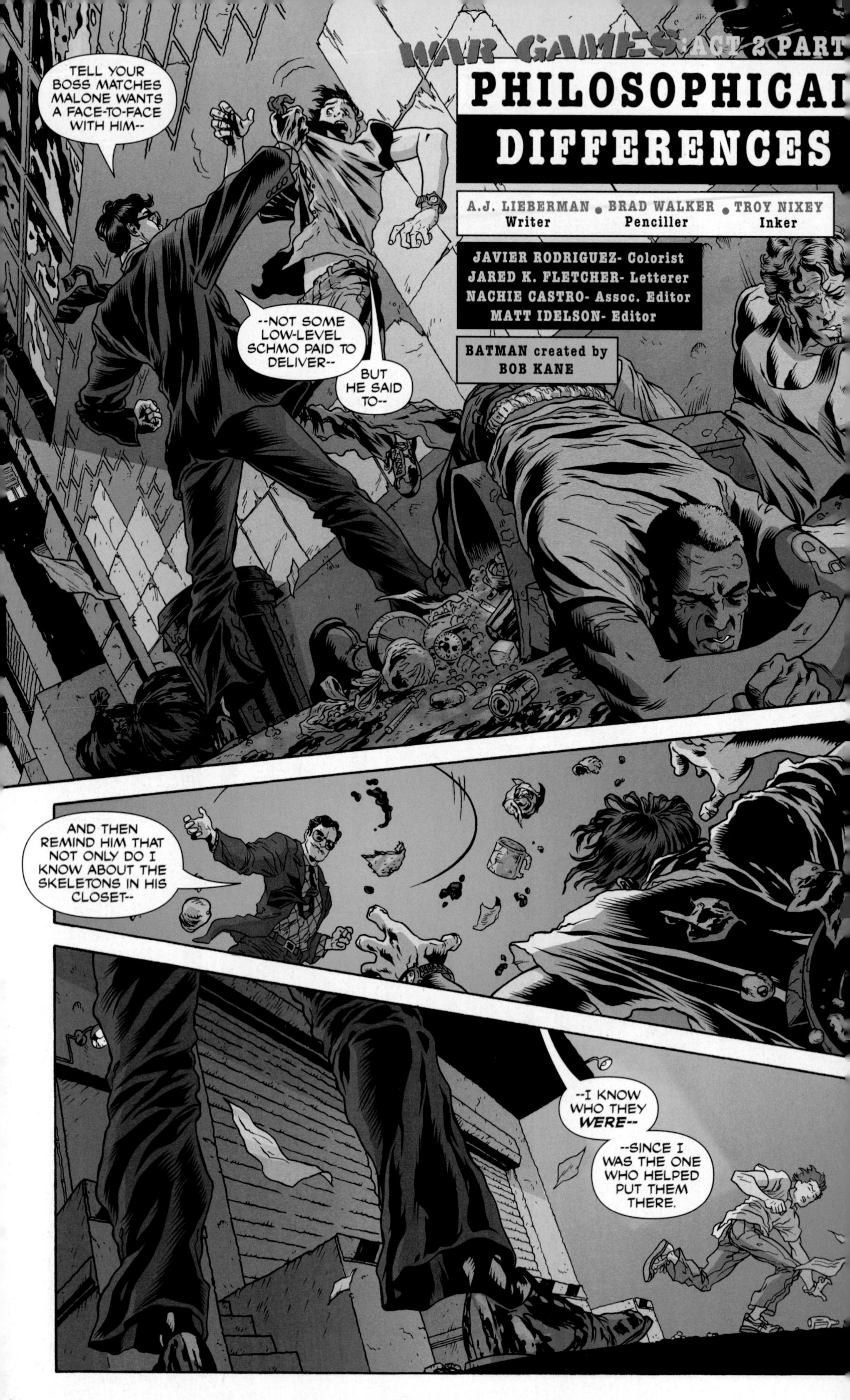
WAR GAMES: ACT 2 PART
PHILOSOPHICAL DIFFERENCES
A.J. LIEBERMAN Writer • BRAD WALKER Penciller • TROY NIXEY Inker
JAVIER RODRIGUEZ- Colorist
JARED K. FLETCHER- Letterer
NACHIE CASTRO- Assoc. Editor
MATT IDELSON- Editor
BATMAN created by BOB KANE
TELL YOUR BOSS MATCHES MALONE WANTS A FACE-TO-FACE WITH HIM--
--NOT SOME LOW-LEVEL SCHMO PAID TO DELIVER--
BUT HE SAID TO--
AND THEN REMIND HIM THAT NOT ONLY DO I KNOW ABOUT THE SKELETONS IN HIS CLOSET--
--I KNOW WHO THEY *WERE*--
--SINCE I WAS THE ONE WHO HELPED PUT THEM THERE.

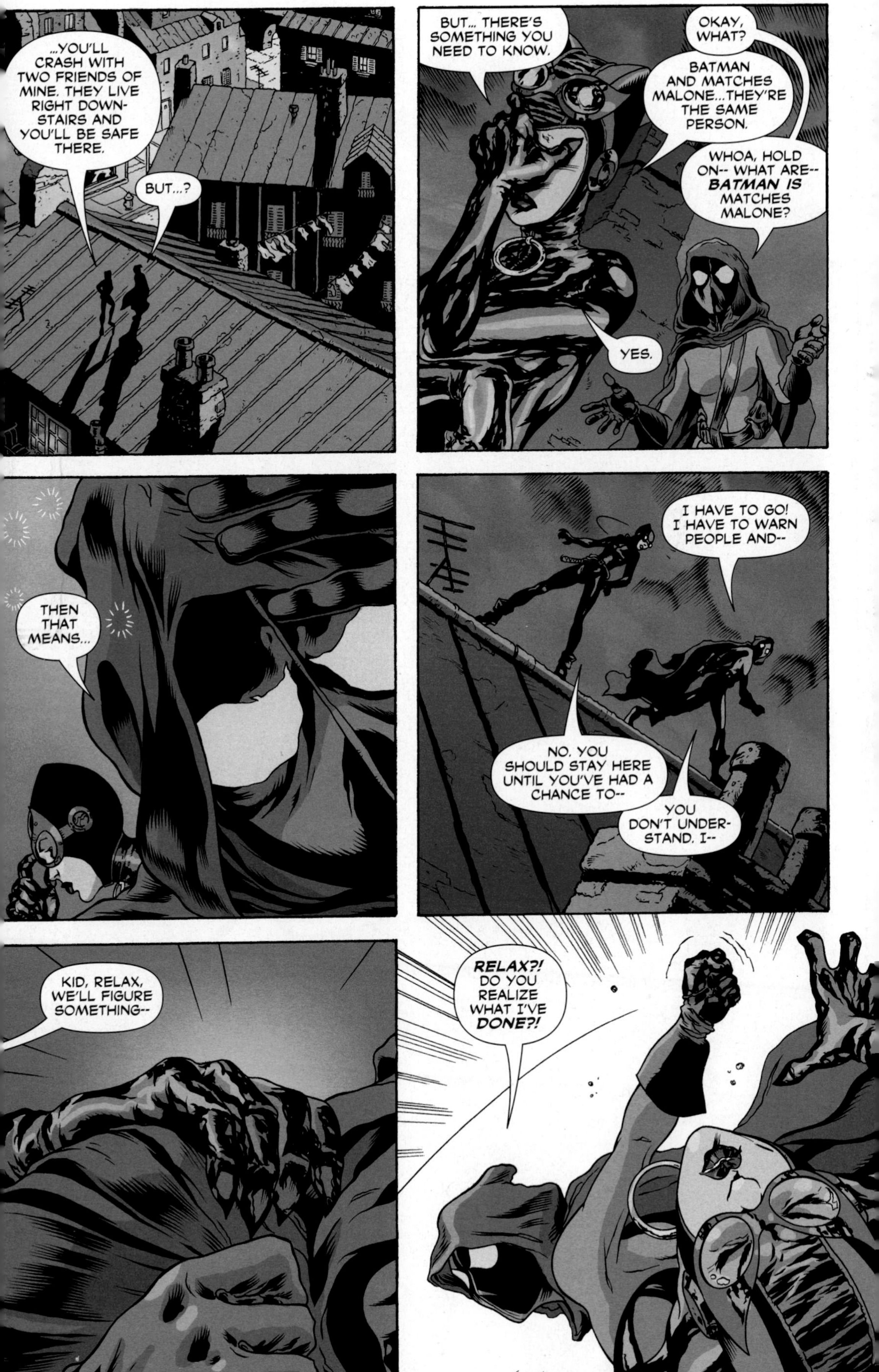
...YOU'LL CRASH WITH TWO FRIENDS OF MINE. THEY LIVE RIGHT DOWN-STAIRS AND YOU'LL BE SAFE THERE.
BUT...?
BUT... THERE'S SOMETHING YOU NEED TO KNOW.
OKAY, WHAT?
BATMAN AND MATCHES MALONE...THEY'RE THE SAME PERSON.
WHOA, HOLD ON-- WHAT ARE-- ***BATMAN IS*** MATCHES MALONE?
YES.
THEN THAT MEANS...
I HAVE TO GO! I HAVE TO WARN PEOPLE AND--
NO. YOU SHOULD STAY HERE UNTIL YOU'VE HAD A CHANCE TO--
YOU DON'T UNDER-STAND. I--
KID, RELAX, WE'LL FIGURE SOMETHING--
RELAX?! DO YOU REALIZE WHAT I'VE ***DONE?!***

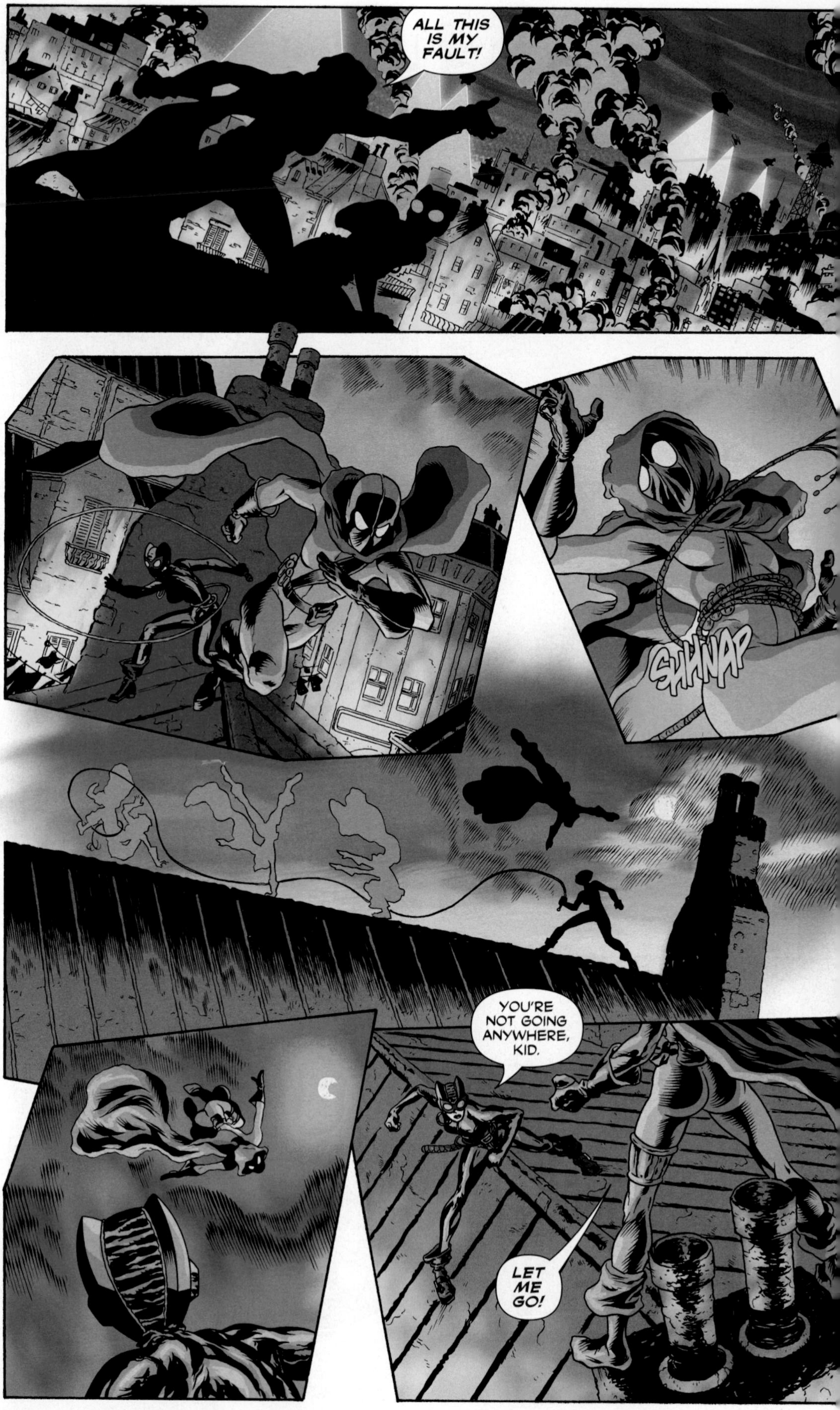
ALL THIS IS MY FAULT!
SHHNAP
YOU'RE NOT GOING ANYWHERE, KID.
LET ME GO!

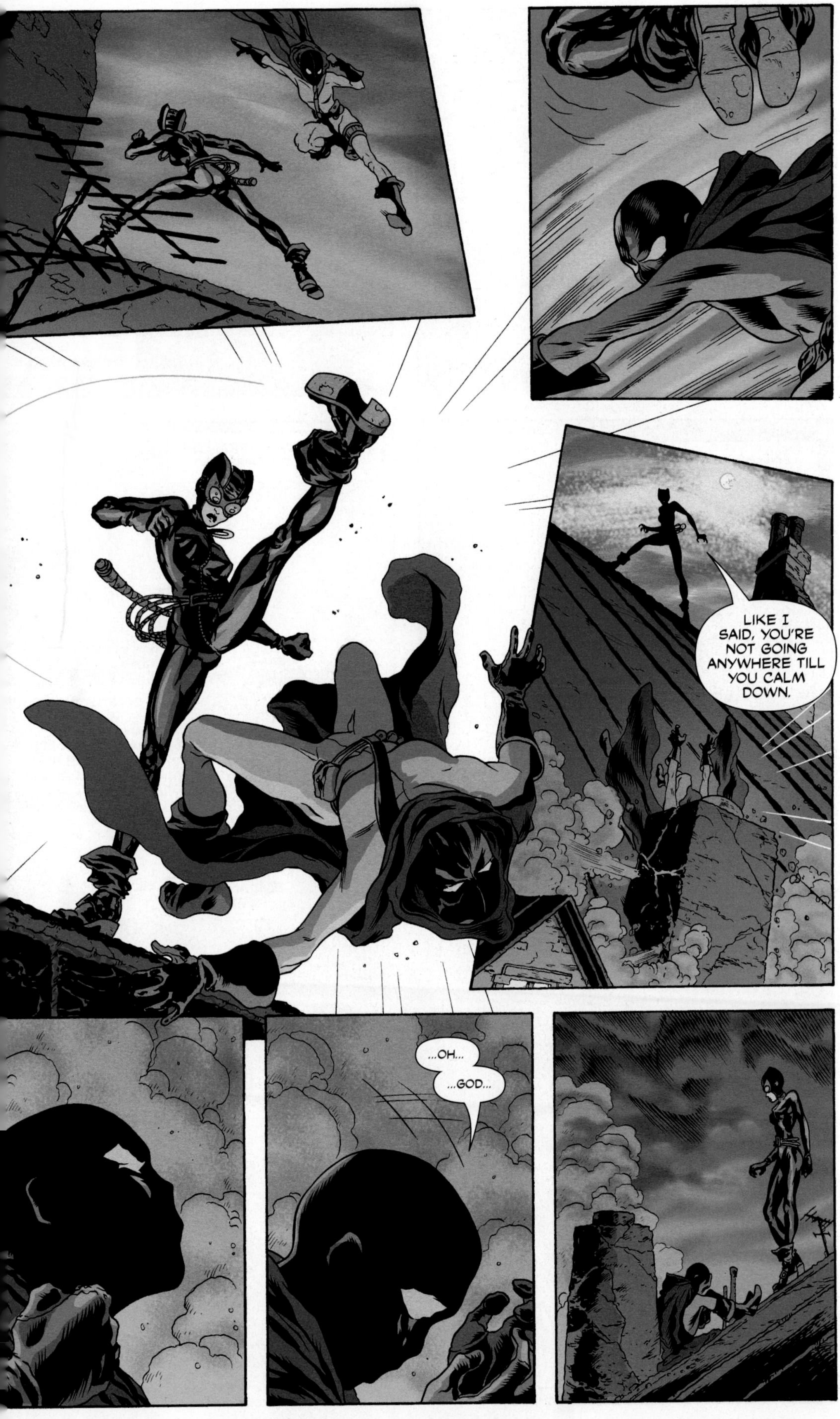
LIKE I SAID, YOU'RE NOT GOING ANYWHERE TILL YOU CALM DOWN.
...OH...
...GOD...

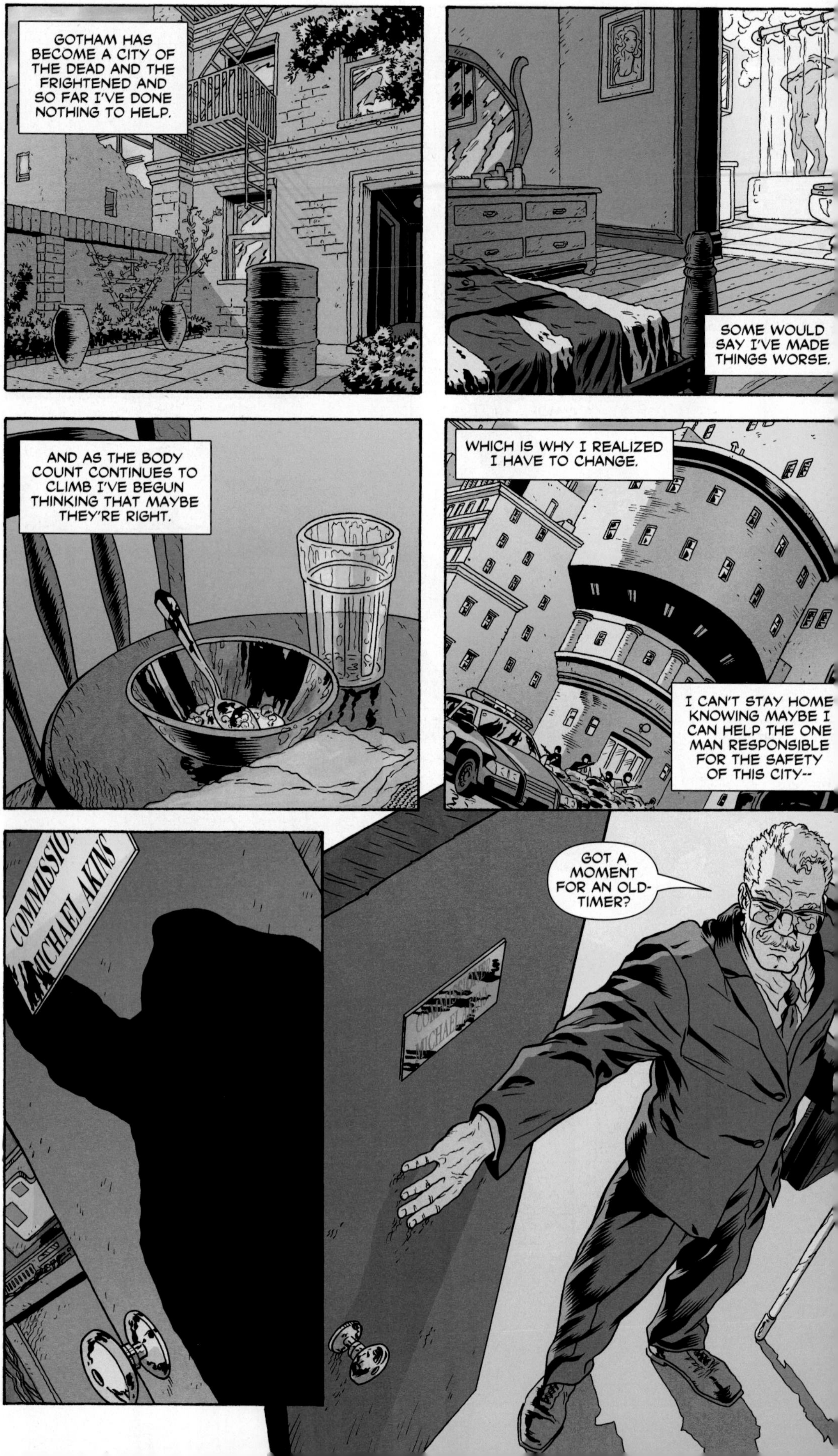

GOTHAM HAS BECOME A CITY OF THE DEAD AND THE FRIGHTENED AND SO FAR I'VE DONE NOTHING TO HELP.
SOME WOULD SAY I'VE MADE THINGS WORSE.
AND AS THE BODY COUNT CONTINUES TO CLIMB I'VE BEGUN THINKING THAT MAYBE THEY'RE RIGHT.
WHICH IS WHY I REALIZED I HAVE TO CHANGE.
I CAN'T STAY HOME KNOWING MAYBE I CAN HELP THE ONE MAN RESPONSIBLE FOR THE SAFETY OF THIS CITY--
COMMISSIONER MICHAEL AKINS
GOT A MOMENT FOR AN OLD-TIMER?

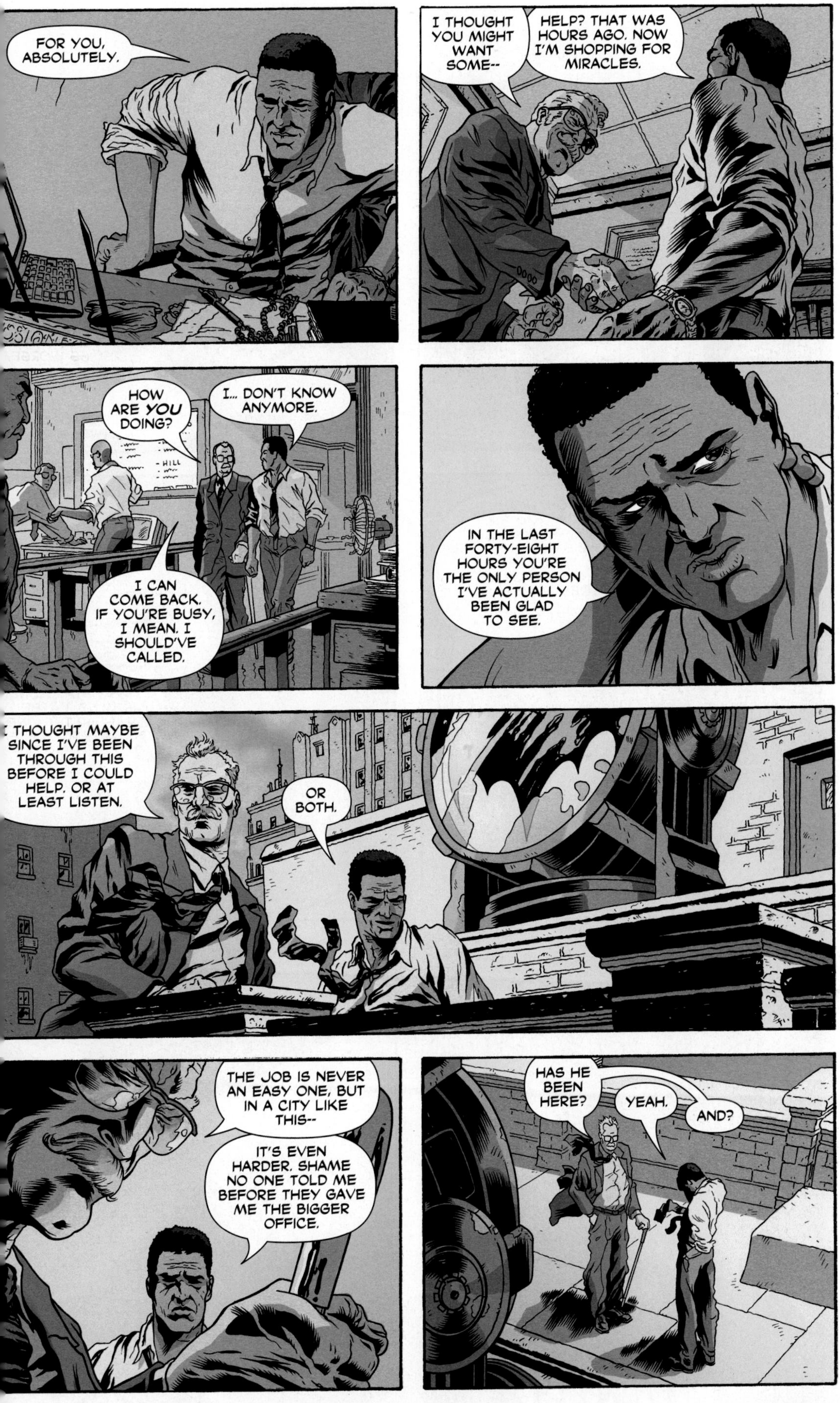
FOR YOU, ABSOLUTELY.
I THOUGHT YOU MIGHT WANT SOME--
HELP? THAT WAS HOURS AGO. NOW I'M SHOPPING FOR MIRACLES.
HOW ARE *YOU* DOING?
I... DON'T KNOW ANYMORE.
I CAN COME BACK. IF YOU'RE BUSY, I MEAN. I SHOULD'VE CALLED.
IN THE LAST FORTY-EIGHT HOURS YOU'RE THE ONLY PERSON I'VE ACTUALLY BEEN GLAD TO SEE.
I THOUGHT MAYBE SINCE I'VE BEEN THROUGH THIS BEFORE I COULD HELP. OR AT LEAST LISTEN.
OR BOTH.
THE JOB IS NEVER AN EASY ONE, BUT IN A CITY LIKE THIS--
IT'S EVEN HARDER. SHAME NO ONE TOLD ME BEFORE THEY GAVE ME THE BIGGER OFFICE.
HAS HE BEEN HERE?
YEAH.
AND?

AND I THOUGHT ABOUT TAKING HIM IN RIGHT THERE AND THEN.

BUT...?

BUT I DECIDED TO YELL AND SCREAM AND WALK AWAY INSTEAD.

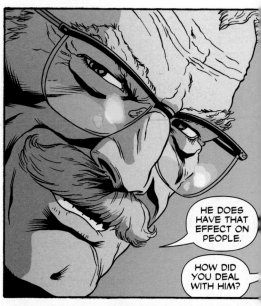

HE DOES HAVE THAT EFFECT ON PEOPLE.

HOW DID YOU DEAL WITH HIM?

AT FIRST IT WAS... DIFFICULT. EXTREMELY DIFFICULT.

LOOK, JIM, I KNOW YOU AND HE ARE... FRIENDS, BUT HE'S... HE'S NOT RIGHT THIS TIME. EVERYTHING I, WE STAND FOR, HE GOES AGAINST.

I'M SORRY.

DON'T BE. I CAN'T TELL YOU HOW MANY TIMES I'VE FELT THE EXACT SAME WAY.

BESIDES, UNDER THE MASK HE'S JUST A MAN, LIKE YOU OR ME.

AND NO MAN, NOT EVEN HIM, IS RIGHT ONE-HUNDRED PERCENT OF THE TIME.

SO, WHAT CAN I DO 'ROUND HERE TO HELP?

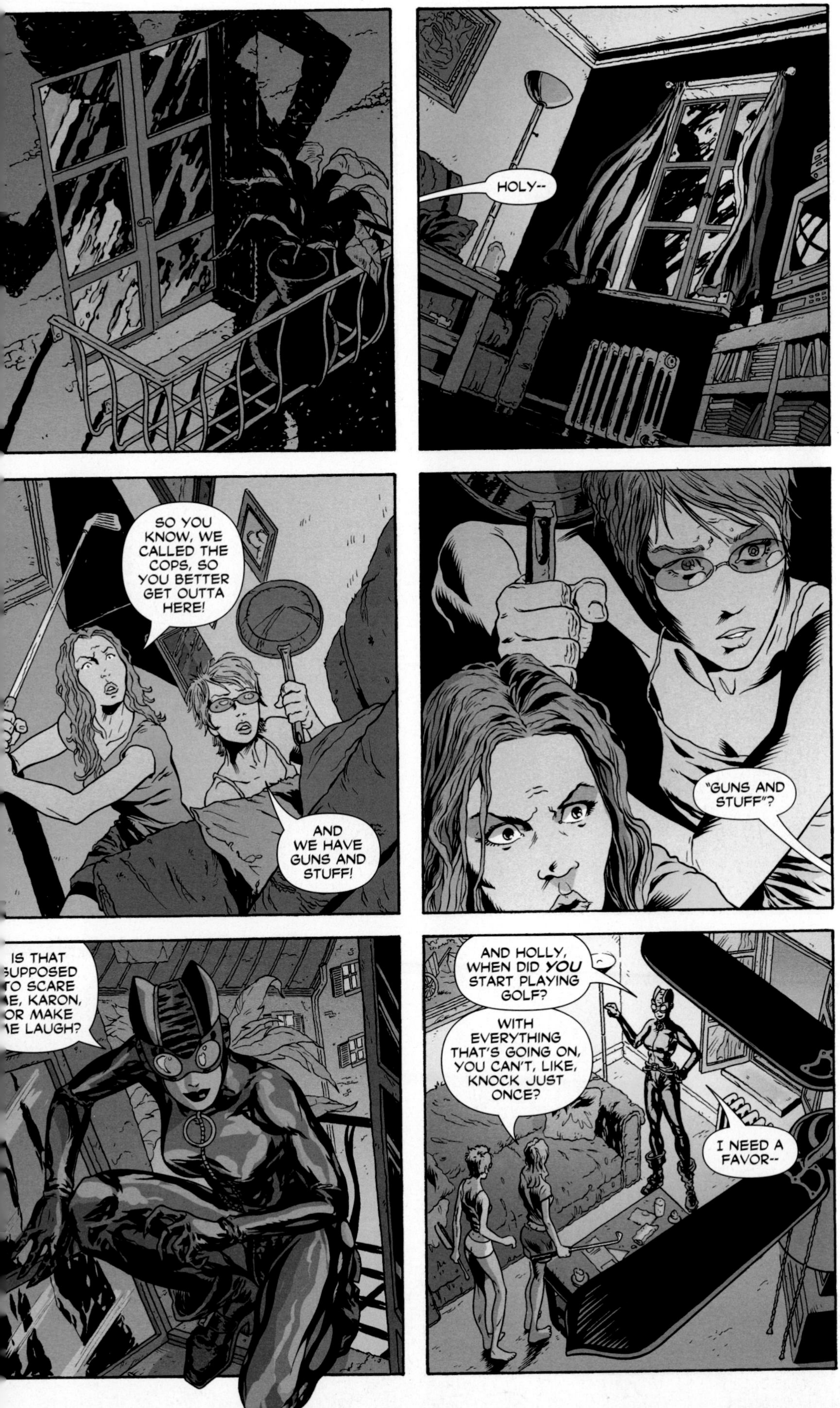
HOLY--
SO YOU KNOW, WE CALLED THE COPS, SO YOU BETTER GET OUTTA HERE!
AND WE HAVE GUNS AND STUFF!
"GUNS AND STUFF"?
IS THAT SUPPOSED TO SCARE ME, KARON, OR MAKE ME LAUGH?
AND HOLLY, WHEN DID *YOU* START PLAYING GOLF?
WITH EVERYTHING THAT'S GOING ON, YOU CAN'T, LIKE, KNOCK JUST ONCE?
I NEED A FAVOR--

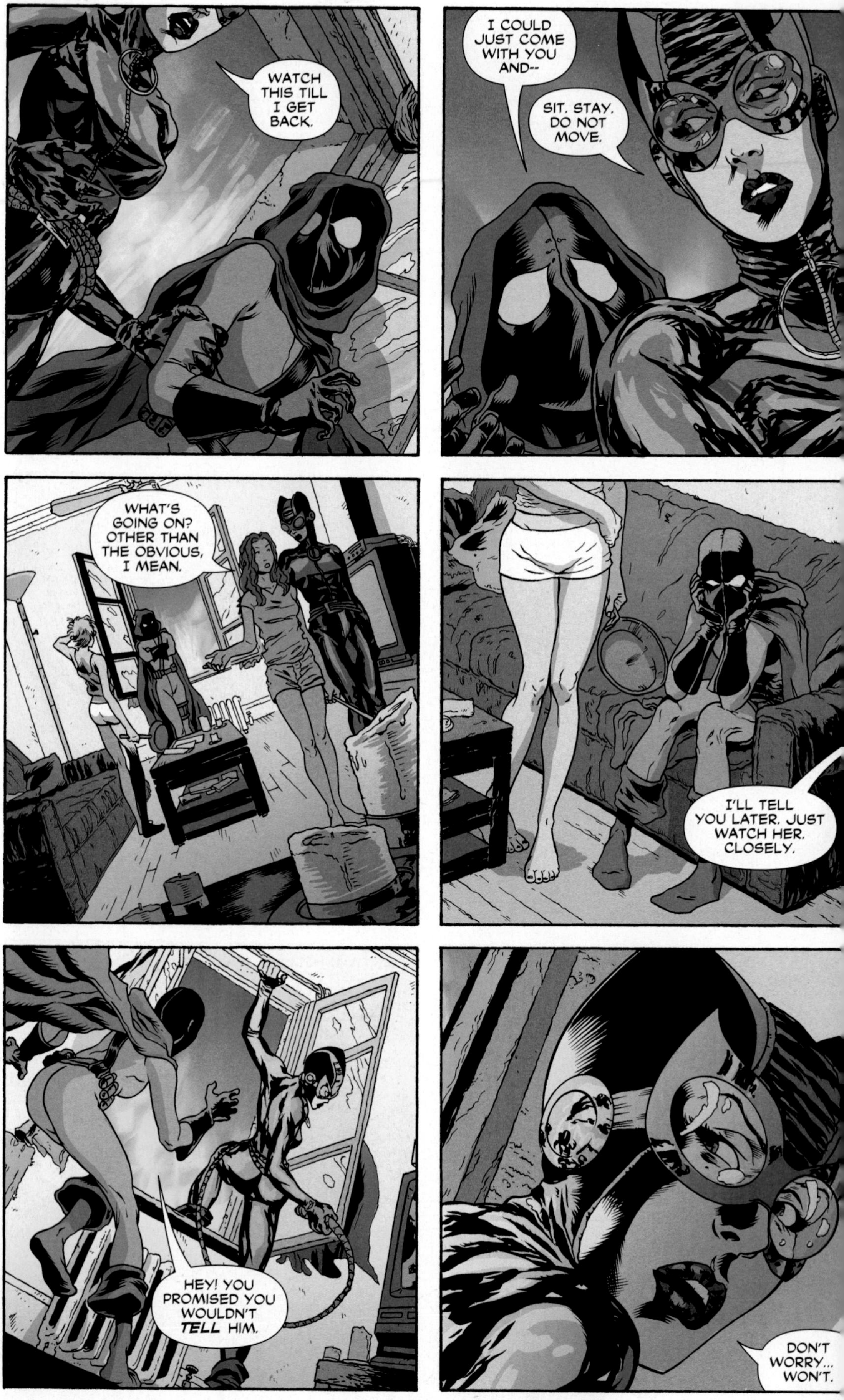

WATCH THIS TILL I GET BACK.
I COULD JUST COME WITH YOU AND--
SIT. STAY. DO NOT MOVE.
WHAT'S GOING ON? OTHER THAN THE OBVIOUS, I MEAN.
I'LL TELL YOU LATER. JUST WATCH HER. CLOSELY.
HEY! YOU PROMISED YOU WOULDN'T TELL HIM.
DON'T WORRY... WON'T.

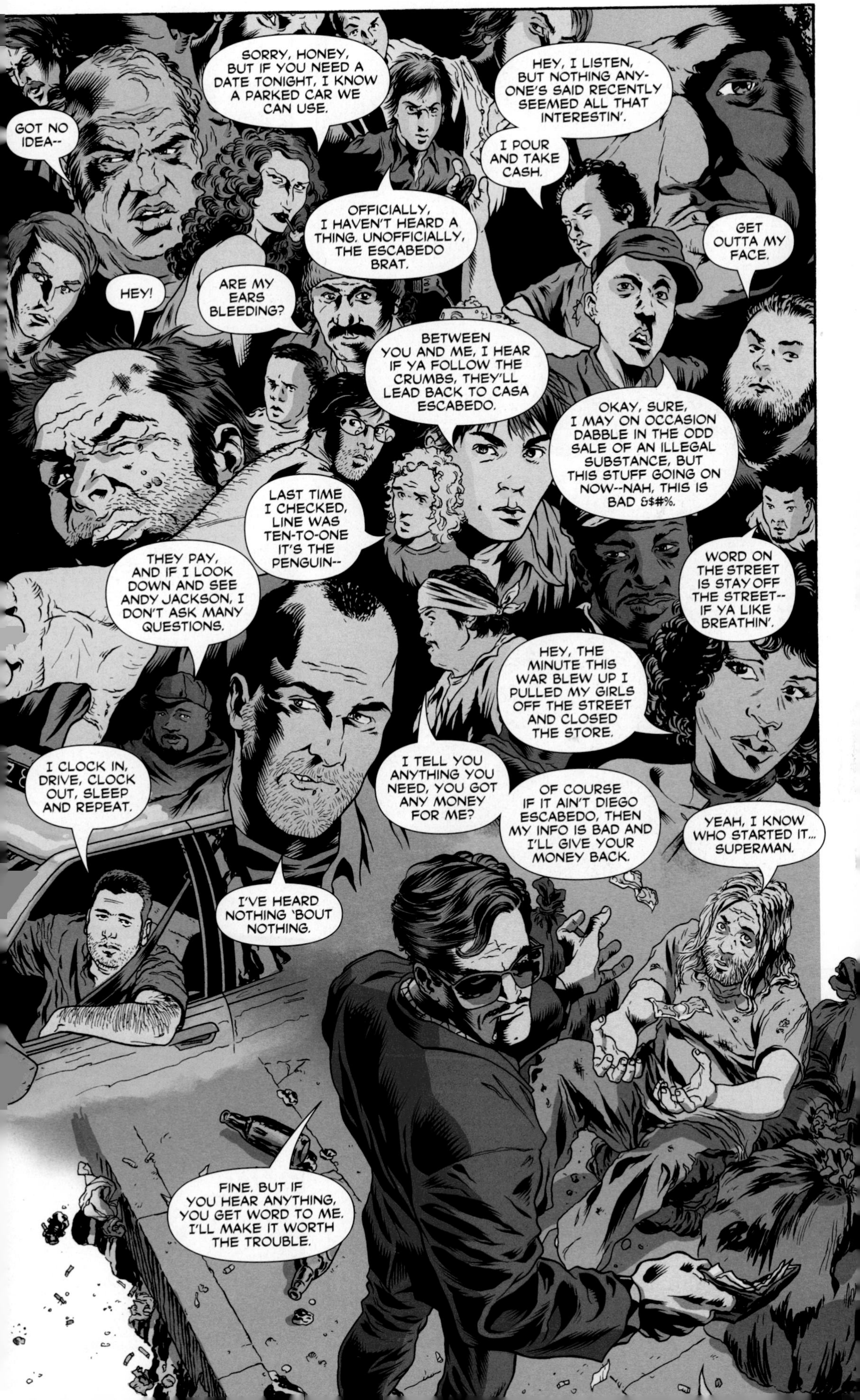
GOT NO IDEA--
SORRY, HONEY, BUT IF YOU NEED A DATE TONIGHT, I KNOW A PARKED CAR WE CAN USE.
HEY, I LISTEN, BUT NOTHING ANYONE'S SAID RECENTLY SEEMED ALL THAT INTERESTIN'.
I POUR AND TAKE CASH.
OFFICIALLY, I HAVEN'T HEARD A THING. UNOFFICIALLY, THE ESCABEDO BRAT.
GET OUTTA MY FACE.
HEY!
ARE MY EARS BLEEDING?
BETWEEN YOU AND ME, I HEAR IF YA FOLLOW THE CRUMBS, THEY'LL LEAD BACK TO CASA ESCABEDO.
OKAY, SURE, I MAY ON OCCASION DABBLE IN THE ODD SALE OF AN ILLEGAL SUBSTANCE, BUT THIS STUFF GOING ON NOW--NAH, THIS IS BAD &$#%.
LAST TIME I CHECKED, LINE WAS TEN-TO-ONE IT'S THE PENGUIN--
THEY PAY, AND IF I LOOK DOWN AND SEE ANDY JACKSON, I DON'T ASK MANY QUESTIONS.
WORD ON THE STREET IS STAY OFF THE STREET--IF YA LIKE BREATHIN'.
HEY, THE MINUTE THIS WAR BLEW UP I PULLED MY GIRLS OFF THE STREET AND CLOSED THE STORE.
I CLOCK IN, DRIVE, CLOCK OUT, SLEEP AND REPEAT.
I TELL YOU ANYTHING YOU NEED, YOU GOT ANY MONEY FOR ME?
OF COURSE IF IT AIN'T DIEGO ESCABEDO, THEN MY INFO IS BAD AND I'LL GIVE YOUR MONEY BACK.
YEAH, I KNOW WHO STARTED IT... SUPERMAN.
I'VE HEARD NOTHING 'BOUT NOTHING.
FINE. BUT IF YOU HEAR ANYTHING, YOU GET WORD TO ME. I'LL MAKE IT WORTH THE TROUBLE.

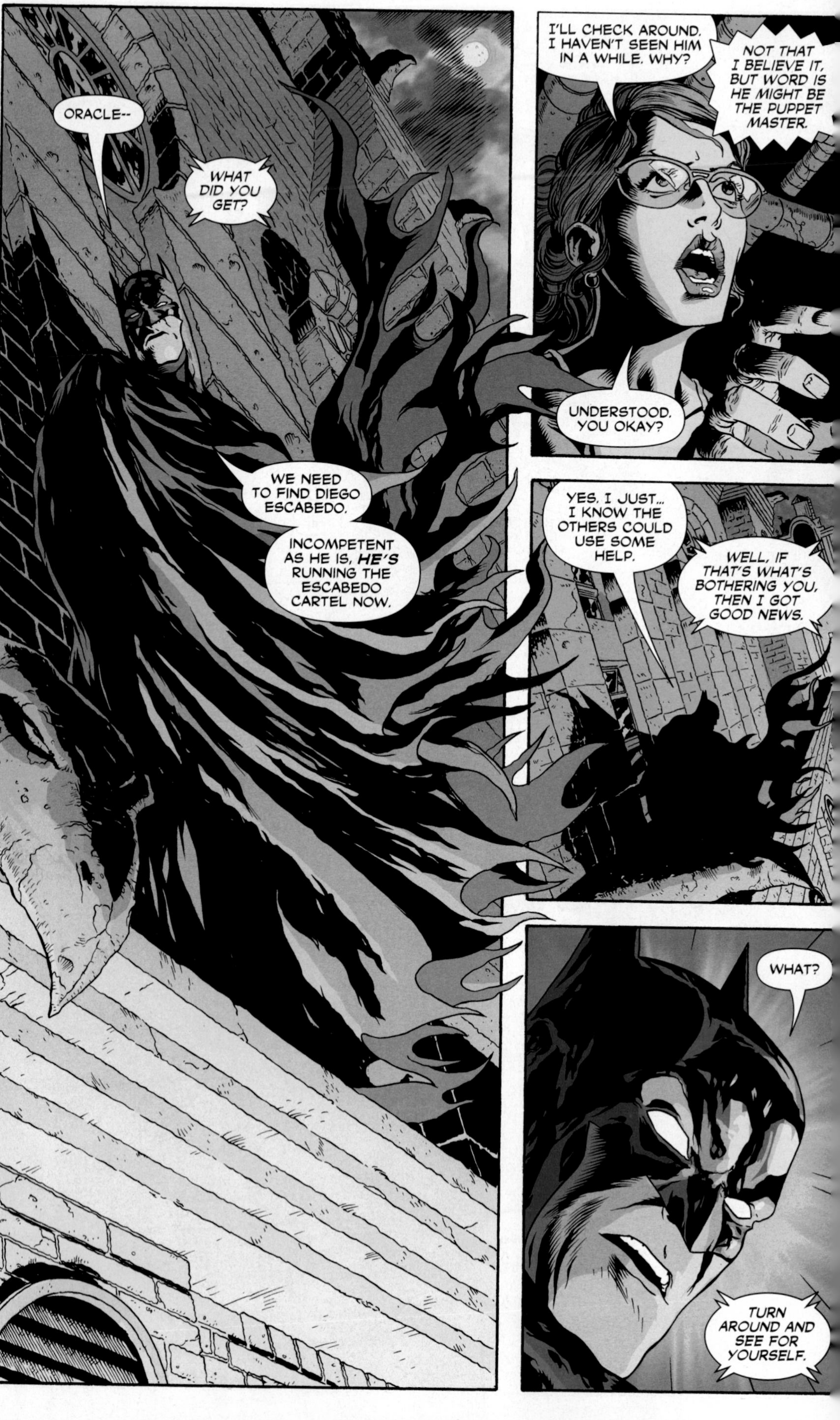
ORACLE--
WHAT DID YOU GET?
I'LL CHECK AROUND. I HAVEN'T SEEN HIM IN A WHILE. WHY?
NOT THAT I BELIEVE IT, BUT WORD IS HE MIGHT BE THE PUPPET MASTER.
WE NEED TO FIND DIEGO ESCABEDO.
INCOMPETENT AS HE IS, ***HE'S*** RUNNING THE ESCABEDO CARTEL NOW.
UNDERSTOOD. YOU OKAY?
YES. I JUST... I KNOW THE OTHERS COULD USE SOME HELP.
WELL, IF THAT'S WHAT'S BOTHERING YOU, THEN I GOT GOOD NEWS.
WHAT?
TURN AROUND AND SEE FOR YOURSELF.

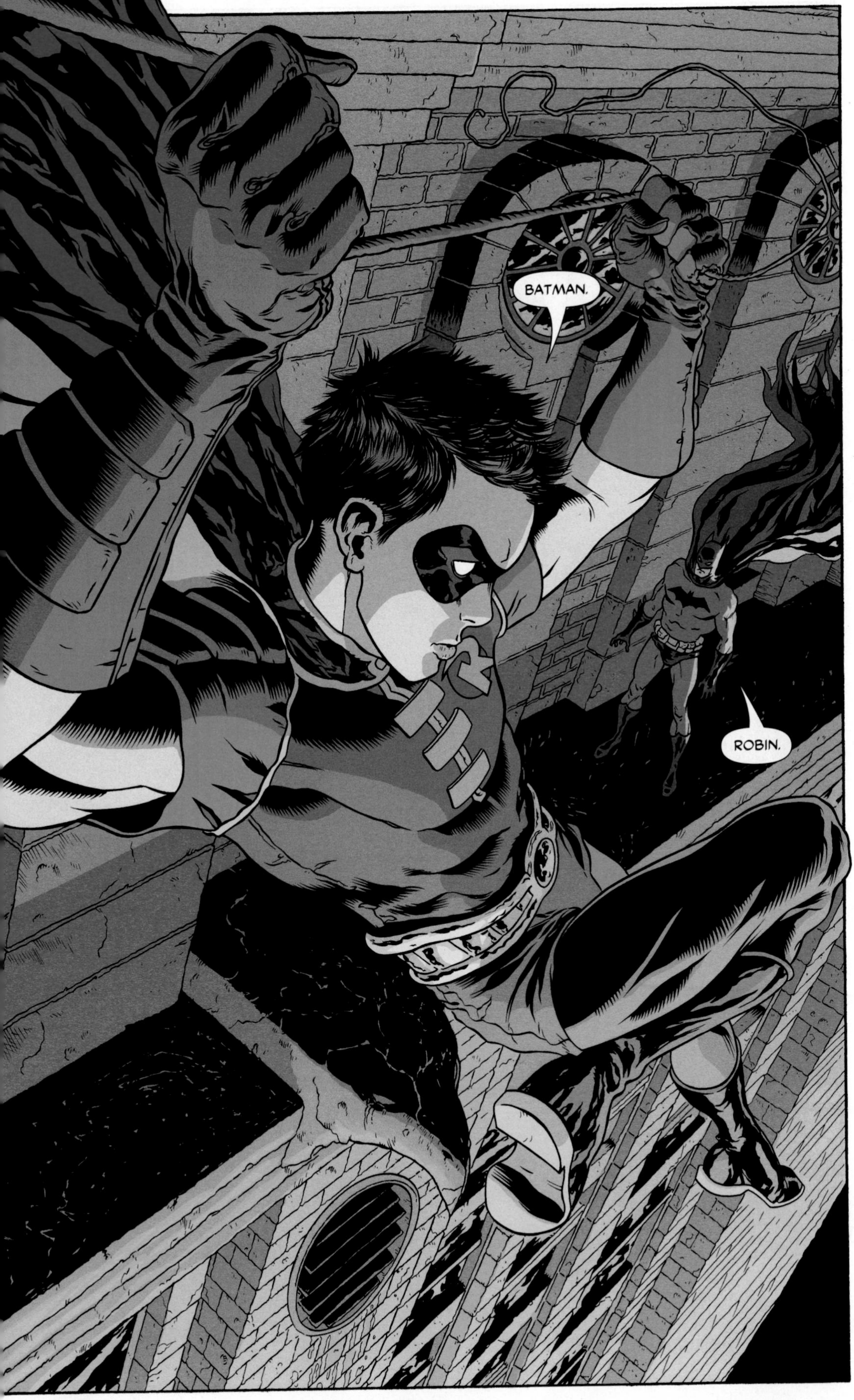
BATMAN.
ROBIN.

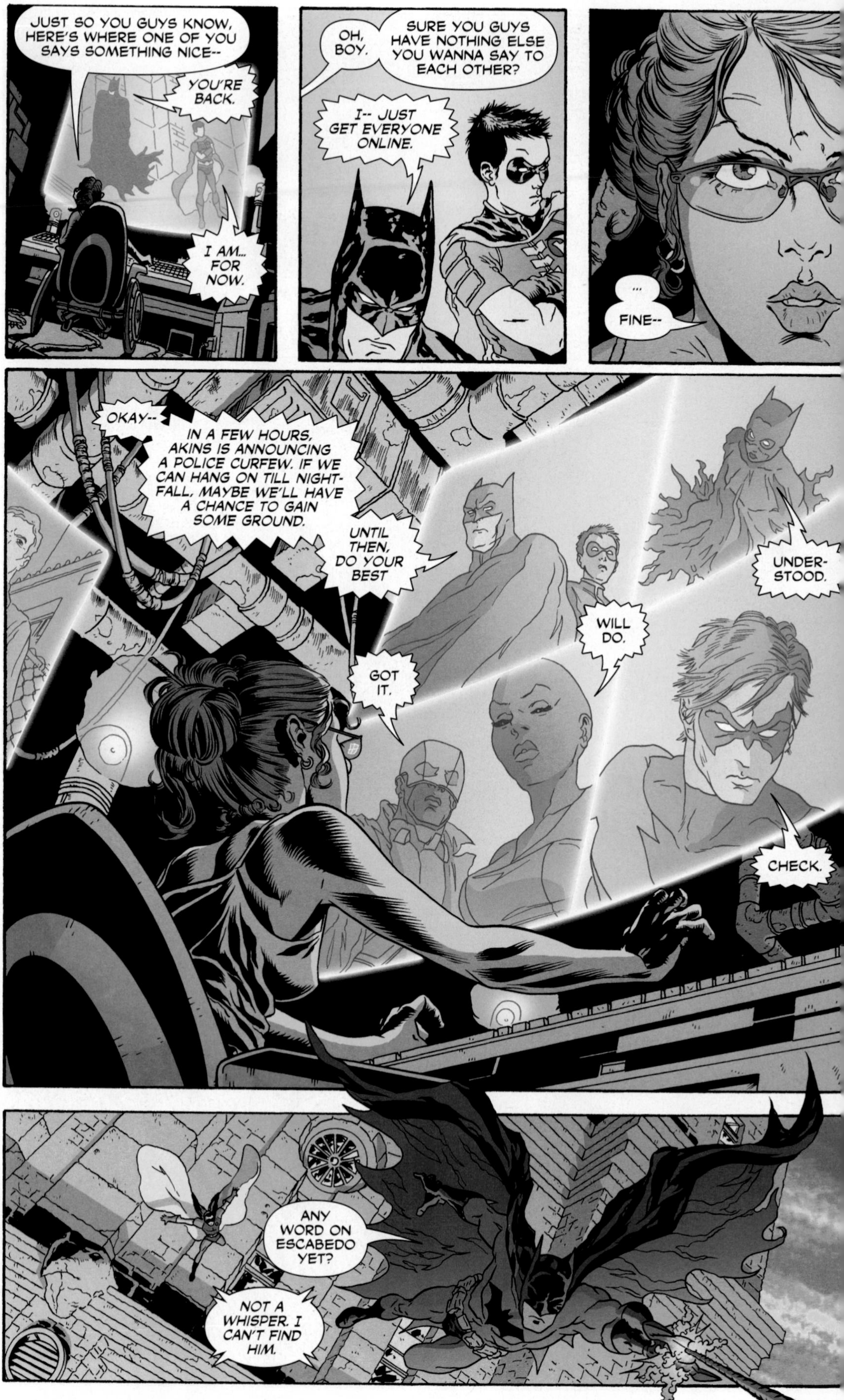
JUST SO YOU GUYS KNOW, HERE'S WHERE ONE OF YOU SAYS SOMETHING NICE--
YOU'RE BACK.
I AM... FOR NOW.
OH, BOY.
SURE YOU GUYS HAVE NOTHING ELSE YOU WANNA SAY TO EACH OTHER?
I-- JUST GET EVERYONE ONLINE.
... FINE--
OKAY--
IN A FEW HOURS, AKINS IS ANNOUNCING A POLICE CURFEW. IF WE CAN HANG ON TILL NIGHT-FALL, MAYBE WE'LL HAVE A CHANCE TO GAIN SOME GROUND.
UNTIL THEN, DO YOUR BEST
UNDER-STOOD.
WILL DO.
GOT IT.
CHECK.
ANY WORD ON ESCABEDO YET?
NOT A WHISPER. I CAN'T FIND HIM.

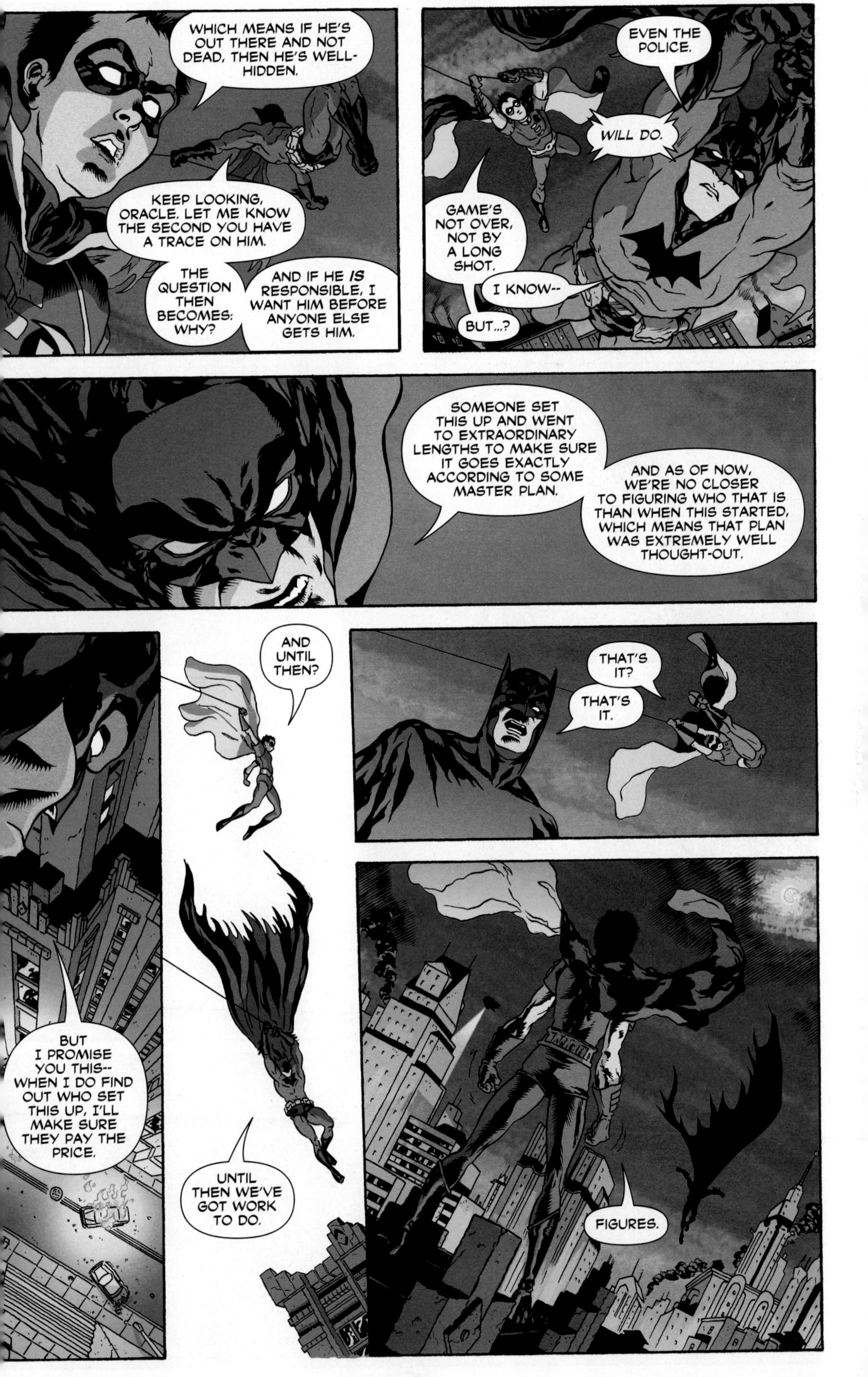
WHICH MEANS IF HE'S OUT THERE AND NOT DEAD, THEN HE'S WELL-HIDDEN.
KEEP LOOKING, ORACLE. LET ME KNOW THE SECOND YOU HAVE A TRACE ON HIM.
THE QUESTION THEN BECOMES: WHY?
AND IF HE *IS* RESPONSIBLE, I WANT HIM BEFORE ANYONE ELSE GETS HIM.
EVEN THE POLICE.
WILL DO.
GAME'S NOT OVER, NOT BY A LONG SHOT.
I KNOW--
BUT...?
SOMEONE SET THIS UP AND WENT TO EXTRAORDINARY LENGTHS TO MAKE SURE IT GOES EXACTLY ACCORDING TO SOME MASTER PLAN.
AND AS OF NOW, WE'RE NO CLOSER TO FIGURING WHO THAT IS THAN WHEN THIS STARTED, WHICH MEANS THAT PLAN WAS EXTREMELY WELL THOUGHT-OUT.
AND UNTIL THEN?
BUT I PROMISE YOU THIS-- WHEN I DO FIND OUT WHO SET THIS UP, I'LL MAKE SURE THEY PAY THE PRICE.
UNTIL THEN WE'VE GOT WORK TO DO.
THAT'S IT?
THAT'S IT.
FIGURES.

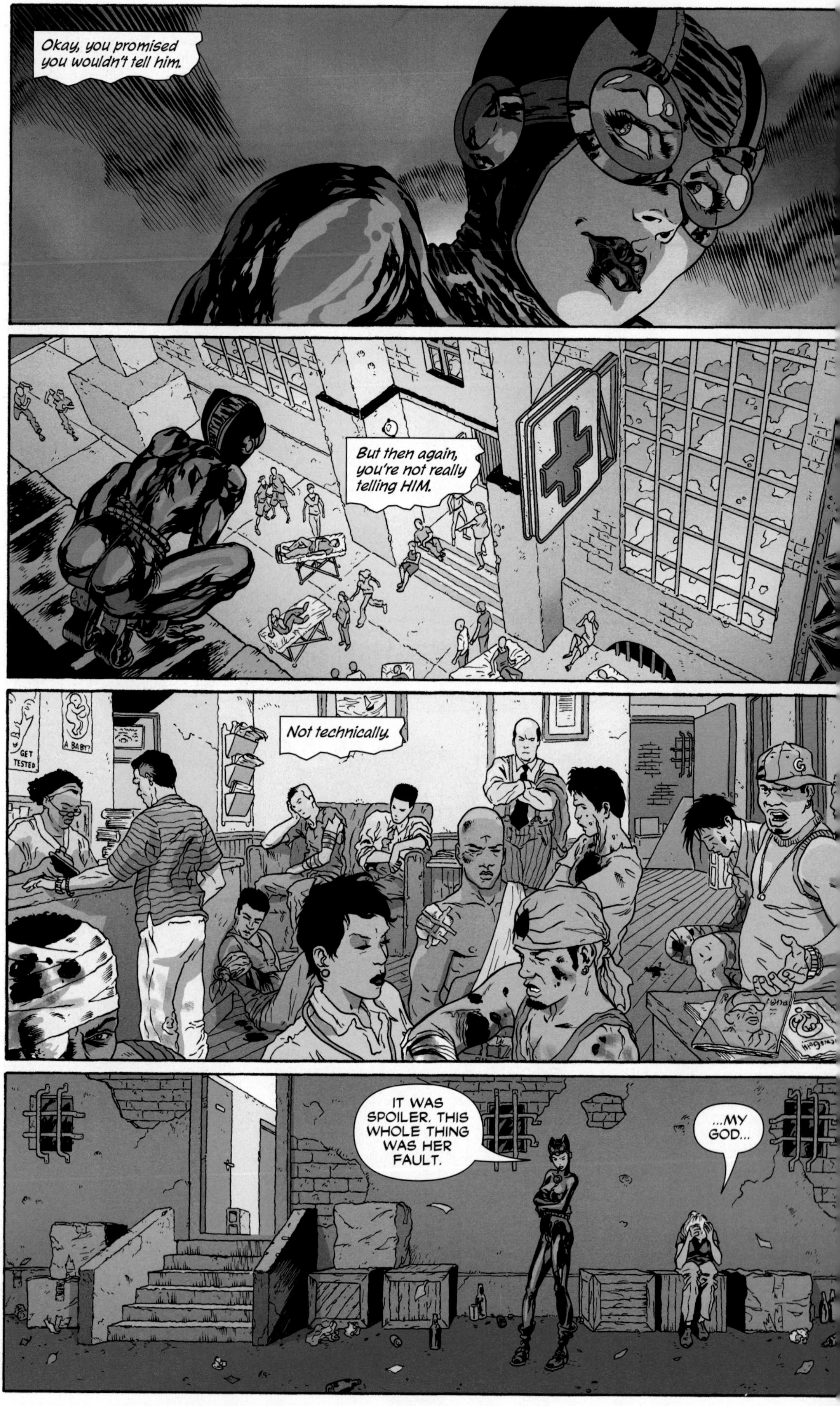
Okay, you promised you wouldn't tell him.
But then again, you're not really telling HIM.
GET TESTED
A BABY?
Not technically.
IT WAS SPOILER. THIS WHOLE THING WAS HER FAULT.
...MY GOD...

...BUT WHY?

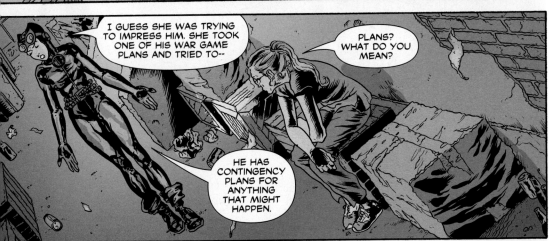

I GUESS SHE WAS TRYING TO IMPRESS HIM. SHE TOOK ONE OF HIS WAR GAME PLANS AND TRIED TO--

PLANS? WHAT DO YOU MEAN?

HE HAS CONTINGENCY PLANS FOR ANYTHING THAT MIGHT HAPPEN.

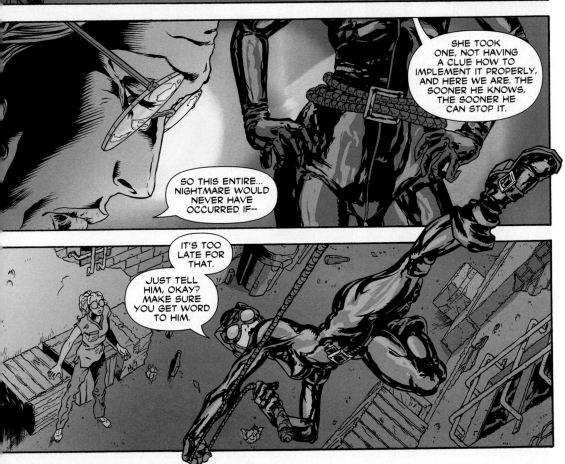

SHE TOOK ONE, NOT HAVING A CLUE HOW TO IMPLEMENT IT PROPERLY, AND HERE WE ARE. THE SOONER HE KNOWS, THE SOONER HE CAN STOP IT.

SO THIS ENTIRE... NIGHTMARE WOULD NEVER HAVE OCCURRED IF--

IT'S TOO LATE FOR THAT.

JUST TELL HIM, OKAY? MAKE SURE YOU GET WORD TO HIM.

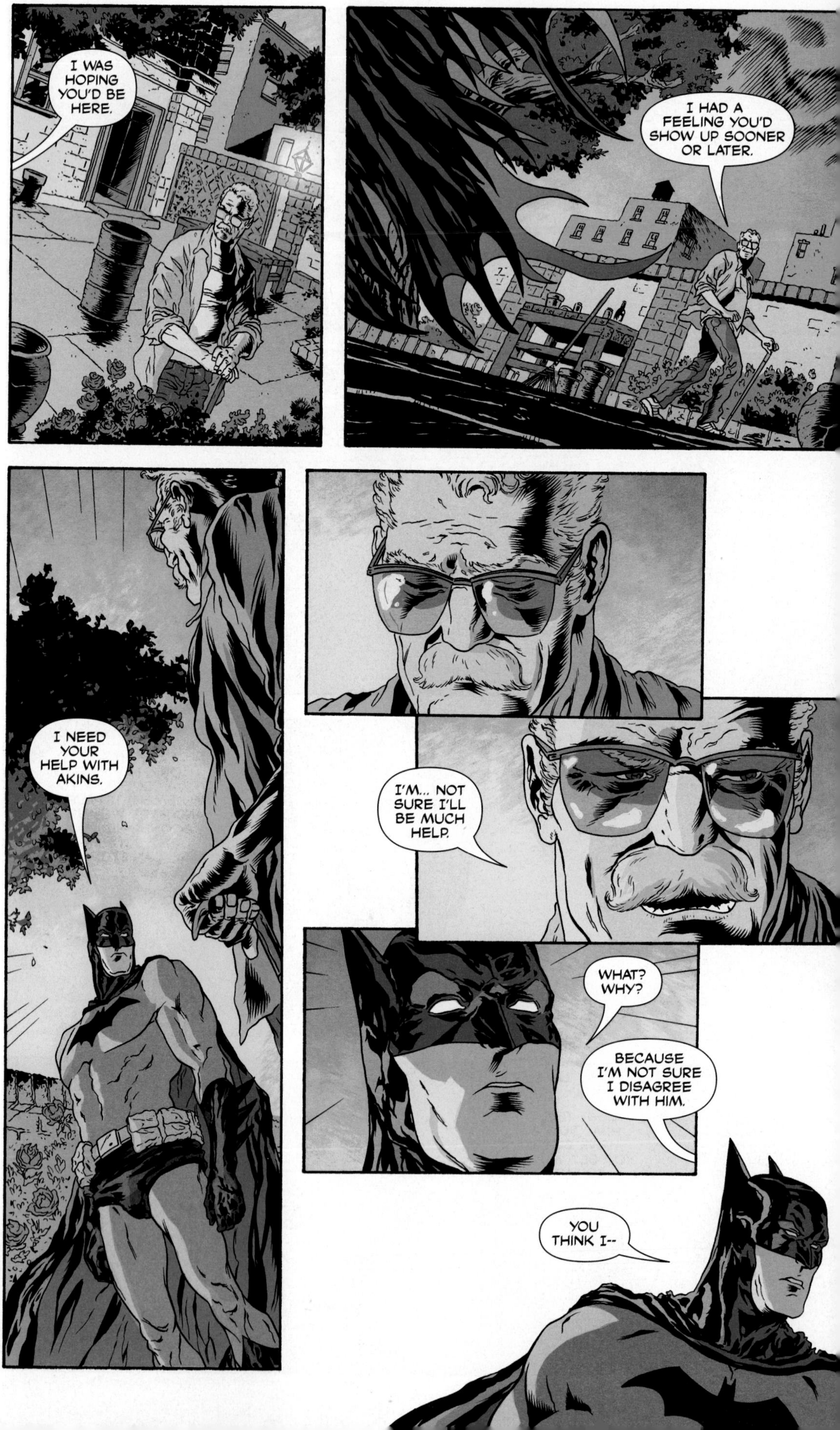
I WAS HOPING YOU'D BE HERE.
I HAD A FEELING YOU'D SHOW UP SOONER OR LATER.
I NEED YOUR HELP WITH AKINS.
I'M... NOT SURE I'LL BE MUCH HELP.
WHAT? WHY?
BECAUSE I'M NOT SURE I DISAGREE WITH HIM.
YOU THINK I--

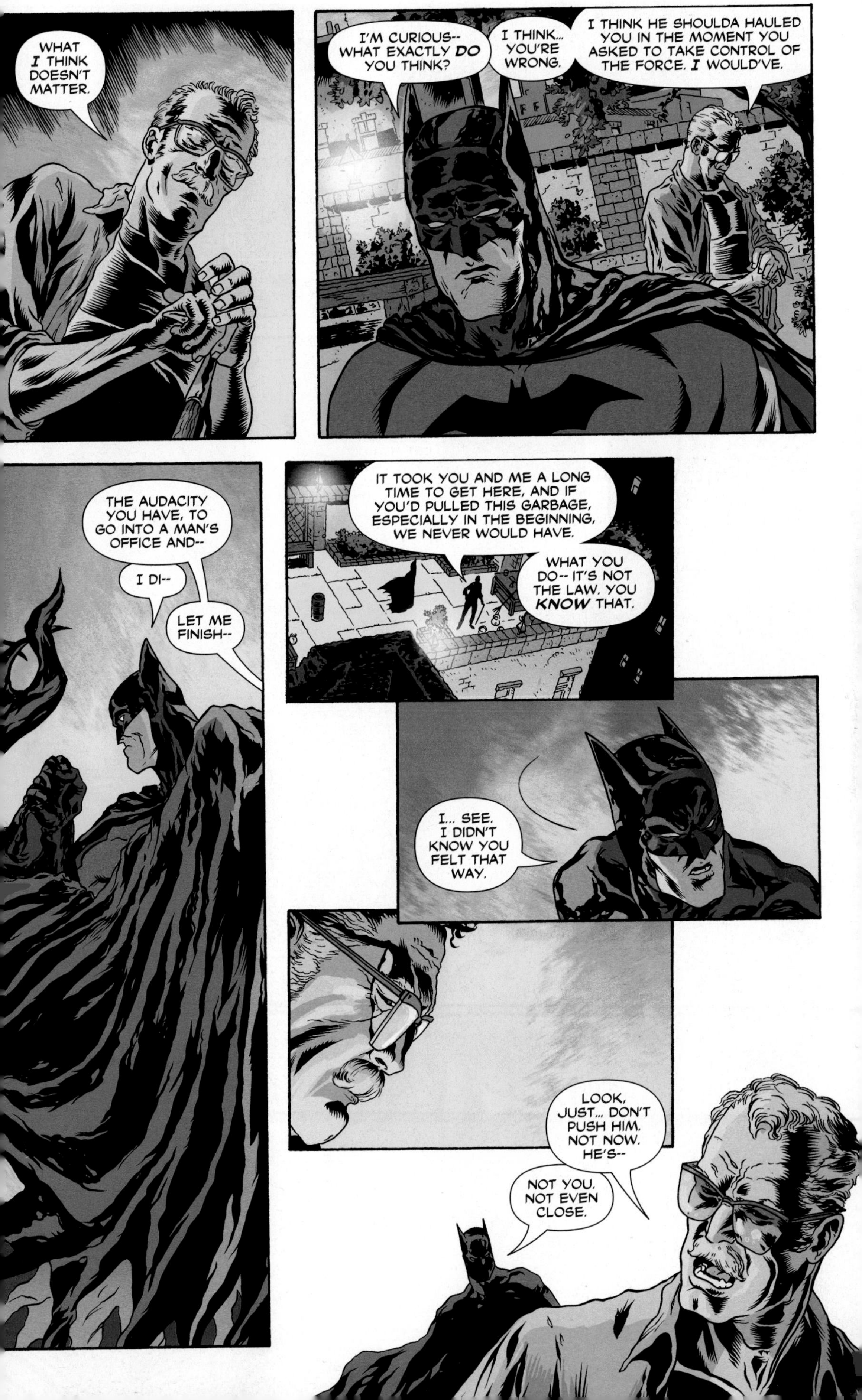
WHAT *I* THINK DOESN'T MATTER.
I'M CURIOUS-- WHAT EXACTLY *DO* YOU THINK?
I THINK... YOU'RE WRONG.
I THINK HE SHOULDA HAULED YOU IN THE MOMENT YOU ASKED TO TAKE CONTROL OF THE FORCE. *I* WOULD'VE.
THE AUDACITY YOU HAVE, TO GO INTO A MAN'S OFFICE AND--
I DI--
LET ME FINISH--
IT TOOK YOU AND ME A LONG TIME TO GET HERE, AND IF YOU'D PULLED THIS GARBAGE, ESPECIALLY IN THE BEGINNING, WE NEVER WOULD HAVE.
WHAT YOU DO-- IT'S NOT THE LAW. YOU *KNOW* THAT.
I... SEE. I DIDN'T KNOW YOU FELT THAT WAY.
LOOK, JUST... DON'T PUSH HIM. NOT NOW. HE'S--
NOT YOU. NOT EVEN CLOSE.

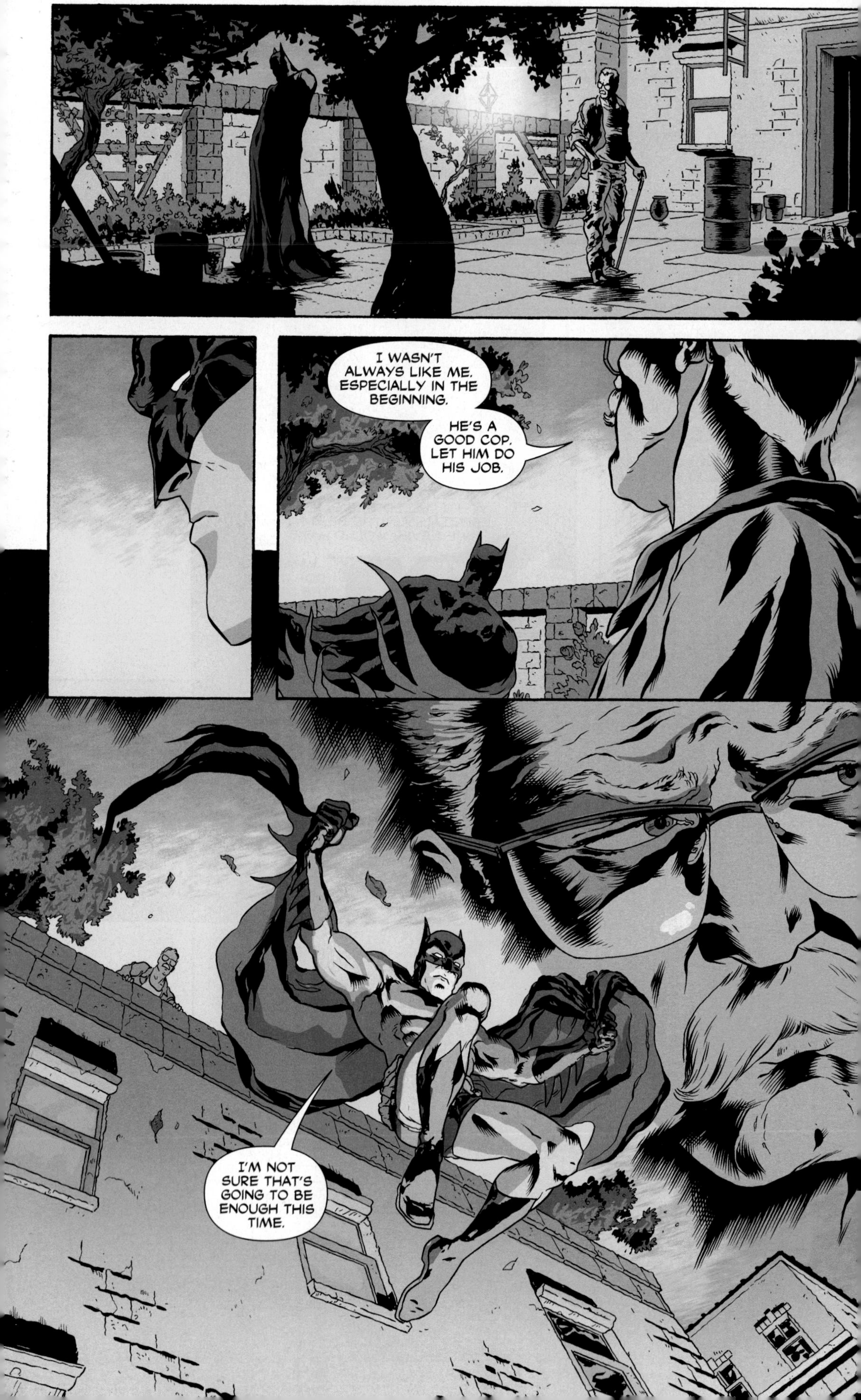
I WASN'T ALWAYS LIKE ME. ESPECIALLY IN THE BEGINNING.
HE'S A GOOD COP. LET HIM DO HIS JOB.
I'M NOT SURE THAT'S GOING TO BE ENOUGH THIS TIME.

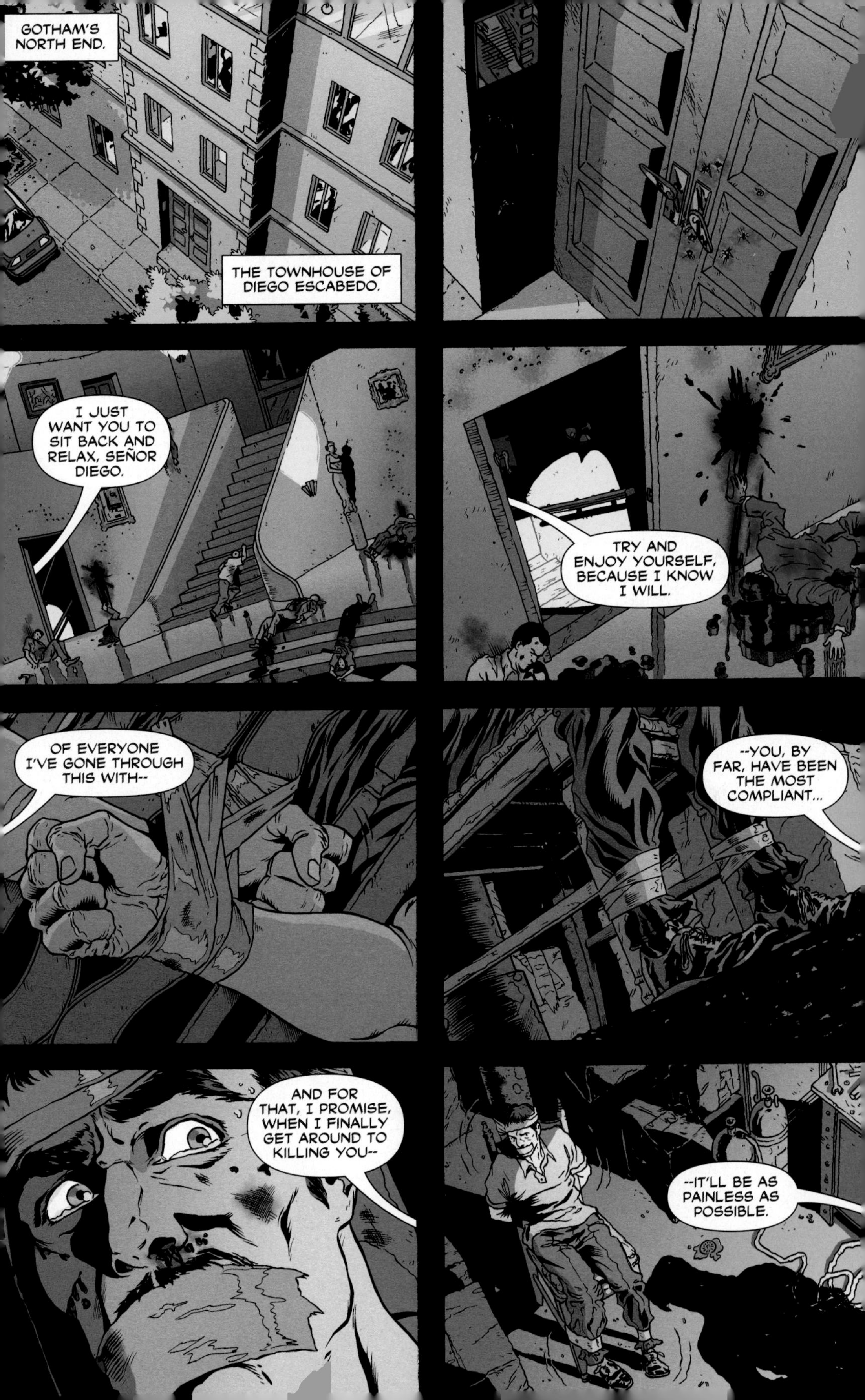
GOTHAM'S NORTH END.
THE TOWNHOUSE OF DIEGO ESCABEDO.
I JUST WANT YOU TO SIT BACK AND RELAX, SEÑOR DIEGO.
TRY AND ENJOY YOURSELF, BECAUSE I KNOW I WILL.
OF EVERYONE I'VE GONE THROUGH THIS WITH--
--YOU, BY FAR, HAVE BEEN THE MOST COMPLIANT...
AND FOR THAT, I PROMISE, WHEN I FINALLY GET AROUND TO KILLING YOU--
--IT'LL BE AS PAINLESS AS POSSIBLE.

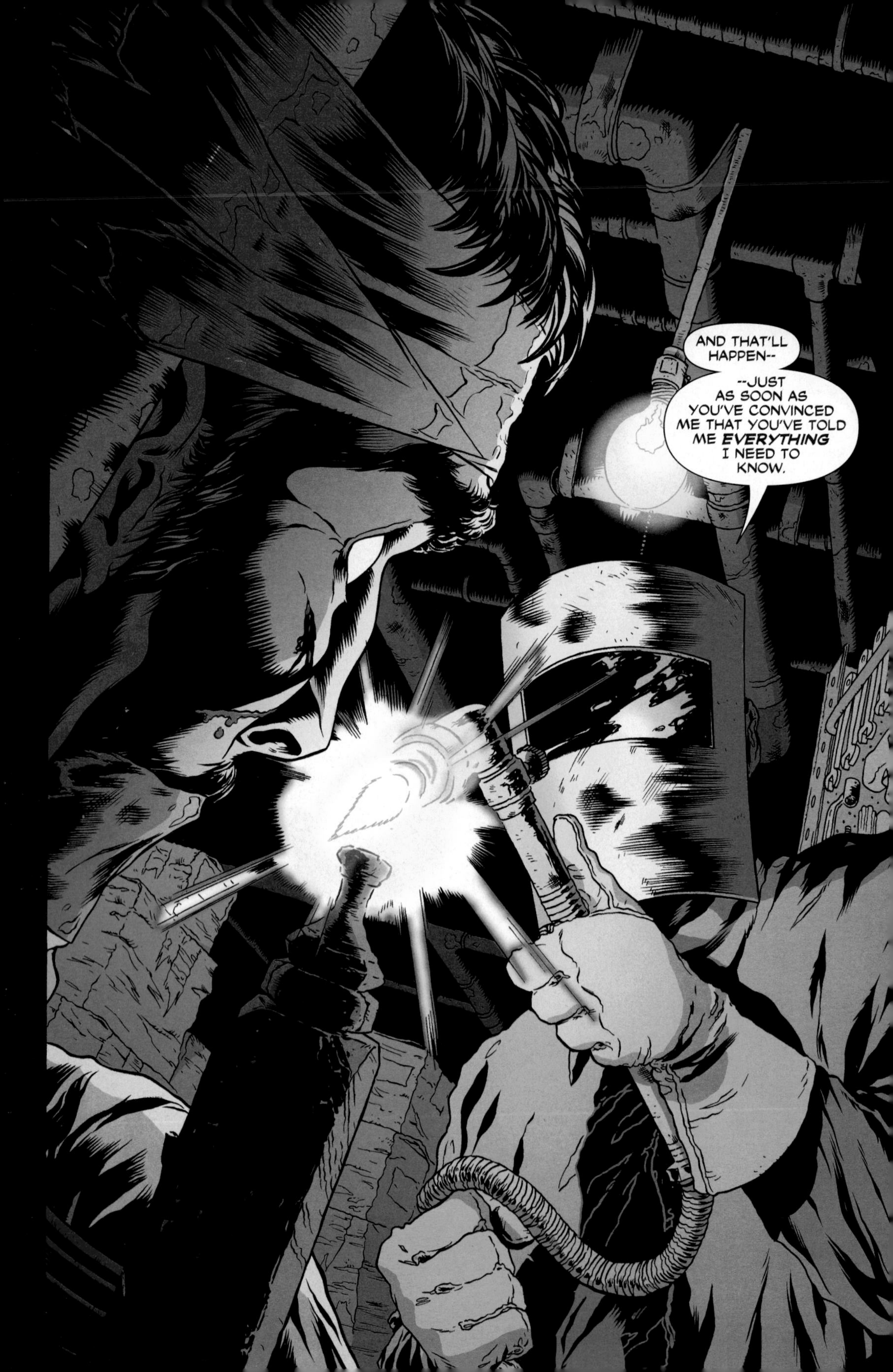
AND THAT'LL HAPPEN--
--JUST AS SOON AS YOU'VE CONVINCED ME THAT YOU'VE TOLD ME *EVERYTHING* I NEED TO KNOW.

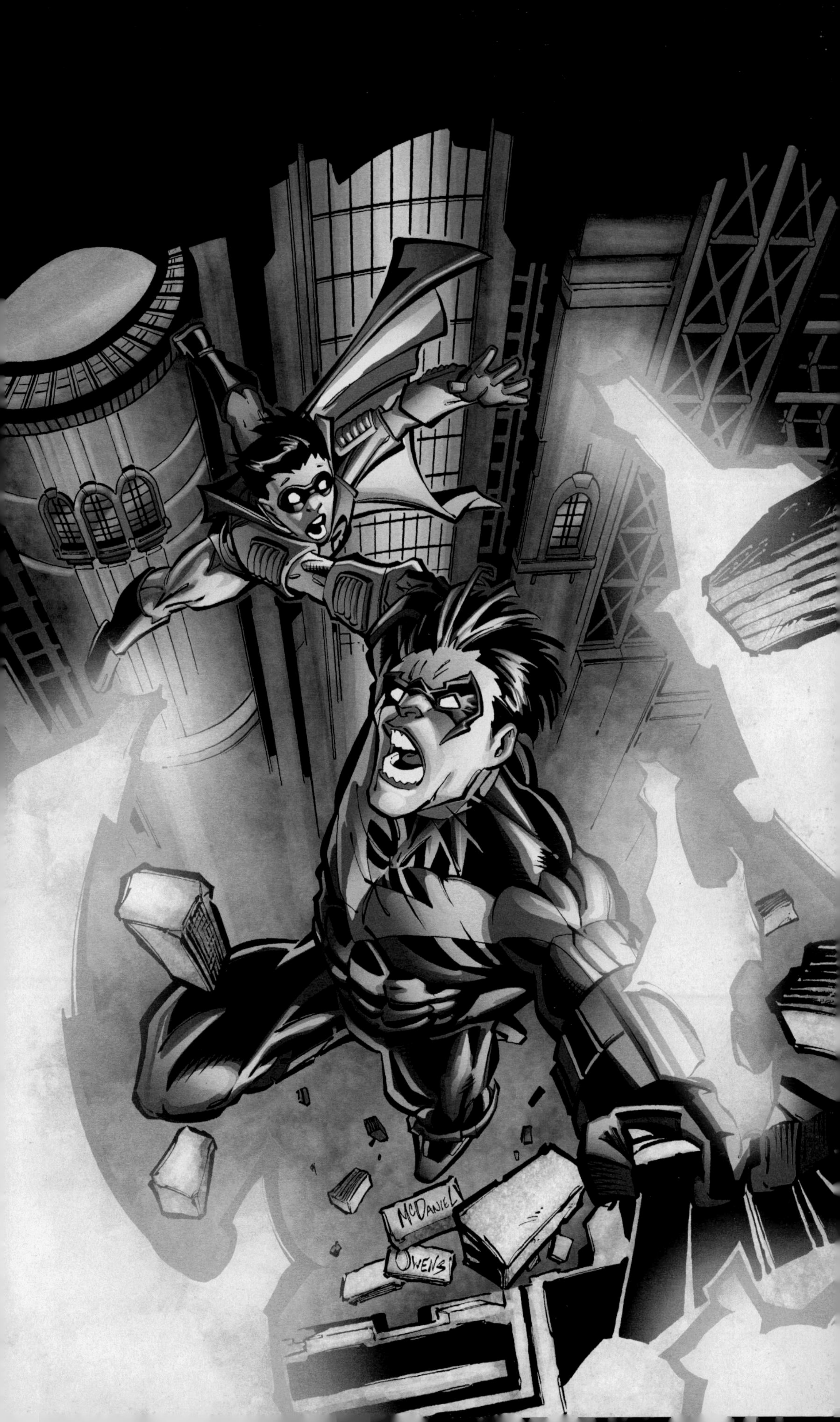
McDANIEL
OWENS

COVER ART BY
SCOTT MCDANIEL,
ANDY OWENS,
& NATHAN EYRING

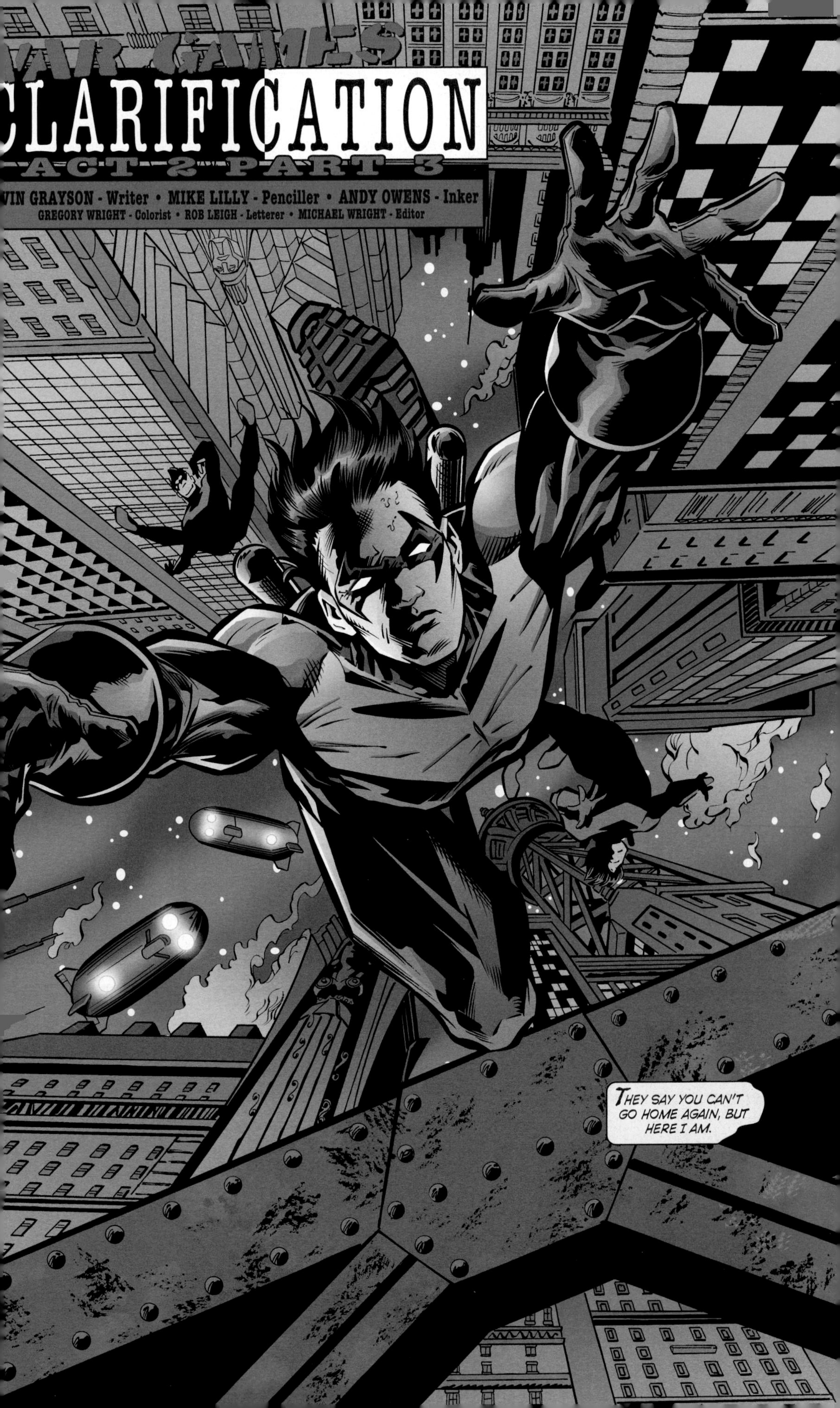

WAR GAMES
CLARIFICATION
ACT 2 PART 3
VIN GRAYSON - Writer • MIKE LILLY - Penciller • ANDY OWENS - Inker
GREGORY WRIGHT - Colorist • ROB LEIGH - Letterer • MICHAEL WRIGHT - Editor
THEY SAY YOU CAN'T GO HOME AGAIN, BUT HERE I AM.

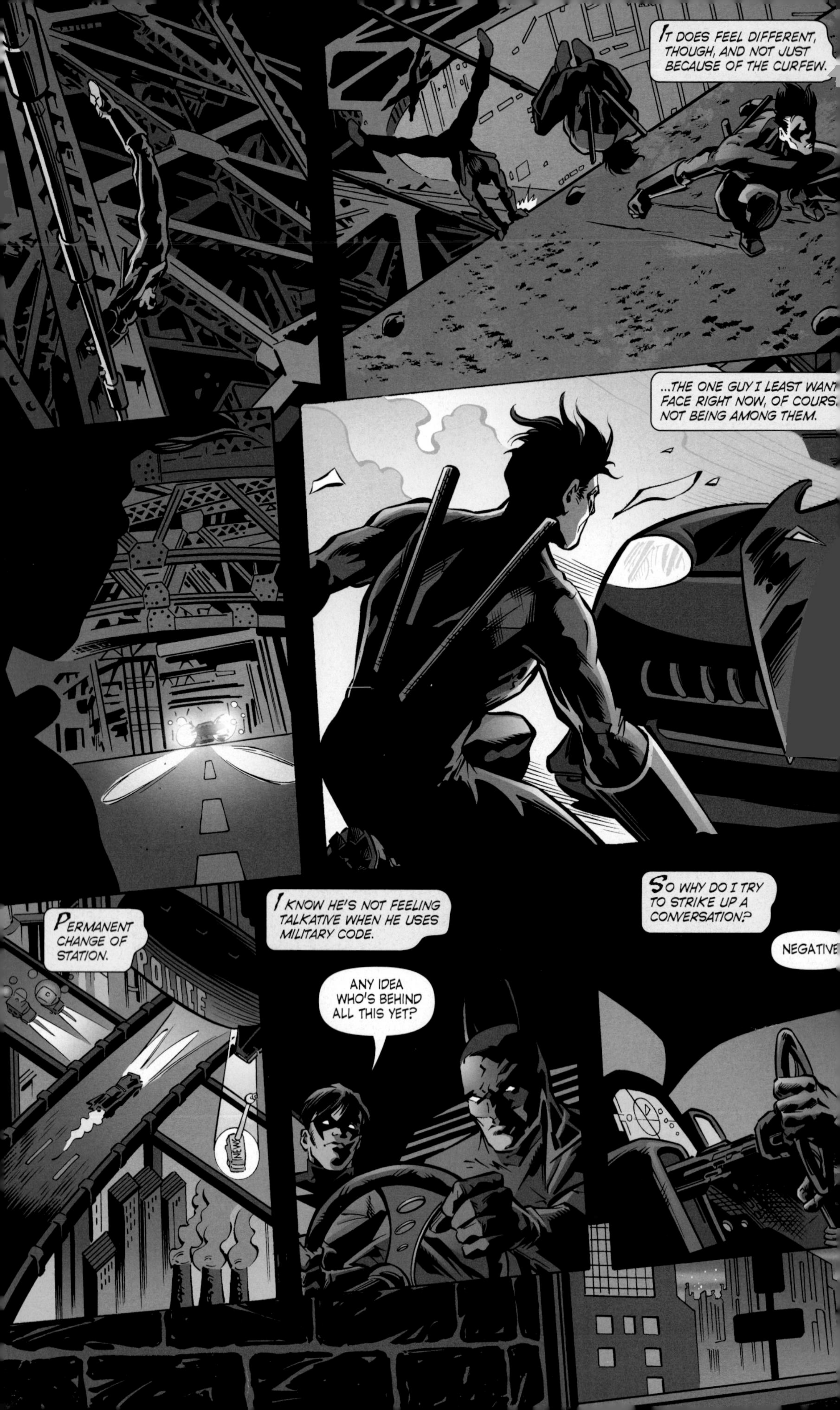
IT DOES FEEL DIFFERENT, THOUGH, AND NOT JUST BECAUSE OF THE CURFEW.
...THE ONE GUY I LEAST WANT FACE RIGHT NOW, OF COURS NOT BEING AMONG THEM.
PERMANENT CHANGE OF STATION.
POLICE
NEWS
I KNOW HE'S NOT FEELING TALKATIVE WHEN HE USES MILITARY CODE.
ANY IDEA WHO'S BEHIND ALL THIS YET?
SO WHY DO I TRY TO STRIKE UP A CONVERSATION?
NEGATIVE

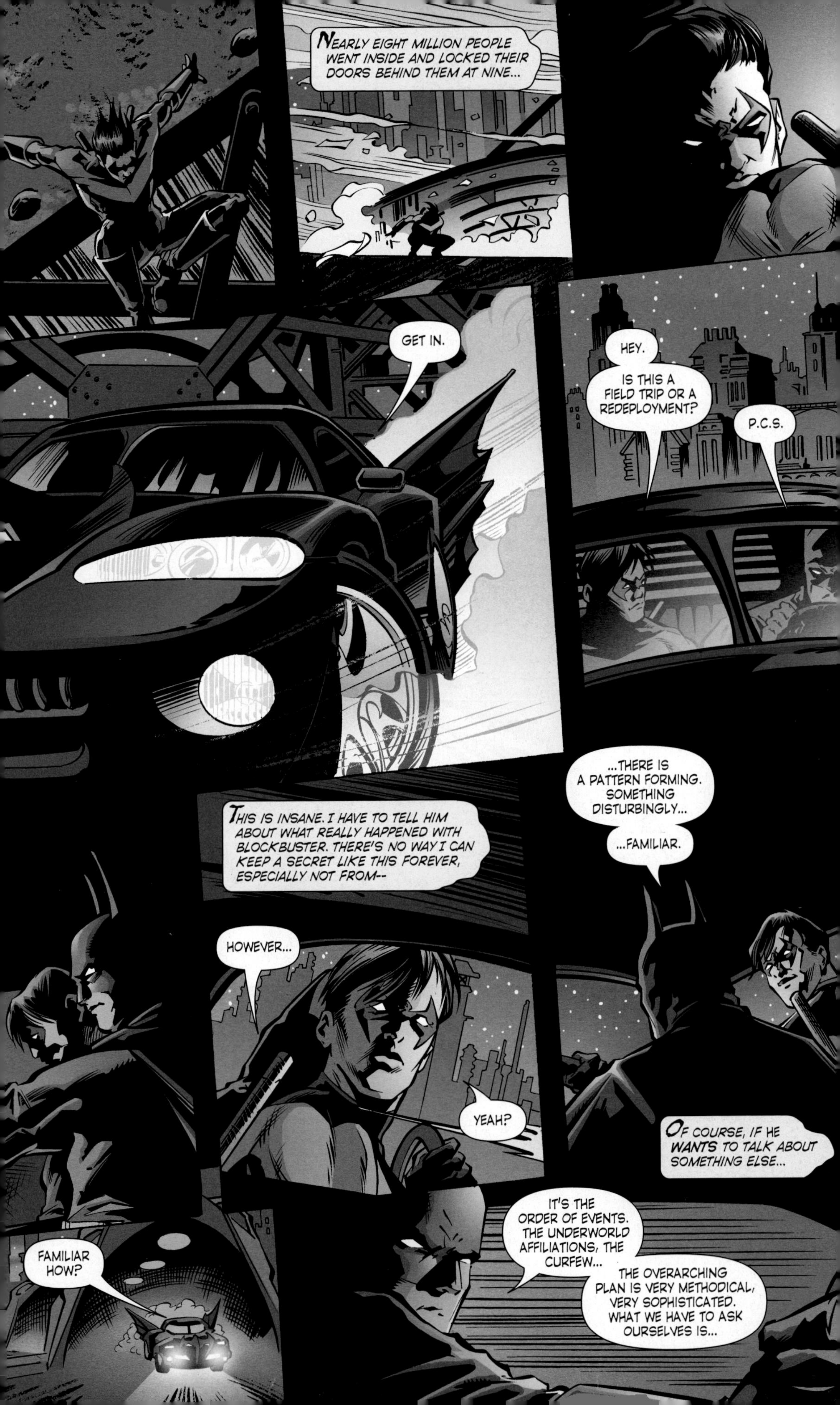
NEARLY EIGHT MILLION PEOPLE WENT INSIDE AND LOCKED THEIR DOORS BEHIND THEM AT NINE...
GET IN.
HEY.
IS THIS A FIELD TRIP OR A REDEPLOYMENT?
P.C.S.
THIS IS INSANE. I HAVE TO TELL HIM ABOUT WHAT REALLY HAPPENED WITH BLOCKBUSTER. THERE'S NO WAY I CAN KEEP A SECRET LIKE THIS FOREVER, ESPECIALLY NOT FROM--
HOWEVER...
YEAH?
...THERE IS A PATTERN FORMING. SOMETHING DISTURBINGLY...
...FAMILIAR.
OF COURSE, IF HE WANTS TO TALK ABOUT SOMETHING ELSE...
FAMILIAR HOW?
IT'S THE ORDER OF EVENTS. THE UNDERWORLD AFFILIATIONS, THE CURFEW...
THE OVERARCHING PLAN IS VERY METHODICAL, VERY SOPHISTICATED. WHAT WE HAVE TO ASK OURSELVES IS...

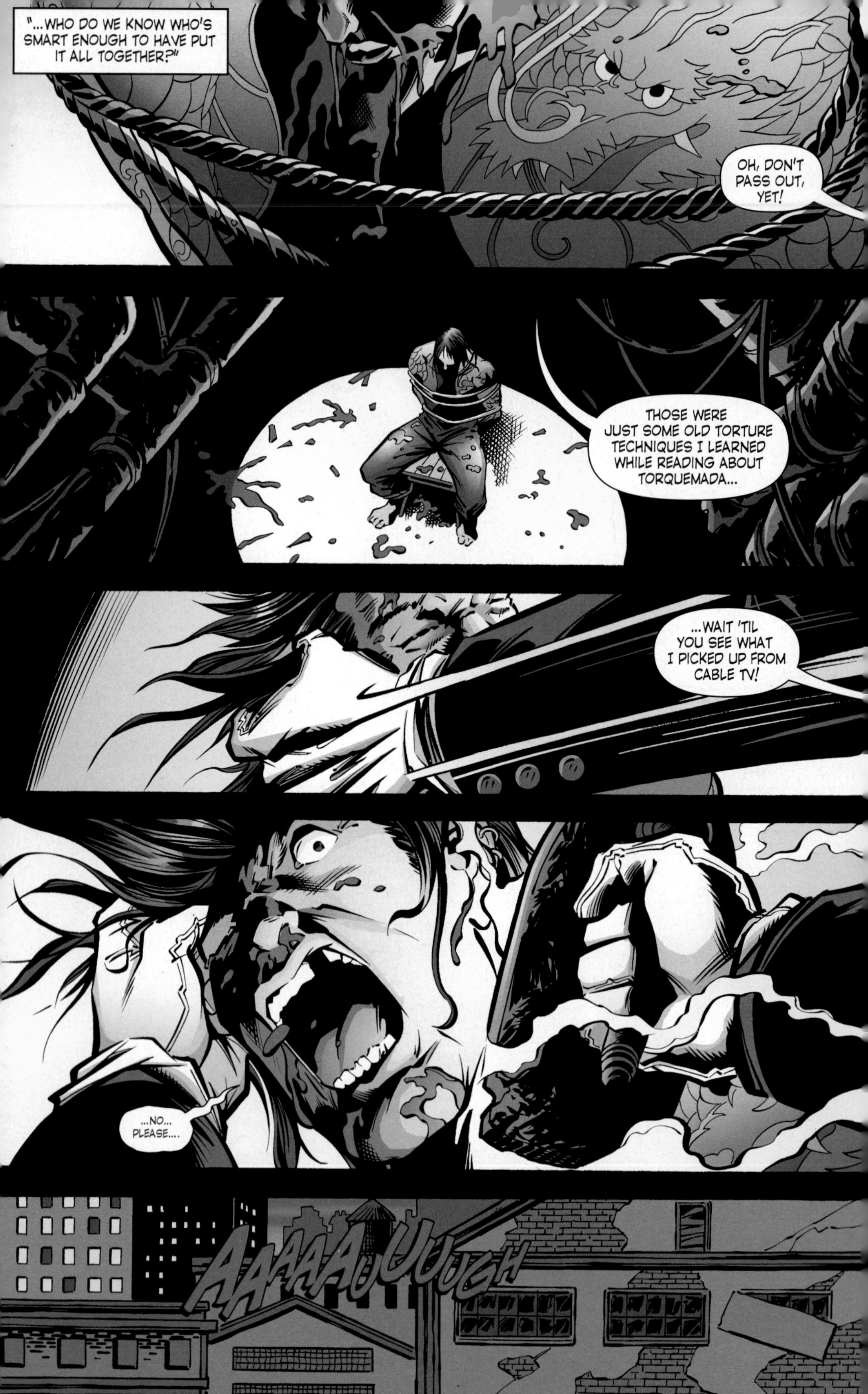
"...WHO DO WE KNOW WHO'S SMART ENOUGH TO HAVE PUT IT ALL TOGETHER?"
OH, DON'T PASS OUT, YET!
THOSE WERE JUST SOME OLD TORTURE TECHNIQUES I LEARNED WHILE READING ABOUT TORQUEMADA...
...WAIT 'TIL YOU SEE WHAT I PICKED UP FROM CABLE TV!
...NO... PLEASE....
AAAAAUUUGH

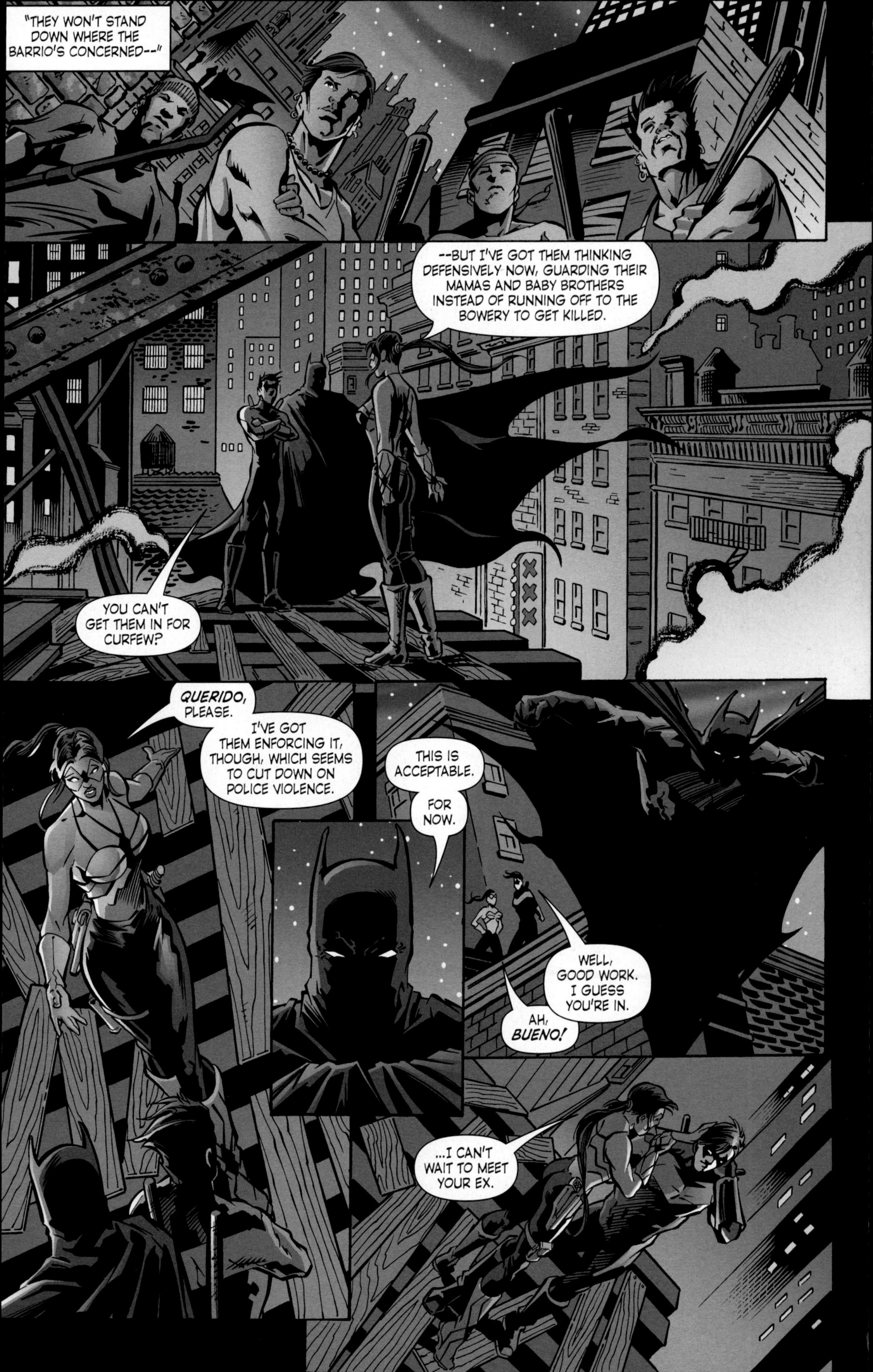
"THEY WON'T STAND DOWN WHERE THE BARRIO'S CONCERNED--"
--BUT I'VE GOT THEM THINKING DEFENSIVELY NOW, GUARDING THEIR MAMAS AND BABY BROTHERS INSTEAD OF RUNNING OFF TO THE BOWERY TO GET KILLED.
YOU CAN'T GET THEM IN FOR CURFEW?
QUERIDO, PLEASE.
I'VE GOT THEM ENFORCING IT, THOUGH, WHICH SEEMS TO CUT DOWN ON POLICE VIOLENCE.
THIS IS ACCEPTABLE.
FOR NOW.
WELL, GOOD WORK. I GUESS YOU'RE IN.
AH, *BUENO!*
...I CAN'T WAIT TO MEET YOUR EX.

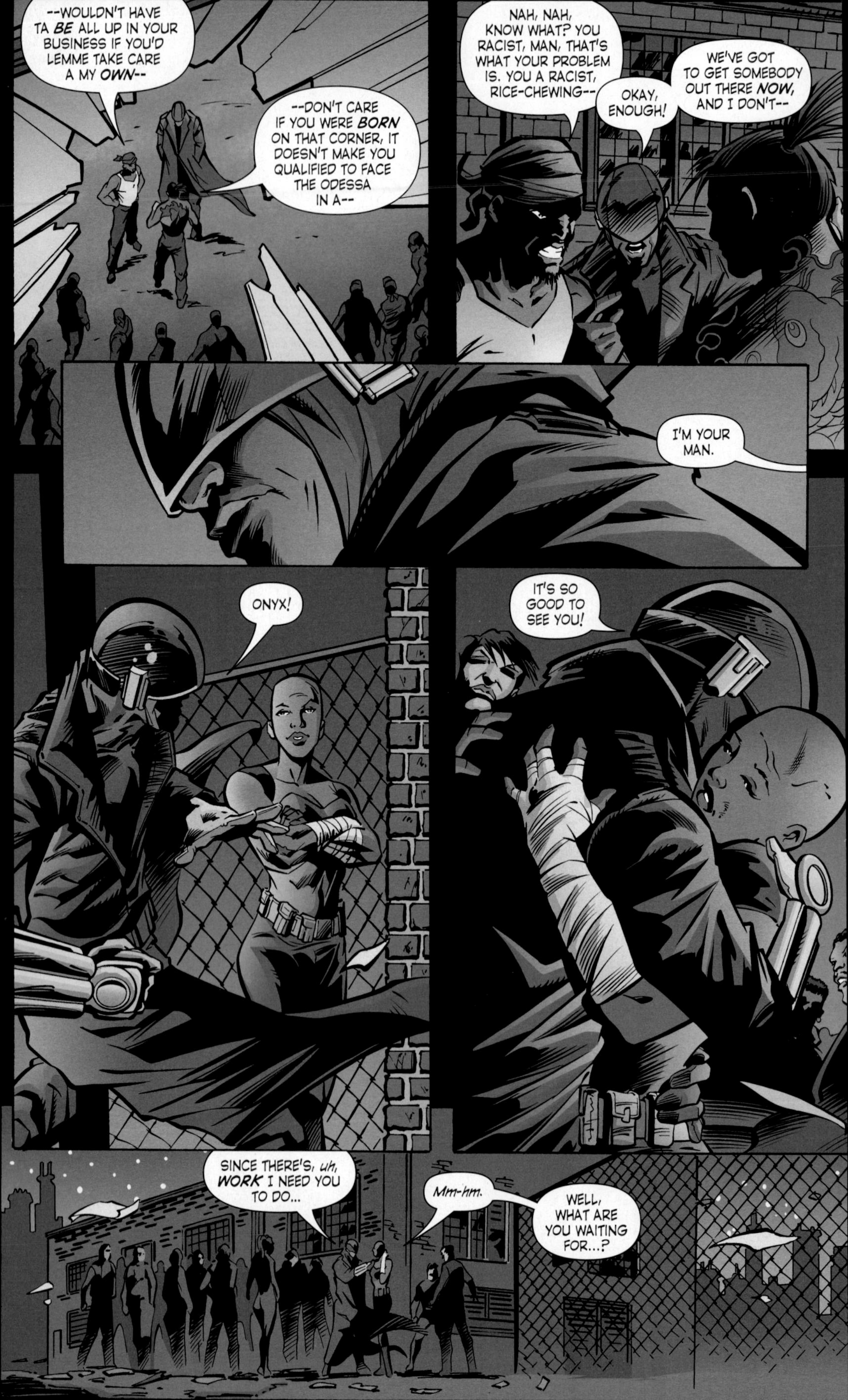
--WOULDN'T HAVE TA *BE* ALL UP IN YOUR BUSINESS IF YOU'D LEMME TAKE CARE A MY *OWN*--
--DON'T CARE IF YOU WERE *BORN* ON THAT CORNER, IT DOESN'T MAKE YOU QUALIFIED TO FACE THE ODESSA IN A--
NAH, NAH, KNOW WHAT? YOU RACIST, MAN, THAT'S WHAT YOUR PROBLEM IS. YOU A RACIST, RICE-CHEWING--
OKAY, ENOUGH!
WE'VE GOT TO GET SOMEBODY OUT THERE *NOW*, AND I DON'T--
I'M YOUR MAN.
ONYX!
IT'S SO GOOD TO SEE YOU!
SINCE THERE'S, *uh*, ***WORK*** I NEED YOU TO DO...
Mm-hm.
WELL, WHAT ARE YOU WAITING FOR...?

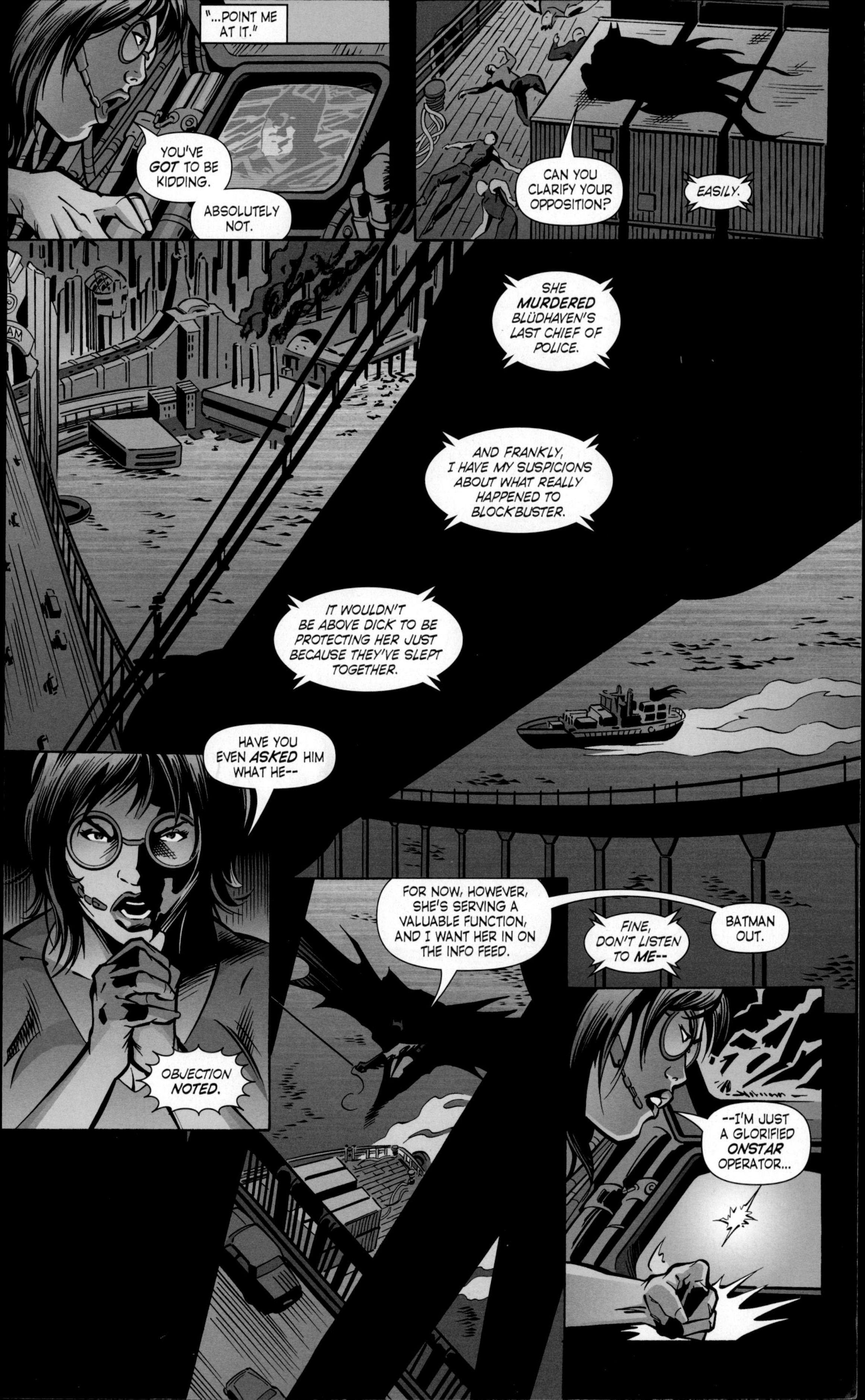
"...POINT ME AT IT."
YOU'VE GOT TO BE KIDDING.
ABSOLUTELY NOT.
CAN YOU CLARIFY YOUR OPPOSITION?
EASILY.
SHE MURDERED BLÜDHAVEN'S LAST CHIEF OF POLICE.
AND FRANKLY, I HAVE MY SUSPICIONS ABOUT WHAT REALLY HAPPENED TO BLOCKBUSTER.
IT WOULDN'T BE ABOVE DICK TO BE PROTECTING HER JUST BECAUSE THEY'VE SLEPT TOGETHER.
HAVE YOU EVEN ASKED HIM WHAT HE--
OBJECTION NOTED.
FOR NOW, HOWEVER, SHE'S SERVING A VALUABLE FUNCTION, AND I WANT HER IN ON THE INFO FEED.
BATMAN OUT.
FINE, DON'T LISTEN TO ME--
--I'M JUST A GLORIFIED ONSTAR OPERATOR...

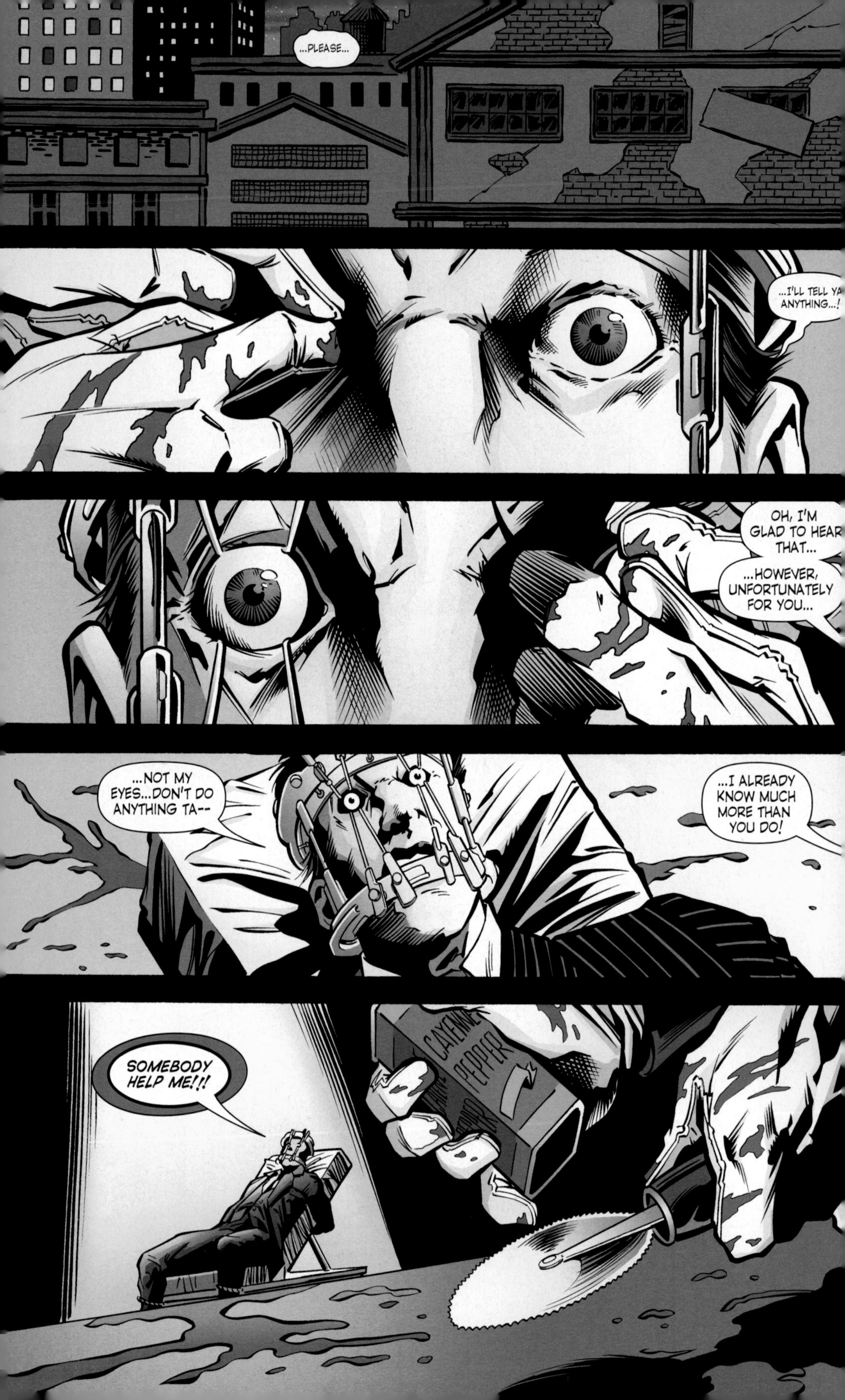
...PLEASE...
...I'LL TELL YA ANYTHING...!
OH, I'M GLAD TO HEAR THAT...
...HOWEVER, UNFORTUNATELY FOR YOU...
...NOT MY EYES...DON'T DO ANYTHING TA--
...I ALREADY KNOW MUCH MORE THAN YOU DO!
SOMEBODY HELP ME!!!
CAYENNE PEPPER

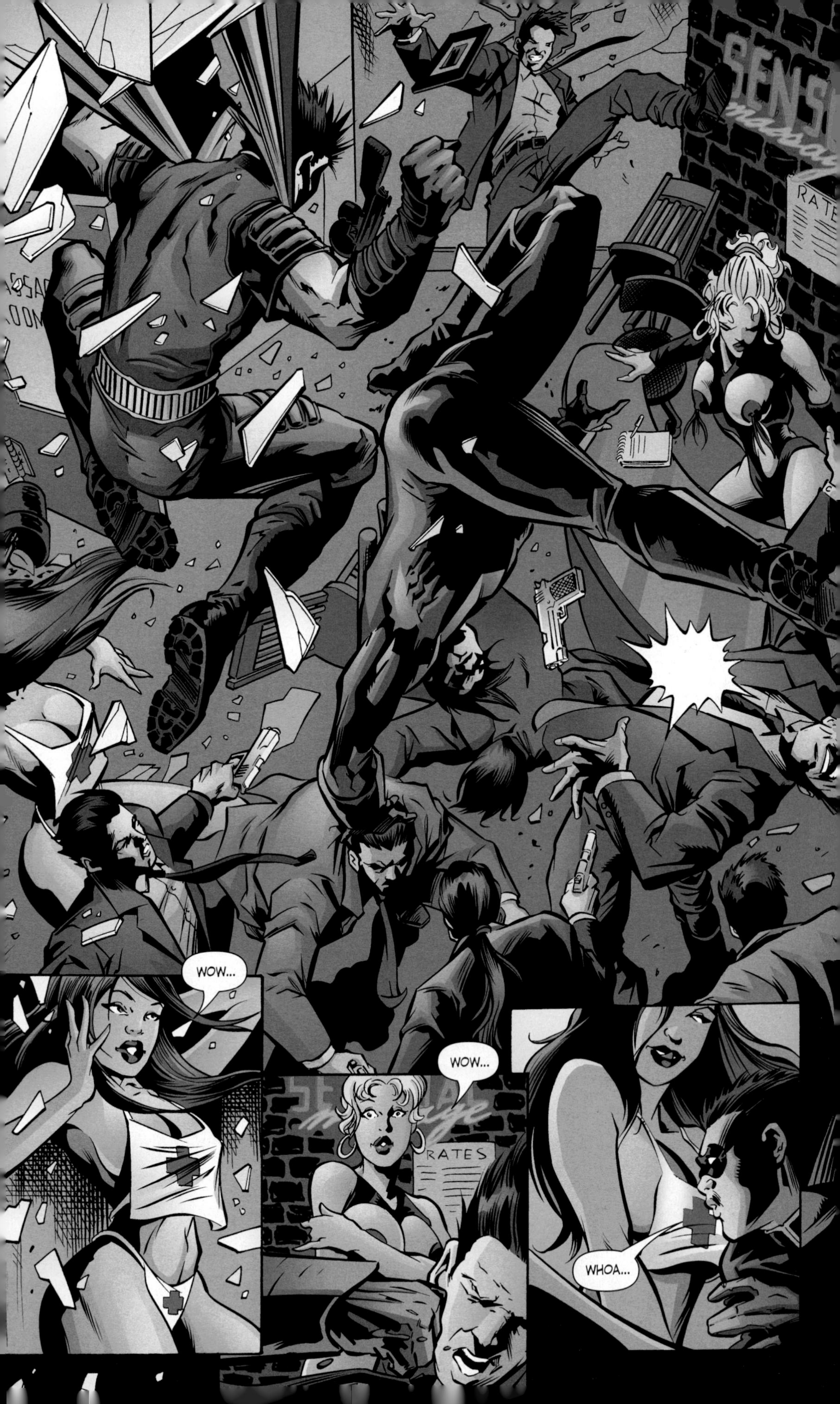
WOW...
WOW...
RATES
WHOA...

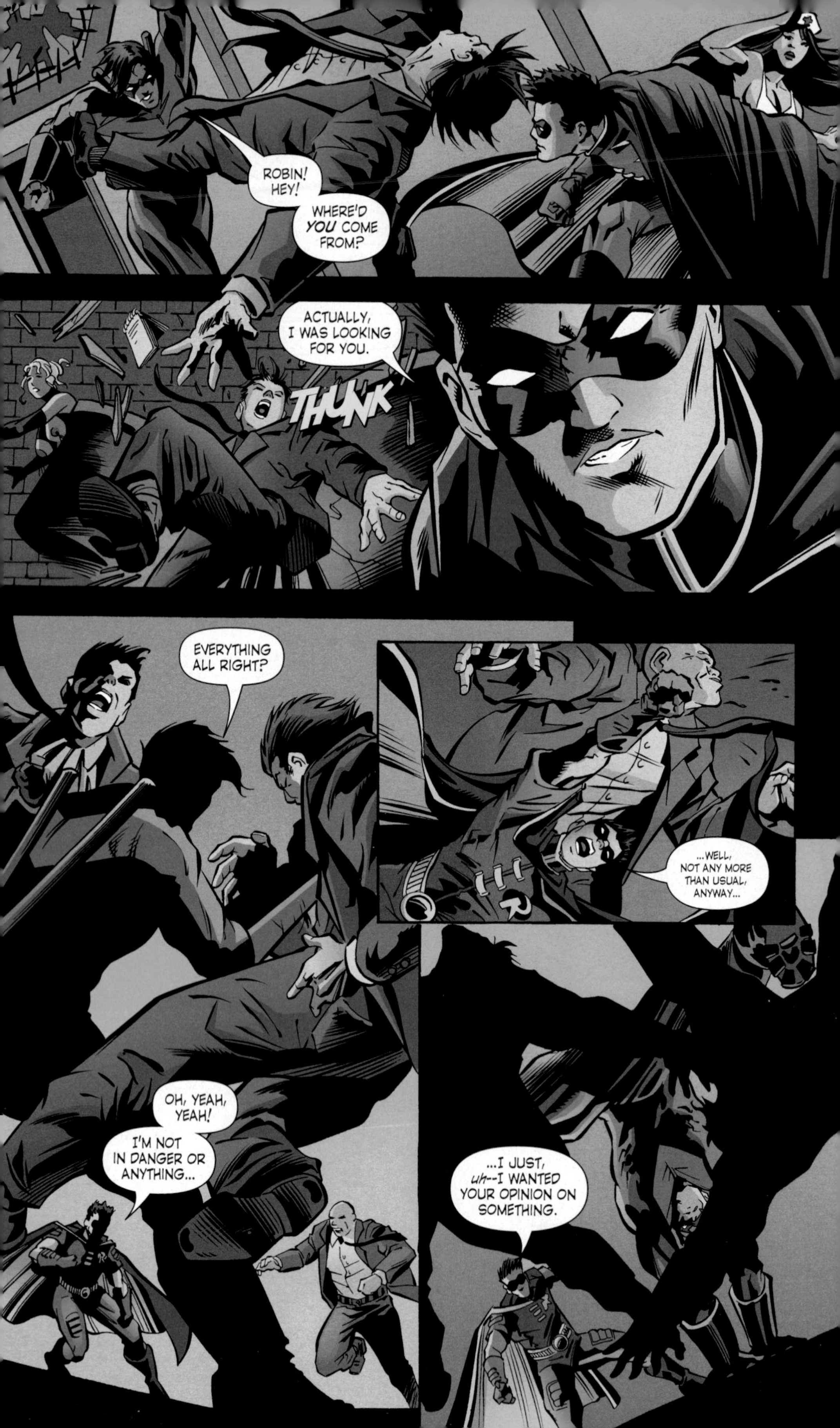
ROBIN! HEY!
WHERE'D YOU COME FROM?
ACTUALLY, I WAS LOOKING FOR YOU.
THUNK
EVERYTHING ALL RIGHT?
...WELL, NOT ANY MORE THAN USUAL, ANYWAY...
OH, YEAH, YEAH!
I'M NOT IN DANGER OR ANYTHING...
...I JUST, uh--I WANTED YOUR OPINION ON SOMETHING.

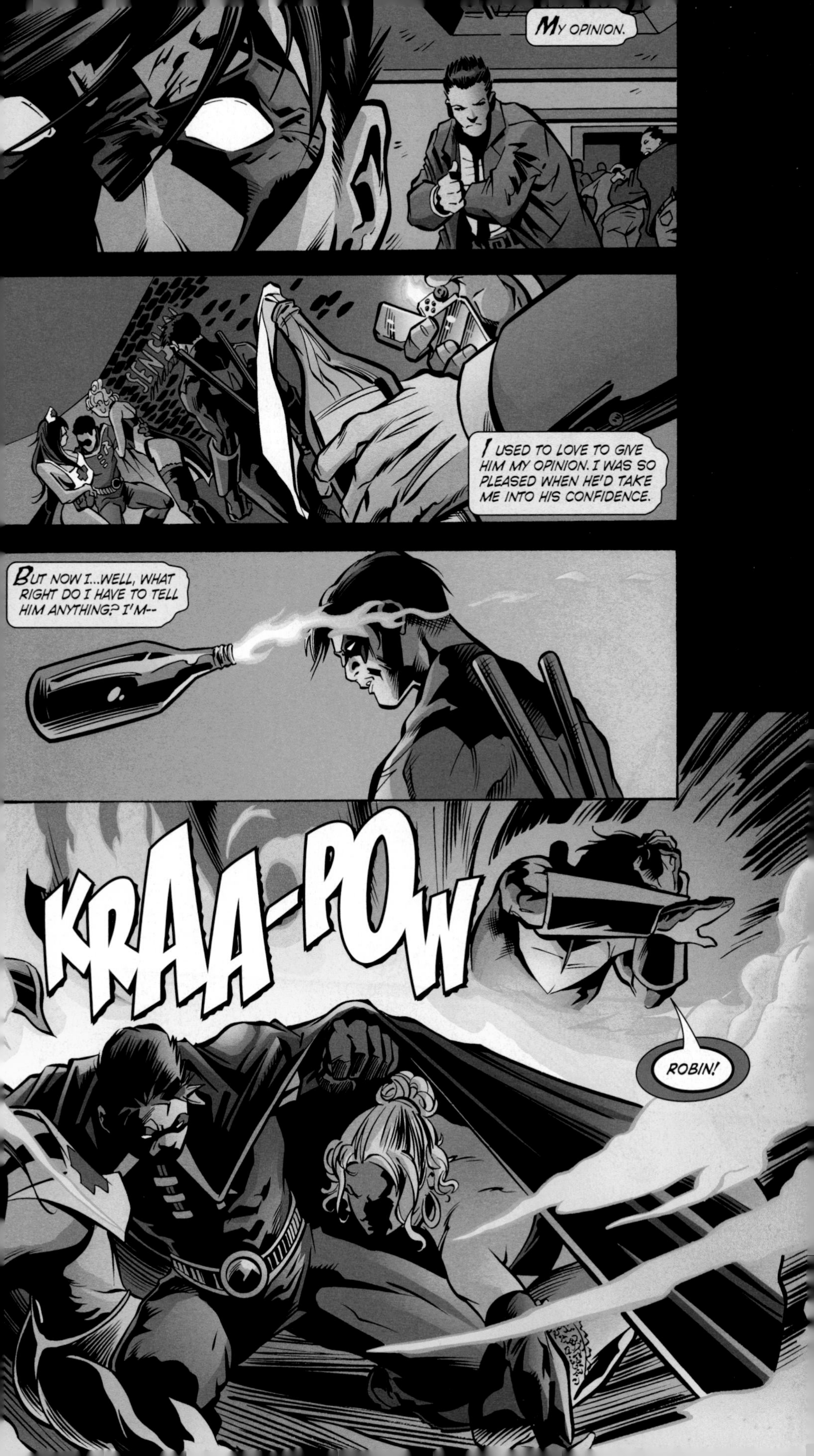
MY OPINION.
I USED TO LOVE TO GIVE HIM MY OPINION. I WAS SO PLEASED WHEN HE'D TAKE ME INTO HIS CONFIDENCE.
BUT NOW I...WELL, WHAT RIGHT DO I HAVE TO TELL HIM ANYTHING? I'M--
KRAA-POW
ROBIN!

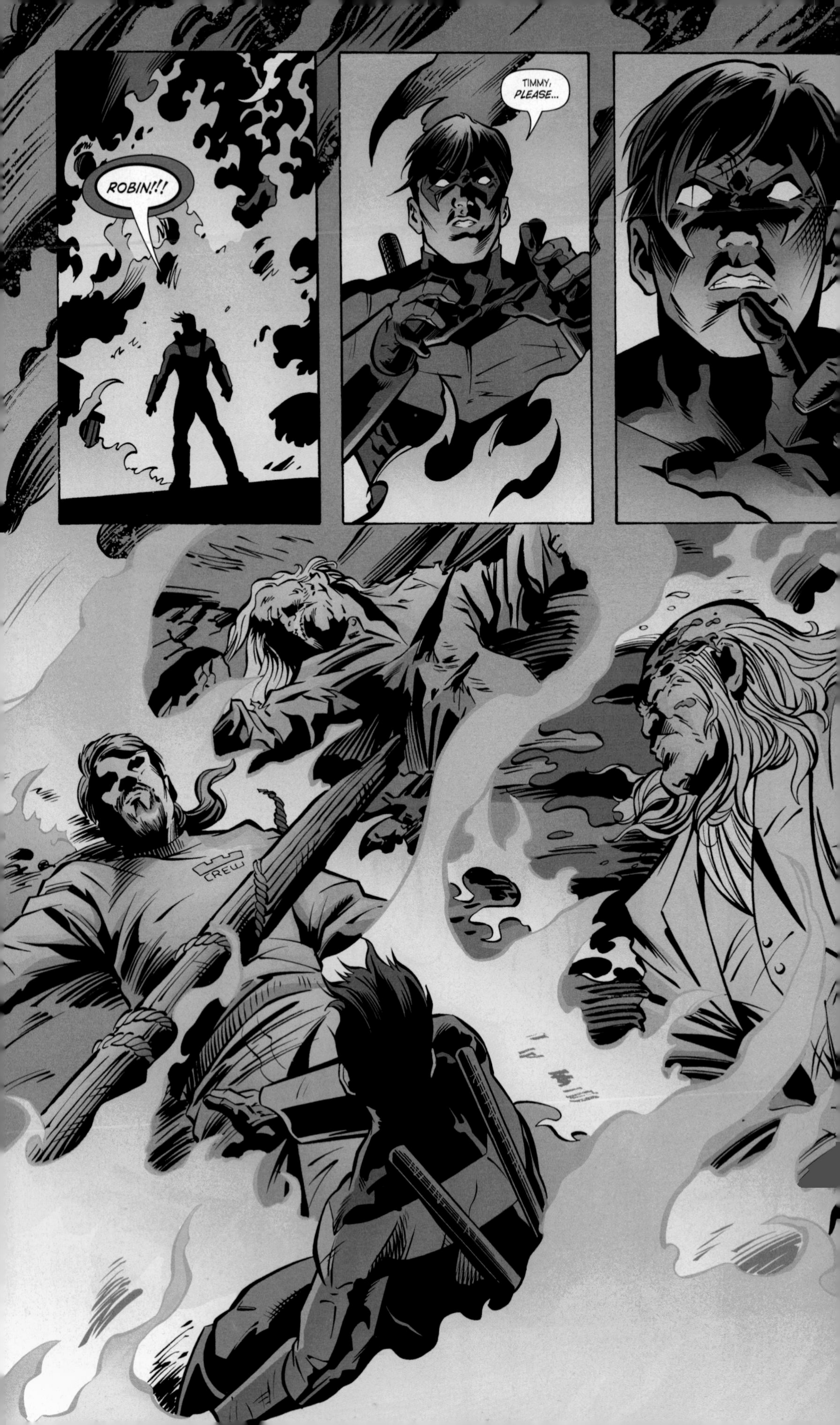
ROBIN!!!
TIMMY, PLEASE...
CREW

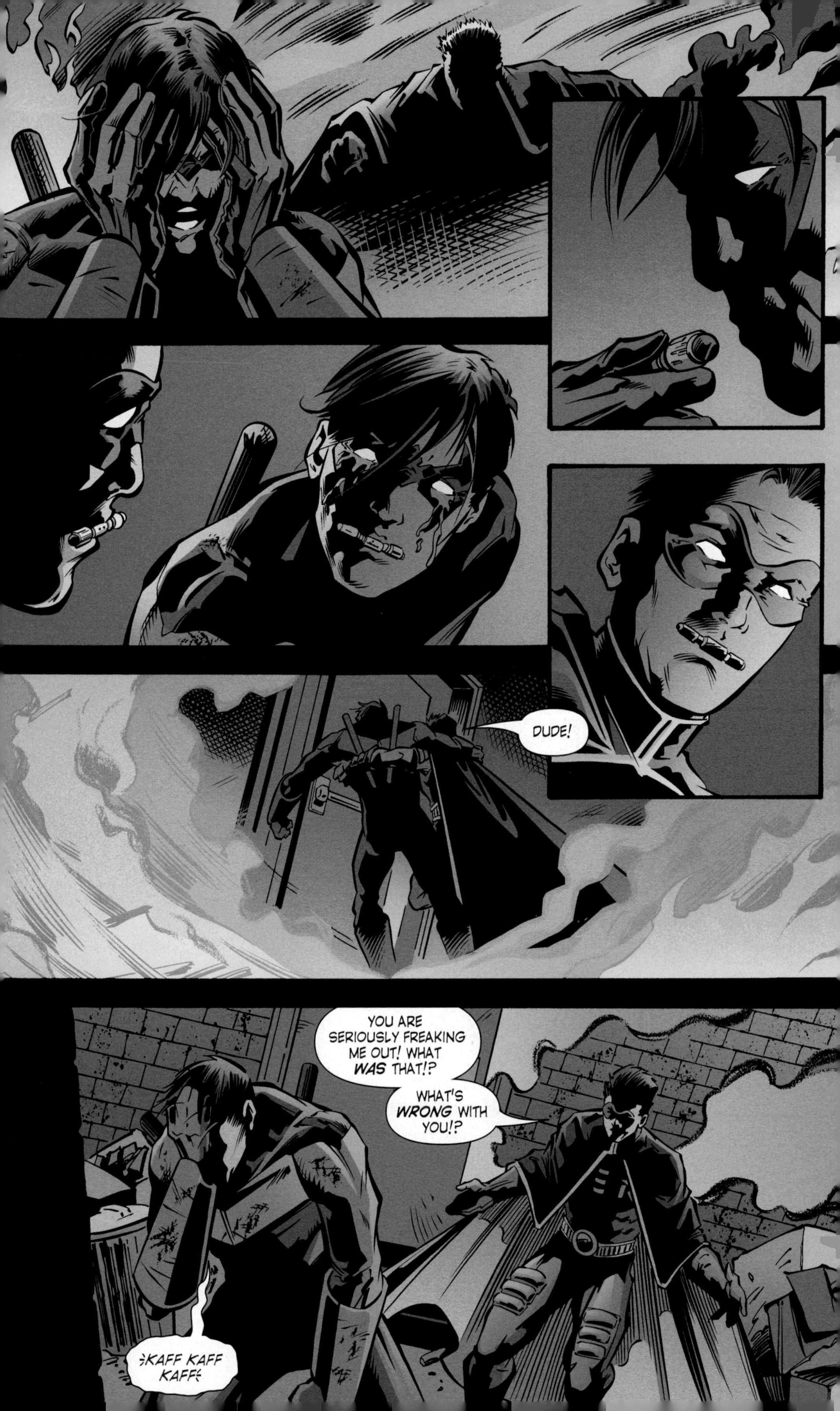
DUDE!
YOU ARE SERIOUSLY FREAKING ME OUT! WHAT WAS THAT!?
WHAT'S WRONG WITH YOU!?
KAFF KAFF KAFF

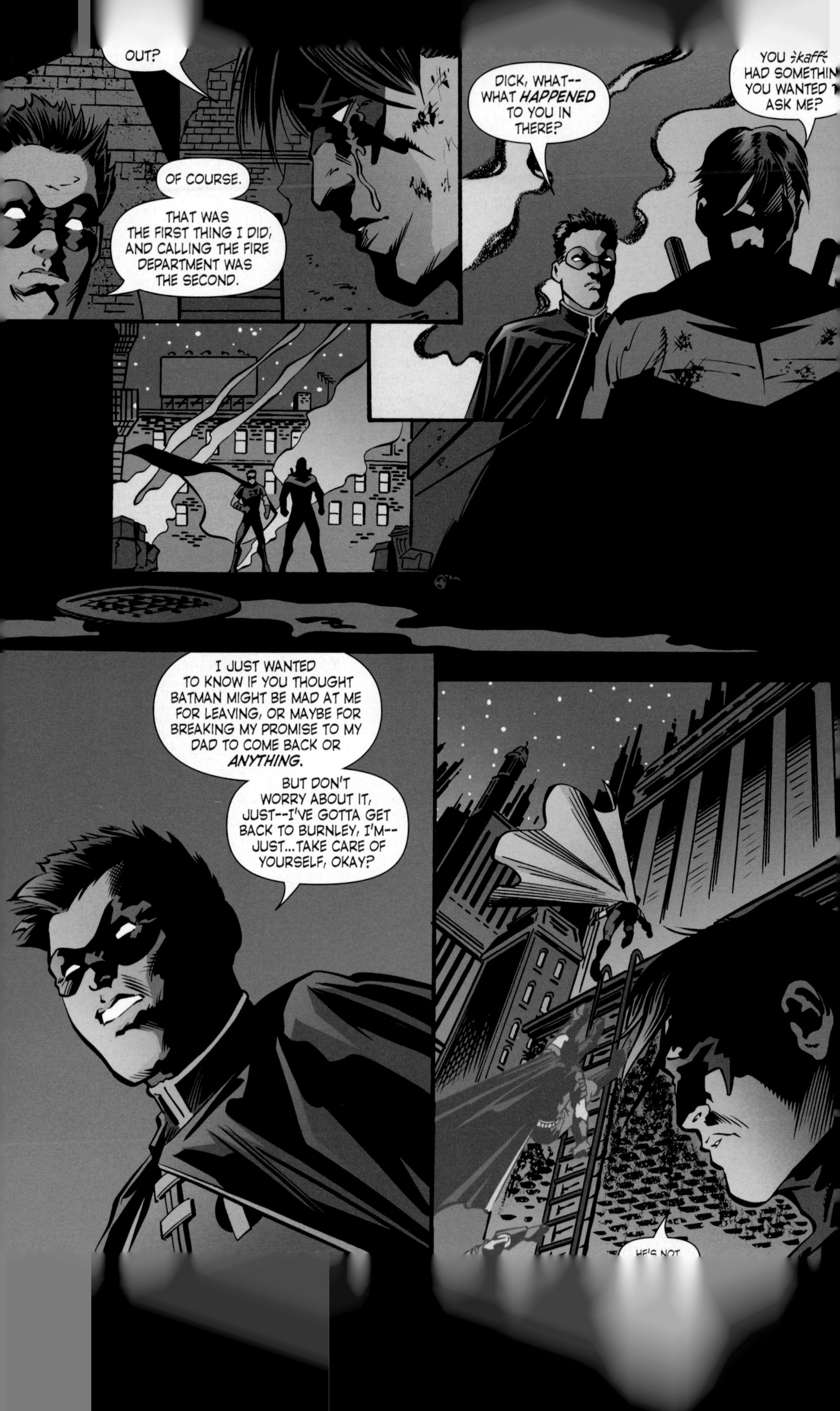

OUT?
OF COURSE.
THAT WAS THE FIRST THING I DID, AND CALLING THE FIRE DEPARTMENT WAS THE SECOND.
DICK, WHAT-- WHAT *HAPPENED* TO YOU IN THERE?
YOU *kaff* HAD SOMETHIN YOU WANTED T ASK ME?
I JUST WANTED TO KNOW IF YOU THOUGHT BATMAN MIGHT BE MAD AT ME FOR LEAVING, OR MAYBE FOR BREAKING MY PROMISE TO MY DAD TO COME BACK OR *ANYTHING*.
BUT DON'T WORRY ABOUT IT, JUST--I'VE GOTTA GET BACK TO BURNLEY, I'M-- JUST...TAKE CARE OF YOURSELF, OKAY?

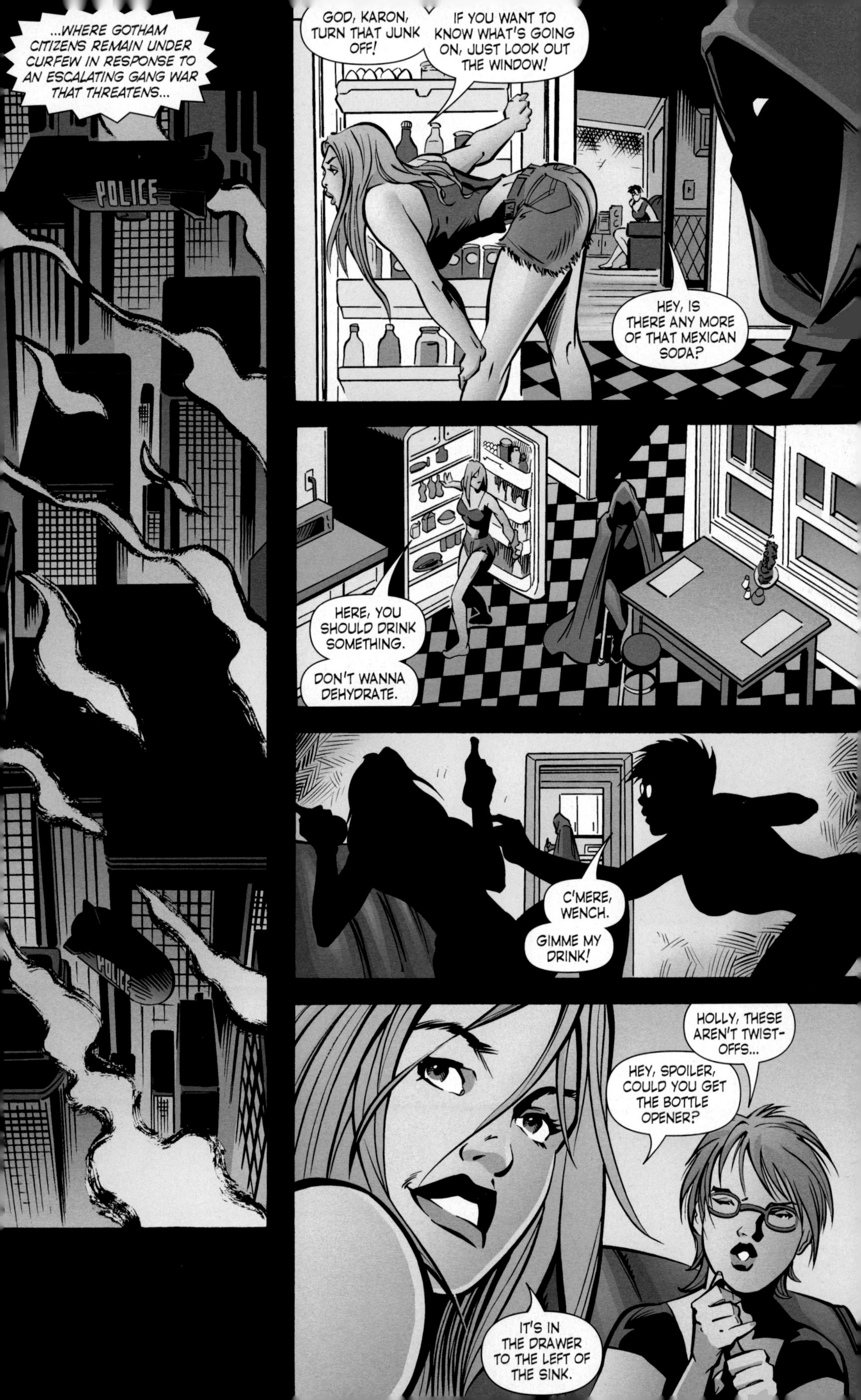
...WHERE GOTHAM CITIZENS REMAIN UNDER CURFEW IN RESPONSE TO AN ESCALATING GANG WAR THAT THREATENS...
POLICE
POLICE
GOD, KARON, TURN THAT JUNK OFF!
IF YOU WANT TO KNOW WHAT'S GOING ON, JUST LOOK OUT THE WINDOW!
HEY, IS THERE ANY MORE OF THAT MEXICAN SODA?
HERE, YOU SHOULD DRINK SOMETHING.
DON'T WANNA DEHYDRATE.
C'MERE, WENCH.
GIMME MY DRINK!
HOLLY, THESE AREN'T TWIST-OFFS...
HEY, SPOILER, COULD YOU GET THE BOTTLE OPENER?
IT'S IN THE DRAWER TO THE LEFT OF THE SINK.

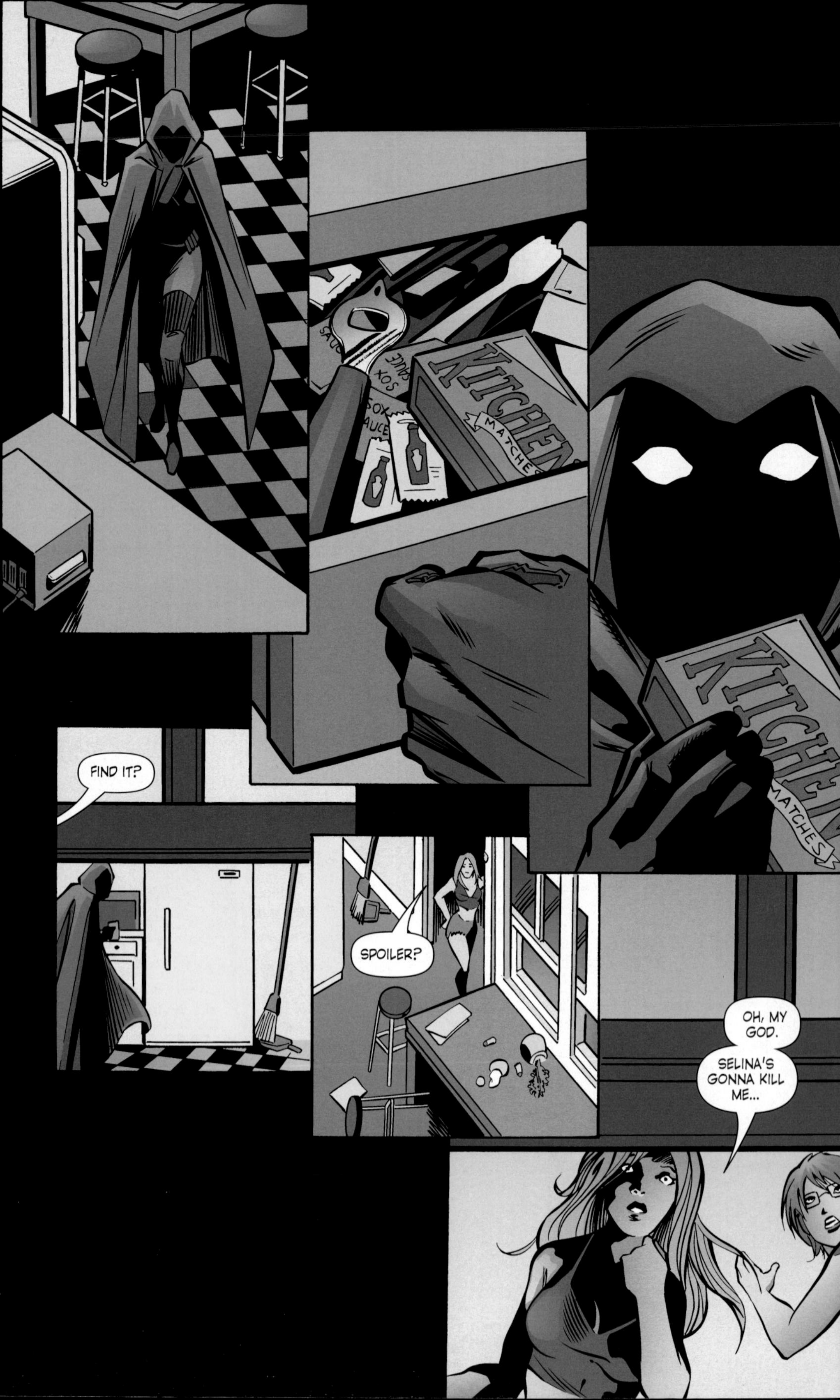
KITCHEN MATCHES
SOX SAUCE
KITCHEN MATCHES
FIND IT?
SPOILER?
OH, MY GOD.
SELINA'S GONNA KILL ME...

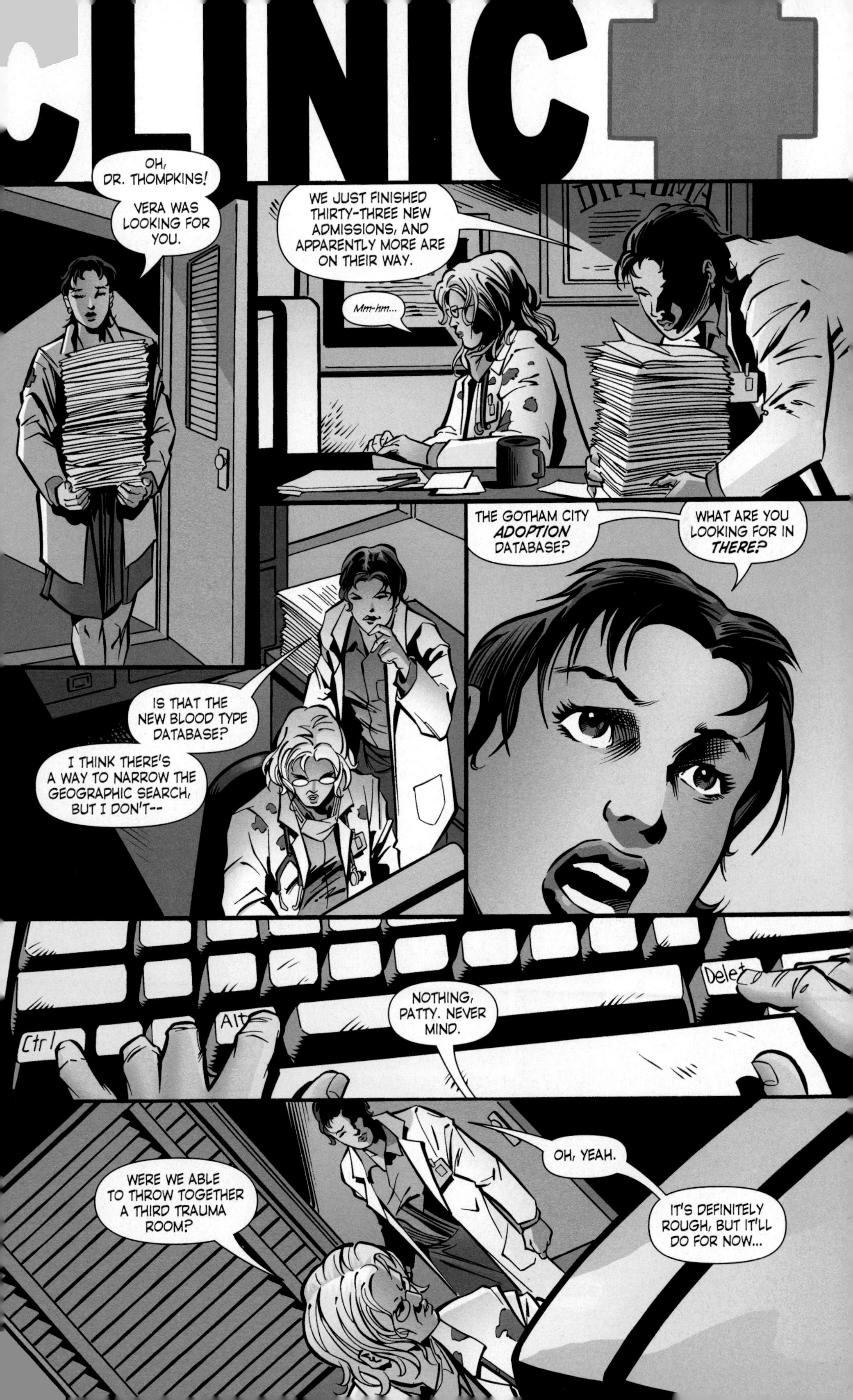
CLINIC
OH, DR. THOMPKINS!
VERA WAS LOOKING FOR YOU.
WE JUST FINISHED THIRTY-THREE NEW ADMISSIONS, AND APPARENTLY MORE ARE ON THEIR WAY.
Mm-hm...
IS THAT THE NEW BLOOD TYPE DATABASE?
I THINK THERE'S A WAY TO NARROW THE GEOGRAPHIC SEARCH, BUT I DON'T--
THE GOTHAM CITY ADOPTION DATABASE?
WHAT ARE YOU LOOKING FOR IN THERE?
Ctrl
Alt
Delete
NOTHING, PATTY. NEVER MIND.
WERE WE ABLE TO THROW TOGETHER A THIRD TRAUMA ROOM?
OH, YEAH.
IT'S DEFINITELY ROUGH, BUT IT'LL DO FOR NOW...

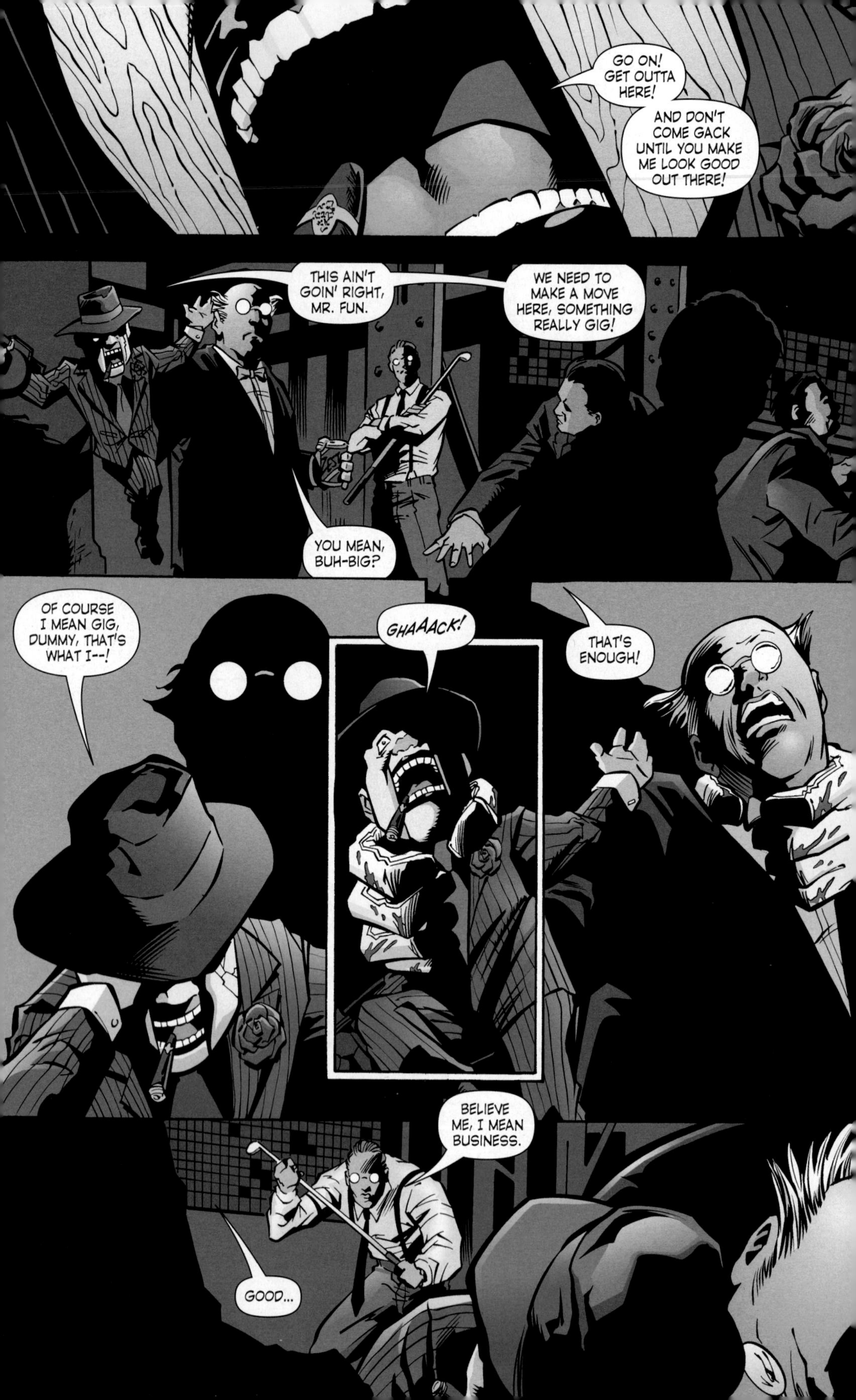
GO ON! GET OUTTA HERE!
AND DON'T COME GACK UNTIL YOU MAKE ME LOOK GOOD OUT THERE!
THIS AIN'T GOIN' RIGHT, MR. FUN.
WE NEED TO MAKE A MOVE HERE, SOMETHING REALLY GIG!
YOU MEAN, BUH-BIG?
OF COURSE I MEAN GIG, DUMMY, THAT'S WHAT I--!
GHAAACK!
THAT'S ENOUGH!
BELIEVE ME, I MEAN BUSINESS.
GOOD...

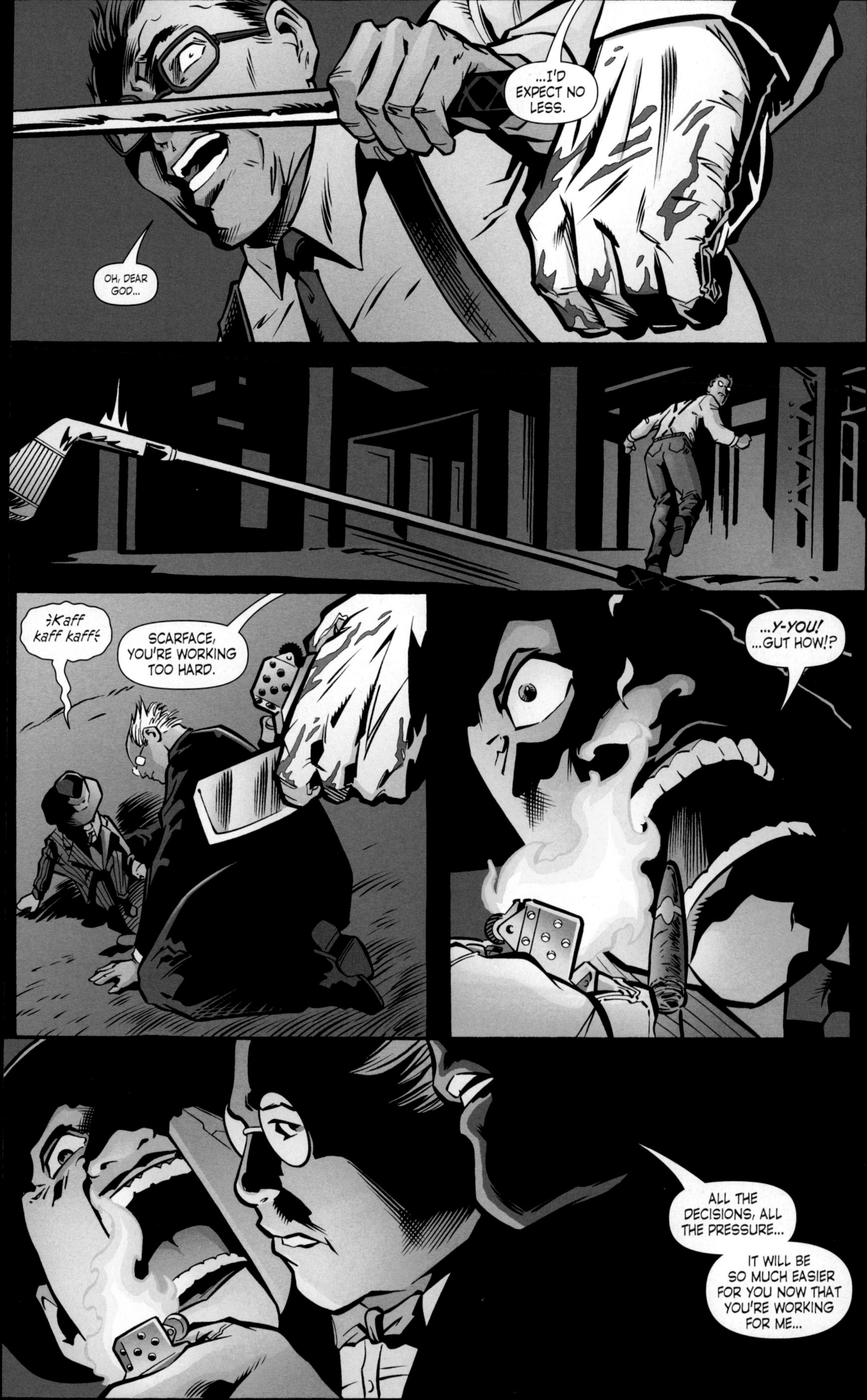
...I'D EXPECT NO LESS.
OH, DEAR GOD...
⊰Kaff kaff kaff⊱
SCARFACE, YOU'RE WORKING TOO HARD.
...Y-YOU! ...GUT HOW!?
ALL THE DECISIONS, ALL THE PRESSURE...
IT WILL BE SO MUCH EASIER FOR YOU NOW THAT YOU'RE WORKING FOR ME...

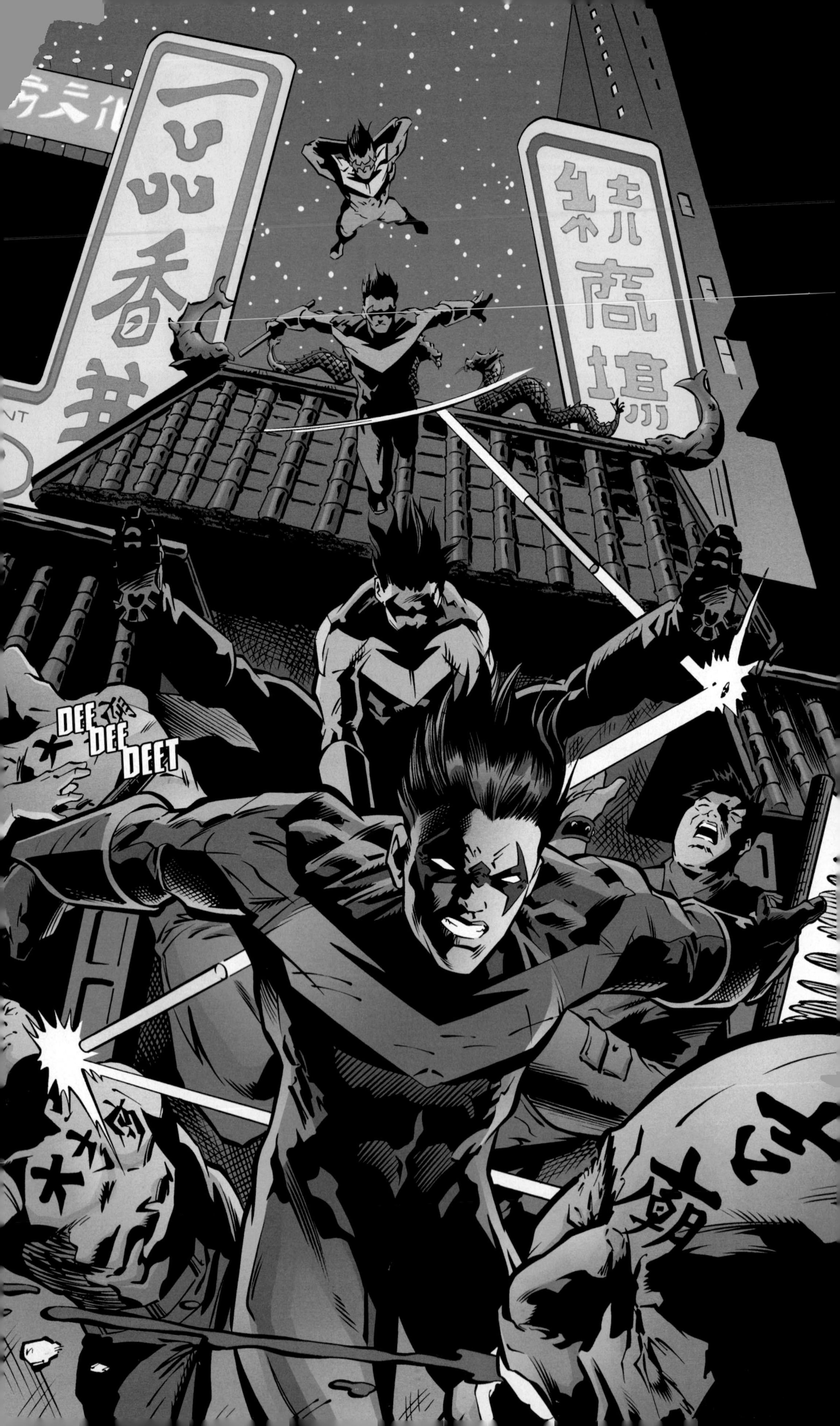
DEE DEE DEET

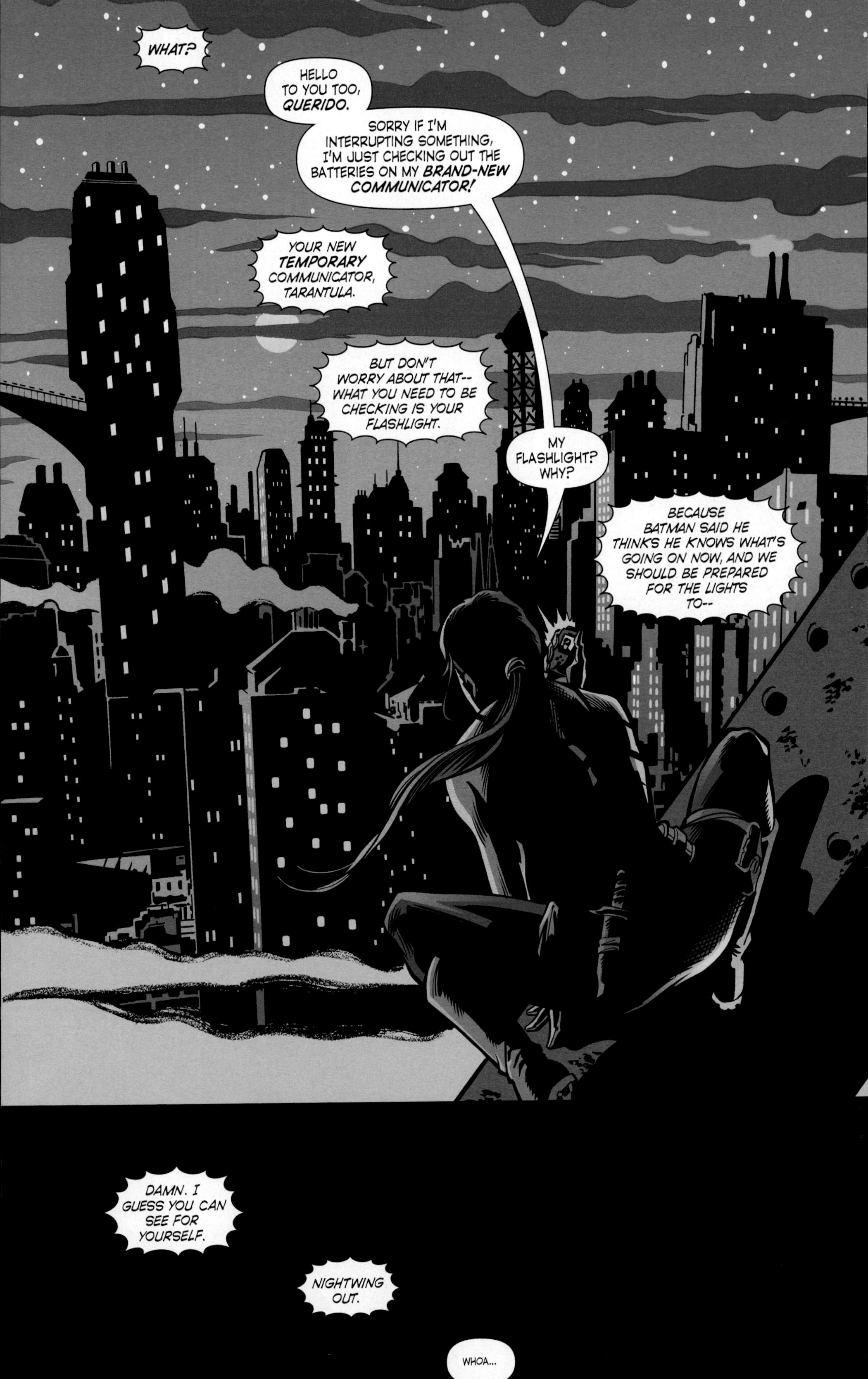
WHAT?
HELLO TO YOU TOO, QUERIDO.
SORRY IF I'M INTERRUPTING SOMETHING, I'M JUST CHECKING OUT THE BATTERIES ON MY BRAND-NEW COMMUNICATOR!
YOUR NEW TEMPORARY COMMUNICATOR, TARANTULA.
BUT DON'T WORRY ABOUT THAT-- WHAT YOU NEED TO BE CHECKING IS YOUR FLASHLIGHT.
MY FLASHLIGHT? WHY?
BECAUSE BATMAN SAID HE THINKS HE KNOWS WHAT'S GOING ON NOW, AND WE SHOULD BE PREPARED FOR THE LIGHTS TO--
DAMN. I GUESS YOU CAN SEE FOR YOURSELF.
NIGHTWING OUT.
WHOA...

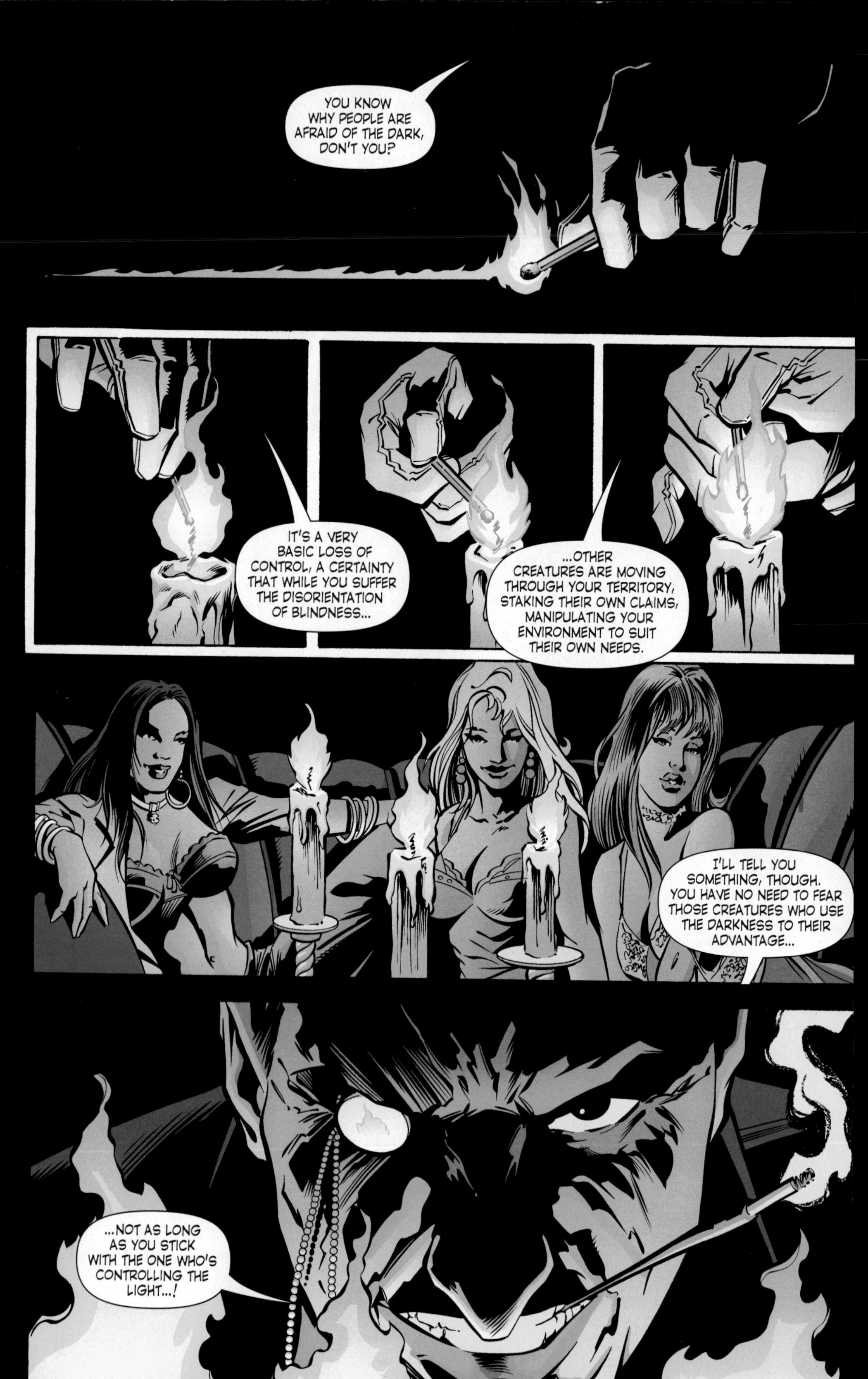
YOU KNOW WHY PEOPLE ARE AFRAID OF THE DARK, DON'T YOU?
IT'S A VERY BASIC LOSS OF CONTROL, A CERTAINTY THAT WHILE YOU SUFFER THE DISORIENTATION OF BLINDNESS...
...OTHER CREATURES ARE MOVING THROUGH YOUR TERRITORY, STAKING THEIR OWN CLAIMS, MANIPULATING YOUR ENVIRONMENT TO SUIT THEIR OWN NEEDS.
I'LL TELL YOU SOMETHING, THOUGH. YOU HAVE NO NEED TO FEAR THOSE CREATURES WHO USE THE DARKNESS TO THEIR ADVANTAGE...
...NOT AS LONG AS YOU STICK WITH THE ONE WHO'S CONTROLLING THE LIGHT...!

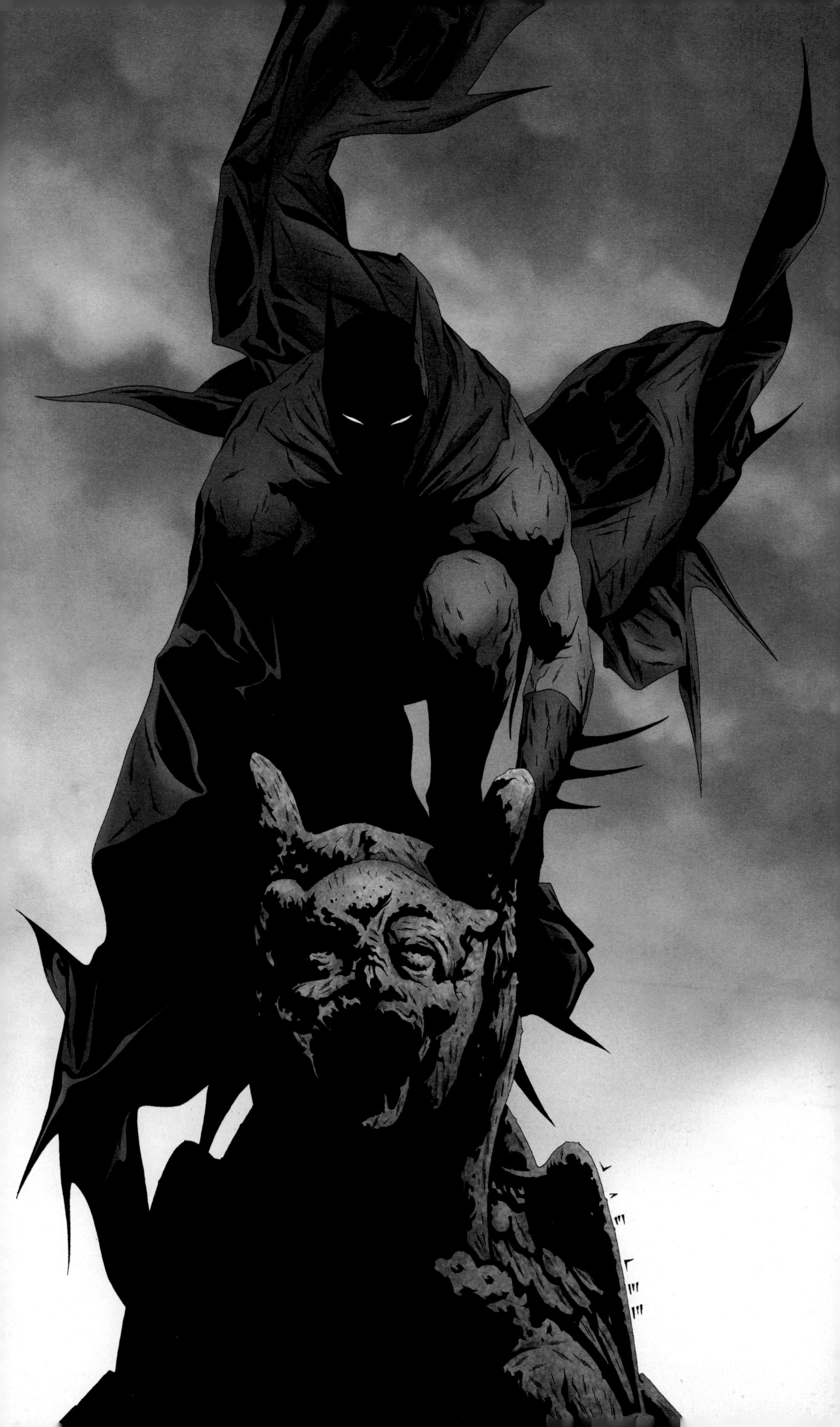

COVER ART BY
JAE LEE & JUNE CHUNG

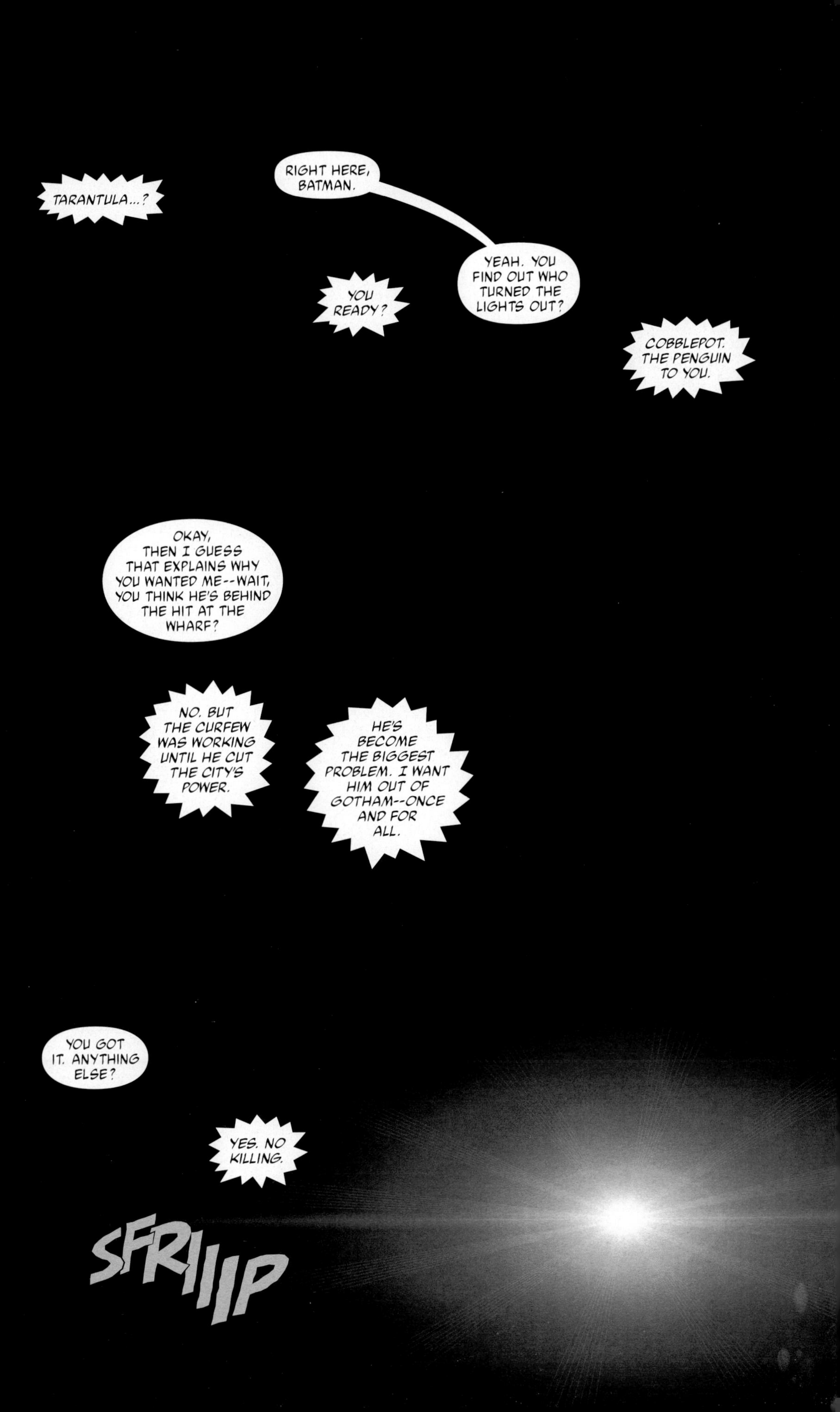
TARANTULA...?
RIGHT HERE, BATMAN.
YEAH. YOU FIND OUT WHO TURNED THE LIGHTS OUT?
YOU READY?
COBBLEPOT. THE PENGUIN TO YOU.
OKAY, THEN I GUESS THAT EXPLAINS WHY YOU WANTED ME--WAIT, YOU THINK HE'S BEHIND THE HIT AT THE WHARF?
NO. BUT THE CURFEW WAS WORKING UNTIL HE CUT THE CITY'S POWER.
HE'S BECOME THE BIGGEST PROBLEM. I WANT HIM OUT OF GOTHAM--ONCE AND FOR ALL.
YOU GOT IT. ANYTHING ELSE?
YES. NO KILLING.
SFRIIIP

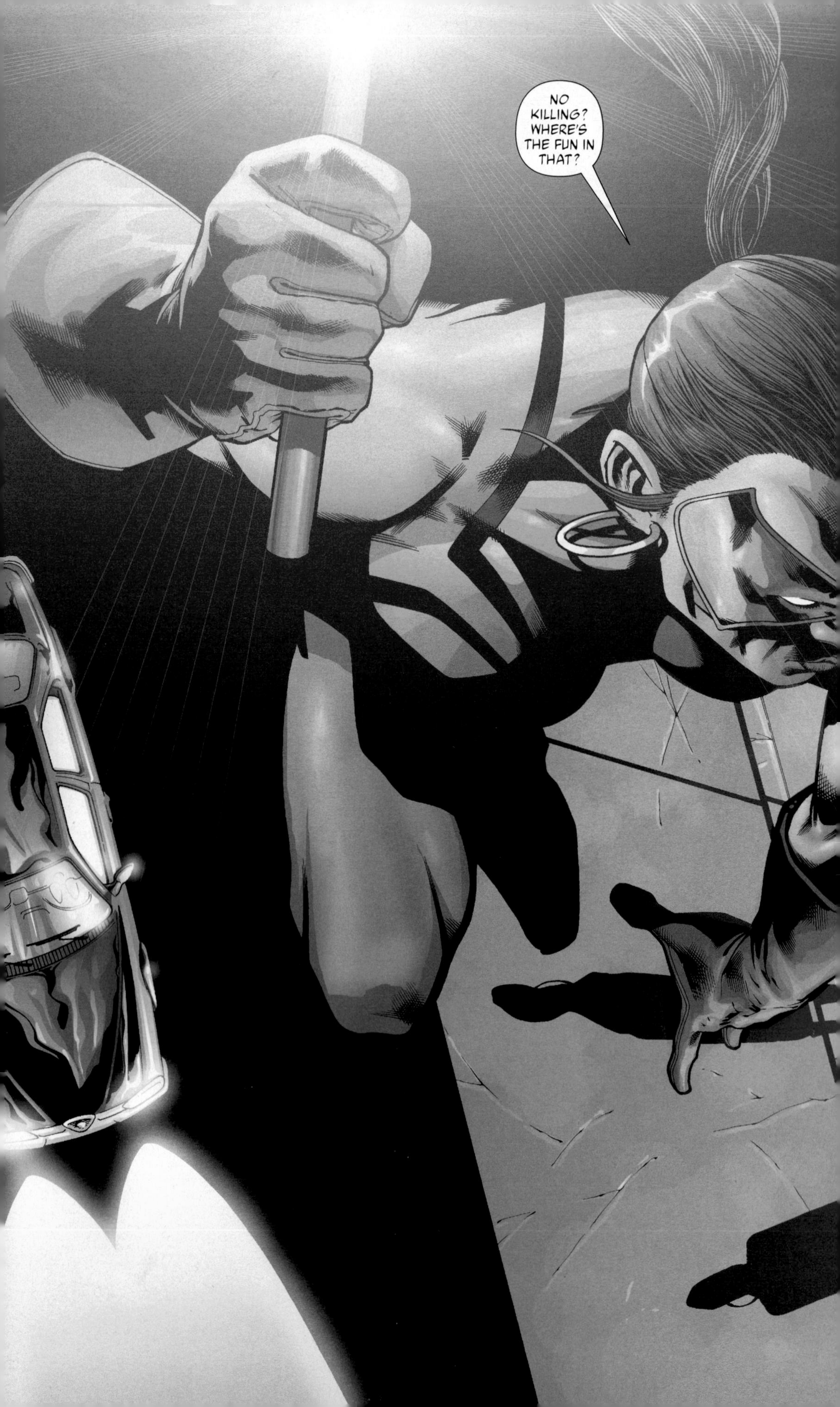
NO KILLING? WHERE'S THE FUN IN THAT?

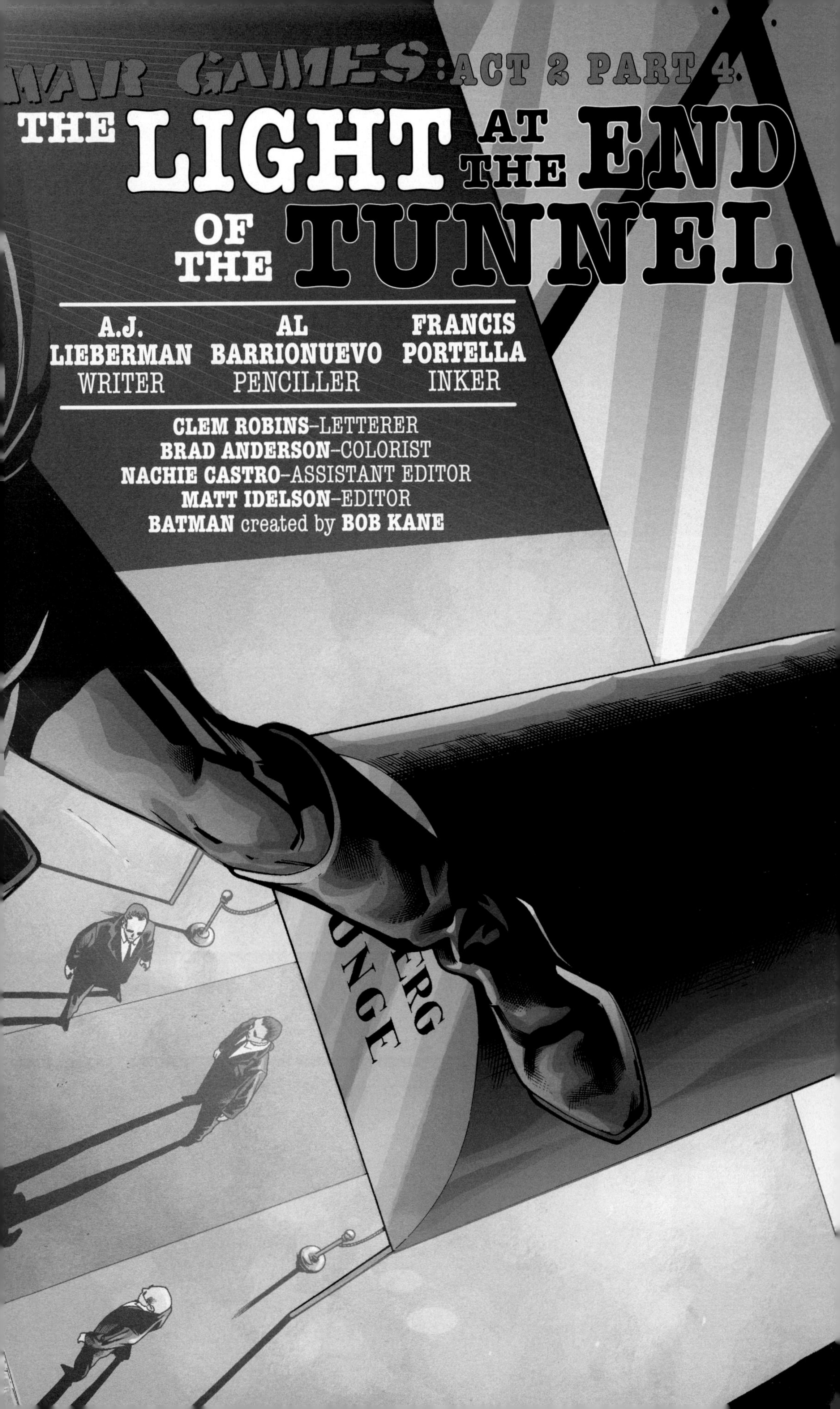
WAR GAMES: ACT 2 PART 4
THE LIGHT AT THE END OF THE TUNNEL
A.J. LIEBERMAN WRITER
AL BARRIONUEVO PENCILLER
FRANCIS PORTELLA INKER
CLEM ROBINS–LETTERER
BRAD ANDERSON–COLORIST
NACHIE CASTRO–ASSISTANT EDITOR
MATT IDELSON–EDITOR
BATMAN created by BOB KANE

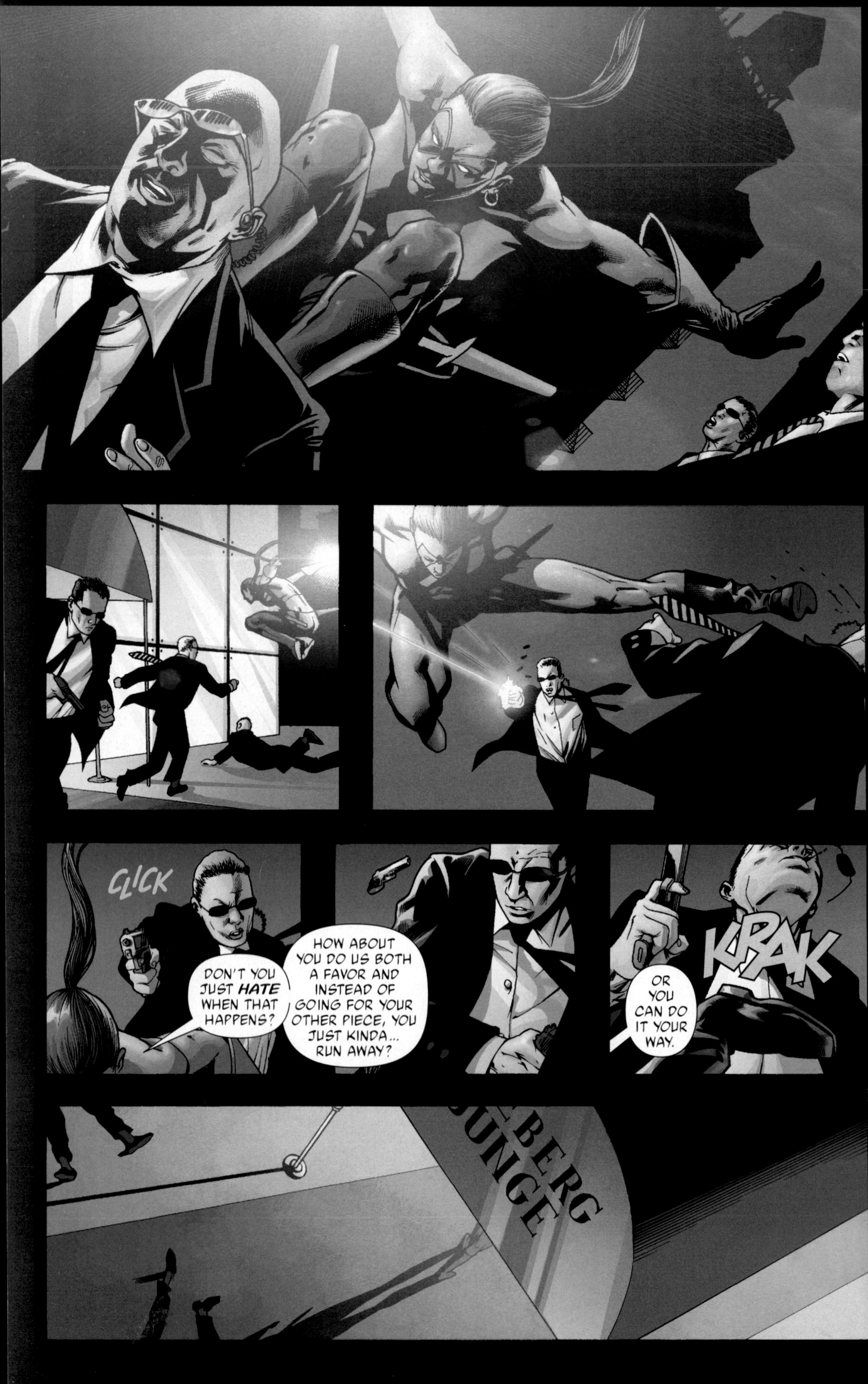
CLICK
DON'T YOU JUST HATE WHEN THAT HAPPENS?
HOW ABOUT YOU DO US BOTH A FAVOR AND INSTEAD OF GOING FOR YOUR OTHER PIECE, YOU JUST KINDA... RUN AWAY?
KRAK
OR YOU CAN DO IT YOUR WAY.
BERG
UNGE

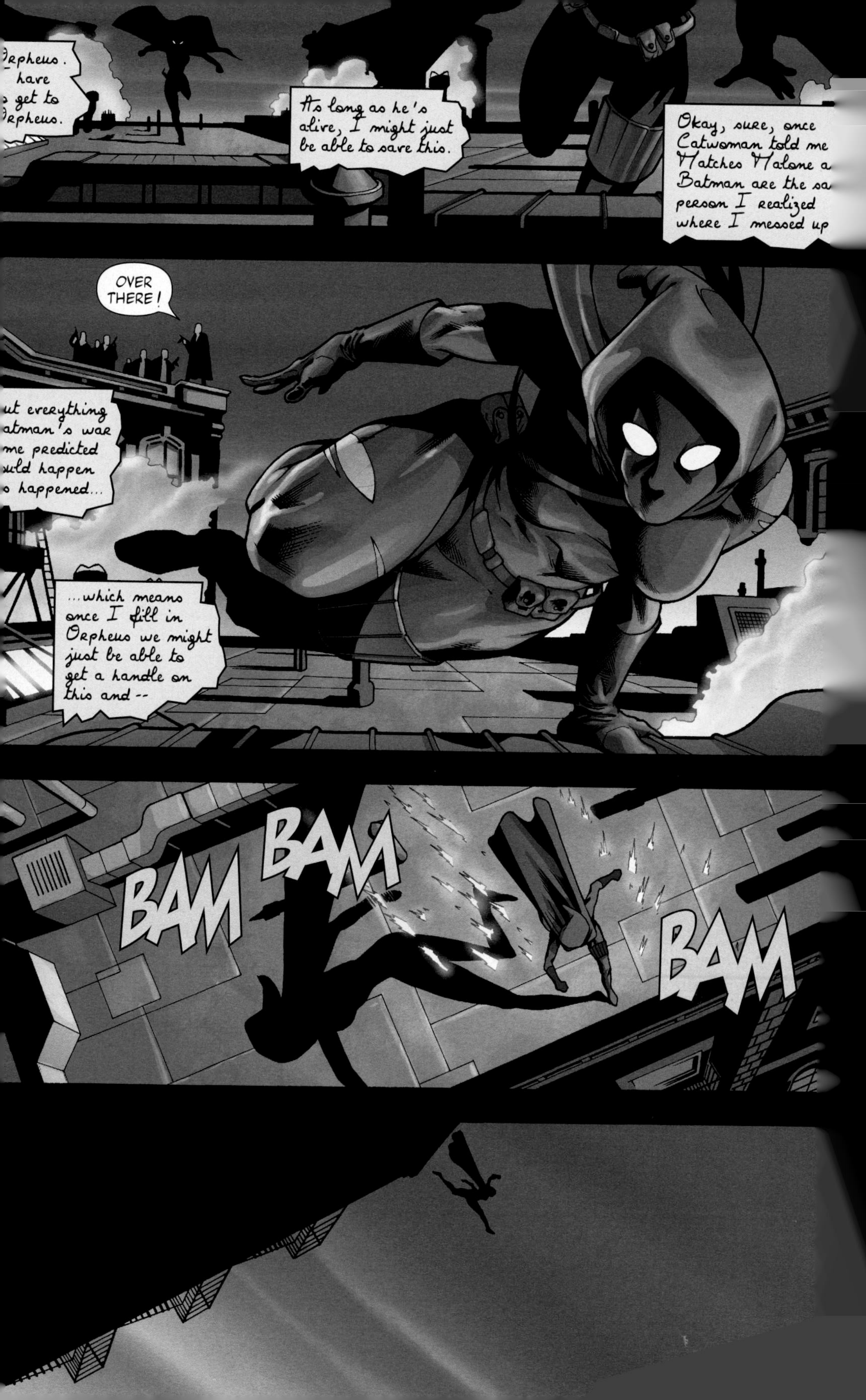
Orpheus. have get to Orpheus.
As long as he's alive, I might just be able to save this.
Okay, sure, once Catwoman told me Matches Malone a Batman are the sa person I realized where I messed up
OVER THERE!
ut everything atman's war me predicted uld happen happened...
...which means once I fill in Orpheus we might just be able to get a handle on this and --
BAM
BAM
BAM

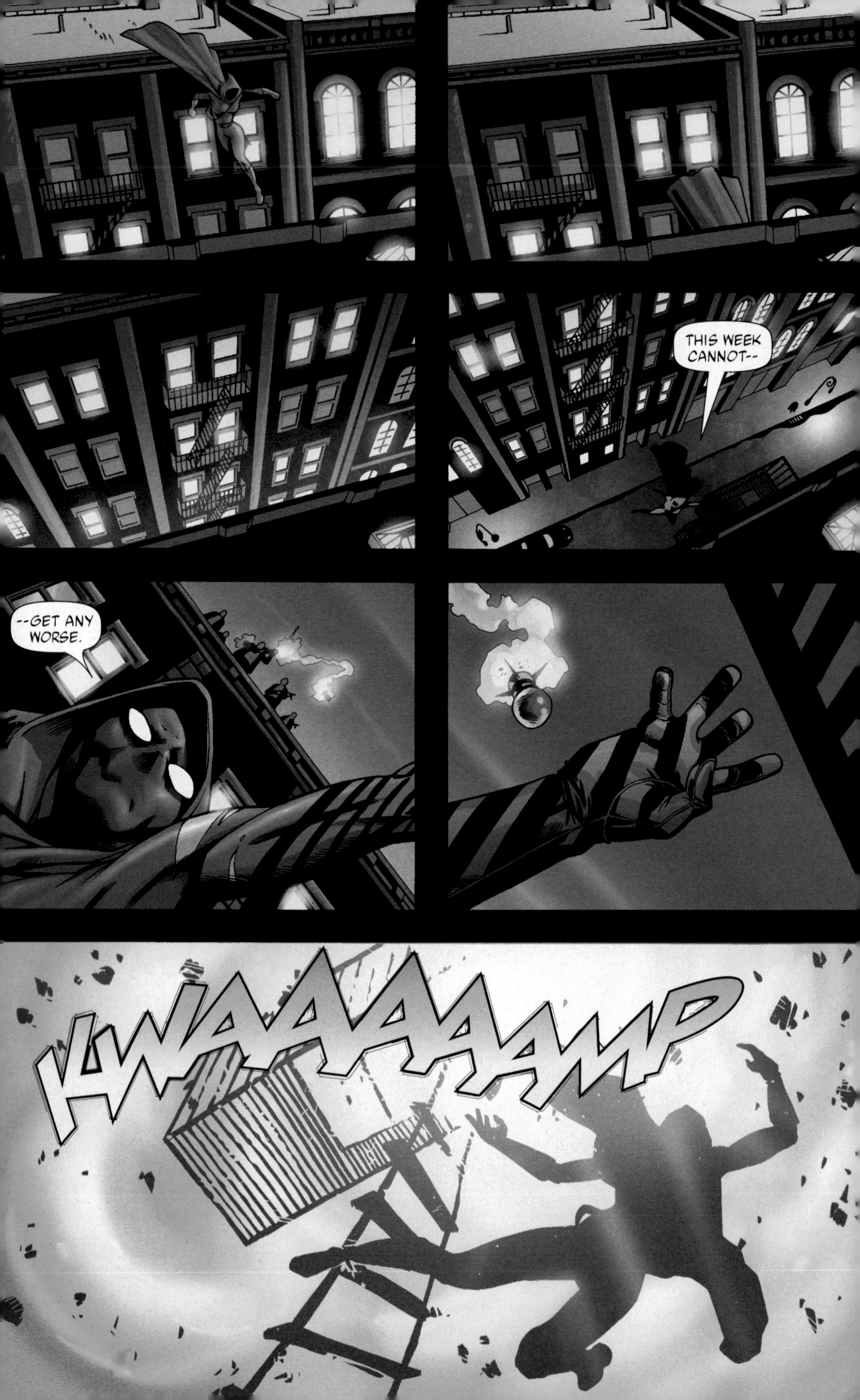
THIS WEEK CANNOT--
--GET ANY WORSE.
KWAAAAAMP

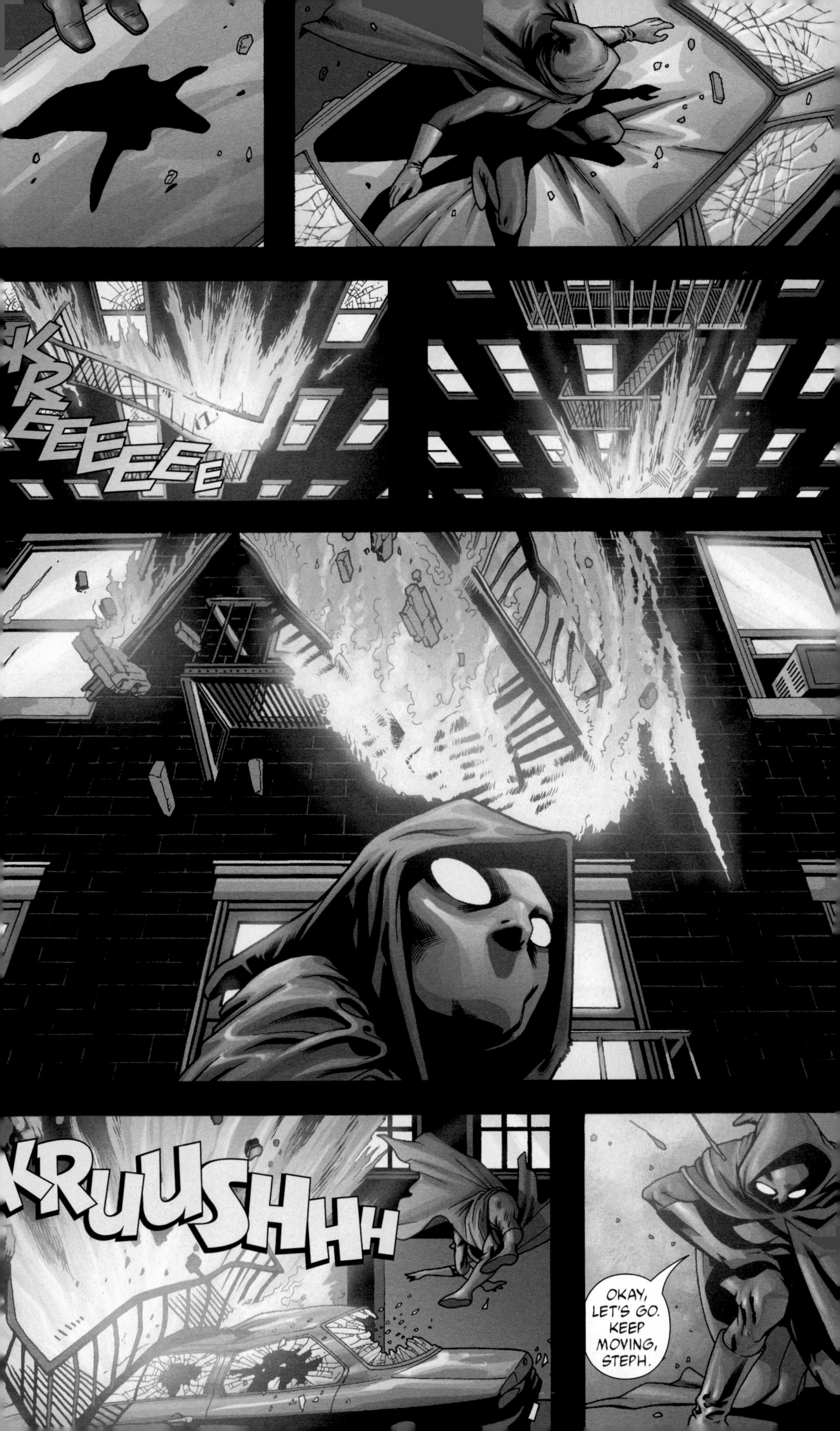
KREEEEEE
KRUUSHHH
OKAY, LET'S GO. KEEP MOVING, STEPH.

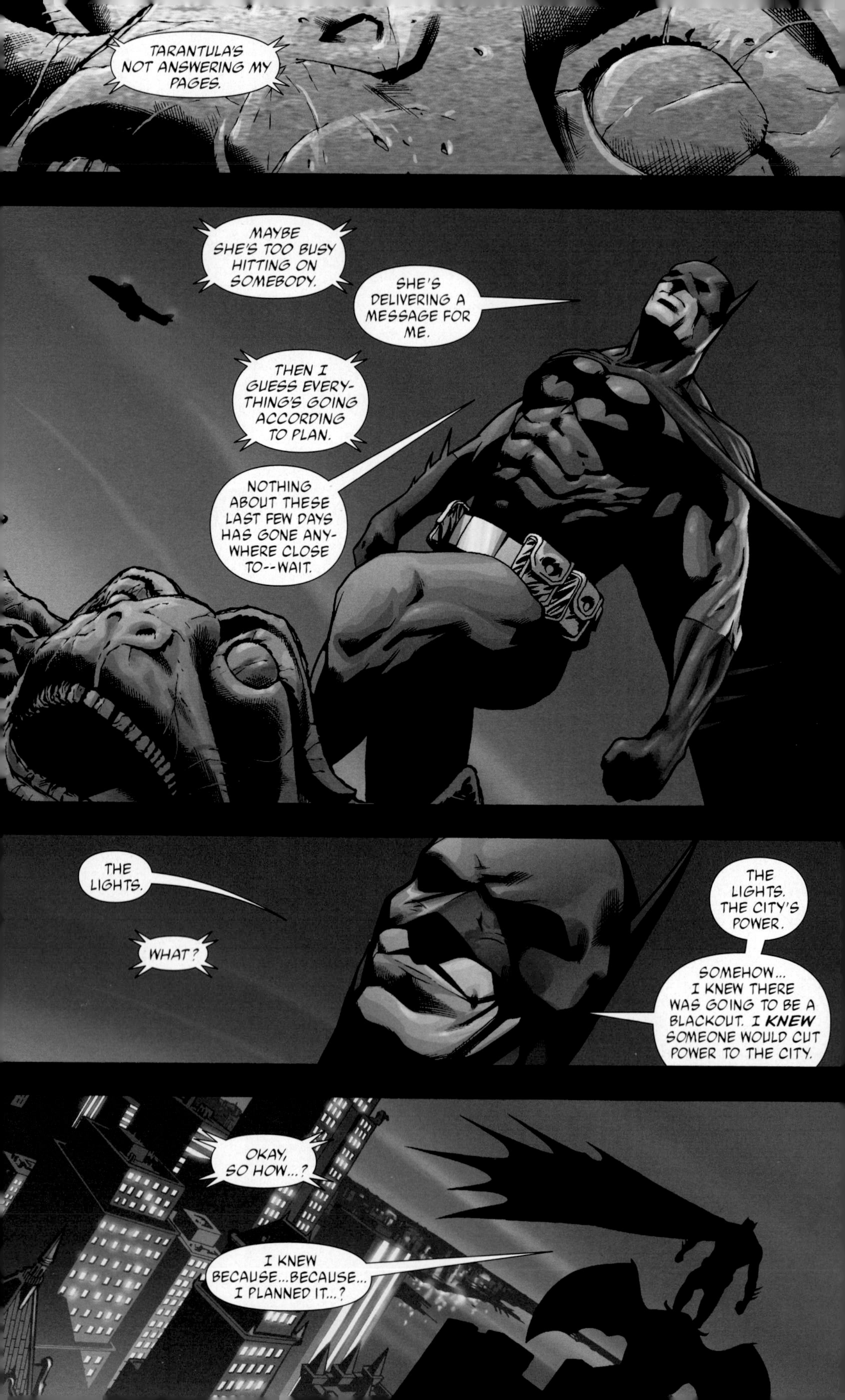
TARANTULA'S NOT ANSWERING MY PAGES.
MAYBE SHE'S TOO BUSY HITTING ON SOMEBODY.
SHE'S DELIVERING A MESSAGE FOR ME.
THEN I GUESS EVERY-THING'S GOING ACCORDING TO PLAN.
NOTHING ABOUT THESE LAST FEW DAYS HAS GONE ANY-WHERE CLOSE TO--WAIT.
THE LIGHTS.
WHAT?
THE LIGHTS. THE CITY'S POWER.
SOMEHOW... I KNEW THERE WAS GOING TO BE A BLACKOUT. I **KNEW** SOMEONE WOULD CUT POWER TO THE CITY.
OKAY, SO HOW...?
I KNEW BECAUSE...BECAUSE... I PLANNED IT...?

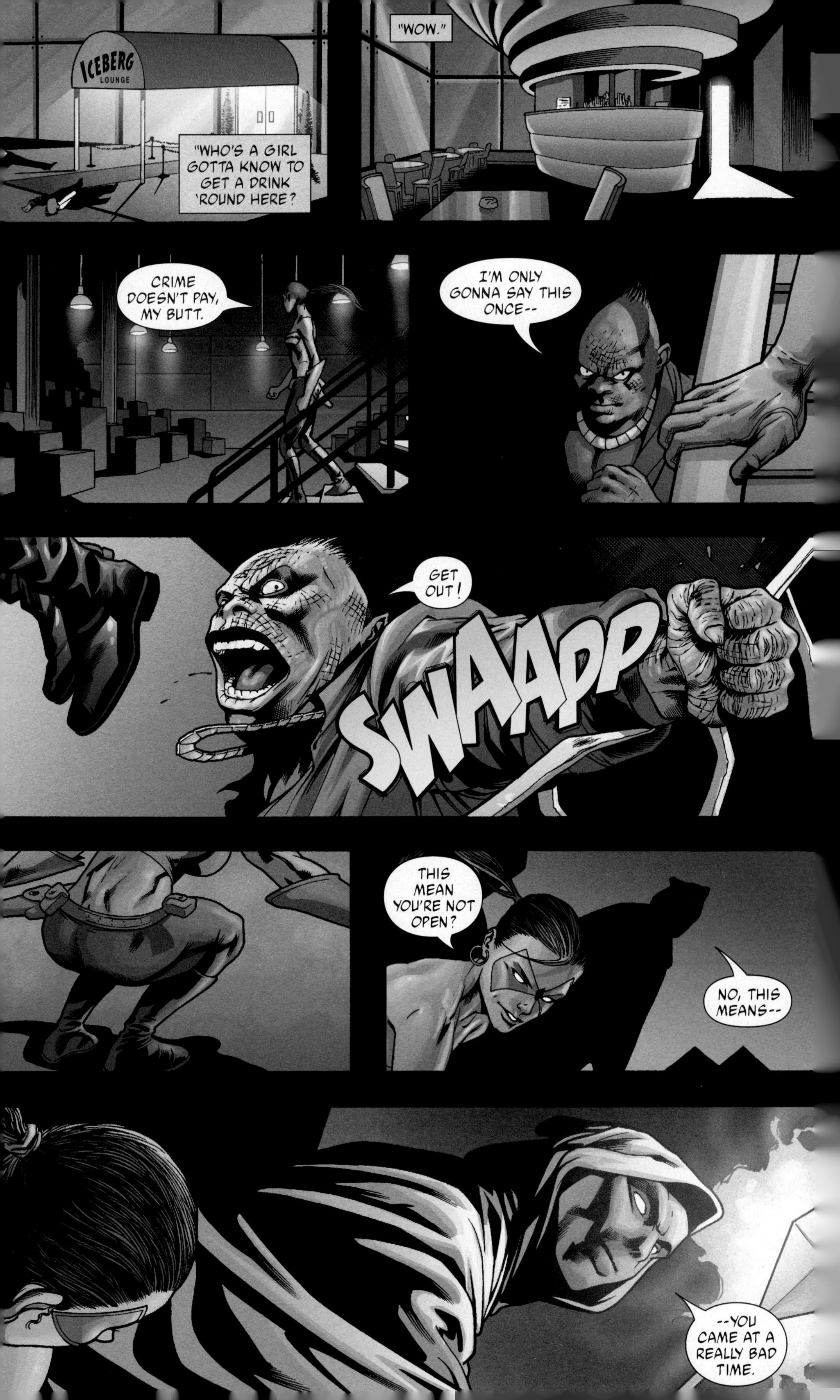

ICEBERG LOUNGE
"WHO'S A GIRL GOTTA KNOW TO GET A DRINK 'ROUND HERE?
"WOW."
CRIME DOESN'T PAY, MY BUTT.
I'M ONLY GONNA SAY THIS ONCE--
GET OUT!
SWAAPP
THIS MEAN YOU'RE NOT OPEN?
NO, THIS MEANS--
--YOU CAME AT A REALLY BAD TIME.

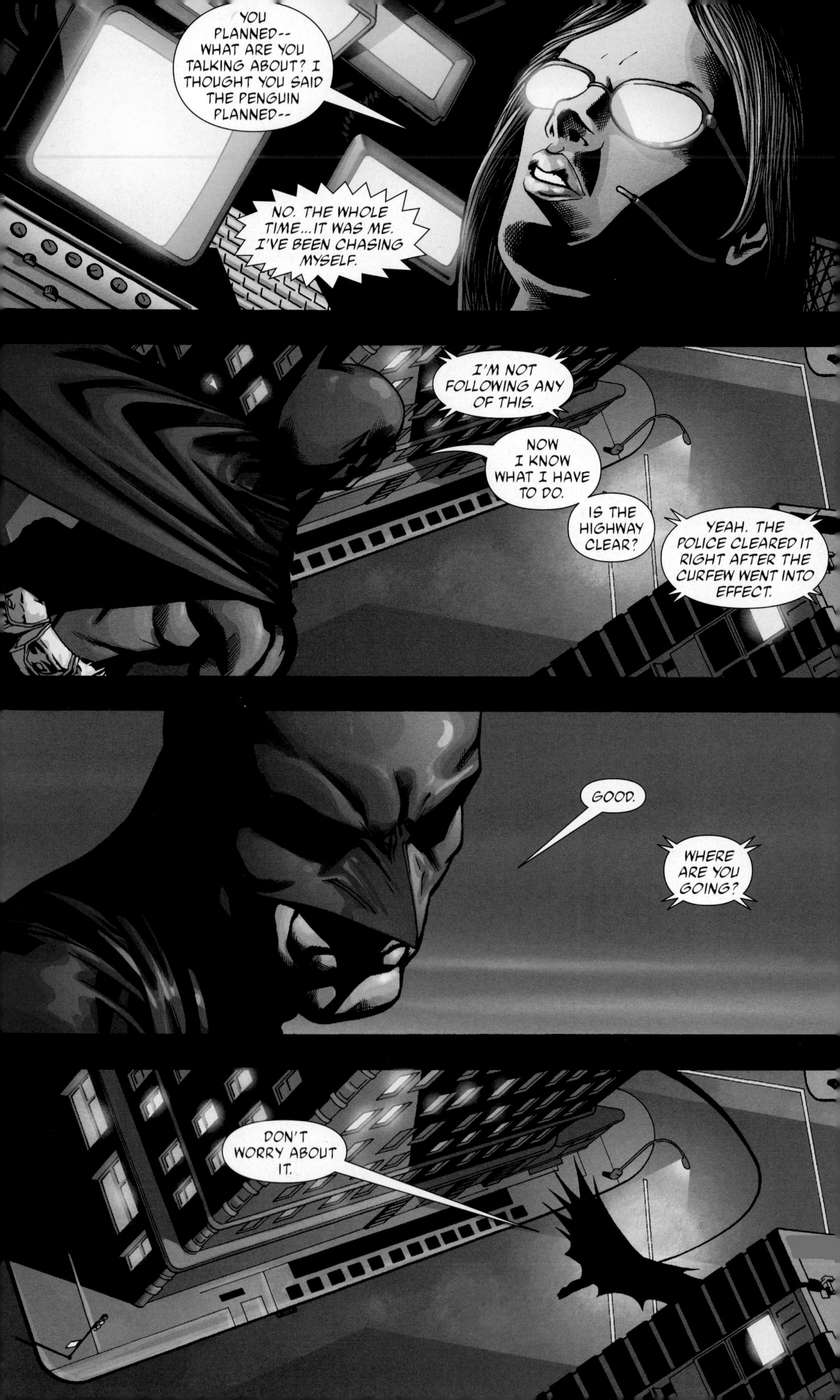
YOU PLANNED-- WHAT ARE YOU TALKING ABOUT? I THOUGHT YOU SAID THE PENGUIN PLANNED--
NO. THE WHOLE TIME...IT WAS ME. I'VE BEEN CHASING MYSELF.
I'M NOT FOLLOWING ANY OF THIS.
NOW I KNOW WHAT I HAVE TO DO.
IS THE HIGHWAY CLEAR?
YEAH. THE POLICE CLEARED IT RIGHT AFTER THE CURFEW WENT INTO EFFECT.
GOOD.
WHERE ARE YOU GOING?
DON'T WORRY ABOUT IT.

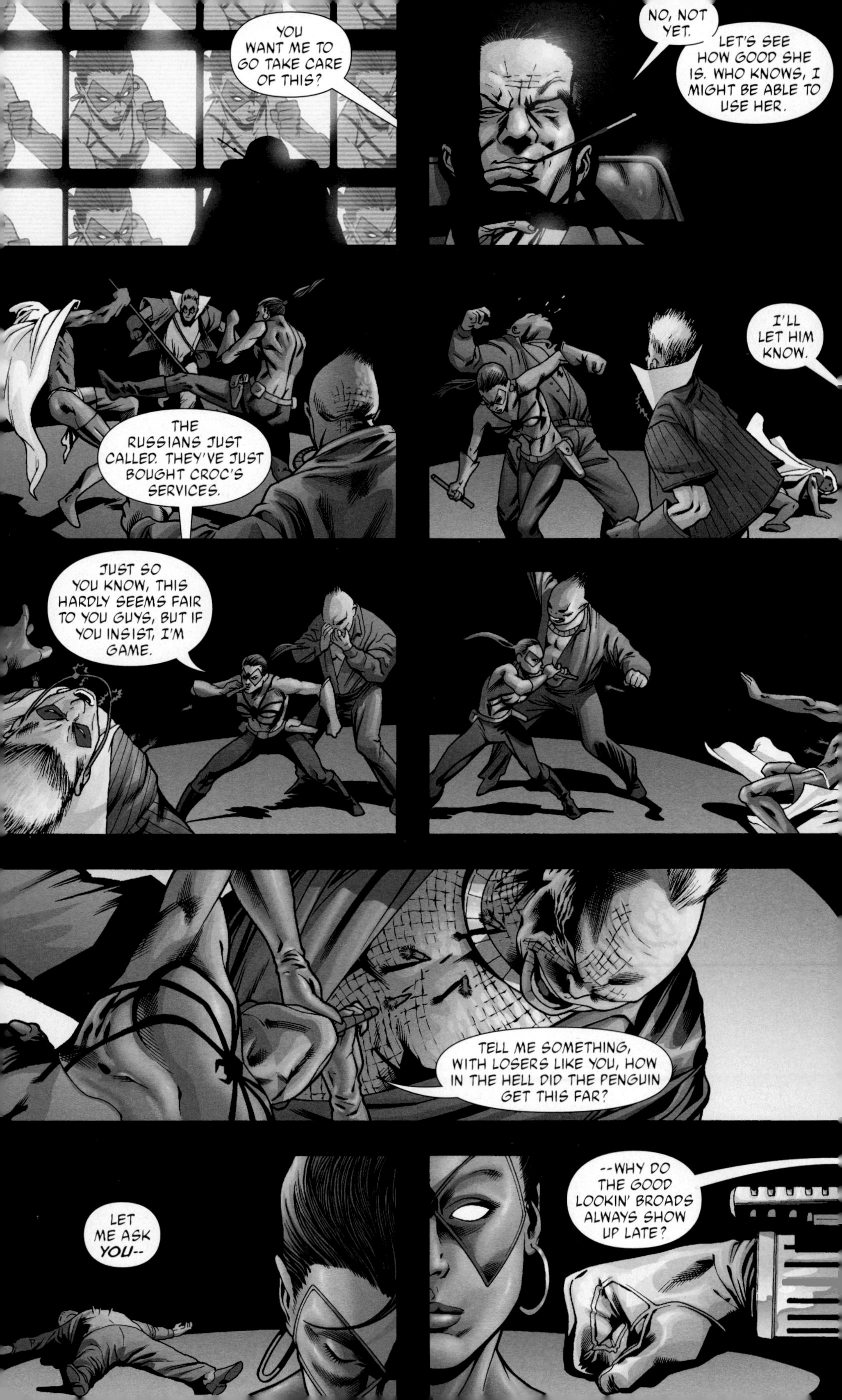
YOU WANT ME TO GO TAKE CARE OF THIS?
NO, NOT YET.
LET'S SEE HOW GOOD SHE IS. WHO KNOWS, I MIGHT BE ABLE TO USE HER.
THE RUSSIANS JUST CALLED. THEY'VE JUST BOUGHT CROC'S SERVICES.
I'LL LET HIM KNOW.
JUST SO YOU KNOW, THIS HARDLY SEEMS FAIR TO YOU GUYS, BUT IF YOU INSIST, I'M GAME.
TELL ME SOMETHING, WITH LOSERS LIKE YOU, HOW IN THE HELL DID THE PENGUIN GET THIS FAR?
LET ME ASK *YOU*--
--WHY DO THE GOOD LOOKIN' BROADS ALWAYS SHOW UP LATE?

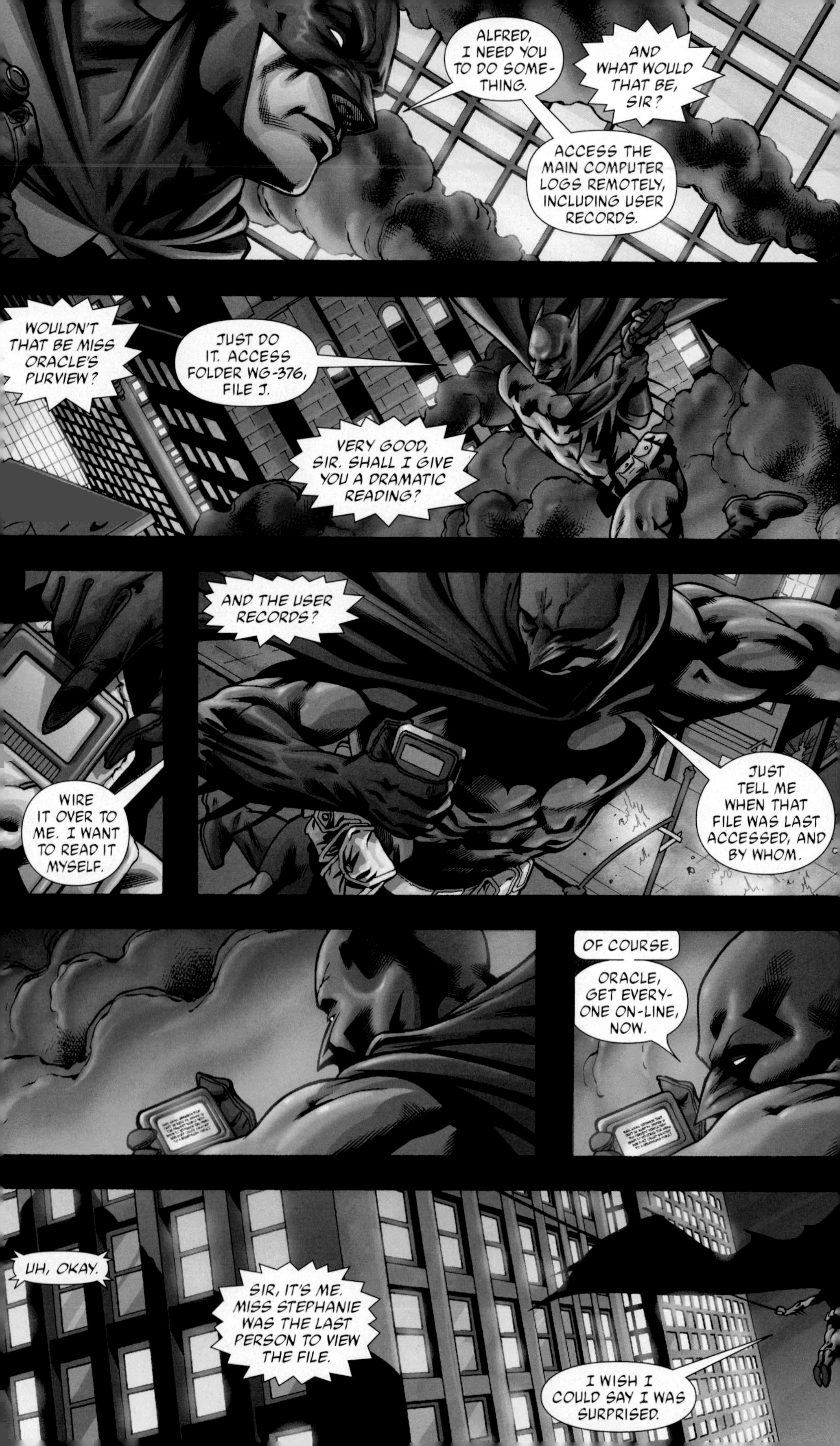
ALFRED, I NEED YOU TO DO SOME-THING.
AND WHAT WOULD THAT BE, SIR?
ACCESS THE MAIN COMPUTER LOGS REMOTELY, INCLUDING USER RECORDS.
WOULDN'T THAT BE MISS ORACLE'S PURVIEW?
JUST DO IT. ACCESS FOLDER WG-376, FILE J.
VERY GOOD, SIR. SHALL I GIVE YOU A DRAMATIC READING?
AND THE USER RECORDS?
WIRE IT OVER TO ME. I WANT TO READ IT MYSELF.
JUST TELL ME WHEN THAT FILE WAS LAST ACCESSED, AND BY WHOM.
OF COURSE.
ORACLE, GET EVERY-ONE ON-LINE, NOW.
UH, OKAY.
SIR, IT'S ME. MISS STEPHANIE WAS THE LAST PERSON TO VIEW THE FILE.
I WISH I COULD SAY I WAS SURPRISED.

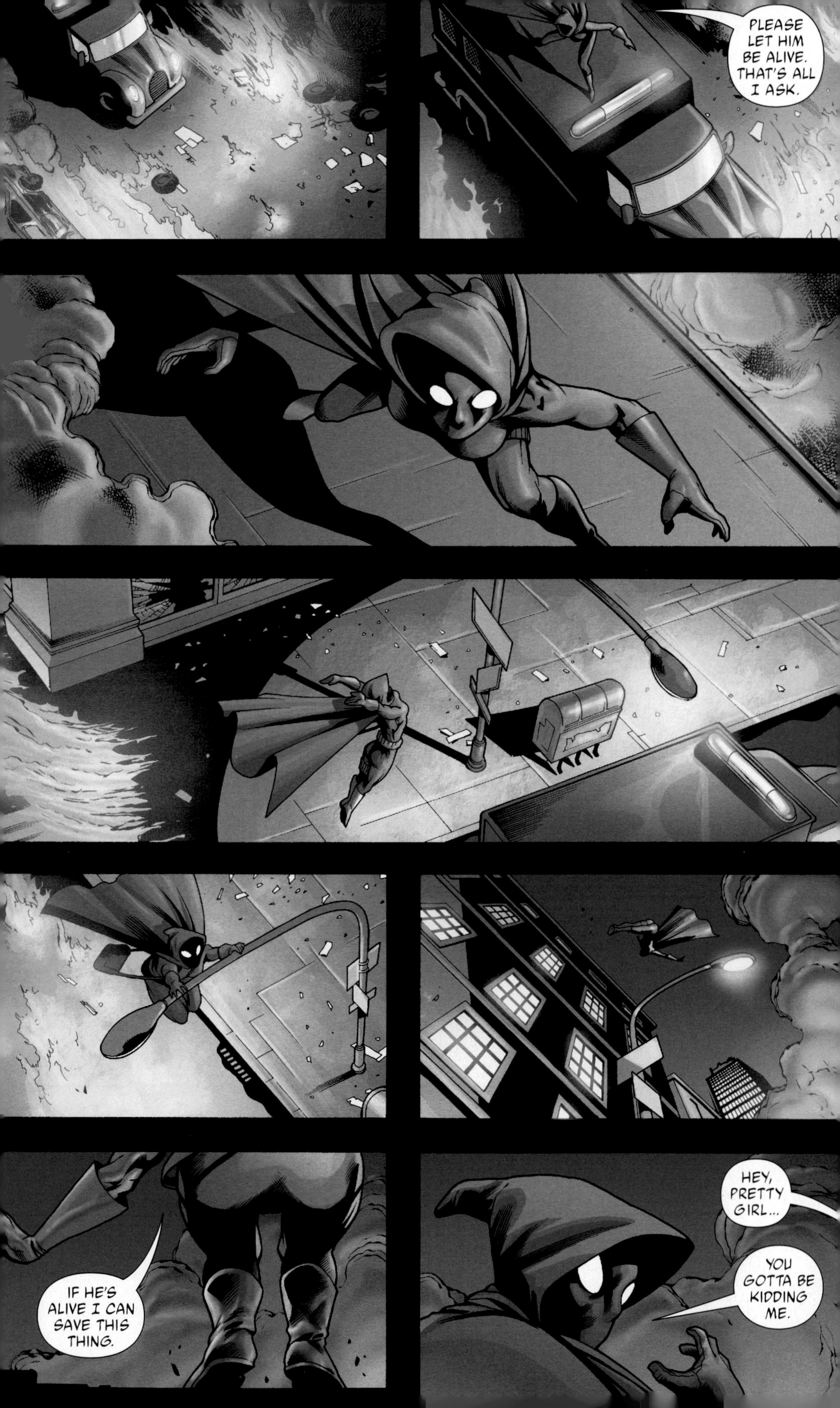
PLEASE LET HIM BE ALIVE. THAT'S ALL I ASK.
IF HE'S ALIVE I CAN SAVE THIS THING.
HEY, PRETTY GIRL...
YOU GOTTA BE KIDDING ME.

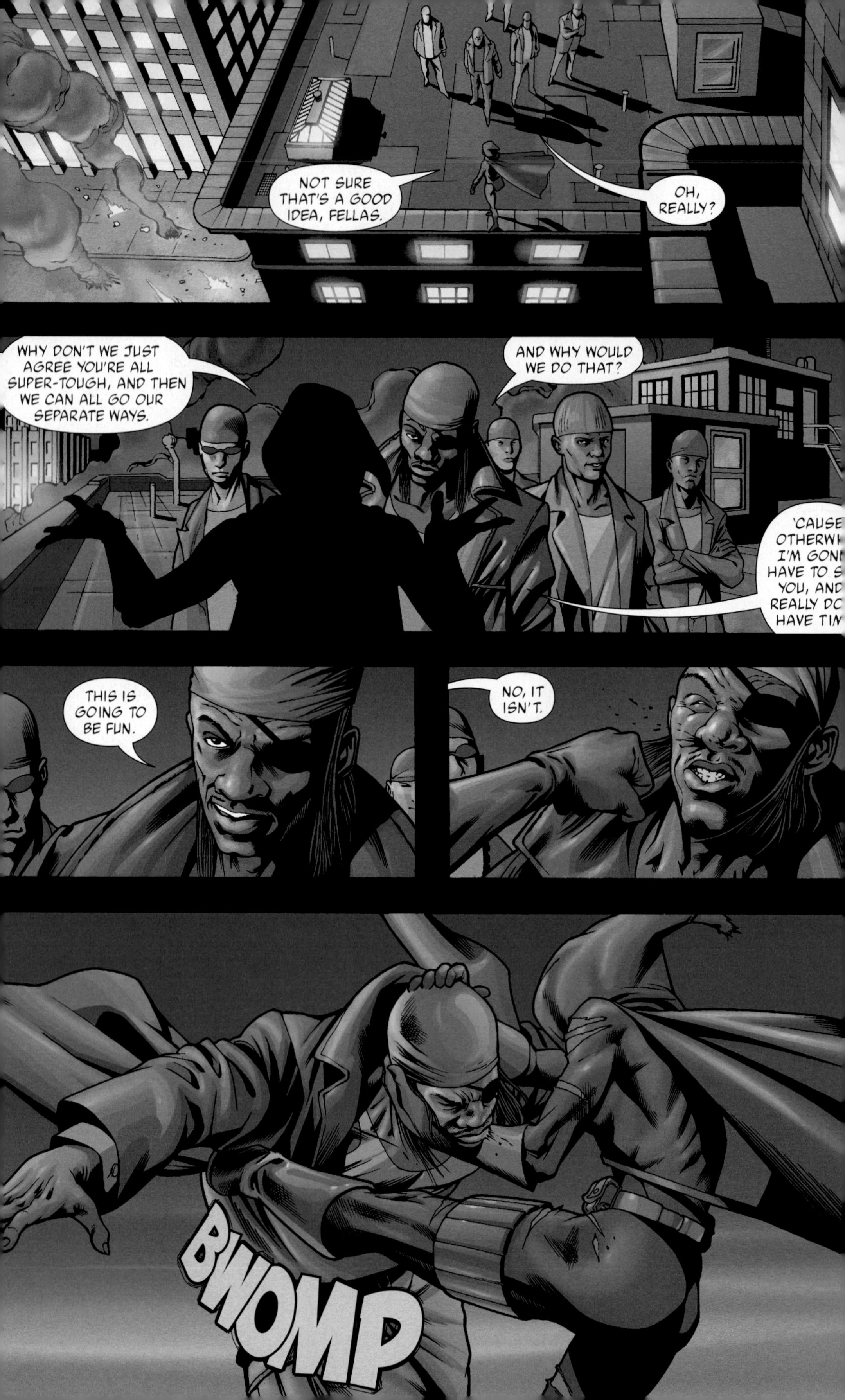
NOT SURE THAT'S A GOOD IDEA, FELLAS.
OH, REALLY?
WHY DON'T WE JUST AGREE YOU'RE ALL SUPER-TOUGH, AND THEN WE CAN ALL GO OUR SEPARATE WAYS.
AND WHY WOULD WE DO THAT?
THIS IS GOING TO BE FUN.
NO, IT ISN'T.
BWOMP

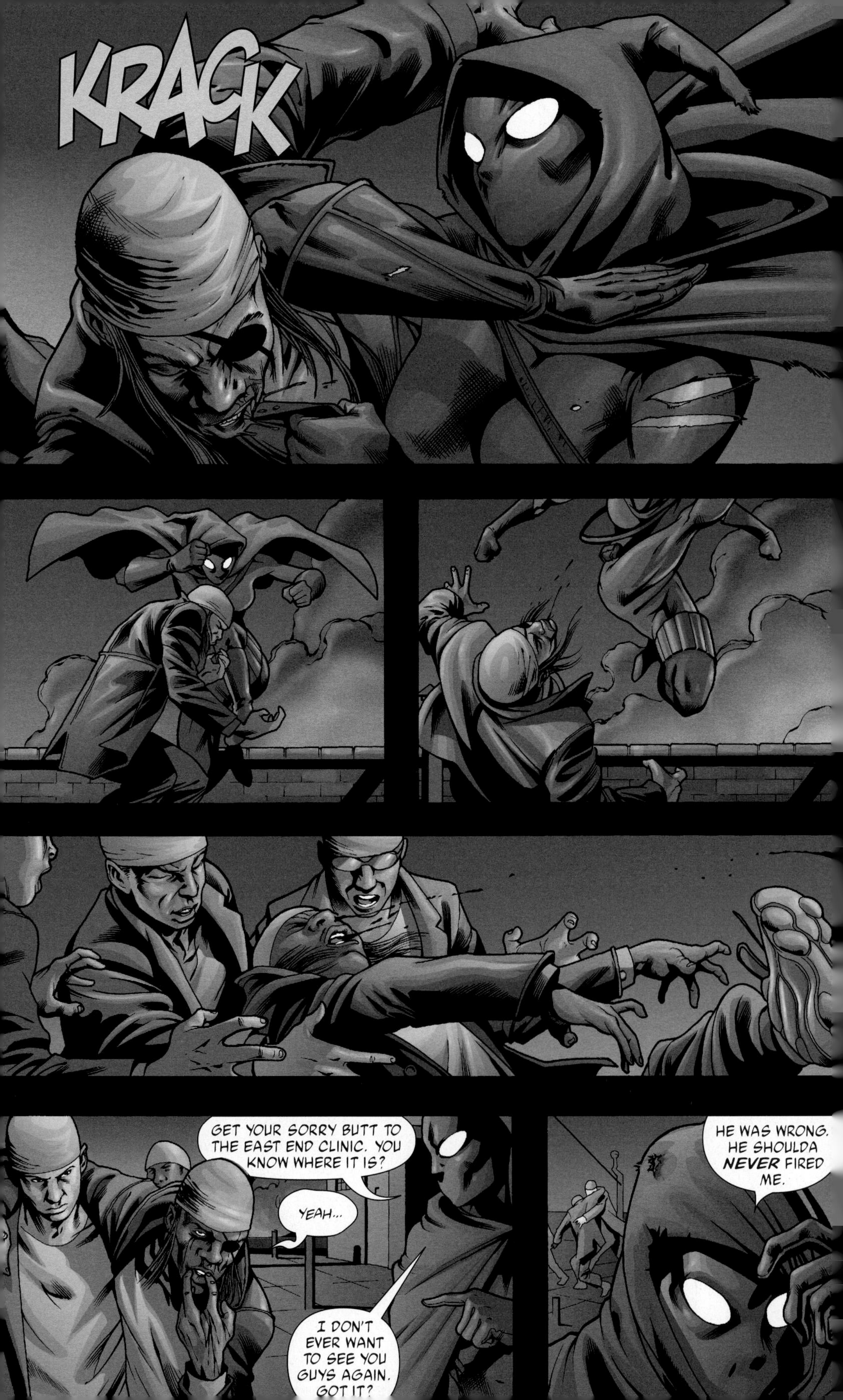
KRACK
GET YOUR SORRY BUTT TO THE EAST END CLINIC. YOU KNOW WHERE IT IS?
YEAH...
I DON'T EVER WANT TO SEE YOU GUYS AGAIN. GOT IT?
HE WAS WRONG. HE SHOULDA NEVER FIRED ME.

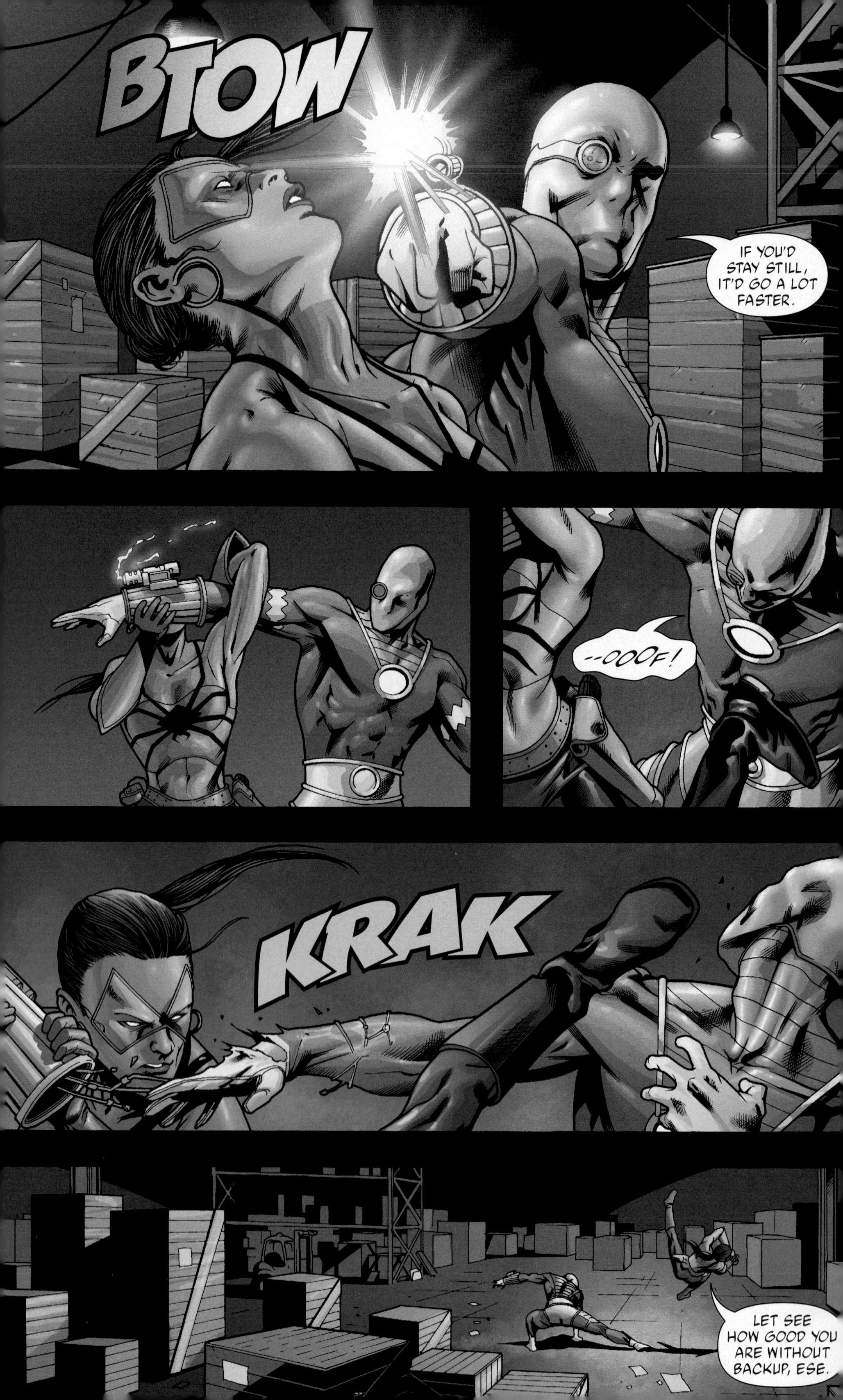
BTOW
IF YOU'D STAY STILL, IT'D GO A LOT FASTER.
--OOOF!
KRAK
LET SEE HOW GOOD YOU ARE WITHOUT BACKUP, ESE.

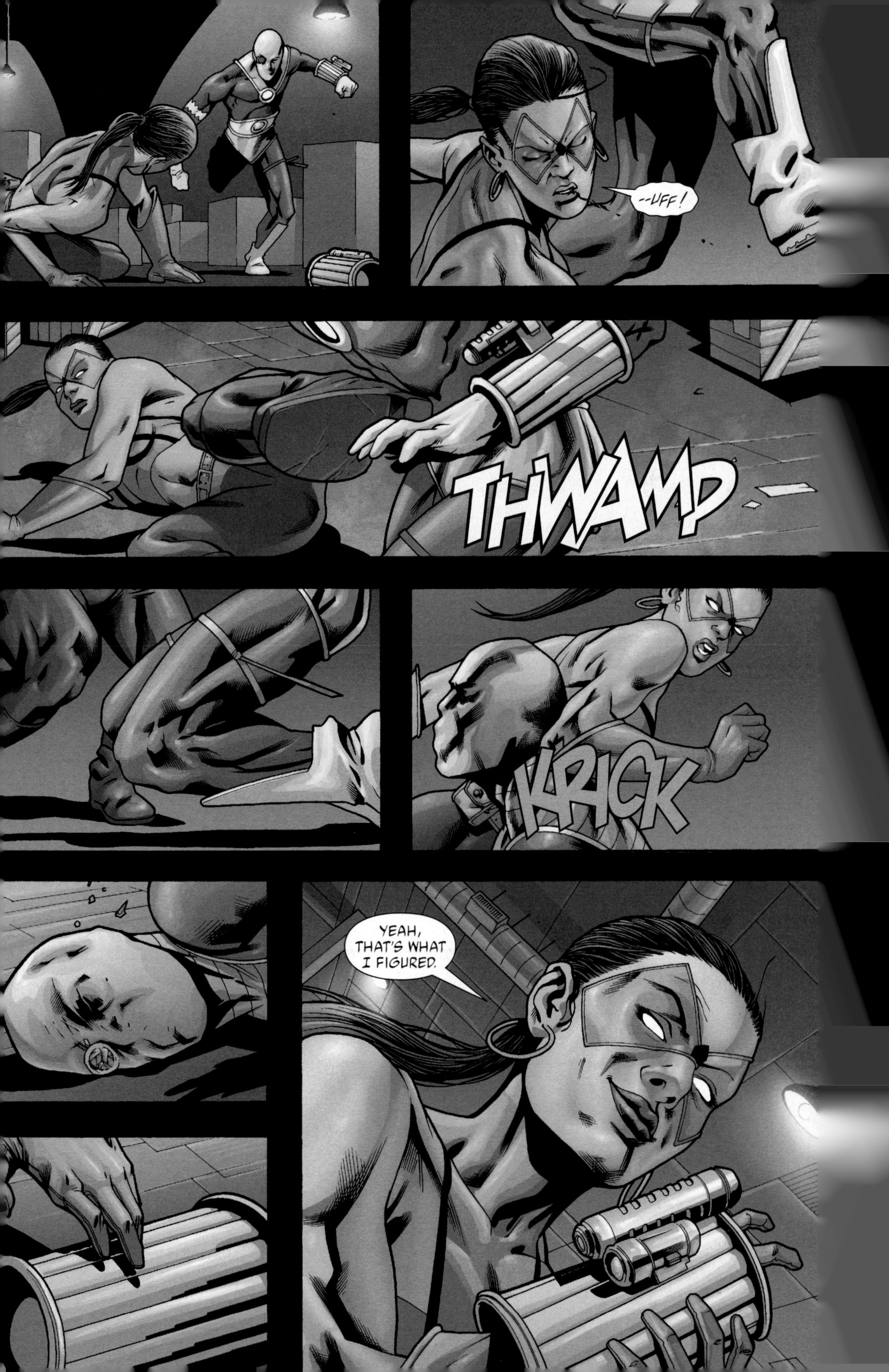
--UFF!
THWAMP
KRICK
YEAH, THAT'S WHAT I FIGURED.

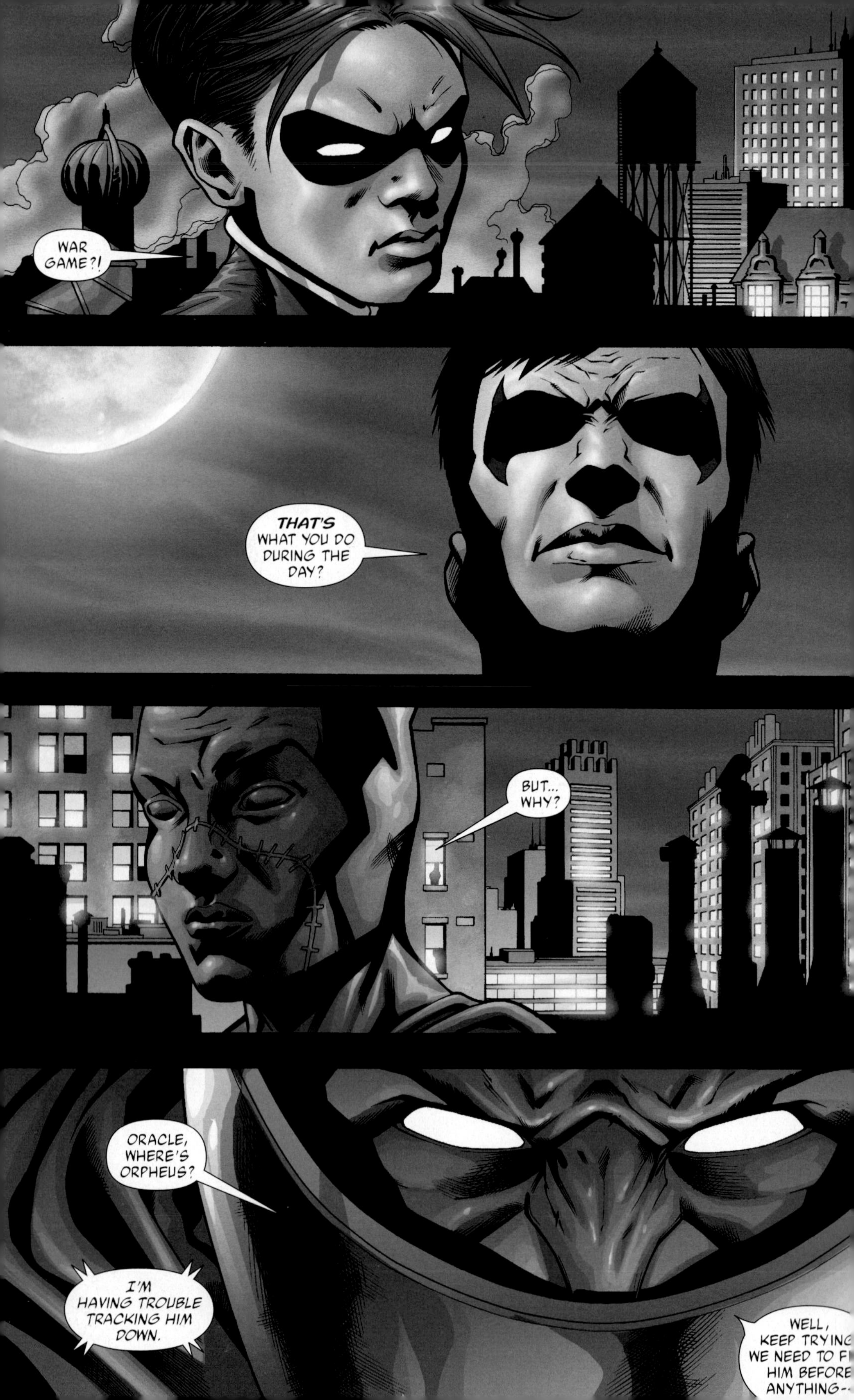
WAR GAME?!
THAT'S WHAT YOU DO DURING THE DAY?
BUT... WHY?
ORACLE, WHERE'S ORPHEUS?
I'M HAVING TROUBLE TRACKING HIM DOWN.
WELL, KEEP TRYING

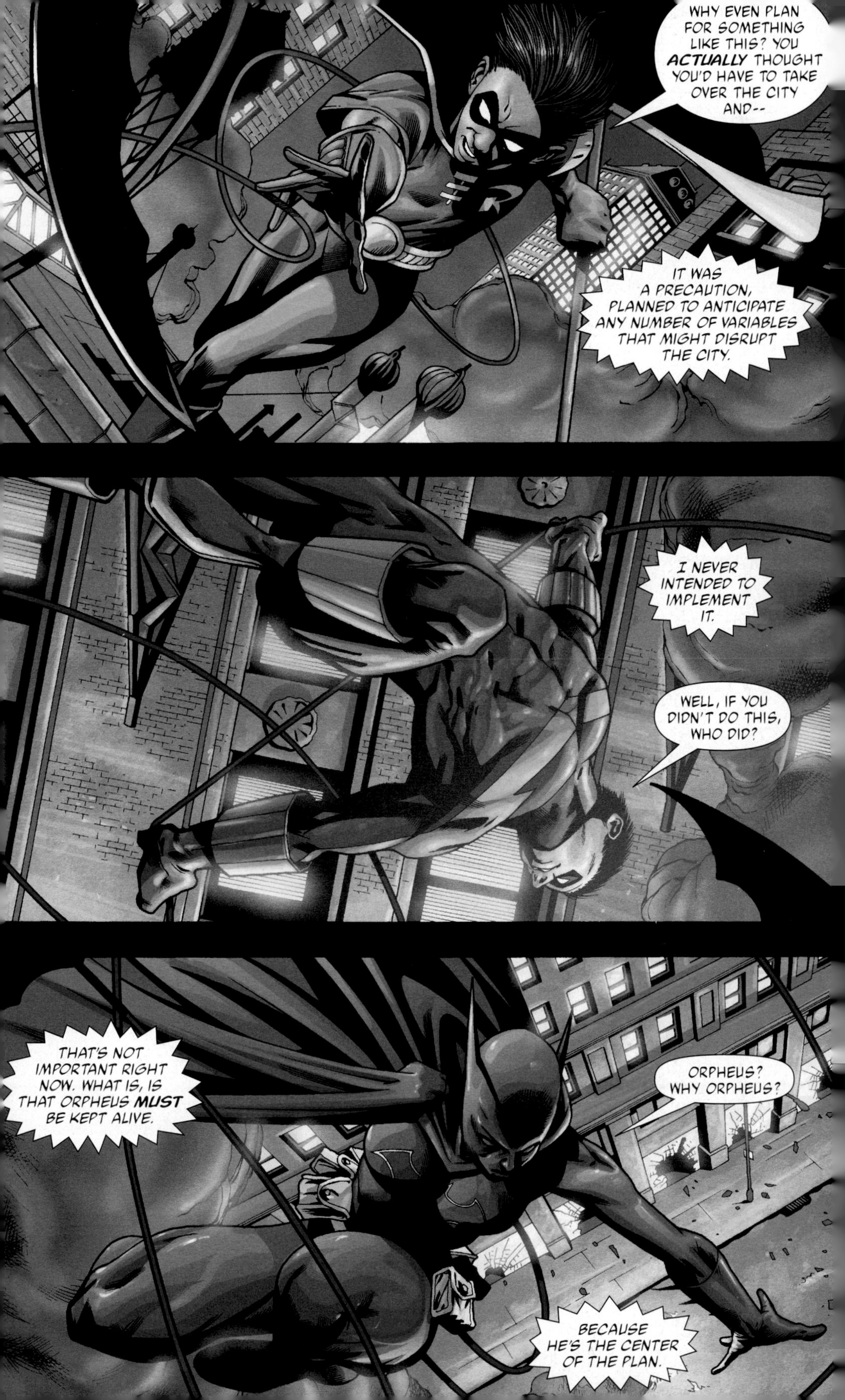
WHY EVEN PLAN FOR SOMETHING LIKE THIS? YOU **ACTUALLY** THOUGHT YOU'D HAVE TO TAKE OVER THE CITY AND--
IT WAS A PRECAUTION, PLANNED TO ANTICIPATE ANY NUMBER OF VARIABLES THAT MIGHT DISRUPT THE CITY.
I NEVER INTENDED TO IMPLEMENT IT.
WELL, IF YOU DIDN'T DO THIS, WHO DID?
THAT'S NOT IMPORTANT RIGHT NOW. WHAT IS, IS THAT ORPHEUS **MUST** BE KEPT ALIVE.
ORPHEUS? WHY ORPHEUS?
BECAUSE HE'S THE CENTER OF THE PLAN.

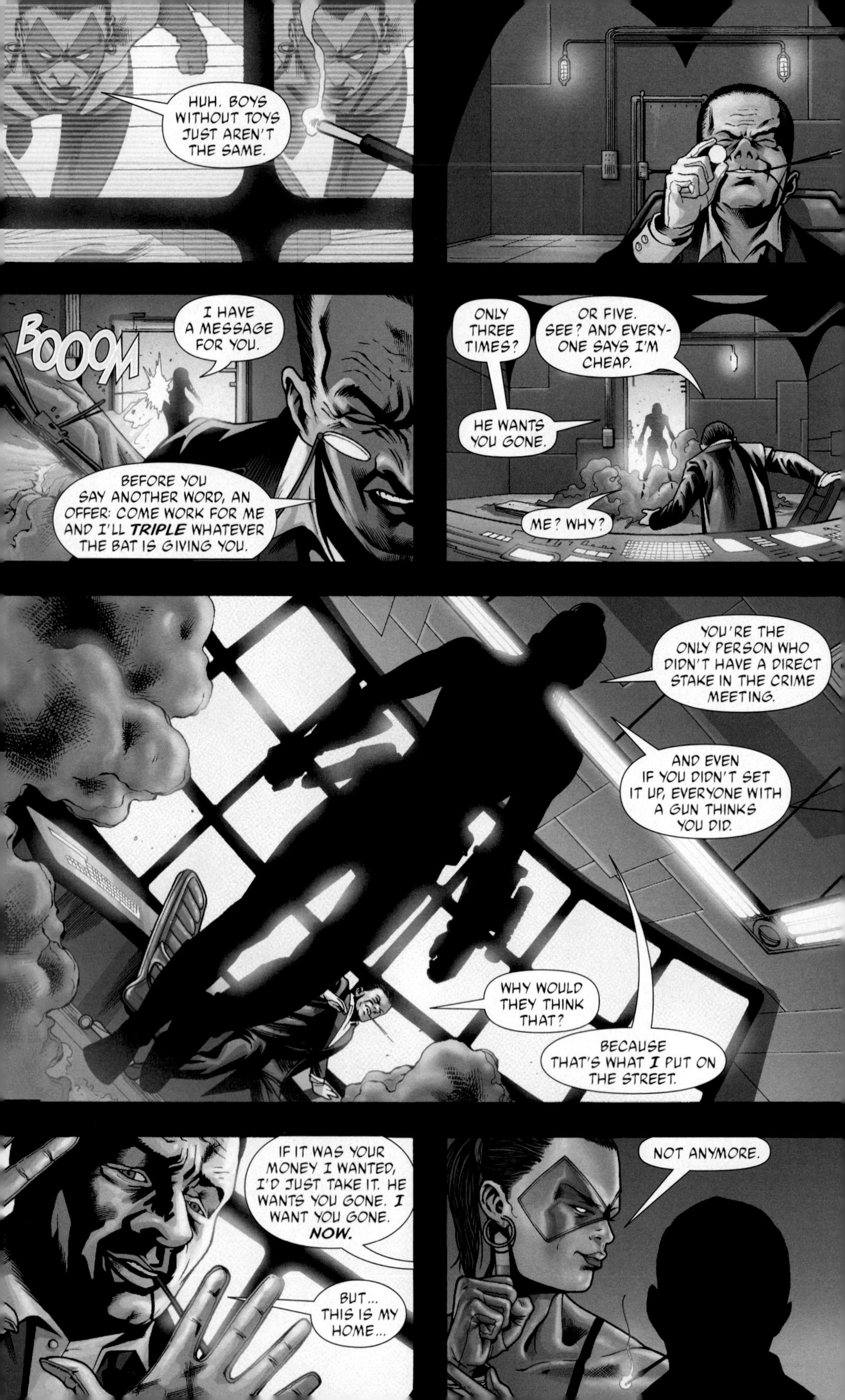
HUH. BOYS WITHOUT TOYS JUST AREN'T THE SAME.
BOOOM
I HAVE A MESSAGE FOR YOU.
BEFORE YOU SAY ANOTHER WORD, AN OFFER: COME WORK FOR ME AND I'LL *TRIPLE* WHATEVER THE BAT IS GIVING YOU.
ONLY THREE TIMES?
OR FIVE. SEE? AND EVERYONE SAYS I'M CHEAP.
HE WANTS YOU GONE.
ME? WHY?
YOU'RE THE ONLY PERSON WHO DIDN'T HAVE A DIRECT STAKE IN THE CRIME MEETING.
AND EVEN IF YOU DIDN'T SET IT UP, EVERYONE WITH A GUN THINKS YOU DID.
WHY WOULD THEY THINK THAT?
BECAUSE THAT'S WHAT *I* PUT ON THE STREET.
IF IT WAS YOUR MONEY I WANTED, I'D JUST TAKE IT. HE WANTS YOU GONE. *I* WANT YOU GONE. **NOW.**
BUT... THIS IS MY HOME...
NOT ANYMORE.

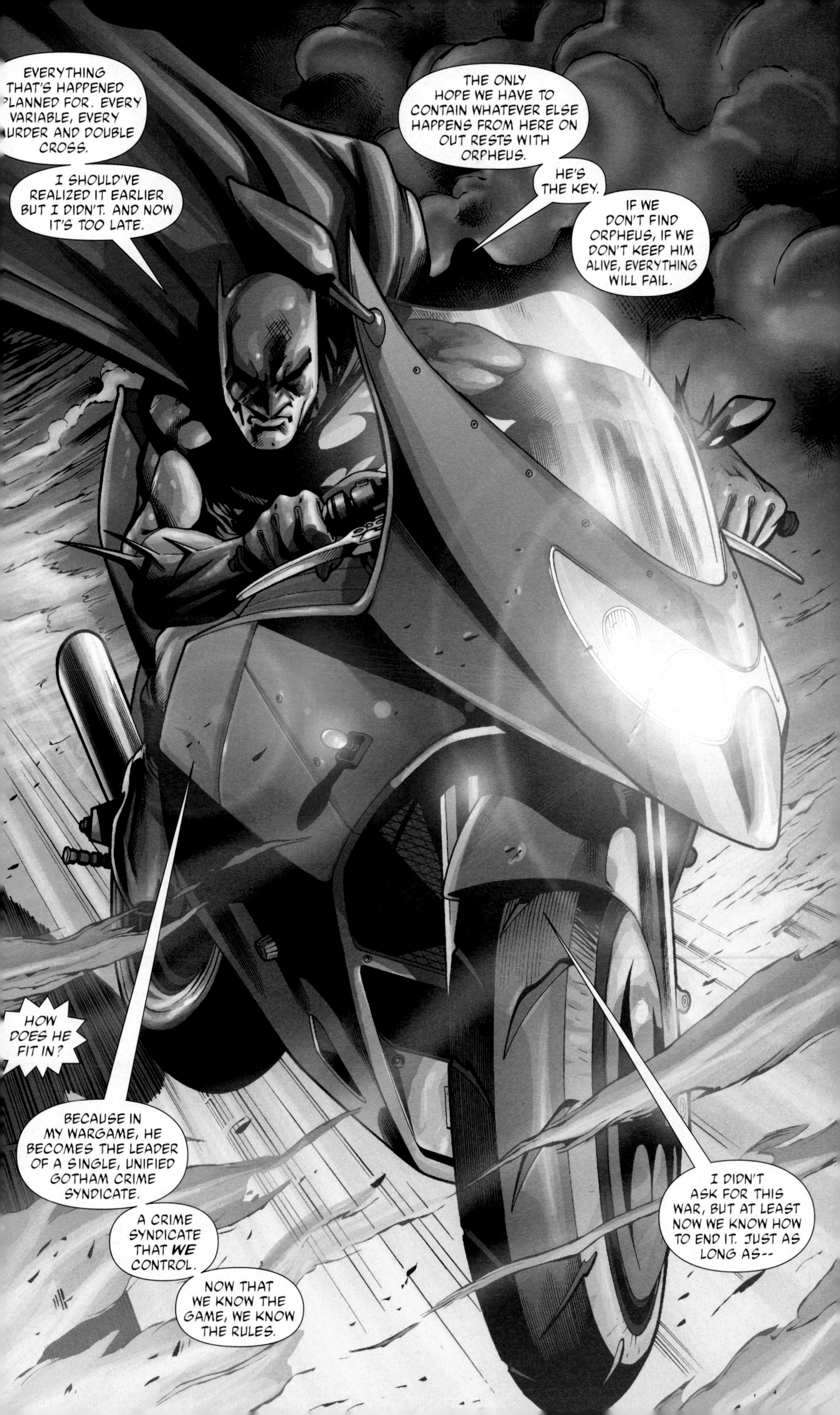
EVERYTHING THAT'S HAPPENED PLANNED FOR. EVERY VARIABLE, EVERY URDER AND DOUBLE CROSS.
I SHOULD'VE REALIZED IT EARLIER BUT I DIDN'T. AND NOW IT'S TOO LATE.
THE ONLY HOPE WE HAVE TO CONTAIN WHATEVER ELSE HAPPENS FROM HERE ON OUT RESTS WITH ORPHEUS.
HE'S THE KEY.
IF WE DON'T FIND ORPHEUS, IF WE DON'T KEEP HIM ALIVE, EVERYTHING WILL FAIL.
HOW DOES HE FIT IN?
BECAUSE IN MY WARGAME, HE BECOMES THE LEADER OF A SINGLE, UNIFIED GOTHAM CRIME SYNDICATE.
A CRIME SYNDICATE THAT *WE* CONTROL.
NOW THAT WE KNOW THE GAME, WE KNOW THE RULES.
I DIDN'T ASK FOR THIS WAR, BUT AT LEAST NOW WE KNOW HOW TO END IT. JUST AS LONG AS--

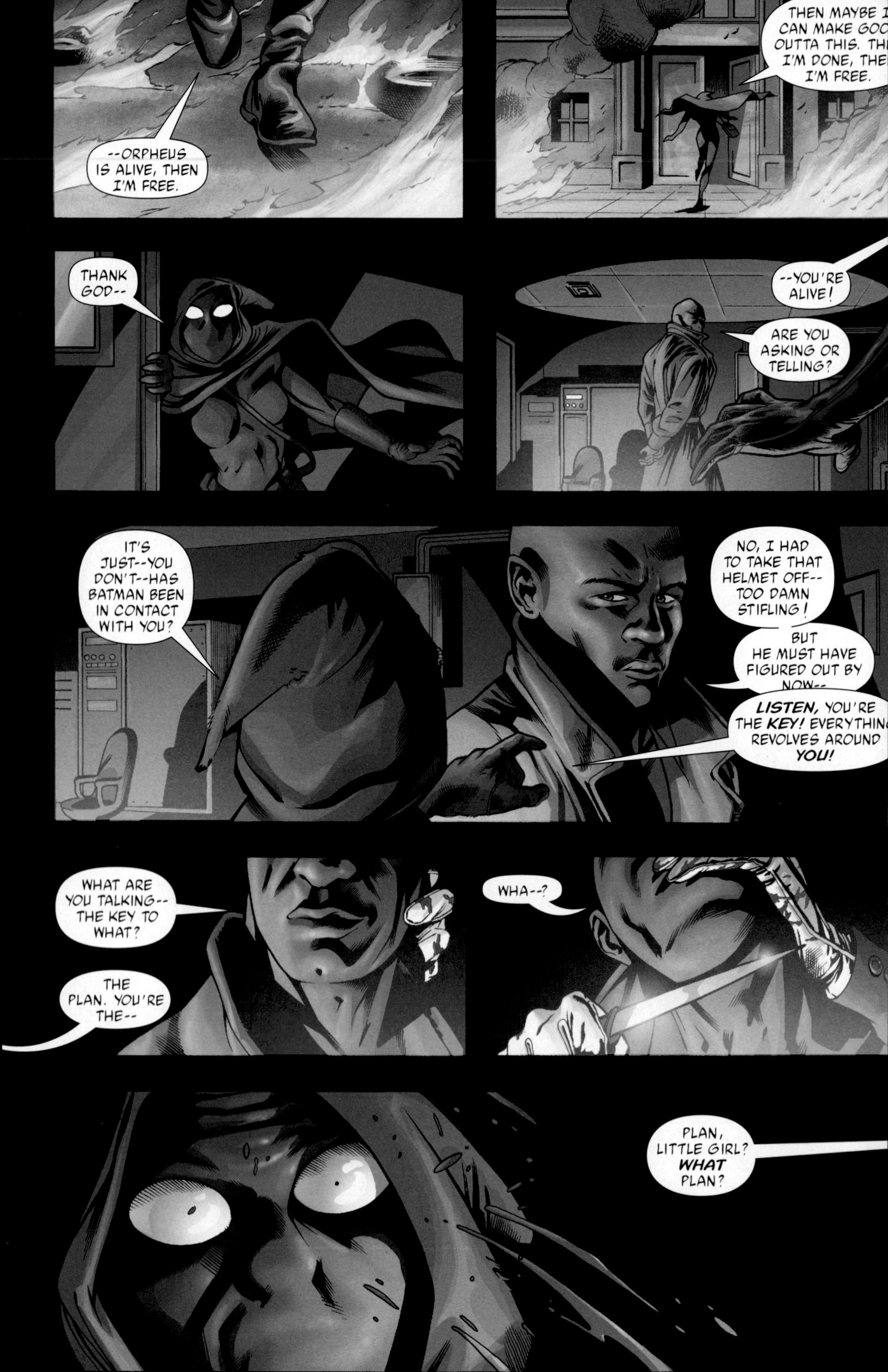
--ORPHEUS IS ALIVE, THEN I'M FREE.
THEN MAYBE I CAN MAKE GOO OUTTA THIS. TH I'M DONE, THE I'M FREE.
THANK GOD--
--YOU'RE ALIVE!
ARE YOU ASKING OR TELLING?
IT'S JUST--YOU DON'T--HAS BATMAN BEEN IN CONTACT WITH YOU?
NO, I HAD TO TAKE THAT HELMET OFF--TOO DAMN STIFLING!
BUT HE MUST HAVE FIGURED OUT BY NOW--
LISTEN, YOU'RE THE **KEY!** EVERYTHIN REVOLVES AROUND **YOU!**
WHAT ARE YOU TALKING--THE KEY TO WHAT?
THE PLAN. YOU'RE THE--
WHA--?
PLAN, LITTLE GIRL? **WHAT** PLAN?

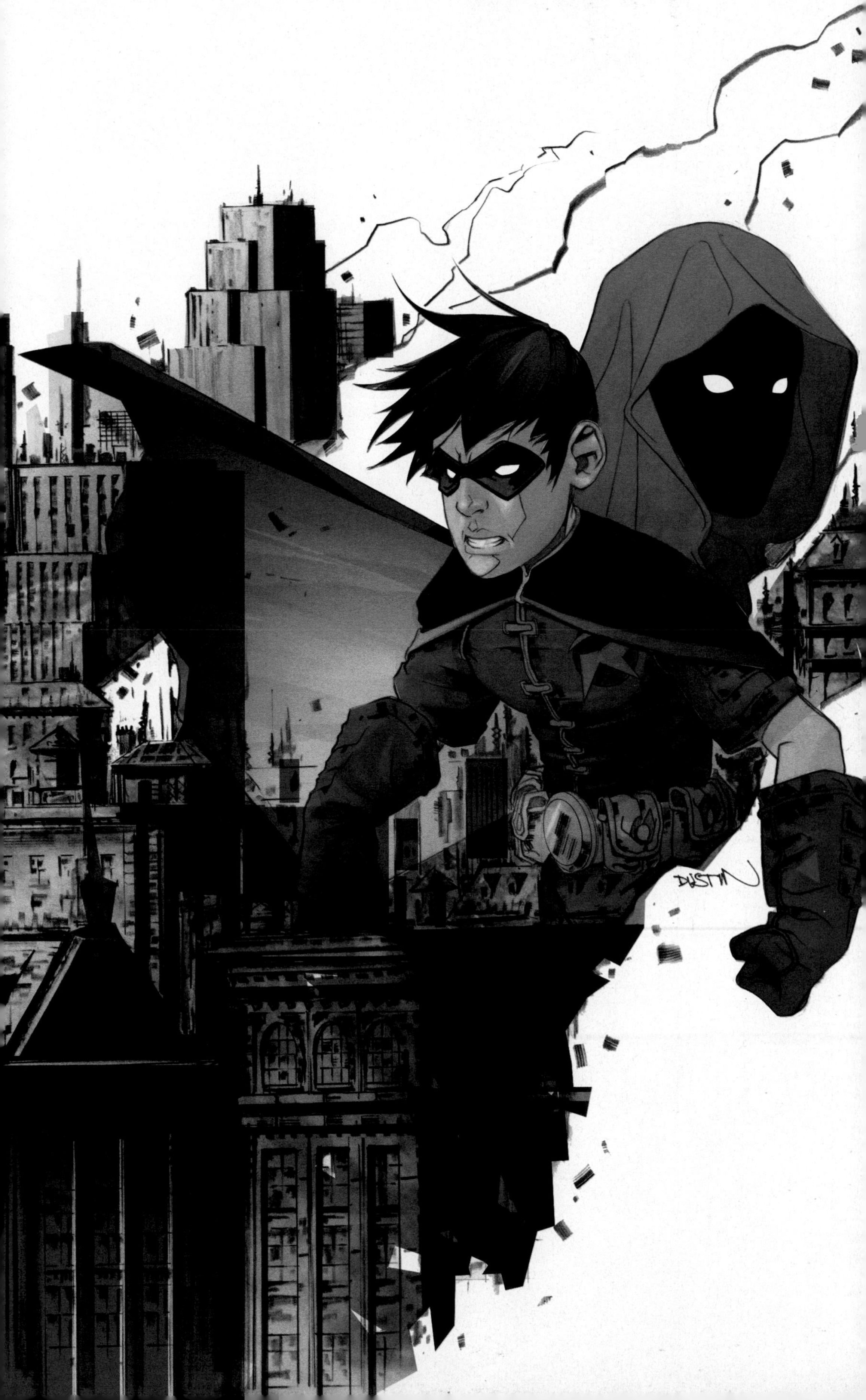
DUSTIN

COVER ART BY
DUSTIN NGUYEN

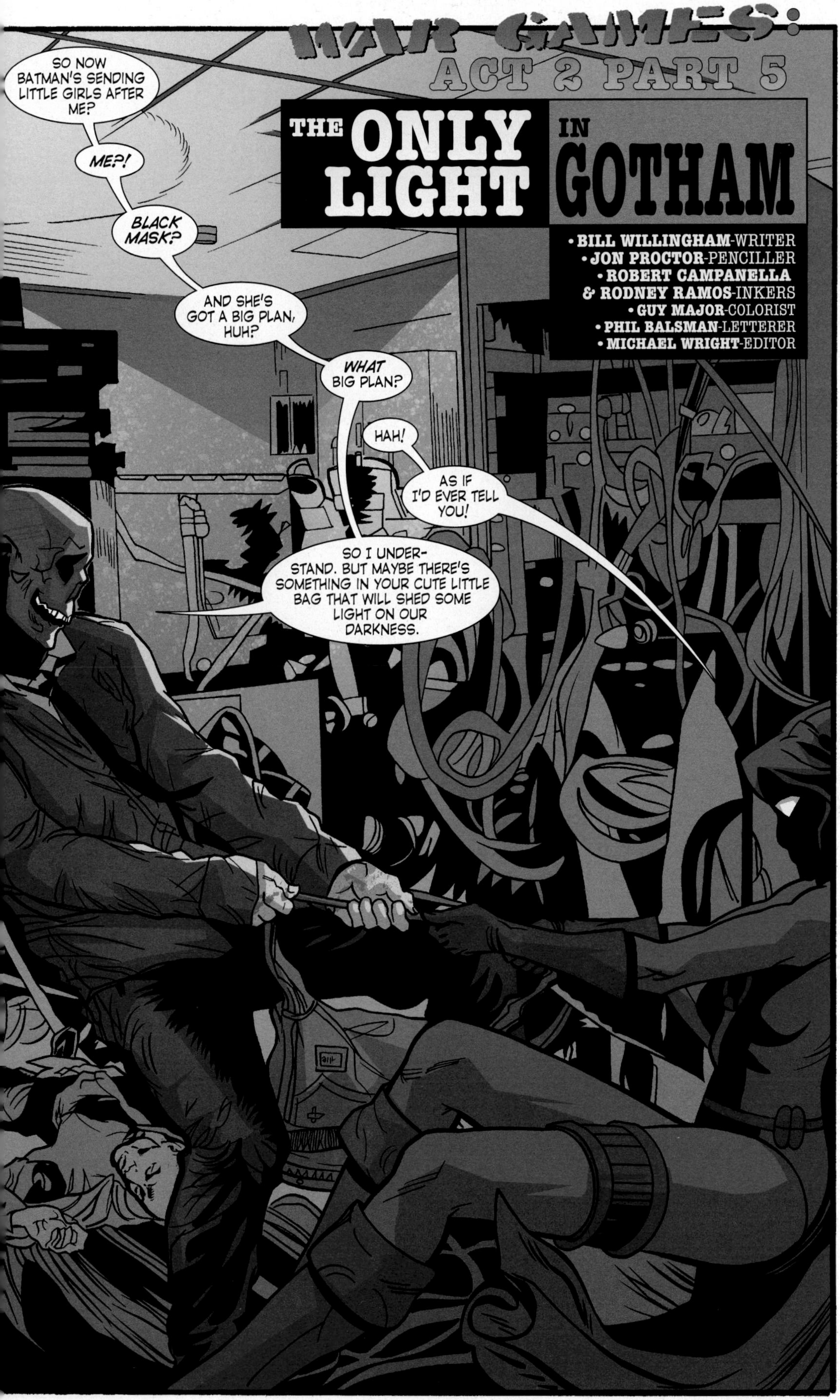
WAR GAMES:
ACT 2 PART 5
THE ONLY LIGHT IN GOTHAM
•BILL WILLINGHAM-WRITER
•JON PROCTOR-PENCILLER
•ROBERT CAMPANELLA & RODNEY RAMOS-INKERS
•GUY MAJOR-COLORIST
•PHIL BALSMAN-LETTERER
•MICHAEL WRIGHT-EDITOR
SO NOW BATMAN'S SENDING LITTLE GIRLS AFTER ME?
ME?!
BLACK MASK?
AND SHE'S GOT A BIG PLAN, HUH?
WHAT BIG PLAN?
HAH!
AS IF I'D EVER TELL YOU!
SO I UNDERSTAND. BUT MAYBE THERE'S SOMETHING IN YOUR CUTE LITTLE BAG THAT WILL SHED SOME LIGHT ON OUR DARKNESS.

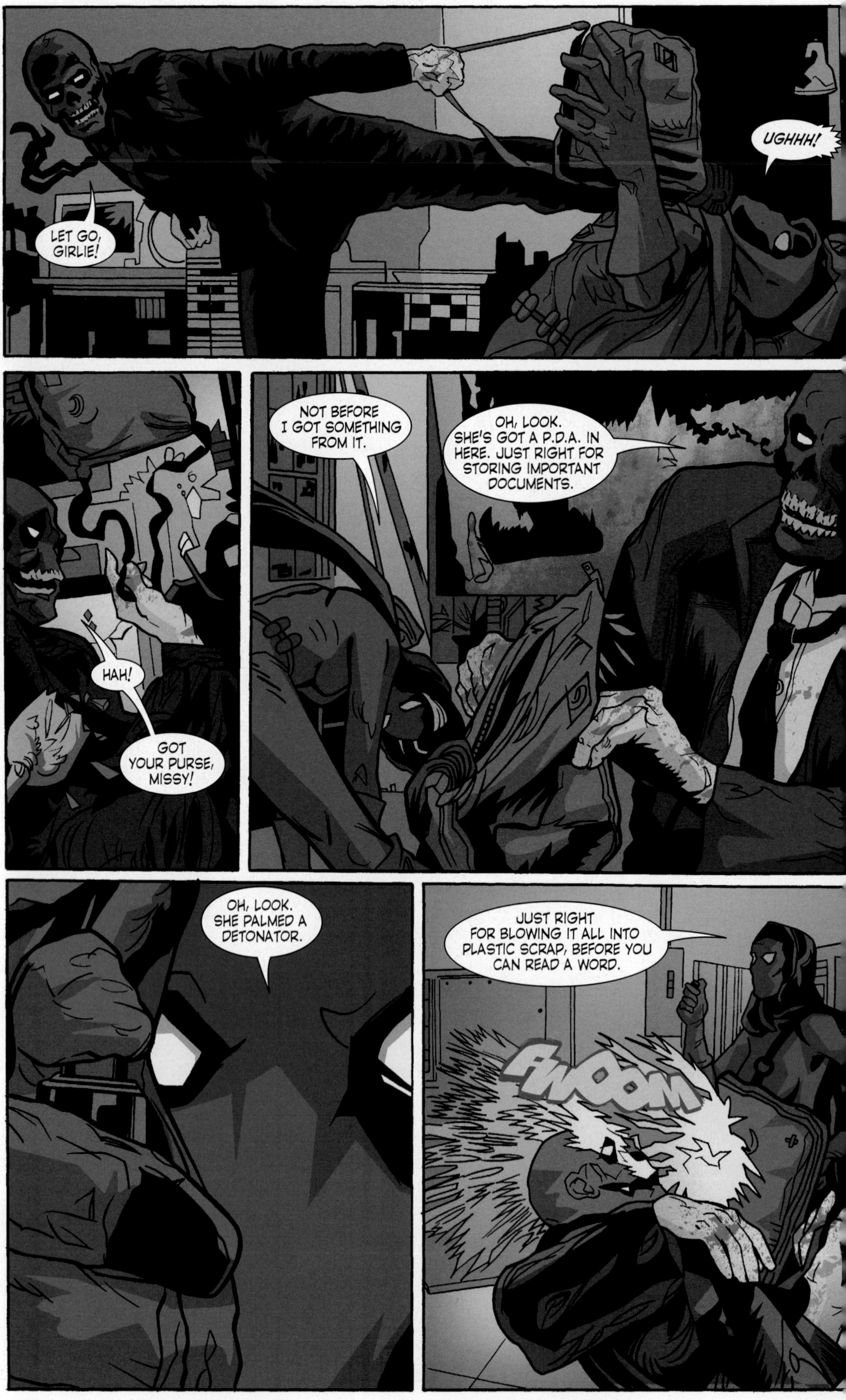
UGHHH!
LET GO, GIRLIE!
HAH!
GOT YOUR PURSE, MISSY!
NOT BEFORE I GOT SOMETHING FROM IT.
OH, LOOK. SHE'S GOT A P.D.A. IN HERE. JUST RIGHT FOR STORING IMPORTANT DOCUMENTS.
OH, LOOK. SHE PALMED A DETONATOR.
JUST RIGHT FOR BLOWING IT ALL INTO PLASTIC SCRAP, BEFORE YOU CAN READ A WORD.
FWOOM

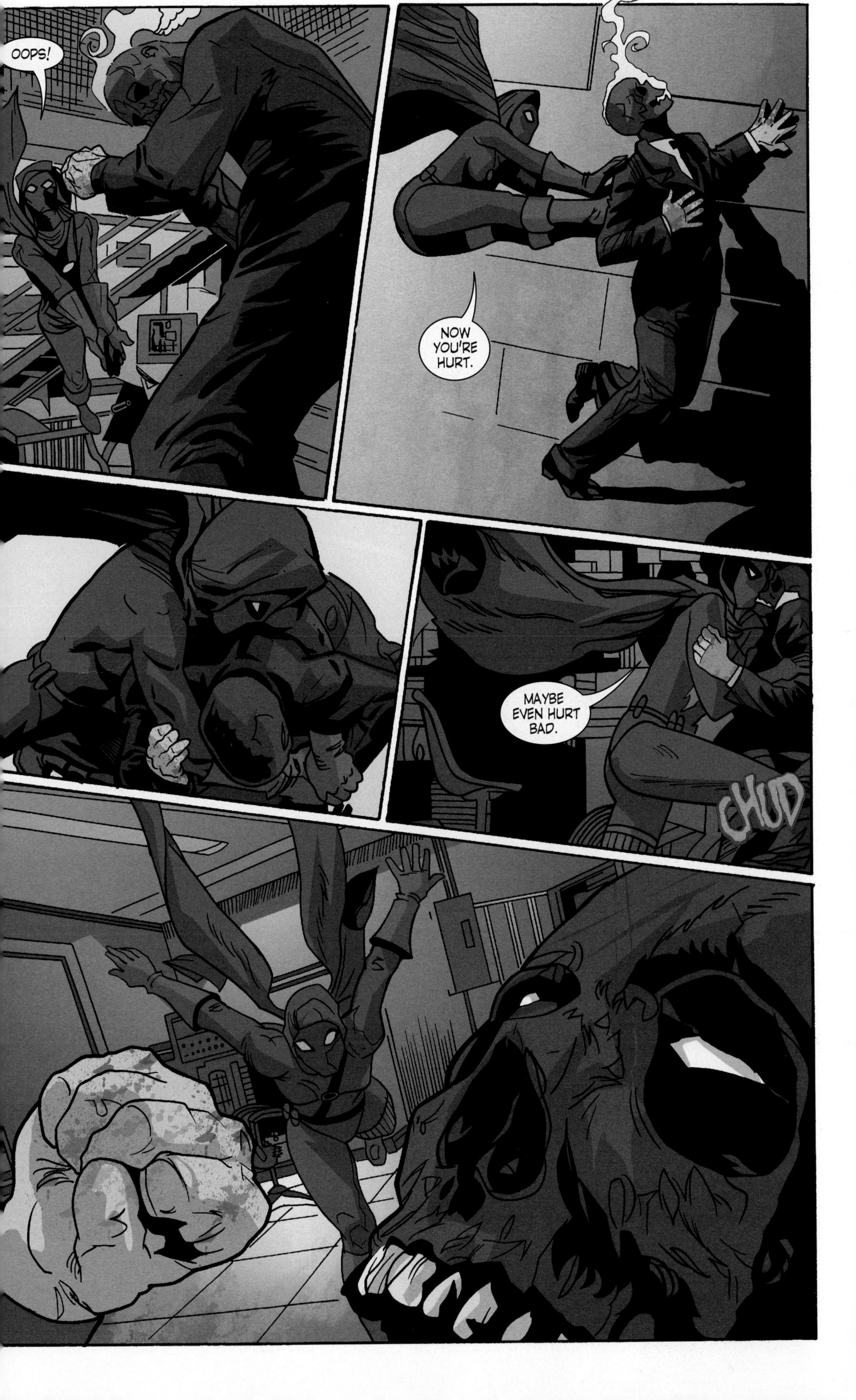
OOPS!
NOW YOU'RE HURT.
MAYBE EVEN HURT BAD.
CHUD

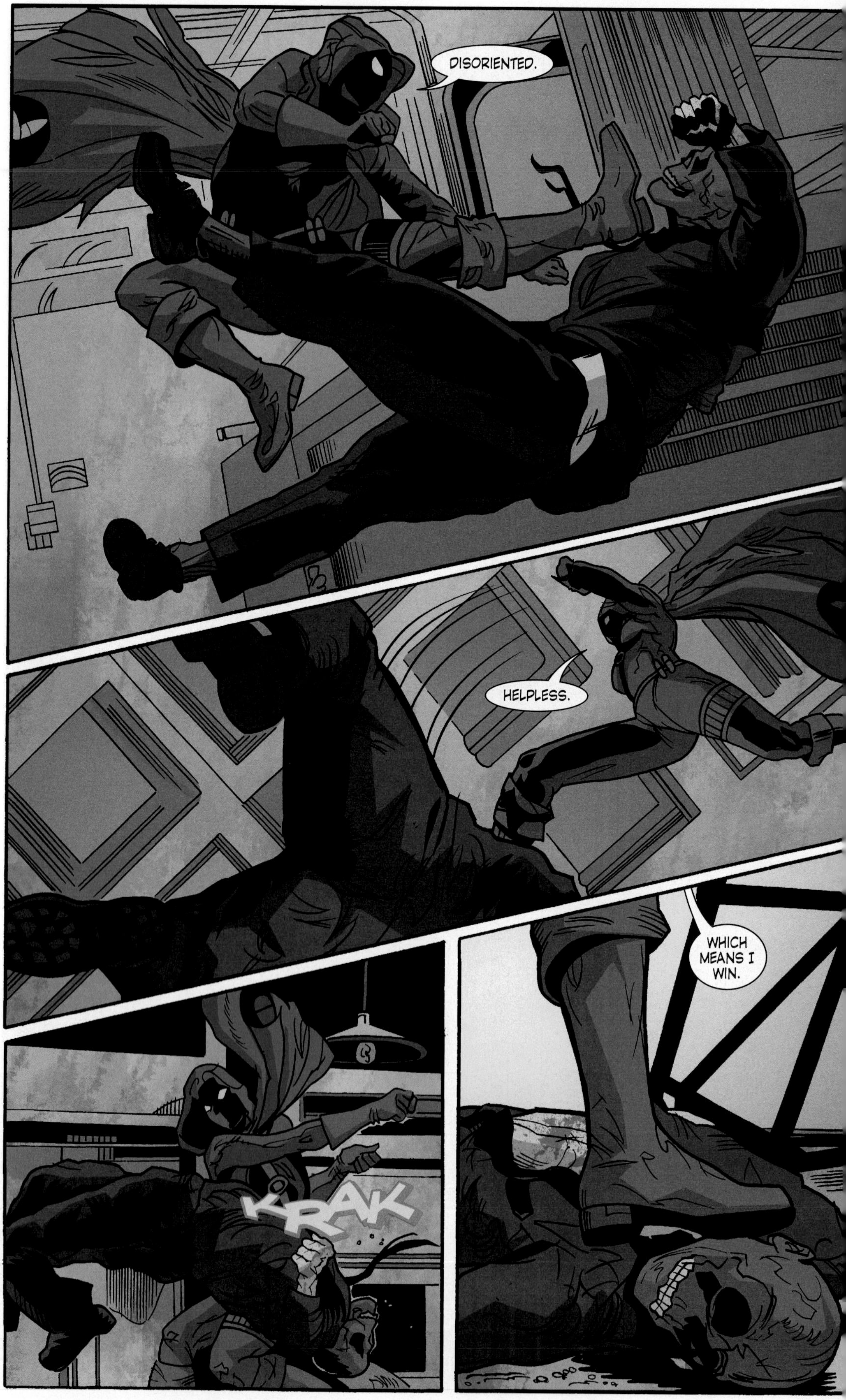
DISORIENTED.
HELPLESS.
KRAK
WHICH MEANS I WIN.

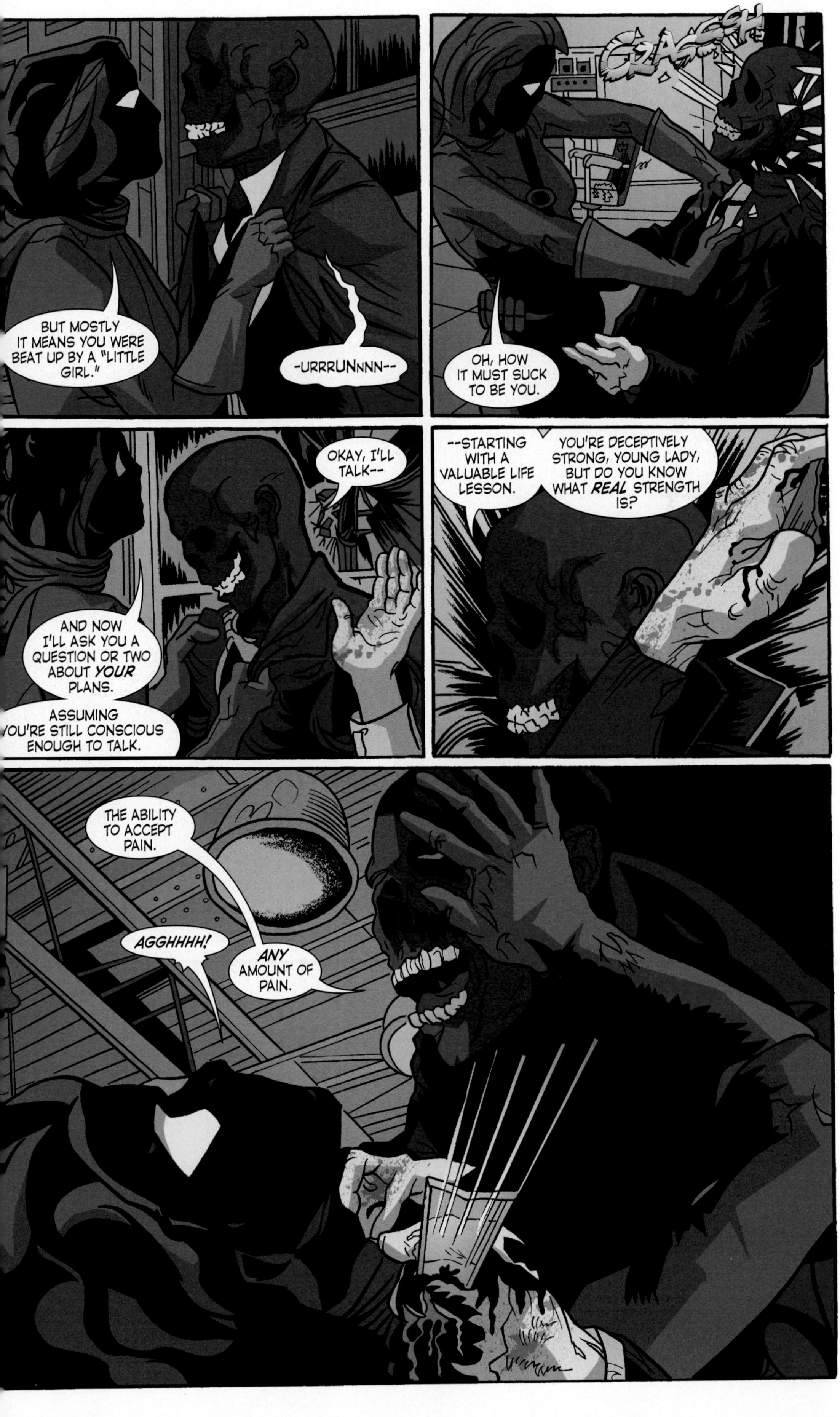
BUT MOSTLY IT MEANS YOU WERE BEAT UP BY A "LITTLE GIRL."
-URRRUNNNN--
OH, HOW IT MUST SUCK TO BE YOU.
AND NOW I'LL ASK YOU A QUESTION OR TWO ABOUT YOUR PLANS.
ASSUMING YOU'RE STILL CONSCIOUS ENOUGH TO TALK.
OKAY, I'LL TALK--
--STARTING WITH A VALUABLE LIFE LESSON.
YOU'RE DECEPTIVELY STRONG, YOUNG LADY, BUT DO YOU KNOW WHAT REAL STRENGTH IS?
THE ABILITY TO ACCEPT PAIN.
AGGHHHH!
ANY AMOUNT OF PAIN.

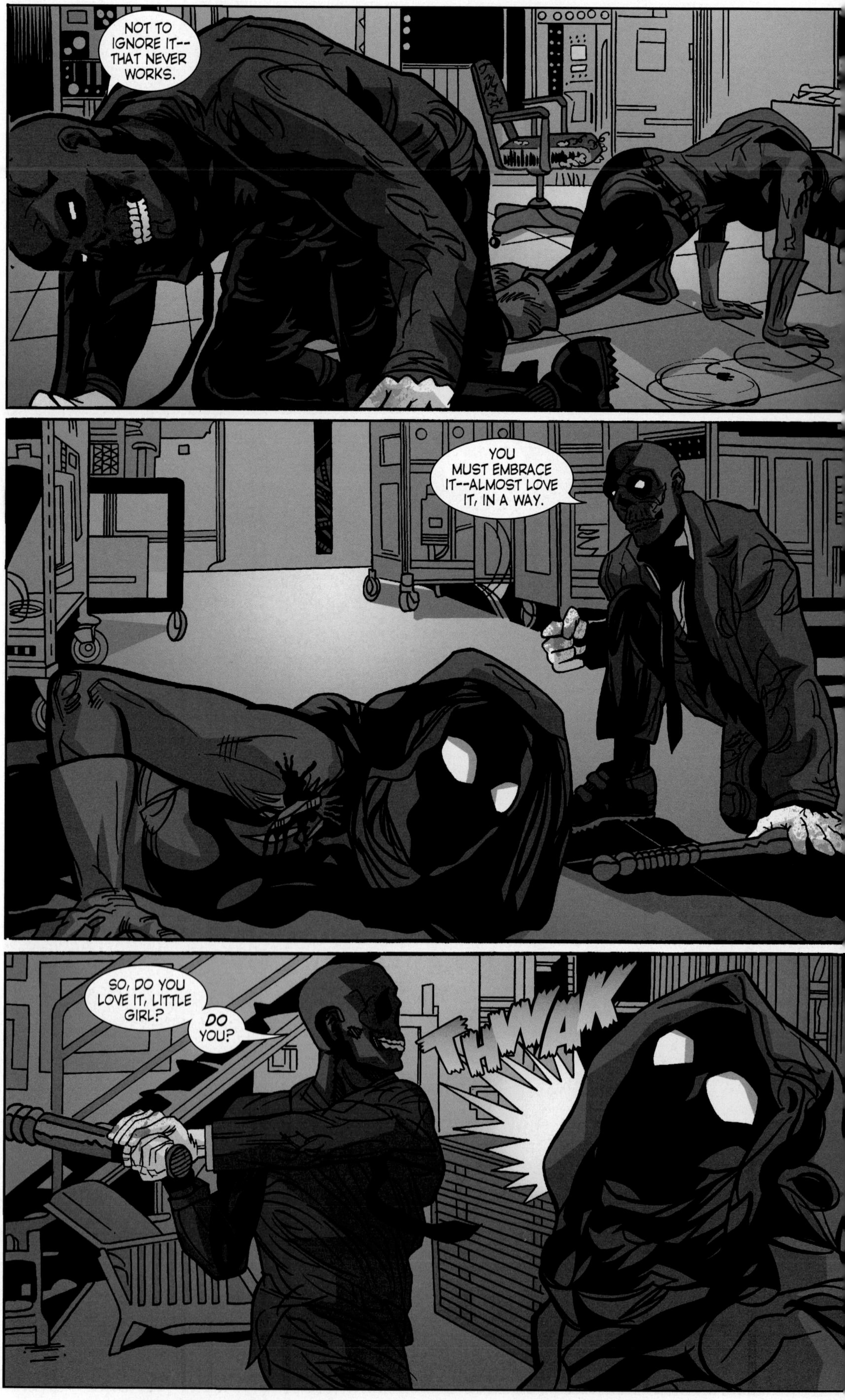
NOT TO IGNORE IT-- THAT NEVER WORKS.
YOU MUST EMBRACE IT--ALMOST LOVE IT, IN A WAY.
SO, DO YOU LOVE IT, LITTLE GIRL?
DO YOU?
THWAK

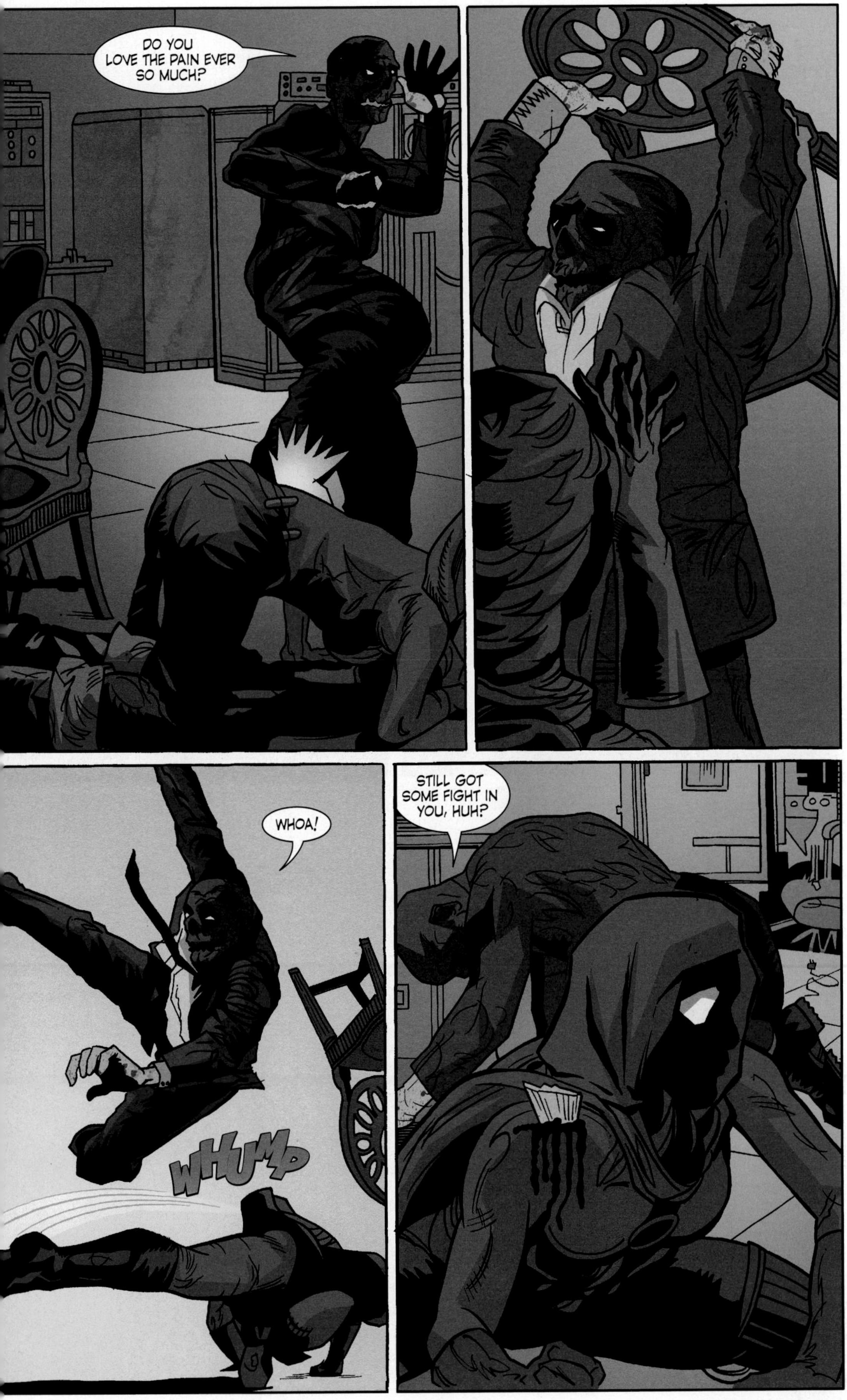
DO YOU LOVE THE PAIN EVER SO MUCH?
WHOA!
WHUMP
STILL GOT SOME FIGHT IN YOU, HUH?

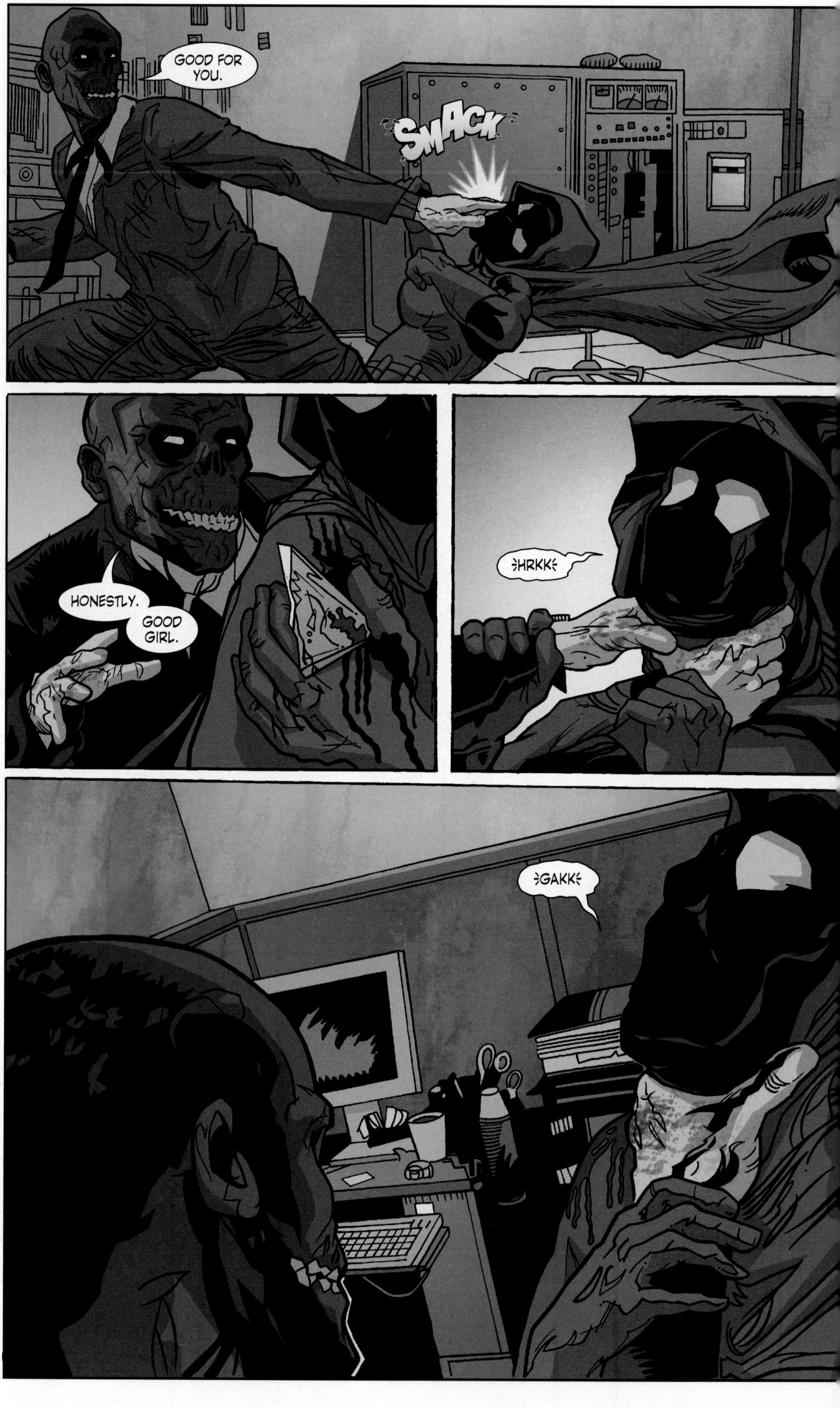
GOOD FOR YOU.
SMACK
HONESTLY.
GOOD GIRL.
HRKK
GAKK

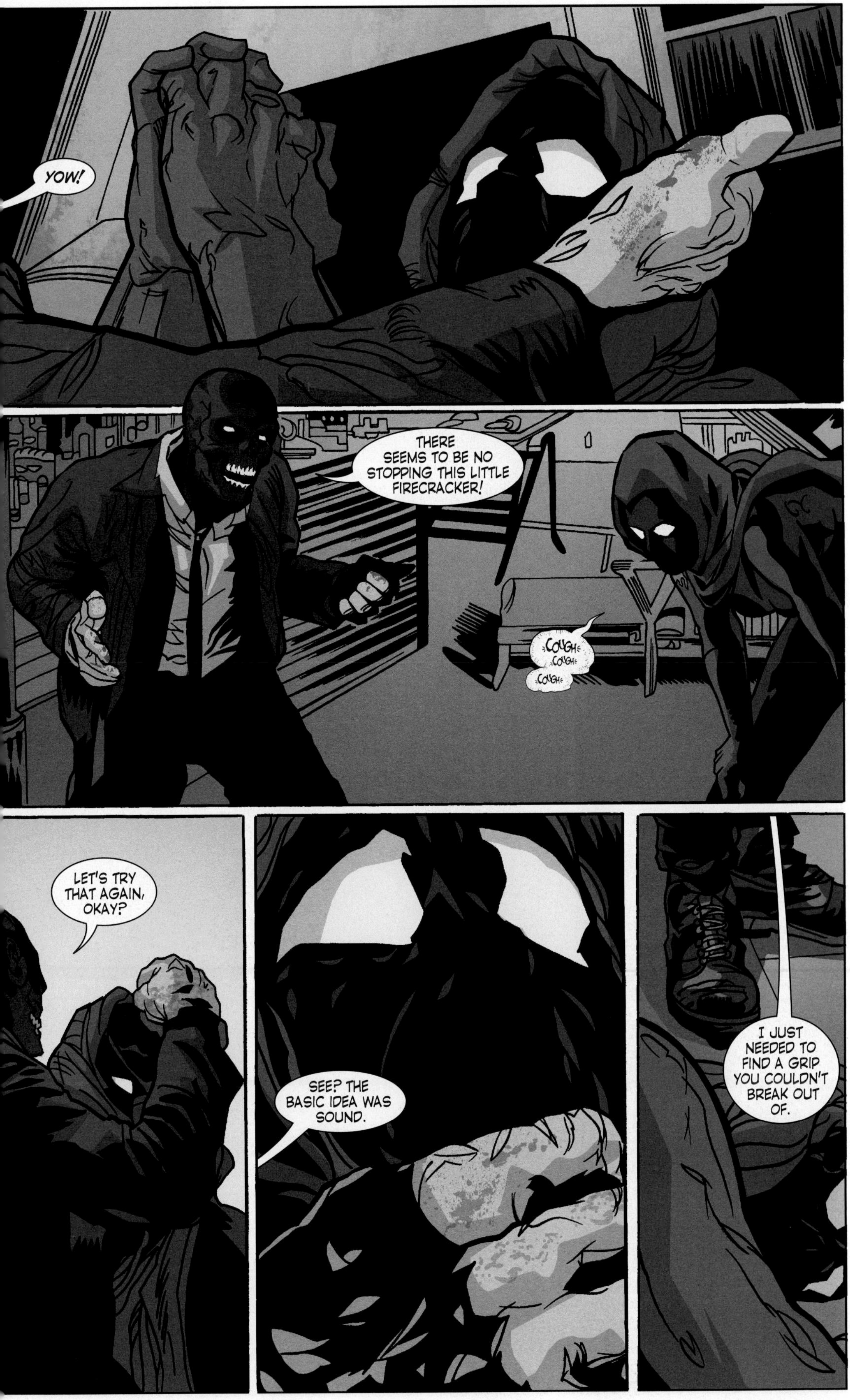
YOW!
THERE SEEMS TO BE NO STOPPING THIS LITTLE FIRECRACKER!
COUGH COUGH COUGH COUGH
LET'S TRY THAT AGAIN, OKAY?
SEE? THE BASIC IDEA WAS SOUND.
I JUST NEEDED TO FIND A GRIP YOU COULDN'T BREAK OUT OF.

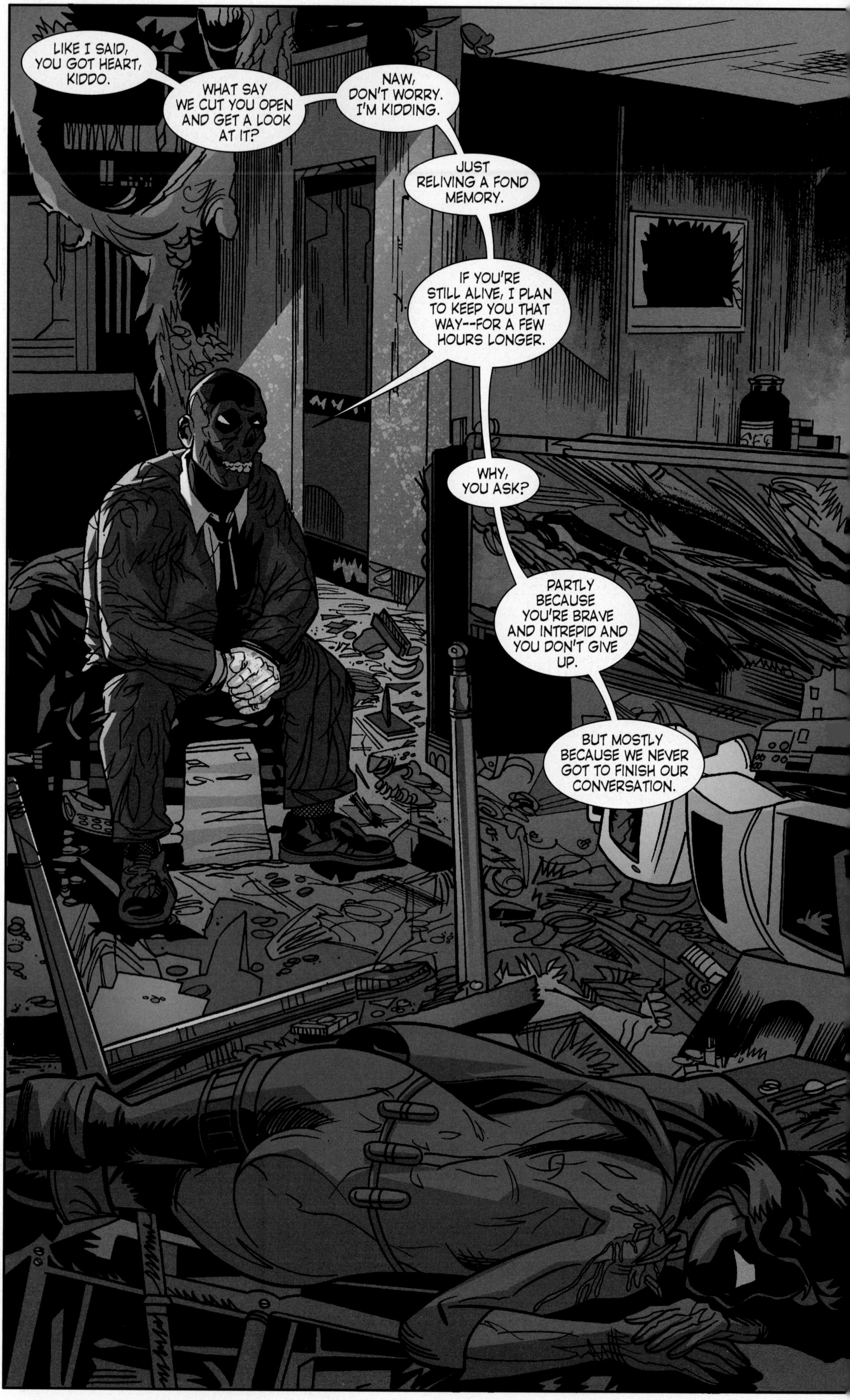
LIKE I SAID, YOU GOT HEART, KIDDO.
WHAT SAY WE CUT YOU OPEN AND GET A LOOK AT IT?
NAW, DON'T WORRY. I'M KIDDING.
JUST RELIVING A FOND MEMORY.
IF YOU'RE STILL ALIVE, I PLAN TO KEEP YOU THAT WAY--FOR A FEW HOURS LONGER.
WHY, YOU ASK?
PARTLY BECAUSE YOU'RE BRAVE AND INTREPID AND YOU DON'T GIVE UP.
BUT MOSTLY BECAUSE WE NEVER GOT TO FINISH OUR CONVERSATION.

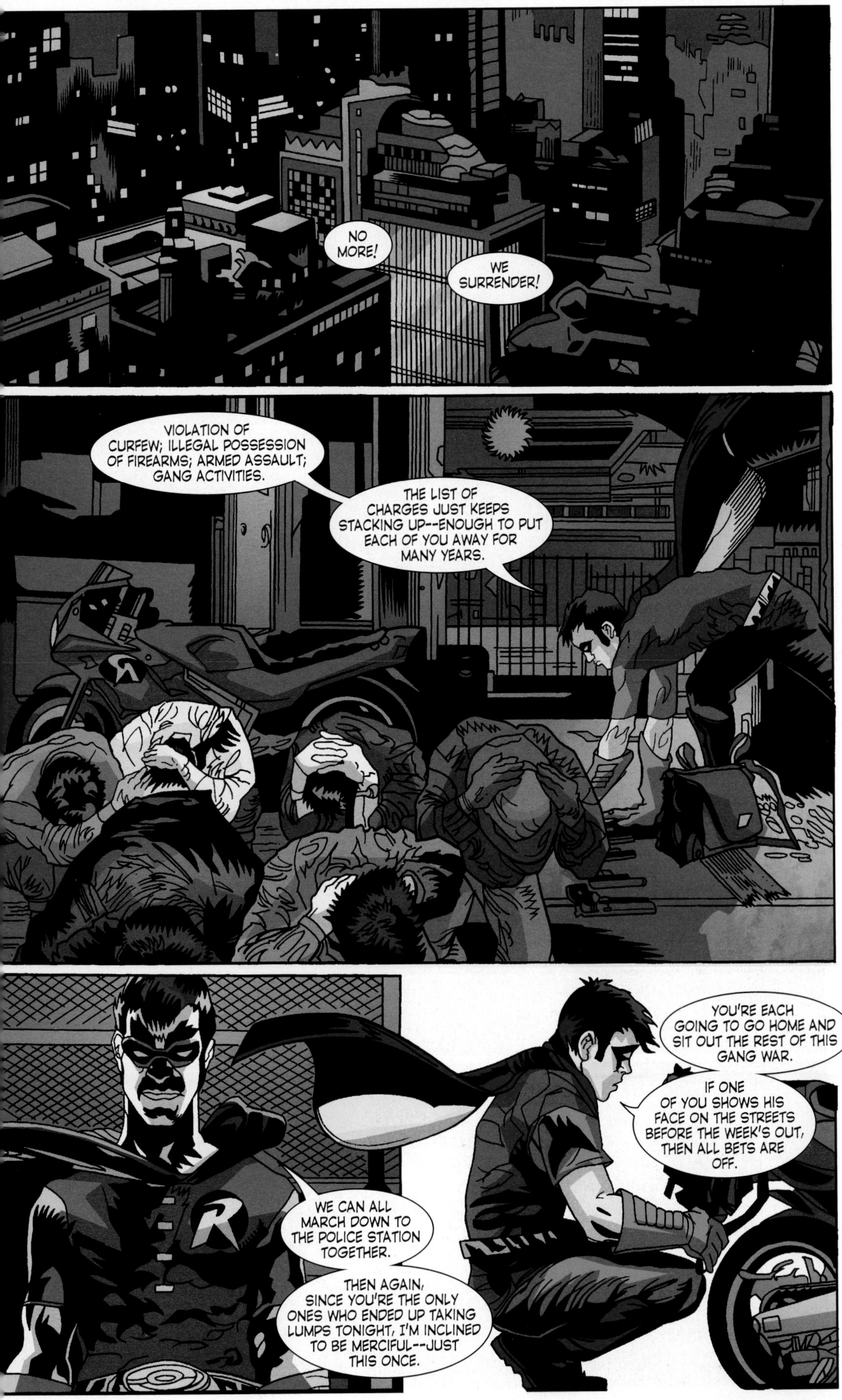
NO MORE!
WE SURRENDER!
VIOLATION OF CURFEW; ILLEGAL POSSESSION OF FIREARMS; ARMED ASSAULT; GANG ACTIVITIES.
THE LIST OF CHARGES JUST KEEPS STACKING UP--ENOUGH TO PUT EACH OF YOU AWAY FOR MANY YEARS.
WE CAN ALL MARCH DOWN TO THE POLICE STATION TOGETHER.
THEN AGAIN, SINCE YOU'RE THE ONLY ONES WHO ENDED UP TAKING LUMPS TONIGHT, I'M INCLINED TO BE MERCIFUL--JUST THIS ONCE.
YOU'RE EACH GOING TO GO HOME AND SIT OUT THE REST OF THIS GANG WAR.
IF ONE OF YOU SHOWS HIS FACE ON THE STREETS BEFORE THE WEEK'S OUT, THEN ALL BETS ARE OFF.

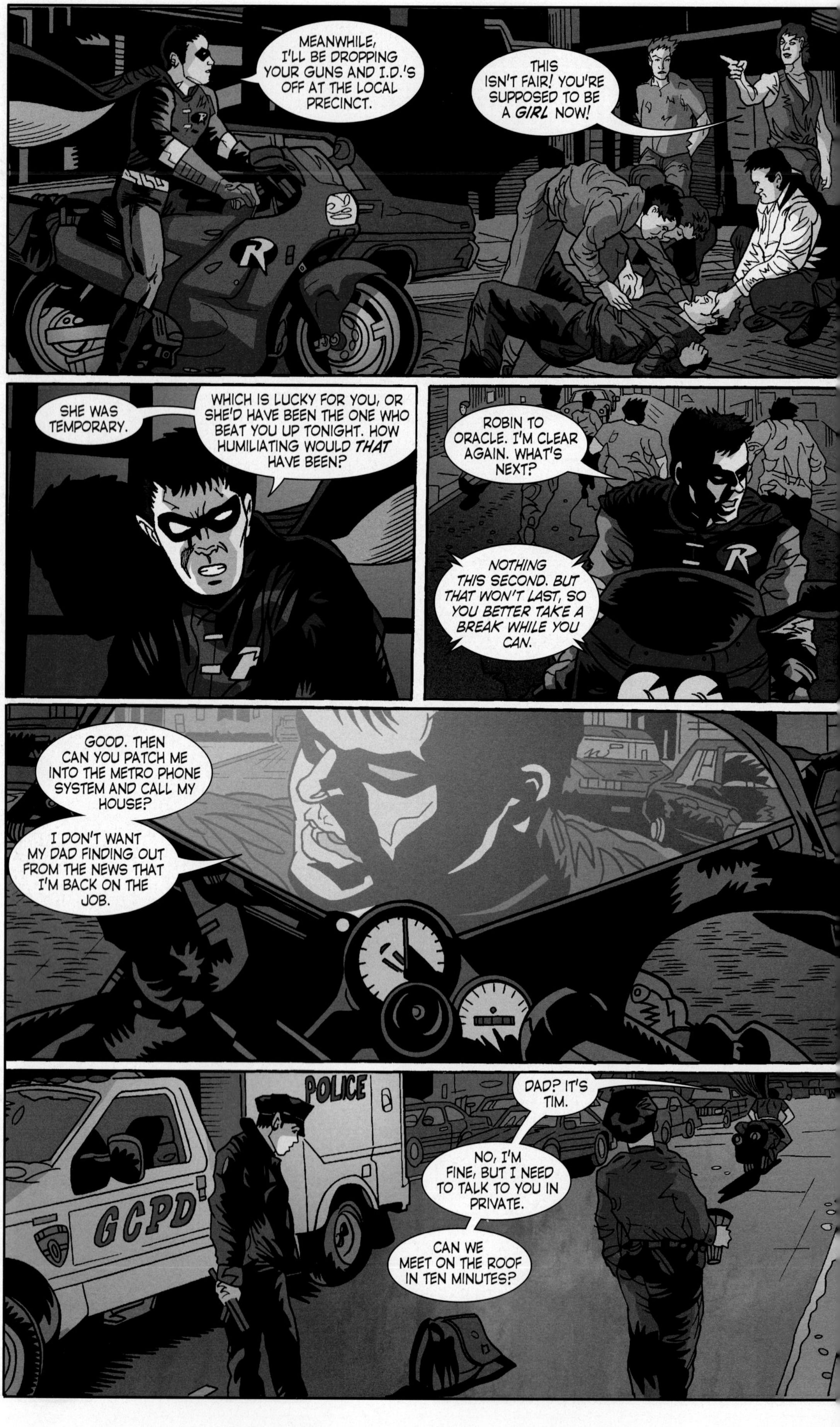
MEANWHILE, I'LL BE DROPPING YOUR GUNS AND I.D.'S OFF AT THE LOCAL PRECINCT.
THIS ISN'T FAIR! YOU'RE SUPPOSED TO BE A *GIRL* NOW!
SHE WAS TEMPORARY.
WHICH IS LUCKY FOR YOU, OR SHE'D HAVE BEEN THE ONE WHO BEAT YOU UP TONIGHT. HOW HUMILIATING WOULD *THAT* HAVE BEEN?
ROBIN TO ORACLE. I'M CLEAR AGAIN. WHAT'S NEXT?
NOTHING THIS SECOND. BUT THAT WON'T LAST, SO YOU BETTER TAKE A BREAK WHILE YOU CAN.
GOOD. THEN CAN YOU PATCH ME INTO THE METRO PHONE SYSTEM AND CALL MY HOUSE?
I DON'T WANT MY DAD FINDING OUT FROM THE NEWS THAT I'M BACK ON THE JOB.
POLICE
GCPD
DAD? IT'S TIM.
NO, I'M FINE, BUT I NEED TO TALK TO YOU IN PRIVATE.
CAN WE MEET ON THE ROOF IN TEN MINUTES?

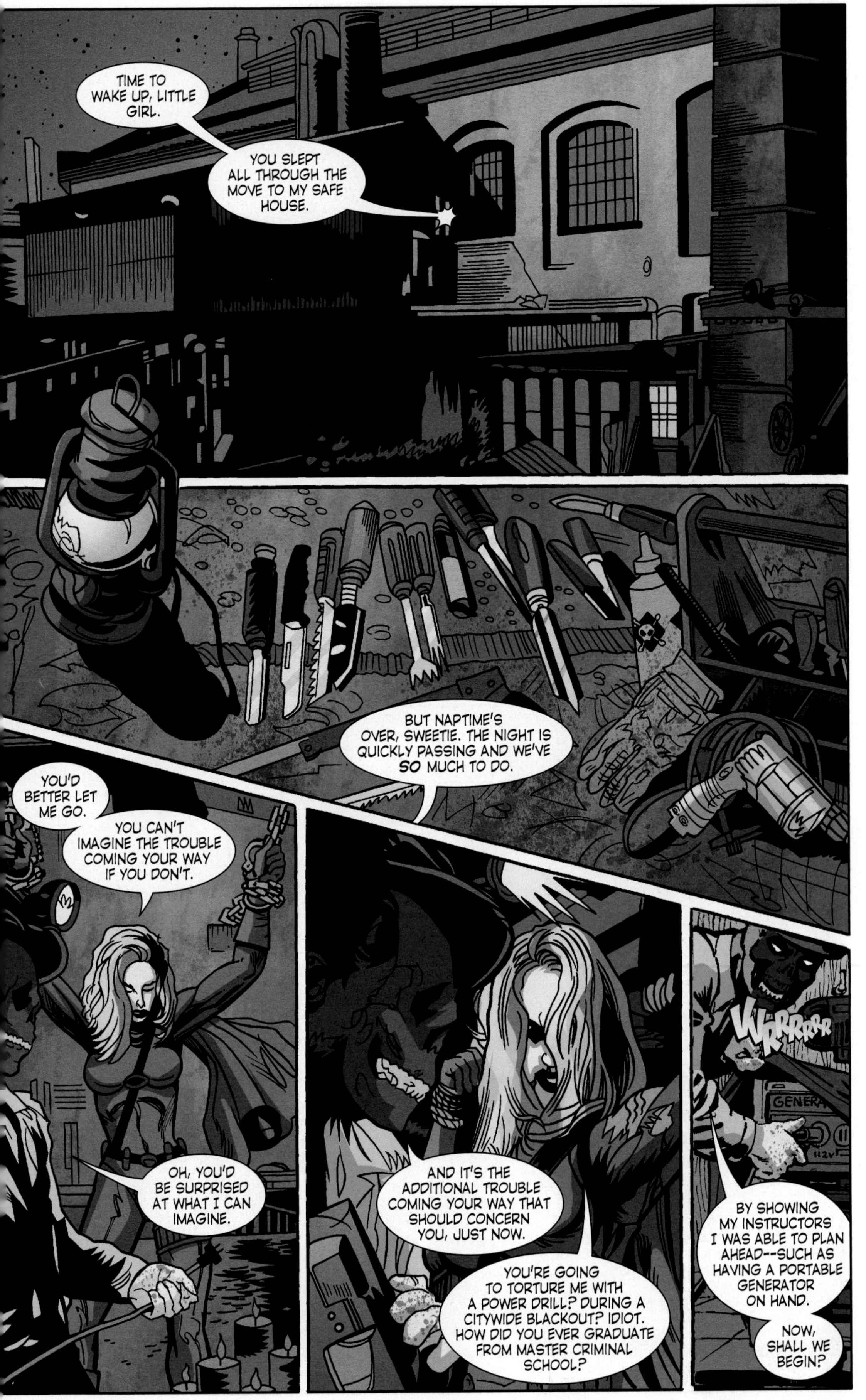
TIME TO WAKE UP, LITTLE GIRL.
YOU SLEPT ALL THROUGH THE MOVE TO MY SAFE HOUSE.
BUT NAPTIME'S OVER, SWEETIE. THE NIGHT IS QUICKLY PASSING AND WE'VE SO MUCH TO DO.
YOU'D BETTER LET ME GO.
YOU CAN'T IMAGINE THE TROUBLE COMING YOUR WAY IF YOU DON'T.
OH, YOU'D BE SURPRISED AT WHAT I CAN IMAGINE.
AND IT'S THE ADDITIONAL TROUBLE COMING YOUR WAY THAT SHOULD CONCERN YOU, JUST NOW.
YOU'RE GOING TO TORTURE ME WITH A POWER DRILL? DURING A CITYWIDE BLACKOUT? IDIOT. HOW DID YOU EVER GRADUATE FROM MASTER CRIMINAL SCHOOL?
WRRRRRR
BY SHOWING MY INSTRUCTORS I WAS ABLE TO PLAN AHEAD--SUCH AS HAVING A PORTABLE GENERATOR ON HAND.
NOW, SHALL WE BEGIN?

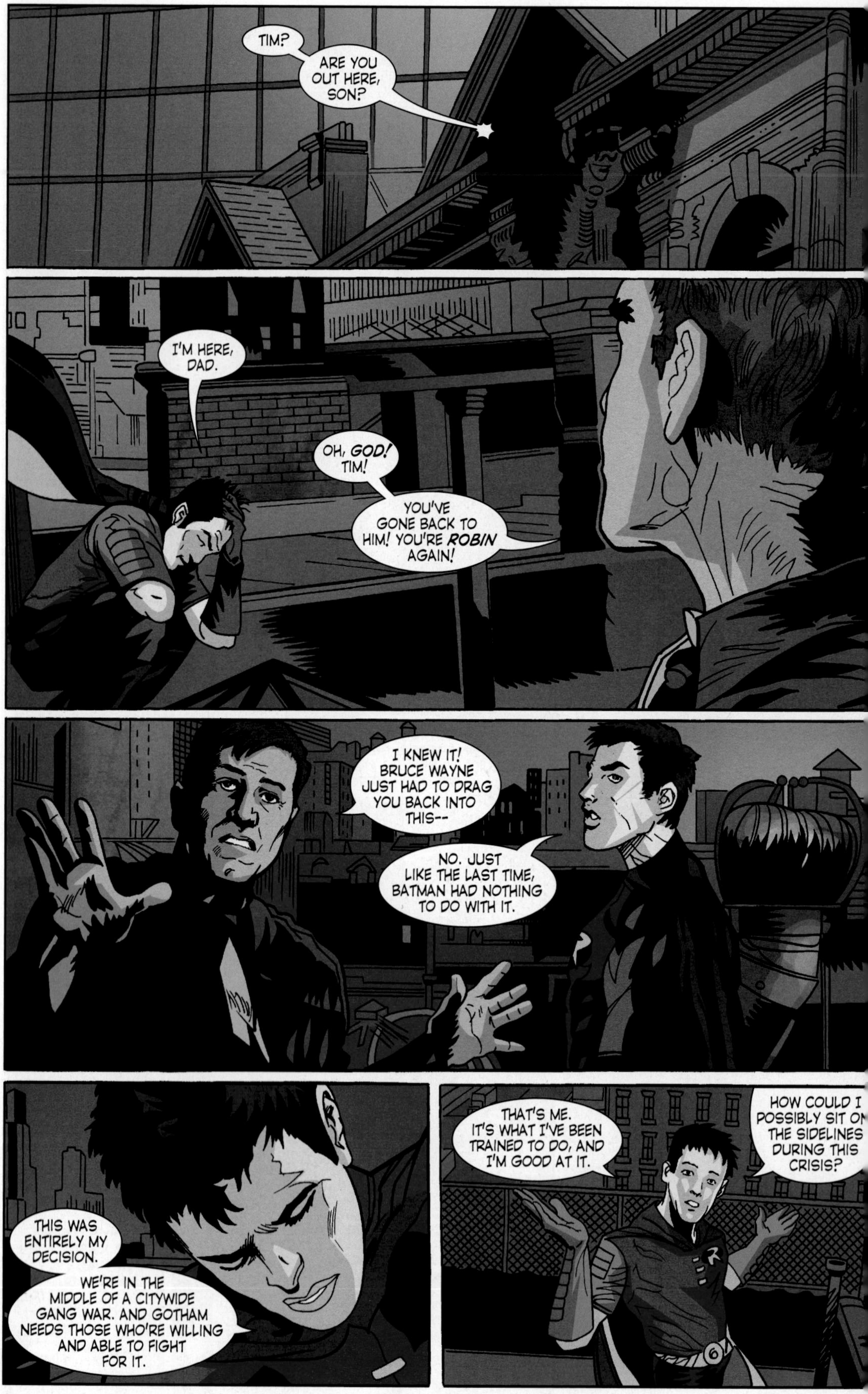
TIM?
ARE YOU OUT HERE, SON?
I'M HERE, DAD.
OH, GOD! TIM!
YOU'VE GONE BACK TO HIM! YOU'RE ROBIN AGAIN!
I KNEW IT! BRUCE WAYNE JUST HAD TO DRAG YOU BACK INTO THIS--
NO. JUST LIKE THE LAST TIME, BATMAN HAD NOTHING TO DO WITH IT.
THIS WAS ENTIRELY MY DECISION.
WE'RE IN THE MIDDLE OF A CITYWIDE GANG WAR. AND GOTHAM NEEDS THOSE WHO'RE WILLING AND ABLE TO FIGHT FOR IT.
THAT'S ME. IT'S WHAT I'VE BEEN TRAINED TO DO, AND I'M GOOD AT IT.
HOW COULD I POSSIBLY SIT ON THE SIDELINES DURING THIS CRISIS?

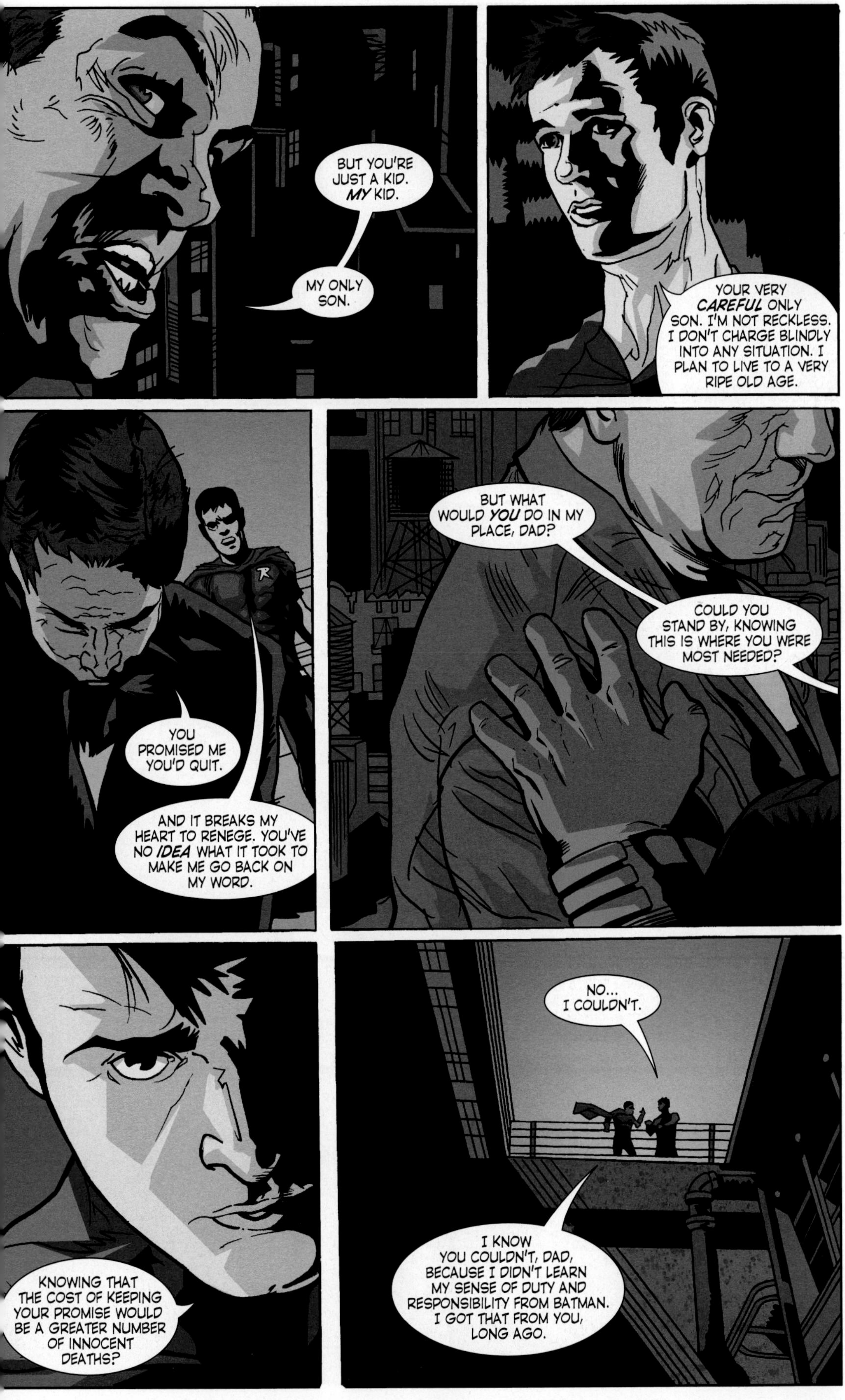
BUT YOU'RE JUST A KID. *MY* KID.
MY ONLY SON.
YOUR VERY *CAREFUL* ONLY SON. I'M NOT RECKLESS. I DON'T CHARGE BLINDLY INTO ANY SITUATION. I PLAN TO LIVE TO A VERY RIPE OLD AGE.
YOU PROMISED ME YOU'D QUIT.
AND IT BREAKS MY HEART TO RENEGE. YOU'VE NO *IDEA* WHAT IT TOOK TO MAKE ME GO BACK ON MY WORD.
BUT WHAT WOULD *YOU* DO IN MY PLACE, DAD?
COULD YOU STAND BY, KNOWING THIS IS WHERE YOU WERE MOST NEEDED?
KNOWING THAT THE COST OF KEEPING YOUR PROMISE WOULD BE A GREATER NUMBER OF INNOCENT DEATHS?
NO... I COULDN'T.
I KNOW YOU COULDN'T, DAD, BECAUSE I DIDN'T LEARN MY SENSE OF DUTY AND RESPONSIBILITY FROM BATMAN. I GOT THAT FROM YOU, LONG AGO.

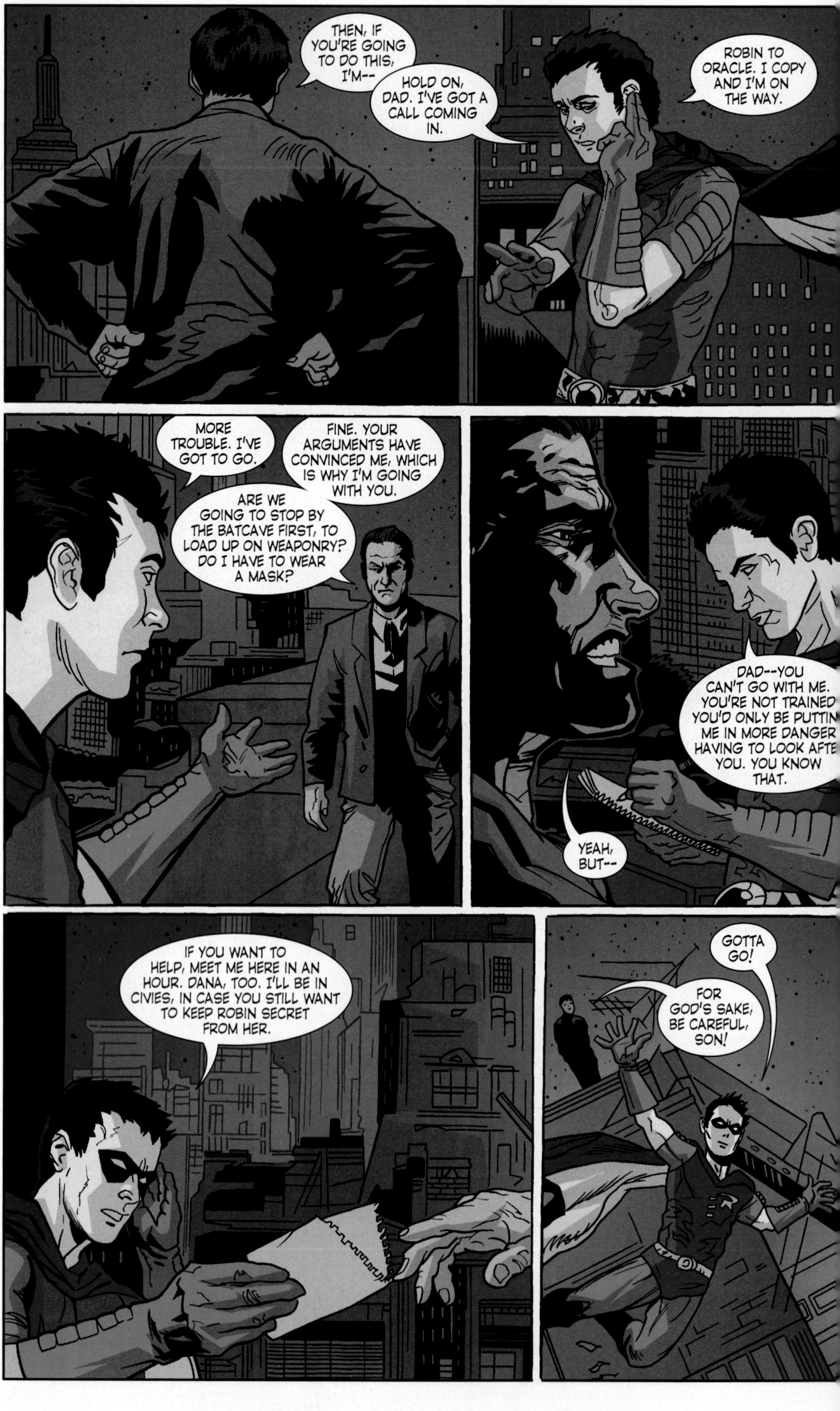
THEN, IF YOU'RE GOING TO DO THIS, I'M--
HOLD ON, DAD. I'VE GOT A CALL COMING IN.
ROBIN TO ORACLE. I COPY AND I'M ON THE WAY.
MORE TROUBLE. I'VE GOT TO GO.
FINE. YOUR ARGUMENTS HAVE CONVINCED ME, WHICH IS WHY I'M GOING WITH YOU.
ARE WE GOING TO STOP BY THE BATCAVE FIRST, TO LOAD UP ON WEAPONRY? DO I HAVE TO WEAR A MASK?
DAD--YOU CAN'T GO WITH ME. YOU'RE NOT TRAINED YOU'D ONLY BE PUTTIN ME IN MORE DANGER HAVING TO LOOK AFTE YOU. YOU KNOW THAT.
YEAH, BUT--
IF YOU WANT TO HELP, MEET ME HERE IN AN HOUR. DANA, TOO. I'LL BE IN CIVIES, IN CASE YOU STILL WANT TO KEEP ROBIN SECRET FROM HER.
GOTTA GO!
FOR GOD'S SAKE, BE CAREFUL, SON!

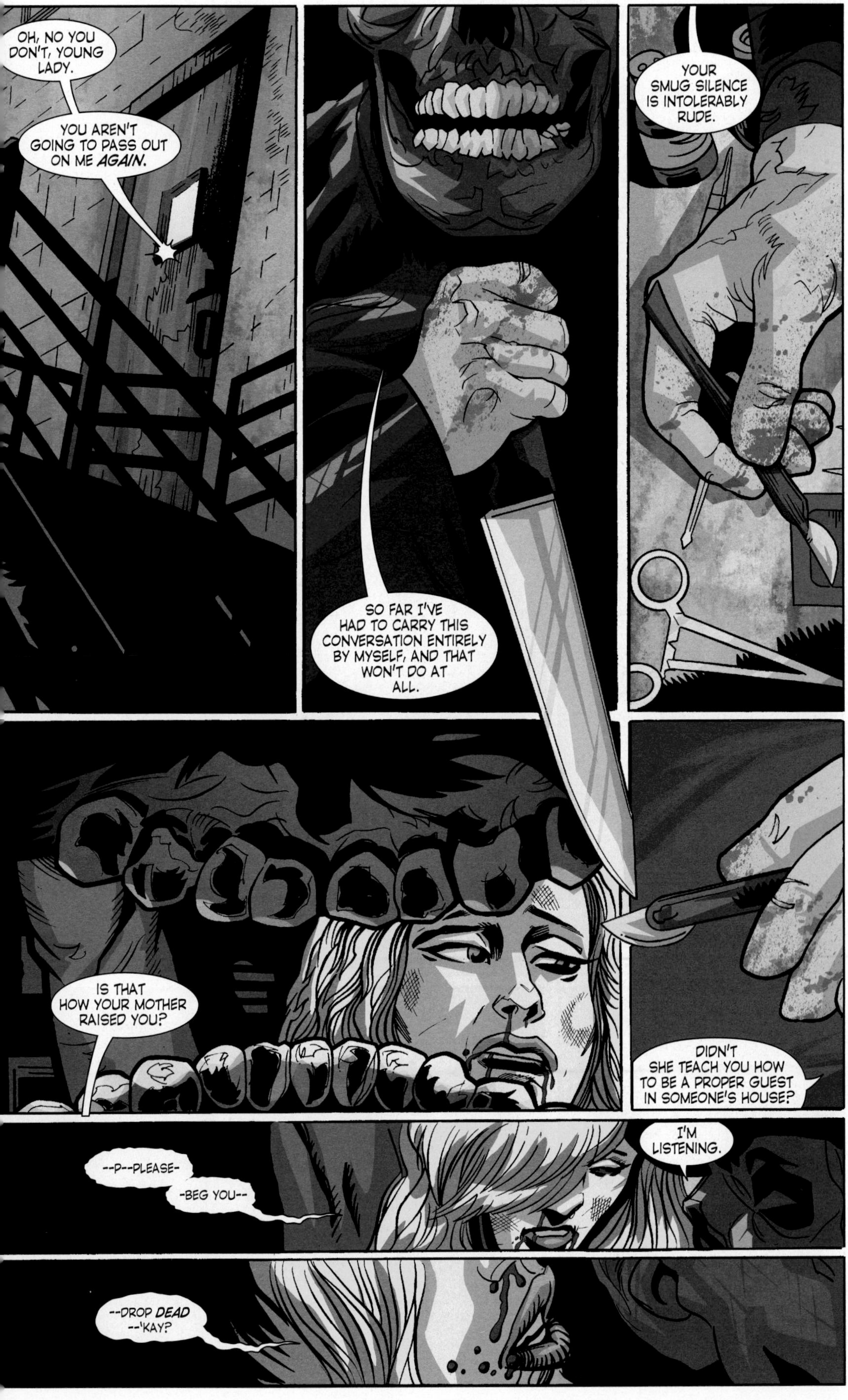
OH, NO YOU DON'T, YOUNG LADY.
YOU AREN'T GOING TO PASS OUT ON ME AGAIN.
SO FAR I'VE HAD TO CARRY THIS CONVERSATION ENTIRELY BY MYSELF, AND THAT WON'T DO AT ALL.
YOUR SMUG SILENCE IS INTOLERABLY RUDE.
IS THAT HOW YOUR MOTHER RAISED YOU?
DIDN'T SHE TEACH YOU HOW TO BE A PROPER GUEST IN SOMEONE'S HOUSE?
--P--PLEASE-
-BEG YOU--
I'M LISTENING.
--DROP DEAD --'KAY?

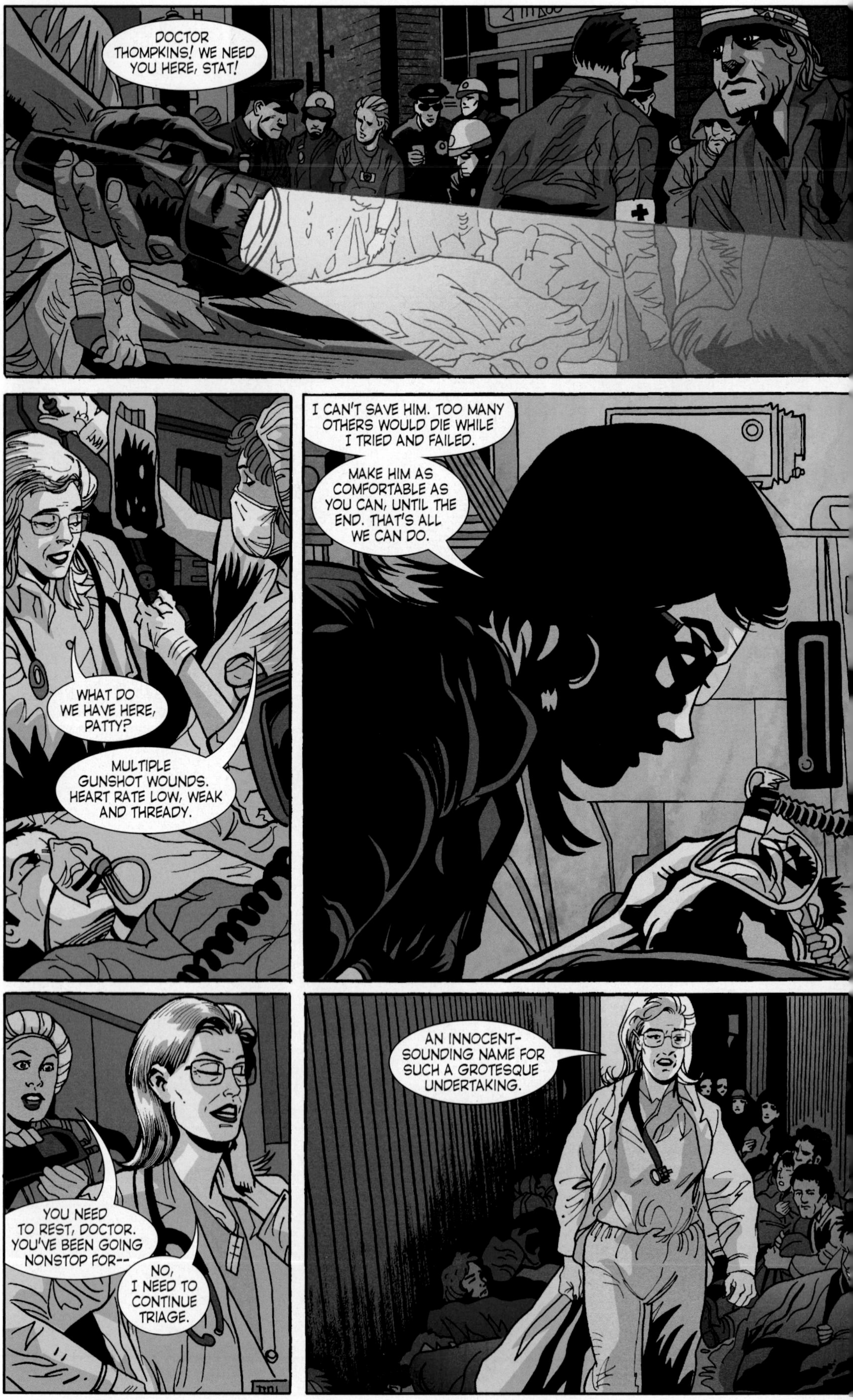
DOCTOR THOMPKINS! WE NEED YOU HERE, STAT!
WHAT DO WE HAVE HERE, PATTY?
MULTIPLE GUNSHOT WOUNDS. HEART RATE LOW, WEAK AND THREADY.
I CAN'T SAVE HIM. TOO MANY OTHERS WOULD DIE WHILE I TRIED AND FAILED.
MAKE HIM AS COMFORTABLE AS YOU CAN, UNTIL THE END. THAT'S ALL WE CAN DO.
YOU NEED TO REST, DOCTOR. YOU'VE BEEN GOING NONSTOP FOR--
NO, I NEED TO CONTINUE TRIAGE.
AN INNOCENT-SOUNDING NAME FOR SUCH A GROTESQUE UNDERTAKING.

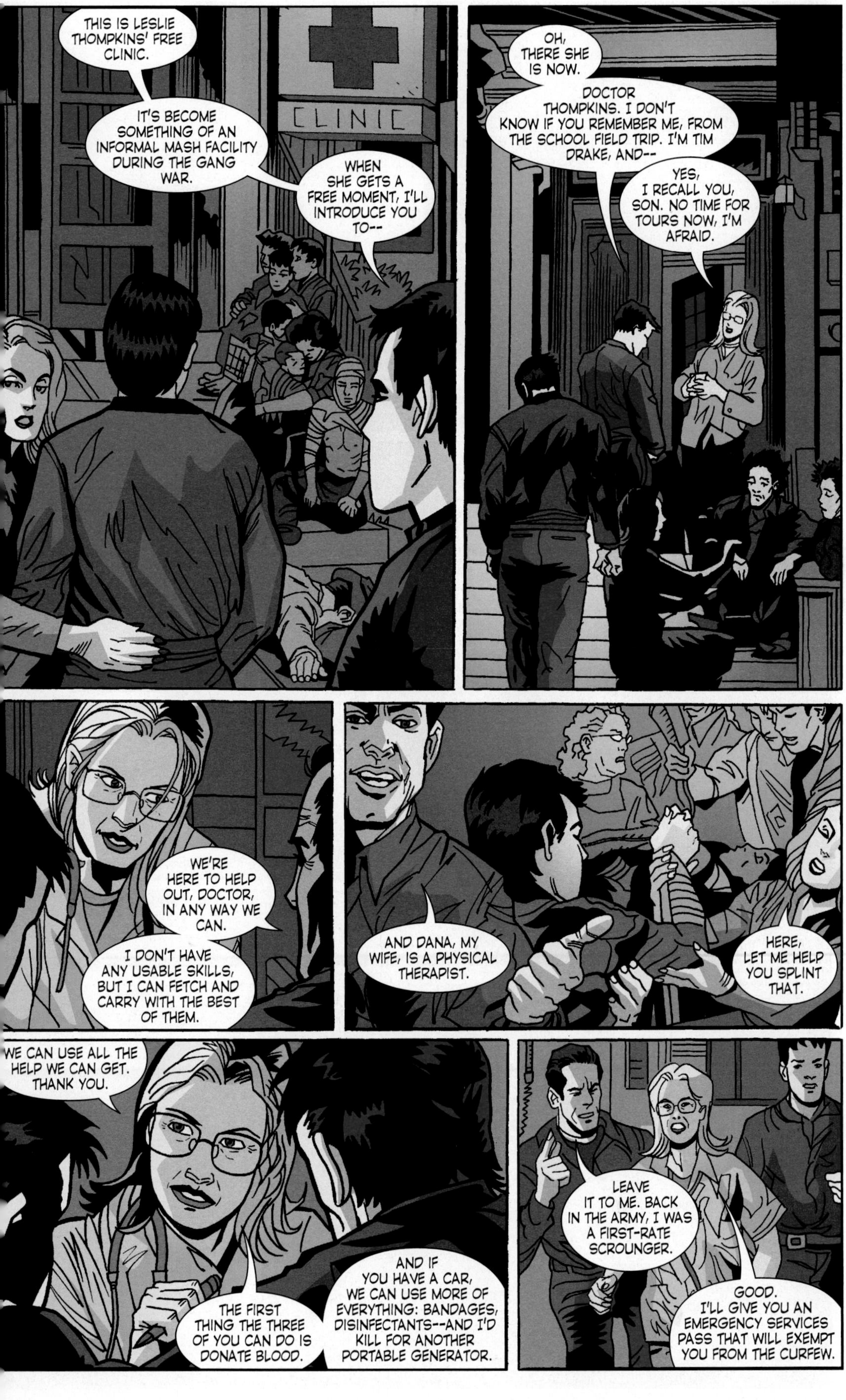
THIS IS LESLIE THOMPKINS' FREE CLINIC.
CLINIC
IT'S BECOME SOMETHING OF AN INFORMAL MASH FACILITY DURING THE GANG WAR.
WHEN SHE GETS A FREE MOMENT, I'LL INTRODUCE YOU TO--
OH, THERE SHE IS NOW.
DOCTOR THOMPKINS. I DON'T KNOW IF YOU REMEMBER ME, FROM THE SCHOOL FIELD TRIP. I'M TIM DRAKE, AND--
YES, I RECALL YOU, SON. NO TIME FOR TOURS NOW, I'M AFRAID.
WE'RE HERE TO HELP OUT, DOCTOR, IN ANY WAY WE CAN.
I DON'T HAVE ANY USABLE SKILLS, BUT I CAN FETCH AND CARRY WITH THE BEST OF THEM.
AND DANA, MY WIFE, IS A PHYSICAL THERAPIST.
HERE, LET ME HELP YOU SPLINT THAT.
WE CAN USE ALL THE HELP WE CAN GET. THANK YOU.
THE FIRST THING THE THREE OF YOU CAN DO IS DONATE BLOOD.
AND IF YOU HAVE A CAR, WE CAN USE MORE OF EVERYTHING: BANDAGES, DISINFECTANTS--AND I'D KILL FOR ANOTHER PORTABLE GENERATOR.
LEAVE IT TO ME. BACK IN THE ARMY, I WAS A FIRST-RATE SCROUNGER.
GOOD. I'LL GIVE YOU AN EMERGENCY SERVICES PASS THAT WILL EXEMPT YOU FROM THE CURFEW.

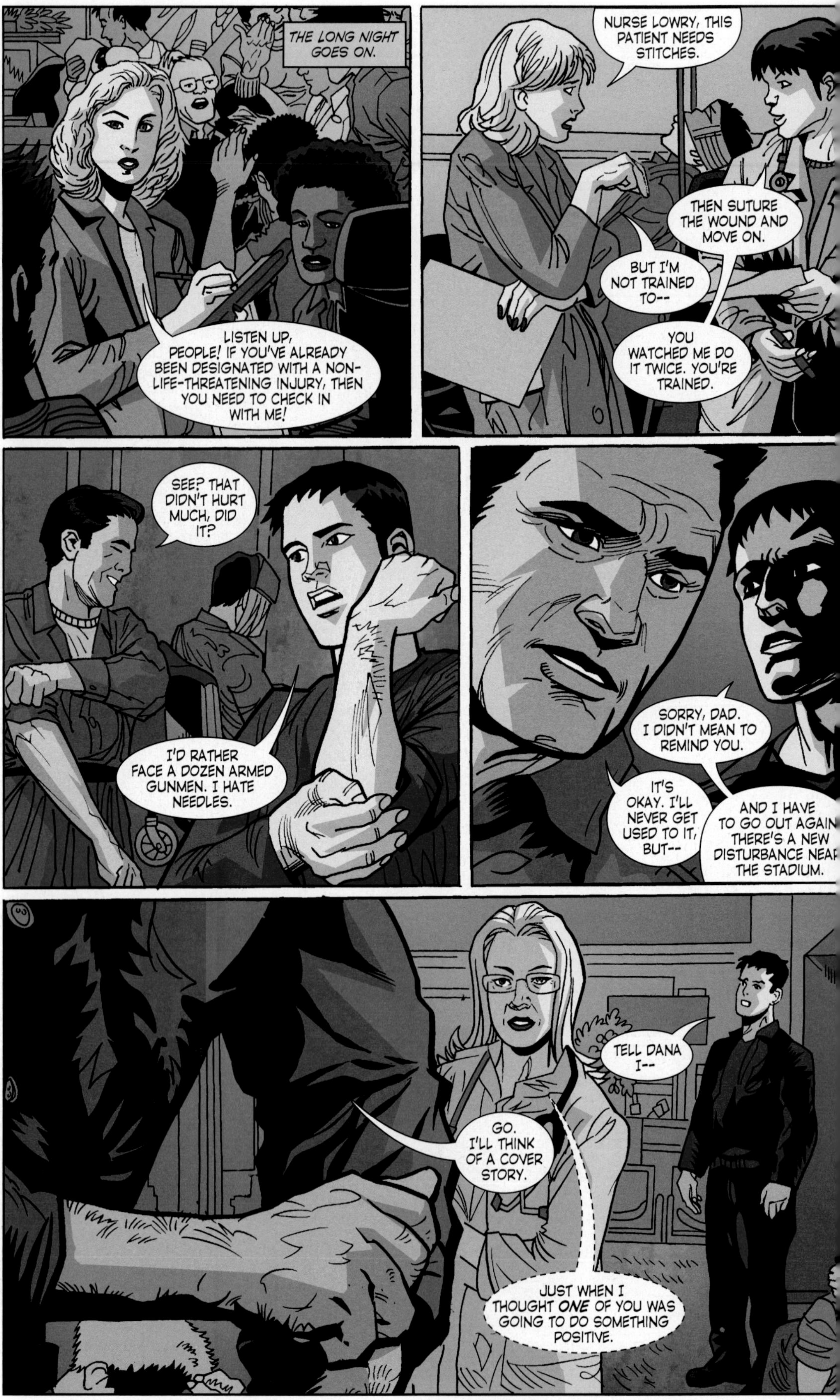
THE LONG NIGHT GOES ON.
LISTEN UP, PEOPLE! IF YOU'VE ALREADY BEEN DESIGNATED WITH A NON-LIFE-THREATENING INJURY, THEN YOU NEED TO CHECK IN WITH ME!
NURSE LOWRY, THIS PATIENT NEEDS STITCHES.
THEN SUTURE THE WOUND AND MOVE ON.
BUT I'M NOT TRAINED TO--
YOU WATCHED ME DO IT TWICE. YOU'RE TRAINED.
SEE? THAT DIDN'T HURT MUCH, DID IT?
I'D RATHER FACE A DOZEN ARMED GUNMEN. I HATE NEEDLES.
SORRY, DAD. I DIDN'T MEAN TO REMIND YOU.
IT'S OKAY. I'LL NEVER GET USED TO IT, BUT--
AND I HAVE TO GO OUT AGAIN THERE'S A NEW DISTURBANCE NEAR THE STADIUM.
TELL DANA I--
GO. I'LL THINK OF A COVER STORY.
JUST WHEN I THOUGHT ONE OF YOU WAS GOING TO DO SOMETHING POSITIVE.

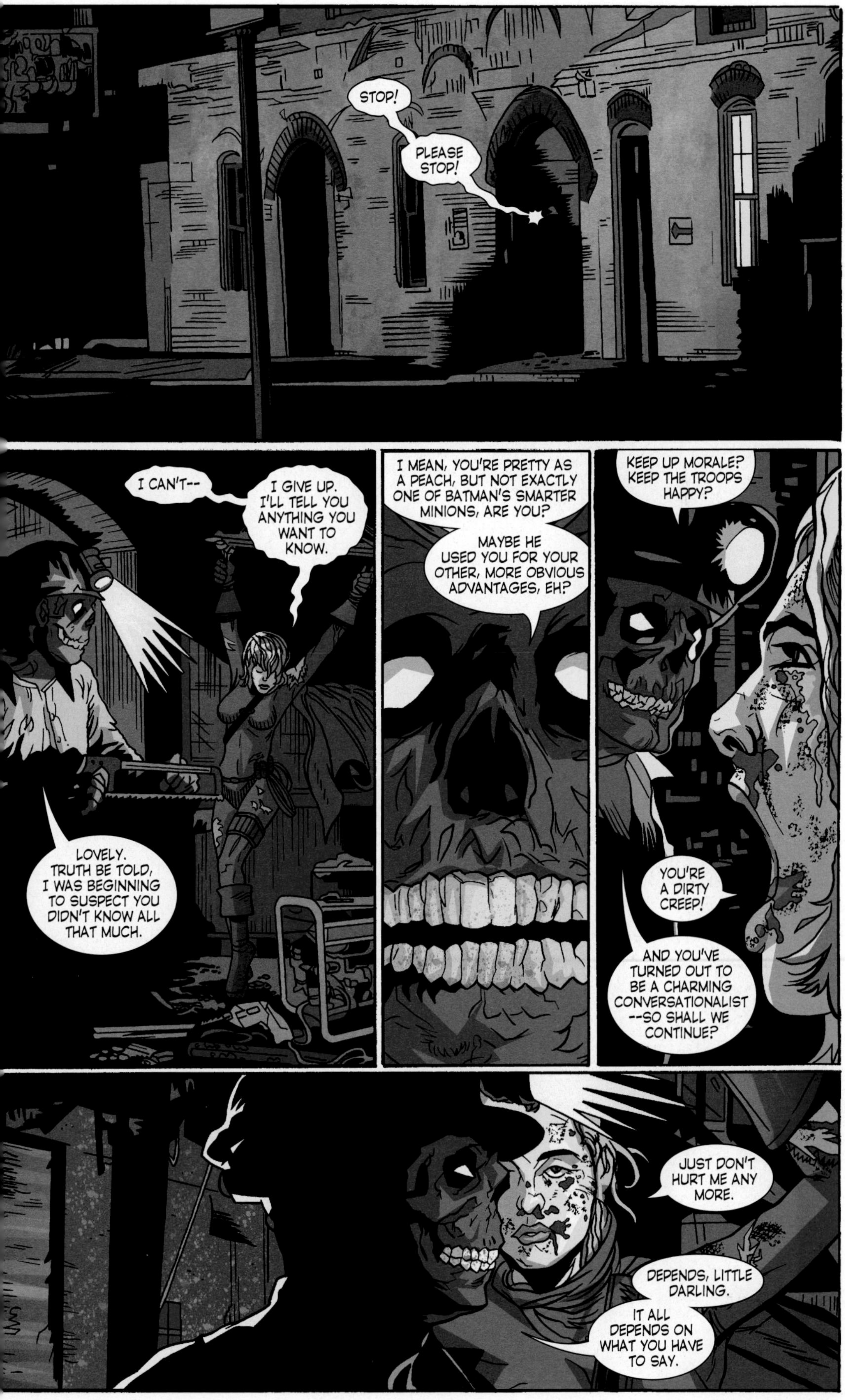
STOP!
PLEASE STOP!
I CAN'T--
I GIVE UP. I'LL TELL YOU ANYTHING YOU WANT TO KNOW.
LOVELY. TRUTH BE TOLD, I WAS BEGINNING TO SUSPECT YOU DIDN'T KNOW ALL THAT MUCH.
I MEAN, YOU'RE PRETTY AS A PEACH, BUT NOT EXACTLY ONE OF BATMAN'S SMARTER MINIONS, ARE YOU?
MAYBE HE USED YOU FOR YOUR OTHER, MORE OBVIOUS ADVANTAGES, EH?
KEEP UP MORALE? KEEP THE TROOPS HAPPY?
YOU'RE A DIRTY CREEP!
AND YOU'VE TURNED OUT TO BE A CHARMING CONVERSATIONALIST --SO SHALL WE CONTINUE?
JUST DON'T HURT ME ANY MORE.
DEPENDS, LITTLE DARLING.
IT ALL DEPENDS ON WHAT YOU HAVE TO SAY.

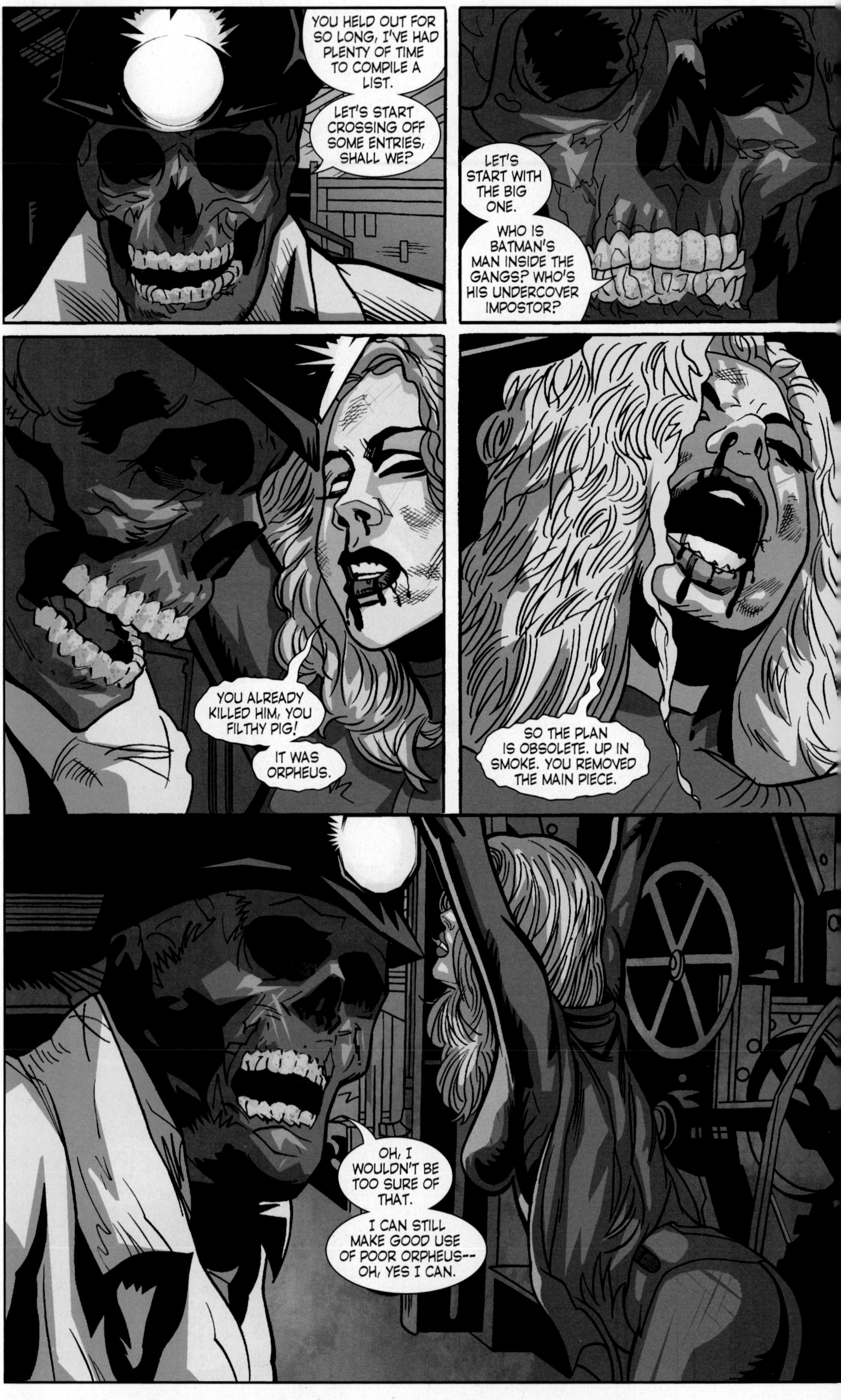
YOU HELD OUT FOR SO LONG, I'VE HAD PLENTY OF TIME TO COMPILE A LIST.
LET'S START CROSSING OFF SOME ENTRIES, SHALL WE?
LET'S START WITH THE BIG ONE.
WHO IS BATMAN'S MAN INSIDE THE GANGS? WHO'S HIS UNDERCOVER IMPOSTOR?
YOU ALREADY KILLED HIM, YOU FILTHY PIG!
IT WAS ORPHEUS.
SO THE PLAN IS OBSOLETE. UP IN SMOKE. YOU REMOVED THE MAIN PIECE.
OH, I WOULDN'T BE TOO SURE OF THAT.
I CAN STILL MAKE GOOD USE OF POOR ORPHEUS--OH, YES I CAN.

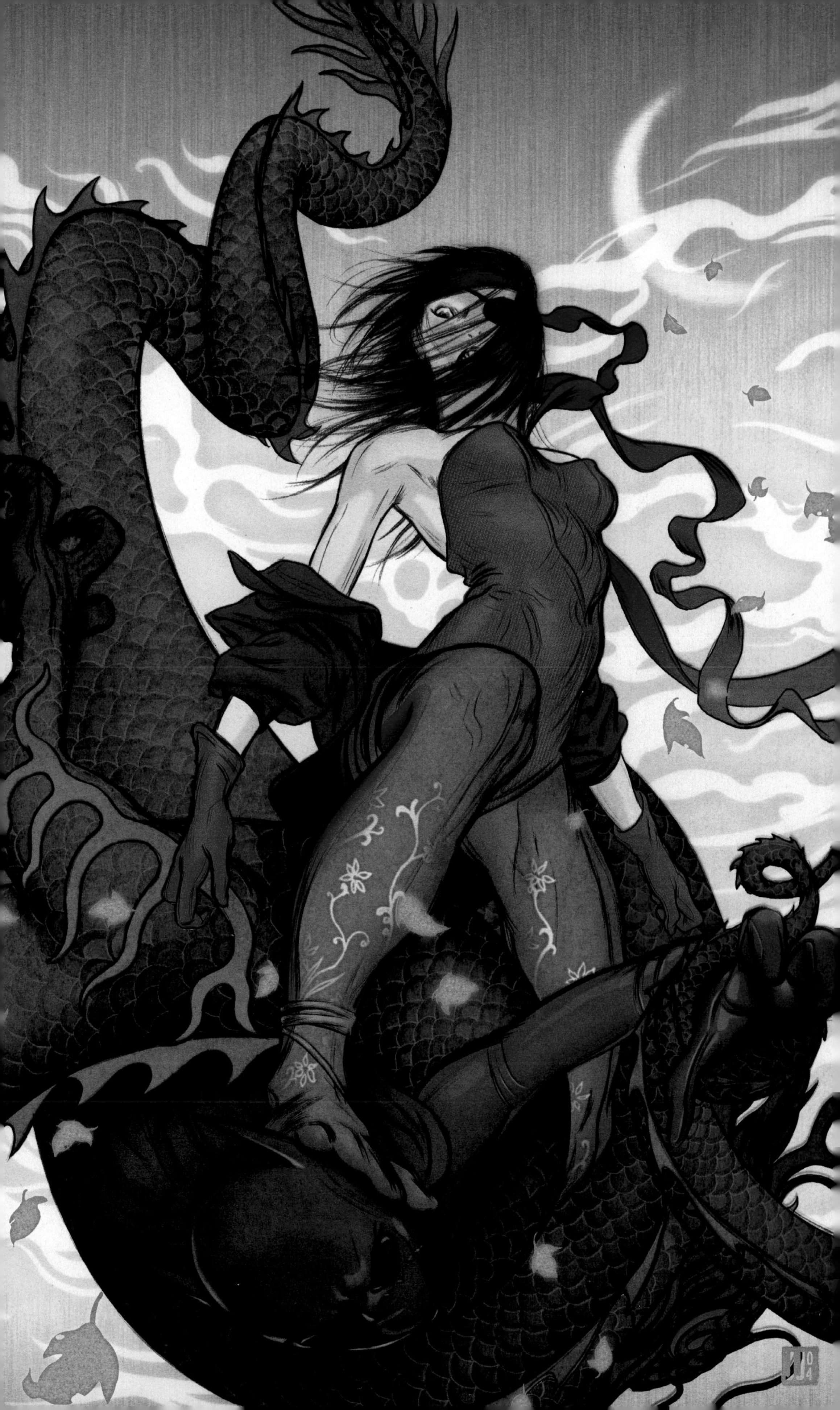

COVER ART BY
JAMES JEAN

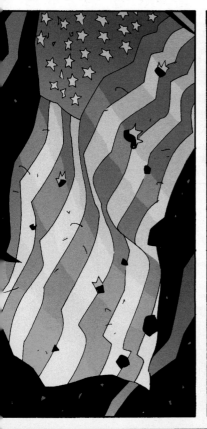

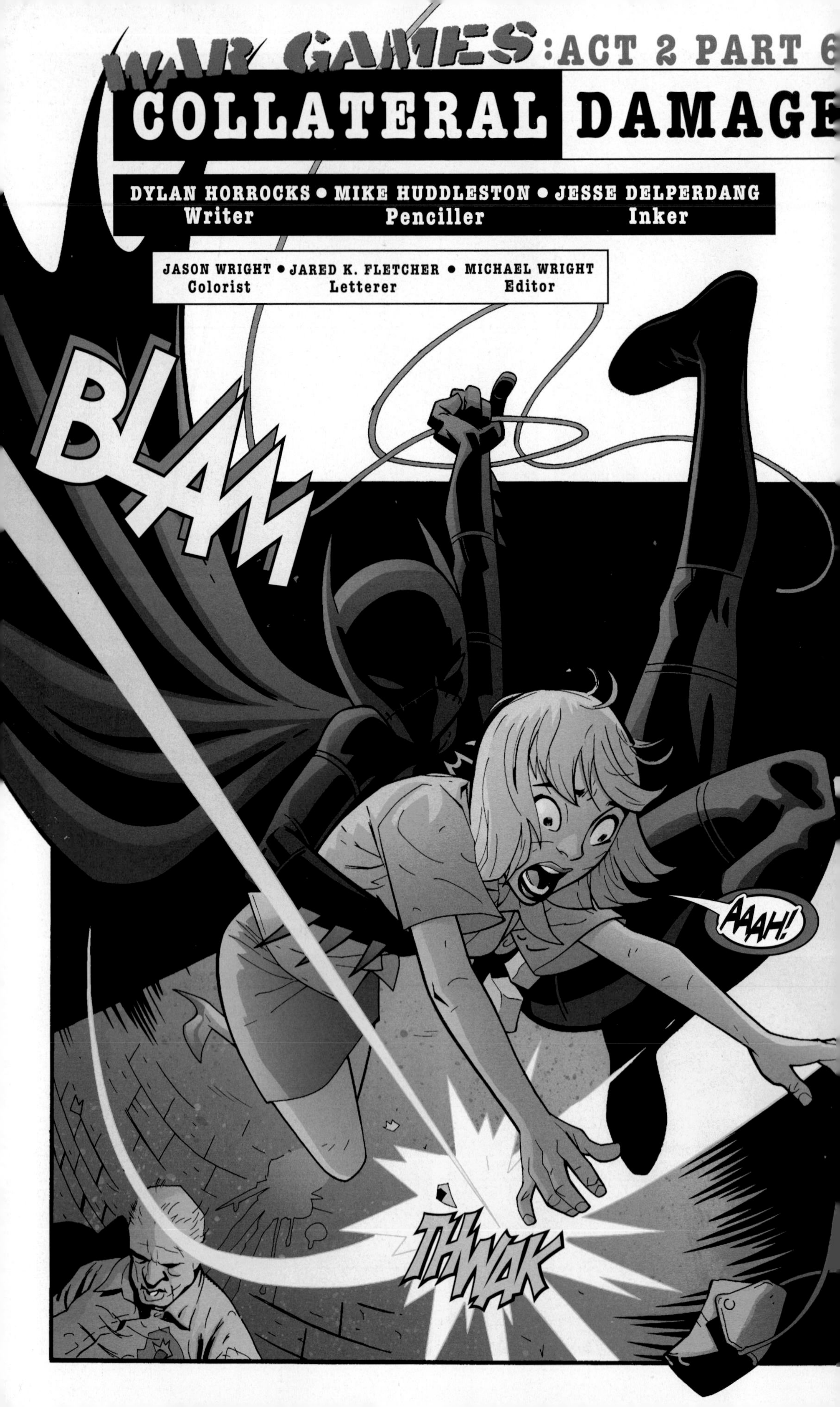
WAR GAMES: ACT 2 PART 6
COLLATERAL DAMAGE
DYLAN HORROCKS • MIKE HUDDLESTON • JESSE DELPERDANG
Writer Penciller Inker
JASON WRIGHT • JARED K. FLETCHER • MICHAEL WRIGHT
Colorist Letterer Editor
BLAM
AAAH!
THWAK

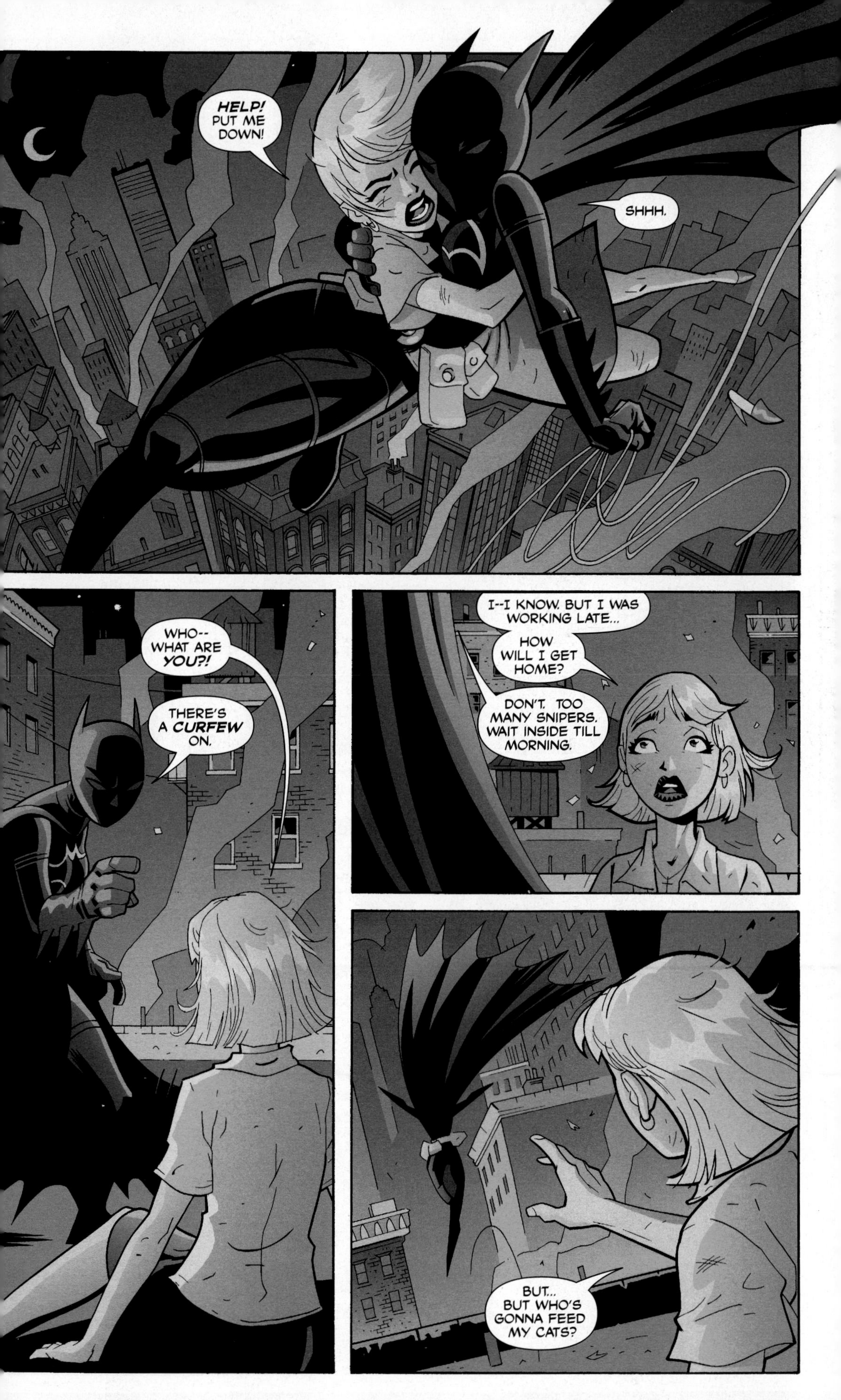
HELP! PUT ME DOWN!
SHHH.
WHO-- WHAT ARE YOU?!
THERE'S A CURFEW ON.
I--I KNOW. BUT I WAS WORKING LATE...
HOW WILL I GET HOME?
DON'T. TOO MANY SNIPERS. WAIT INSIDE TILL MORNING.
BUT... BUT WHO'S GONNA FEED MY CATS?

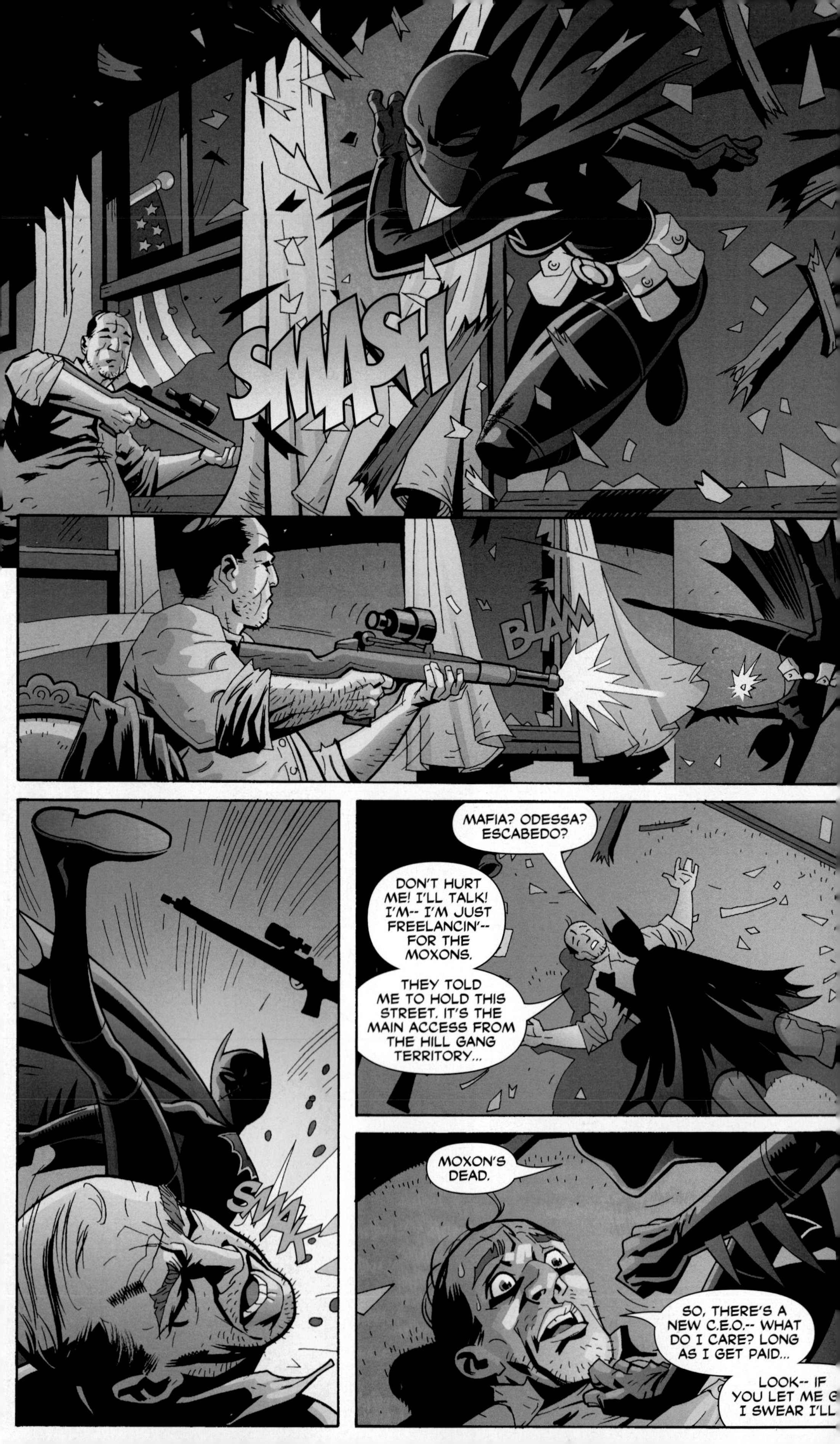

SMASH
BLAM
SMAK
MAFIA? ODESSA? ESCABEDO?
DON'T HURT ME! I'LL TALK! I'M-- I'M JUST FREELANCIN'-- FOR THE MOXONS.
THEY TOLD ME TO HOLD THIS STREET. IT'S THE MAIN ACCESS FROM THE HILL GANG TERRITORY...
MOXON'S DEAD.
SO, THERE'S A NEW C.E.O.-- WHAT DO I CARE? LONG AS I GET PAID...
LOOK-- IF YOU LET ME
I SWEAR I'LL

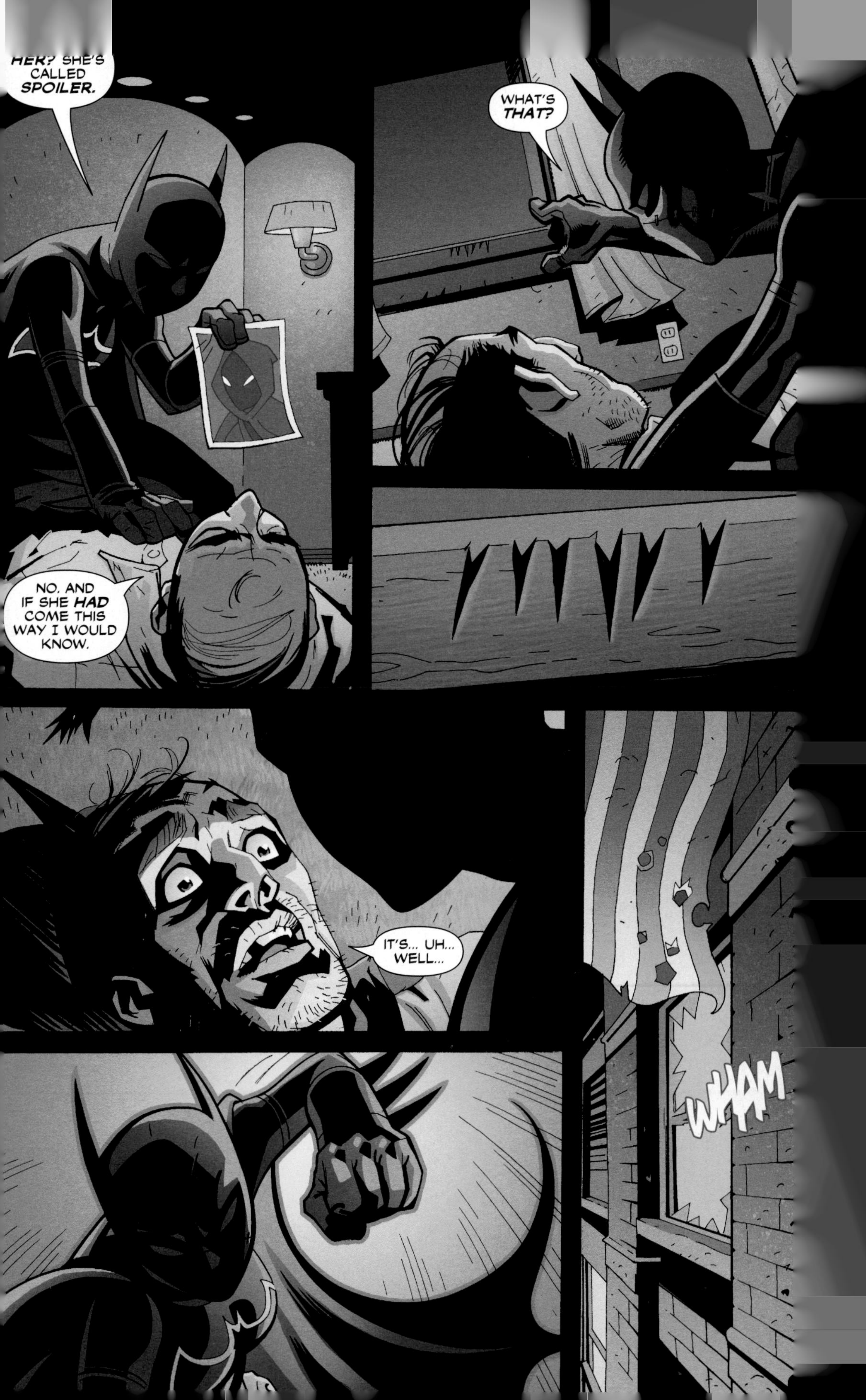
HER? SHE'S CALLED SPOILER.
WHAT'S THAT?
NO. AND IF SHE HAD COME THIS WAY I WOULD KNOW.
IT'S... UH... WELL...
WHAM

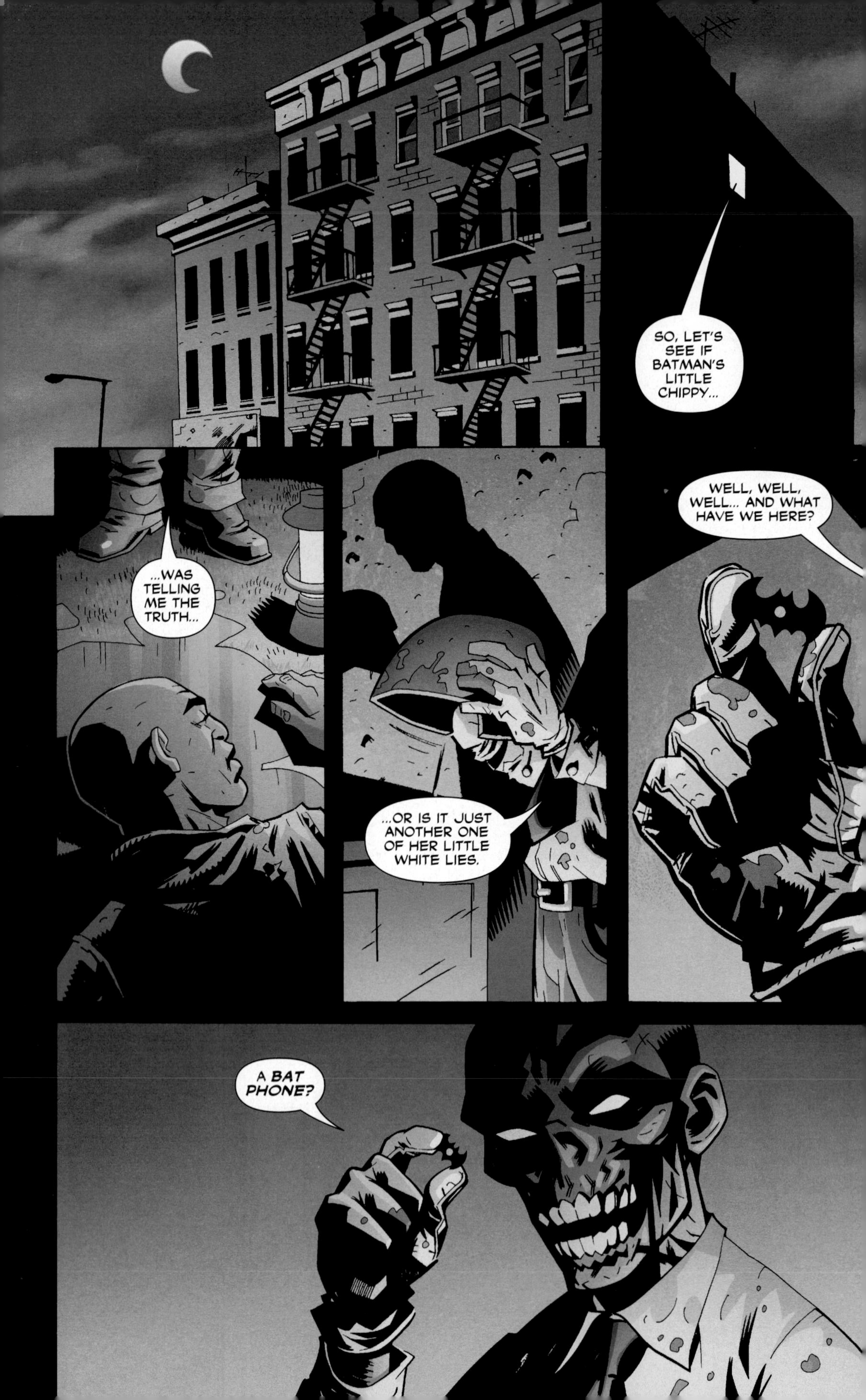
SO, LET'S SEE IF BATMAN'S LITTLE CHIPPY...
...WAS TELLING ME THE TRUTH...
...OR IS IT JUST ANOTHER ONE OF HER LITTLE WHITE LIES.
WELL, WELL, WELL... AND WHAT HAVE WE HERE?
A BAT PHONE?

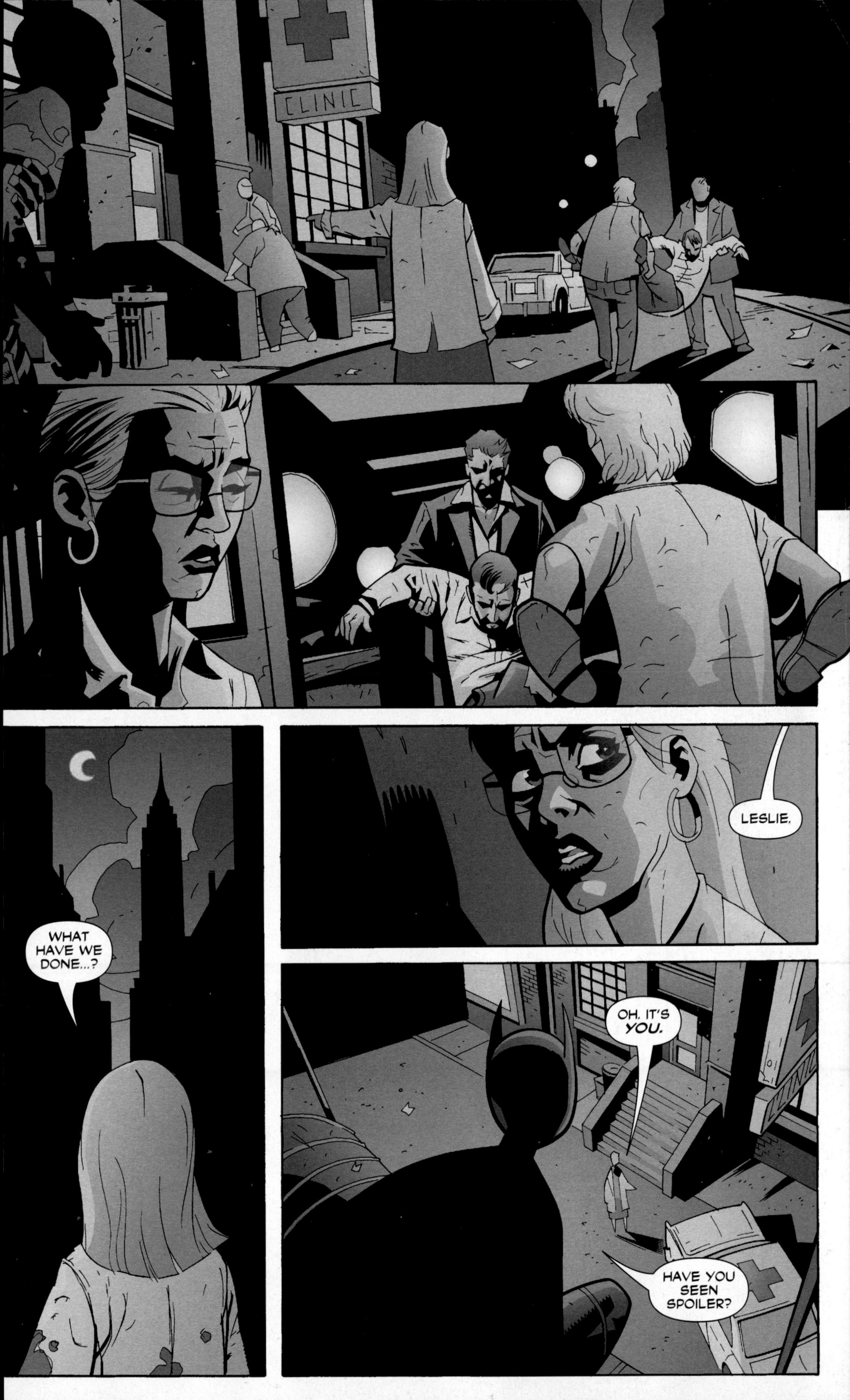
CLINIC
LESLIE.
WHAT HAVE WE DONE...?
OH, IT'S YOU.
HAVE YOU SEEN SPOILER?
CLINIC

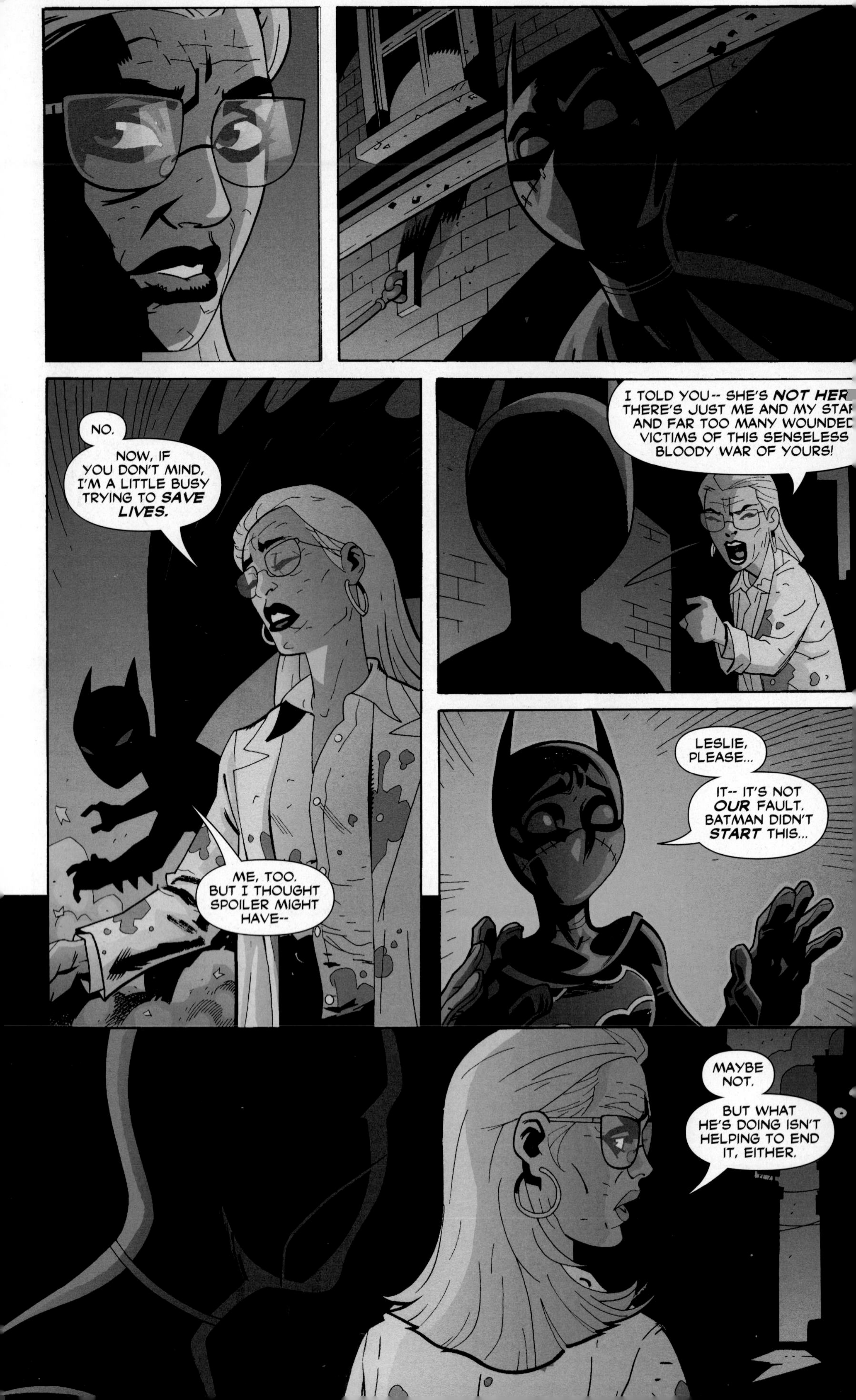
NO.
NOW, IF YOU DON'T MIND, I'M A LITTLE BUSY TRYING TO SAVE LIVES.
ME, TOO. BUT I THOUGHT SPOILER MIGHT HAVE--
I TOLD YOU-- SHE'S NOT HER
THERE'S JUST ME AND MY STAF
AND FAR TOO MANY WOUNDED
VICTIMS OF THIS SENSELESS
BLOODY WAR OF YOURS!
LESLIE, PLEASE...
IT-- IT'S NOT OUR FAULT. BATMAN DIDN'T START THIS...
MAYBE NOT.
BUT WHAT HE'S DOING ISN'T HELPING TO END IT, EITHER.

MOVE FAST, MY GHOST DRAGONS! SECURE THE AREA!

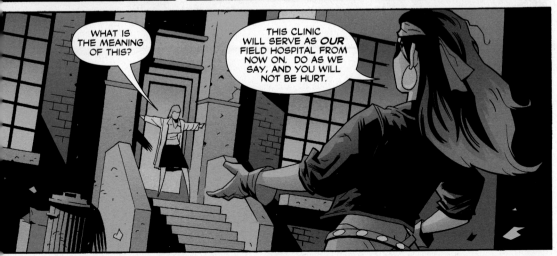

WHAT IS THE MEANING OF THIS?

THIS CLINIC WILL SERVE AS *OUR* FIELD HOSPITAL FROM NOW ON. DO AS WE SAY, AND YOU WILL NOT BE HURT.

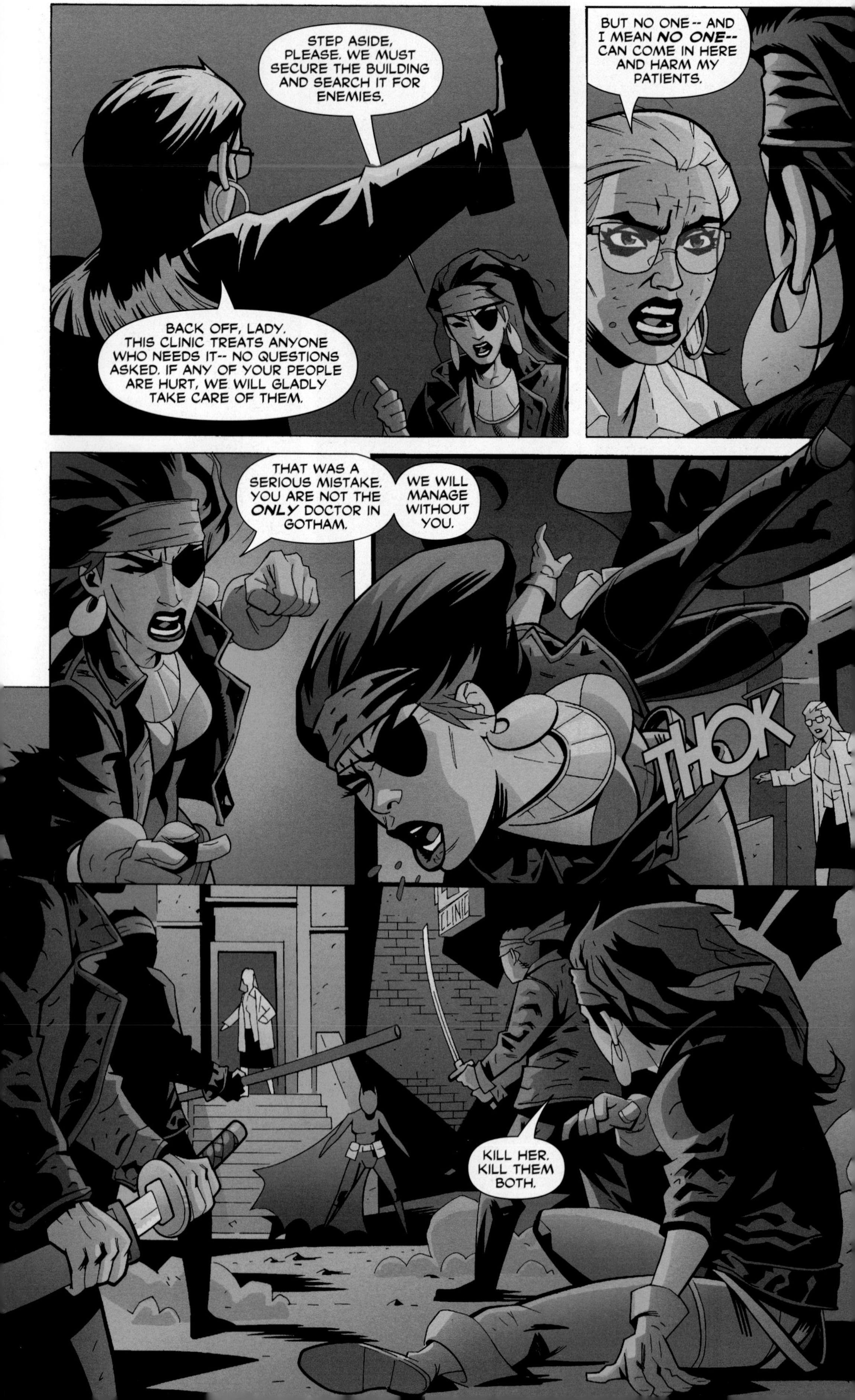
STEP ASIDE, PLEASE. WE MUST SECURE THE BUILDING AND SEARCH IT FOR ENEMIES.
BACK OFF, LADY. THIS CLINIC TREATS ANYONE WHO NEEDS IT-- NO QUESTIONS ASKED. IF ANY OF YOUR PEOPLE ARE HURT, WE WILL GLADLY TAKE CARE OF THEM.
BUT NO ONE -- AND I MEAN NO ONE-- CAN COME IN HERE AND HARM MY PATIENTS.
THAT WAS A SERIOUS MISTAKE. YOU ARE NOT THE ONLY DOCTOR IN GOTHAM.
WE WILL MANAGE WITHOUT YOU.
THOK
CLINIC
KILL HER. KILL THEM BOTH.

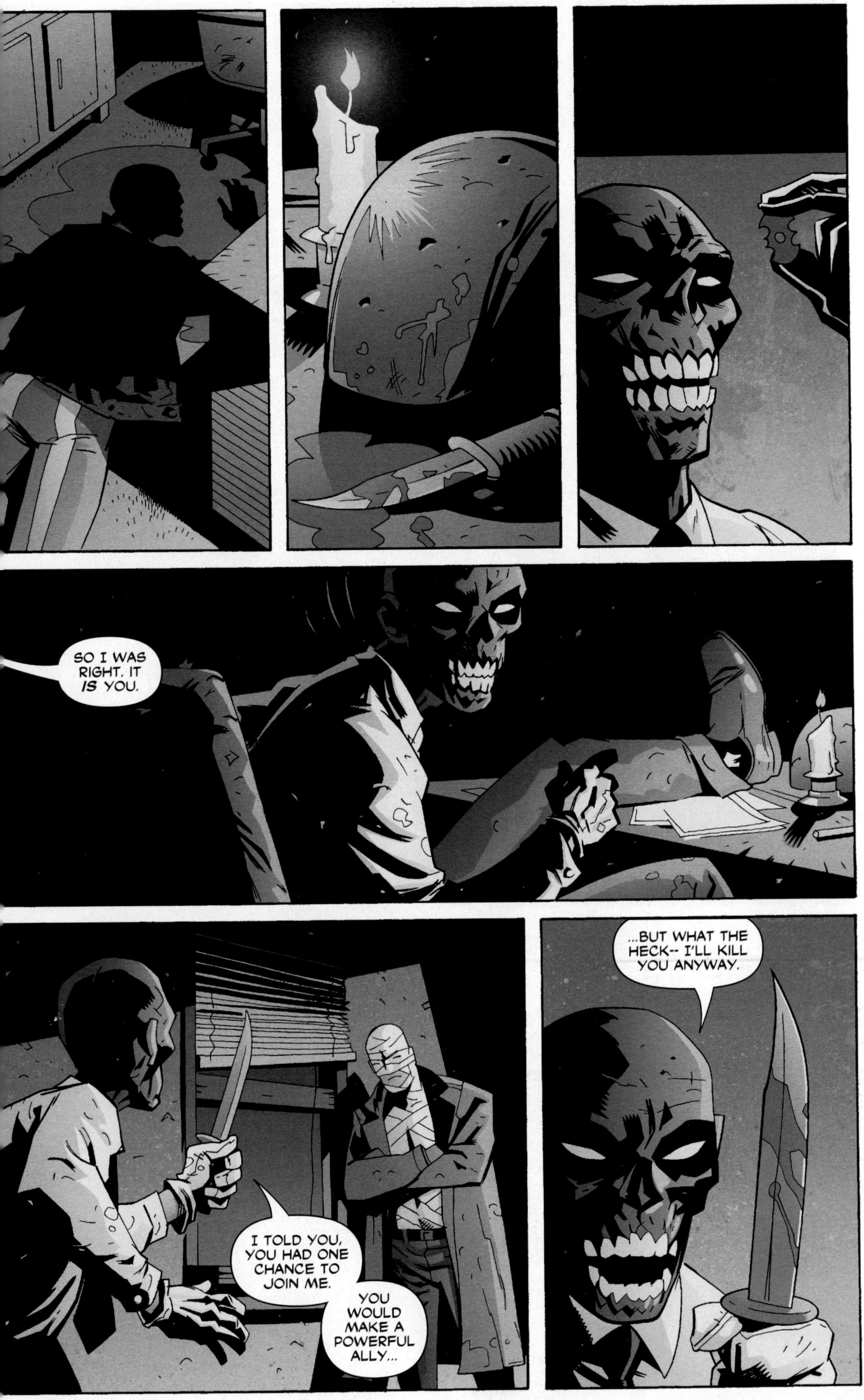
SO I WAS RIGHT. IT *IS* YOU.
I TOLD YOU, YOU HAD ONE CHANCE TO JOIN ME.
YOU WOULD MAKE A POWERFUL ALLY...
...BUT WHAT THE HECK-- I'LL KILL YOU ANYWAY.

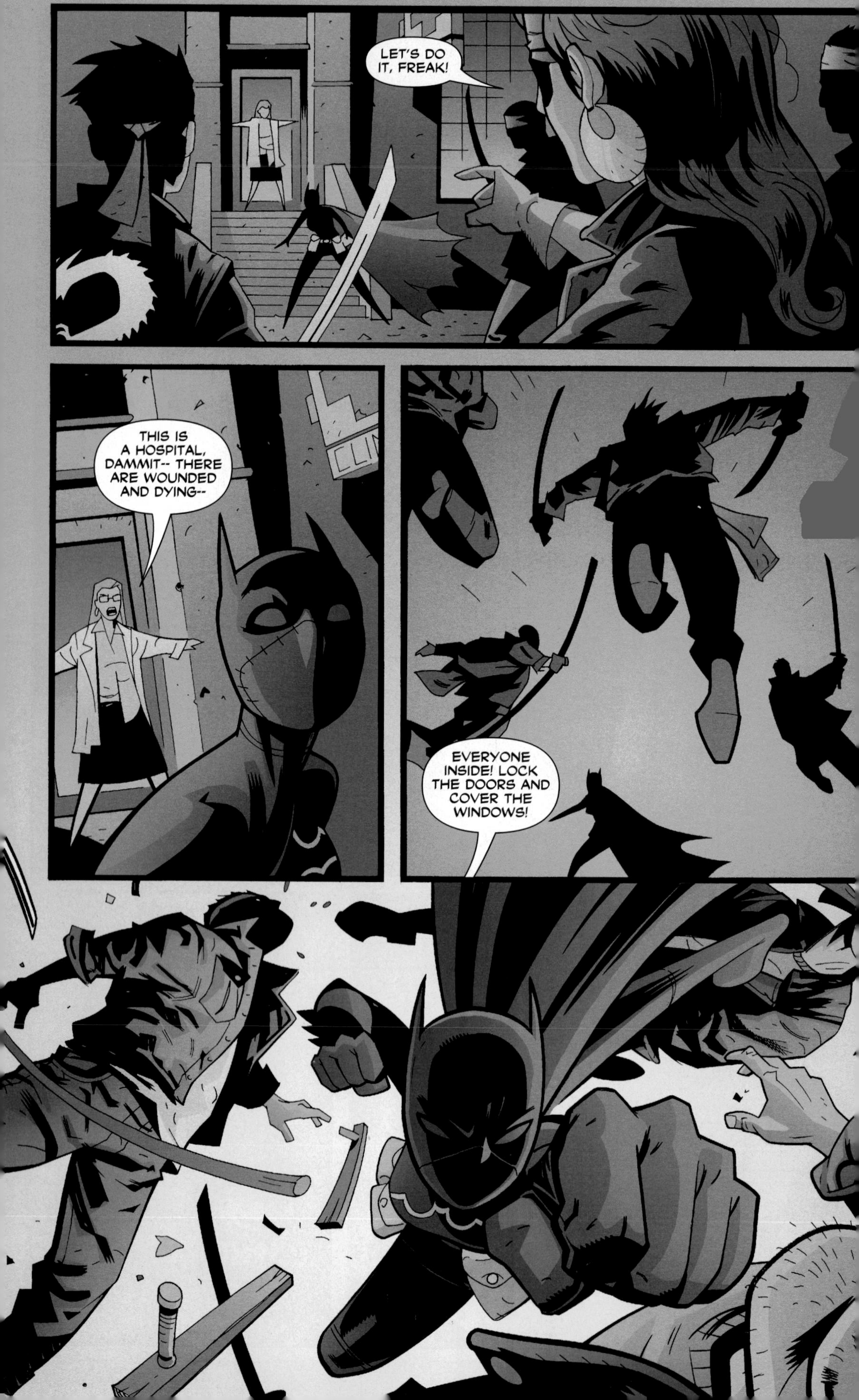
LET'S DO IT, FREAK!
THIS IS A HOSPITAL, DAMMIT-- THERE ARE WOUNDED AND DYING--
EVERYONE INSIDE! LOCK THE DOORS AND COVER THE WINDOWS!

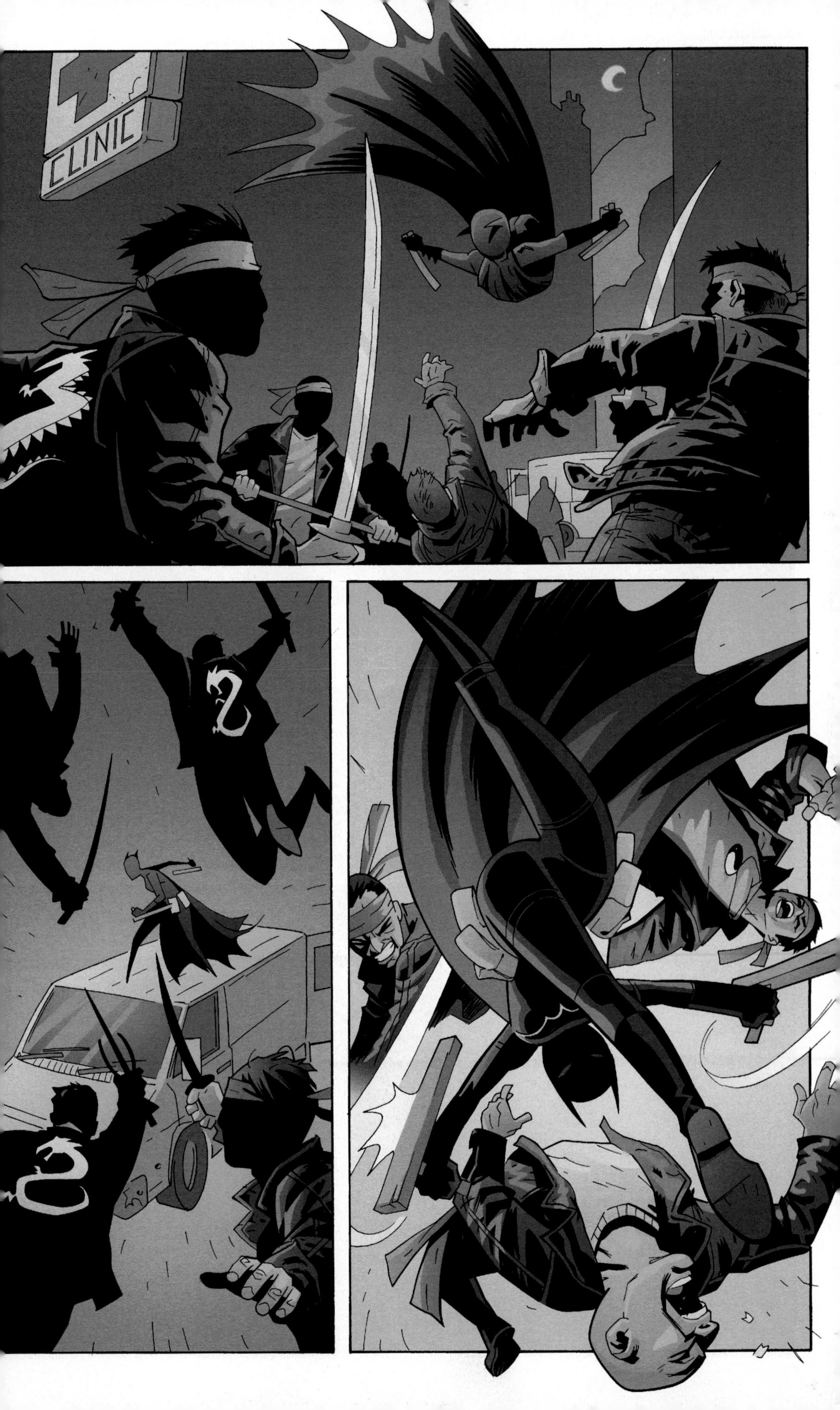
CLINIC

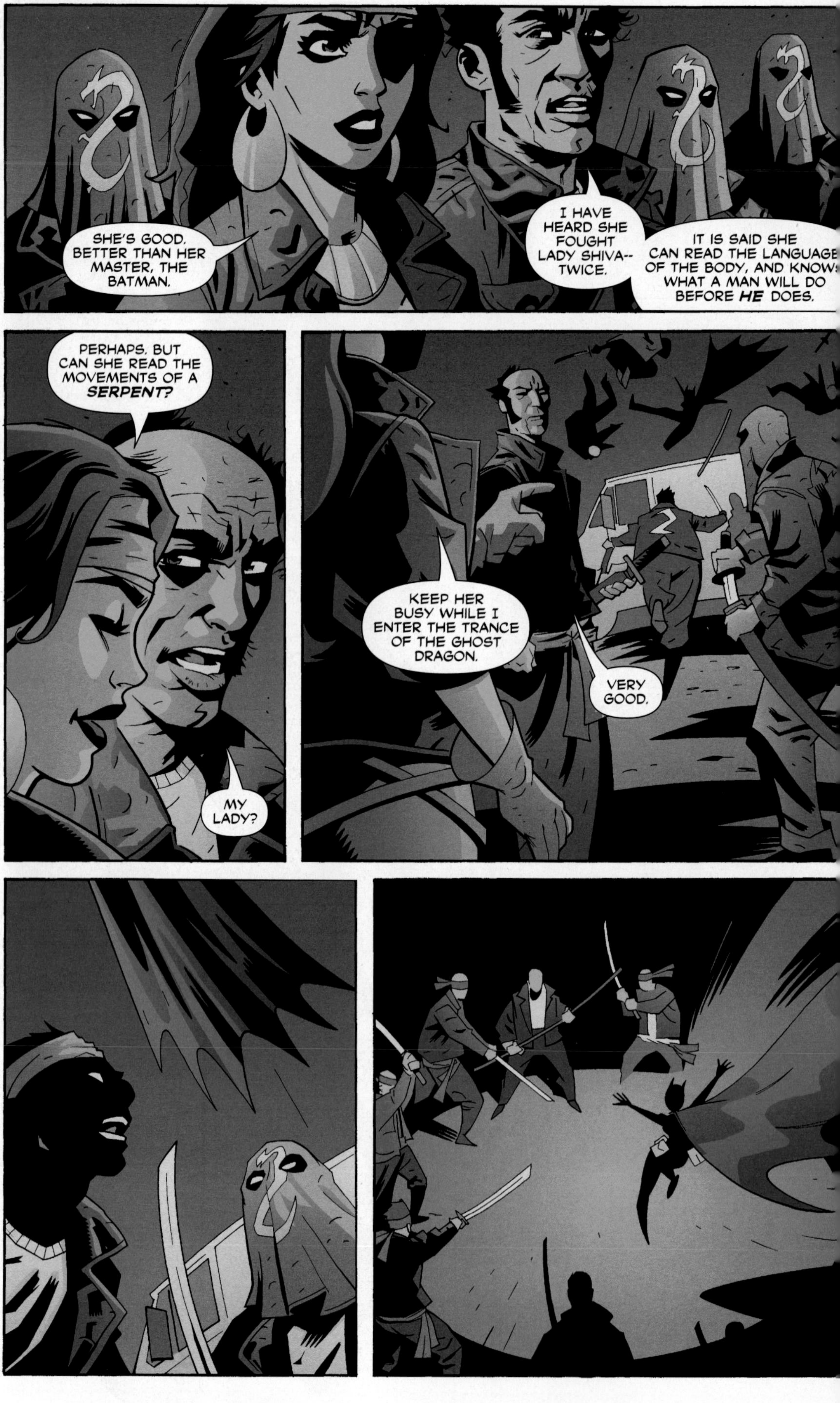
SHE'S GOOD. BETTER THAN HER MASTER, THE BATMAN.
I HAVE HEARD SHE FOUGHT LADY SHIVA-- TWICE.
IT IS SAID SHE CAN READ THE LANGUAGE OF THE BODY, AND KNOWS WHAT A MAN WILL DO BEFORE *HE* DOES.
PERHAPS. BUT CAN SHE READ THE MOVEMENTS OF A *SERPENT?*
MY LADY?
KEEP HER BUSY WHILE I ENTER THE TRANCE OF THE GHOST DRAGON.
VERY GOOD.

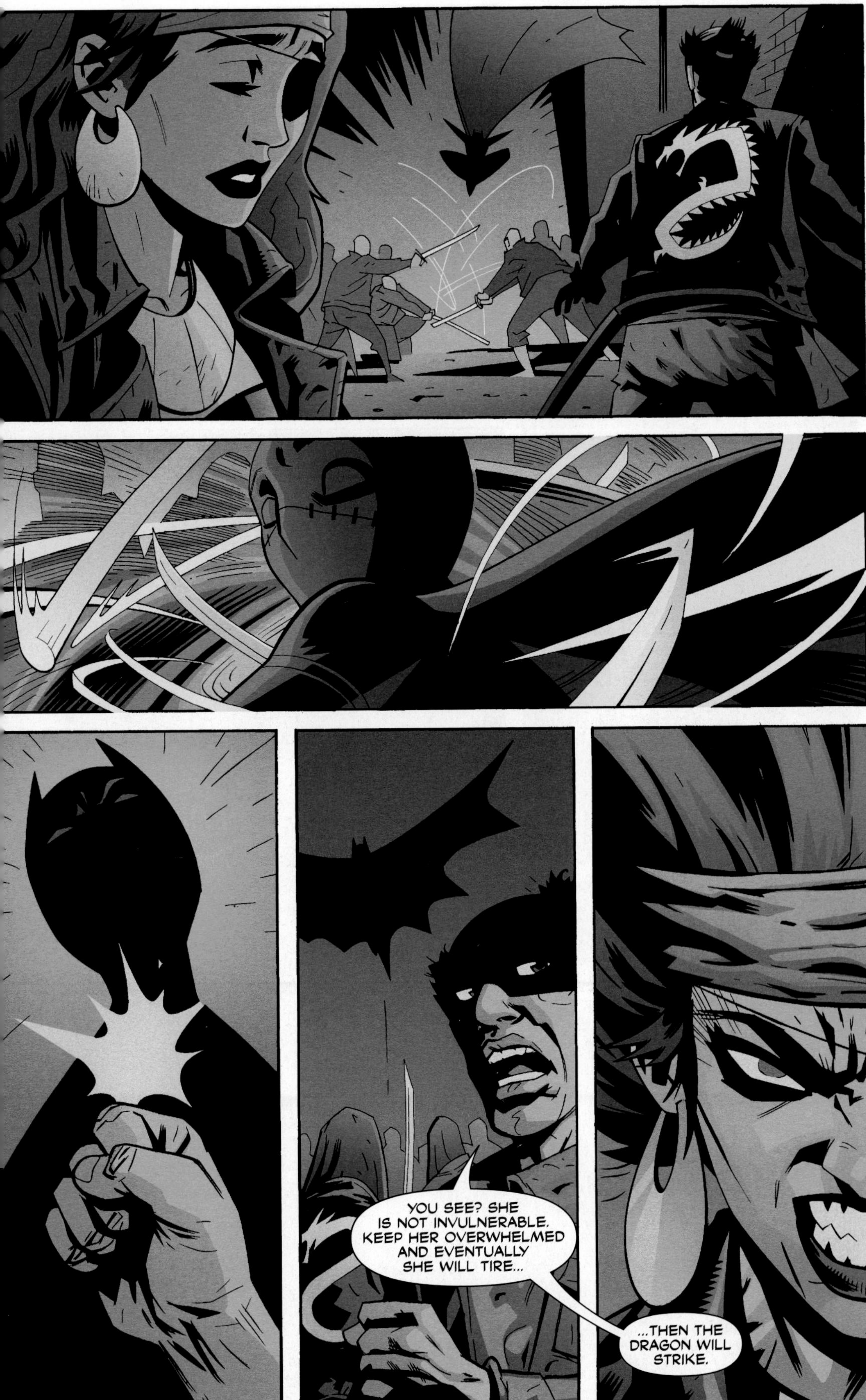
YOU SEE? SHE IS NOT INVULNERABLE. KEEP HER OVERWHELMED AND EVENTUALLY SHE WILL TIRE...
...THEN THE DRAGON WILL STRIKE.

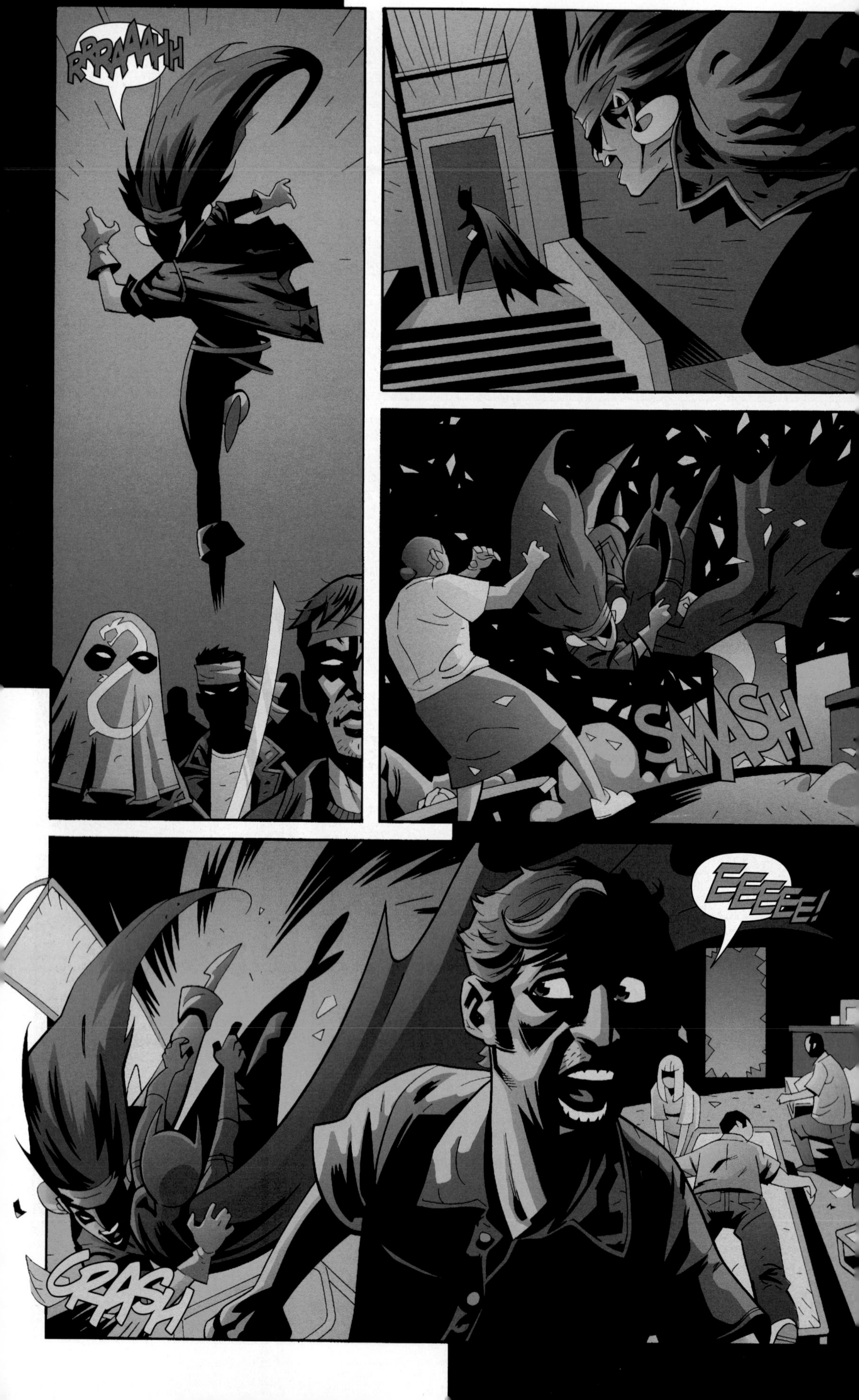
RRRAAAHH
SMASH
EEEEEE!
CRASH

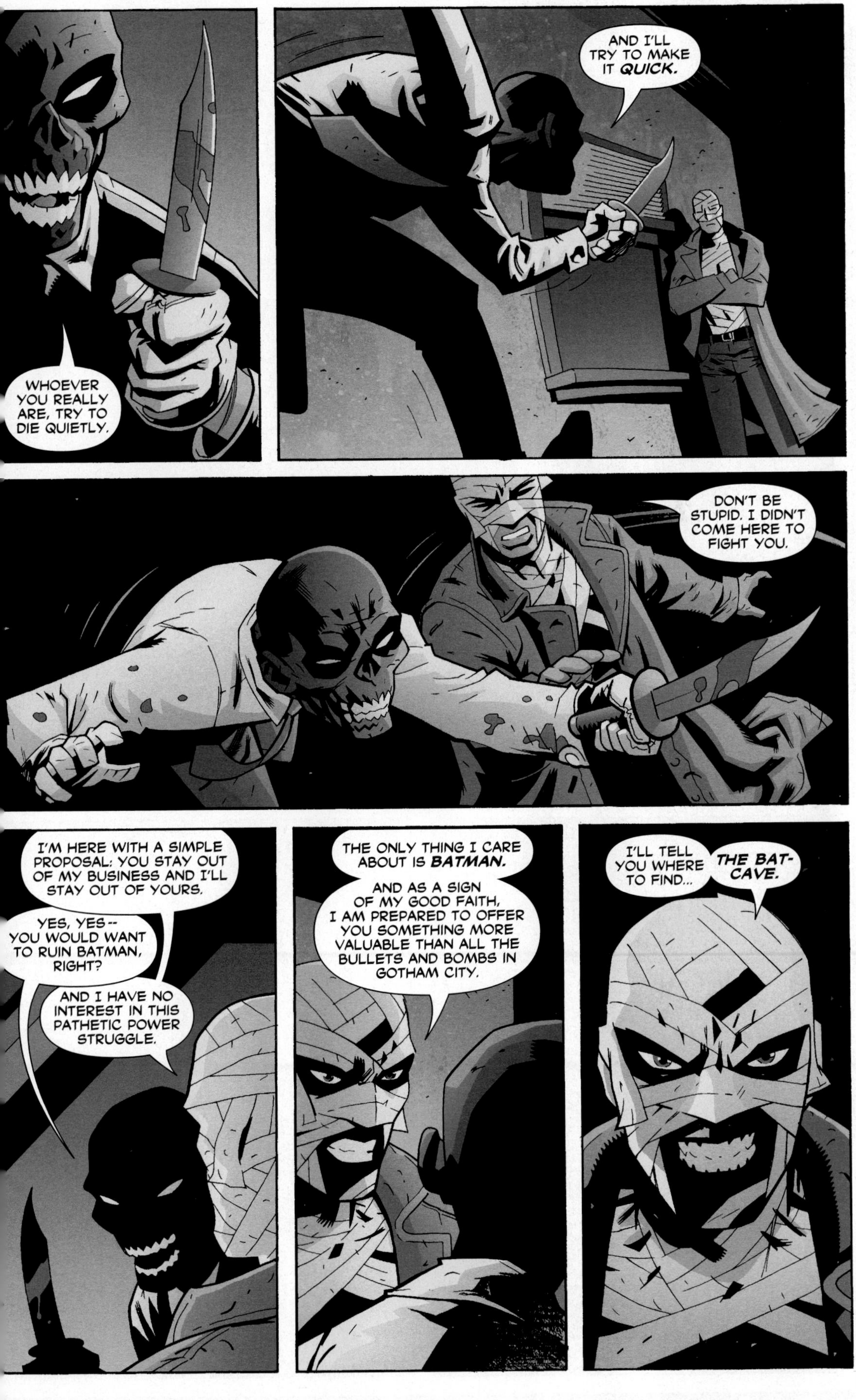
WHOEVER YOU REALLY ARE, TRY TO DIE QUIETLY.
AND I'LL TRY TO MAKE IT QUICK.
DON'T BE STUPID. I DIDN'T COME HERE TO FIGHT YOU.
I'M HERE WITH A SIMPLE PROPOSAL: YOU STAY OUT OF MY BUSINESS AND I'LL STAY OUT OF YOURS.
YES, YES-- YOU WOULD WANT TO RUIN BATMAN, RIGHT?
AND I HAVE NO INTEREST IN THIS PATHETIC POWER STRUGGLE.
THE ONLY THING I CARE ABOUT IS BATMAN.
AND AS A SIGN OF MY GOOD FAITH, I AM PREPARED TO OFFER YOU SOMETHING MORE VALUABLE THAN ALL THE BULLETS AND BOMBS IN GOTHAM CITY.
I'LL TELL YOU WHERE TO FIND...
THE BAT-CAVE.

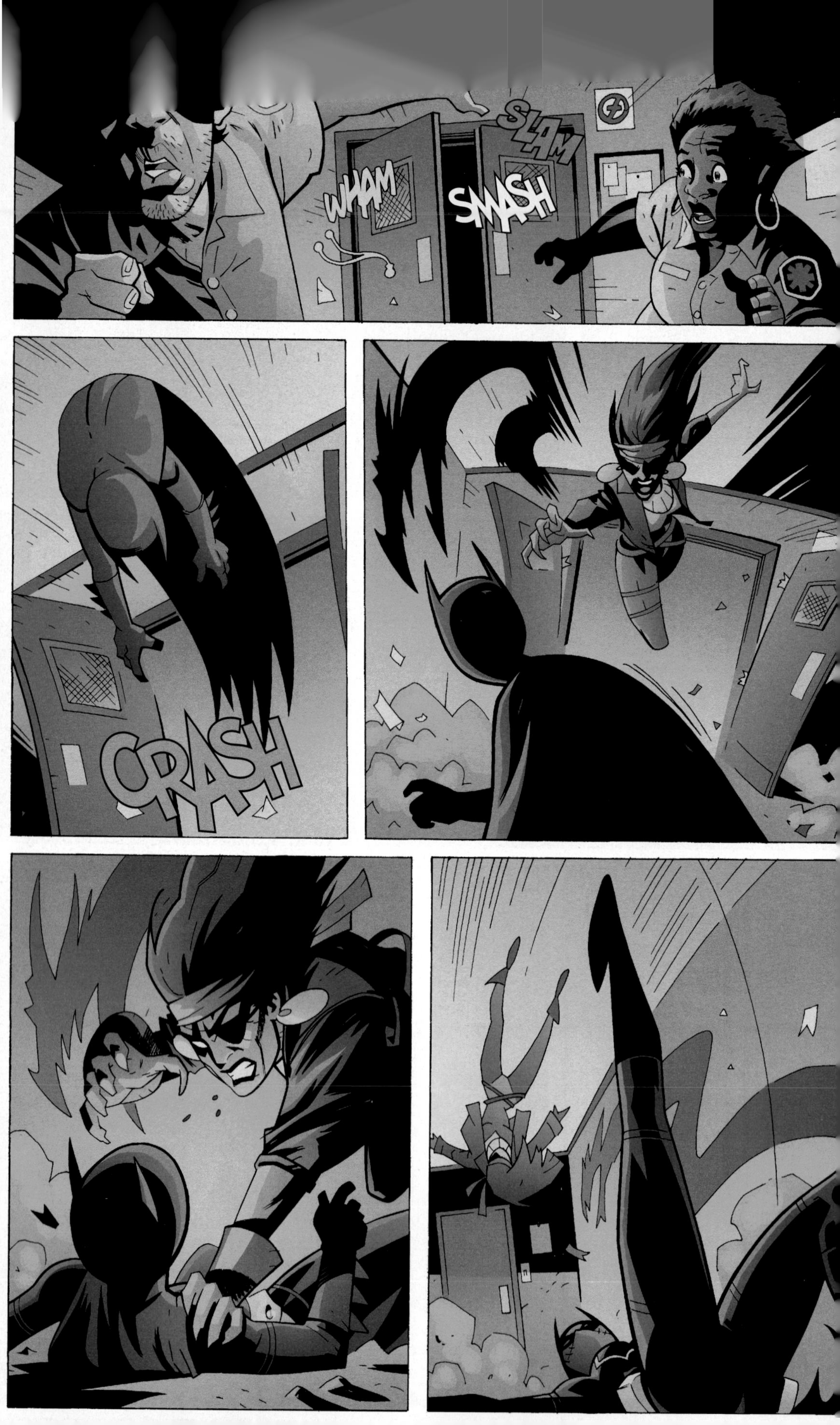
SLAM
WHAM
SMASH
CRASH

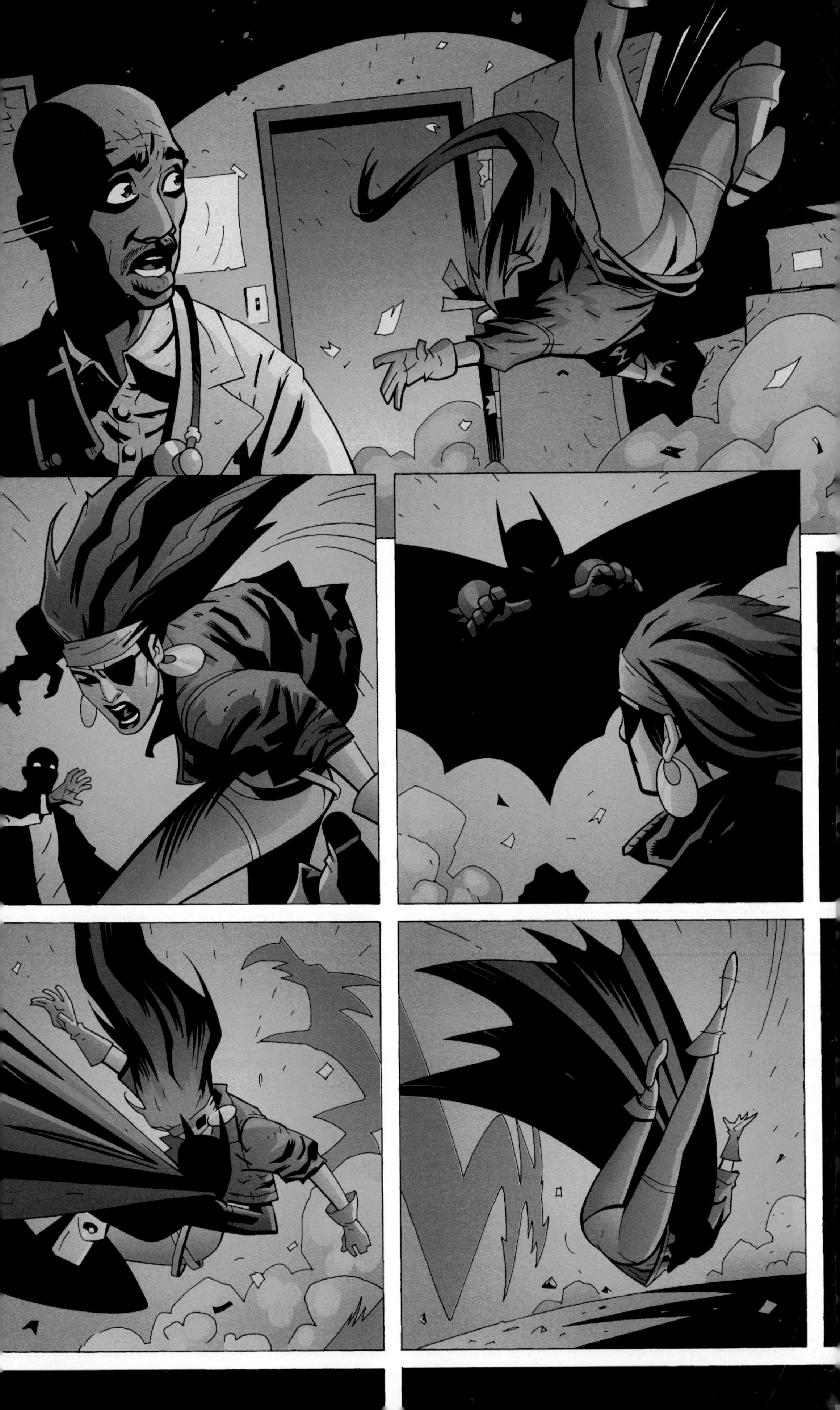

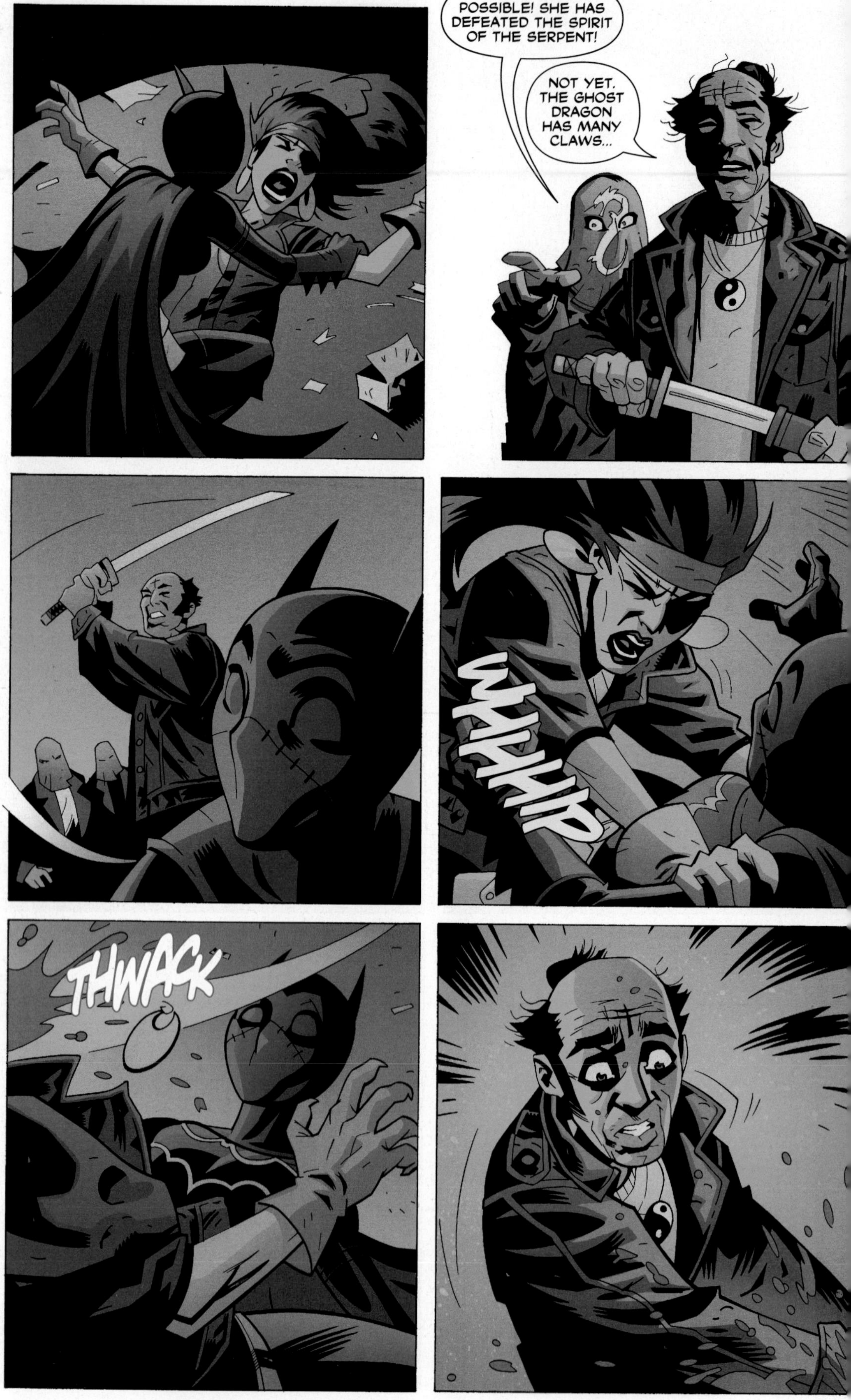

IT-- IT IS NOT POSSIBLE! SHE HAS DEFEATED THE SPIRIT OF THE SERPENT!
NOT YET. THE GHOST DRAGON HAS MANY CLAWS...
WHHHIP
THWACK

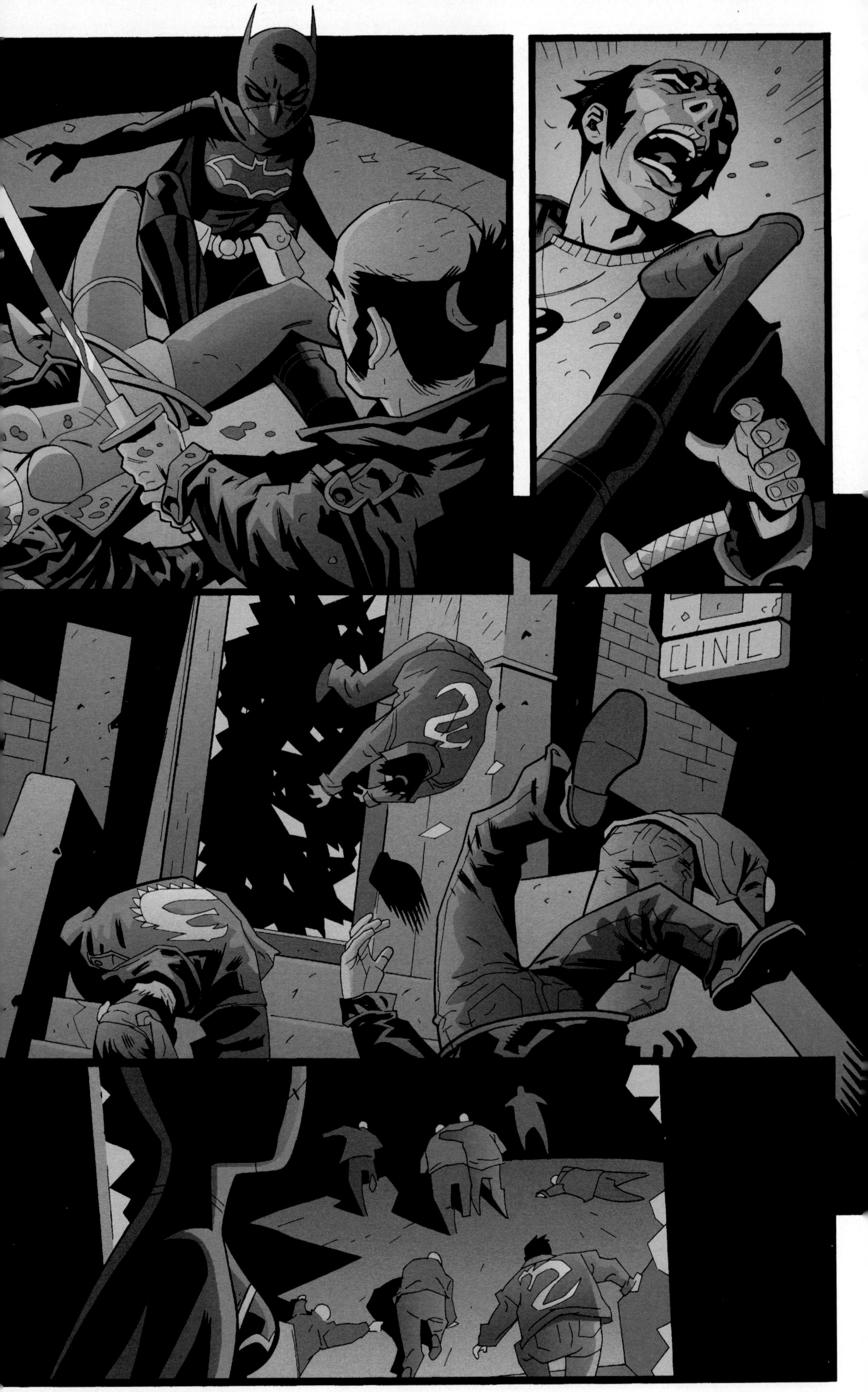
CLINIC

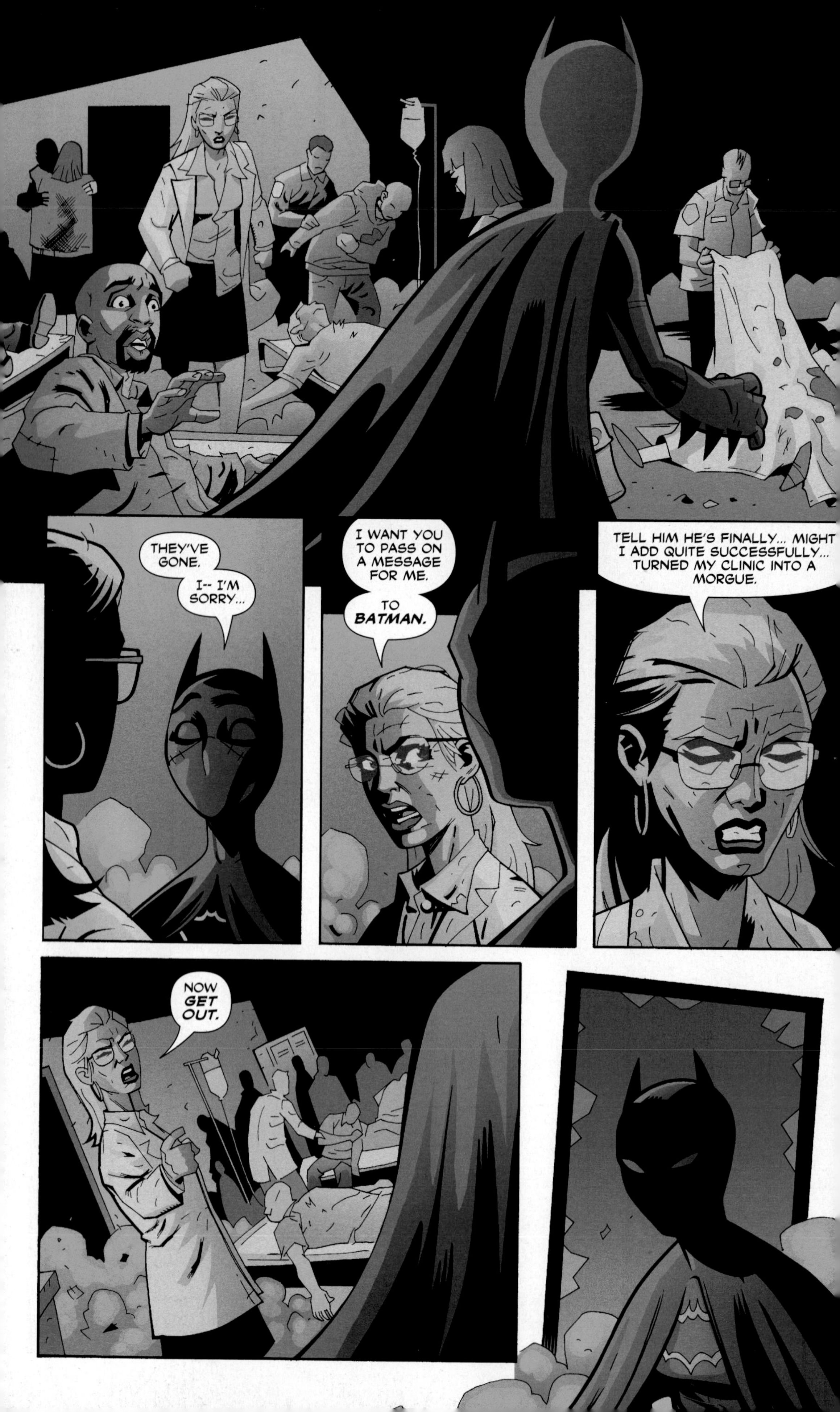
THEY'VE GONE.
I-- I'M SORRY...
I WANT YOU TO PASS ON A MESSAGE FOR ME.
TO BATMAN.
TELL HIM HE'S FINALLY... MIGHT I ADD QUITE SUCCESSFULLY... TURNED MY CLINIC INTO A MORGUE.
NOW GET OUT.

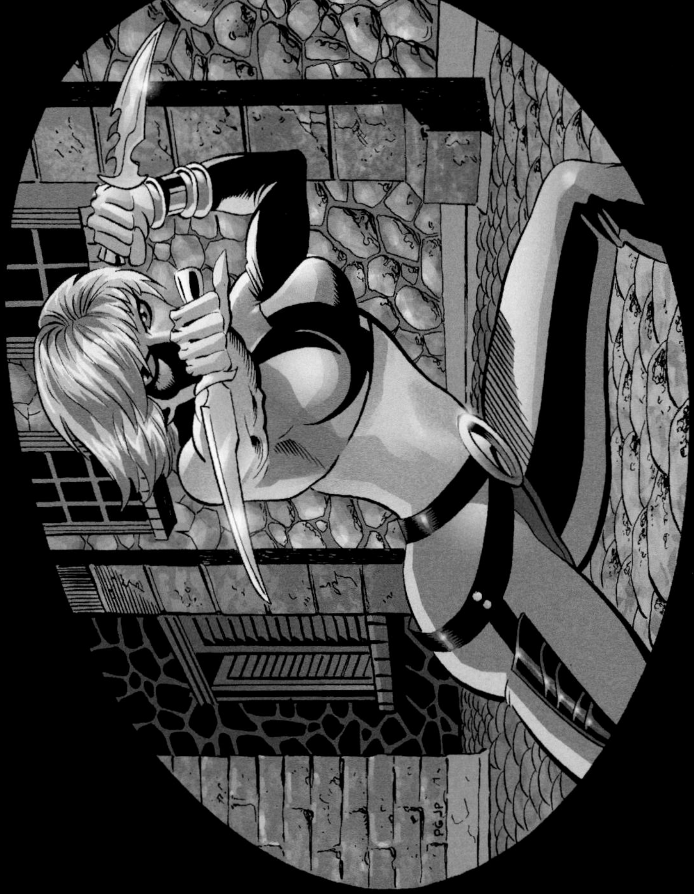

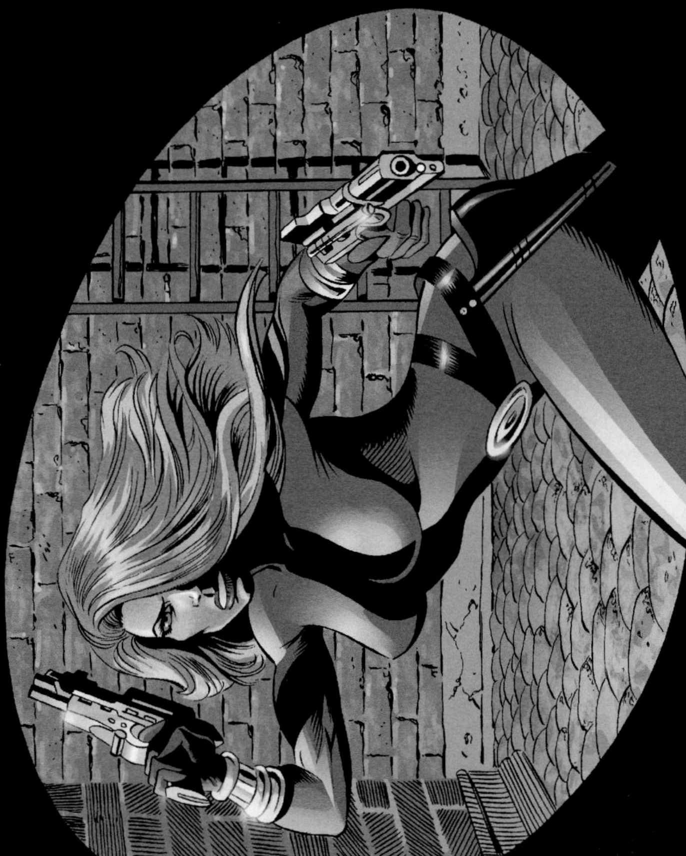

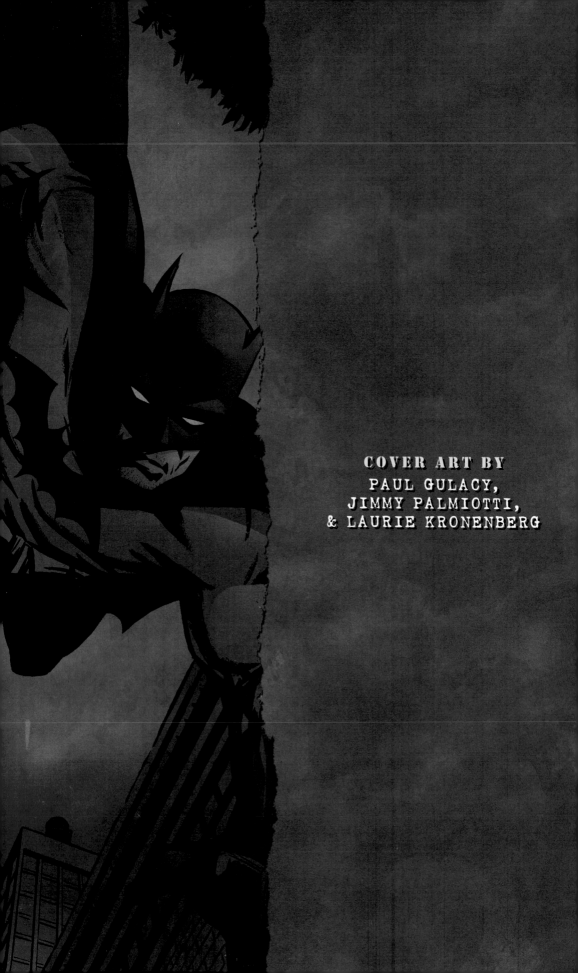

COVER ART BY
PAUL GULACY,
JIMMY PALMIOTTI,
& LAURIE KRONENBERG

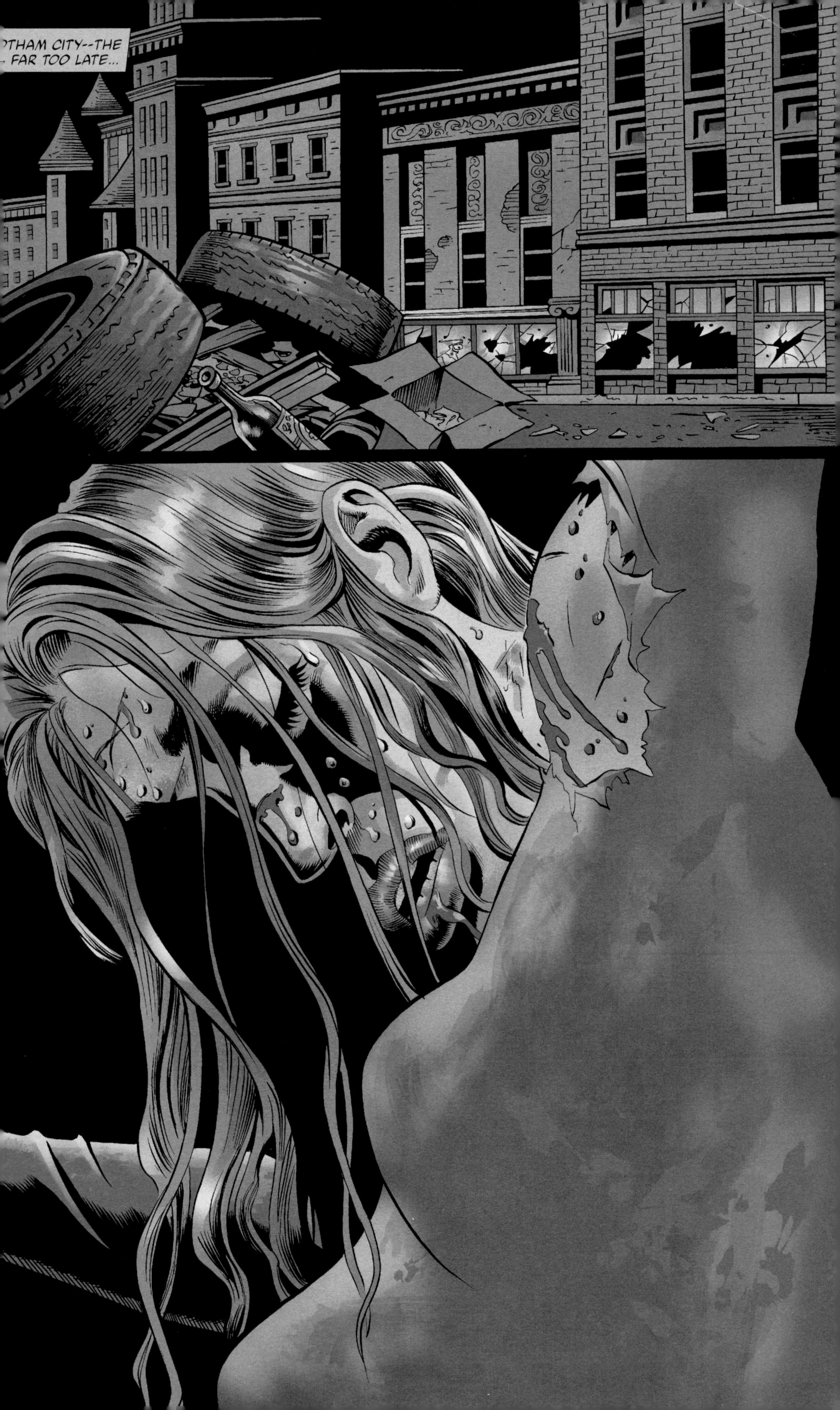

OTHAM CITY--THE
FAR TOO LATE...

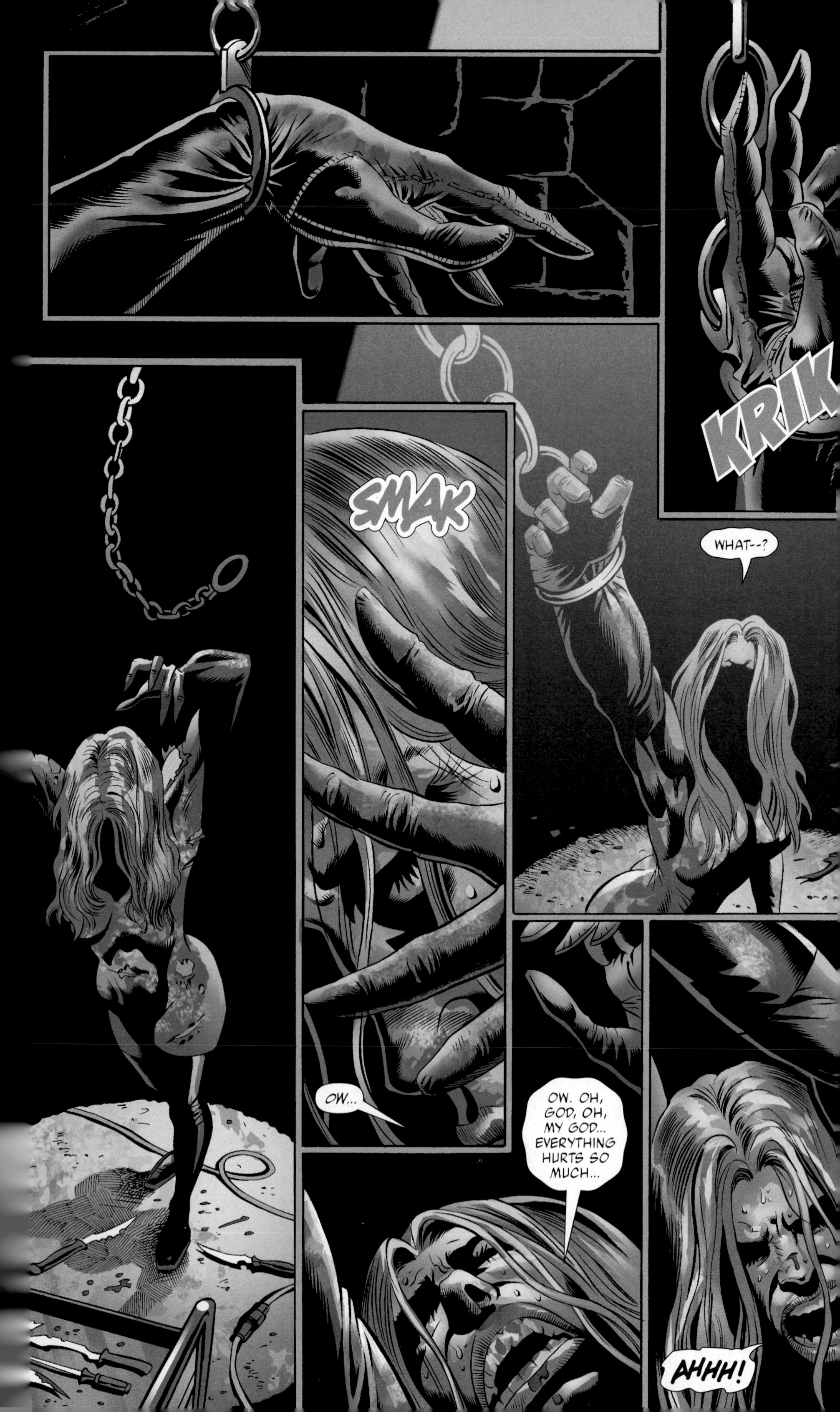
KRIK
SMAK
WHAT--?
OW...
OW. OH, GOD, OH, MY GOD... EVERYTHING HURTS SO MUCH...
AHHH!

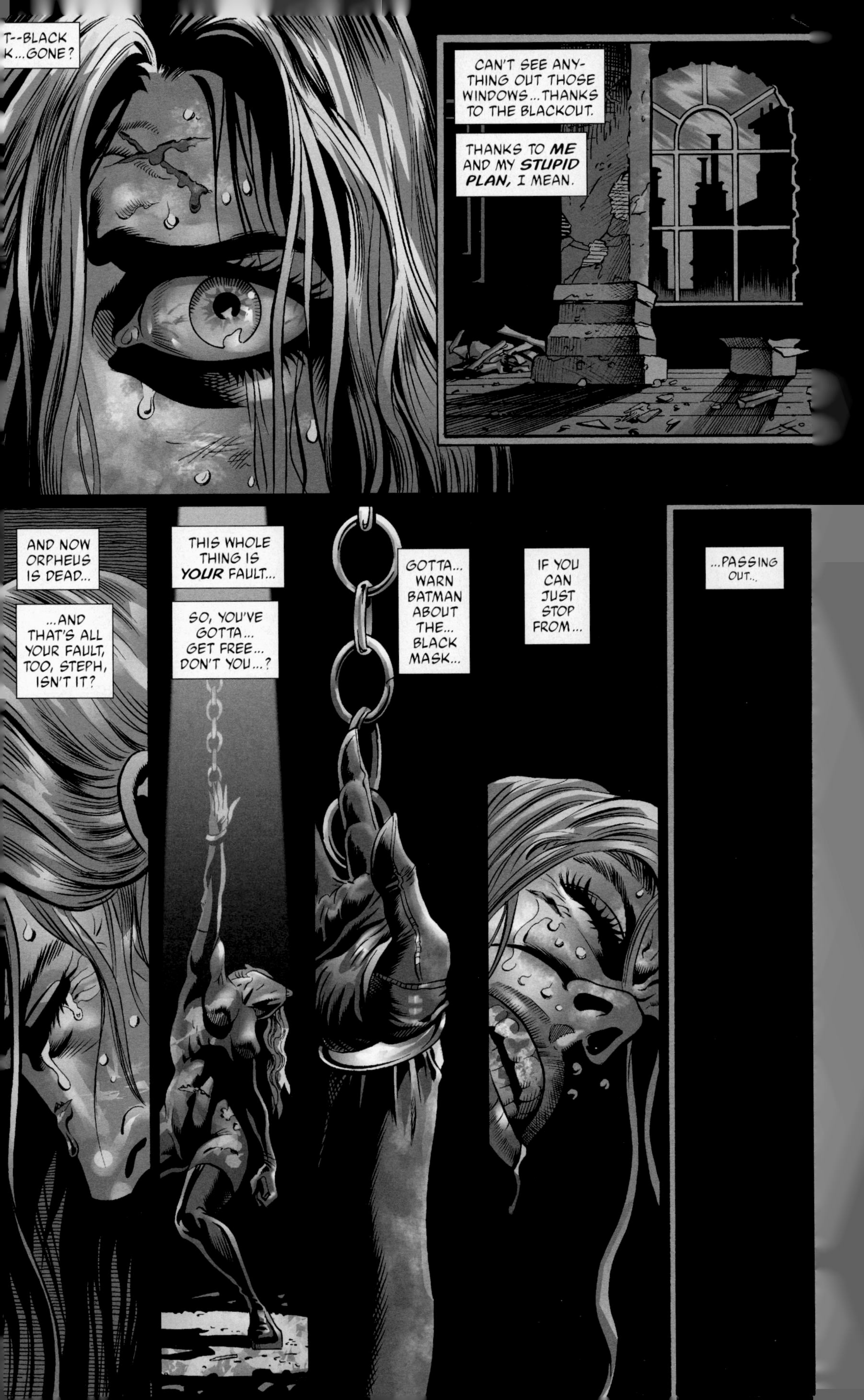
T--BLACK
K...GONE?
CAN'T SEE ANYTHING OUT THOSE WINDOWS...THANKS TO THE BLACKOUT.
THANKS TO ME AND MY STUPID PLAN, I MEAN.
AND NOW ORPHEUS IS DEAD...
...AND THAT'S ALL YOUR FAULT, TOO, STEPH, ISN'T IT?
THIS WHOLE THING IS YOUR FAULT...
SO, YOU'VE GOTTA... GET FREE... DON'T YOU...?
GOTTA... WARN BATMAN ABOUT THE... BLACK MASK...
IF YOU CAN JUST STOP FROM...
...PASSING OUT...

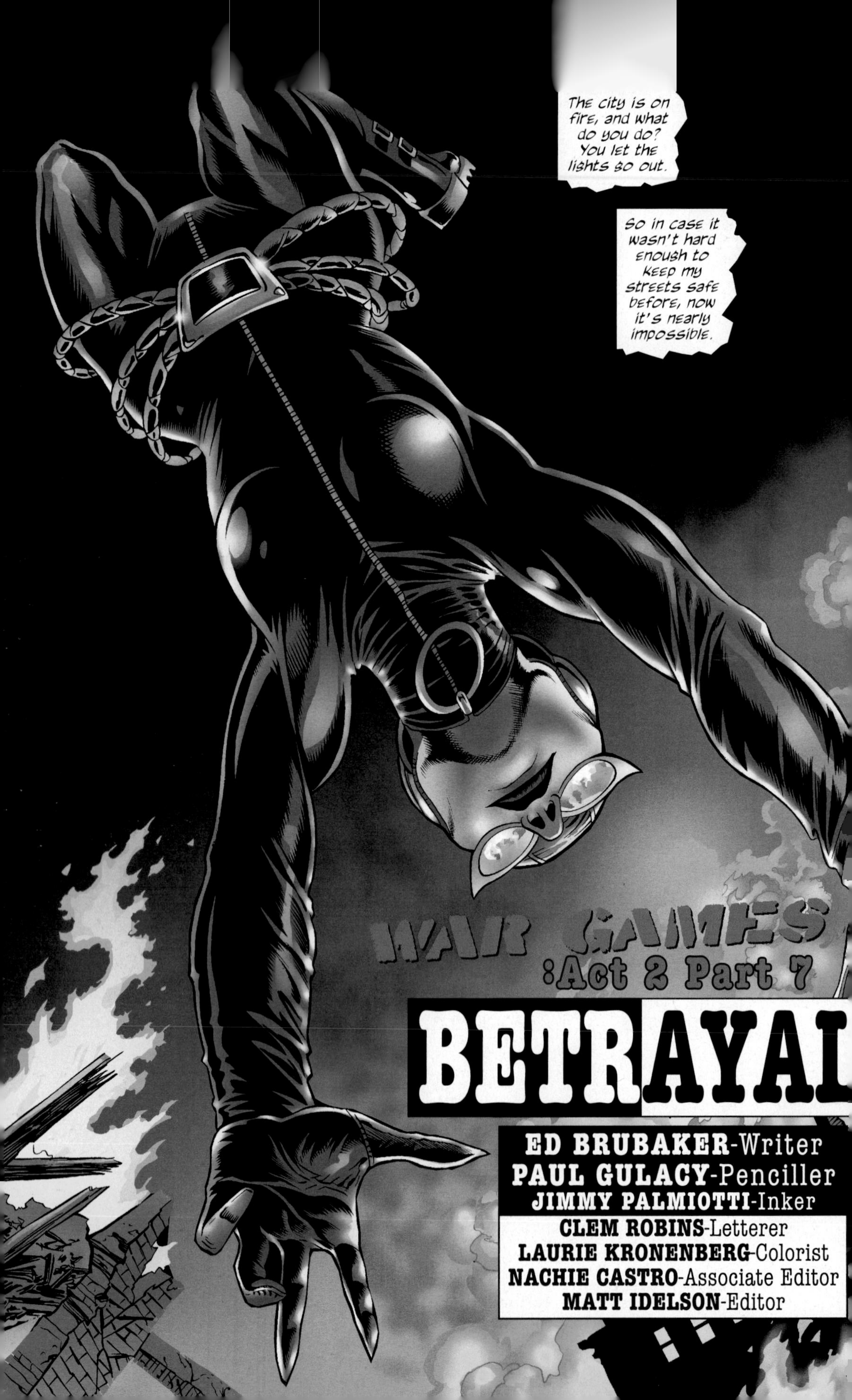

The city is on fire, and what do you do? You let the lights go out.
So in case it wasn't hard enough to keep my streets safe before, now it's nearly impossible.
WAR GAMES
:Act 2 Part 7
BETRAYAL
ED BRUBAKER-Writer
PAUL GULACY-Penciller
JIMMY PALMIOTTI-Inker
CLEM ROBINS-Letterer
LAURIE KRONENBERG-Colorist
NACHIE CASTRO-Associate Editor
MATT IDELSON-Editor

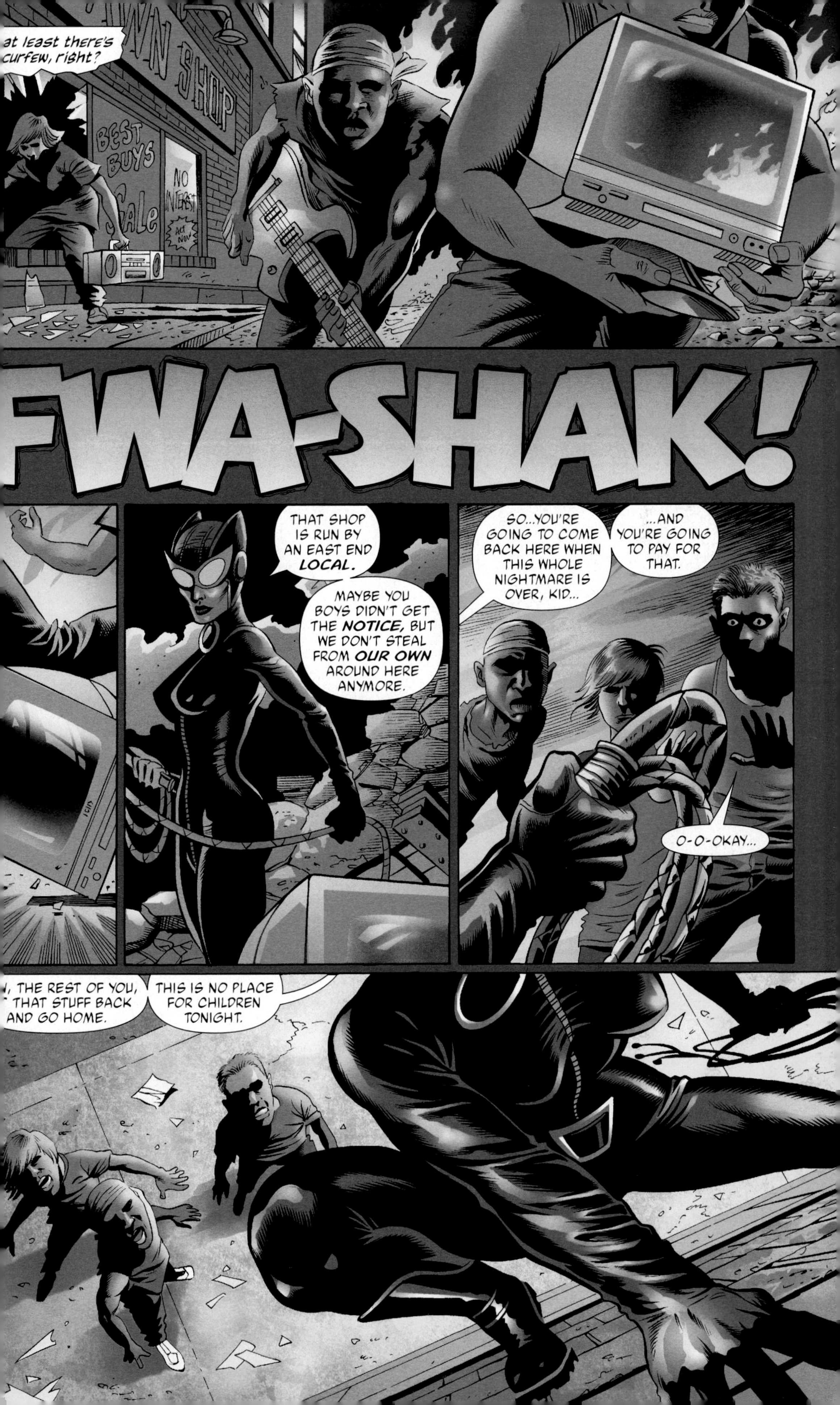
at least there's
curfew, right?
BEST BUYS Sale
NO INTEREST
ACT NOW
FWA-SHAK!
THAT SHOP IS RUN BY AN EAST END LOCAL.
MAYBE YOU BOYS DIDN'T GET THE NOTICE, BUT WE DON'T STEAL FROM OUR OWN AROUND HERE ANYMORE.
SO...YOU'RE GOING TO COME BACK HERE WHEN THIS WHOLE NIGHTMARE IS OVER, KID...
...AND YOU'RE GOING TO PAY FOR THAT.
O-O-OKAY...
THE REST OF YOU,
THAT STUFF BACK AND GO HOME.
THIS IS NO PLACE FOR CHILDREN TONIGHT.

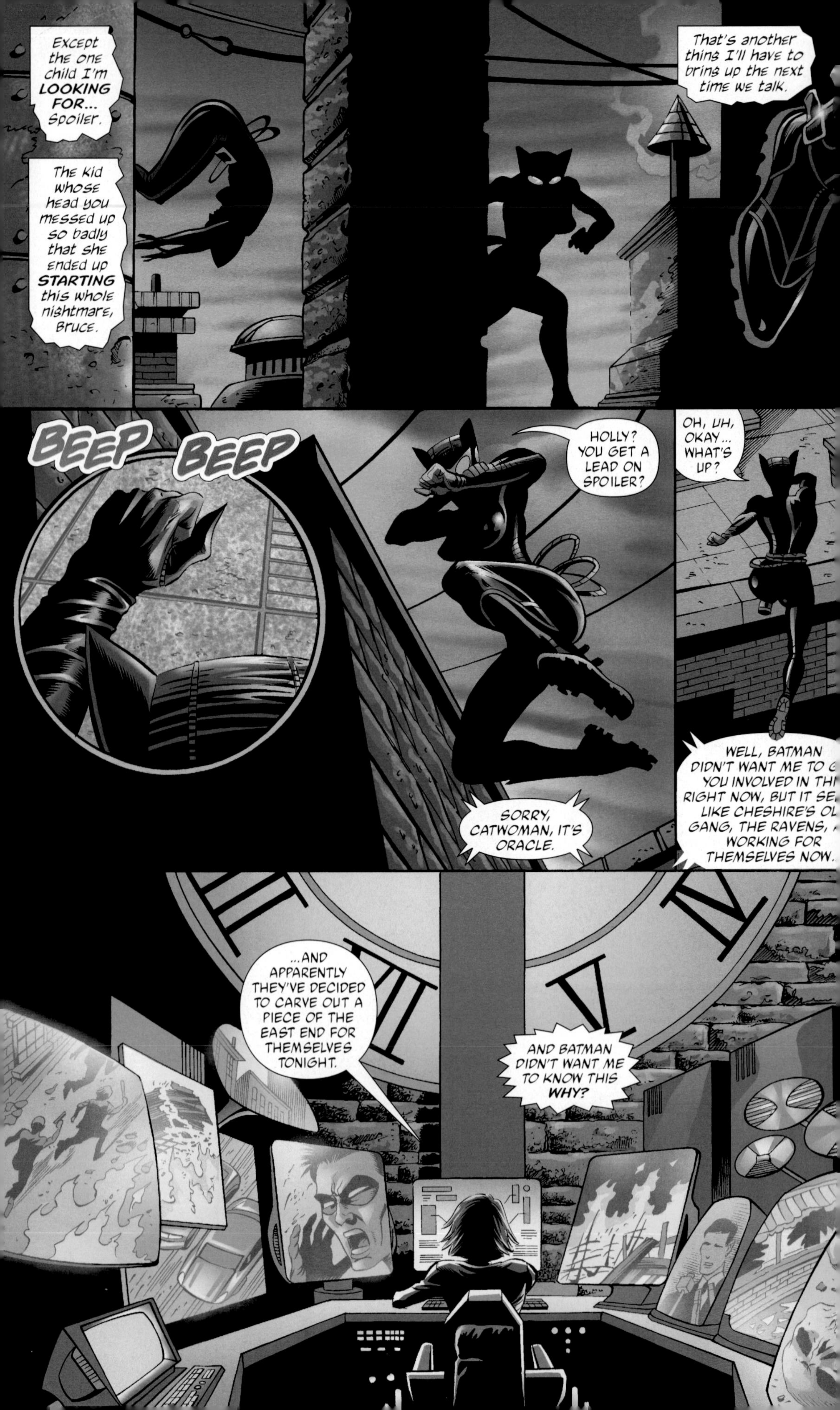

Except the one child I'm LOOKING FOR... Spoiler.
The kid whose head you messed up so badly that she ended up STARTING this whole nightmare, Bruce.
That's another thing I'll have to bring up the next time we talk.
BEEP BEEP
HOLLY? YOU GET A LEAD ON SPOILER?
SORRY, CATWOMAN, IT'S ORACLE.
OH, UH, OKAY... WHAT'S UP?
WELL, BATMAN DIDN'T WANT ME TO G YOU INVOLVED IN THI RIGHT NOW, BUT IT SE LIKE CHESHIRE'S OL GANG, THE RAVENS, WORKING FOR THEMSELVES NOW.
...AND APPARENTLY THEY'VE DECIDED TO CARVE OUT A PIECE OF THE EAST END FOR THEMSELVES TONIGHT.
AND BATMAN DIDN'T WANT ME TO KNOW THIS WHY?

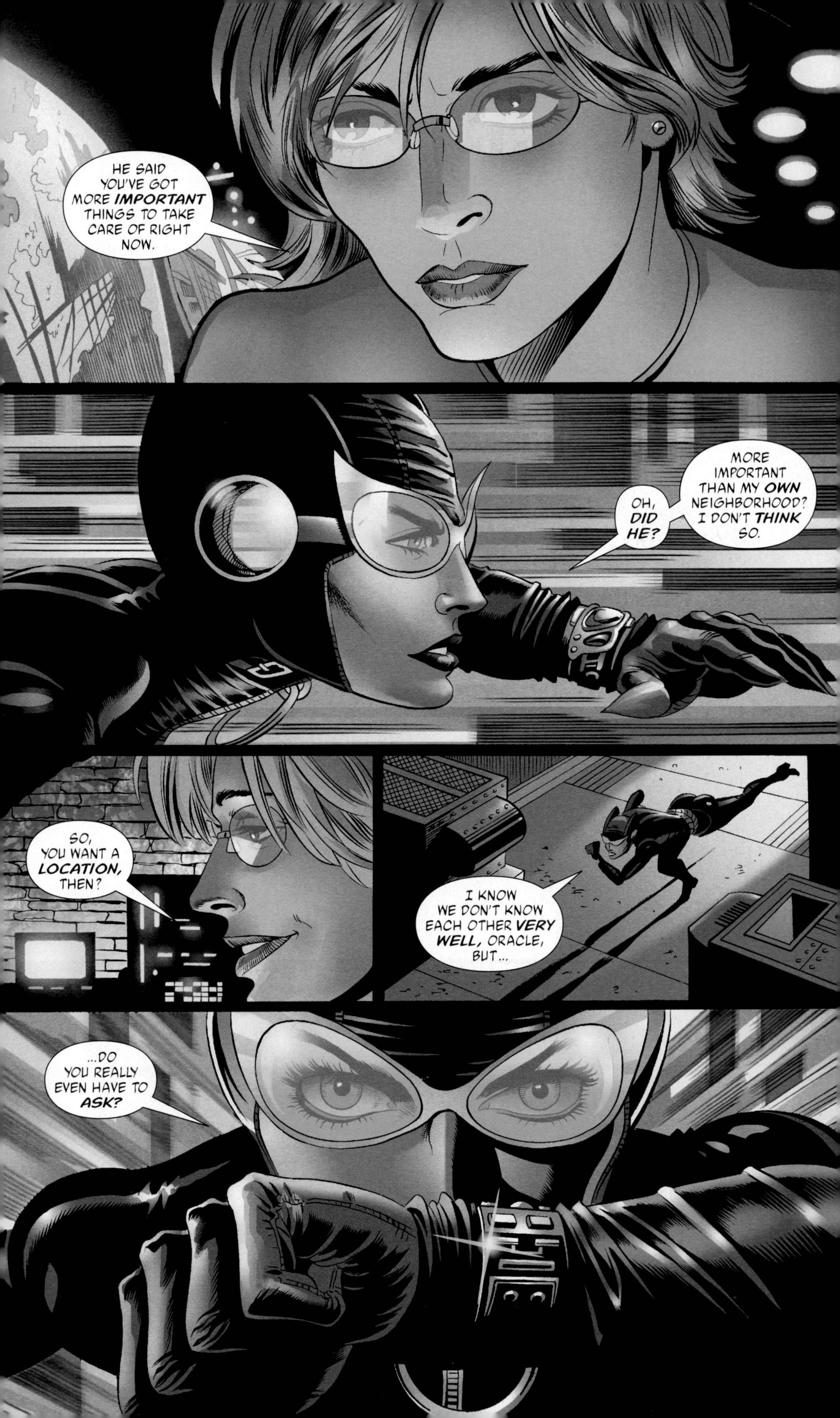
HE SAID YOU'VE GOT MORE IMPORTANT THINGS TO TAKE CARE OF RIGHT NOW.
OH, DID HE?
MORE IMPORTANT THAN MY OWN NEIGHBORHOOD? I DON'T THINK SO.
SO, YOU WANT A LOCATION, THEN?
I KNOW WE DON'T KNOW EACH OTHER VERY WELL, ORACLE, BUT...
...DO YOU REALLY EVEN HAVE TO ASK?

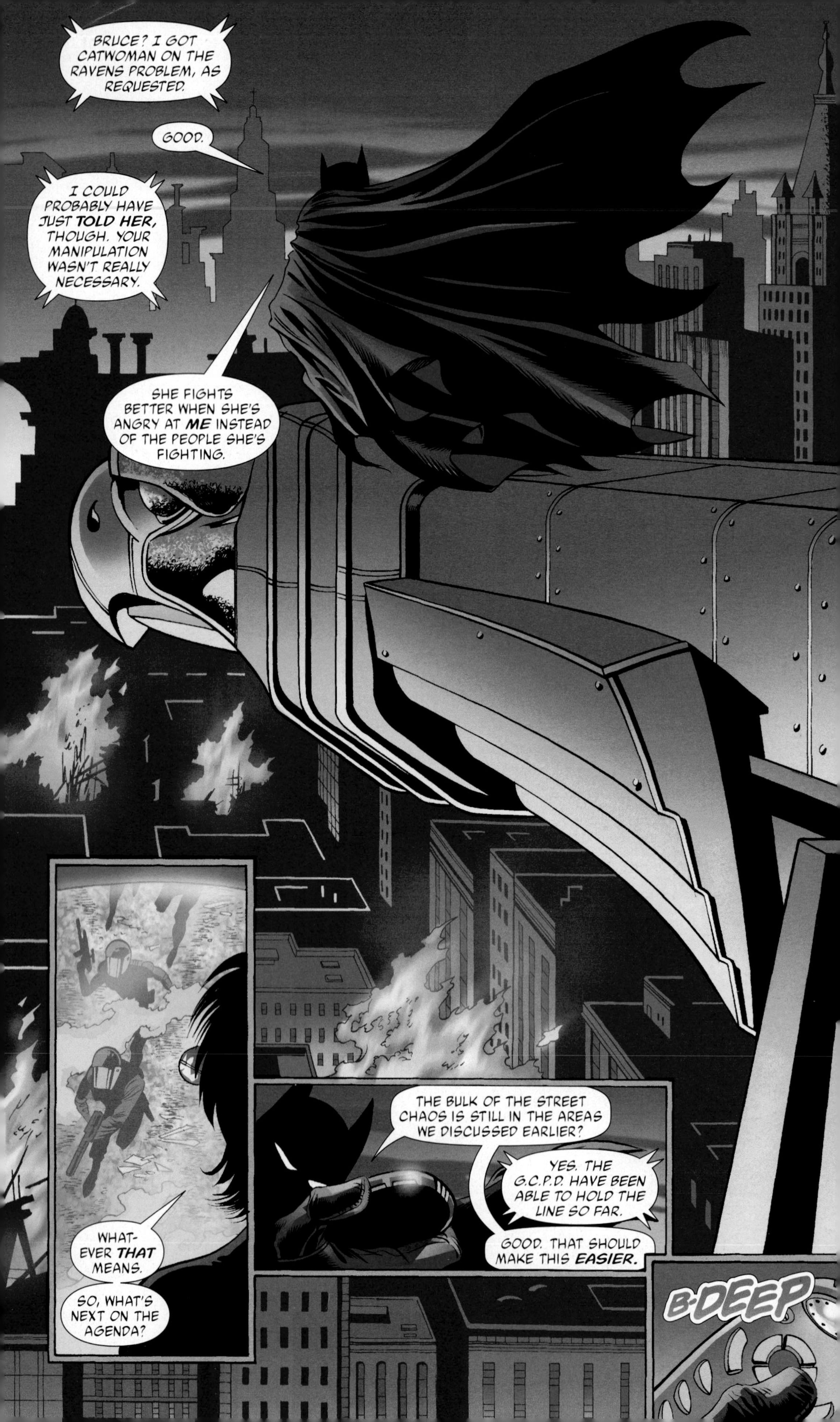
BRUCE? I GOT CATWOMAN ON THE RAVENS PROBLEM, AS REQUESTED.
GOOD.
I COULD PROBABLY HAVE JUST TOLD HER, THOUGH. YOUR MANIPULATION WASN'T REALLY NECESSARY.
SHE FIGHTS BETTER WHEN SHE'S ANGRY AT ME INSTEAD OF THE PEOPLE SHE'S FIGHTING.
WHAT-EVER THAT MEANS.
SO, WHAT'S NEXT ON THE AGENDA?
THE BULK OF THE STREET CHAOS IS STILL IN THE AREAS WE DISCUSSED EARLIER?
YES. THE G.C.P.D. HAVE BEEN ABLE TO HOLD THE LINE SO FAR.
GOOD. THAT SHOULD MAKE THIS EASIER.
B-DEEP

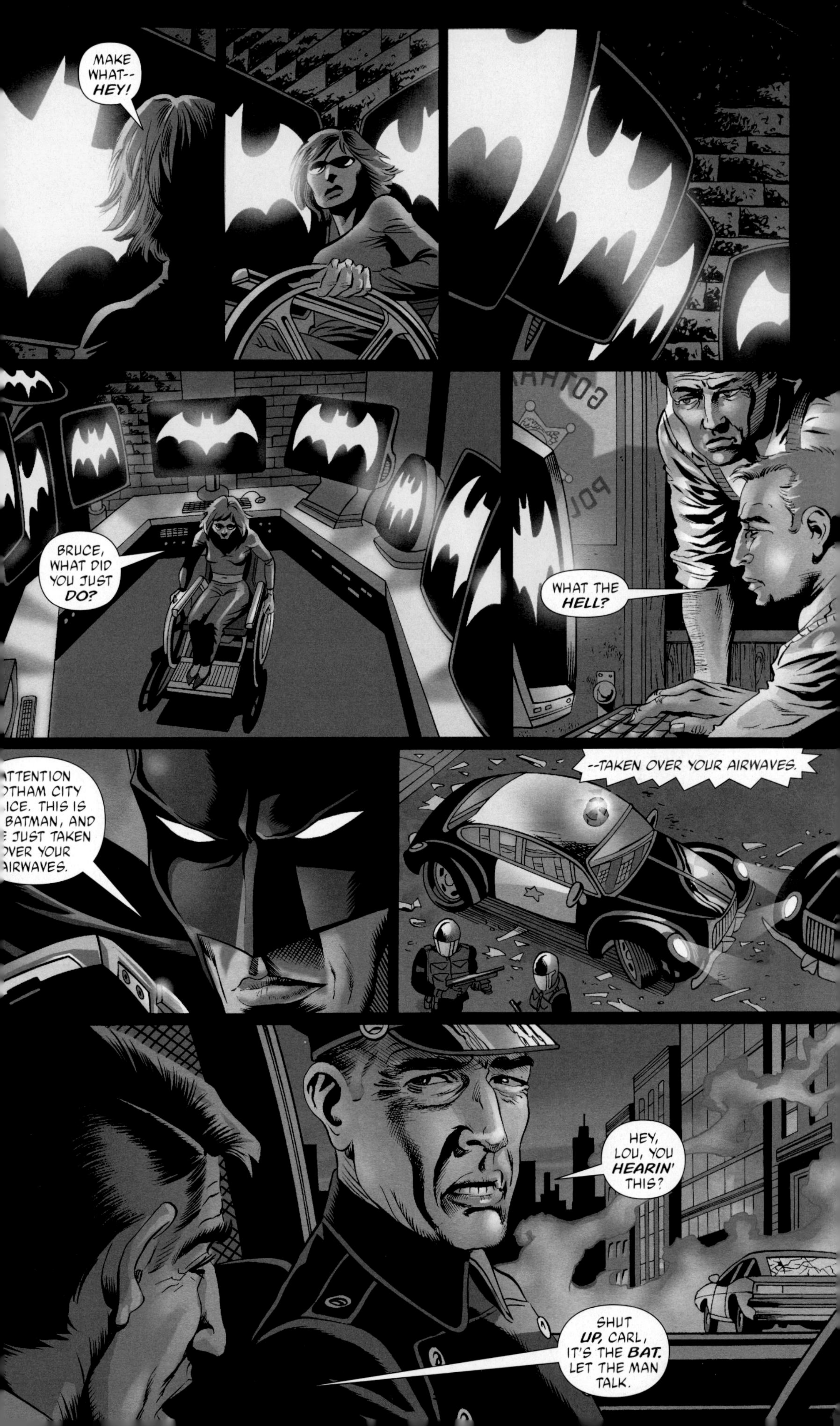
MAKE WHAT-- HEY!
BRUCE, WHAT DID YOU JUST DO?
WHAT THE HELL?
ATTENTION OTHAM CITY ICE. THIS IS BATMAN, AND E JUST TAKEN OVER YOUR AIRWAVES.
--TAKEN OVER YOUR AIRWAVES.
HEY, LOU, YOU HEARIN' THIS?
SHUT UP, CARL, IT'S THE BAT. LET THE MAN TALK.

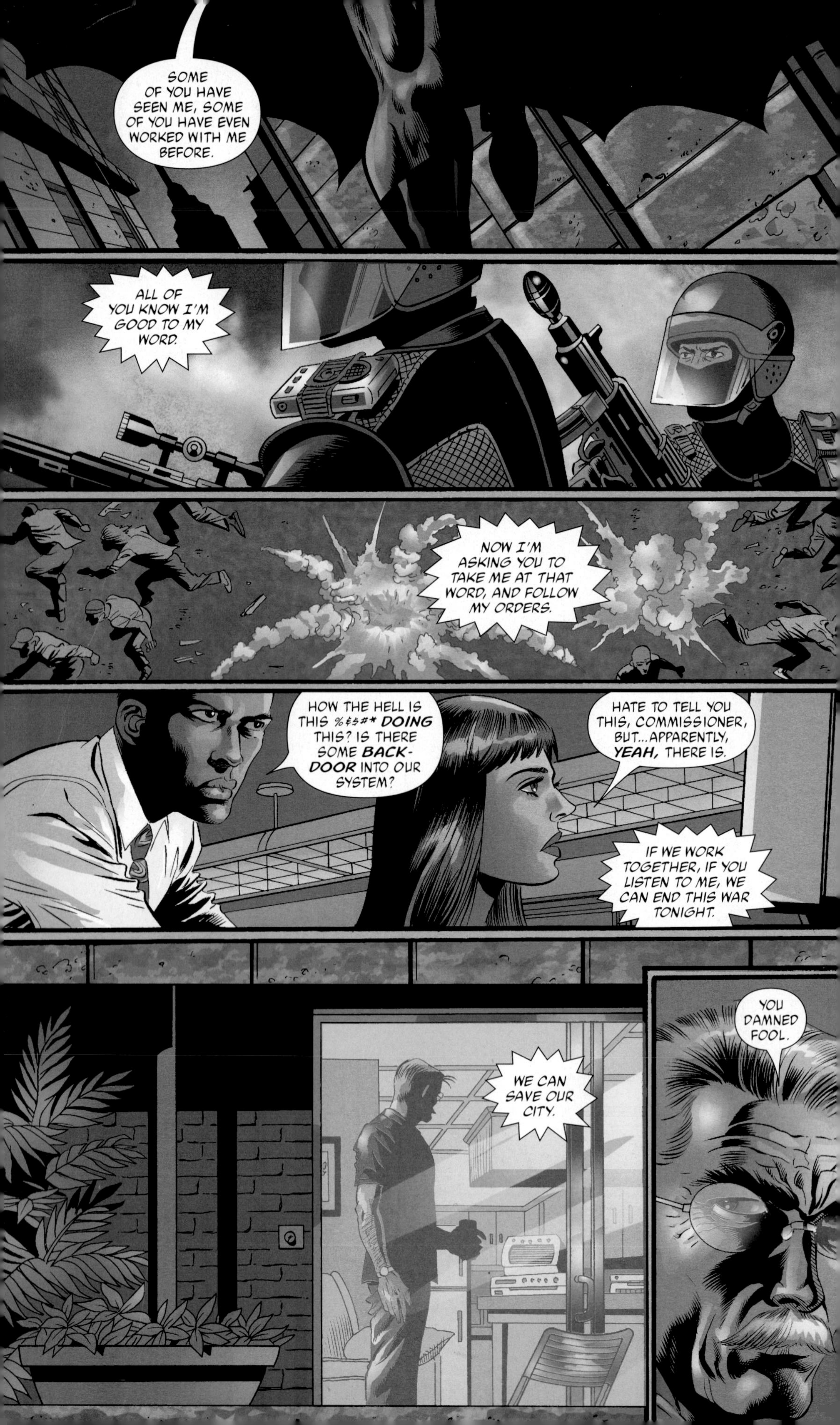

SOME OF YOU HAVE SEEN ME, SOME OF YOU HAVE EVEN WORKED WITH ME BEFORE.
ALL OF YOU KNOW I'M GOOD TO MY WORD.
NOW I'M ASKING YOU TO TAKE ME AT THAT WORD, AND FOLLOW MY ORDERS.
HOW THE HELL IS THIS %$$#* DOING THIS? IS THERE SOME BACK-DOOR INTO OUR SYSTEM?
HATE TO TELL YOU THIS, COMMISSIONER, BUT...APPARENTLY, YEAH, THERE IS.
IF WE WORK TOGETHER, IF YOU LISTEN TO ME, WE CAN END THIS WAR TONIGHT.
WE CAN SAVE OUR CITY.
YOU DAMNED FOOL.

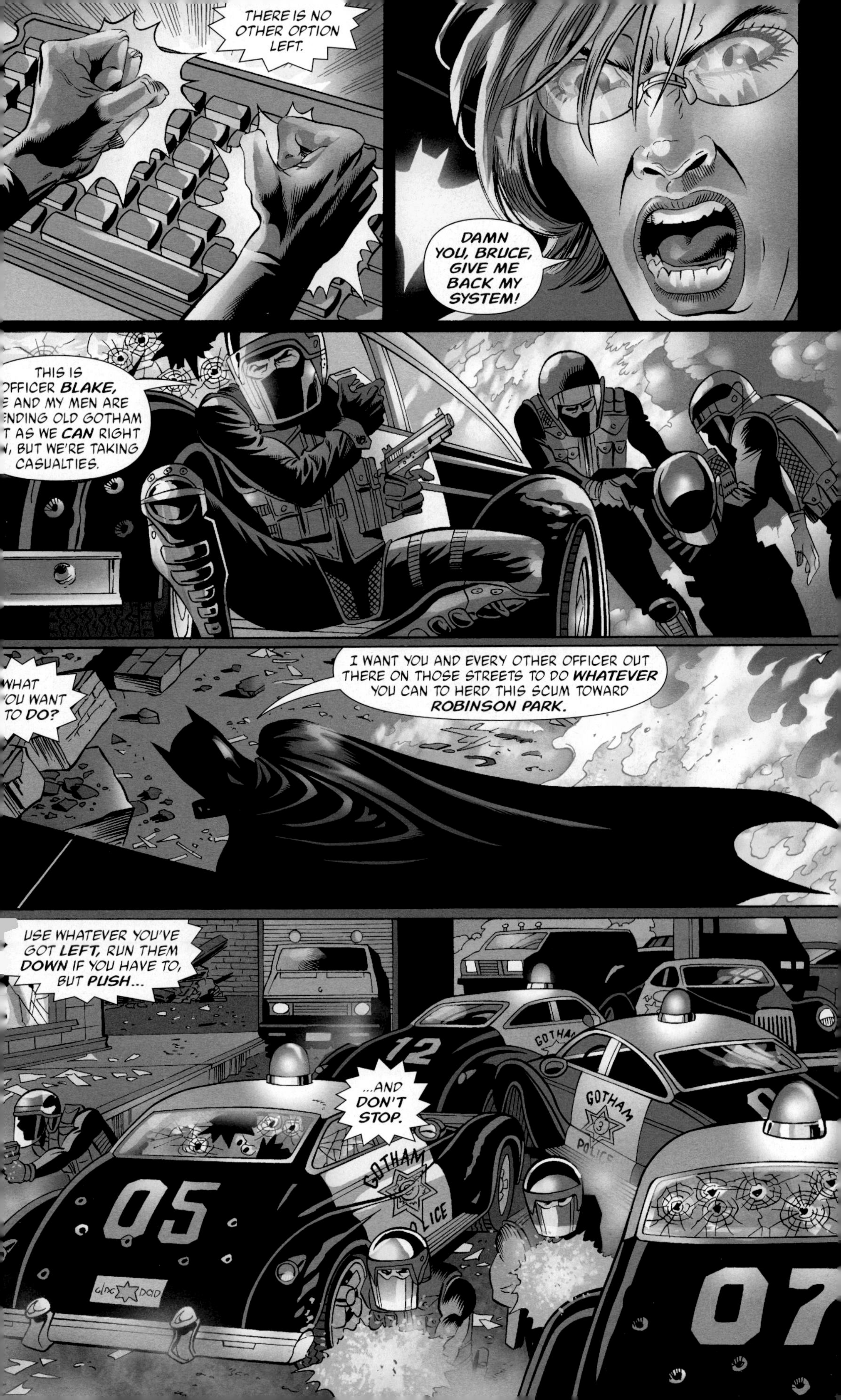
THERE IS NO OTHER OPTION LEFT.
DAMN YOU, BRUCE, GIVE ME BACK MY SYSTEM!
THIS IS OFFICER BLAKE, E AND MY MEN ARE ENDING OLD GOTHAM T AS WE CAN RIGHT , BUT WE'RE TAKING CASUALTIES.
WHAT YOU WANT TO DO?
I WANT YOU AND EVERY OTHER OFFICER OUT THERE ON THOSE STREETS TO DO WHATEVER YOU CAN TO HERD THIS SCUM TOWARD ROBINSON PARK.
USE WHATEVER YOU'VE GOT LEFT, RUN THEM DOWN IF YOU HAVE TO, BUT PUSH...
...AND DON'T STOP.
12
GOTHAM
GOTHAM 3 POLICE
GOTHAM POLICE
05
07

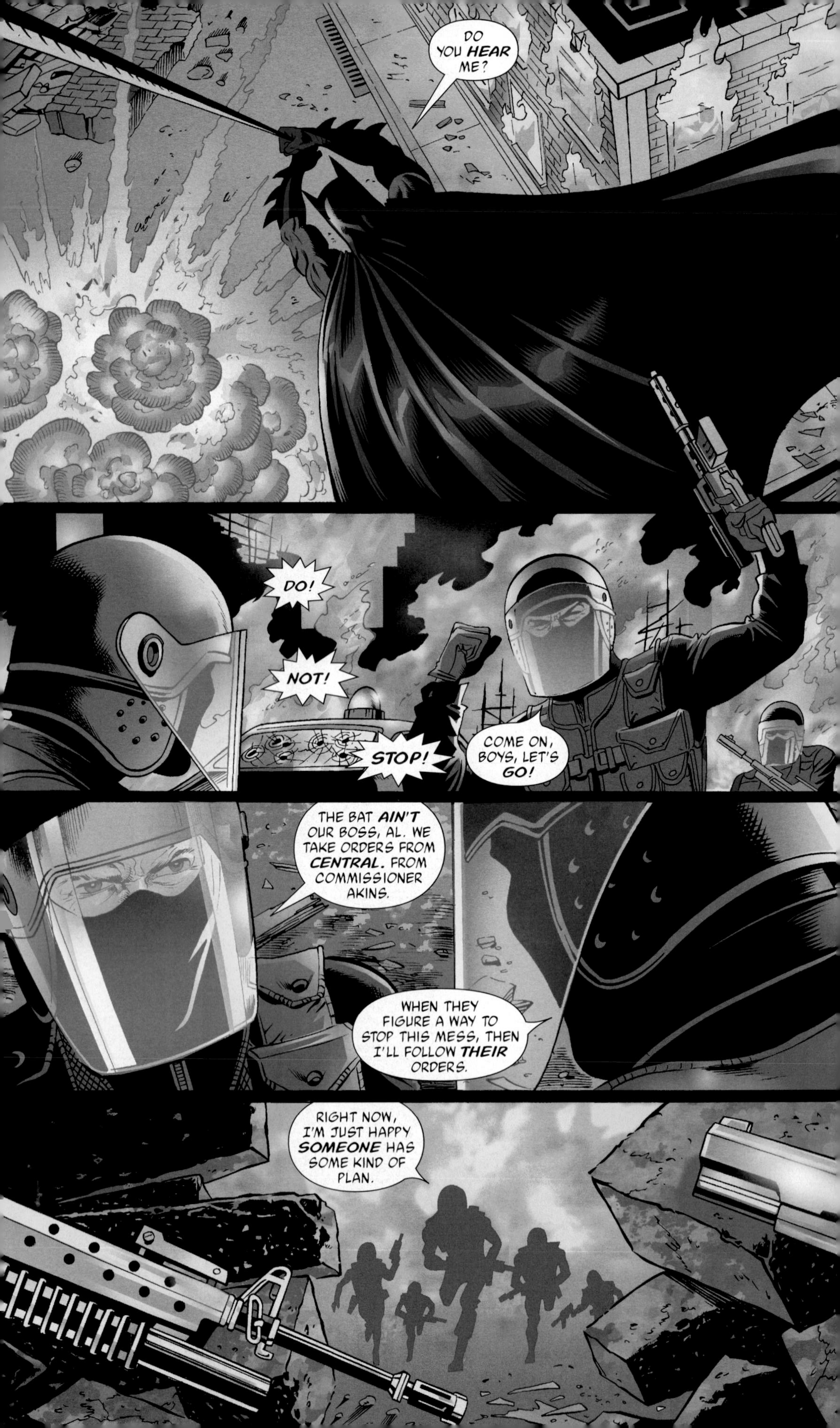
DO YOU HEAR ME?
DO!
NOT!
STOP!
COME ON, BOYS, LET'S GO!
THE BAT AIN'T OUR BOSS, AL. WE TAKE ORDERS FROM CENTRAL. FROM COMMISSIONER AKINS.
WHEN THEY FIGURE A WAY TO STOP THIS MESS, THEN I'LL FOLLOW THEIR ORDERS.
RIGHT NOW, I'M JUST HAPPY SOMEONE HAS SOME KIND OF PLAN.

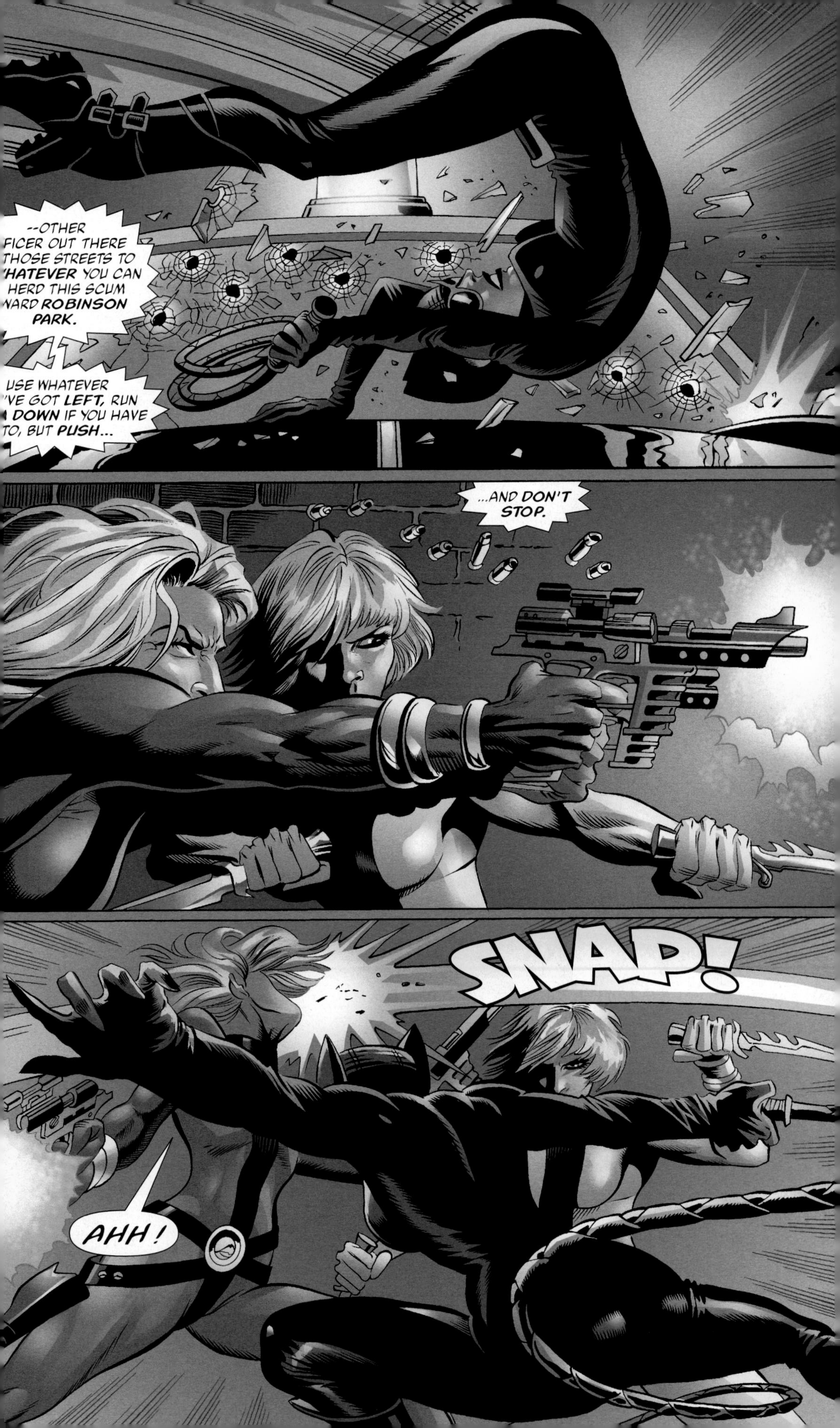
--OTHER FICER OUT THERE THOSE STREETS TO HATEVER YOU CAN HERD THIS SCUM WARD ROBINSON PARK.
USE WHATEVER 'VE GOT LEFT, RUN DOWN IF YOU HAVE TO, BUT PUSH...
...AND DON'T STOP.
SNAP!
AHH!

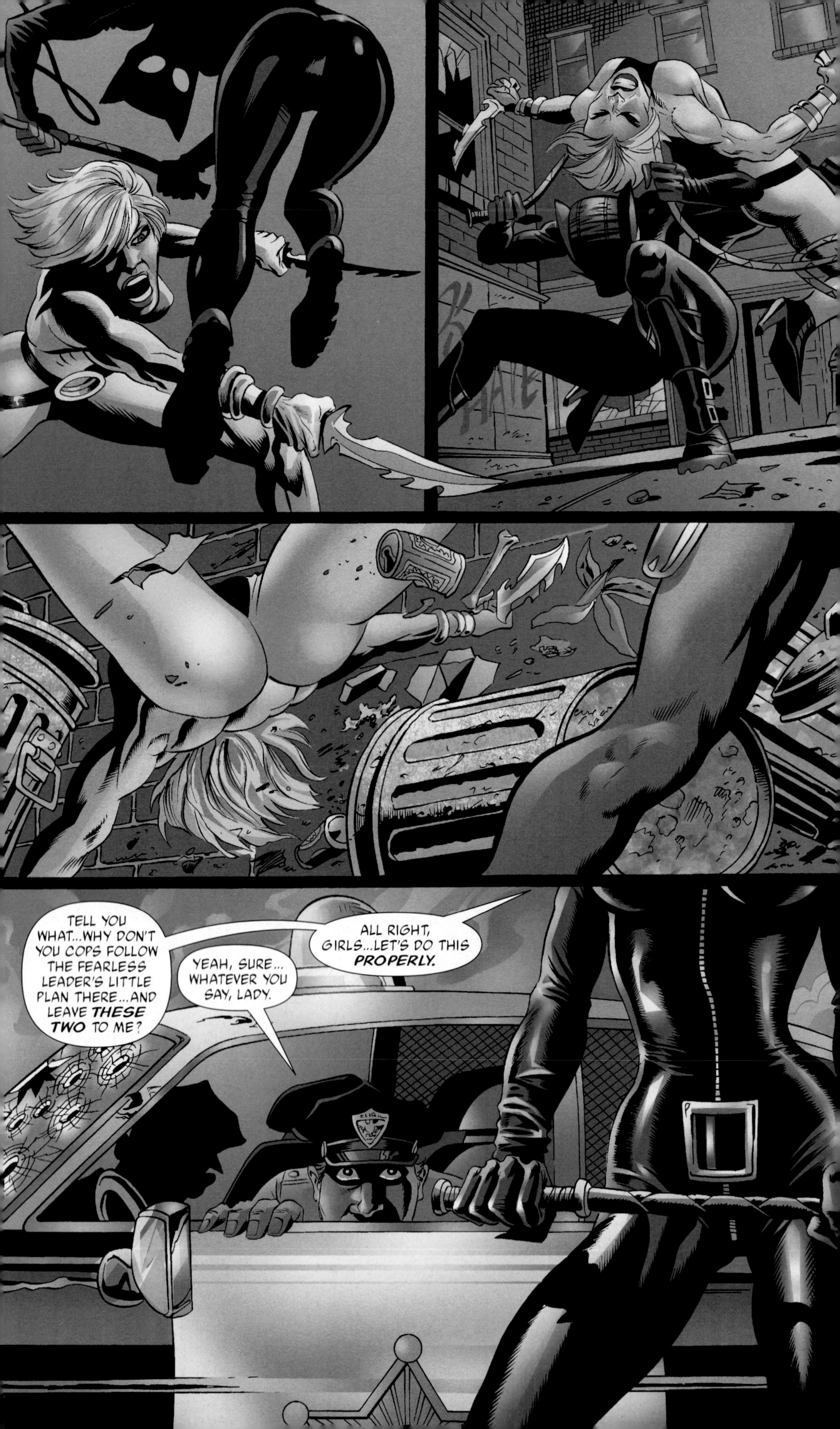
TELL YOU WHAT...WHY DON'T YOU COPS FOLLOW THE FEARLESS LEADER'S LITTLE PLAN THERE...AND LEAVE **THESE TWO** TO ME?
YEAH, SURE... WHATEVER YOU SAY, LADY.
ALL RIGHT, GIRLS...LET'S DO THIS **PROPERLY.**

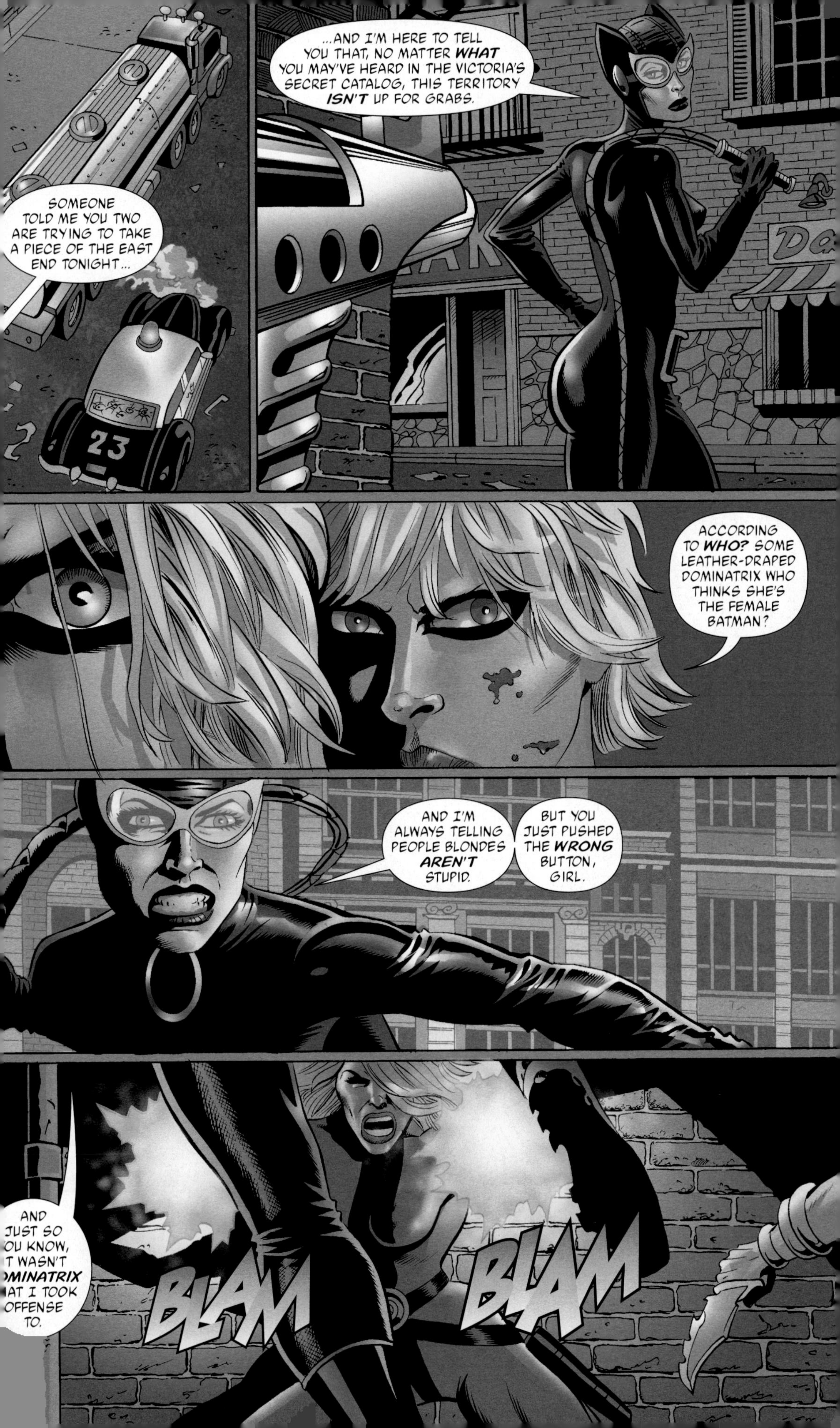

SOMEONE TOLD ME YOU TWO ARE TRYING TO TAKE A PIECE OF THE EAST END TONIGHT...
...AND I'M HERE TO TELL YOU THAT, NO MATTER WHAT YOU MAY'VE HEARD IN THE VICTORIA'S SECRET CATALOG, THIS TERRITORY ISN'T UP FOR GRABS.
23
ACCORDING TO WHO? SOME LEATHER-DRAPED DOMINATRIX WHO THINKS SHE'S THE FEMALE BATMAN?
AND I'M ALWAYS TELLING PEOPLE BLONDES AREN'T STUPID.
BUT YOU JUST PUSHED THE WRONG BUTTON, GIRL.
AND JUST SO OU KNOW, T WASN'T OMINATRIX AT I TOOK OFFENSE TO.
BLAM
BLAM

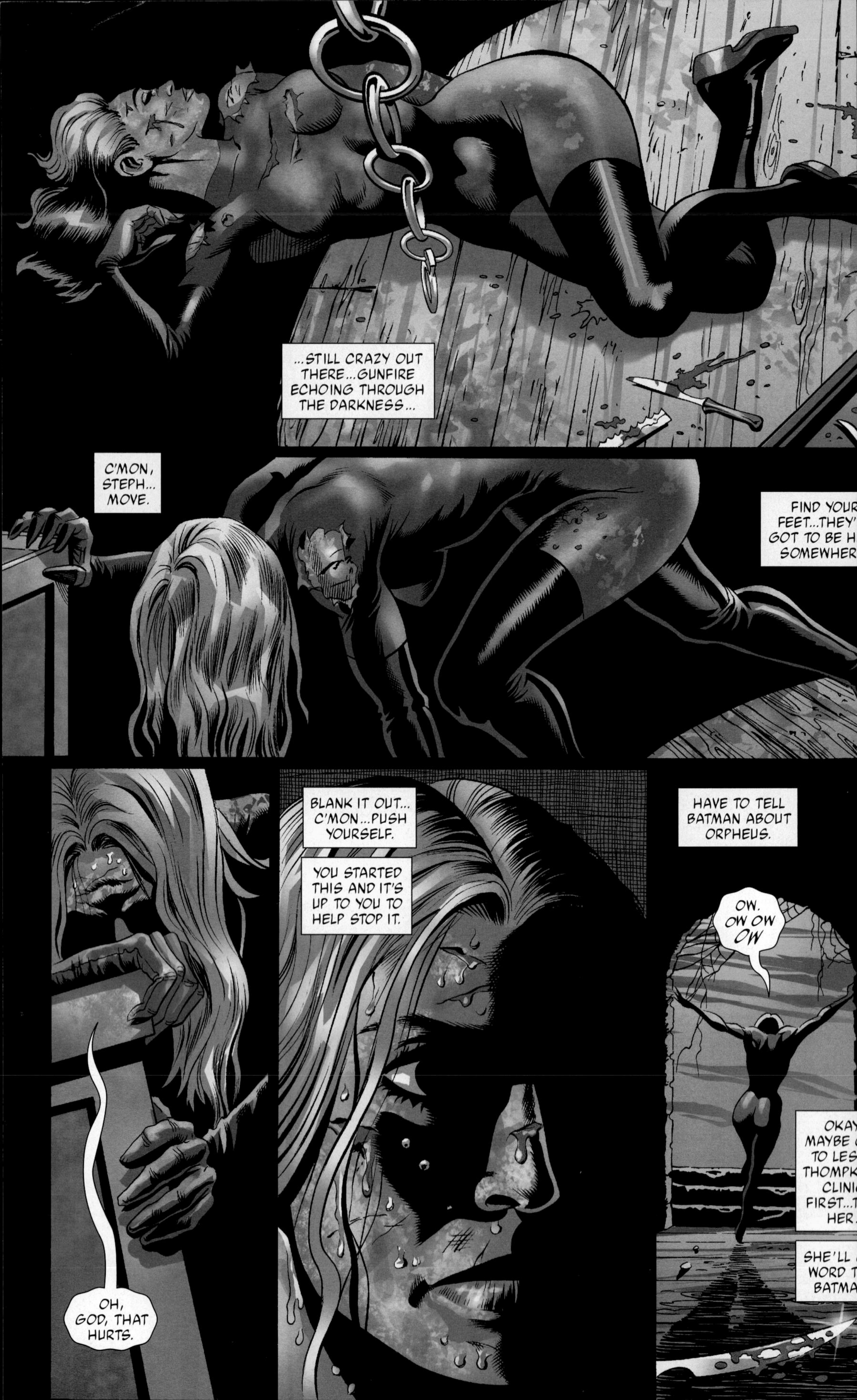
...STILL CRAZY OUT THERE...GUNFIRE ECHOING THROUGH THE DARKNESS...
C'MON, STEPH... MOVE.
FIND YOUR FEET...THEY' GOT TO BE H SOMEWHER
OH, GOD, THAT HURTS.
BLANK IT OUT... C'MON...PUSH YOURSELF.
YOU STARTED THIS AND IT'S UP TO YOU TO HELP STOP IT.
HAVE TO TELL BATMAN ABOUT ORPHEUS.
OW. OW OW OW
OKAY MAYBE TO LES THOMPK CLINI FIRST...T HER.
SHE'LL WORD T BATMA

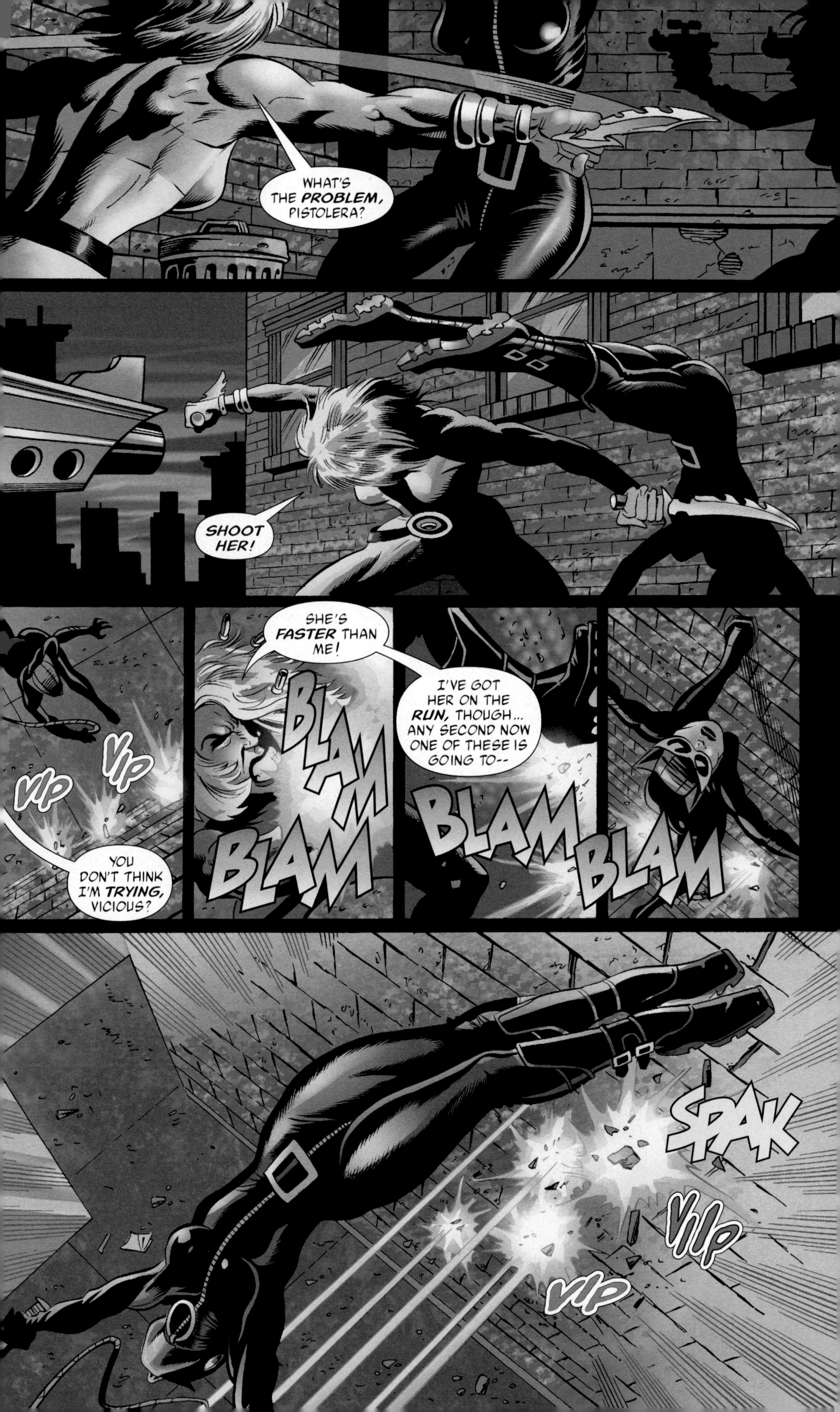
WHAT'S THE PROBLEM, PISTOLERA?
SHOOT HER!
VIP
VIP
YOU DON'T THINK I'M TRYING, VICIOUS?
SHE'S FASTER THAN ME!
BLAM
BLAM
I'VE GOT HER ON THE RUN, THOUGH... ANY SECOND NOW ONE OF THESE IS GOING TO--
BLAM
BLAM
SPAK
VIP
VIP

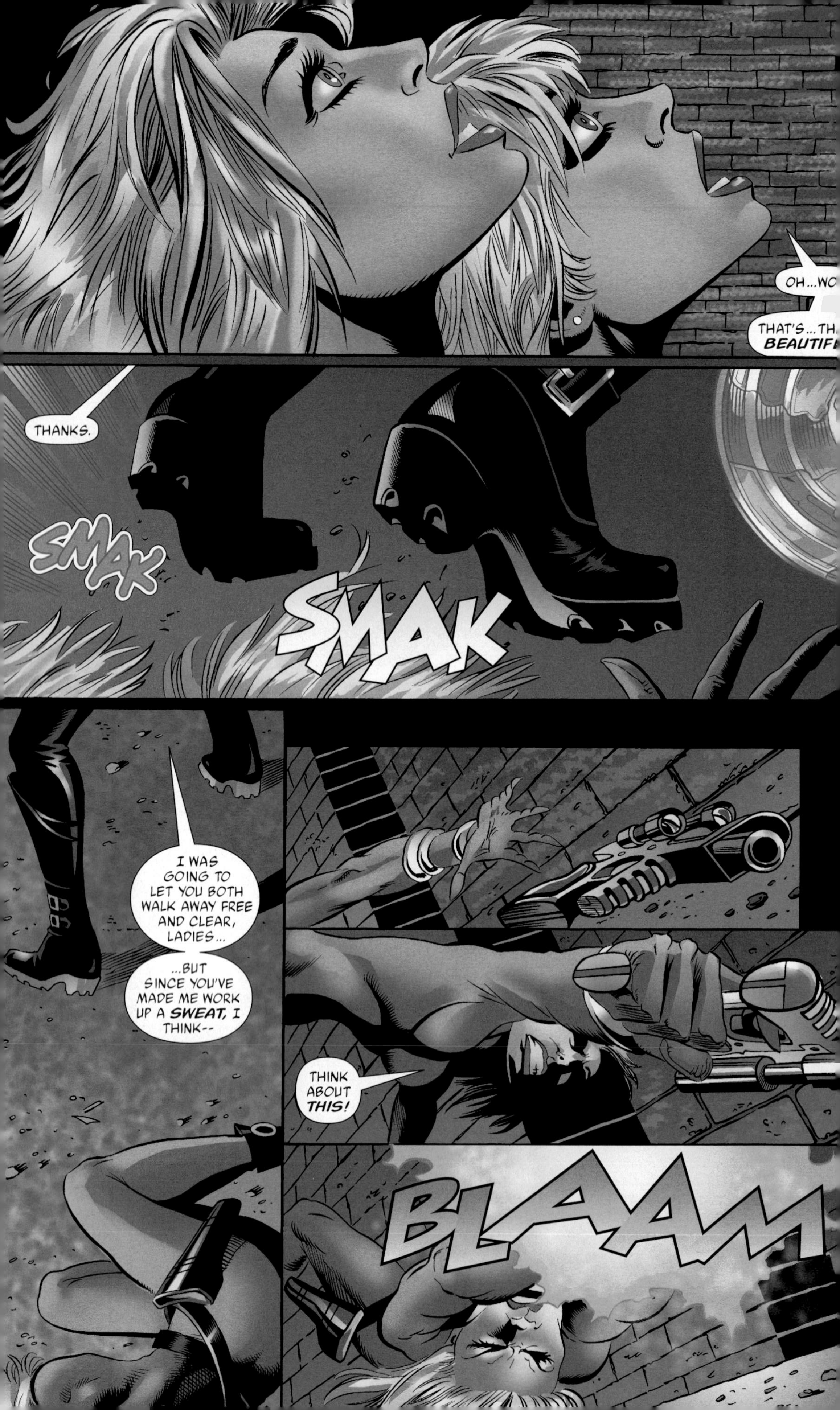
OH...WO
THAT'S...TH BEAUTIF
THANKS.
SMAK
SMAK
I WAS GOING TO LET YOU BOTH WALK AWAY FREE AND CLEAR, LADIES...
...BUT SINCE YOU'VE MADE ME WORK UP A SWEAT, I THINK--
THINK ABOUT THIS!
BLAAM

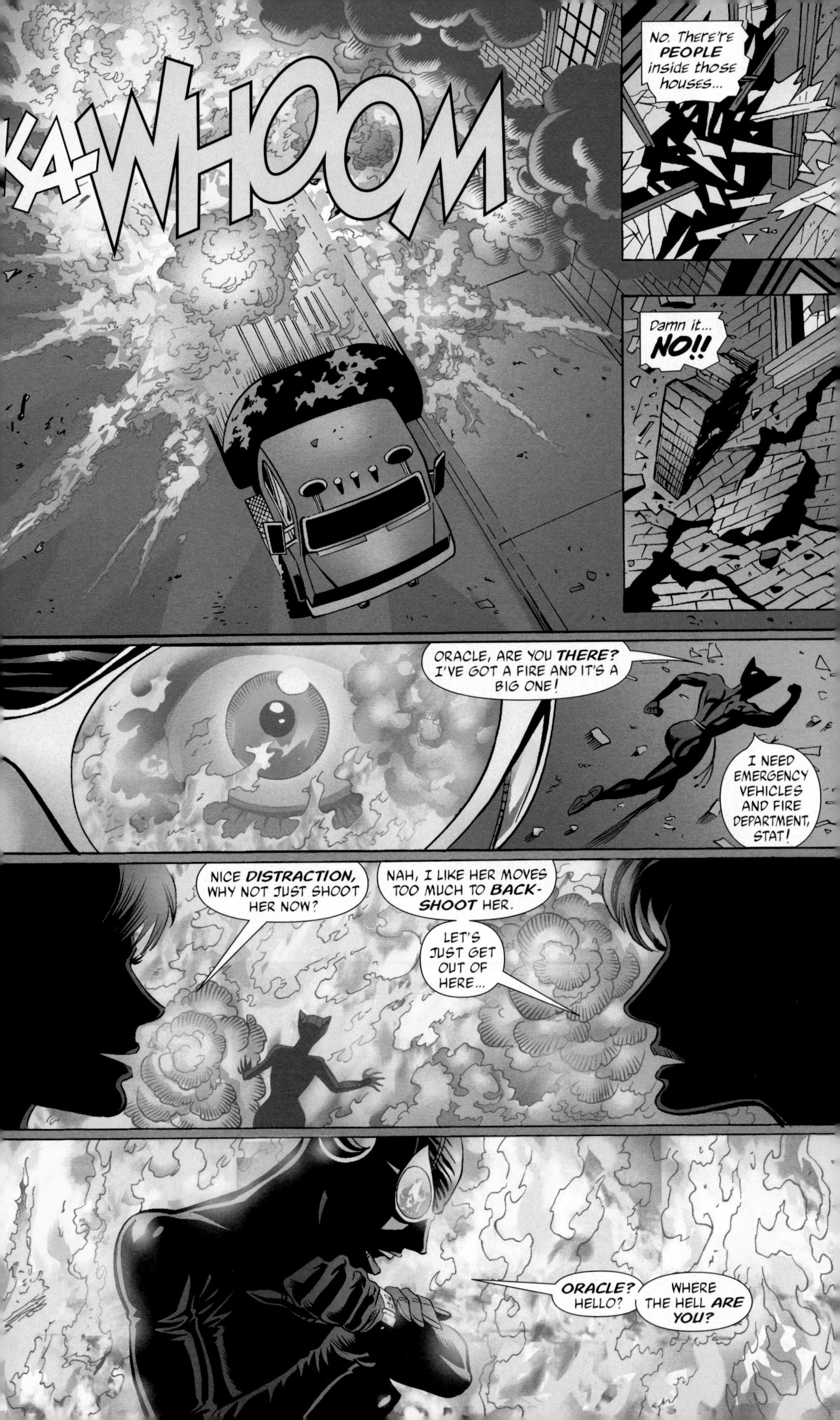
KA-WHOOM
No. There're PEOPLE inside those houses...
Damn it... NO!!
ORACLE, ARE YOU THERE? I'VE GOT A FIRE AND IT'S A BIG ONE!
I NEED EMERGENCY VEHICLES AND FIRE DEPARTMENT, STAT!
NICE DISTRACTION, WHY NOT JUST SHOOT HER NOW?
NAH, I LIKE HER MOVES TOO MUCH TO BACK-SHOOT HER.
LET'S JUST GET OUT OF HERE...
ORACLE? HELLO?
WHERE THE HELL ARE YOU?

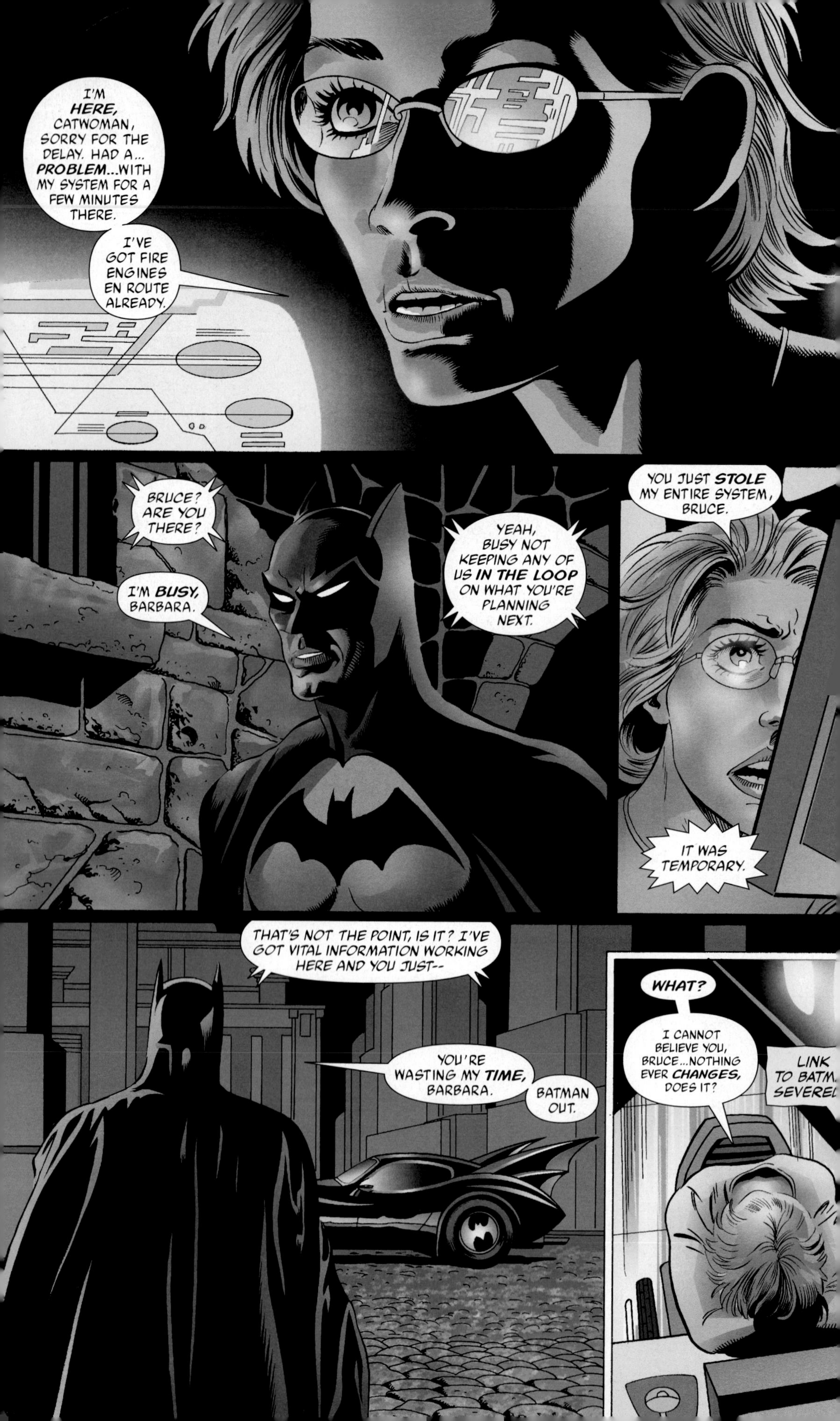
I'M HERE, CATWOMAN, SORRY FOR THE DELAY. HAD A... PROBLEM...WITH MY SYSTEM FOR A FEW MINUTES THERE.
I'VE GOT FIRE ENGINES EN ROUTE ALREADY.
BRUCE? ARE YOU THERE?
I'M BUSY, BARBARA.
YEAH, BUSY NOT KEEPING ANY OF US IN THE LOOP ON WHAT YOU'RE PLANNING NEXT.
YOU JUST STOLE MY ENTIRE SYSTEM, BRUCE.
IT WAS TEMPORARY.
THAT'S NOT THE POINT, IS IT? I'VE GOT VITAL INFORMATION WORKING HERE AND YOU JUST--
YOU'RE WASTING MY TIME, BARBARA.
BATMAN OUT.
WHAT?
I CANNOT BELIEVE YOU, BRUCE...NOTHING EVER CHANGES, DOES IT?
LINK TO BATM SEVERE

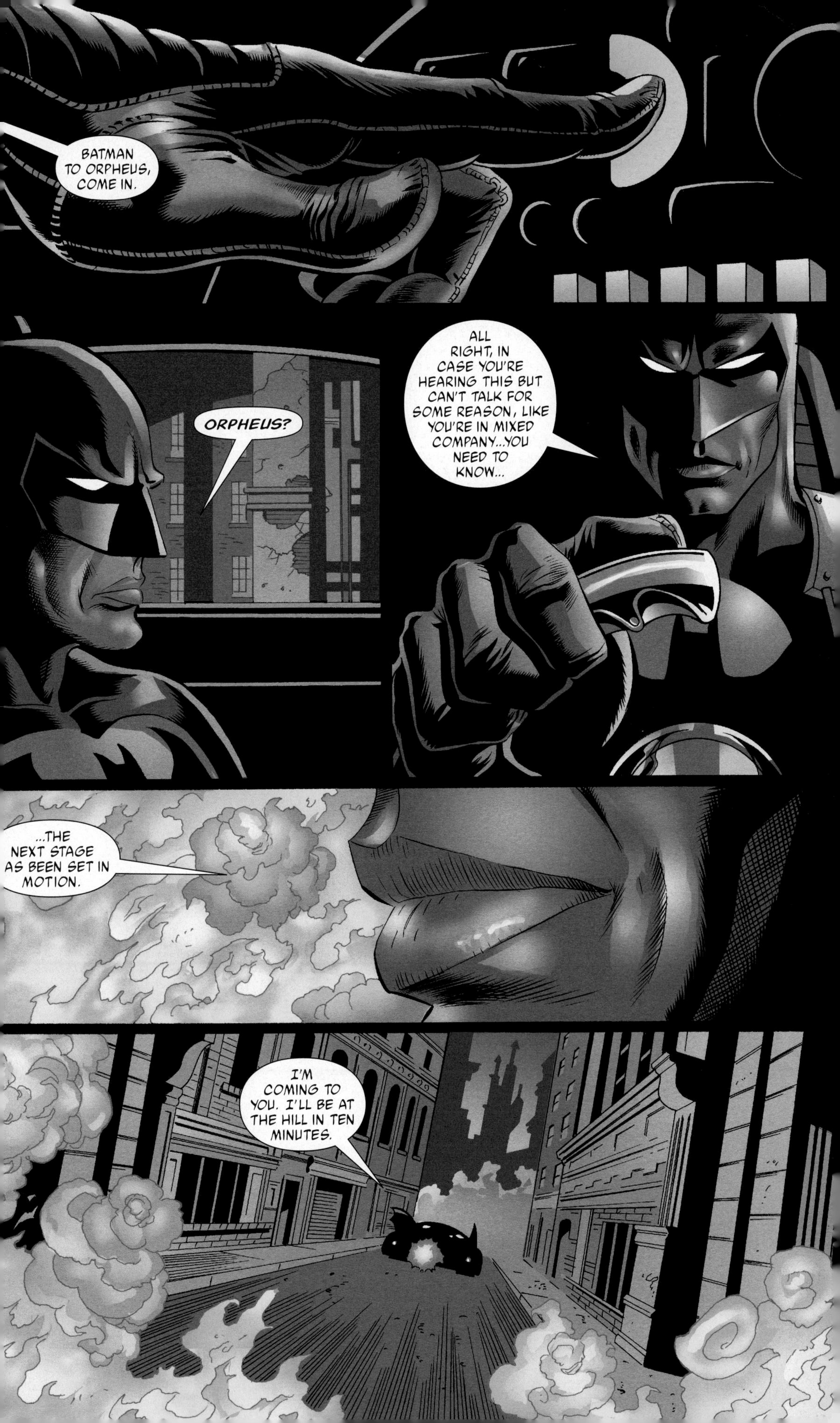
BATMAN TO ORPHEUS, COME IN.
ORPHEUS?
ALL RIGHT, IN CASE YOU'RE HEARING THIS BUT CAN'T TALK FOR SOME REASON, LIKE YOU'RE IN MIXED COMPANY...YOU NEED TO KNOW...
...THE NEXT STAGE AS BEEN SET IN MOTION.
I'M COMING TO YOU. I'LL BE AT THE HILL IN TEN MINUTES.

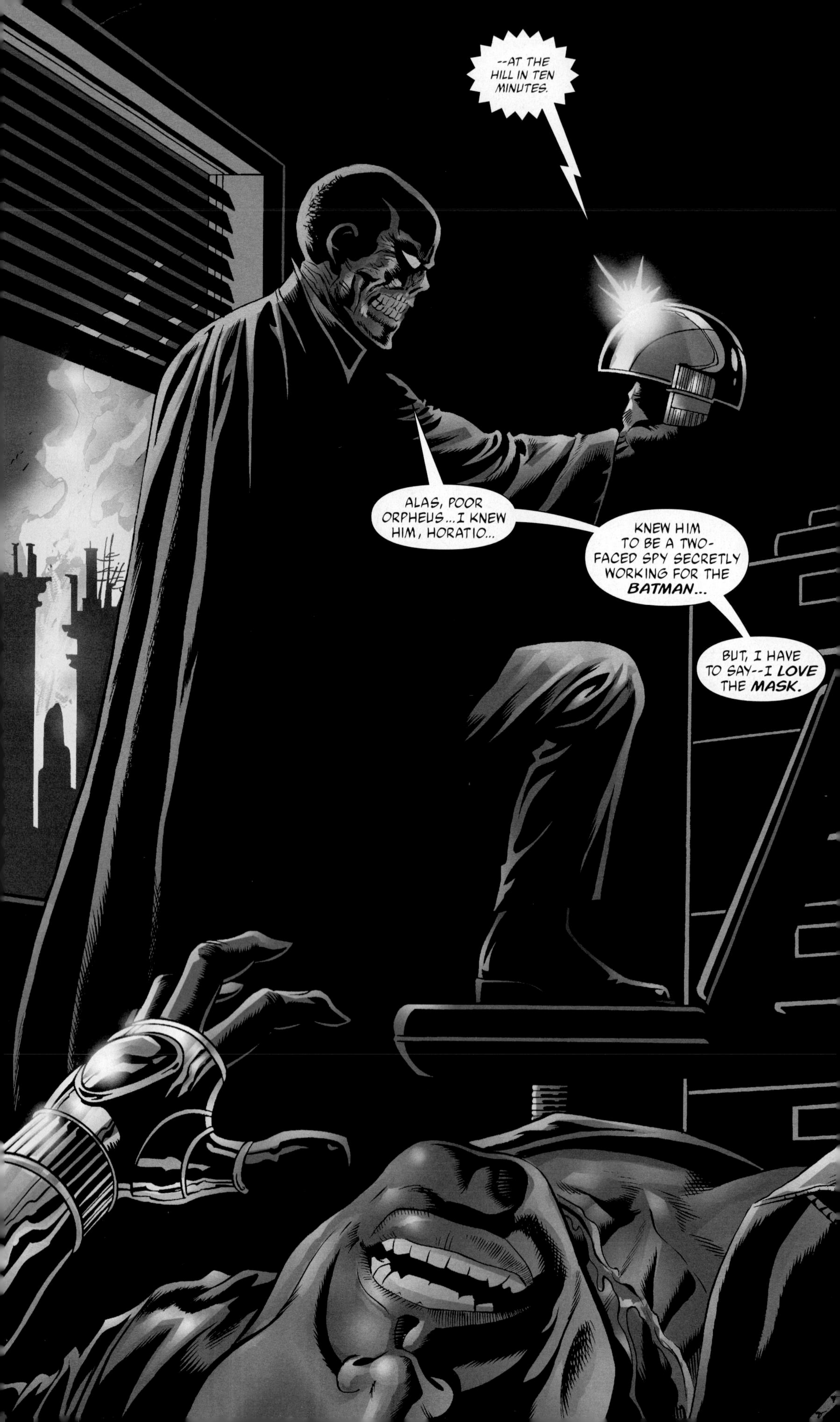
--AT THE HILL IN TEN MINUTES.
ALAS, POOR ORPHEUS...I KNEW HIM, HORATIO...
KNEW HIM TO BE A TWO-FACED SPY SECRETLY WORKING FOR THE BATMAN...
BUT, I HAVE TO SAY--I LOVE THE MASK.

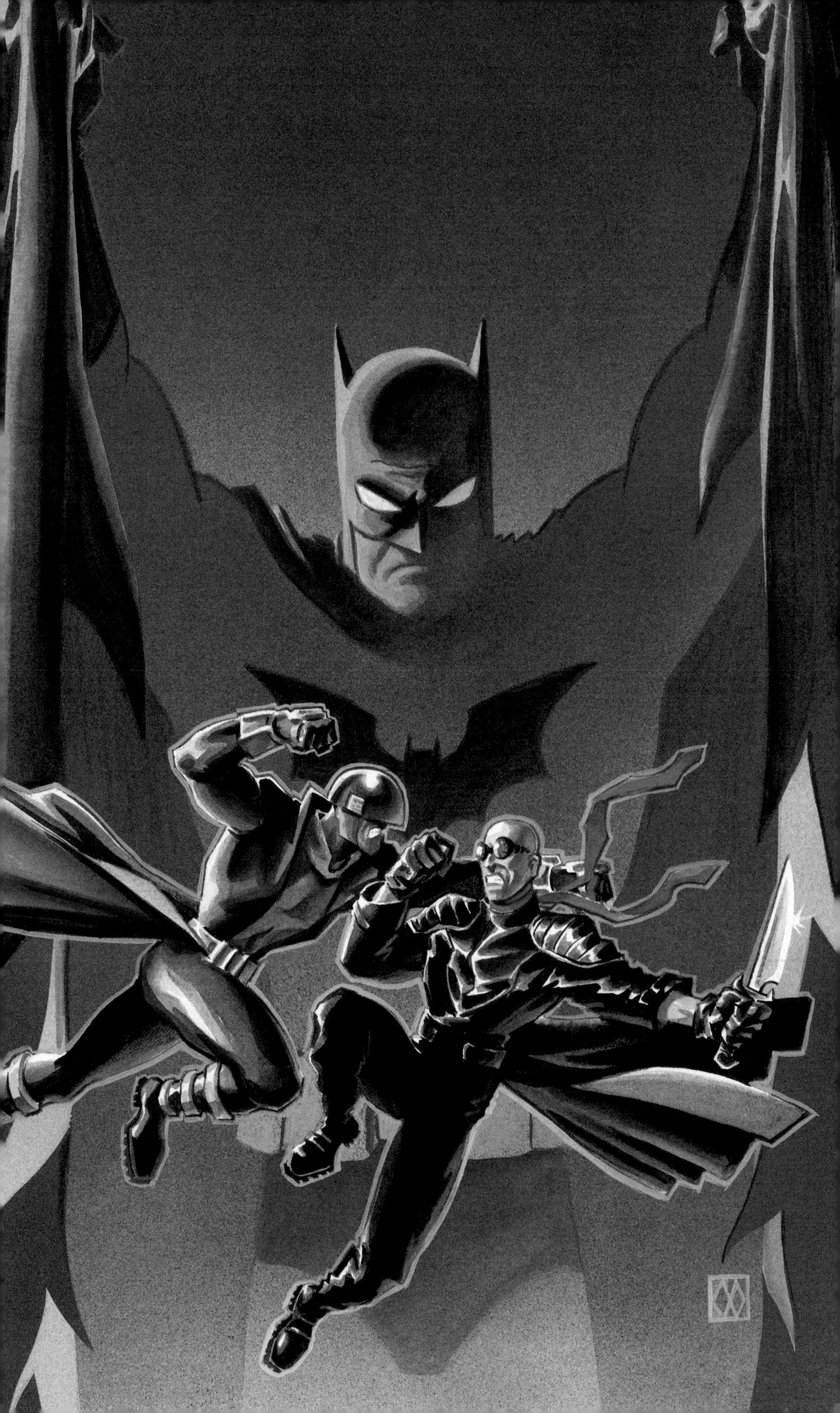

COVER ART BY
MATT WAGNER

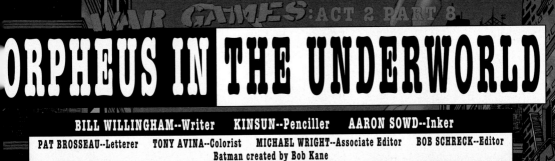

ORPHEUS IN THE UNDERWORLD

BILL WILLINGHAM--Writer   KINSUN--Penciller   AARON SOWD--Inker

PAT BROSSEAU--Letterer   TONY AVINA--Colorist   MICHAEL WRIGHT--Associate Editor   BOB SCHRECK--Editor

Batman created by Bob Kane

BATMAN TO ORPHEUS.

PICK UP, IF YOU'RE OUT THERE.

BATMAN TO ORACLE. I'M NOT GETTING *ANY* RESPONSE FROM ORPHEUS. CAN *YOU* GET THROUGH?

I'M TRYING TO RAISE HIM-- TOO. SO FAR-- NO LUCK.

KEEP TRYING. I'M ON MY WAY UP TO THE HILL TO CHECK ON HIM IN PERSON.

TOO MUCH DEPENDS ON *HIM* NOW.

HE'S THE KEY TO ENDING THIS GANG WAR WITH A MINIMUM OF ADDITIONAL BLOODSHED.

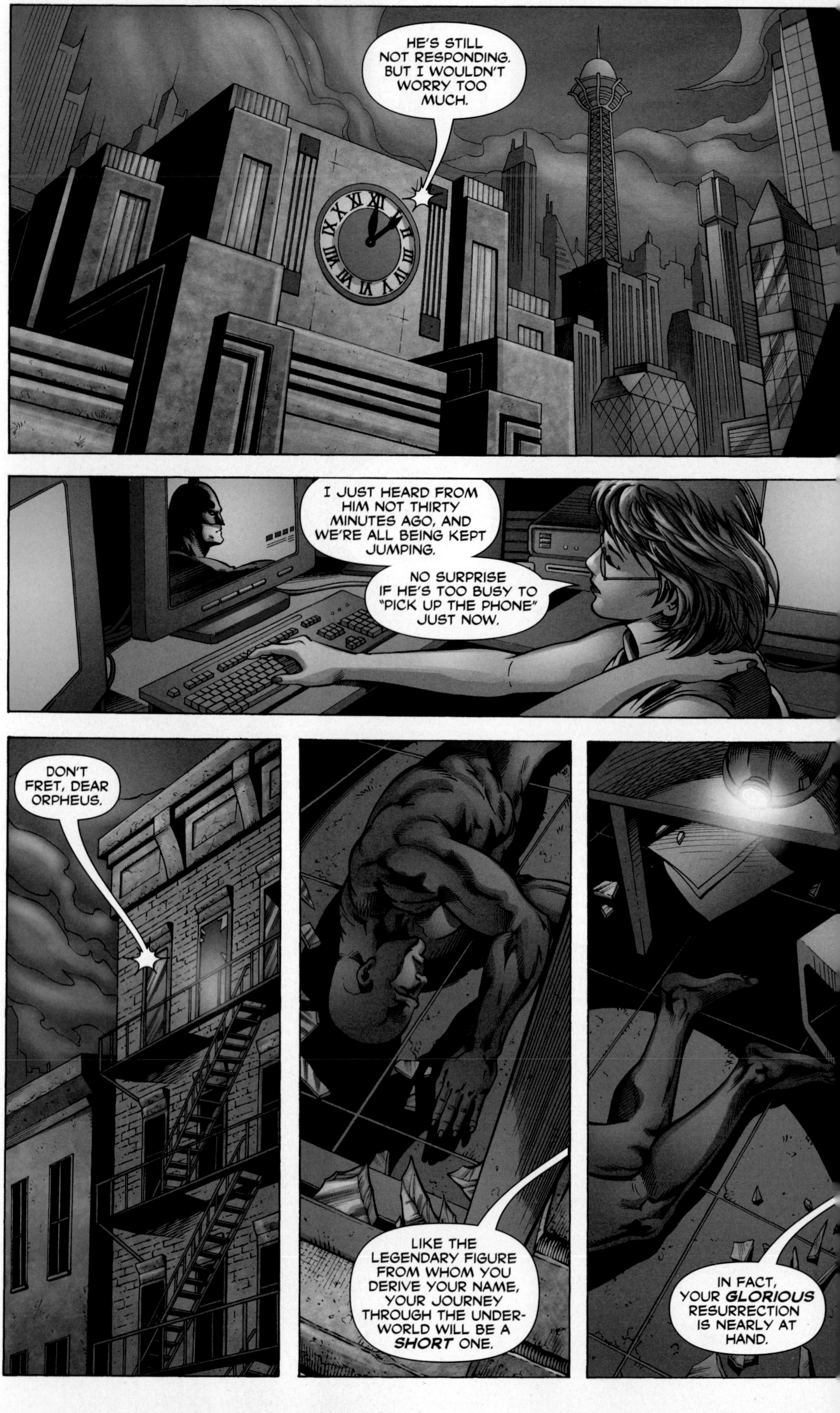
HE'S STILL NOT RESPONDING. BUT I WOULDN'T WORRY TOO MUCH.
I JUST HEARD FROM HIM NOT THIRTY MINUTES AGO, AND WE'RE ALL BEING KEPT JUMPING.
NO SURPRISE IF HE'S TOO BUSY TO "PICK UP THE PHONE" JUST NOW.
DON'T FRET, DEAR ORPHEUS.
LIKE THE LEGENDARY FIGURE FROM WHOM YOU DERIVE YOUR NAME, YOUR JOURNEY THROUGH THE UNDER-WORLD WILL BE A SHORT ONE.
IN FACT, YOUR GLORIOUS RESURRECTION IS NEARLY AT HAND.

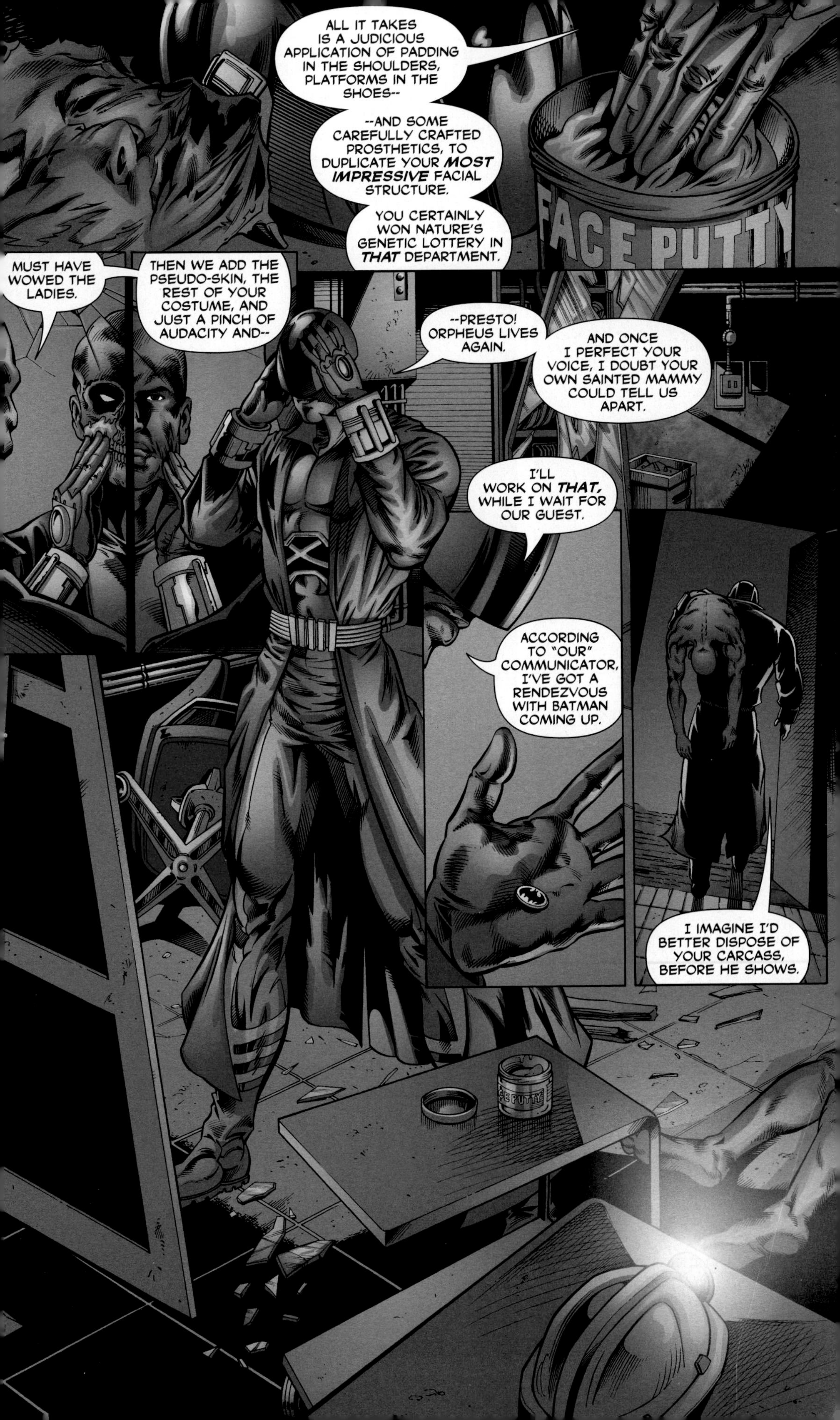
ALL IT TAKES IS A JUDICIOUS APPLICATION OF PADDING IN THE SHOULDERS, PLATFORMS IN THE SHOES--
--AND SOME CAREFULLY CRAFTED PROSTHETICS, TO DUPLICATE YOUR *MOST IMPRESSIVE* FACIAL STRUCTURE.
YOU CERTAINLY WON NATURE'S GENETIC LOTTERY IN *THAT* DEPARTMENT.
FACE PUTTY
MUST HAVE WOWED THE LADIES.
THEN WE ADD THE PSEUDO-SKIN, THE REST OF YOUR COSTUME, AND JUST A PINCH OF AUDACITY AND--
--PRESTO! ORPHEUS LIVES AGAIN.
AND ONCE I PERFECT YOUR VOICE, I DOUBT YOUR OWN SAINTED MAMMY COULD TELL US APART.
I'LL WORK ON *THAT,* WHILE I WAIT FOR OUR GUEST.
ACCORDING TO "OUR" COMMUNICATOR, I'VE GOT A RENDEZVOUS WITH BATMAN COMING UP.
I IMAGINE I'D BETTER DISPOSE OF YOUR CARCASS, BEFORE HE SHOWS.

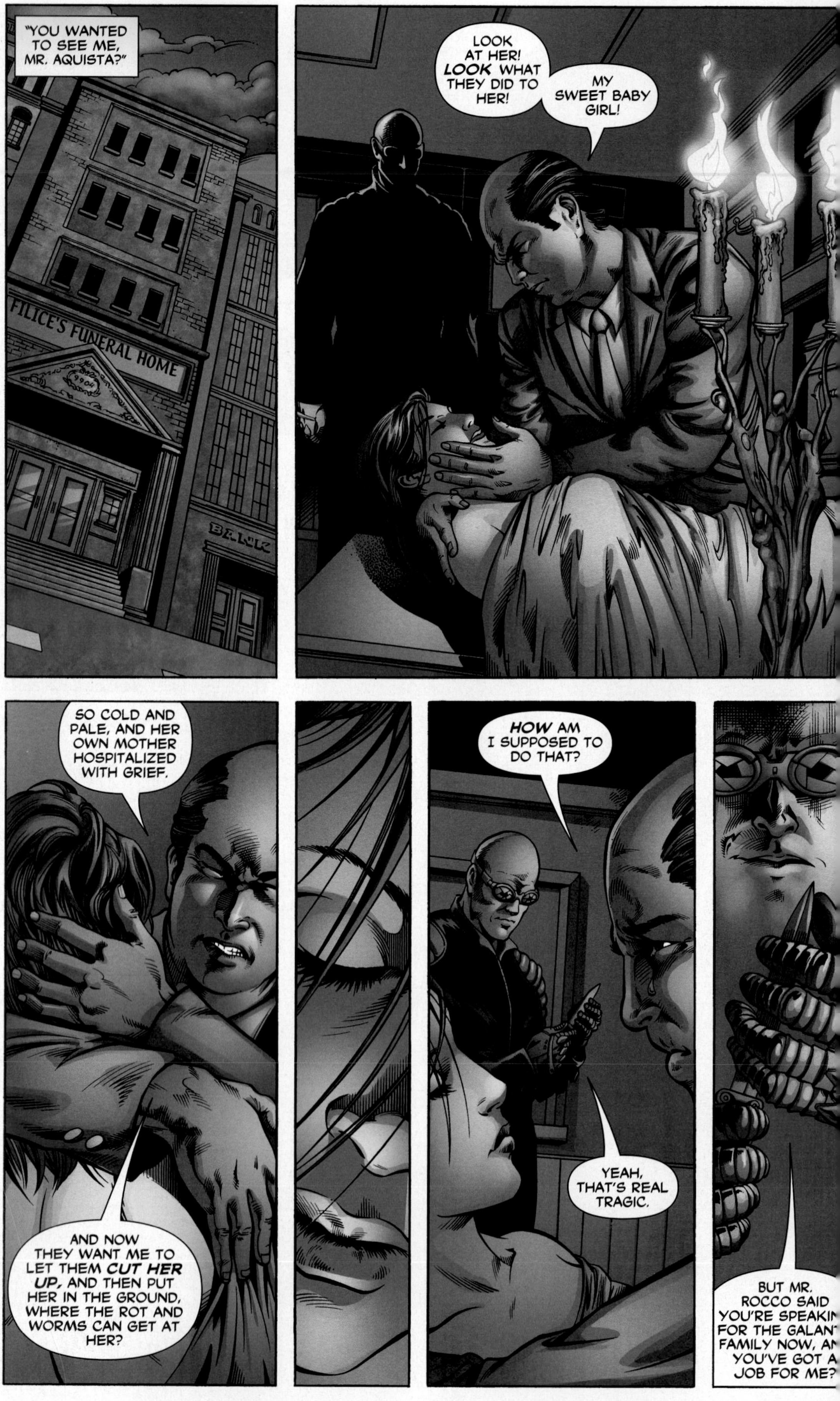
"YOU WANTED TO SEE ME, MR. AQUISTA?"
FILICE'S FUNERAL HOME
BANK
LOOK AT HER! LOOK WHAT THEY DID TO HER!
MY SWEET BABY GIRL!
SO COLD AND PALE, AND HER OWN MOTHER HOSPITALIZED WITH GRIEF.
AND NOW THEY WANT ME TO LET THEM CUT HER UP, AND THEN PUT HER IN THE GROUND, WHERE THE ROT AND WORMS CAN GET AT HER?
HOW AM I SUPPOSED TO DO THAT?
YEAH, THAT'S REAL TRAGIC.
BUT MR. ROCCO SAID YOU'RE SPEAKIN FOR THE GALAN FAMILY NOW, AN YOU'VE GOT A JOB FOR ME?

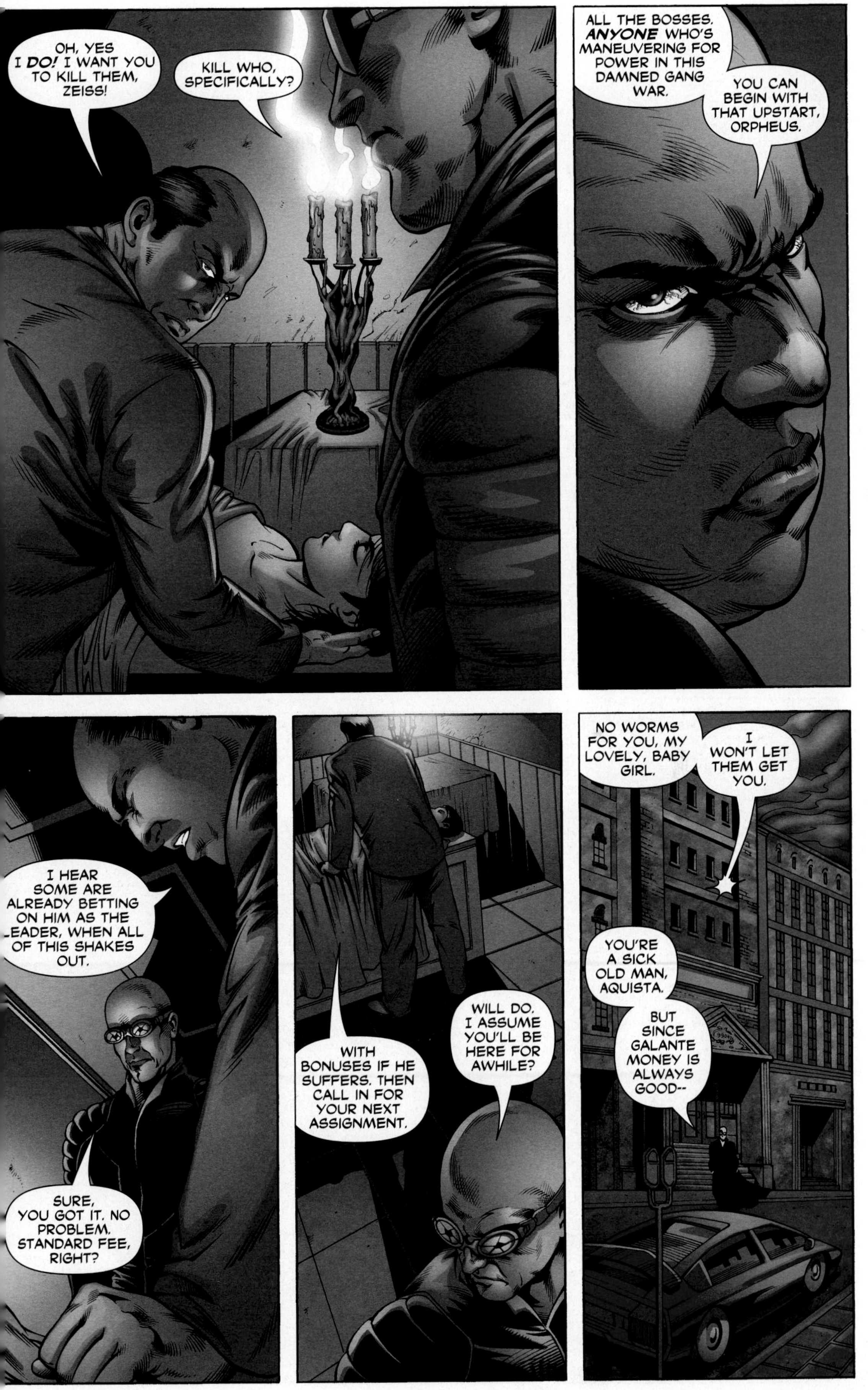
OH, YES I DO! I WANT YOU TO KILL THEM, ZEISS!
KILL WHO, SPECIFICALLY?
ALL THE BOSSES. ANYONE WHO'S MANEUVERING FOR POWER IN THIS DAMNED GANG WAR.
YOU CAN BEGIN WITH THAT UPSTART, ORPHEUS.
I HEAR SOME ARE ALREADY BETTING ON HIM AS THE LEADER, WHEN ALL OF THIS SHAKES OUT.
SURE, YOU GOT IT. NO PROBLEM. STANDARD FEE, RIGHT?
WITH BONUSES IF HE SUFFERS. THEN CALL IN FOR YOUR NEXT ASSIGNMENT.
WILL DO. I ASSUME YOU'LL BE HERE FOR AWHILE?
NO WORMS FOR YOU, MY LOVELY, BABY GIRL.
I WON'T LET THEM GET YOU.
YOU'RE A SICK OLD MAN, AQUISTA.
BUT SINCE GALANTE MONEY IS ALWAYS GOOD--

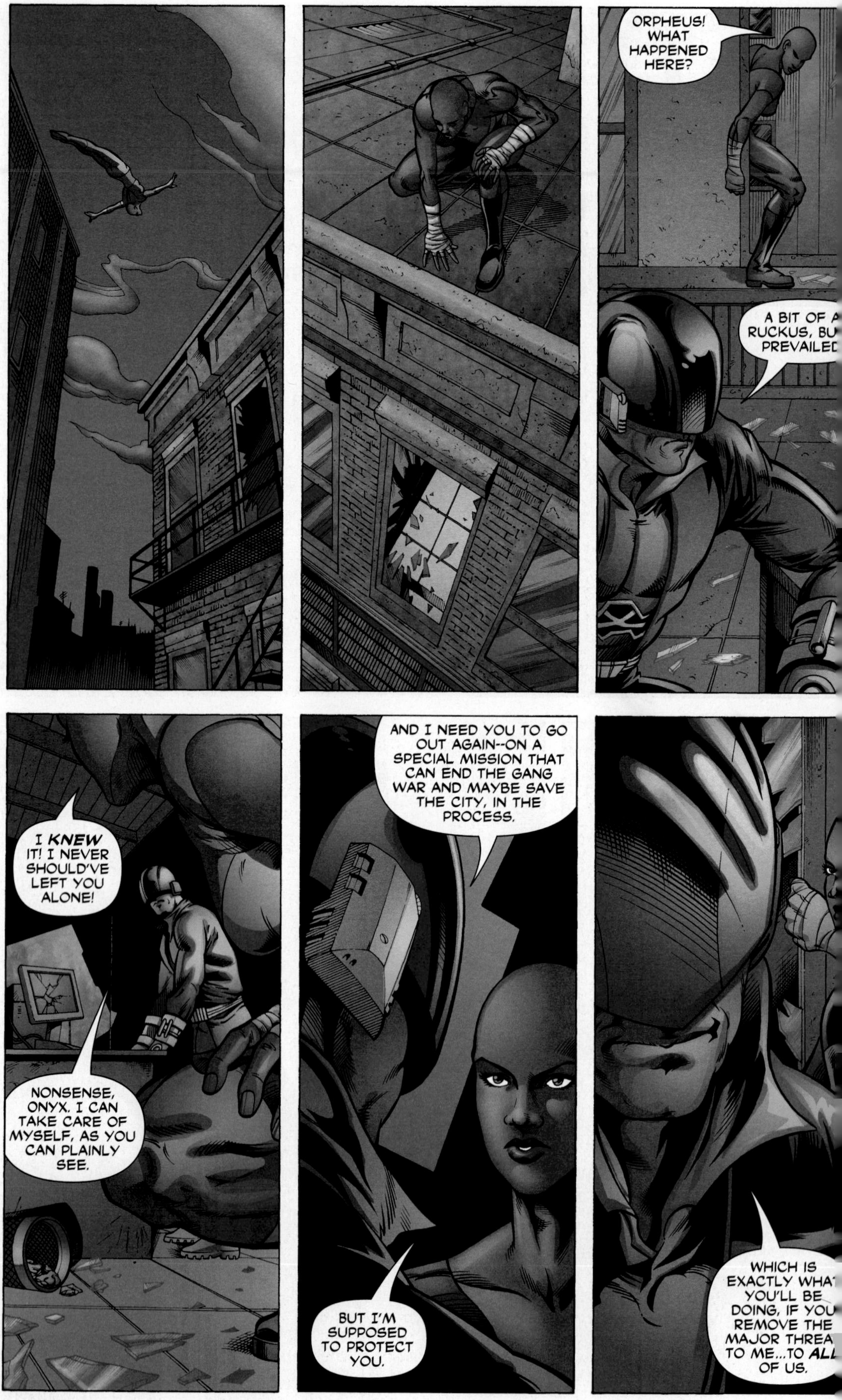
ORPHEUS! WHAT HAPPENED HERE?
A BIT OF A RUCKUS, BU PREVAILED
I KNEW IT! I NEVER SHOULD'VE LEFT YOU ALONE!
NONSENSE, ONYX. I CAN TAKE CARE OF MYSELF, AS YOU CAN PLAINLY SEE.
AND I NEED YOU TO GO OUT AGAIN--ON A SPECIAL MISSION THAT CAN END THE GANG WAR AND MAYBE SAVE THE CITY, IN THE PROCESS.
BUT I'M SUPPOSED TO PROTECT YOU.
WHICH IS EXACTLY WHA YOU'LL BE DOING, IF YOU REMOVE THE MAJOR THREA TO ME...TO ALL OF US.

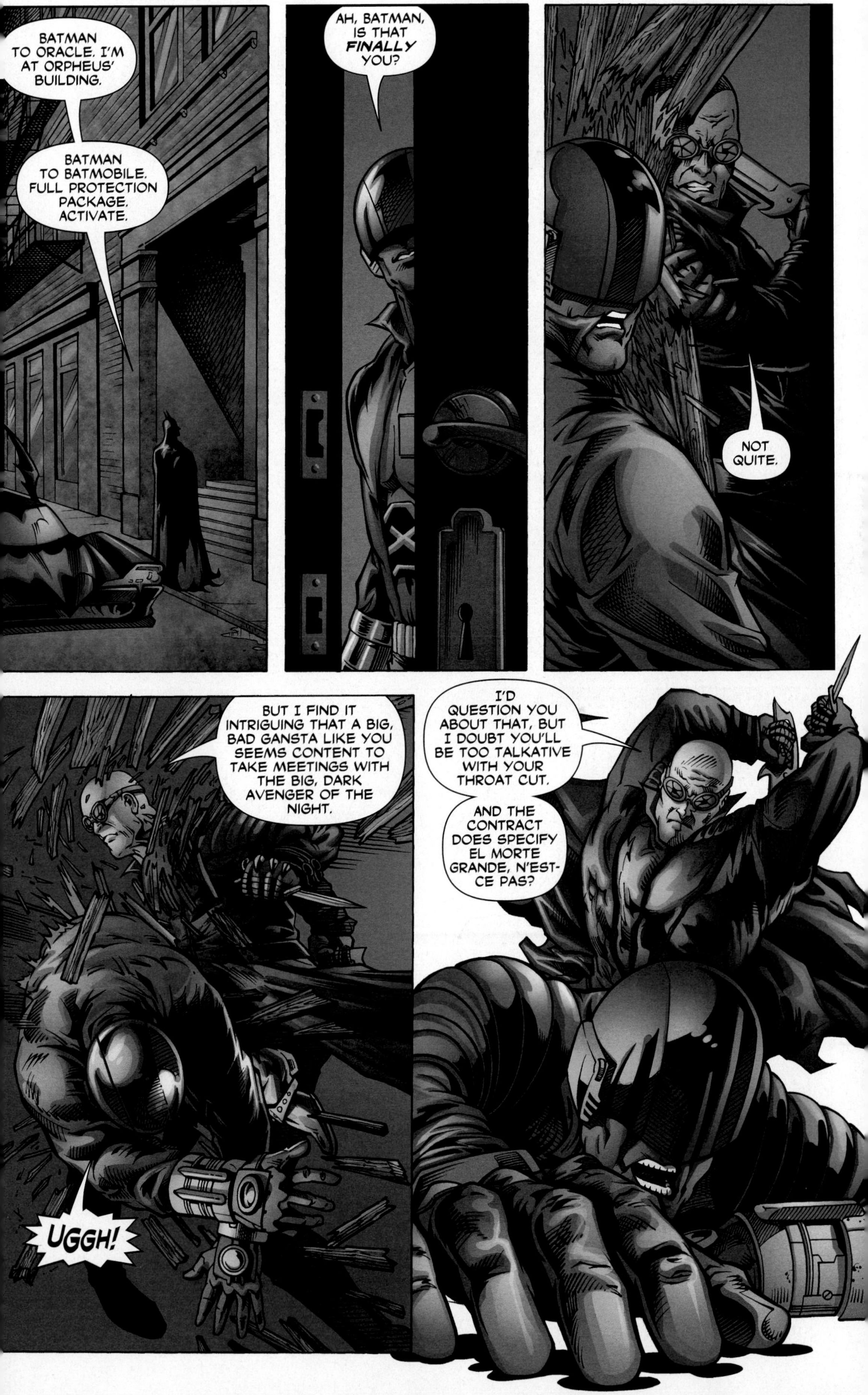
BATMAN TO ORACLE. I'M AT ORPHEUS' BUILDING.
BATMAN TO BATMOBILE. FULL PROTECTION PACKAGE. ACTIVATE.
AH, BATMAN, IS THAT *FINALLY* YOU?
NOT QUITE.
BUT I FIND IT INTRIGUING THAT A BIG, BAD GANSTA LIKE YOU SEEMS CONTENT TO TAKE MEETINGS WITH THE BIG, DARK AVENGER OF THE NIGHT.
UGGH!
I'D QUESTION YOU ABOUT THAT, BUT I DOUBT YOU'LL BE TOO TALKATIVE WITH YOUR THROAT CUT.
AND THE CONTRACT DOES SPECIFY EL MORTE GRANDE, N'EST-CE PAS?

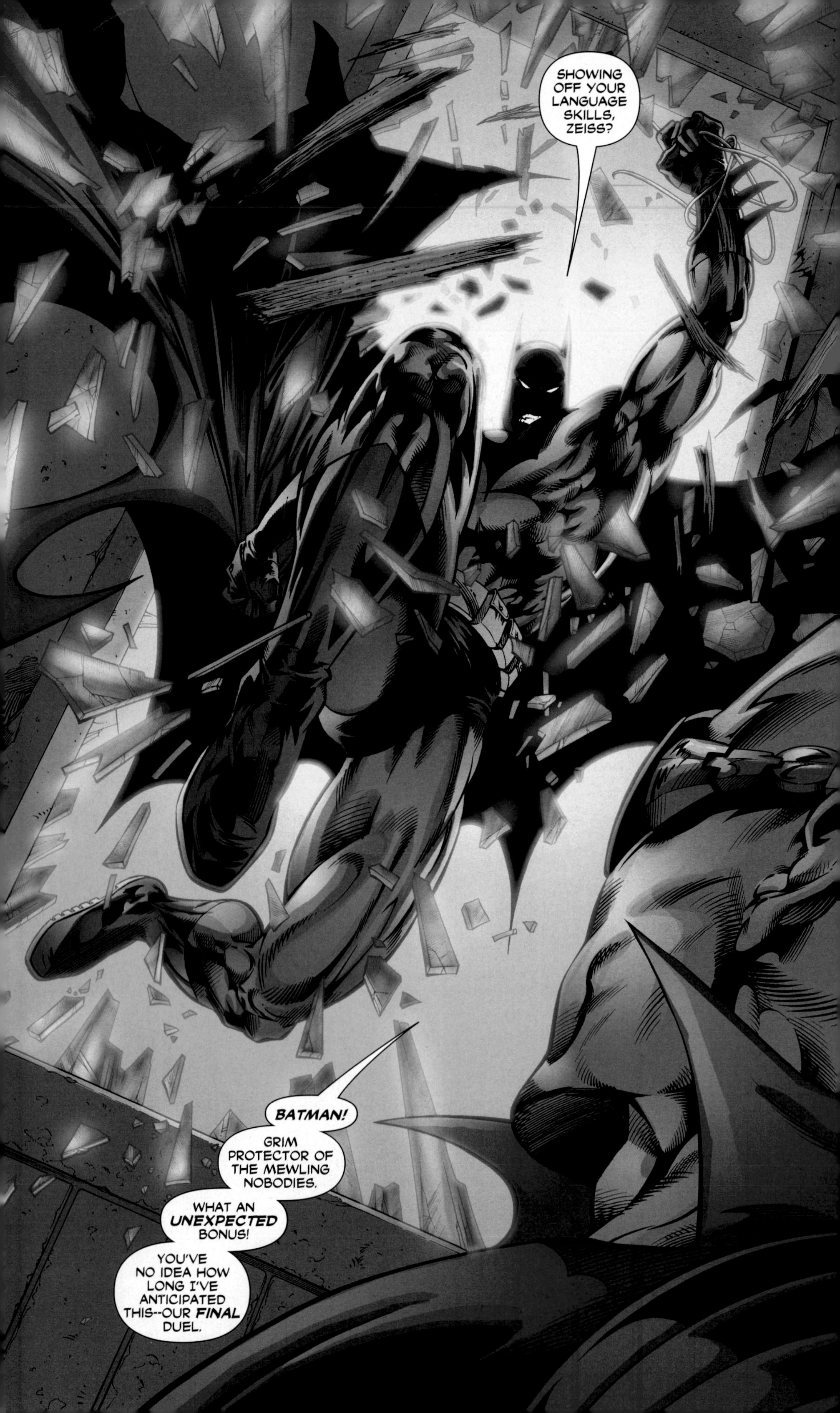
SHOWING OFF YOUR LANGUAGE SKILLS, ZEISS?
BATMAN!
GRIM PROTECTOR OF THE MEWLING NOBODIES.
WHAT AN UNEXPECTED BONUS!
YOU'VE NO IDEA HOW LONG I'VE ANTICIPATED THIS--OUR FINAL DUEL.

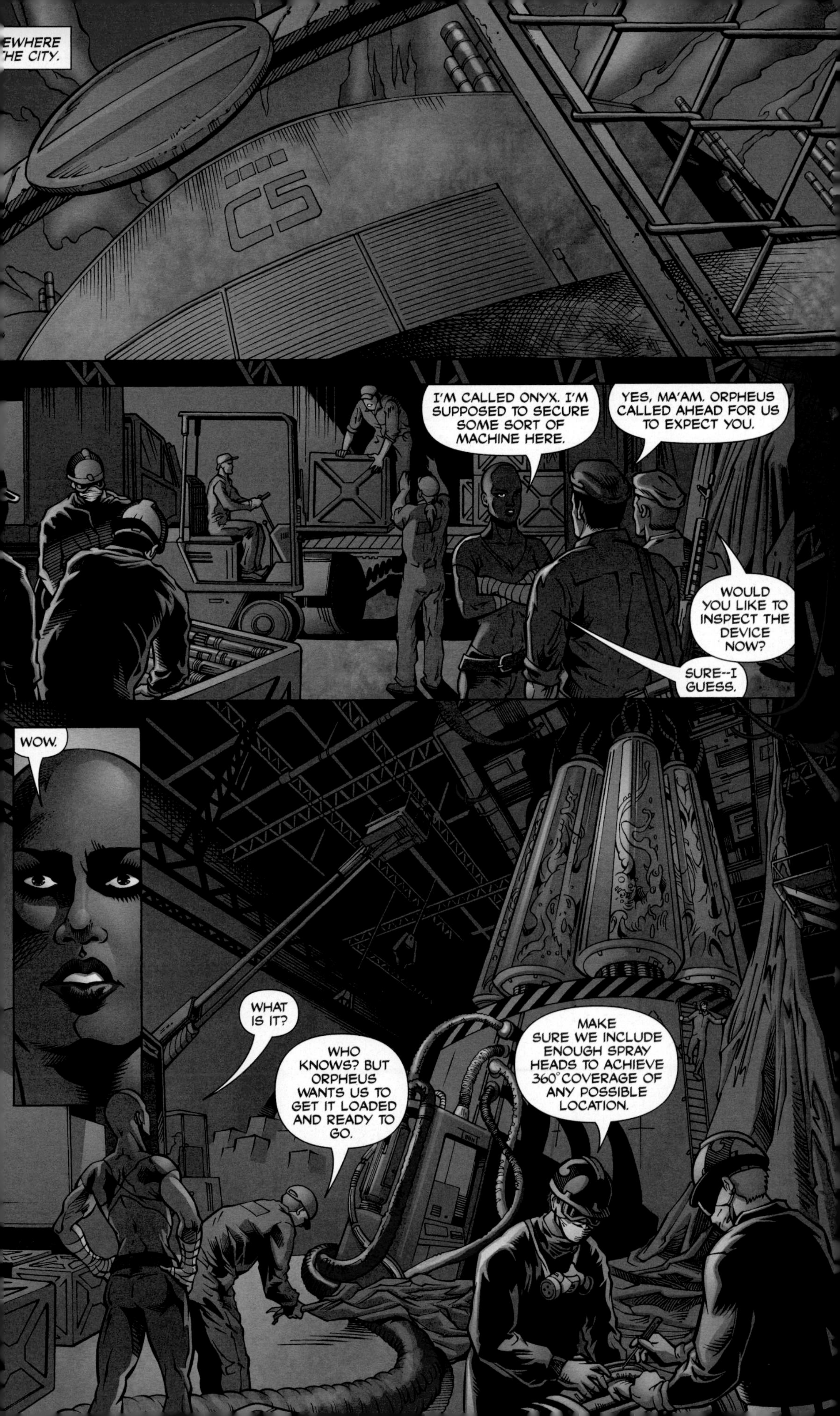

EWHERE
HE CITY.
I'M CALLED ONYX. I'M SUPPOSED TO SECURE SOME SORT OF MACHINE HERE.
YES, MA'AM. ORPHEUS CALLED AHEAD FOR US TO EXPECT YOU.
WOULD YOU LIKE TO INSPECT THE DEVICE NOW?
SURE--I GUESS.
WOW.
WHAT IS IT?
WHO KNOWS? BUT ORPHEUS WANTS US TO GET IT LOADED AND READY TO GO.
MAKE SURE WE INCLUDE ENOUGH SPRAY HEADS TO ACHIEVE 360° COVERAGE OF ANY POSSIBLE LOCATION.

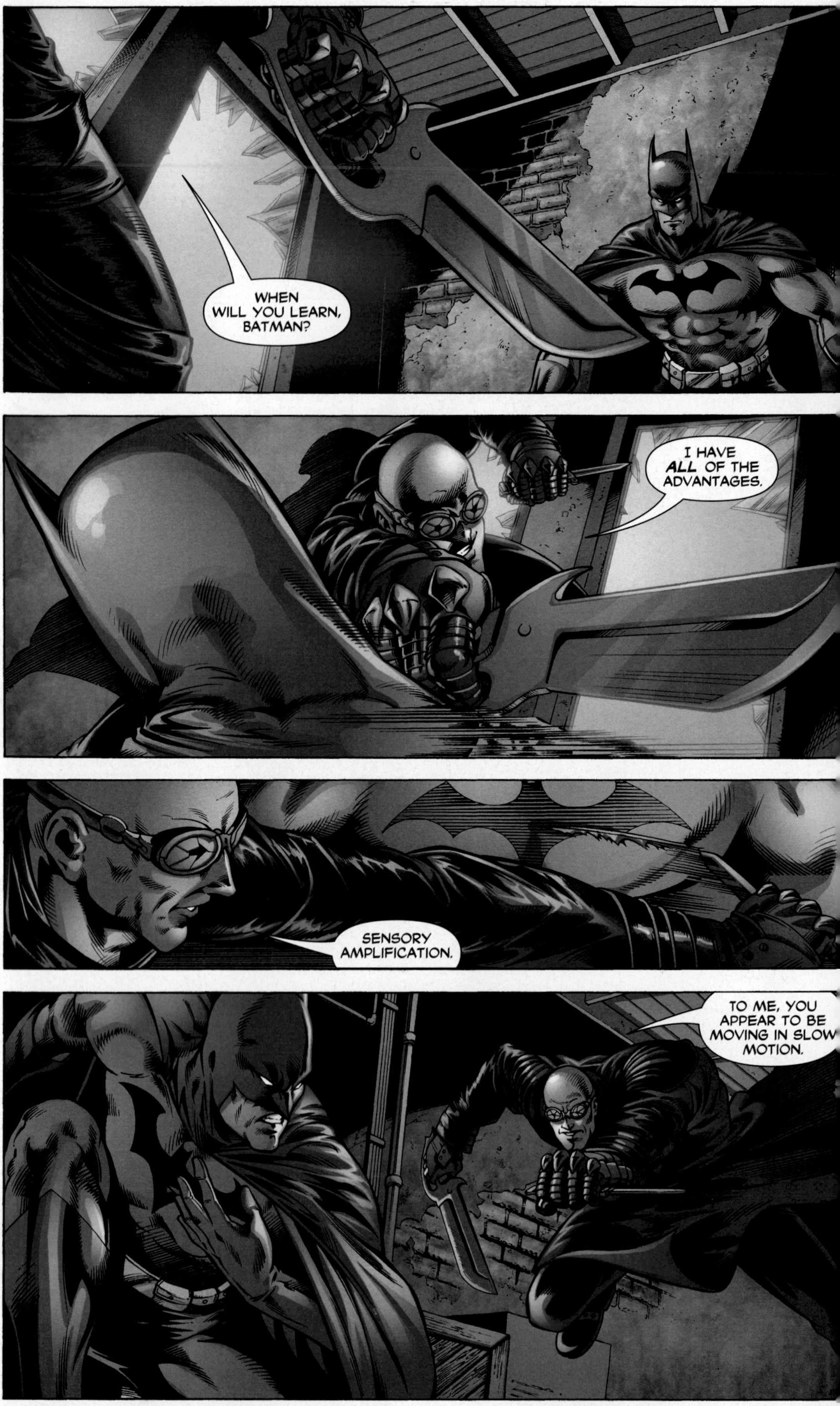
WHEN WILL YOU LEARN, BATMAN?
I HAVE ALL OF THE ADVANTAGES.
SENSORY AMPLIFICATION.
TO ME, YOU APPEAR TO BE MOVING IN SLOW MOTION.

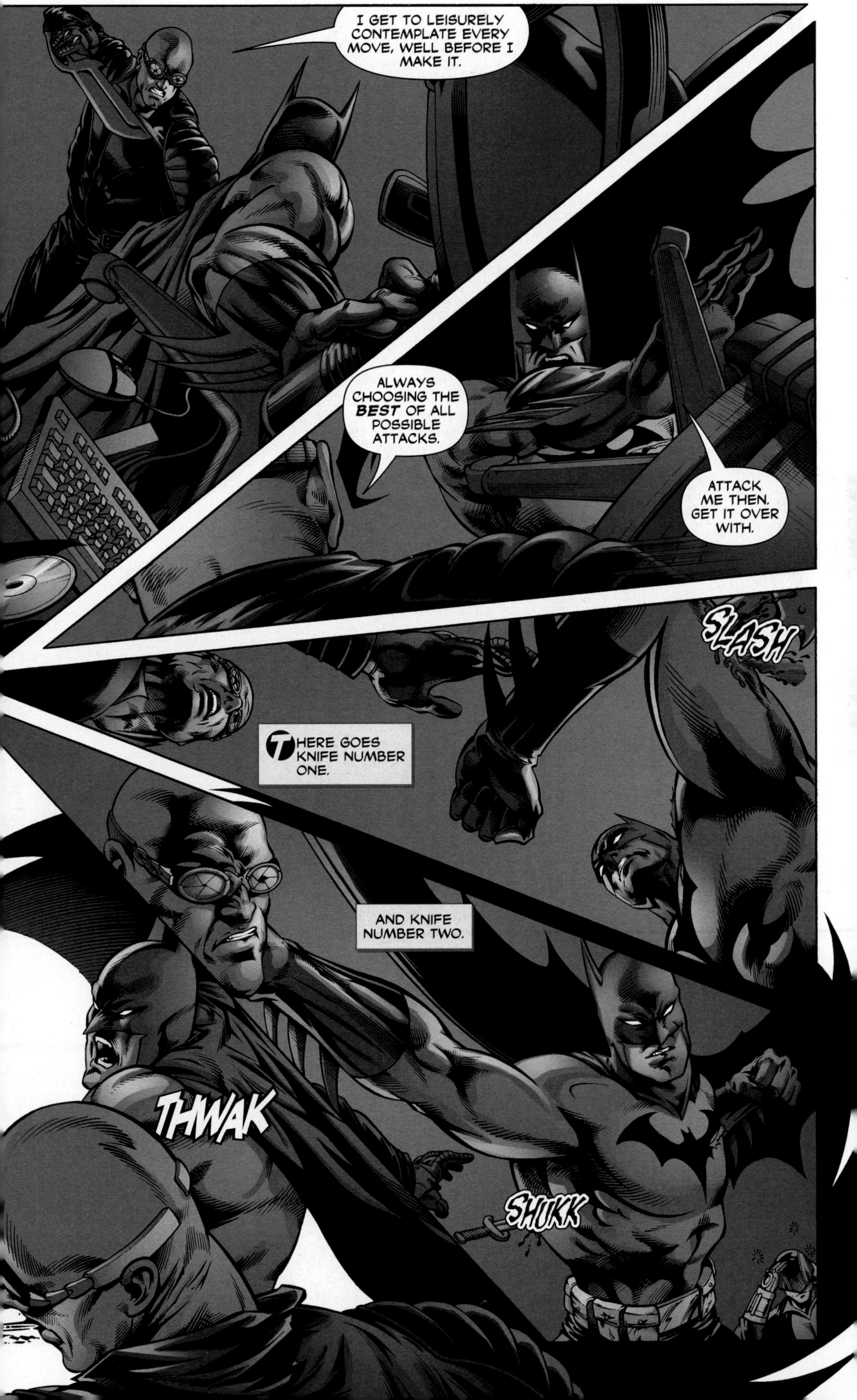
I GET TO LEISURELY CONTEMPLATE EVERY MOVE, WELL BEFORE I MAKE IT.
ALWAYS CHOOSING THE *BEST* OF ALL POSSIBLE ATTACKS.
ATTACK ME THEN. GET IT OVER WITH.
SLASH
THERE GOES KNIFE NUMBER ONE.
AND KNIFE NUMBER TWO.
THWAK
SHUKK

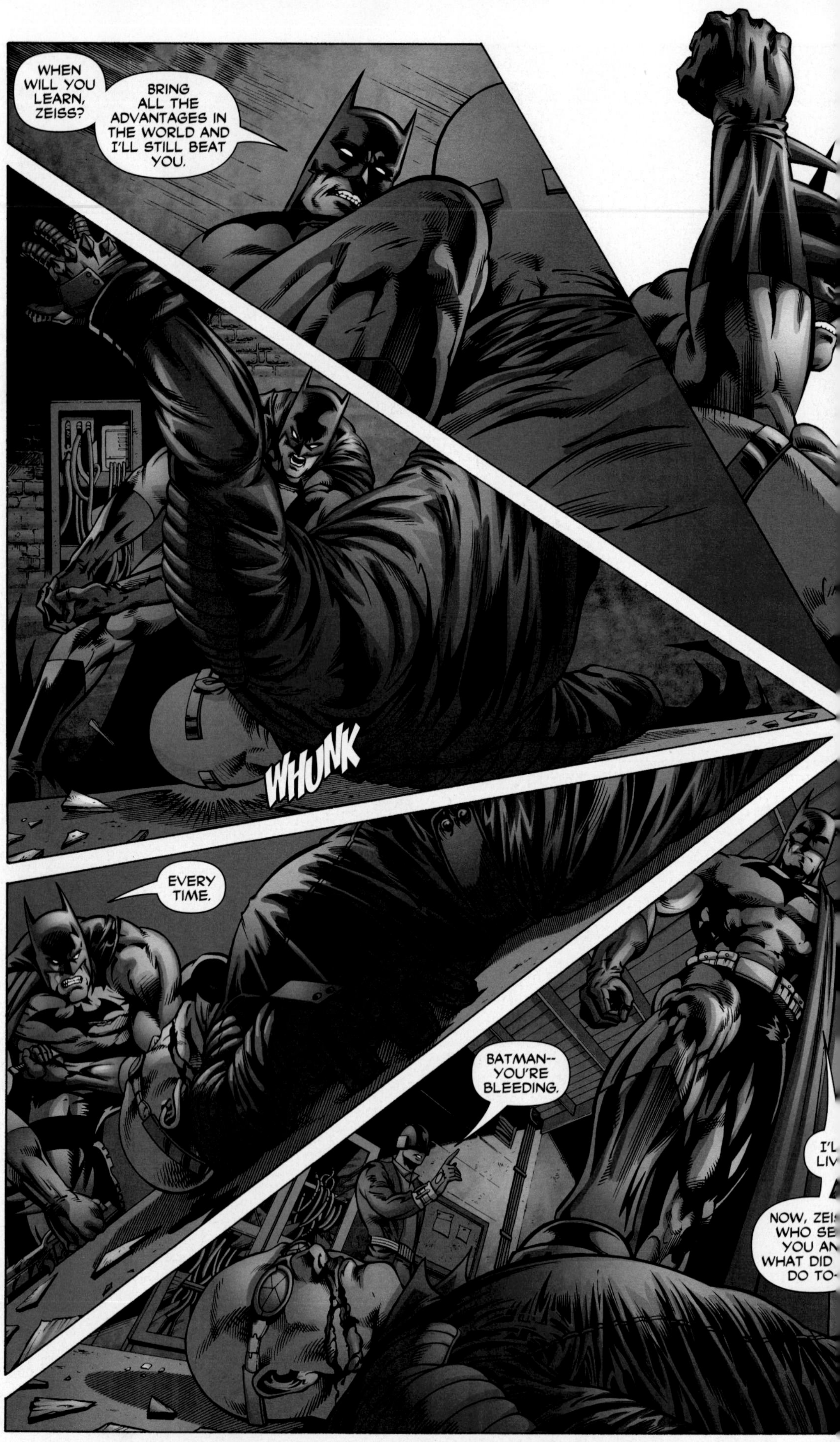
WHEN WILL YOU LEARN, ZEISS?
BRING ALL THE ADVANTAGES IN THE WORLD AND I'LL STILL BEAT YOU.
WHUNK
EVERY TIME.
BATMAN-- YOU'RE BLEEDING.

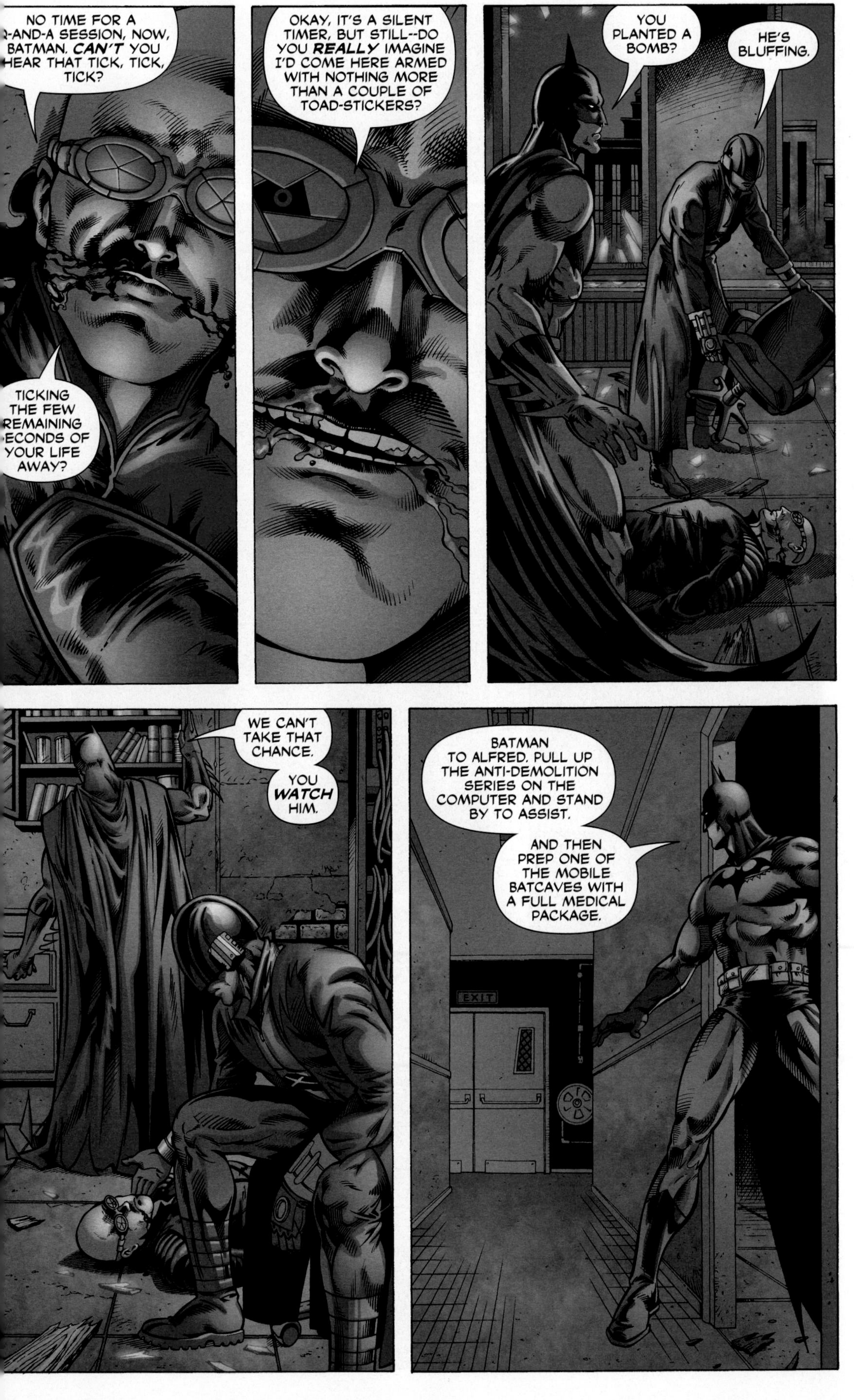
NO TIME FOR A Q-AND-A SESSION, NOW, BATMAN. CAN'T YOU HEAR THAT TICK, TICK, TICK?
TICKING THE FEW REMAINING SECONDS OF YOUR LIFE AWAY?
OKAY, IT'S A SILENT TIMER, BUT STILL--DO YOU REALLY IMAGINE I'D COME HERE ARMED WITH NOTHING MORE THAN A COUPLE OF TOAD-STICKERS?
YOU PLANTED A BOMB?
HE'S BLUFFING.
WE CAN'T TAKE THAT CHANCE.
YOU WATCH HIM.
BATMAN TO ALFRED. PULL UP THE ANTI-DEMOLITION SERIES ON THE COMPUTER AND STAND BY TO ASSIST.
AND THEN PREP ONE OF THE MOBILE BATCAVES WITH A FULL MEDICAL PACKAGE.
EXIT

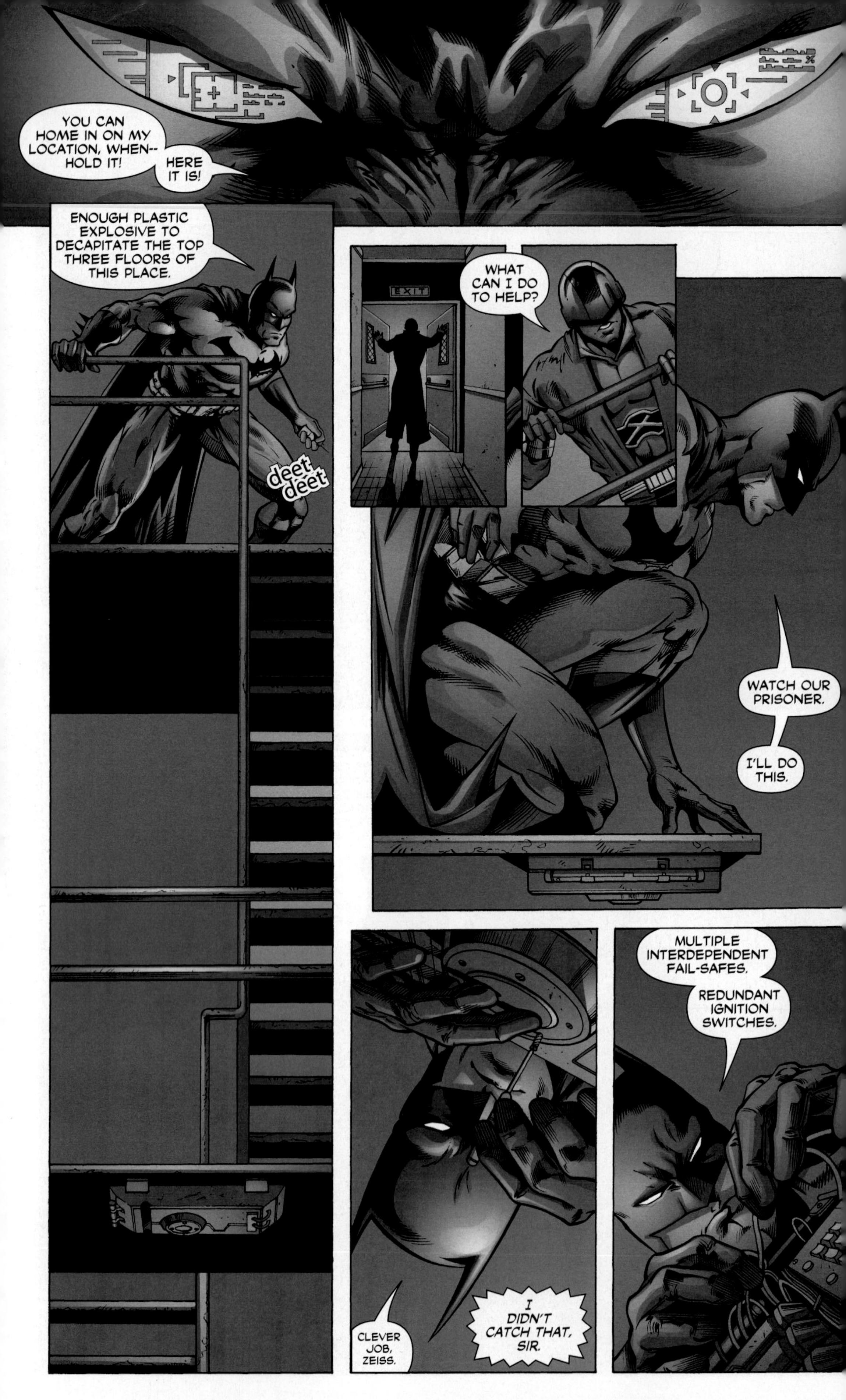
YOU CAN HOME IN ON MY LOCATION, WHEN-- HOLD IT!
HERE IT IS!
ENOUGH PLASTIC EXPLOSIVE TO DECAPITATE THE TOP THREE FLOORS OF THIS PLACE.
deet deet
EXIT
WHAT CAN I DO TO HELP?
WATCH OUR PRISONER.
I'LL DO THIS.
MULTIPLE INTERDEPENDENT FAIL-SAFES.
REDUNDANT IGNITION SWITCHES.
CLEVER JOB, ZEISS.
I DIDN'T CATCH THAT, SIR.

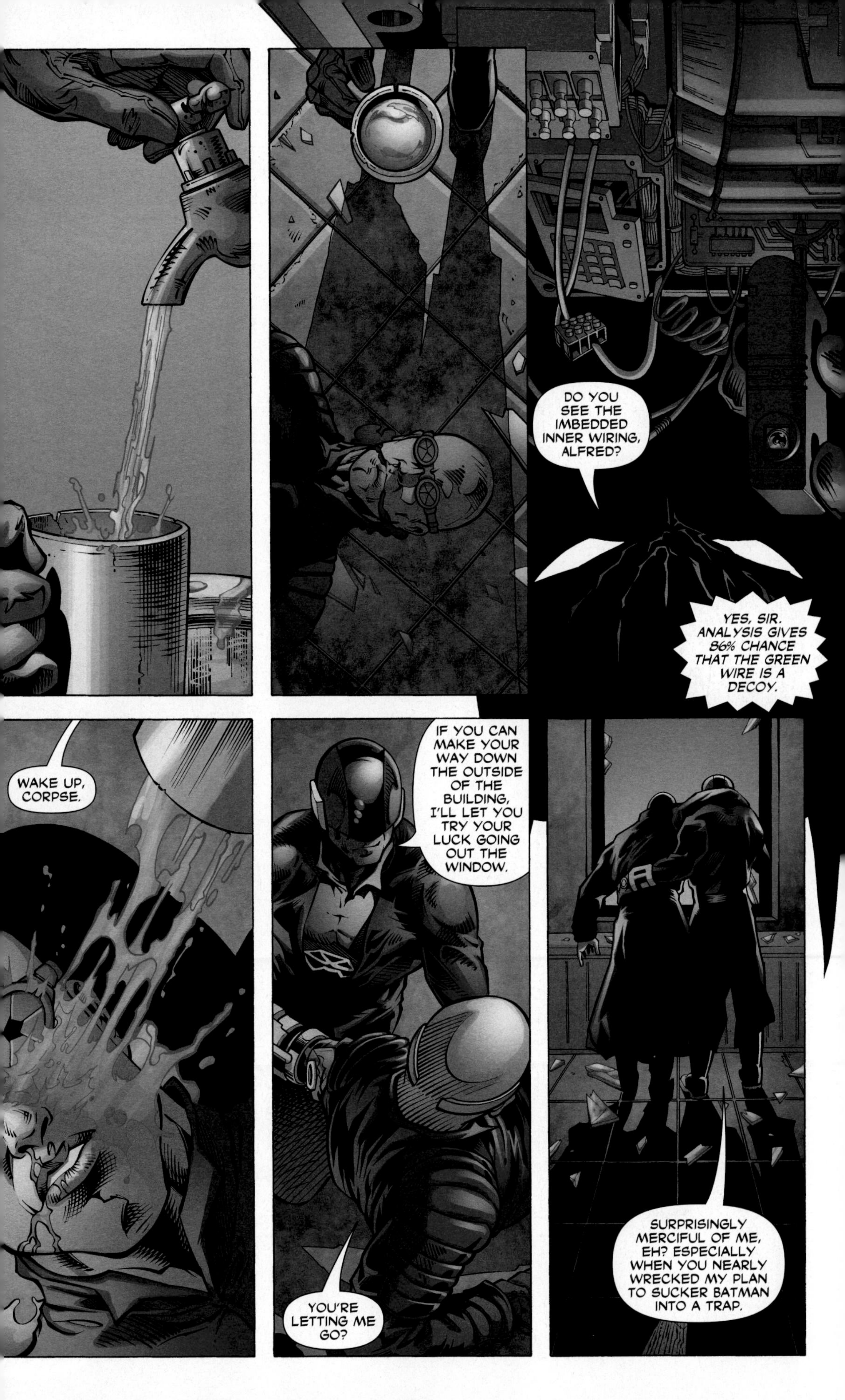
DO YOU SEE THE IMBEDDED INNER WIRING, ALFRED?
YES, SIR. ANALYSIS GIVES 86% CHANCE THAT THE GREEN WIRE IS A DECOY.
WAKE UP, CORPSE.
IF YOU CAN MAKE YOUR WAY DOWN THE OUTSIDE OF THE BUILDING, I'LL LET YOU TRY YOUR LUCK GOING OUT THE WINDOW.
YOU'RE LETTING ME GO?
SURPRISINGLY MERCIFUL OF ME, EH? ESPECIALLY WHEN YOU NEARLY WRECKED MY PLAN TO SUCKER BATMAN INTO A TRAP.

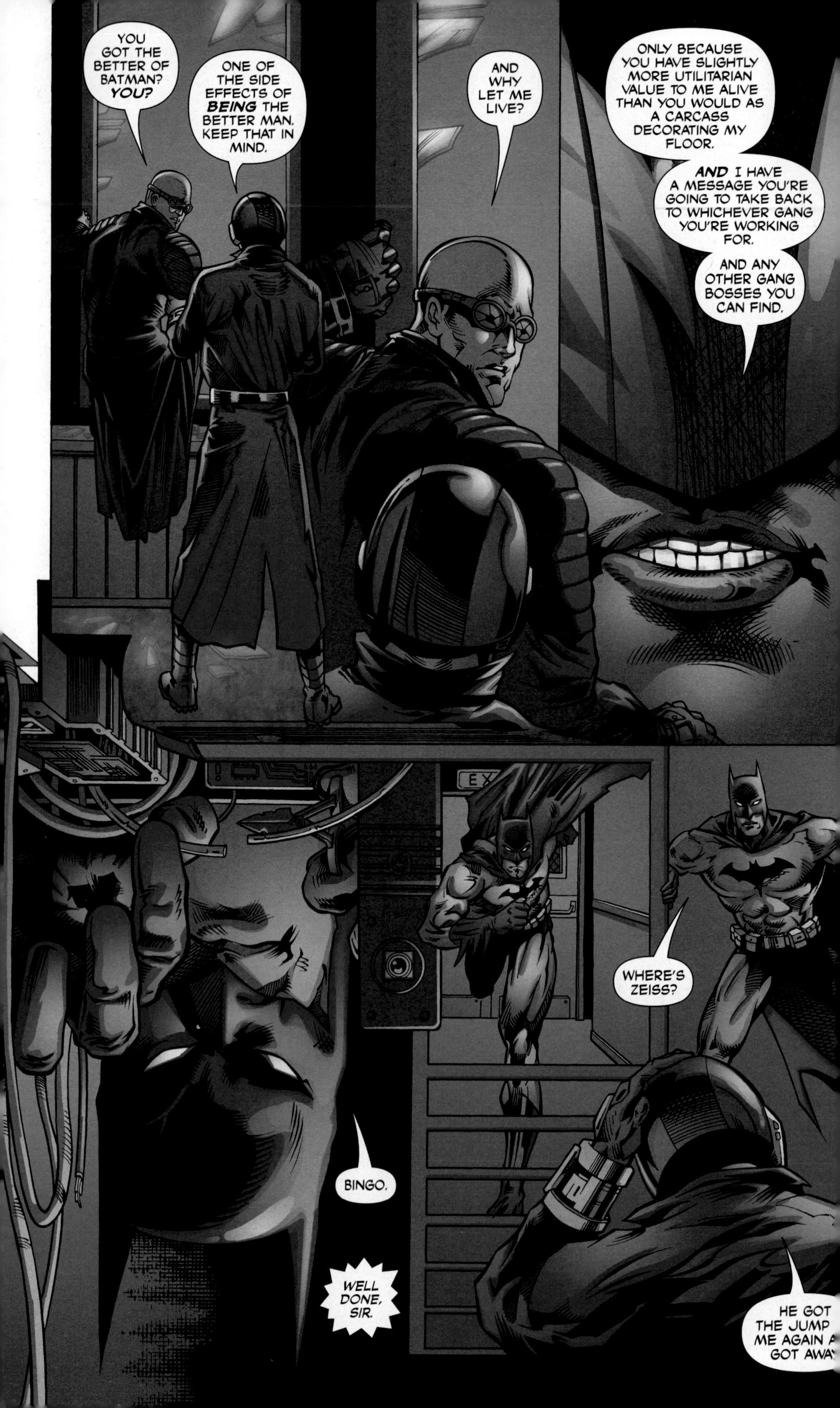
YOU GOT THE BETTER OF BATMAN? YOU?
ONE OF THE SIDE EFFECTS OF BEING THE BETTER MAN. KEEP THAT IN MIND.
AND WHY LET ME LIVE?
ONLY BECAUSE YOU HAVE SLIGHTLY MORE UTILITARIAN VALUE TO ME ALIVE THAN YOU WOULD AS A CARCASS DECORATING MY FLOOR.
AND I HAVE A MESSAGE YOU'RE GOING TO TAKE BACK TO WHICHEVER GANG YOU'RE WORKING FOR.
AND ANY OTHER GANG BOSSES YOU CAN FIND.
BINGO.
WELL DONE, SIR.
WHERE'S ZEISS?
HE GOT THE JUMP ME AGAIN A GOT AWA

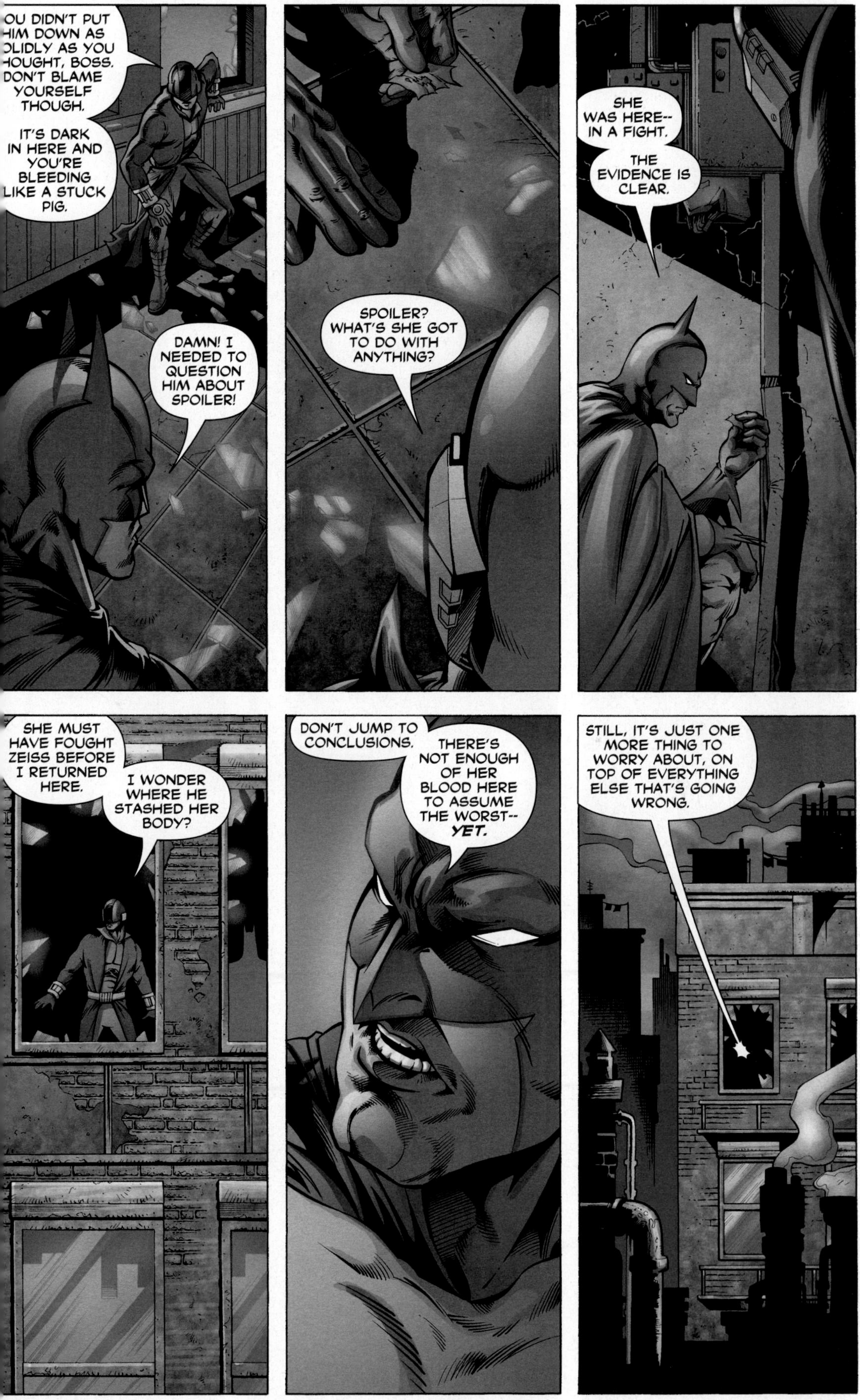

OU DIDN'T PUT HIM DOWN AS OLIDLY AS YOU HOUGHT, BOSS. DON'T BLAME YOURSELF THOUGH.
IT'S DARK IN HERE AND YOU'RE BLEEDING LIKE A STUCK PIG.
DAMN! I NEEDED TO QUESTION HIM ABOUT SPOILER!
SPOILER? WHAT'S SHE GOT TO DO WITH ANYTHING?
SHE WAS HERE-- IN A FIGHT.
THE EVIDENCE IS CLEAR.
SHE MUST HAVE FOUGHT ZEISS BEFORE I RETURNED HERE.
I WONDER WHERE HE STASHED HER BODY?
DON'T JUMP TO CONCLUSIONS.
THERE'S NOT ENOUGH OF HER BLOOD HERE TO ASSUME THE WORST-- *YET.*
STILL, IT'S JUST ONE MORE THING TO WORRY ABOUT, ON TOP OF EVERYTHING ELSE THAT'S GOING WRONG.

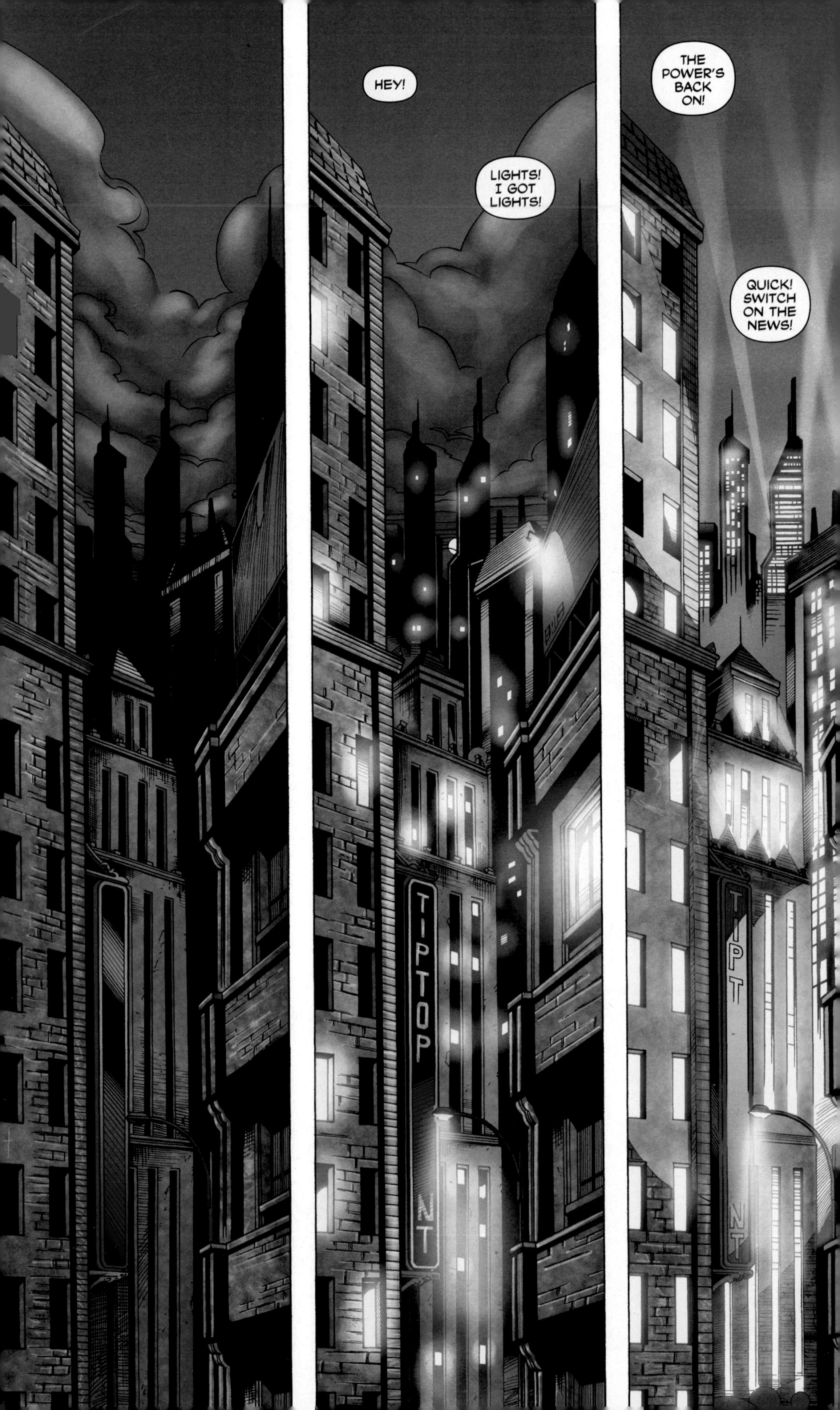

HEY!
LIGHTS! I GOT LIGHTS!
THE POWER'S BACK ON!
QUICK! SWITCH ON THE NEWS!
TIPTOP
NT

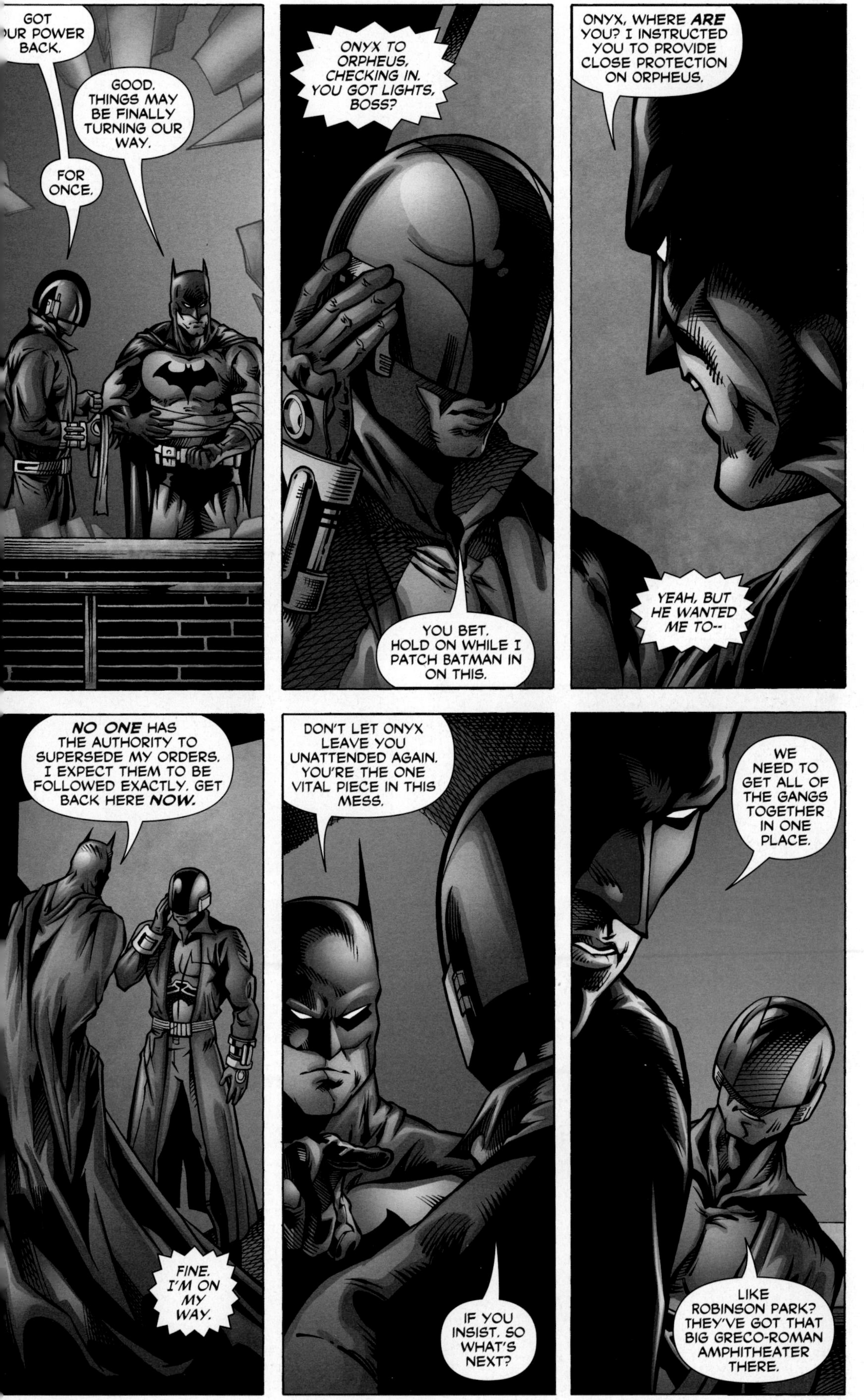
GOT
UR POWER BACK.
GOOD. THINGS MAY BE FINALLY TURNING OUR WAY.
FOR ONCE.
ONYX TO ORPHEUS, CHECKING IN. YOU GOT LIGHTS, BOSS?
YOU BET. HOLD ON WHILE I PATCH BATMAN IN ON THIS.
ONYX, WHERE ARE YOU? I INSTRUCTED YOU TO PROVIDE CLOSE PROTECTION ON ORPHEUS.
YEAH, BUT HE WANTED ME TO--
NO ONE HAS THE AUTHORITY TO SUPERSEDE MY ORDERS. I EXPECT THEM TO BE FOLLOWED EXACTLY. GET BACK HERE NOW.
FINE. I'M ON MY WAY.
DON'T LET ONYX LEAVE YOU UNATTENDED AGAIN. YOU'RE THE ONE VITAL PIECE IN THIS MESS.
IF YOU INSIST. SO WHAT'S NEXT?
WE NEED TO GET ALL OF THE GANGS TOGETHER IN ONE PLACE.
LIKE ROBINSON PARK? THEY'VE GOT THAT BIG GRECO-ROMAN AMPHITHEATER THERE.

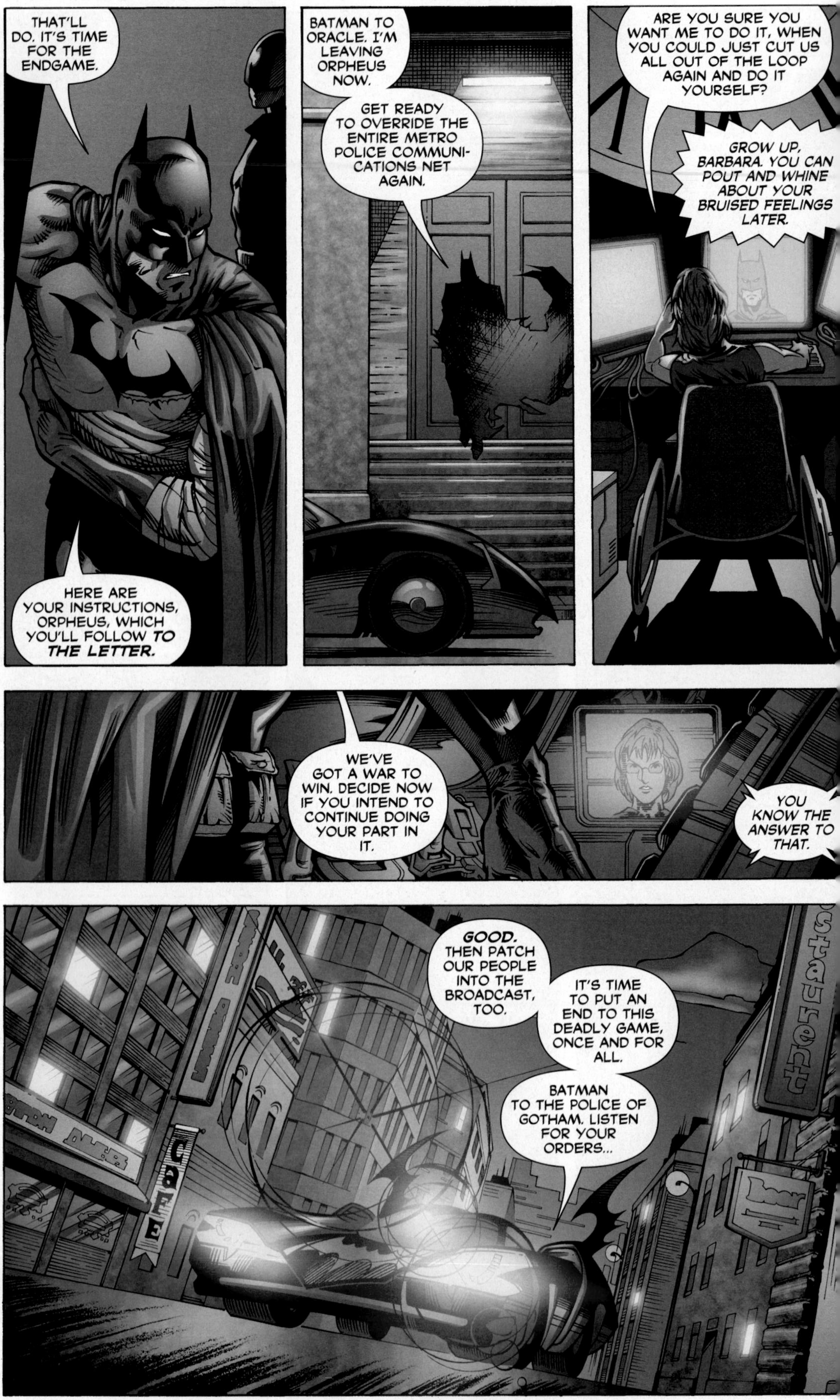

THAT'LL DO. IT'S TIME FOR THE ENDGAME.
HERE ARE YOUR INSTRUCTIONS, ORPHEUS, WHICH YOU'LL FOLLOW *TO THE LETTER.*
BATMAN TO ORACLE. I'M LEAVING ORPHEUS NOW.
GET READY TO OVERRIDE THE ENTIRE METRO POLICE COMMUNICATIONS NET AGAIN.
ARE YOU SURE YOU WANT ME TO DO IT, WHEN YOU COULD JUST CUT US ALL OUT OF THE LOOP AGAIN AND DO IT YOURSELF?
GROW UP, BARBARA. YOU CAN POUT AND WHINE ABOUT YOUR BRUISED FEELINGS LATER.
WE'VE GOT A WAR TO WIN. DECIDE NOW IF YOU INTEND TO CONTINUE DOING YOUR PART IN IT.
YOU KNOW THE ANSWER TO THAT.
GOOD. THEN PATCH OUR PEOPLE INTO THE BROADCAST, TOO.
IT'S TIME TO PUT AN END TO THIS DEADLY GAME, ONCE AND FOR ALL.
BATMAN TO THE POLICE OF GOTHAM. LISTEN FOR YOUR ORDERS...
CAFE

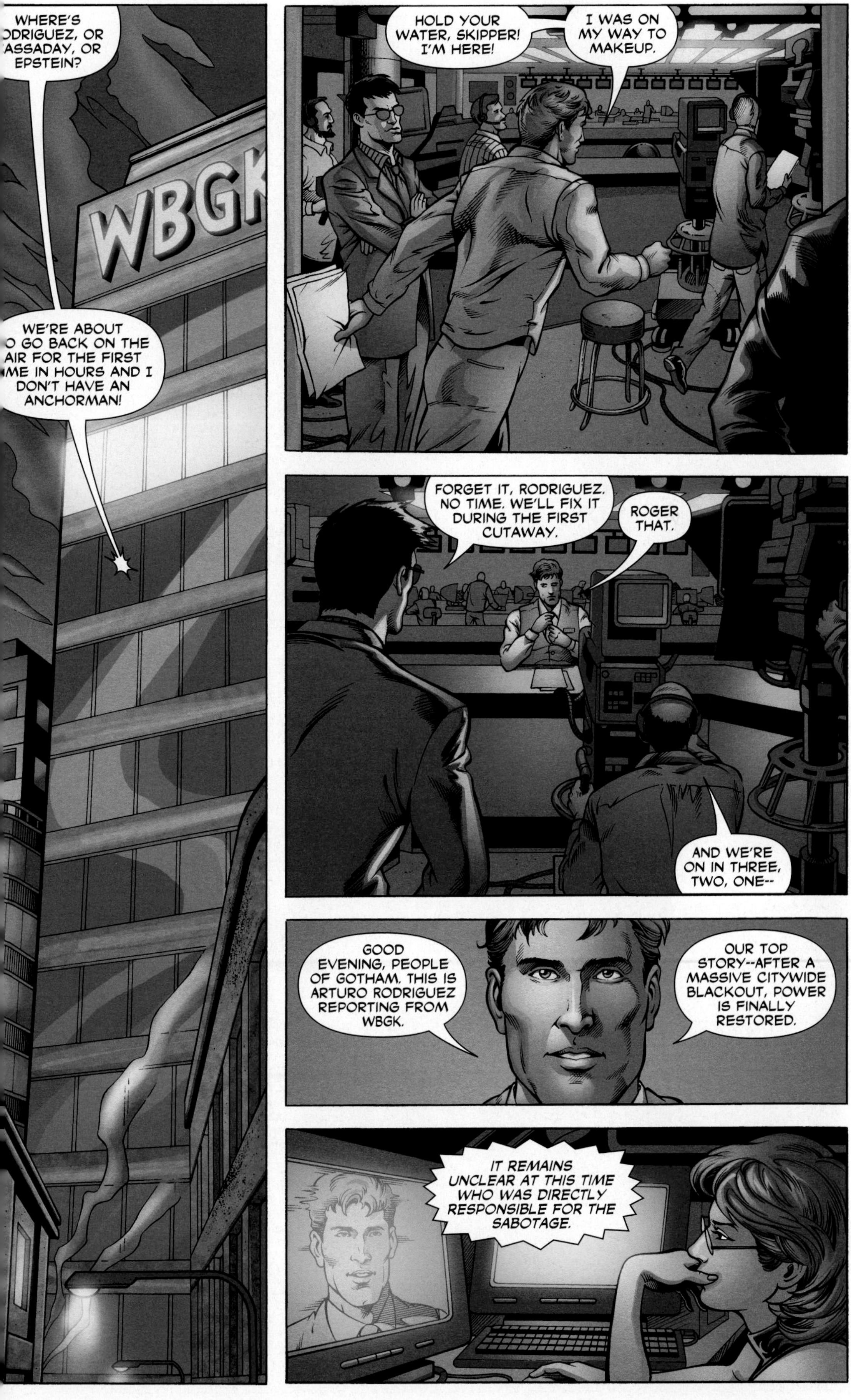

WHERE'S
ODRIGUEZ, OR
ASSADAY, OR
EPSTEIN?
WE'RE ABOUT
O GO BACK ON THE
AIR FOR THE FIRST
ME IN HOURS AND I
DON'T HAVE AN
ANCHORMAN!
WBGK
HOLD YOUR WATER, SKIPPER! I'M HERE!
I WAS ON MY WAY TO MAKEUP.
FORGET IT, RODRIGUEZ. NO TIME. WE'LL FIX IT DURING THE FIRST CUTAWAY.
ROGER THAT.
AND WE'RE ON IN THREE, TWO, ONE--
GOOD EVENING, PEOPLE OF GOTHAM. THIS IS ARTURO RODRIGUEZ REPORTING FROM WBGK.
OUR TOP STORY--AFTER A MASSIVE CITYWIDE BLACKOUT, POWER IS FINALLY RESTORED.
IT REMAINS UNCLEAR AT THIS TIME WHO WAS DIRECTLY RESPONSIBLE FOR THE SABOTAGE.

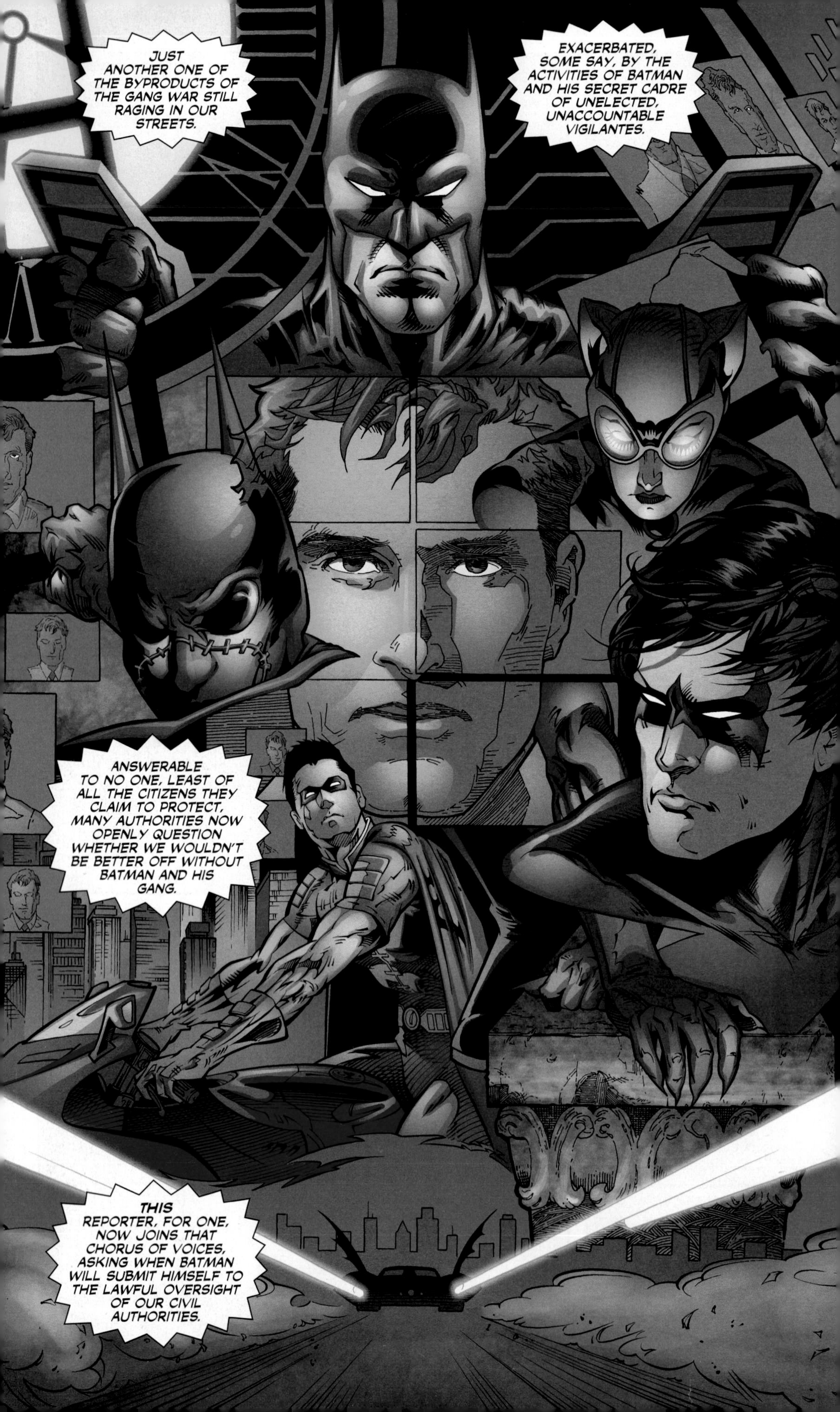
JUST ANOTHER ONE OF THE BYPRODUCTS OF THE GANG WAR STILL RAGING IN OUR STREETS.
EXACERBATED, SOME SAY, BY THE ACTIVITIES OF BATMAN AND HIS SECRET CADRE OF UNELECTED, UNACCOUNTABLE VIGILANTES.
ANSWERABLE TO NO ONE, LEAST OF ALL THE CITIZENS THEY CLAIM TO PROTECT, MANY AUTHORITIES NOW OPENLY QUESTION WHETHER WE WOULDN'T BE BETTER OFF WITHOUT BATMAN AND HIS GANG.
THIS REPORTER, FOR ONE, NOW JOINS THAT CHORUS OF VOICES, ASKING WHEN BATMAN WILL SUBMIT HIMSELF TO THE LAWFUL OVERSIGHT OF OUR CIVIL AUTHORITIES.

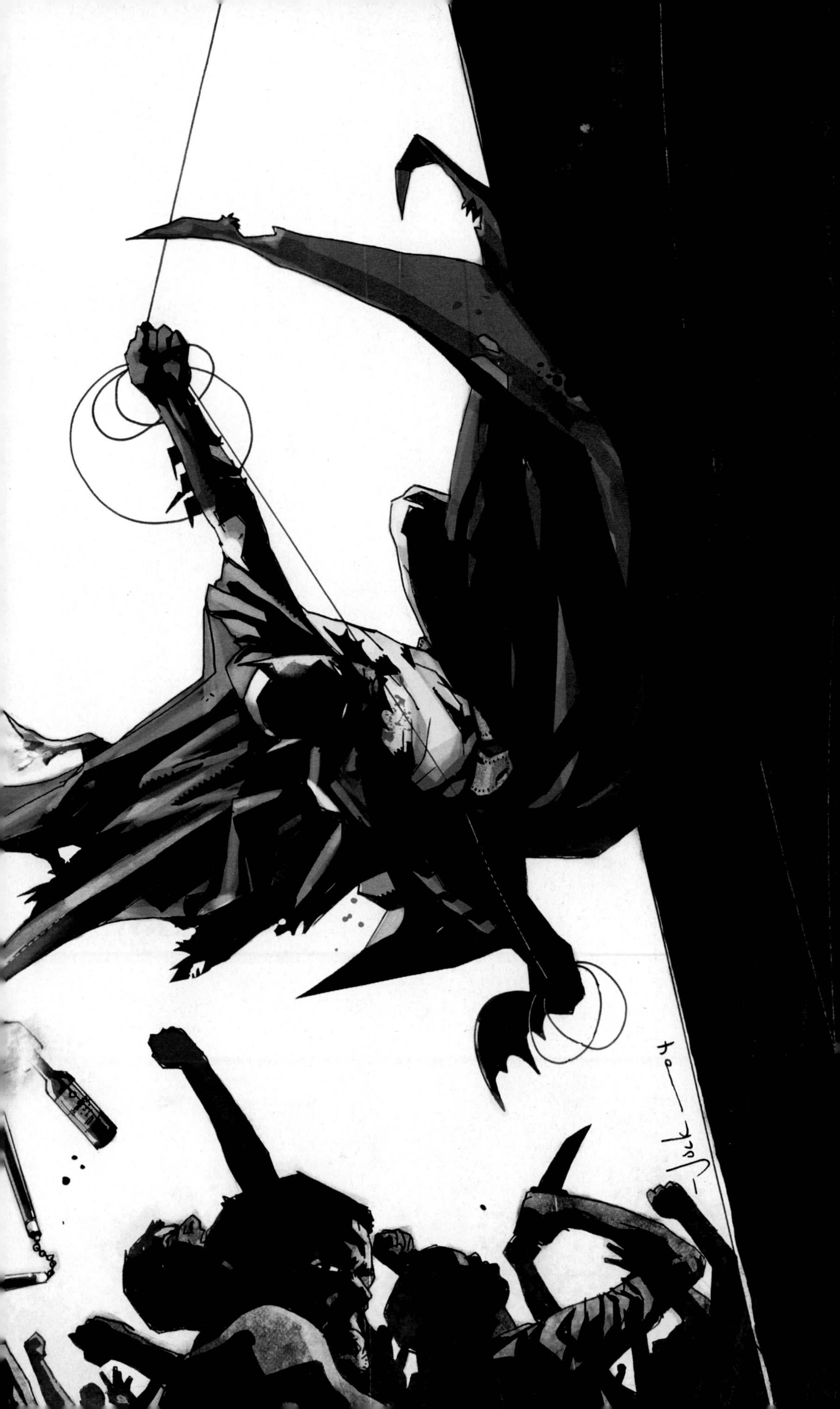
Jock

COVER ART BY
JOCK

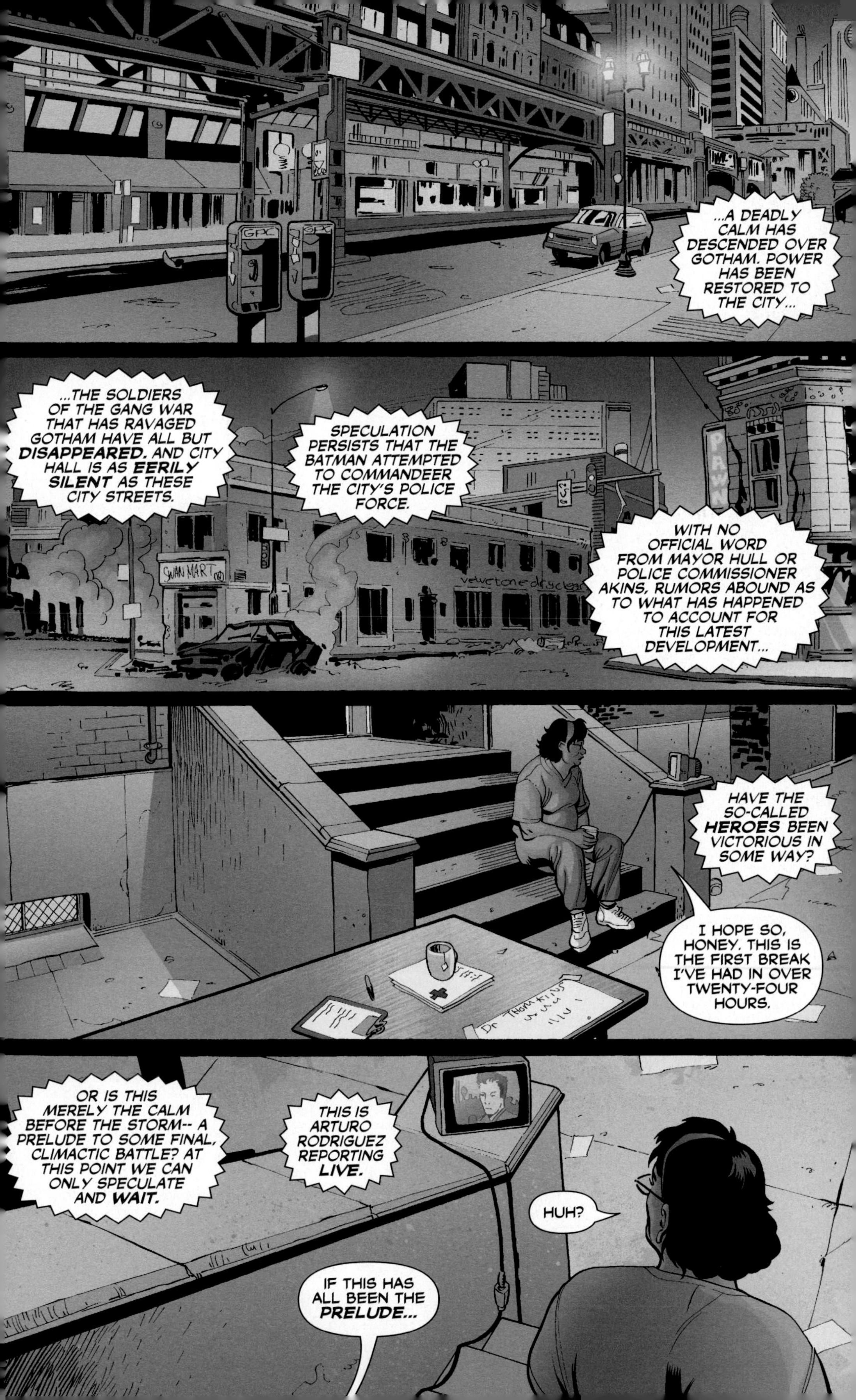
GPC
GPC
...A DEADLY CALM HAS DESCENDED OVER GOTHAM. POWER HAS BEEN RESTORED TO THE CITY...
...THE SOLDIERS OF THE GANG WAR THAT HAS RAVAGED GOTHAM HAVE ALL BUT DISAPPEARED. AND CITY HALL IS AS EERILY SILENT AS THESE CITY STREETS.
SPECULATION PERSISTS THAT THE BATMAN ATTEMPTED TO COMMANDEER THE CITY'S POLICE FORCE.
SWAN MART
PAWN
WITH NO OFFICIAL WORD FROM MAYOR HULL OR POLICE COMMISSIONER AKINS, RUMORS ABOUND AS TO WHAT HAS HAPPENED TO ACCOUNT FOR THIS LATEST DEVELOPMENT...
HAVE THE SO-CALLED HEROES BEEN VICTORIOUS IN SOME WAY?
I HOPE SO, HONEY. THIS IS THE FIRST BREAK I'VE HAD IN OVER TWENTY-FOUR HOURS.
OR IS THIS MERELY THE CALM BEFORE THE STORM-- A PRELUDE TO SOME FINAL, CLIMACTIC BATTLE? AT THIS POINT WE CAN ONLY SPECULATE AND WAIT.
THIS IS ARTURO RODRIGUEZ REPORTING LIVE.
HUH?
IF THIS HAS ALL BEEN THE PRELUDE...

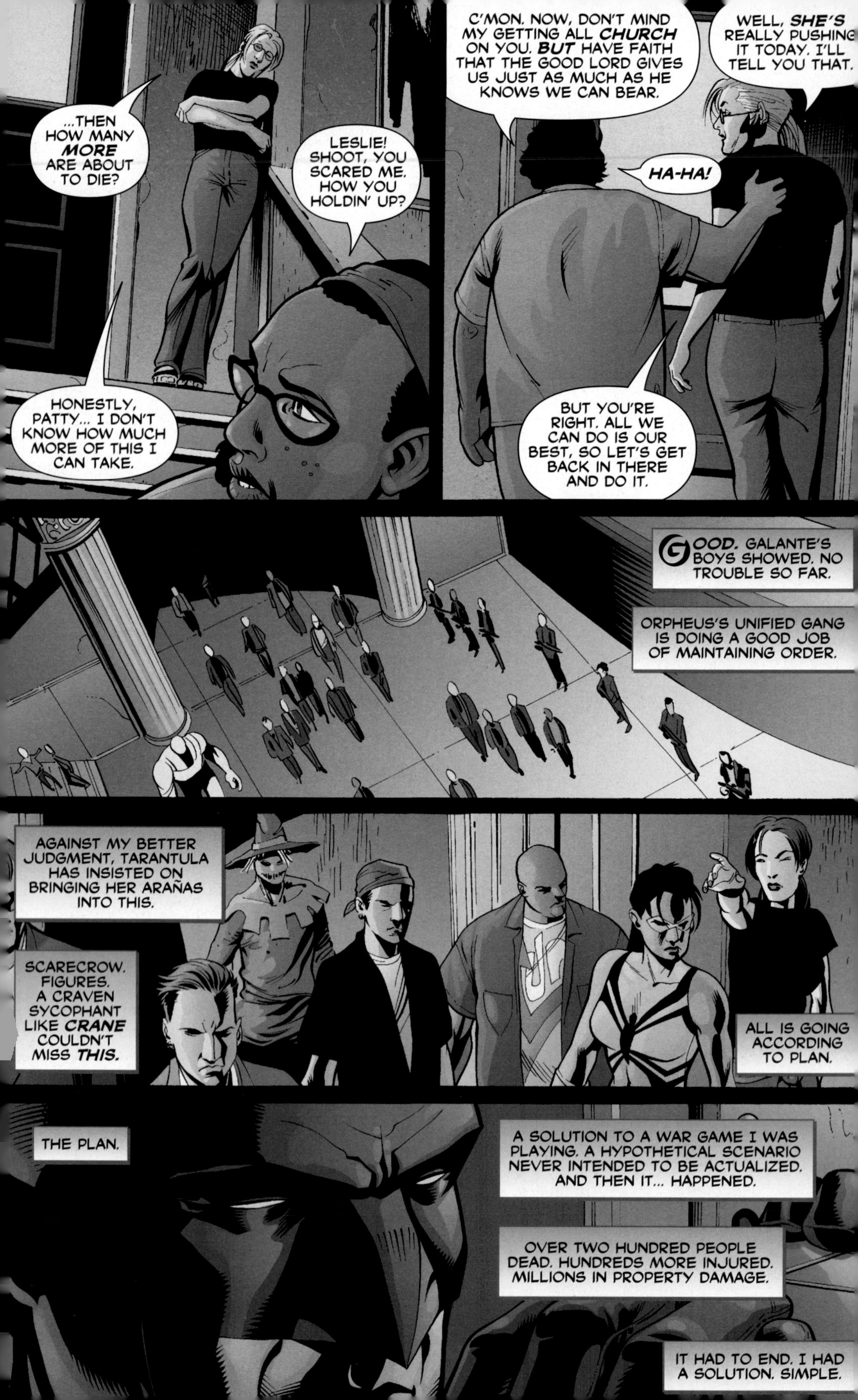
...THEN HOW MANY MORE ARE ABOUT TO DIE?
LESLIE! SHOOT, YOU SCARED ME. HOW YOU HOLDIN' UP?
HONESTLY, PATTY... I DON'T KNOW HOW MUCH MORE OF THIS I CAN TAKE.
C'MON. NOW, DON'T MIND MY GETTING ALL CHURCH ON YOU. BUT HAVE FAITH THAT THE GOOD LORD GIVES US JUST AS MUCH AS HE KNOWS WE CAN BEAR.
WELL, SHE'S REALLY PUSHING IT TODAY. I'LL TELL YOU THAT.
HA-HA!
BUT YOU'RE RIGHT. ALL WE CAN DO IS OUR BEST, SO LET'S GET BACK IN THERE AND DO IT.
GOOD. GALANTE'S BOYS SHOWED. NO TROUBLE SO FAR.
ORPHEUS'S UNIFIED GANG IS DOING A GOOD JOB OF MAINTAINING ORDER.
AGAINST MY BETTER JUDGMENT, TARANTULA HAS INSISTED ON BRINGING HER ARAÑAS INTO THIS.
SCARECROW. FIGURES. A CRAVEN SYCOPHANT LIKE CRANE COULDN'T MISS THIS.
ALL IS GOING ACCORDING TO PLAN.
THE PLAN.
A SOLUTION TO A WAR GAME I WAS PLAYING. A HYPOTHETICAL SCENARIO NEVER INTENDED TO BE ACTUALIZED. AND THEN IT... HAPPENED.
OVER TWO HUNDRED PEOPLE DEAD. HUNDREDS MORE INJURED. MILLIONS IN PROPERTY DAMAGE.
IT HAD TO END. I HAD A SOLUTION. SIMPLE.

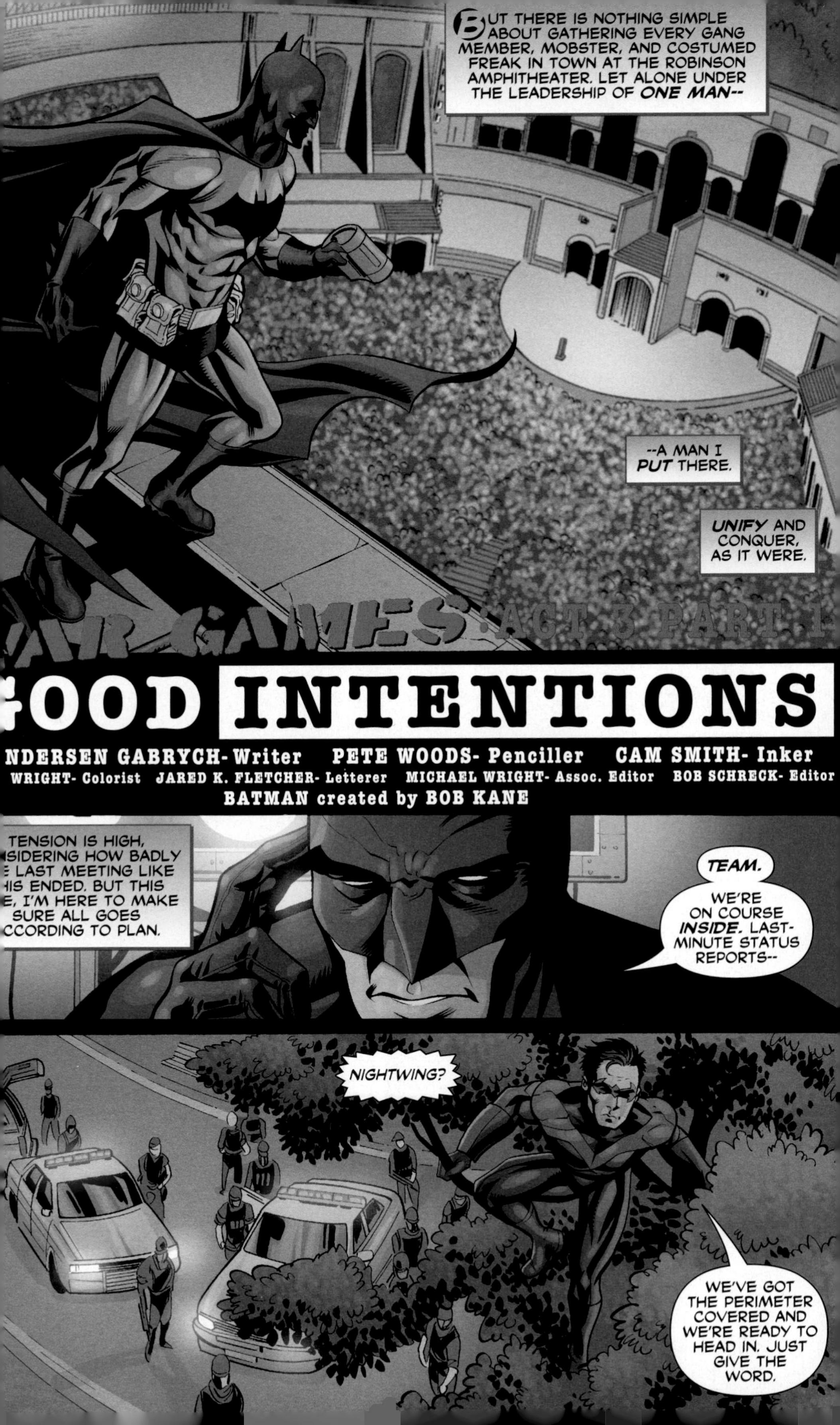
BUT THERE IS NOTHING SIMPLE ABOUT GATHERING EVERY GANG MEMBER, MOBSTER, AND COSTUMED FREAK IN TOWN AT THE ROBINSON AMPHITHEATER. LET ALONE UNDER THE LEADERSHIP OF ONE MAN--
--A MAN I PUT THERE.
UNIFY AND CONQUER, AS IT WERE.
AR GAMES: ACT 3 PART 1
OOD INTENTIONS
NDERSEN GABRYCH- Writer PETE WOODS- Penciller CAM SMITH- Inker
WRIGHT- Colorist JARED K. FLETCHER- Letterer MICHAEL WRIGHT- Assoc. Editor BOB SCHRECK- Editor
BATMAN created by BOB KANE
TENSION IS HIGH, SIDERING HOW BADLY E LAST MEETING LIKE HIS ENDED. BUT THIS E, I'M HERE TO MAKE SURE ALL GOES CCORDING TO PLAN.
TEAM.
WE'RE ON COURSE INSIDE. LAST-MINUTE STATUS REPORTS--
NIGHTWING?
WE'VE GOT THE PERIMETER COVERED AND WE'RE READY TO HEAD IN. JUST GIVE THE WORD.

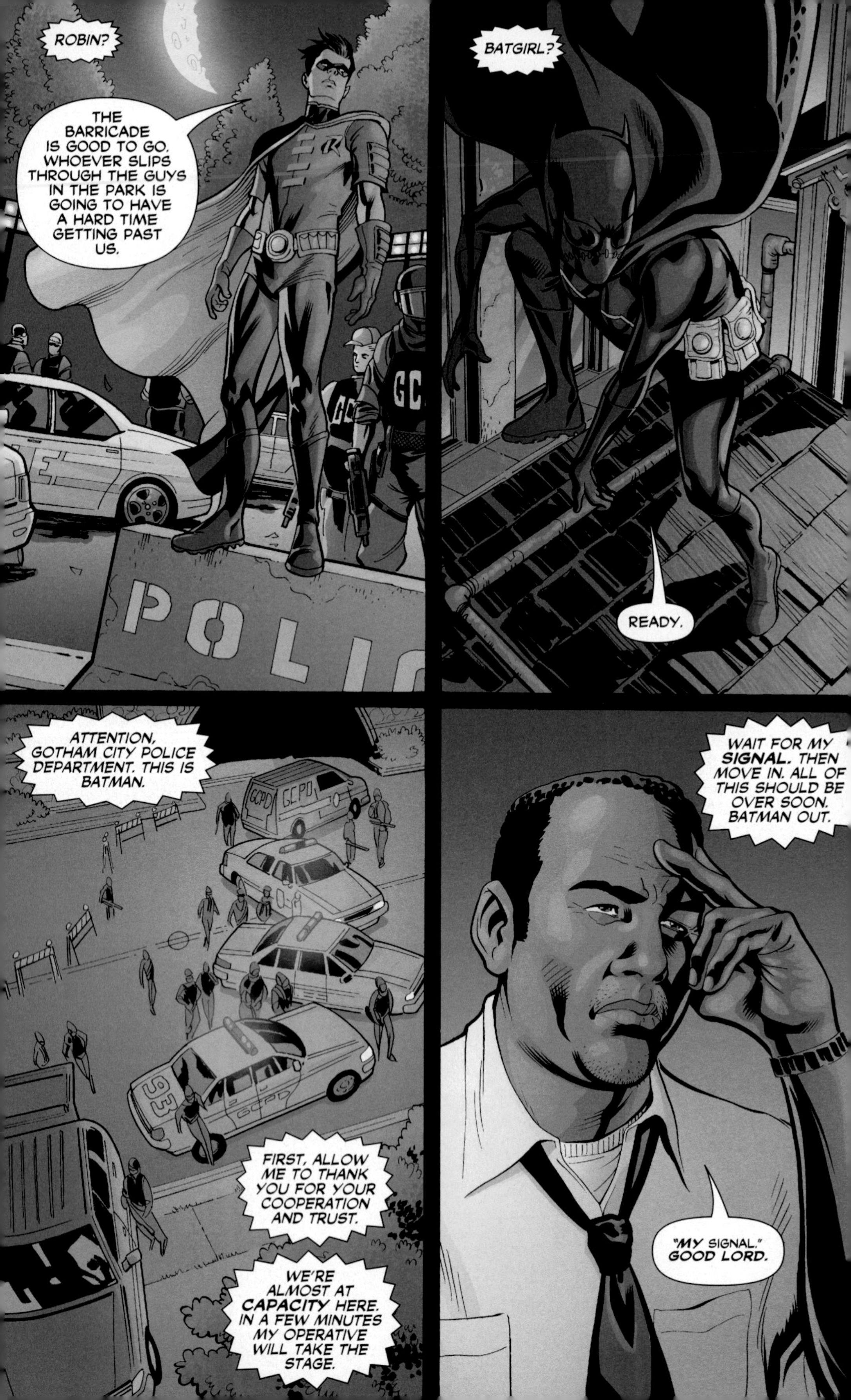
ROBIN?
THE BARRICADE IS GOOD TO GO. WHOEVER SLIPS THROUGH THE GUYS IN THE PARK IS GOING TO HAVE A HARD TIME GETTING PAST US.
POLIC
BATGIRL?
READY.
ATTENTION, GOTHAM CITY POLICE DEPARTMENT. THIS IS BATMAN.
GCPD
FIRST, ALLOW ME TO THANK YOU FOR YOUR COOPERATION AND TRUST.
WE'RE ALMOST AT CAPACITY HERE. IN A FEW MINUTES MY OPERATIVE WILL TAKE THE STAGE.
WAIT FOR MY SIGNAL. THEN MOVE IN. ALL OF THIS SHOULD BE OVER SOON. BATMAN OUT.
"MY SIGNAL." GOOD LORD.

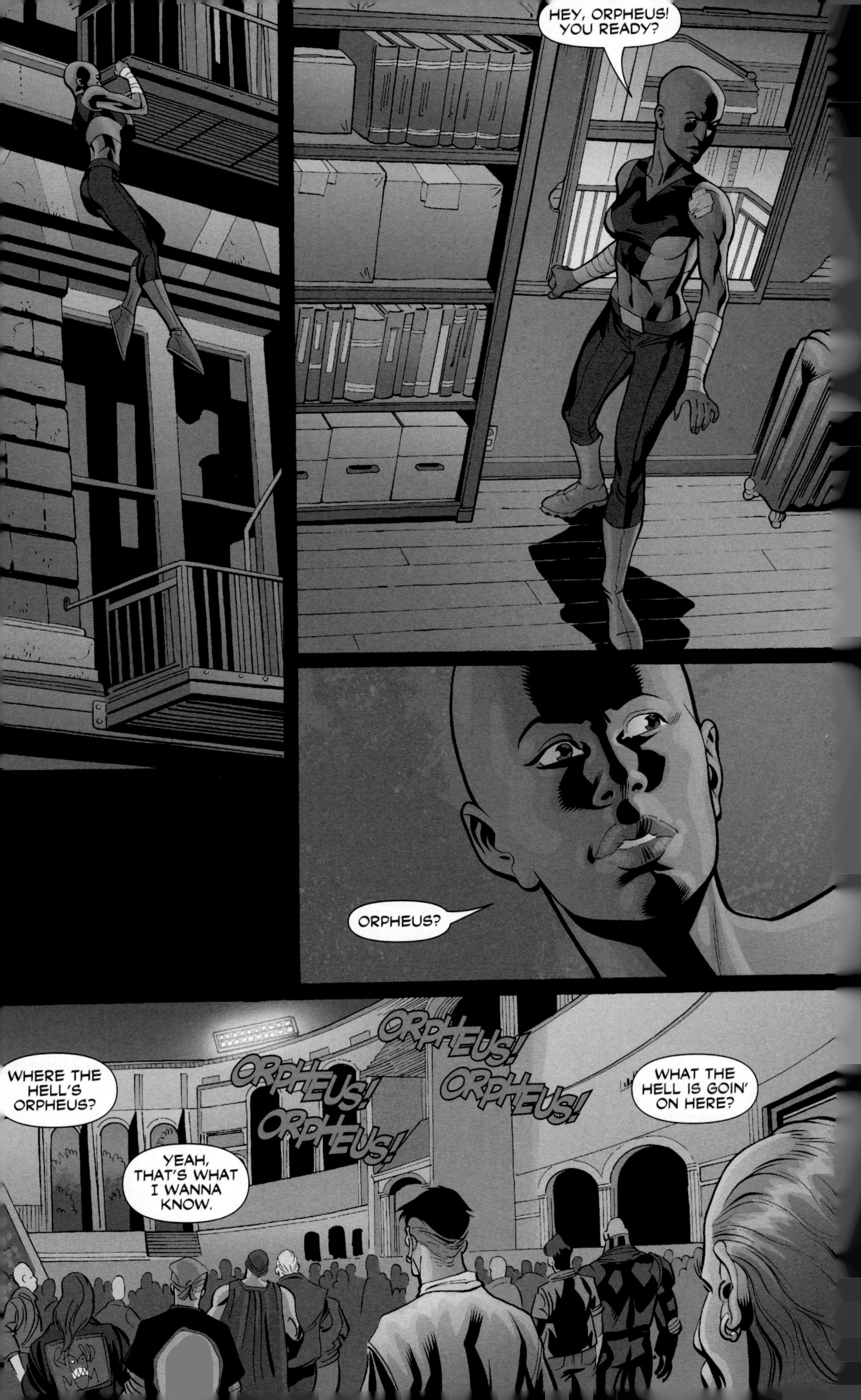
HEY, ORPHEUS! YOU READY?
ORPHEUS?
WHERE THE HELL'S ORPHEUS?
ORPHEUS! ORPHEUS! ORPHEUS! ORPHEUS!
YEAH, THAT'S WHAT I WANNA KNOW.
WHAT THE HELL IS GOIN' ON HERE?

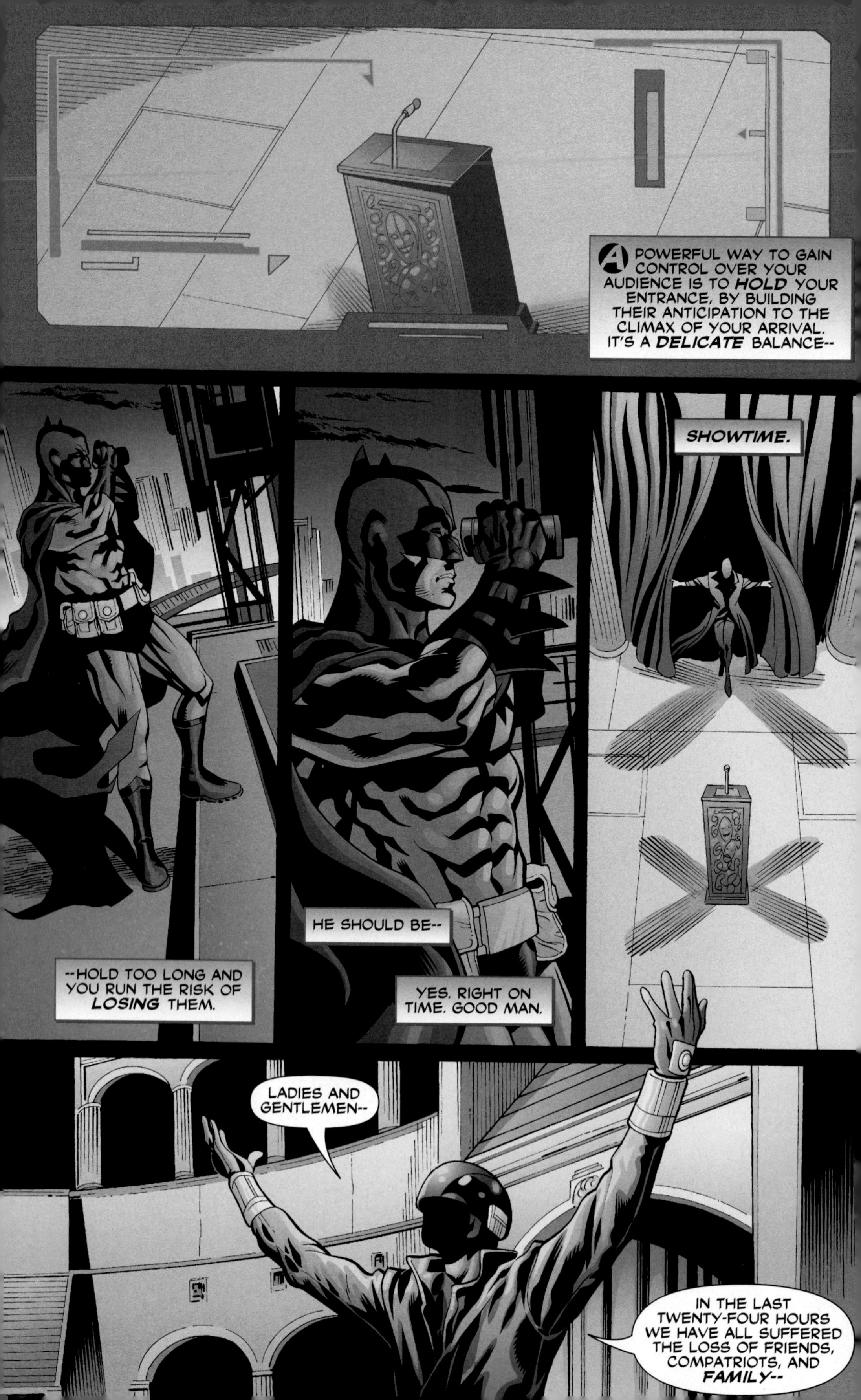
A POWERFUL WAY TO GAIN CONTROL OVER YOUR AUDIENCE IS TO HOLD YOUR ENTRANCE, BY BUILDING THEIR ANTICIPATION TO THE CLIMAX OF YOUR ARRIVAL. IT'S A DELICATE BALANCE--
--HOLD TOO LONG AND YOU RUN THE RISK OF LOSING THEM.
HE SHOULD BE--
YES. RIGHT ON TIME. GOOD MAN.
SHOWTIME.
LADIES AND GENTLEMEN--
IN THE LAST TWENTY-FOUR HOURS WE HAVE ALL SUFFERED THE LOSS OF FRIENDS, COMPATRIOTS, AND FAMILY--

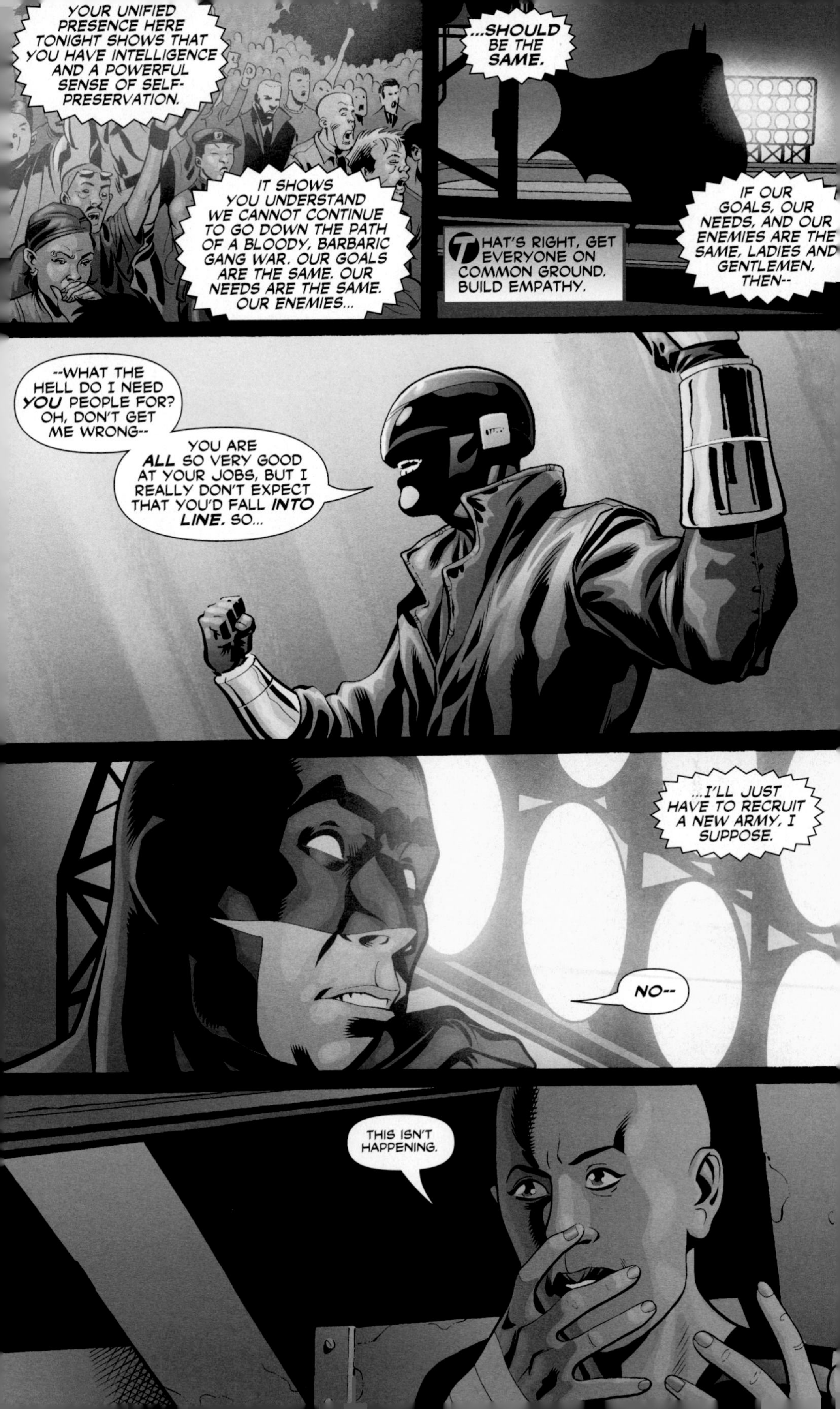
YOUR UNIFIED PRESENCE HERE TONIGHT SHOWS THAT YOU HAVE INTELLIGENCE AND A POWERFUL SENSE OF SELF-PRESERVATION.
IT SHOWS YOU UNDERSTAND WE CANNOT CONTINUE TO GO DOWN THE PATH OF A BLOODY, BARBARIC GANG WAR. OUR GOALS ARE THE SAME. OUR NEEDS ARE THE SAME. OUR ENEMIES...
...SHOULD BE THE SAME.
THAT'S RIGHT, GET EVERYONE ON COMMON GROUND. BUILD EMPATHY.
IF OUR GOALS, OUR NEEDS, AND OUR ENEMIES ARE THE SAME, LADIES AND GENTLEMEN, THEN--
--WHAT THE HELL DO I NEED YOU PEOPLE FOR? OH, DON'T GET ME WRONG--
YOU ARE ALL SO VERY GOOD AT YOUR JOBS, BUT I REALLY DON'T EXPECT THAT YOU'D FALL INTO LINE. SO...
...I'LL JUST HAVE TO RECRUIT A NEW ARMY, I SUPPOSE.
NO--
THIS ISN'T HAPPENING.

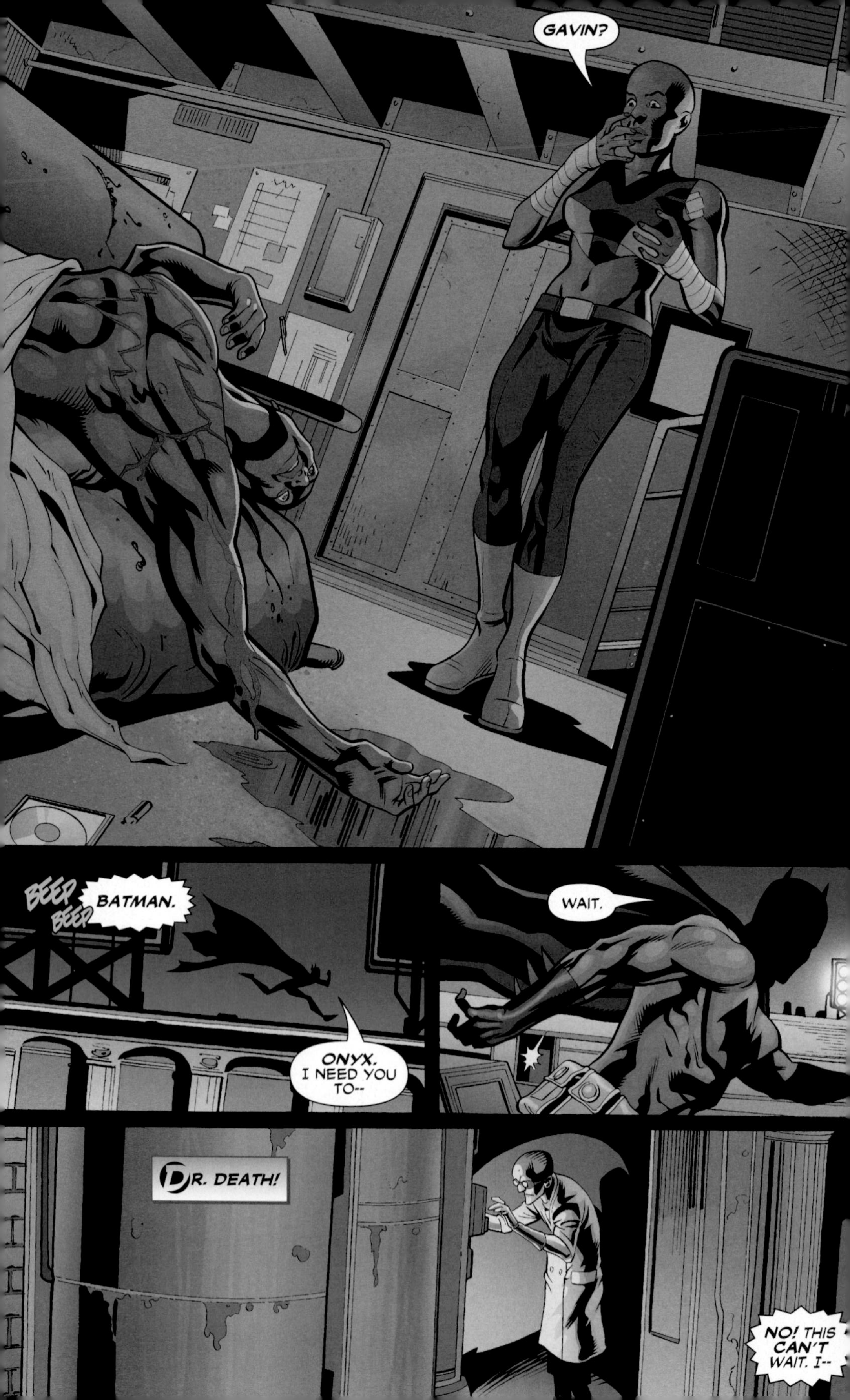
GAVIN?
BEEP BEEP
BATMAN.
ONYX. I NEED YOU TO--
WAIT.
DR. DEATH!
NO! THIS CAN'T WAIT. I--

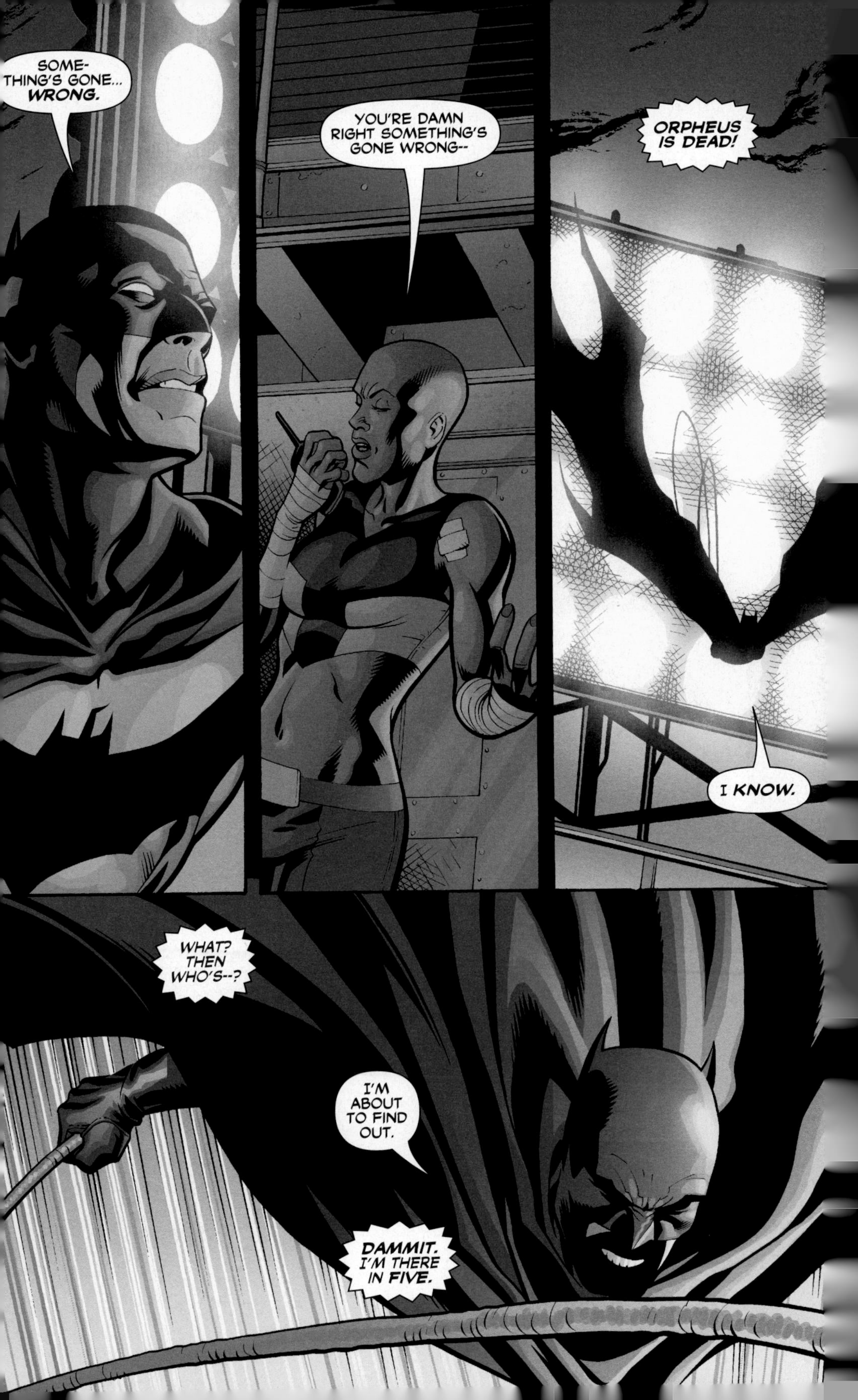
SOME-
THING'S GONE...
WRONG.
YOU'RE DAMN
RIGHT SOMETHING'S
GONE WRONG--
ORPHEUS
IS DEAD!
I KNOW.
WHAT?
THEN
WHO'S--?
I'M
ABOUT
TO FIND
OUT.
DAMMIT.
I'M THERE
IN FIVE.

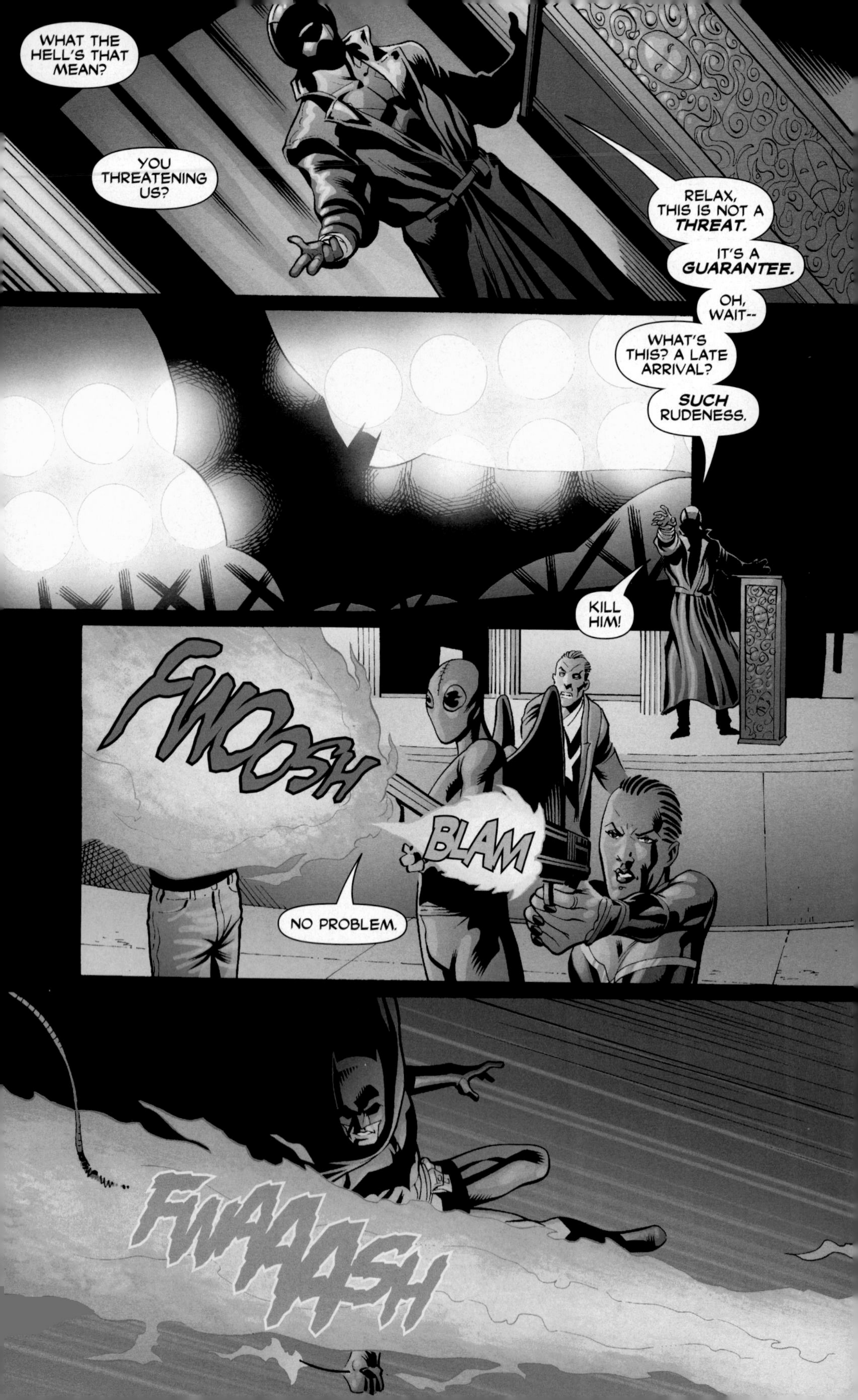
WHAT THE HELL'S THAT MEAN?
YOU THREATENING US?
RELAX, THIS IS NOT A THREAT.
IT'S A GUARANTEE.
OH, WAIT--
WHAT'S THIS? A LATE ARRIVAL?
SUCH RUDENESS.
KILL HIM!
FWOOSH
BLAM
NO PROBLEM.
FWAAASH

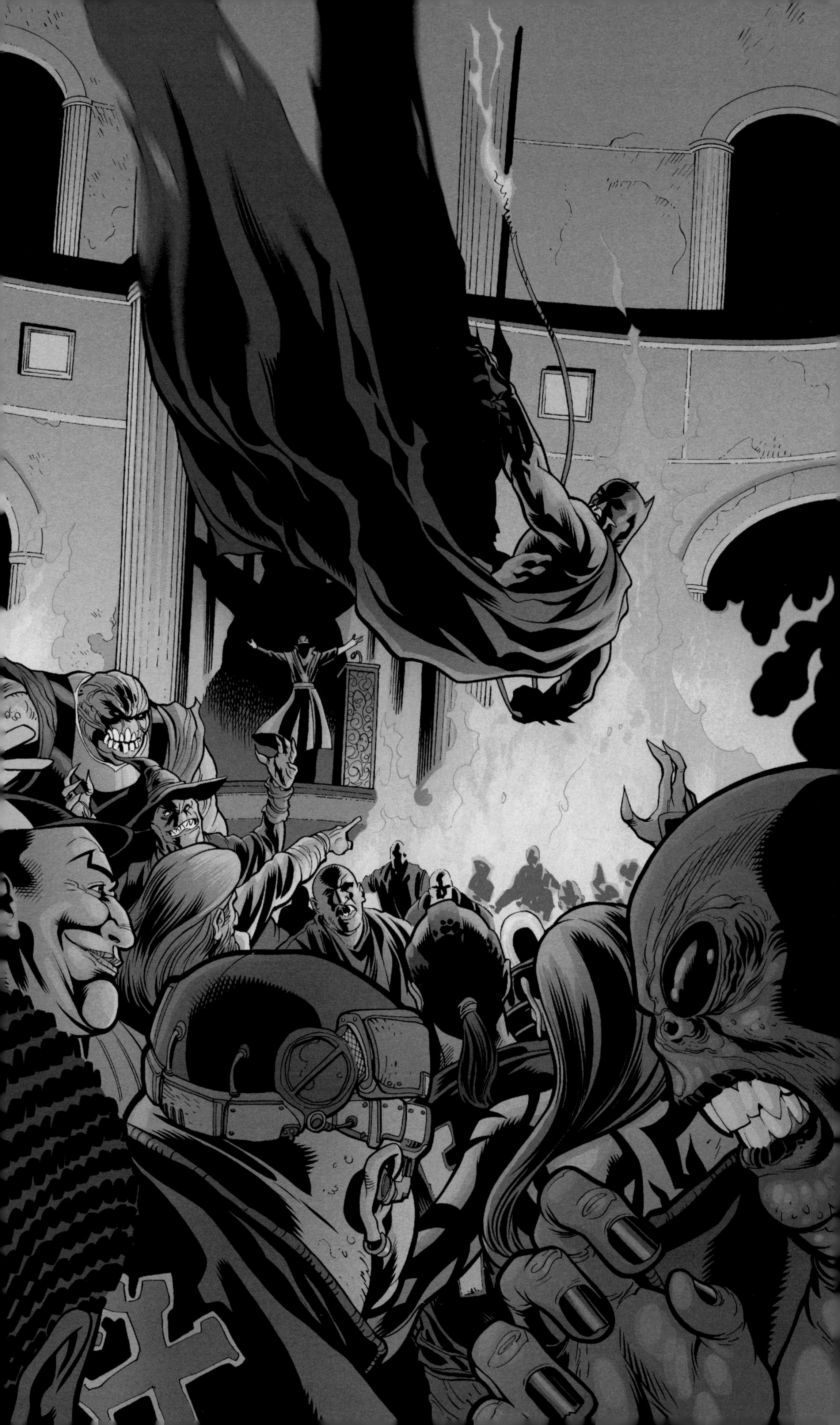

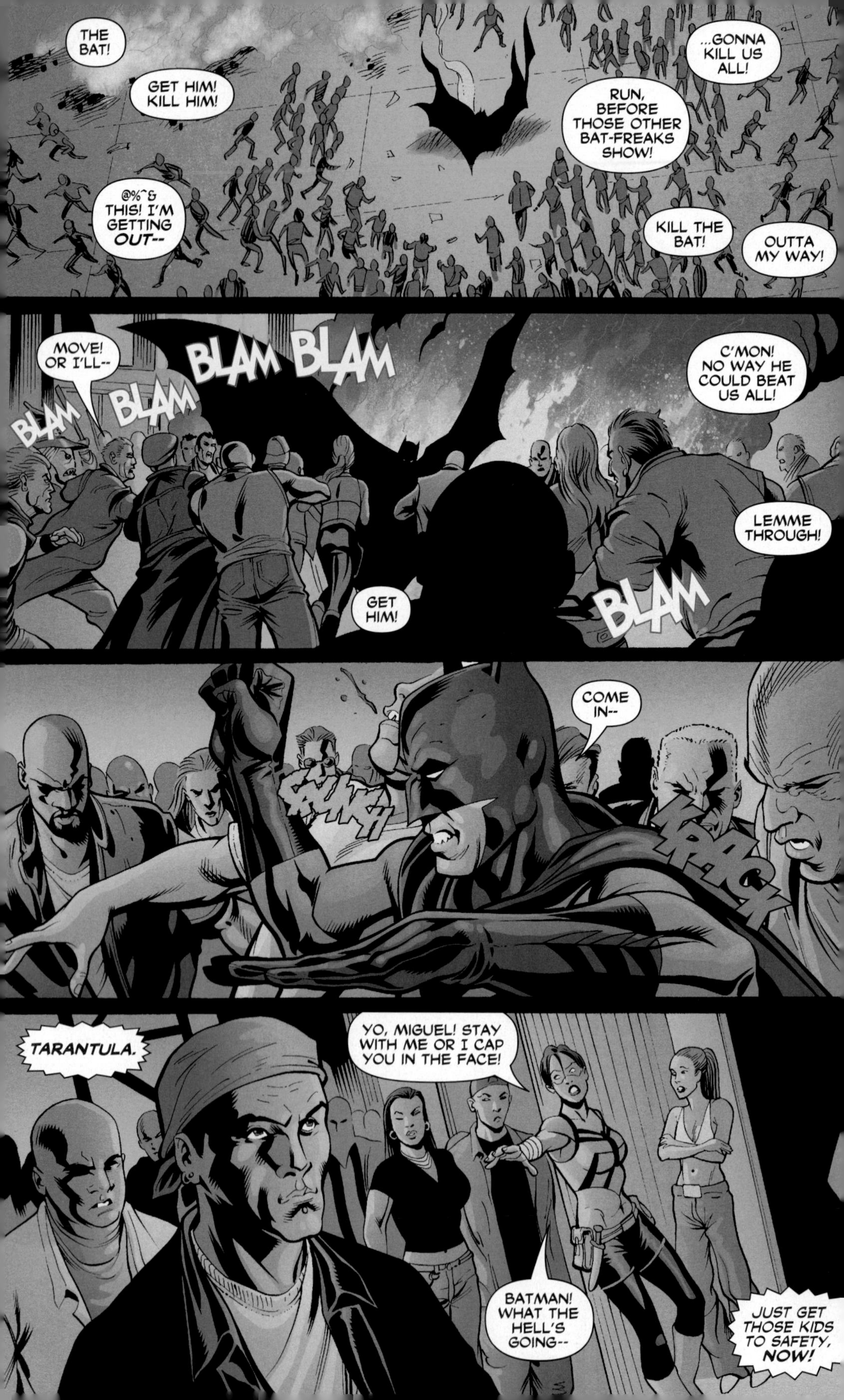
THE BAT!
GET HIM! KILL HIM!
@%^& THIS! I'M GETTING OUT--
...GONNA KILL US ALL!
RUN, BEFORE THOSE OTHER BAT-FREAKS SHOW!
KILL THE BAT!
OUTTA MY WAY!
MOVE! OR I'LL--
BLAM
BLAM
BLAM
BLAM
C'MON! NO WAY HE COULD BEAT US ALL!
LEMME THROUGH!
GET HIM!
BLAM
COME IN--
TARANTULA.
YO, MIGUEL! STAY WITH ME OR I CAP YOU IN THE FACE!
BATMAN! WHAT THE HELL'S GOING--
JUST GET THOSE KIDS TO SAFETY, NOW!

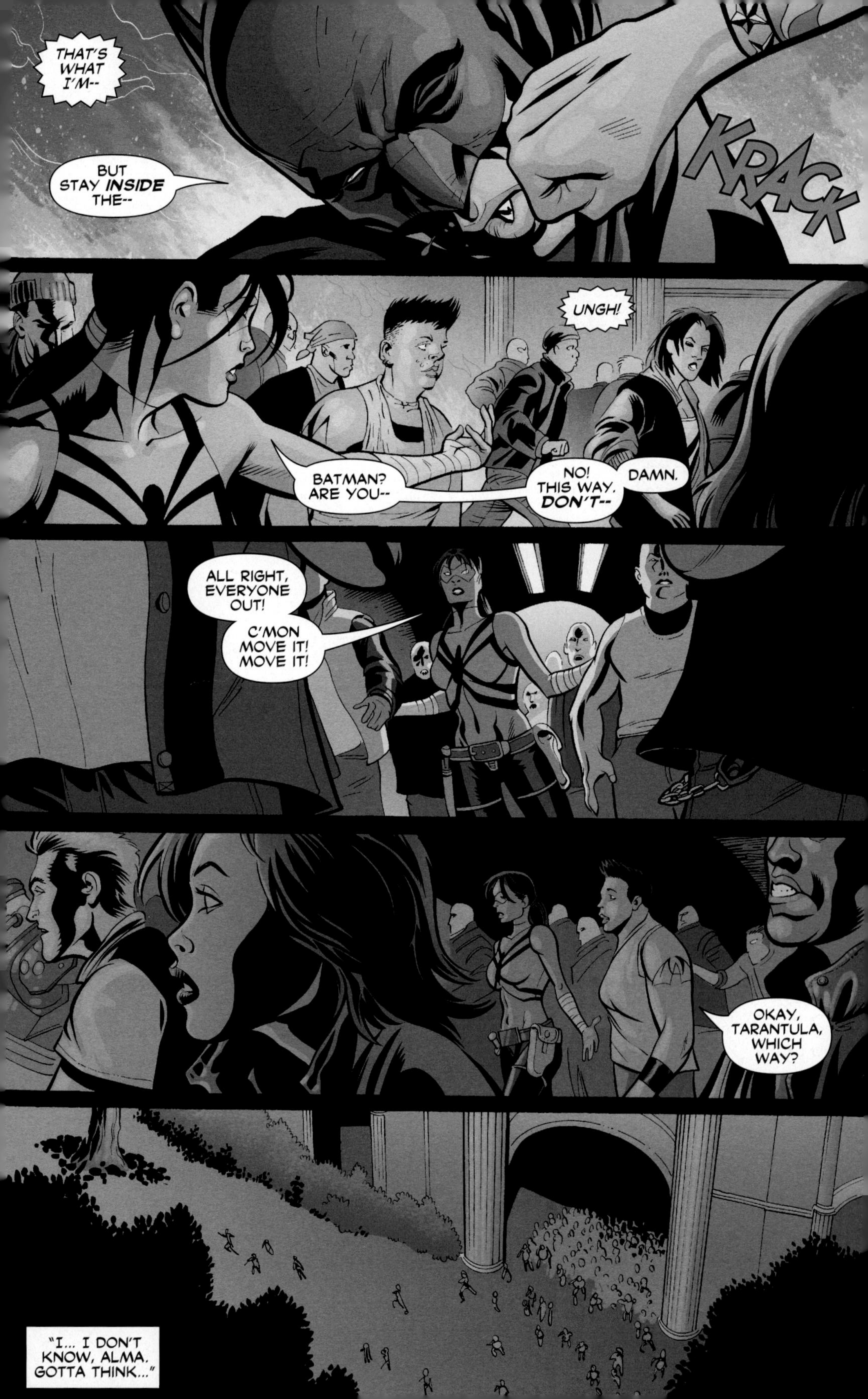
THAT'S WHAT I'M--
BUT STAY INSIDE THE--
KRACK
UNGH!
BATMAN? ARE YOU--
NO! THIS WAY. DON'T--
DAMN.
ALL RIGHT, EVERYONE OUT!
C'MON MOVE IT! MOVE IT!
OKAY, TARANTULA, WHICH WAY?
"I... I DON'T KNOW, ALMA. GOTTA THINK..."

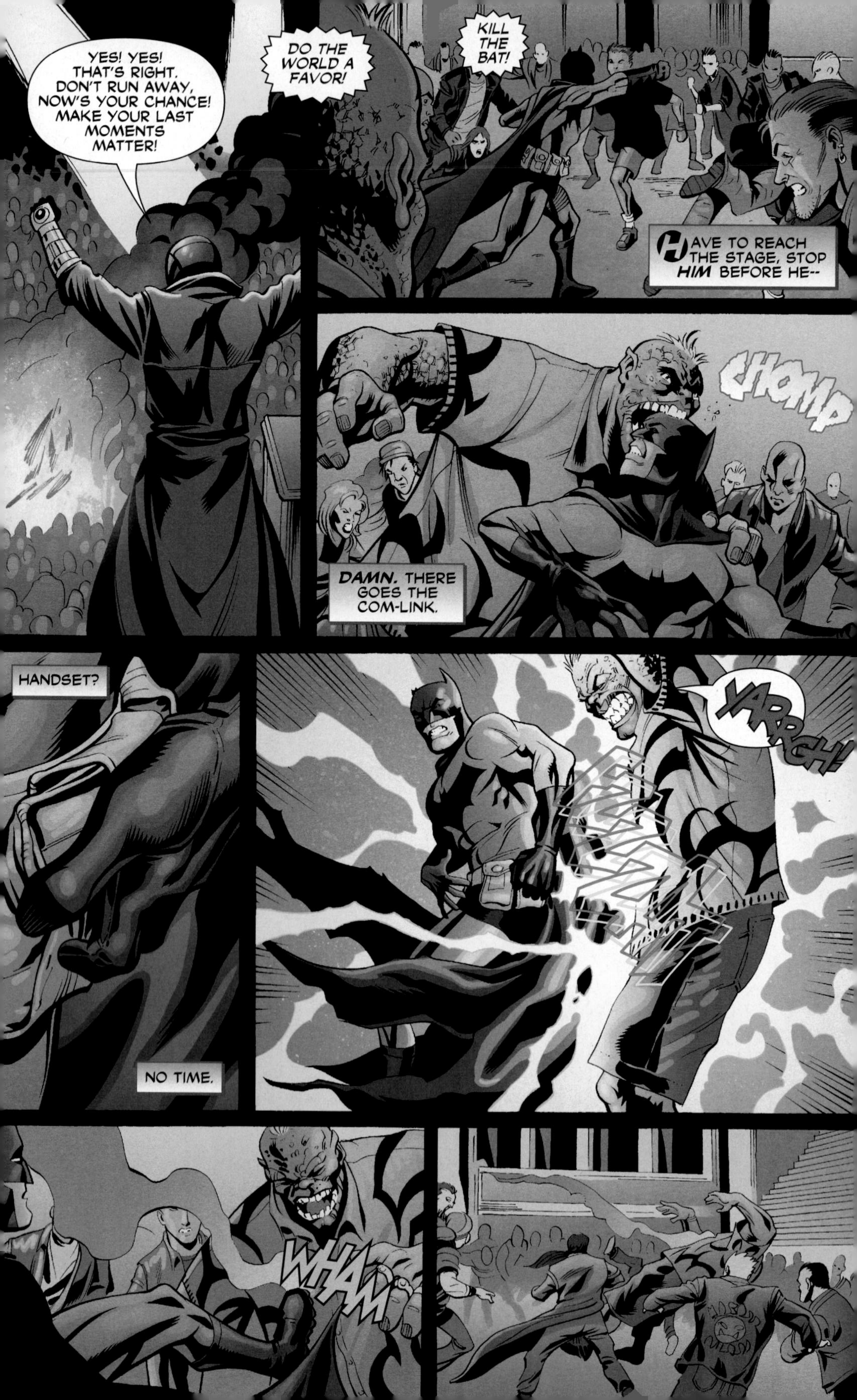
YES! YES! THAT'S RIGHT. DON'T RUN AWAY, NOW'S YOUR CHANCE! MAKE YOUR LAST MOMENTS MATTER!
DO THE WORLD A FAVOR!
KILL THE BAT!
HAVE TO REACH THE STAGE, STOP HIM BEFORE HE--
CHOMP
DAMN. THERE GOES THE COM-LINK.
HANDSET?
NO TIME.
YARRGH!
WHAM

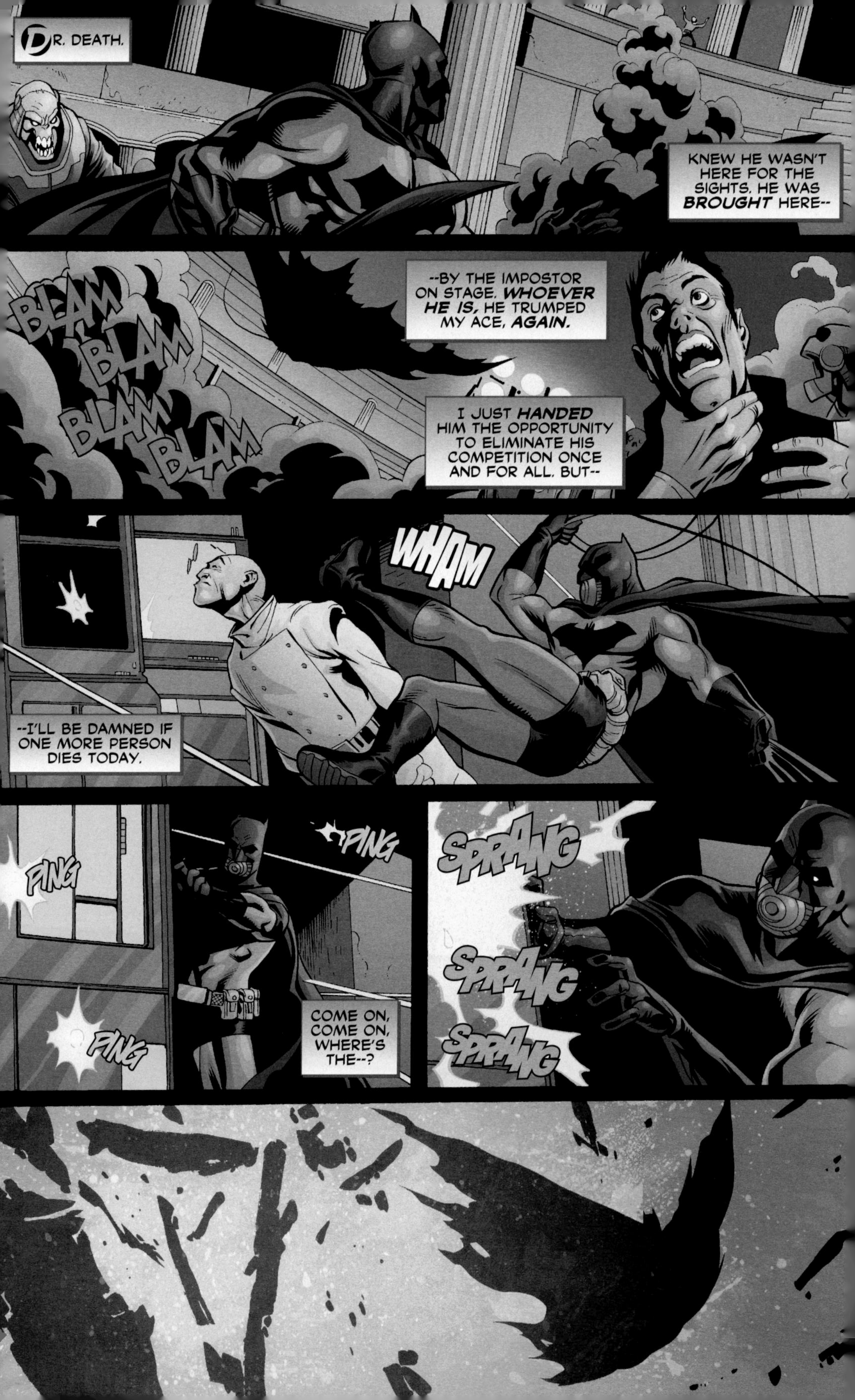

DR. DEATH.
KNEW HE WASN'T HERE FOR THE SIGHTS. HE WAS BROUGHT HERE--
BLAM BLAM BLAM BLAM
--BY THE IMPOSTOR ON STAGE. WHOEVER HE IS, HE TRUMPED MY ACE, AGAIN.
I JUST HANDED HIM THE OPPORTUNITY TO ELIMINATE HIS COMPETITION ONCE AND FOR ALL. BUT--
WHAM
--I'LL BE DAMNED IF ONE MORE PERSON DIES TODAY.
PING
PING
PING
COME ON, COME ON, WHERE'S THE--?
SPRANG
SPRANG
SPRANG

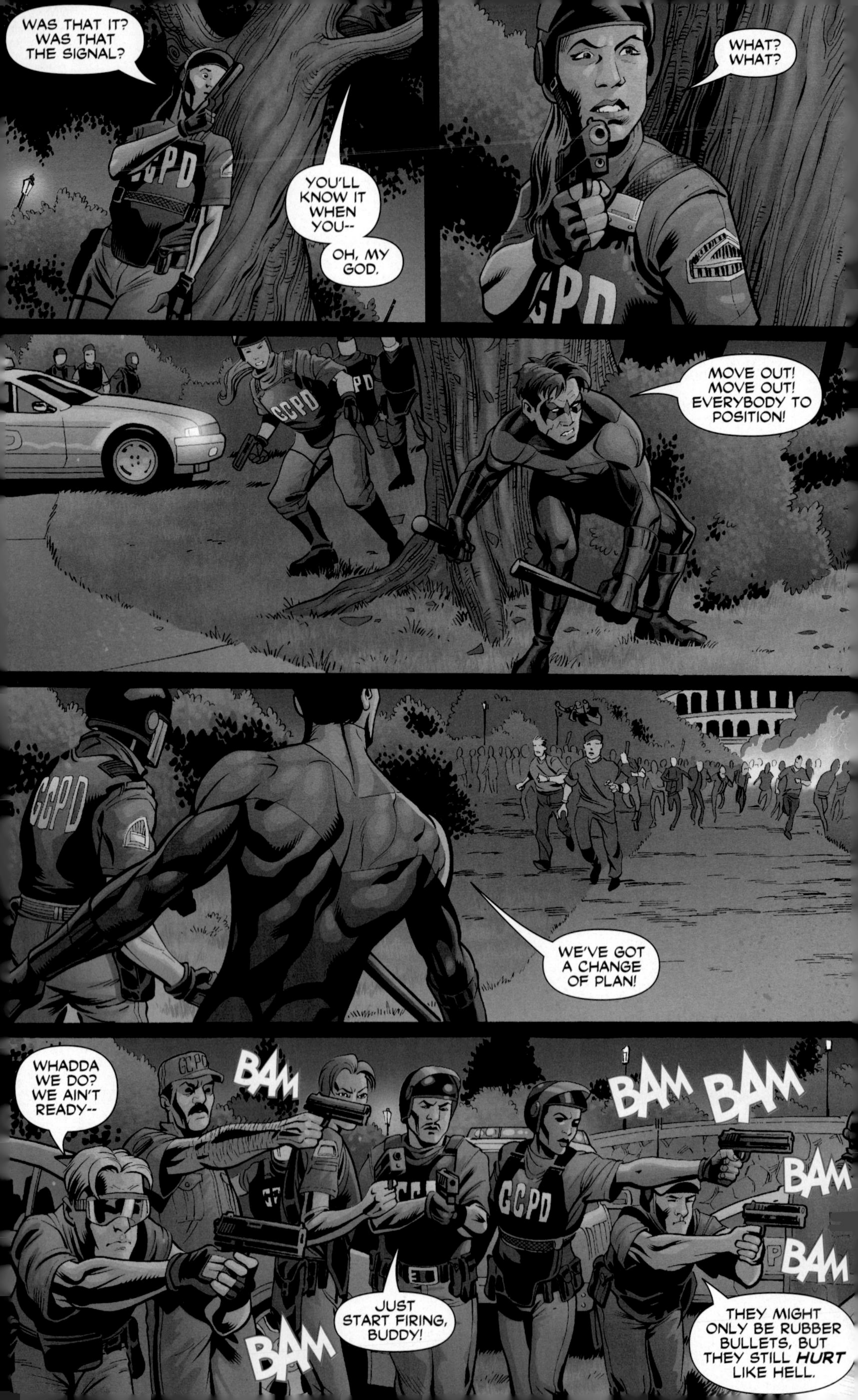
WAS THAT IT? WAS THAT THE SIGNAL?
YOU'LL KNOW IT WHEN YOU--
OH, MY GOD.
WHAT? WHAT?
MOVE OUT! MOVE OUT! EVERYBODY TO POSITION!
WE'VE GOT A CHANGE OF PLAN!
WHADDA WE DO? WE AIN'T READY--
BAM
BAM BAM
BAM
BAM
BAM
JUST START FIRING, BUDDY!
THEY MIGHT ONLY BE RUBBER BULLETS, BUT THEY STILL *HURT* LIKE HELL.

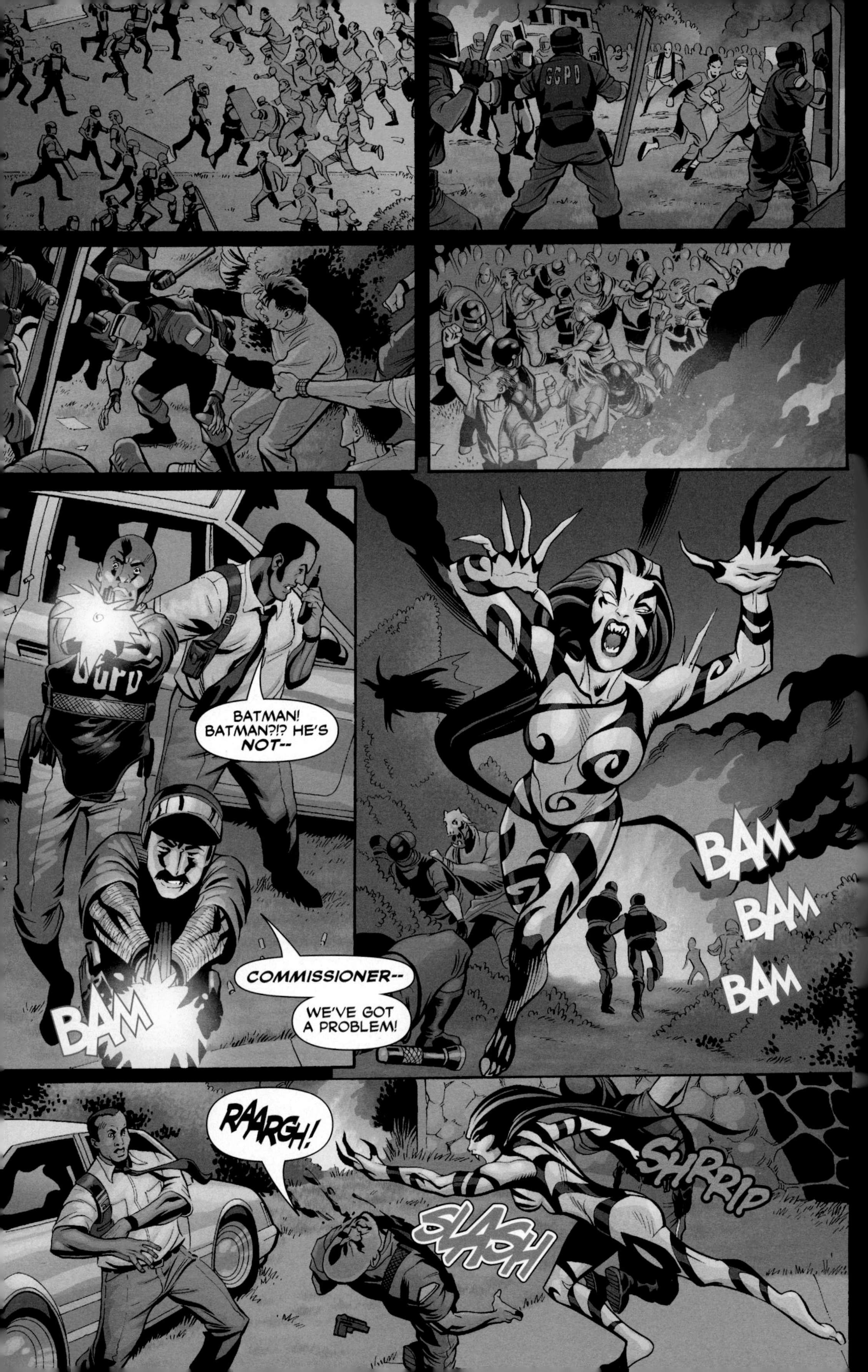
GCPD
BATMAN! BATMAN?!? HE'S NOT--
COMMISSIONER--
WE'VE GOT A PROBLEM!
BAM
BAM
BAM
BAM
RAARGH!
SHRRIP
SLASH

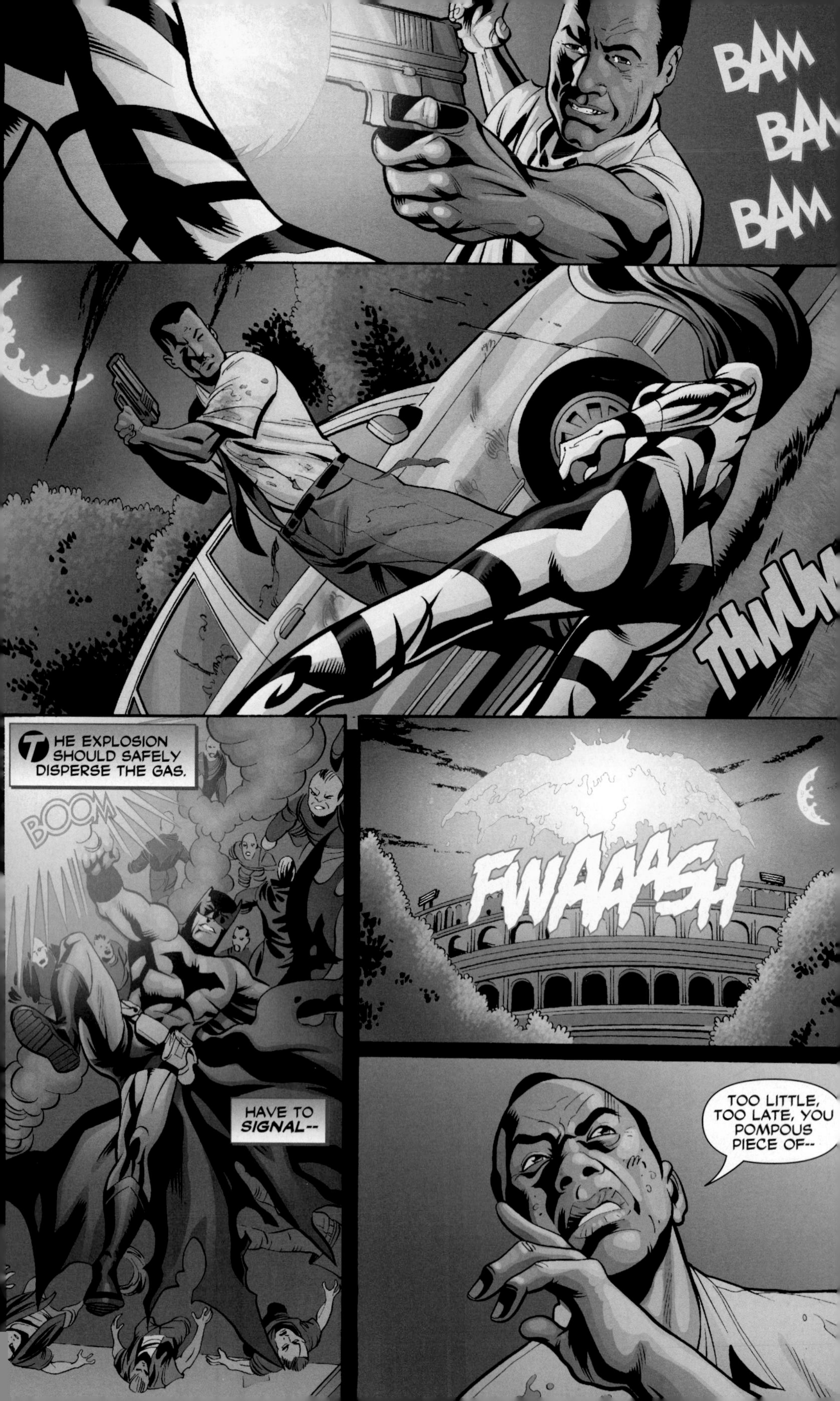
BAM
BAM
BAM
THWUMP
THE EXPLOSION SHOULD SAFELY DISPERSE THE GAS.
BOOM
FWAAASH
HAVE TO SIGNAL--
TOO LITTLE, TOO LATE, YOU POMPOUS PIECE OF--

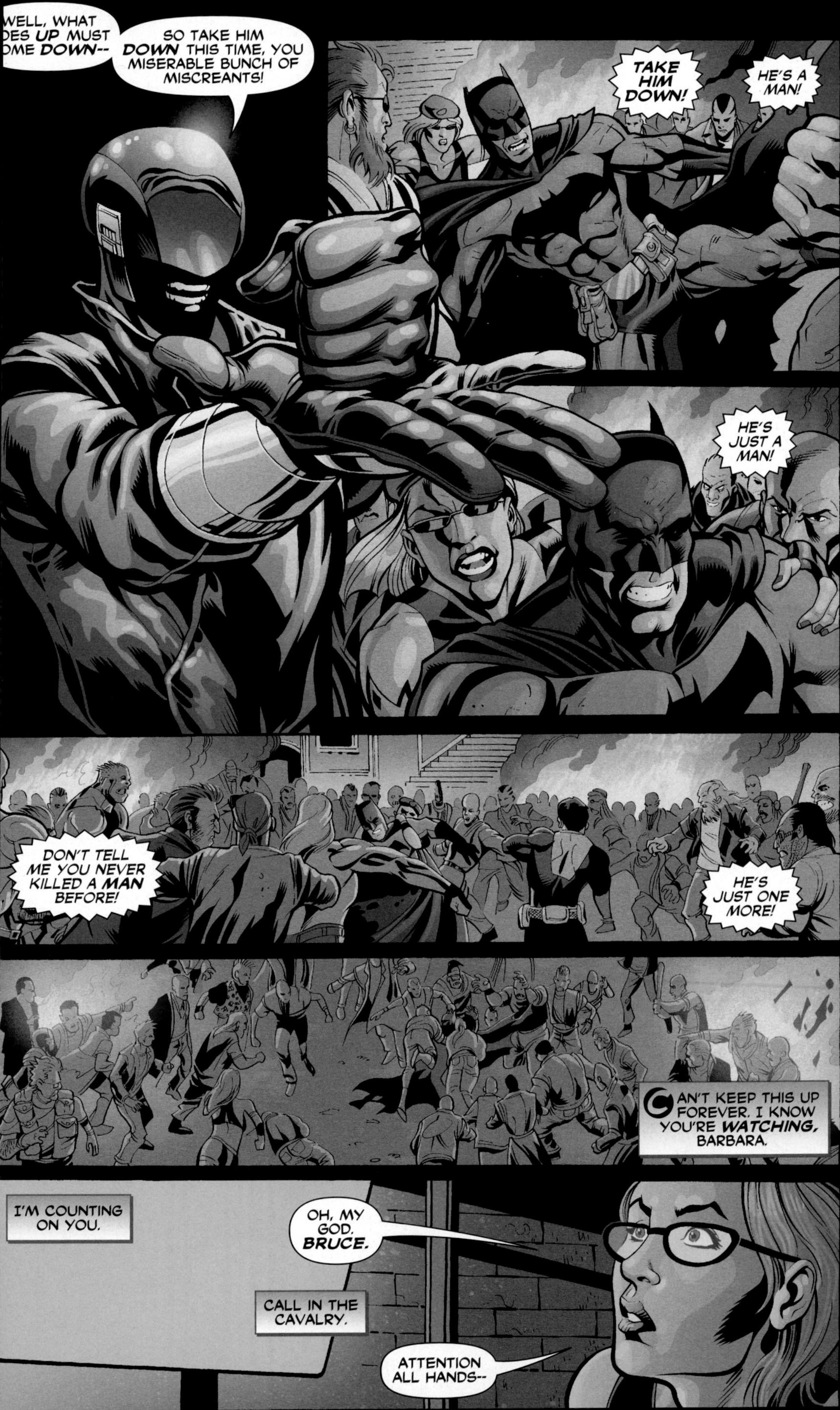
WELL, WHAT
DES UP MUST
OME DOWN--
SO TAKE HIM DOWN THIS TIME, YOU MISERABLE BUNCH OF MISCREANTS!
TAKE HIM DOWN!
HE'S A MAN!
HE'S JUST A MAN!
DON'T TELL ME YOU NEVER KILLED A MAN BEFORE!
HE'S JUST ONE MORE!
CAN'T KEEP THIS UP FOREVER. I KNOW YOU'RE WATCHING, BARBARA.
I'M COUNTING ON YOU.
OH, MY GOD. BRUCE.
CALL IN THE CAVALRY.
ATTENTION ALL HANDS--

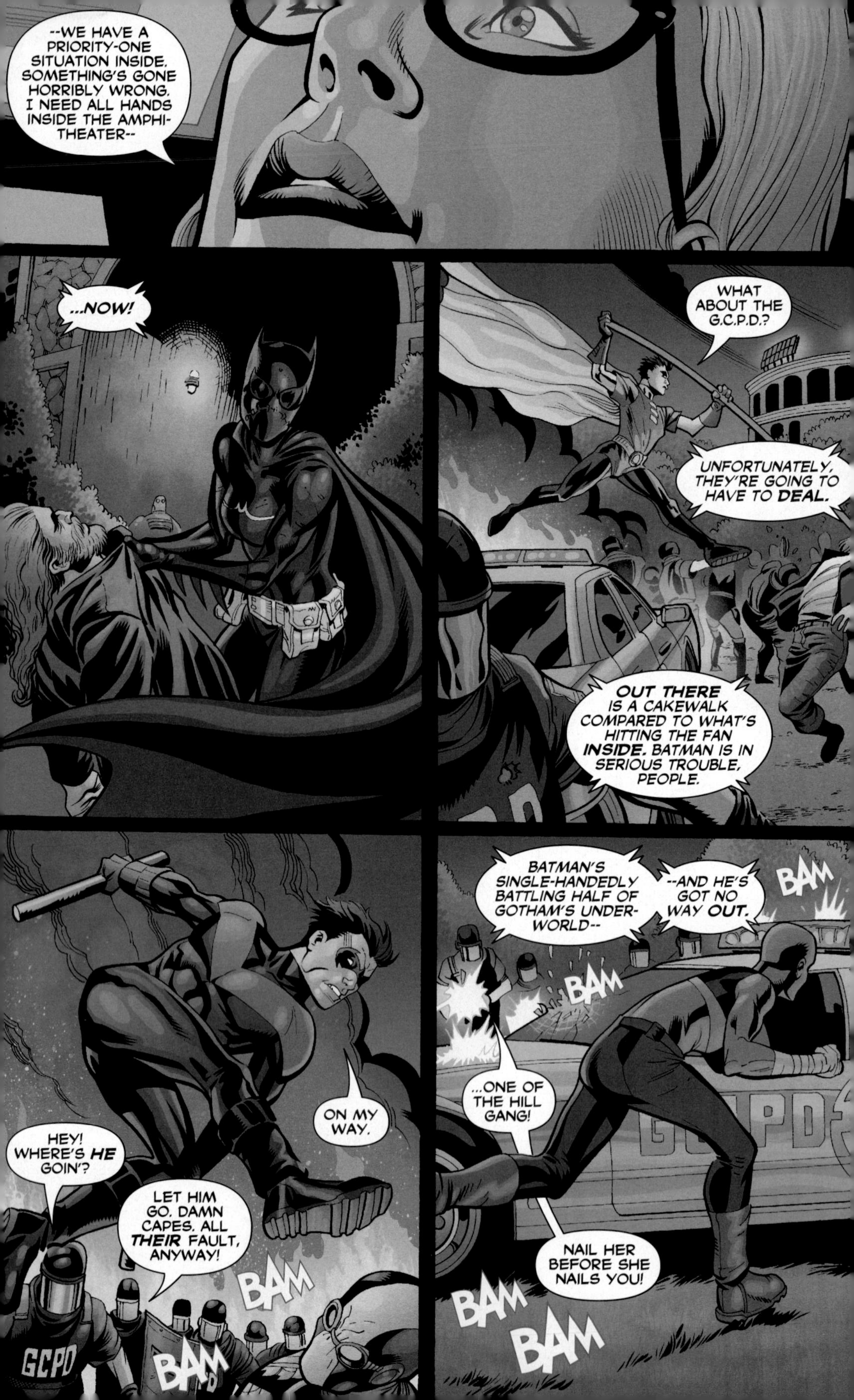
--WE HAVE A PRIORITY-ONE SITUATION INSIDE. SOMETHING'S GONE HORRIBLY WRONG. I NEED ALL HANDS INSIDE THE AMPHI-THEATER--
...NOW!
WHAT ABOUT THE G.C.P.D.?
UNFORTUNATELY, THEY'RE GOING TO HAVE TO DEAL.
OUT THERE IS A CAKEWALK COMPARED TO WHAT'S HITTING THE FAN INSIDE. BATMAN IS IN SERIOUS TROUBLE, PEOPLE.
ON MY WAY.
HEY! WHERE'S HE GOIN'?
LET HIM GO. DAMN CAPES. ALL THEIR FAULT, ANYWAY!
BAM
BAM
GCPD
BATMAN'S SINGLE-HANDEDLY BATTLING HALF OF GOTHAM'S UNDER-WORLD--
--AND HE'S GOT NO WAY OUT.
BAM
BAM
...ONE OF THE HILL GANG!
NAIL HER BEFORE SHE NAILS YOU!
BAM
BAM
GCPD

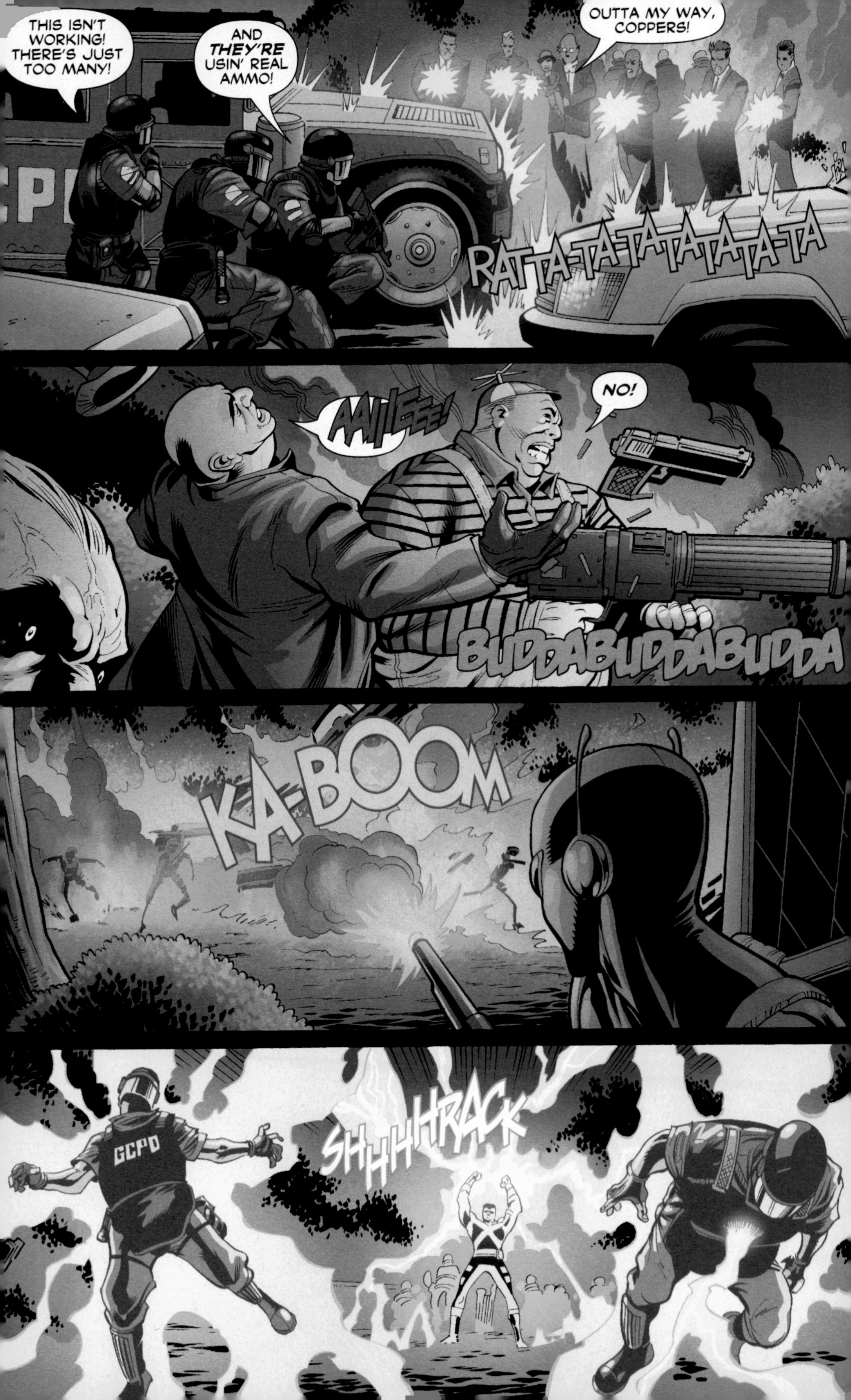
THIS ISN'T WORKING! THERE'S JUST TOO MANY!
AND THEY'RE USIN' REAL AMMO!
OUTTA MY WAY, COPPERS!
RATTA-TA-TA-TA-TA-TA-TA-TA
AAIIEEE!
NO!
BUDDABUDDABUDDA
KA-BOOM
GCPD
SHHHHRACK

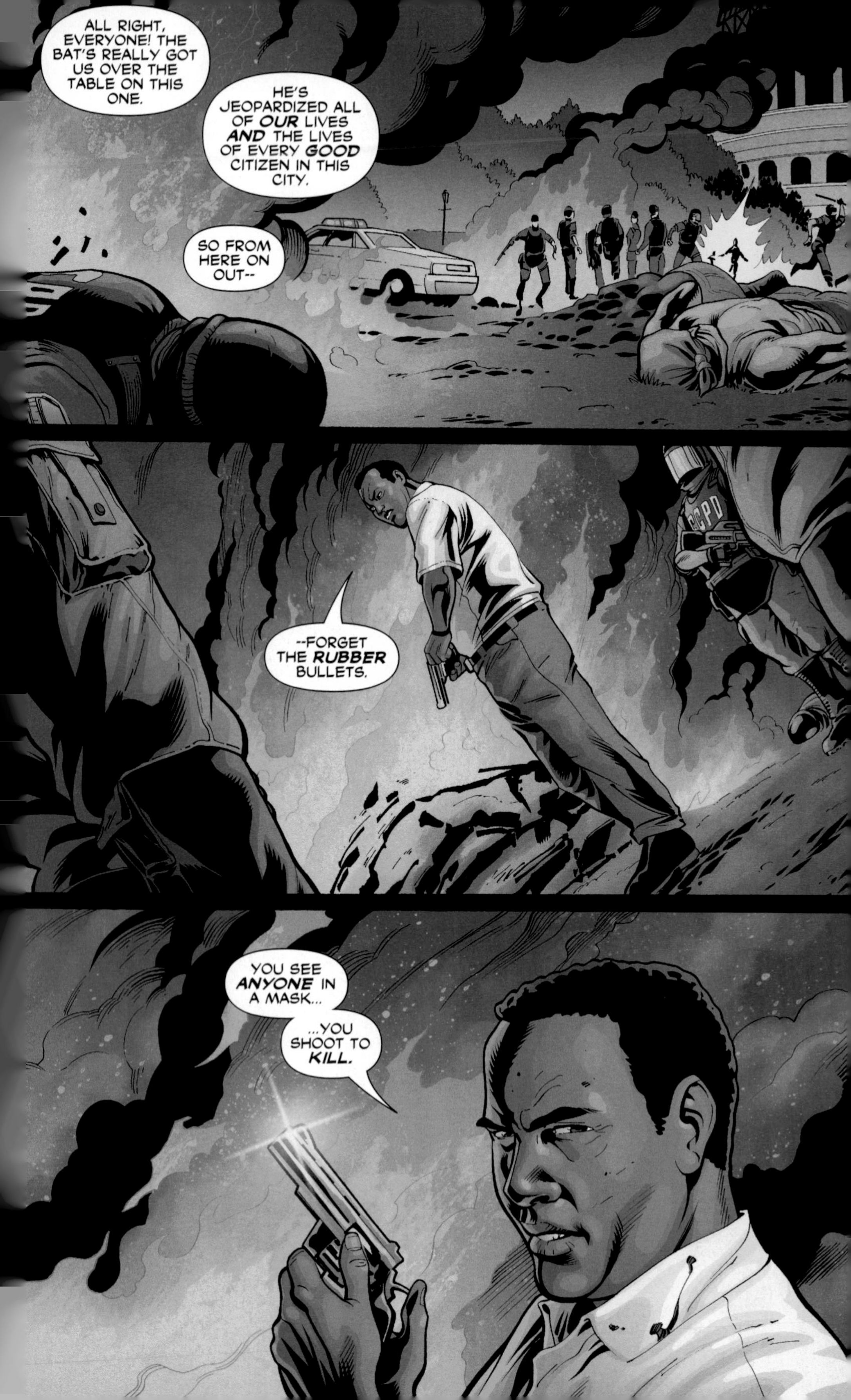
ALL RIGHT, EVERYONE! THE BAT'S REALLY GOT US OVER THE TABLE ON THIS ONE.
HE'S JEOPARDIZED ALL OF OUR LIVES AND THE LIVES OF EVERY GOOD CITIZEN IN THIS CITY.
SO FROM HERE ON OUT--
--FORGET THE RUBBER BULLETS.
YOU SEE ANYONE IN A MASK...
...YOU SHOOT TO KILL.

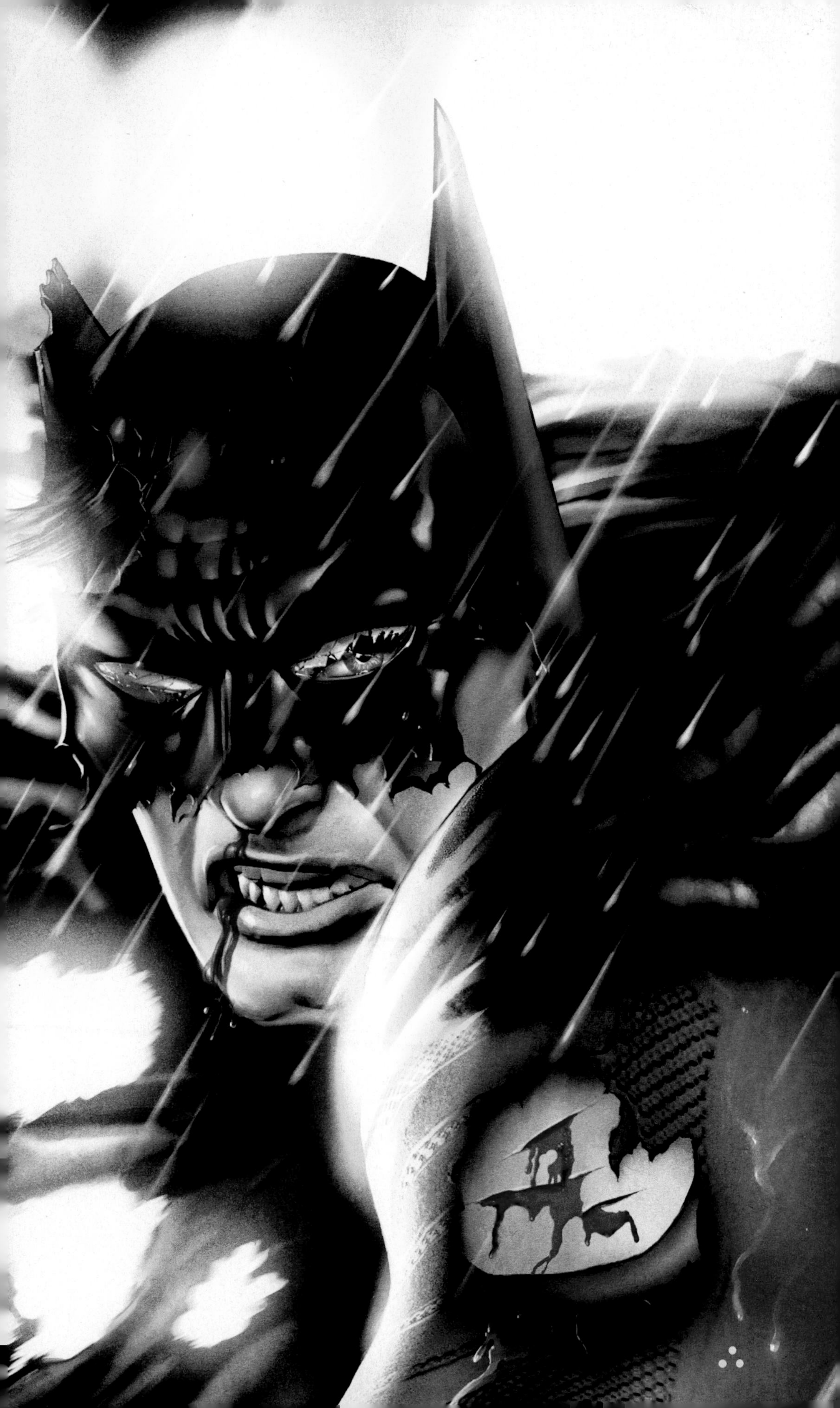

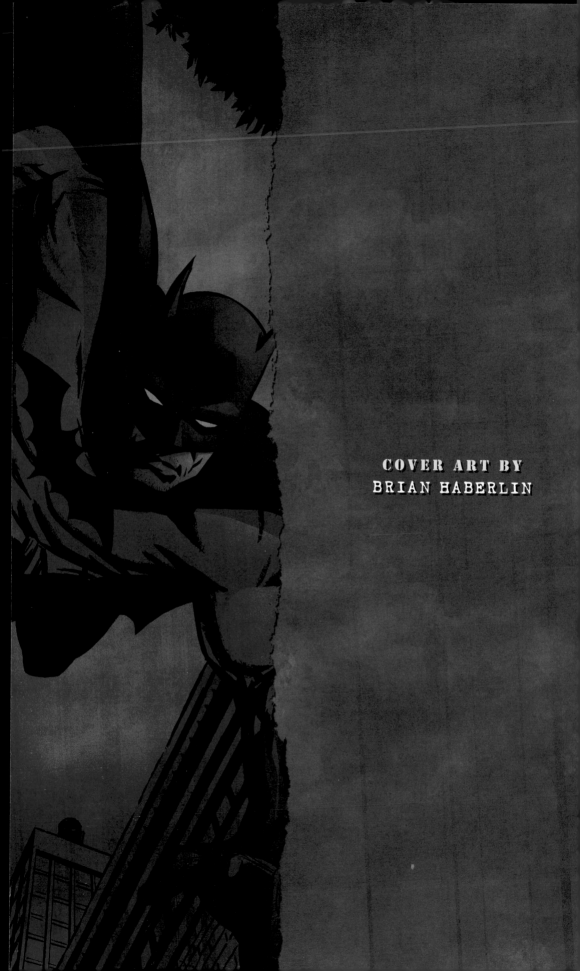

COVER ART BY
BRIAN HABERLIN

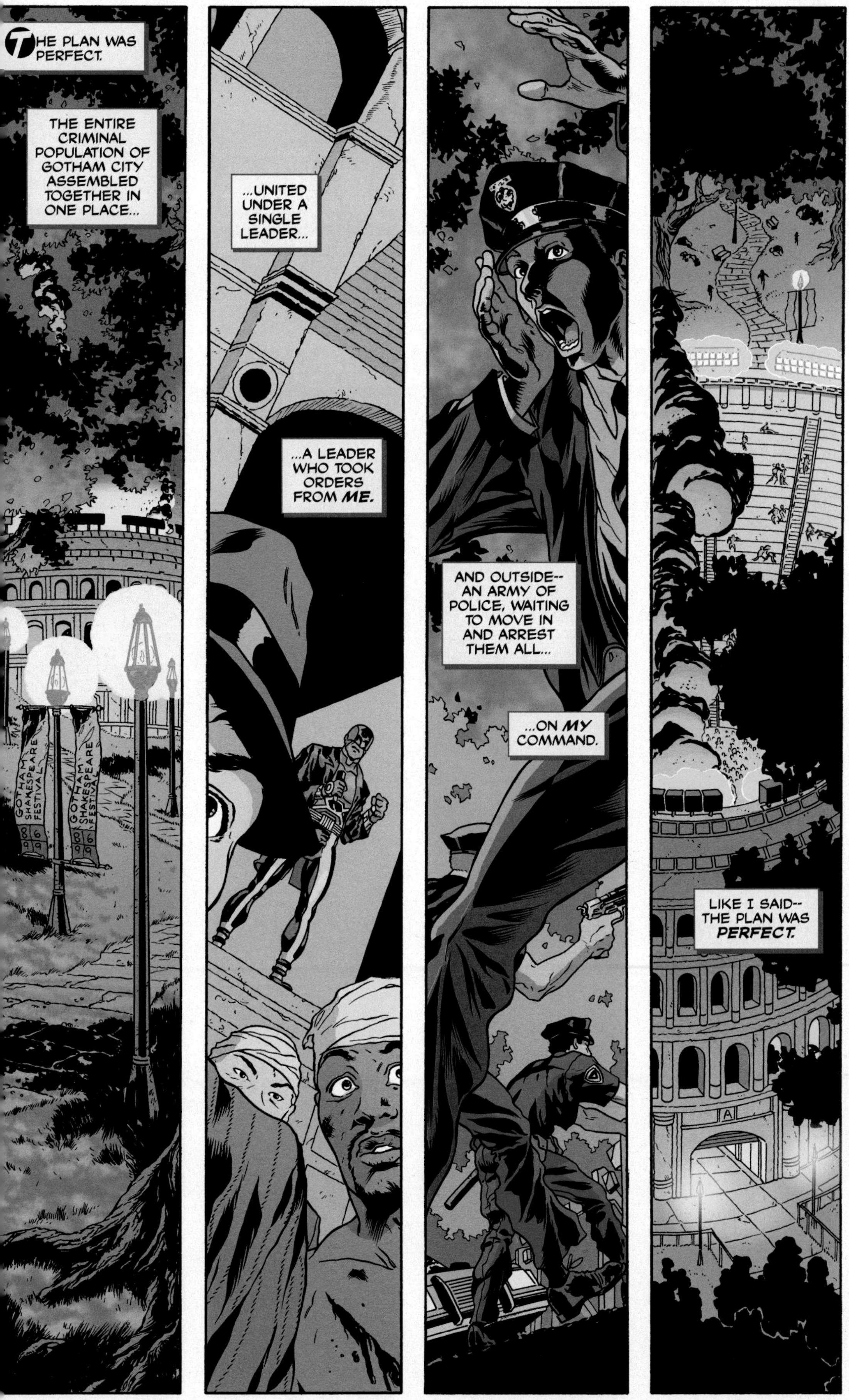
THE PLAN WAS PERFECT.
THE ENTIRE CRIMINAL POPULATION OF GOTHAM CITY ASSEMBLED TOGETHER IN ONE PLACE...
GOTHAM SHAKESPEARE FESTIVAL 8 6 9 9
GOTHAM SHAKESPEARE FESTIVAL 8 6 9 9
...UNITED UNDER A SINGLE LEADER...
...A LEADER WHO TOOK ORDERS FROM ME.
AND OUTSIDE-- AN ARMY OF POLICE, WAITING TO MOVE IN AND ARREST THEM ALL...
...ON MY COMMAND.
LIKE I SAID-- THE PLAN WAS PERFECT.

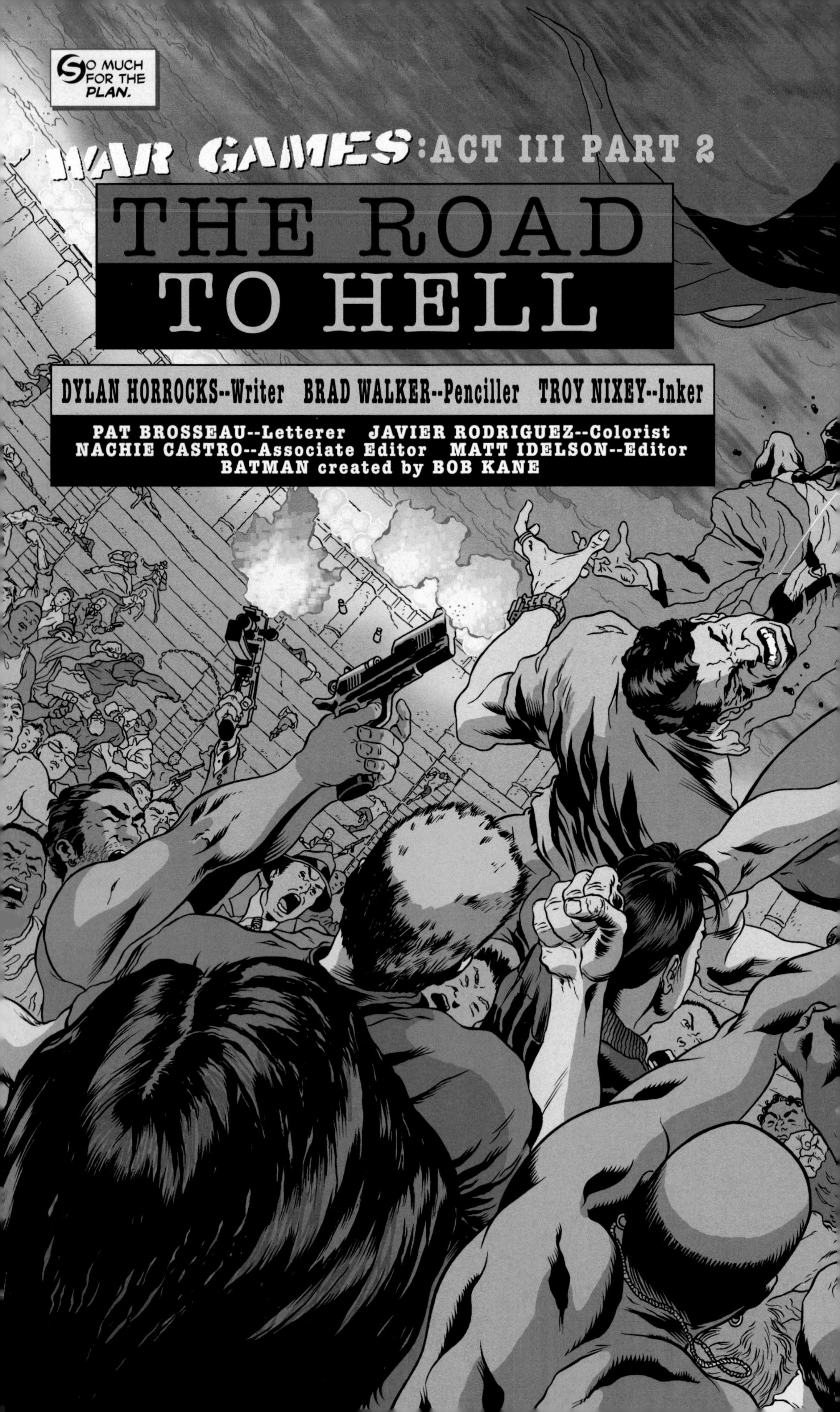

SO MUCH FOR THE PLAN.
WAR GAMES: ACT III PART 2
THE ROAD TO HELL
DYLAN HORROCKS--Writer BRAD WALKER--Penciller TROY NIXEY--Inker
PAT BROSSEAU--Letterer JAVIER RODRIGUEZ--Colorist
NACHIE CASTRO--Associate Editor MATT IDELSON--Editor
BATMAN created by BOB KANE

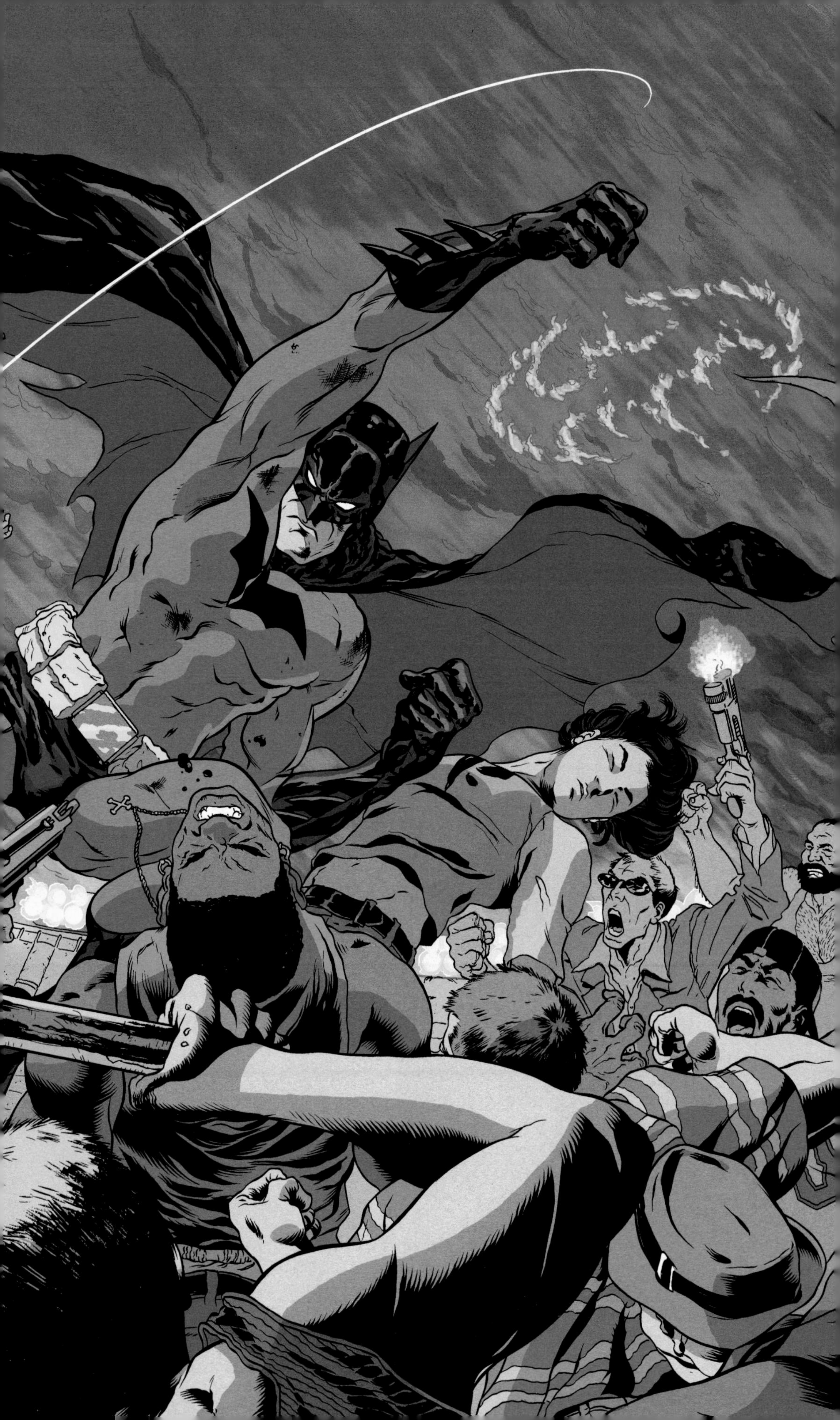

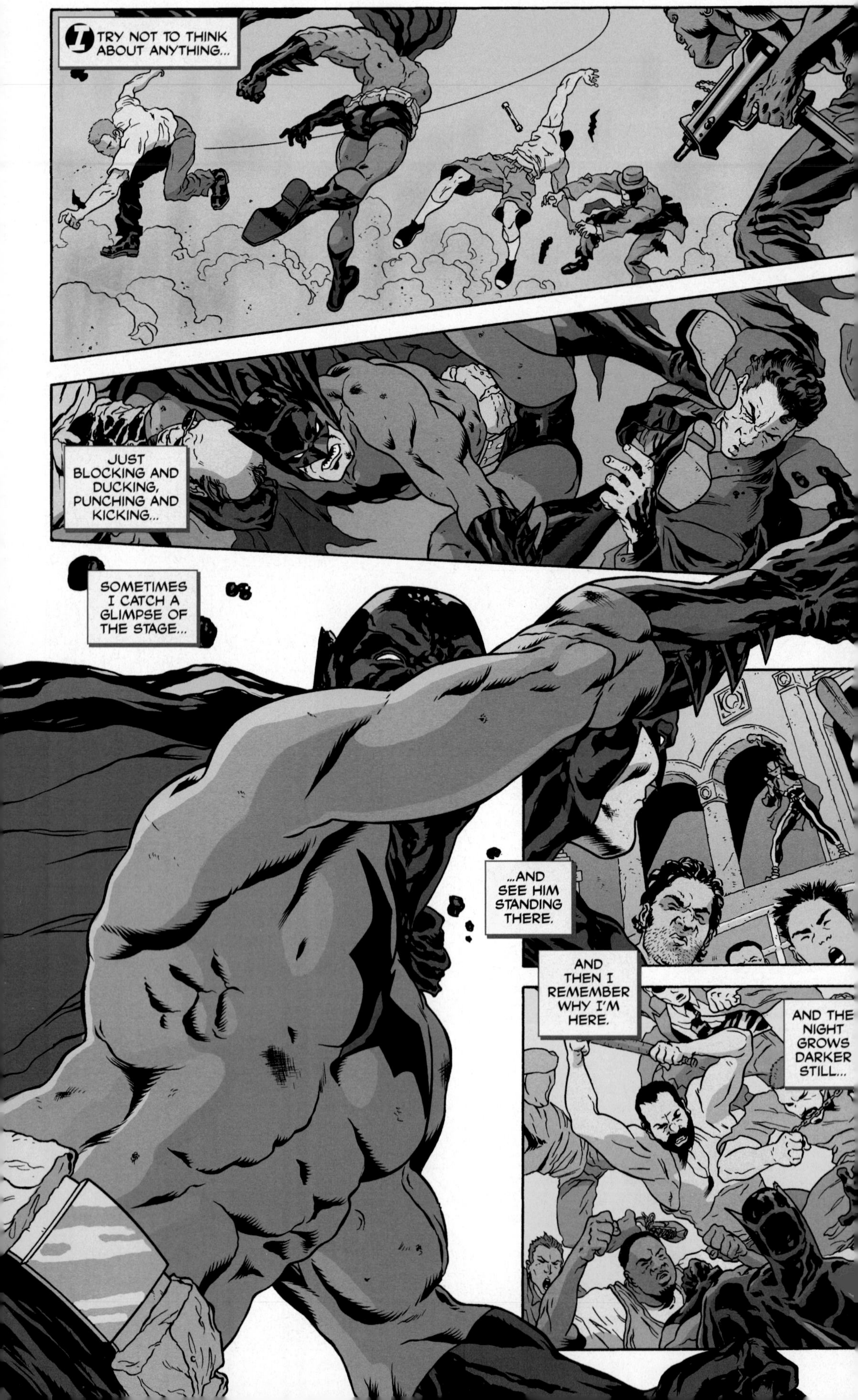
I TRY NOT TO THINK ABOUT ANYTHING...
JUST BLOCKING AND DUCKING, PUNCHING AND KICKING...
SOMETIMES I CATCH A GLIMPSE OF THE STAGE...
...AND SEE HIM STANDING THERE.
AND THEN I REMEMBER WHY I'M HERE.
AND THE NIGHT GROWS DARKER STILL...

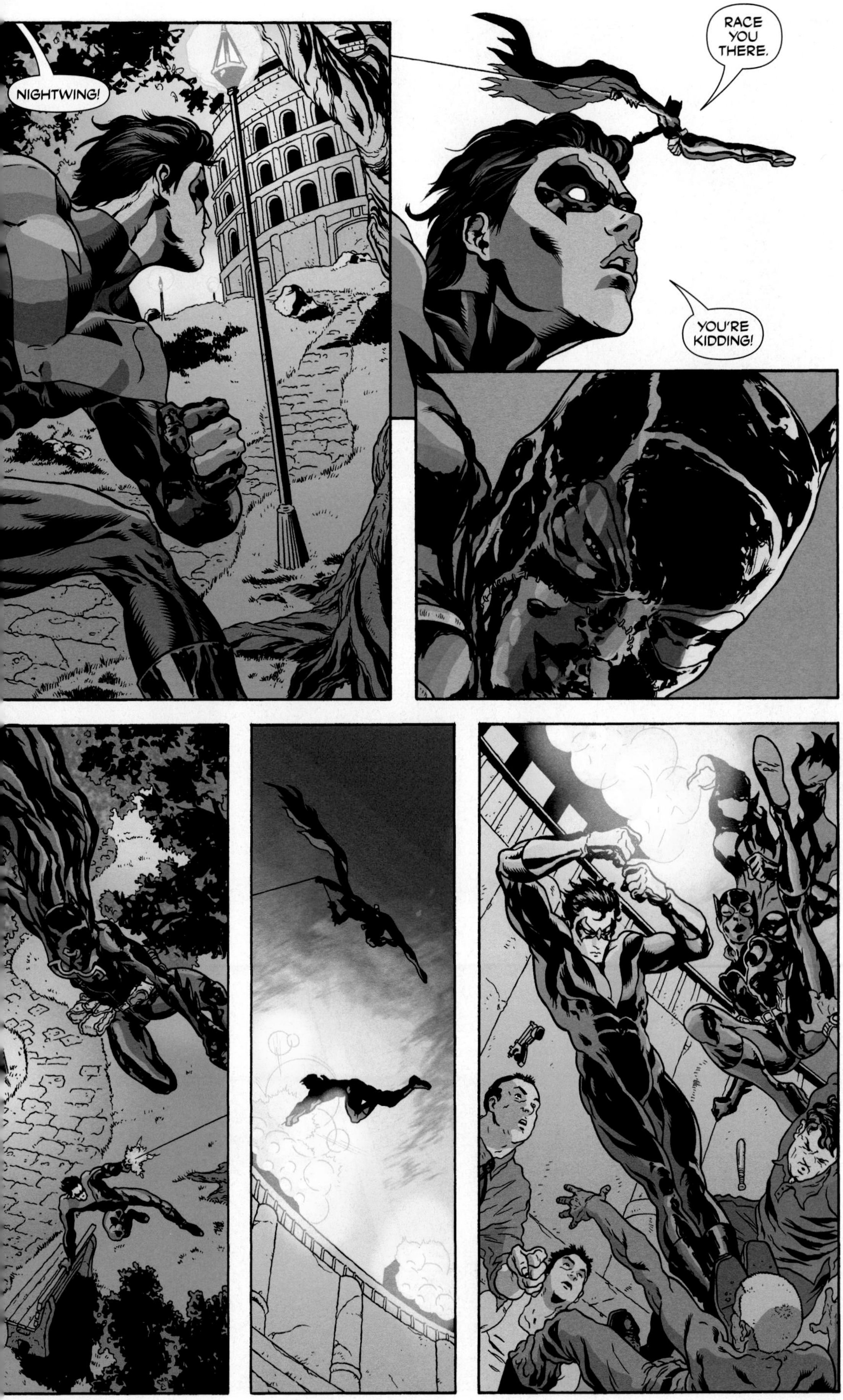
NIGHTWING!
RACE YOU THERE.
YOU'RE KIDDING!

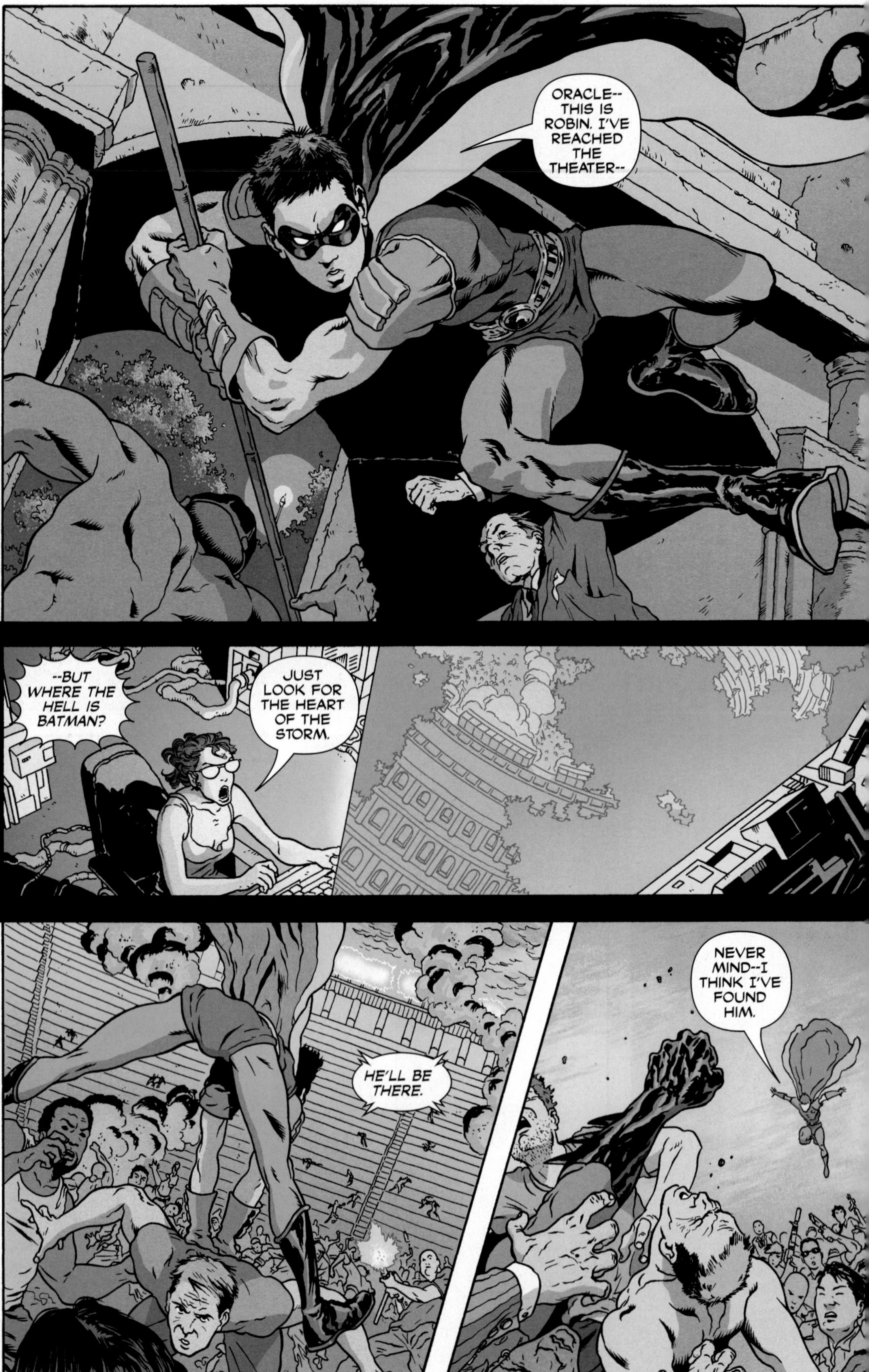
ORACLE-- THIS IS ROBIN. I'VE REACHED THE THEATER--
--BUT WHERE THE HELL IS BATMAN?
JUST LOOK FOR THE HEART OF THE STORM.
HE'LL BE THERE.
NEVER MIND--I THINK I'VE FOUND HIM.

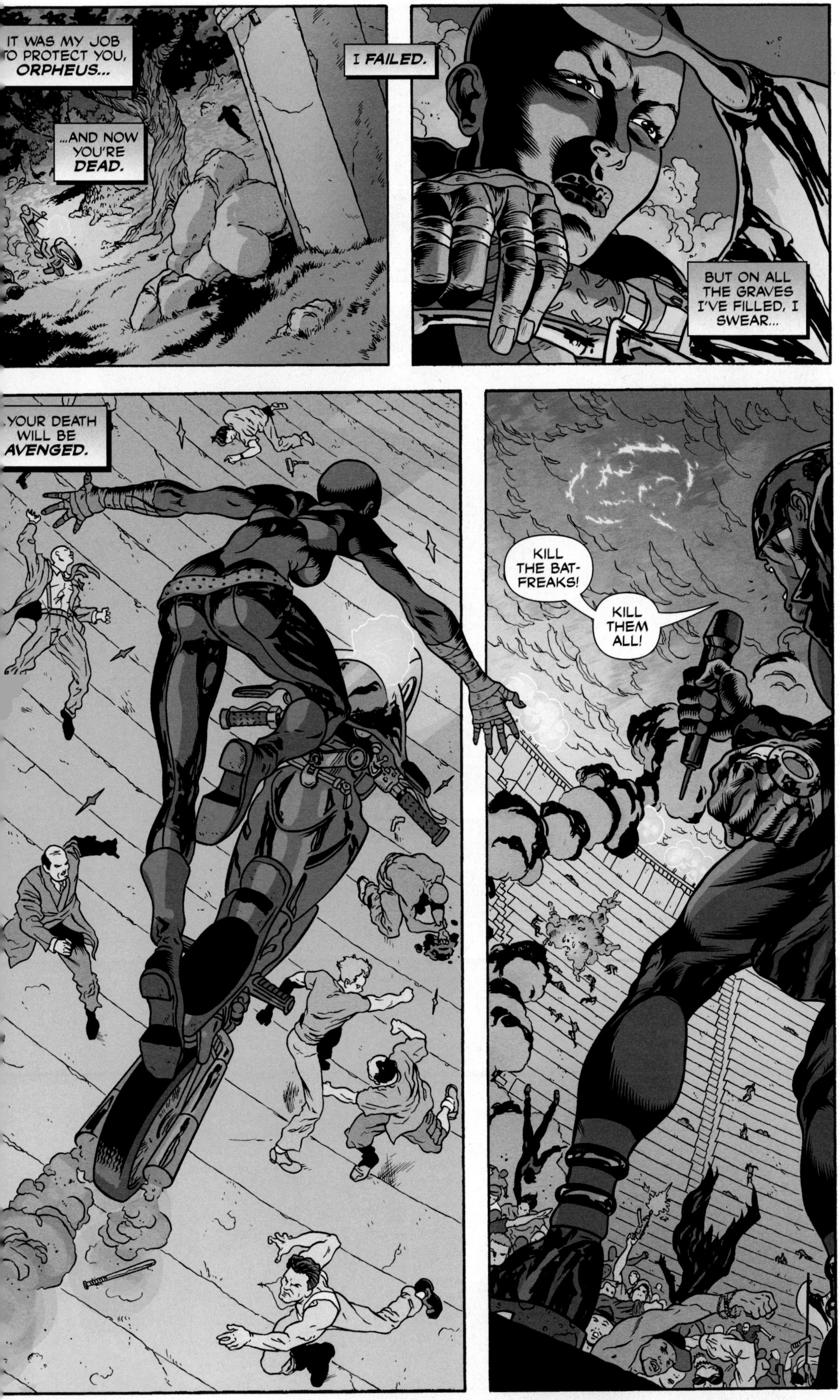
IT WAS MY JOB TO PROTECT YOU, ORPHEUS...
...AND NOW YOU'RE DEAD.
I FAILED.
BUT ON ALL THE GRAVES I'VE FILLED, I SWEAR...
YOUR DEATH WILL BE AVENGED.
KILL THE BAT-FREAKS!
KILL THEM ALL!

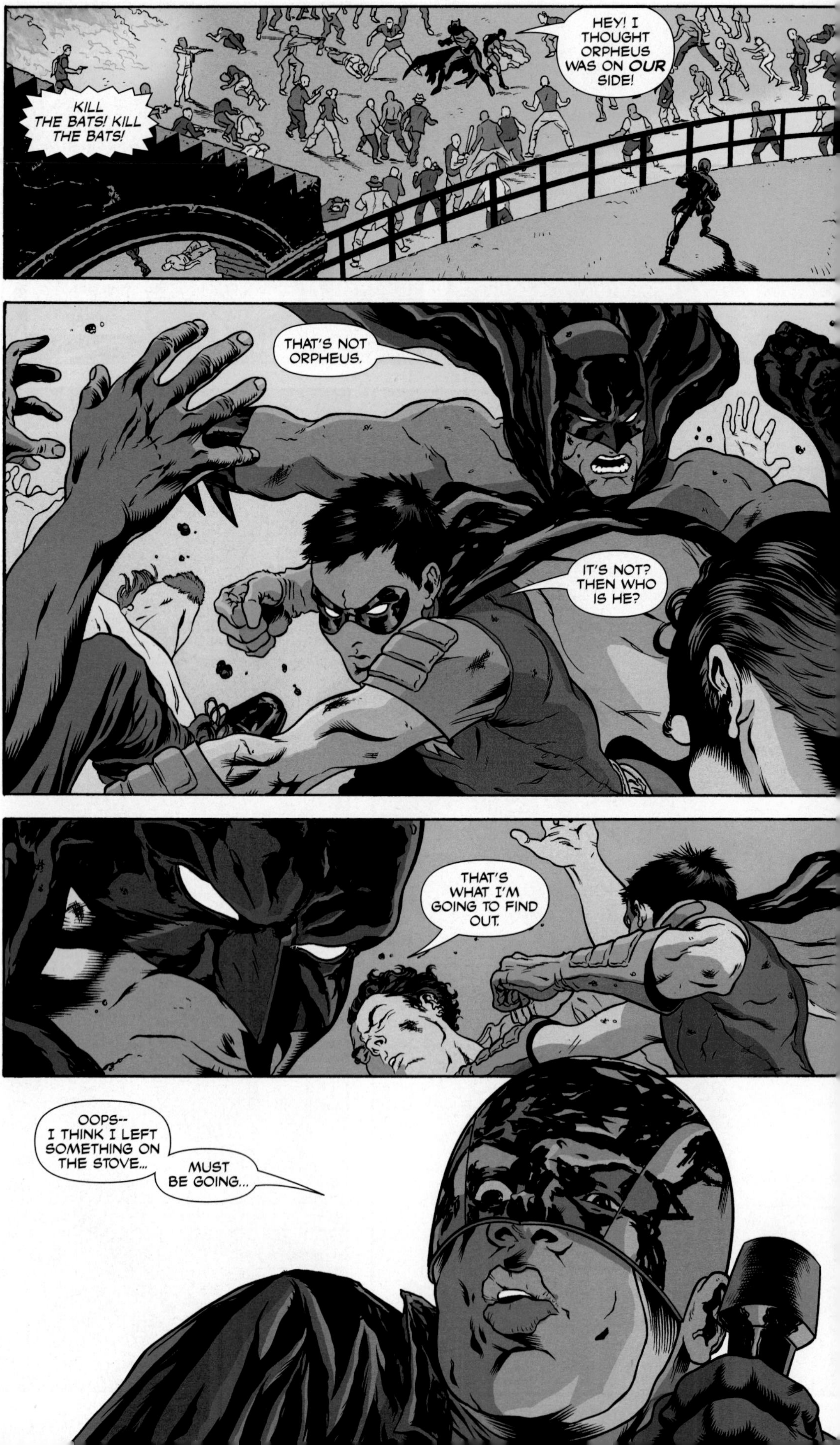
KILL THE BATS! KILL THE BATS!
HEY! I THOUGHT ORPHEUS WAS ON OUR SIDE!
THAT'S NOT ORPHEUS.
IT'S NOT? THEN WHO IS HE?
THAT'S WHAT I'M GOING TO FIND OUT.
OOPS-- I THINK I LEFT SOMETHING ON THE STOVE...
MUST BE GOING...

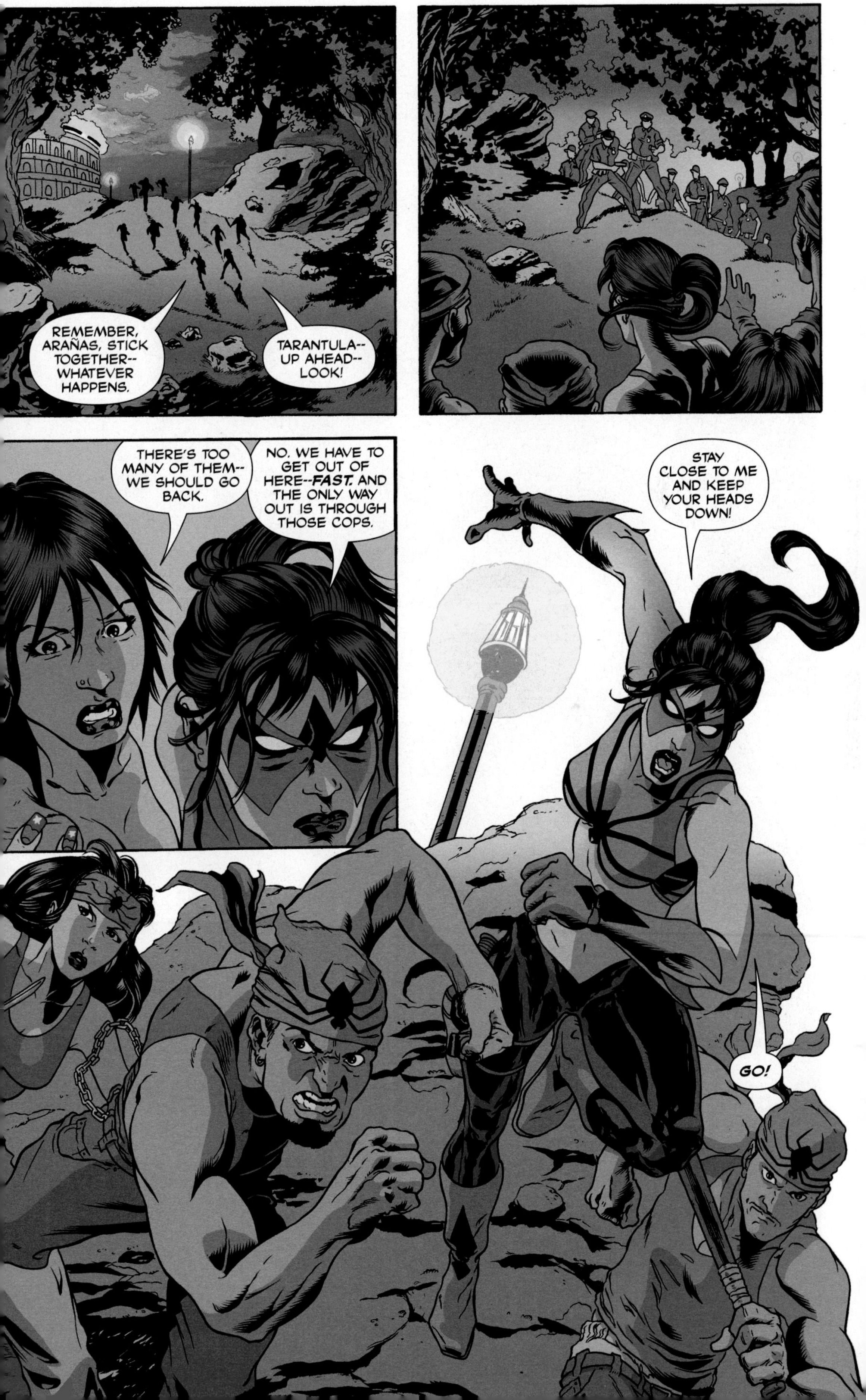

REMEMBER, ARAÑAS, STICK TOGETHER--WHATEVER HAPPENS.
TARANTULA--UP AHEAD--LOOK!
THERE'S TOO MANY OF THEM--WE SHOULD GO BACK.
NO. WE HAVE TO GET OUT OF HERE--**FAST.** AND THE ONLY WAY OUT IS THROUGH THOSE COPS.
STAY CLOSE TO ME AND KEEP YOUR HEADS DOWN!
GO!

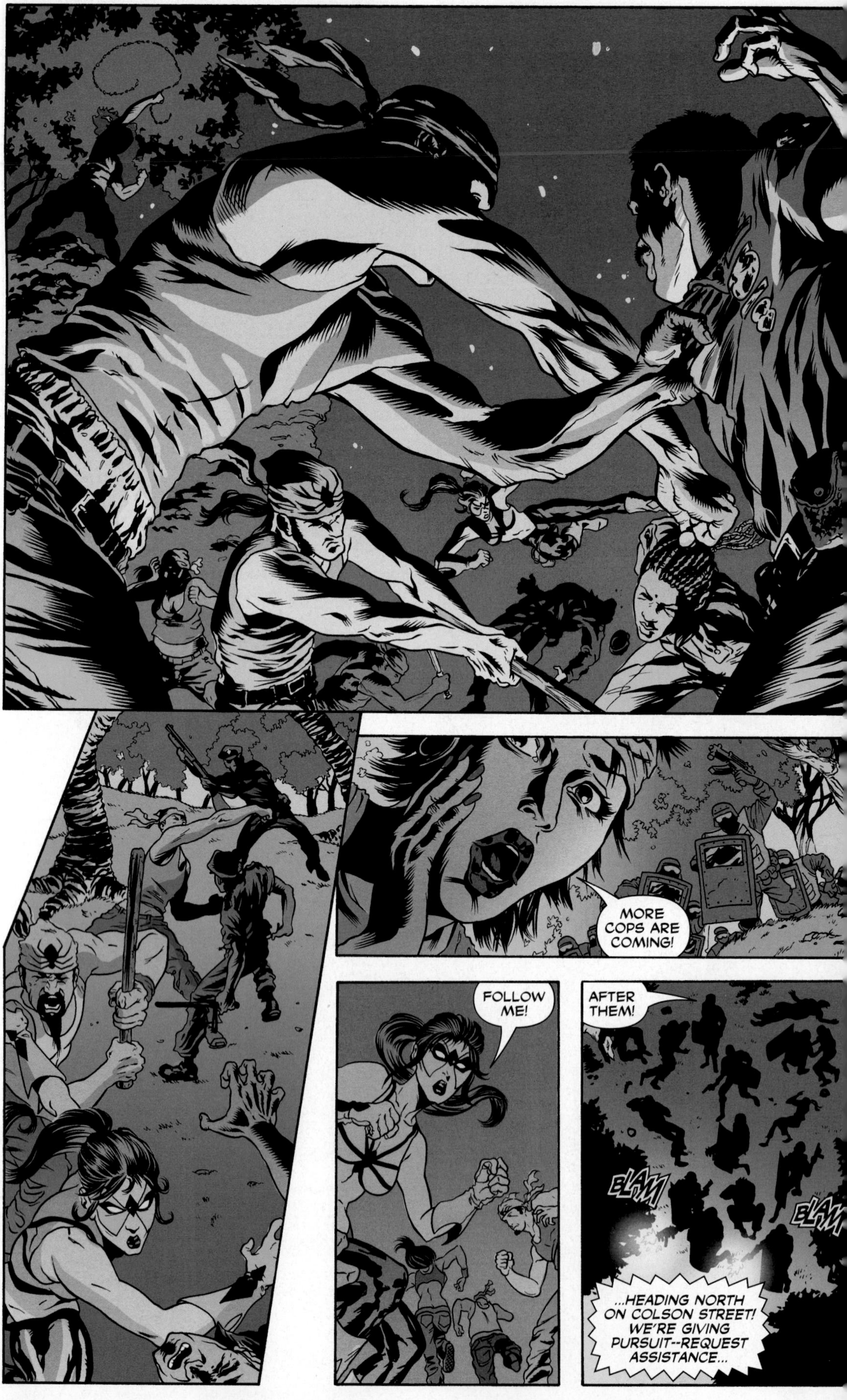
MORE COPS ARE COMING!
FOLLOW ME!
AFTER THEM!
BLAM
BLAM
...HEADING NORTH ON COLSON STREET! WE'RE GIVING PURSUIT--REQUEST ASSISTANCE...

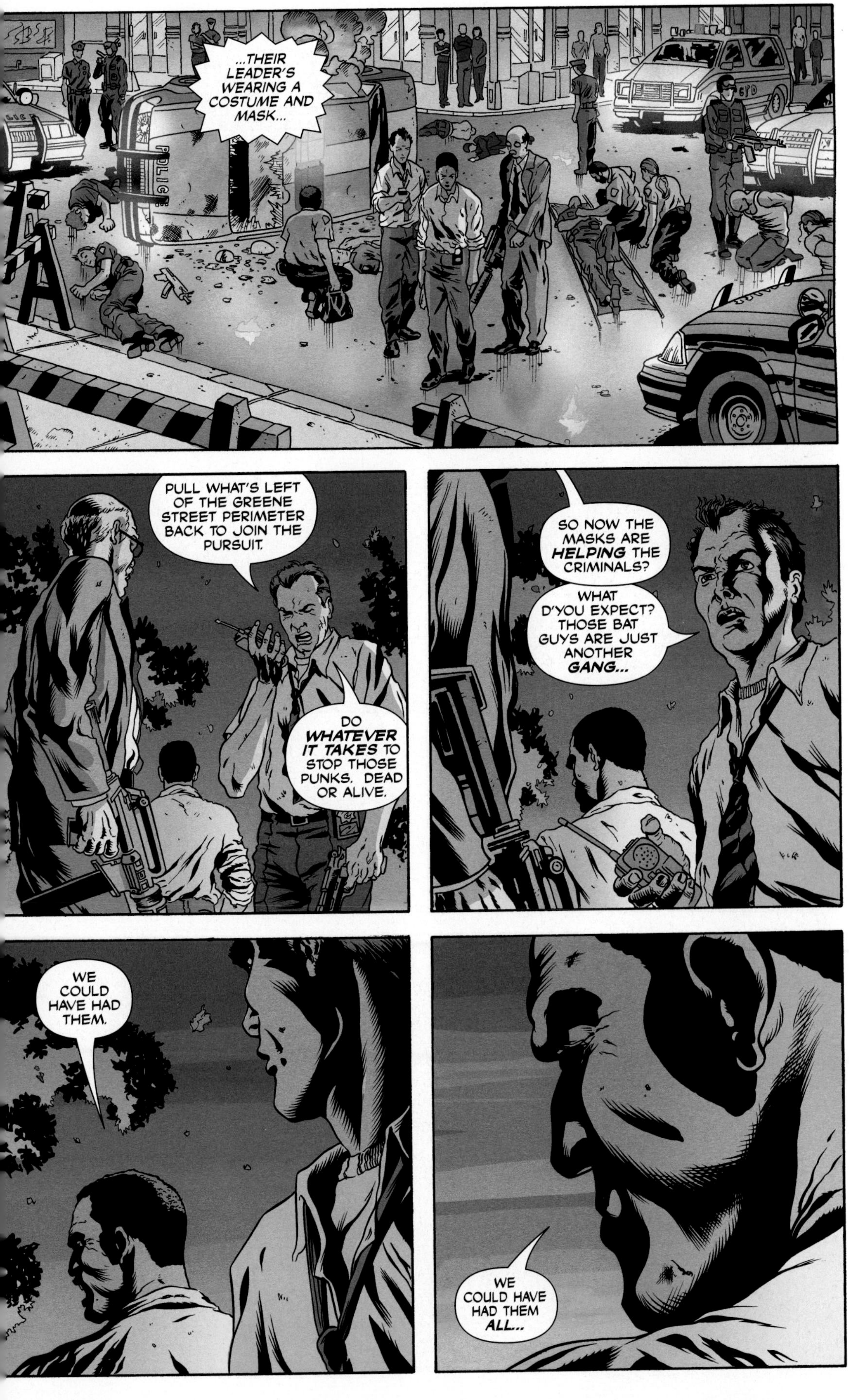
...THEIR LEADER'S WEARING A COSTUME AND MASK...
PULL WHAT'S LEFT OF THE GREENE STREET PERIMETER BACK TO JOIN THE PURSUIT.
DO WHATEVER IT TAKES TO STOP THOSE PUNKS. DEAD OR ALIVE.
SO NOW THE MASKS ARE HELPING THE CRIMINALS?
WHAT D'YOU EXPECT? THOSE BAT GUYS ARE JUST ANOTHER GANG...
WE COULD HAVE HAD THEM.
WE COULD HAVE HAD THEM ALL...

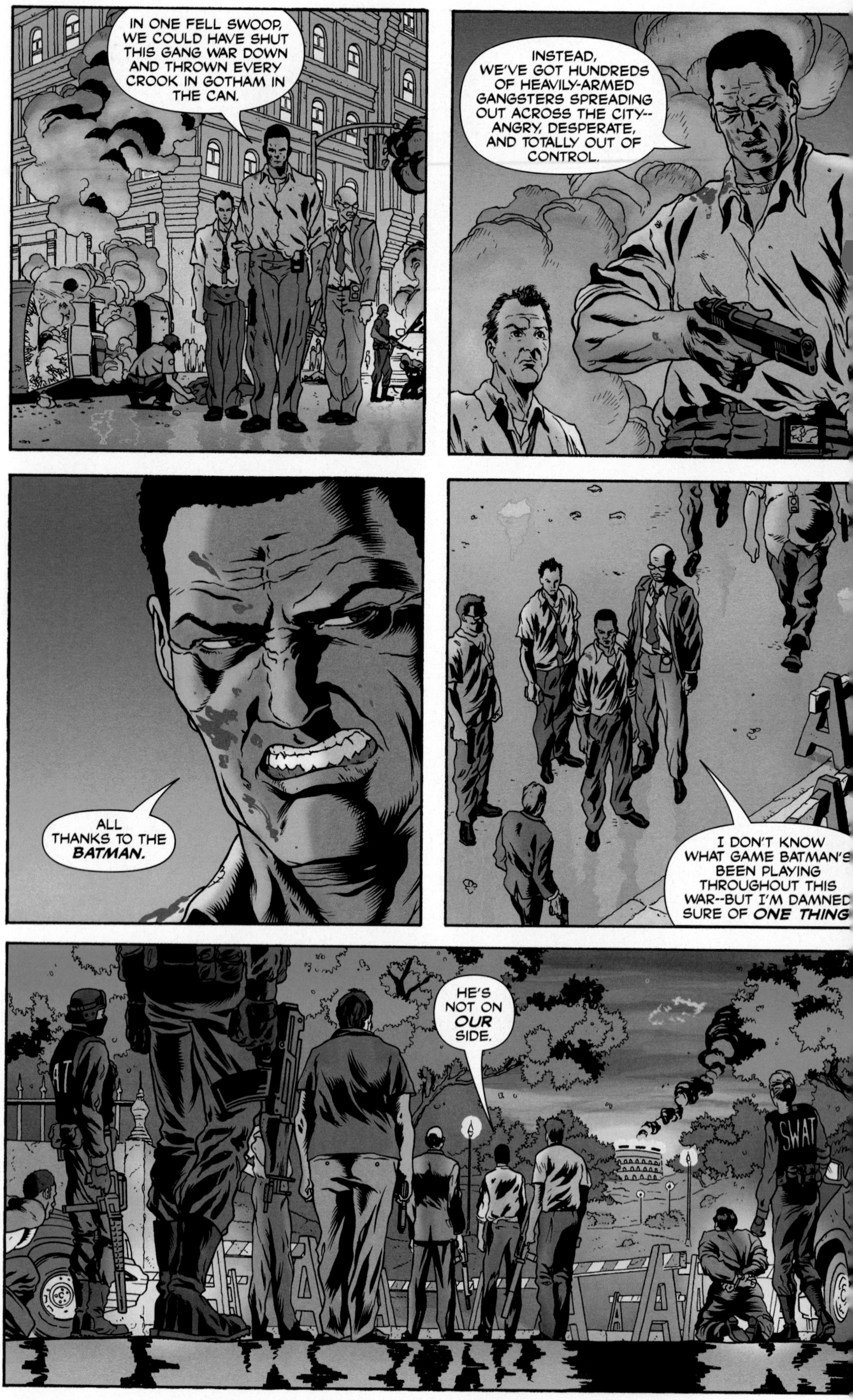
IN ONE FELL SWOOP, WE COULD HAVE SHUT THIS GANG WAR DOWN AND THROWN EVERY CROOK IN GOTHAM IN THE CAN.
INSTEAD, WE'VE GOT HUNDREDS OF HEAVILY-ARMED GANGSTERS SPREADING OUT ACROSS THE CITY-- ANGRY, DESPERATE, AND TOTALLY OUT OF CONTROL.
ALL THANKS TO THE BATMAN.
I DON'T KNOW WHAT GAME BATMAN'S BEEN PLAYING THROUGHOUT THIS WAR--BUT I'M DAMNED SURE OF ONE THING
HE'S NOT ON OUR SIDE.
SWAT

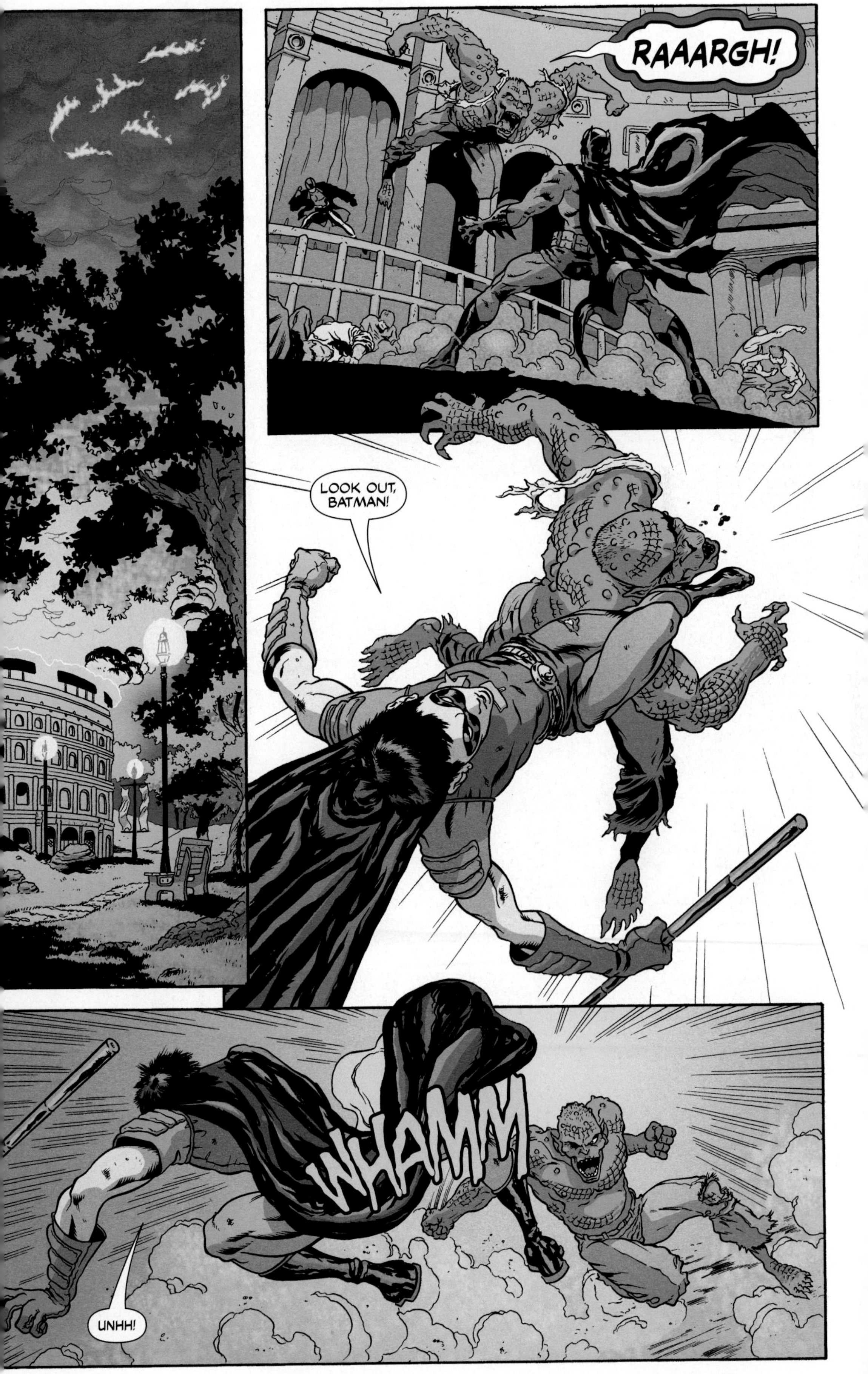
RAAARGH!
LOOK OUT, BATMAN!
WHAMM
UNHH!

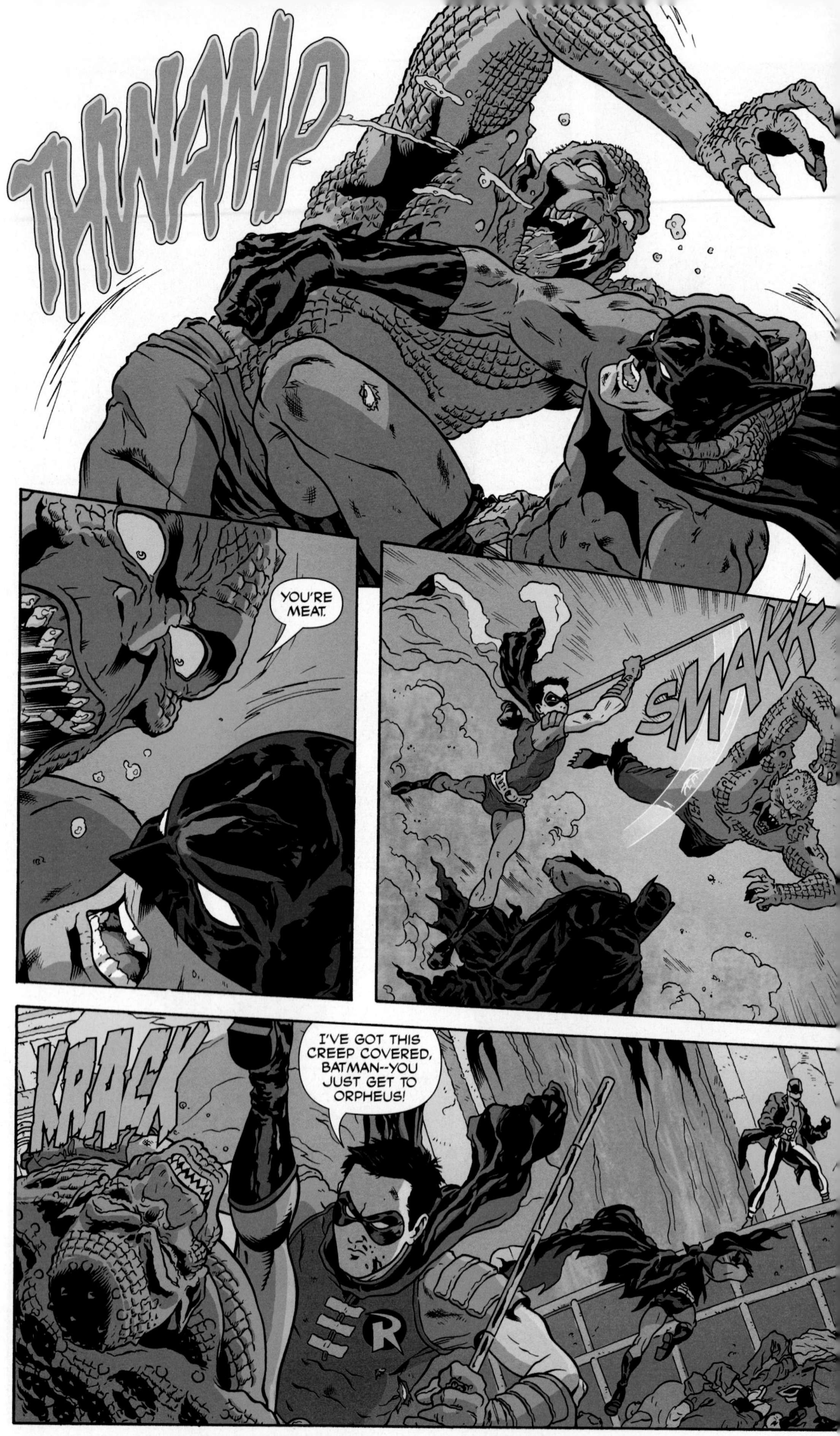
THWAMP
YOU'RE MEAT.
SMAKK
KRACK
I'VE GOT THIS CREEP COVERED, BATMAN--YOU JUST GET TO ORPHEUS!

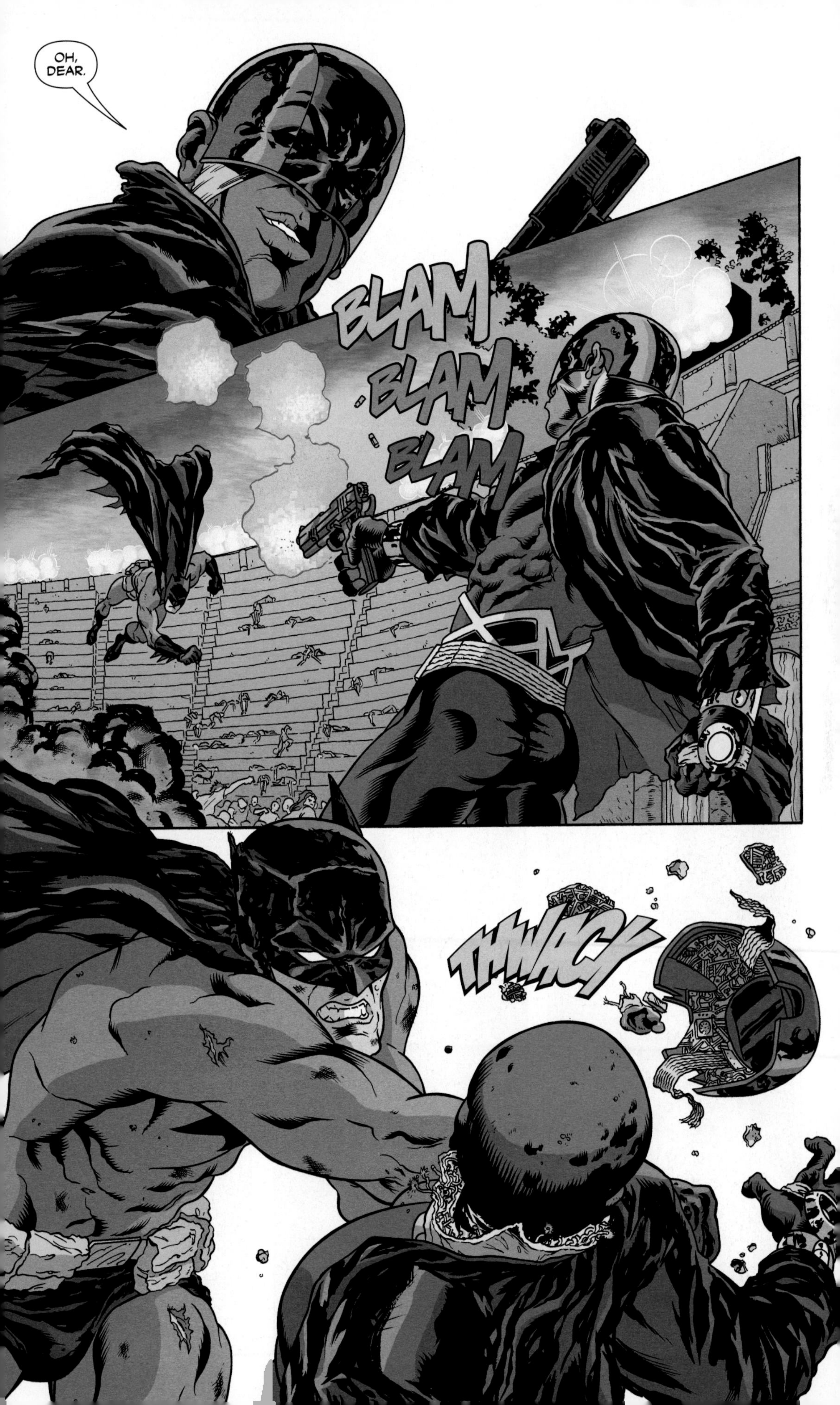
OH, DEAR.
BLAM
BLAM
BLAM
THWACK

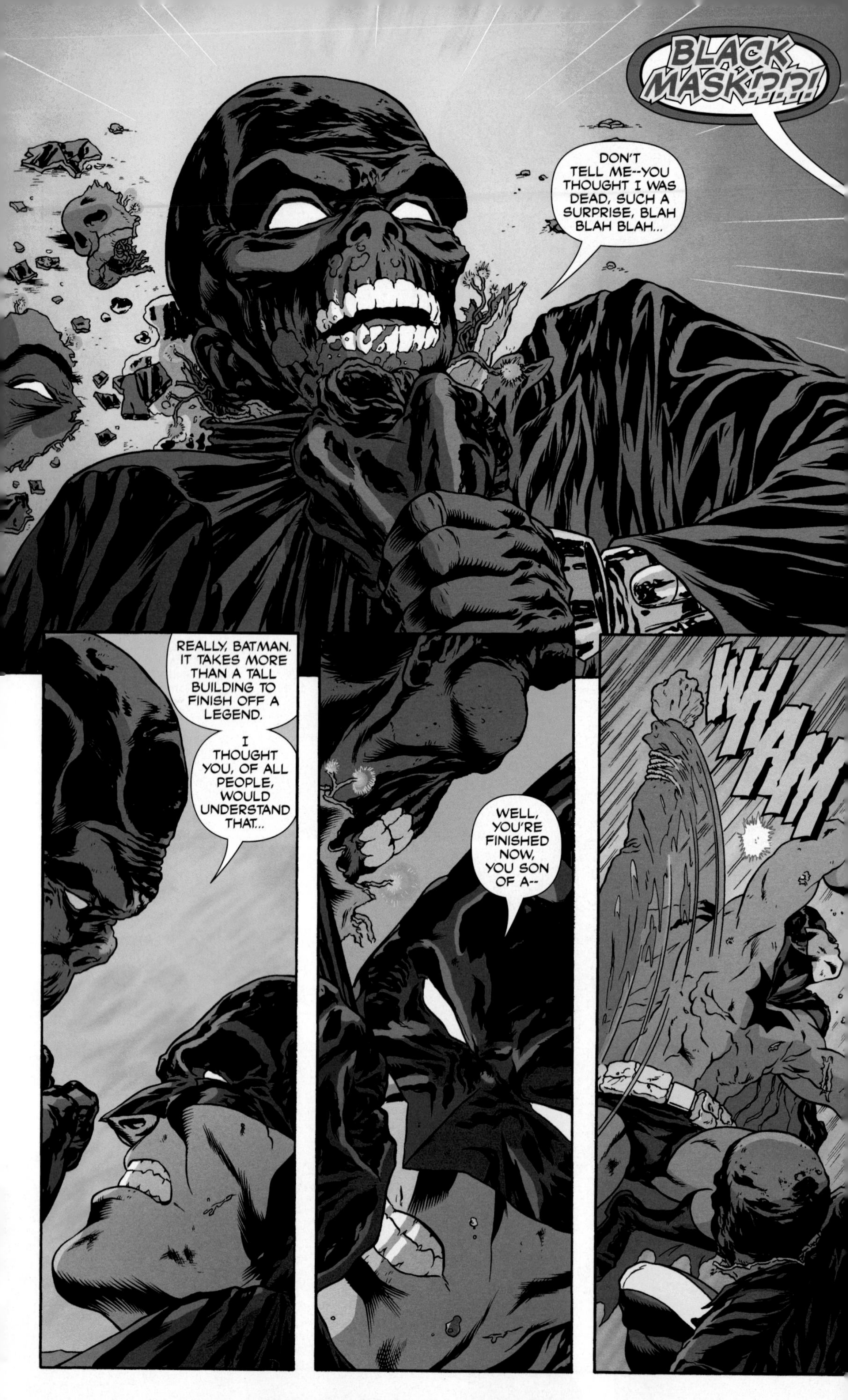
BLACK MASK!?!?!
DON'T TELL ME--YOU THOUGHT I WAS DEAD, SUCH A SURPRISE, BLAH BLAH BLAH...
REALLY, BATMAN. IT TAKES MORE THAN A TALL BUILDING TO FINISH OFF A LEGEND.
I THOUGHT YOU, OF ALL PEOPLE, WOULD UNDERSTAND THAT...
WELL, YOU'RE FINISHED NOW, YOU SON OF A--
WHAM

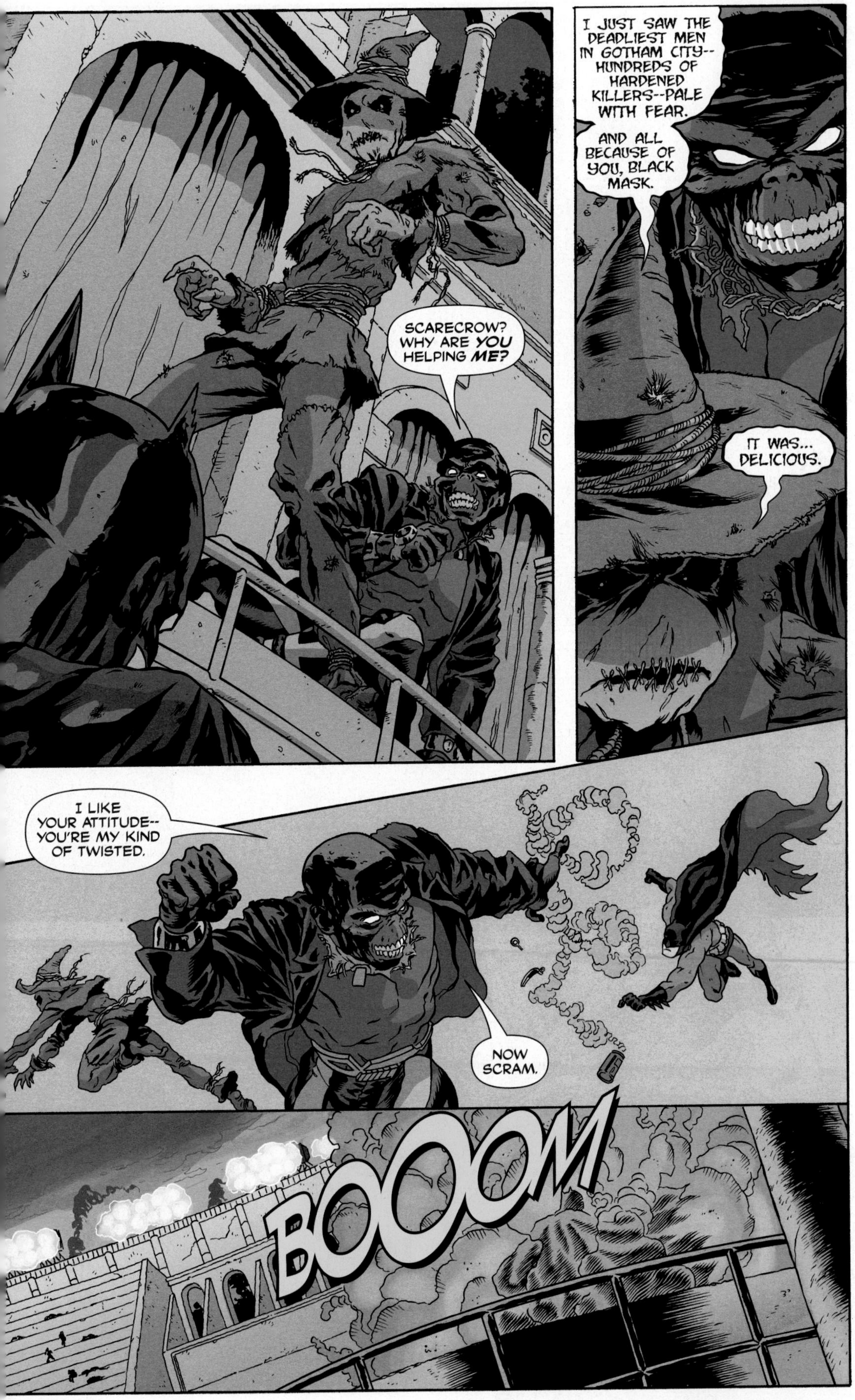
SCARECROW? WHY ARE YOU HELPING ME?
I JUST SAW THE DEADLIEST MEN IN GOTHAM CITY-- HUNDREDS OF HARDENED KILLERS--PALE WITH FEAR.
AND ALL BECAUSE OF YOU, BLACK MASK.
IT WAS... DELICIOUS.
I LIKE YOUR ATTITUDE-- YOU'RE MY KIND OF TWISTED.
NOW SCRAM.
BOOOM

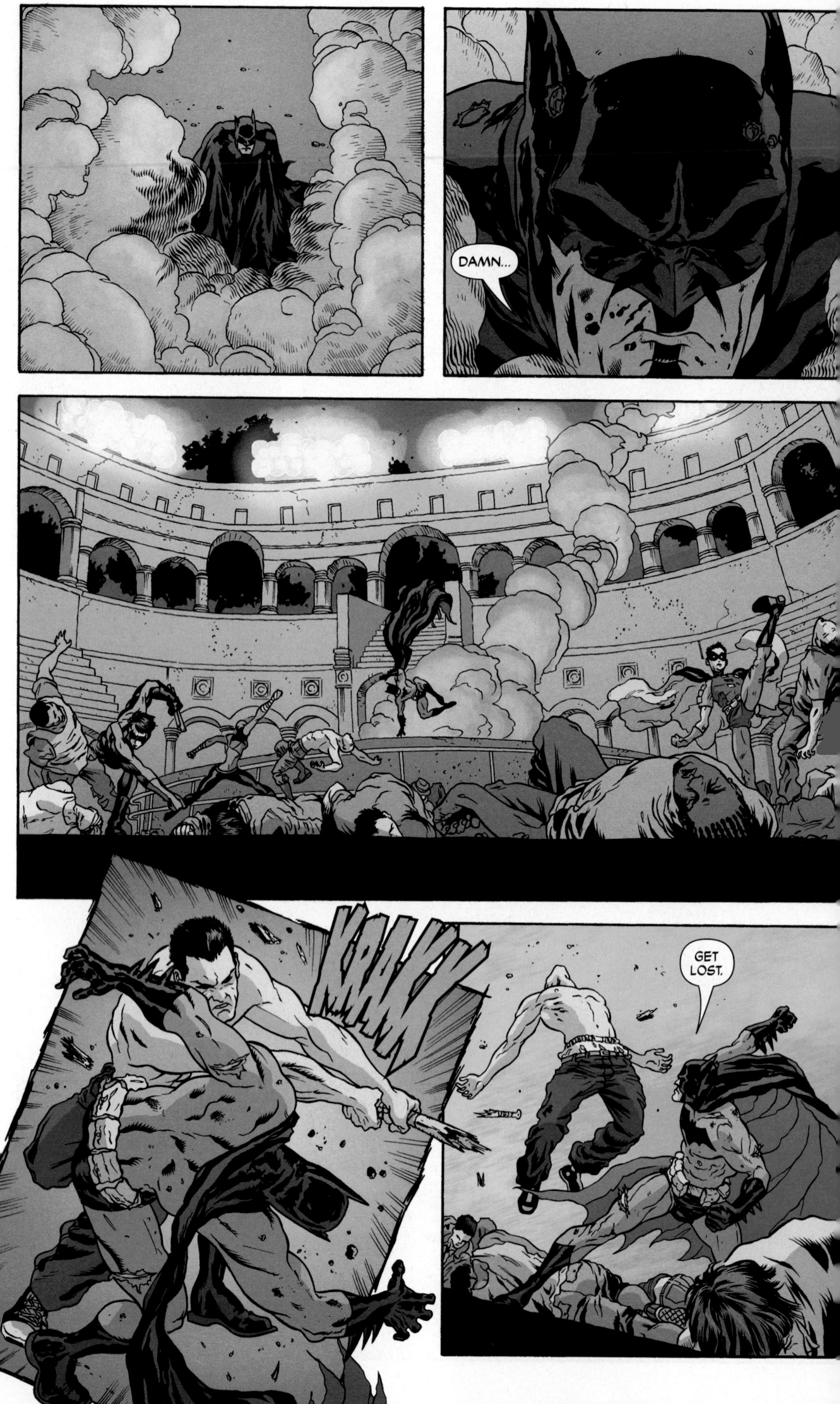
DAMN...
KRAKK
GET LOST.

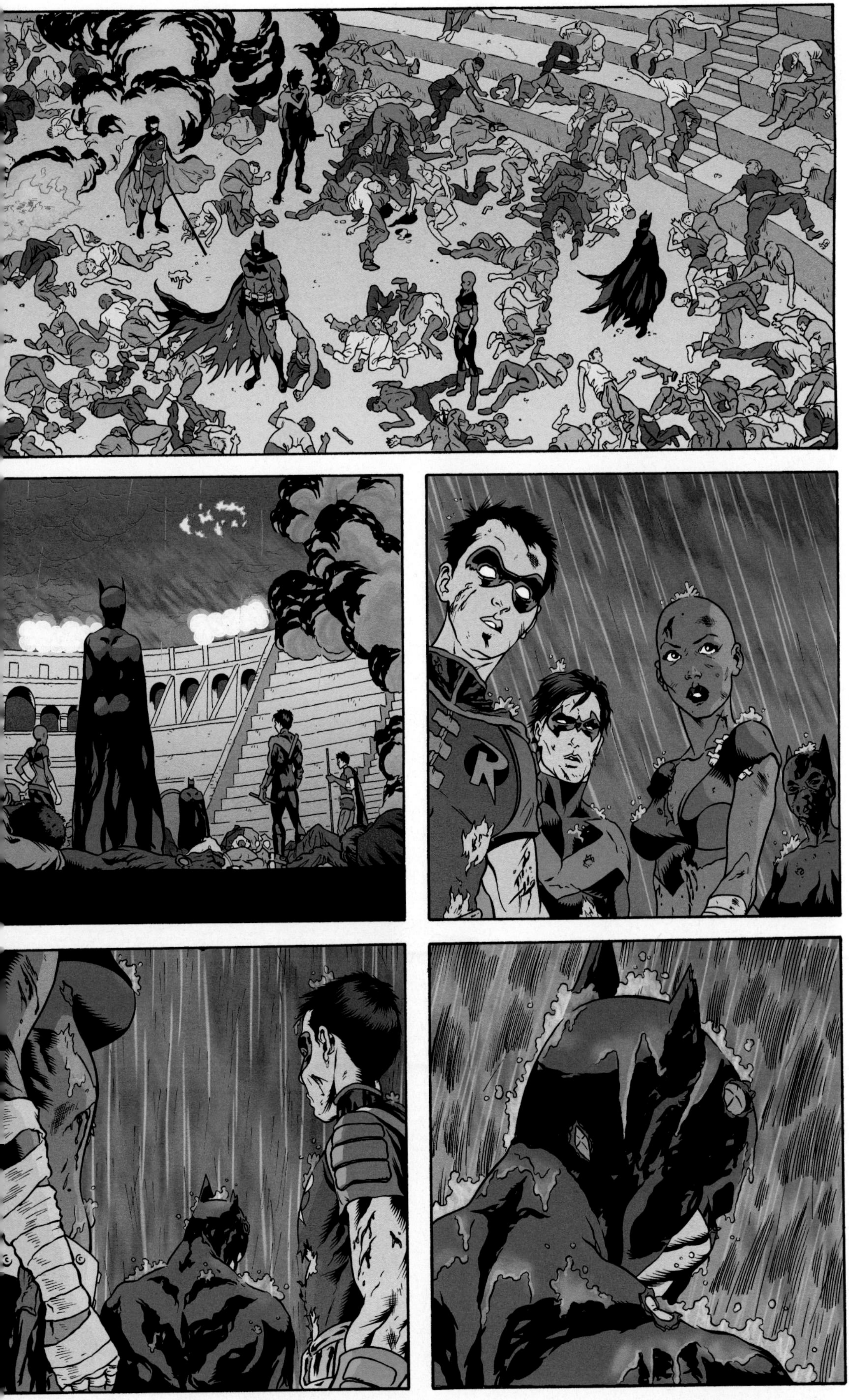

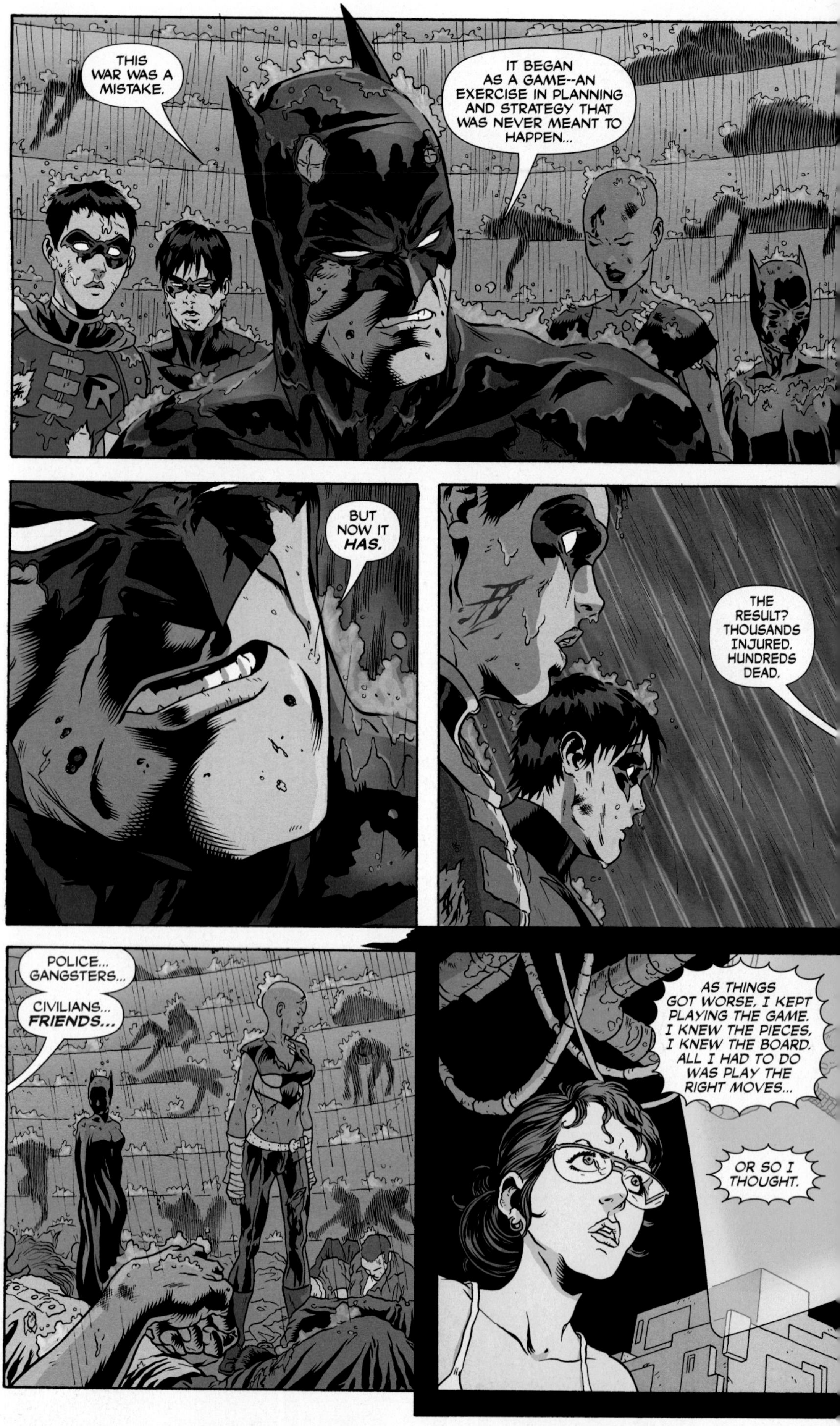
THIS WAR WAS A MISTAKE.
IT BEGAN AS A GAME--AN EXERCISE IN PLANNING AND STRATEGY THAT WAS NEVER MEANT TO HAPPEN...
BUT NOW IT HAS.
THE RESULT? THOUSANDS INJURED. HUNDREDS DEAD.
POLICE... GANGSTERS...
CIVILIANS... FRIENDS...
AS THINGS GOT WORSE, I KEPT PLAYING THE GAME. I KNEW THE PIECES, I KNEW THE BOARD. ALL I HAD TO DO WAS PLAY THE RIGHT MOVES...
OR SO I THOUGHT.

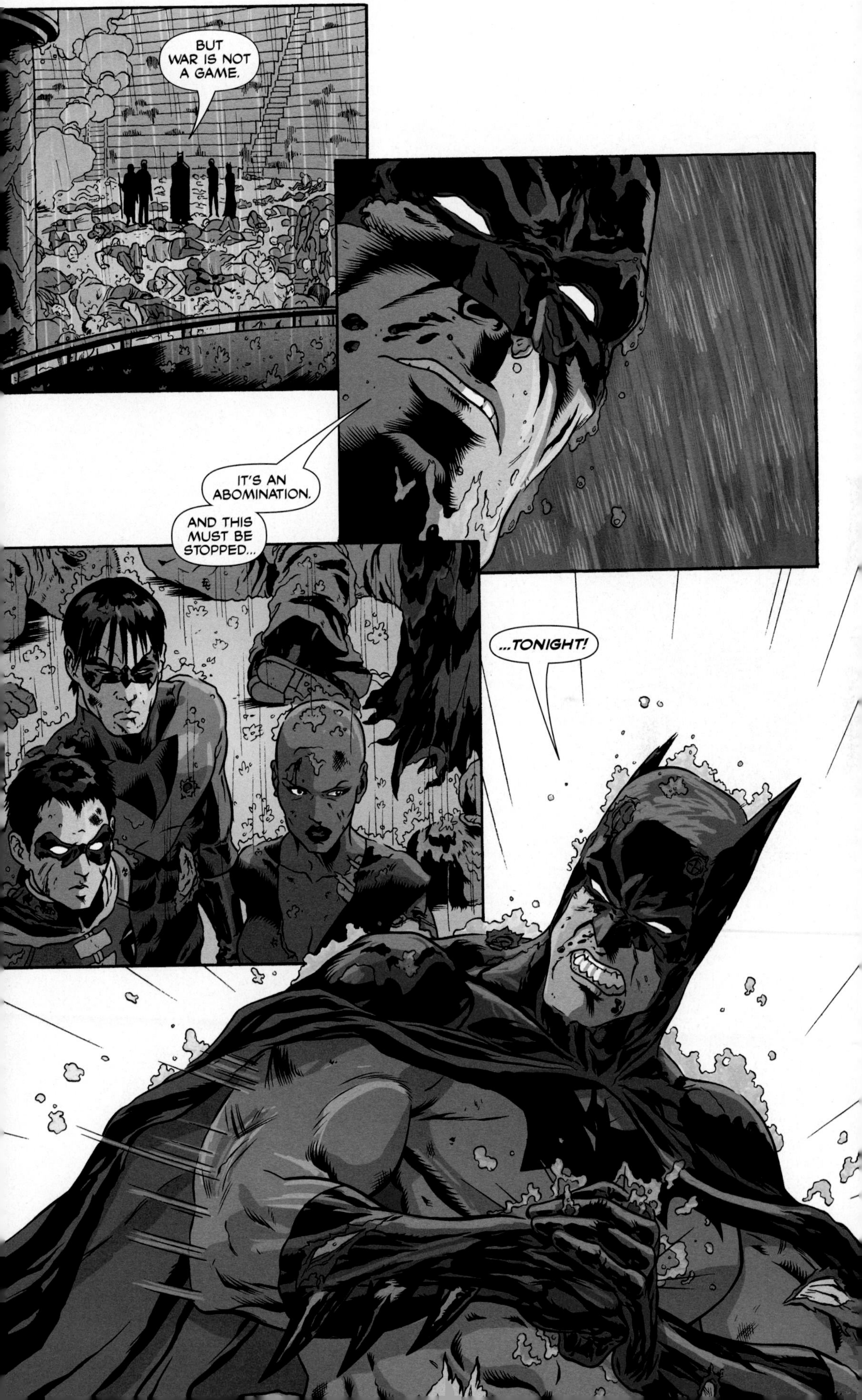
BUT WAR IS NOT A GAME.
IT'S AN ABOMINATION.
AND THIS MUST BE STOPPED...
...TONIGHT!

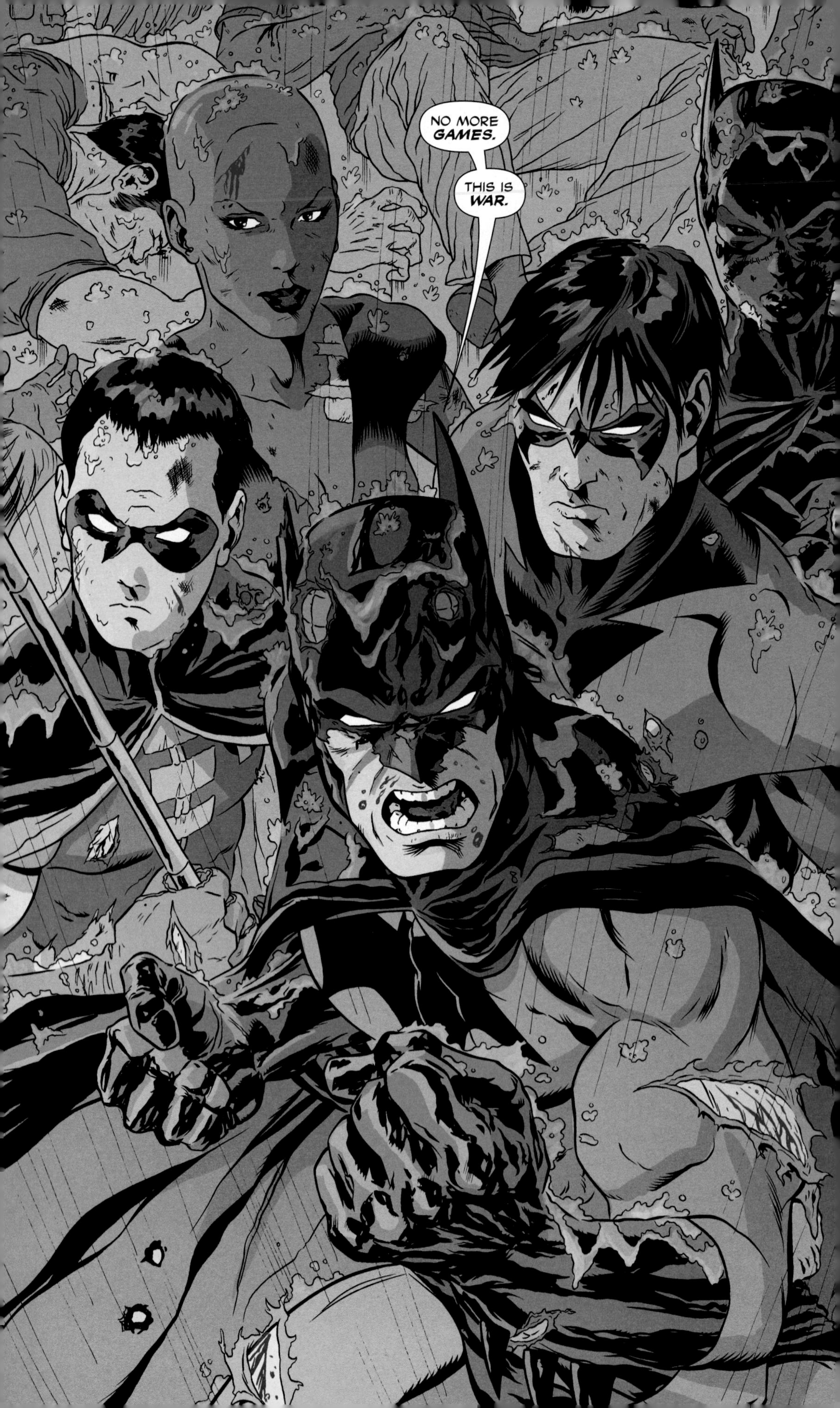
NO MORE GAMES.
THIS IS WAR.

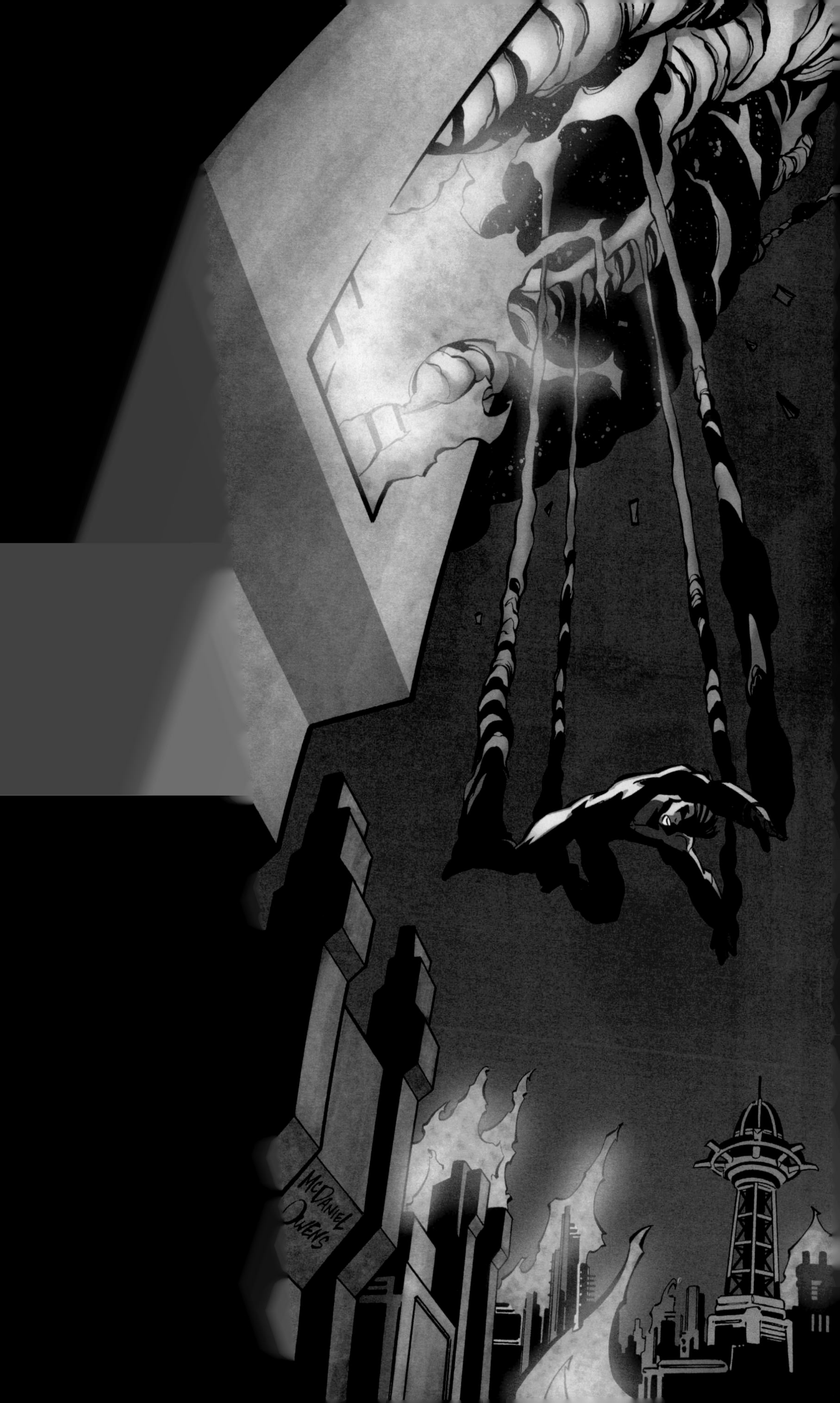
McDaniel
Owens

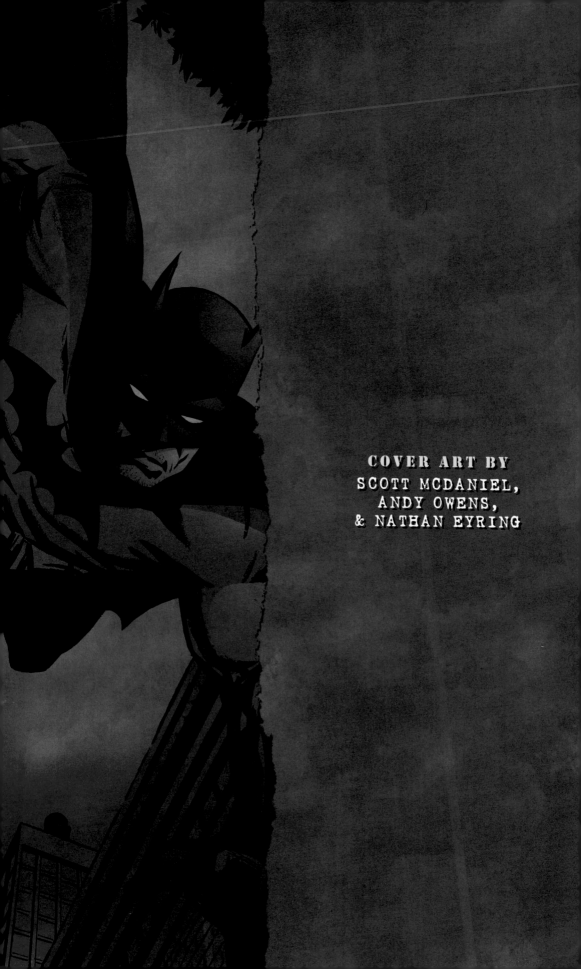

COVER ART BY
SCOTT MCDANIEL,
ANDY OWENS,
& NATHAN EYRING

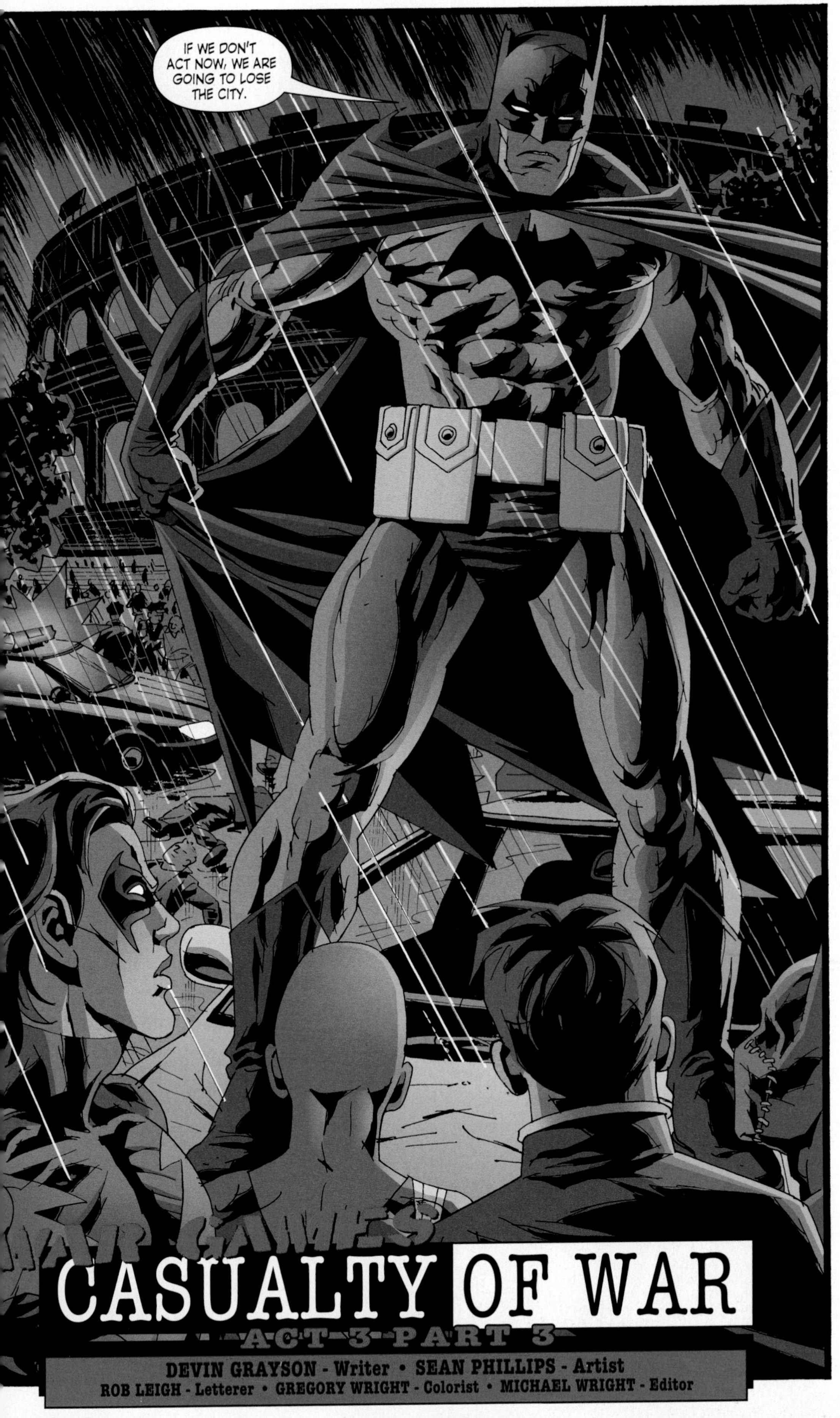
IF WE DON'T ACT NOW, WE ARE GOING TO LOSE THE CITY.
CASUALTY OF WAR
ACT 3 PART 3
DEVIN GRAYSON - Writer • SEAN PHILLIPS - Artist
ROB LEIGH - Letterer • GREGORY WRIGHT - Colorist • MICHAEL WRIGHT - Editor

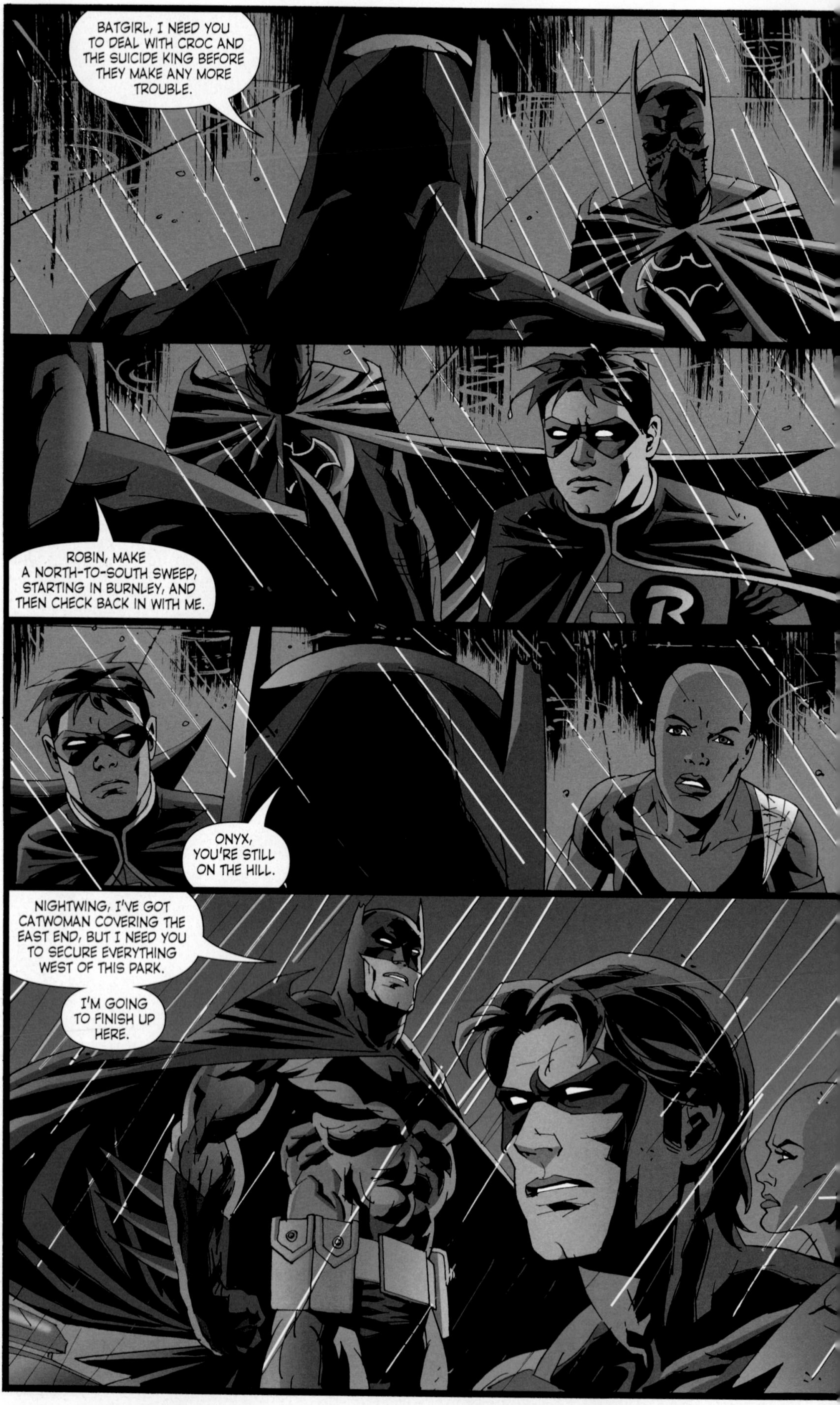
BATGIRL, I NEED YOU TO DEAL WITH CROC AND THE SUICIDE KING BEFORE THEY MAKE ANY MORE TROUBLE.
ROBIN, MAKE A NORTH-TO-SOUTH SWEEP, STARTING IN BURNLEY, AND THEN CHECK BACK IN WITH ME.
ONYX, YOU'RE STILL ON THE HILL.
NIGHTWING, I'VE GOT CATWOMAN COVERING THE EAST END, BUT I NEED YOU TO SECURE EVERYTHING WEST OF THIS PARK.
I'M GOING TO FINISH UP HERE.

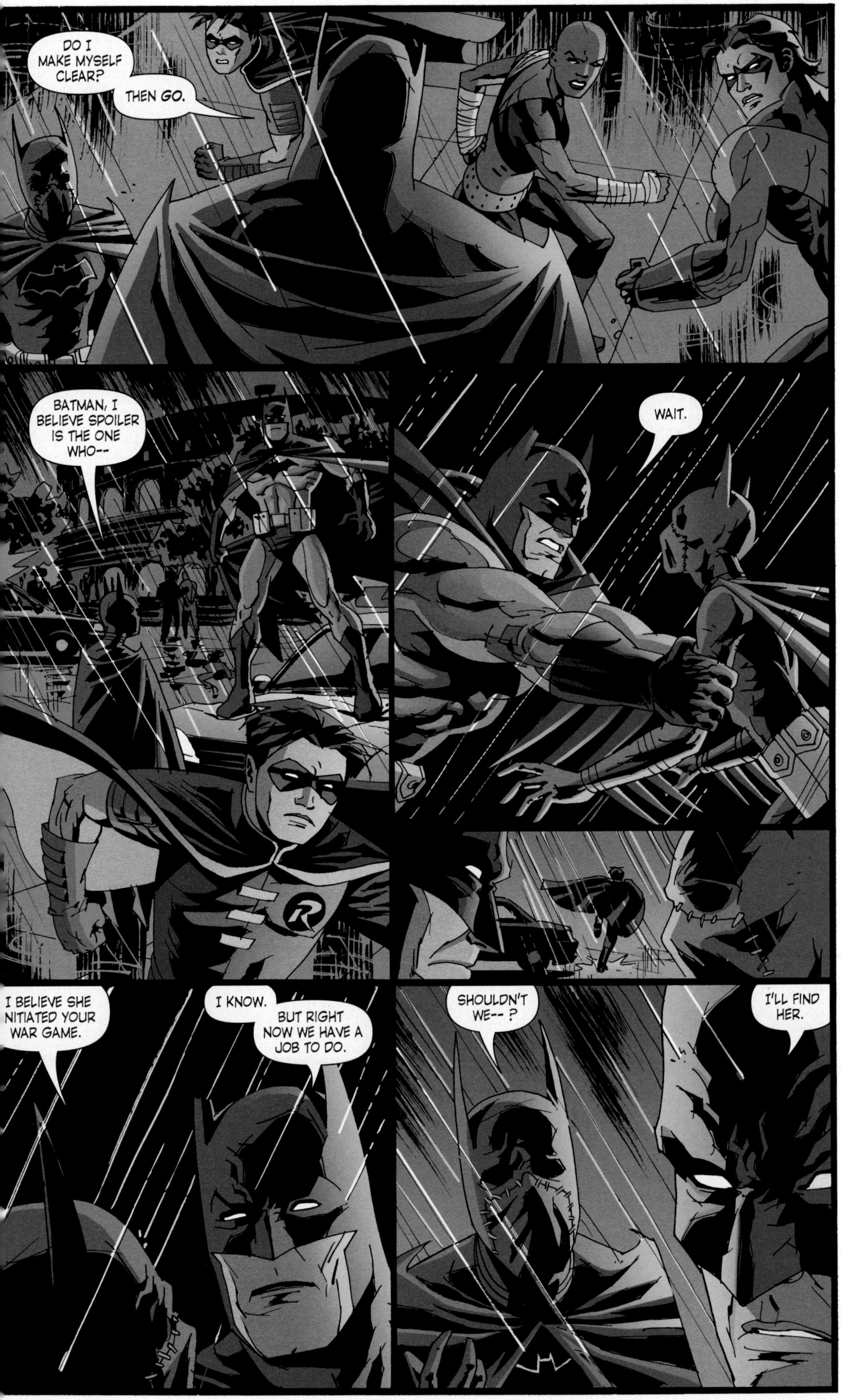

DO I MAKE MYSELF CLEAR?
THEN GO.
BATMAN, I BELIEVE SPOILER IS THE ONE WHO--
WAIT.
I BELIEVE SHE NITIATED YOUR WAR GAME.
I KNOW.
BUT RIGHT NOW WE HAVE A JOB TO DO.
SHOULDN'T WE-- ?
I'LL FIND HER.

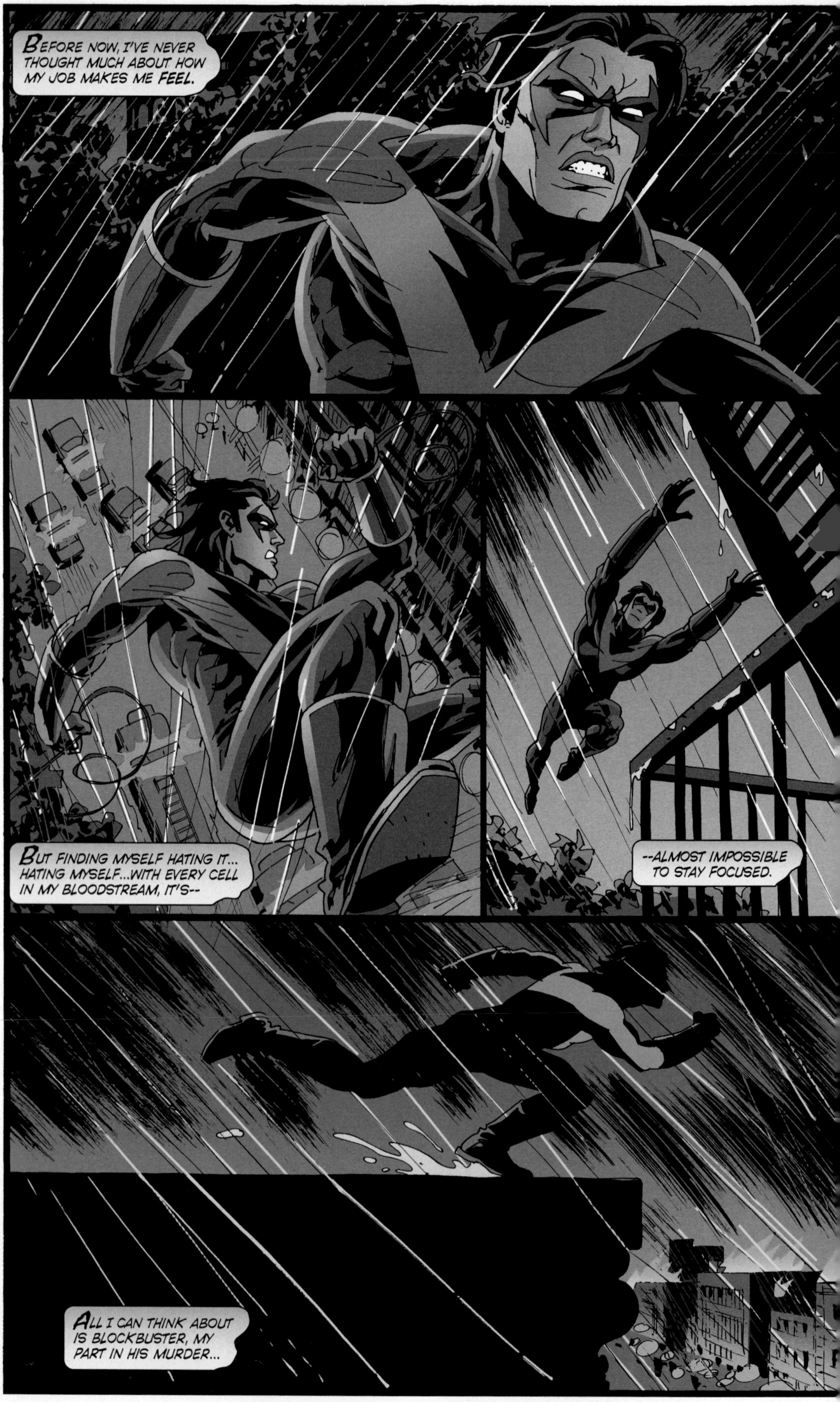
BEFORE NOW, I'VE NEVER THOUGHT MUCH ABOUT HOW MY JOB MAKES ME FEEL.
BUT FINDING MYSELF HATING IT... HATING MYSELF...WITH EVERY CELL IN MY BLOODSTREAM, IT'S--
--ALMOST IMPOSSIBLE TO STAY FOCUSED.
ALL I CAN THINK ABOUT IS BLOCKBUSTER, MY PART IN HIS MURDER...

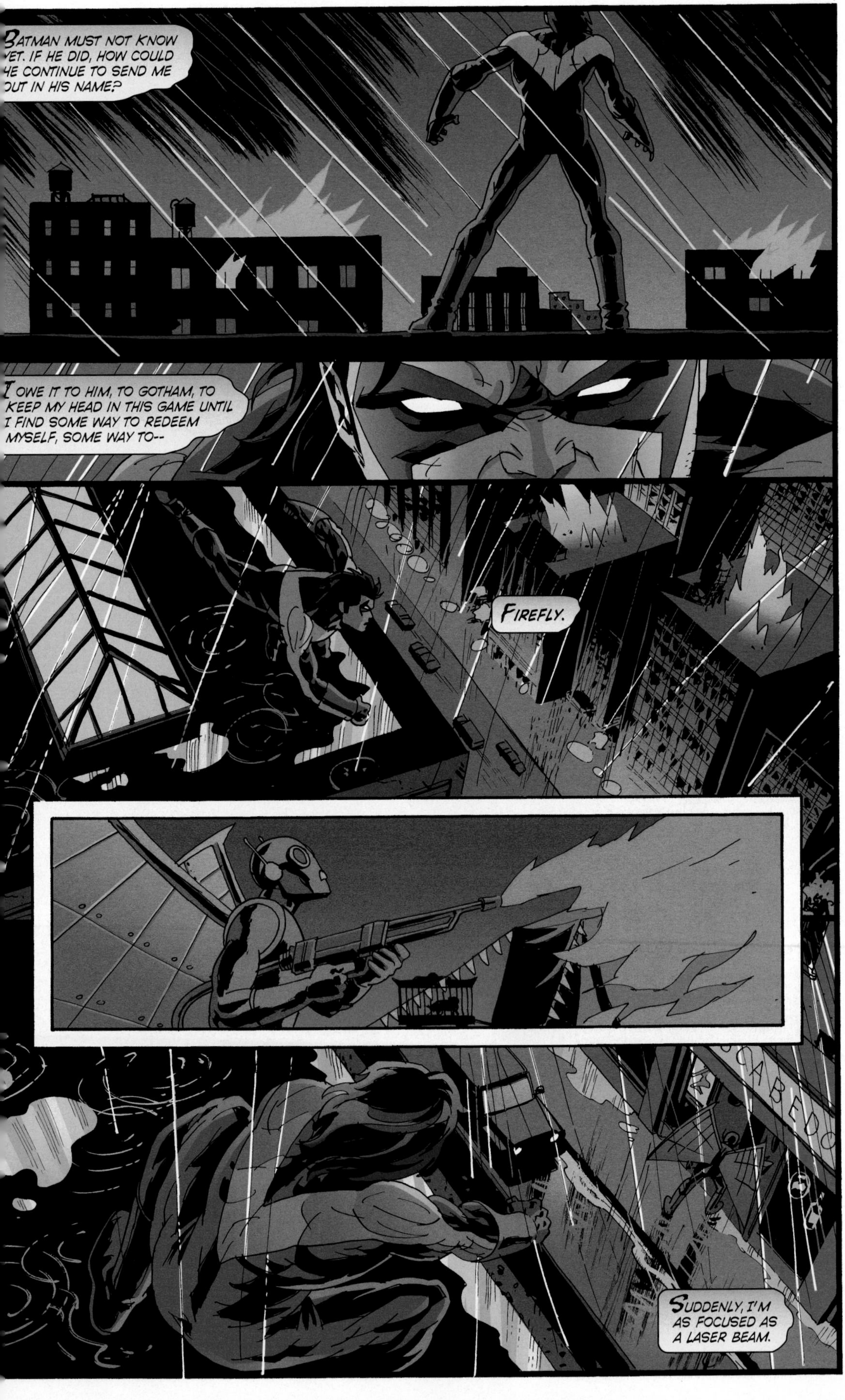
BATMAN MUST NOT KNOW YET. IF HE DID, HOW COULD HE CONTINUE TO SEND ME OUT IN HIS NAME?
I OWE IT TO HIM, TO GOTHAM, TO KEEP MY HEAD IN THIS GAME UNTIL I FIND SOME WAY TO REDEEM MYSELF, SOME WAY TO--
FIREFLY.
SUDDENLY, I'M AS FOCUSED AS A LASER BEAM.

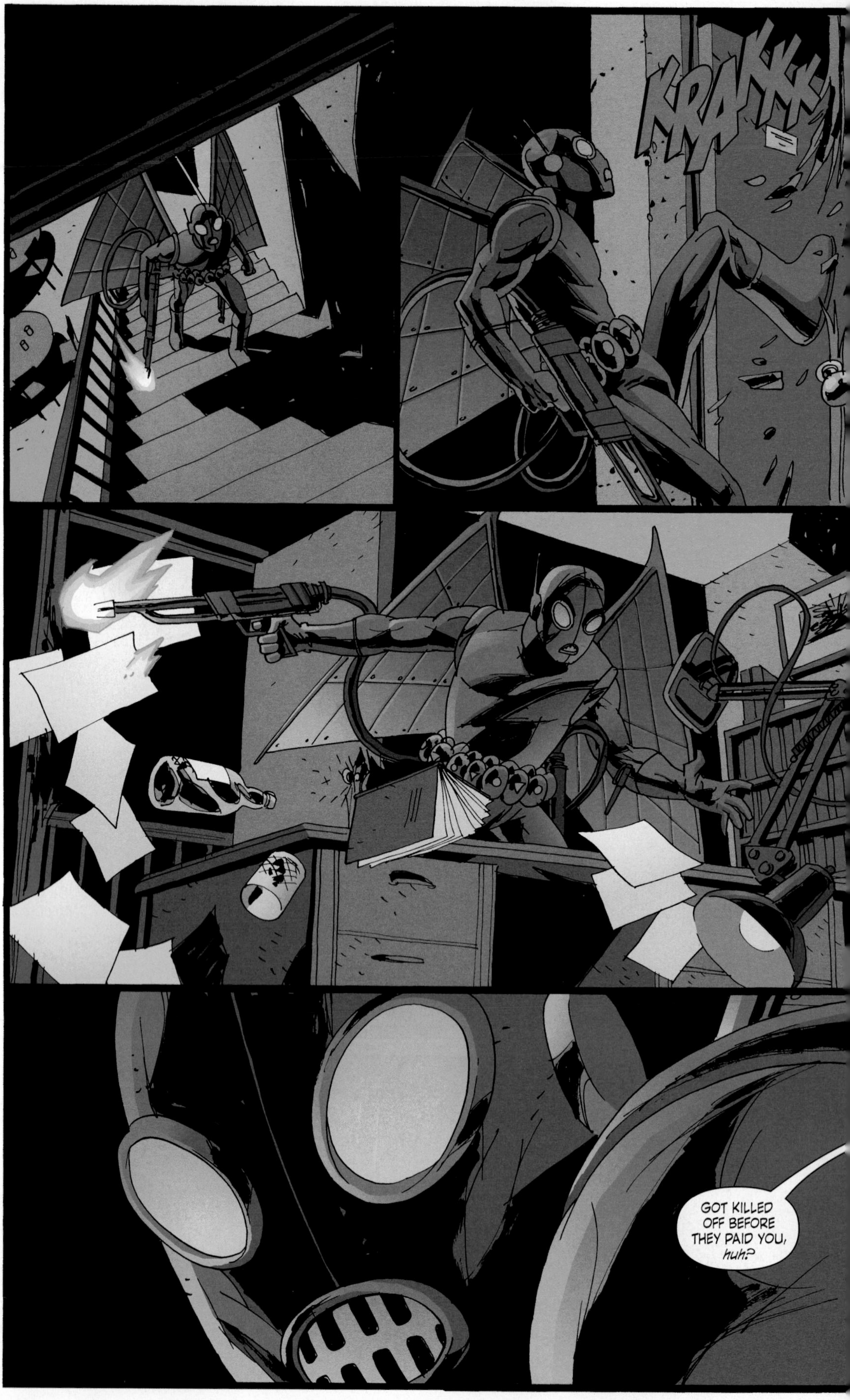
KRAKKK
GOT KILLED OFF BEFORE THEY PAID YOU, *huh?*

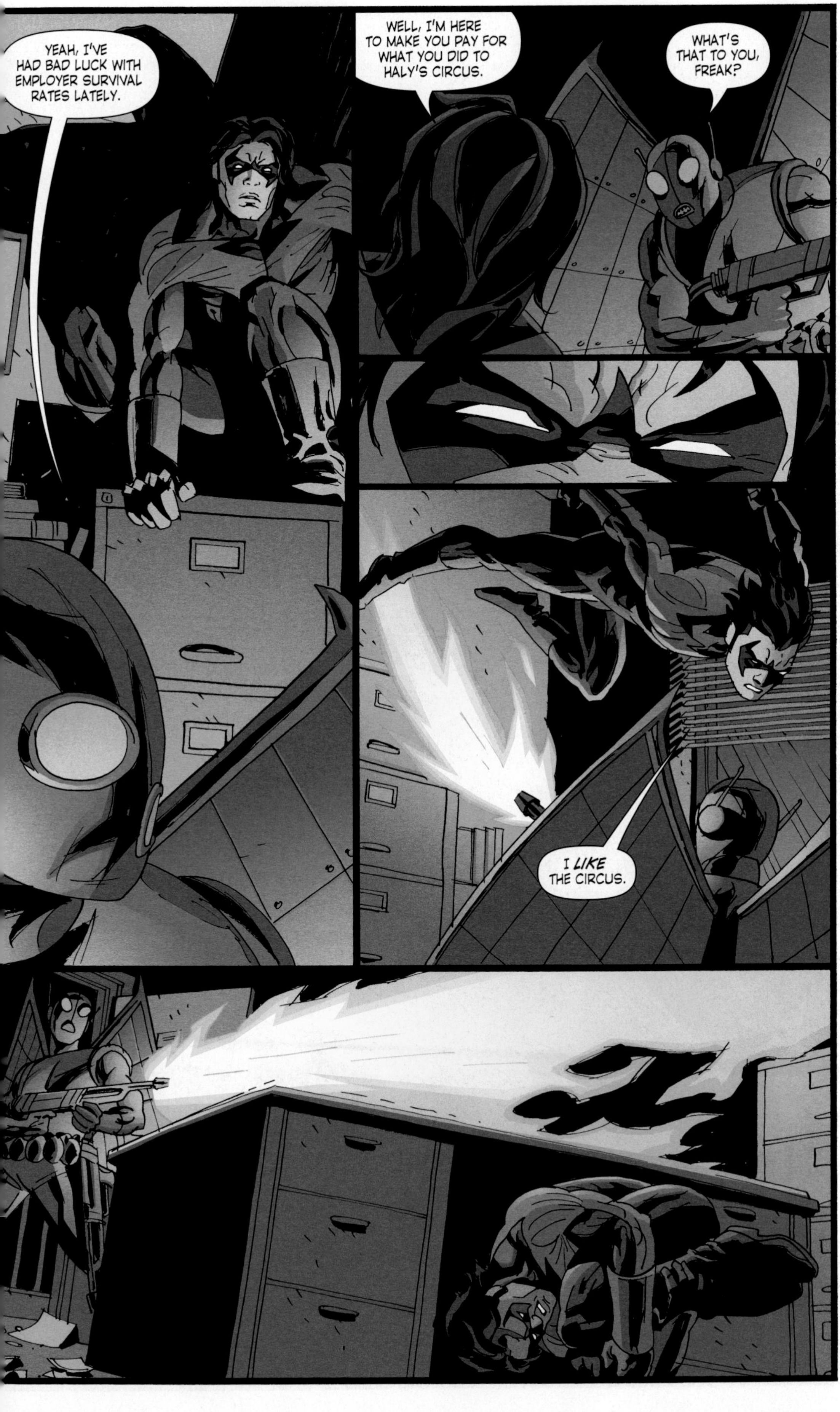
YEAH, I'VE HAD BAD LUCK WITH EMPLOYER SURVIVAL RATES LATELY.
WELL, I'M HERE TO MAKE YOU PAY FOR WHAT YOU DID TO HALY'S CIRCUS.
WHAT'S THAT TO YOU, FREAK?
I LIKE THE CIRCUS.

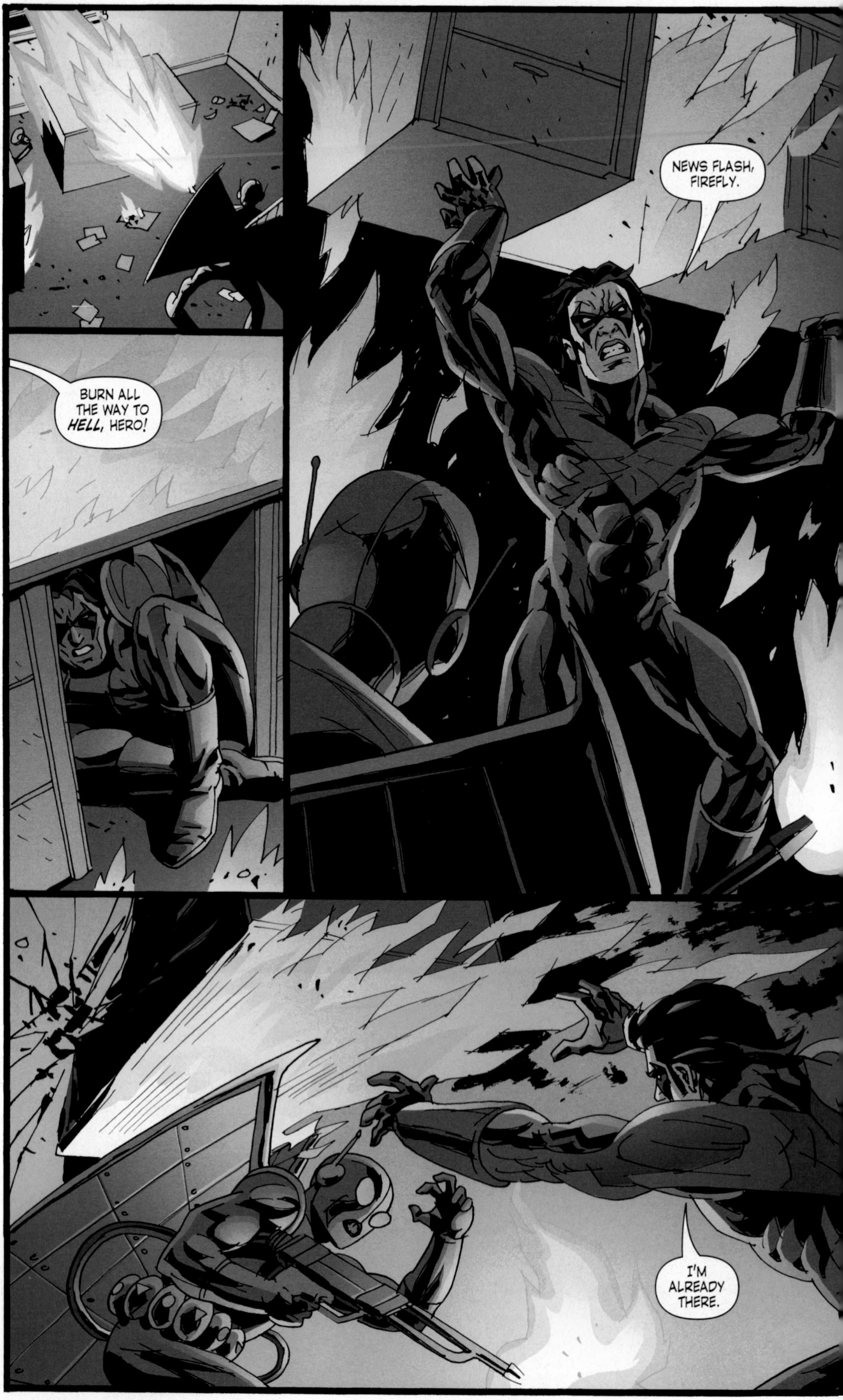
NEWS FLASH, FIREFLY.
BURN ALL THE WAY TO HELL, HERO!
I'M ALREADY THERE.

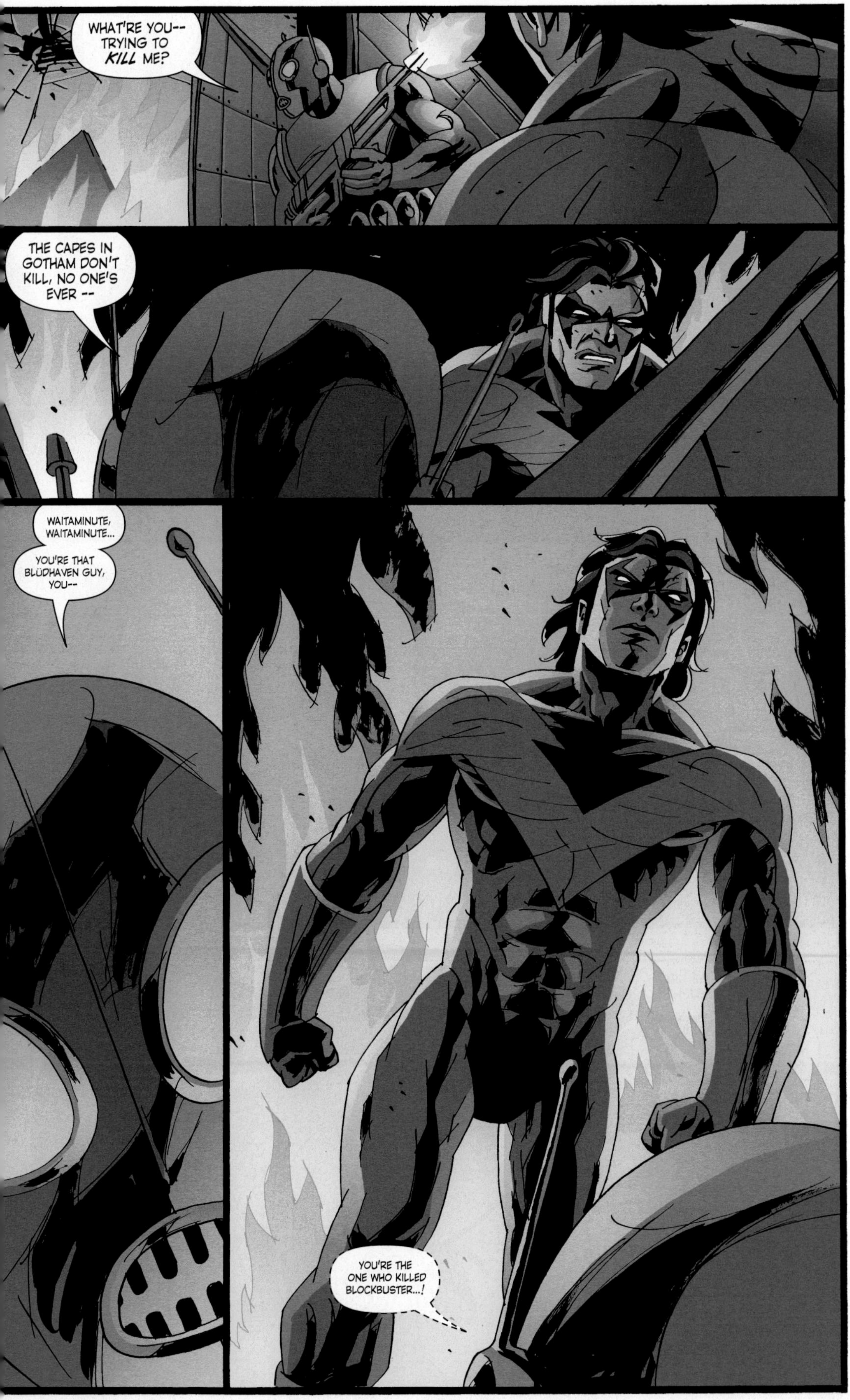
WHAT'RE YOU-- TRYING TO KILL ME?
THE CAPES IN GOTHAM DON'T KILL, NO ONE'S EVER --
WAITAMINUTE, WAITAMINUTE...
YOU'RE THAT BLÜDHAVEN GUY, YOU--
YOU'RE THE ONE WHO KILLED BLOCKBUSTER...!

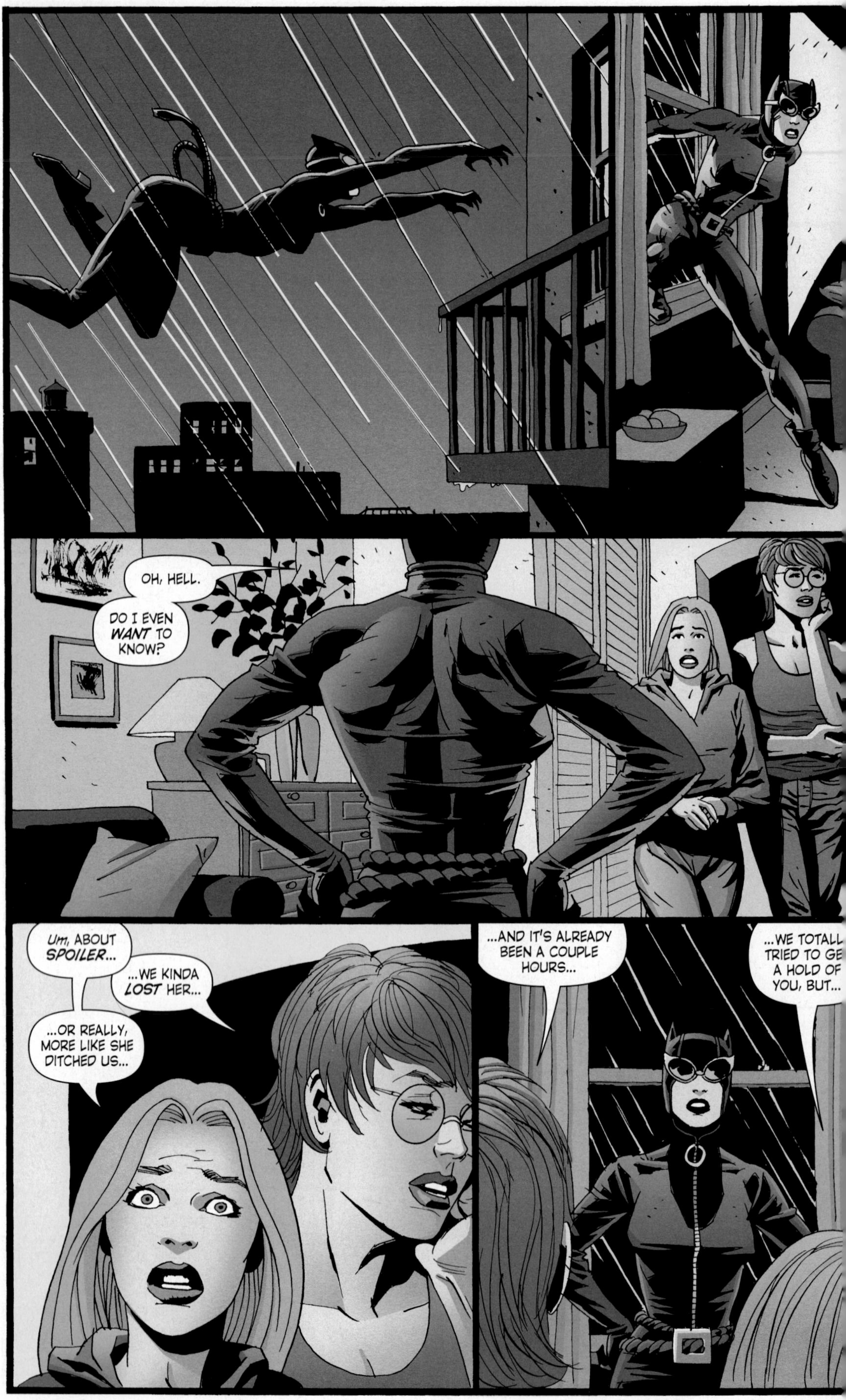

OH, HELL.
DO I EVEN *WANT* TO KNOW?
Um, ABOUT *SPOILER*...
...WE KINDA *LOST* HER...
...OR REALLY, MORE LIKE SHE DITCHED US...
...AND IT'S ALREADY BEEN A COUPLE HOURS...
...WE TOTALL TRIED TO GE A HOLD OF YOU, BUT...

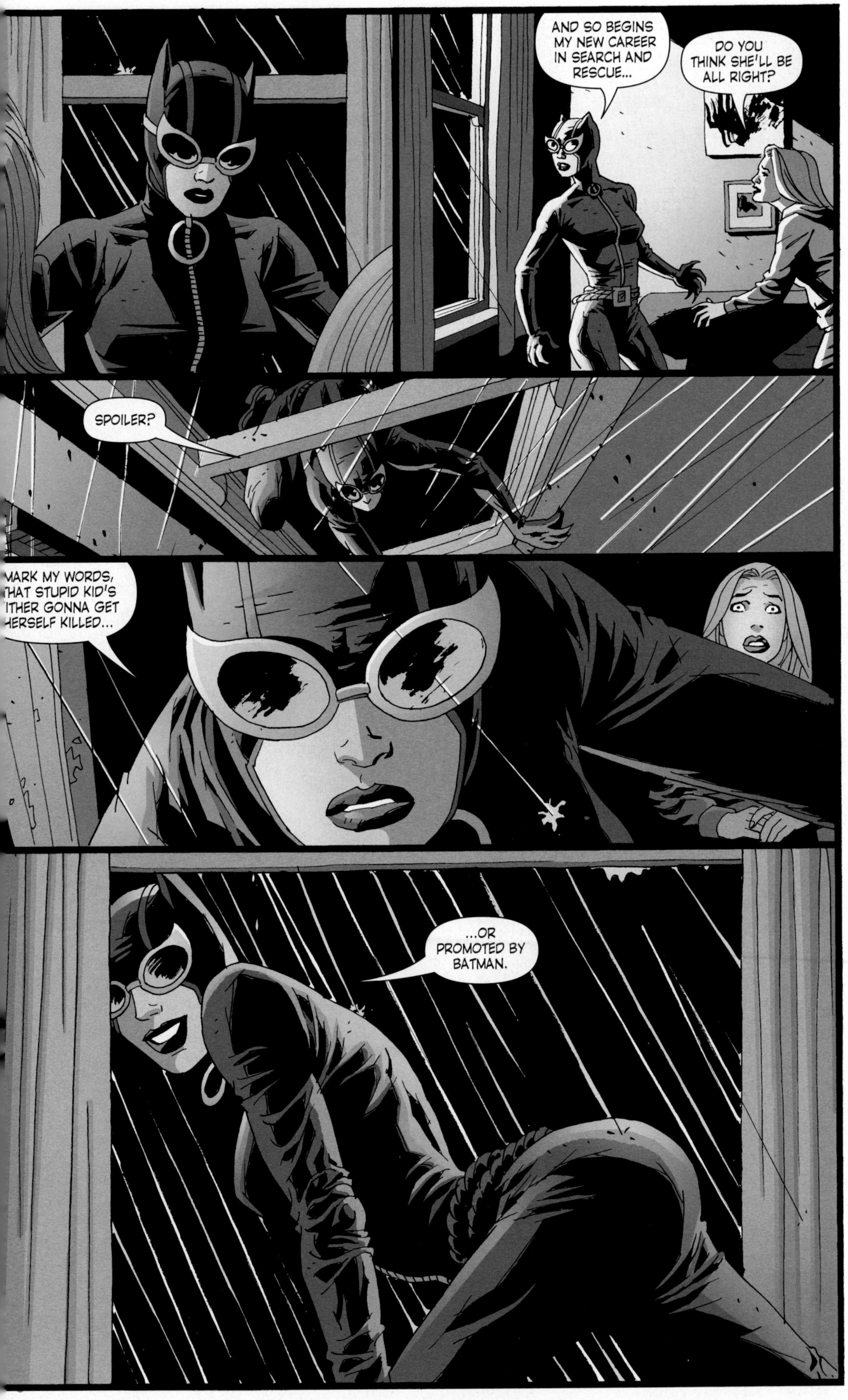
AND SO BEGINS MY NEW CAREER IN SEARCH AND RESCUE...
DO YOU THINK SHE'LL BE ALL RIGHT?
SPOILER?
MARK MY WORDS, THAT STUPID KID'S EITHER GONNA GET HERSELF KILLED...
...OR PROMOTED BY BATMAN.

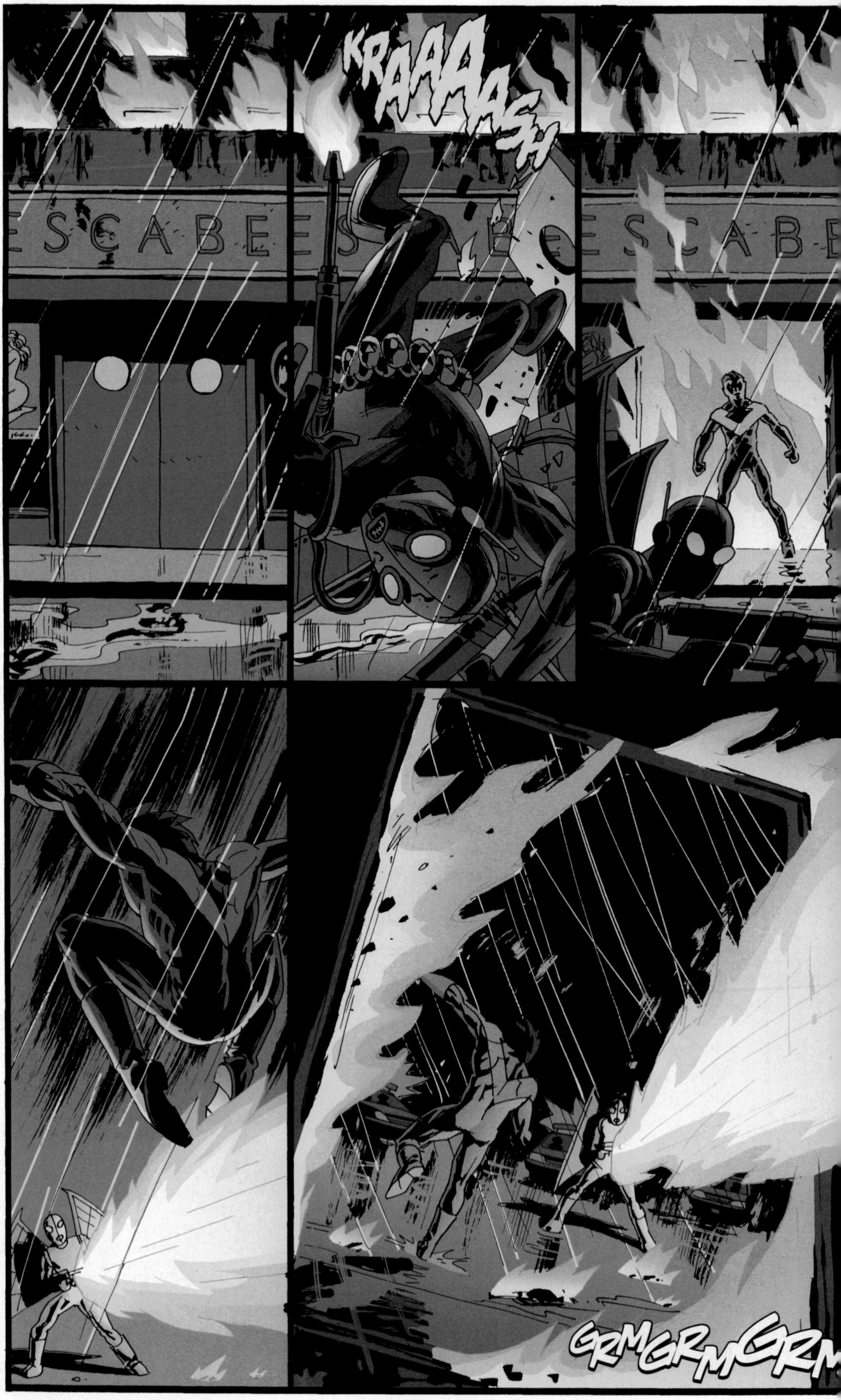

ESCABE
KRAAAAASH
ESCABE
GRMGRMGRM

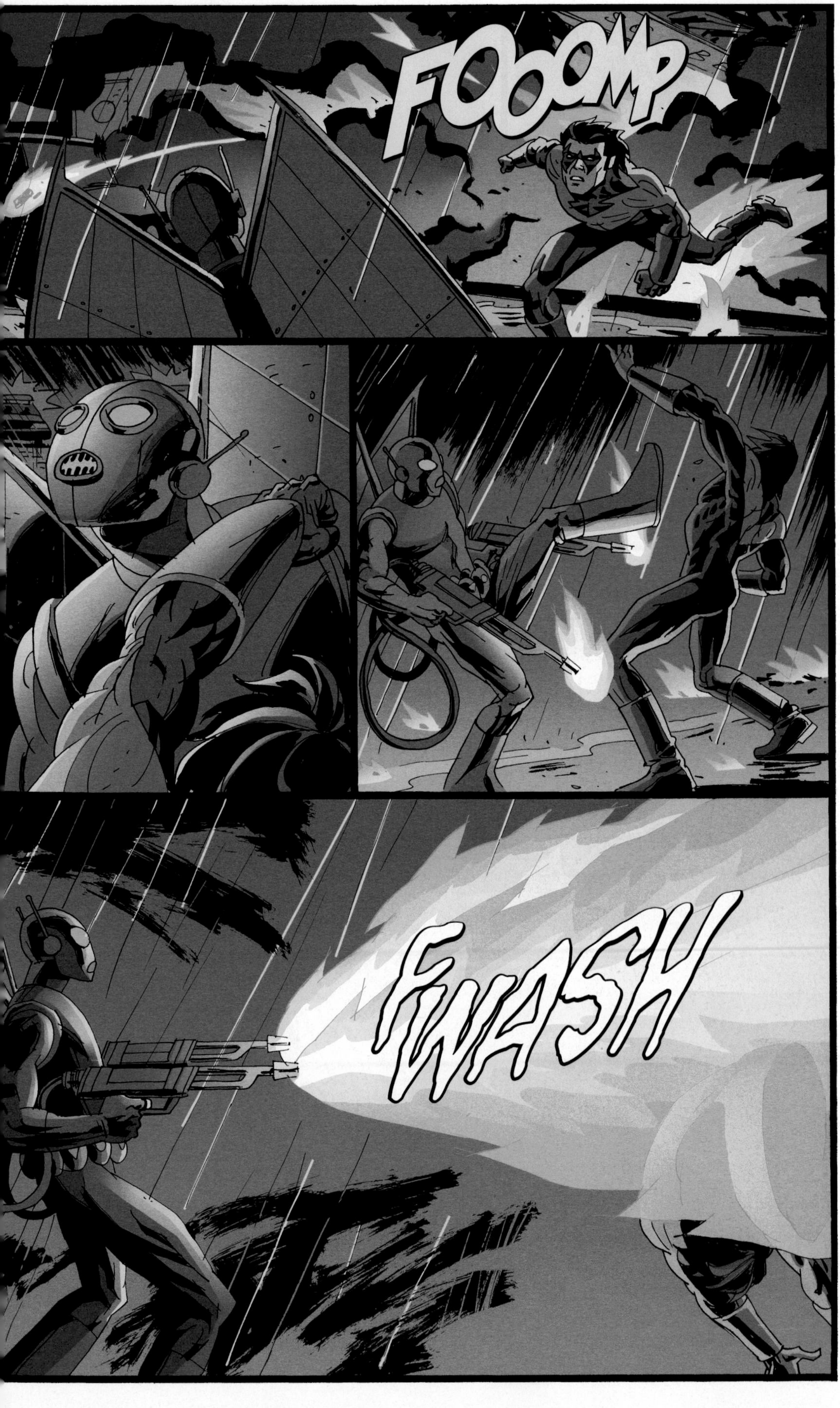
FOOOMP
FWASH

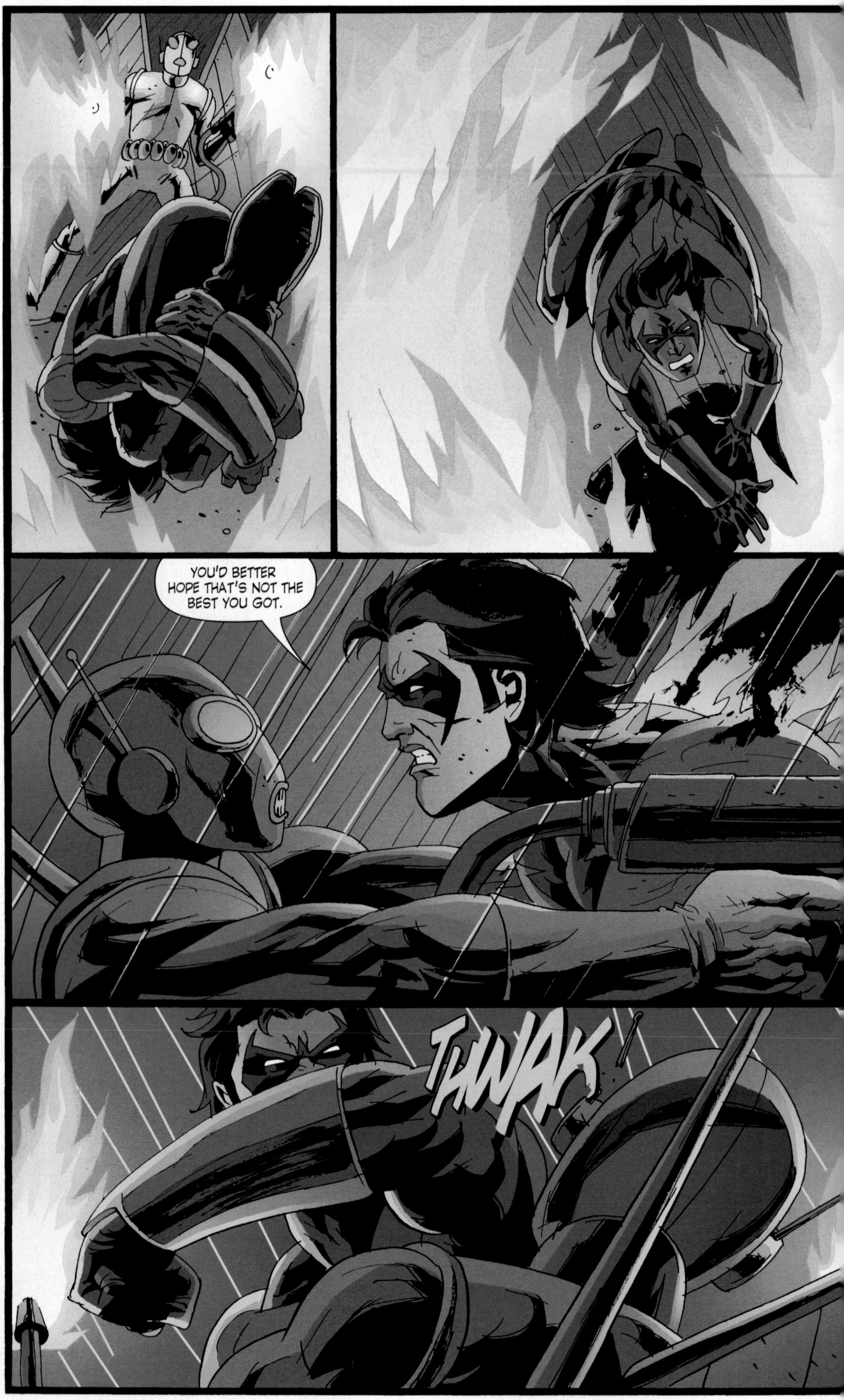
YOU'D BETTER HOPE THAT'S NOT THE BEST YOU GOT.
THWAK

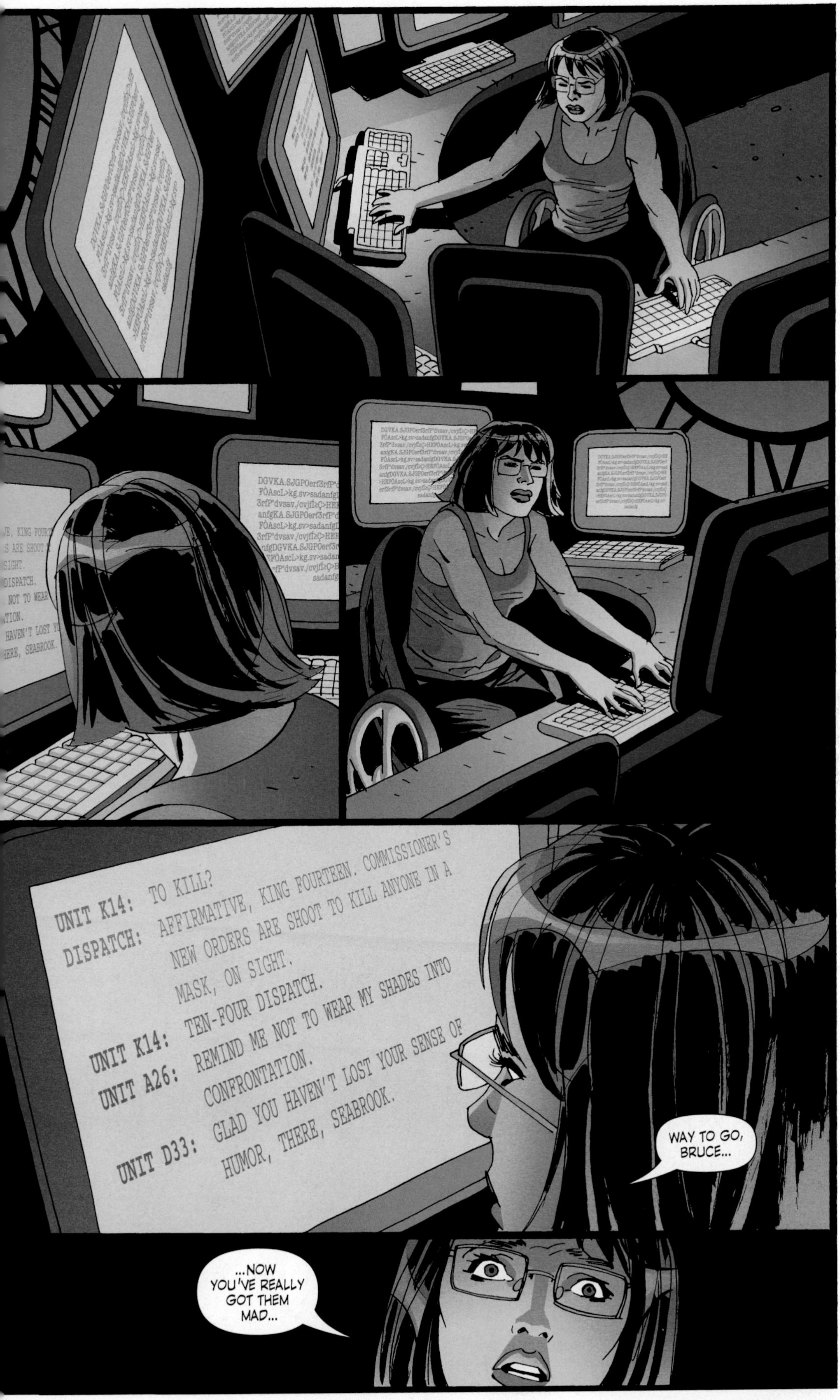
UNIT K14: TO KILL?
DISPATCH: AFFIRMATIVE, KING FOURTEEN. COMMISSIONER'S NEW ORDERS ARE SHOOT TO KILL ANYONE IN A MASK, ON SIGHT.
UNIT K14: TEN-FOUR DISPATCH.
UNIT A26: REMIND ME NOT TO WEAR MY SHADES INTO CONFRONTATION.
UNIT D33: GLAD YOU HAVEN'T LOST YOUR SENSE OF HUMOR, THERE, SEABROOK.
WAY TO GO, BRUCE...
...NOW YOU'VE REALLY GOT THEM MAD...

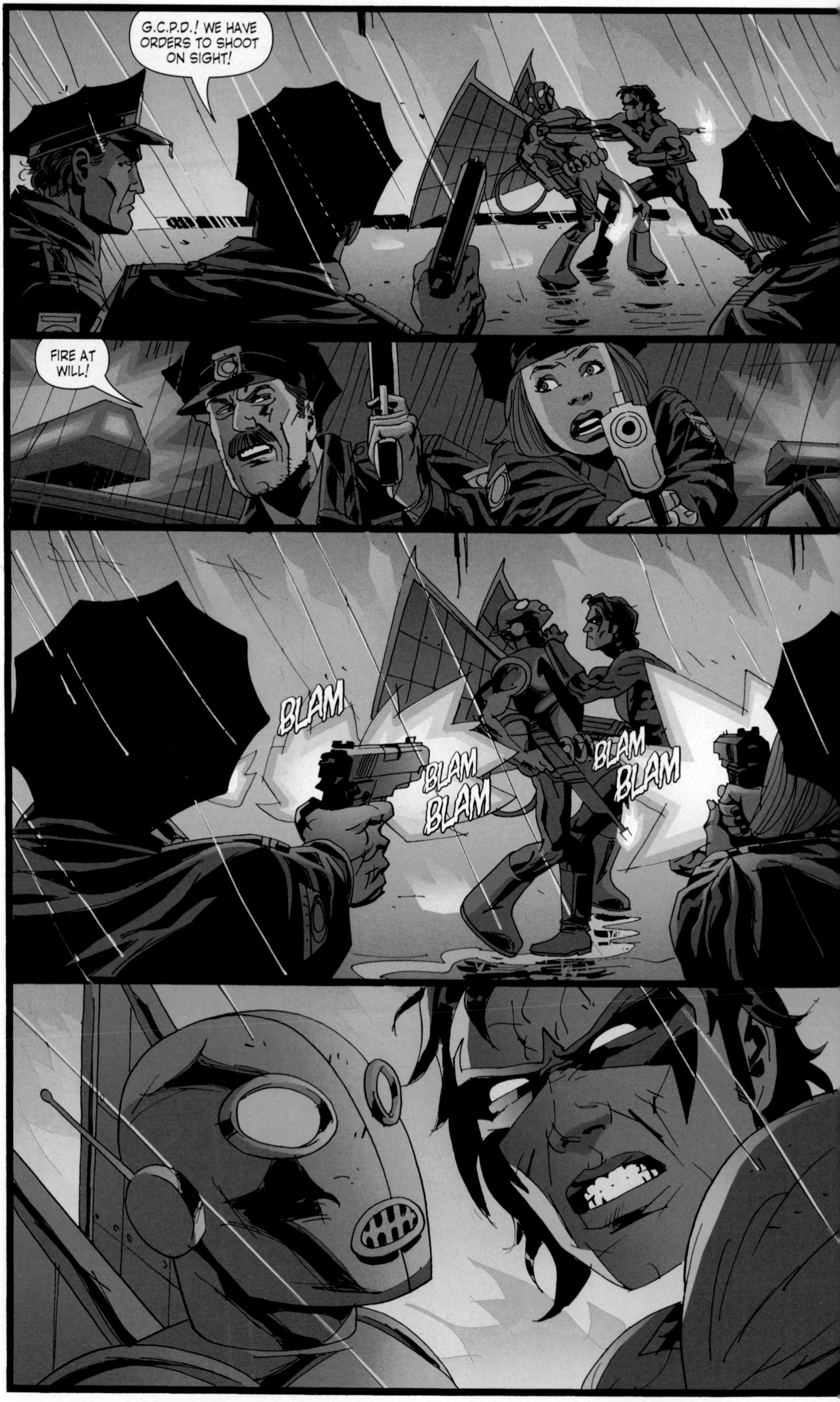
G.C.P.D.! WE HAVE ORDERS TO SHOOT ON SIGHT!
FIRE AT WILL!
BLAM
BLAM BLAM
BLAM BLAM

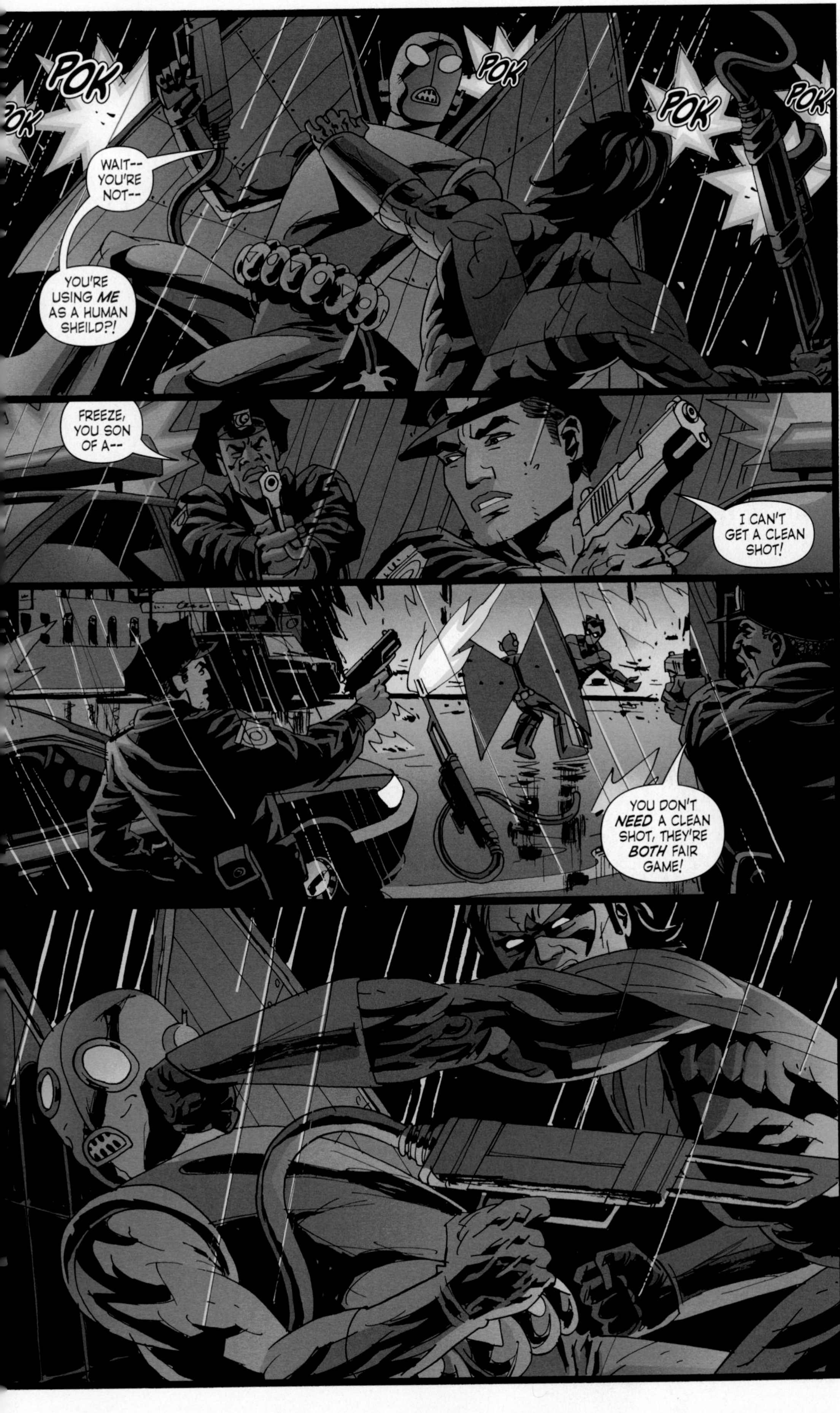
POK
POK
POK
POK
POK
WAIT-- YOU'RE NOT--
YOU'RE USING ME AS A HUMAN SHEILD?!
FREEZE, YOU SON OF A--
I CAN'T GET A CLEAN SHOT!
YOU DON'T NEED A CLEAN SHOT, THEY'RE BOTH FAIR GAME!

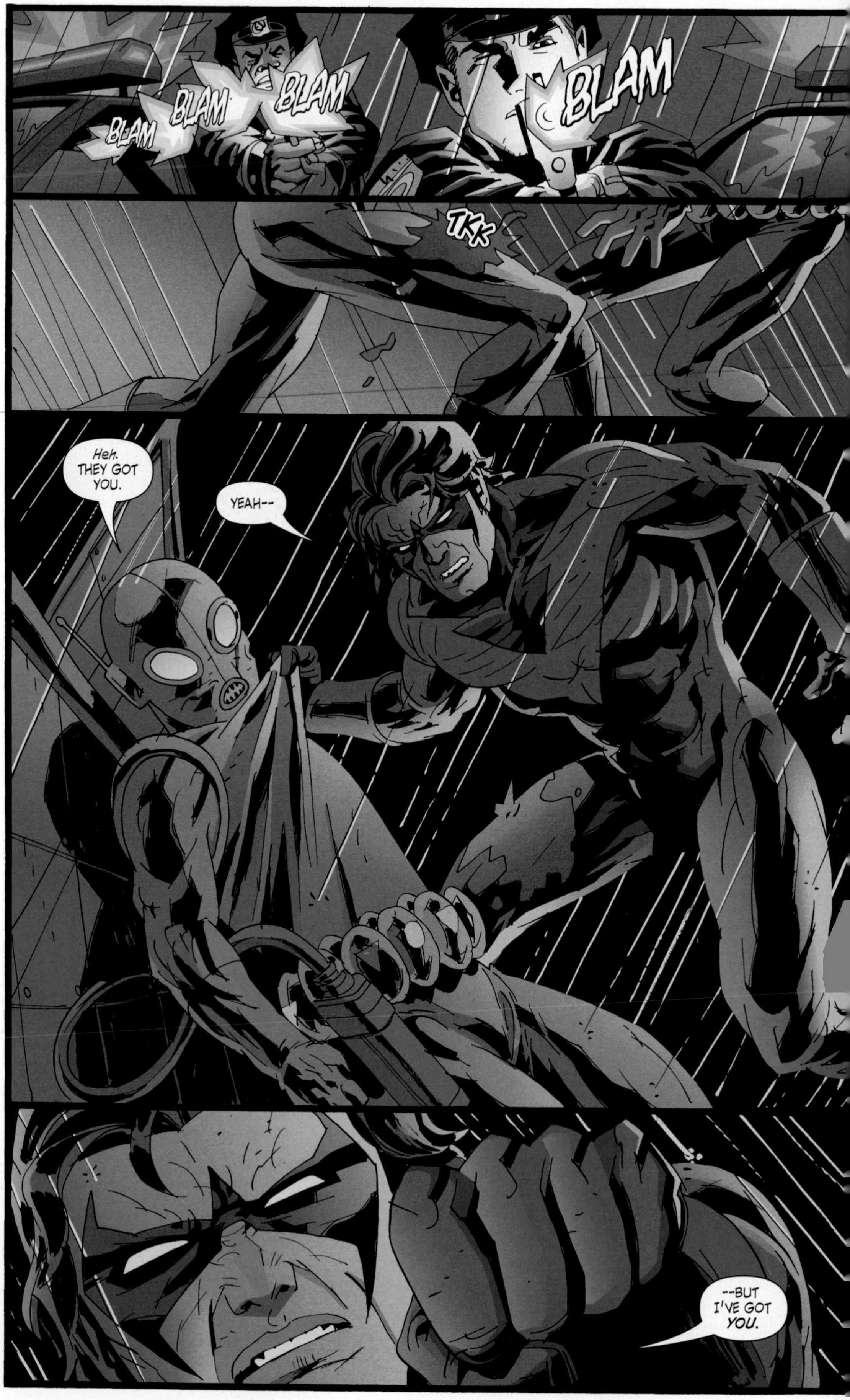
BLAM
BLAM
BLAM
BLAM
TKK
Heh. THEY GOT YOU.
YEAH--
--BUT I'VE GOT YOU.

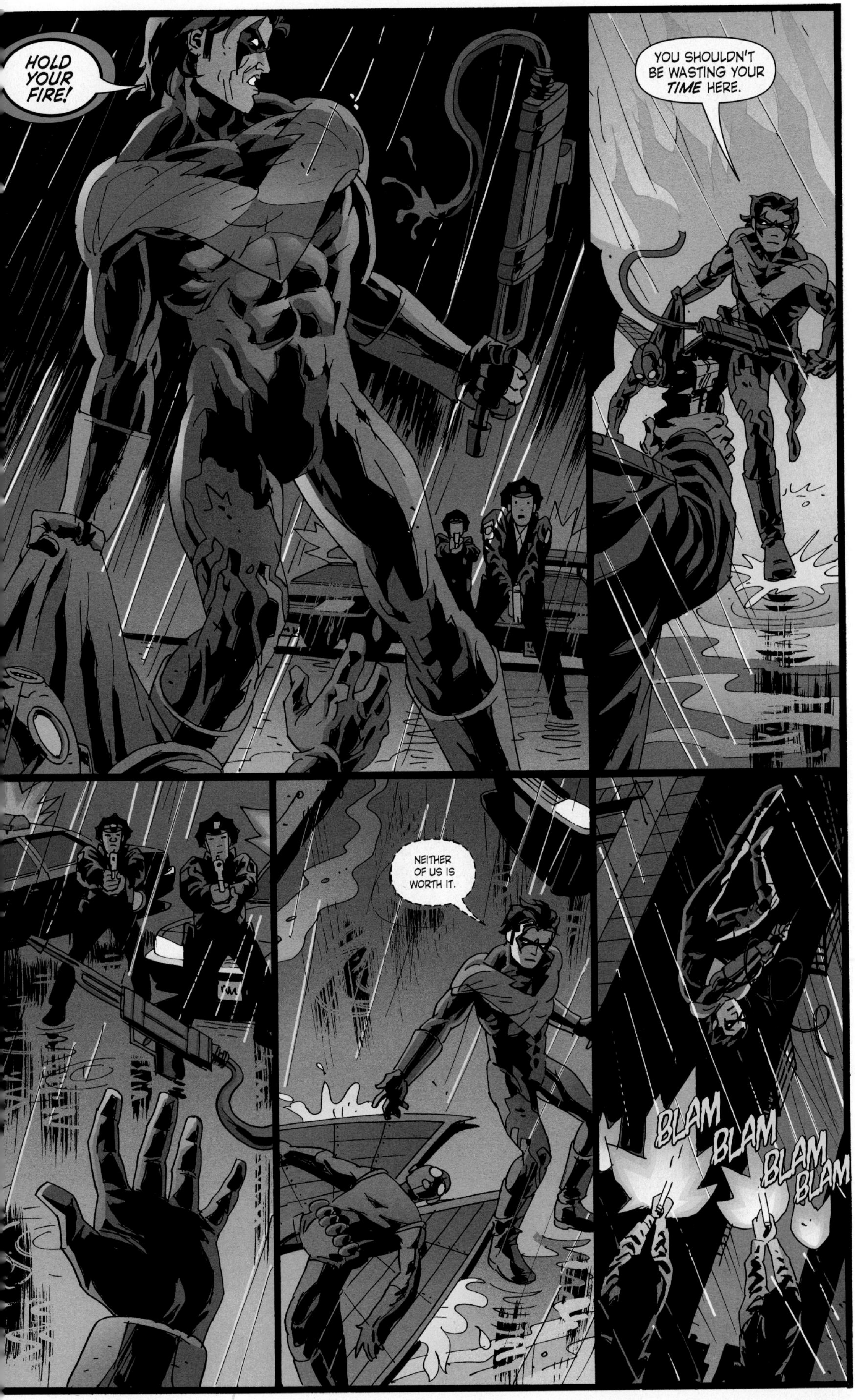
HOLD YOUR FIRE!
YOU SHOULDN'T BE WASTING YOUR TIME HERE.
NEITHER OF US IS WORTH IT.
BLAM
BLAM
BLAM
BLAM

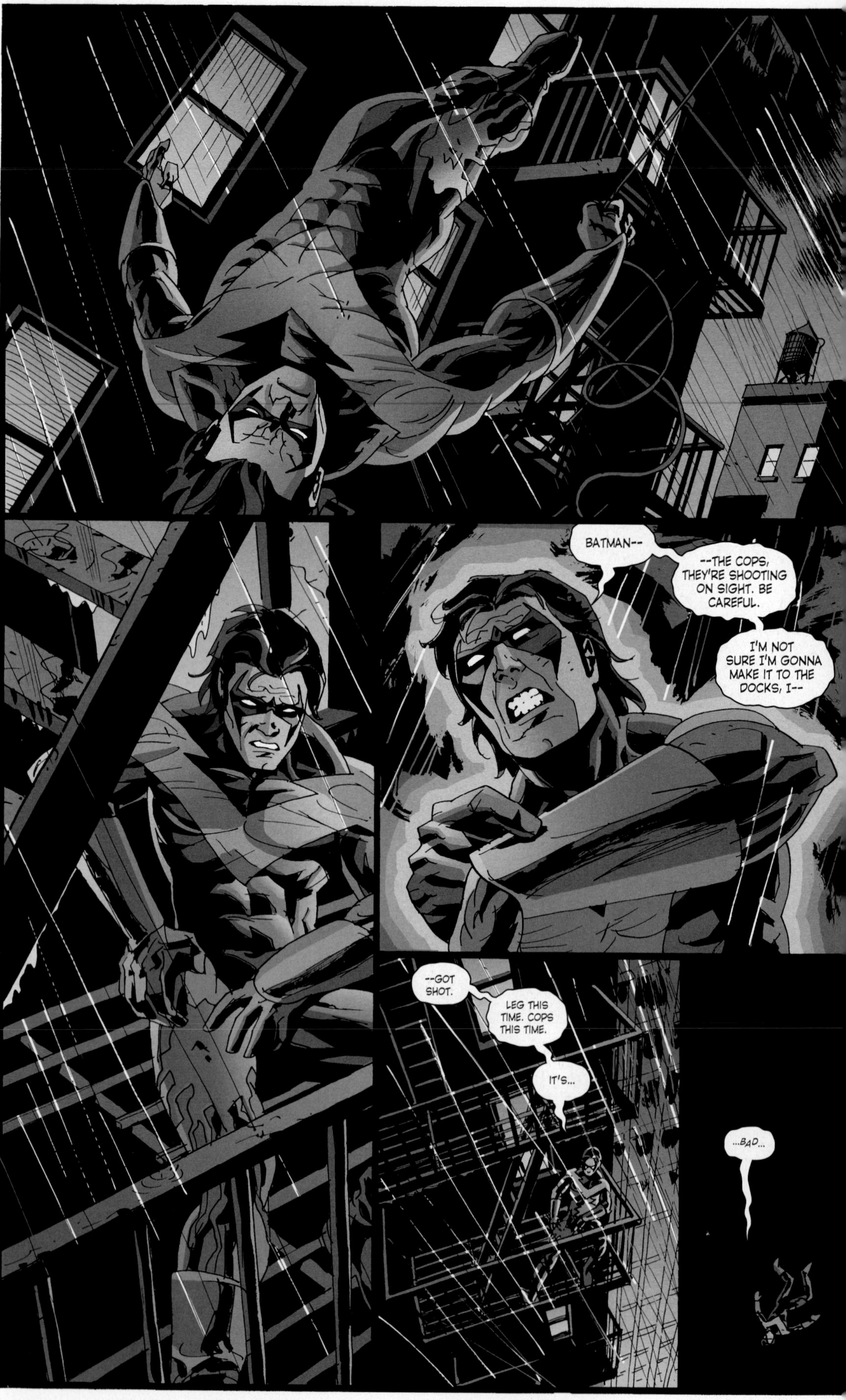
BATMAN--
--THE COPS, THEY'RE SHOOTING ON SIGHT. BE CAREFUL.
I'M NOT SURE I'M GONNA MAKE IT TO THE DOCKS, I--
--GOT SHOT.
LEG THIS TIME. COPS THIS TIME.
IT'S...
...BAD...

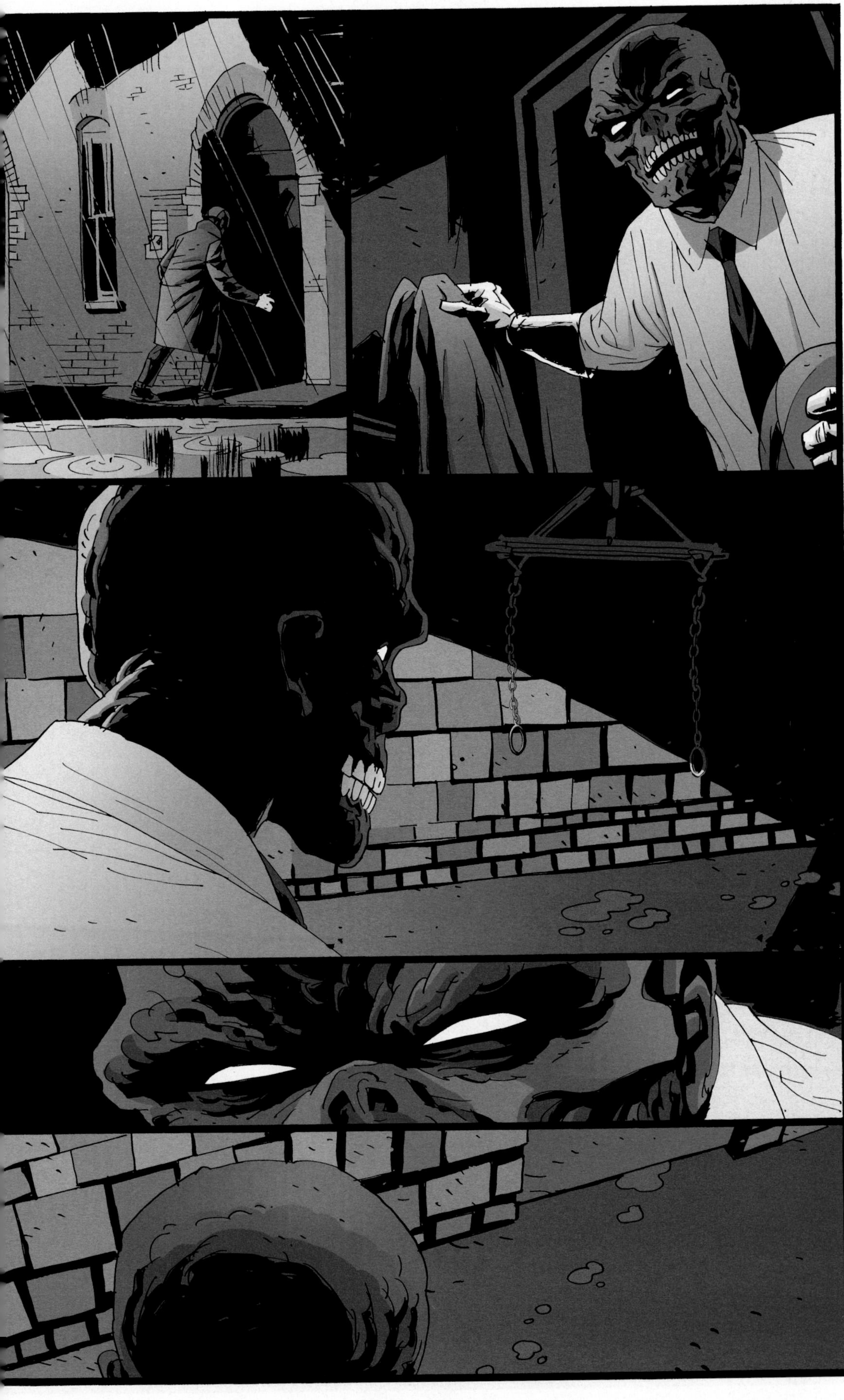

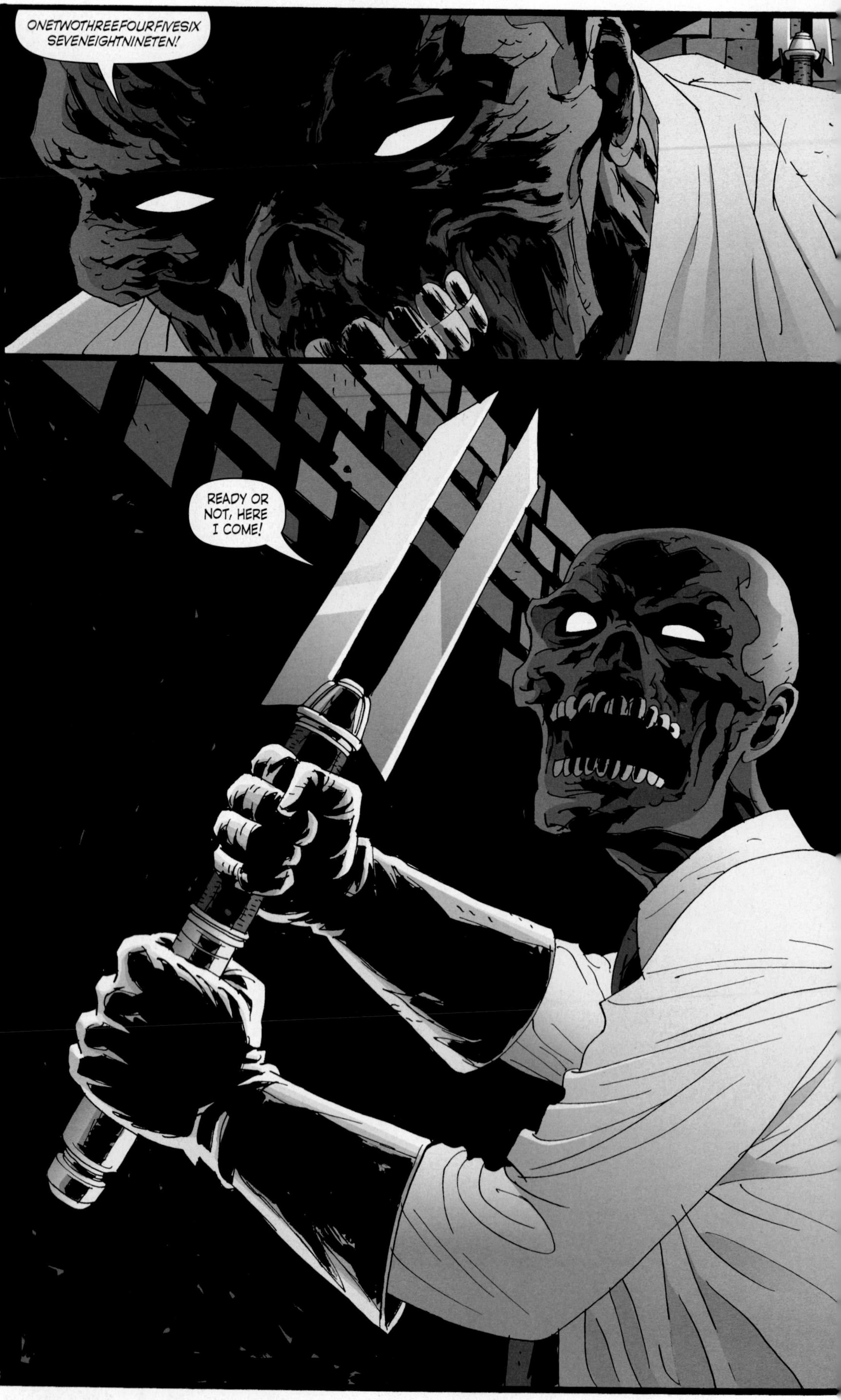
ONETWOTHREEFOURFIVESIX SEVENEIGHTNINETEN!
READY OR NOT, HERE I COME!

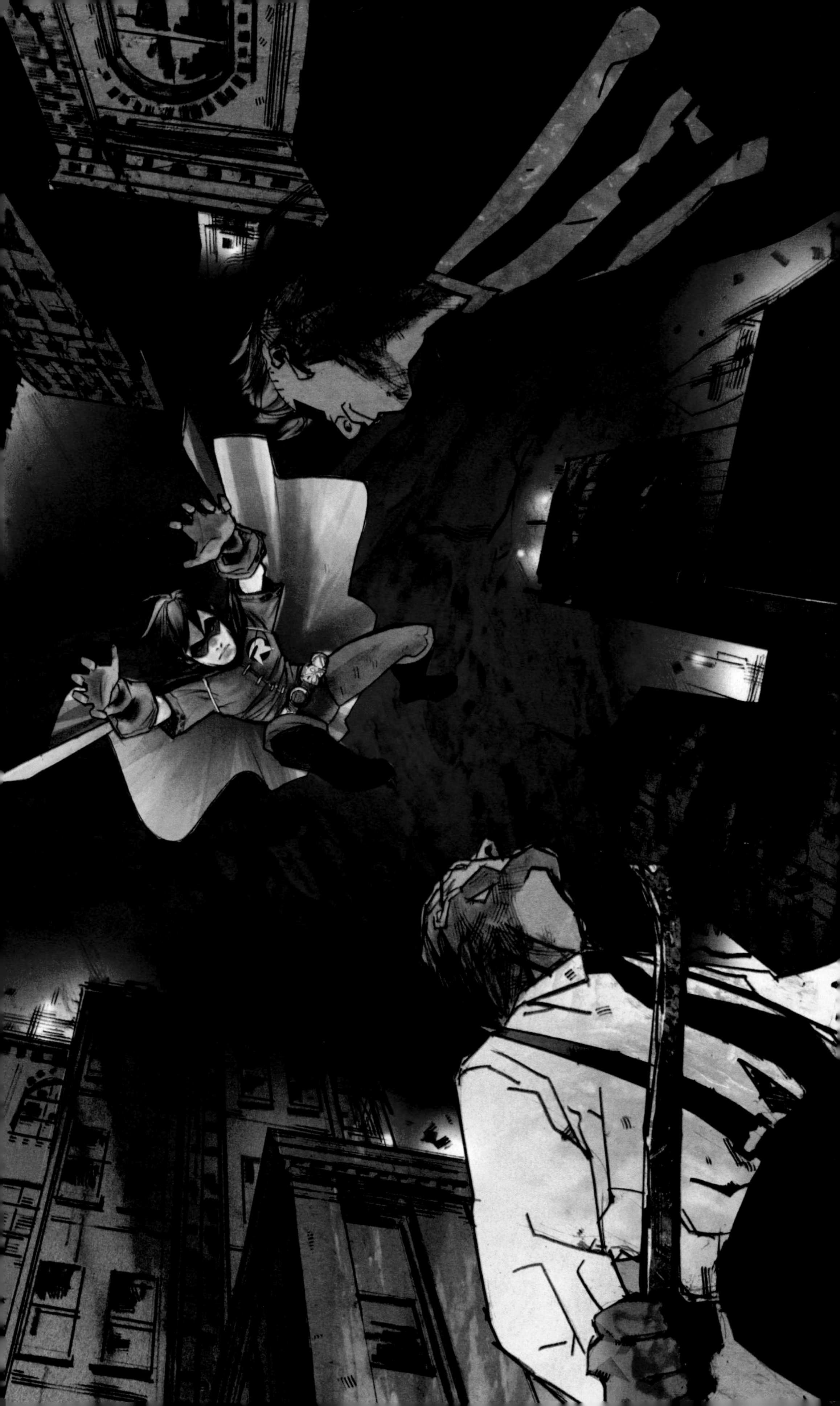

COVER ART BY
DUSTIN NGUYEN

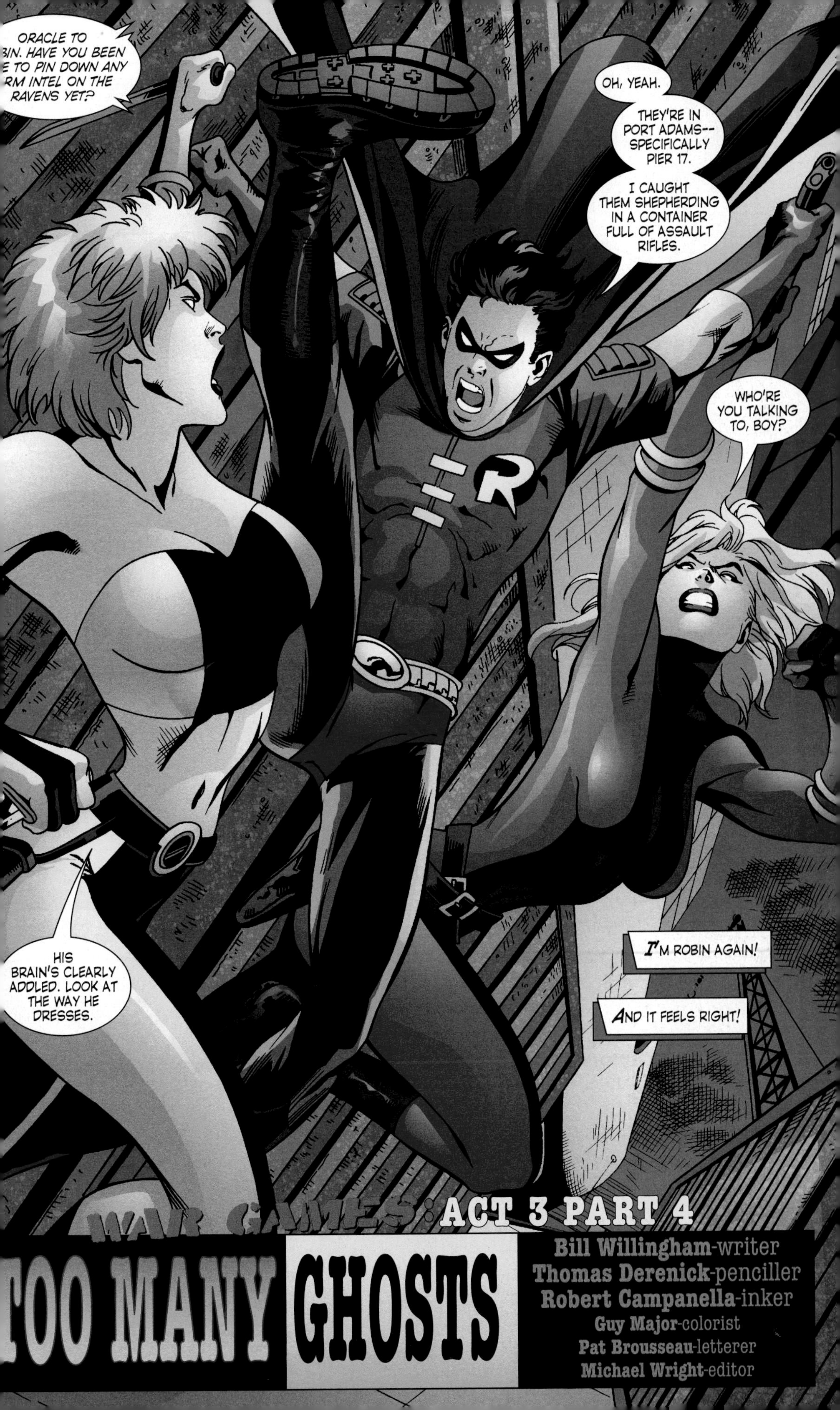
ORACLE TO BIN. HAVE YOU BEEN E TO PIN DOWN ANY RM INTEL ON THE RAVENS YET?
OH, YEAH.
THEY'RE IN PORT ADAMS-- SPECIFICALLY PIER 17.
I CAUGHT THEM SHEPHERDING IN A CONTAINER FULL OF ASSAULT RIFLES.
WHO'RE YOU TALKING TO, BOY?
HIS BRAIN'S CLEARLY ADDLED. LOOK AT THE WAY HE DRESSES.
I'M ROBIN AGAIN!
AND IT FEELS RIGHT!
WAR GAMES: ACT 3 PART 4
TOO MANY GHOSTS
Bill Willingham-writer
Thomas Derenick-penciller
Robert Campanella-inker
Guy Major-colorist
Pat Brousseau-letterer
Michael Wright-editor

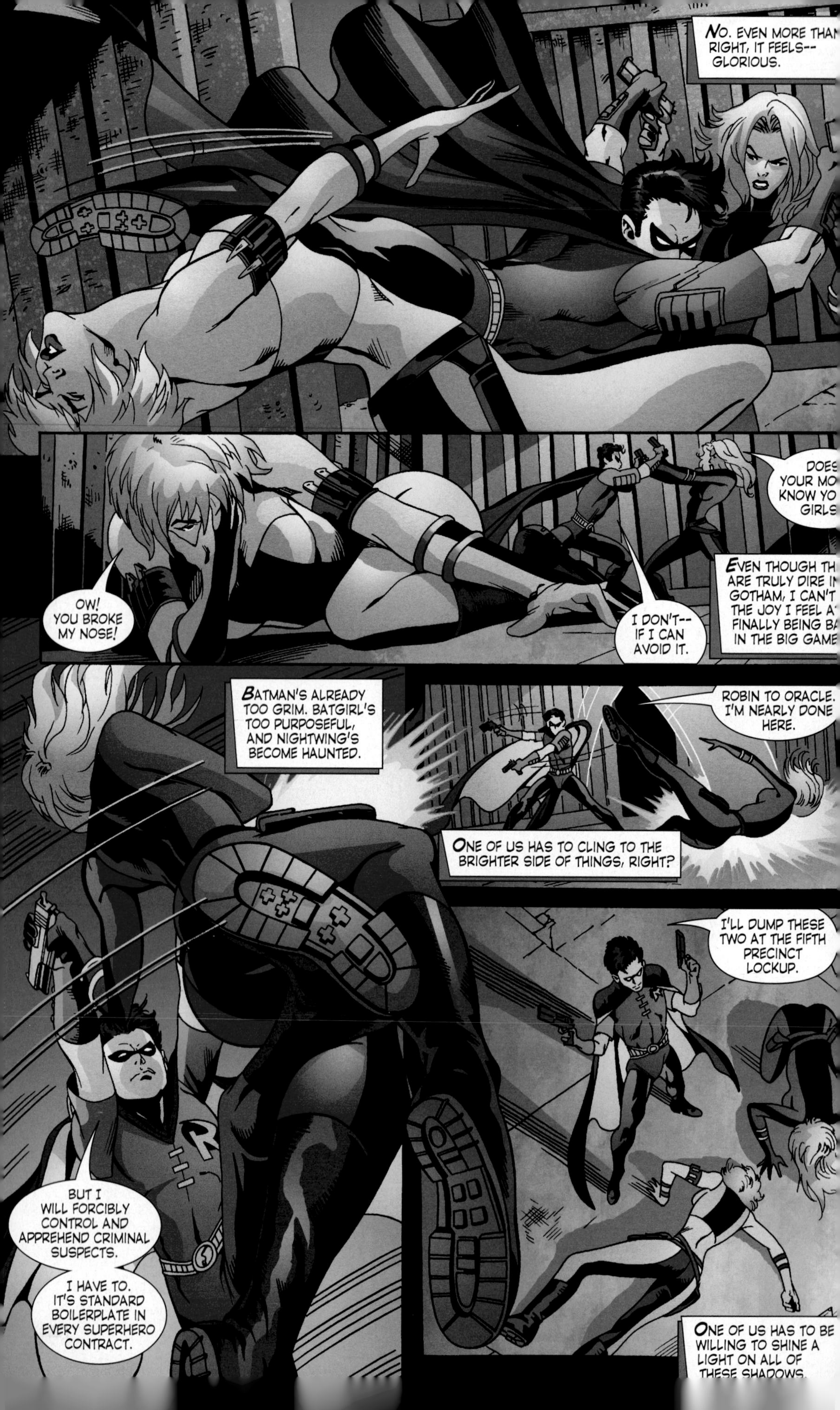
NO. EVEN MORE THAN RIGHT, IT FEELS-- GLORIOUS.
DOES YOUR MO KNOW YO GIRLS
OW! YOU BROKE MY NOSE!
I DON'T-- IF I CAN AVOID IT.
EVEN THOUGH TH ARE TRULY DIRE I GOTHAM, I CAN'T THE JOY I FEEL A FINALLY BEING BA IN THE BIG GAME
BATMAN'S ALREADY TOO GRIM. BATGIRL'S TOO PURPOSEFUL, AND NIGHTWING'S BECOME HAUNTED.
ROBIN TO ORACLE. I'M NEARLY DONE HERE.
ONE OF US HAS TO CLING TO THE BRIGHTER SIDE OF THINGS, RIGHT?
I'LL DUMP THESE TWO AT THE FIFTH PRECINCT LOCKUP.
BUT I WILL FORCIBLY CONTROL AND APPREHEND CRIMINAL SUSPECTS.
I HAVE TO. IT'S STANDARD BOILERPLATE IN EVERY SUPERHERO CONTRACT.
ONE OF US HAS TO BE WILLING TO SHINE A LIGHT ON ALL OF THESE SHADOWS.

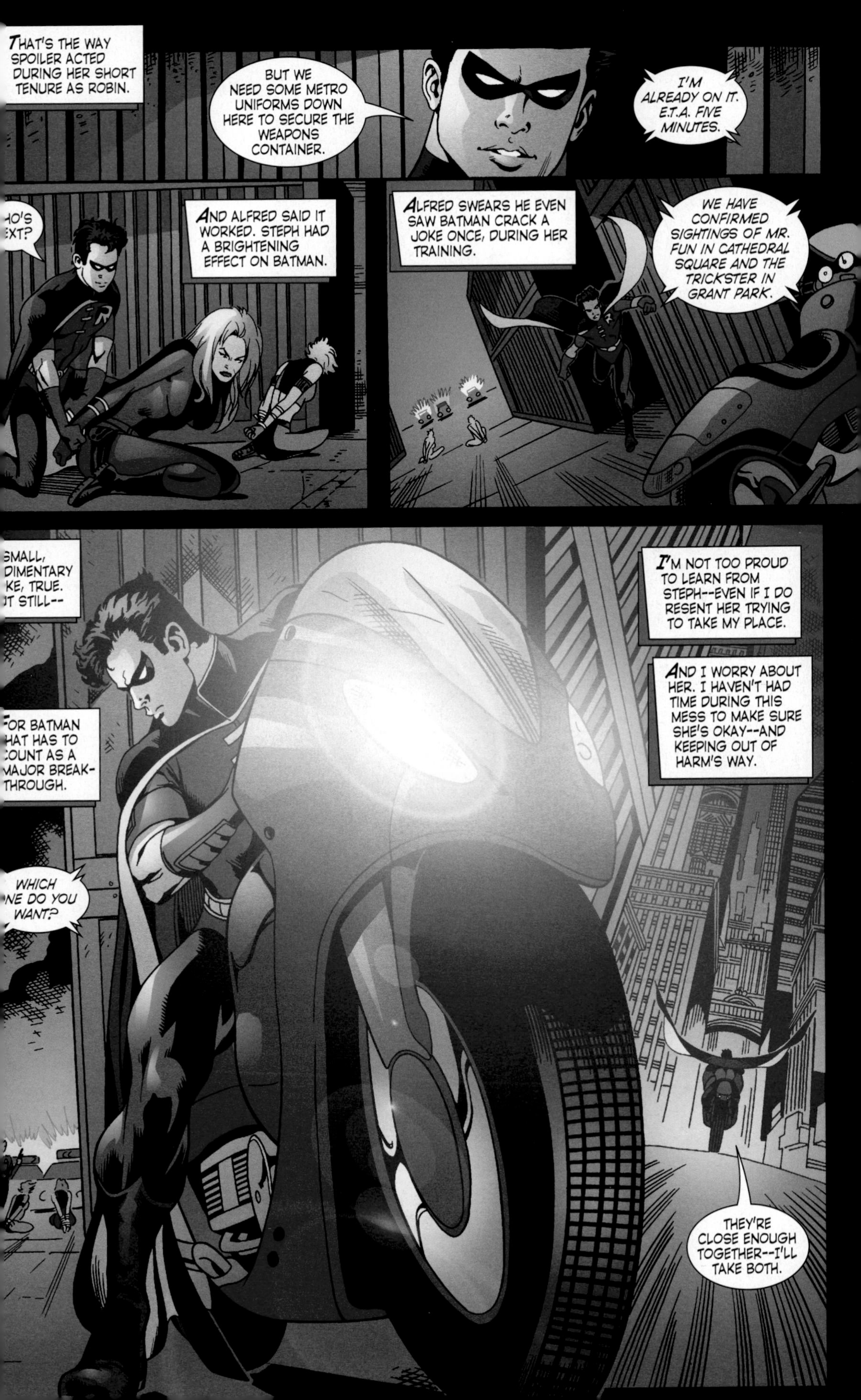
THAT'S THE WAY SPOILER ACTED DURING HER SHORT TENURE AS ROBIN.
BUT WE NEED SOME METRO UNIFORMS DOWN HERE TO SECURE THE WEAPONS CONTAINER.
I'M ALREADY ON IT. E.T.A. FIVE MINUTES.
AND ALFRED SAID IT WORKED. STEPH HAD A BRIGHTENING EFFECT ON BATMAN.
ALFRED SWEARS HE EVEN SAW BATMAN CRACK A JOKE ONCE, DURING HER TRAINING.
WE HAVE CONFIRMED SIGHTINGS OF MR. FUN IN CATHEDRAL SQUARE AND THE TRICKSTER IN GRANT PARK.
I'M NOT TOO PROUD TO LEARN FROM STEPH--EVEN IF I DO RESENT HER TRYING TO TAKE MY PLACE.
AND I WORRY ABOUT HER. I HAVEN'T HAD TIME DURING THIS MESS TO MAKE SURE SHE'S OKAY--AND KEEPING OUT OF HARM'S WAY.
WHICH
THEY'RE CLOSE ENOUGH TOGETHER--I'LL TAKE BOTH.

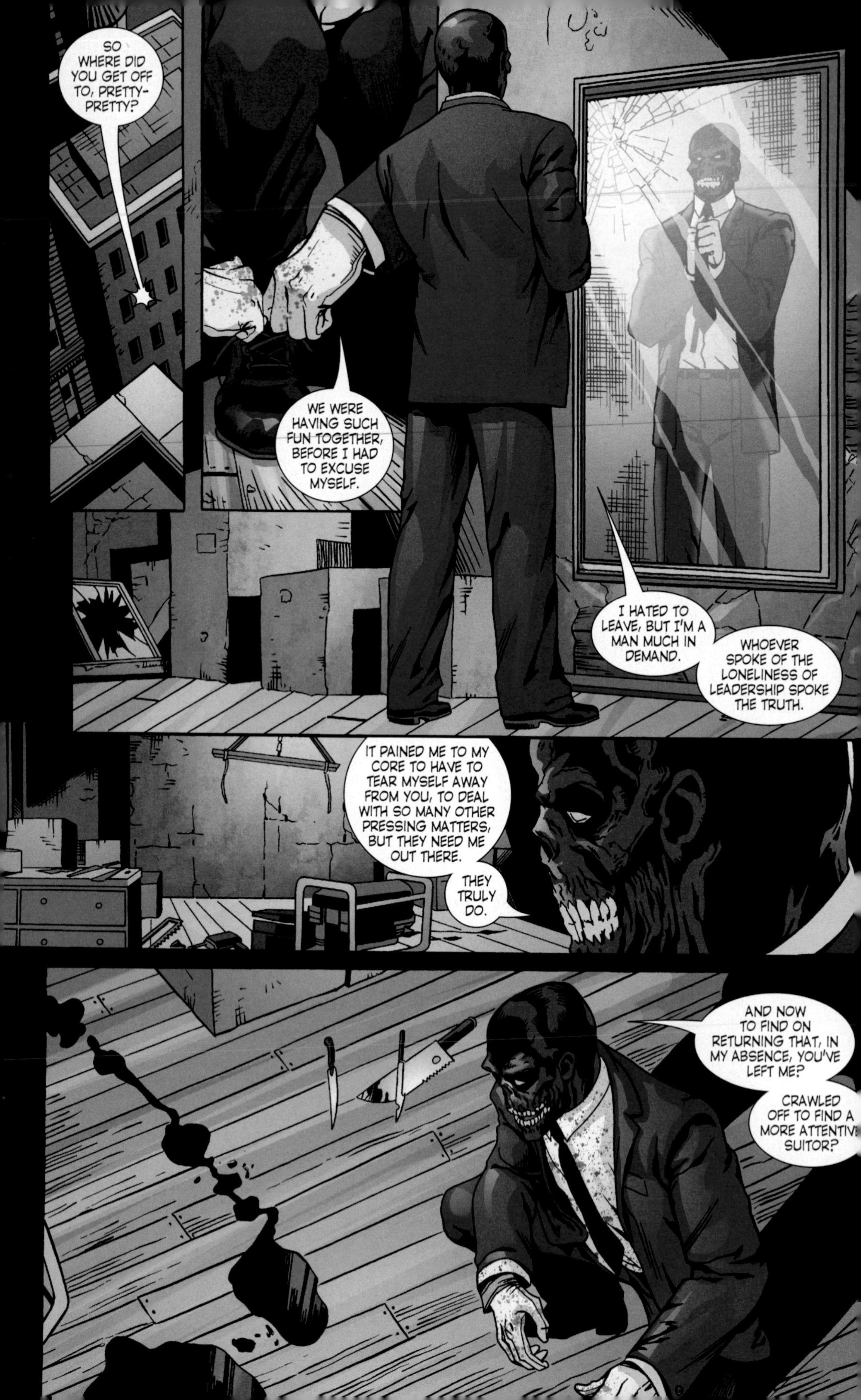
SO WHERE DID YOU GET OFF TO, PRETTY-PRETTY?
WE WERE HAVING SUCH FUN TOGETHER, BEFORE I HAD TO EXCUSE MYSELF.
I HATED TO LEAVE, BUT I'M A MAN MUCH IN DEMAND.
WHOEVER SPOKE OF THE LONELINESS OF LEADERSHIP SPOKE THE TRUTH.
IT PAINED ME TO MY CORE TO HAVE TO TEAR MYSELF AWAY FROM YOU, TO DEAL WITH SO MANY OTHER PRESSING MATTERS, BUT THEY NEED ME OUT THERE.
THEY TRULY DO.
AND NOW TO FIND ON RETURNING THAT, IN MY ABSENCE, YOU'VE LEFT ME?
CRAWLED OFF TO FIND A MORE ATTENTIVE SUITOR?

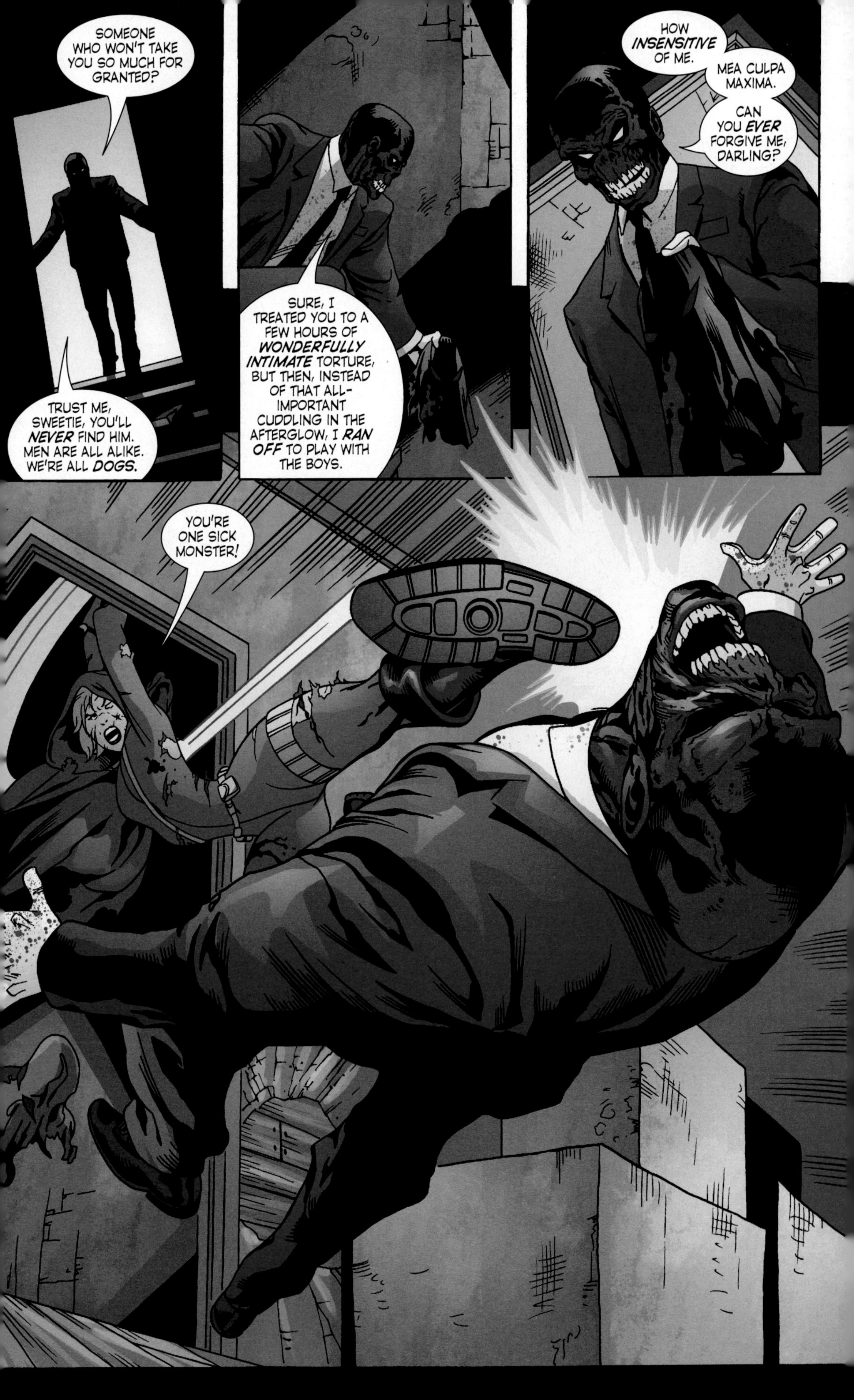
SOMEONE WHO WON'T TAKE YOU SO MUCH FOR GRANTED?
TRUST ME, SWEETIE, YOU'LL NEVER FIND HIM. MEN ARE ALL ALIKE. WE'RE ALL DOGS.
SURE, I TREATED YOU TO A FEW HOURS OF WONDERFULLY INTIMATE TORTURE, BUT THEN, INSTEAD OF THAT ALL-IMPORTANT CUDDLING IN THE AFTERGLOW, I RAN OFF TO PLAY WITH THE BOYS.
HOW INSENSITIVE OF ME.
MEA CULPA MAXIMA.
CAN YOU EVER FORGIVE ME, DARLING?
YOU'RE ONE SICK MONSTER!

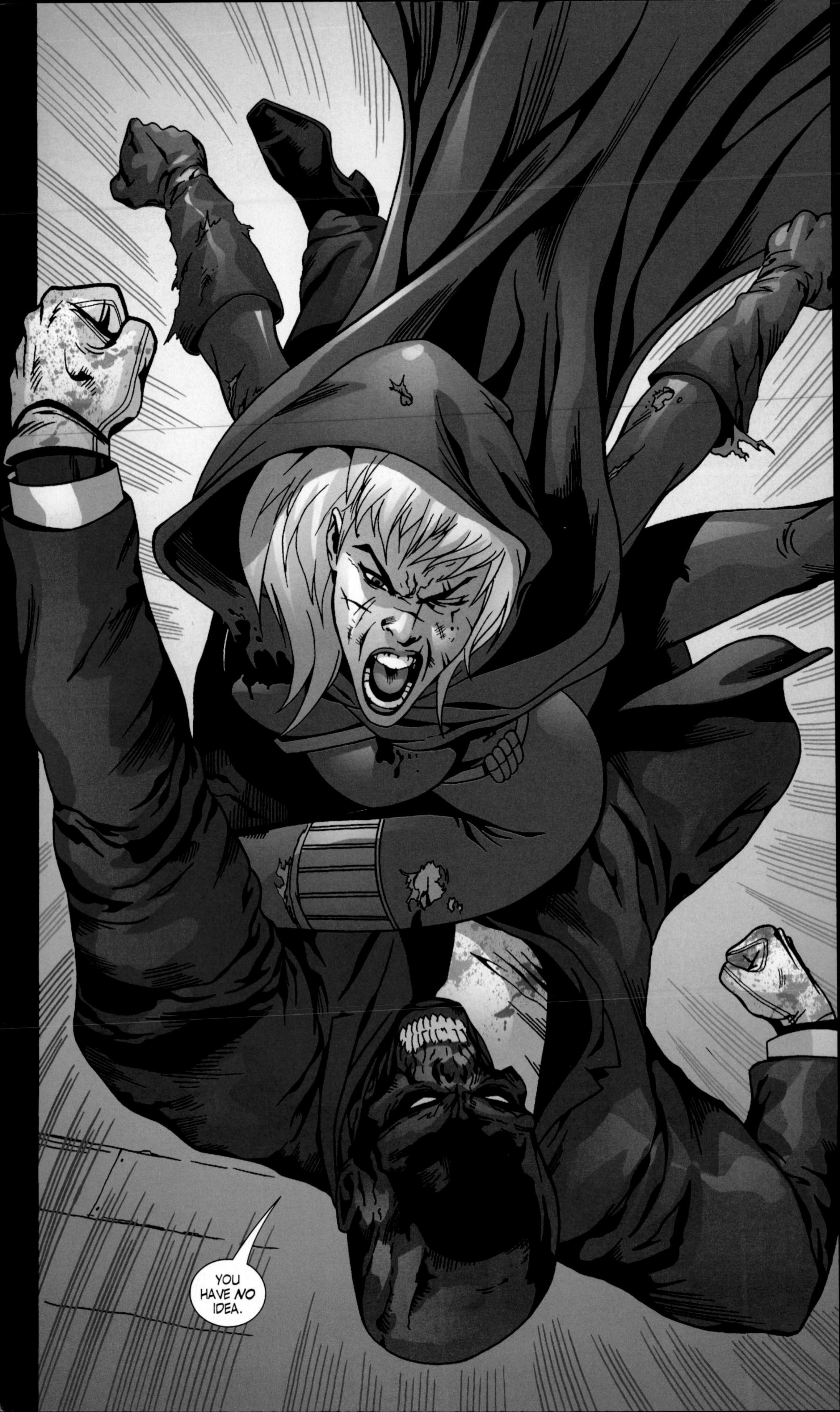
YOU HAVE *NO* IDEA.

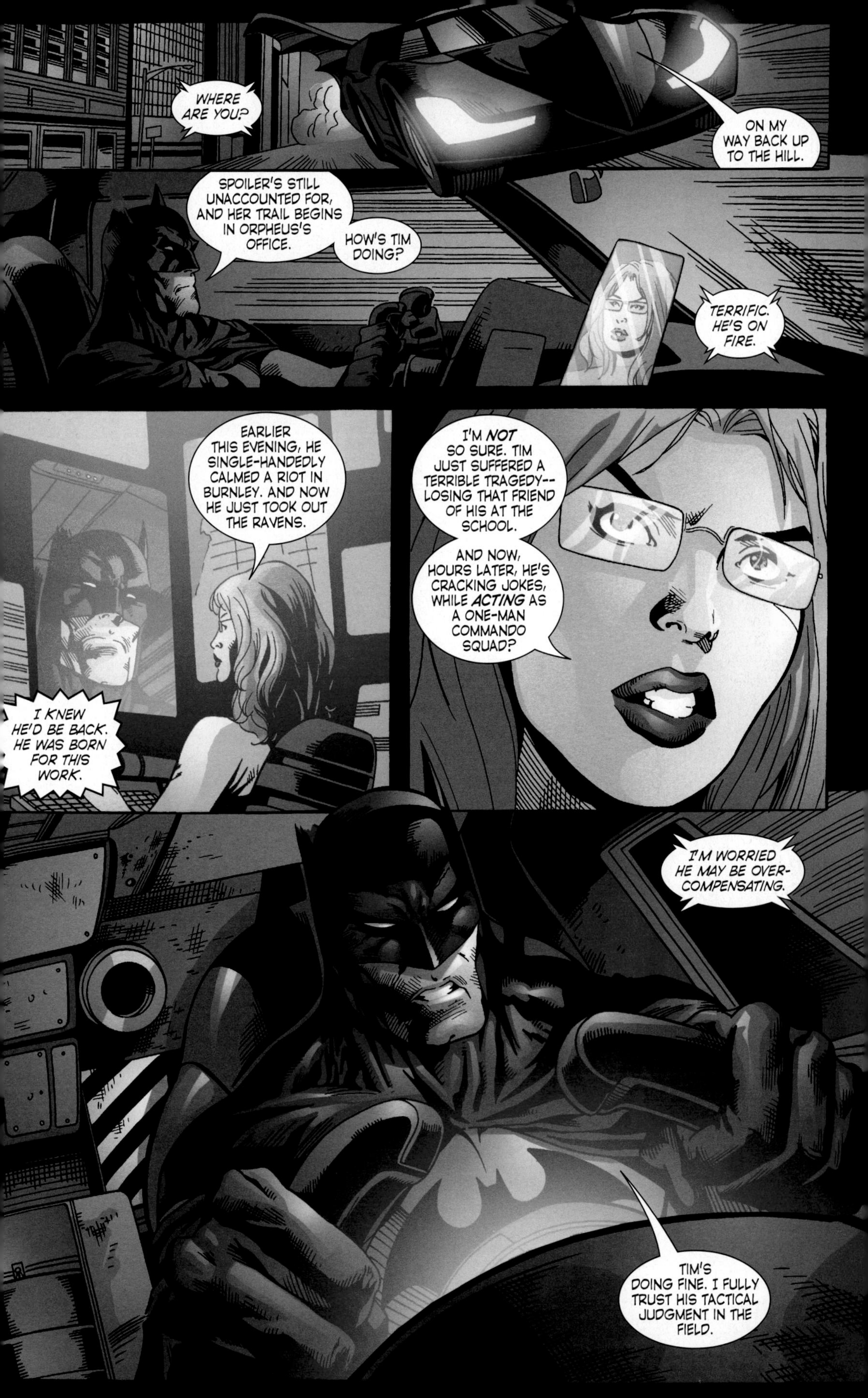
WHERE ARE YOU?
ON MY WAY BACK UP TO THE HILL.
SPOILER'S STILL UNACCOUNTED FOR, AND HER TRAIL BEGINS IN ORPHEUS'S OFFICE.
HOW'S TIM DOING?
TERRIFIC. HE'S ON FIRE.
EARLIER THIS EVENING, HE SINGLE-HANDEDLY CALMED A RIOT IN BURNLEY. AND NOW HE JUST TOOK OUT THE RAVENS.
I KNEW HE'D BE BACK. HE WAS BORN FOR THIS WORK.
I'M NOT SO SURE. TIM JUST SUFFERED A TERRIBLE TRAGEDY--LOSING THAT FRIEND OF HIS AT THE SCHOOL.
AND NOW, HOURS LATER, HE'S CRACKING JOKES, WHILE ACTING AS A ONE-MAN COMMANDO SQUAD?
I'M WORRIED HE MAY BE OVER-COMPENSATING.
TIM'S DOING FINE. I FULLY TRUST HIS TACTICAL JUDGMENT IN THE FIELD.

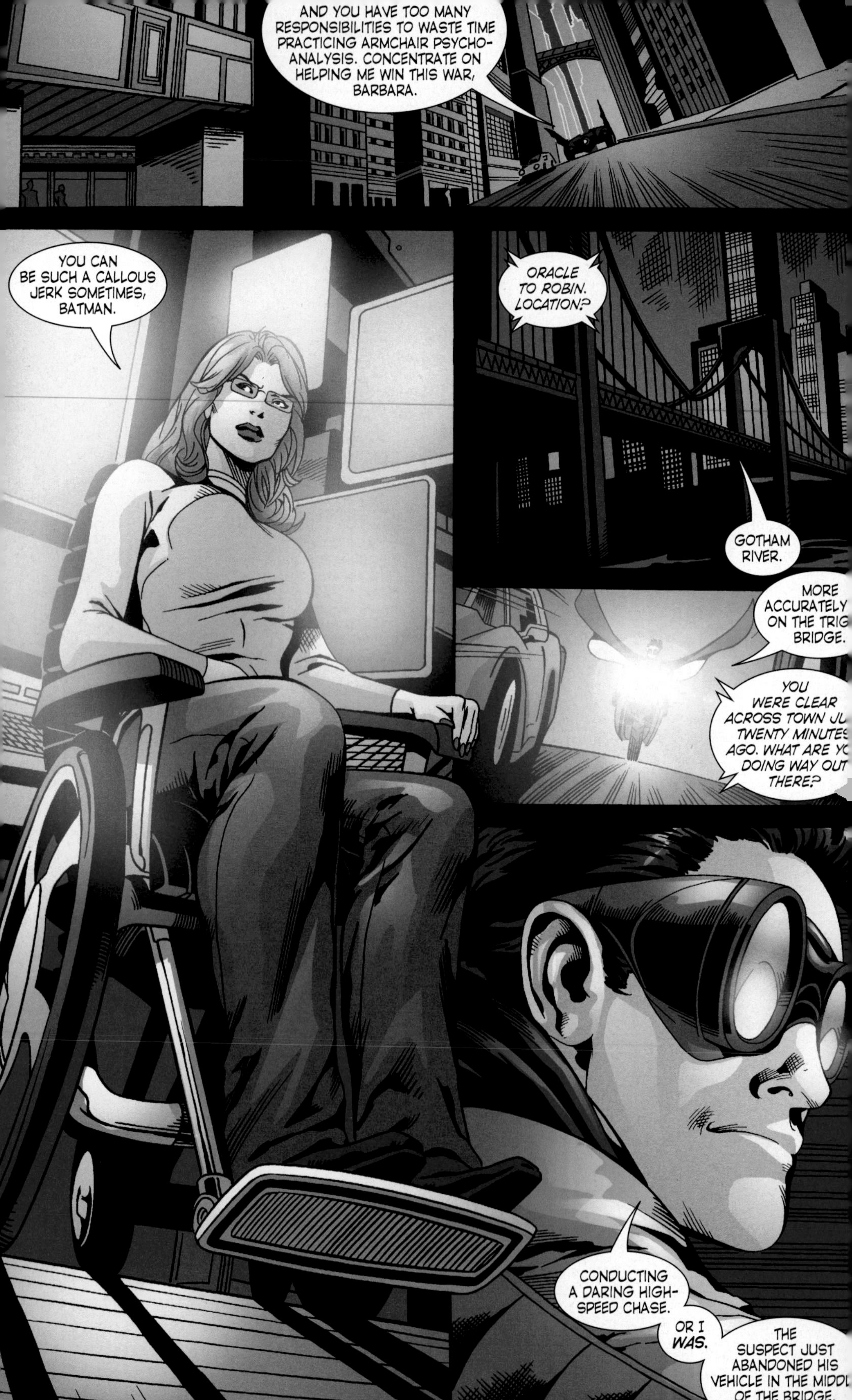
AND YOU HAVE TOO MANY RESPONSIBILITIES TO WASTE TIME PRACTICING ARMCHAIR PSYCHO-ANALYSIS. CONCENTRATE ON HELPING ME WIN THIS WAR, BARBARA.
YOU CAN BE SUCH A CALLOUS JERK SOMETIMES, BATMAN.
ORACLE TO ROBIN. LOCATION?
GOTHAM RIVER.
MORE ACCURATELY ON THE TRIG BRIDGE.
YOU WERE CLEAR ACROSS TOWN JU TWENTY MINUTES AGO. WHAT ARE YO DOING WAY OUT THERE?
CONDUCTING A DARING HIGH-SPEED CHASE.
OR I *WAS.*
THE SUSPECT JUST ABANDONED HIS VEHICLE IN THE MIDDL OF THE BRIDGE.

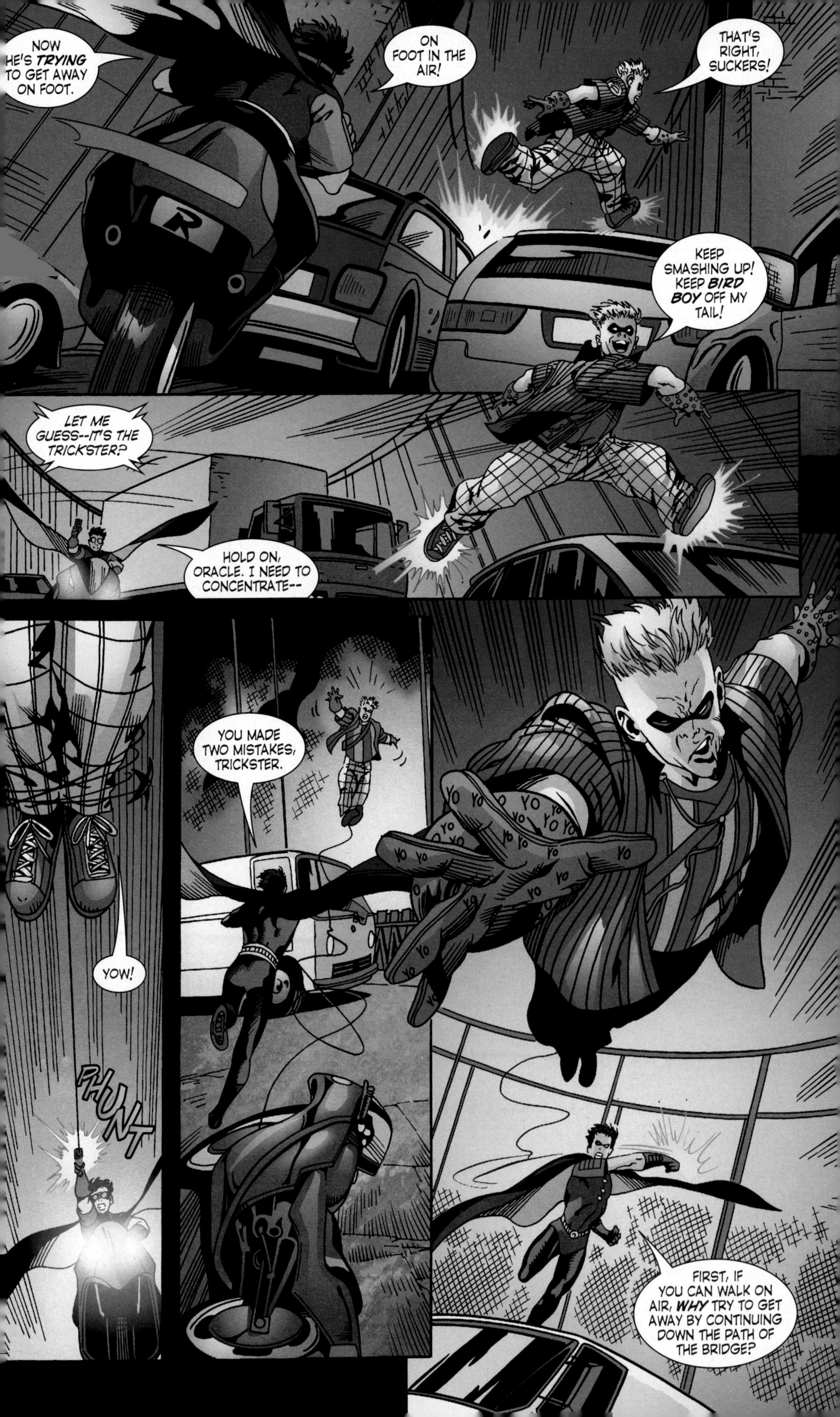
NOW HE'S *TRYING* TO GET AWAY ON FOOT.
ON FOOT IN THE AIR!
THAT'S RIGHT, SUCKERS!
KEEP SMASHING UP! KEEP *BIRD BOY* OFF MY TAIL!
LET ME GUESS--IT'S THE TRICKSTER?
HOLD ON, ORACLE. I NEED TO CONCENTRATE--
PHUNT
YOW!
YOU MADE TWO MISTAKES, TRICKSTER.
FIRST, IF YOU CAN WALK ON AIR, *WHY* TRY TO GET AWAY BY CONTINUING DOWN THE PATH OF THE BRIDGE?

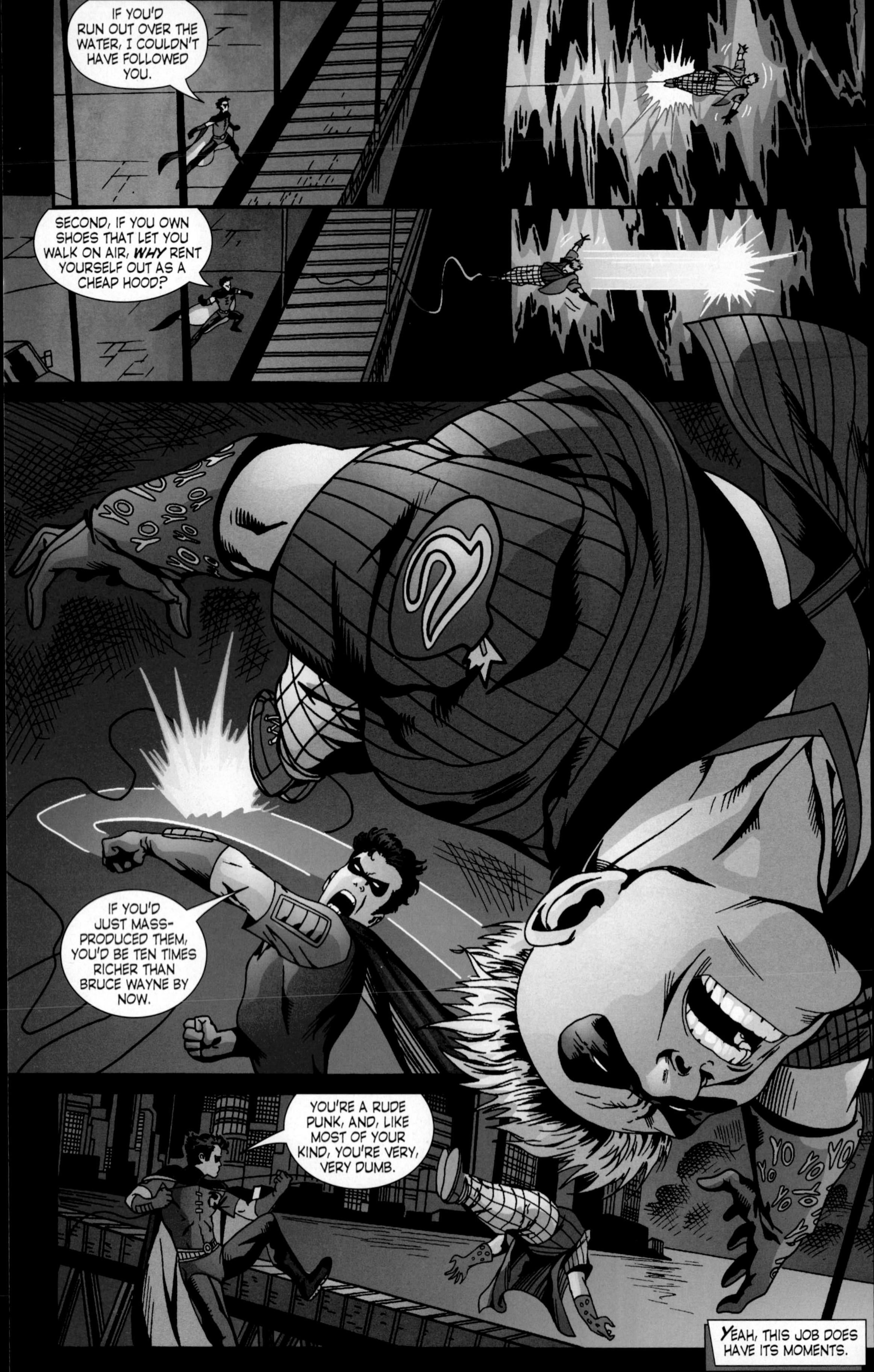
IF YOU'D RUN OUT OVER THE WATER, I COULDN'T HAVE FOLLOWED YOU.
SECOND, IF YOU OWN SHOES THAT LET YOU WALK ON AIR, WHY RENT YOURSELF OUT AS A CHEAP HOOD?
YO YO YO
IF YOU'D JUST MASS-PRODUCED THEM, YOU'D BE TEN TIMES RICHER THAN BRUCE WAYNE BY NOW.
YOU'RE A RUDE PUNK, AND, LIKE MOST OF YOUR KIND, YOU'RE VERY, VERY DUMB.
YEAH, THIS JOB DOES HAVE ITS MOMENTS.

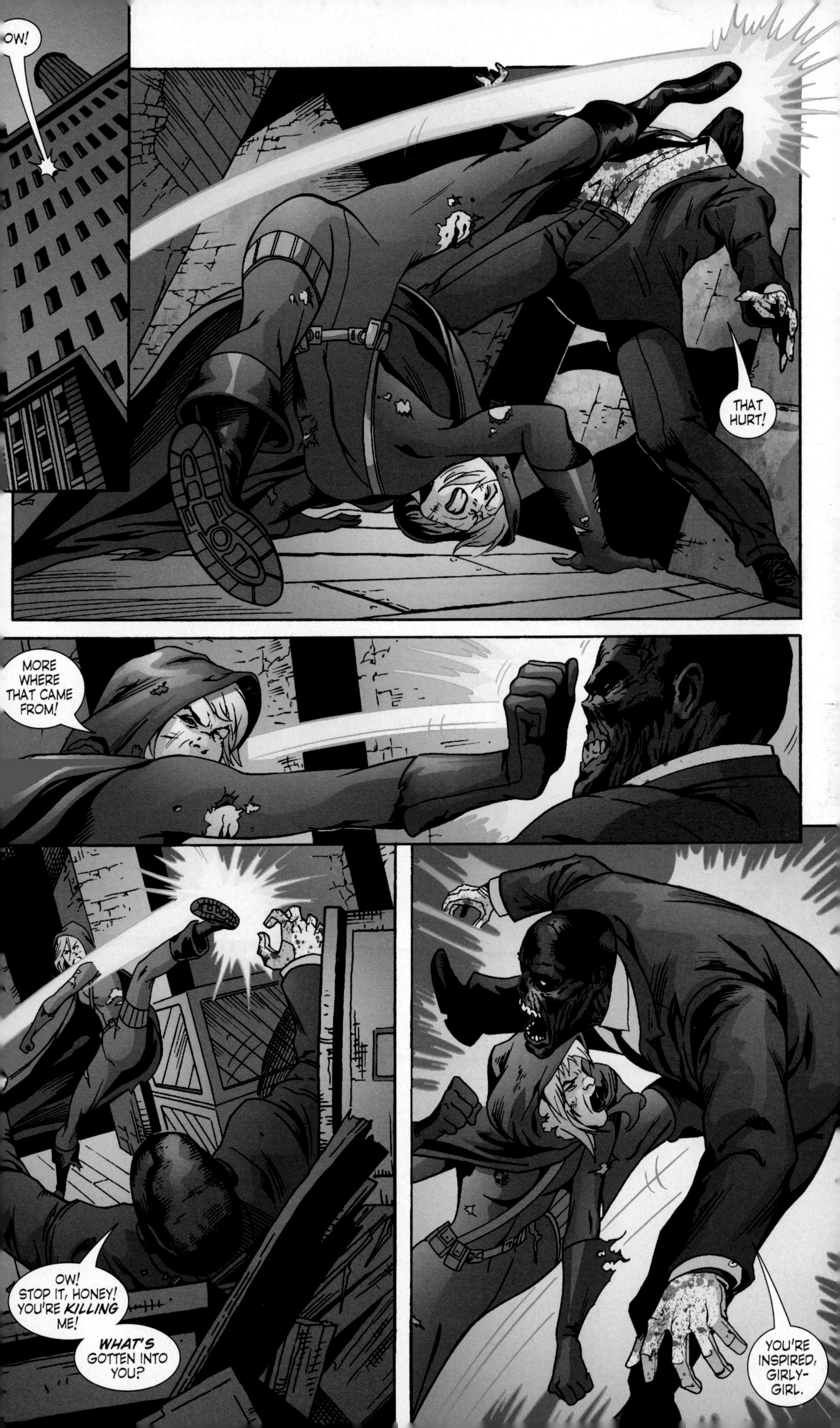
OW!
THAT HURT!
MORE WHERE THAT CAME FROM!
OW! STOP IT, HONEY! YOU'RE *KILLING* ME!
WHAT'S GOTTEN INTO YOU?
YOU'RE INSPIRED, GIRLY-GIRL.

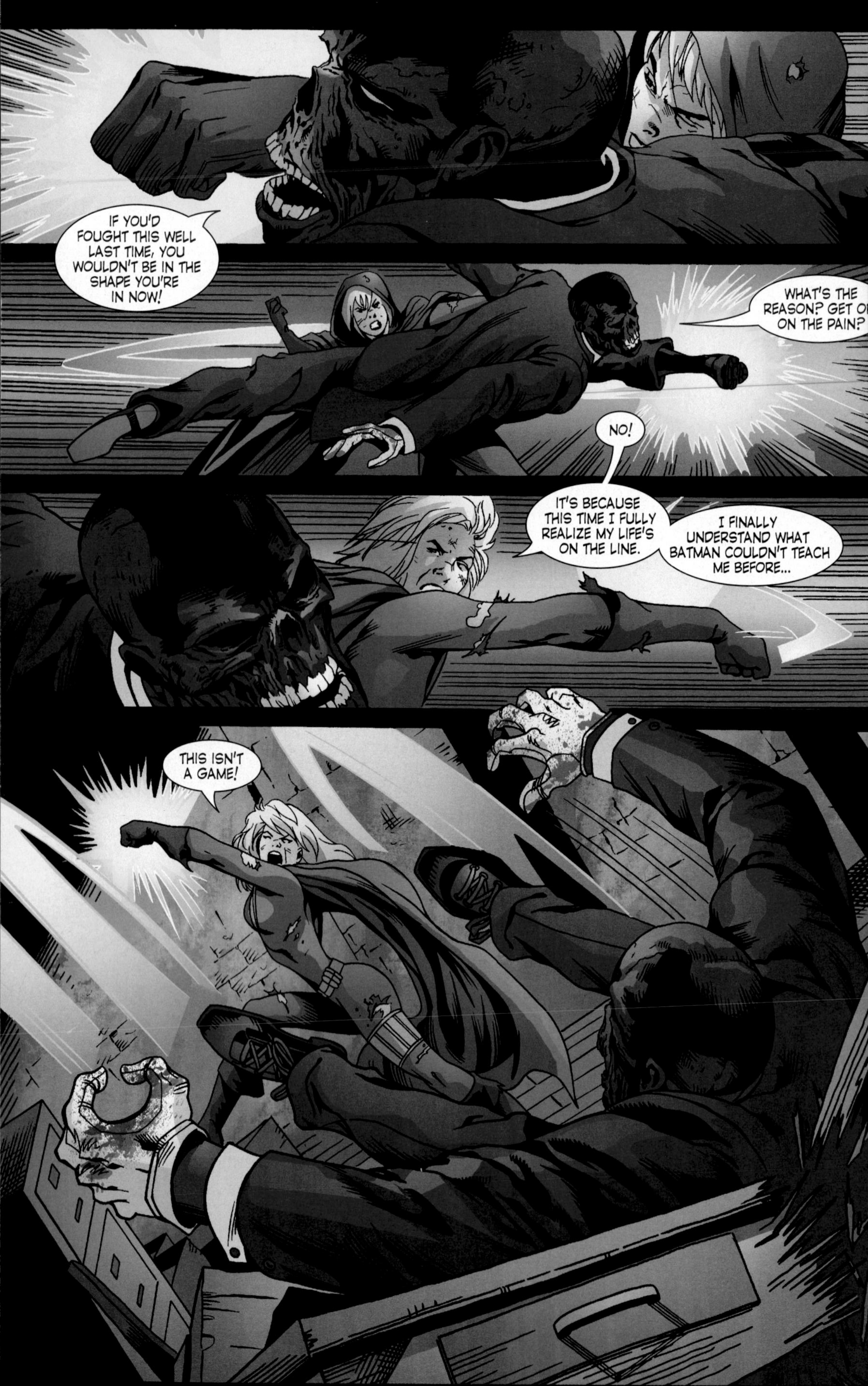
IF YOU'D FOUGHT THIS WELL LAST TIME, YOU WOULDN'T BE IN THE SHAPE YOU'RE IN NOW!
WHAT'S THE REASON? GET O ON THE PAIN?
NO!
IT'S BECAUSE THIS TIME I FULLY REALIZE MY LIFE'S ON THE LINE.
I FINALLY UNDERSTAND WHAT BATMAN COULDN'T TEACH ME BEFORE...
THIS ISN'T A GAME!

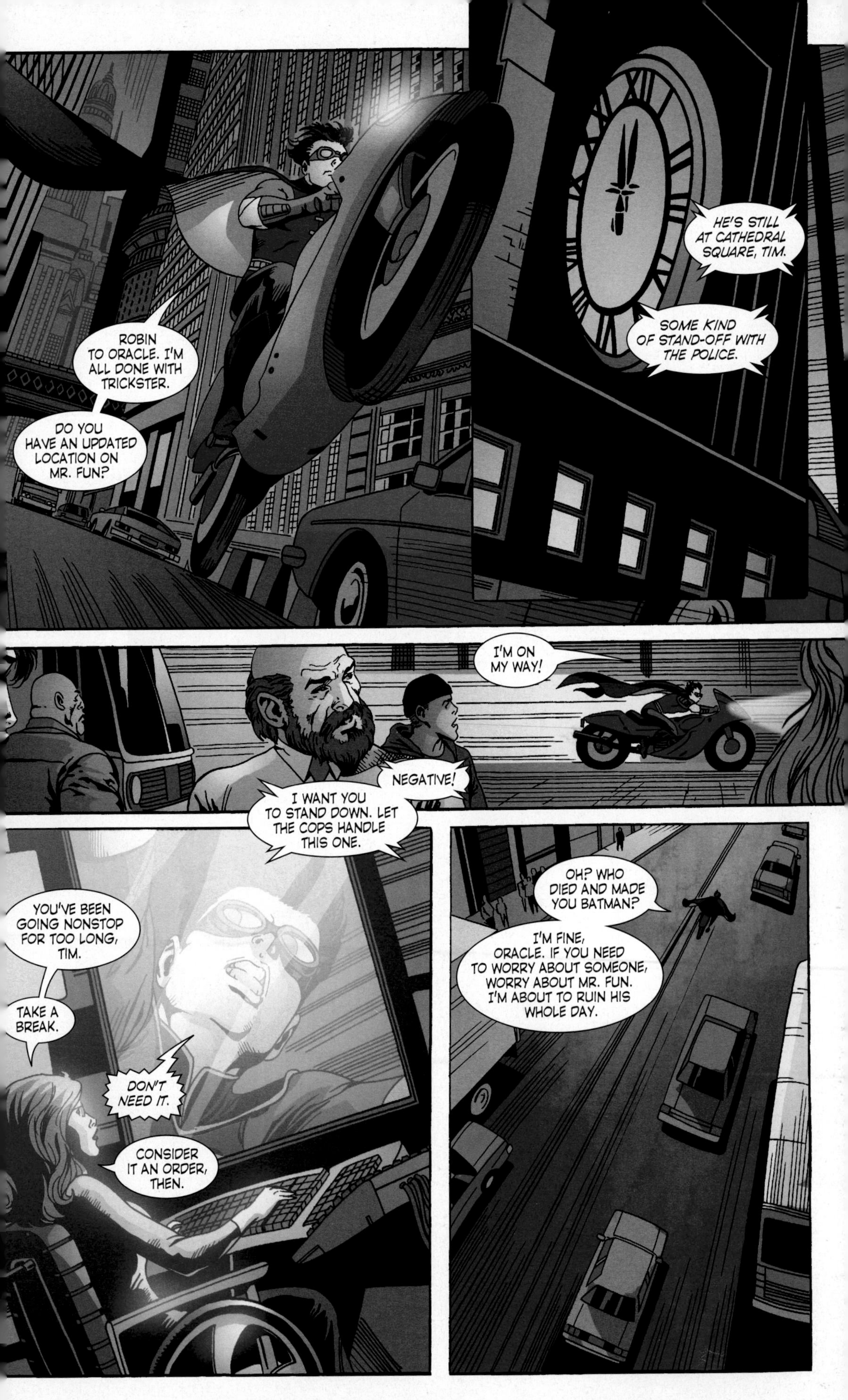
ROBIN TO ORACLE. I'M ALL DONE WITH TRICKSTER.
DO YOU HAVE AN UPDATED LOCATION ON MR. FUN?
HE'S STILL AT CATHEDRAL SQUARE, TIM.
SOME KIND OF STAND-OFF WITH THE POLICE.
I'M ON MY WAY!
NEGATIVE!
I WANT YOU TO STAND DOWN. LET THE COPS HANDLE THIS ONE.
YOU'VE BEEN GOING NONSTOP FOR TOO LONG, TIM.
TAKE A BREAK.
DON'T NEED IT.
CONSIDER IT AN ORDER, THEN.
OH? WHO DIED AND MADE YOU BATMAN?
I'M FINE, ORACLE. IF YOU NEED TO WORRY ABOUT SOMEONE, WORRY ABOUT MR. FUN. I'M ABOUT TO RUIN HIS WHOLE DAY.

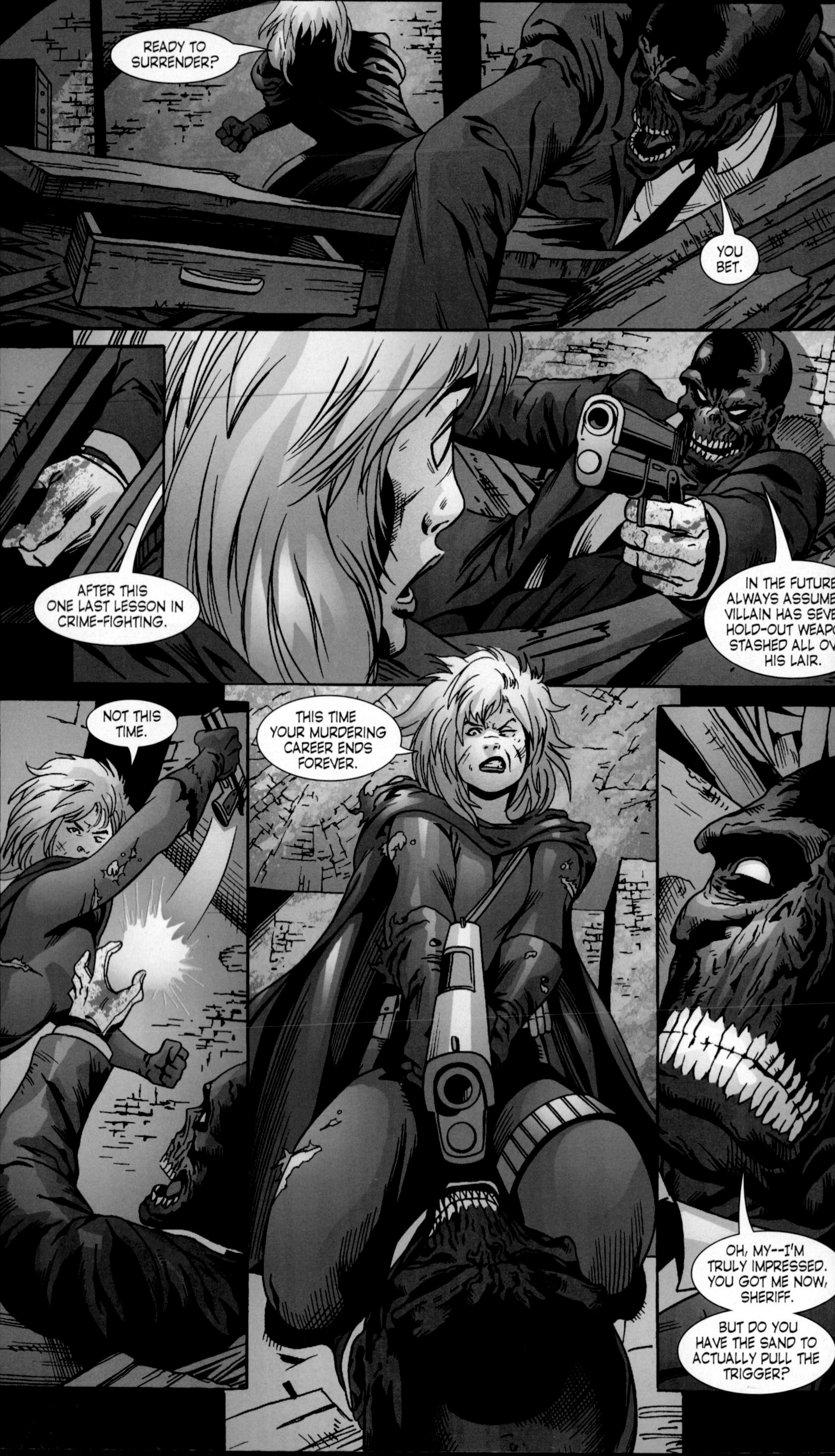
READY TO SURRENDER?
YOU BET.
AFTER THIS ONE LAST LESSON IN CRIME-FIGHTING.
IN THE FUTURE ALWAYS ASSUME VILLAIN HAS SEVE HOLD-OUT WEAPO STASHED ALL OV HIS LAIR.
NOT THIS TIME.
THIS TIME YOUR MURDERING CAREER ENDS FOREVER.
OH, MY--I'M TRULY IMPRESSED. YOU GOT ME NOW, SHERIFF.
BUT DO YOU HAVE THE SAND TO ACTUALLY PULL THE TRIGGER?

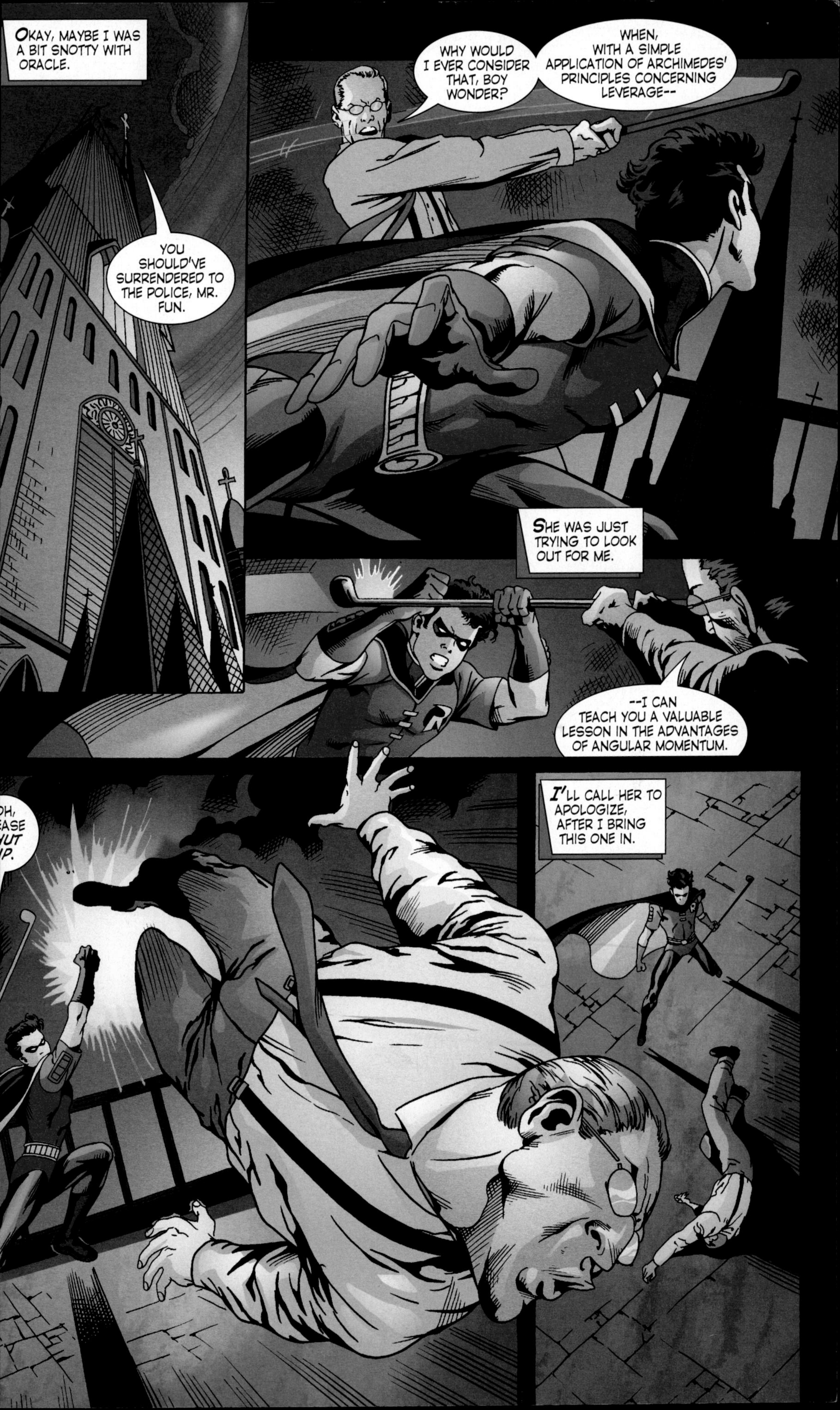

OKAY, MAYBE I WAS A BIT SNOTTY WITH ORACLE.
YOU SHOULD'VE SURRENDERED TO THE POLICE, MR. FUN.
WHY WOULD I EVER CONSIDER THAT, BOY WONDER?
WHEN, WITH A SIMPLE APPLICATION OF ARCHIMEDES' PRINCIPLES CONCERNING LEVERAGE--
SHE WAS JUST TRYING TO LOOK OUT FOR ME.
--I CAN TEACH YOU A VALUABLE LESSON IN THE ADVANTAGES OF ANGULAR MOMENTUM.
OH, EASE HUT UP.
I'LL CALL HER TO APOLOGIZE, AFTER I BRING THIS ONE IN.

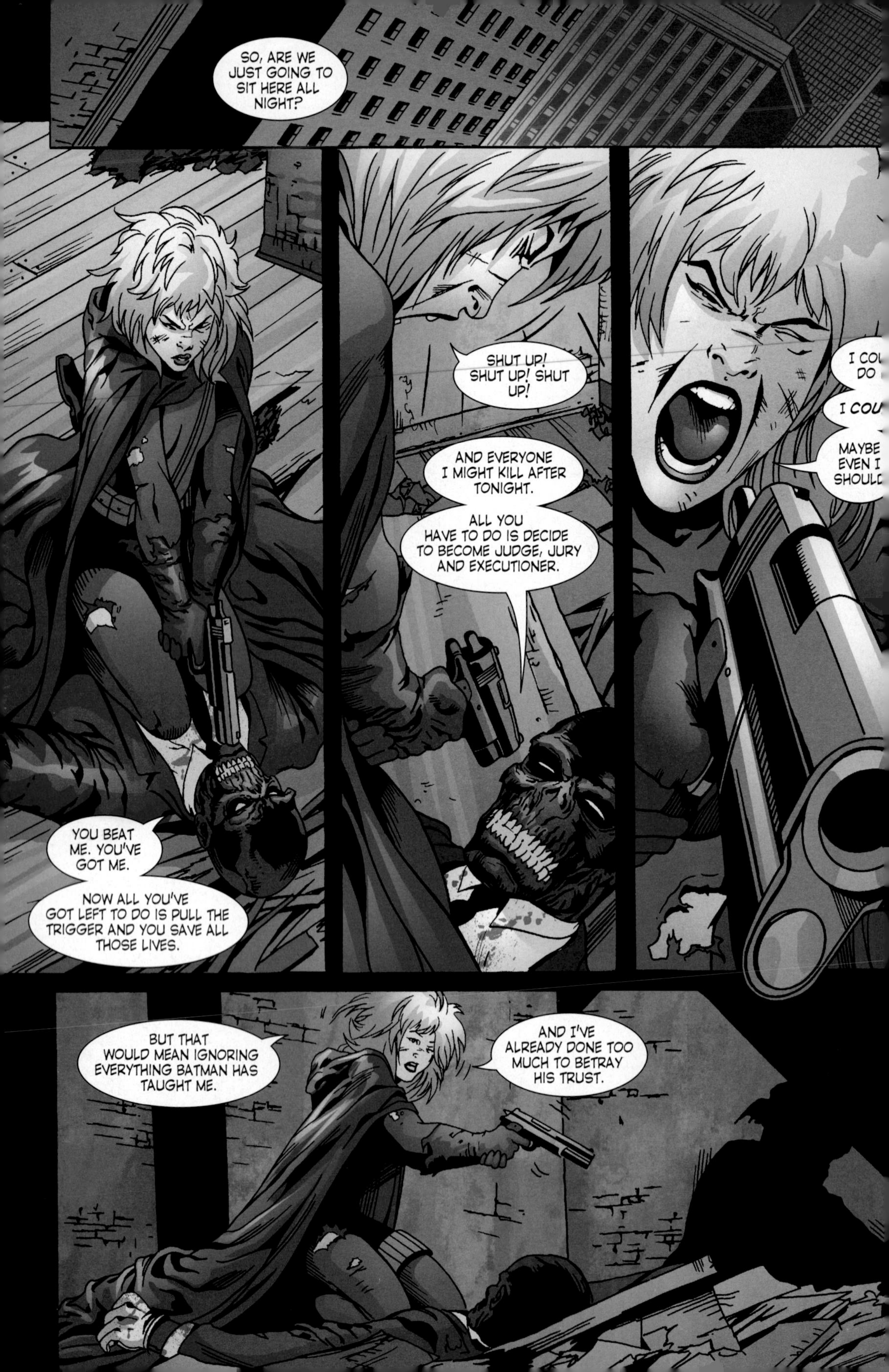
SO, ARE WE JUST GOING TO SIT HERE ALL NIGHT?
YOU BEAT ME. YOU'VE GOT ME.
NOW ALL YOU'VE GOT LEFT TO DO IS PULL THE TRIGGER AND YOU SAVE ALL THOSE LIVES.
SHUT UP! SHUT UP! SHUT UP!
AND EVERYONE I MIGHT KILL AFTER TONIGHT.
ALL YOU HAVE TO DO IS DECIDE TO BECOME JUDGE, JURY AND EXECUTIONER.
I COU DO
I COU
MAYBE EVEN I SHOULD
BUT THAT WOULD MEAN IGNORING EVERYTHING BATMAN HAS TAUGHT ME.
AND I'VE ALREADY DONE TOO MUCH TO BETRAY HIS TRUST.

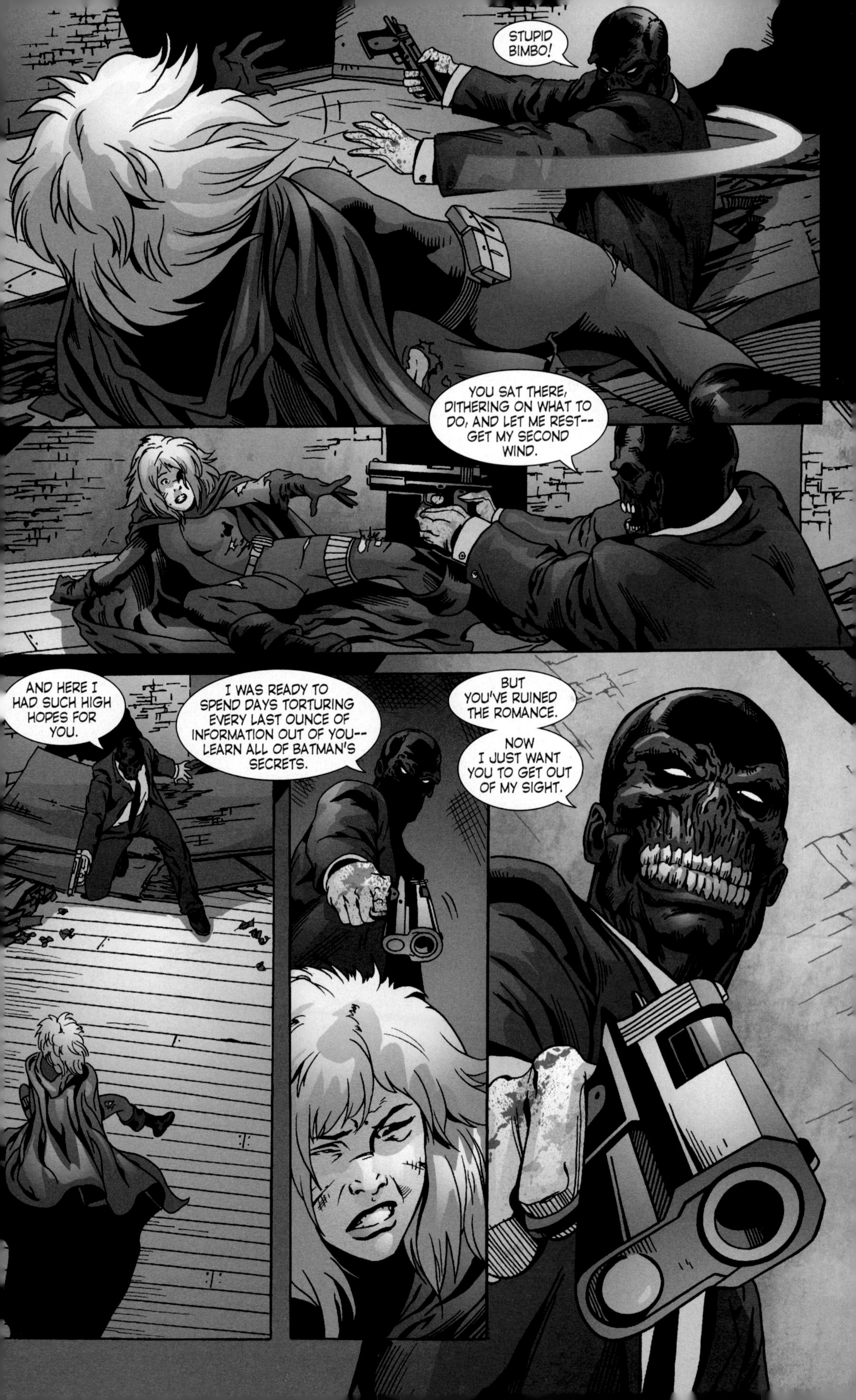
STUPID BIMBO!
YOU SAT THERE, DITHERING ON WHAT TO DO, AND LET ME REST-- GET MY SECOND WIND.
AND HERE I HAD SUCH HIGH HOPES FOR YOU.
I WAS READY TO SPEND DAYS TORTURING EVERY LAST OUNCE OF INFORMATION OUT OF YOU-- LEARN ALL OF BATMAN'S SECRETS.
BUT YOU'VE RUINED THE ROMANCE.
NOW I JUST WANT YOU TO GET OUT OF MY SIGHT.

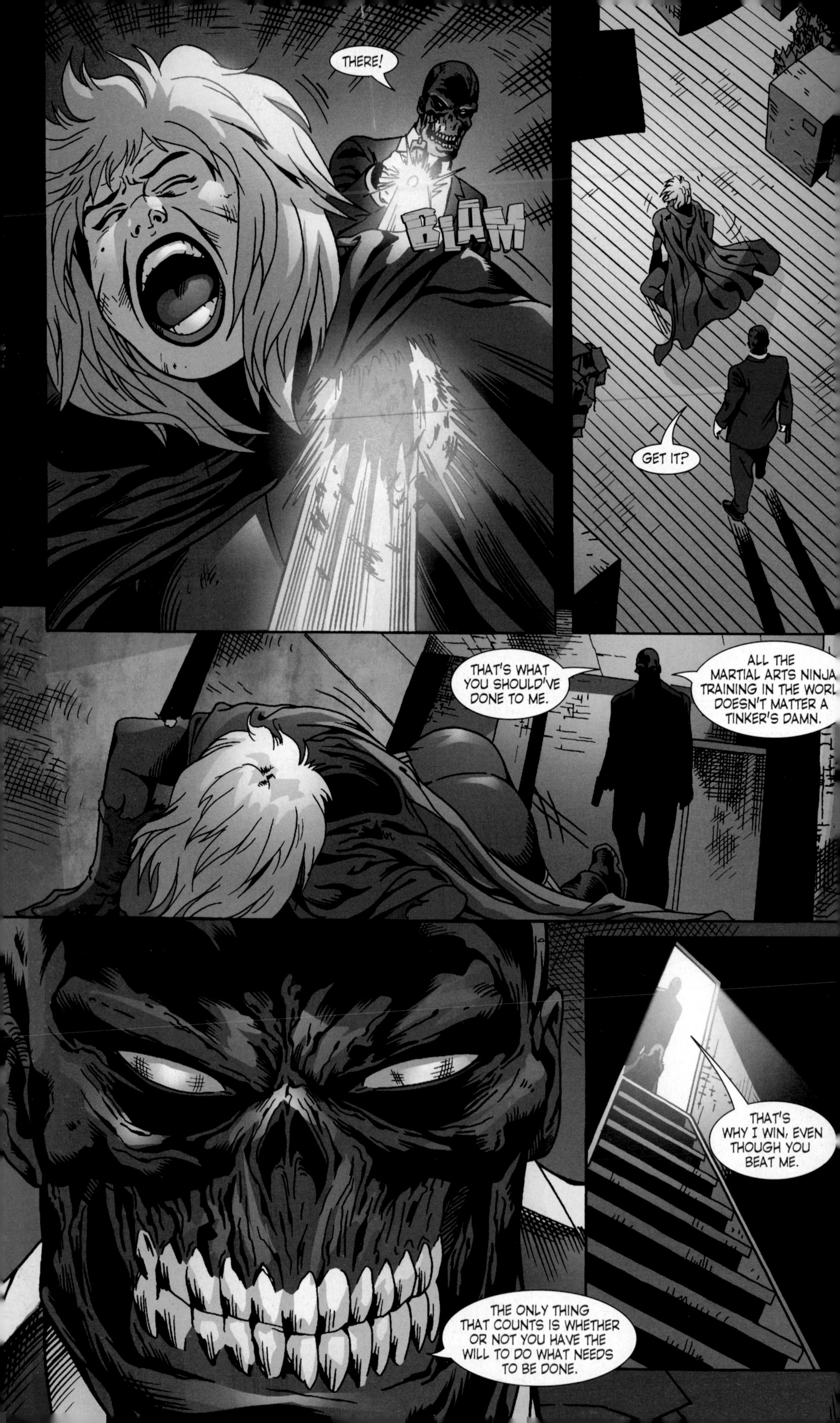
THERE!
BLAM
GET IT?
THAT'S WHAT YOU SHOULD'VE DONE TO ME.
ALL THE MARTIAL ARTS NINJA TRAINING IN THE WORL DOESN'T MATTER A TINKER'S DAMN.
THE ONLY THING THAT COUNTS IS WHETHER OR NOT YOU HAVE THE WILL TO DO WHAT NEEDS TO BE DONE.
THAT'S WHY I WIN, EVEN THOUGH YOU BEAT ME.

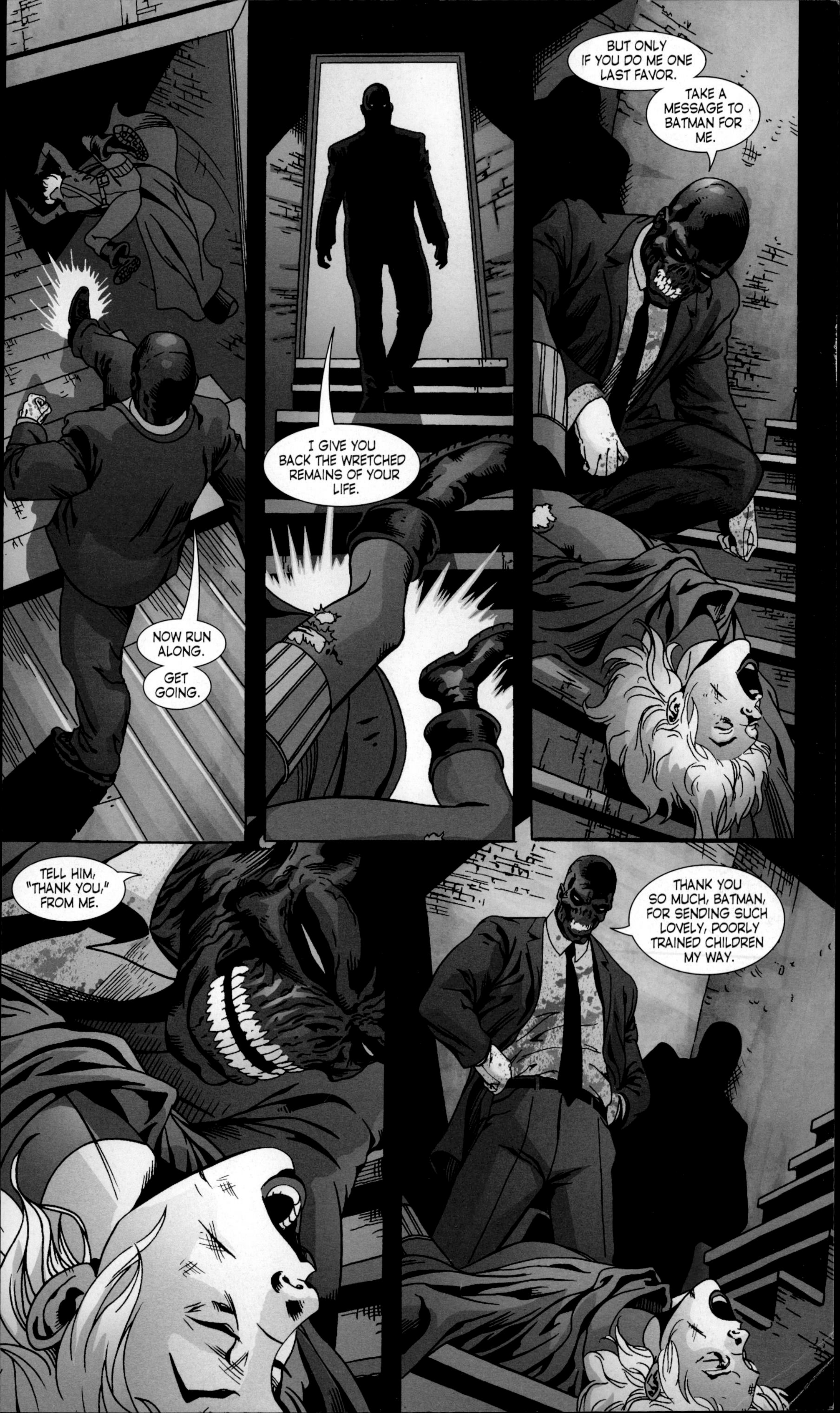
NOW RUN ALONG.
GET GOING.
I GIVE YOU BACK THE WRETCHED REMAINS OF YOUR LIFE.
BUT ONLY IF YOU DO ME ONE LAST FAVOR.
TAKE A MESSAGE TO BATMAN FOR ME.
TELL HIM, "THANK YOU," FROM ME.
THANK YOU SO MUCH, BATMAN, FOR SENDING SUCH LOVELY, POORLY TRAINED CHILDREN MY WAY.

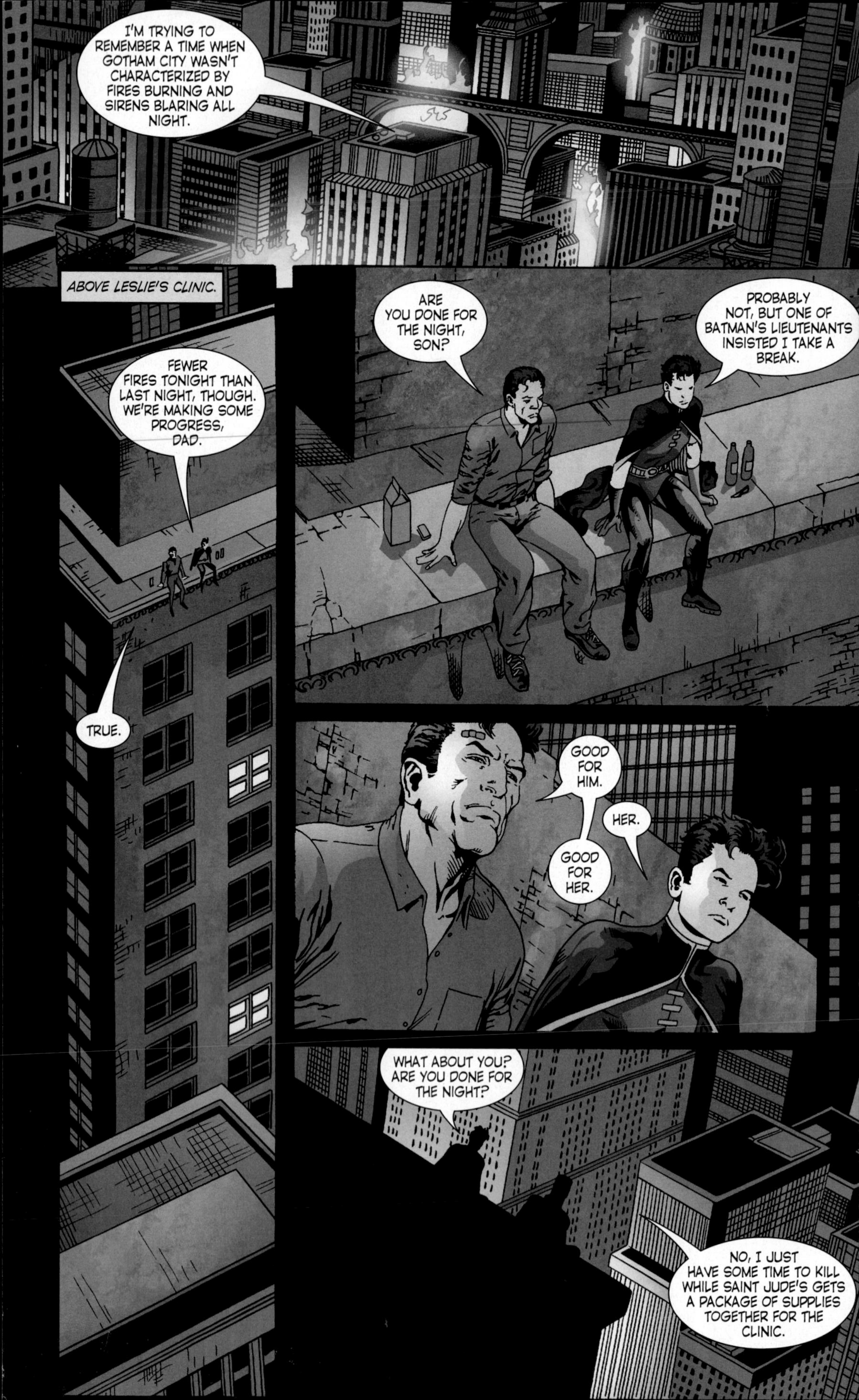
I'M TRYING TO REMEMBER A TIME WHEN GOTHAM CITY WASN'T CHARACTERIZED BY FIRES BURNING AND SIRENS BLARING ALL NIGHT.
ABOVE LESLIE'S CLINIC.
FEWER FIRES TONIGHT THAN LAST NIGHT, THOUGH. WE'RE MAKING SOME PROGRESS, DAD.
TRUE.
ARE YOU DONE FOR THE NIGHT, SON?
PROBABLY NOT, BUT ONE OF BATMAN'S LIEUTENANTS INSISTED I TAKE A BREAK.
GOOD FOR HIM.
HER.
GOOD FOR HER.
WHAT ABOUT YOU? ARE YOU DONE FOR THE NIGHT?
NO, I JUST HAVE SOME TIME TO KILL WHILE SAINT JUDE'S GETS A PACKAGE OF SUPPLIES TOGETHER FOR THE CLINIC.

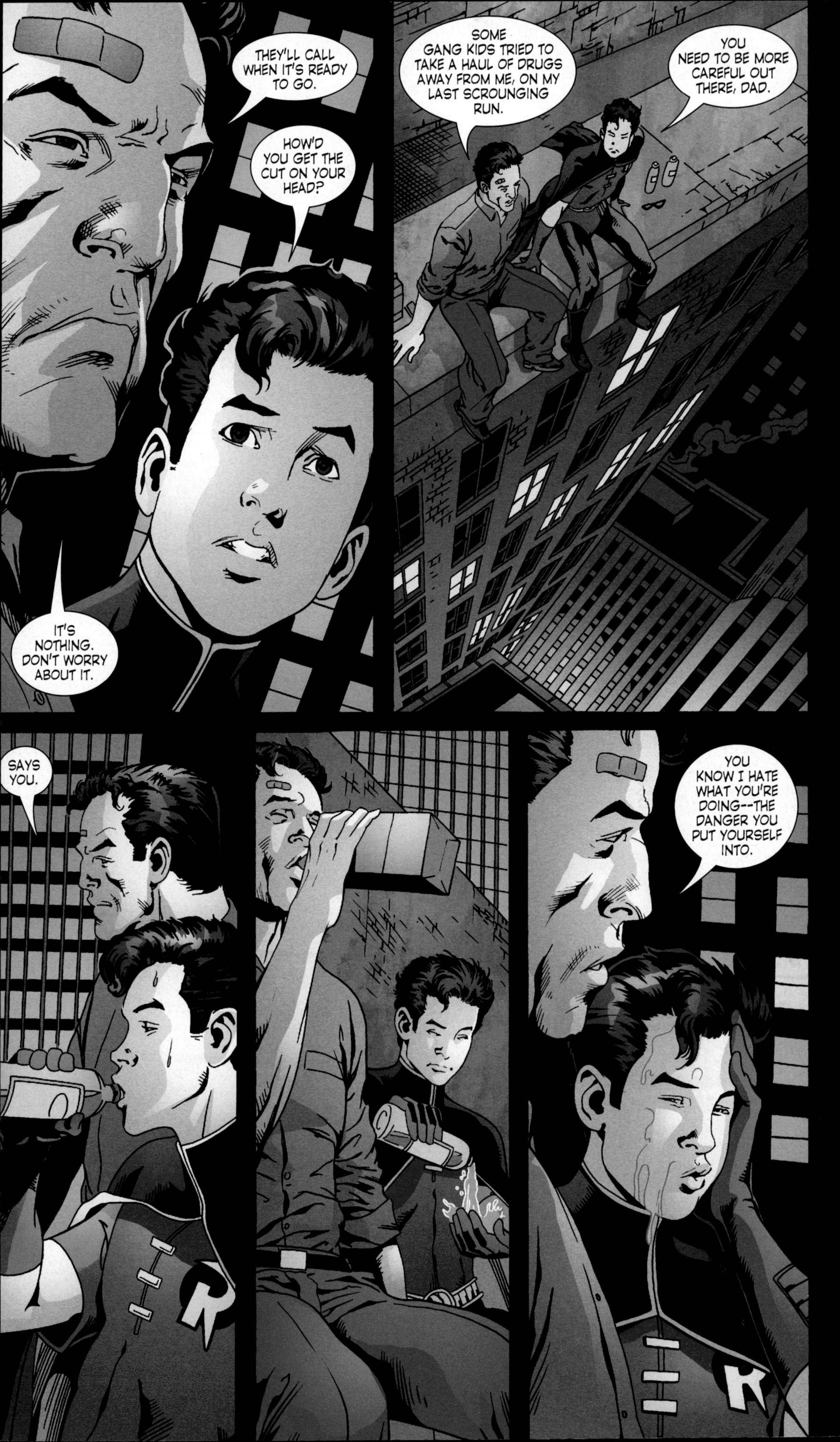
THEY'LL CALL WHEN IT'S READY TO GO.
HOW'D YOU GET THE CUT ON YOUR HEAD?
IT'S NOTHING. DON'T WORRY ABOUT IT.
SOME GANG KIDS TRIED TO TAKE A HAUL OF DRUGS AWAY FROM ME, ON MY LAST SCROUNGING RUN.
YOU NEED TO BE MORE CAREFUL OUT THERE, DAD.
SAYS YOU.
YOU KNOW I HATE WHAT YOU'RE DOING--THE DANGER YOU PUT YOURSELF INTO.

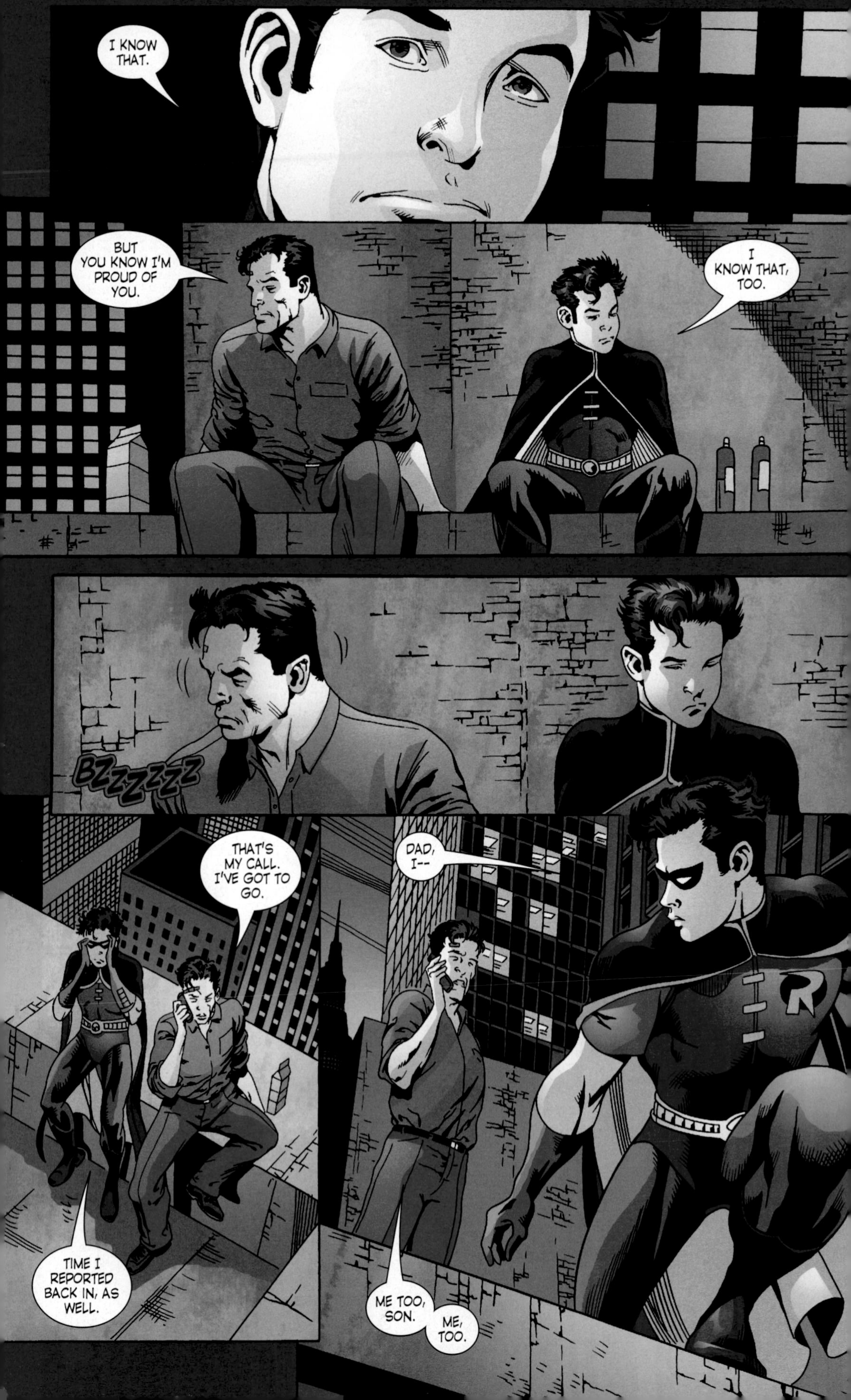
I KNOW THAT.
BUT YOU KNOW I'M PROUD OF YOU.
I KNOW THAT, TOO.
BZZZZZZZ
THAT'S MY CALL. I'VE GOT TO GO.
TIME I REPORTED BACK IN, AS WELL.
DAD, I--
ME TOO, SON.
ME, TOO.

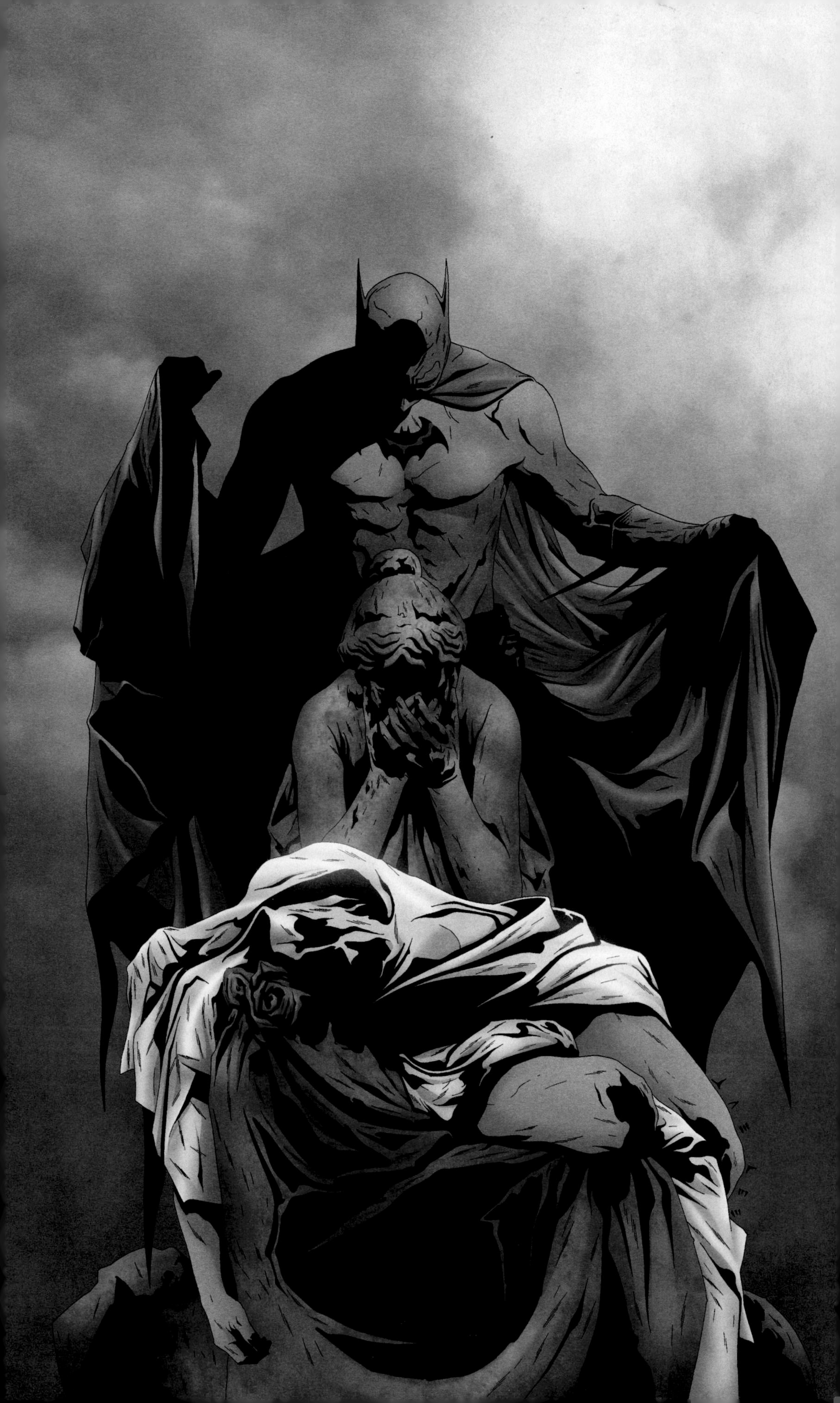

COVER ART BY
JAE LEE & JUNE CHUNG

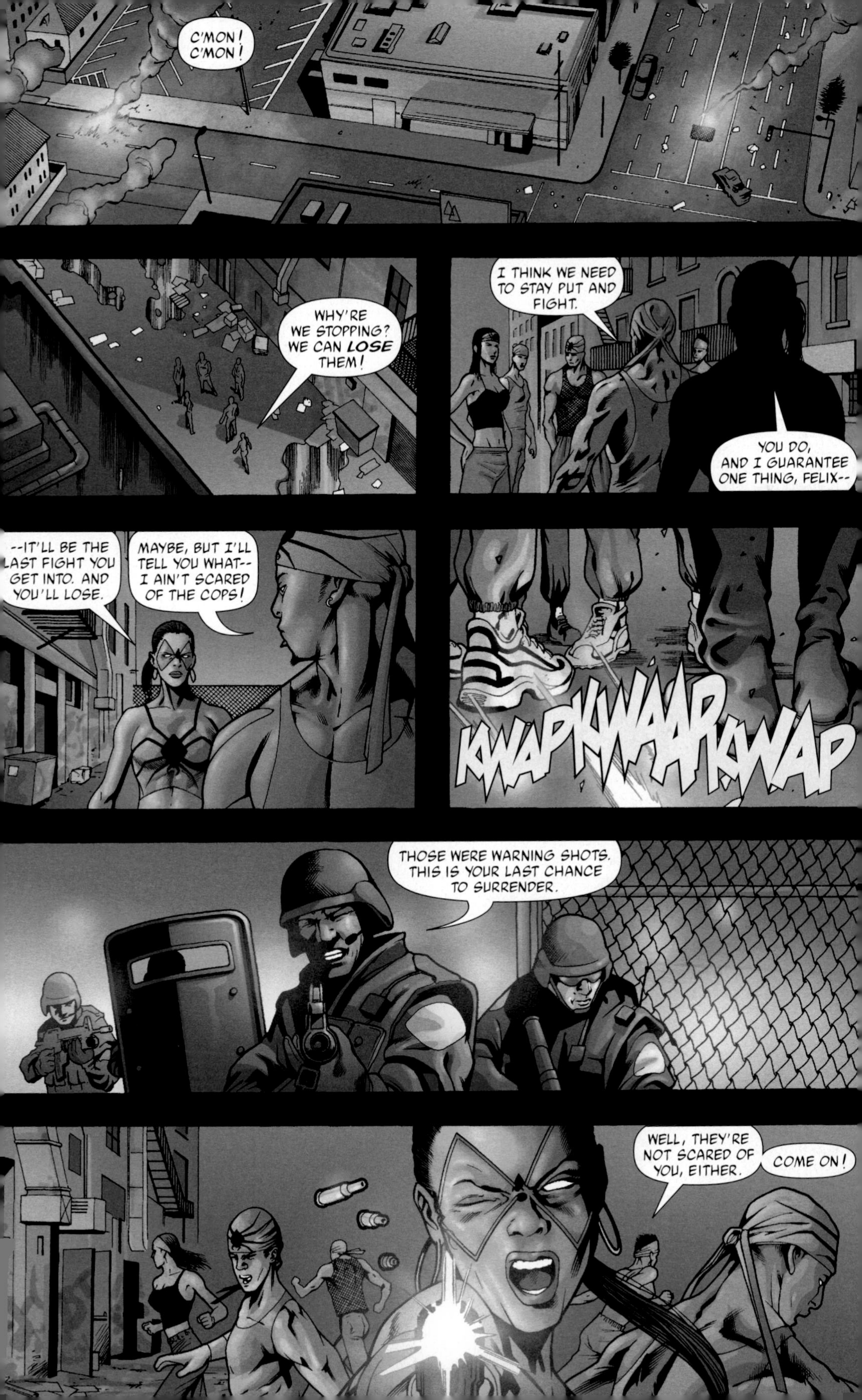
C'MON! C'MON!
WHY'RE WE STOPPING? WE CAN LOSE THEM!
I THINK WE NEED TO STAY PUT AND FIGHT.
YOU DO, AND I GUARANTEE ONE THING, FELIX--
--IT'LL BE THE LAST FIGHT YOU GET INTO. AND YOU'LL LOSE.
MAYBE, BUT I'LL TELL YOU WHAT-- I AIN'T SCARED OF THE COPS!
KWAP KWAAP KWAP
THOSE WERE WARNING SHOTS. THIS IS YOUR LAST CHANCE TO SURRENDER.
WELL, THEY'RE NOT SCARED OF YOU, EITHER.
COME ON!

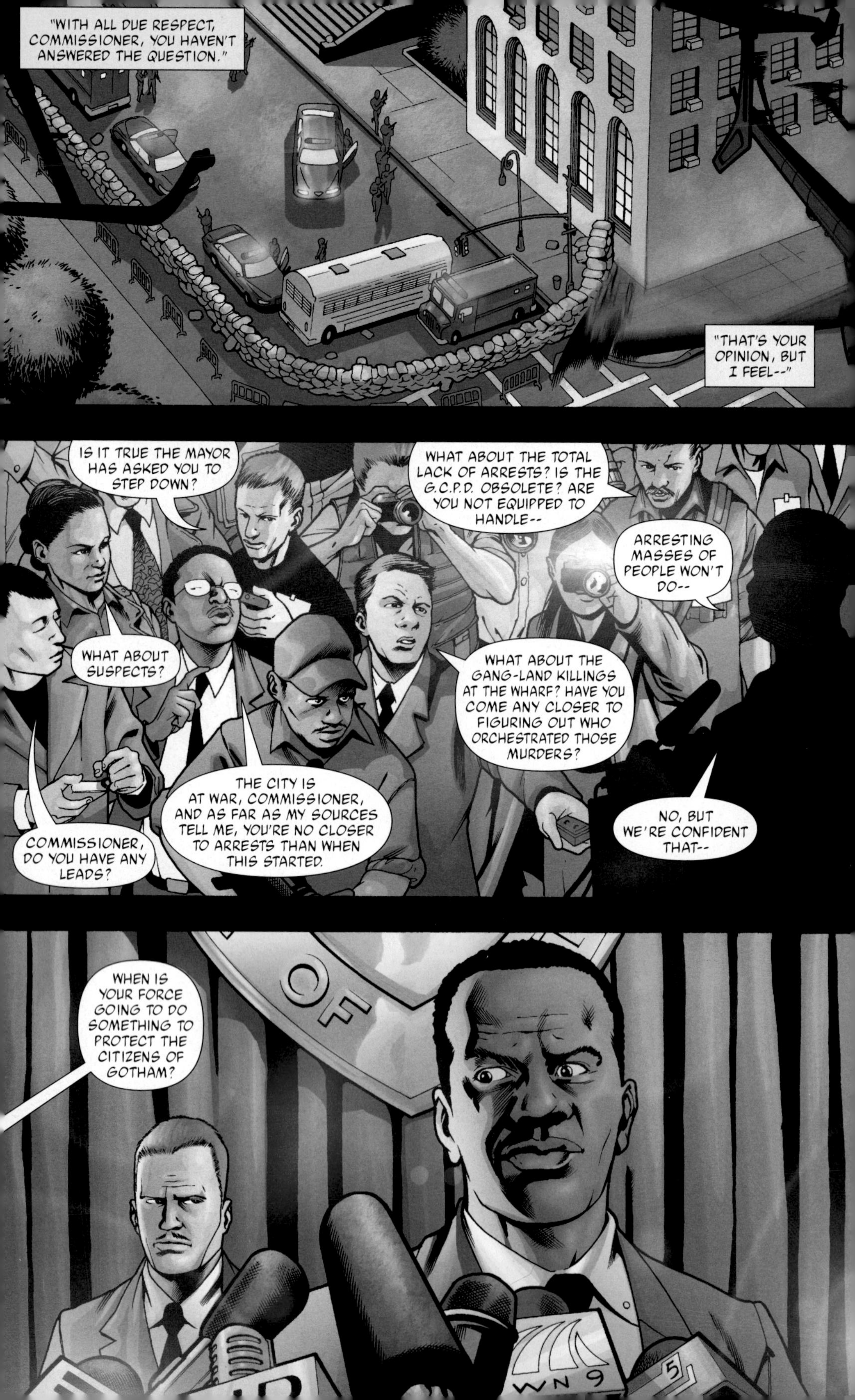
"WITH ALL DUE RESPECT, COMMISSIONER, YOU HAVEN'T ANSWERED THE QUESTION."
"THAT'S YOUR OPINION, BUT I FEEL--"
IS IT TRUE THE MAYOR HAS ASKED YOU TO STEP DOWN?
WHAT ABOUT THE TOTAL LACK OF ARRESTS? IS THE G.C.P.D. OBSOLETE? ARE YOU NOT EQUIPPED TO HANDLE--
ARRESTING MASSES OF PEOPLE WON'T DO--
WHAT ABOUT SUSPECTS?
WHAT ABOUT THE GANG-LAND KILLINGS AT THE WHARF? HAVE YOU COME ANY CLOSER TO FIGURING OUT WHO ORCHESTRATED THOSE MURDERS?
COMMISSIONER, DO YOU HAVE ANY LEADS?
THE CITY IS AT WAR, COMMISSIONER, AND AS FAR AS MY SOURCES TELL ME, YOU'RE NO CLOSER TO ARRESTS THAN WHEN THIS STARTED.
NO, BUT WE'RE CONFIDENT THAT--
WHEN IS YOUR FORCE GOING TO DO SOMETHING TO PROTECT THE CITIZENS OF GOTHAM?

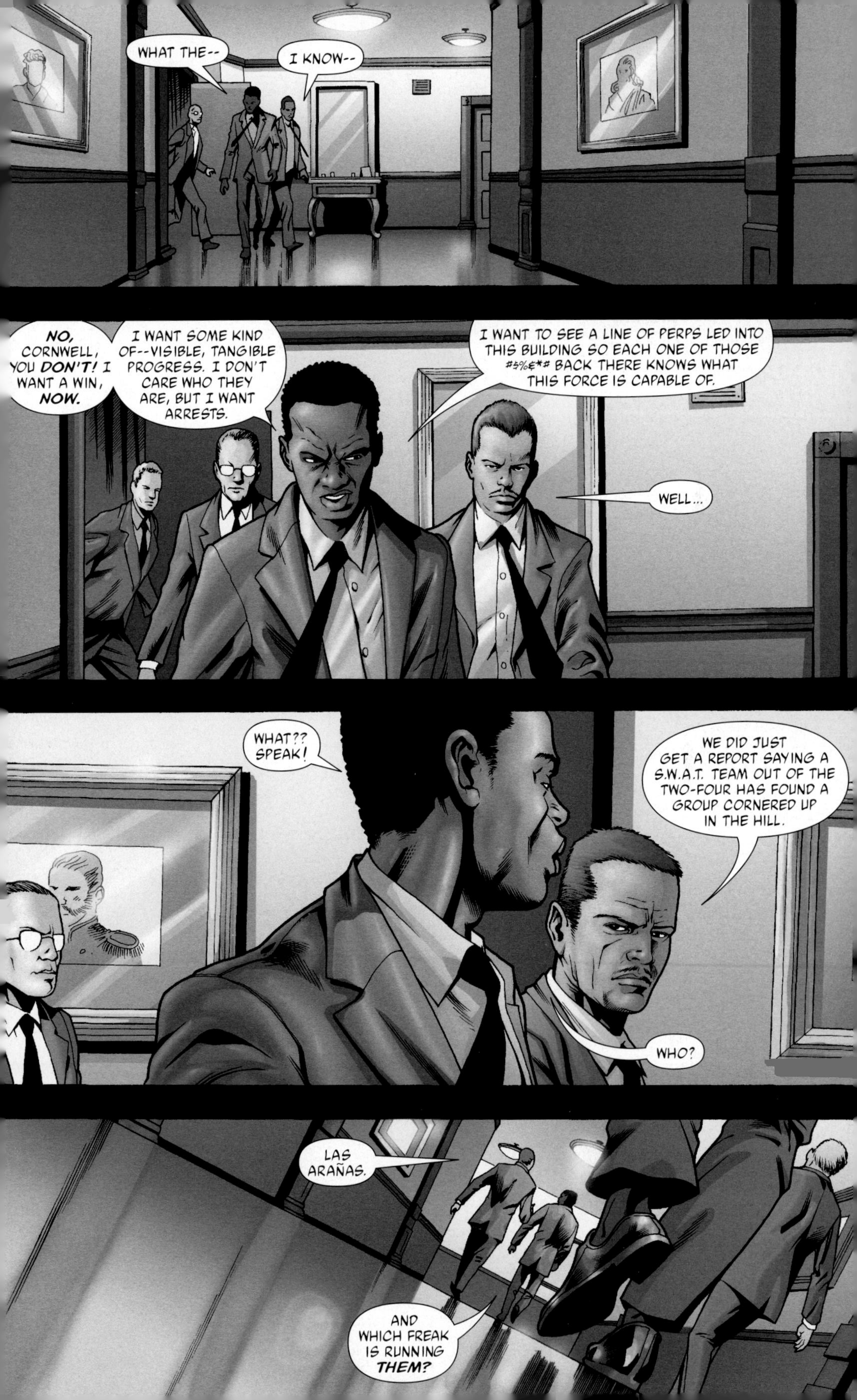
WHAT THE--
I KNOW--
NO, CORNWELL, YOU DON'T! I WANT A WIN, NOW.
I WANT SOME KIND OF--VISIBLE, TANGIBLE PROGRESS. I DON'T CARE WHO THEY ARE, BUT I WANT ARRESTS.
I WANT TO SEE A LINE OF PERPS LED INTO THIS BUILDING SO EACH ONE OF THOSE #$%&*# BACK THERE KNOWS WHAT THIS FORCE IS CAPABLE OF.
WELL...
WHAT?? SPEAK!
WE DID JUST GET A REPORT SAYING A S.W.A.T. TEAM OUT OF THE TWO-FOUR HAS FOUND A GROUP CORNERED UP IN THE HILL.
WHO?
LAS ARAÑAS.
AND WHICH FREAK IS RUNNING THEM?

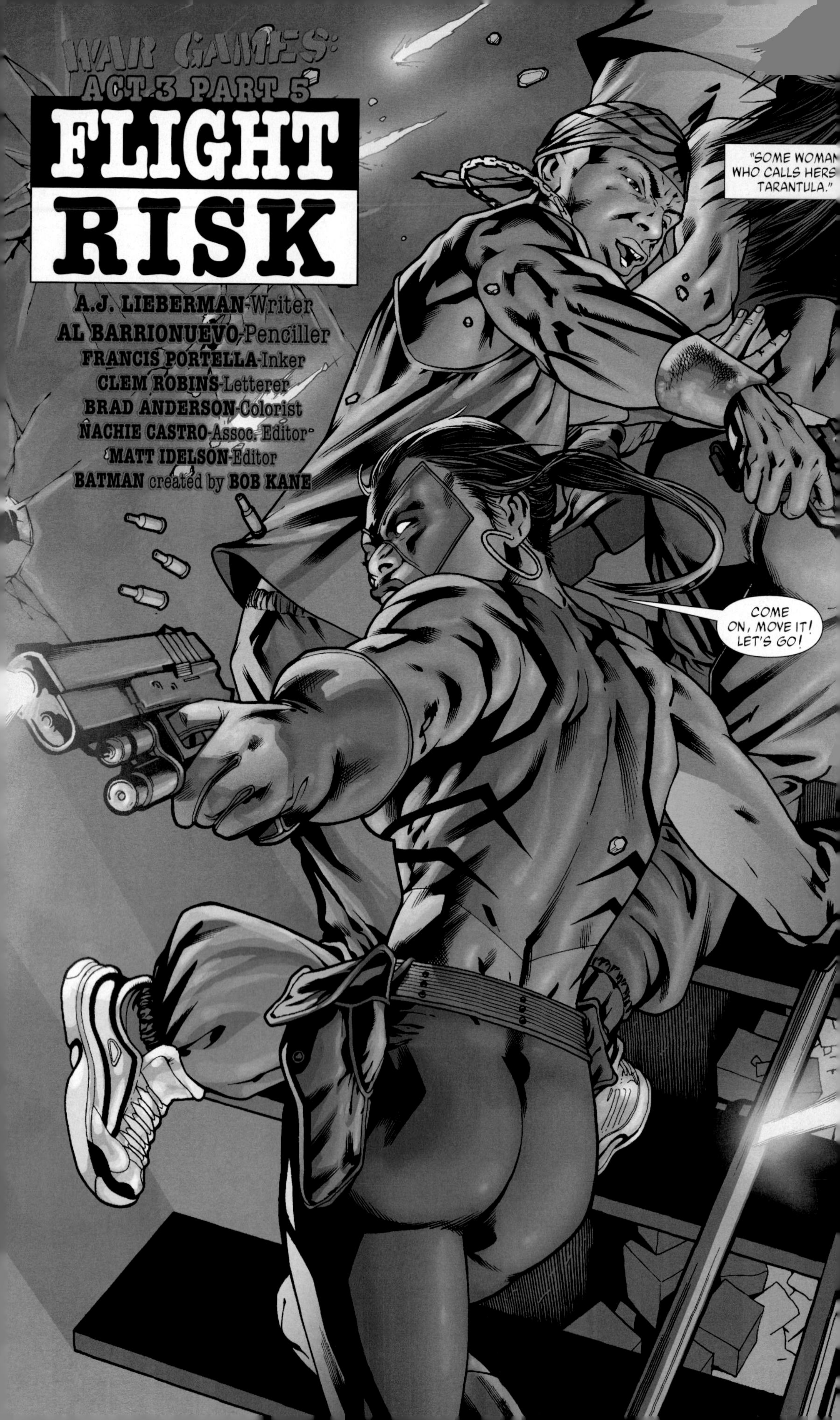

WAR GAMES:
ACT 3 PART 5
FLIGHT RISK
A.J. LIEBERMAN-Writer
AL BARRIONUEVO-Penciller
FRANCIS PORTELLA-Inker
CLEM ROBINS-Letterer
BRAD ANDERSON-Colorist
ÑACHIE CASTRO-Assoc. Editor
MATT IDELSON-Editor
BATMAN created by BOB KANE
"SOME WOMAN WHO CALLS HERS TARANTULA."
COME ON, MOVE IT! LET'S GO!

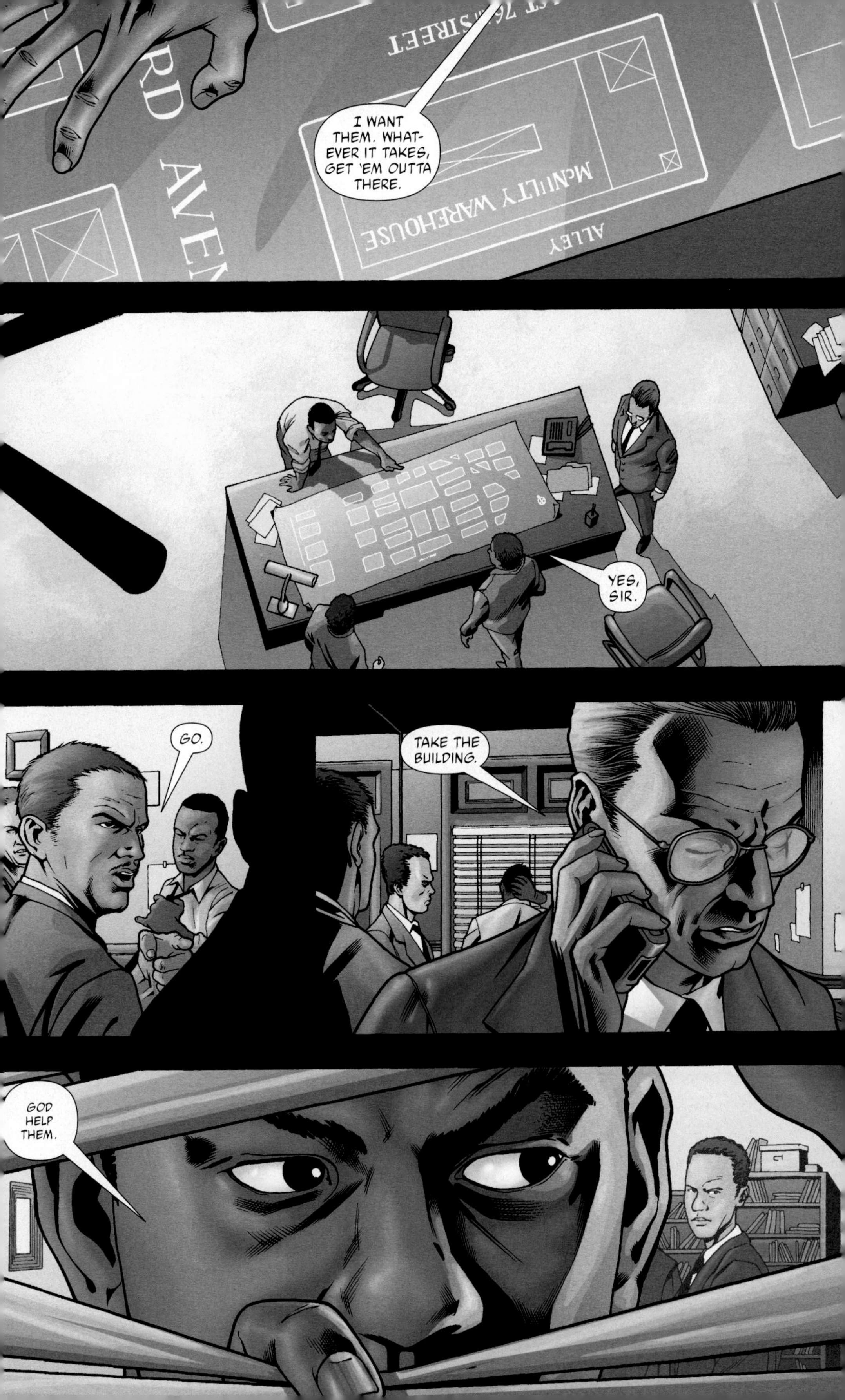
I WANT THEM. WHAT-EVER IT TAKES, GET 'EM OUTTA THERE.
YES, SIR.
GO.
TAKE THE BUILDING.
GOD HELP THEM.

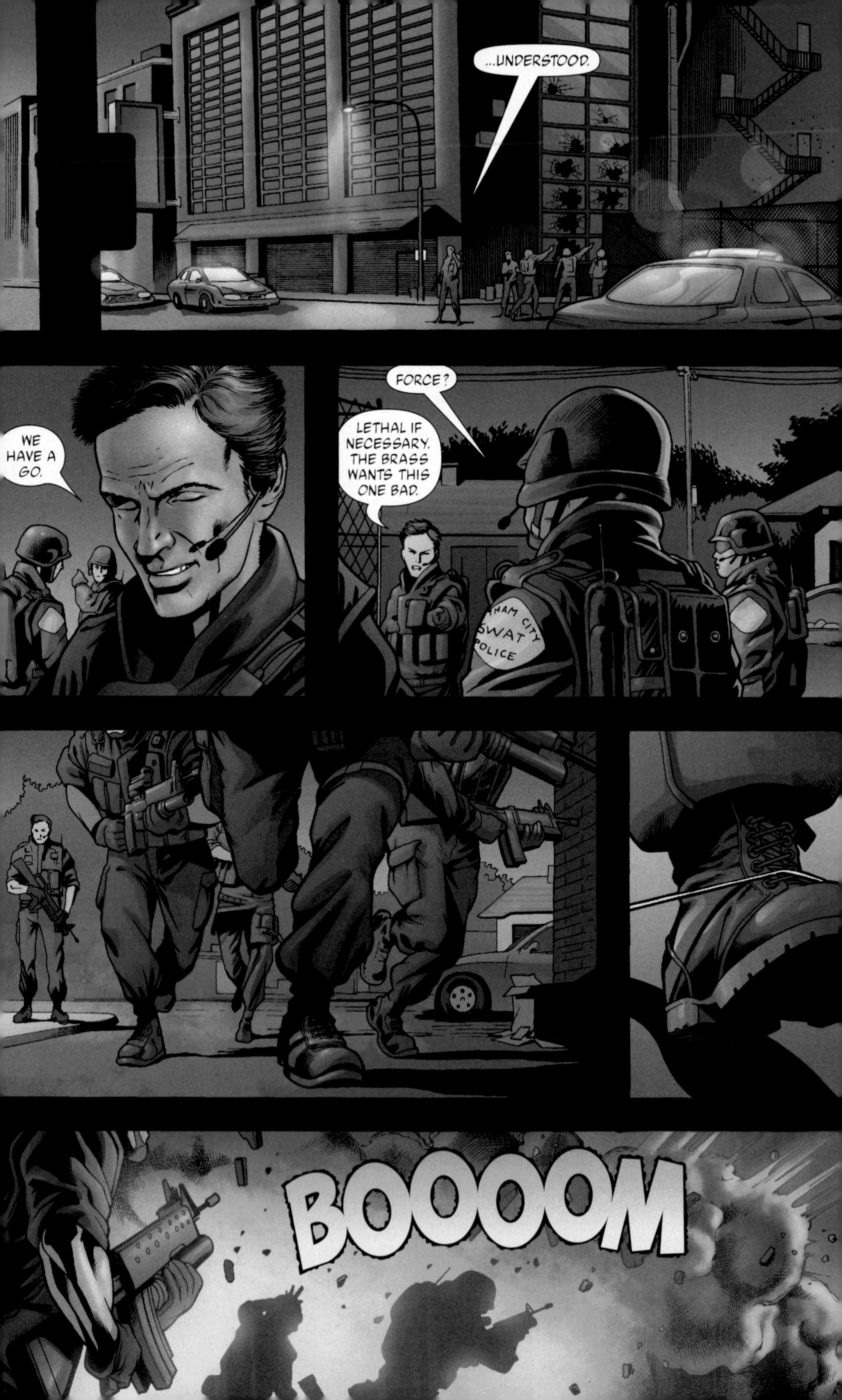

...UNDERSTOOD.
WE HAVE A GO.
FORCE?
LETHAL IF NECESSARY. THE BRASS WANTS THIS ONE BAD.
SWAT
POLICE
BOOOOM

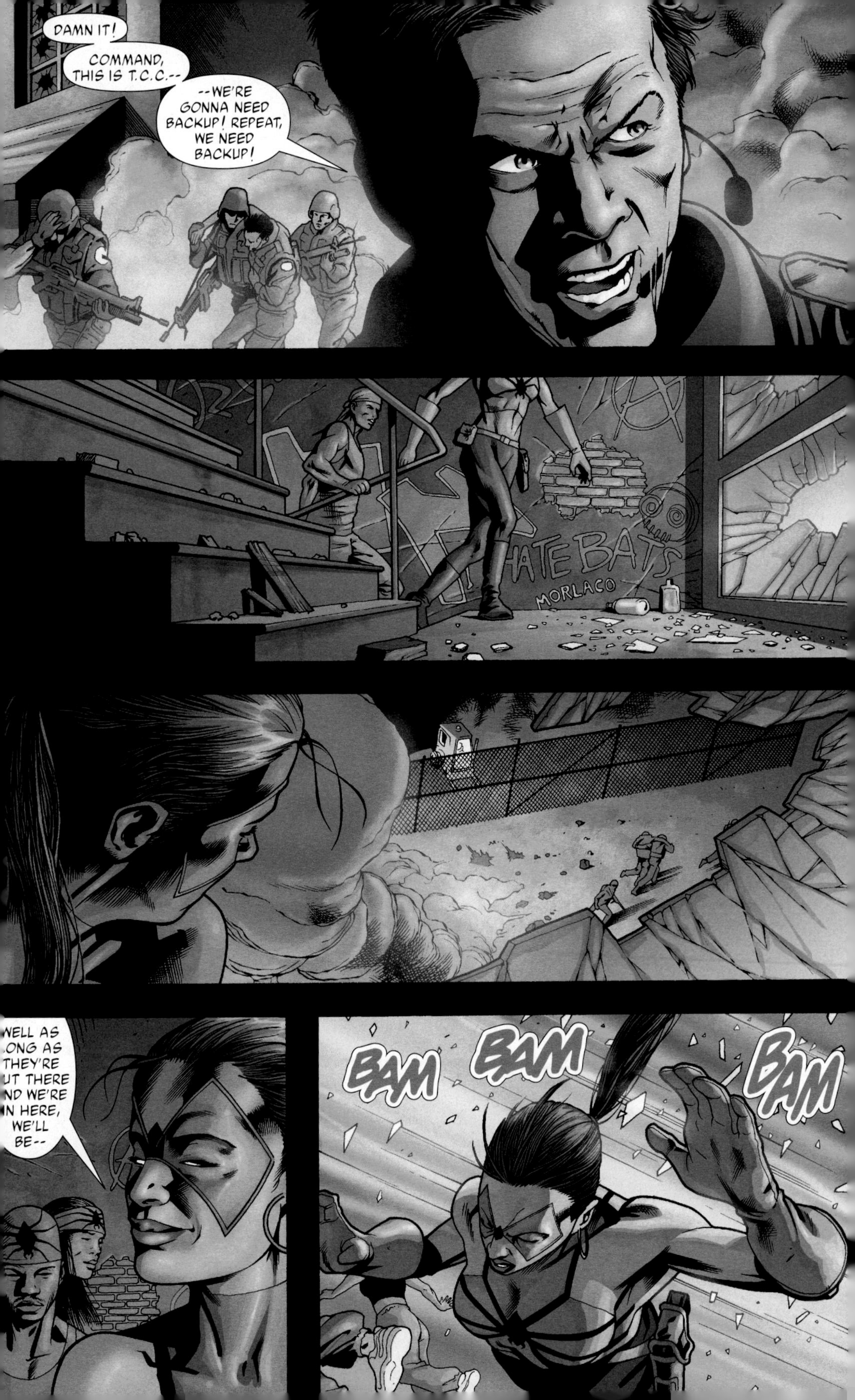

DAMN IT!
COMMAND, THIS IS T.C.C.--
--WE'RE GONNA NEED BACKUP! REPEAT, WE NEED BACKUP!
HATE BATS
MORLACO
WELL AS ONG AS THEY'RE UT THERE ND WE'RE N HERE, WE'LL BE--
BAM
BAM
BAM

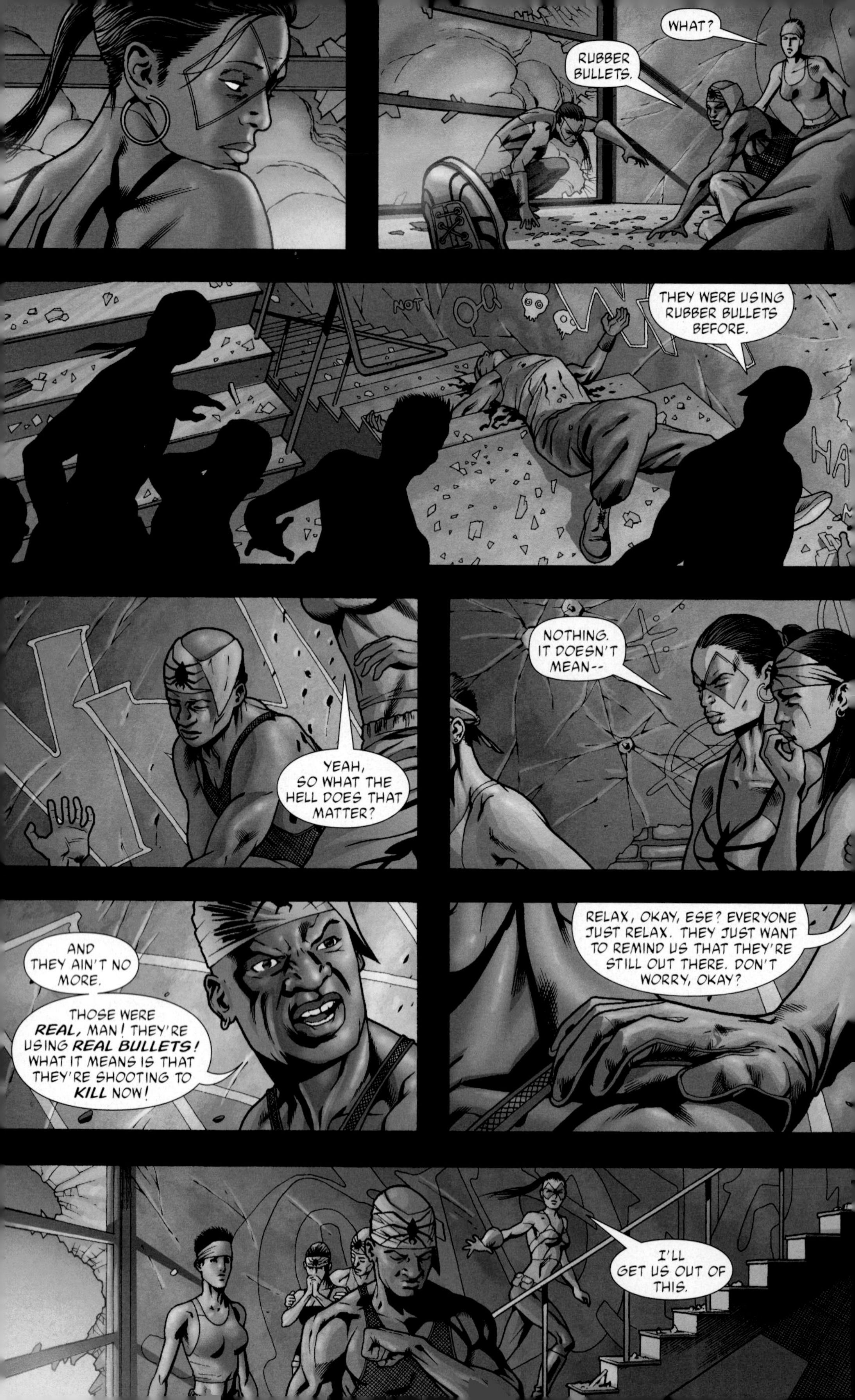
WHAT?
RUBBER BULLETS.
THEY WERE USING RUBBER BULLETS BEFORE.
NOT
YEAH, SO WHAT THE HELL DOES THAT MATTER?
NOTHING. IT DOESN'T MEAN--
AND THEY AIN'T NO MORE.
THOSE WERE **REAL**, MAN! THEY'RE USING **REAL BULLETS**! WHAT IT MEANS IS THAT THEY'RE SHOOTING TO **KILL** NOW!
RELAX, OKAY, ESE? EVERYONE JUST RELAX. THEY JUST WANT TO REMIND US THAT THEY'RE STILL OUT THERE. DON'T WORRY, OKAY?
I'LL GET US OUT OF THIS.

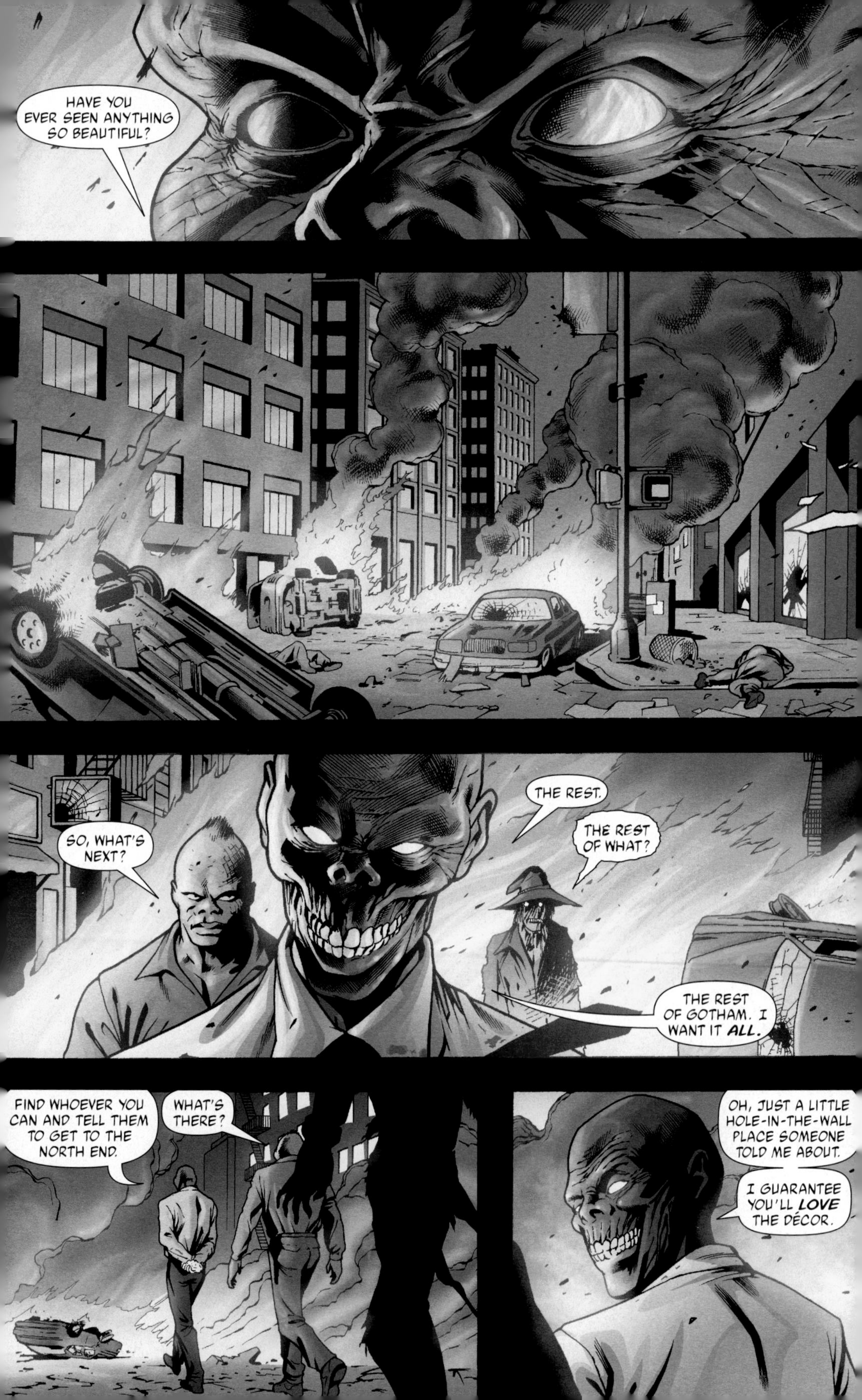
HAVE YOU EVER SEEN ANYTHING SO BEAUTIFUL?
SO, WHAT'S NEXT?
THE REST.
THE REST OF WHAT?
THE REST OF GOTHAM. I WANT IT **ALL.**
FIND WHOEVER YOU CAN AND TELL THEM TO GET TO THE NORTH END.
WHAT'S THERE?
OH, JUST A LITTLE HOLE-IN-THE-WALL PLACE SOMEONE TOLD ME ABOUT.
I GUARANTEE YOU'LL **LOVE** THE DÉCOR.

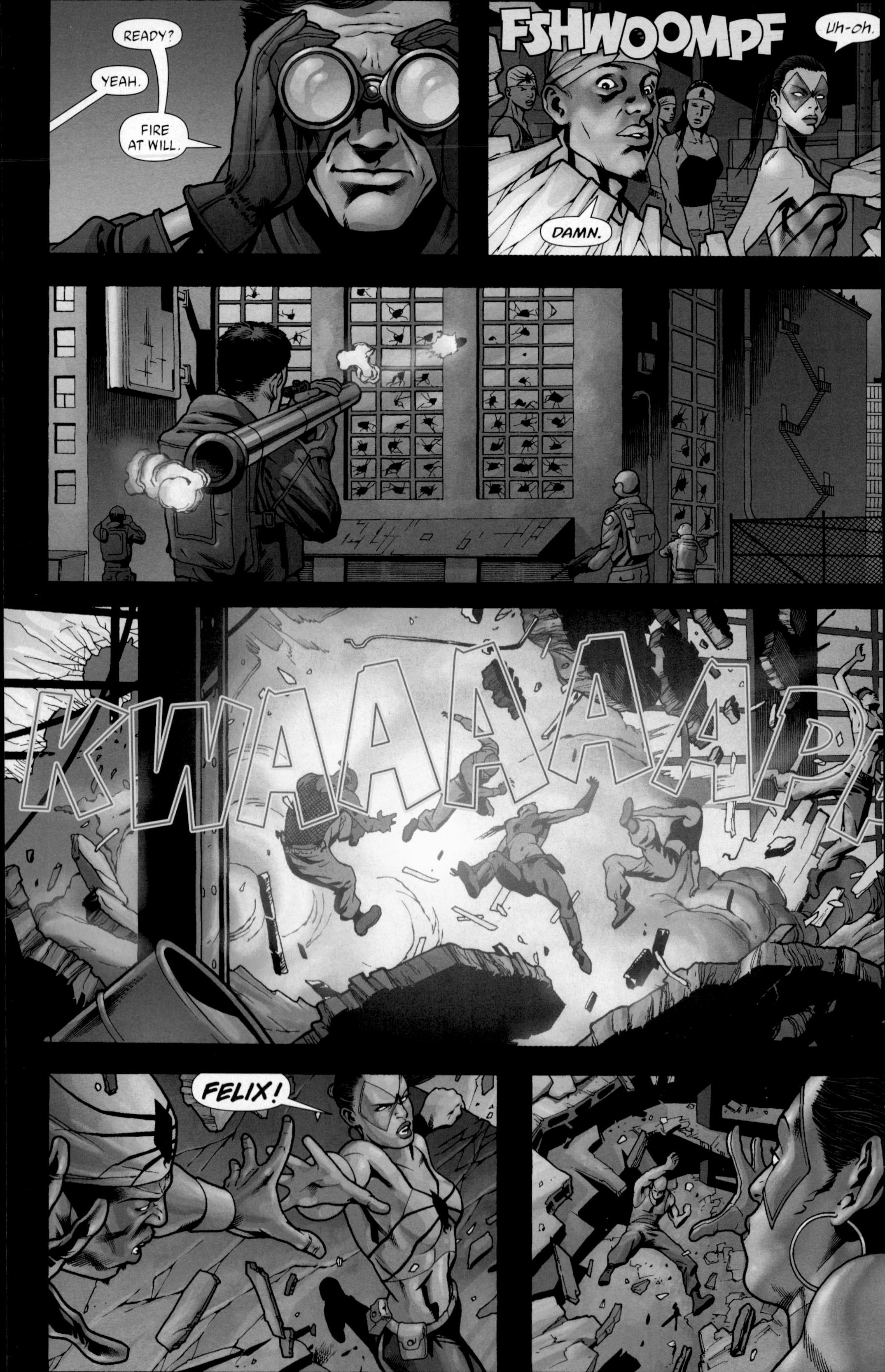
READY?
YEAH.
FIRE AT WILL.
FSHWOOMPF
Uh-oh.
DAMN.
KWAAAAAP
FELIX!

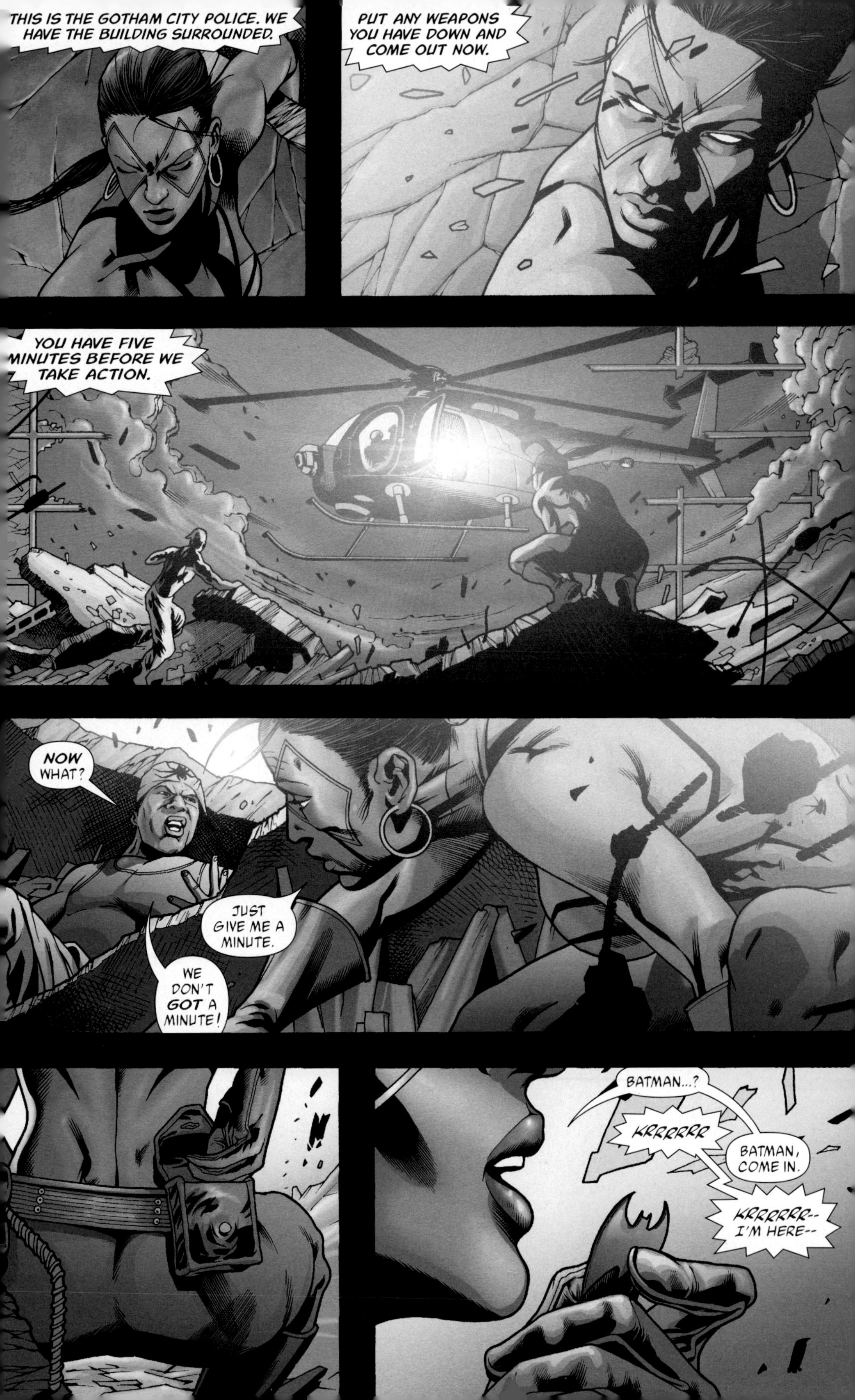
THIS IS THE GOTHAM CITY POLICE. WE HAVE THE BUILDING SURROUNDED.
PUT ANY WEAPONS YOU HAVE DOWN AND COME OUT NOW.
YOU HAVE FIVE MINUTES BEFORE WE TAKE ACTION.
NOW WHAT?
JUST GIVE ME A MINUTE.
WE DON'T GOT A MINUTE!
BATMAN...?
KRRRRRR
BATMAN, COME IN.
KRRRRRR-- I'M HERE--

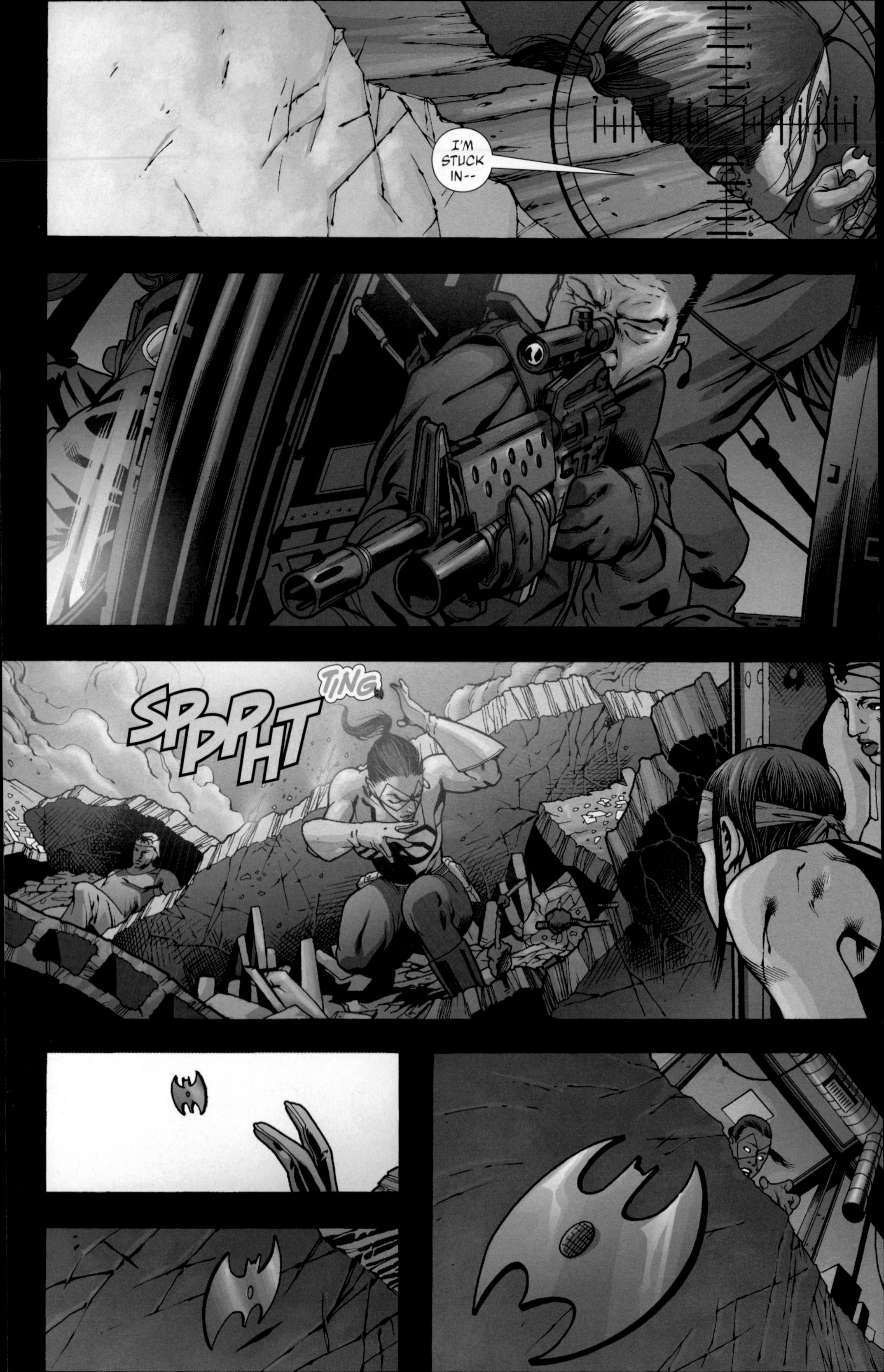
I'M STUCK IN--
SPDPHT
TING

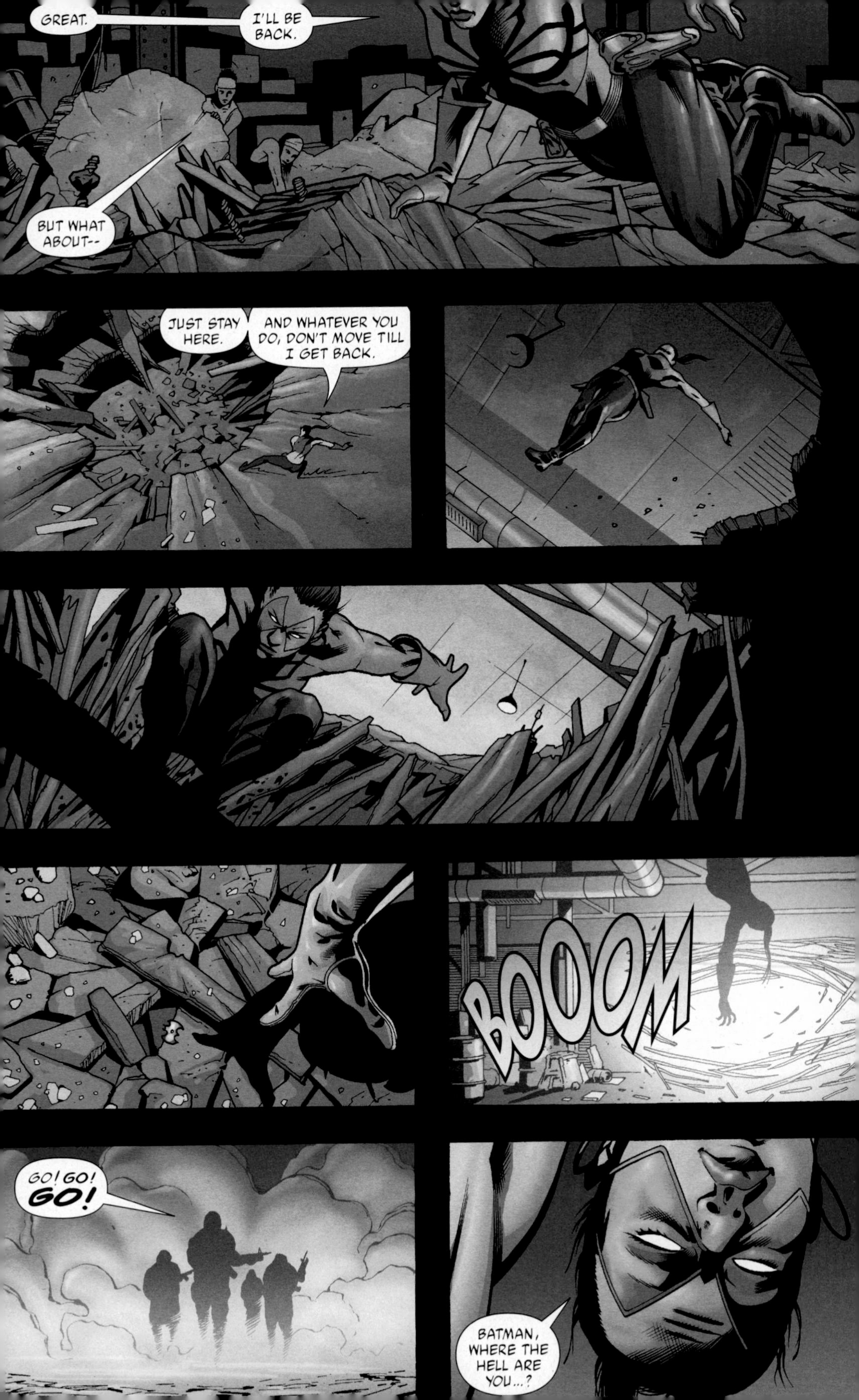
GREAT.
I'LL BE BACK.
BUT WHAT ABOUT--
JUST STAY HERE.
AND WHATEVER YOU DO, DON'T MOVE TILL I GET BACK.
BOOOM
GO! GO! GO!
BATMAN, WHERE THE HELL ARE YOU...?

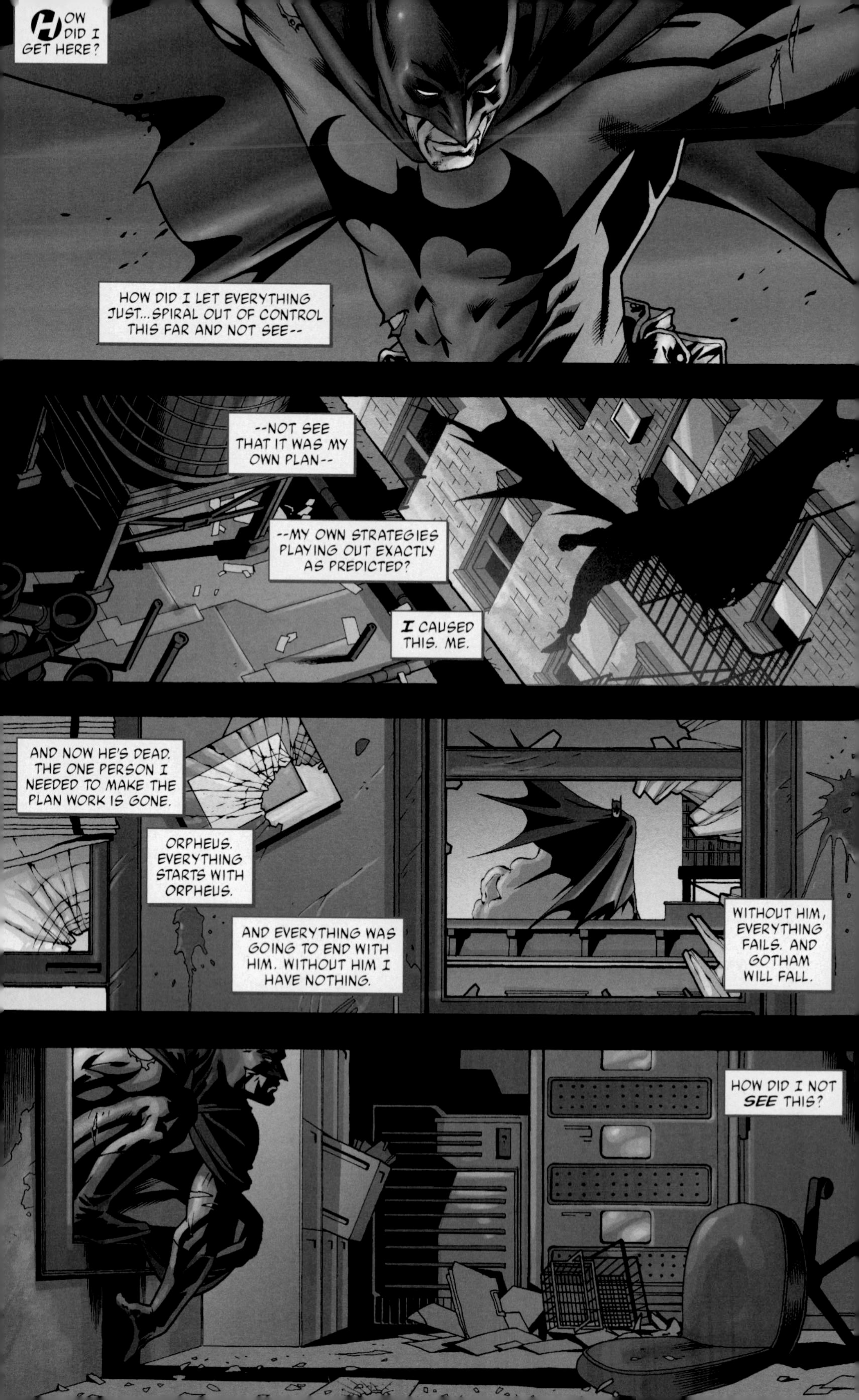
HOW DID I GET HERE?
HOW DID I LET EVERYTHING JUST...SPIRAL OUT OF CONTROL THIS FAR AND NOT SEE--
--NOT SEE THAT IT WAS MY OWN PLAN--
--MY OWN STRATEGIES PLAYING OUT EXACTLY AS PREDICTED?
I CAUSED THIS. ME.
AND NOW HE'S DEAD. THE ONE PERSON I NEEDED TO MAKE THE PLAN WORK IS GONE.
ORPHEUS. EVERYTHING STARTS WITH ORPHEUS.
AND EVERYTHING WAS GOING TO END WITH HIM. WITHOUT HIM I HAVE NOTHING.
WITHOUT HIM, EVERYTHING FAILS. AND GOTHAM WILL FALL.
HOW DID I NOT SEE THIS?

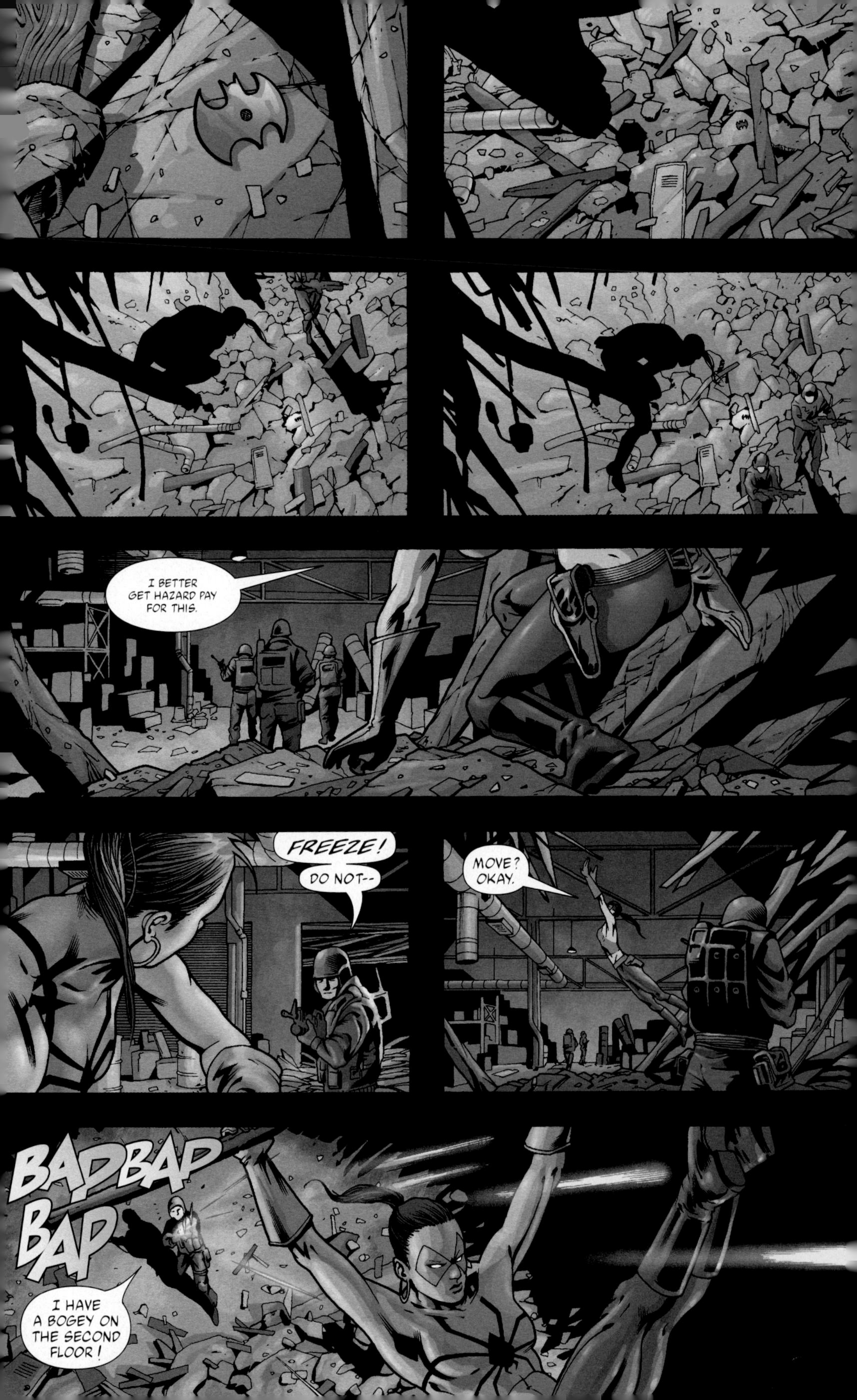
I BETTER GET HAZARD PAY FOR THIS.
FREEZE!
DO NOT--
MOVE? OKAY.
BADBAP BAP
I HAVE A BOGEY ON THE SECOND FLOOR!

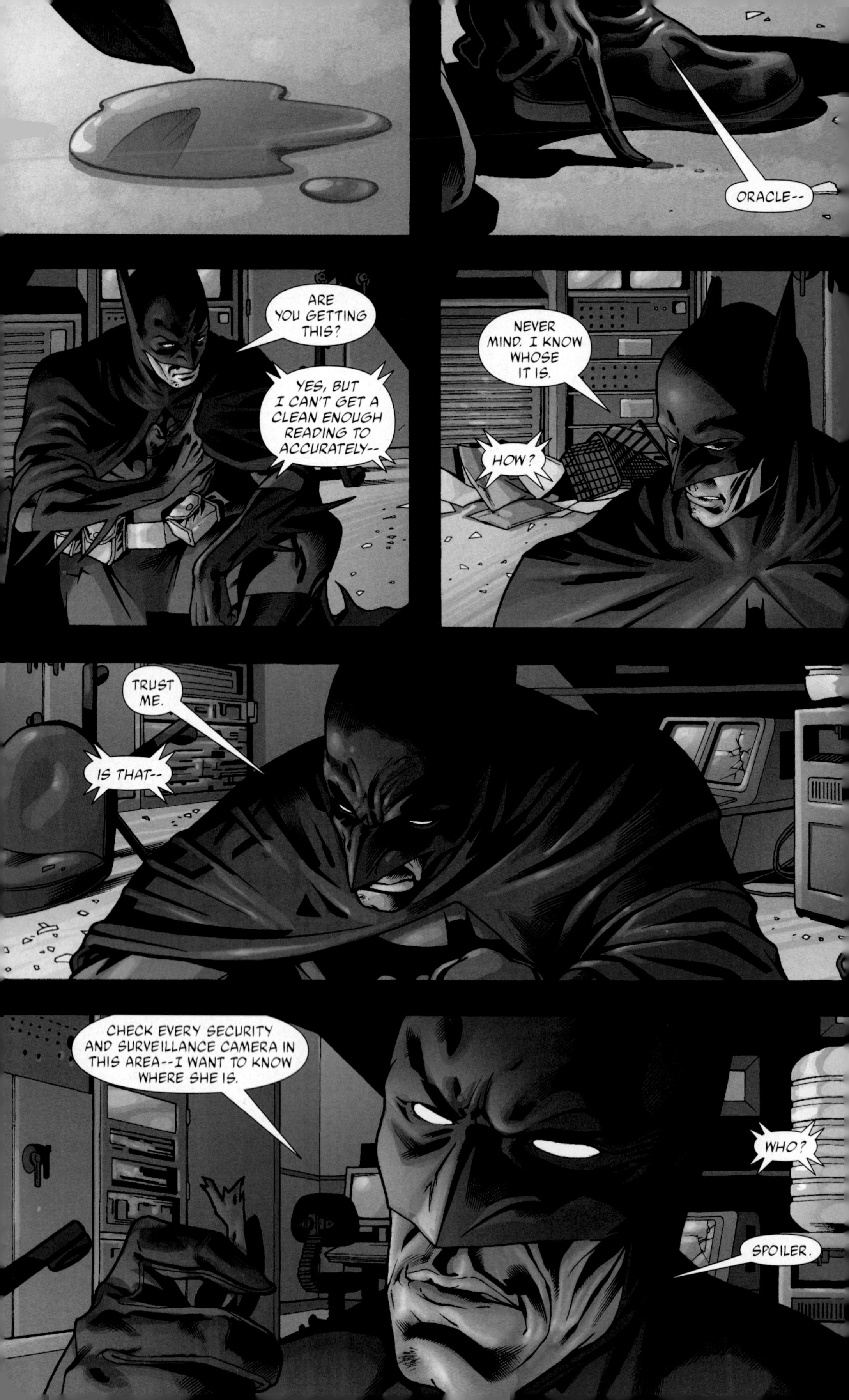
ORACLE--
ARE YOU GETTING THIS?
YES, BUT I CAN'T GET A CLEAN ENOUGH READING TO ACCURATELY--
NEVER MIND. I KNOW WHOSE IT IS.
HOW?
TRUST ME.
IS THAT--
CHECK EVERY SECURITY AND SURVEILLANCE CAMERA IN THIS AREA--I WANT TO KNOW WHERE SHE IS.
WHO?
SPOILER.

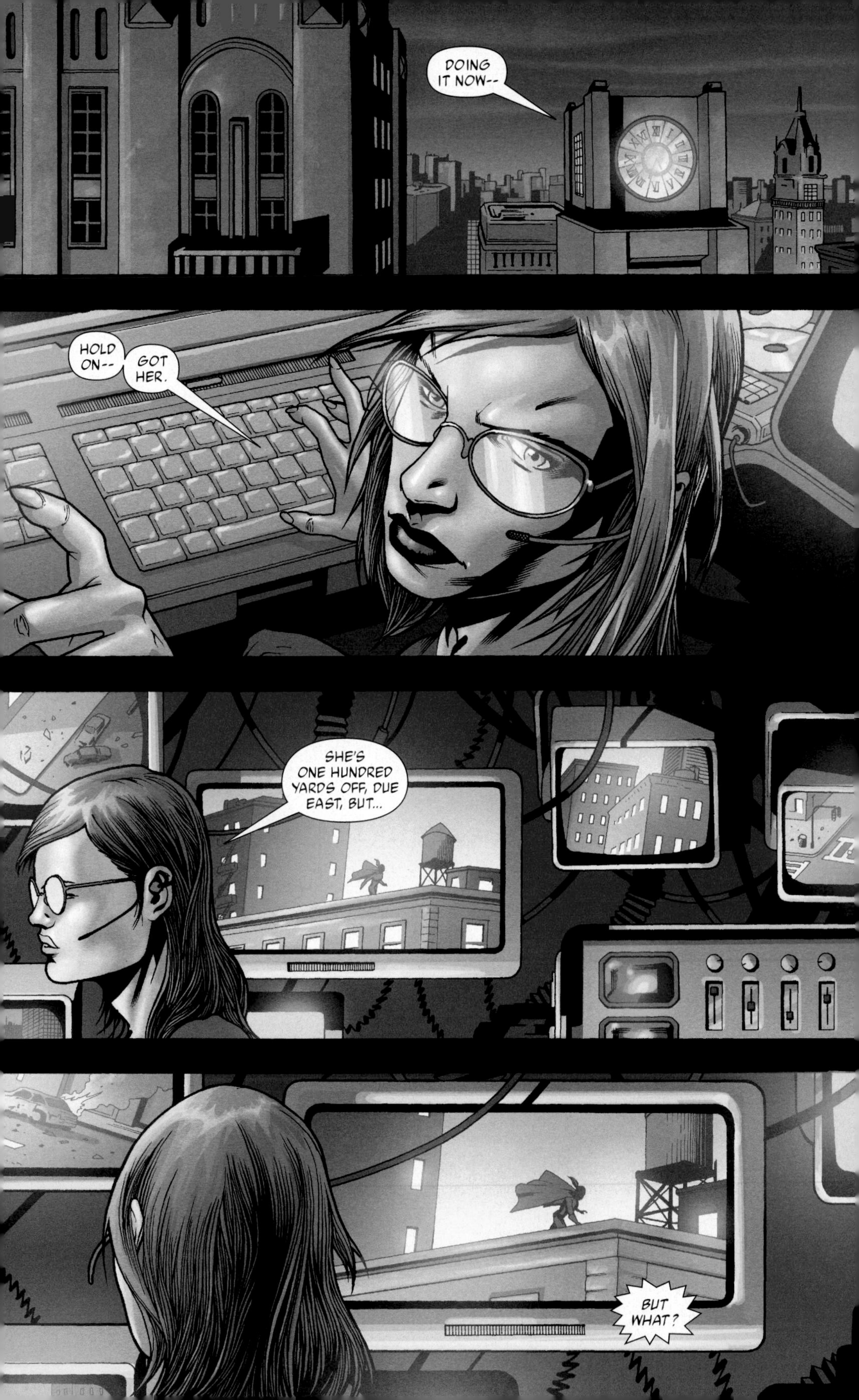
DOING IT NOW--
HOLD ON--
GOT HER.
SHE'S ONE HUNDRED YARDS OFF, DUE EAST, BUT...
BUT WHAT?

SHE DOESN'T LOOK GOOD.

I...

I...I TRIED...

I TRIED... TO STOP...

IT'S ALL RIGHT. EVERY-THING'S ALL RIGHT.

I JU WANTE HEL

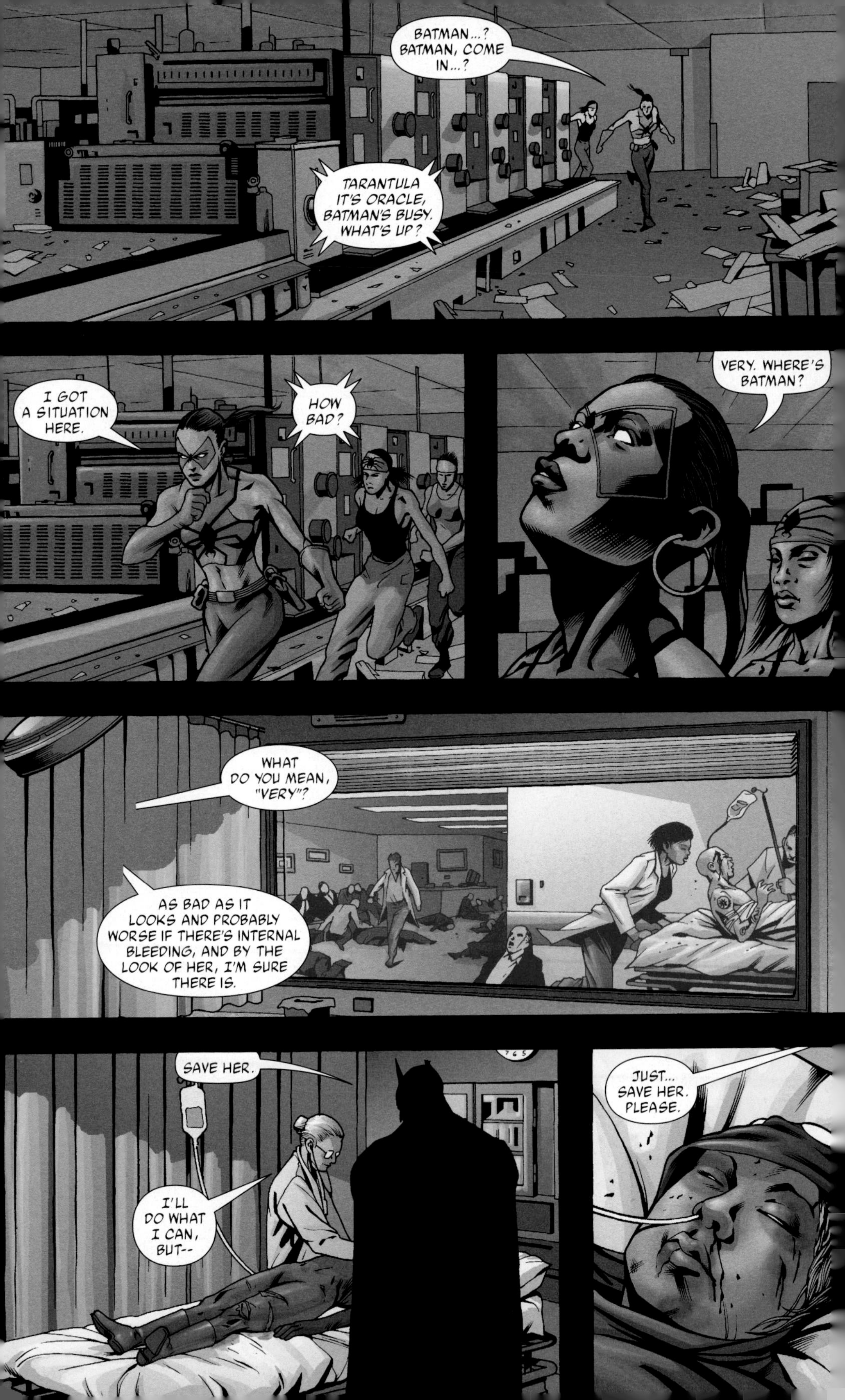
BATMAN...? BATMAN, COME IN...?
TARANTULA IT'S ORACLE, BATMAN'S BUSY. WHAT'S UP?
I GOT A SITUATION HERE.
HOW BAD?
VERY. WHERE'S BATMAN?
WHAT DO YOU MEAN, "VERY"?
AS BAD AS IT LOOKS AND PROBABLY WORSE IF THERE'S INTERNAL BLEEDING, AND BY THE LOOK OF HER, I'M SURE THERE IS.
SAVE HER.
I'LL DO WHAT I CAN, BUT--
JUST... SAVE HER. PLEASE.

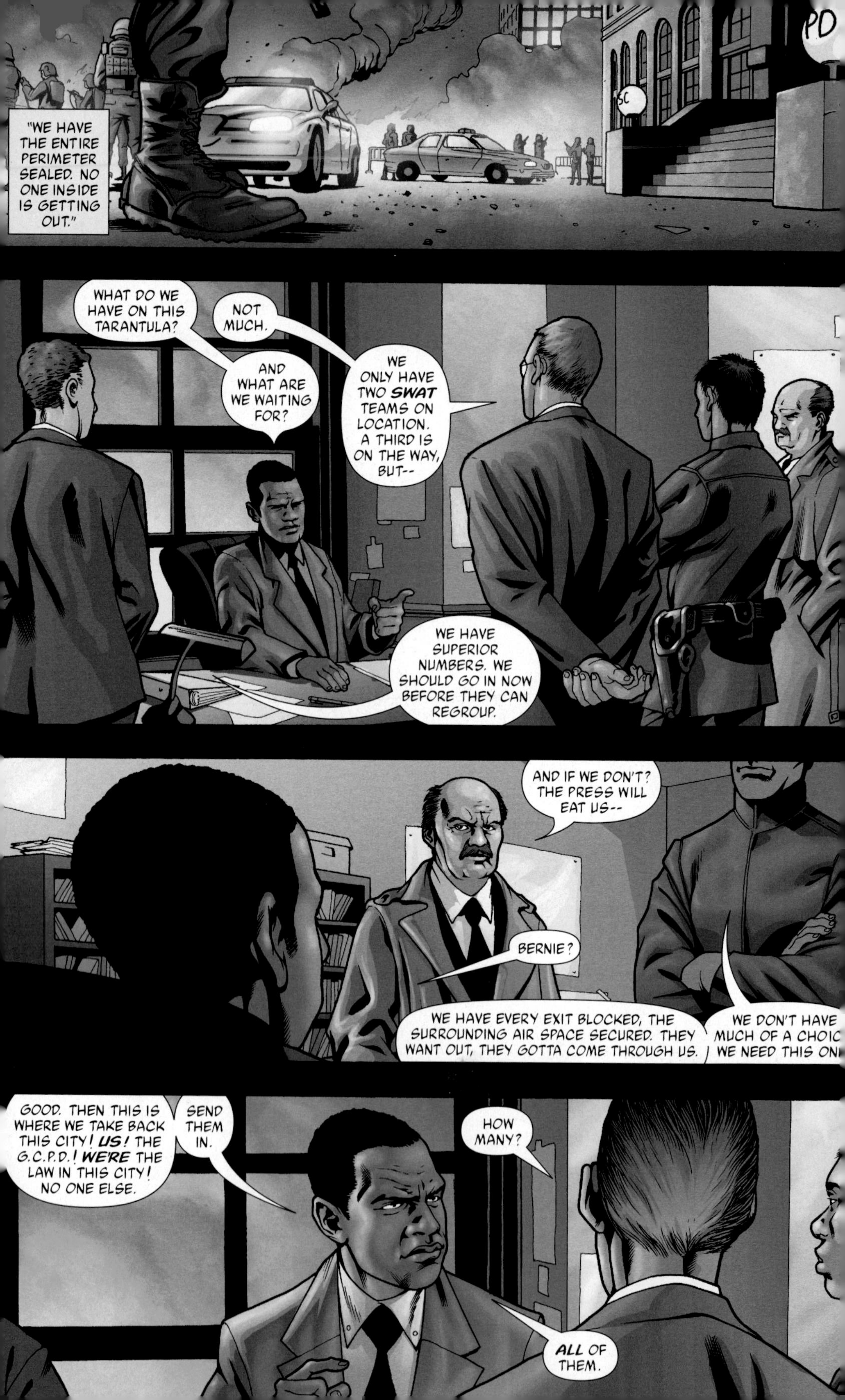
PD
SC
"WE HAVE THE ENTIRE PERIMETER SEALED. NO ONE INSIDE IS GETTING OUT."
WHAT DO WE HAVE ON THIS TARANTULA?
NOT MUCH.
AND WHAT ARE WE WAITING FOR?
WE ONLY HAVE TWO SWAT TEAMS ON LOCATION. A THIRD IS ON THE WAY, BUT--
WE HAVE SUPERIOR NUMBERS. WE SHOULD GO IN NOW BEFORE THEY CAN REGROUP.
AND IF WE DON'T? THE PRESS WILL EAT US--
BERNIE?
WE HAVE EVERY EXIT BLOCKED, THE SURROUNDING AIR SPACE SECURED. THEY WANT OUT, THEY GOTTA COME THROUGH US.
WE DON'T HAVE MUCH OF A CHOIC WE NEED THIS ON
GOOD. THEN THIS IS WHERE WE TAKE BACK THIS CITY! US! THE G.C.P.D.! WE'RE THE LAW IN THIS CITY! NO ONE ELSE.
SEND THEM IN.
HOW MANY?
ALL OF THEM.

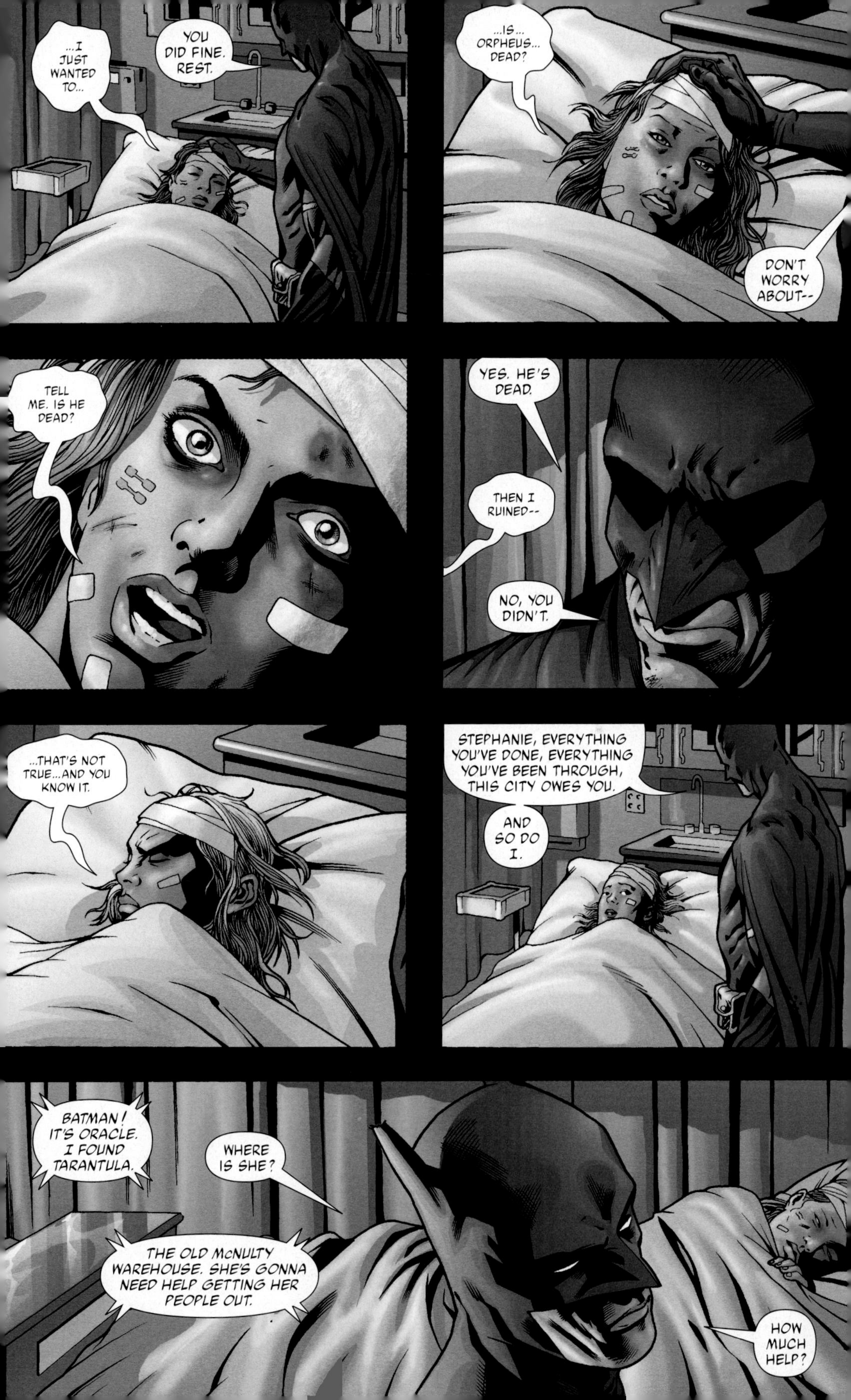
...I JUST WANTED TO...
YOU DID FINE. REST.
...IS... ORPHEUS... DEAD?
DON'T WORRY ABOUT--
TELL ME. IS HE DEAD?
YES. HE'S DEAD.
THEN I RUINED--
NO, YOU DIDN'T.
...THAT'S NOT TRUE...AND YOU KNOW IT.
STEPHANIE, EVERYTHING YOU'VE DONE, EVERYTHING YOU'VE BEEN THROUGH, THIS CITY OWES YOU.
AND SO DO I.
BATMAN! IT'S ORACLE. I FOUND TARANTULA.
WHERE IS SHE?
THE OLD McNULTY WAREHOUSE. SHE'S GONNA NEED HELP GETTING HER PEOPLE OUT.
HOW MUCH HELP?

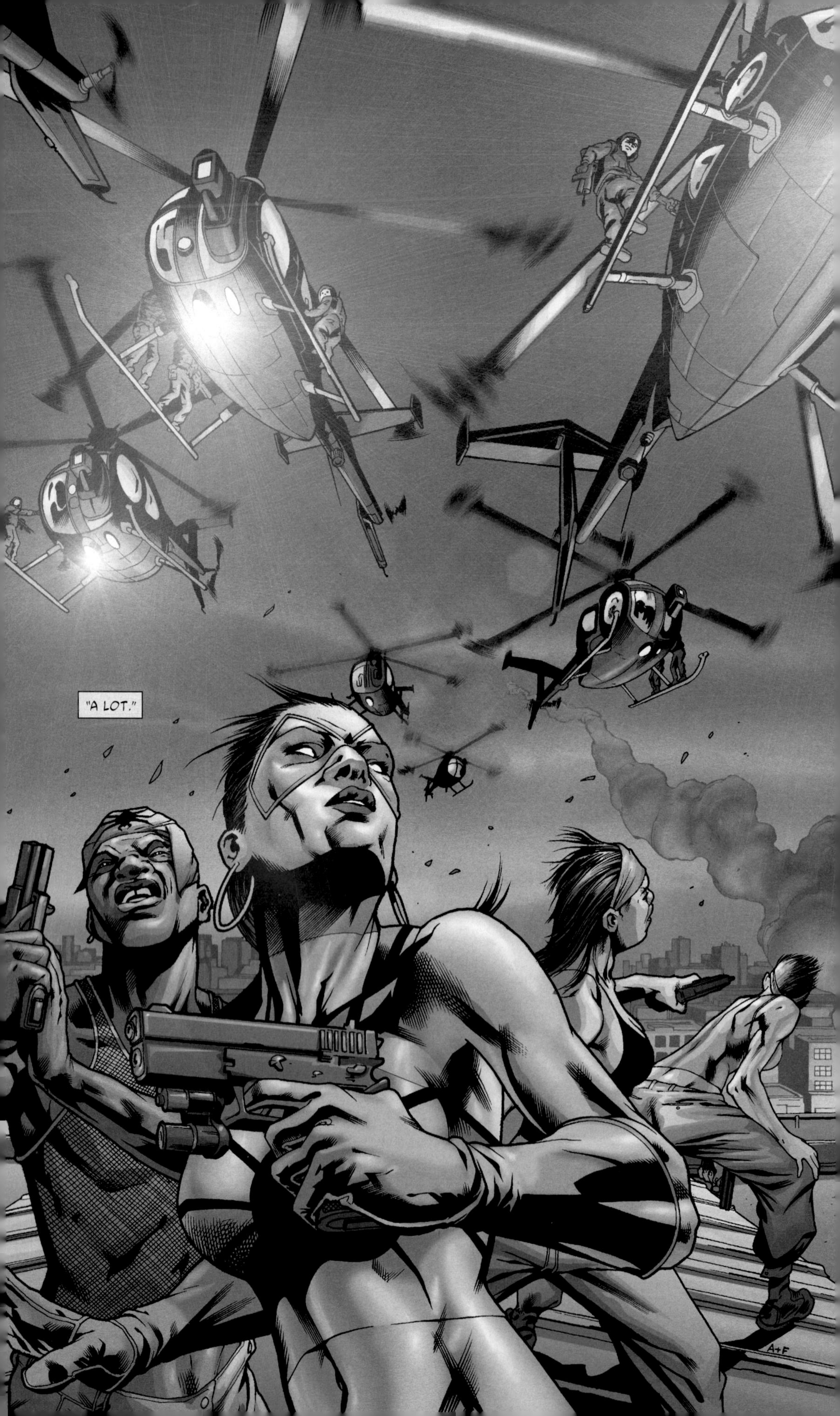
"A LOT."
A+F

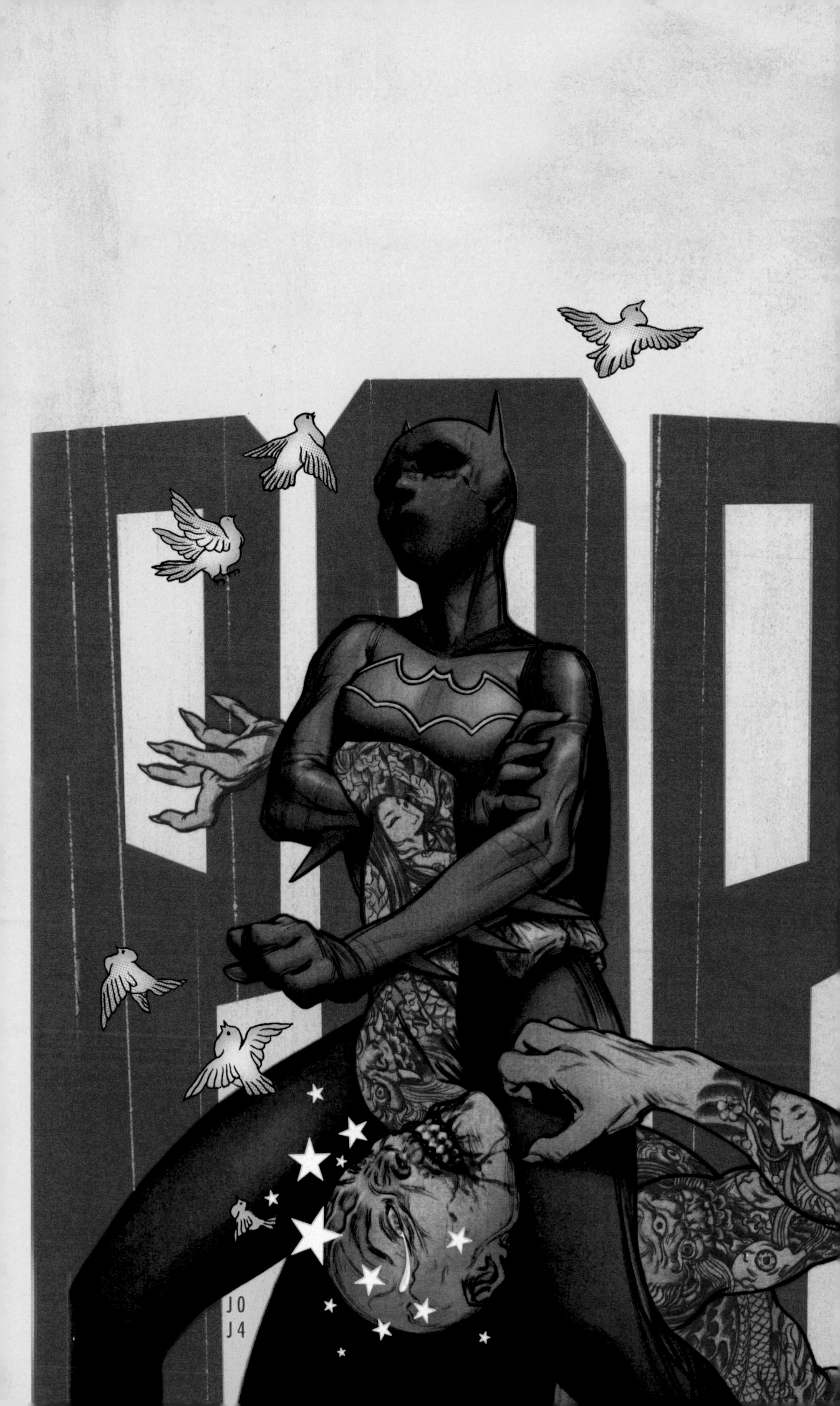
JO
J4

COVER ART BY
JAMES JEAN

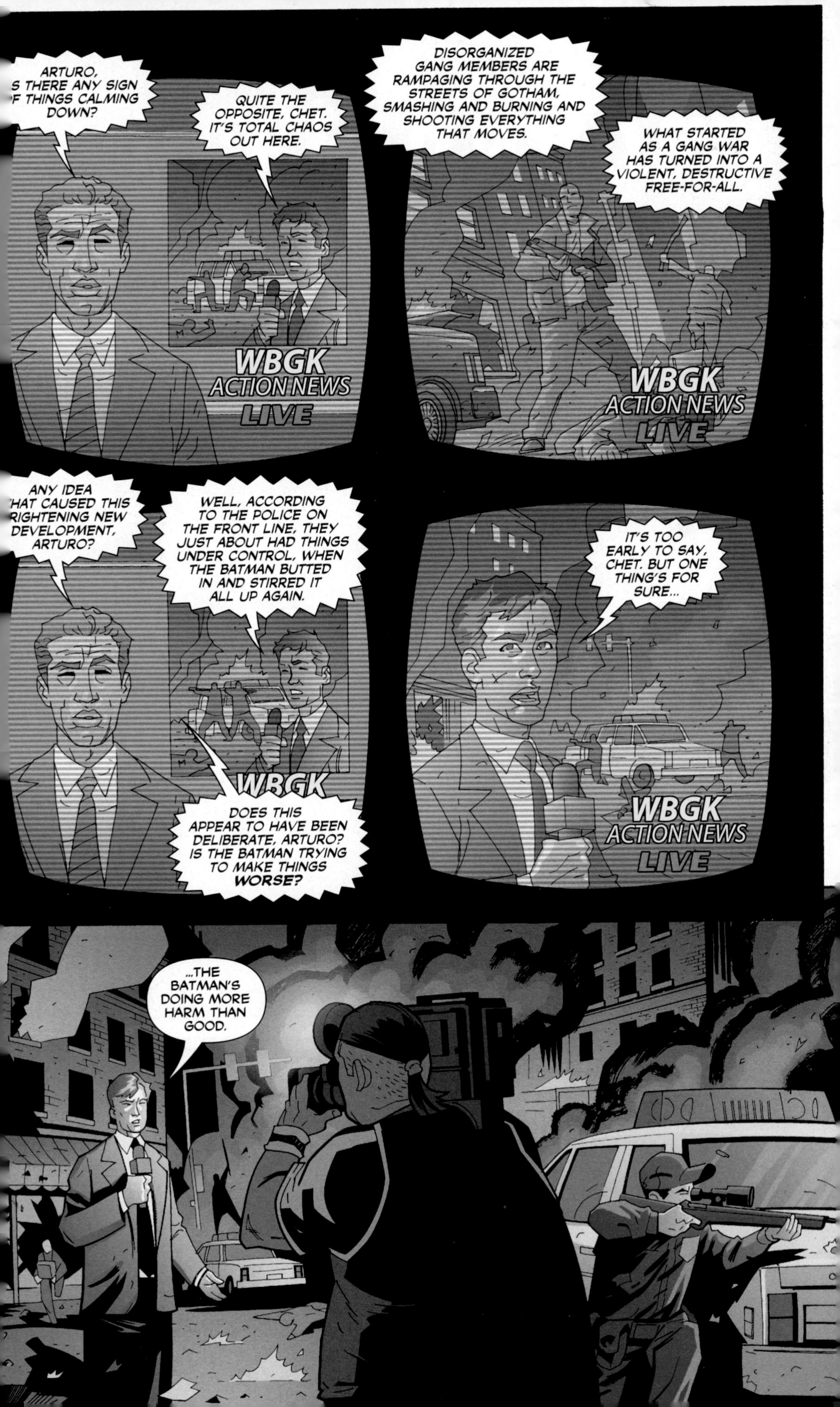
ARTURO, S THERE ANY SIGN F THINGS CALMING DOWN?
QUITE THE OPPOSITE, CHET. IT'S TOTAL CHAOS OUT HERE.
WBGK ACTION NEWS LIVE
DISORGANIZED GANG MEMBERS ARE RAMPAGING THROUGH THE STREETS OF GOTHAM, SMASHING AND BURNING AND SHOOTING EVERYTHING THAT MOVES.
WHAT STARTED AS A GANG WAR HAS TURNED INTO A VIOLENT, DESTRUCTIVE FREE-FOR-ALL.
WBGK ACTION NEWS LIVE
ANY IDEA HAT CAUSED THIS RIGHTENING NEW DEVELOPMENT, ARTURO?
WELL, ACCORDING TO THE POLICE ON THE FRONT LINE, THEY JUST ABOUT HAD THINGS UNDER CONTROL, WHEN THE BATMAN BUTTED IN AND STIRRED IT ALL UP AGAIN.
WBGK
DOES THIS APPEAR TO HAVE BEEN DELIBERATE, ARTURO? IS THE BATMAN TRYING TO MAKE THINGS **WORSE?**
IT'S TOO EARLY TO SAY, CHET. BUT ONE THING'S FOR SURE...
WBGK ACTION NEWS LIVE
...THE BATMAN'S DOING MORE HARM THAN GOOD.

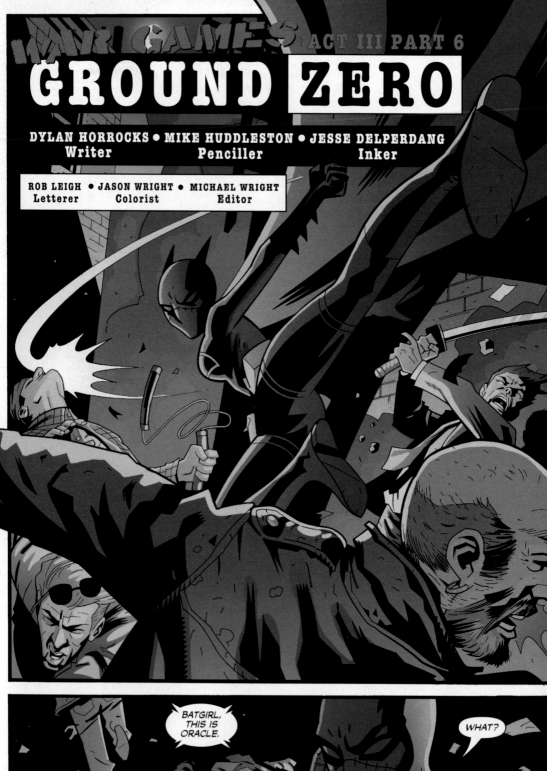

GROUND ZERO

DYLAN HORROCKS • **MIKE HUDDLESTON** • **JESSE DELPERDANG**
Writer — Penciller — Inker

ROB LEIGH • **JASON WRIGHT** • **MICHAEL WRIGHT**
Letterer — Colorist — Editor

BATGIRL, THIS IS ORACLE.

WHAT?

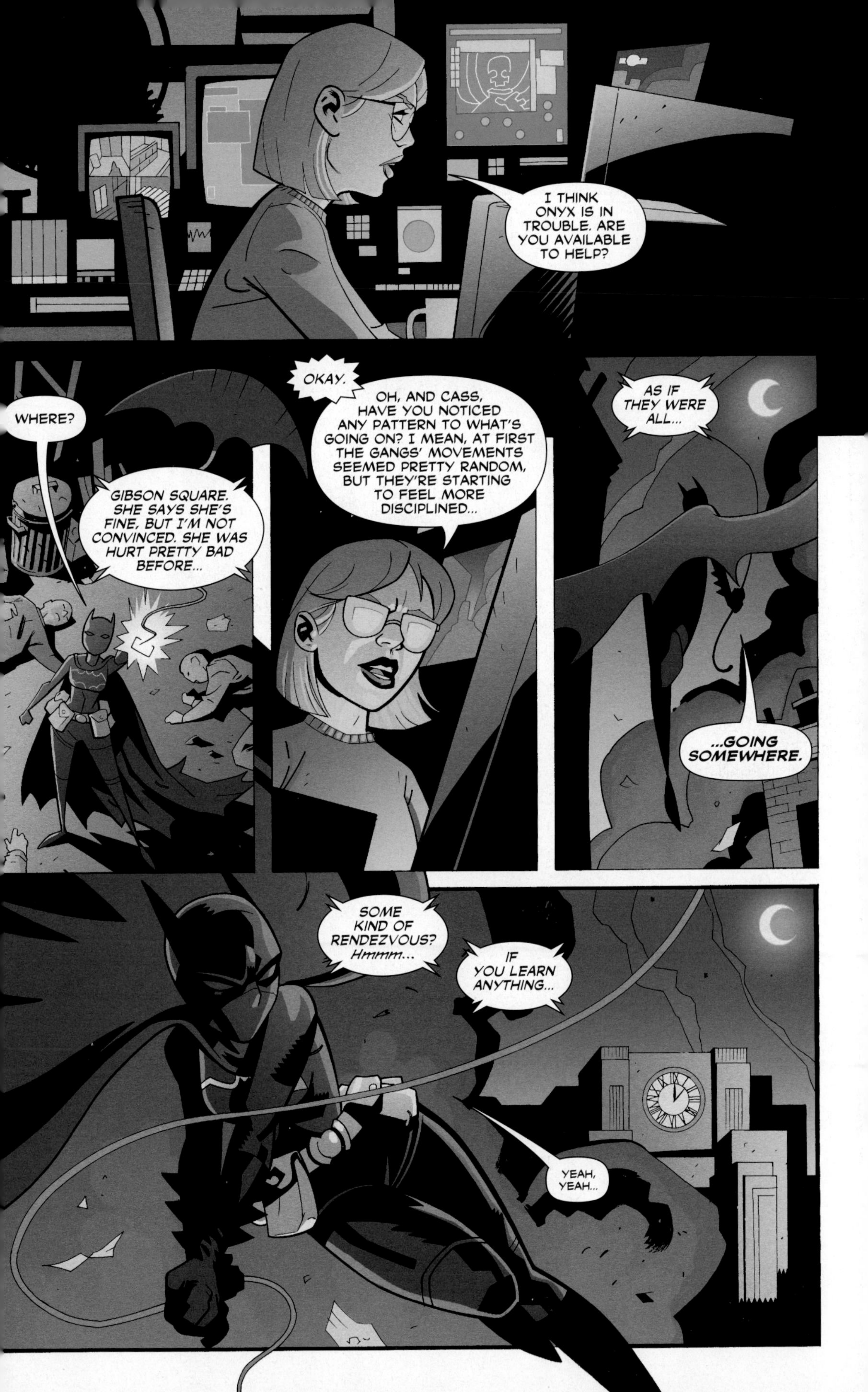
I THINK ONYX IS IN TROUBLE. ARE YOU AVAILABLE TO HELP?
WHERE?
GIBSON SQUARE. SHE SAYS SHE'S FINE, BUT I'M NOT CONVINCED. SHE WAS HURT PRETTY BAD BEFORE...
OKAY.
OH, AND CASS, HAVE YOU NOTICED ANY PATTERN TO WHAT'S GOING ON? I MEAN, AT FIRST THE GANGS' MOVEMENTS SEEMED PRETTY RANDOM, BUT THEY'RE STARTING TO FEEL MORE DISCIPLINED...
AS IF THEY WERE ALL...
...GOING SOMEWHERE.
SOME KIND OF RENDEZVOUS? Hmmm...
IF YOU LEARN ANYTHING...
YEAH, YEAH...

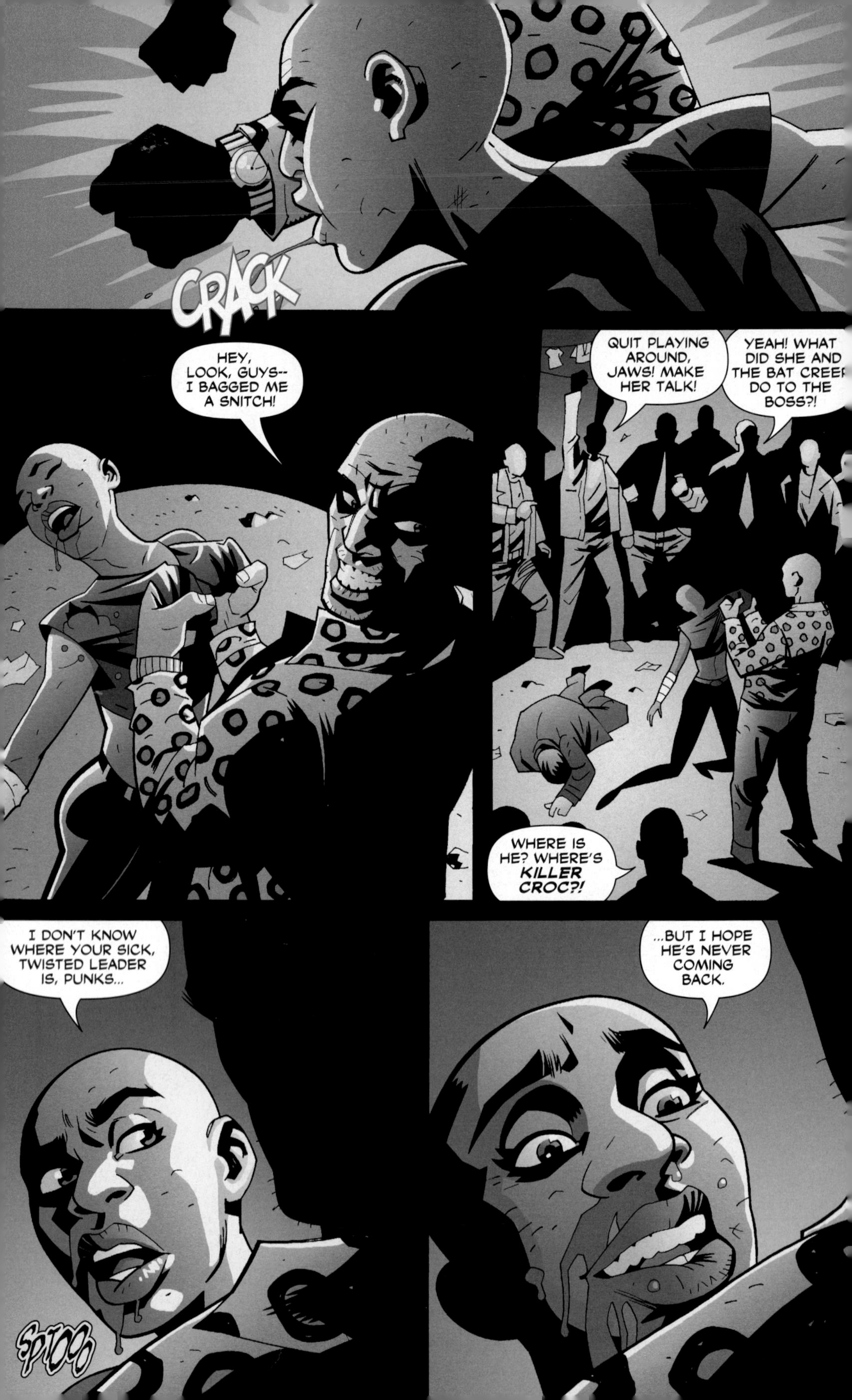
CRACK
HEY, LOOK, GUYS-- I BAGGED ME A SNITCH!
QUIT PLAYING AROUND, JAWS! MAKE HER TALK!
YEAH! WHAT DID SHE AND THE BAT CREEP DO TO THE BOSS?!
WHERE IS HE? WHERE'S KILLER CROC?!
I DON'T KNOW WHERE YOUR SICK, TWISTED LEADER IS, PUNKS...
SPTOOO
...BUT I HOPE HE'S NEVER COMING BACK.

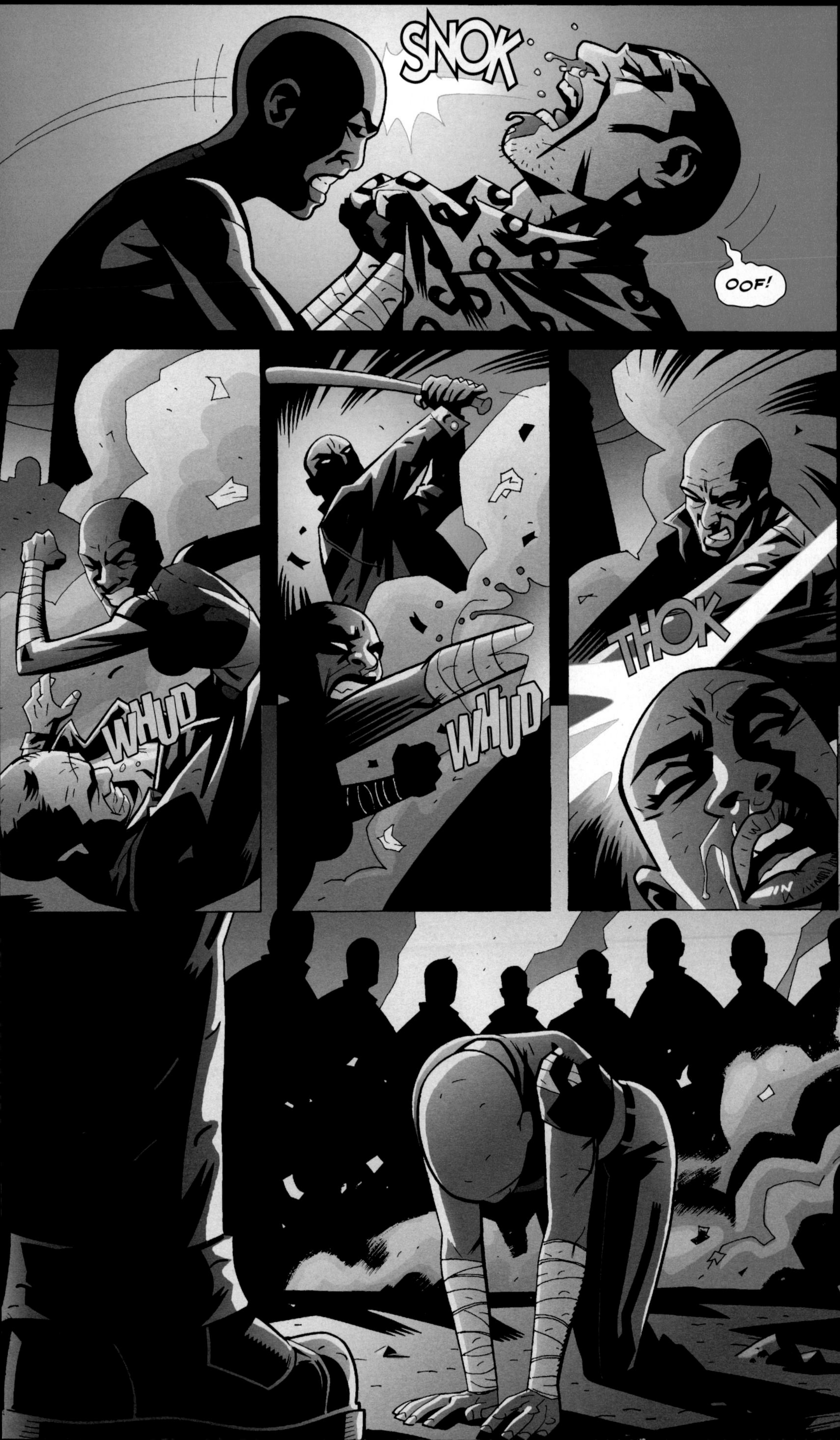
SNOK
OOF!
WHUD
WHUD
THOK

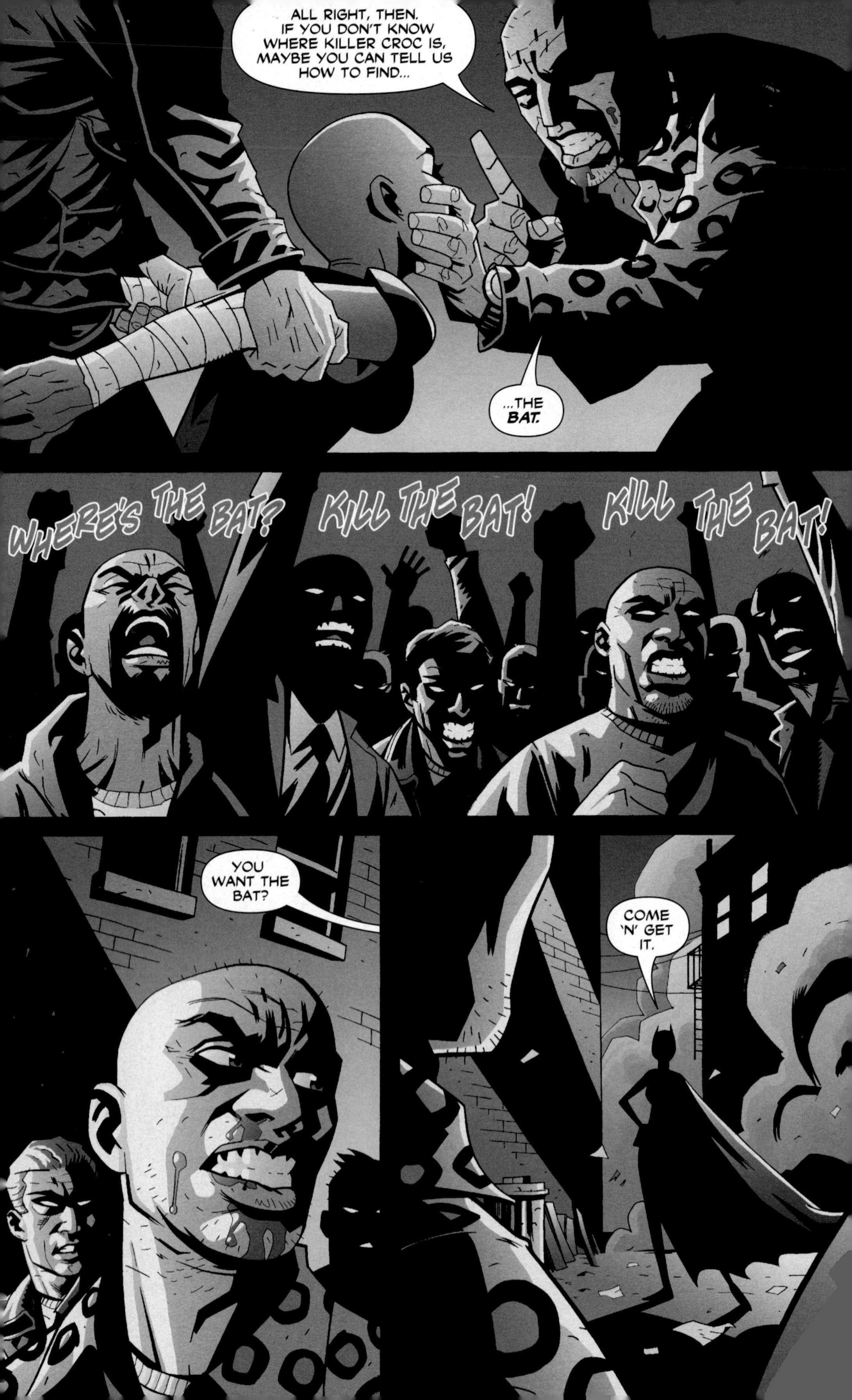
ALL RIGHT, THEN. IF YOU DON'T KNOW WHERE KILLER CROC IS, MAYBE YOU CAN TELL US HOW TO FIND...
...THE BAT.
WHERE'S THE BAT?
KILL THE BAT!
KILL THE BAT!
YOU WANT THE BAT?
COME 'N' GET IT.

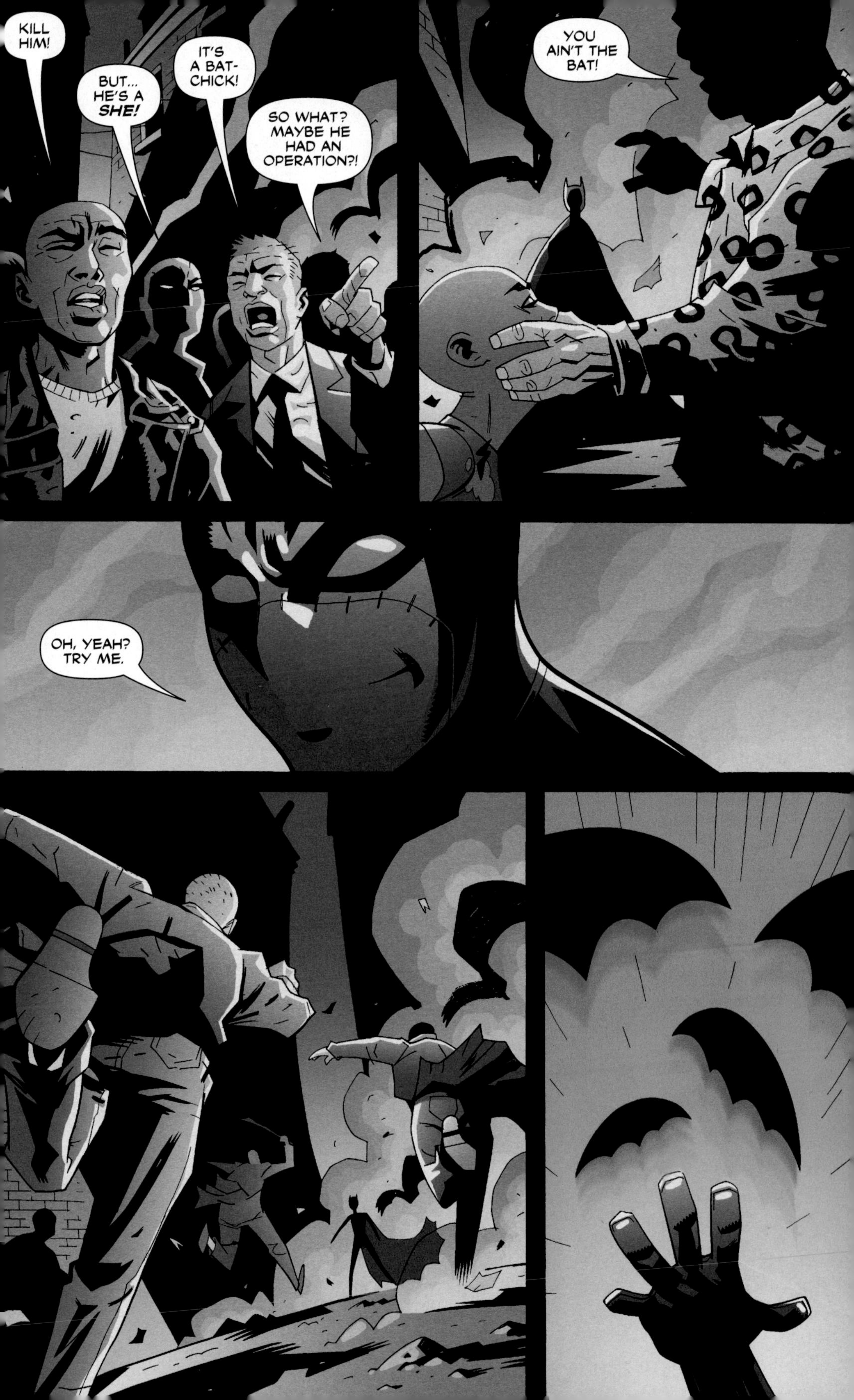
KILL HIM!
BUT... HE'S A *SHE!*
IT'S A BAT-CHICK!
SO WHAT? MAYBE HE HAD AN OPERATION?!
YOU AIN'T THE BAT!
OH, YEAH? TRY ME.

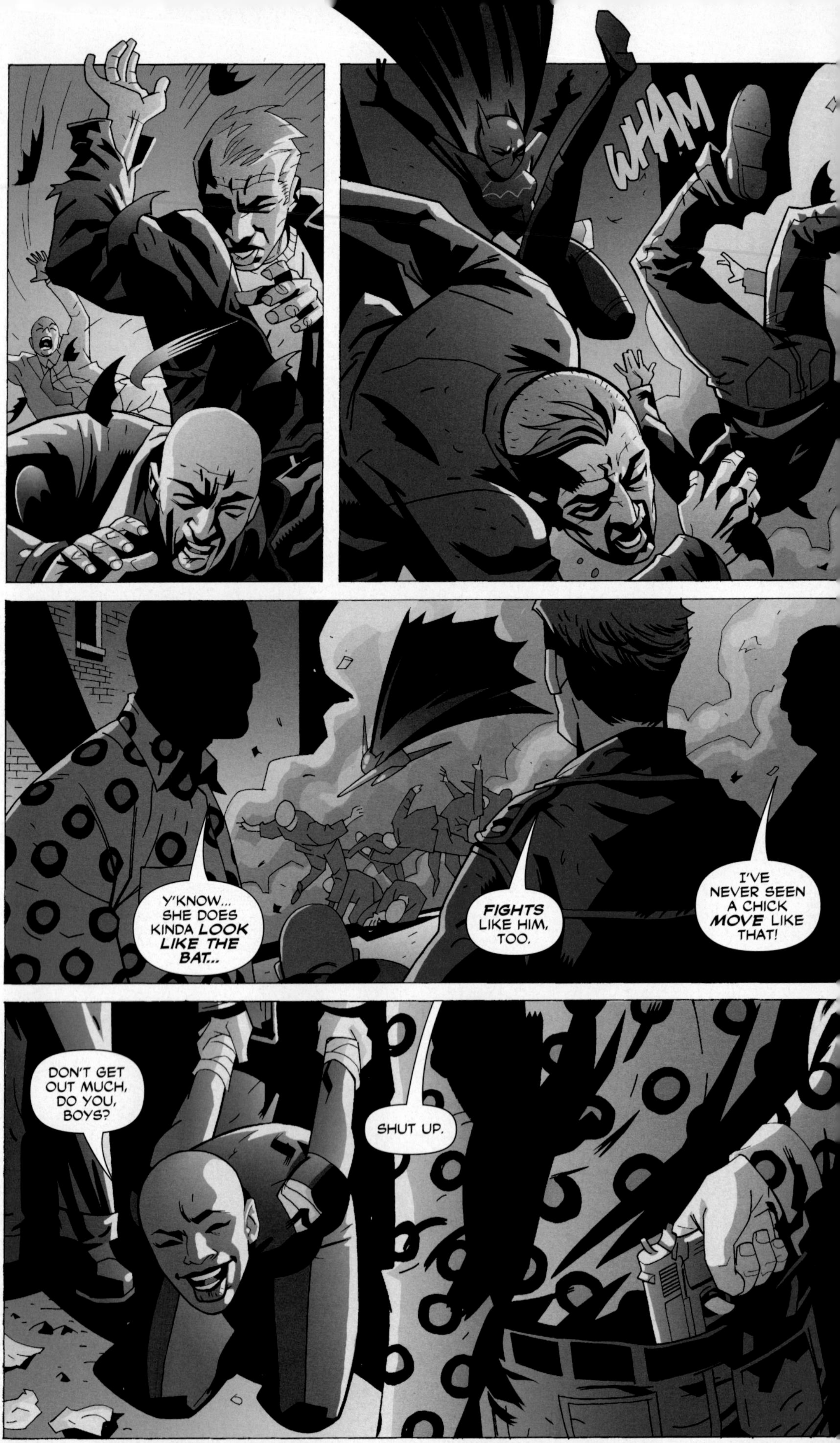
WHAM
Y'KNOW... SHE DOES KINDA LOOK LIKE THE BAT...
FIGHTS LIKE HIM, TOO.
I'VE NEVER SEEN A CHICK MOVE LIKE THAT!
DON'T GET OUT MUCH, DO YOU, BOYS?
SHUT UP.

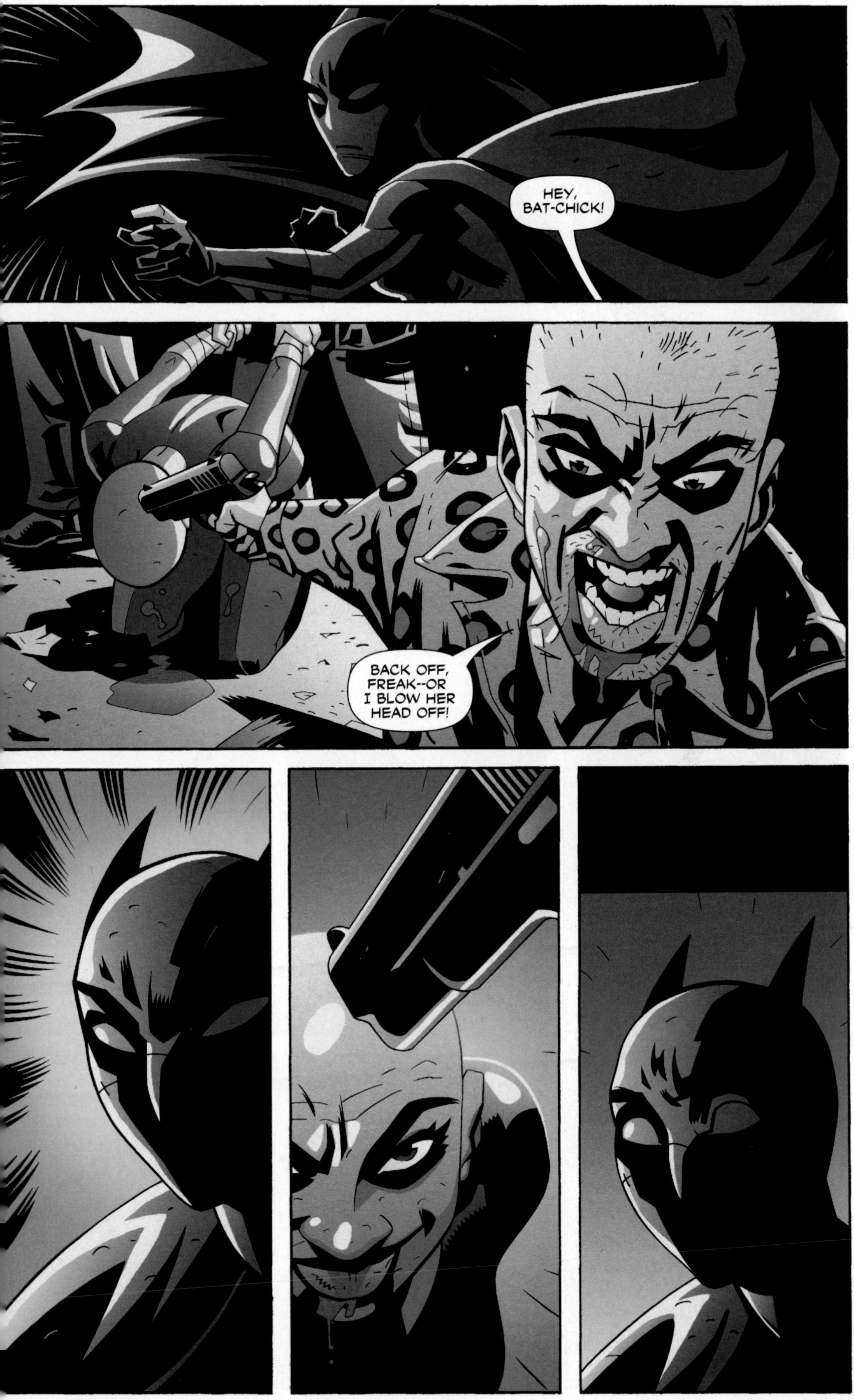
HEY, BAT-CHICK!
BACK OFF, FREAK--OR I BLOW HER HEAD OFF!

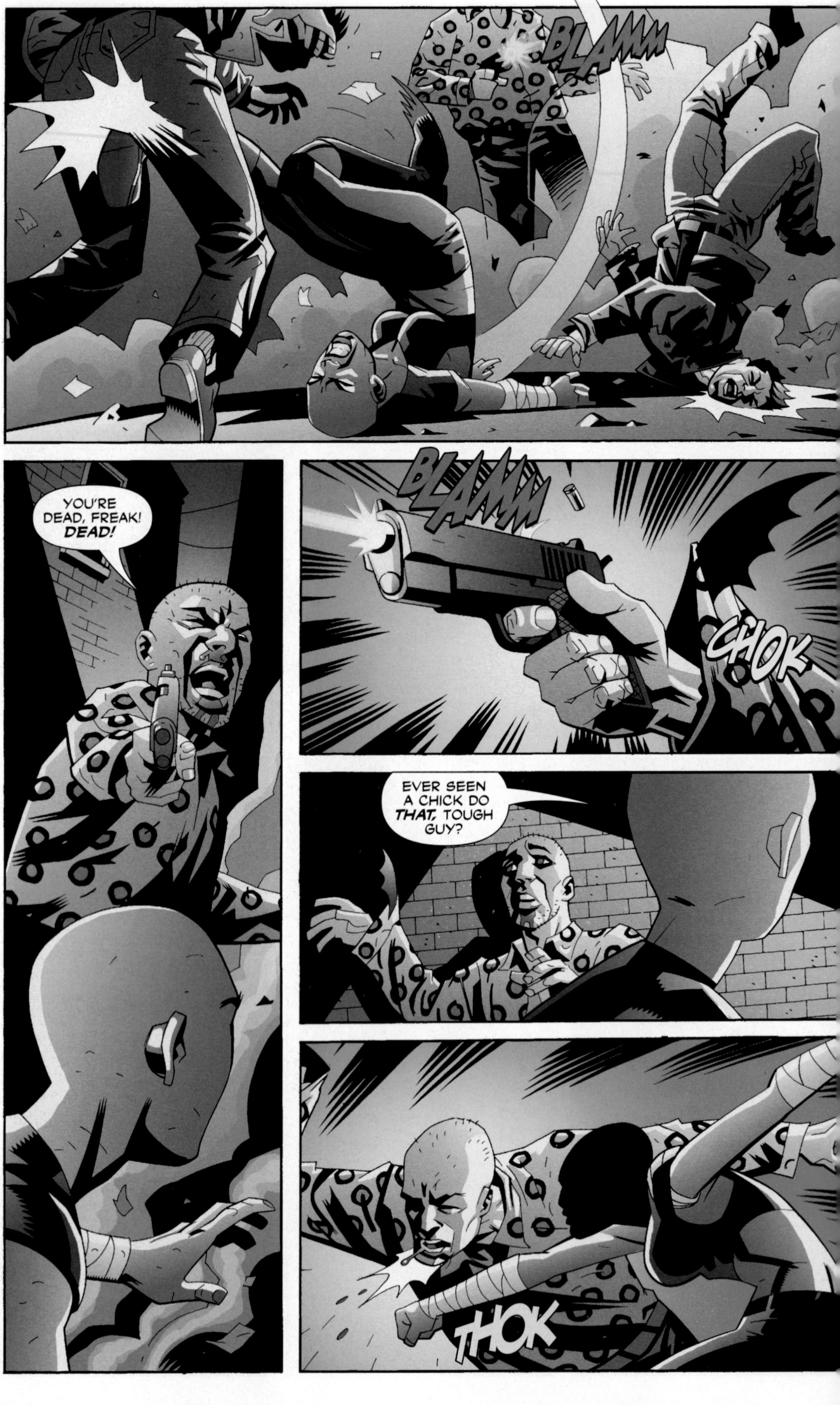
BLAMM
YOU'RE DEAD, FREAK! **DEAD!**
BLAMM
CHOK
EVER SEEN A CHICK DO ***THAT,*** TOUGH GUY?
THOK

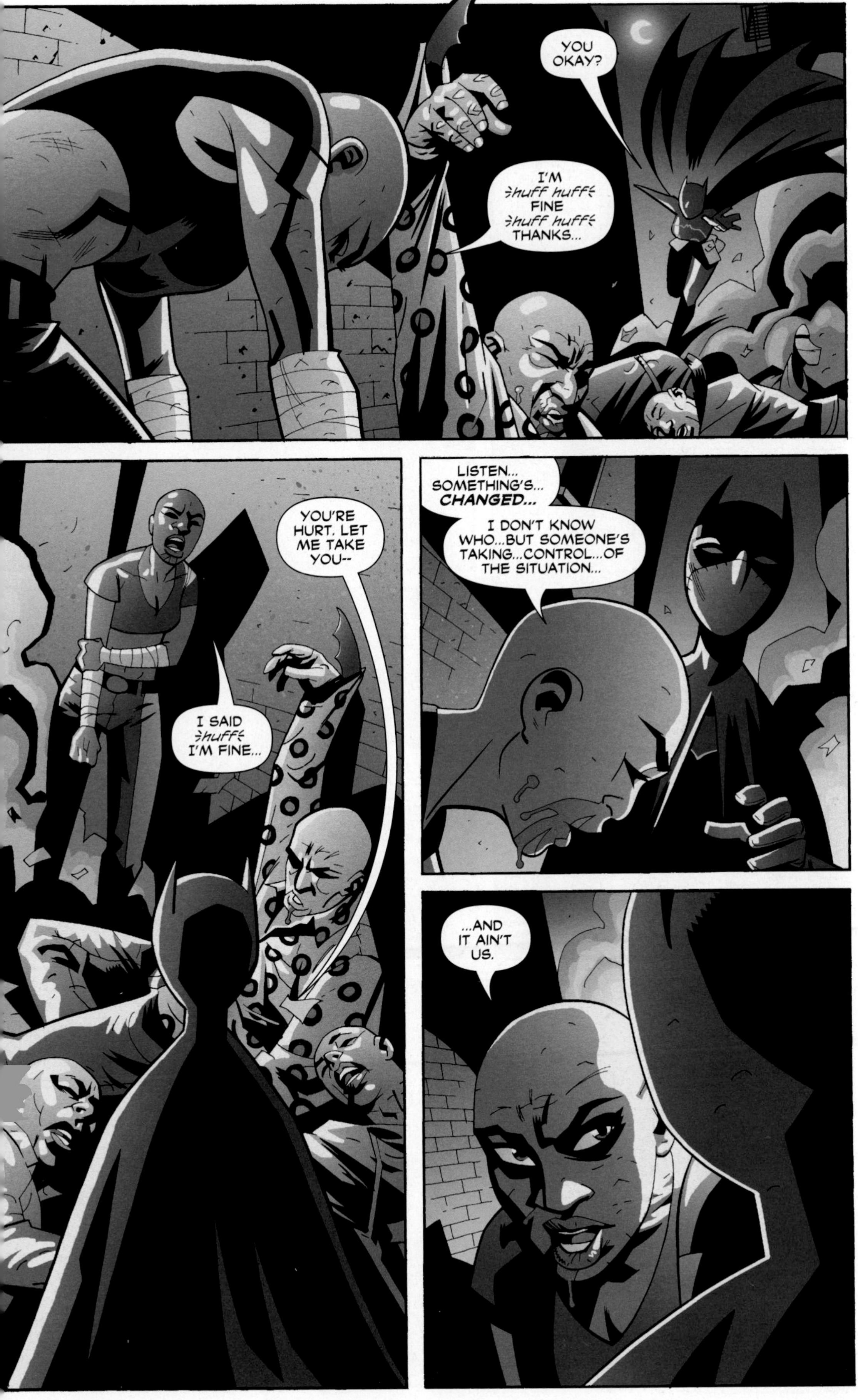

YOU OKAY?
I'M ≥huff huff≤ FINE ≥huff huff≤ THANKS...
YOU'RE HURT. LET ME TAKE YOU--
I SAID ≥huff≤ I'M FINE...
LISTEN... SOMETHING'S... CHANGED...
I DON'T KNOW WHO...BUT SOMEONE'S TAKING...CONTROL...OF THE SITUATION...
...AND IT AIN'T US.

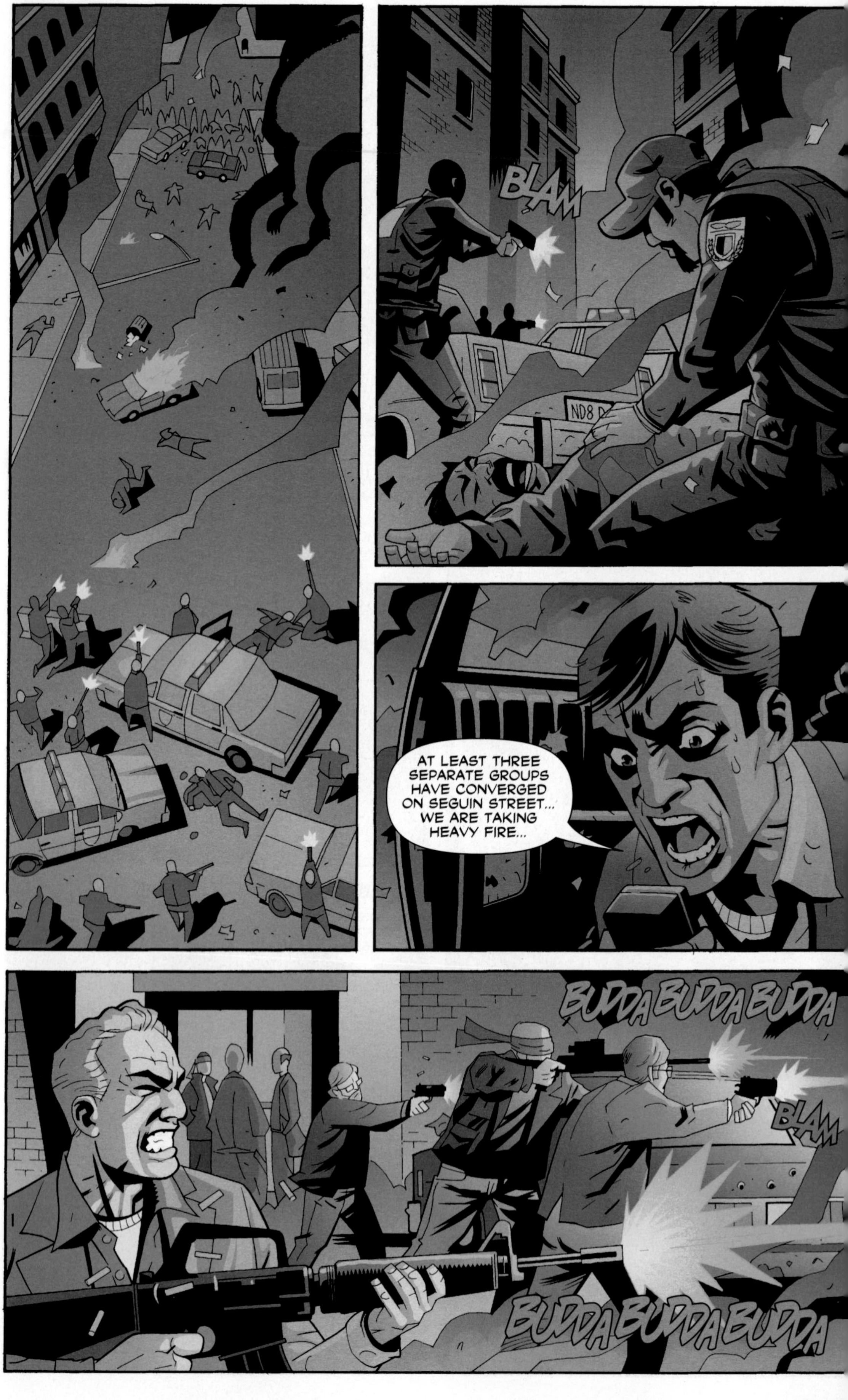
BLAM
ND8
AT LEAST THREE SEPARATE GROUPS HAVE CONVERGED ON SEGUIN STREET... WE ARE TAKING HEAVY FIRE...
BUDDA BUDDA BUDDA
BLAM
BUDDA BUDDA BUDDA

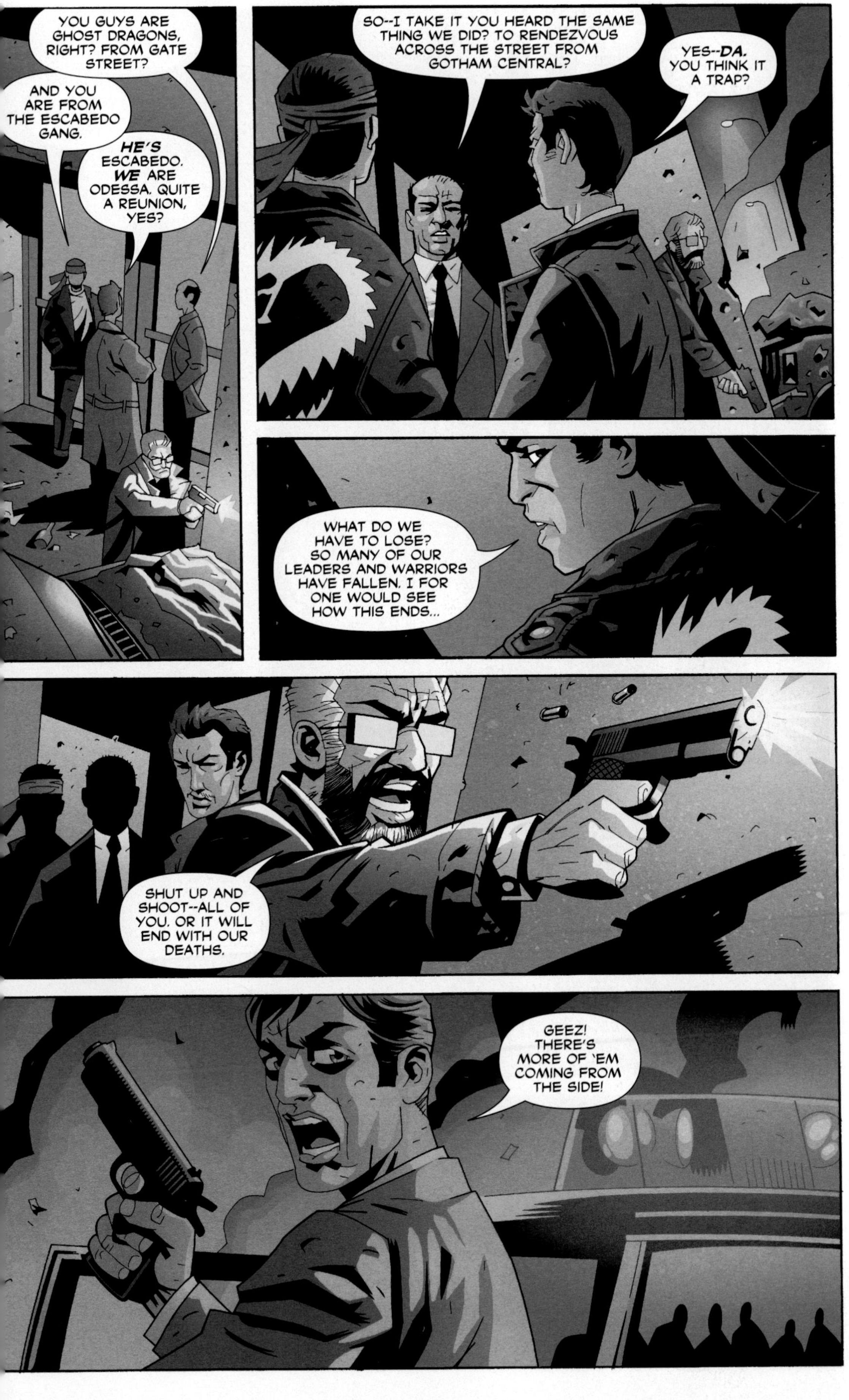
YOU GUYS ARE GHOST DRAGONS, RIGHT? FROM GATE STREET?
AND YOU ARE FROM THE ESCABEDO GANG.
HE'S ESCABEDO. WE ARE ODESSA. QUITE A REUNION, YES?
SO--I TAKE IT YOU HEARD THE SAME THING WE DID? TO RENDEZVOUS ACROSS THE STREET FROM GOTHAM CENTRAL?
YES--DA. YOU THINK IT A TRAP?
WHAT DO WE HAVE TO LOSE? SO MANY OF OUR LEADERS AND WARRIORS HAVE FALLEN. I FOR ONE WOULD SEE HOW THIS ENDS...
SHUT UP AND SHOOT--ALL OF YOU. OR IT WILL END WITH OUR DEATHS.
GEEZ! THERE'S MORE OF 'EM COMING FROM THE SIDE!

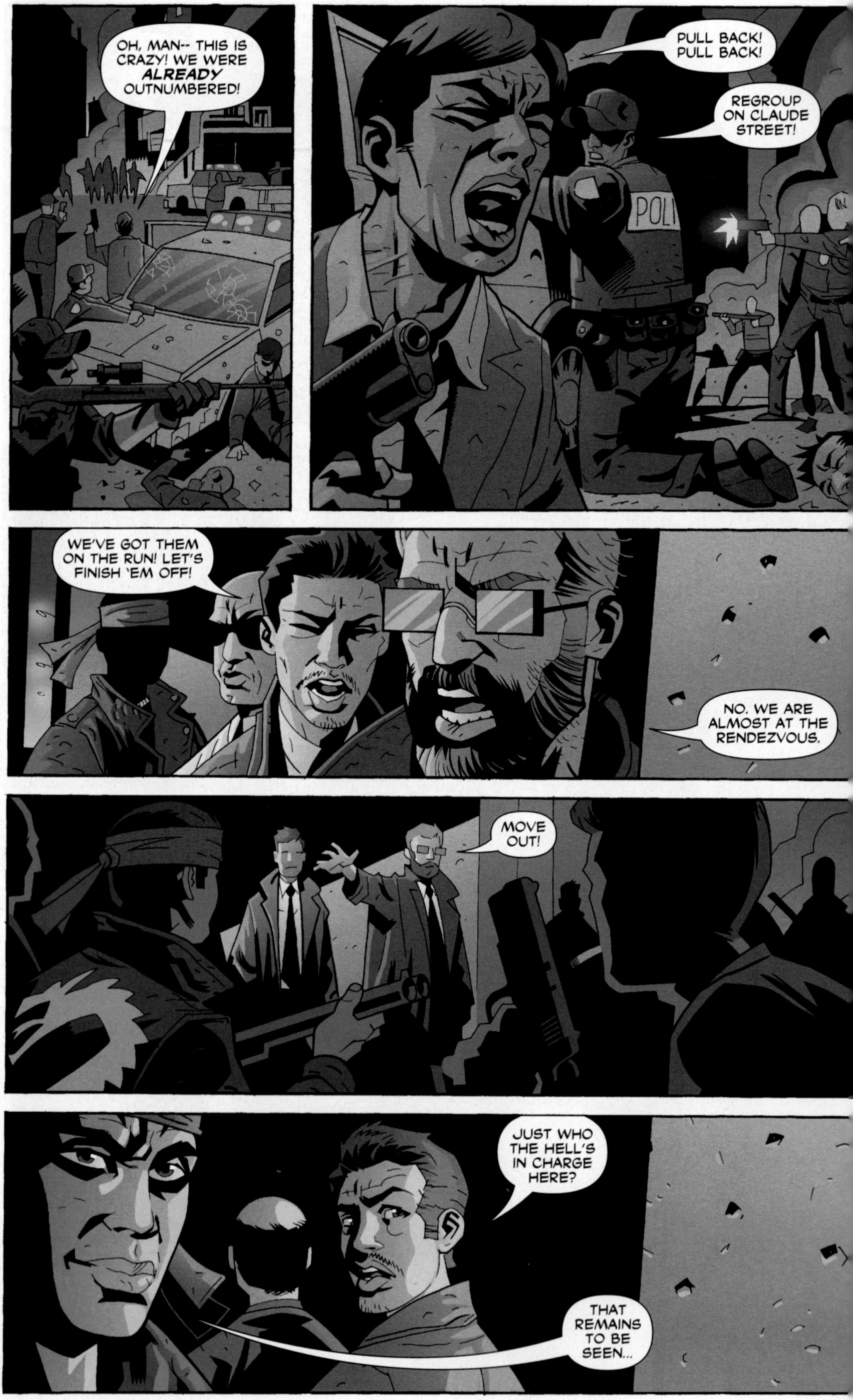
OH, MAN-- THIS IS CRAZY! WE WERE *ALREADY* OUTNUMBERED!
PULL BACK! PULL BACK!
REGROUP ON CLAUDE STREET!
POLI
WE'VE GOT THEM ON THE RUN! LET'S FINISH 'EM OFF!
NO. WE ARE ALMOST AT THE RENDEZVOUS.
MOVE OUT!
JUST WHO THE HELL'S IN CHARGE HERE?
THAT REMAINS TO BE SEEN...

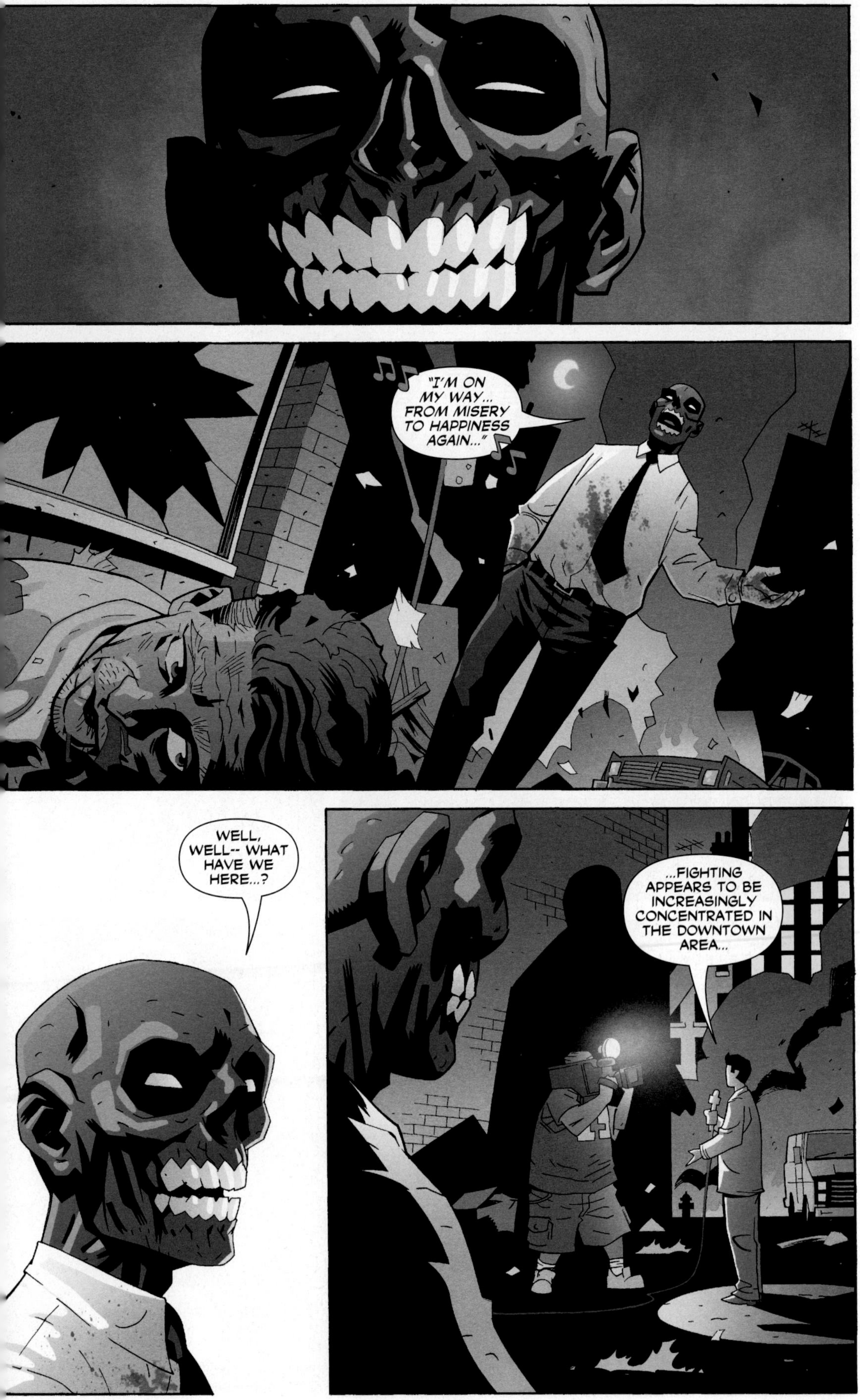
"I'M ON MY WAY... FROM MISERY TO HAPPINESS AGAIN..."
WELL, WELL-- WHAT HAVE WE HERE...?
...FIGHTING APPEARS TO BE INCREASINGLY CONCENTRATED IN THE DOWNTOWN AREA...

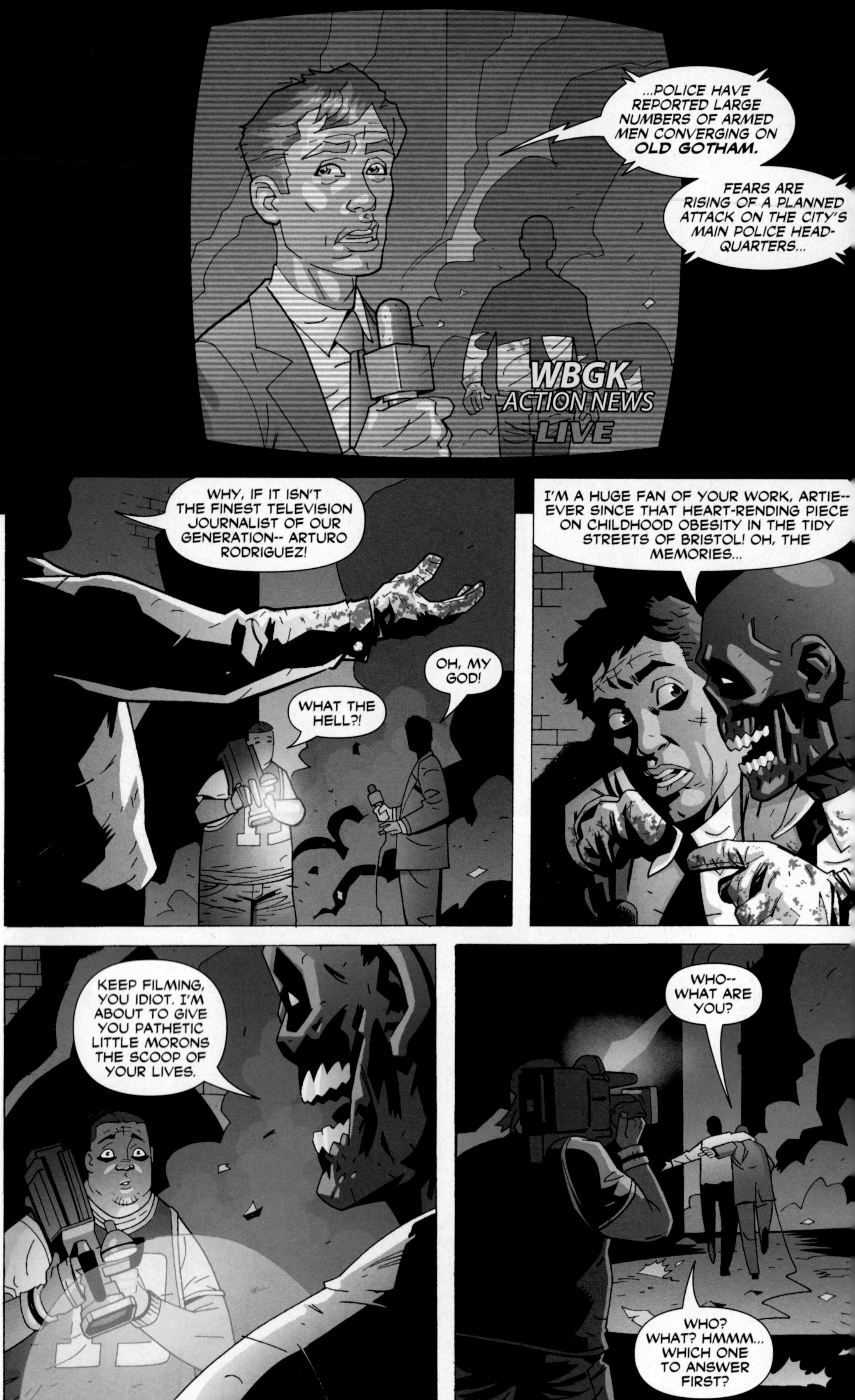
...POLICE HAVE REPORTED LARGE NUMBERS OF ARMED MEN CONVERGING ON **OLD GOTHAM.**
FEARS ARE RISING OF A PLANNED ATTACK ON THE CITY'S MAIN POLICE HEAD-QUARTERS...
WBGK
ACTION NEWS
LIVE
WHY, IF IT ISN'T THE FINEST TELEVISION JOURNALIST OF OUR GENERATION-- ARTURO RODRIGUEZ!
WHAT THE HELL?!
OH, MY GOD!
I'M A HUGE FAN OF YOUR WORK, ARTIE-- EVER SINCE THAT HEART-RENDING PIECE ON CHILDHOOD OBESITY IN THE TIDY STREETS OF BRISTOL! OH, THE MEMORIES...
KEEP FILMING, YOU IDIOT. I'M ABOUT TO GIVE YOU PATHETIC LITTLE MORONS THE SCOOP OF YOUR LIVES.
WHO-- WHAT ARE YOU?
WHO? WHAT? HMMM... WHICH ONE TO ANSWER FIRST?

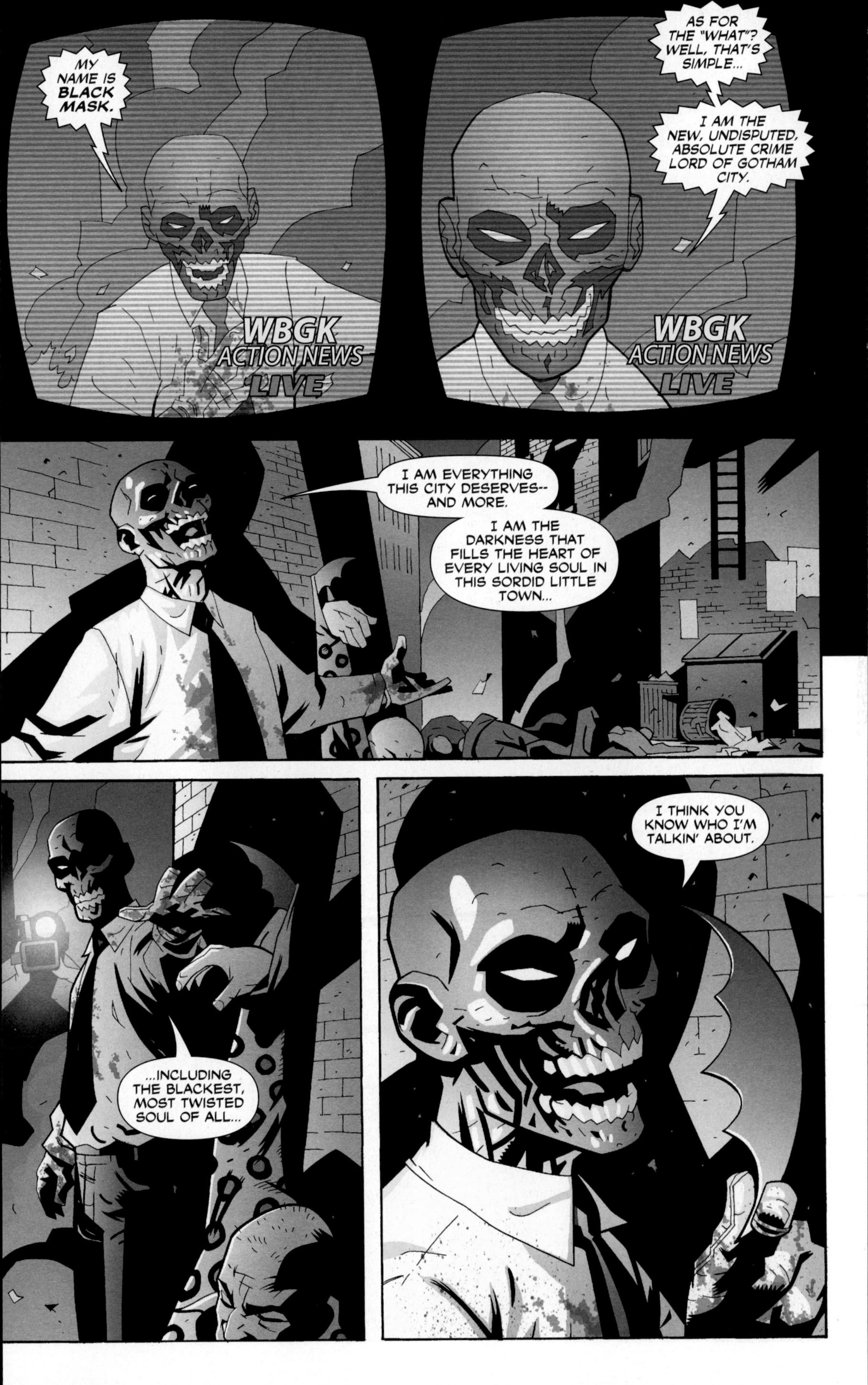
MY NAME IS BLACK MASK.
WBGK ACTION NEWS LIVE
AS FOR THE "WHAT"? WELL, THAT'S SIMPLE...
I AM THE NEW, UNDISPUTED, ABSOLUTE CRIME LORD OF GOTHAM CITY.
WBGK ACTION NEWS LIVE
I AM EVERYTHING THIS CITY DESERVES-- AND MORE.
I AM THE DARKNESS THAT FILLS THE HEART OF EVERY LIVING SOUL IN THIS SORDID LITTLE TOWN...
...INCLUDING THE BLACKEST, MOST TWISTED SOUL OF ALL...
I THINK YOU KNOW WHO I'M TALKIN' ABOUT.

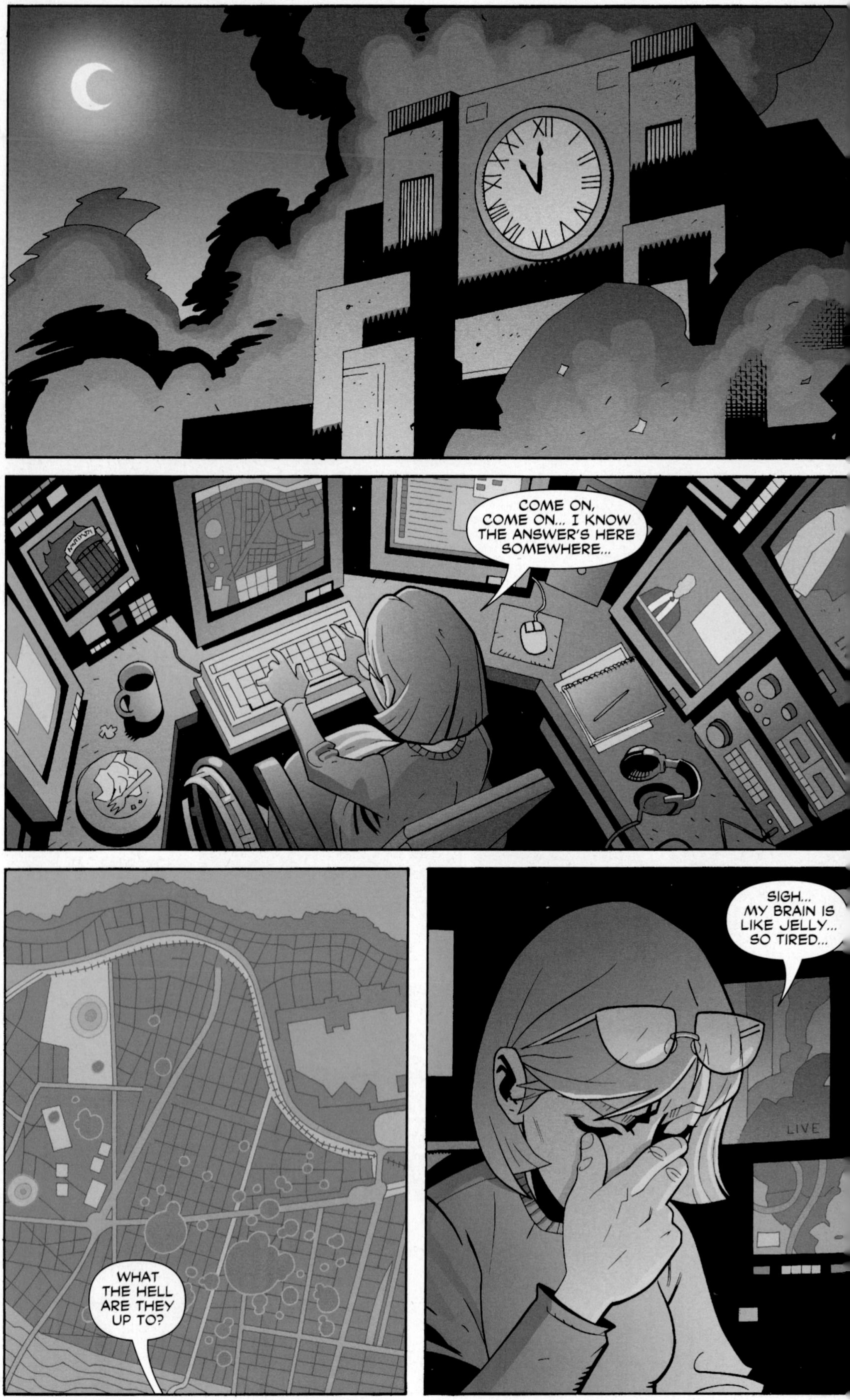
COME ON, COME ON... I KNOW THE ANSWER'S HERE SOMEWHERE...
WHAT THE HELL ARE THEY UP TO?
SIGH... MY BRAIN IS LIKE JELLY... SO TIRED...
LIVE

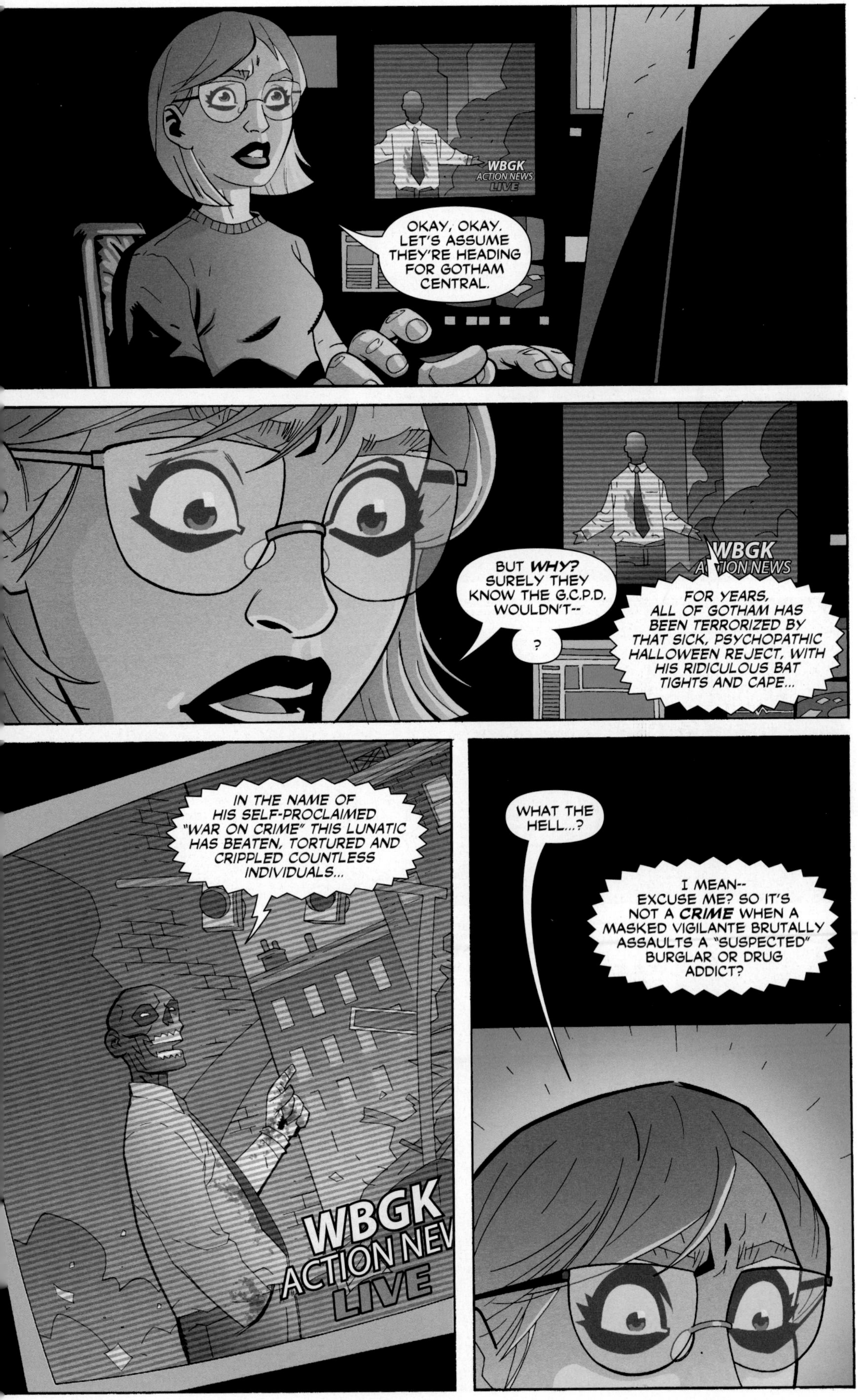
WBGK
ACTION NEWS
LIVE
OKAY, OKAY. LET'S ASSUME THEY'RE HEADING FOR GOTHAM CENTRAL.
WBGK
ACTION NEWS
BUT WHY? SURELY THEY KNOW THE G.C.P.D. WOULDN'T--
?
FOR YEARS, ALL OF GOTHAM HAS BEEN TERRORIZED BY THAT SICK, PSYCHOPATHIC HALLOWEEN REJECT, WITH HIS RIDICULOUS BAT TIGHTS AND CAPE...
IN THE NAME OF HIS SELF-PROCLAIMED "WAR ON CRIME" THIS LUNATIC HAS BEATEN, TORTURED AND CRIPPLED COUNTLESS INDIVIDUALS...
WBGK
ACTION NEW
LIVE
WHAT THE HELL...?
I MEAN-- EXCUSE ME? SO IT'S NOT A CRIME WHEN A MASKED VIGILANTE BRUTALLY ASSAULTS A "SUSPECTED" BURGLAR OR DRUG ADDICT?

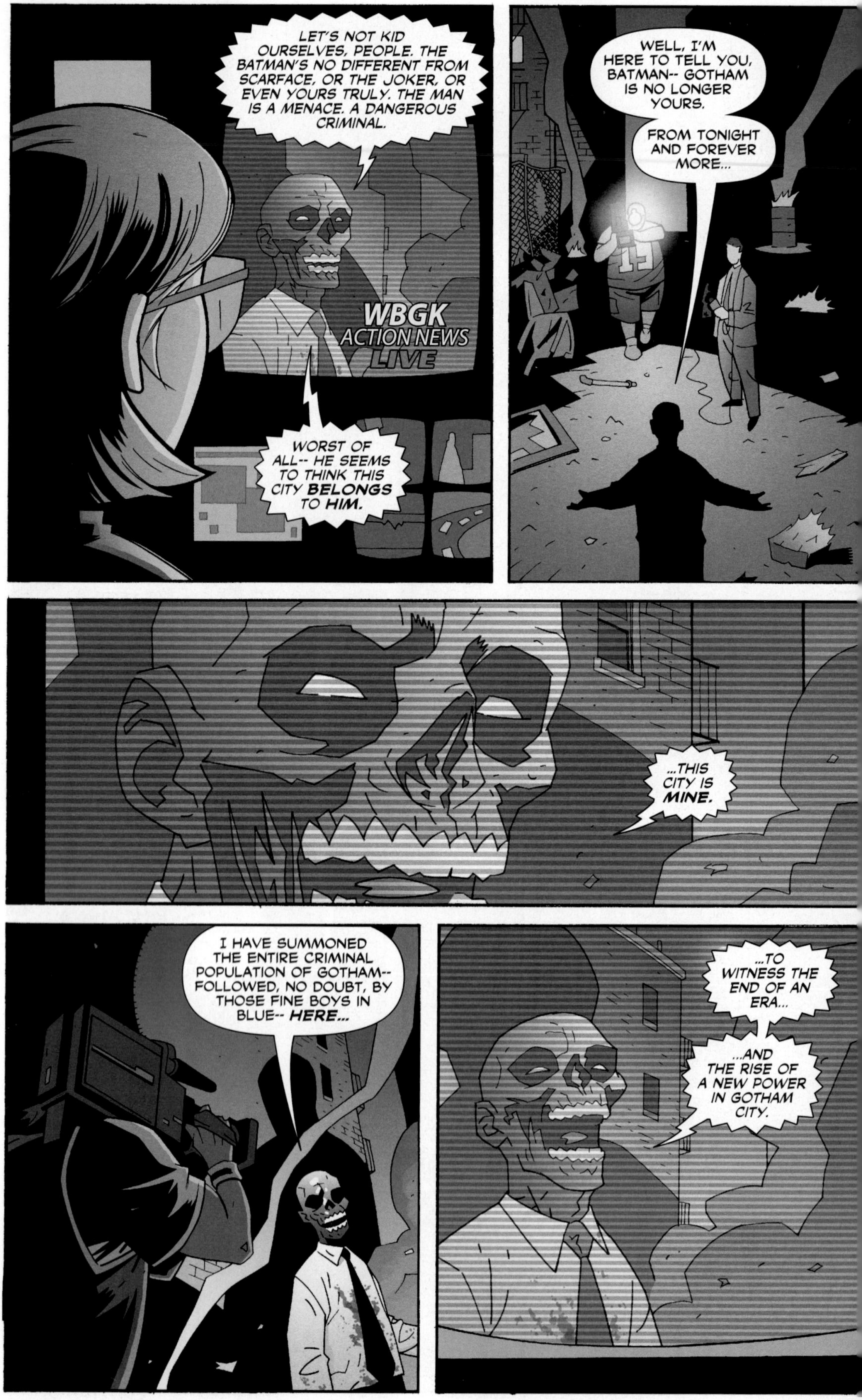

LET'S NOT KID OURSELVES, PEOPLE. THE BATMAN'S NO DIFFERENT FROM SCARFACE, OR THE JOKER, OR EVEN YOURS TRULY. THE MAN IS A MENACE. A DANGEROUS CRIMINAL.
WBGK ACTION NEWS LIVE
WORST OF ALL-- HE SEEMS TO THINK THIS CITY BELONGS TO HIM.
WELL, I'M HERE TO TELL YOU, BATMAN-- GOTHAM IS NO LONGER YOURS.
FROM TONIGHT AND FOREVER MORE...
...THIS CITY IS MINE.
I HAVE SUMMONED THE ENTIRE CRIMINAL POPULATION OF GOTHAM-- FOLLOWED, NO DOUBT, BY THOSE FINE BOYS IN BLUE-- HERE...
...TO WITNESS THE END OF AN ERA...
...AND THE RISE OF A NEW POWER IN GOTHAM CITY.

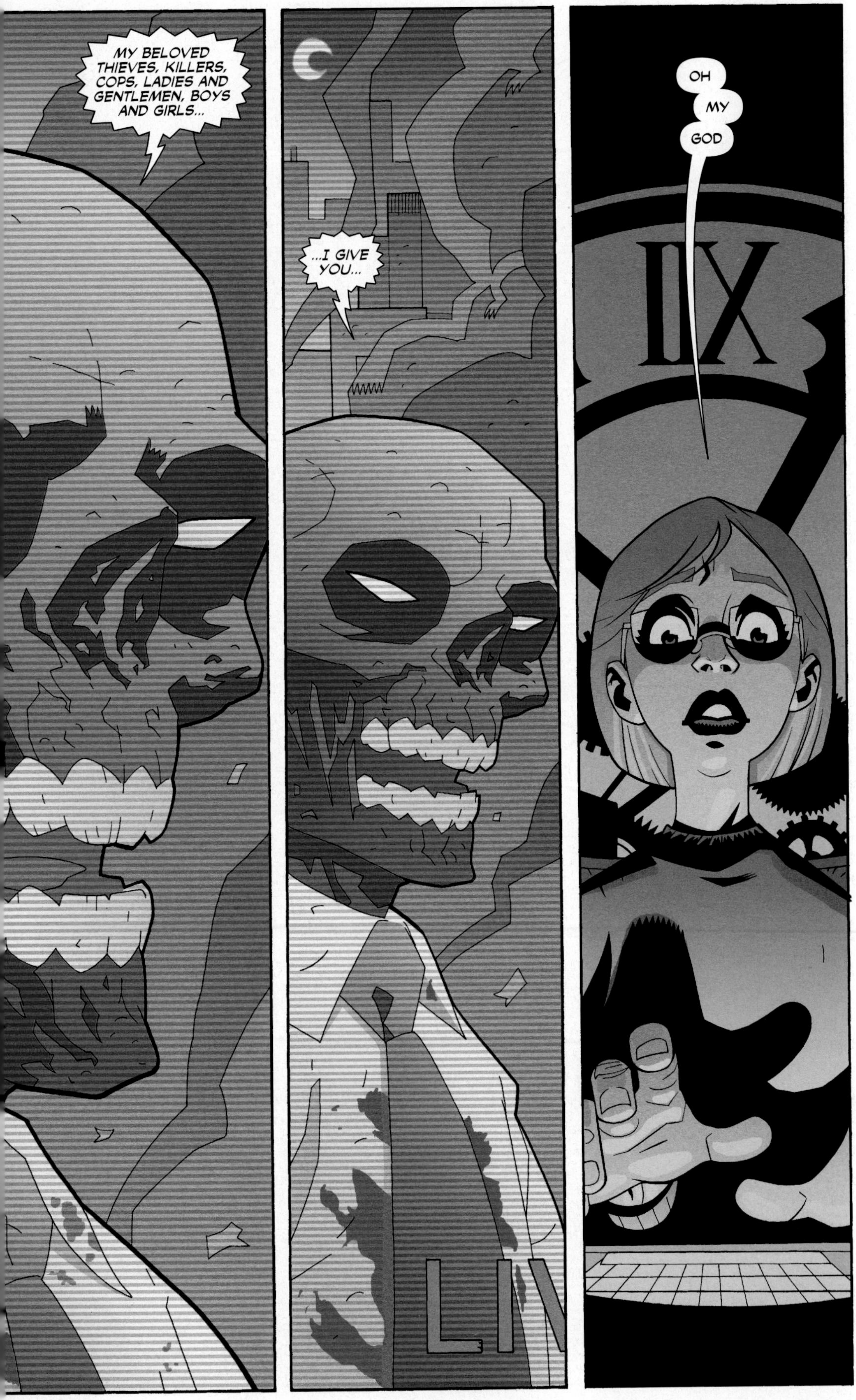
MY BELOVED THIEVES, KILLERS, COPS, LADIES AND GENTLEMEN, BOYS AND GIRLS...
...I GIVE YOU...
OH
MY
GOD

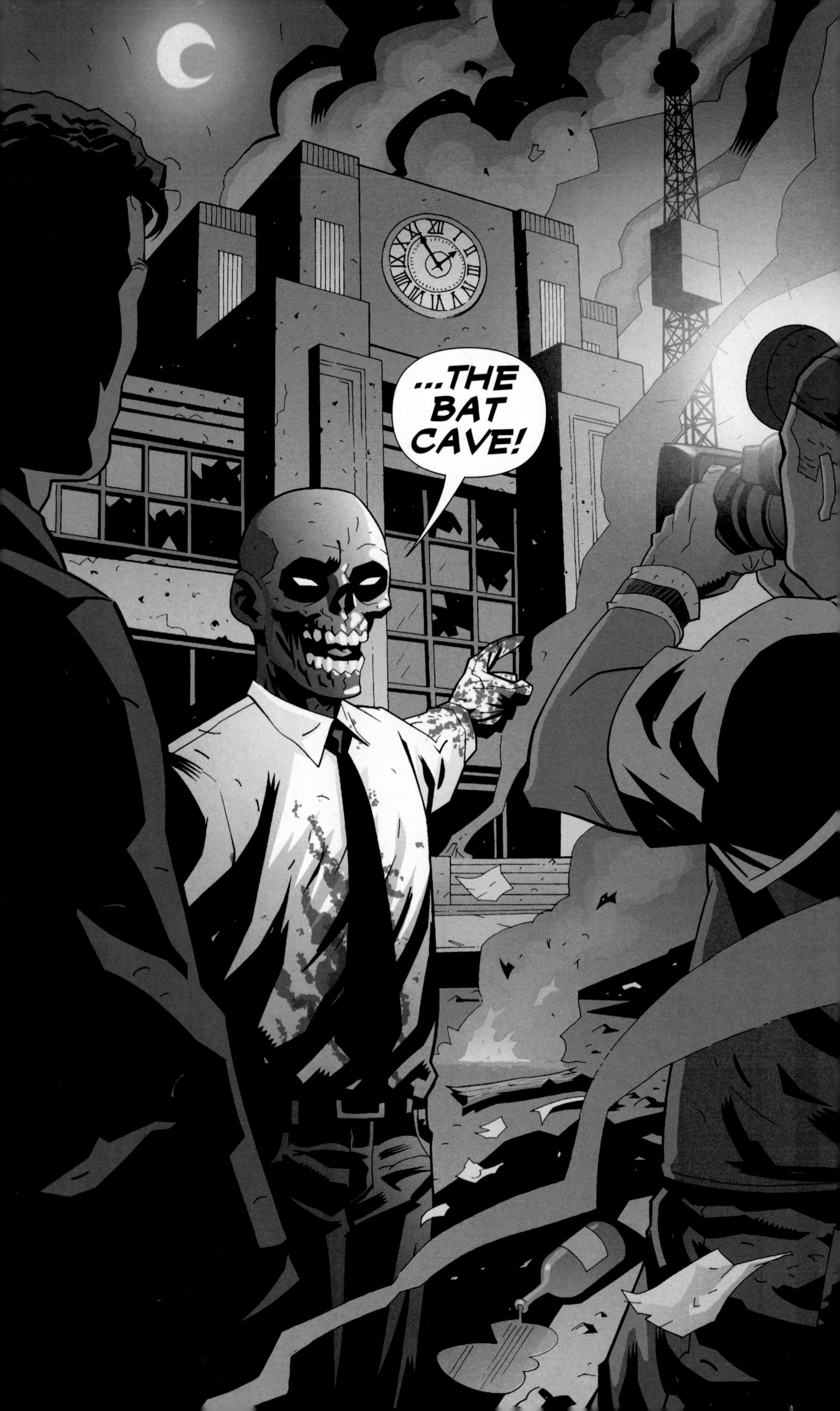
...THE BAT CAVE!

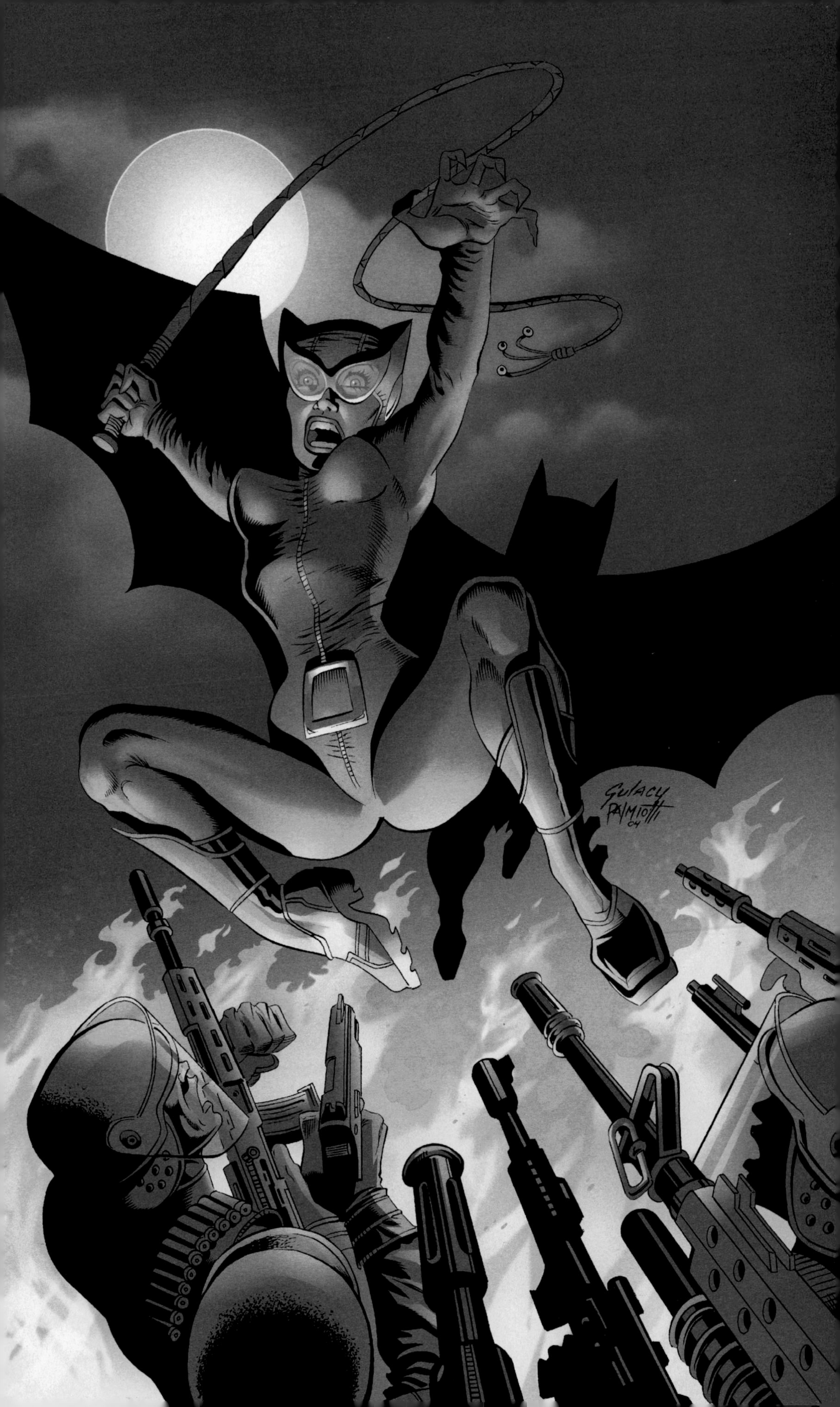
GULACY
PALMIOTTI
04

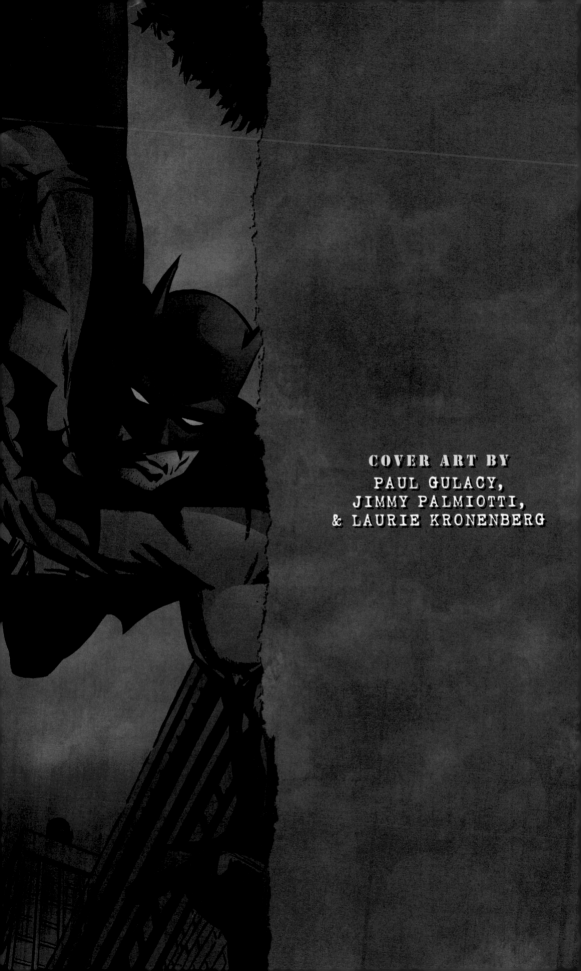

COVER ART BY
PAUL GULACY,
JIMMY PALMIOTTI,
& LAURIE KRONENBERG

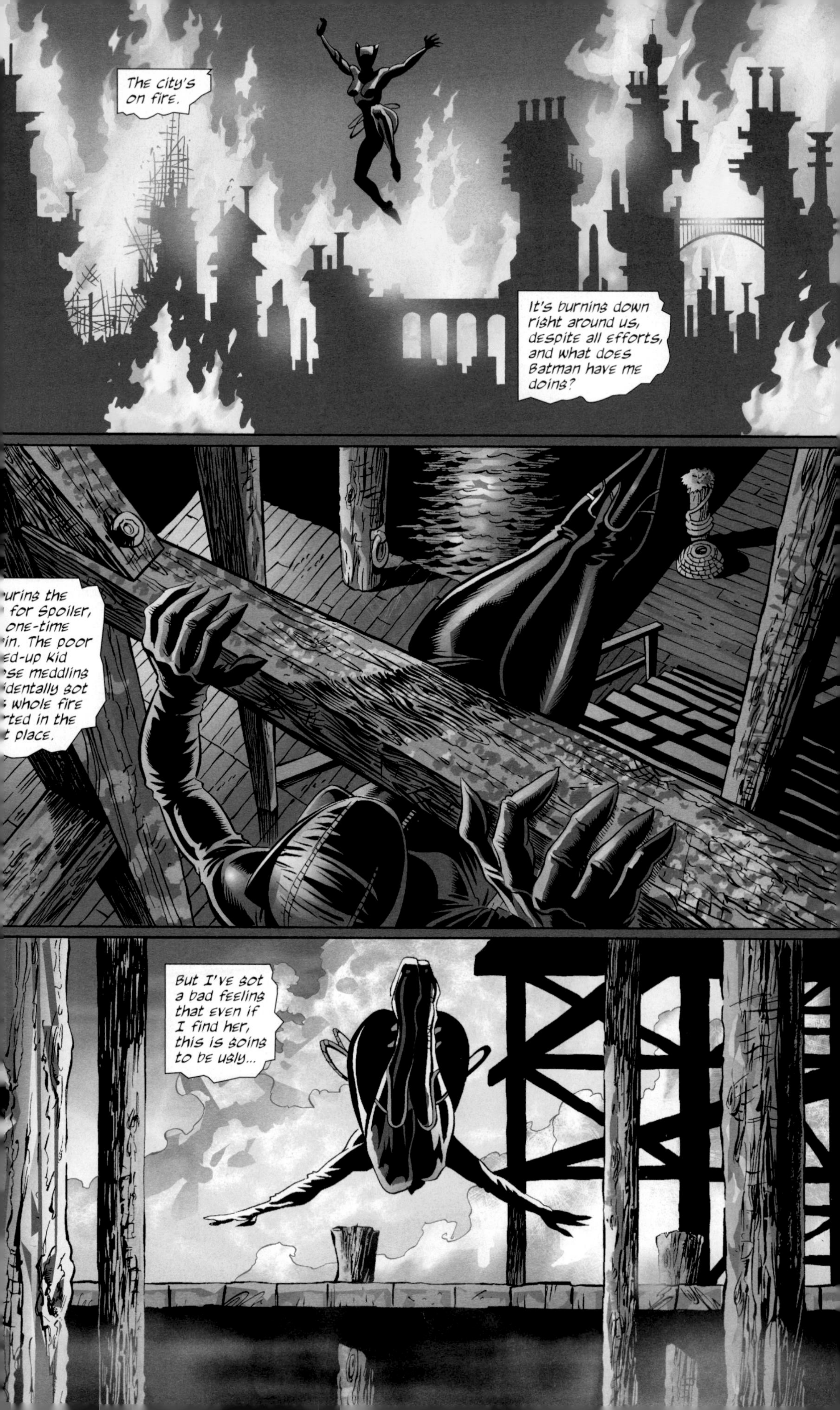

The city's on fire.
It's burning down right around us, despite all efforts, and what does Batman have me doing?
for Spoiler, one-time The poor kid whole fire in the place.
But I've got a bad feeling that even if I find her, this is going to be ugly...

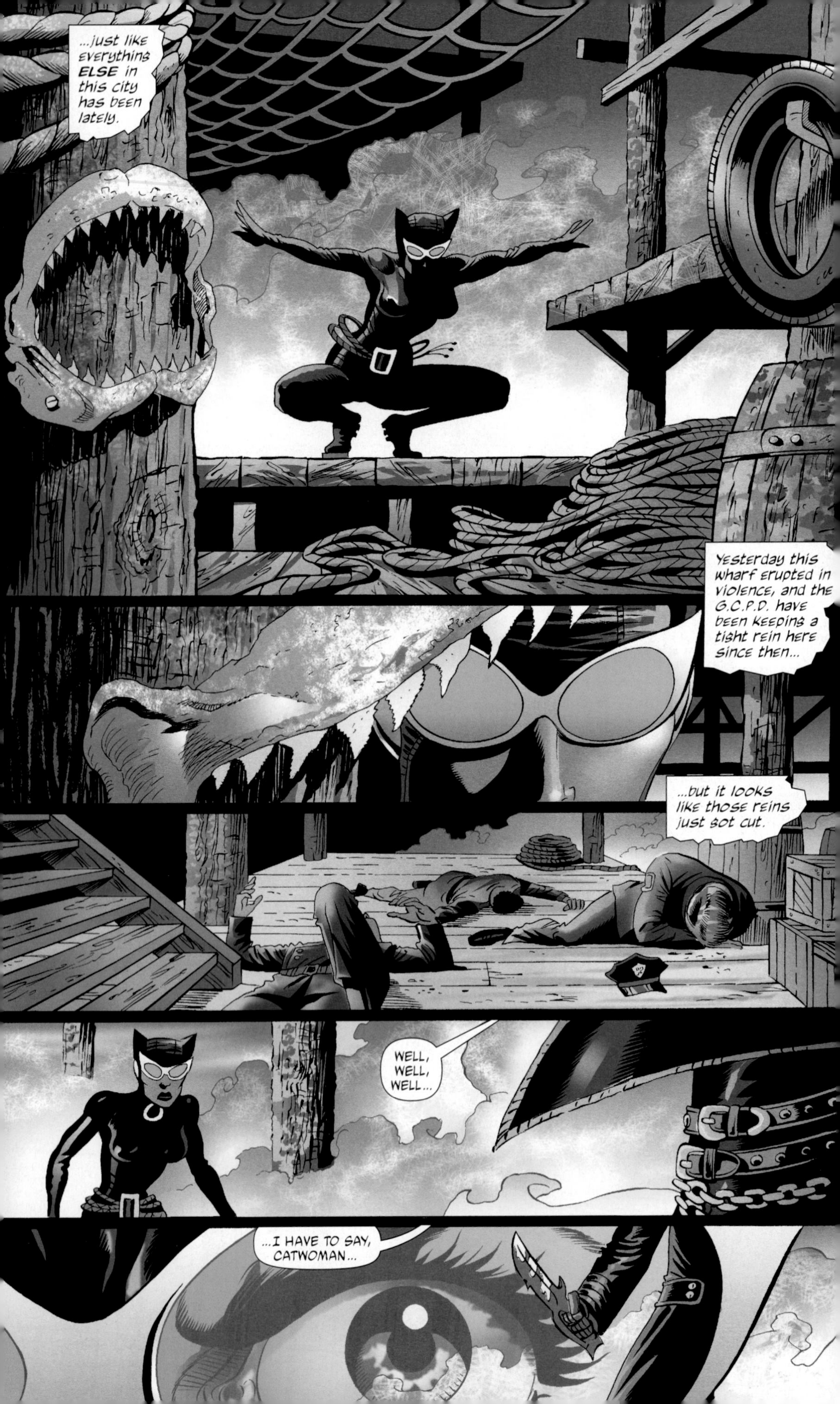

...just like everything ELSE in this city has been lately.
Yesterday this wharf erupted in violence, and the G.C.P.D. have been keeping a tight rein here since then...
...but it looks like those reins just got cut.
WELL, WELL, WELL...
...I HAVE TO SAY, CATWOMAN...

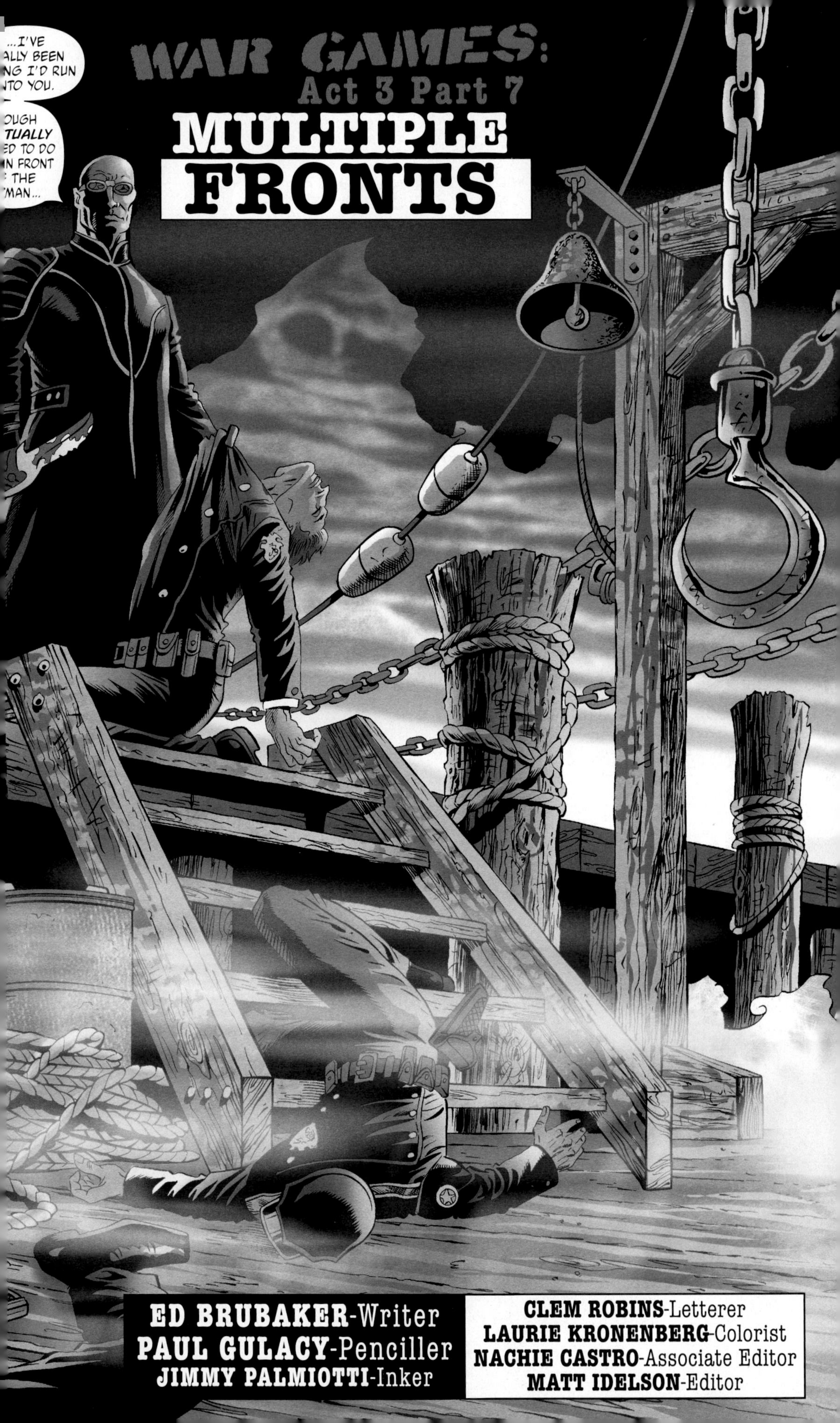
...I'VE
ALLY BEEN
NG I'D RUN
NTO YOU.
OUGH
TUALLY
ED TO DO
N FRONT
THE
MAN...
WAR GAMES:
Act 3 Part 7
MULTIPLE FRONTS
ED BRUBAKER-Writer
PAUL GULACY-Penciller
JIMMY PALMIOTTI-Inker
CLEM ROBINS-Letterer
LAURIE KRONENBERG-Colorist
NACHIE CASTRO-Associate Editor
MATT IDELSON-Editor

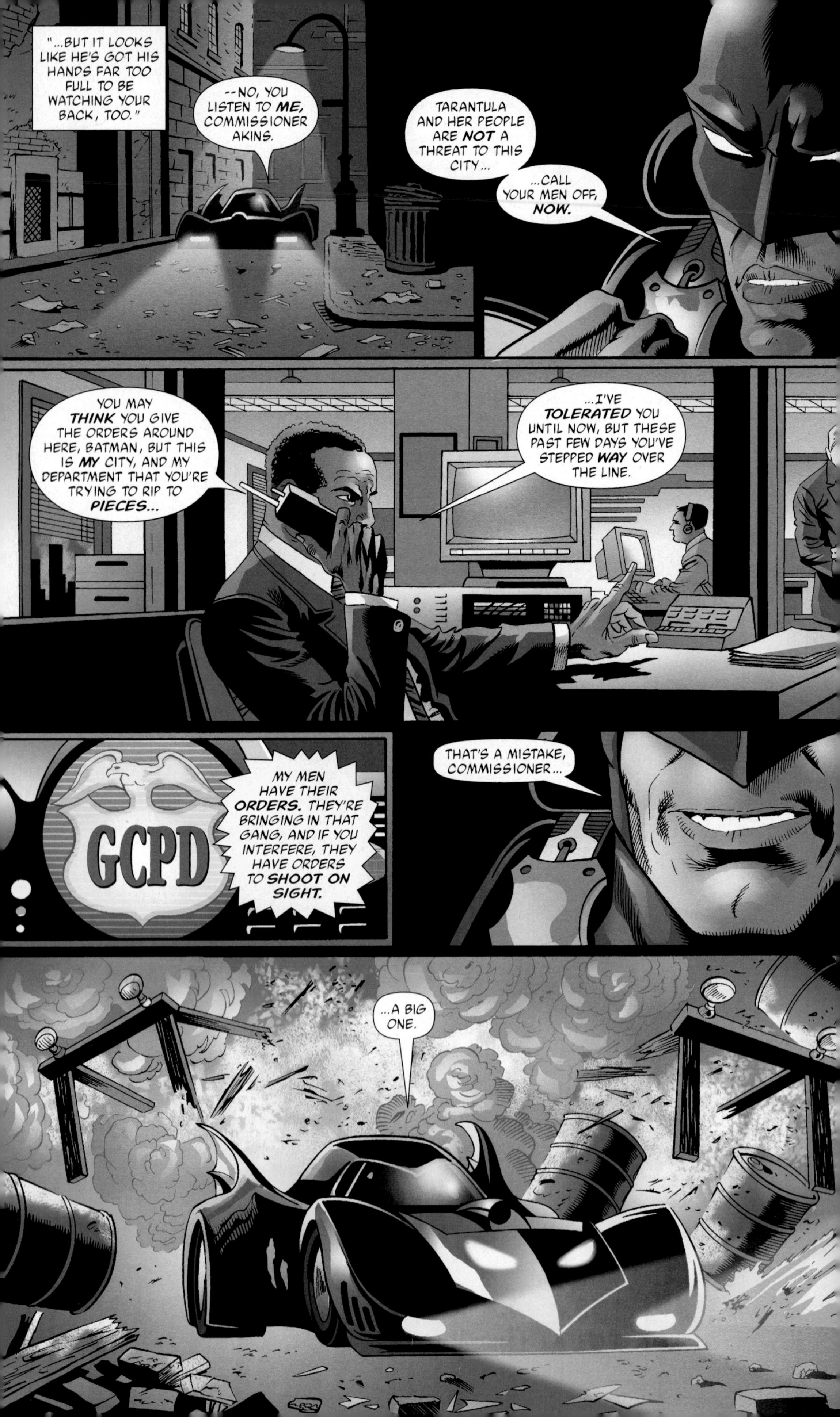
"...BUT IT LOOKS LIKE HE'S GOT HIS HANDS FAR TOO FULL TO BE WATCHING YOUR BACK, TOO."
--NO, YOU LISTEN TO ME, COMMISSIONER AKINS.
TARANTULA AND HER PEOPLE ARE NOT A THREAT TO THIS CITY...
...CALL YOUR MEN OFF, NOW.
YOU MAY THINK YOU GIVE THE ORDERS AROUND HERE, BATMAN, BUT THIS IS MY CITY, AND MY DEPARTMENT THAT YOU'RE TRYING TO RIP TO PIECES...
...I'VE TOLERATED YOU UNTIL NOW, BUT THESE PAST FEW DAYS YOU'VE STEPPED WAY OVER THE LINE.
GCPD
MY MEN HAVE THEIR ORDERS. THEY'RE BRINGING IN THAT GANG, AND IF YOU INTERFERE, THEY HAVE ORDERS TO SHOOT ON SIGHT.
THAT'S A MISTAKE, COMMISSIONER...
...A BIG ONE.

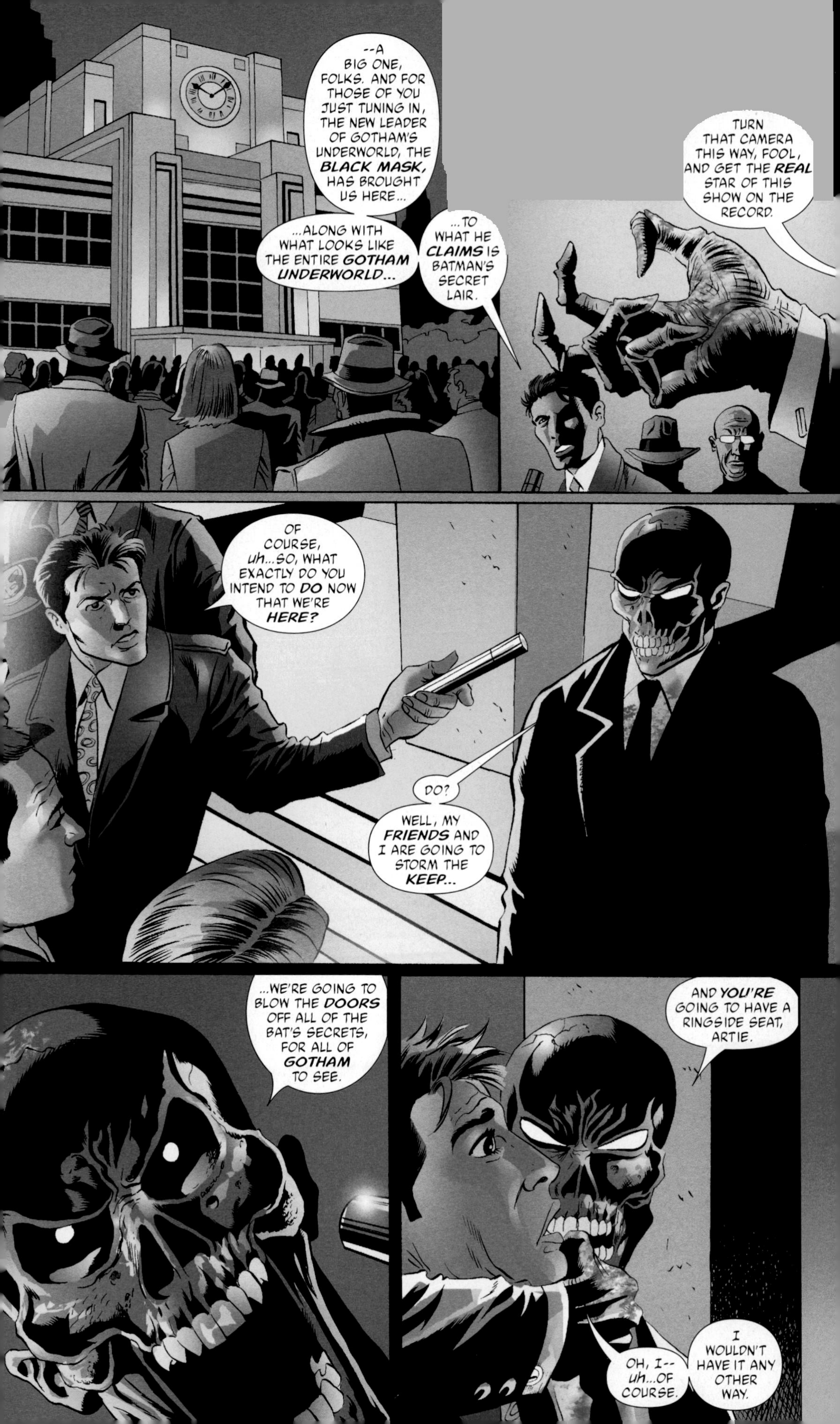
--A BIG ONE, FOLKS. AND FOR THOSE OF YOU JUST TUNING IN, THE NEW LEADER OF GOTHAM'S UNDERWORLD, THE BLACK MASK, HAS BROUGHT US HERE...
...ALONG WITH WHAT LOOKS LIKE THE ENTIRE GOTHAM UNDERWORLD...
...TO WHAT HE CLAIMS IS BATMAN'S SECRET LAIR.
TURN THAT CAMERA THIS WAY, FOOL, AND GET THE REAL STAR OF THIS SHOW ON THE RECORD.
OF COURSE, uh...SO, WHAT EXACTLY DO YOU INTEND TO DO NOW THAT WE'RE HERE?
DO?
WELL, MY FRIENDS AND I ARE GOING TO STORM THE KEEP...
...WE'RE GOING TO BLOW THE DOORS OFF ALL OF THE BAT'S SECRETS, FOR ALL OF GOTHAM TO SEE.
AND YOU'RE GOING TO HAVE A RINGSIDE SEAT, ARTIE.
OH, I--uh...OF COURSE.
I WOULDN'T HAVE IT ANY OTHER WAY.

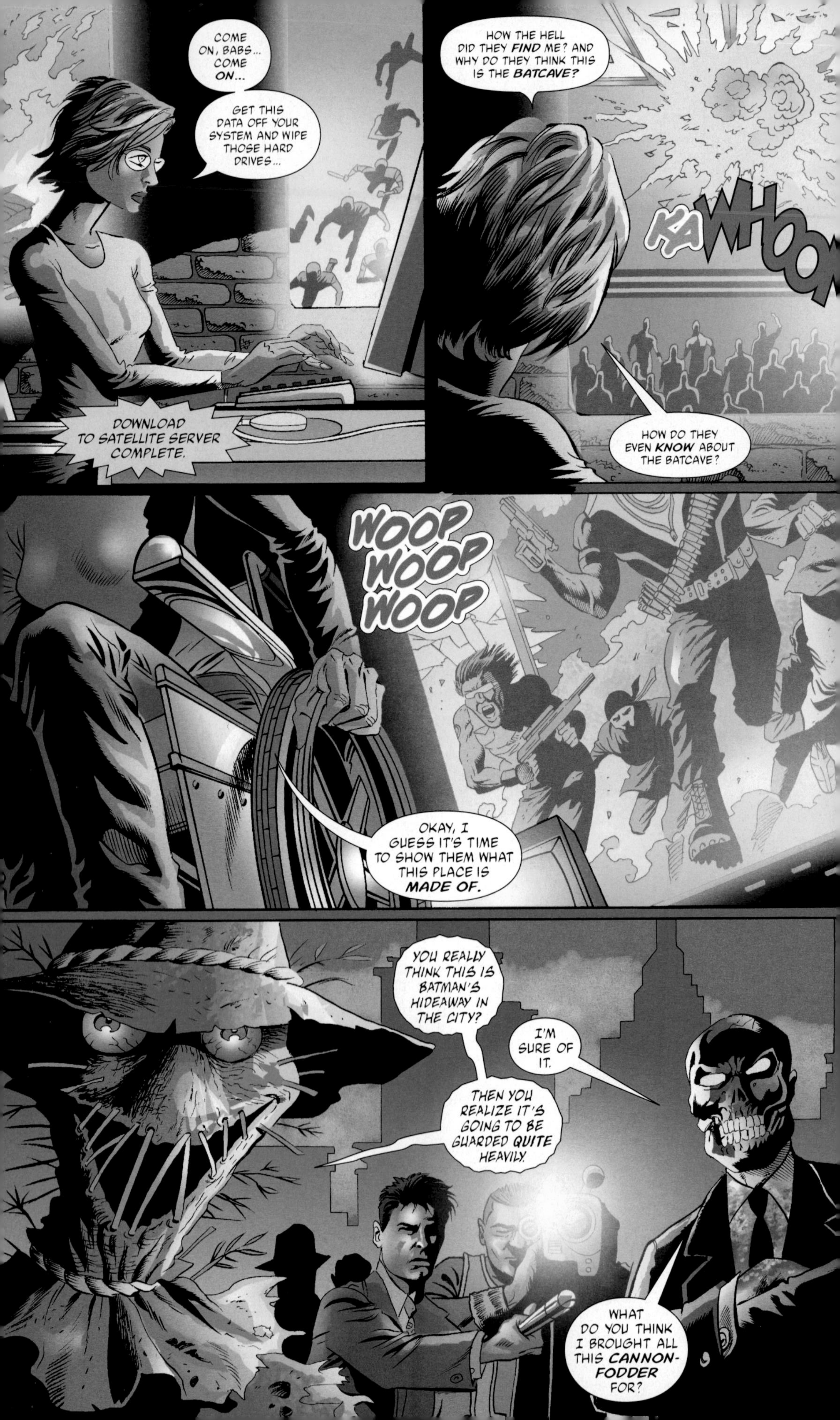

COME ON, BABS... COME ON...
GET THIS DATA OFF YOUR SYSTEM AND WIPE THOSE HARD DRIVES...
DOWNLOAD TO SATELLITE SERVER COMPLETE.
HOW THE HELL DID THEY FIND ME? AND WHY DO THEY THINK THIS IS THE BATCAVE?
KAWHOOM
HOW DO THEY EVEN KNOW ABOUT THE BATCAVE?
WOOP WOOP WOOP
OKAY, I GUESS IT'S TIME TO SHOW THEM WHAT THIS PLACE IS MADE OF.
YOU REALLY THINK THIS IS BATMAN'S HIDEAWAY IN THE CITY?
I'M SURE OF IT.
THEN YOU REALIZE IT'S GOING TO BE GUARDED QUITE HEAVILY.
WHAT DO YOU THINK I BROUGHT ALL THIS CANNON-FODDER FOR?

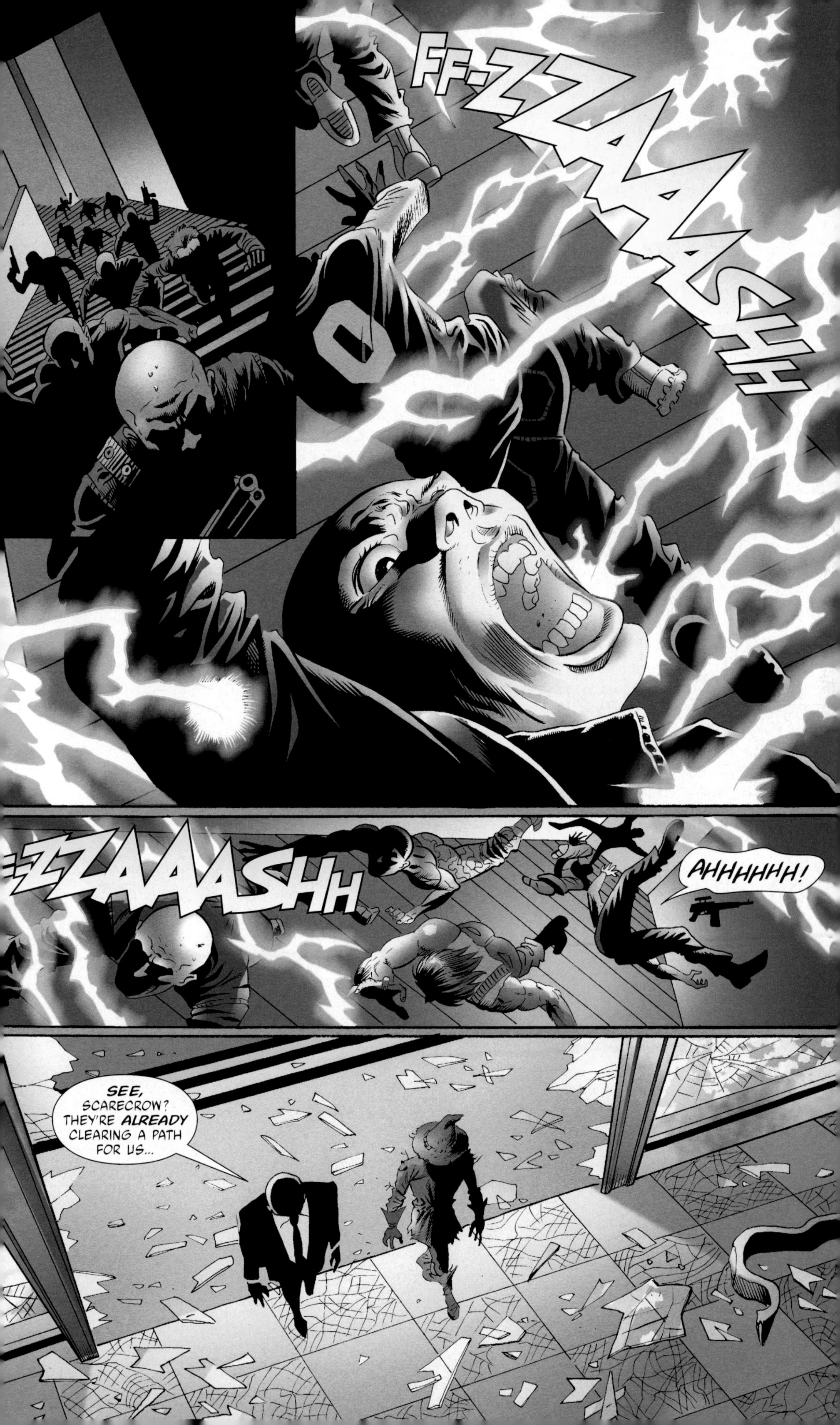
FF-ZZAAASHH
ZZAAASHH
AHHHHHH!
SEE, SCARECROW? THEY'RE ALREADY CLEARING A PATH FOR US...

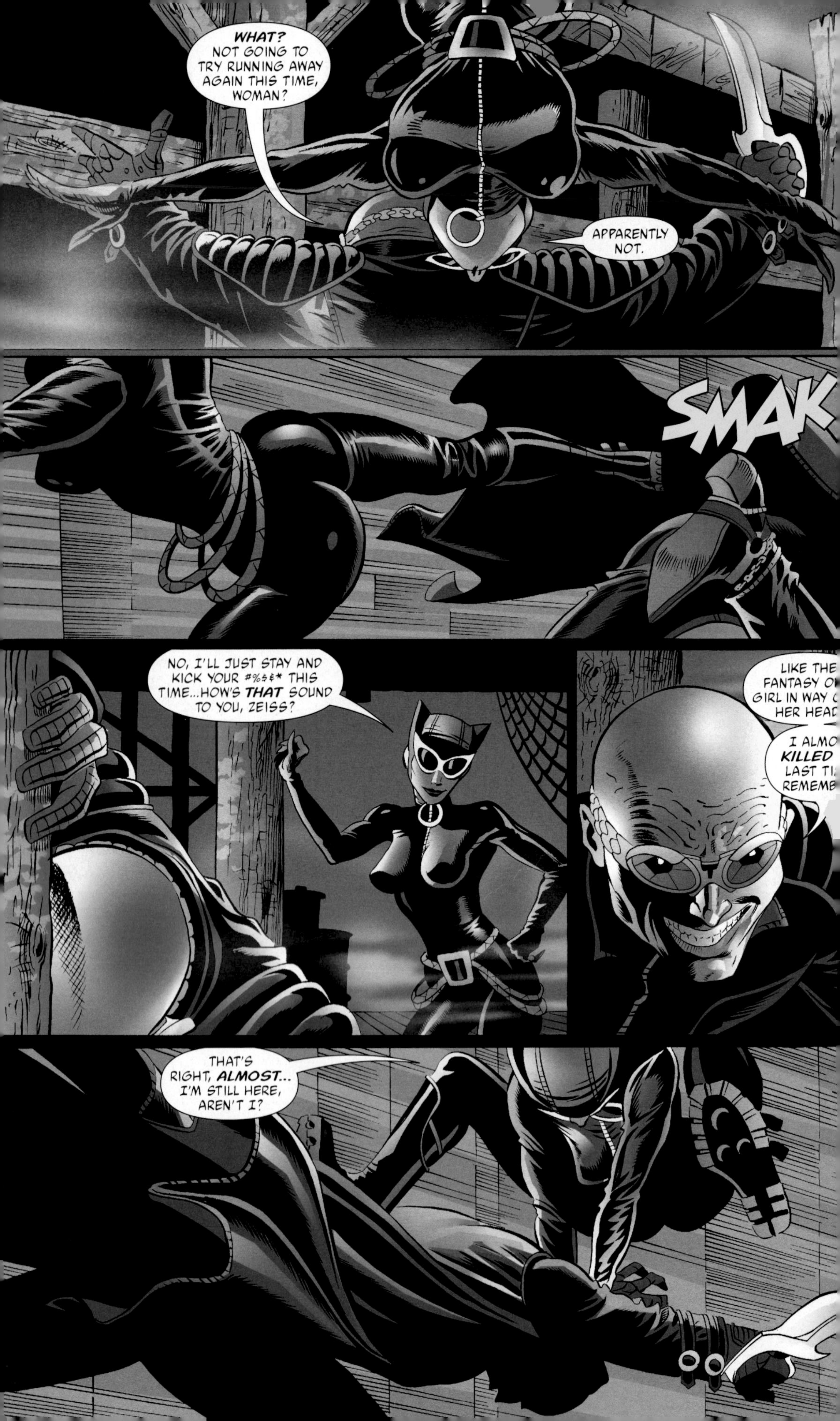
WHAT? NOT GOING TO TRY RUNNING AWAY AGAIN THIS TIME, WOMAN?
APPARENTLY NOT.
SMAK
NO, I'LL JUST STAY AND KICK YOUR #%$&* THIS TIME...HOW'S THAT SOUND TO YOU, ZEISS?
LIKE THE FANTASY O GIRL IN WAY HER HEAD
I ALMO KILLED LAST TI. REMEMB
THAT'S RIGHT, ALMOST... I'M STILL HERE, AREN'T I?

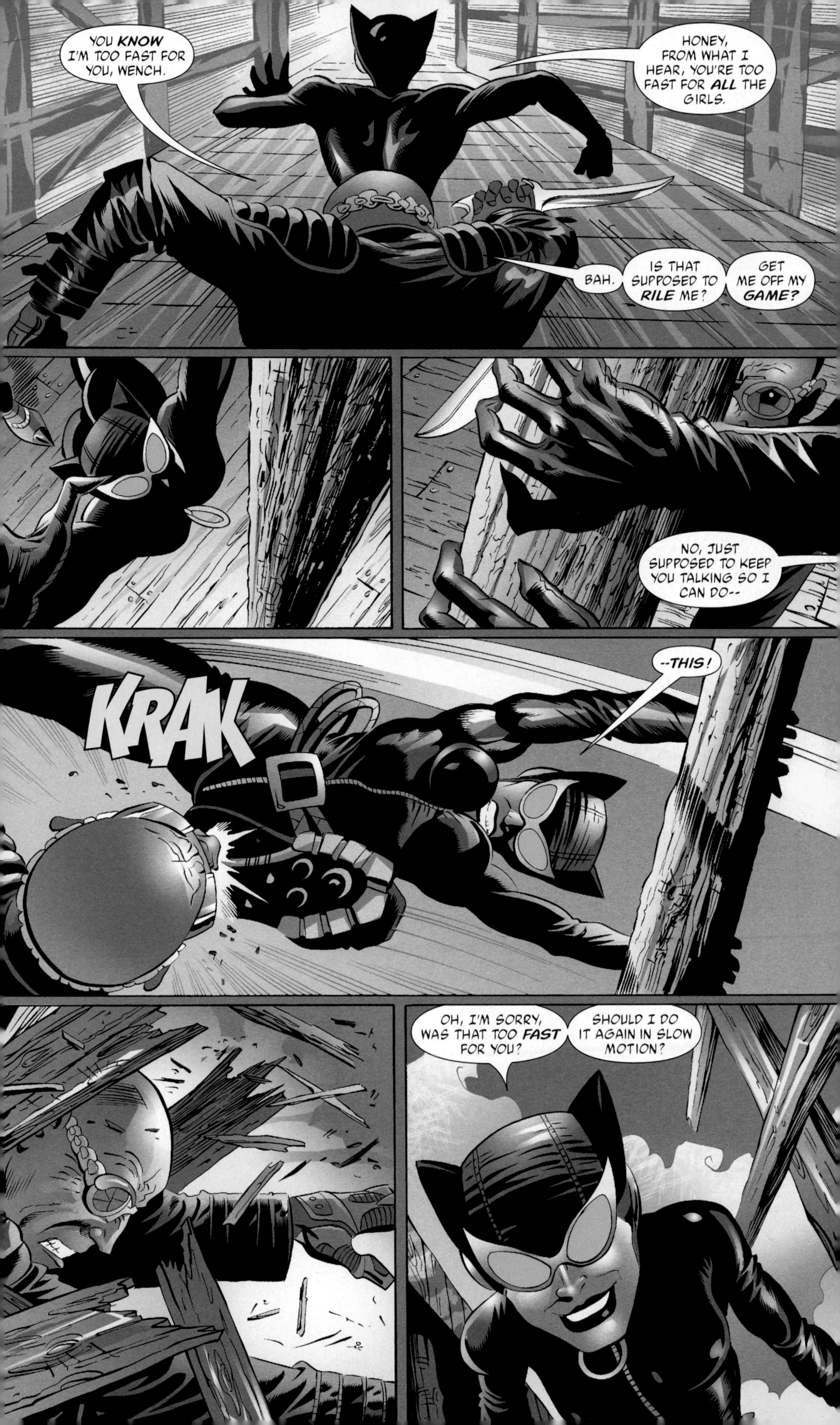
YOU KNOW I'M TOO FAST FOR YOU, WENCH.
HONEY, FROM WHAT I HEAR, YOU'RE TOO FAST FOR ALL THE GIRLS.
BAH.
IS THAT SUPPOSED TO RILE ME?
GET ME OFF MY GAME?
NO, JUST SUPPOSED TO KEEP YOU TALKING SO I CAN DO--
KRAK
--THIS!
OH, I'M SORRY, WAS THAT TOO FAST FOR YOU?
SHOULD I DO IT AGAIN IN SLOW MOTION?

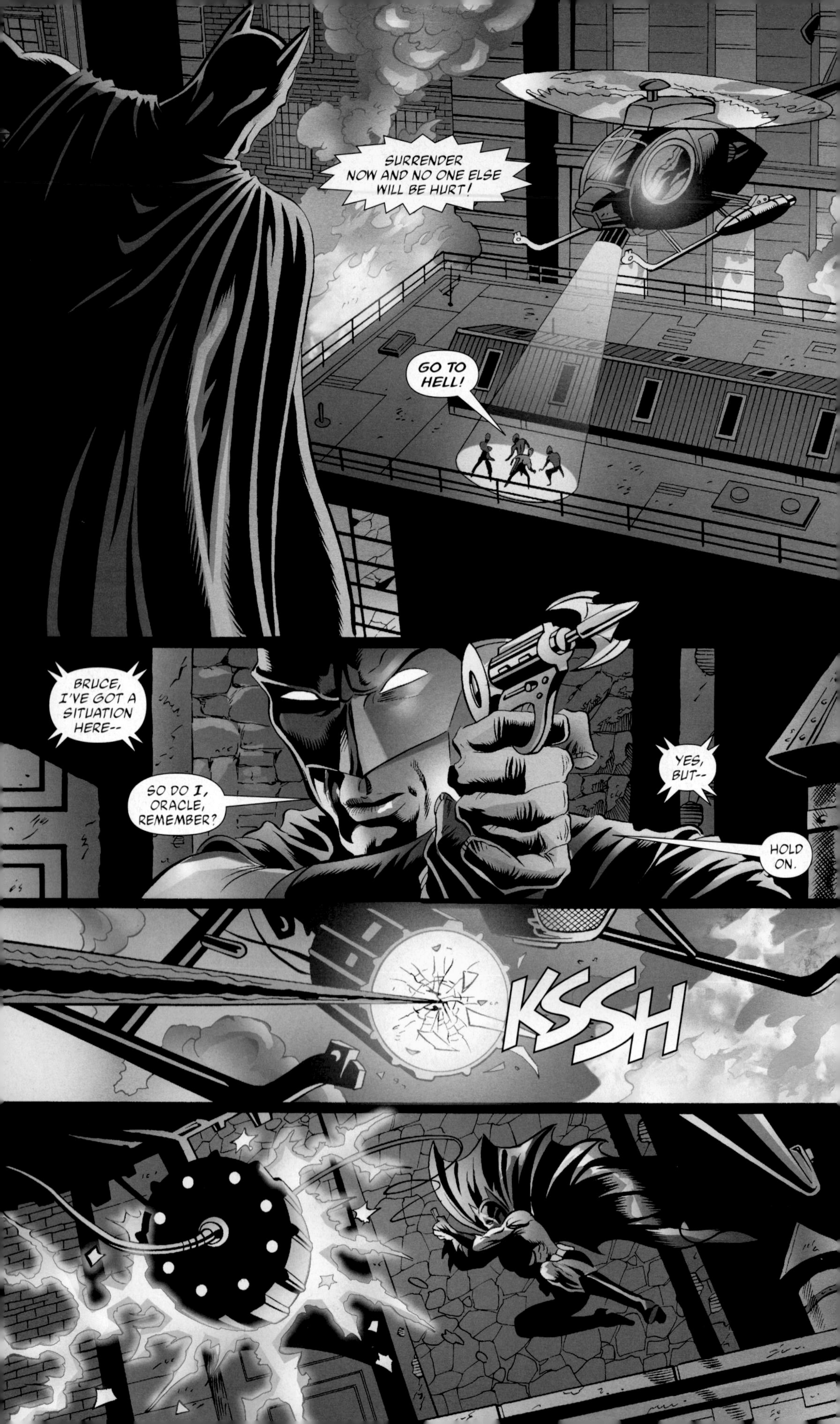

SURRENDER NOW AND NO ONE ELSE WILL BE HURT!
GO TO HELL!
BRUCE, I'VE GOT A SITUATION HERE--
SO DO I, ORACLE, REMEMBER?
YES, BUT--
HOLD ON.
KSSH

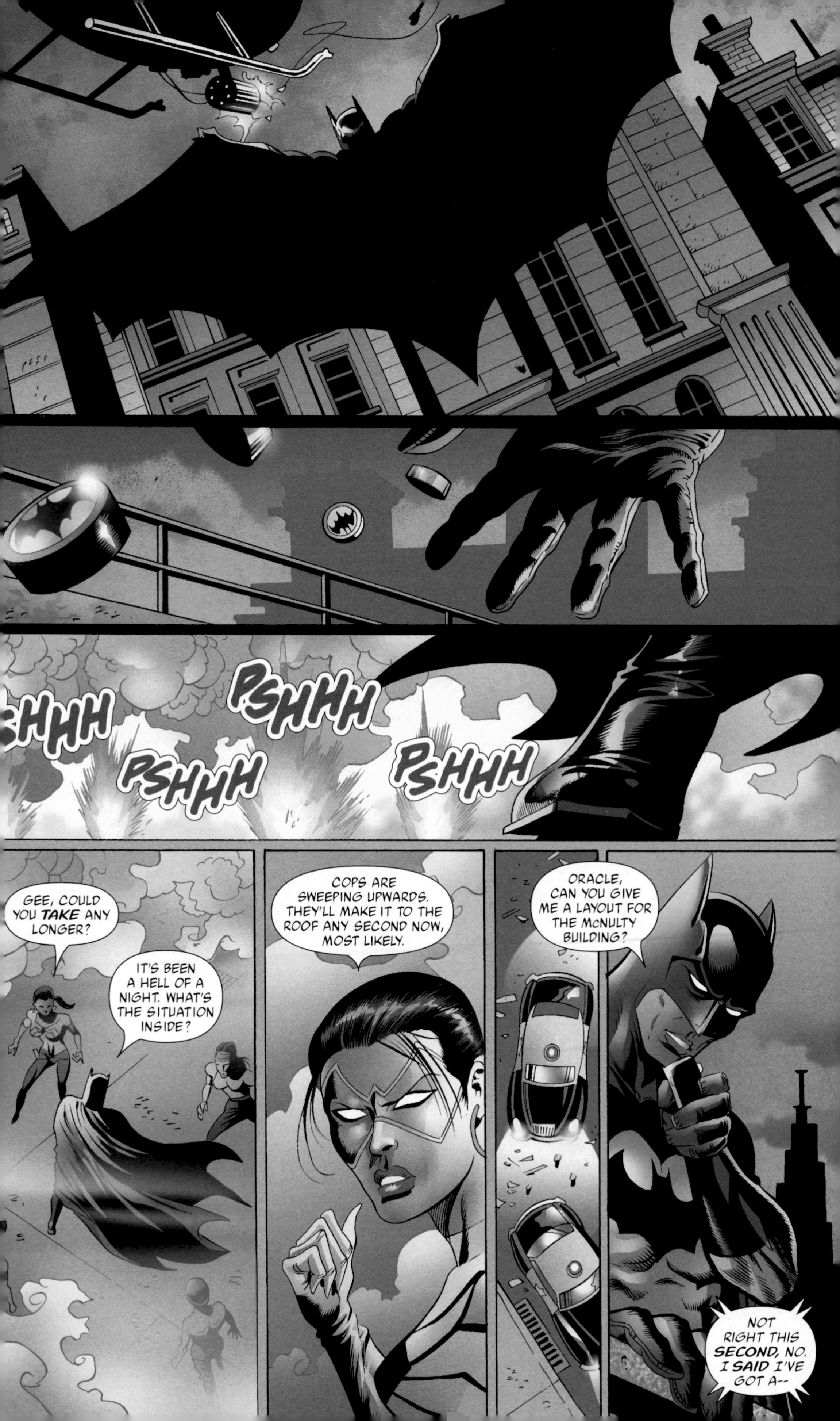

SHHH
PSHHH
PSHHH
PSHHH
GEE, COULD YOU *TAKE* ANY LONGER?
IT'S BEEN A HELL OF A NIGHT. WHAT'S THE SITUATION INSIDE?
COPS ARE SWEEPING UPWARDS. THEY'LL MAKE IT TO THE ROOF ANY SECOND NOW, MOST LIKELY.
ORACLE, CAN YOU GIVE ME A LAYOUT FOR THE McNULTY BUILDING?
NOT RIGHT THIS *SECOND*, NO. *I SAID* I'VE GOT A--

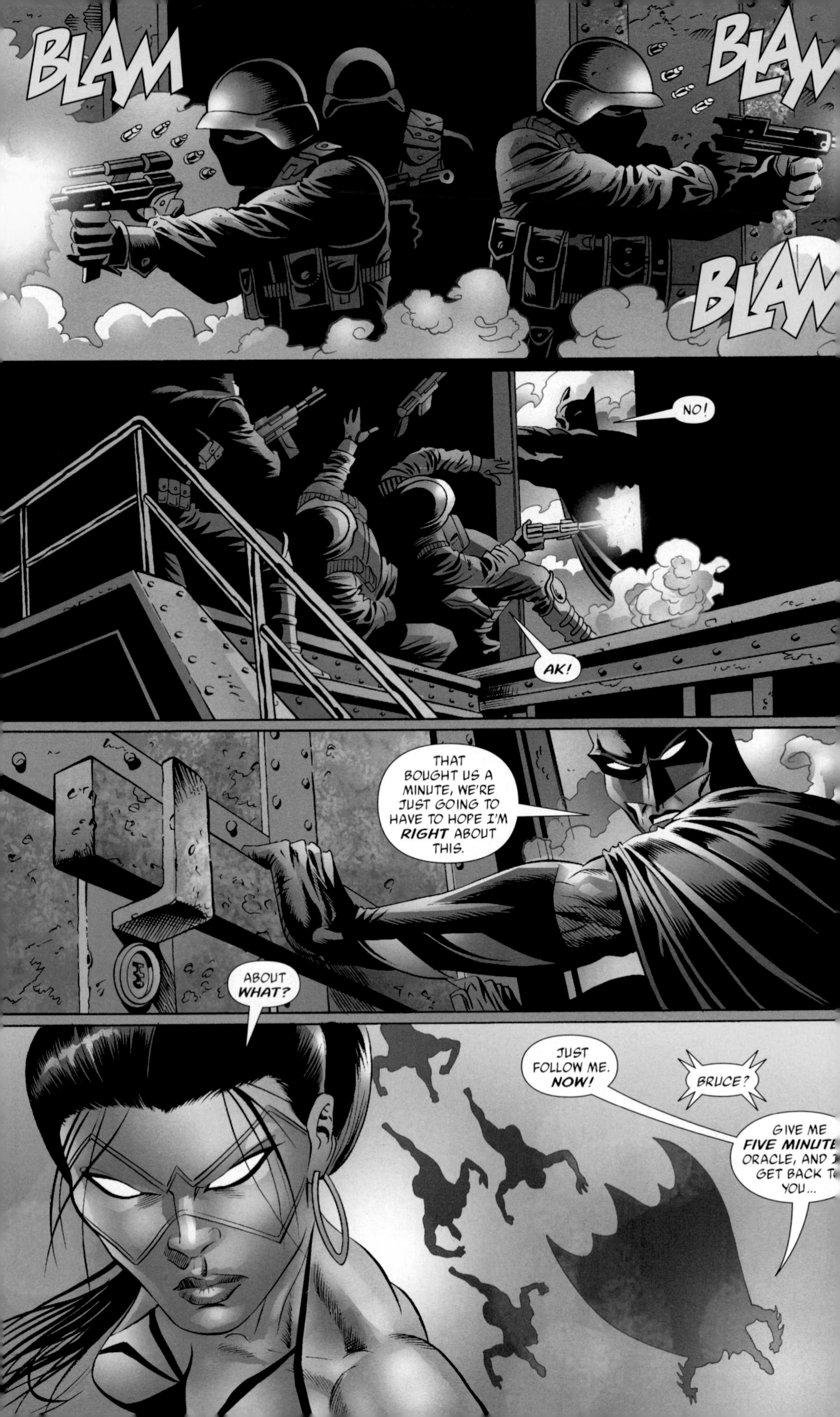
BLAM
BLAM
BLAM
NO!
AK!
THAT BOUGHT US A MINUTE, WE'RE JUST GOING TO HAVE TO HOPE I'M **RIGHT** ABOUT THIS.
ABOUT **WHAT?**
JUST FOLLOW ME. **NOW!**
BRUCE?
GIVE ME **FIVE MINUTE** ORACLE, AND I GET BACK T YOU...

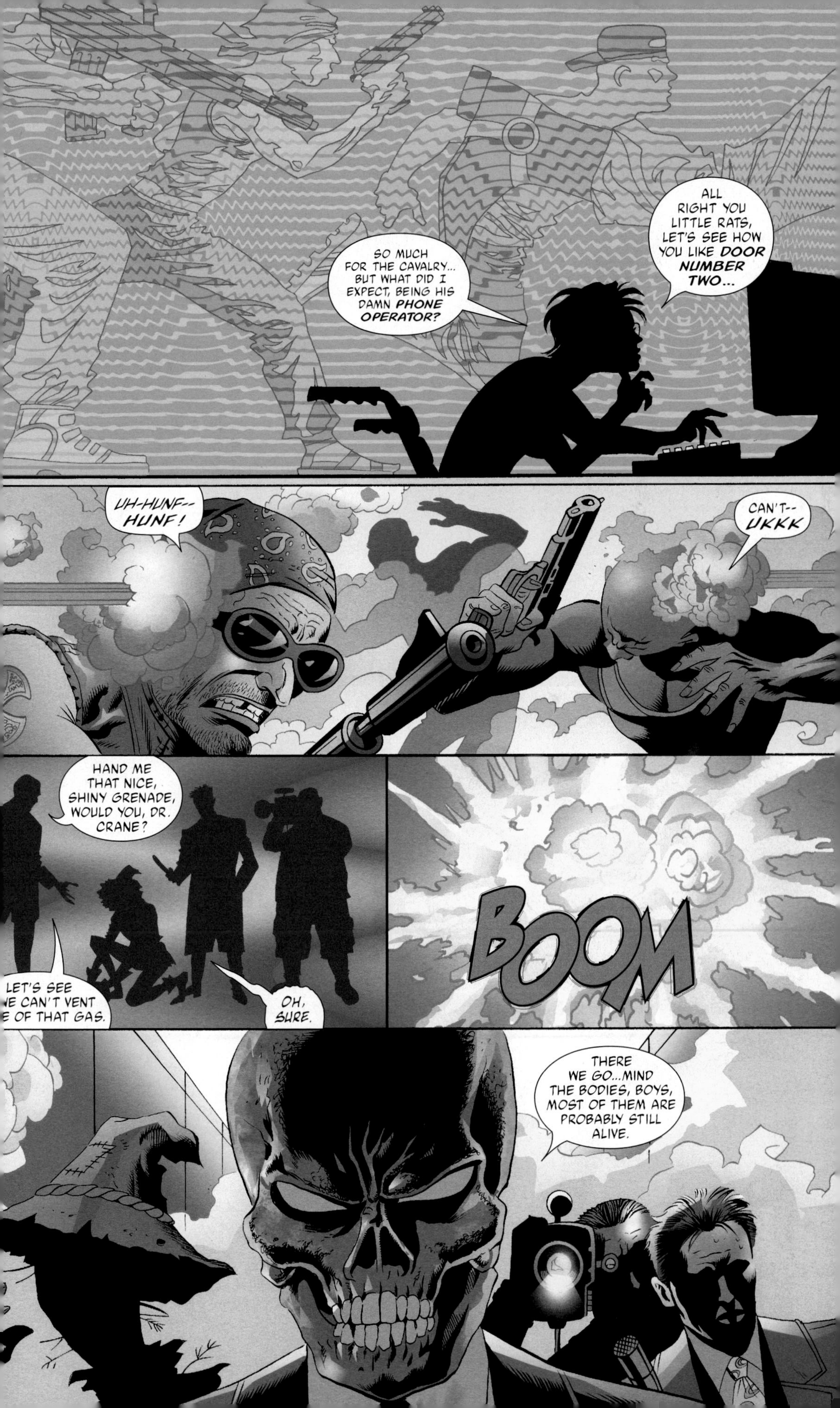
SO MUCH FOR THE CAVALRY... BUT WHAT DID I EXPECT, BEING HIS DAMN PHONE OPERATOR?
ALL RIGHT YOU LITTLE RATS, LET'S SEE HOW YOU LIKE DOOR NUMBER TWO...
UH-HUNF-- HUNF!
CAN'T-- UKKK
HAND ME THAT NICE, SHINY GRENADE, WOULD YOU, DR. CRANE?
LET'S SEE WE CAN'T VENT E OF THAT GAS.
OH, SURE.
BOOM
THERE WE GO...MIND THE BODIES, BOYS, MOST OF THEM ARE PROBABLY STILL ALIVE.

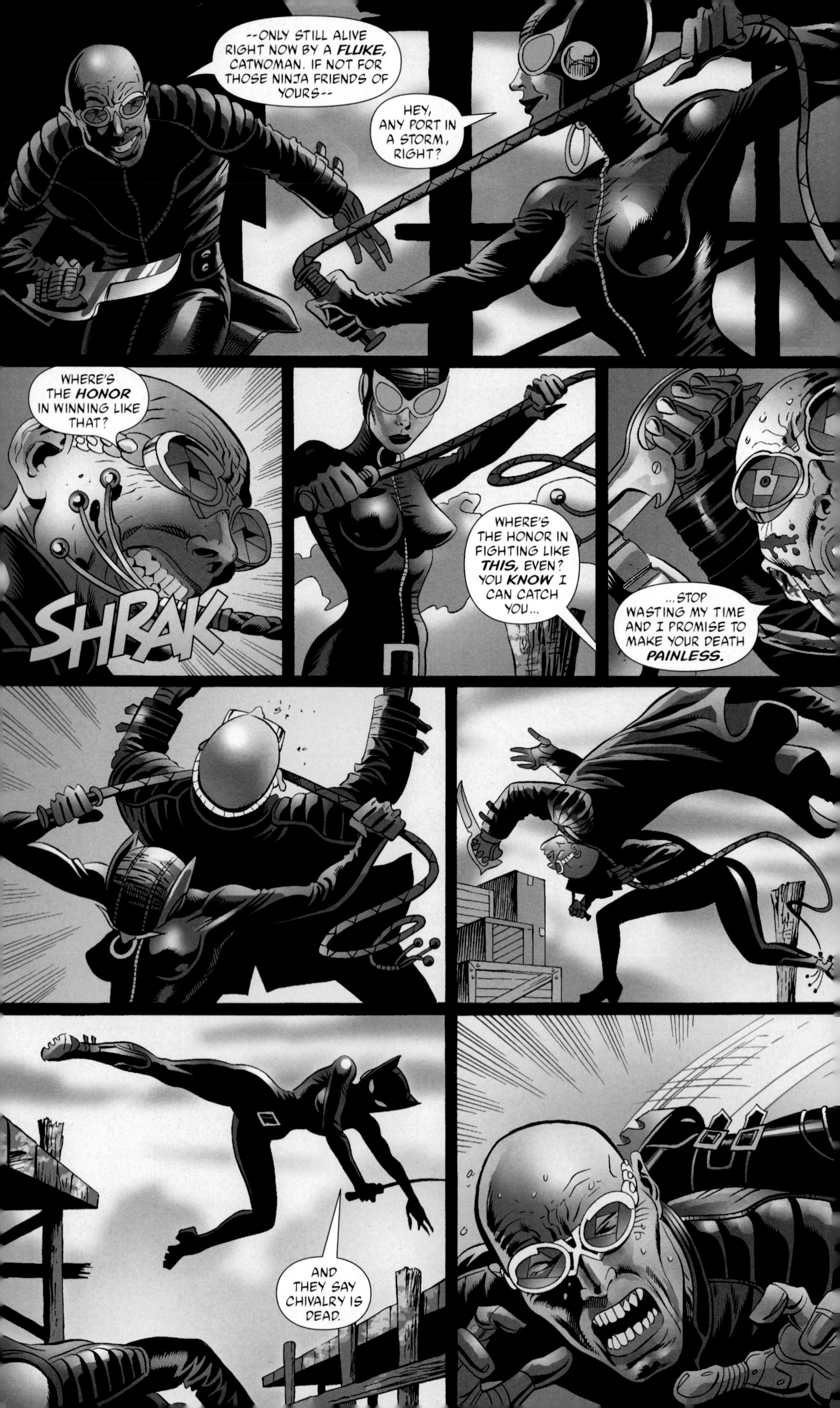
--ONLY STILL ALIVE RIGHT NOW BY A FLUKE, CATWOMAN. IF NOT FOR THOSE NINJA FRIENDS OF YOURS--
HEY, ANY PORT IN A STORM, RIGHT?
WHERE'S THE HONOR IN WINNING LIKE THAT?
SHRAK
WHERE'S THE HONOR IN FIGHTING LIKE THIS, EVEN? YOU KNOW I CAN CATCH YOU...
...STOP WASTING MY TIME AND I PROMISE TO MAKE YOUR DEATH PAINLESS.
AND THEY SAY CHIVALRY IS DEAD.

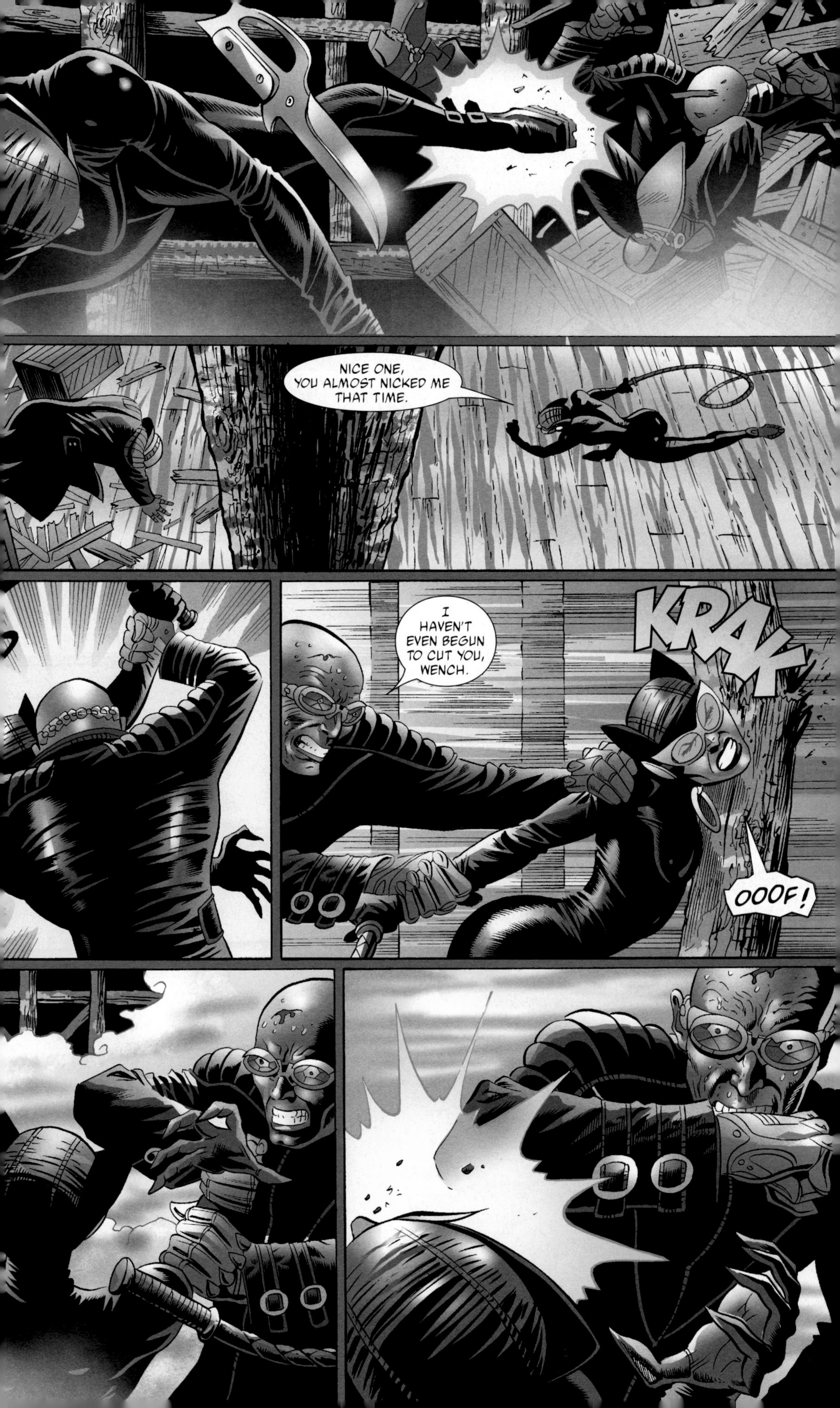

NICE ONE, YOU ALMOST NICKED ME THAT TIME.
I HAVEN'T EVEN BEGUN TO CUT YOU, WENCH.
KRAK
OOOF!

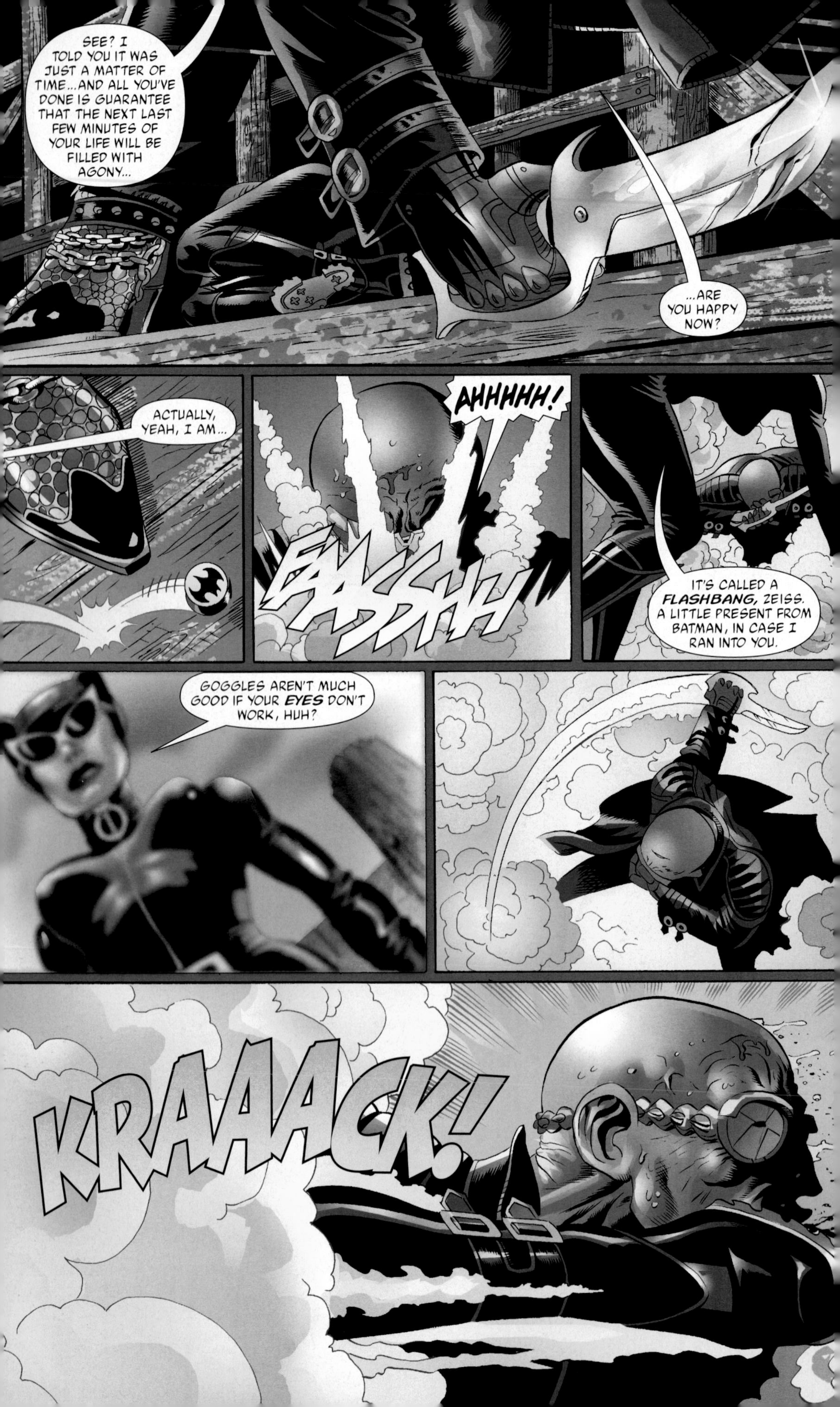
SEE? I TOLD YOU IT WAS JUST A MATTER OF TIME...AND ALL YOU'VE DONE IS GUARANTEE THAT THE NEXT LAST FEW MINUTES OF YOUR LIFE WILL BE FILLED WITH AGONY...
...ARE YOU HAPPY NOW?
ACTUALLY, YEAH, I AM...
AHHHHH!
FASSHH
IT'S CALLED A FLASHBANG, ZEISS. A LITTLE PRESENT FROM BATMAN, IN CASE I RAN INTO YOU.
GOGGLES AREN'T MUCH GOOD IF YOUR EYES DON'T WORK, HUH?
KRAAACK!

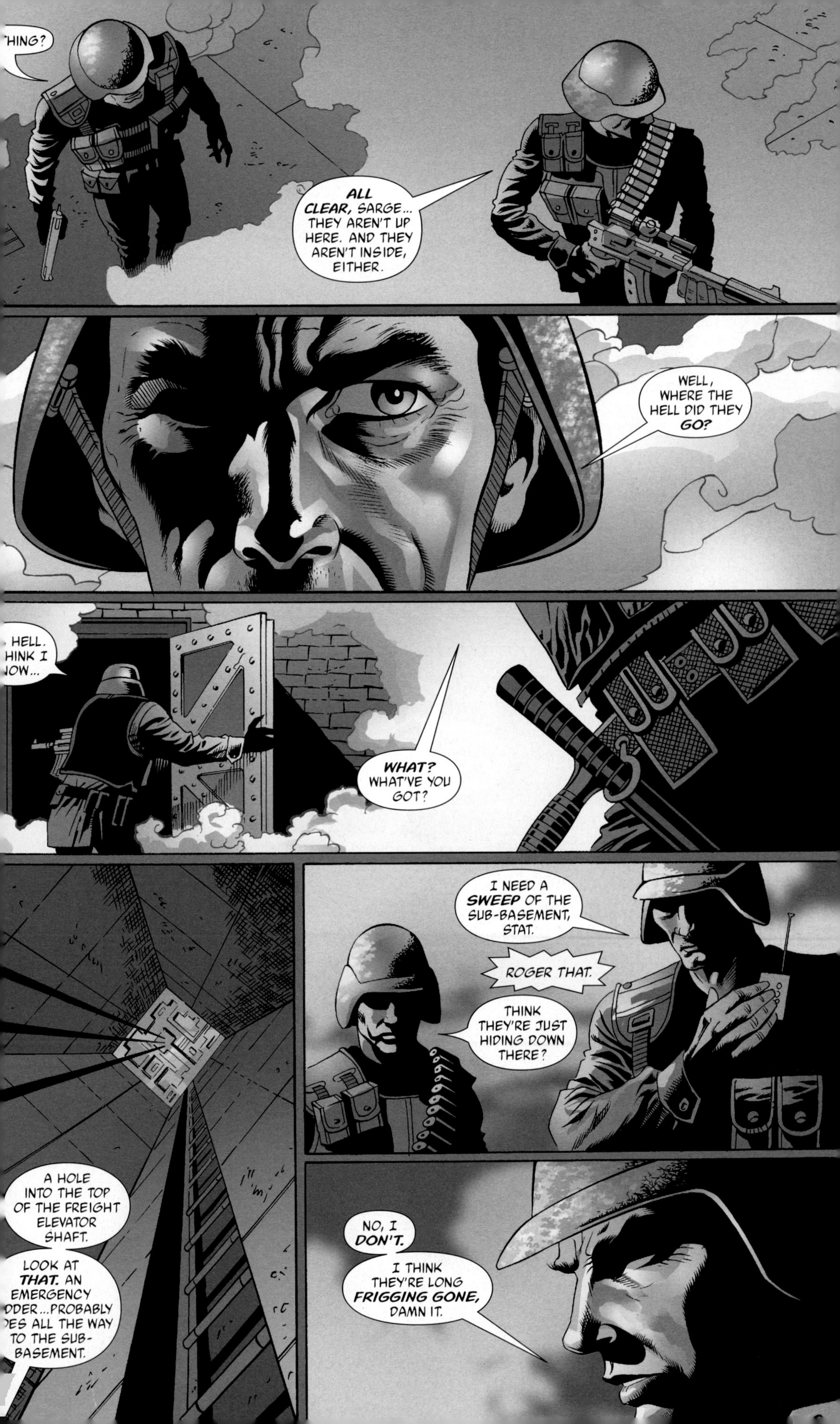
'HING?
ALL CLEAR, SARGE... THEY AREN'T UP HERE. AND THEY AREN'T INSIDE, EITHER.
WELL, WHERE THE HELL DID THEY GO?
HELL. HINK I OW...
WHAT? WHAT'VE YOU GOT?
A HOLE INTO THE TOP OF THE FREIGHT ELEVATOR SHAFT.
LOOK AT THAT. AN EMERGENCY DDER...PROBABLY ES ALL THE WAY TO THE SUB-BASEMENT.
I NEED A SWEEP OF THE SUB-BASEMENT, STAT.
ROGER THAT.
THINK THEY'RE JUST HIDING DOWN THERE?
NO, I DON'T.
I THINK THEY'RE LONG FRIGGING GONE, DAMN IT.

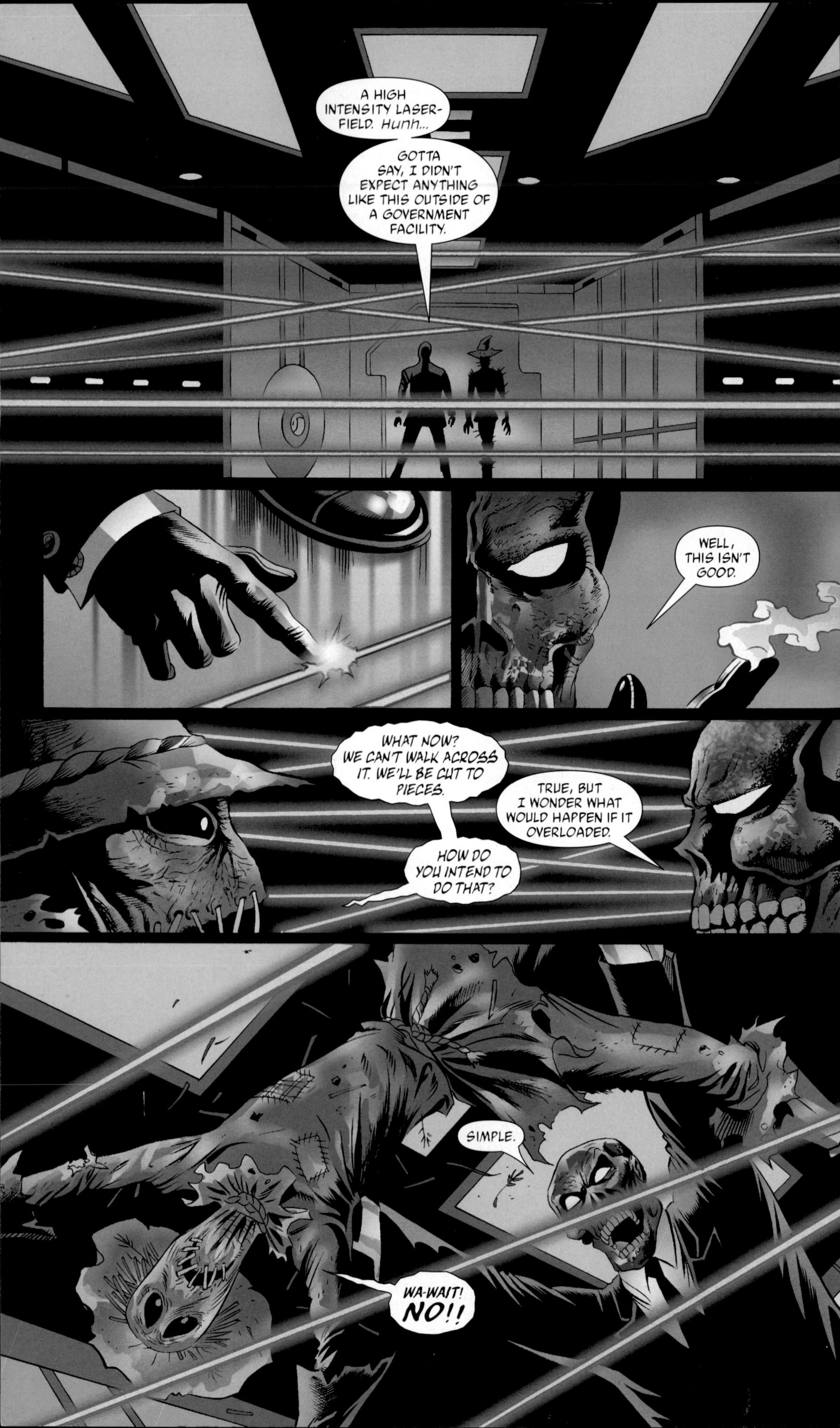
A HIGH INTENSITY LASER-FIELD. *Hunh...*
GOTTA SAY, I DIDN'T EXPECT ANYTHING LIKE THIS OUTSIDE OF A GOVERNMENT FACILITY.
WELL, THIS ISN'T GOOD.
WHAT NOW? WE CAN'T WALK ACROSS IT. WE'LL BE CUT TO PIECES.
TRUE, BUT I WONDER WHAT WOULD HAPPEN IF IT OVERLOADED.
HOW DO YOU INTEND TO DO THAT?
SIMPLE.
WA-WAIT! **NO!!**

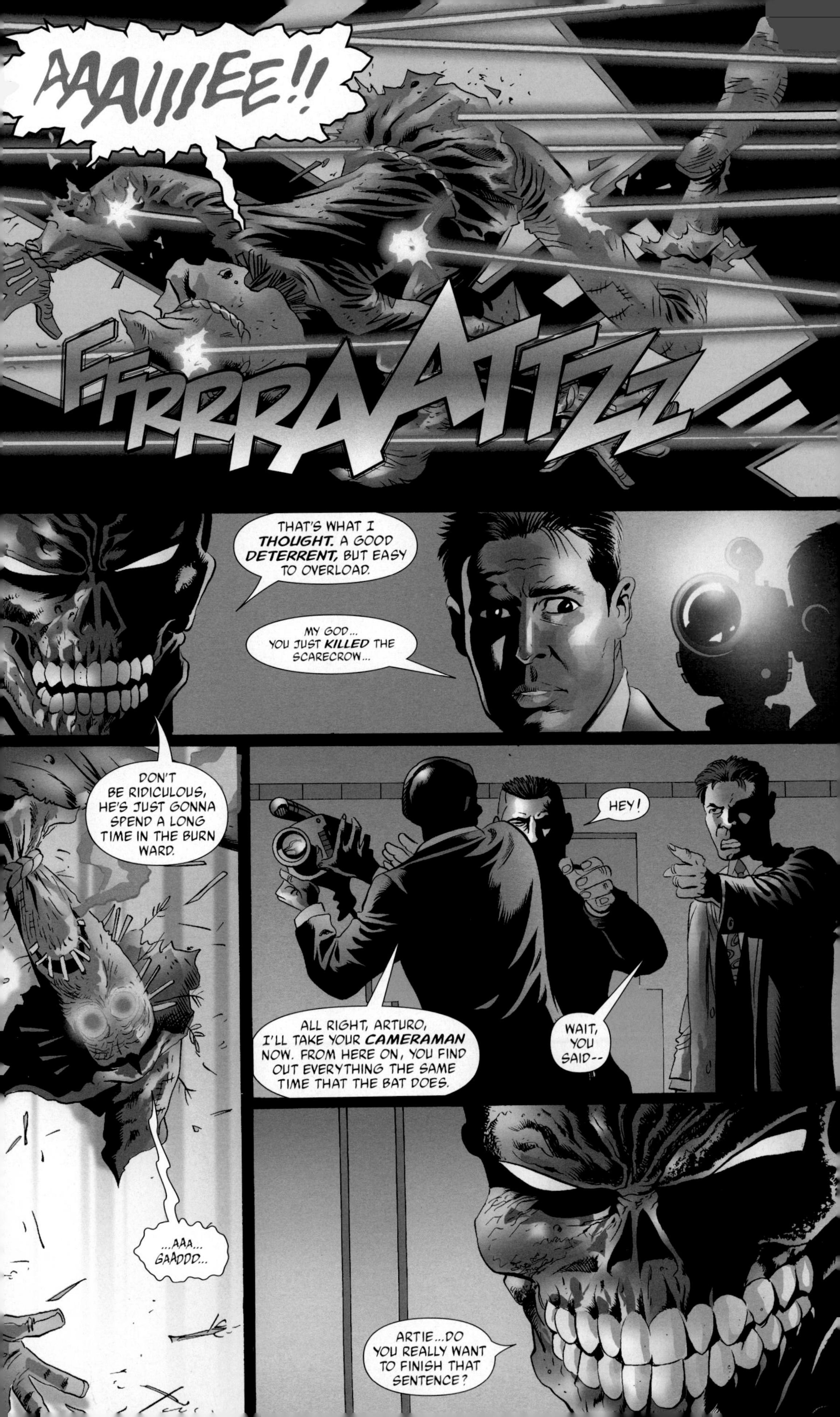
AAAIIIEE!!
FFRRRAATTZZ
THAT'S WHAT I THOUGHT. A GOOD DETERRENT, BUT EASY TO OVERLOAD.
MY GOD... YOU JUST KILLED THE SCARECROW...
DON'T BE RIDICULOUS, HE'S JUST GONNA SPEND A LONG TIME IN THE BURN WARD.
HEY!
ALL RIGHT, ARTURO, I'LL TAKE YOUR CAMERAMAN NOW. FROM HERE ON, YOU FIND OUT EVERYTHING THE SAME TIME THAT THE BAT DOES.
WAIT, YOU SAID--
...AAA... GAADDD...
ARTIE...DO YOU REALLY WANT TO FINISH THAT SENTENCE?

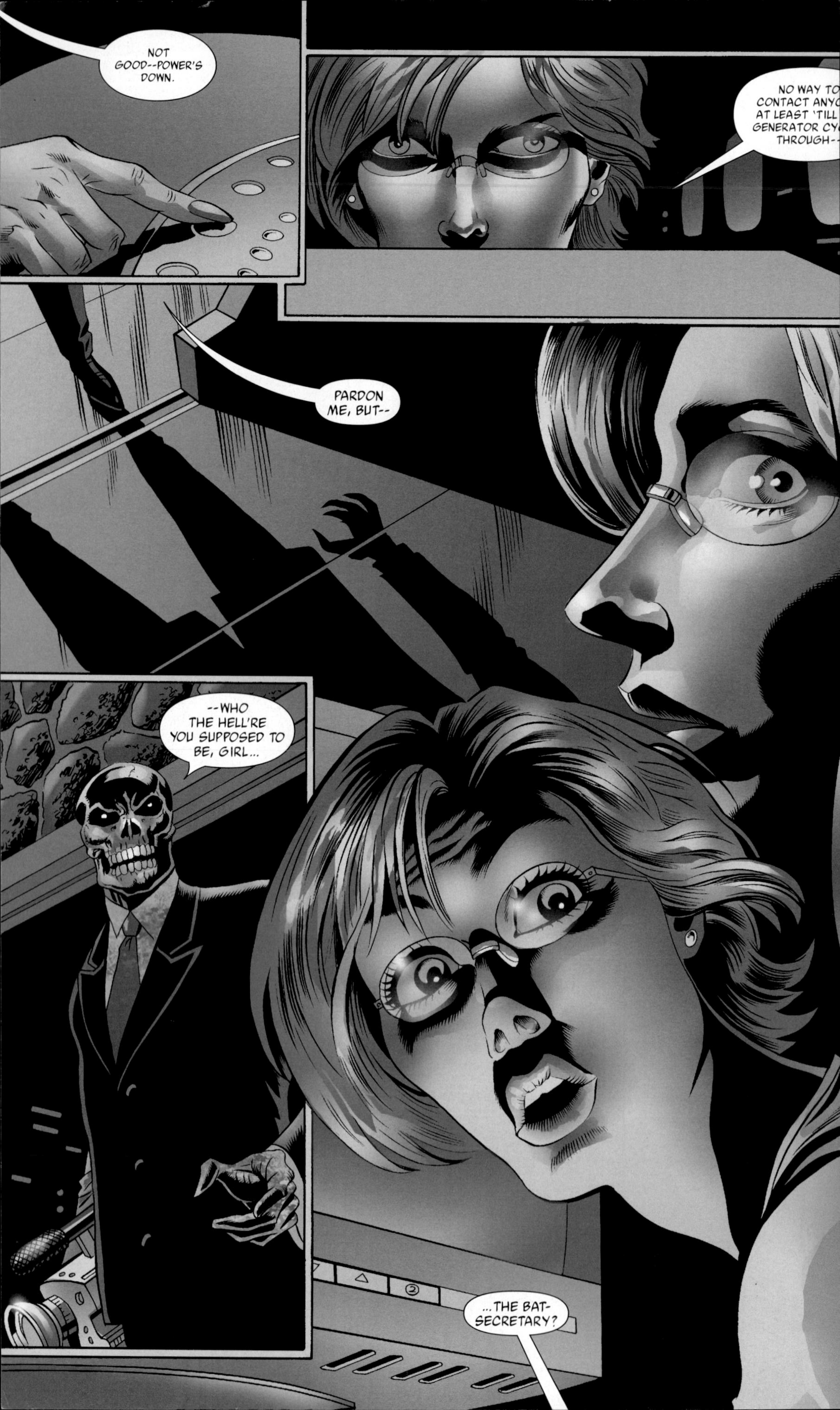
NOT GOOD--POWER'S DOWN.
NO WAY TO CONTACT ANYO AT LEAST 'TILL GENERATOR CY THROUGH--
PARDON ME, BUT--
--WHO THE HELL'RE YOU SUPPOSED TO BE, GIRL...
...THE BAT-SECRETARY?

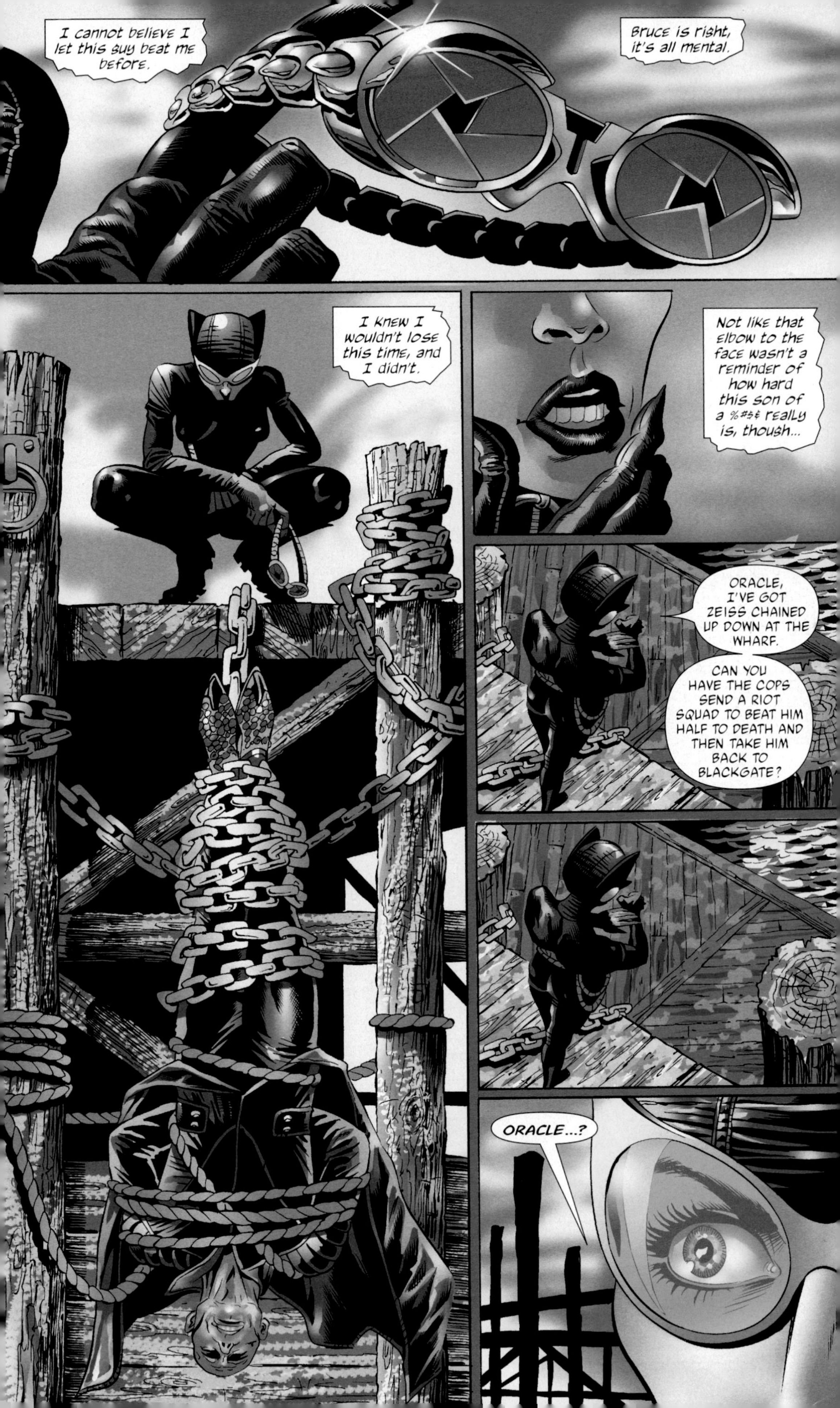

I cannot believe I let this guy beat me before.
Bruce is right, it's all mental.
I knew I wouldn't lose this time, and I didn't.
Not like that elbow to the face wasn't a reminder of how hard this son of a %#$¢ really is, though...
ORACLE, I'VE GOT ZEISS CHAINED UP DOWN AT THE WHARF.
CAN YOU HAVE THE COPS SEND A RIOT SQUAD TO BEAT HIM HALF TO DEATH AND THEN TAKE HIM BACK TO BLACKGATE?
ORACLE...?

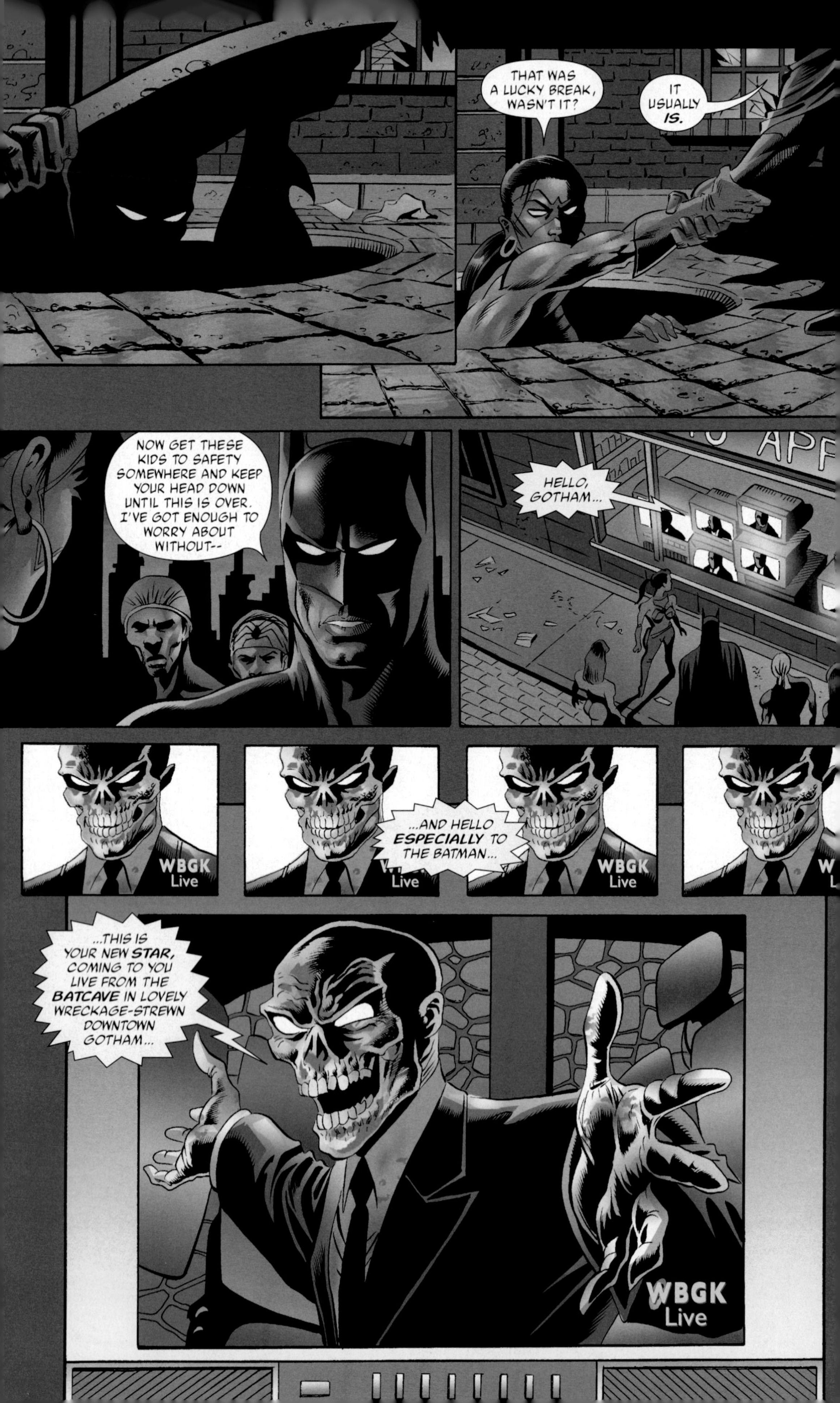

THAT WAS A LUCKY BREAK, WASN'T IT?
IT USUALLY IS.
NOW GET THESE KIDS TO SAFETY SOMEWHERE AND KEEP YOUR HEAD DOWN UNTIL THIS IS OVER. I'VE GOT ENOUGH TO WORRY ABOUT WITHOUT--
HELLO, GOTHAM...
WBGK Live
...AND HELLO ESPECIALLY TO THE BATMAN...
...THIS IS YOUR NEW STAR, COMING TO YOU LIVE FROM THE BATCAVE IN LOVELY WRECKAGE-STREWN DOWNTOWN GOTHAM...
WBGK Live

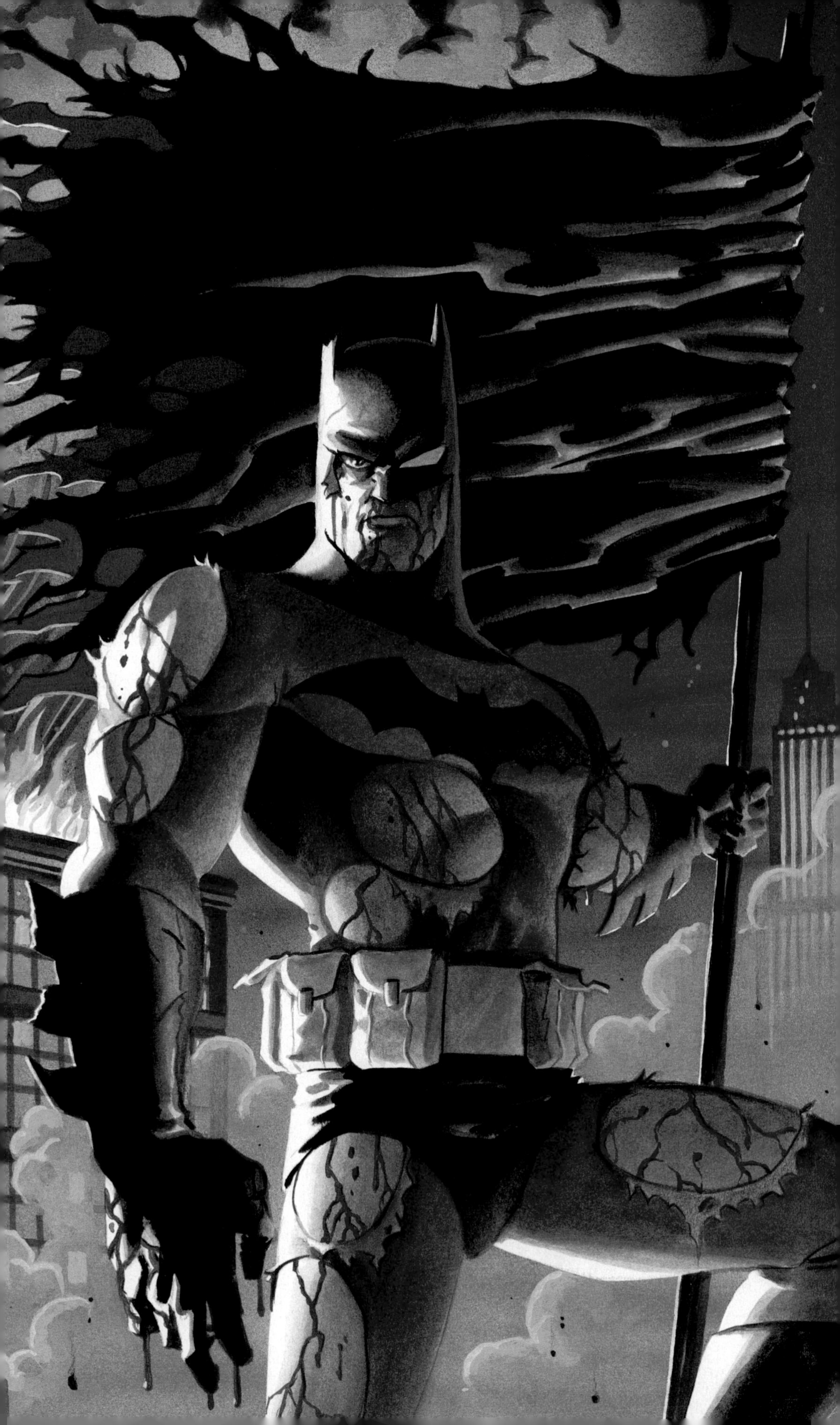

COVER ART BY
MATT WAGNER

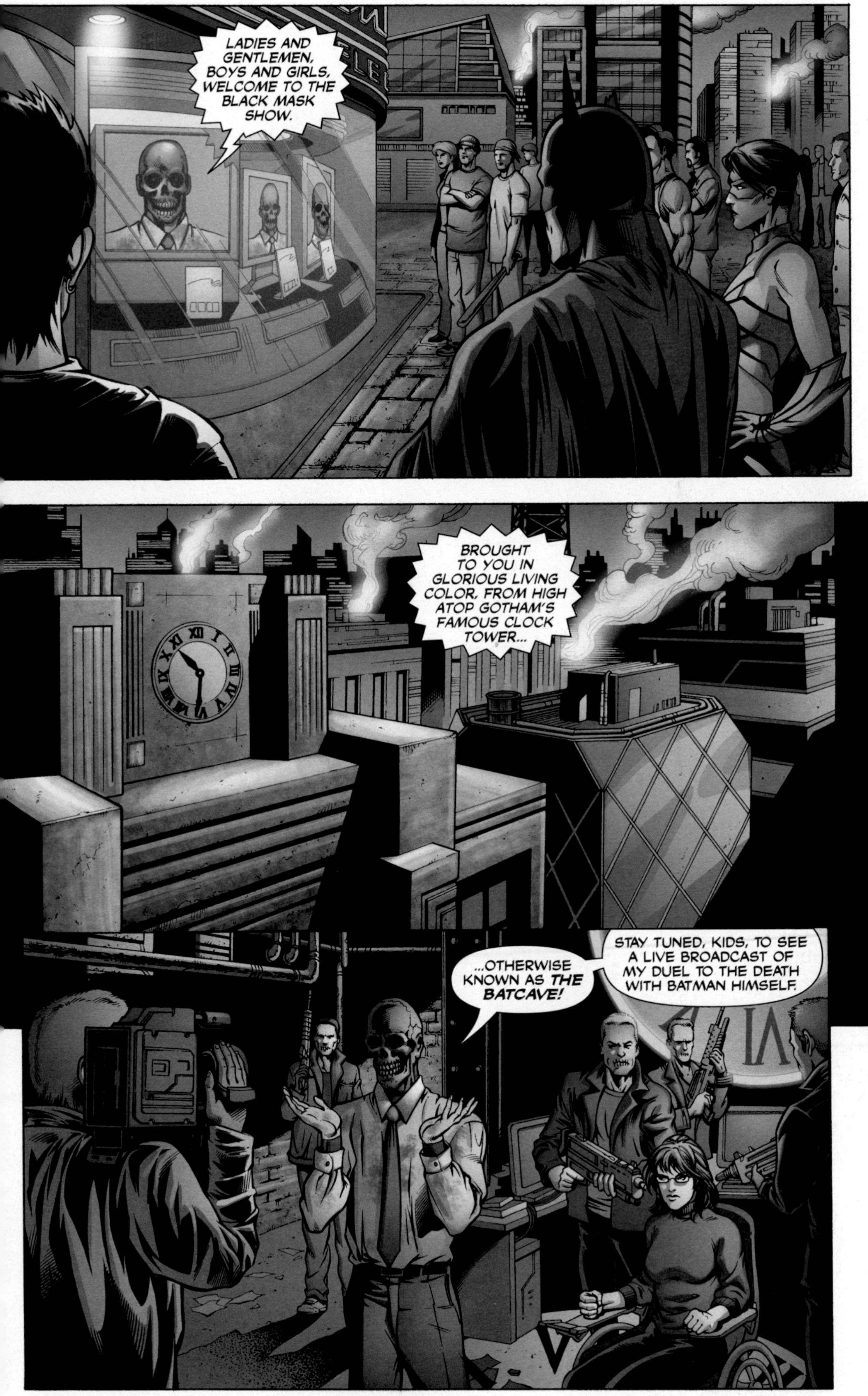
LADIES AND GENTLEMEN, BOYS AND GIRLS, WELCOME TO THE BLACK MASK SHOW.
BROUGHT TO YOU IN GLORIOUS LIVING COLOR, FROM HIGH ATOP GOTHAM'S FAMOUS CLOCK TOWER...
...OTHERWISE KNOWN AS *THE BATCAVE!*
STAY TUNED, KIDS, TO SEE A LIVE BROADCAST OF MY DUEL TO THE DEATH WITH BATMAN HIMSELF.

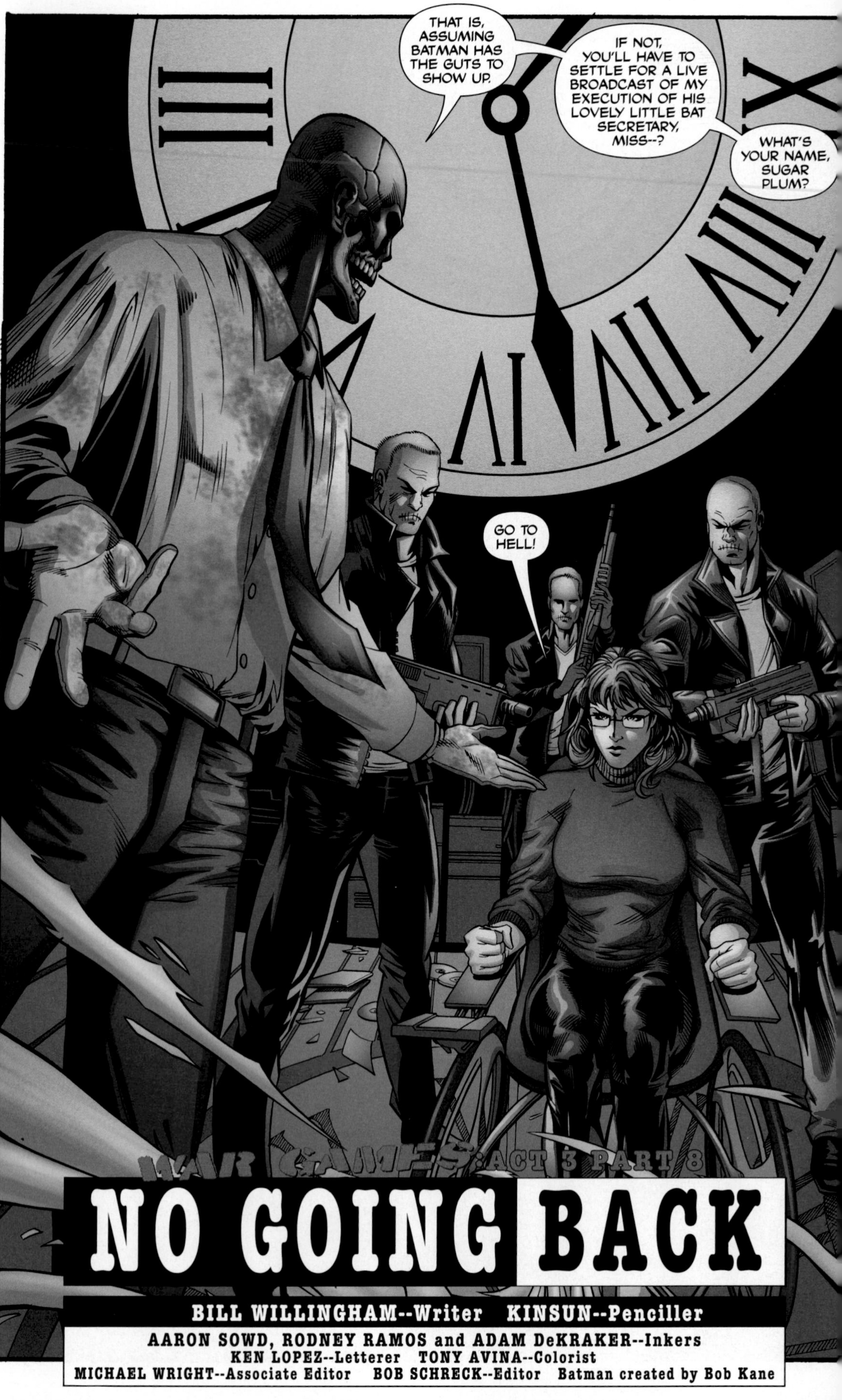
THAT IS, ASSUMING BATMAN HAS THE GUTS TO SHOW UP.
IF NOT, YOU'LL HAVE TO SETTLE FOR A LIVE BROADCAST OF MY EXECUTION OF HIS LOVELY LITTLE BAT SECRETARY, MISS--?
WHAT'S YOUR NAME, SUGAR PLUM?
GO TO HELL!
WAR GAMES: ACT 3 PART 8
NO GOING BACK
BILL WILLINGHAM--Writer KINSUN--Penciller
AARON SOWD, RODNEY RAMOS and ADAM DeKRAKER--Inkers
KEN LOPEZ--Letterer TONY AVINA--Colorist
MICHAEL WRIGHT--Associate Editor BOB SCHRECK--Editor Batman created by Bob Kane

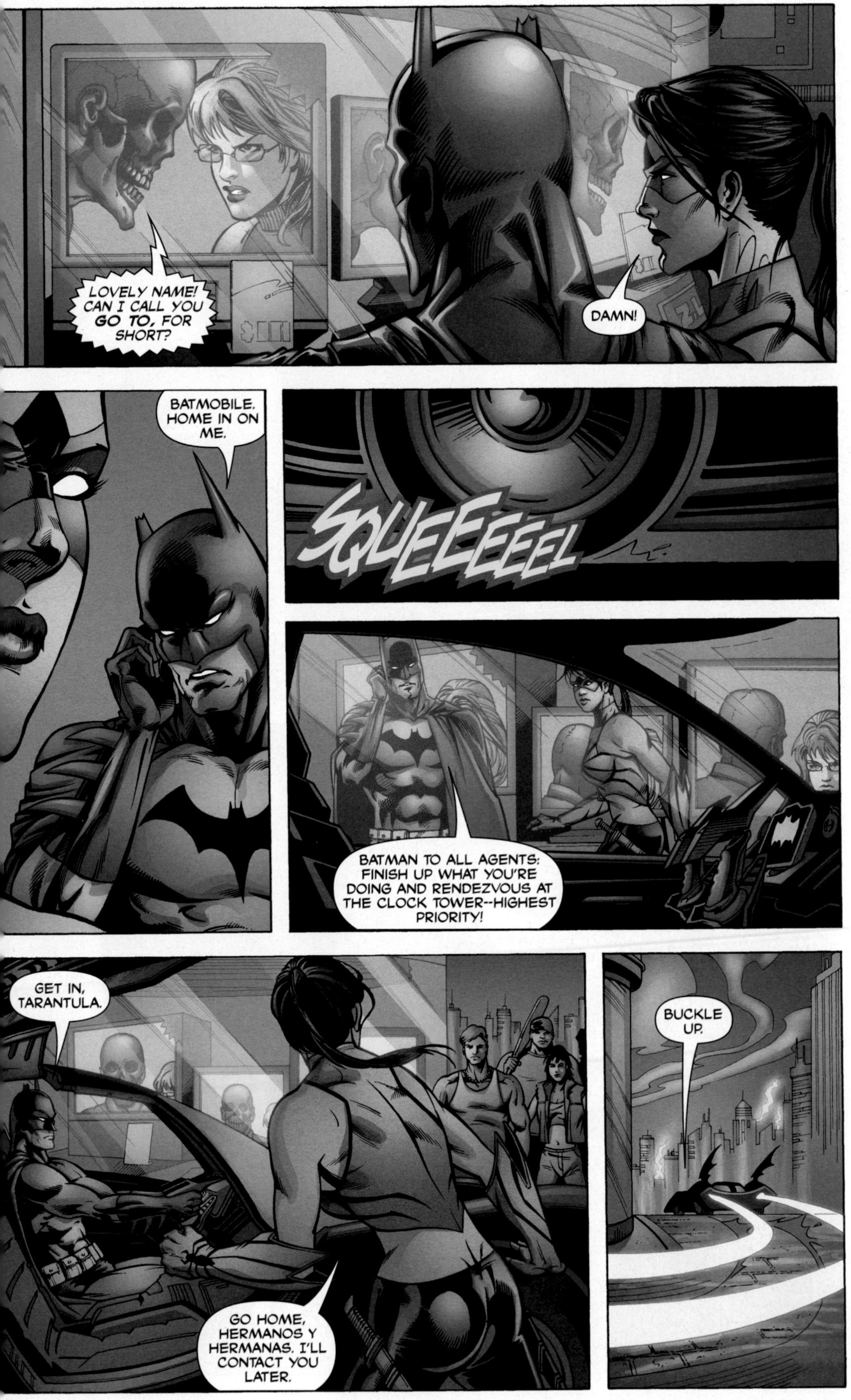
LOVELY NAME! CAN I CALL YOU GO TO, FOR SHORT?
DAMN!
BATMOBILE. HOME IN ON ME.
SQUEEEEEL
BATMAN TO ALL AGENTS: FINISH UP WHAT YOU'RE DOING AND RENDEZVOUS AT THE CLOCK TOWER--HIGHEST PRIORITY!
GET IN, TARANTULA.
GO HOME, HERMANOS Y HERMANAS. I'LL CONTACT YOU LATER.
BUCKLE UP.

MOVE THOSE BARRICADES BACK, CAPTAIN!

I DON'T WANT TO SEE A BYSTANDER WITHIN A CITY BLOCK OF THIS PLACE, IN EVERY DIRECTION!

I'M ON IT, SIR.

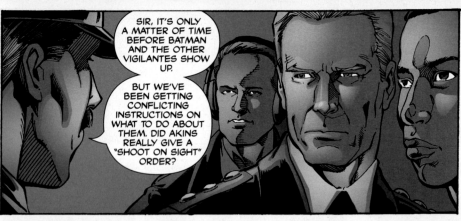

SIR, IT'S ONLY A MATTER OF TIME BEFORE BATMAN AND THE OTHER VIGILANTES SHOW UP.

BUT WE'VE BEEN GETTING CONFLICTING INSTRUCTIONS ON WHAT TO DO ABOUT THEM. DID AKINS REALLY GIVE A "SHOOT ON SIGHT" ORDER?

COMMISSIONER AKINS, I RECOMMEND--

YES, SIR.

YES, SIR. I UNDERSTAND, BUT--

BUT--

NO, COMMISSIONER, I'M NOT REFUSING TO CARRY OUT YOUR ORDERS.

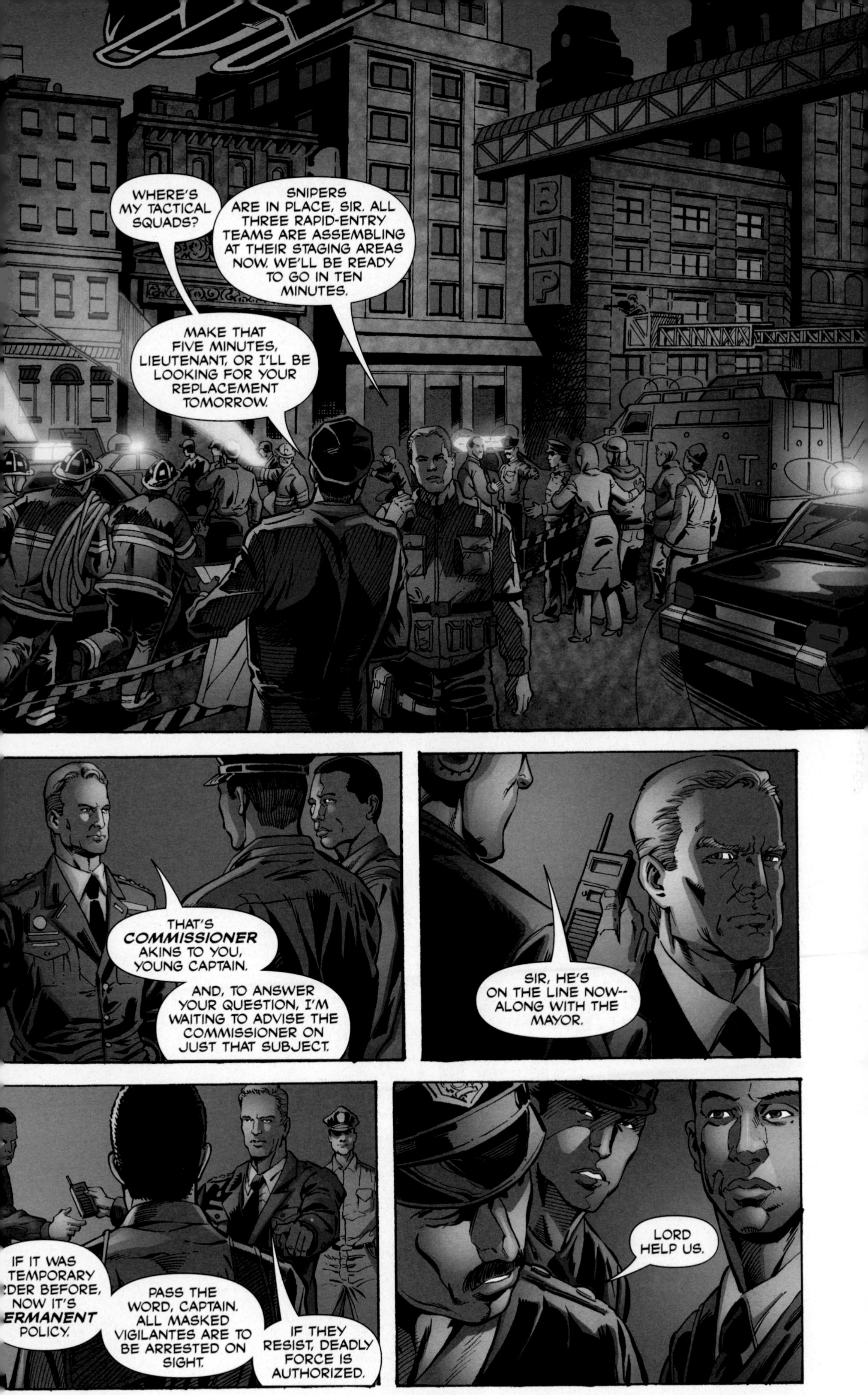
WHERE'S MY TACTICAL SQUADS?
SNIPERS ARE IN PLACE, SIR. ALL THREE RAPID-ENTRY TEAMS ARE ASSEMBLING AT THEIR STAGING AREAS NOW. WE'LL BE READY TO GO IN TEN MINUTES.
MAKE THAT FIVE MINUTES, LIEUTENANT, OR I'LL BE LOOKING FOR YOUR REPLACEMENT TOMORROW.
THAT'S *COMMISSIONER* AKINS TO YOU, YOUNG CAPTAIN.
AND, TO ANSWER YOUR QUESTION, I'M WAITING TO ADVISE THE COMMISSIONER ON JUST THAT SUBJECT.
SIR, HE'S ON THE LINE NOW-- ALONG WITH THE MAYOR.
IF IT WAS TEMPORARY ᴅᴇʀ BEFORE, NOW IT'S *ERMANENT* POLICY.
PASS THE WORD, CAPTAIN. ALL MASKED VIGILANTES ARE TO BE ARRESTED ON SIGHT.
IF THEY RESIST, DEADLY FORCE IS AUTHORIZED.
LORD HELP US.

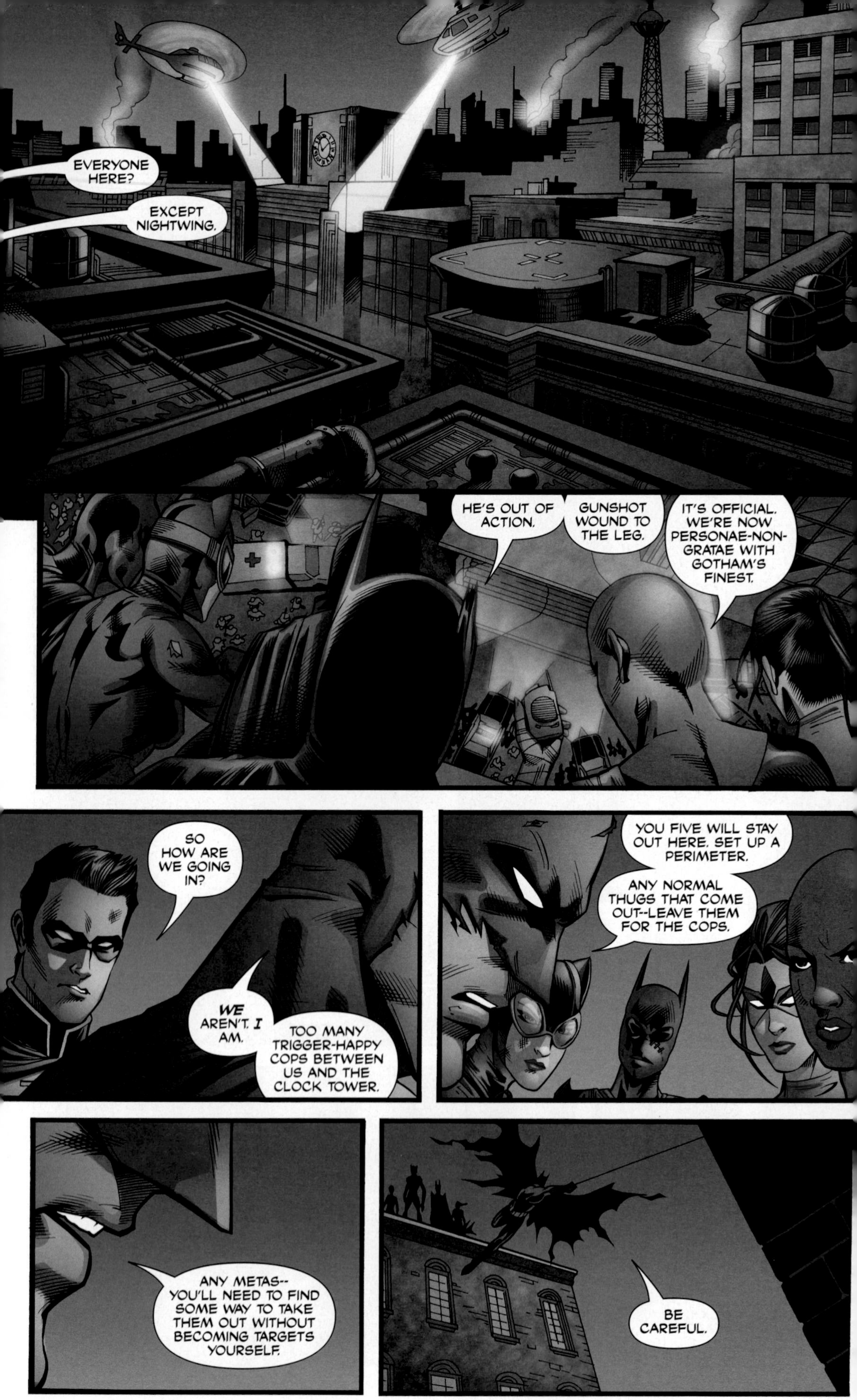
EVERYONE HERE?
EXCEPT NIGHTWING.
HE'S OUT OF ACTION.
GUNSHOT WOUND TO THE LEG.
IT'S OFFICIAL. WE'RE NOW PERSONAE-NON-GRATAE WITH GOTHAM'S FINEST.
SO HOW ARE WE GOING IN?
WE AREN'T. I AM.
TOO MANY TRIGGER-HAPPY COPS BETWEEN US AND THE CLOCK TOWER.
YOU FIVE WILL STAY OUT HERE. SET UP A PERIMETER.
ANY NORMAL THUGS THAT COME OUT--LEAVE THEM FOR THE COPS.
ANY METAS--YOU'LL NEED TO FIND SOME WAY TO TAKE THEM OUT WITHOUT BECOMING TARGETS YOURSELF.
BE CAREFUL.

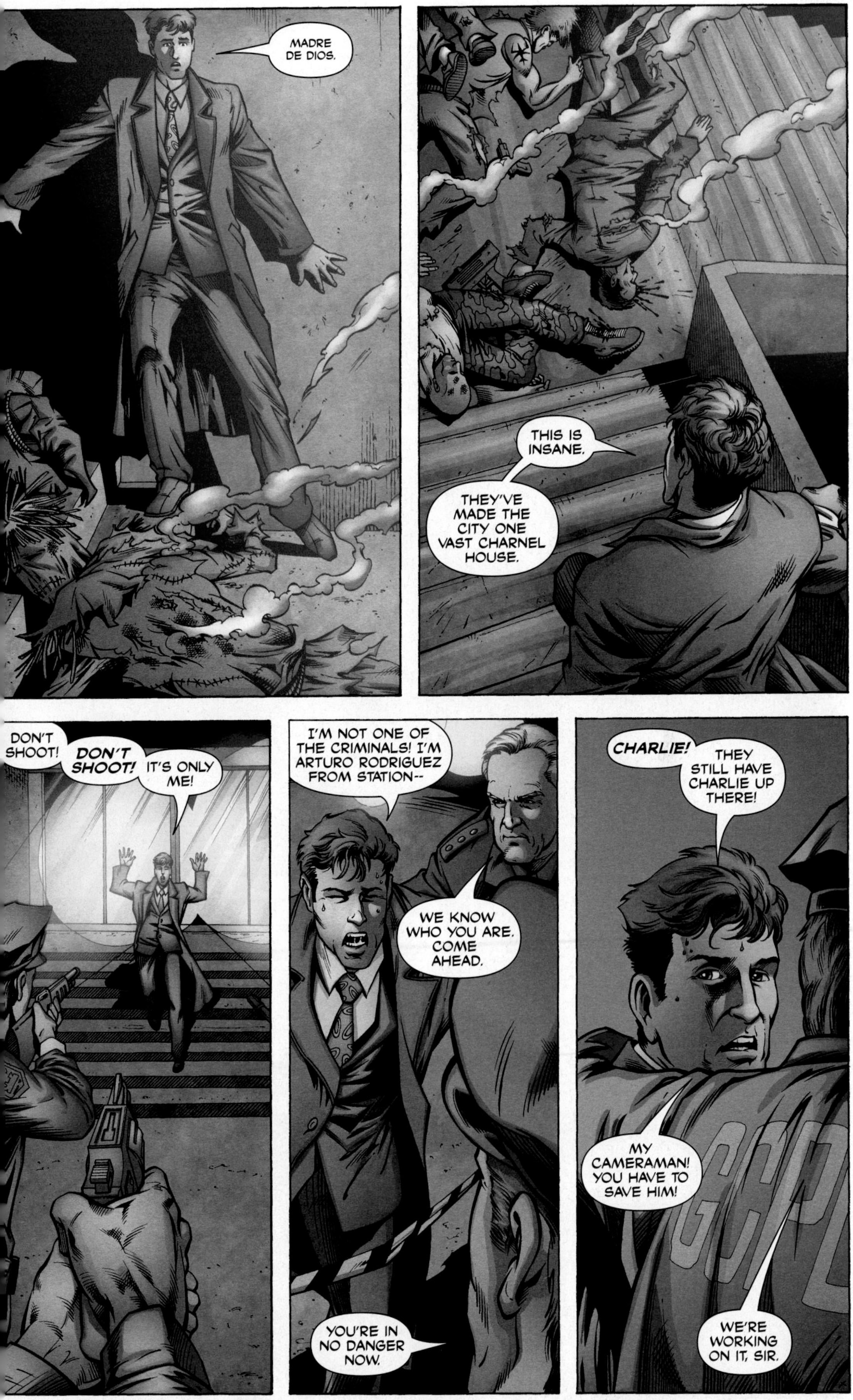

MADRE DE DIOS.
THIS IS INSANE.
THEY'VE MADE THE CITY ONE VAST CHARNEL HOUSE.
DON'T SHOOT!
DON'T SHOOT!
IT'S ONLY ME!
I'M NOT ONE OF THE CRIMINALS! I'M ARTURO RODRIGUEZ FROM STATION--
WE KNOW WHO YOU ARE. COME AHEAD.
YOU'RE IN NO DANGER NOW.
CHARLIE!
THEY STILL HAVE CHARLIE UP THERE!
MY CAMERAMAN! YOU HAVE TO SAVE HIM!
WE'RE WORKING ON IT, SIR.

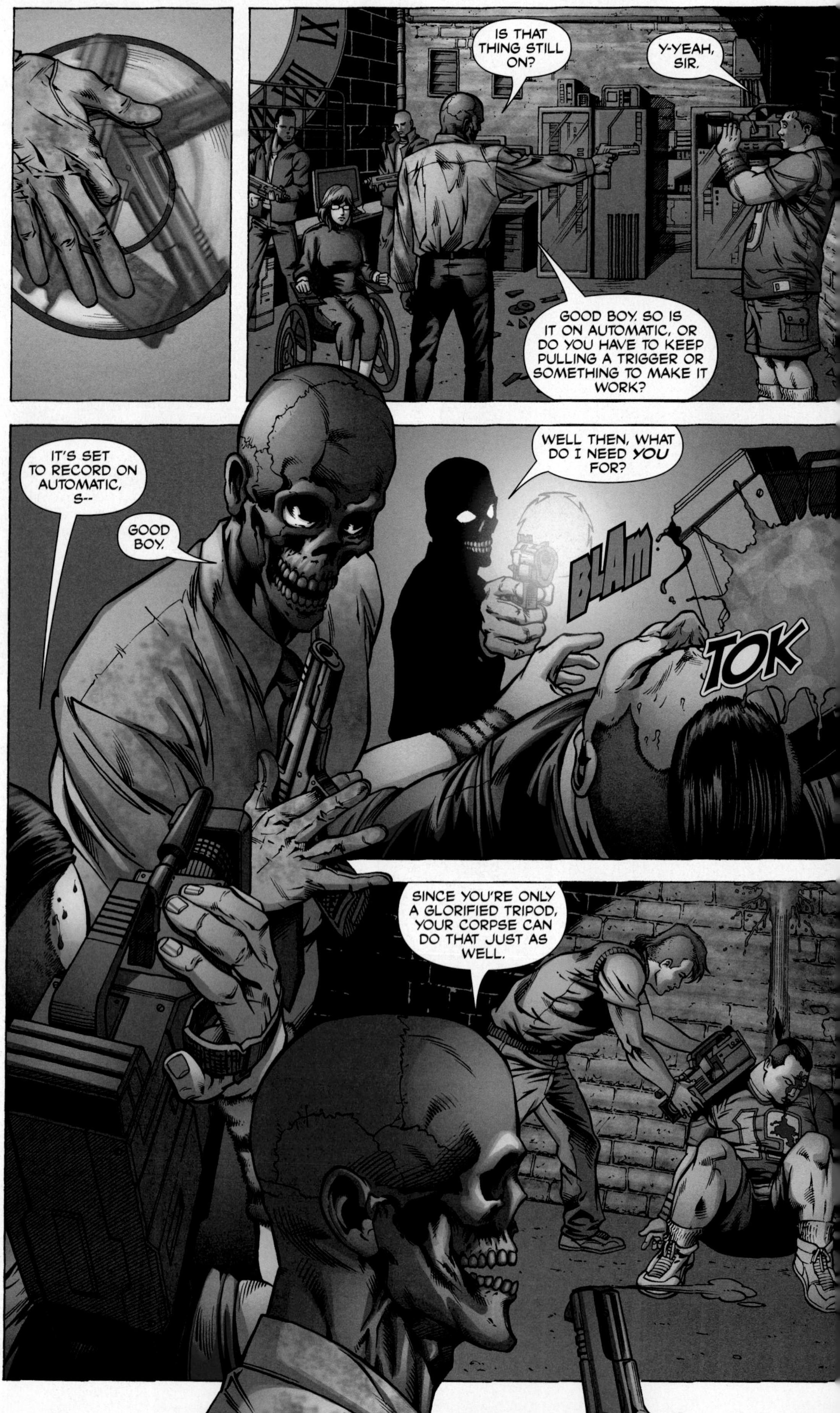
IS THAT THING STILL ON?
Y-YEAH, SIR.
GOOD BOY. SO IS IT ON AUTOMATIC, OR DO YOU HAVE TO KEEP PULLING A TRIGGER OR SOMETHING TO MAKE IT WORK?
IT'S SET TO RECORD ON AUTOMATIC, S--
GOOD BOY.
WELL THEN, WHAT DO I NEED *YOU* FOR?
BLAM
TOK
SINCE YOU'RE ONLY A GLORIFIED TRIPOD, YOUR CORPSE CAN DO THAT JUST AS WELL.

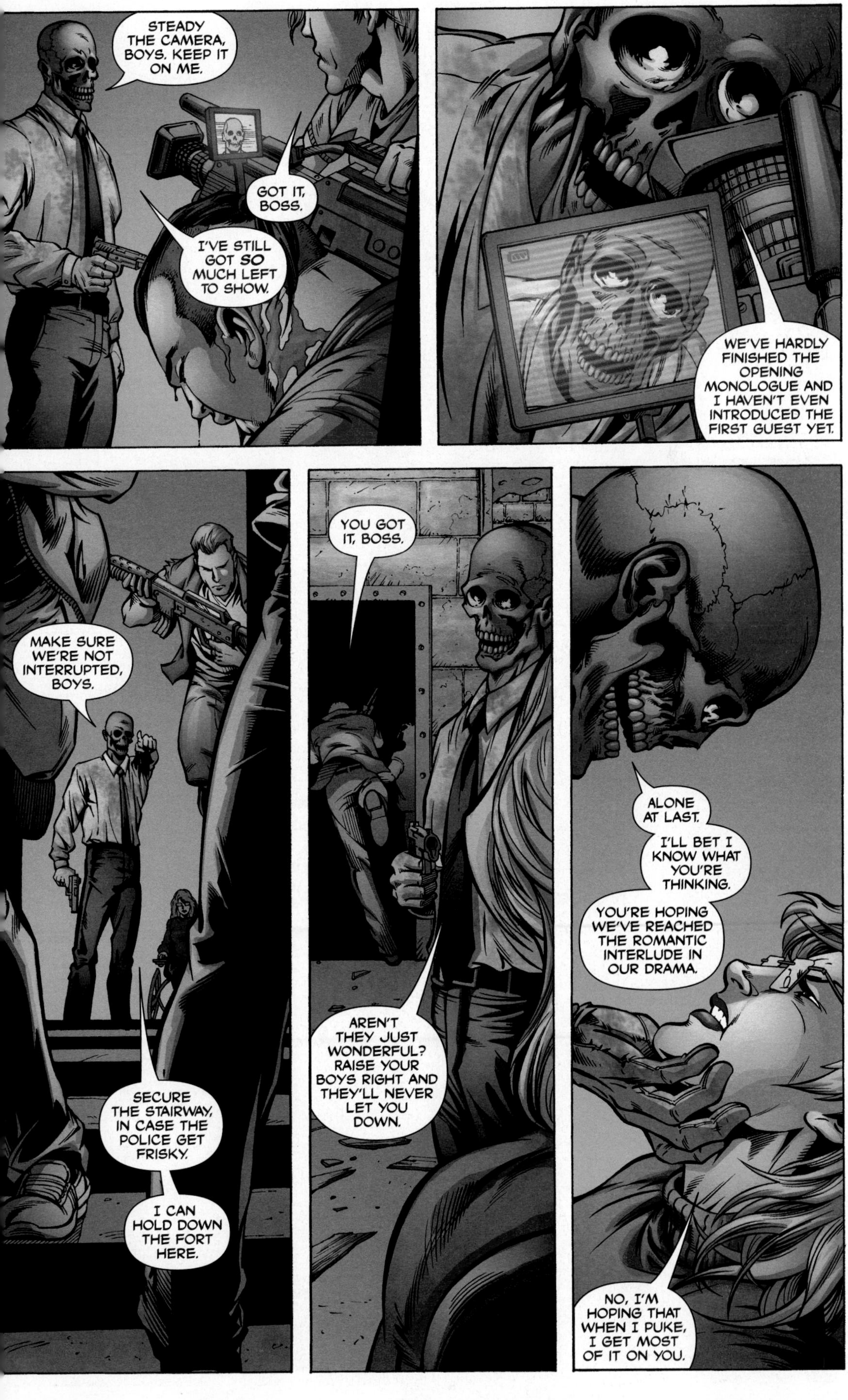

STEADY THE CAMERA, BOYS. KEEP IT ON ME.
GOT IT, BOSS.
I'VE STILL GOT SO MUCH LEFT TO SHOW.
WE'VE HARDLY FINISHED THE OPENING MONOLOGUE AND I HAVEN'T EVEN INTRODUCED THE FIRST GUEST YET.
MAKE SURE WE'RE NOT INTERRUPTED, BOYS.
SECURE THE STAIRWAY, IN CASE THE POLICE GET FRISKY.
I CAN HOLD DOWN THE FORT HERE.
YOU GOT IT, BOSS.
AREN'T THEY JUST WONDERFUL? RAISE YOUR BOYS RIGHT AND THEY'LL NEVER LET YOU DOWN.
ALONE AT LAST.
I'LL BET I KNOW WHAT YOU'RE THINKING.
YOU'RE HOPING WE'VE REACHED THE ROMANTIC INTERLUDE IN OUR DRAMA.
NO, I'M HOPING THAT WHEN I PUKE, I GET MOST OF IT ON YOU.

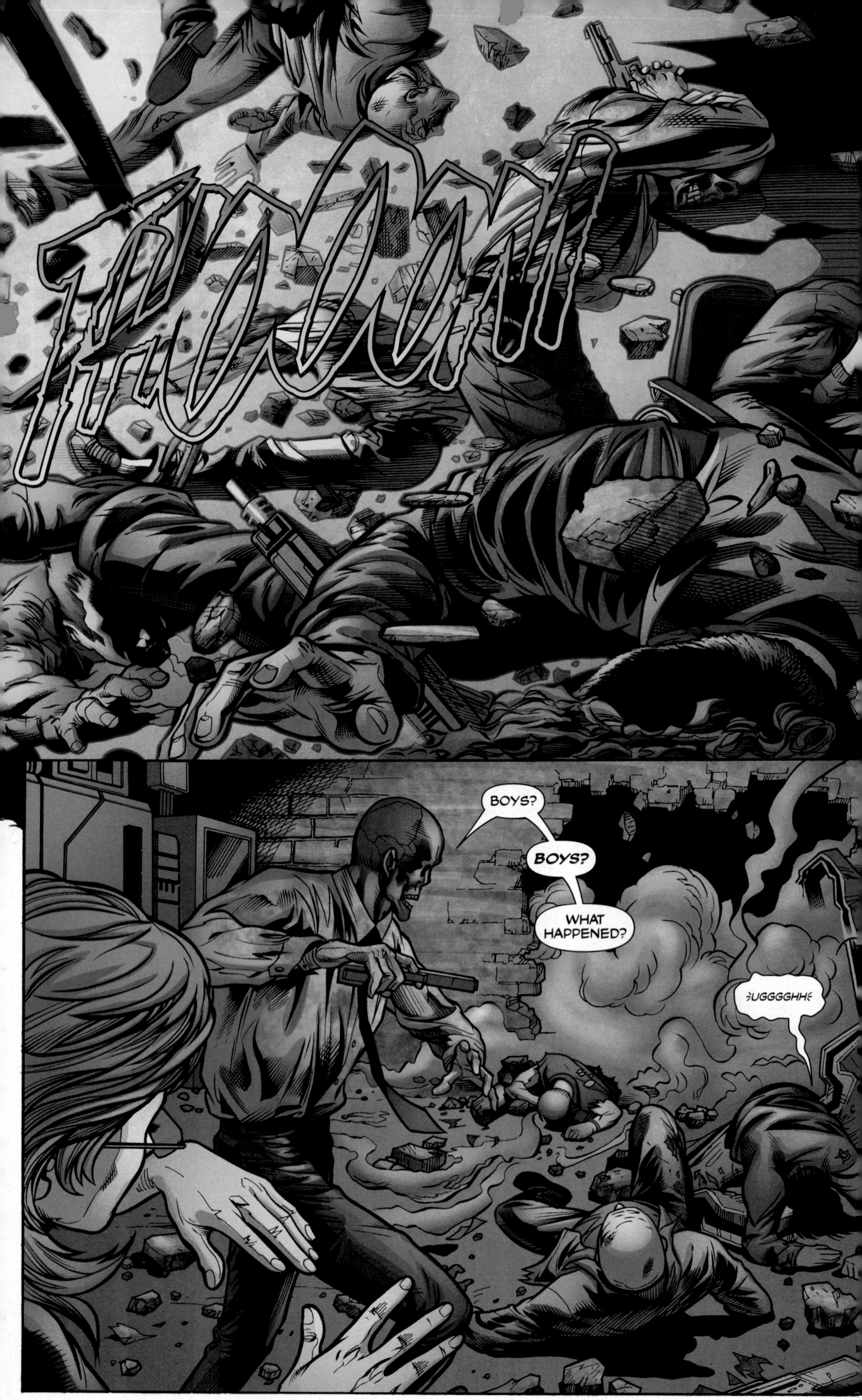
BOYS?
BOYS?
WHAT HAPPENED?
UGGGGHH

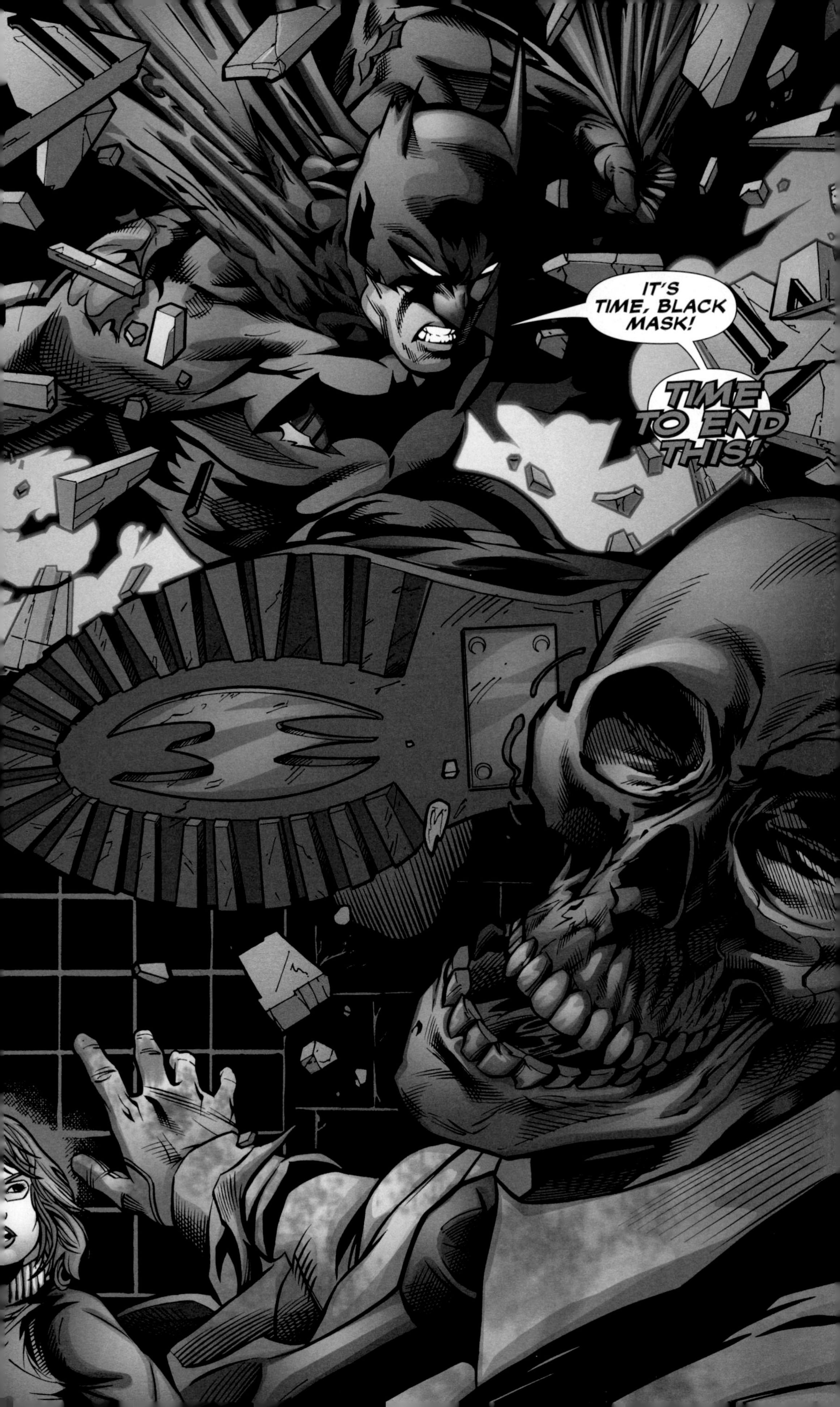
IT'S TIME, BLACK MASK!
TIME TO END THIS!

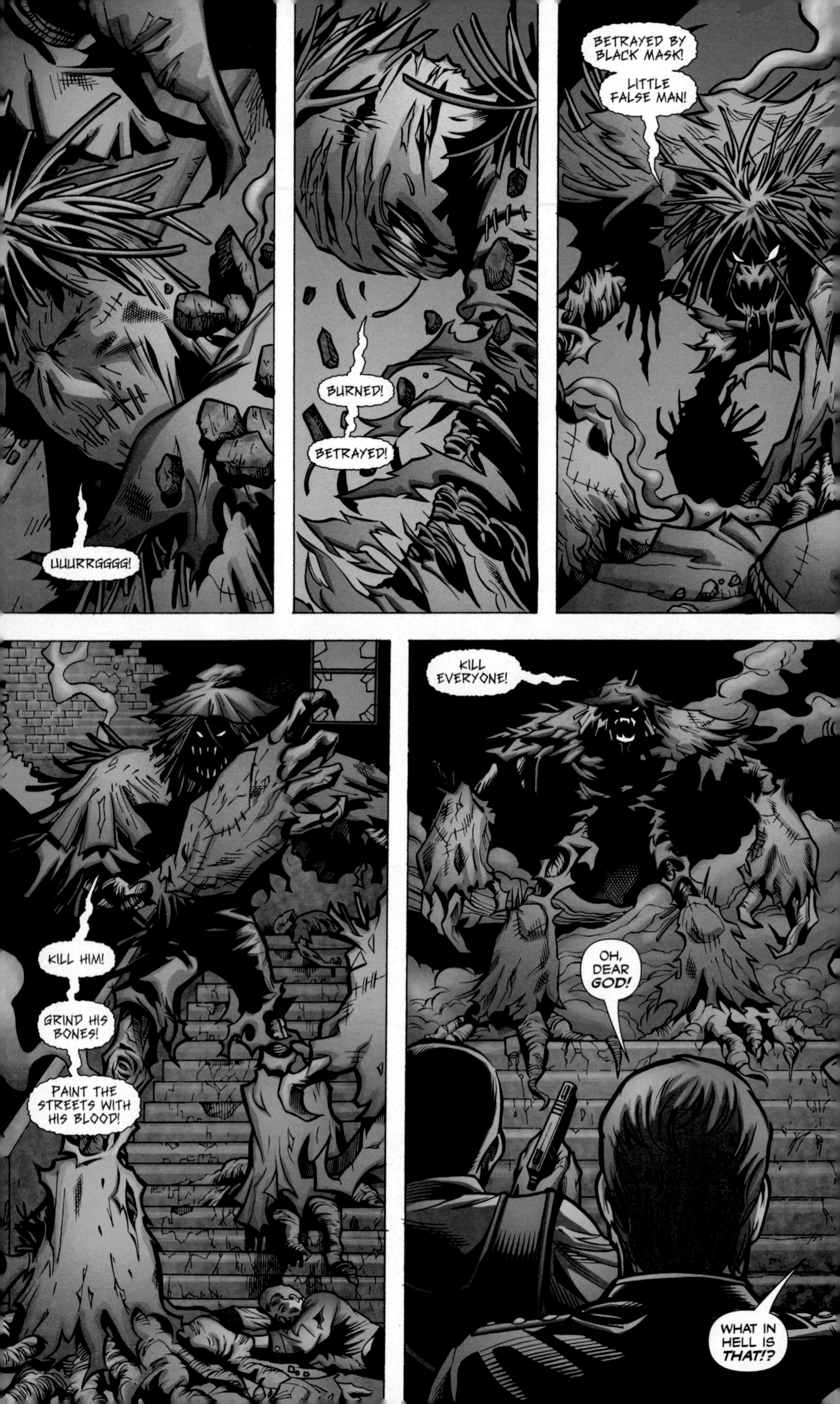

UUURRGGGG!
BURNED!
BETRAYED!
BETRAYED BY BLACK MASK!
LITTLE FALSE MAN!
KILL HIM!
GRIND HIS BONES!
PAINT THE STREETS WITH HIS BLOOD!
KILL EVERYONE!
OH, DEAR GOD!
WHAT IN HELL IS THAT!?

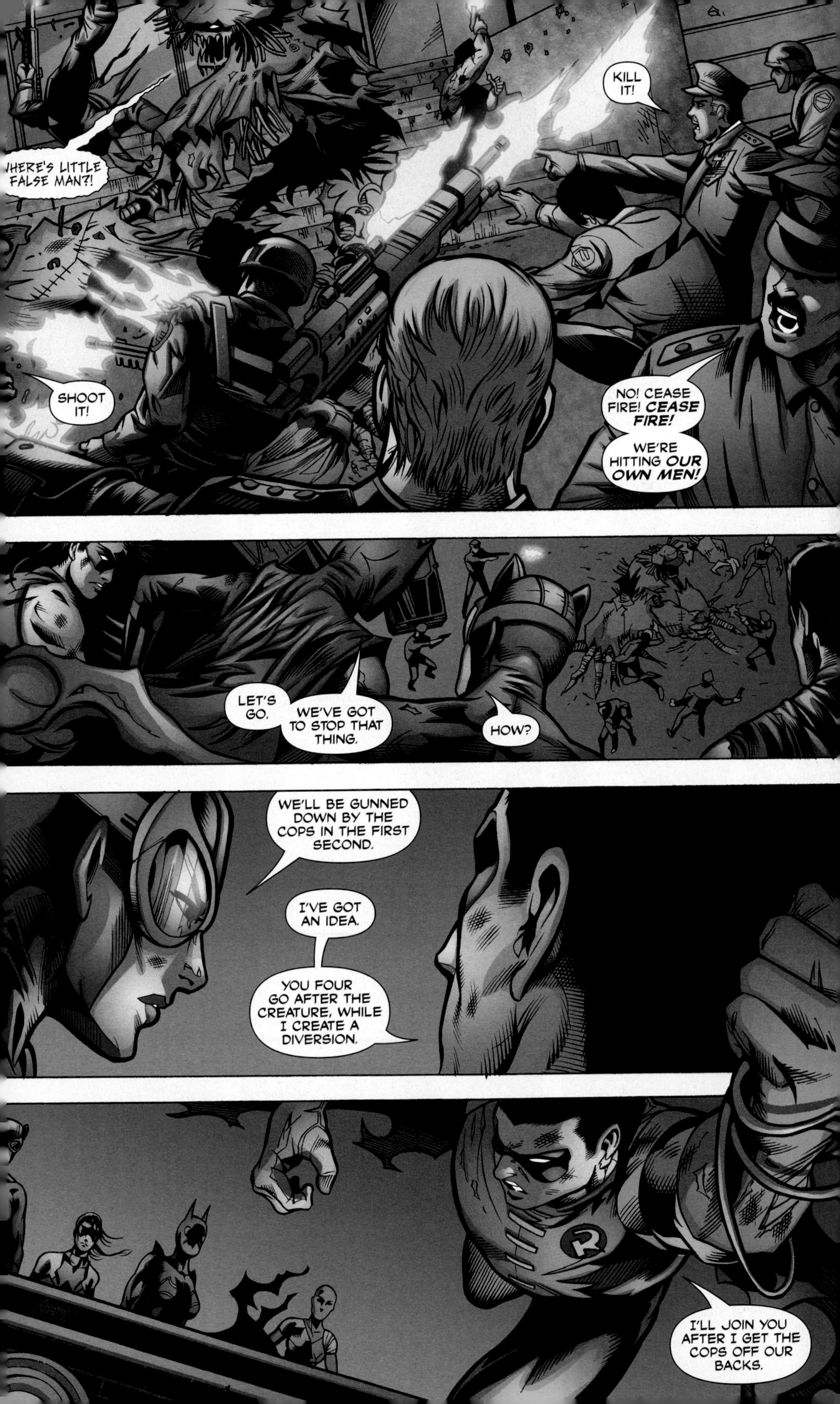
WHERE'S LITTLE FALSE MAN?!
KILL IT!
SHOOT IT!
NO! CEASE FIRE! CEASE FIRE!
WE'RE HITTING OUR OWN MEN!
LET'S GO.
WE'VE GOT TO STOP THAT THING.
HOW?
WE'LL BE GUNNED DOWN BY THE COPS IN THE FIRST SECOND.
I'VE GOT AN IDEA.
YOU FOUR GO AFTER THE CREATURE, WHILE I CREATE A DIVERSION.
I'LL JOIN YOU AFTER I GET THE COPS OFF OUR BACKS.

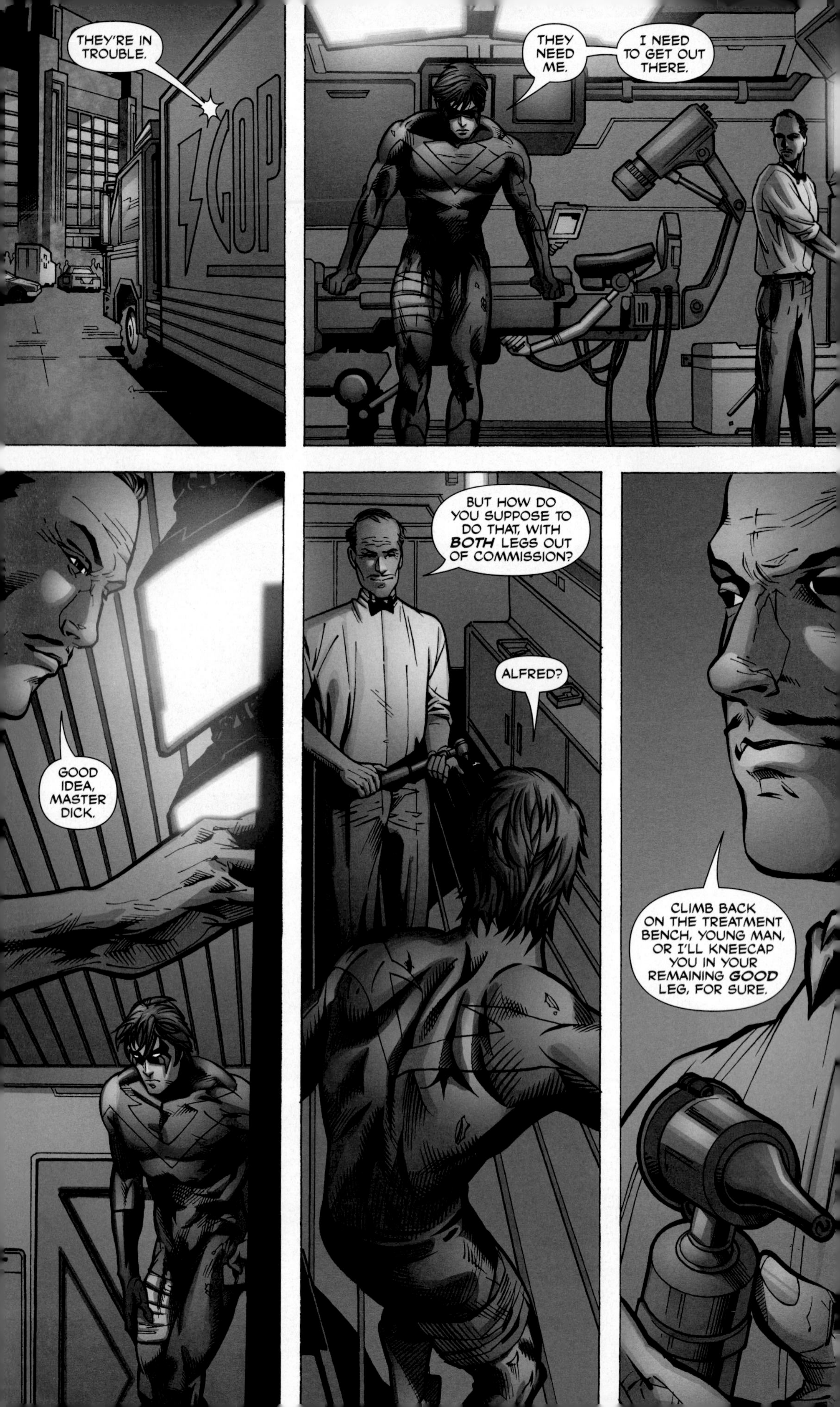
THEY'RE IN TROUBLE.
THEY NEED ME.
I NEED TO GET OUT THERE.
GOOD IDEA, MASTER DICK.
BUT HOW DO YOU SUPPOSE TO DO THAT, WITH *BOTH* LEGS OUT OF COMMISSION?
ALFRED?
CLIMB BACK ON THE TREATMENT BENCH, YOUNG MAN, OR I'LL KNEECAP YOU IN YOUR REMAINING *GOOD* LEG, FOR SURE.

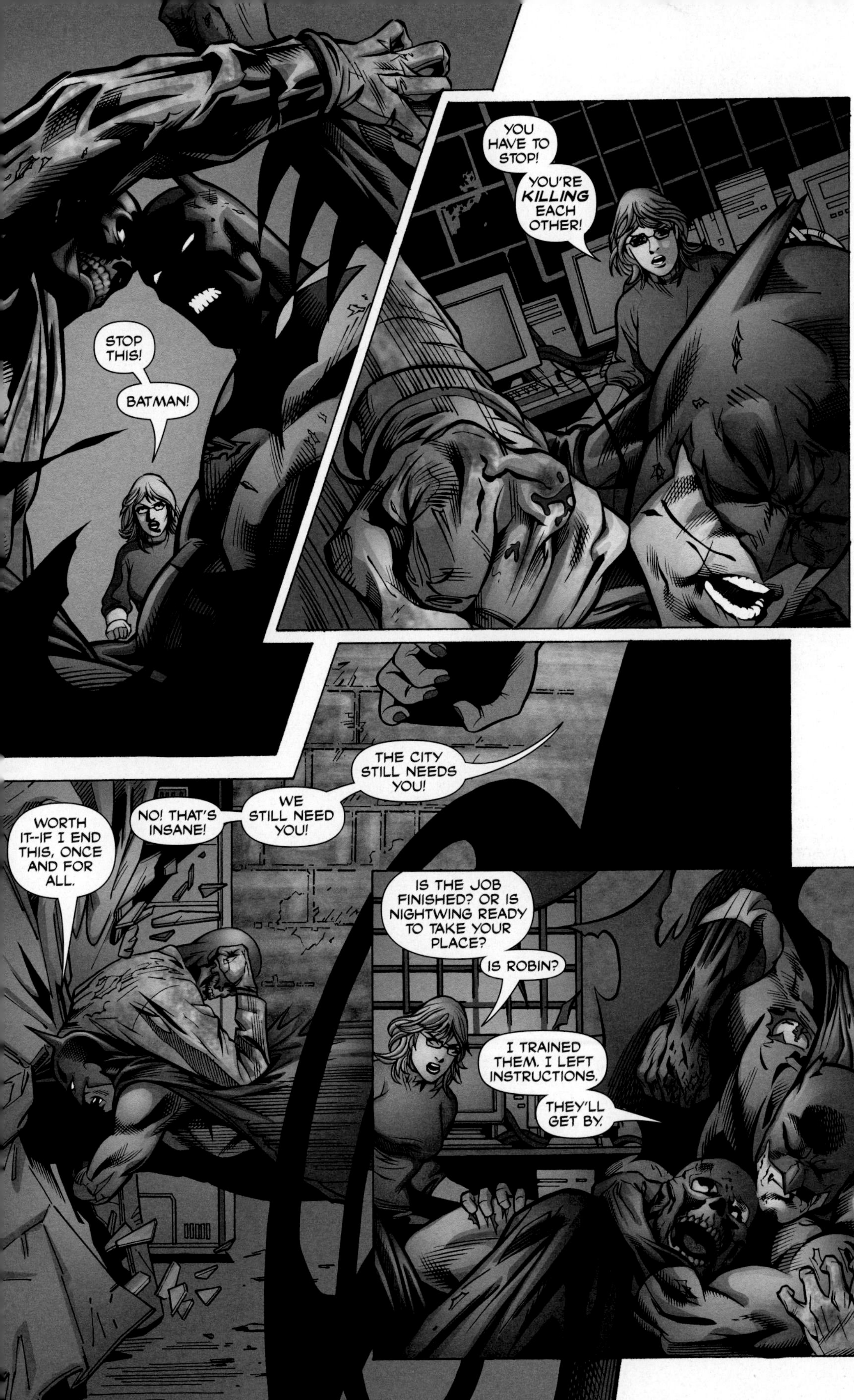
STOP THIS!
BATMAN!
YOU HAVE TO STOP!
YOU'RE KILLING EACH OTHER!
THE CITY STILL NEEDS YOU!
WE STILL NEED YOU!
NO! THAT'S INSANE!
WORTH IT--IF I END THIS, ONCE AND FOR ALL.
IS THE JOB FINISHED? OR IS NIGHTWING READY TO TAKE YOUR PLACE?
IS ROBIN?
I TRAINED THEM. I LEFT INSTRUCTIONS.
THEY'LL GET BY.

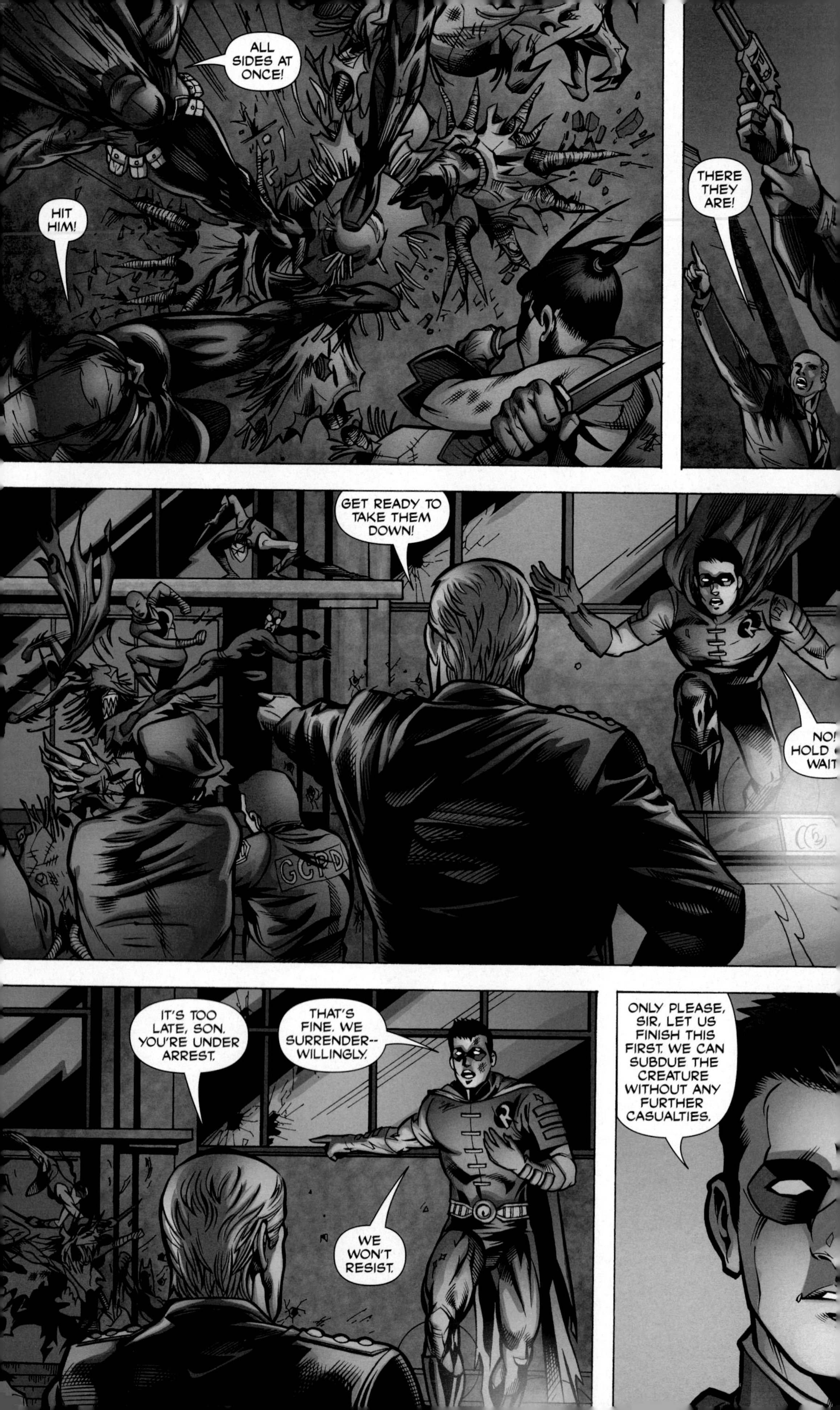
ALL SIDES AT ONCE!
HIT HIM!
THERE THEY ARE!
GET READY TO TAKE THEM DOWN!
NO! HOLD WAIT
IT'S TOO LATE, SON. YOU'RE UNDER ARREST.
THAT'S FINE. WE SURRENDER-- WILLINGLY.
WE WON'T RESIST.
ONLY PLEASE, SIR, LET US FINISH THIS FIRST. WE CAN SUBDUE THE CREATURE WITHOUT ANY FURTHER CASUALTIES.

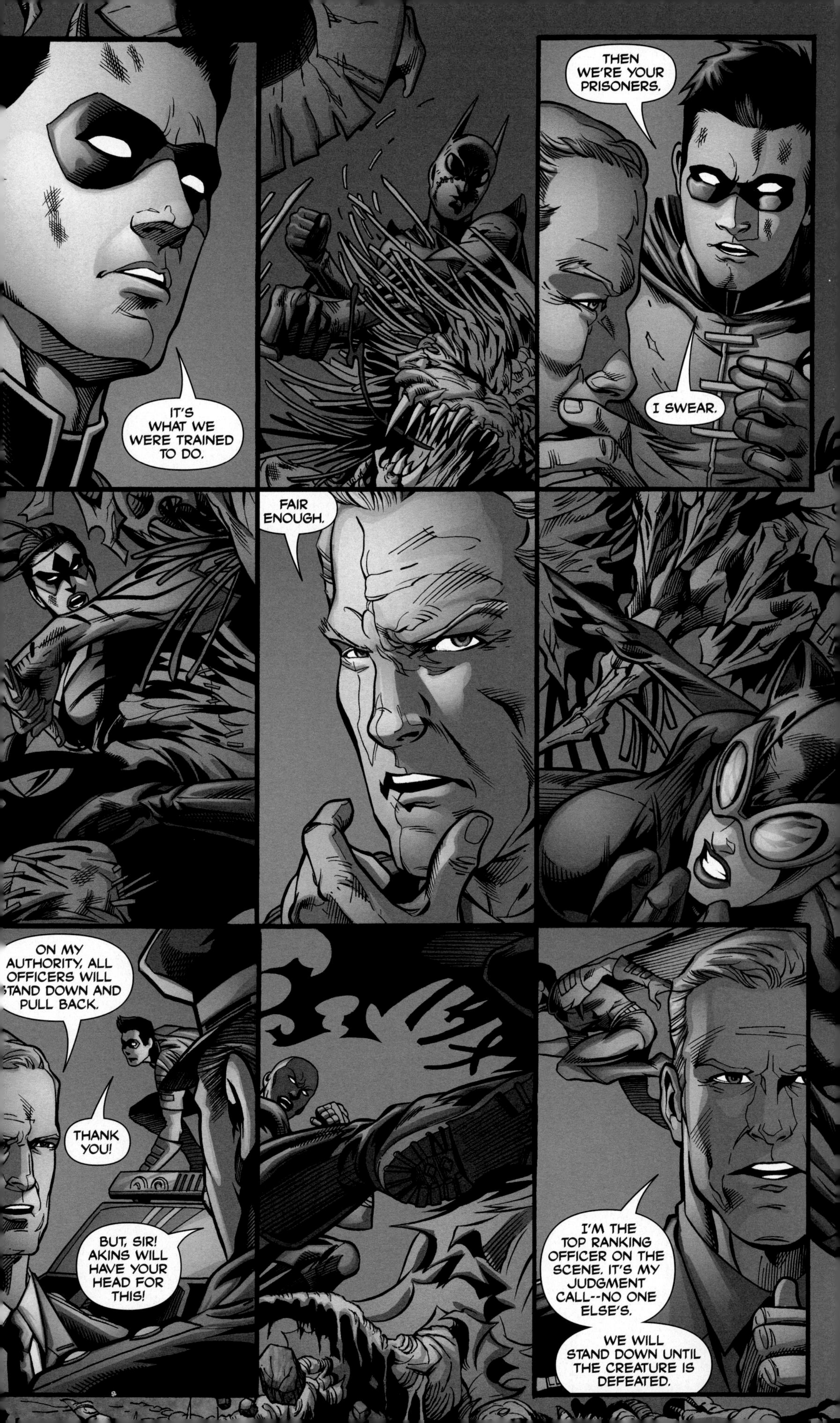
IT'S WHAT WE WERE TRAINED TO DO.
THEN WE'RE YOUR PRISONERS.
I SWEAR.
FAIR ENOUGH.
ON MY AUTHORITY, ALL OFFICERS WILL STAND DOWN AND PULL BACK.
THANK YOU!
BUT, SIR! AKINS WILL HAVE YOUR HEAD FOR THIS!
I'M THE TOP RANKING OFFICER ON THE SCENE. IT'S MY JUDGMENT CALL--NO ONE ELSE'S.
WE WILL STAND DOWN UNTIL THE CREATURE IS DEFEATED.

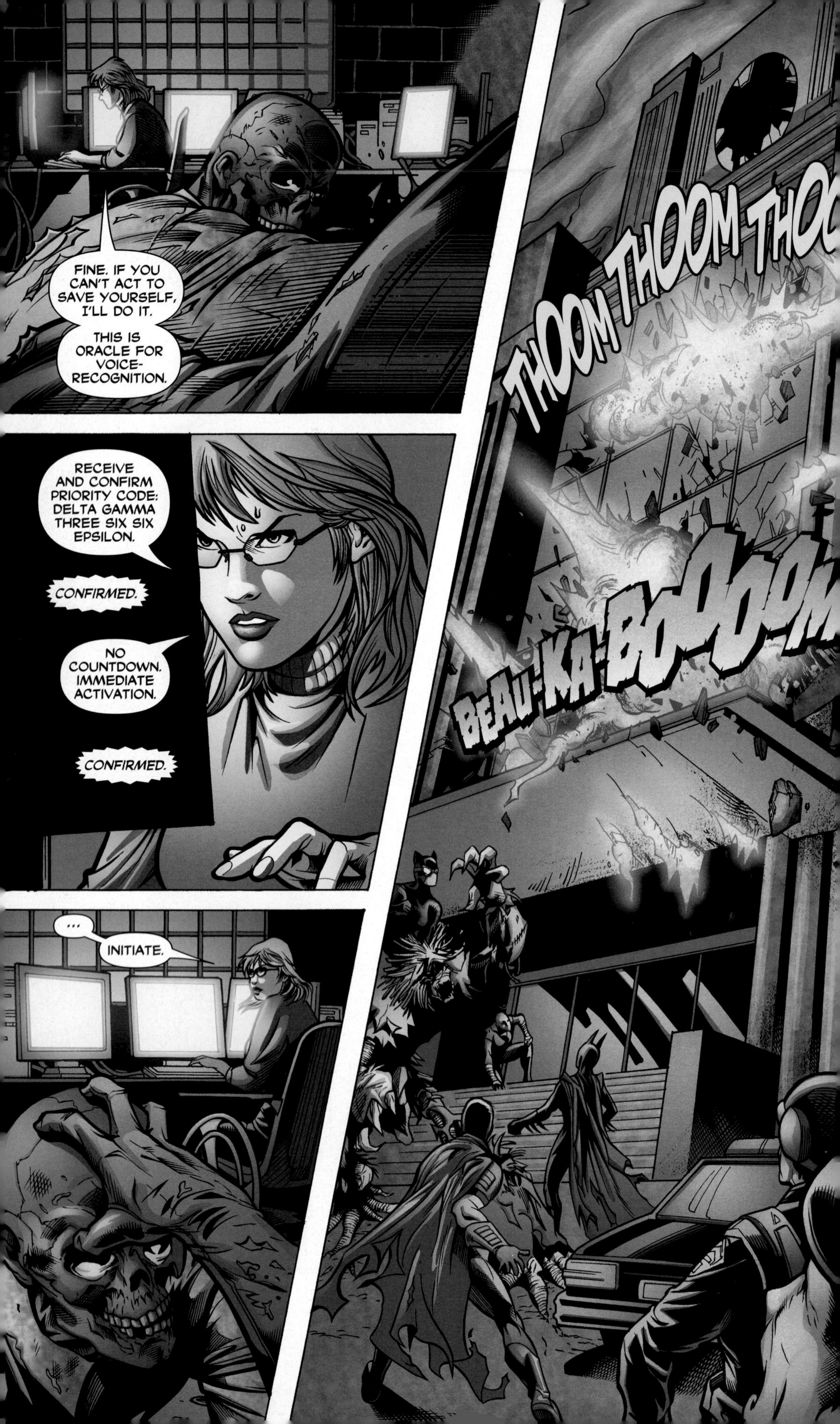
FINE. IF YOU CAN'T ACT TO SAVE YOURSELF, I'LL DO IT.
THIS IS ORACLE FOR VOICE-RECOGNITION.
RECEIVE AND CONFIRM PRIORITY CODE: DELTA GAMMA THREE SIX SIX EPSILON.
CONFIRMED.
NO COUNTDOWN. IMMEDIATE ACTIVATION.
CONFIRMED.
...
INITIATE.
THOOM THOOM THOO
BEAU-KA-BOOOOM

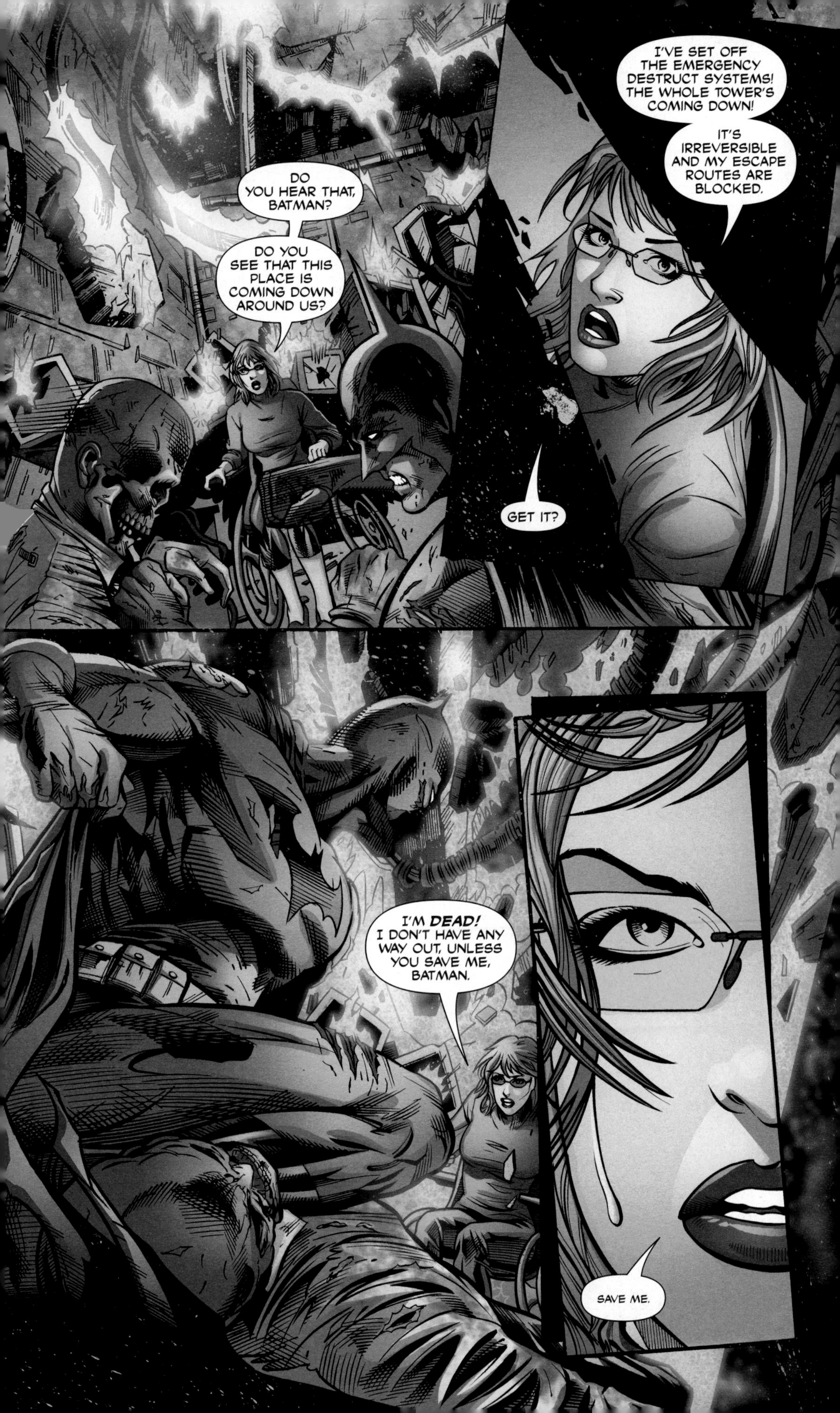
DO YOU HEAR THAT, BATMAN?
DO YOU SEE THAT THIS PLACE IS COMING DOWN AROUND US?
GET IT?
I'VE SET OFF THE EMERGENCY DESTRUCT SYSTEMS! THE WHOLE TOWER'S COMING DOWN!
IT'S IRREVERSIBLE AND MY ESCAPE ROUTES ARE BLOCKED.
I'M *DEAD!* I DON'T HAVE ANY WAY OUT, UNLESS YOU SAVE ME, BATMAN.
SAVE ME.

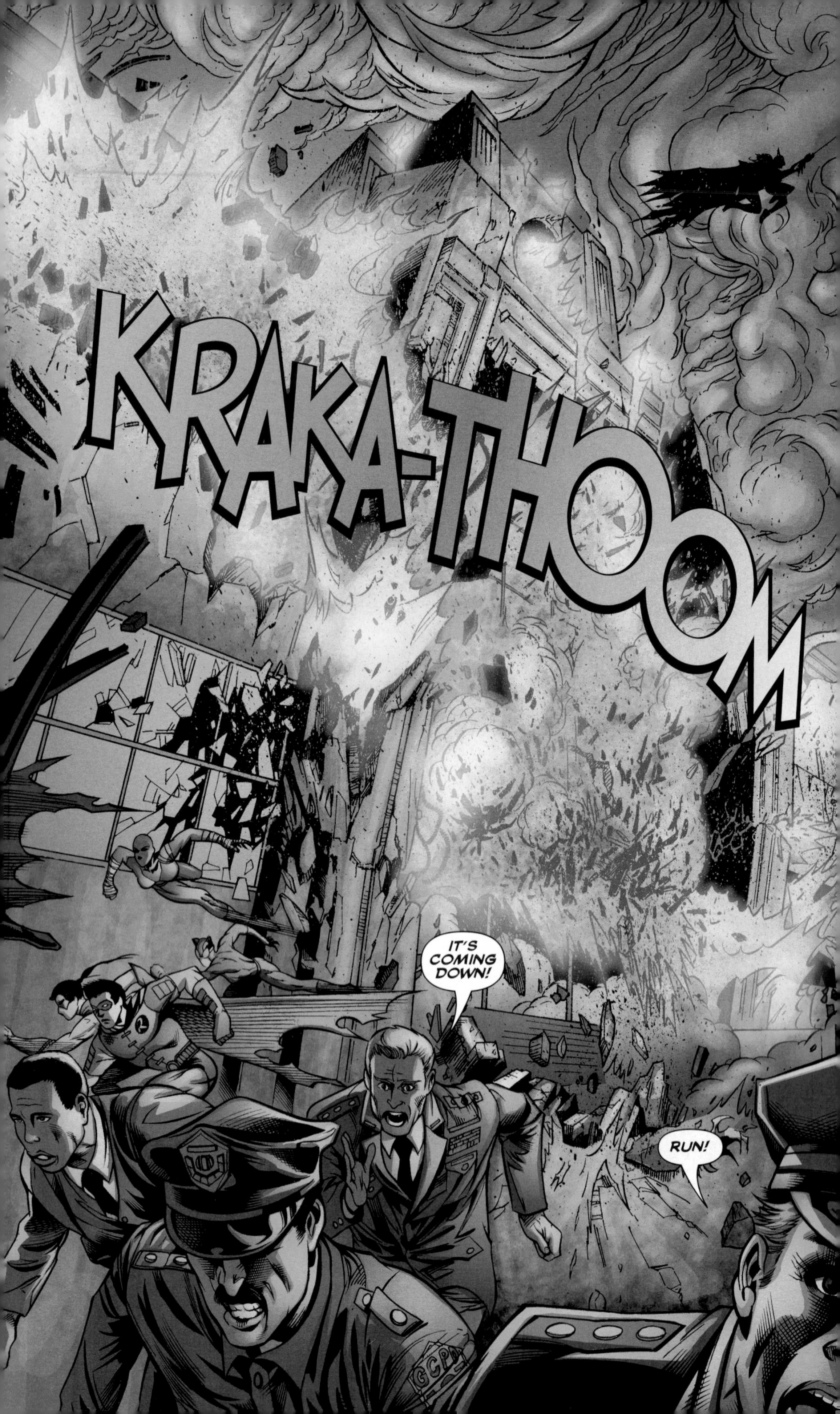
KRAKA-THOOM
IT'S COMING DOWN!
RUN!

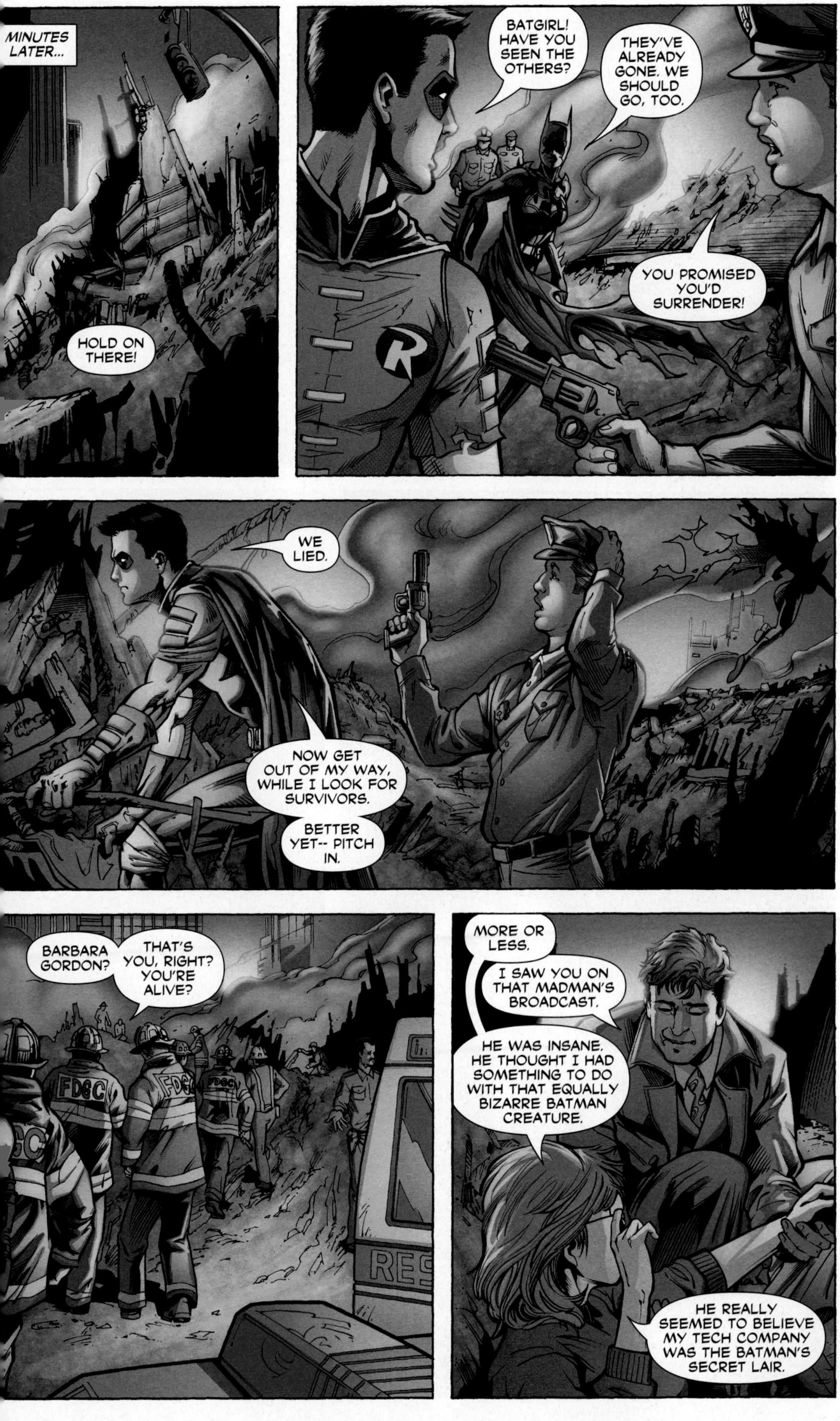
MINUTES LATER...
HOLD ON THERE!
BATGIRL! HAVE YOU SEEN THE OTHERS?
THEY'VE ALREADY GONE. WE SHOULD GO, TOO.
YOU PROMISED YOU'D SURRENDER!
WE LIED.
NOW GET OUT OF MY WAY, WHILE I LOOK FOR SURVIVORS.
BETTER YET-- PITCH IN.
BARBARA GORDON?
THAT'S YOU, RIGHT? YOU'RE ALIVE?
FDGC
FDGC
FDGC
GC
RES
MORE OR LESS.
I SAW YOU ON THAT MADMAN'S BROADCAST.
HE WAS INSANE. HE THOUGHT I HAD SOMETHING TO DO WITH THAT EQUALLY BIZARRE BATMAN CREATURE.
HE REALLY SEEMED TO BELIEVE MY TECH COMPANY WAS THE BATMAN'S SECRET LAIR.

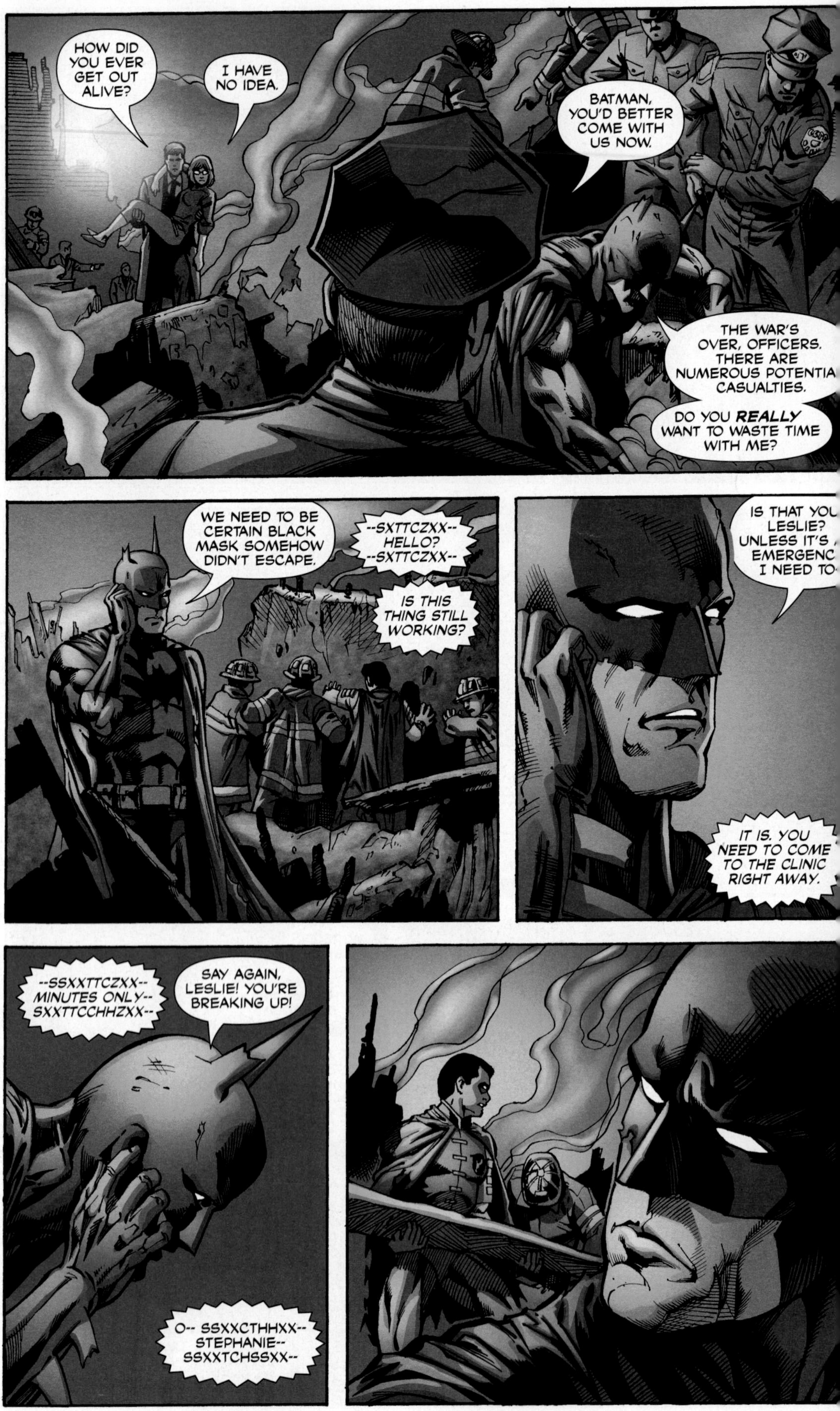
HOW DID YOU EVER GET OUT ALIVE?
I HAVE NO IDEA.
BATMAN, YOU'D BETTER COME WITH US NOW.
THE WAR'S OVER, OFFICERS. THERE ARE NUMEROUS POTENTIA CASUALTIES.
DO YOU REALLY WANT TO WASTE TIME WITH ME?
WE NEED TO BE CERTAIN BLACK MASK SOMEHOW DIDN'T ESCAPE.
--SXTTCZXX-- HELLO? --SXTTCZXX--
IS THIS THING STILL WORKING?
IS THAT YOU LESLIE? UNLESS IT'S EMERGENC I NEED TO
IT IS. YOU NEED TO COME TO THE CLINIC RIGHT AWAY.
--SSXXTTCZXX-- MINUTES ONLY-- SXXTTCCHHZXX--
SAY AGAIN, LESLIE! YOU'RE BREAKING UP!
O-- SSXXCTHHXX-- STEPHANIE-- SSXXTCHSSXX--

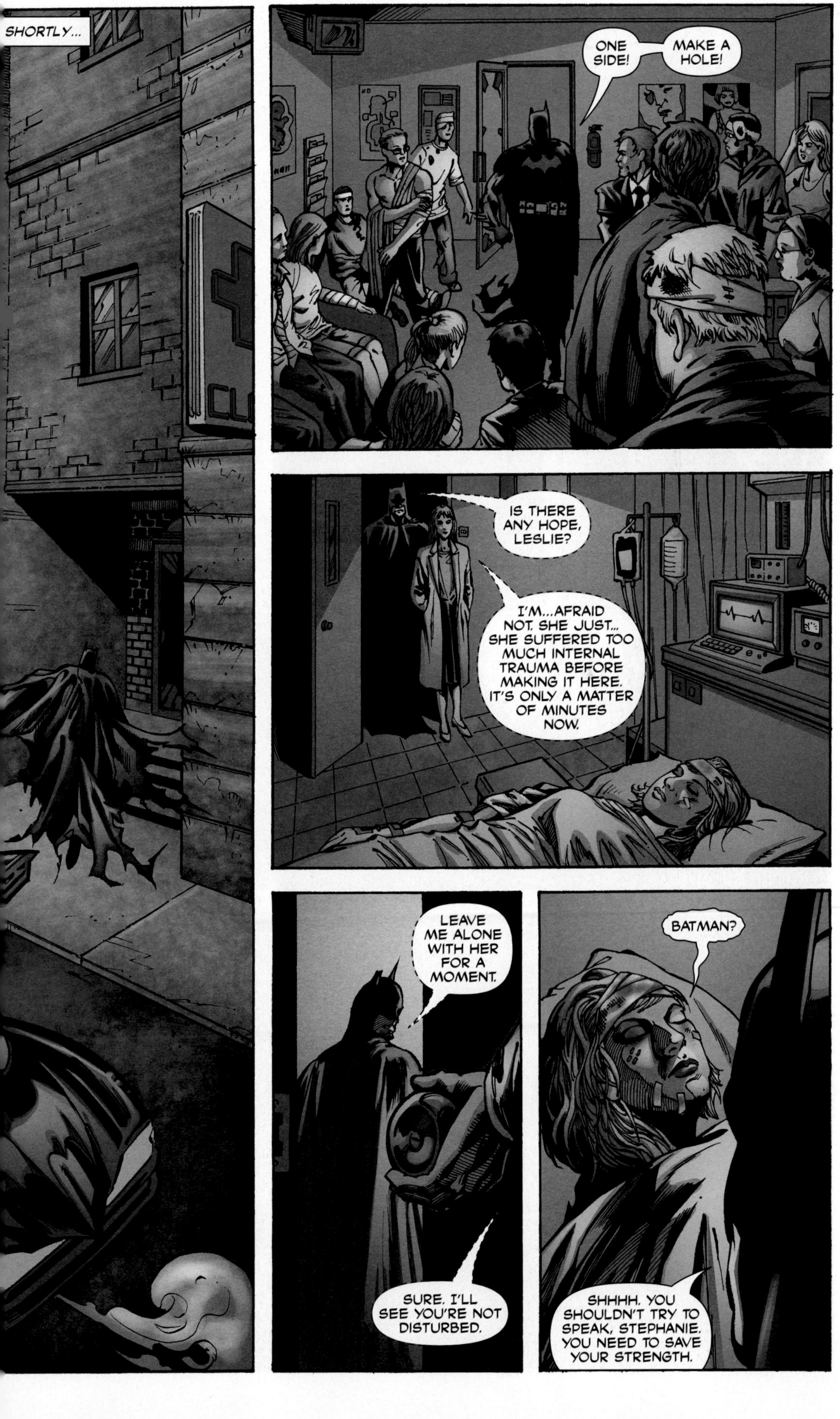
SHORTLY...
ONE SIDE!
MAKE A HOLE!
IS THERE ANY HOPE, LESLIE?
I'M...AFRAID NOT. SHE JUST... SHE SUFFERED TOO MUCH INTERNAL TRAUMA BEFORE MAKING IT HERE. IT'S ONLY A MATTER OF MINUTES NOW.
LEAVE ME ALONE WITH HER FOR A MOMENT.
SURE. I'LL SEE YOU'RE NOT DISTURBED.
BATMAN?
SHHHH. YOU SHOULDN'T TRY TO SPEAK, STEPHANIE. YOU NEED TO SAVE YOUR STRENGTH.

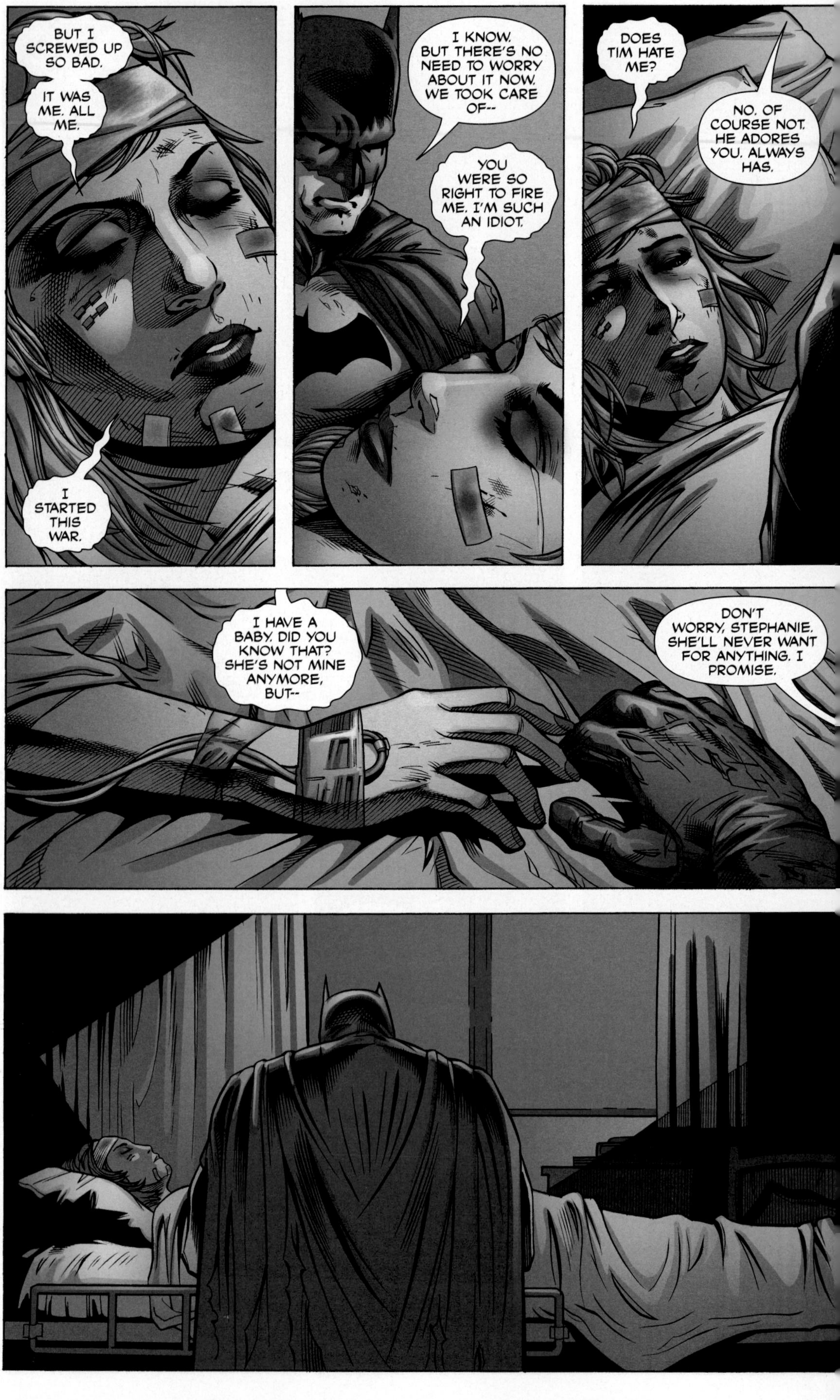
BUT I SCREWED UP SO BAD.
IT WAS ME. ALL ME.
I STARTED THIS WAR.
I KNOW. BUT THERE'S NO NEED TO WORRY ABOUT IT NOW. WE TOOK CARE OF--
YOU WERE SO RIGHT TO FIRE ME. I'M SUCH AN IDIOT.
DOES TIM HATE ME?
NO. OF COURSE NOT. HE ADORES YOU. ALWAYS HAS.
I HAVE A BABY. DID YOU KNOW THAT? SHE'S NOT MINE ANYMORE, BUT--
DON'T WORRY, STEPHANIE. SHE'LL NEVER WANT FOR ANYTHING. I PROMISE.

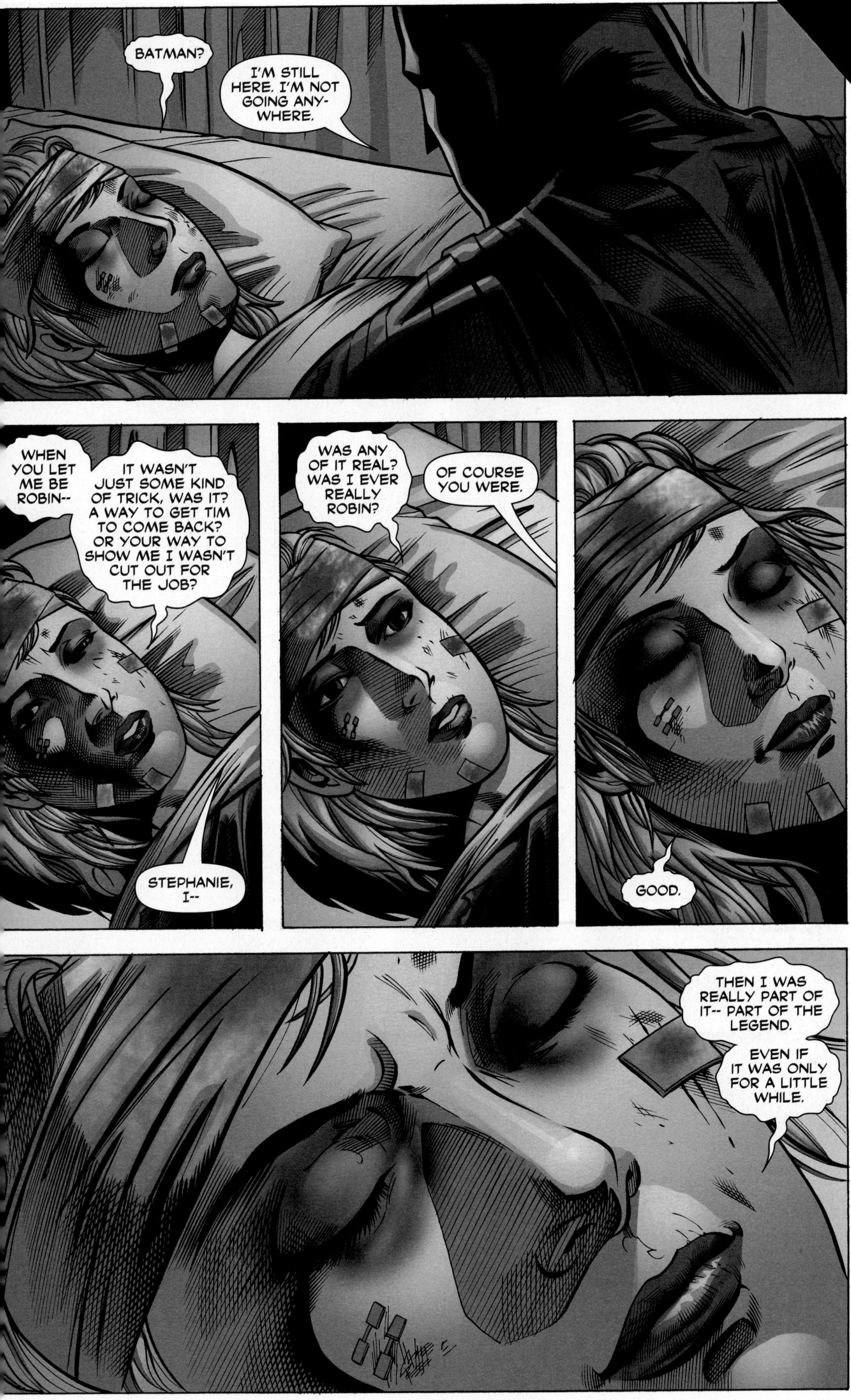
BATMAN?
I'M STILL HERE. I'M NOT GOING ANY-WHERE.
WHEN YOU LET ME BE ROBIN--
IT WASN'T JUST SOME KIND OF TRICK, WAS IT? A WAY TO GET TIM TO COME BACK? OR YOUR WAY TO SHOW ME I WASN'T CUT OUT FOR THE JOB?
STEPHANIE, I--
WAS ANY OF IT REAL? WAS I EVER REALLY ROBIN?
OF COURSE YOU WERE.
GOOD.
THEN I WAS REALLY PART OF IT-- PART OF THE LEGEND.
EVEN IF IT WAS ONLY FOR A LITTLE WHILE.

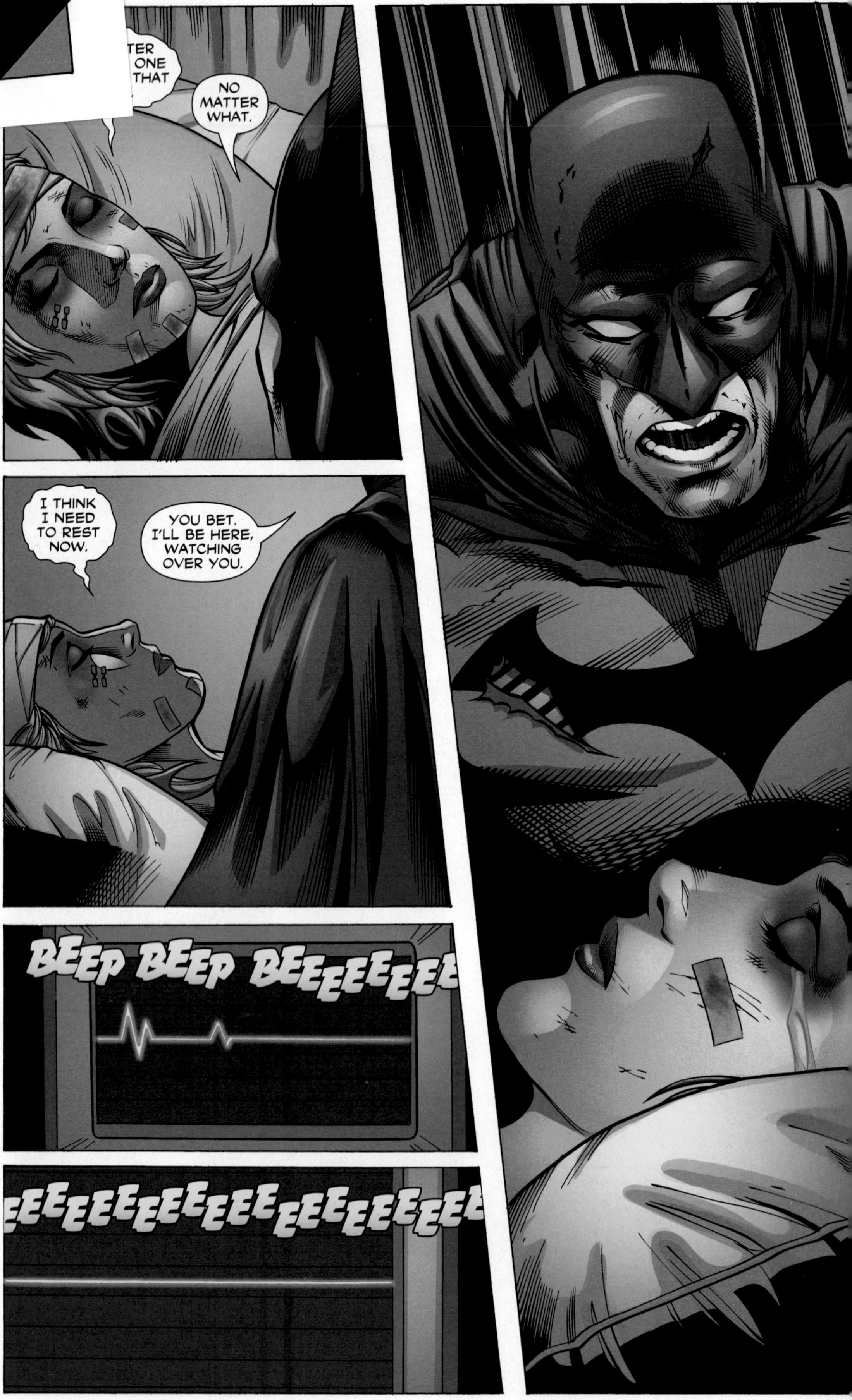

TER ONE THAT
NO MATTER WHAT.
I THINK I NEED TO REST NOW.
YOU BET. I'LL BE HERE, WATCHING OVER YOU.
BEEP BEEP BEEEEEEEE
EEEEEEEEEEEEEEEEEEEEE

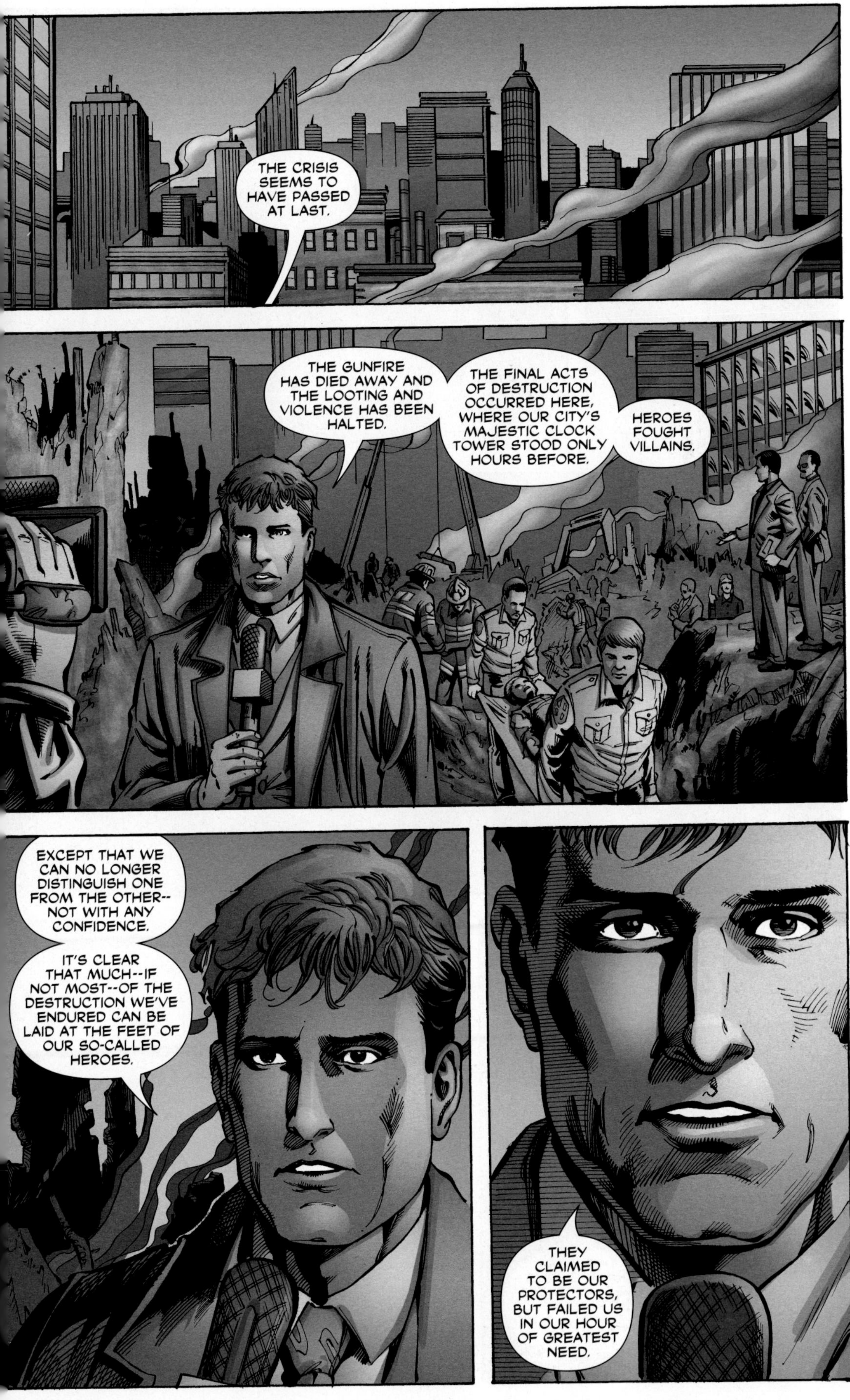

THE CRISIS SEEMS TO HAVE PASSED AT LAST.
THE GUNFIRE HAS DIED AWAY AND THE LOOTING AND VIOLENCE HAS BEEN HALTED.
THE FINAL ACTS OF DESTRUCTION OCCURRED HERE, WHERE OUR CITY'S MAJESTIC CLOCK TOWER STOOD ONLY HOURS BEFORE.
HEROES FOUGHT VILLAINS.
EXCEPT THAT WE CAN NO LONGER DISTINGUISH ONE FROM THE OTHER--NOT WITH ANY CONFIDENCE.
IT'S CLEAR THAT MUCH--IF NOT MOST--OF THE DESTRUCTION WE'VE ENDURED CAN BE LAID AT THE FEET OF OUR SO-CALLED HEROES.
THEY CLAIMED TO BE OUR PROTECTORS, BUT FAILED US IN OUR HOUR OF GREATEST NEED.

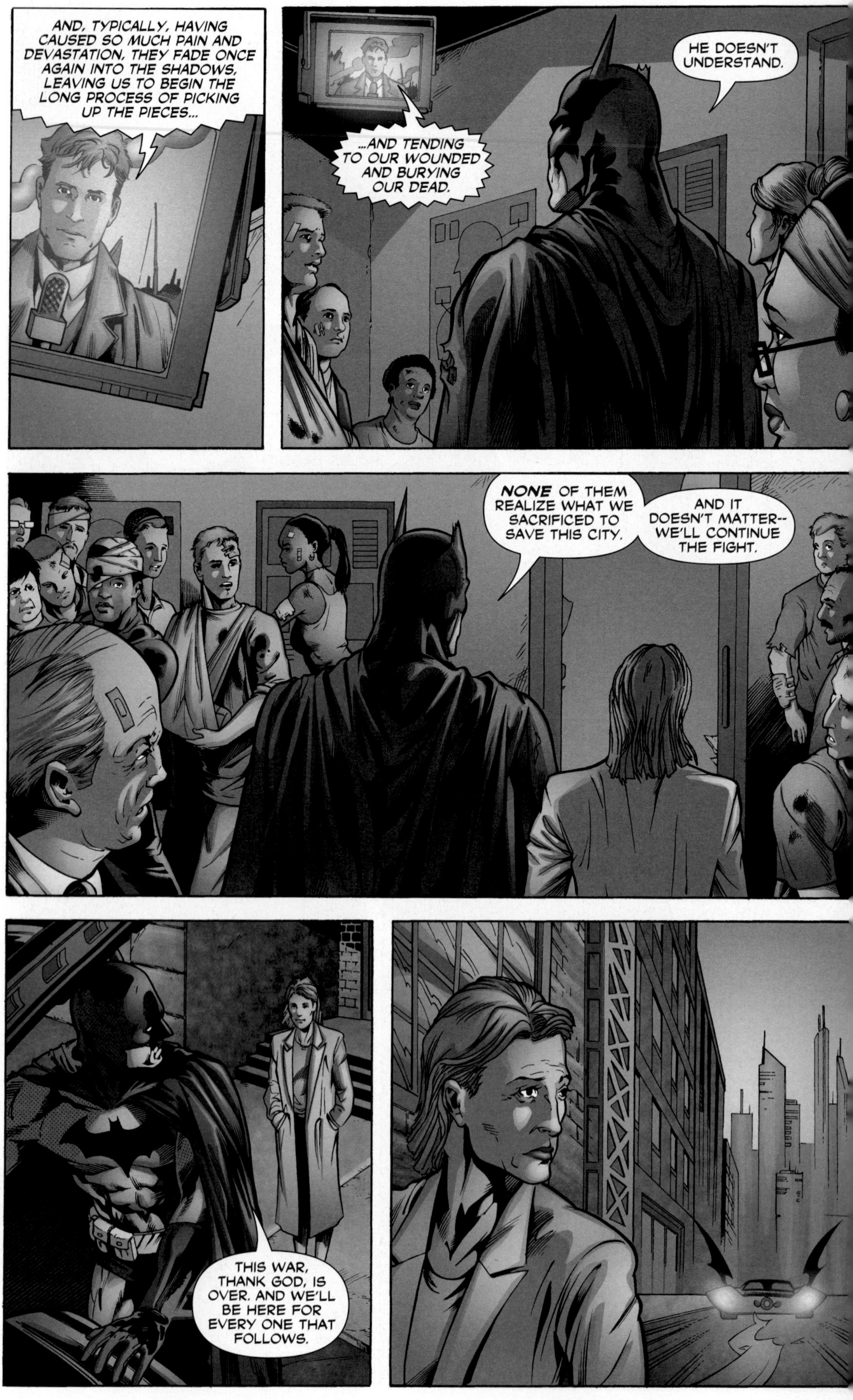
AND, TYPICALLY, HAVING CAUSED SO MUCH PAIN AND DEVASTATION, THEY FADE ONCE AGAIN INTO THE SHADOWS, LEAVING US TO BEGIN THE LONG PROCESS OF PICKING UP THE PIECES...
...AND TENDING TO OUR WOUNDED AND BURYING OUR DEAD.
HE DOESN'T UNDERSTAND.
NONE OF THEM REALIZE WHAT WE SACRIFICED TO SAVE THIS CITY.
AND IT DOESN'T MATTER-- WE'LL CONTINUE THE FIGHT.
THIS WAR, THANK GOD, IS OVER. AND WE'LL BE HERE FOR EVERY ONE THAT FOLLOWS.

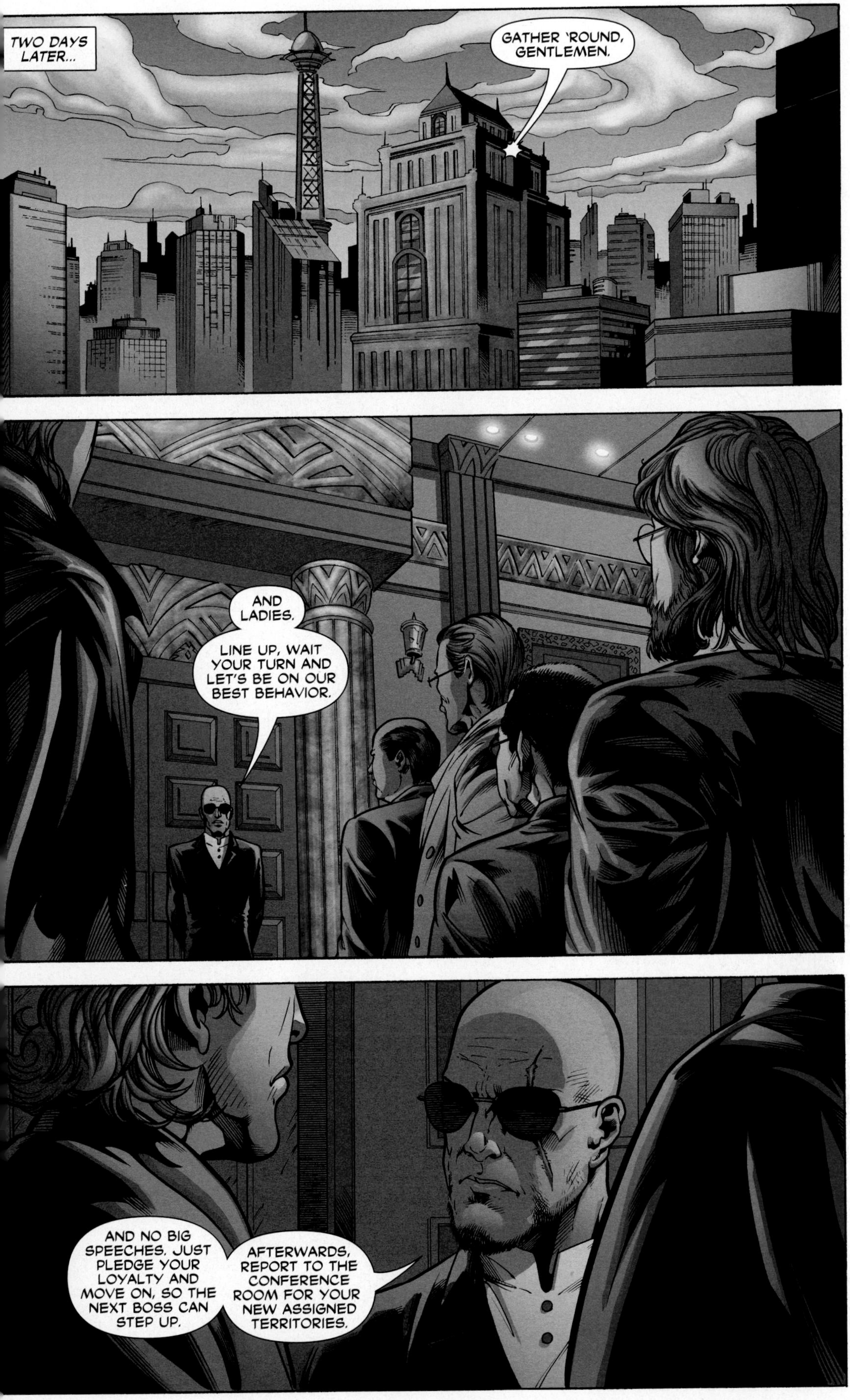
TWO DAYS LATER...
GATHER 'ROUND, GENTLEMEN.
AND LADIES.
LINE UP, WAIT YOUR TURN AND LET'S BE ON OUR BEST BEHAVIOR.
AND NO BIG SPEECHES. JUST PLEDGE YOUR LOYALTY AND MOVE ON, SO THE NEXT BOSS CAN STEP UP.
AFTERWARDS, REPORT TO THE CONFERENCE ROOM FOR YOUR NEW ASSIGNED TERRITORIES.

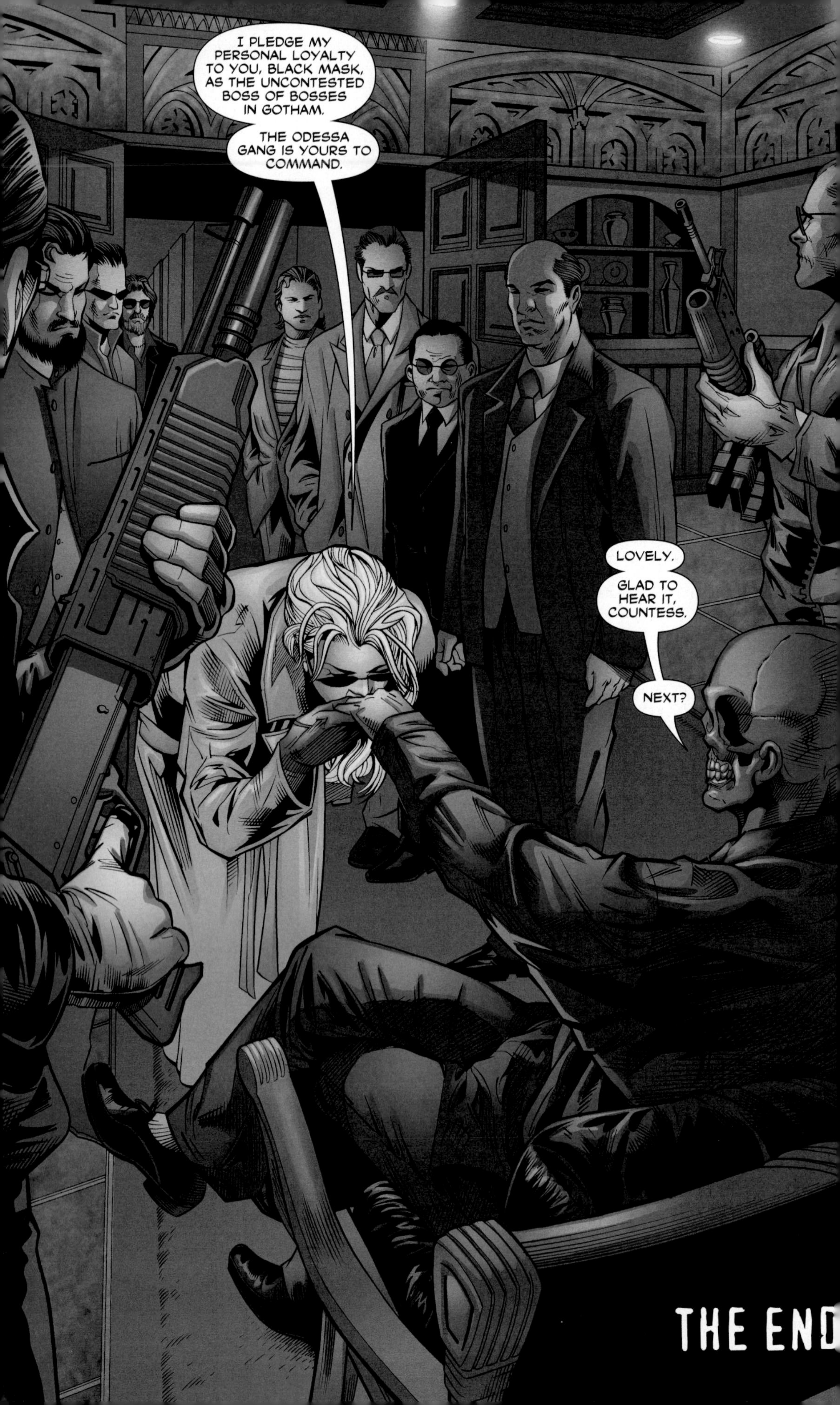
I PLEDGE MY PERSONAL LOYALTY TO YOU, BLACK MASK, AS THE UNCONTESTED BOSS OF BOSSES IN GOTHAM.
THE ODESSA GANG IS YOURS TO COMMAND.
LOVELY.
GLAD TO HEAR IT, COUNTESS.
NEXT?
THE END

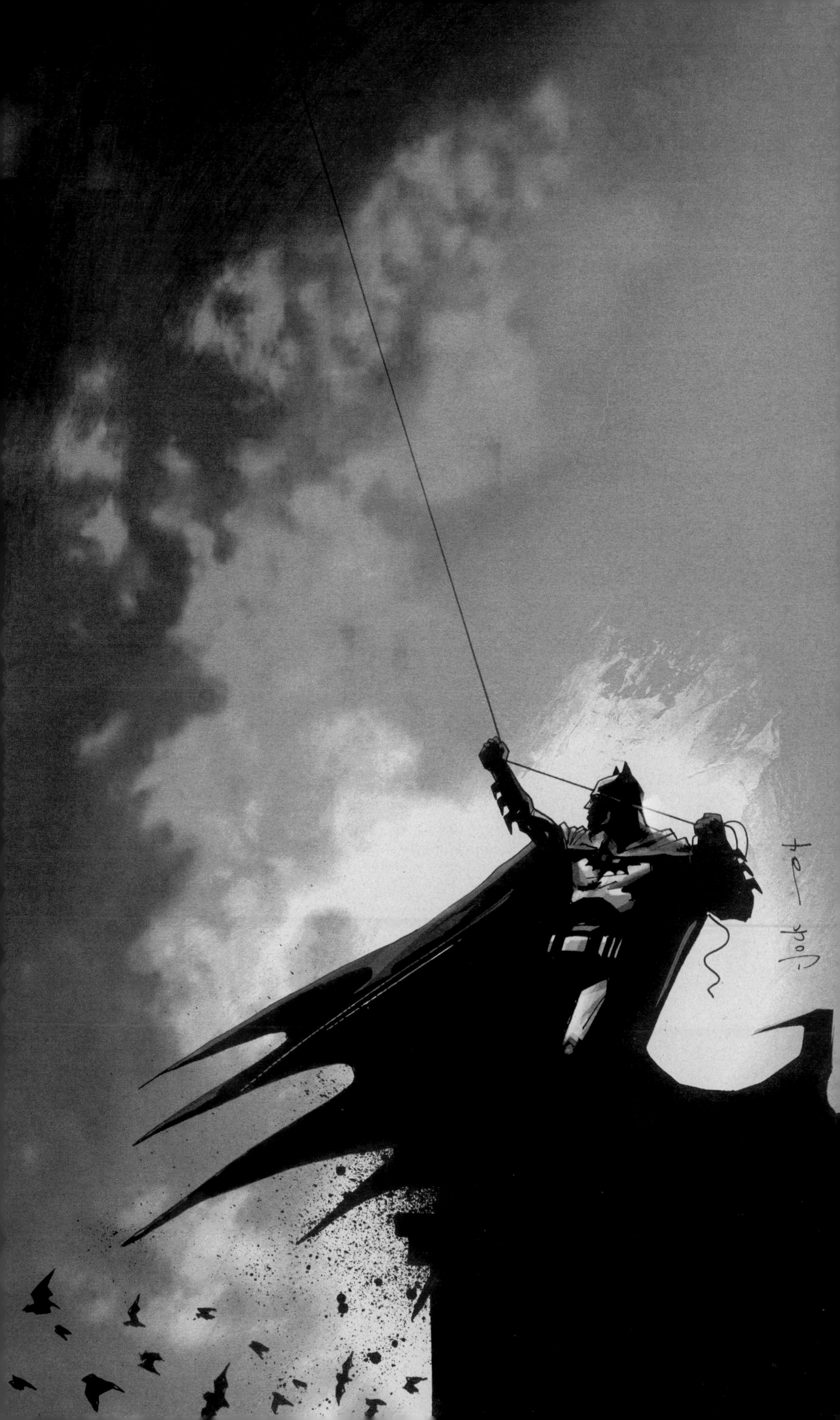

COVER ART BY
JOCK

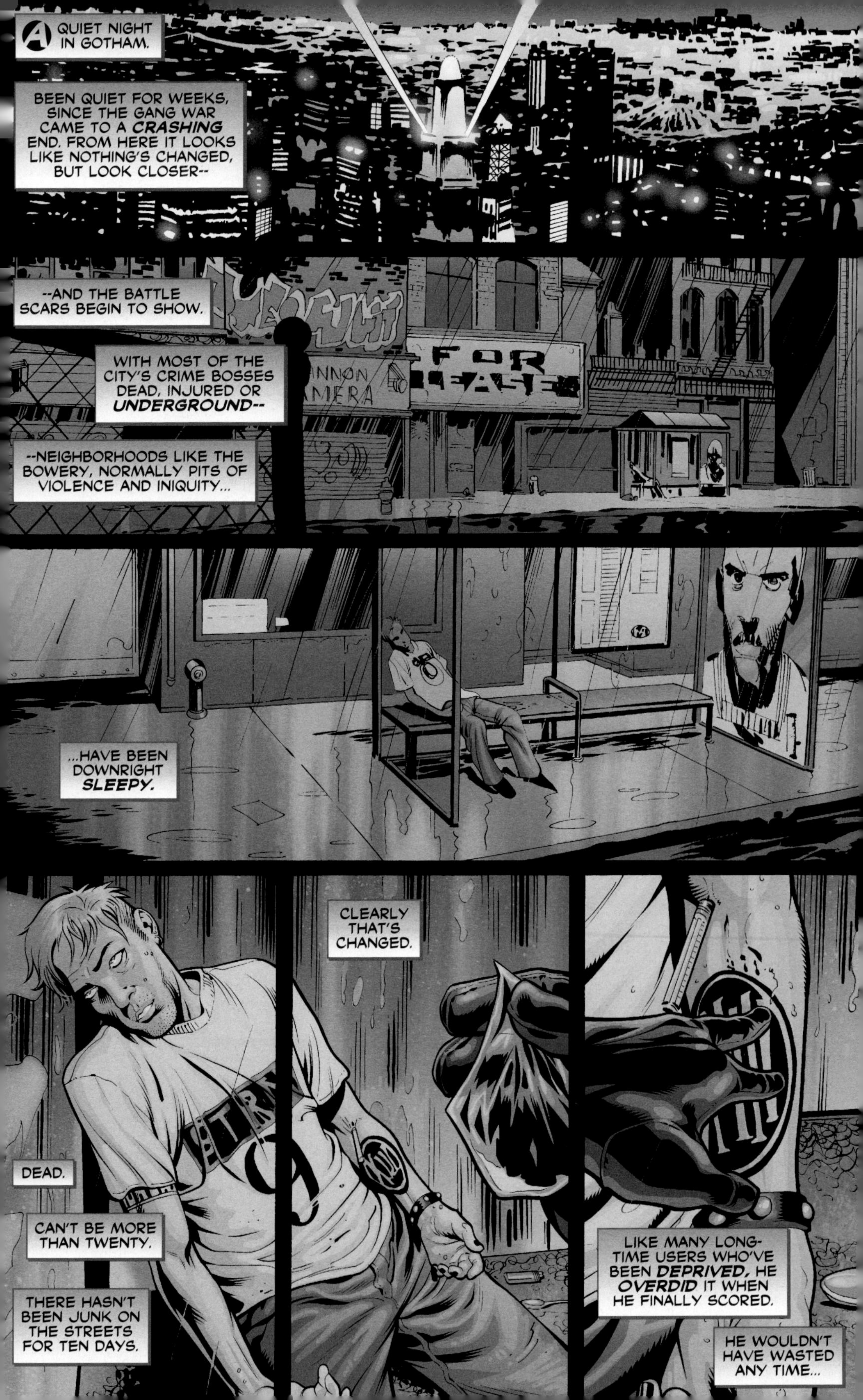
A QUIET NIGHT IN GOTHAM.
BEEN QUIET FOR WEEKS, SINCE THE GANG WAR CAME TO A CRASHING END. FROM HERE IT LOOKS LIKE NOTHING'S CHANGED, BUT LOOK CLOSER--
--AND THE BATTLE SCARS BEGIN TO SHOW.
WITH MOST OF THE CITY'S CRIME BOSSES DEAD, INJURED OR UNDERGROUND--
--NEIGHBORHOODS LIKE THE BOWERY, NORMALLY PITS OF VIOLENCE AND INIQUITY...
FOR
...HAVE BEEN DOWNRIGHT SLEEPY.
DEAD.
CAN'T BE MORE THAN TWENTY.
THERE HASN'T BEEN JUNK ON THE STREETS FOR TEN DAYS.
CLEARLY THAT'S CHANGED.
LIKE MANY LONG-TIME USERS WHO'VE BEEN DEPRIVED, HE OVERDID IT WHEN HE FINALLY SCORED.
HE WOULDN'T HAVE WASTED ANY TIME...

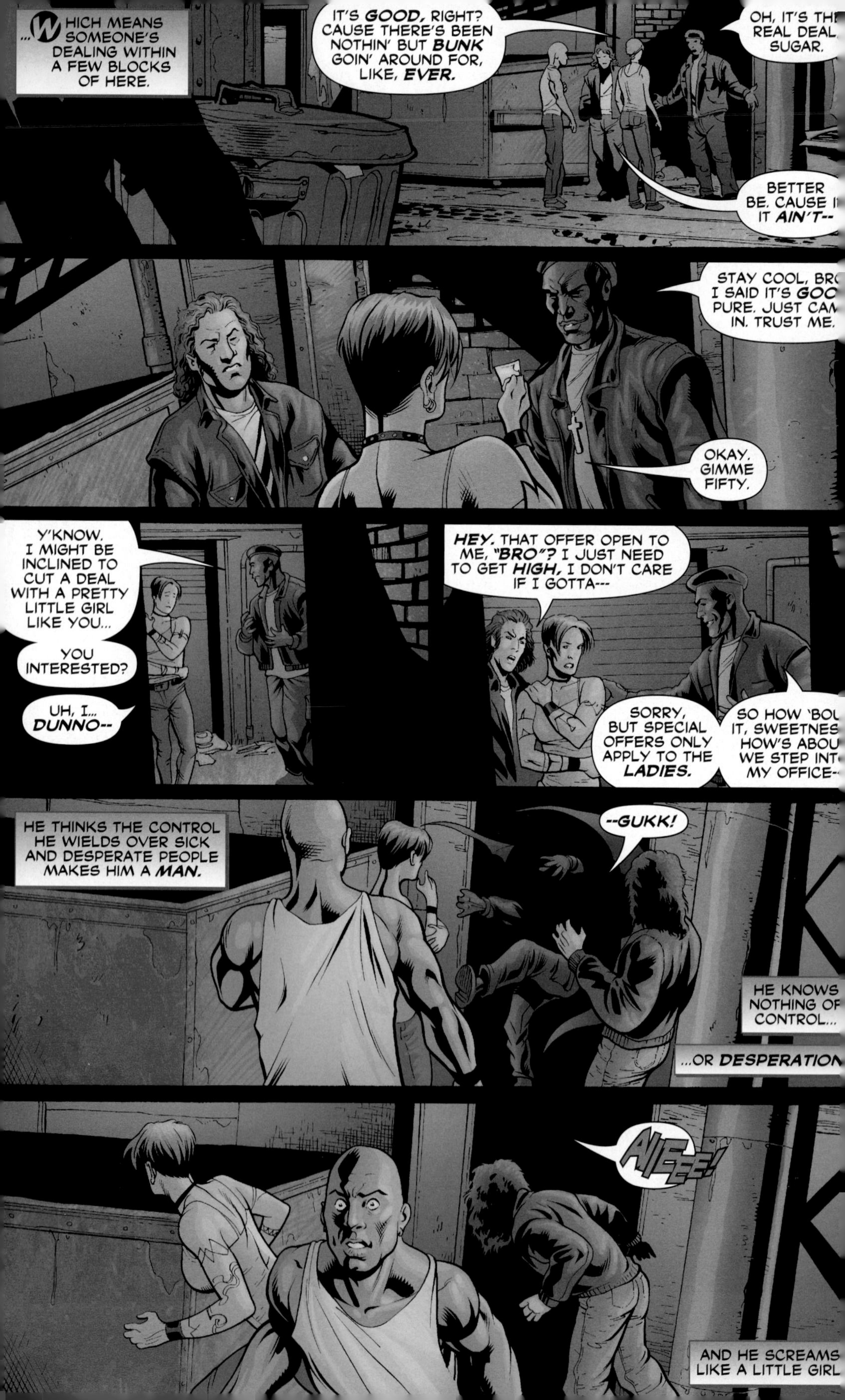

...WHICH MEANS SOMEONE'S DEALING WITHIN A FEW BLOCKS OF HERE.
IT'S GOOD, RIGHT? CAUSE THERE'S BEEN NOTHIN' BUT BUNK GOIN' AROUND FOR, LIKE, EVER.
OH, IT'S THE REAL DEAL, SUGAR.
BETTER BE. CAUSE IF IT AIN'T--
STAY COOL, BRO I SAID IT'S GOOD PURE. JUST CAME IN. TRUST ME.
OKAY. GIMME FIFTY.
Y'KNOW. I MIGHT BE INCLINED TO CUT A DEAL WITH A PRETTY LITTLE GIRL LIKE YOU...
YOU INTERESTED?
UH, I... DUNNO--
HEY. THAT OFFER OPEN TO ME, "BRO"? I JUST NEED TO GET HIGH, I DON'T CARE IF I GOTTA---
SORRY, BUT SPECIAL OFFERS ONLY APPLY TO THE LADIES.
SO HOW 'BOUT IT, SWEETNESS HOW'S ABOUT WE STEP INTO MY OFFICE--
HE THINKS THE CONTROL HE WIELDS OVER SICK AND DESPERATE PEOPLE MAKES HIM A MAN.
--GUKK!
HE KNOWS NOTHING OF CONTROL...
...OR DESPERATION
AIEEE!
AND HE SCREAMS LIKE A LITTLE GIRL

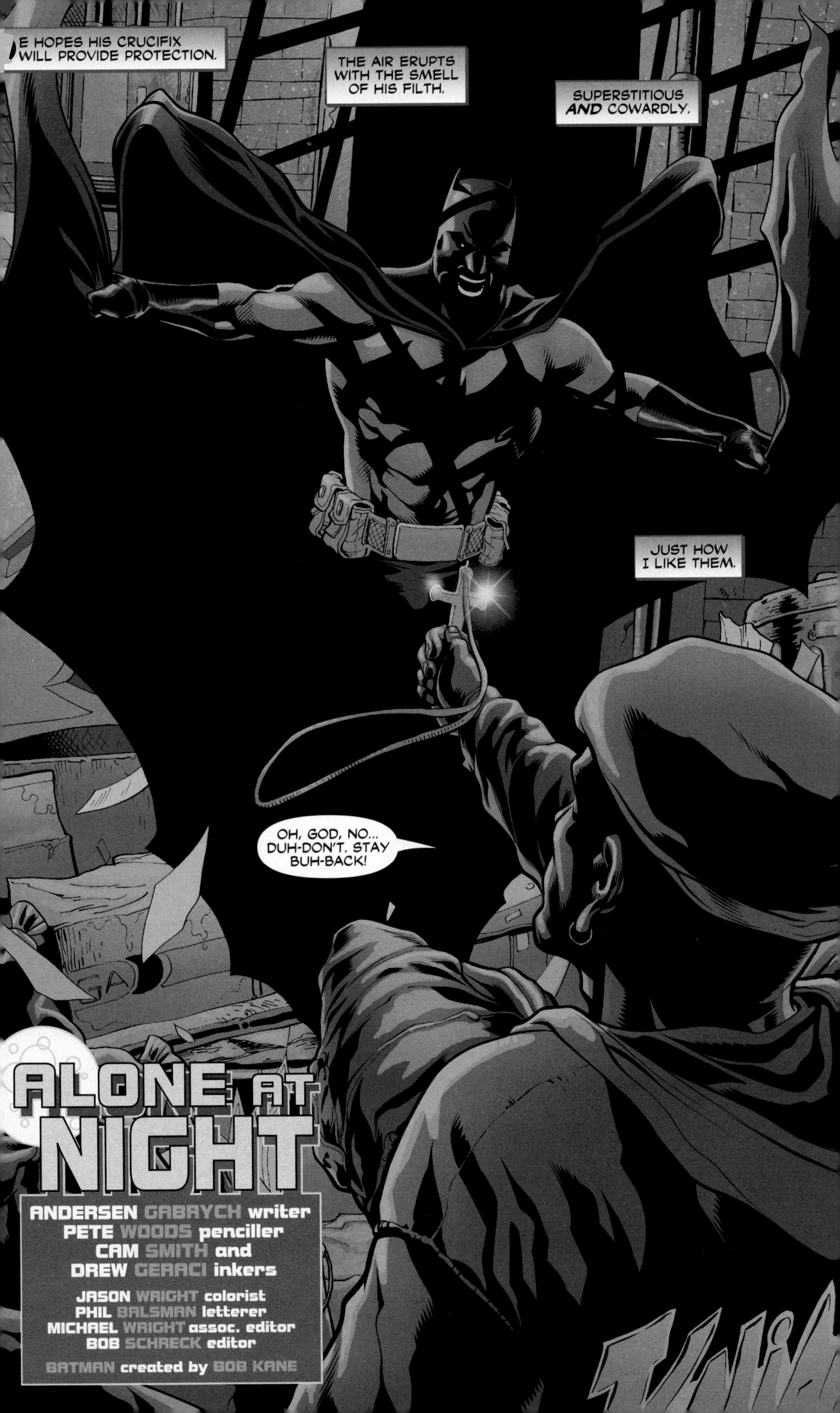
E HOPES HIS CRUCIFIX WILL PROVIDE PROTECTION.
THE AIR ERUPTS WITH THE SMELL OF HIS FILTH.
SUPERSTITIOUS AND COWARDLY.
JUST HOW I LIKE THEM.
OH, GOD, NO... DUH-DON'T. STAY BUH-BACK!
ALONE AT NIGHT
ANDERSEN GABRYCH writer
PETE WOODS penciller
CAM SMITH and
DREW GERACI inkers
JASON WRIGHT colorist
PHIL BALSMAN letterer
MICHAEL WRIGHT assoc. editor
BOB SCHRECK editor
BATMAN created by BOB KANE

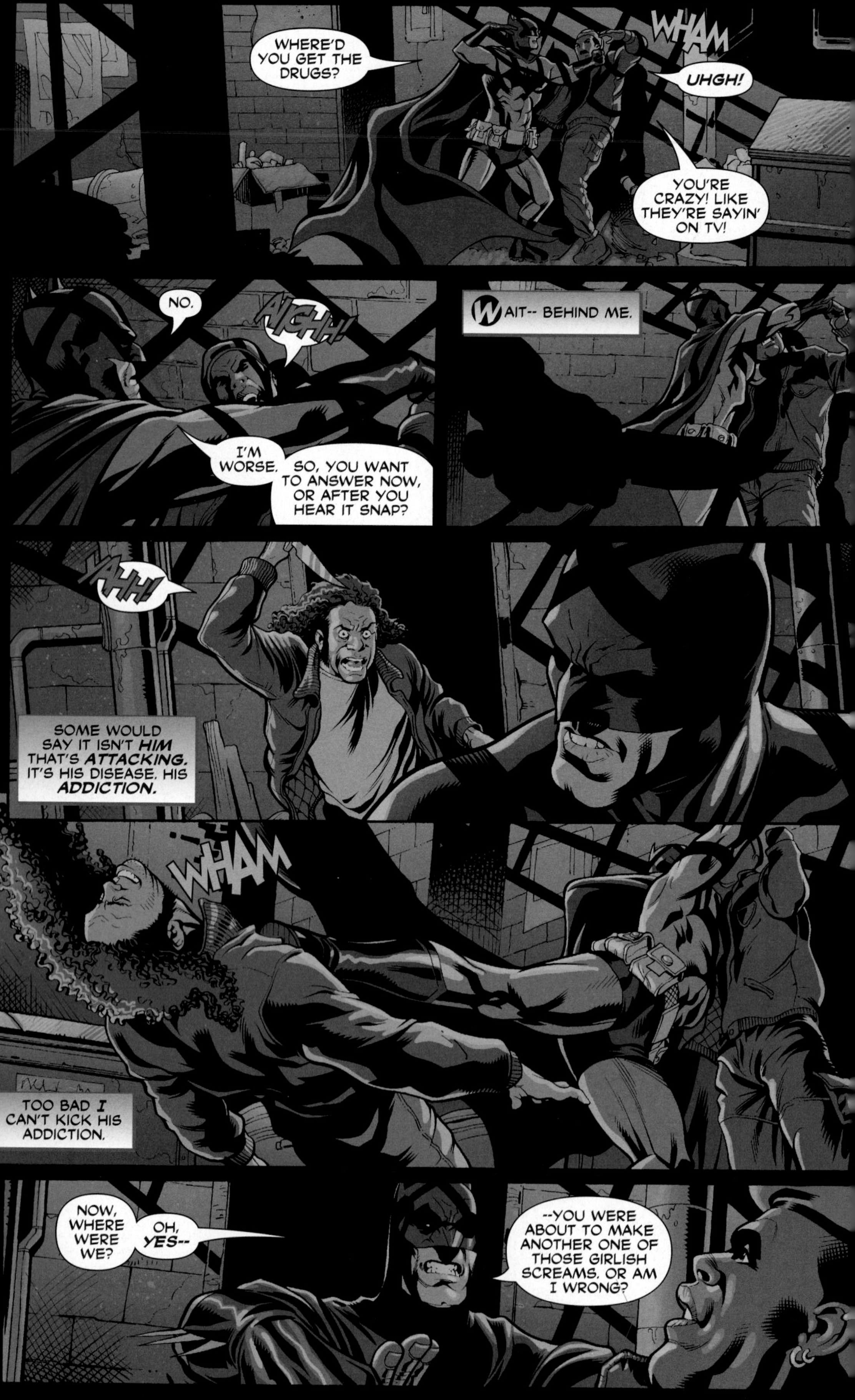
WHERE'D YOU GET THE DRUGS?
WHAM
UHGH!
YOU'RE CRAZY! LIKE THEY'RE SAYIN' ON TV!
NO.
AIGH!
I'M WORSE.
SO, YOU WANT TO ANSWER NOW, OR AFTER YOU HEAR IT SNAP?
WAIT-- BEHIND ME.
YAHH!
SOME WOULD SAY IT ISN'T HIM THAT'S ATTACKING. IT'S HIS DISEASE. HIS ADDICTION.
WHAM
TOO BAD I CAN'T KICK HIS ADDICTION.
NOW, WHERE WERE WE?
OH, YES--
--YOU WERE ABOUT TO MAKE ANOTHER ONE OF THOSE GIRLISH SCREAMS, OR AM I WRONG?

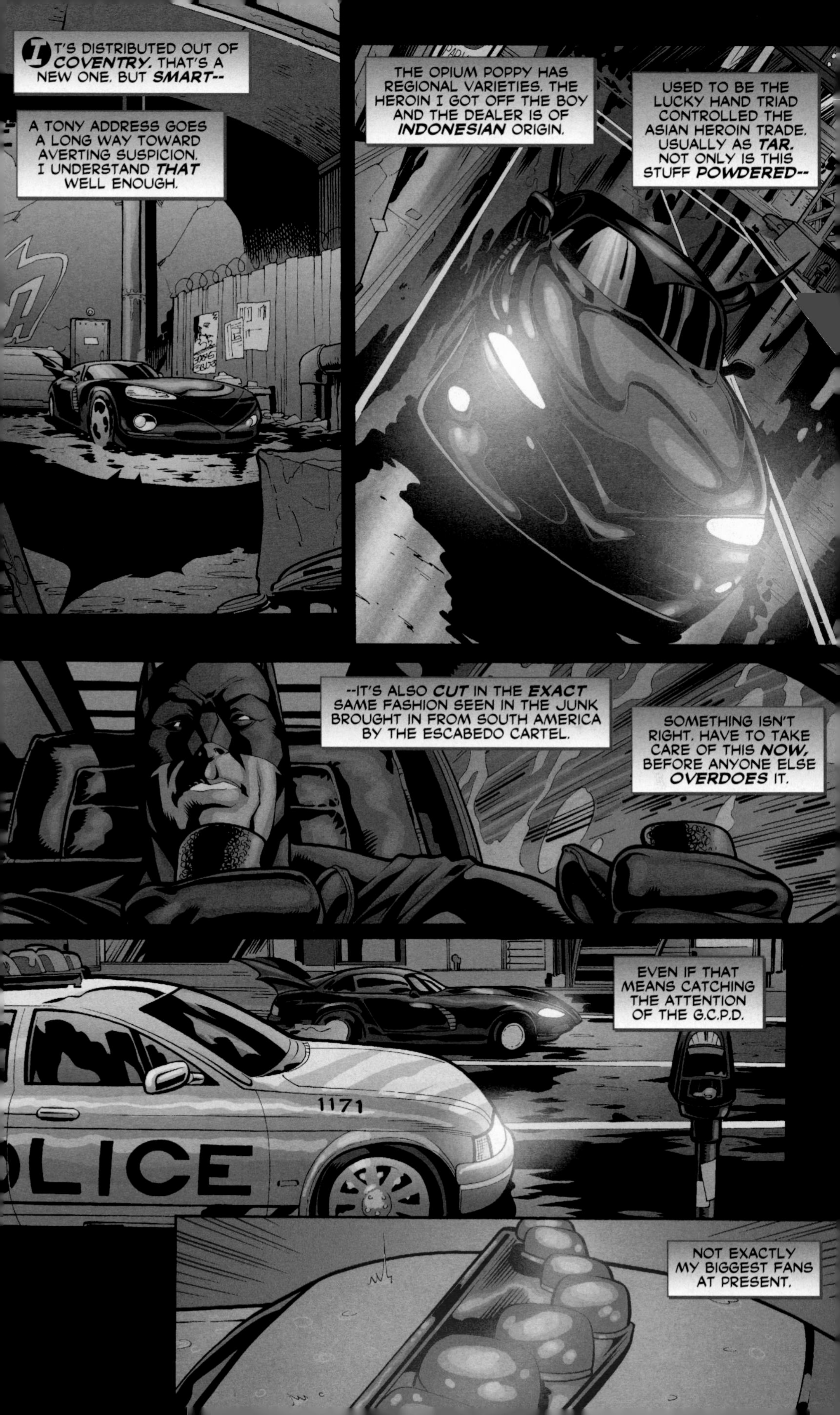
IT'S DISTRIBUTED OUT OF COVENTRY. THAT'S A NEW ONE. BUT SMART--
A TONY ADDRESS GOES A LONG WAY TOWARD AVERTING SUSPICION. I UNDERSTAND THAT WELL ENOUGH.
THE OPIUM POPPY HAS REGIONAL VARIETIES. THE HEROIN I GOT OFF THE BOY AND THE DEALER IS OF INDONESIAN ORIGIN.
USED TO BE THE LUCKY HAND TRIAD CONTROLLED THE ASIAN HEROIN TRADE. USUALLY AS TAR. NOT ONLY IS THIS STUFF POWDERED--
--IT'S ALSO CUT IN THE EXACT SAME FASHION SEEN IN THE JUNK BROUGHT IN FROM SOUTH AMERICA BY THE ESCABEDO CARTEL.
SOMETHING ISN'T RIGHT. HAVE TO TAKE CARE OF THIS NOW, BEFORE ANYONE ELSE OVERDOES IT.
EVEN IF THAT MEANS CATCHING THE ATTENTION OF THE G.C.P.D.
1171
OLICE
NOT EXACTLY MY BIGGEST FANS AT PRESENT.

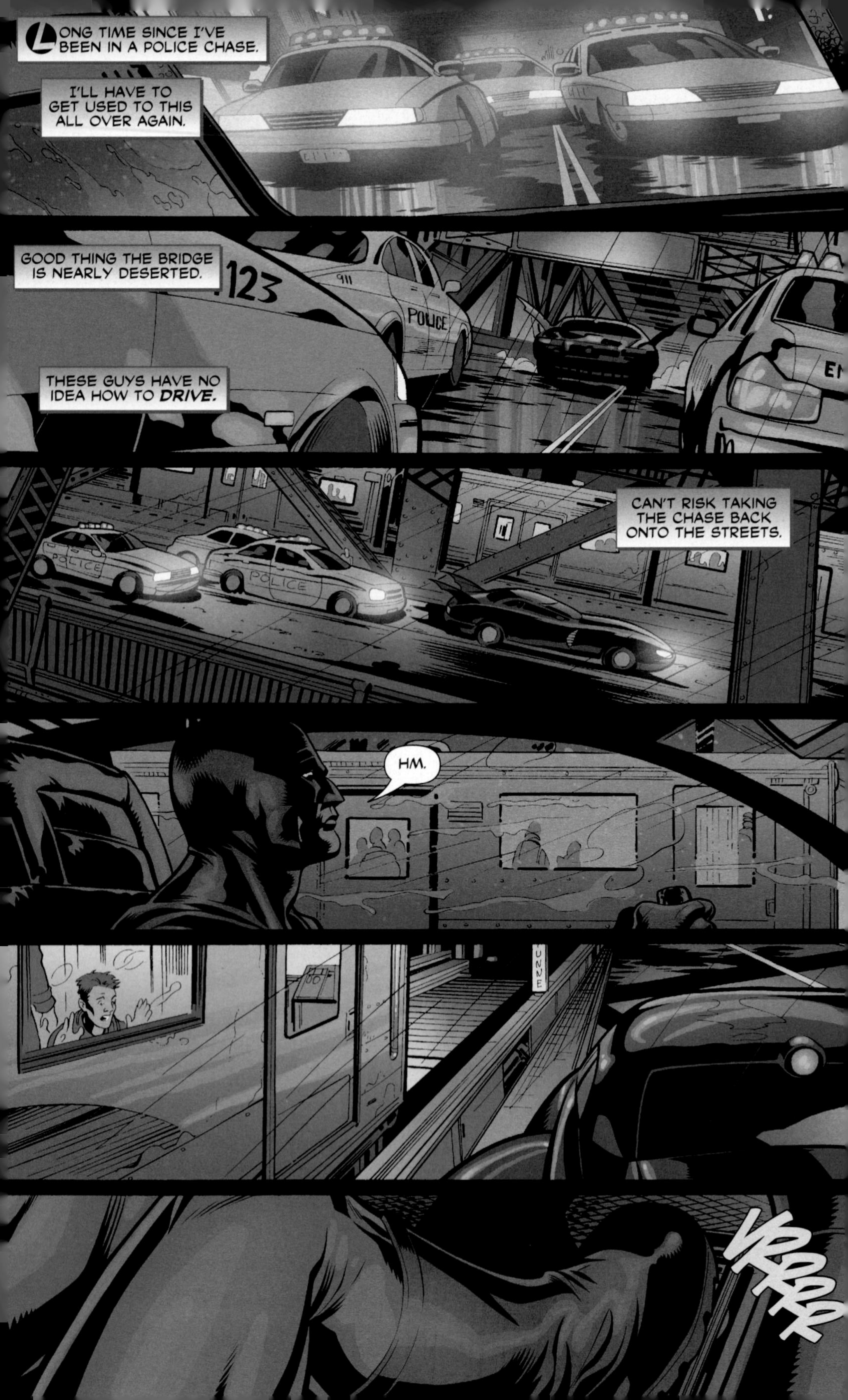
LONG TIME SINCE I'VE BEEN IN A POLICE CHASE.
I'LL HAVE TO GET USED TO THIS ALL OVER AGAIN.
GOOD THING THE BRIDGE IS NEARLY DESERTED.
123
911
POLICE
THESE GUYS HAVE NO IDEA HOW TO DRIVE.
POLICE
POLICE
CAN'T RISK TAKING THE CHASE BACK ONTO THE STREETS.
HM.
VRRRR

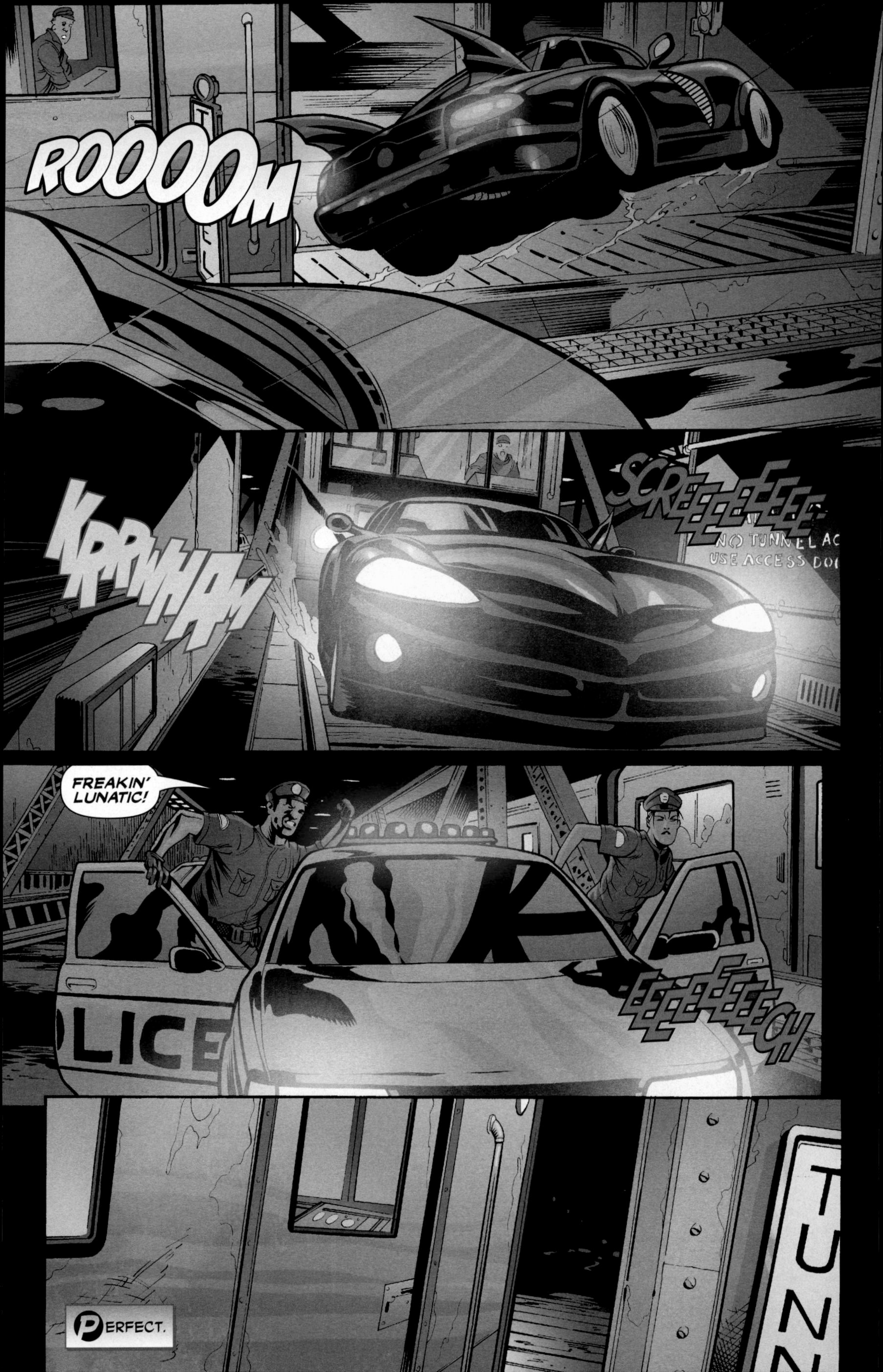
ROOOOM
KRRWHAM
SCREEEEEEEEE-
NO TUNNEL AC
USE ACCESS DO
FREAKIN' LUNATIC!
POLICE
EEEEEEEECH
PERFECT.

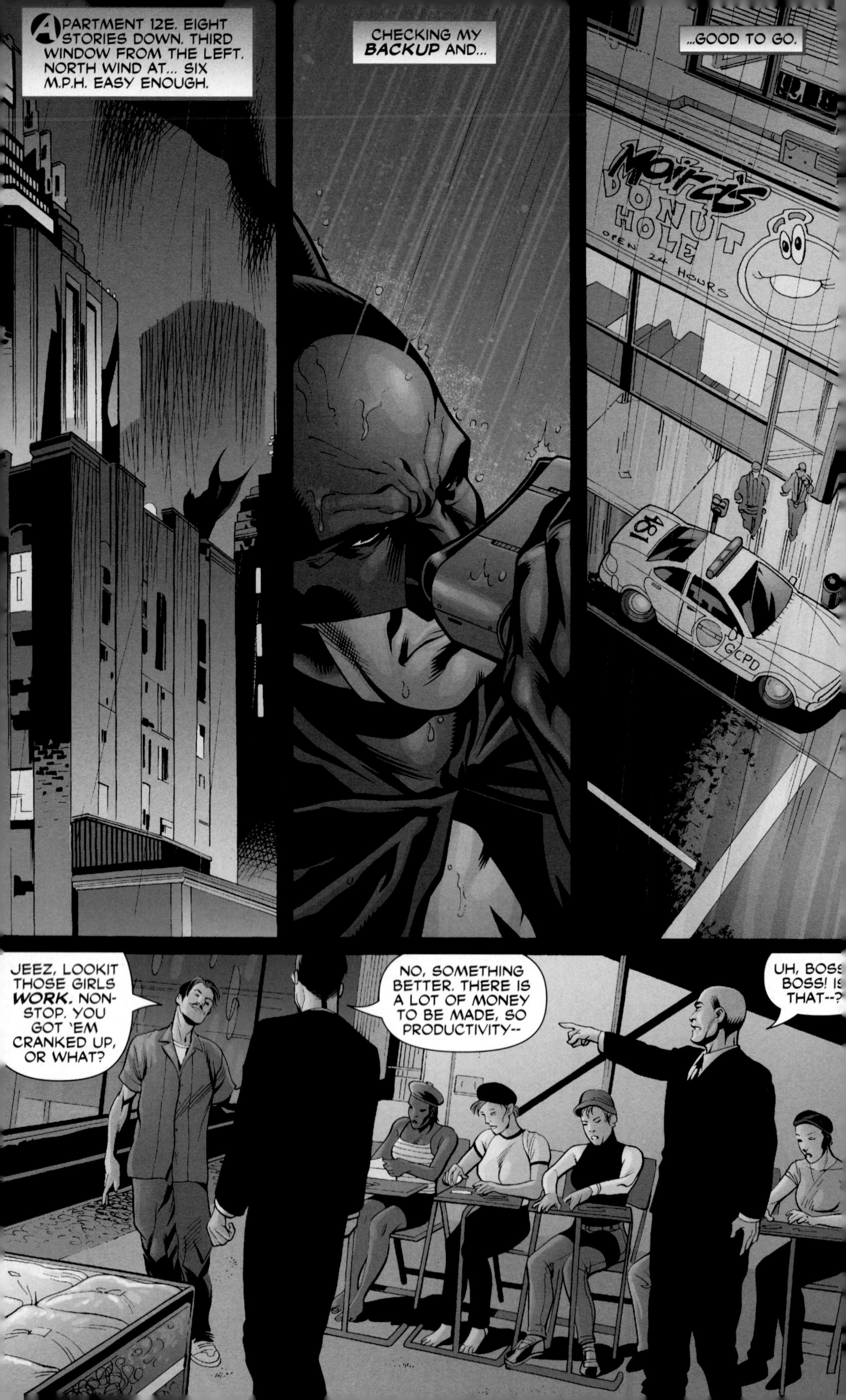
APARTMENT 12E. EIGHT STORIES DOWN. THIRD WINDOW FROM THE LEFT. NORTH WIND AT... SIX M.P.H. EASY ENOUGH.
CHECKING MY BACKUP AND...
...GOOD TO GO.
MAIRA'S DONUT HOLE
OPEN 24 HOURS
481
GCPD
JEEZ, LOOKIT THOSE GIRLS WORK. NON-STOP. YOU GOT 'EM CRANKED UP, OR WHAT?
NO, SOMETHING BETTER. THERE IS A LOT OF MONEY TO BE MADE, SO PRODUCTIVITY--
UH, BOSS BOSS! IS THAT--?

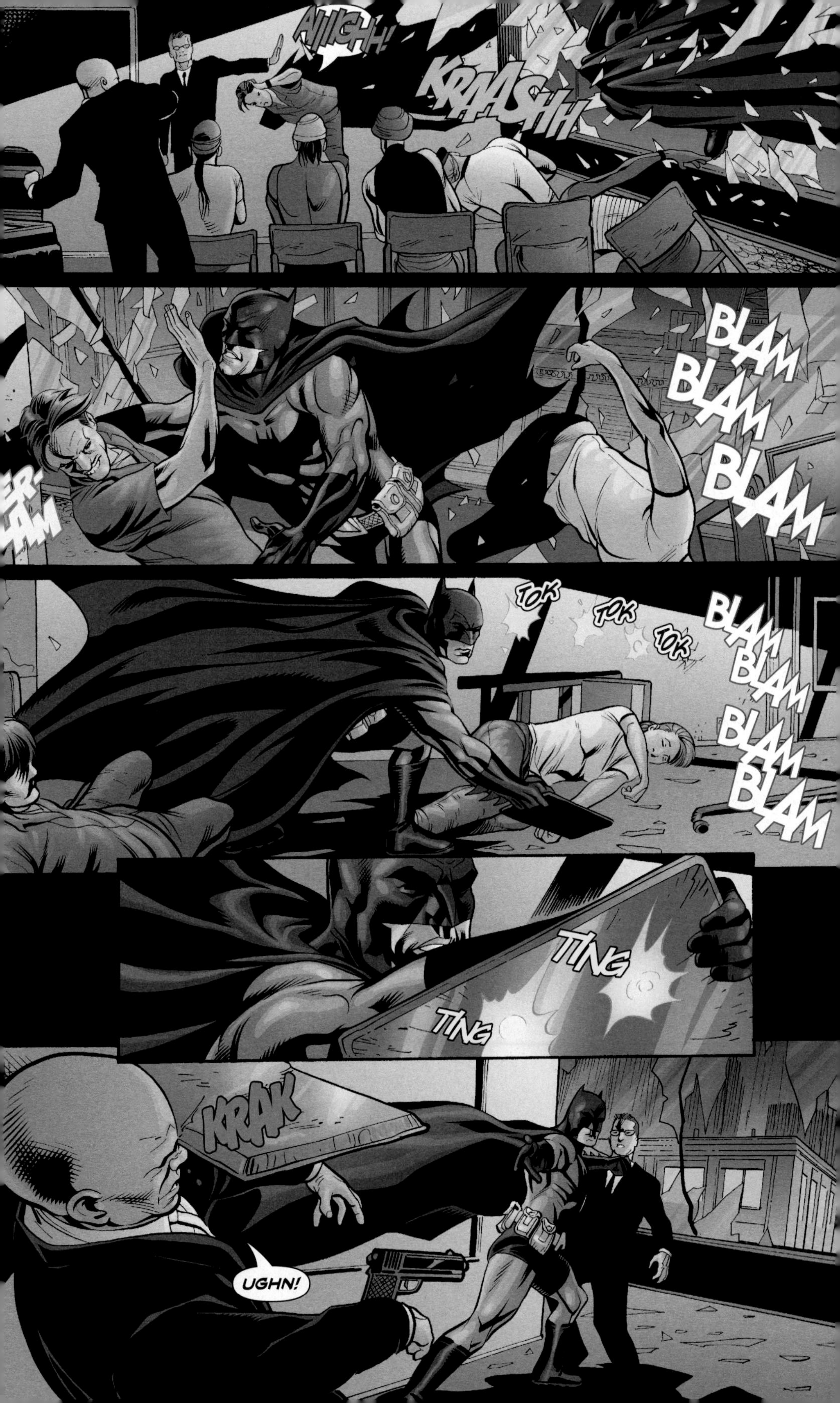
AIIIGH!
KRAASHH
BLAM
BLAM
BLAM
TOK
TOK
TOK
BLAM
BLAM
BLAM
BLAM
TING
TING
KRAK
UGHN!

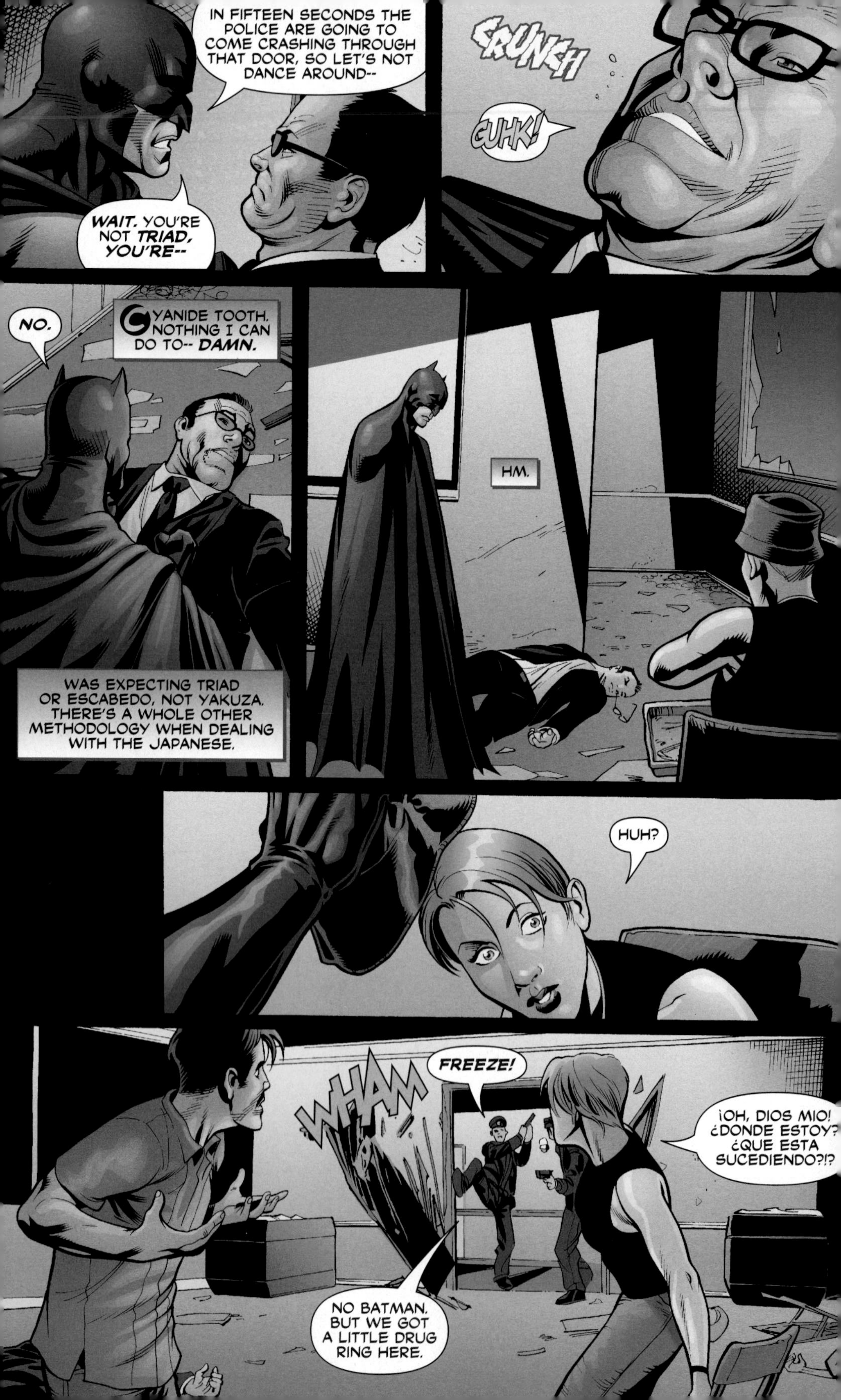
IN FIFTEEN SECONDS THE POLICE ARE GOING TO COME CRASHING THROUGH THAT DOOR, SO LET'S NOT DANCE AROUND--
WAIT. YOU'RE NOT TRIAD, YOU'RE--
CRUNCH
GUHK!
NO.
CYANIDE TOOTH. NOTHING I CAN DO TO-- DAMN.
WAS EXPECTING TRIAD OR ESCABEDO, NOT YAKUZA. THERE'S A WHOLE OTHER METHODOLOGY WHEN DEALING WITH THE JAPANESE.
HM.
HUH?
WHAM
FREEZE!
¡OH, DIOS MIO! ¿DONDE ESTOY? ¿QUE ESTA SUCEDIENDO?!?
NO BATMAN. BUT WE GOT A LITTLE DRUG RING HERE.

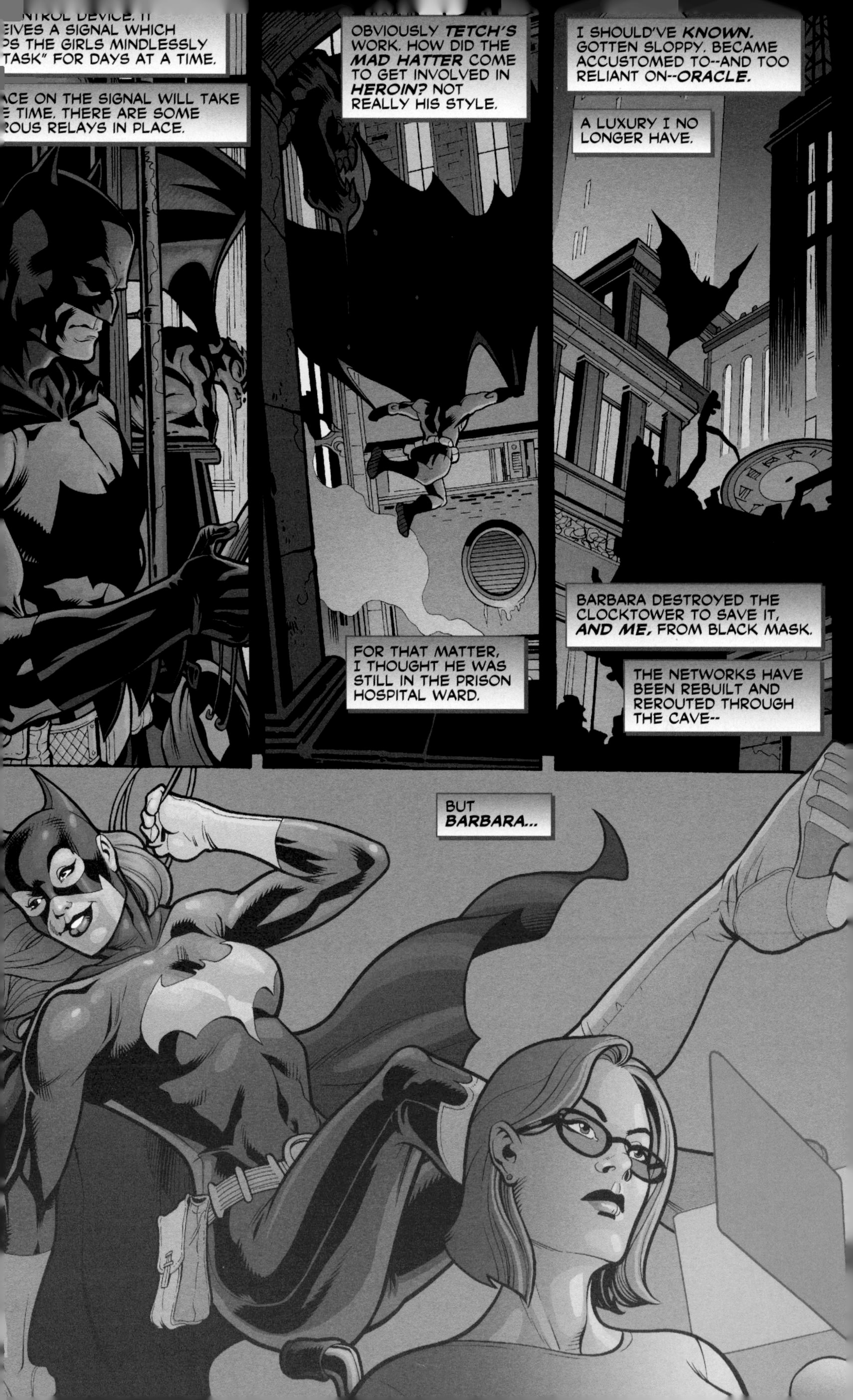

EIVES A SIGNAL WHICH
PS THE GIRLS MINDLESSLY
TASK" FOR DAYS AT A TIME.
ACE ON THE SIGNAL WILL TAKE
E TIME. THERE ARE SOME
ROUS RELAYS IN PLACE.
OBVIOUSLY TETCH'S WORK. HOW DID THE MAD HATTER COME TO GET INVOLVED IN HEROIN? NOT REALLY HIS STYLE.
FOR THAT MATTER, I THOUGHT HE WAS STILL IN THE PRISON HOSPITAL WARD.
I SHOULD'VE KNOWN. GOTTEN SLOPPY. BECAME ACCUSTOMED TO--AND TOO RELIANT ON--ORACLE.
A LUXURY I NO LONGER HAVE.
BARBARA DESTROYED THE CLOCKTOWER TO SAVE IT, AND ME, FROM BLACK MASK.
THE NETWORKS HAVE BEEN REBUILT AND REROUTED THROUGH THE CAVE--
BUT BARBARA...

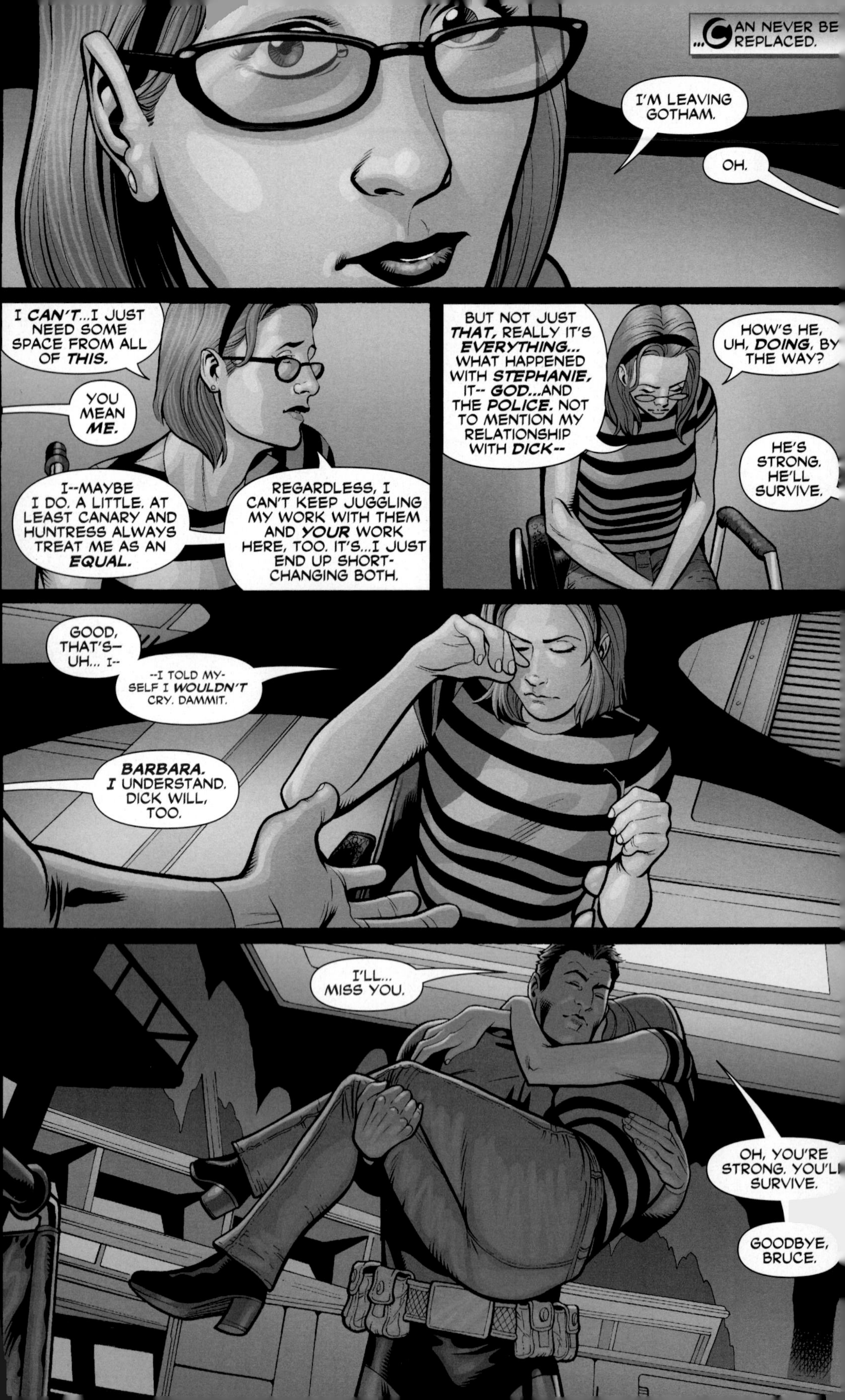
...CAN NEVER BE REPLACED.
I'M LEAVING GOTHAM.
OH.
I CAN'T...I JUST NEED SOME SPACE FROM ALL OF THIS.
YOU MEAN ME.
I--MAYBE I DO. A LITTLE. AT LEAST CANARY AND HUNTRESS ALWAYS TREAT ME AS AN EQUAL.
REGARDLESS, I CAN'T KEEP JUGGLING MY WORK WITH THEM AND YOUR WORK HERE, TOO. IT'S...I JUST END UP SHORT-CHANGING BOTH.
BUT NOT JUST THAT, REALLY IT'S EVERYTHING... WHAT HAPPENED WITH STEPHANIE, IT-- GOD...AND THE POLICE. NOT TO MENTION MY RELATIONSHIP WITH DICK--
HOW'S HE, UH, DOING, BY THE WAY?
HE'S STRONG. HE'LL SURVIVE.
GOOD, THAT'S-- UH... I--
--I TOLD MY-SELF I WOULDN'T CRY. DAMMIT.
BARBARA. I UNDERSTAND. DICK WILL, TOO.
I'LL... MISS YOU.
OH, YOU'RE STRONG. YOU'LL SURVIVE.
GOODBYE, BRUCE.

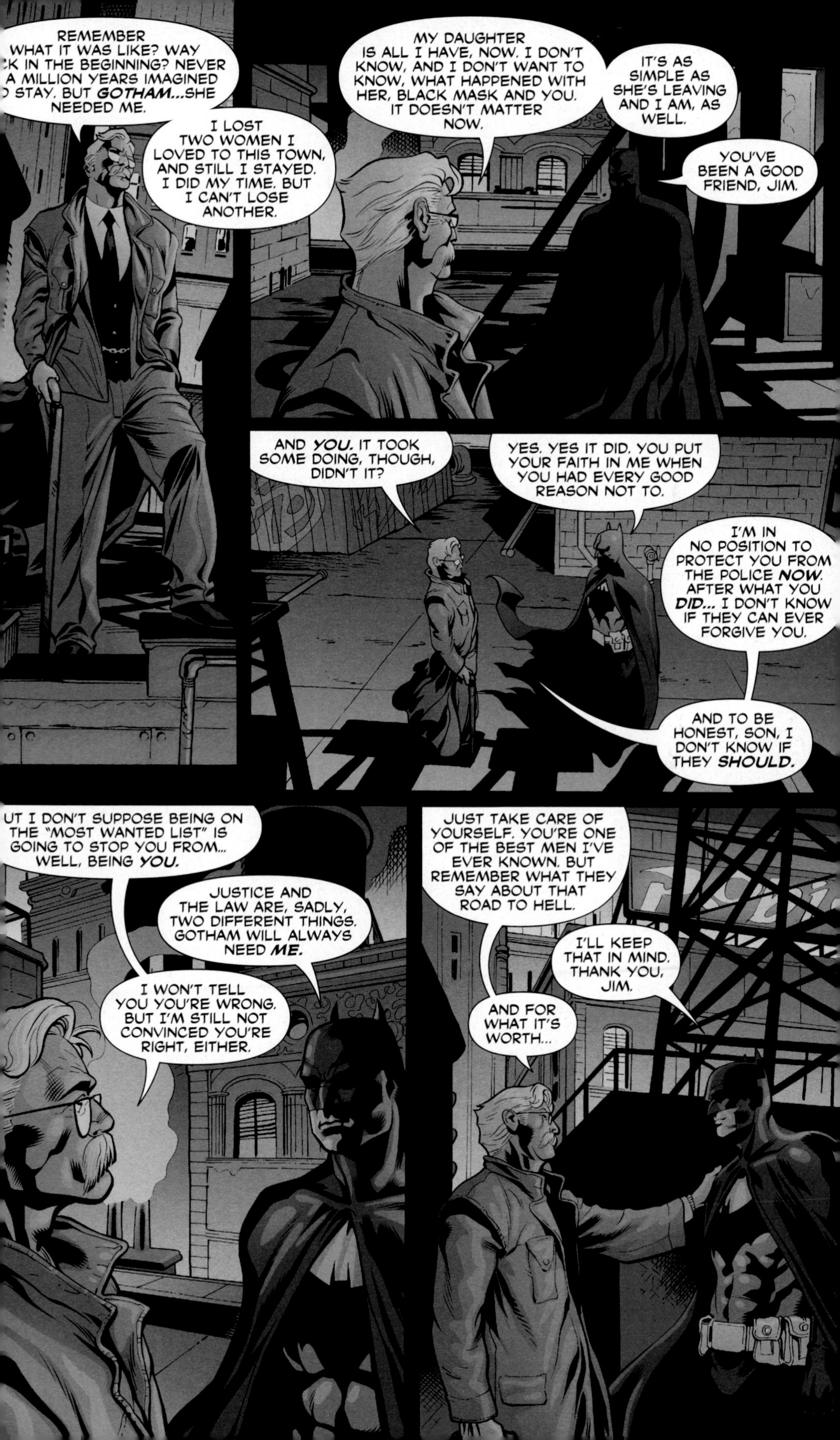

REMEMBER WHAT IT WAS LIKE? WAY CK IN THE BEGINNING? NEVER A MILLION YEARS IMAGINED STAY. BUT GOTHAM...SHE NEEDED ME.
I LOST TWO WOMEN I LOVED TO THIS TOWN, AND STILL I STAYED. I DID MY TIME. BUT I CAN'T LOSE ANOTHER.
MY DAUGHTER IS ALL I HAVE, NOW. I DON'T KNOW, AND I DON'T WANT TO KNOW, WHAT HAPPENED WITH HER, BLACK MASK AND YOU. IT DOESN'T MATTER NOW.
IT'S AS SIMPLE AS SHE'S LEAVING AND I AM, AS WELL.
YOU'VE BEEN A GOOD FRIEND, JIM.
AND YOU. IT TOOK SOME DOING, THOUGH, DIDN'T IT?
YES. YES IT DID. YOU PUT YOUR FAITH IN ME WHEN YOU HAD EVERY GOOD REASON NOT TO.
I'M IN NO POSITION TO PROTECT YOU FROM THE POLICE NOW. AFTER WHAT YOU DID... I DON'T KNOW IF THEY CAN EVER FORGIVE YOU.
AND TO BE HONEST, SON, I DON'T KNOW IF THEY SHOULD.
UT I DON'T SUPPOSE BEING ON THE "MOST WANTED LIST" IS GOING TO STOP YOU FROM... WELL, BEING YOU.
JUSTICE AND THE LAW ARE, SADLY, TWO DIFFERENT THINGS. GOTHAM WILL ALWAYS NEED ME.
I WON'T TELL YOU YOU'RE WRONG. BUT I'M STILL NOT CONVINCED YOU'RE RIGHT, EITHER.
JUST TAKE CARE OF YOURSELF. YOU'RE ONE OF THE BEST MEN I'VE EVER KNOWN. BUT REMEMBER WHAT THEY SAY ABOUT THAT ROAD TO HELL.
AND FOR WHAT IT'S WORTH...
I'LL KEEP THAT IN MIND. THANK YOU, JIM.

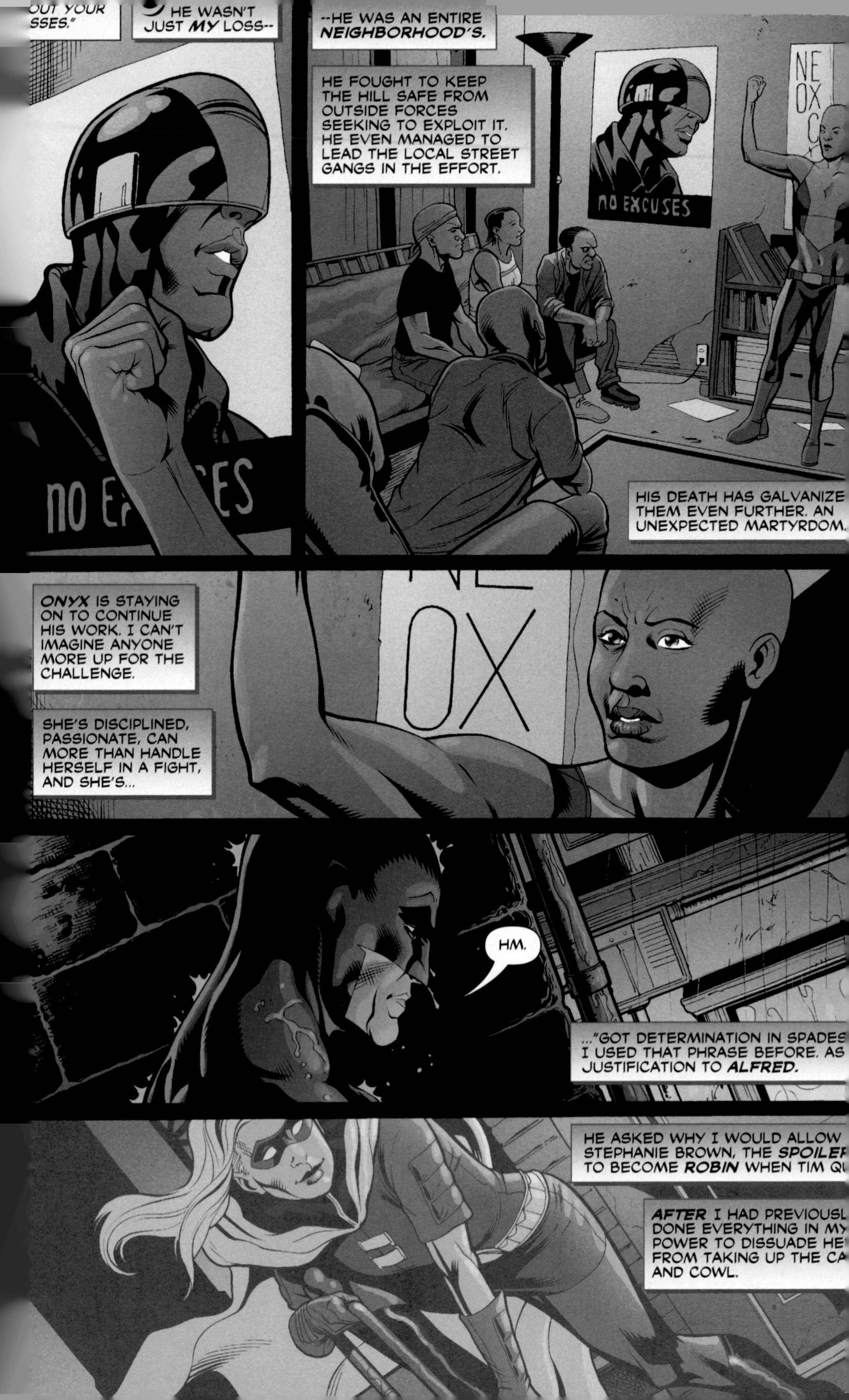

OUT YOUR
SSES."
HE WASN'T JUST MY LOSS--
--HE WAS AN ENTIRE NEIGHBORHOOD'S.
HE FOUGHT TO KEEP THE HILL SAFE FROM OUTSIDE FORCES SEEKING TO EXPLOIT IT. HE EVEN MANAGED TO LEAD THE LOCAL STREET GANGS IN THE EFFORT.
NO EXCUSES
HIS DEATH HAS GALVANIZE THEM EVEN FURTHER. AN UNEXPECTED MARTYRDOM.
ONYX IS STAYING ON TO CONTINUE HIS WORK. I CAN'T IMAGINE ANYONE MORE UP FOR THE CHALLENGE.
SHE'S DISCIPLINED, PASSIONATE, CAN MORE THAN HANDLE HERSELF IN A FIGHT, AND SHE'S...
HM.
..."GOT DETERMINATION IN SPADES I USED THAT PHRASE BEFORE. AS JUSTIFICATION TO ALFRED.
HE ASKED WHY I WOULD ALLOW STEPHANIE BROWN, THE SPOILE TO BECOME ROBIN WHEN TIM QU
AFTER I HAD PREVIOUSL DONE EVERYTHING IN MY POWER TO DISSUADE HE FROM TAKING UP THE CA AND COWL.

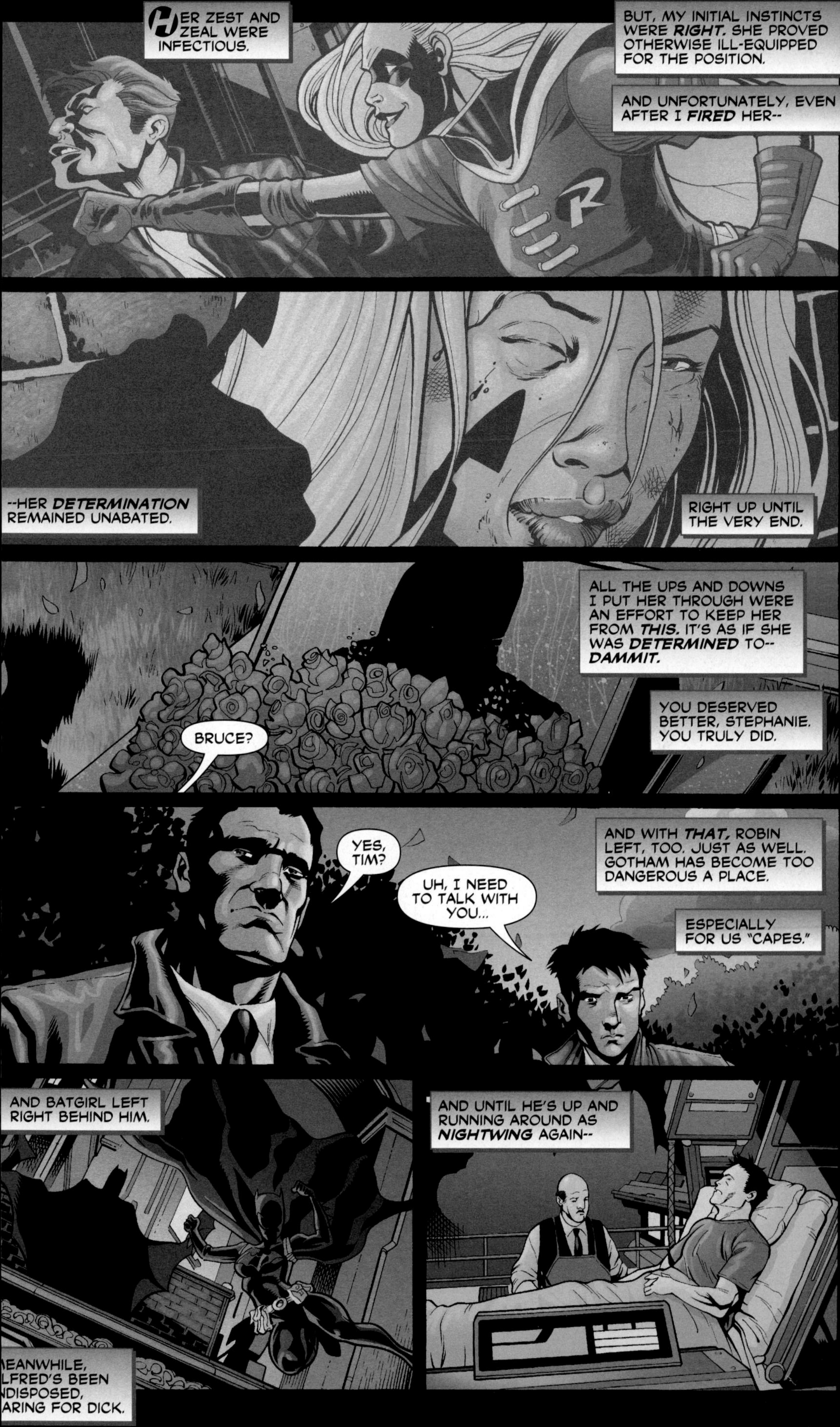
HER ZEST AND ZEAL WERE INFECTIOUS.
BUT, MY INITIAL INSTINCTS WERE RIGHT. SHE PROVED OTHERWISE ILL-EQUIPPED FOR THE POSITION.
AND UNFORTUNATELY, EVEN AFTER I FIRED HER--
--HER DETERMINATION REMAINED UNABATED.
RIGHT UP UNTIL THE VERY END.
ALL THE UPS AND DOWNS I PUT HER THROUGH WERE AN EFFORT TO KEEP HER FROM THIS. IT'S AS IF SHE WAS DETERMINED TO-- DAMMIT.
YOU DESERVED BETTER, STEPHANIE. YOU TRULY DID.
BRUCE?
YES, TIM?
UH, I NEED TO TALK WITH YOU...
AND WITH THAT, ROBIN LEFT, TOO. JUST AS WELL. GOTHAM HAS BECOME TOO DANGEROUS A PLACE.
ESPECIALLY FOR US "CAPES."
AND BATGIRL LEFT RIGHT BEHIND HIM.
EANWHILE, LFRED'S BEEN NDISPOSED, ARING FOR DICK.
AND UNTIL HE'S UP AND RUNNING AROUND AS NIGHTWING AGAIN--

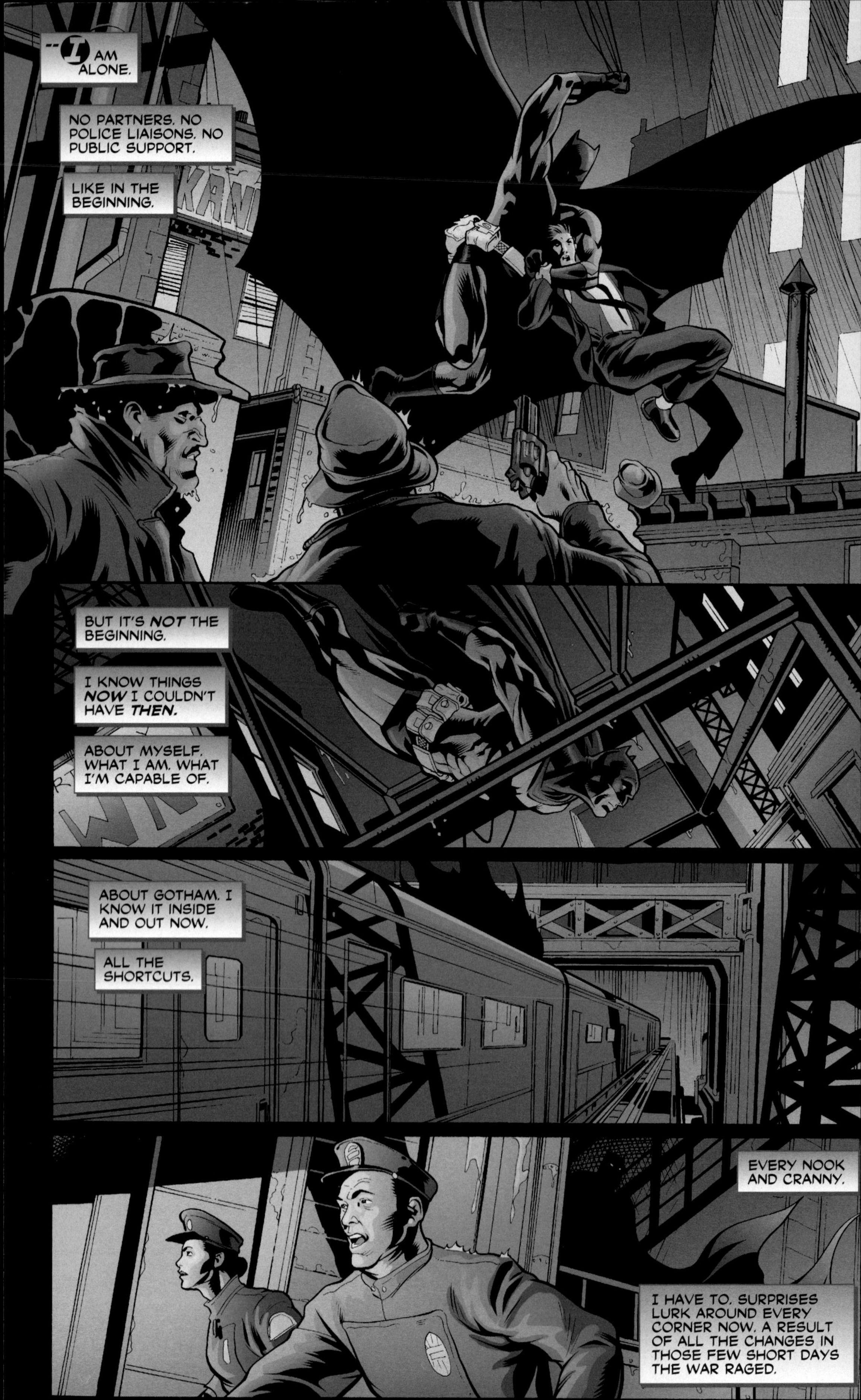
--I AM ALONE.
NO PARTNERS. NO POLICE LIAISONS. NO PUBLIC SUPPORT.
LIKE IN THE BEGINNING.
BUT IT'S *NOT* THE BEGINNING.
I KNOW THINGS *NOW* I COULDN'T HAVE *THEN.*
ABOUT MYSELF. WHAT I AM. WHAT I'M CAPABLE OF.
ABOUT GOTHAM. I KNOW IT INSIDE AND OUT NOW.
ALL THE SHORTCUTS.
EVERY NOOK AND CRANNY.
I HAVE TO. SURPRISES LURK AROUND EVERY CORNER NOW. A RESULT OF ALL THE CHANGES IN THOSE FEW SHORT DAYS THE WAR RAGED.

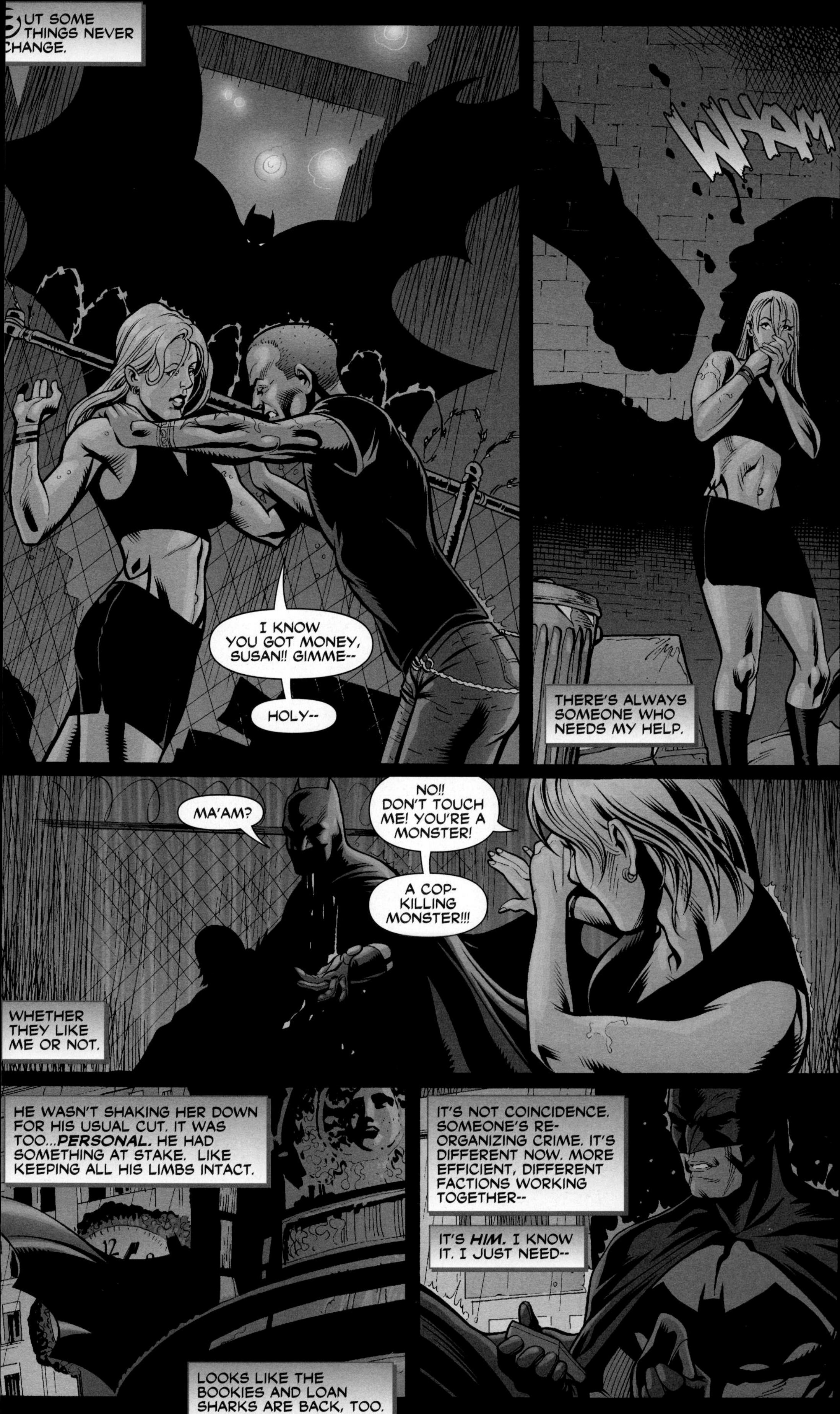
BUT SOME THINGS NEVER CHANGE.
I KNOW YOU GOT MONEY, SUSAN!! GIMME--
HOLY--
WHAM
THERE'S ALWAYS SOMEONE WHO NEEDS MY HELP.
MA'AM?
NO!! DON'T TOUCH ME! YOU'RE A MONSTER!
A COP-KILLING MONSTER!!!
WHETHER THEY LIKE ME OR NOT.
HE WASN'T SHAKING HER DOWN FOR HIS USUAL CUT. IT WAS TOO...PERSONAL. HE HAD SOMETHING AT STAKE. LIKE KEEPING ALL HIS LIMBS INTACT.
LOOKS LIKE THE BOOKIES AND LOAN SHARKS ARE BACK, TOO.
IT'S NOT COINCIDENCE. SOMEONE'S RE-ORGANIZING CRIME. IT'S DIFFERENT NOW. MORE EFFICIENT, DIFFERENT FACTIONS WORKING TOGETHER--
IT'S HIM. I KNOW IT. I JUST NEED--

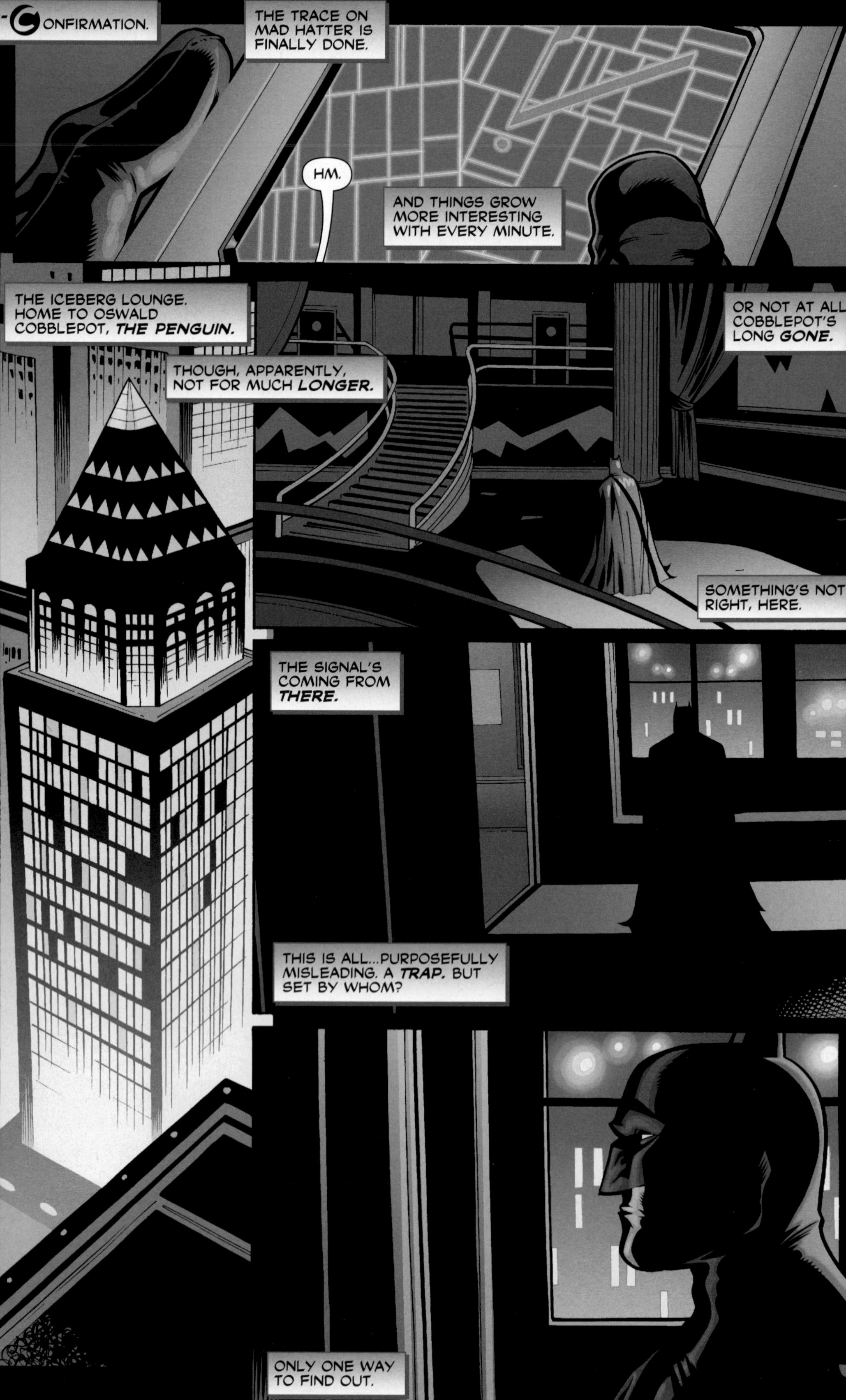
-CONFIRMATION.
THE TRACE ON MAD HATTER IS FINALLY DONE.
HM.
AND THINGS GROW MORE INTERESTING WITH EVERY MINUTE.
THE ICEBERG LOUNGE. HOME TO OSWALD COBBLEPOT, THE PENGUIN.
THOUGH, APPARENTLY, NOT FOR MUCH LONGER.
OR NOT AT ALL. COBBLEPOT'S LONG GONE.
SOMETHING'S NOT RIGHT, HERE.
THE SIGNAL'S COMING FROM THERE.
THIS IS ALL...PURPOSEFULLY MISLEADING. A TRAP. BUT SET BY WHOM?
ONLY ONE WAY TO FIND OUT.

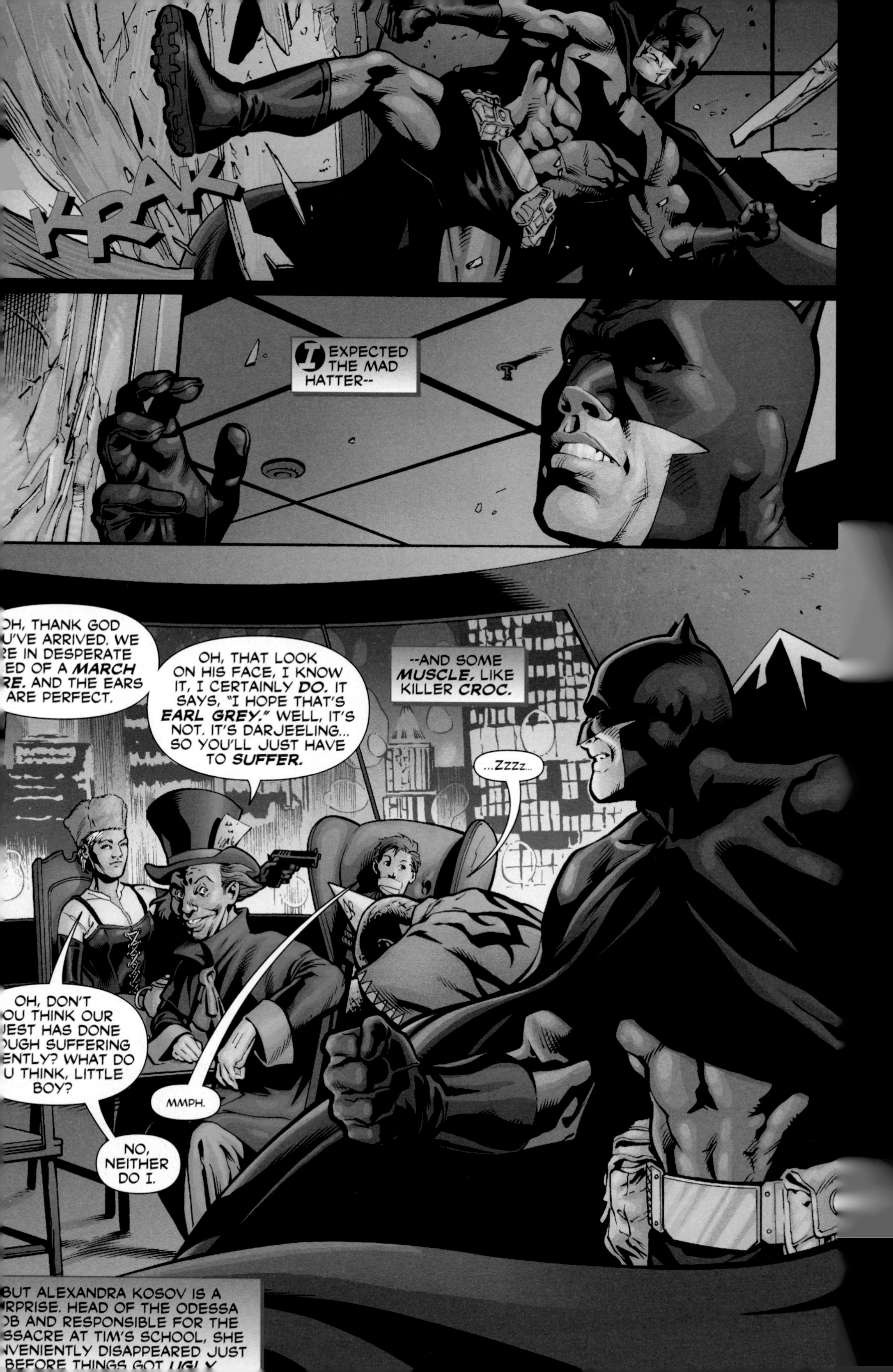
KRAK
I EXPECTED THE MAD HATTER--
OH, THANK GOD U'VE ARRIVED. WE RE IN DESPERATE ED OF A MARCH RE. AND THE EARS ARE PERFECT.
OH, THAT LOOK ON HIS FACE, I KNOW IT, I CERTAINLY DO. IT SAYS, "I HOPE THAT'S EARL GREY." WELL, IT'S NOT. IT'S DARJEELING... SO YOU'LL JUST HAVE TO SUFFER.
--AND SOME MUSCLE, LIKE KILLER CROC.
...Zzzz...
OH, DON'T OU THINK OUR UEST HAS DONE OUGH SUFFERING ENTLY? WHAT DO U THINK, LITTLE BOY?
MMPH.
NO, NEITHER DO I.
BUT ALEXANDRA KOSOV IS A RPRISE. HEAD OF THE ODESSA OB AND RESPONSIBLE FOR THE SSACRE AT TIM'S SCHOOL, SHE NVENIENTLY DISAPPEARED JUST BEFORE THINGS GOT UGLY.

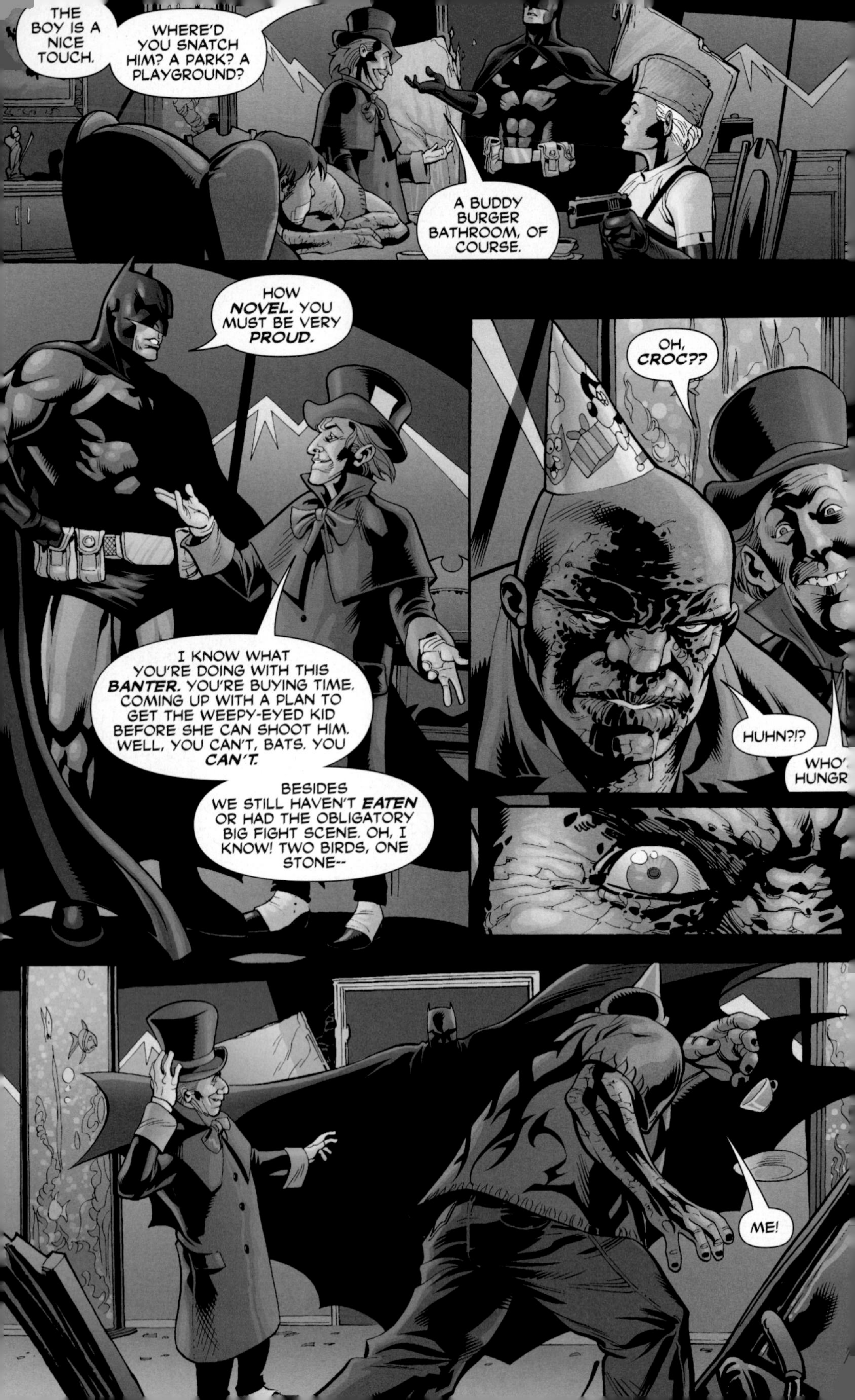
THE BOY IS A NICE TOUCH.
WHERE'D YOU SNATCH HIM? A PARK? A PLAYGROUND?
A BUDDY BURGER BATHROOM, OF COURSE.
HOW NOVEL. YOU MUST BE VERY PROUD.
I KNOW WHAT YOU'RE DOING WITH THIS BANTER. YOU'RE BUYING TIME. COMING UP WITH A PLAN TO GET THE WEEPY-EYED KID BEFORE SHE CAN SHOOT HIM. WELL, YOU CAN'T, BATS. YOU CAN'T.
BESIDES WE STILL HAVEN'T EATEN OR HAD THE OBLIGATORY BIG FIGHT SCENE. OH, I KNOW! TWO BIRDS, ONE STONE--
OH, CROC??
HUHN?!?
ME!

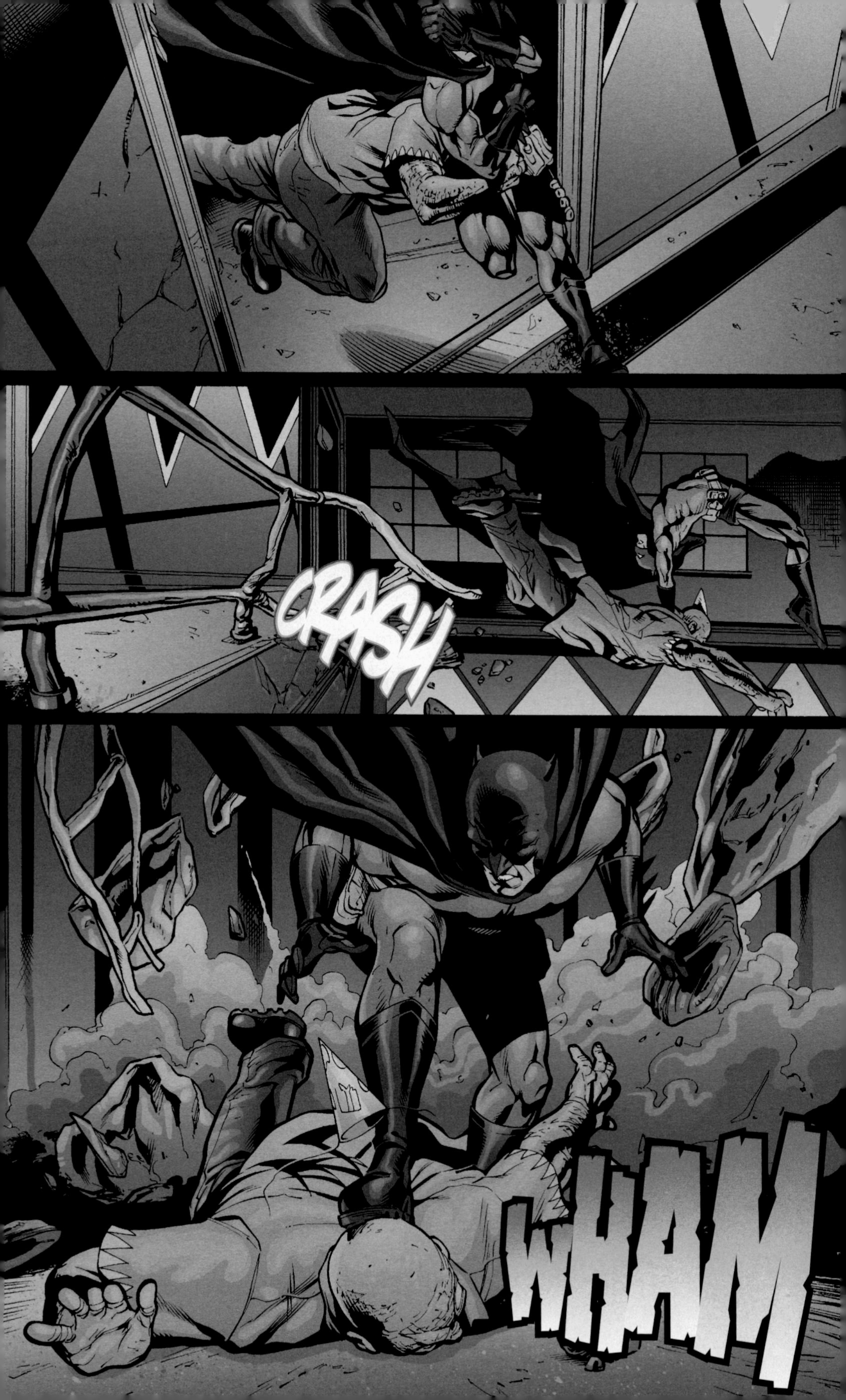
CRASH
WHAM

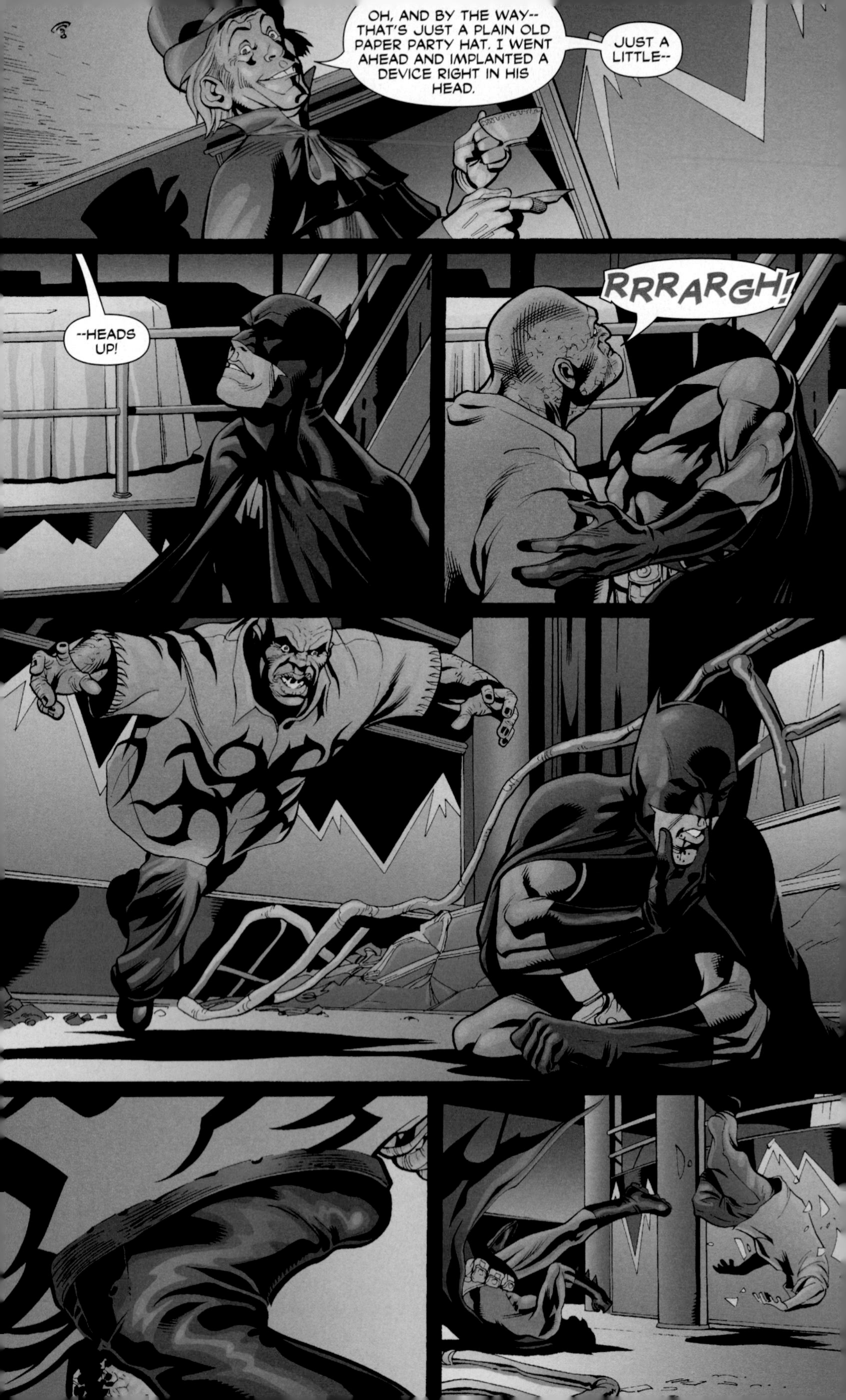
OH, AND BY THE WAY-- THAT'S JUST A PLAIN OLD PAPER PARTY HAT. I WENT AHEAD AND IMPLANTED A DEVICE RIGHT IN HIS HEAD.
JUST A LITTLE--
--HEADS UP!
RRRARGH!

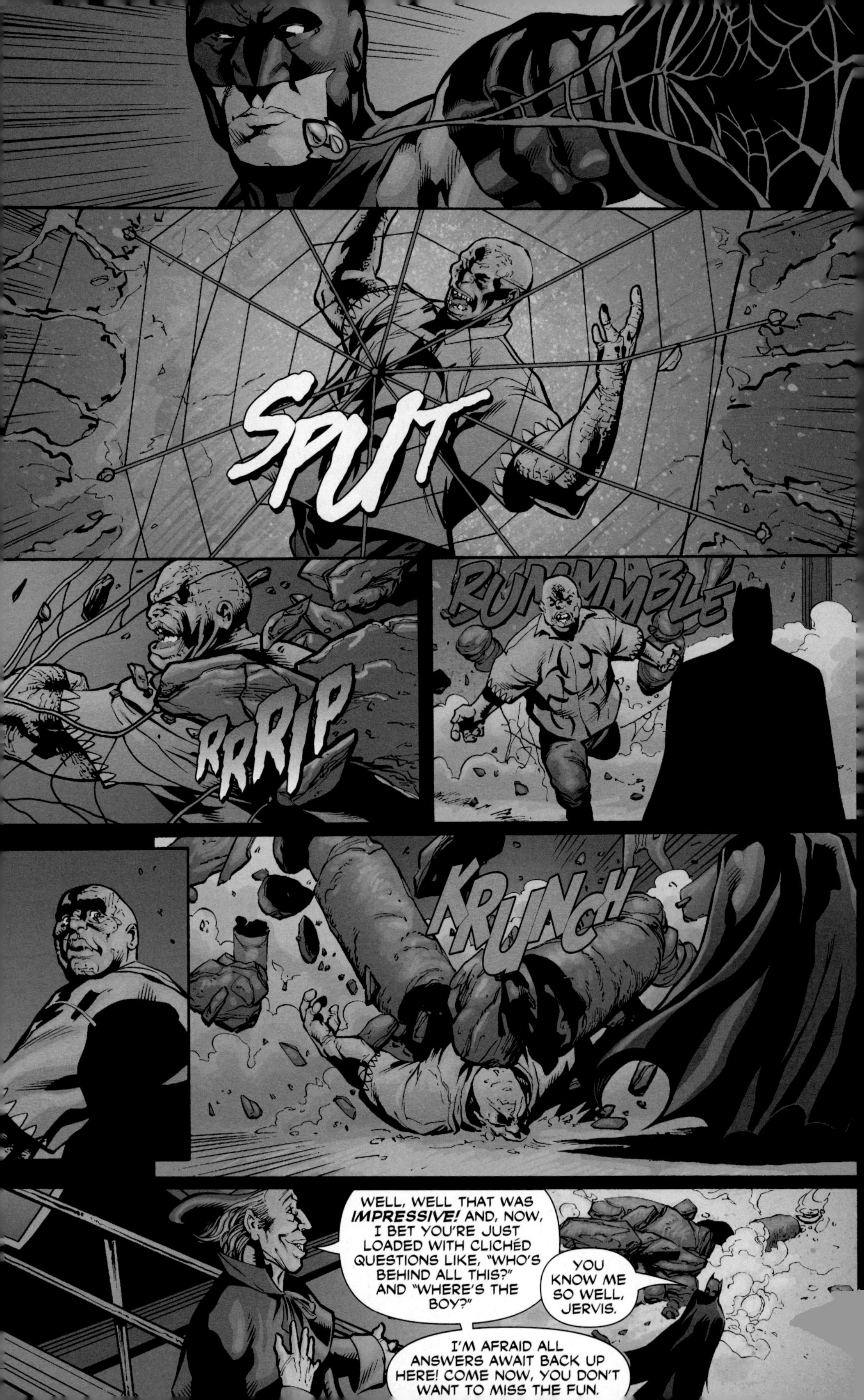
SPLIT
RRRIP
RUMMMBLE
KRUNCH
WELL, WELL THAT WAS *IMPRESSIVE!* AND, NOW, I BET YOU'RE JUST LOADED WITH CLICHÉD QUESTIONS LIKE, "WHO'S BEHIND ALL THIS?" AND "WHERE'S THE BOY?"
YOU KNOW ME SO WELL, JERVIS.
I'M AFRAID ALL ANSWERS AWAIT BACK UP HERE! COME NOW, YOU DON'T WANT TO MISS THE FUN.

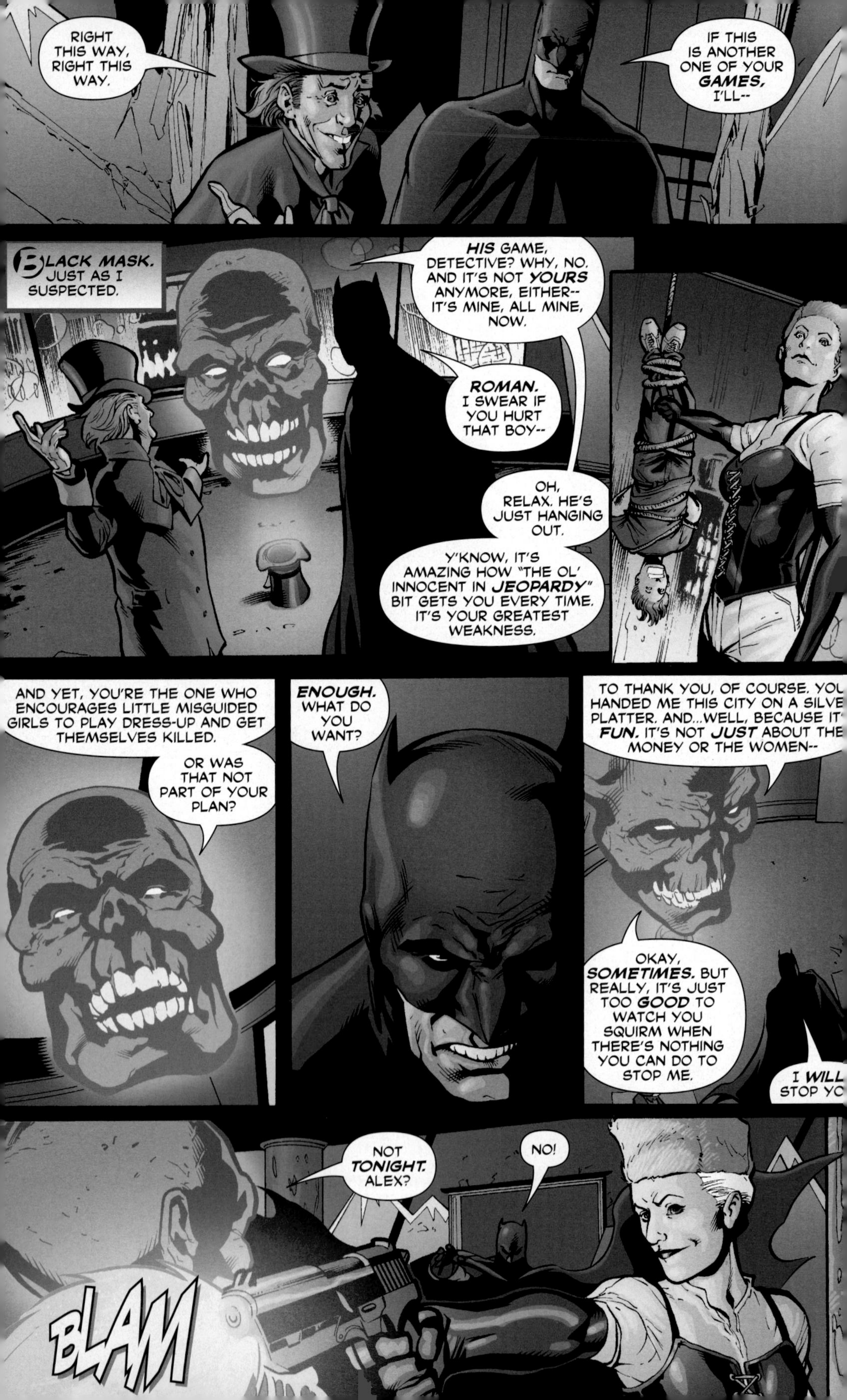
RIGHT THIS WAY, RIGHT THIS WAY.
IF THIS IS ANOTHER ONE OF YOUR GAMES, I'LL--
BLACK MASK. JUST AS I SUSPECTED.
HIS GAME, DETECTIVE? WHY, NO. AND IT'S NOT YOURS ANYMORE, EITHER-- IT'S MINE, ALL MINE, NOW.
ROMAN. I SWEAR IF YOU HURT THAT BOY--
OH, RELAX. HE'S JUST HANGING OUT.
Y'KNOW, IT'S AMAZING HOW "THE OL' INNOCENT IN JEOPARDY" BIT GETS YOU EVERY TIME. IT'S YOUR GREATEST WEAKNESS.
AND YET, YOU'RE THE ONE WHO ENCOURAGES LITTLE MISGUIDED GIRLS TO PLAY DRESS-UP AND GET THEMSELVES KILLED.
OR WAS THAT NOT PART OF YOUR PLAN?
ENOUGH. WHAT DO YOU WANT?
TO THANK YOU, OF COURSE. YOU HANDED ME THIS CITY ON A SILVE PLATTER. AND...WELL, BECAUSE IT' FUN. IT'S NOT JUST ABOUT THE MONEY OR THE WOMEN--
OKAY, SOMETIMES. BUT REALLY, IT'S JUST TOO GOOD TO WATCH YOU SQUIRM WHEN THERE'S NOTHING YOU CAN DO TO STOP ME.
I WILL STOP YO
NOT TONIGHT. ALEX?
NO!
BLAM

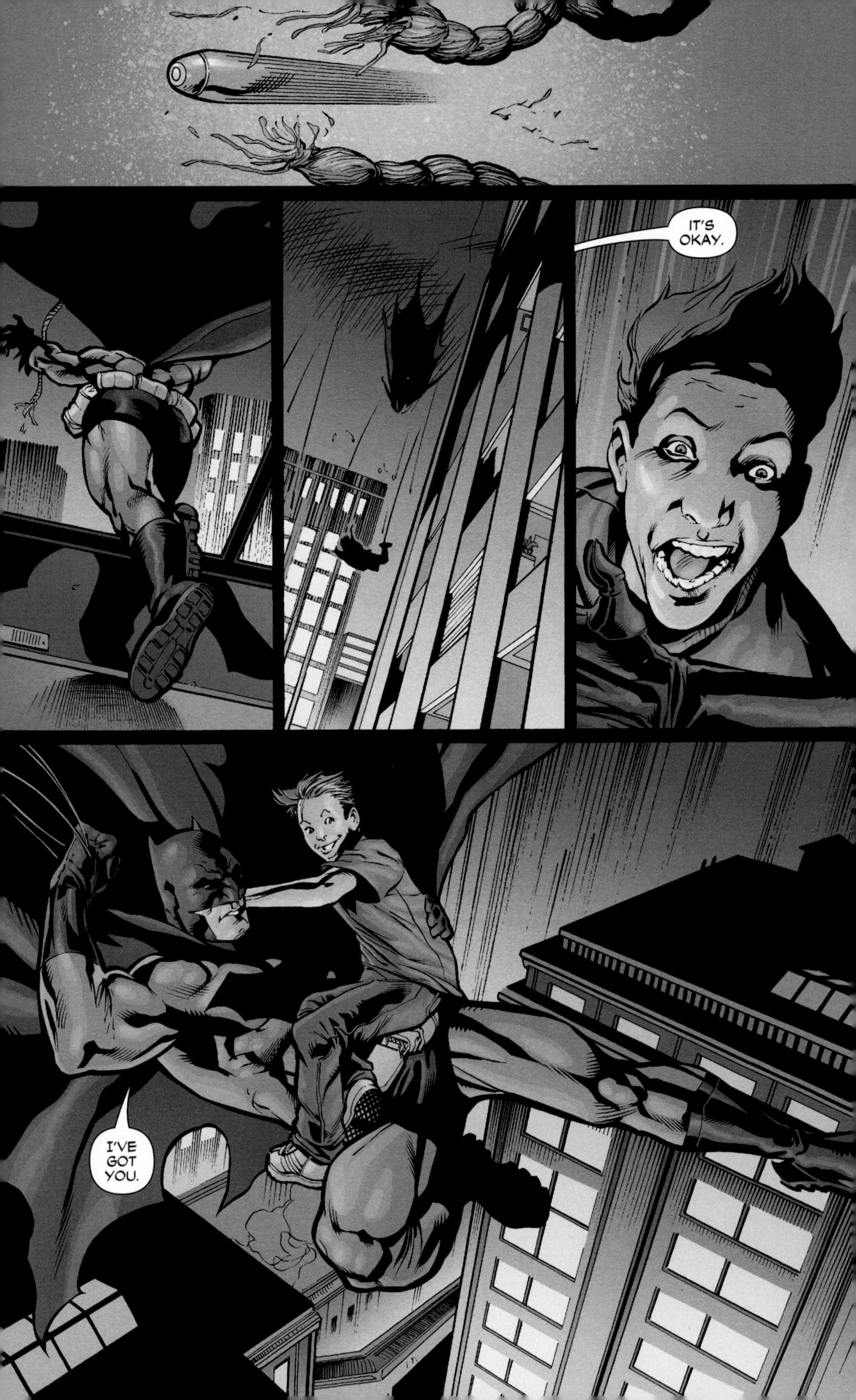
IT'S OKAY.
I'VE GOT YOU.

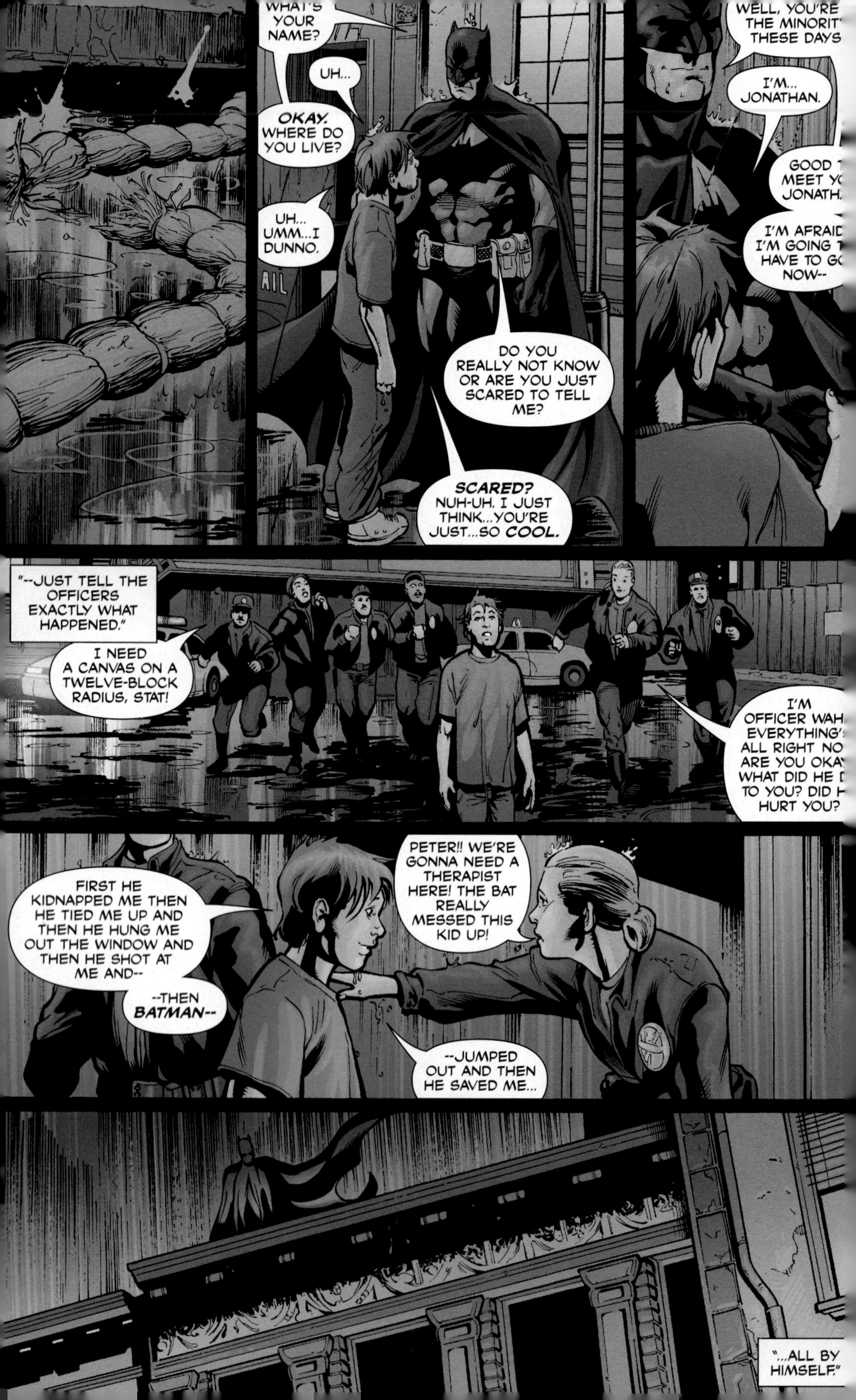
WHAT'S YOUR NAME?
UH...
OKAY. WHERE DO YOU LIVE?
UH... UMM...I DUNNO.
DO YOU REALLY NOT KNOW OR ARE YOU JUST SCARED TO TELL ME?
SCARED? NUH-UH. I JUST THINK...YOU'RE JUST...SO COOL.
WELL, YOU'RE THE MINORIT THESE DAYS
I'M... JONATHAN.
GOOD T MEET YO JONATH.
I'M AFRAID I'M GOING T HAVE TO GO NOW--
"--JUST TELL THE OFFICERS EXACTLY WHAT HAPPENED."
I NEED A CANVAS ON A TWELVE-BLOCK RADIUS, STAT!
I'M OFFICER WAH EVERYTHING'S ALL RIGHT NO ARE YOU OKAY WHAT DID HE D TO YOU? DID H HURT YOU?
FIRST HE KIDNAPPED ME THEN HE TIED ME UP AND THEN HE HUNG ME OUT THE WINDOW AND THEN HE SHOT AT ME AND--
--THEN BATMAN--
PETER!! WE'RE GONNA NEED A THERAPIST HERE! THE BAT REALLY MESSED THIS KID UP!
--JUMPED OUT AND THEN HE SAVED ME...
"...ALL BY HIMSELF."

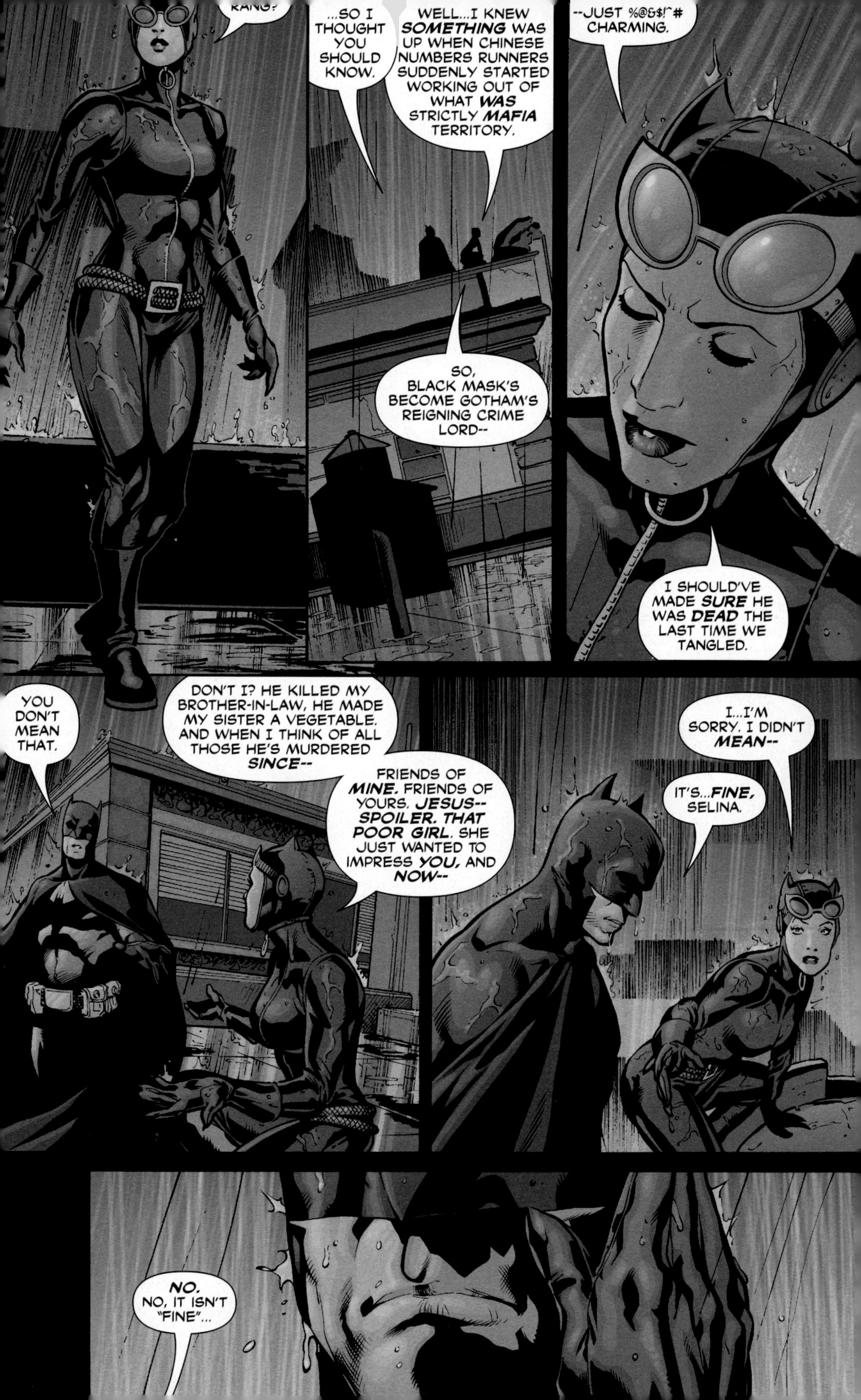

RANG?
...SO I THOUGHT YOU SHOULD KNOW.
WELL...I KNEW **SOMETHING** WAS UP WHEN CHINESE NUMBERS RUNNERS SUDDENLY STARTED WORKING OUT OF WHAT **WAS** STRICTLY **MAFIA** TERRITORY.
SO, BLACK MASK'S BECOME GOTHAM'S REIGNING CRIME LORD--
--JUST %@&$!^# CHARMING.
I SHOULD'VE MADE **SURE** HE WAS **DEAD** THE LAST TIME WE TANGLED.
YOU DON'T MEAN THAT.
DON'T I? HE KILLED MY BROTHER-IN-LAW, HE MADE MY SISTER A VEGETABLE. AND WHEN I THINK OF ALL THOSE HE'S MURDERED **SINCE--**
FRIENDS OF **MINE.** FRIENDS OF YOURS. **JESUS-- SPOILER. THAT POOR GIRL.** SHE JUST WANTED TO IMPRESS **YOU,** AND **NOW--**
I...I'M SORRY. I DIDN'T **MEAN--**
IT'S...**FINE,** SELINA.
NO. NO, IT ISN'T "FINE"...

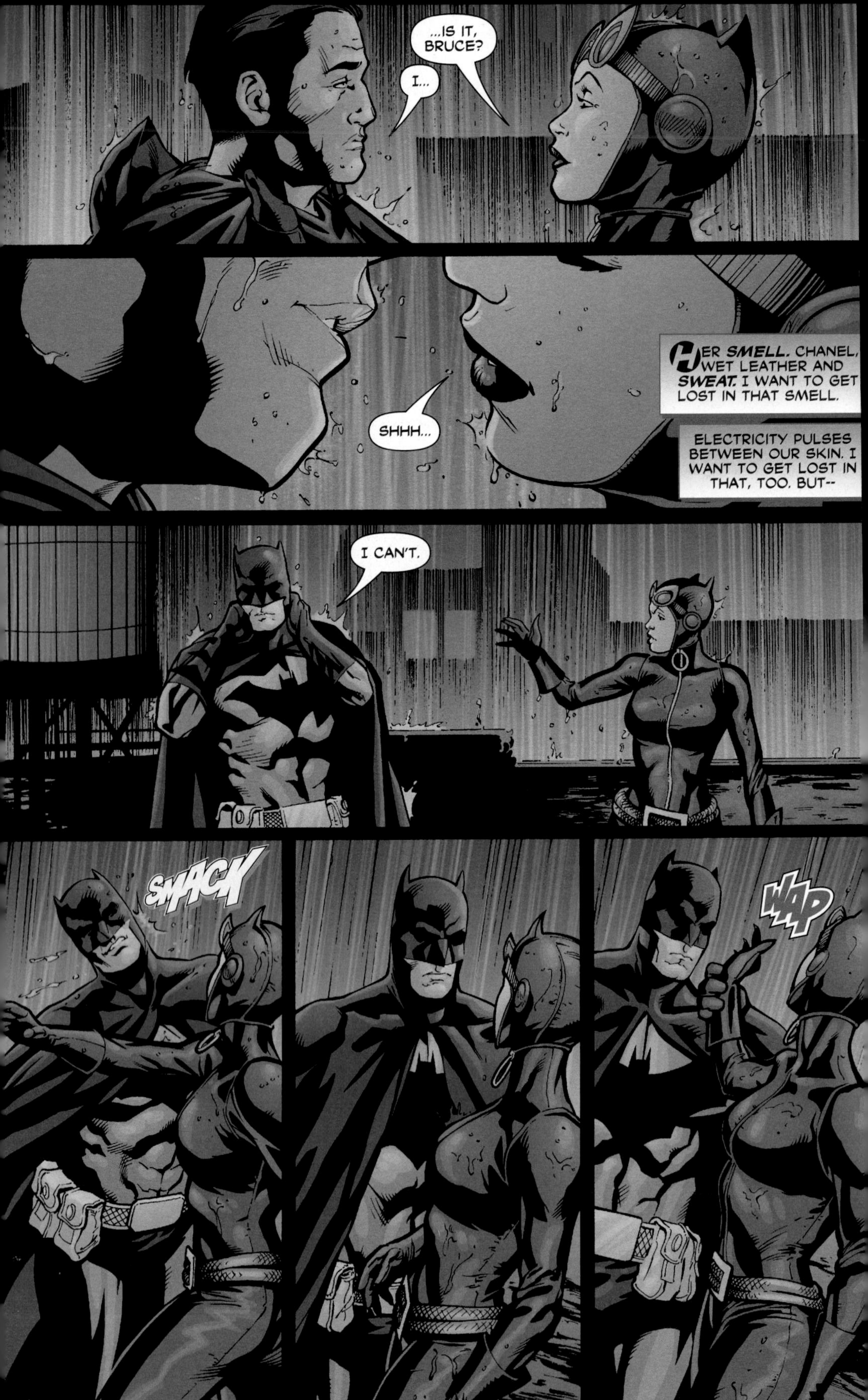
...IS IT, BRUCE?
I...
HER SMELL. CHANEL, WET LEATHER AND SWEAT. I WANT TO GET LOST IN THAT SMELL.
SHHH...
ELECTRICITY PULSES BETWEEN OUR SKIN. I WANT TO GET LOST IN THAT, TOO. BUT--
I CAN'T.
SMACK
WAP

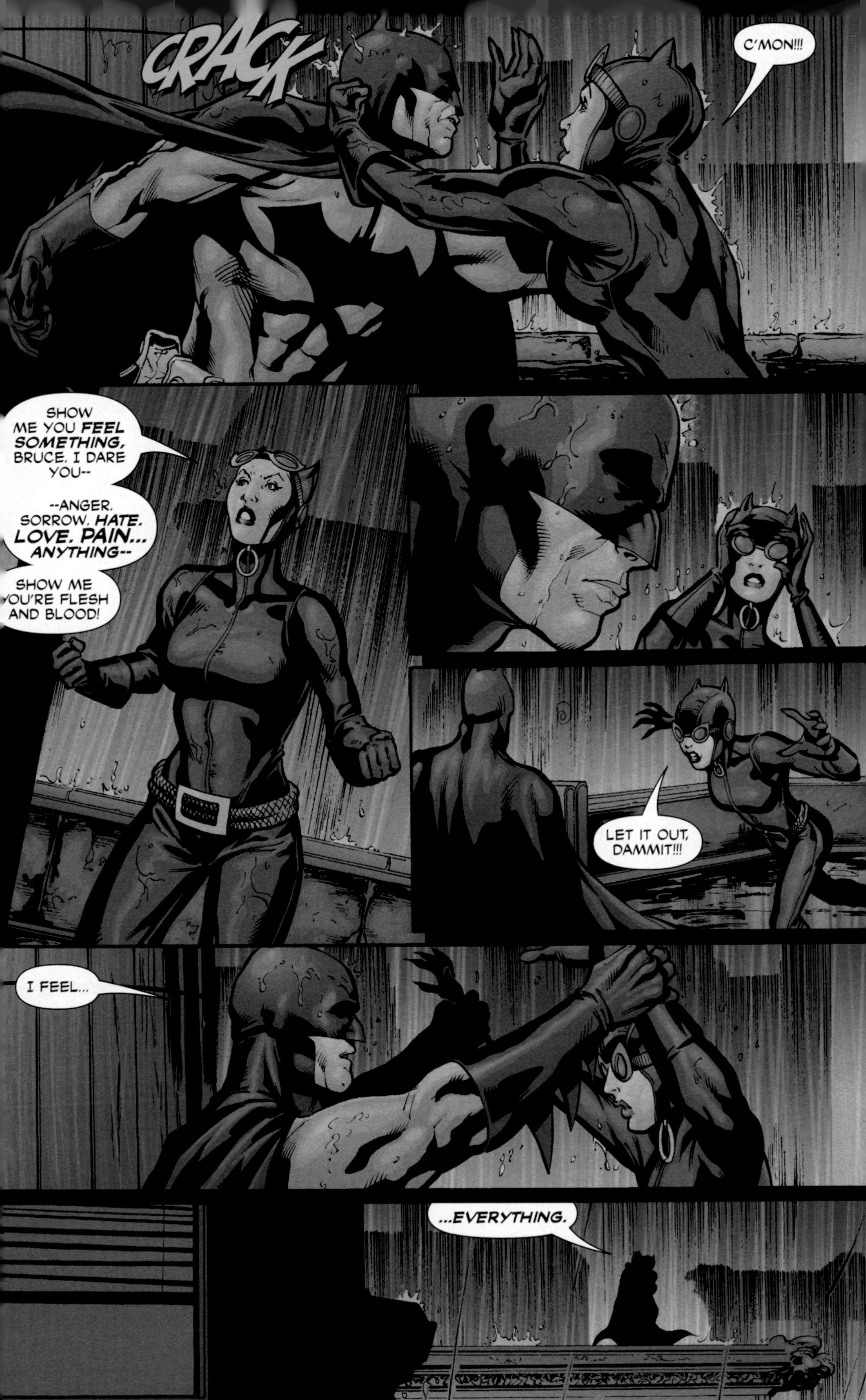

CRACK
C'MON!!!
SHOW ME YOU **FEEL SOMETHING,** BRUCE. I DARE YOU--
--ANGER. SORROW. **HATE. LOVE. PAIN... ANYTHING--**
SHOW ME YOU'RE FLESH AND BLOOD!
LET IT OUT, DAMMIT!!!
I FEEL...
...EVERYTHING.

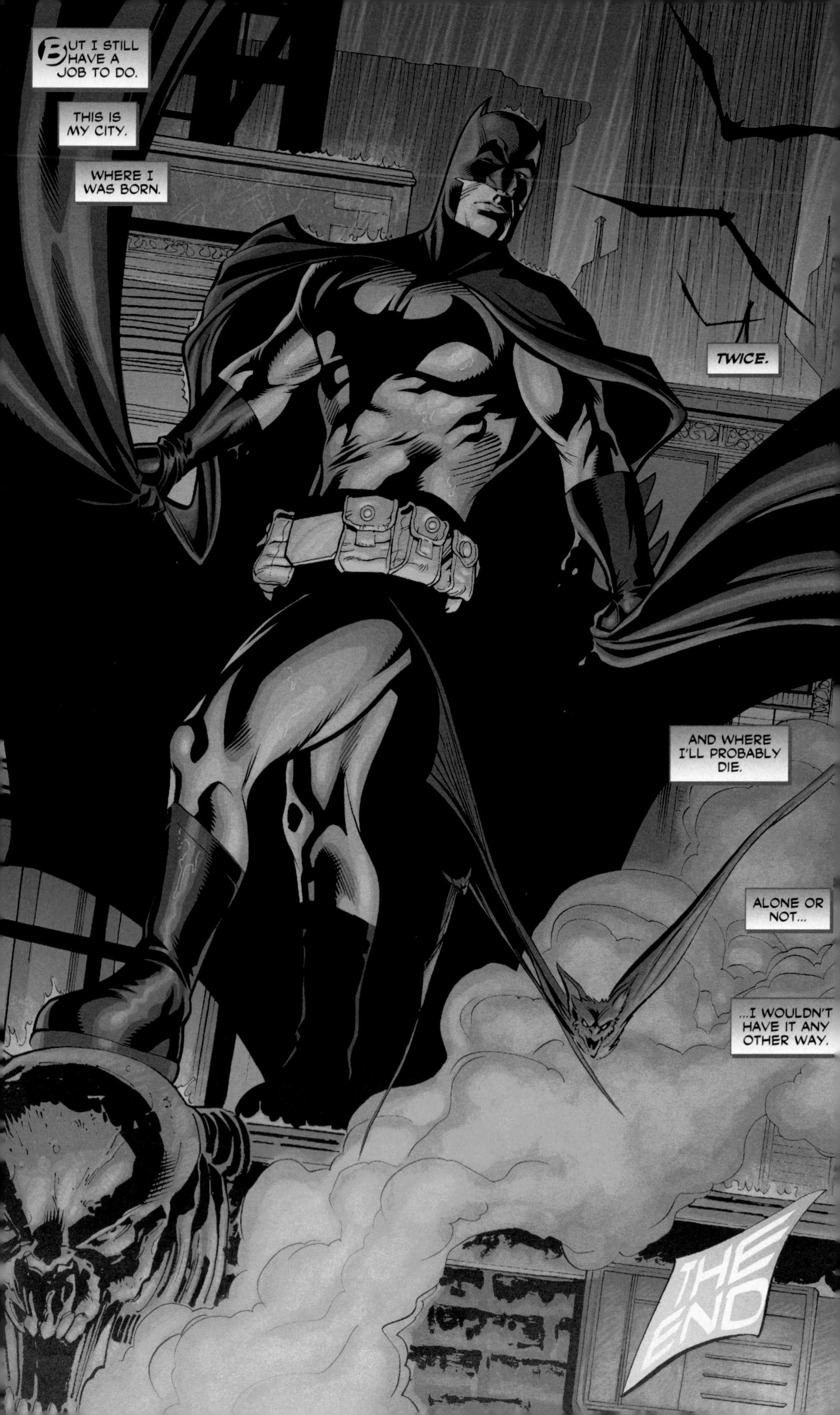
BUT I STILL HAVE A JOB TO DO.
THIS IS MY CITY.
WHERE I WAS BORN.
TWICE.
AND WHERE I'LL PROBABLY DIE.
ALONE OR NOT...
...I WOULDN'T HAVE IT ANY OTHER WAY.
THE END

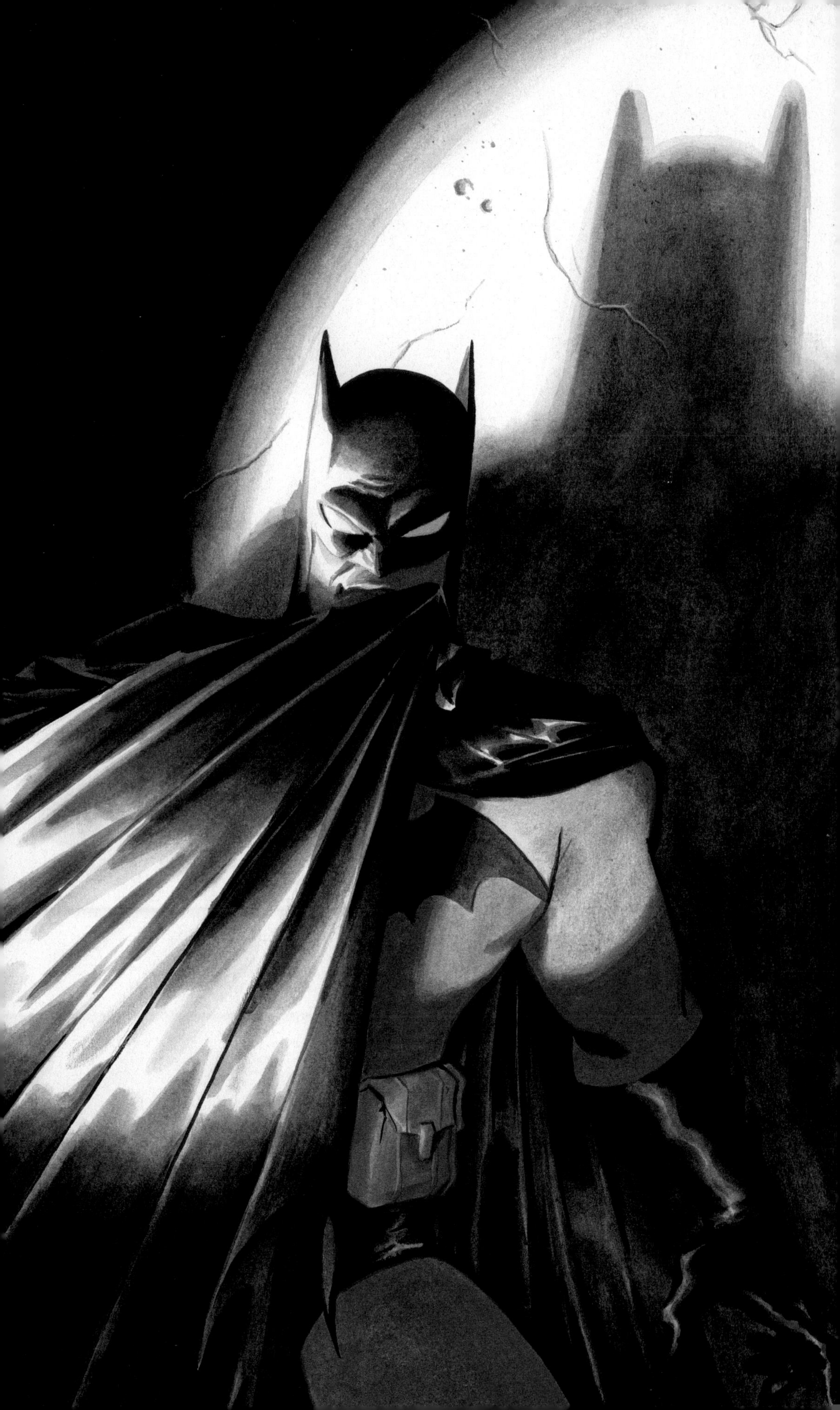

COVER ART BY
MATT WAGNER

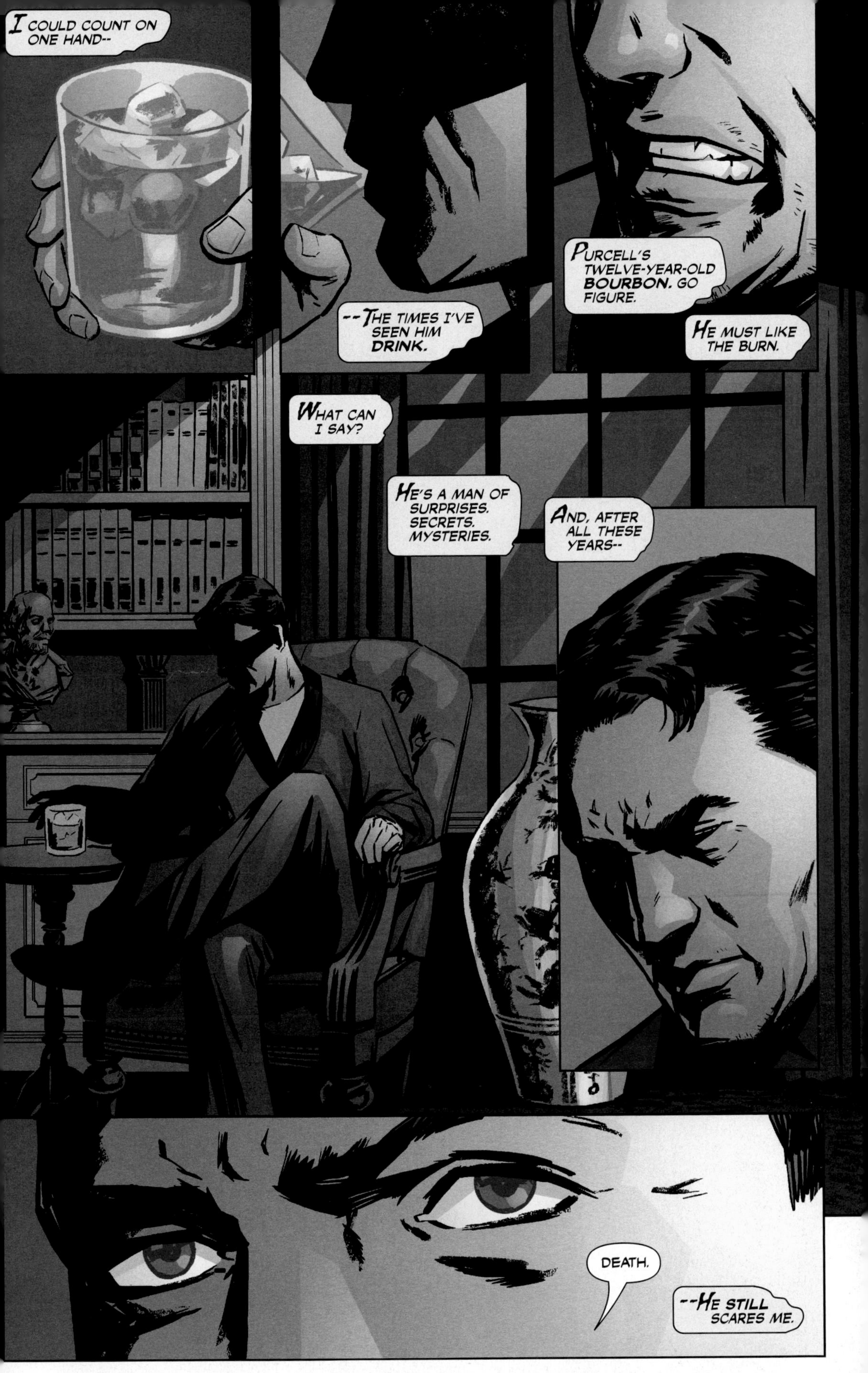
I COULD COUNT ON ONE HAND--
--THE TIMES I'VE SEEN HIM DRINK.
PURCELL'S TWELVE-YEAR-OLD BOURBON. GO FIGURE.
HE MUST LIKE THE BURN.
WHAT CAN I SAY?
HE'S A MAN OF SURPRISES. SECRETS. MYSTERIES.
AND, AFTER ALL THESE YEARS--
DEATH.
--HE STILL SCARES ME.

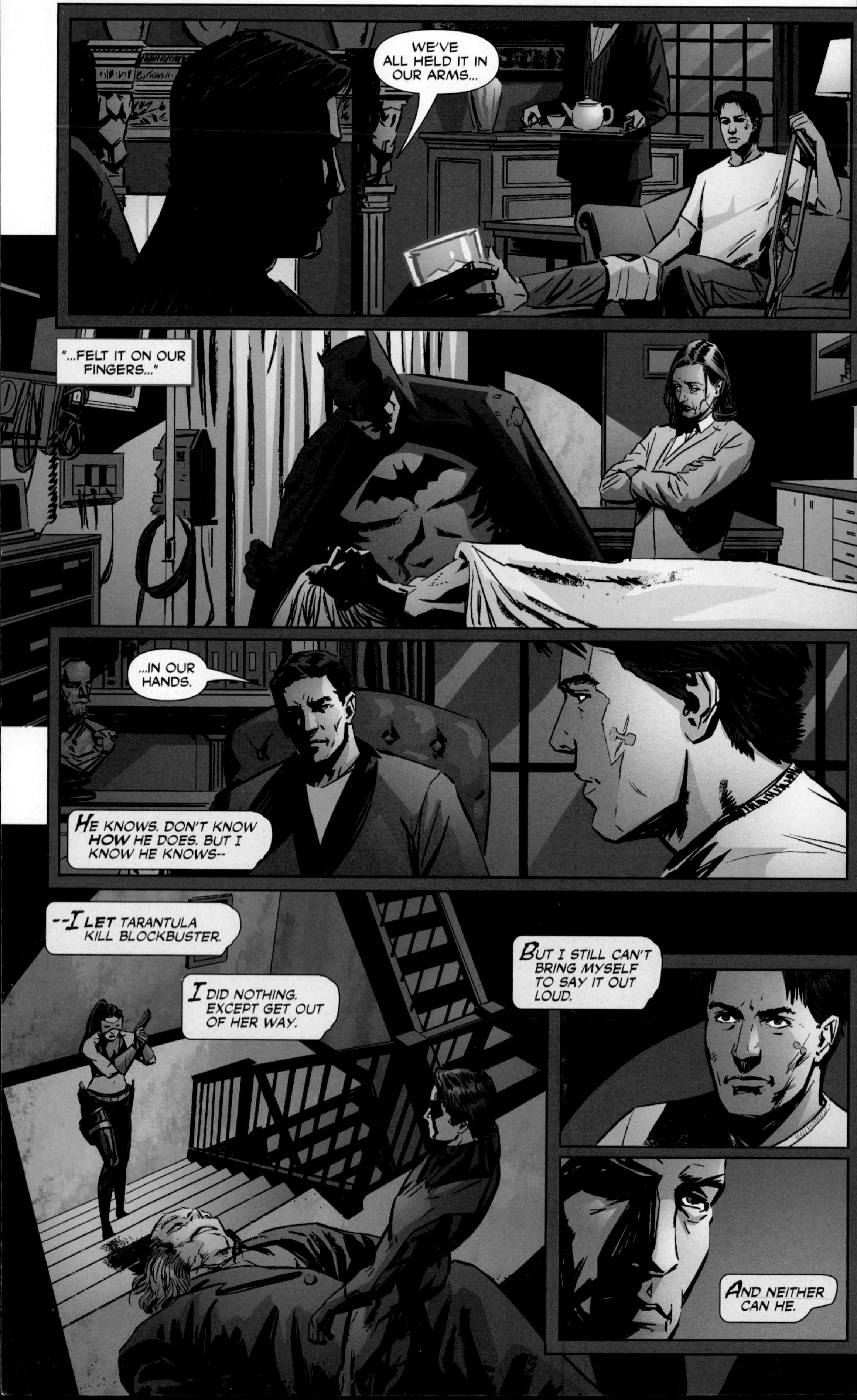

WE'VE ALL HELD IT IN OUR ARMS...
"...FELT IT ON OUR FINGERS..."
...IN OUR HANDS.
HE KNOWS. DON'T KNOW HOW HE DOES. BUT I KNOW HE KNOWS--
--I LET TARANTULA KILL BLOCKBUSTER.
I DID NOTHING. EXCEPT GET OUT OF HER WAY.
BUT I STILL CAN'T BRING MYSELF TO SAY IT OUT LOUD.
AND NEITHER CAN HE.

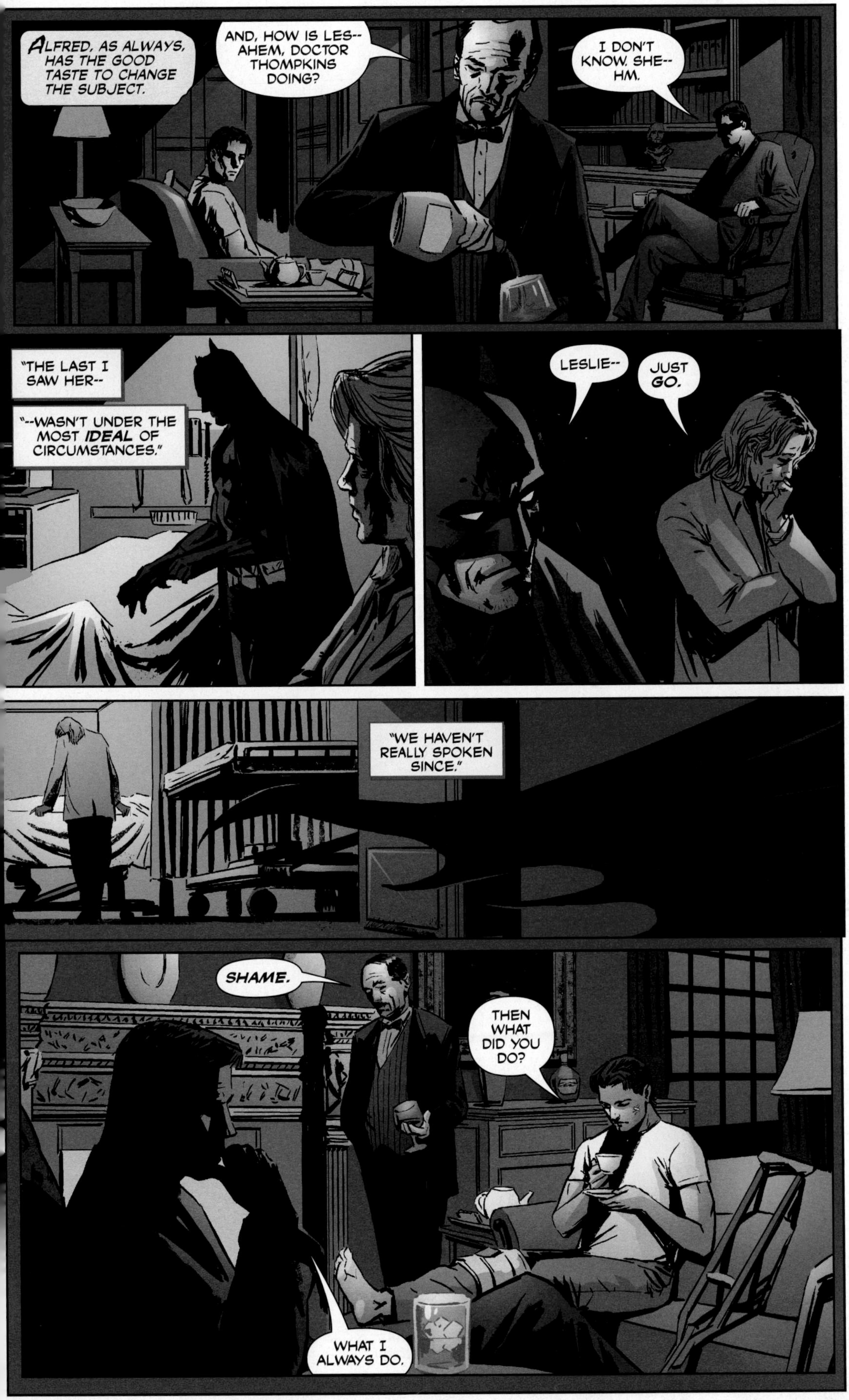
ALFRED, AS ALWAYS, HAS THE GOOD TASTE TO CHANGE THE SUBJECT.
AND, HOW IS LES-- AHEM, DOCTOR THOMPKINS DOING?
I DON'T KNOW. SHE-- HM.
"THE LAST I SAW HER--
"--WASN'T UNDER THE MOST IDEAL OF CIRCUMSTANCES."
LESLIE--
JUST GO.
"WE HAVEN'T REALLY SPOKEN SINCE."
SHAME.
THEN WHAT DID YOU DO?
WHAT I ALWAYS DO.

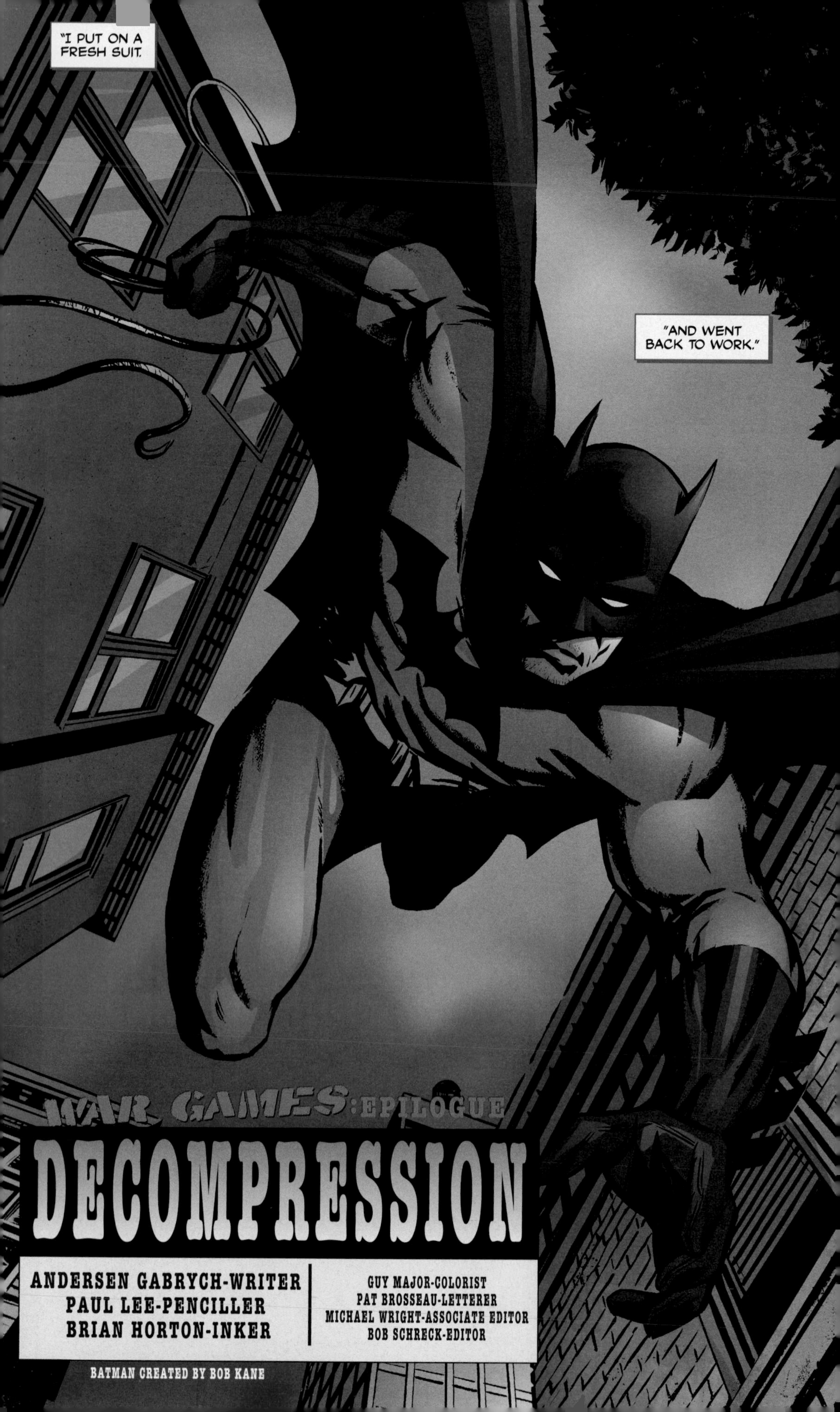
"I PUT ON A FRESH SUIT.
"AND WENT BACK TO WORK."
WAR GAMES: EPILOGUE
DECOMPRESSION
ANDERSEN GABRYCH-WRITER
PAUL LEE-PENCILLER
BRIAN HORTON-INKER
GUY MAJOR-COLORIST
PAT BROSSEAU-LETTERER
MICHAEL WRIGHT-ASSOCIATE EDITOR
BOB SCHRECK-EDITOR
BATMAN CREATED BY BOB KANE

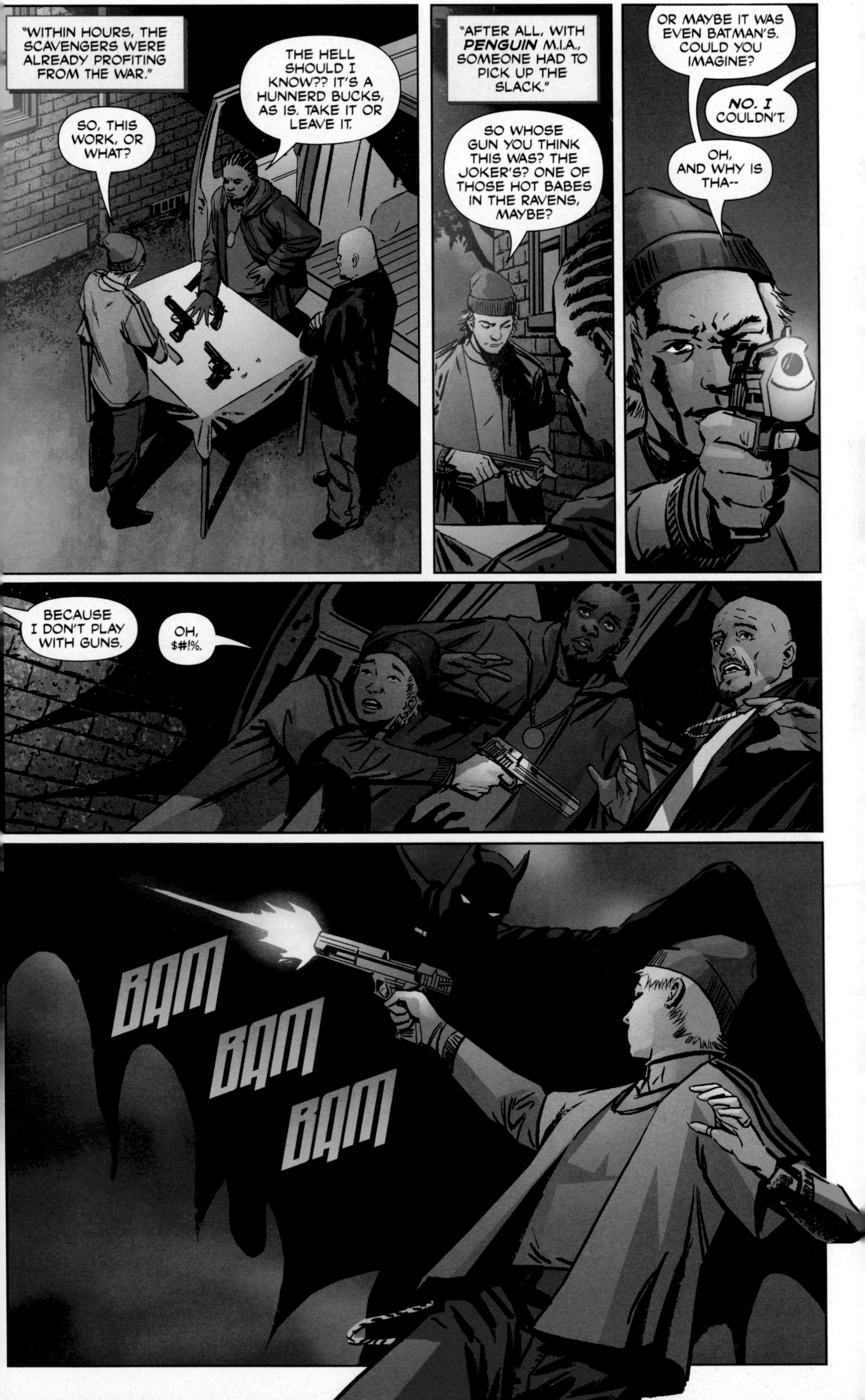
"WITHIN HOURS, THE SCAVENGERS WERE ALREADY PROFITING FROM THE WAR."
SO, THIS WORK, OR WHAT?
THE HELL SHOULD I KNOW?? IT'S A HUNNERD BUCKS, AS IS. TAKE IT OR LEAVE IT.
"AFTER ALL, WITH PENGUIN M.I.A., SOMEONE HAD TO PICK UP THE SLACK."
SO WHOSE GUN YOU THINK THIS WAS? THE JOKER'S? ONE OF THOSE HOT BABES IN THE RAVENS, MAYBE?
OR MAYBE IT WAS EVEN BATMAN'S. COULD YOU IMAGINE?
NO. I COULDN'T.
OH, AND WHY IS THA--
BECAUSE I DON'T PLAY WITH GUNS.
OH, $#!%.
BAM
BAM
BAM

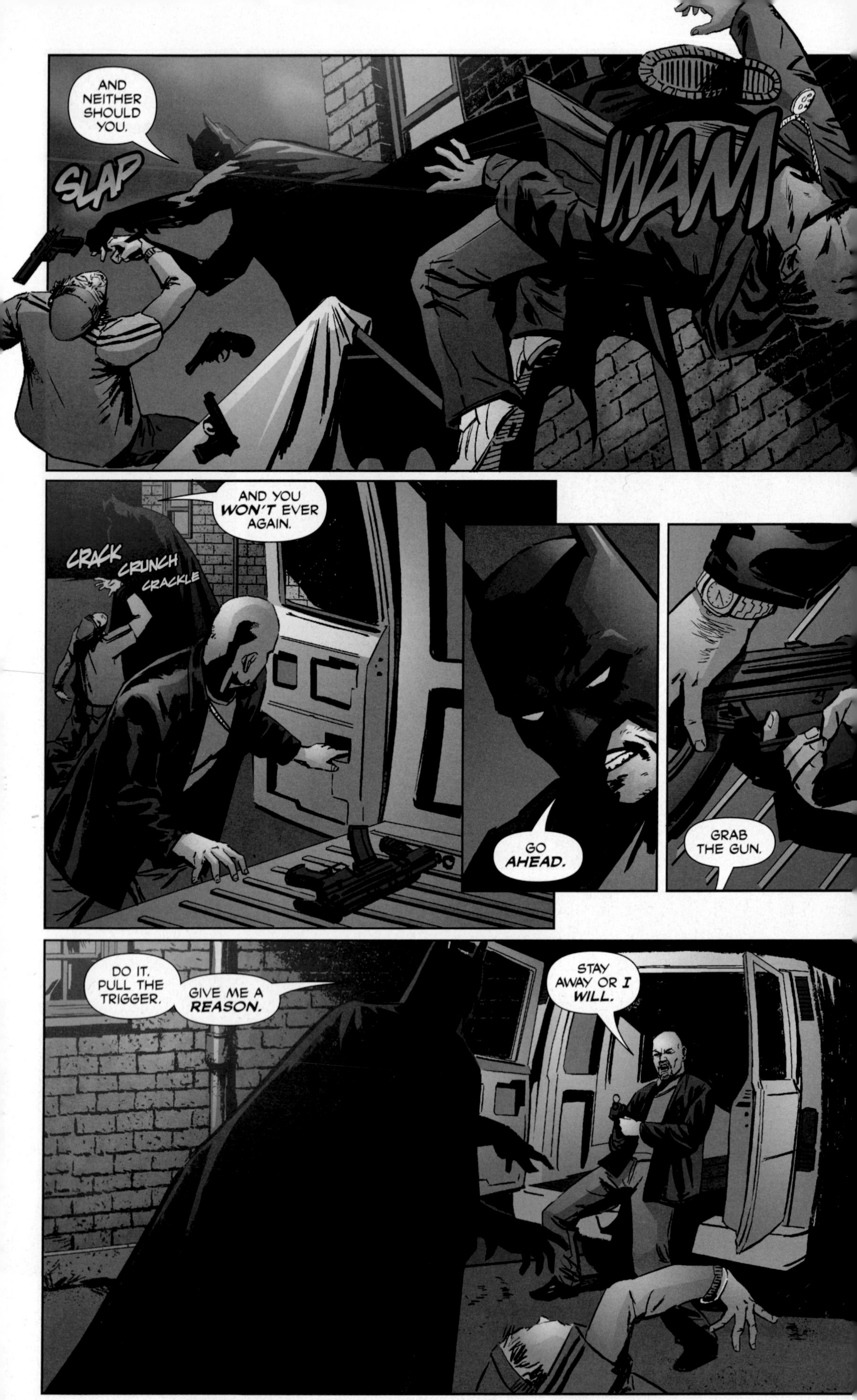

AND NEITHER SHOULD YOU.
SLAP
WAM
AND YOU WON'T EVER AGAIN.
CRACK
CRUNCH
CRACKLE
GO AHEAD.
GRAB THE GUN.
DO IT. PULL THE TRIGGER.
GIVE ME A REASON.
STAY AWAY OR I WILL.

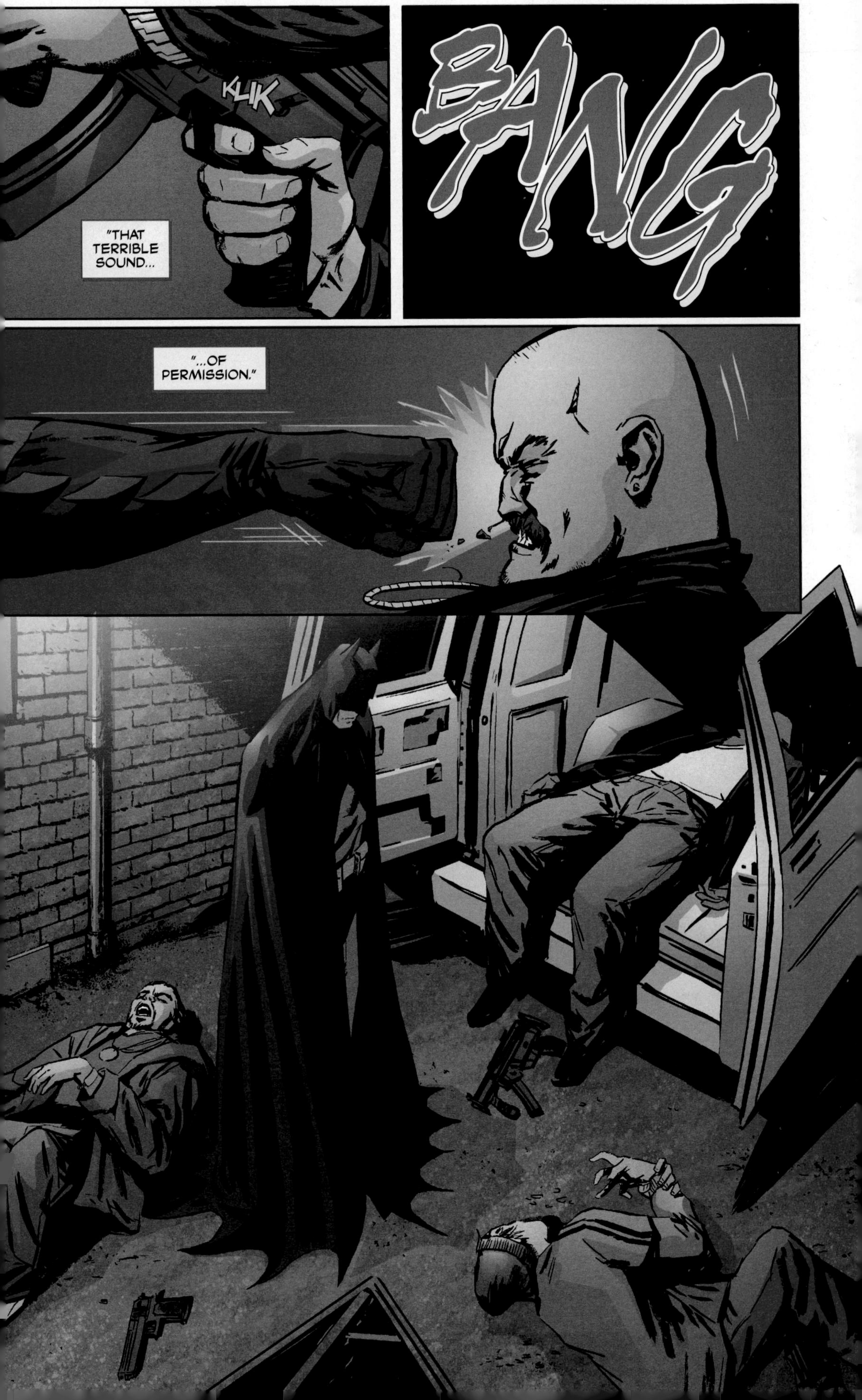
KLIK
"THAT TERRIBLE SOUND...
BANG
"...OF PERMISSION."

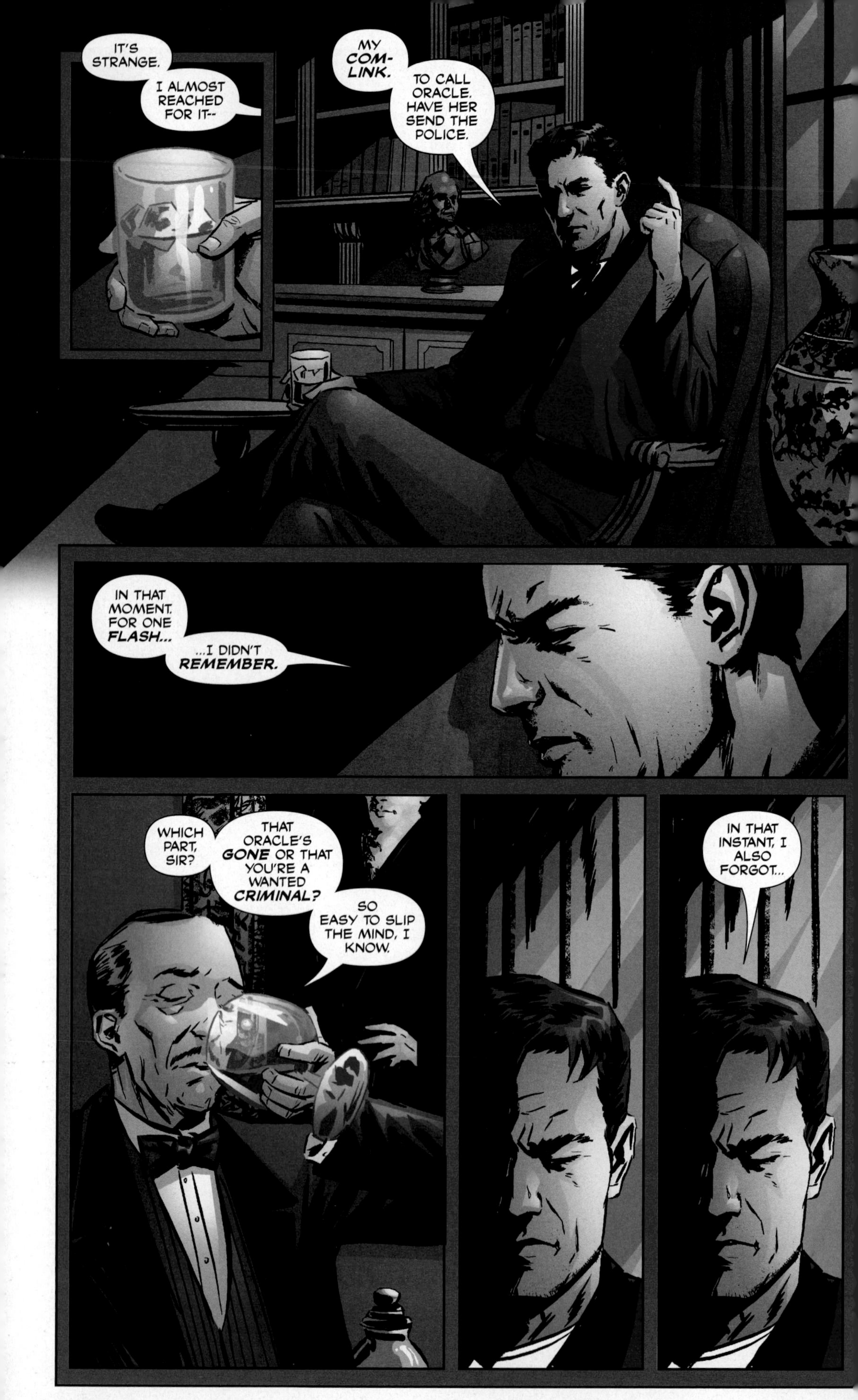
IT'S STRANGE.
I ALMOST REACHED FOR IT--
MY COM-LINK.
TO CALL ORACLE. HAVE HER SEND THE POLICE.
IN THAT MOMENT. FOR ONE FLASH...
...I DIDN'T REMEMBER.
WHICH PART, SIR?
THAT ORACLE'S GONE OR THAT YOU'RE A WANTED CRIMINAL?
SO EASY TO SLIP THE MIND, I KNOW.
IN THAT INSTANT, I ALSO FORGOT...

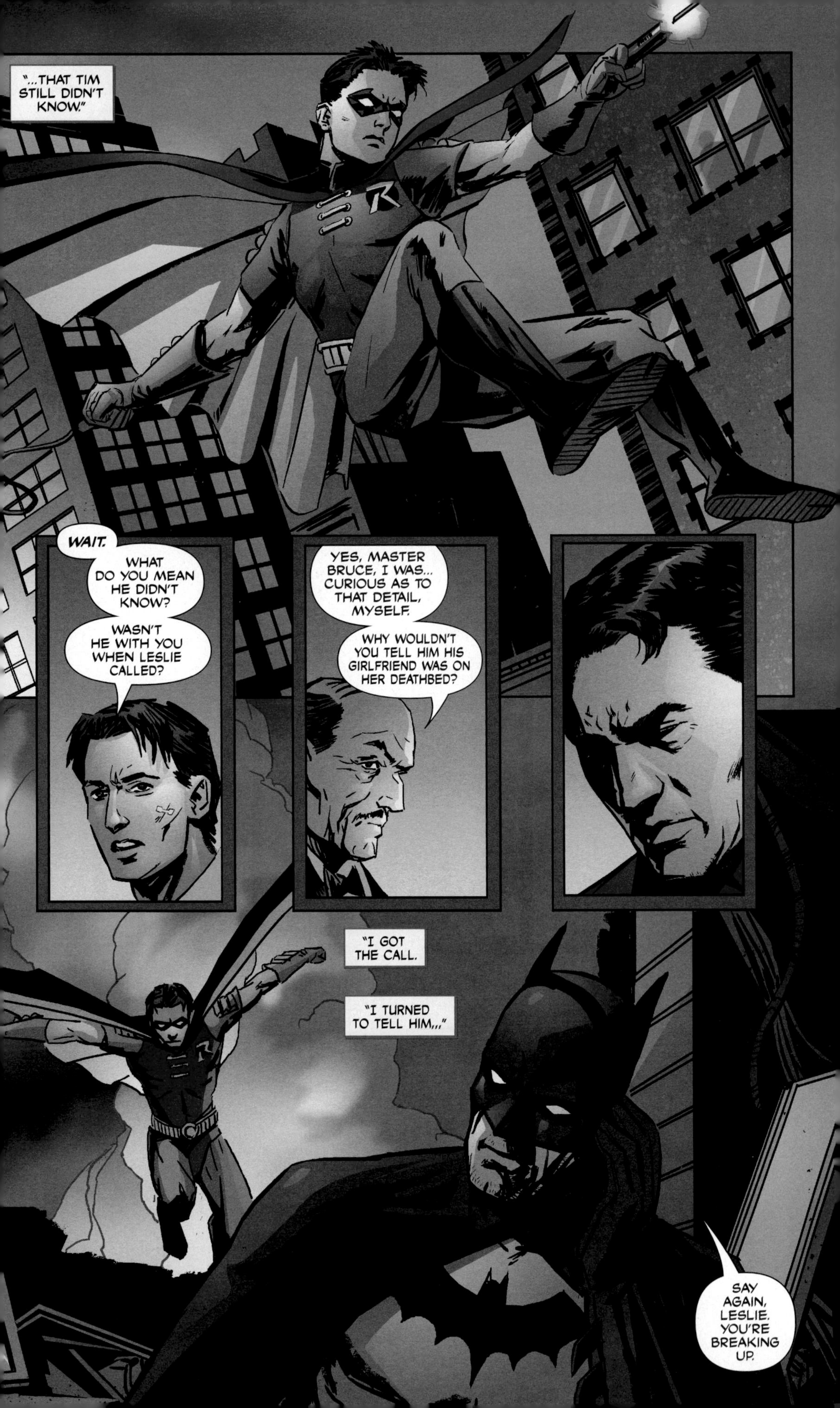
"...THAT TIM STILL DIDN'T KNOW."
WAIT.
WHAT DO YOU MEAN HE DIDN'T KNOW?
WASN'T HE WITH YOU WHEN LESLIE CALLED?
YES, MASTER BRUCE, I WAS... CURIOUS AS TO THAT DETAIL, MYSELF.
WHY WOULDN'T YOU TELL HIM HIS GIRLFRIEND WAS ON HER DEATHBED?
"I GOT THE CALL.
"I TURNED TO TELL HIM...
SAY AGAIN, LESLIE. YOU'RE BREAKING UP.

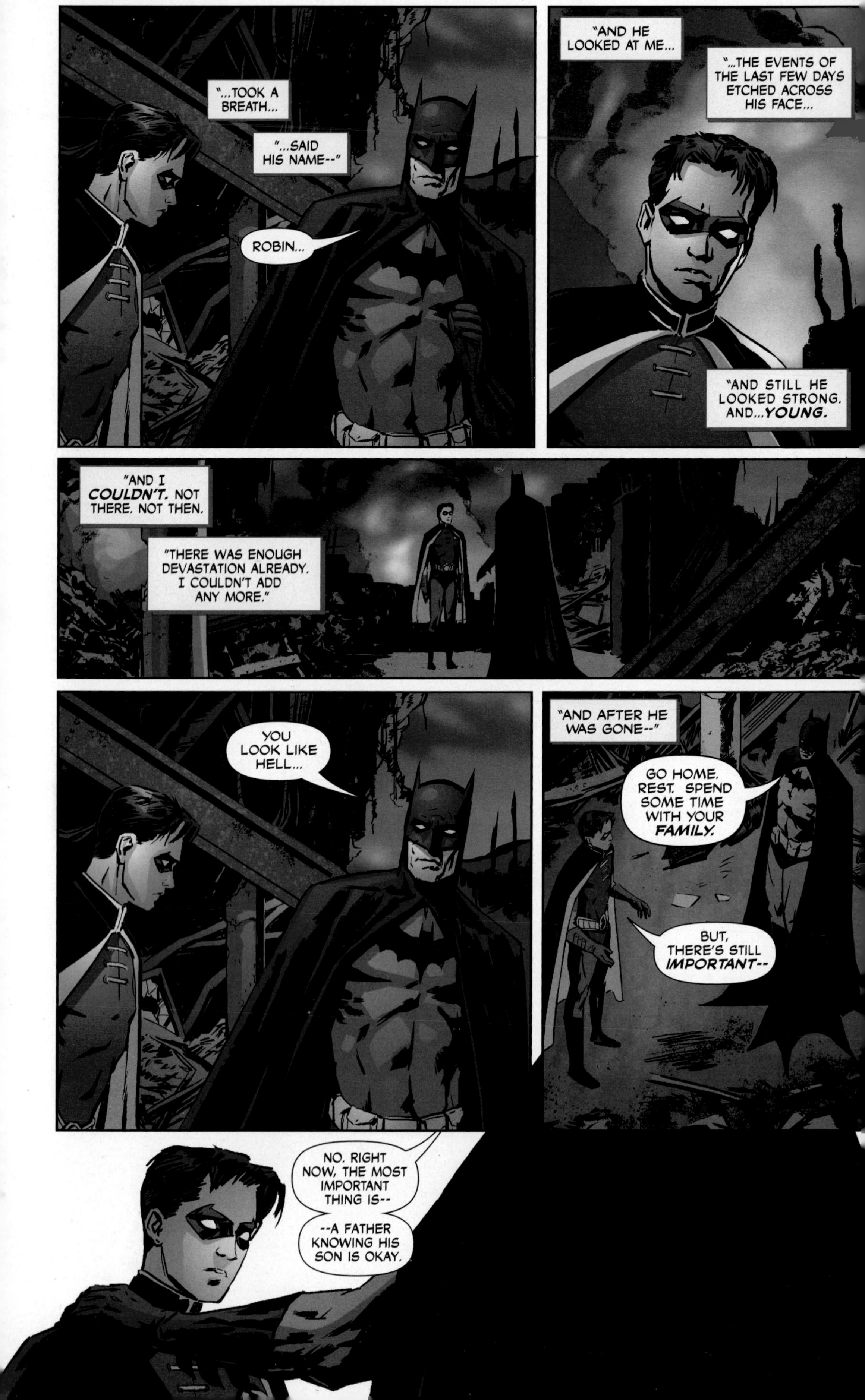
"...TOOK A BREATH...
"...SAID HIS NAME--"
ROBIN...
"AND HE LOOKED AT ME...
"...THE EVENTS OF THE LAST FEW DAYS ETCHED ACROSS HIS FACE...
"AND STILL HE LOOKED STRONG. AND...YOUNG.
"AND I COULDN'T. NOT THERE. NOT THEN.
"THERE WAS ENOUGH DEVASTATION ALREADY. I COULDN'T ADD ANY MORE."
YOU LOOK LIKE HELL...
"AND AFTER HE WAS GONE--"
GO HOME. REST. SPEND SOME TIME WITH YOUR FAMILY.
BUT, THERE'S STILL IMPORTANT--
NO. RIGHT NOW, THE MOST IMPORTANT THING IS--
--A FATHER KNOWING HIS SON IS OKAY.

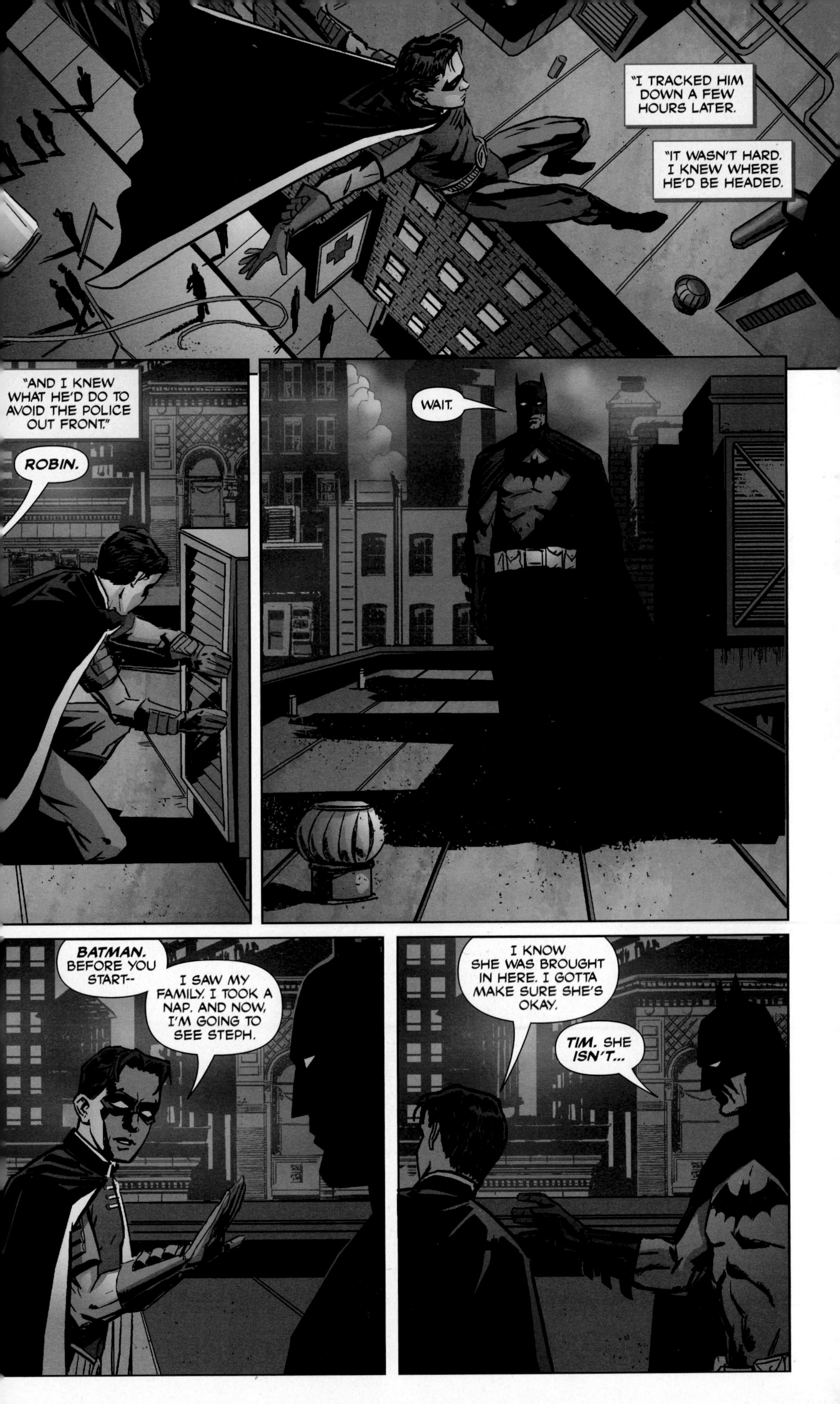
"I TRACKED HIM DOWN A FEW HOURS LATER.
"IT WASN'T HARD. I KNEW WHERE HE'D BE HEADED.
"AND I KNEW WHAT HE'D DO TO AVOID THE POLICE OUT FRONT."
ROBIN.
WAIT.
BATMAN. BEFORE YOU START--
I SAW MY FAMILY. I TOOK A NAP. AND NOW, I'M GOING TO SEE STEPH.
I KNOW SHE WAS BROUGHT IN HERE. I GOTTA MAKE SURE SHE'S OKAY.
TIM. SHE ISN'T...

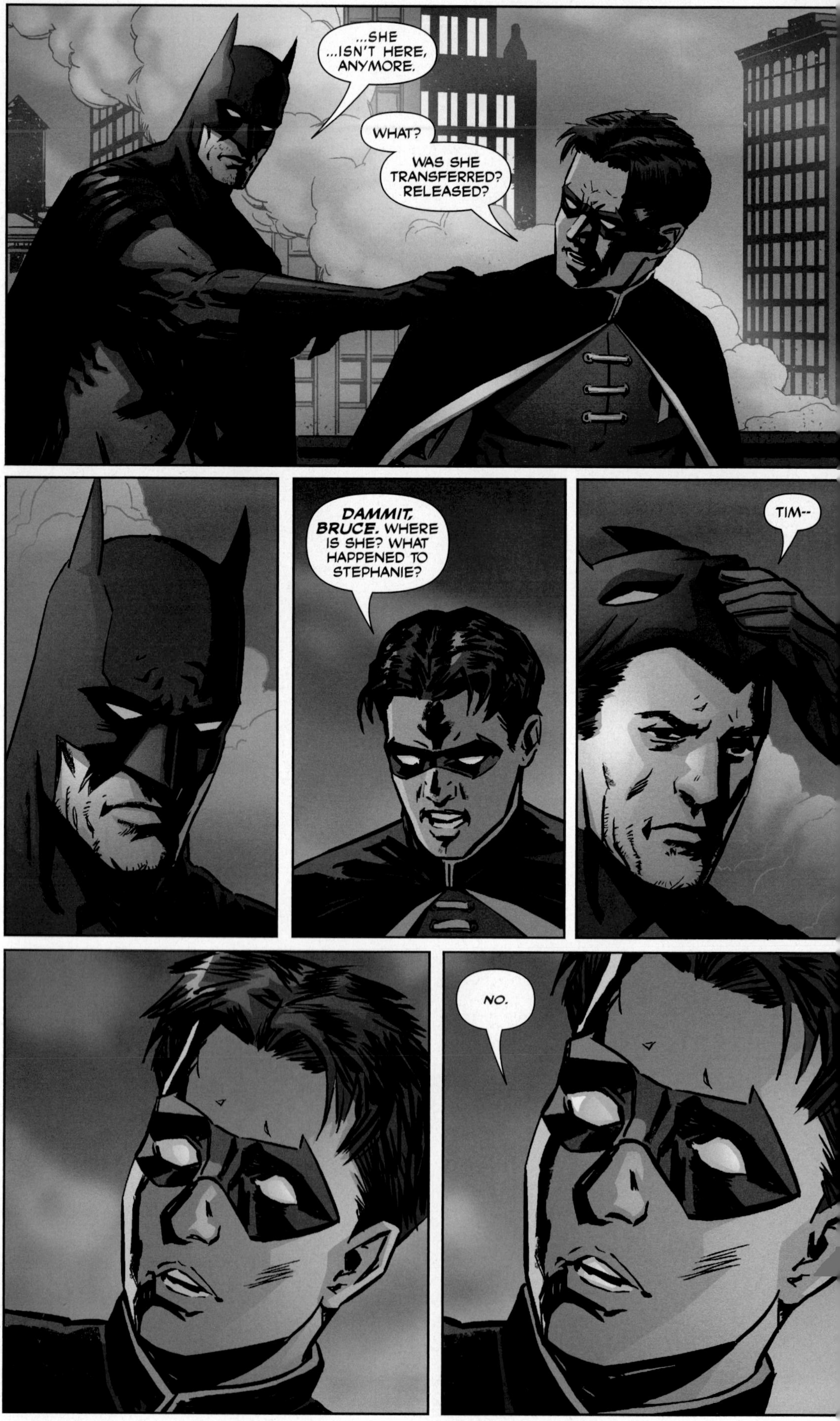
...SHE ...ISN'T HERE, ANYMORE.
WHAT?
WAS SHE TRANSFERRED? RELEASED?
DAMMIT, BRUCE. WHERE IS SHE? WHAT HAPPENED TO STEPHANIE?
TIM--
NO.

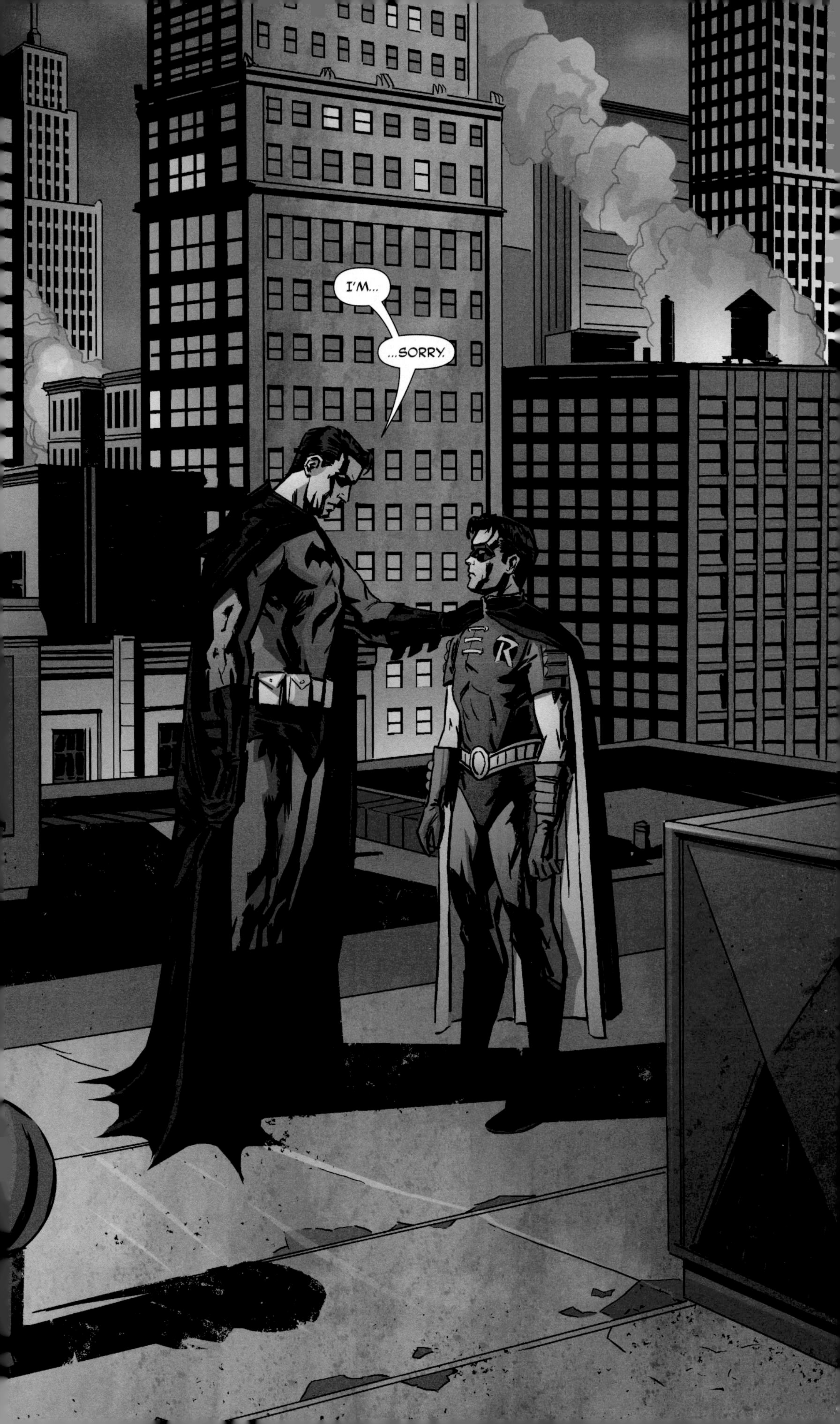
I'M...
...SORRY.

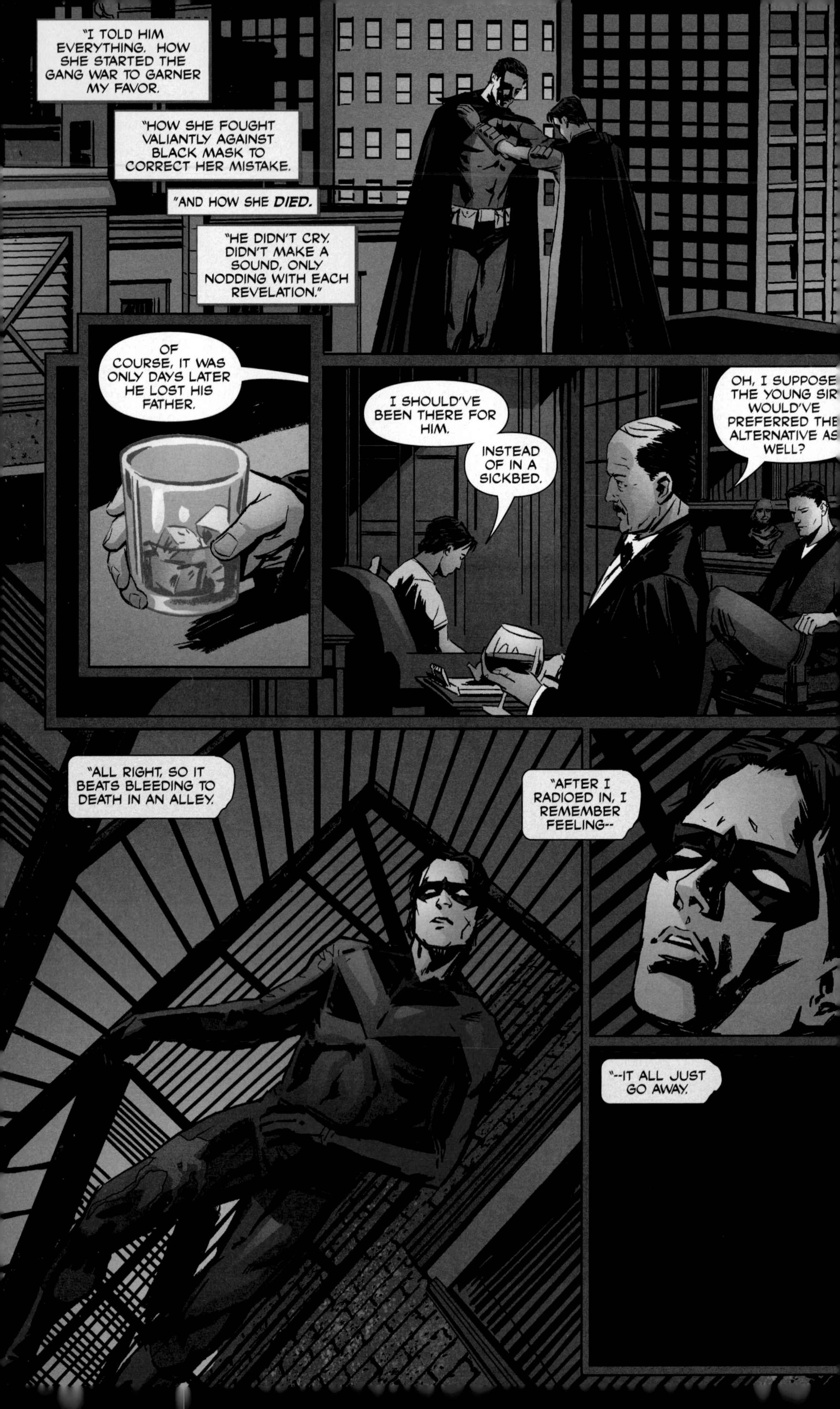
"I TOLD HIM EVERYTHING. HOW SHE STARTED THE GANG WAR TO GARNER MY FAVOR.
"HOW SHE FOUGHT VALIANTLY AGAINST BLACK MASK TO CORRECT HER MISTAKE.
"AND HOW SHE *DIED.*
"HE DIDN'T CRY. DIDN'T MAKE A SOUND, ONLY NODDING WITH EACH REVELATION."
OF COURSE, IT WAS ONLY DAYS LATER HE LOST HIS FATHER.
I SHOULD'VE BEEN THERE FOR HIM.
INSTEAD OF IN A SICKBED.
OH, I SUPPOSE THE YOUNG SIR WOULD'VE PREFERRED THE ALTERNATIVE AS WELL?
"ALL RIGHT, SO IT BEATS BLEEDING TO DEATH IN AN ALLEY.
"AFTER I RADIOED IN, I REMEMBER FEELING--
"--IT ALL JUST GO AWAY.

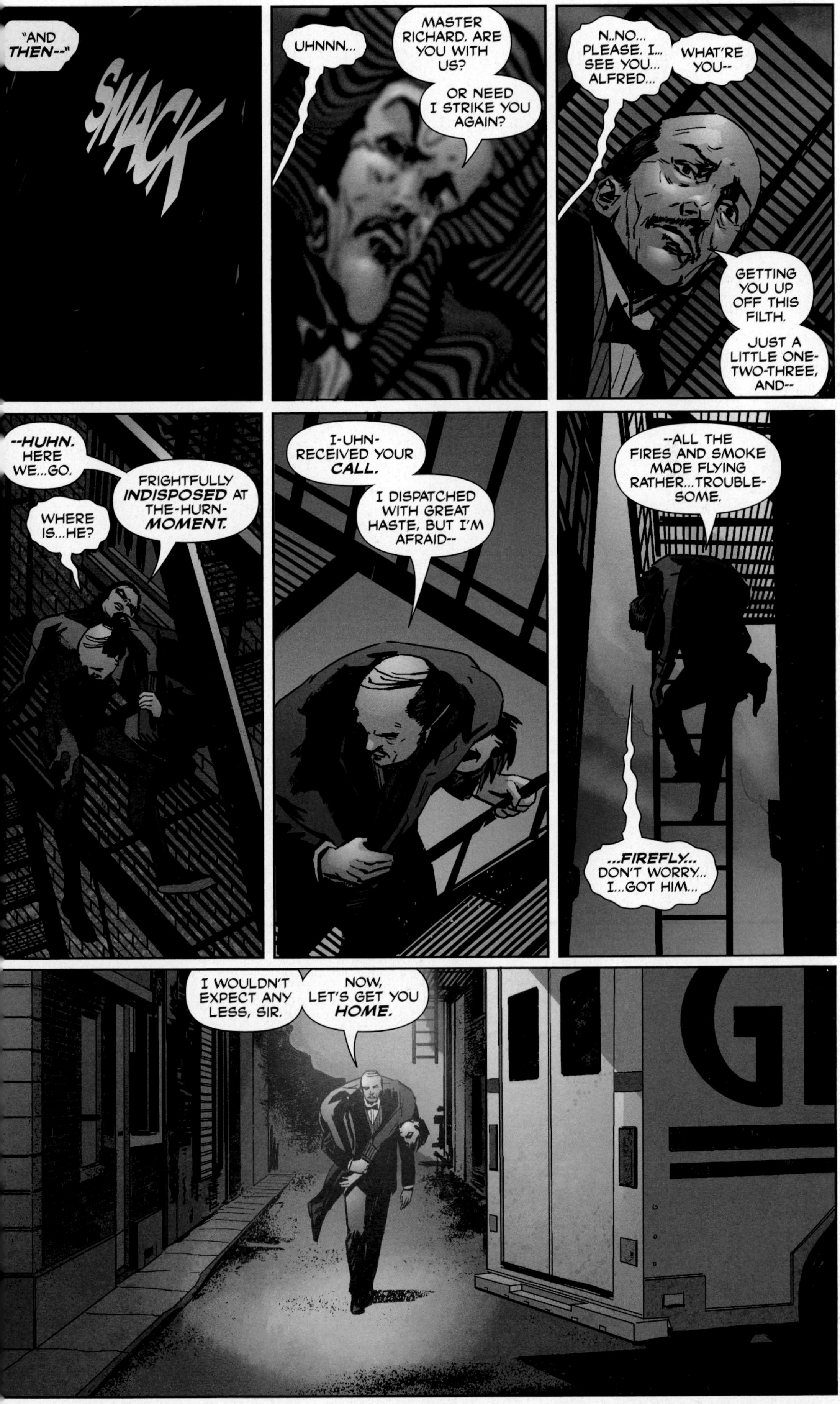

"AND *THEN--*"
SMACK
UHNNN...
MASTER RICHARD, ARE YOU WITH US?
OR NEED I STRIKE YOU AGAIN?
N..NO... PLEASE. I... SEE YOU... ALFRED...
WHAT'RE YOU--
GETTING YOU UP OFF THIS FILTH.
JUST A LITTLE ONE-TWO-THREE, AND--
--HUHN. HERE WE...GO.
WHERE IS...HE?
FRIGHTFULLY *INDISPOSED* AT THE-HURN-*MOMENT.*
I-UHN-RECEIVED YOUR *CALL.*
I DISPATCHED WITH GREAT HASTE, BUT I'M AFRAID--
--ALL THE FIRES AND SMOKE MADE FLYING RATHER...TROUBLE-SOME.
...FIREFLY... DON'T WORRY... I...GOT HIM...
I WOULDN'T EXPECT ANY LESS, SIR.
NOW, LET'S GET YOU *HOME.*

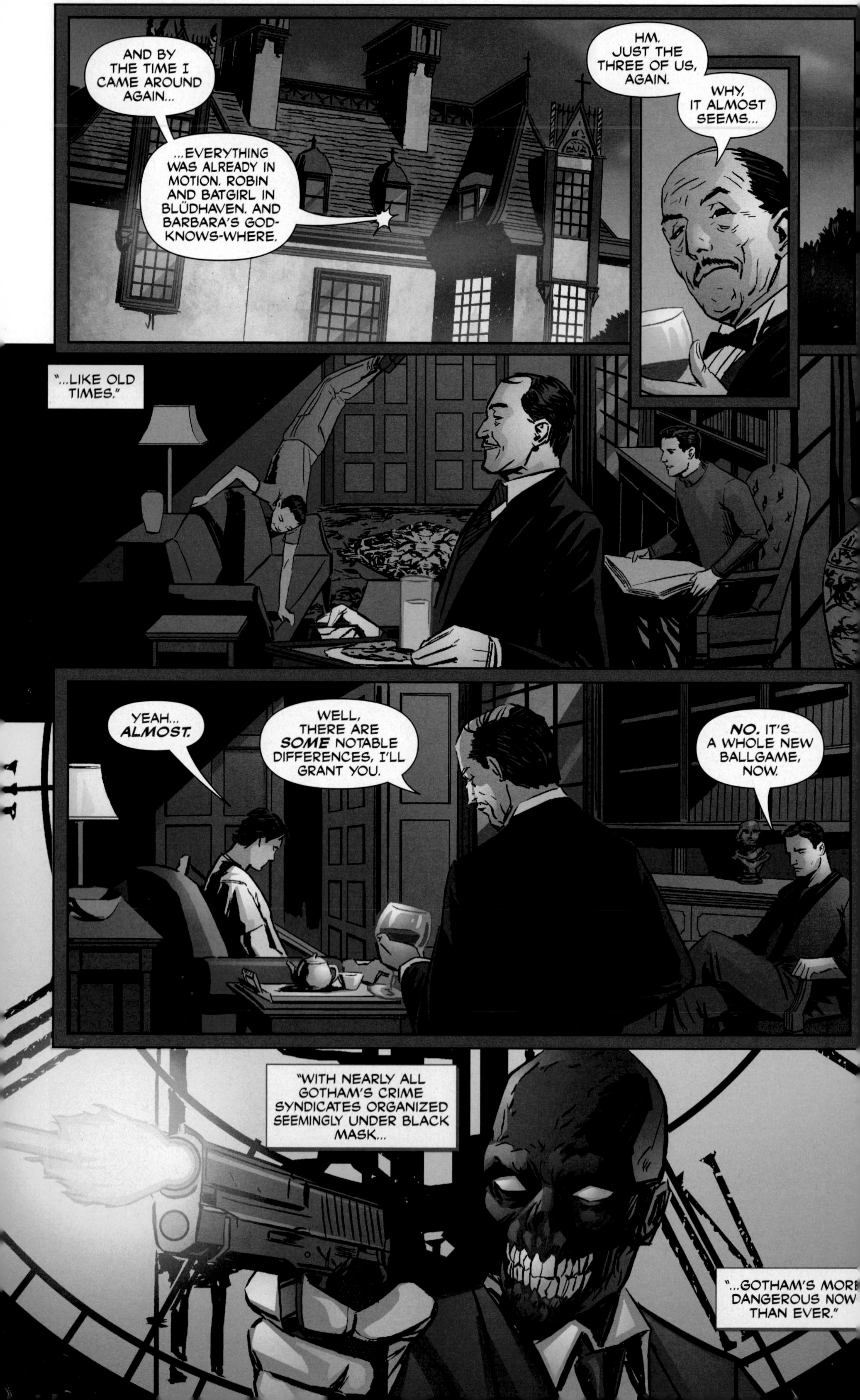
AND BY THE TIME I CAME AROUND AGAIN...
...EVERYTHING WAS ALREADY IN MOTION. ROBIN AND BATGIRL IN BLÜDHAVEN. AND BARBARA'S GOD-KNOWS-WHERE.
HM. JUST THE THREE OF US, AGAIN.
WHY, IT ALMOST SEEMS...
"...LIKE OLD TIMES."
YEAH... ALMOST.
WELL, THERE ARE SOME NOTABLE DIFFERENCES, I'LL GRANT YOU.
NO. IT'S A WHOLE NEW BALLGAME, NOW.
"WITH NEARLY ALL GOTHAM'S CRIME SYNDICATES ORGANIZED SEEMINGLY UNDER BLACK MASK...
"...GOTHAM'S MOR DANGEROUS NOW THAN EVER."

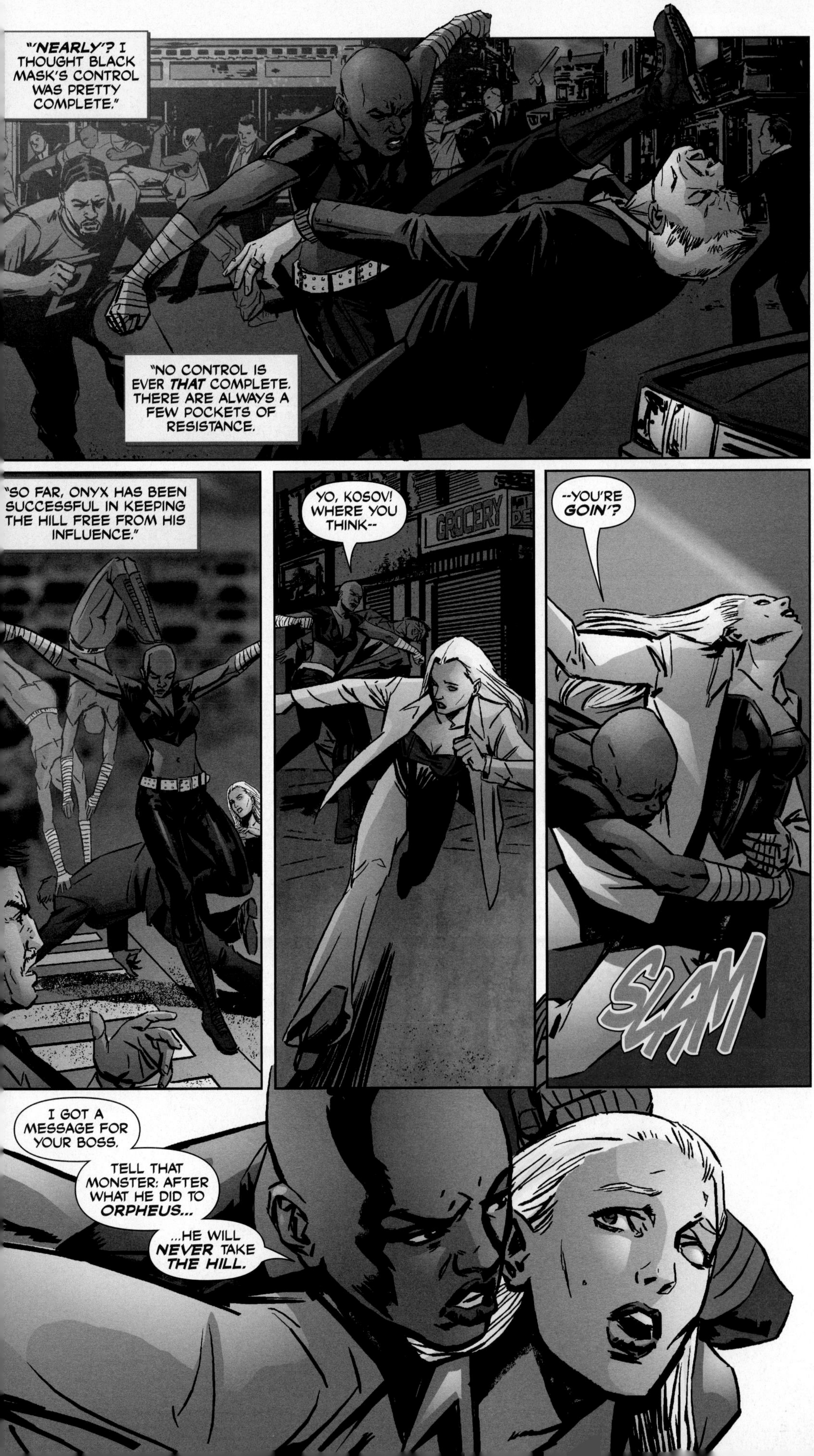
"'NEARLY'? I THOUGHT BLACK MASK'S CONTROL WAS PRETTY COMPLETE."
"NO CONTROL IS EVER THAT COMPLETE. THERE ARE ALWAYS A FEW POCKETS OF RESISTANCE.
"SO FAR, ONYX HAS BEEN SUCCESSFUL IN KEEPING THE HILL FREE FROM HIS INFLUENCE."
YO, KOSOV! WHERE YOU THINK--
GROCERY
--YOU'RE GOIN'?
SLAM
I GOT A MESSAGE FOR YOUR BOSS.
TELL THAT MONSTER: AFTER WHAT HE DID TO ORPHEUS...
...HE WILL NEVER TAKE THE HILL.

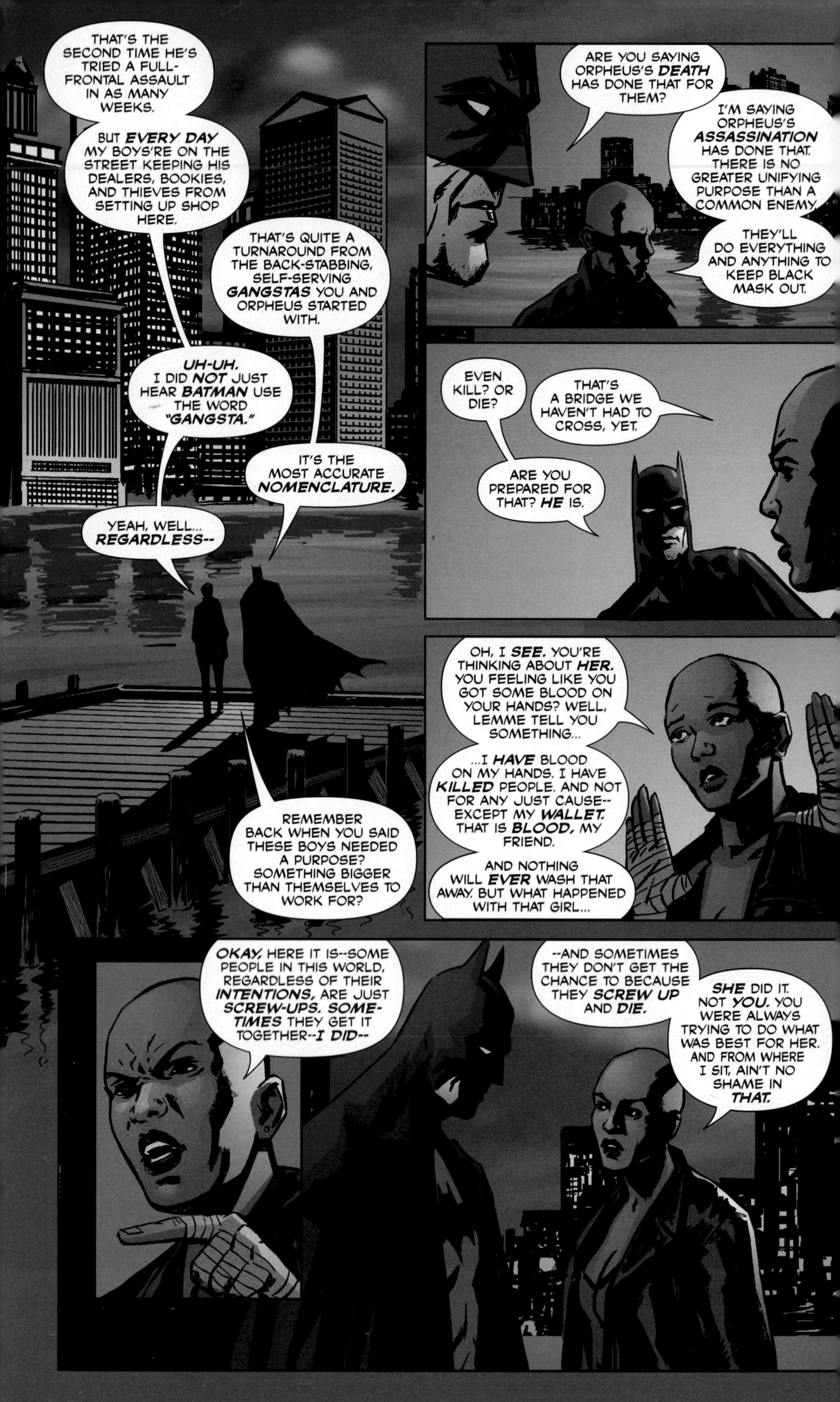

THAT'S THE SECOND TIME HE'S TRIED A FULL-FRONTAL ASSAULT IN AS MANY WEEKS.
BUT EVERY DAY MY BOYS'RE ON THE STREET KEEPING HIS DEALERS, BOOKIES, AND THIEVES FROM SETTING UP SHOP HERE.
THAT'S QUITE A TURNAROUND FROM THE BACK-STABBING, SELF-SERVING GANGSTAS YOU AND ORPHEUS STARTED WITH.
UH-UH. I DID NOT JUST HEAR BATMAN USE THE WORD "GANGSTA."
IT'S THE MOST ACCURATE NOMENCLATURE.
YEAH, WELL... REGARDLESS--
REMEMBER BACK WHEN YOU SAID THESE BOYS NEEDED A PURPOSE? SOMETHING BIGGER THAN THEMSELVES TO WORK FOR?
ARE YOU SAYING ORPHEUS'S DEATH HAS DONE THAT FOR THEM?
I'M SAYING ORPHEUS'S ASSASSINATION HAS DONE THAT. THERE IS NO GREATER UNIFYING PURPOSE THAN A COMMON ENEMY.
THEY'LL DO EVERYTHING AND ANYTHING TO KEEP BLACK MASK OUT.
EVEN KILL? OR DIE?
THAT'S A BRIDGE WE HAVEN'T HAD TO CROSS, YET.
ARE YOU PREPARED FOR THAT? HE IS.
OH, I SEE. YOU'RE THINKING ABOUT HER. YOU FEELING LIKE YOU GOT SOME BLOOD ON YOUR HANDS? WELL, LEMME TELL YOU SOMETHING...
...I HAVE BLOOD ON MY HANDS. I HAVE KILLED PEOPLE. AND NOT FOR ANY JUST CAUSE-- EXCEPT MY WALLET. THAT IS BLOOD, MY FRIEND.
AND NOTHING WILL EVER WASH THAT AWAY. BUT WHAT HAPPENED WITH THAT GIRL...
OKAY. HERE IT IS--SOME PEOPLE IN THIS WORLD, REGARDLESS OF THEIR INTENTIONS, ARE JUST SCREW-UPS. SOMETIMES THEY GET IT TOGETHER--I DID--
--AND SOMETIMES THEY DON'T GET THE CHANCE TO BECAUSE THEY SCREW UP AND DIE.
SHE DID IT. NOT YOU. YOU WERE ALWAYS TRYING TO DO WHAT WAS BEST FOR HER. AND FROM WHERE I SIT, AIN'T NO SHAME IN THAT.

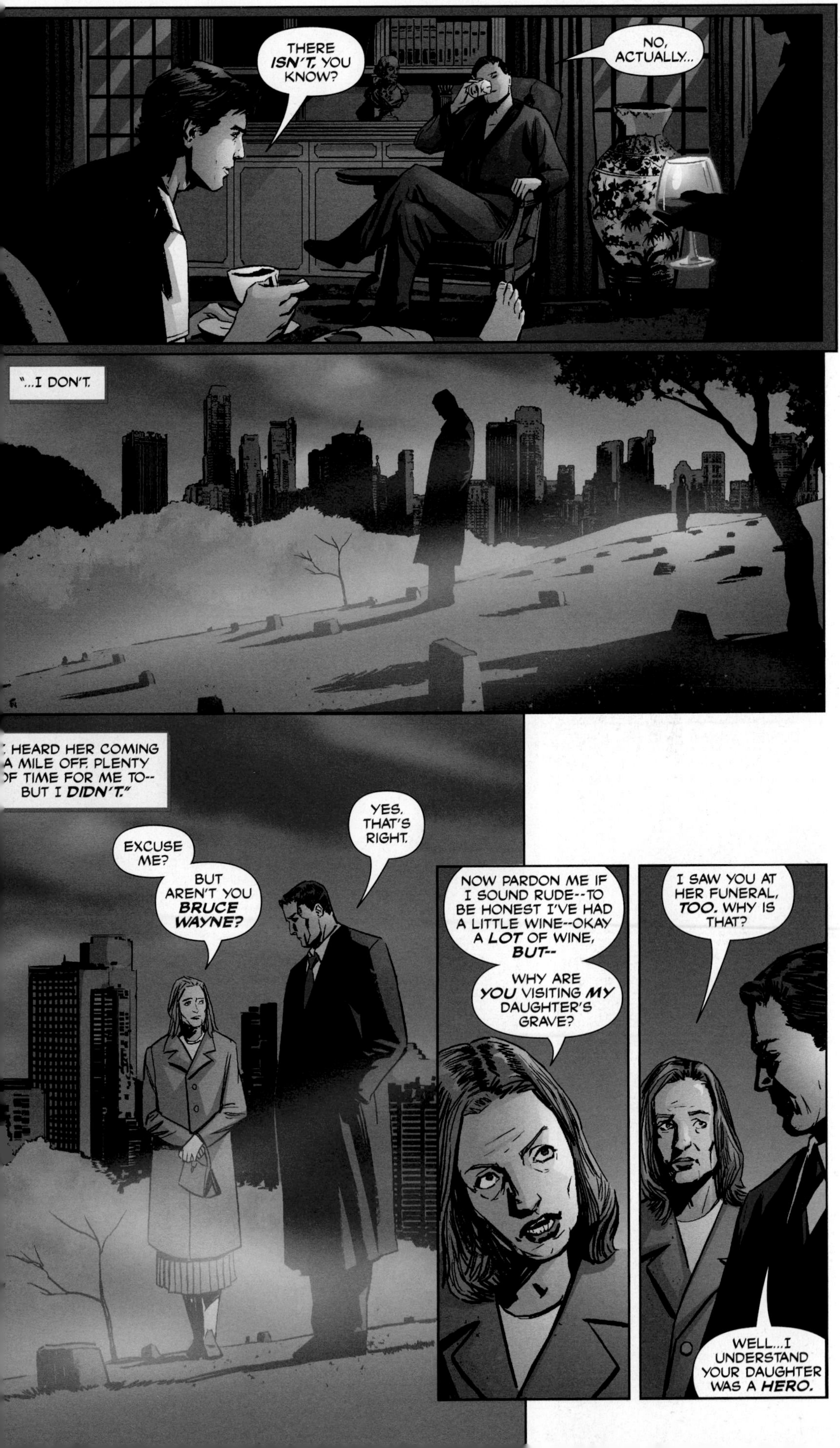
THERE ISN'T, YOU KNOW?
NO, ACTUALLY...
"...I DON'T.
HEARD HER COMING A MILE OFF. PLENTY OF TIME FOR ME TO-- BUT I DIDN'T."
EXCUSE ME?
BUT AREN'T YOU BRUCE WAYNE?
YES. THAT'S RIGHT.
NOW PARDON ME IF I SOUND RUDE--TO BE HONEST I'VE HAD A LITTLE WINE--OKAY A LOT OF WINE, BUT--
WHY ARE YOU VISITING MY DAUGHTER'S GRAVE?
I SAW YOU AT HER FUNERAL, TOO. WHY IS THAT?
WELL...I UNDERSTAND YOUR DAUGHTER WAS A HERO.

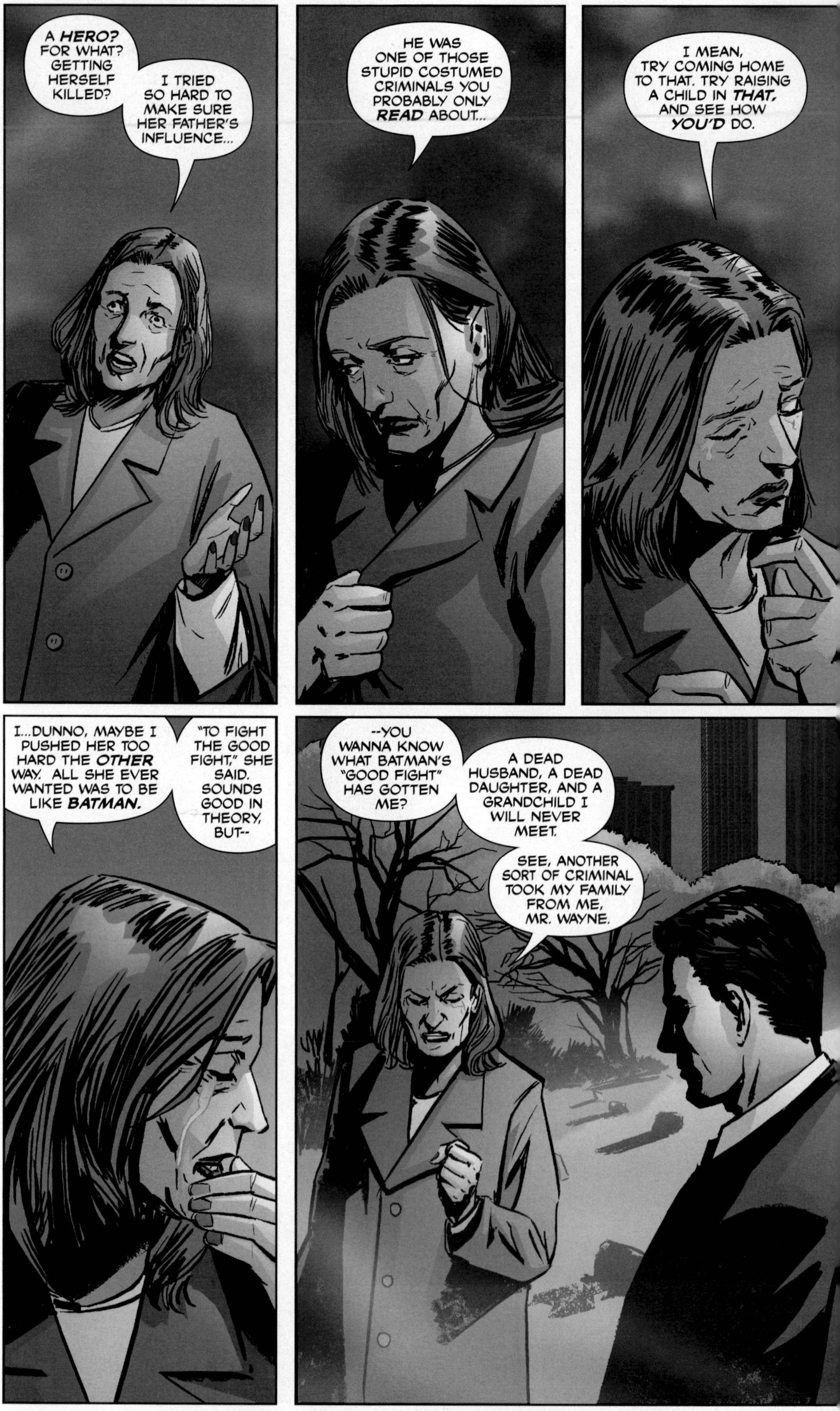
A HERO? FOR WHAT? GETTING HERSELF KILLED?
I TRIED SO HARD TO MAKE SURE HER FATHER'S INFLUENCE...
HE WAS ONE OF THOSE STUPID COSTUMED CRIMINALS YOU PROBABLY ONLY READ ABOUT...
I MEAN, TRY COMING HOME TO THAT. TRY RAISING A CHILD IN THAT, AND SEE HOW YOU'D DO.
I...DUNNO, MAYBE I PUSHED HER TOO HARD THE OTHER WAY. ALL SHE EVER WANTED WAS TO BE LIKE BATMAN.
"TO FIGHT THE GOOD FIGHT," SHE SAID. SOUNDS GOOD IN THEORY, BUT--
--YOU WANNA KNOW WHAT BATMAN'S "GOOD FIGHT" HAS GOTTEN ME?
A DEAD HUSBAND, A DEAD DAUGHTER, AND A GRANDCHILD I WILL NEVER MEET.
SEE, ANOTHER SORT OF CRIMINAL TOOK MY FAMILY FROM ME, MR. WAYNE.

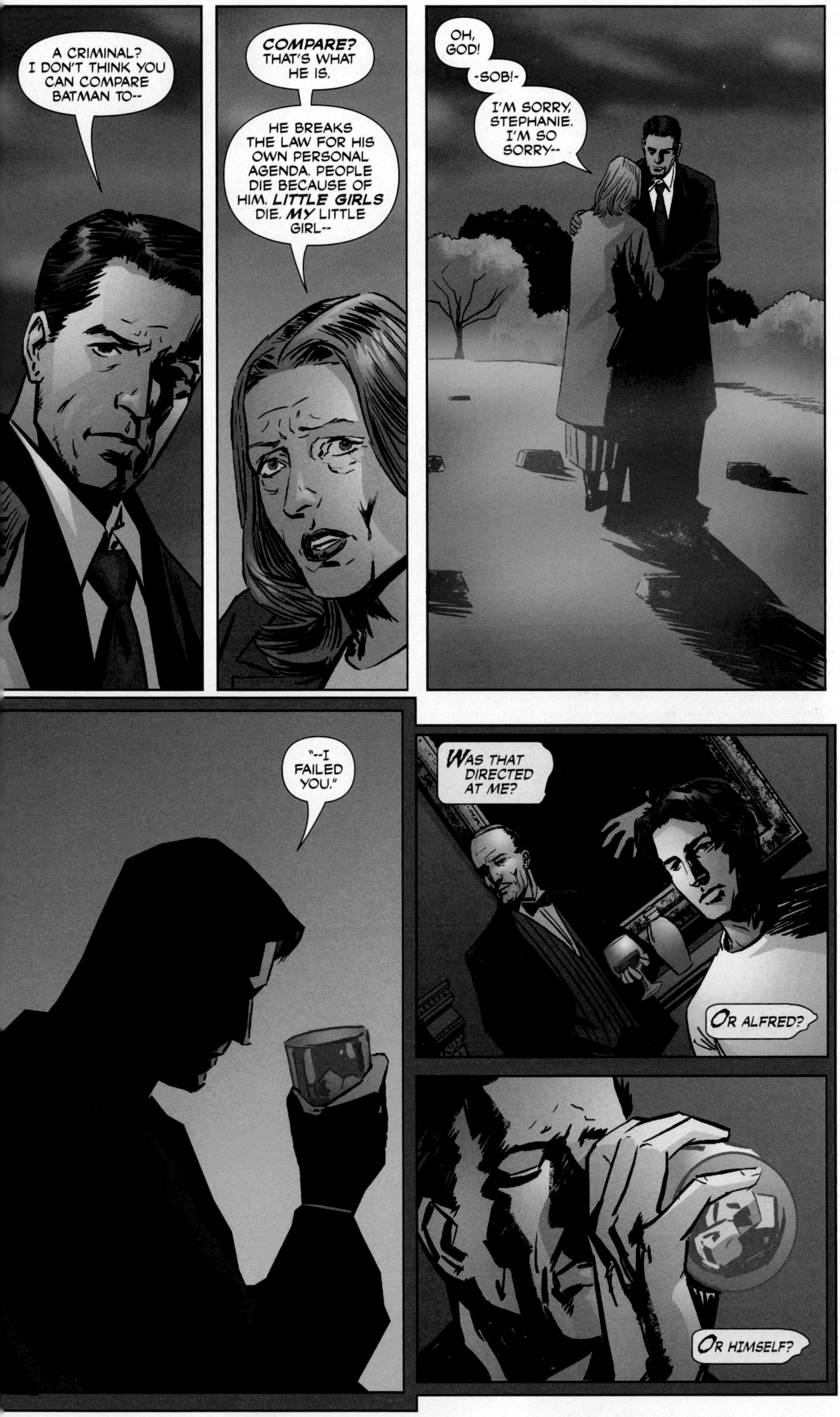
A CRIMINAL? I DON'T THINK YOU CAN COMPARE BATMAN TO--
COMPARE? THAT'S WHAT HE IS.
HE BREAKS THE LAW FOR HIS OWN PERSONAL AGENDA. PEOPLE DIE BECAUSE OF HIM. LITTLE GIRLS DIE. MY LITTLE GIRL--
OH, GOD!
-SOB!-
I'M SORRY, STEPHANIE. I'M SO SORRY--
"--I FAILED YOU."
WAS THAT DIRECTED AT ME?
OR ALFRED?
OR HIMSELF?

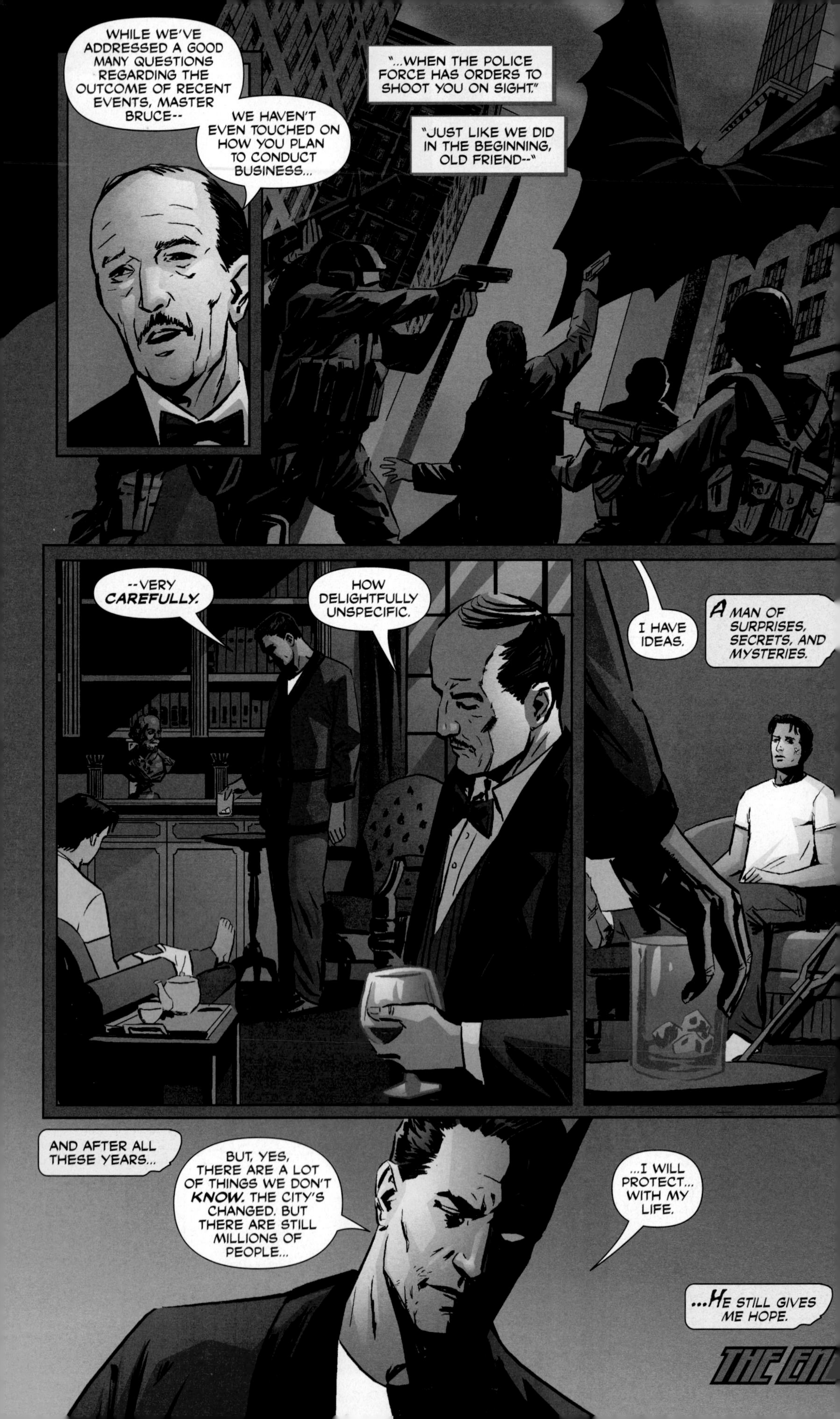
WHILE WE'VE ADDRESSED A GOOD MANY QUESTIONS REGARDING THE OUTCOME OF RECENT EVENTS, MASTER BRUCE--
WE HAVEN'T EVEN TOUCHED ON HOW YOU PLAN TO CONDUCT BUSINESS...
"...WHEN THE POLICE FORCE HAS ORDERS TO SHOOT YOU ON SIGHT."
"JUST LIKE WE DID IN THE BEGINNING, OLD FRIEND--"
--VERY *CAREFULLY.*
HOW DELIGHTFULLY UNSPECIFIC.
I HAVE IDEAS.
A MAN OF SURPRISES, SECRETS, AND MYSTERIES.
AND AFTER ALL THESE YEARS...
BUT, YES, THERE ARE A LOT OF THINGS WE DON'T *KNOW.* THE CITY'S CHANGED. BUT THERE ARE STILL MILLIONS OF PEOPLE...
...I WILL PROTECT... WITH MY LIFE.
...HE STILL GIVES ME HOPE.

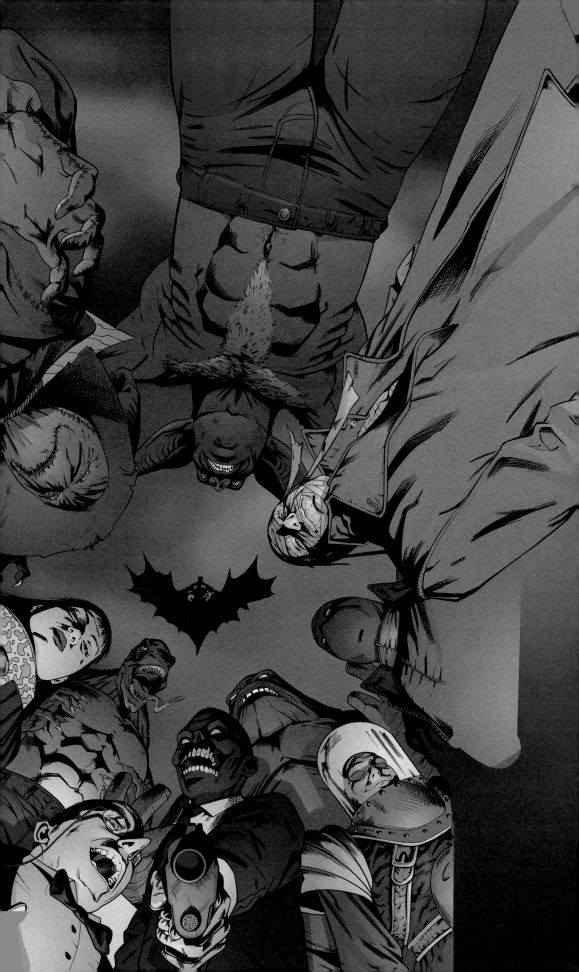

COVER ART BY
AL BARRIONUEVO,
BIT,
& GUY MAJOR

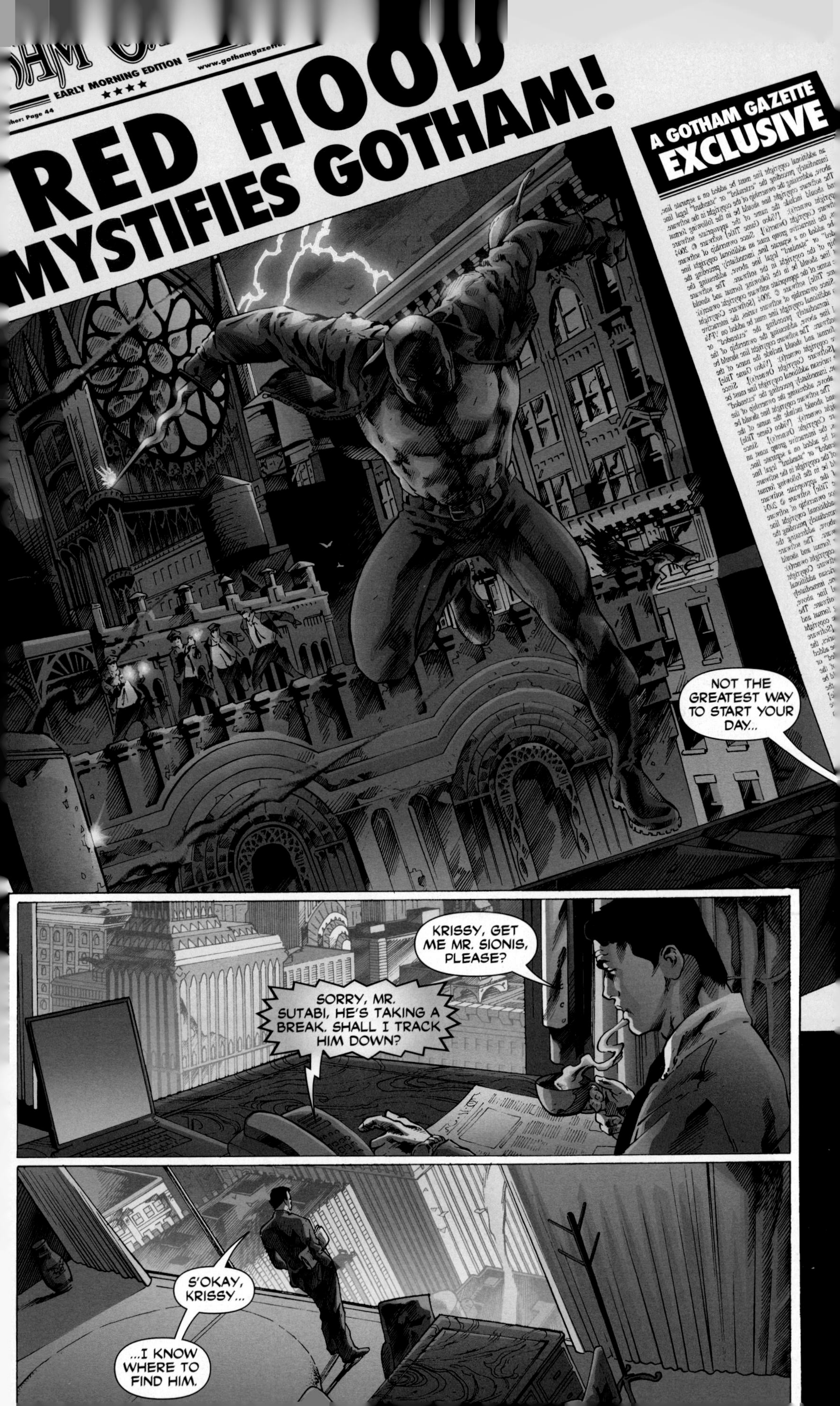
EARLY MORNING EDITION
www.gothamgazette
RED HOOD MYSTIFIES GOTHAM!
A GOTHAM GAZETTE EXCLUSIVE
NOT THE GREATEST WAY TO START YOUR DAY...
KRISSY, GET ME MR. SIONIS, PLEASE?
SORRY, MR. SUTABI, HE'S TAKING A BREAK. SHALL I TRACK HIM DOWN?
S'OKAY, KRISSY...
...I KNOW WHERE TO FIND HIM.

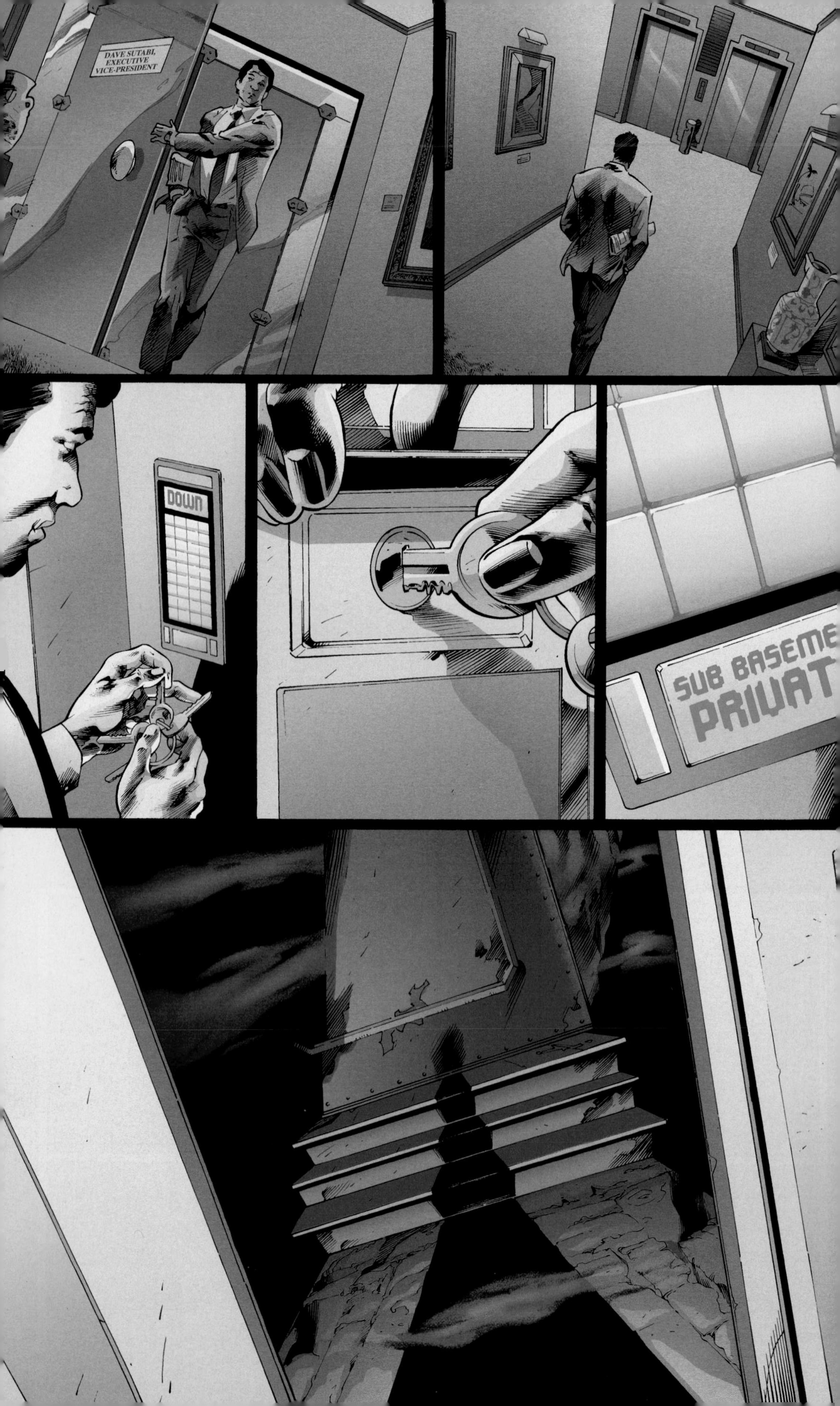
DAVE SUTABI, EXECUTIVE VICE-PRESIDENT
DOWN
SUB BASEME
PRIVAT

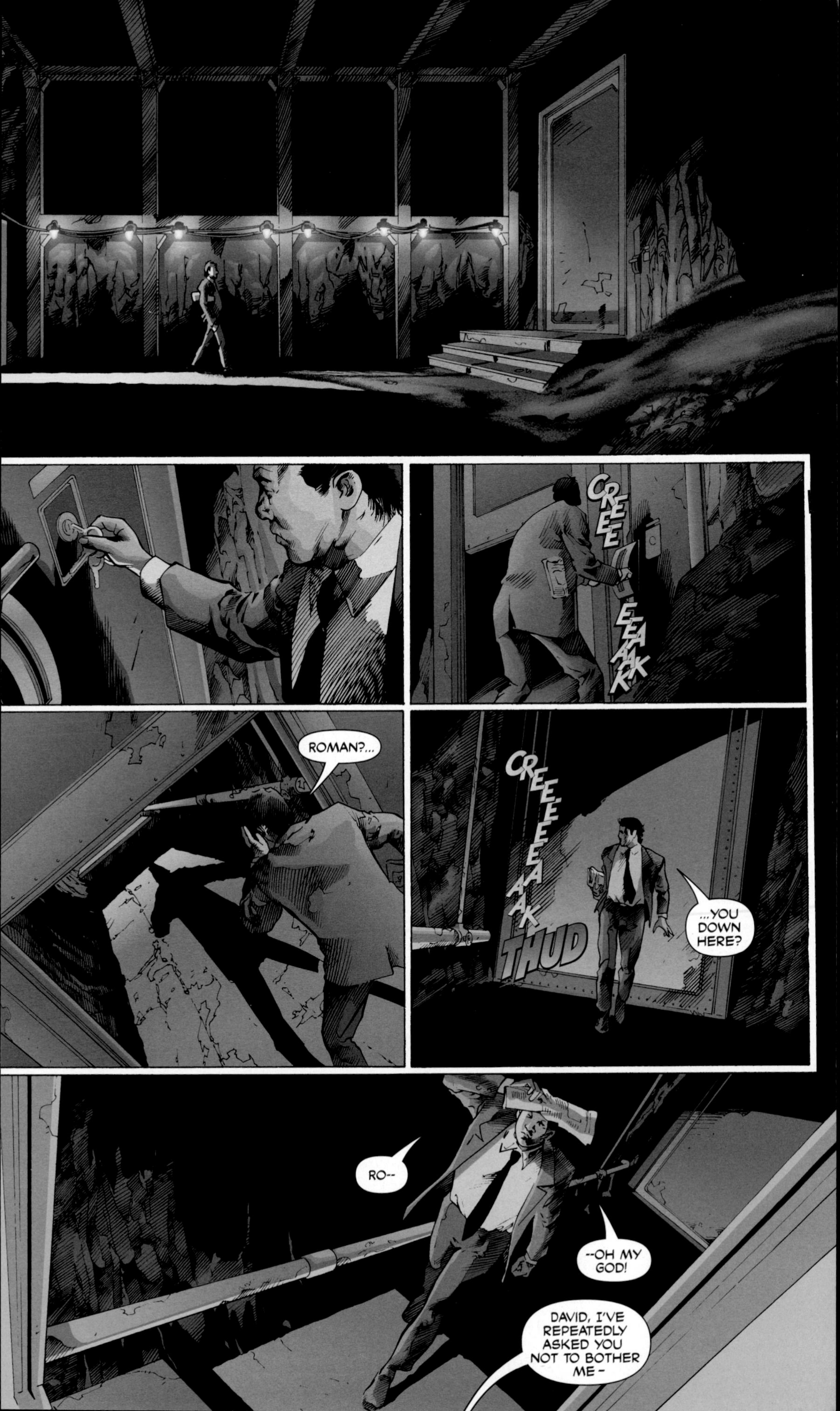
CREEEEAAK
ROMAN?...
CREEEEEEAAK
THUD
...YOU DOWN HERE?
RO--
--OH MY GOD!
DAVID, I'VE REPEATEDLY ASKED YOU NOT TO BOTHER ME -

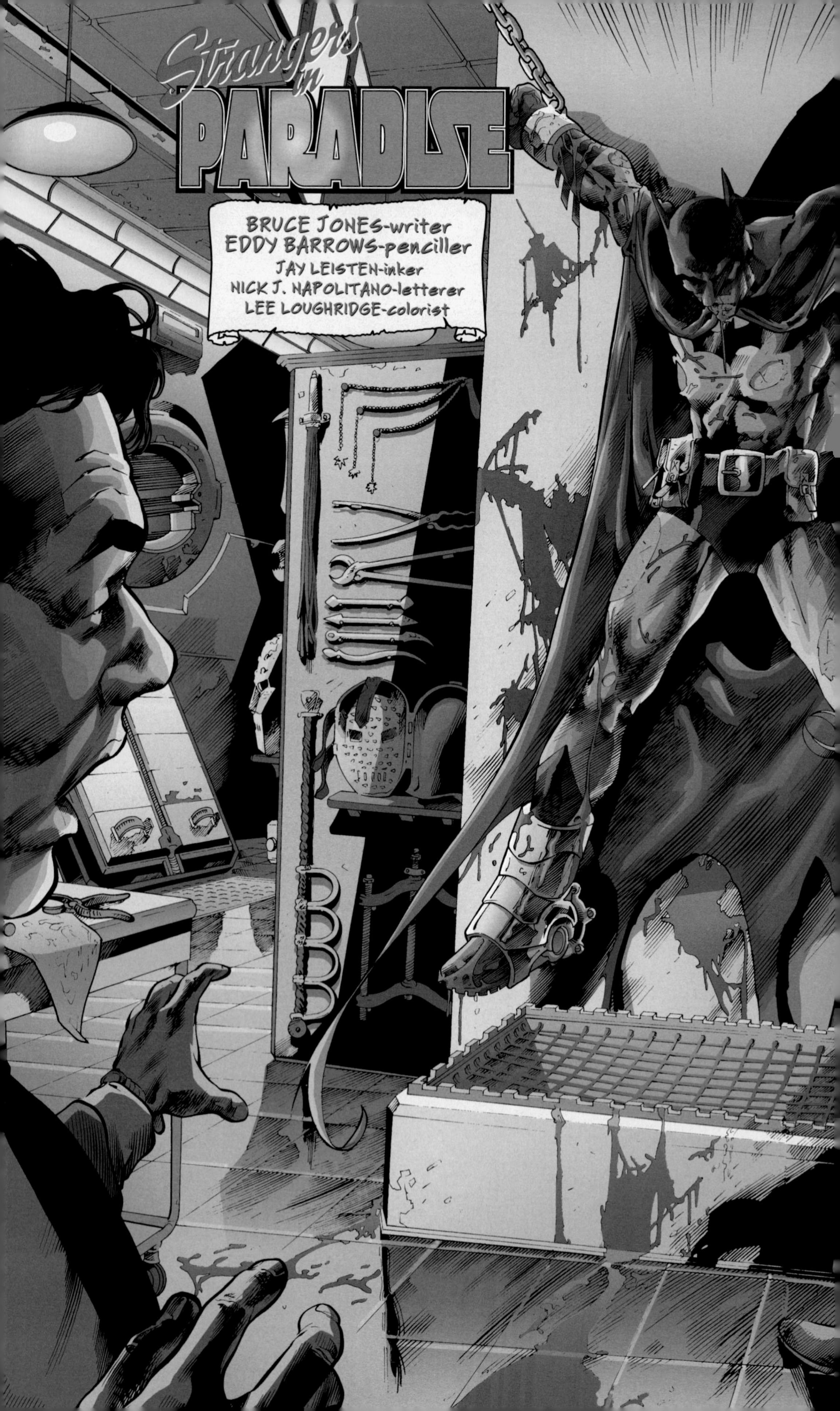
Strangers in PARADISE
BRUCE JONES-writer
EDDY BARROWS-penciller
JAY LEISTEN-inker
NICK J. NAPOLITANO-letterer
LEE LOUGHRIDGE-colorist

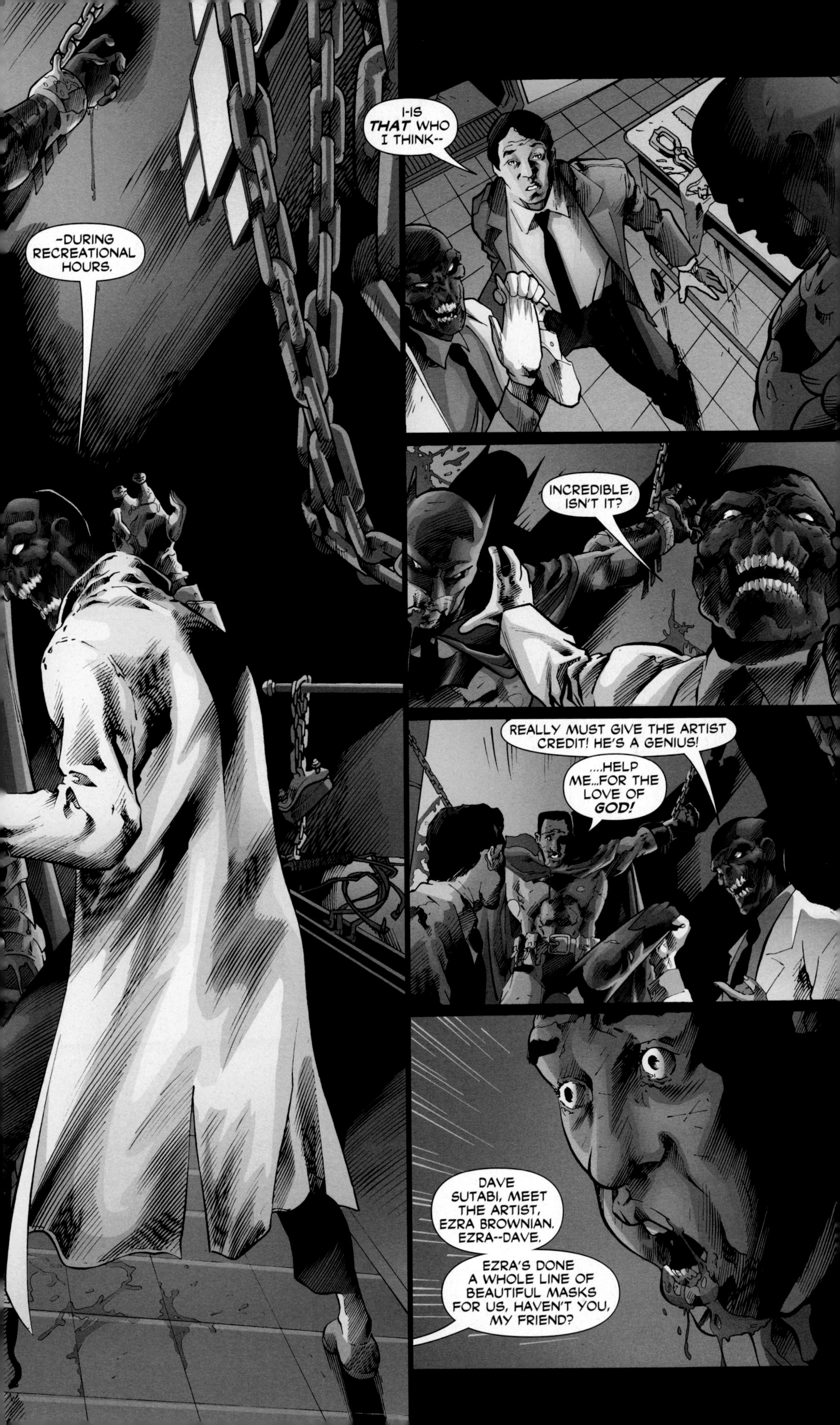

-DURING RECREATIONAL HOURS.
I-IS **THAT** WHO I THINK--
INCREDIBLE, ISN'T IT?
REALLY MUST GIVE THE ARTIST CREDIT! HE'S A GENIUS!
....HELP ME...FOR THE LOVE OF **GOD!**
DAVE SUTABI, MEET THE ARTIST, EZRA BROWNIAN. EZRA--DAVE.
EZRA'S DONE A WHOLE LINE OF BEAUTIFUL MASKS FOR US, HAVEN'T YOU, MY FRIEND?

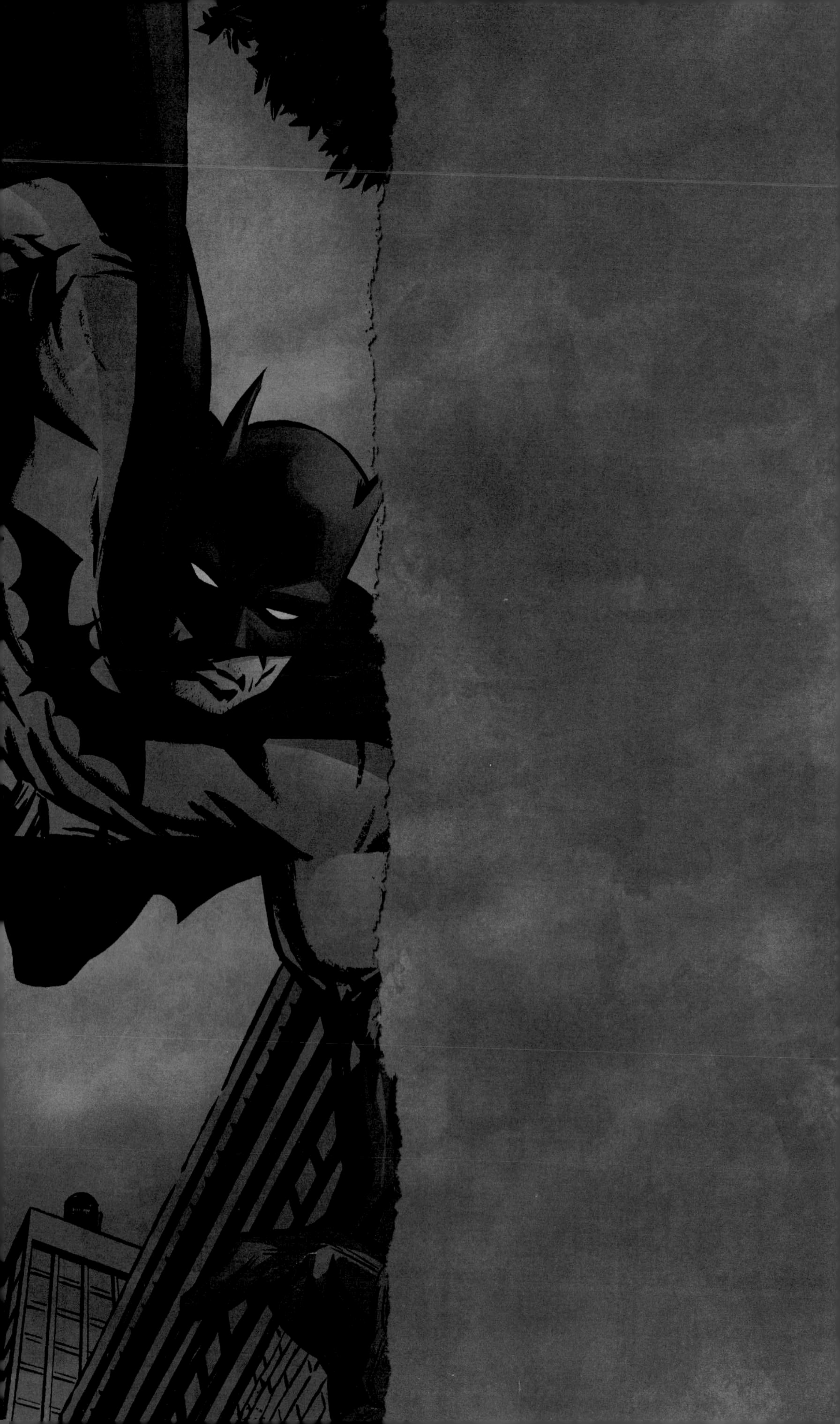

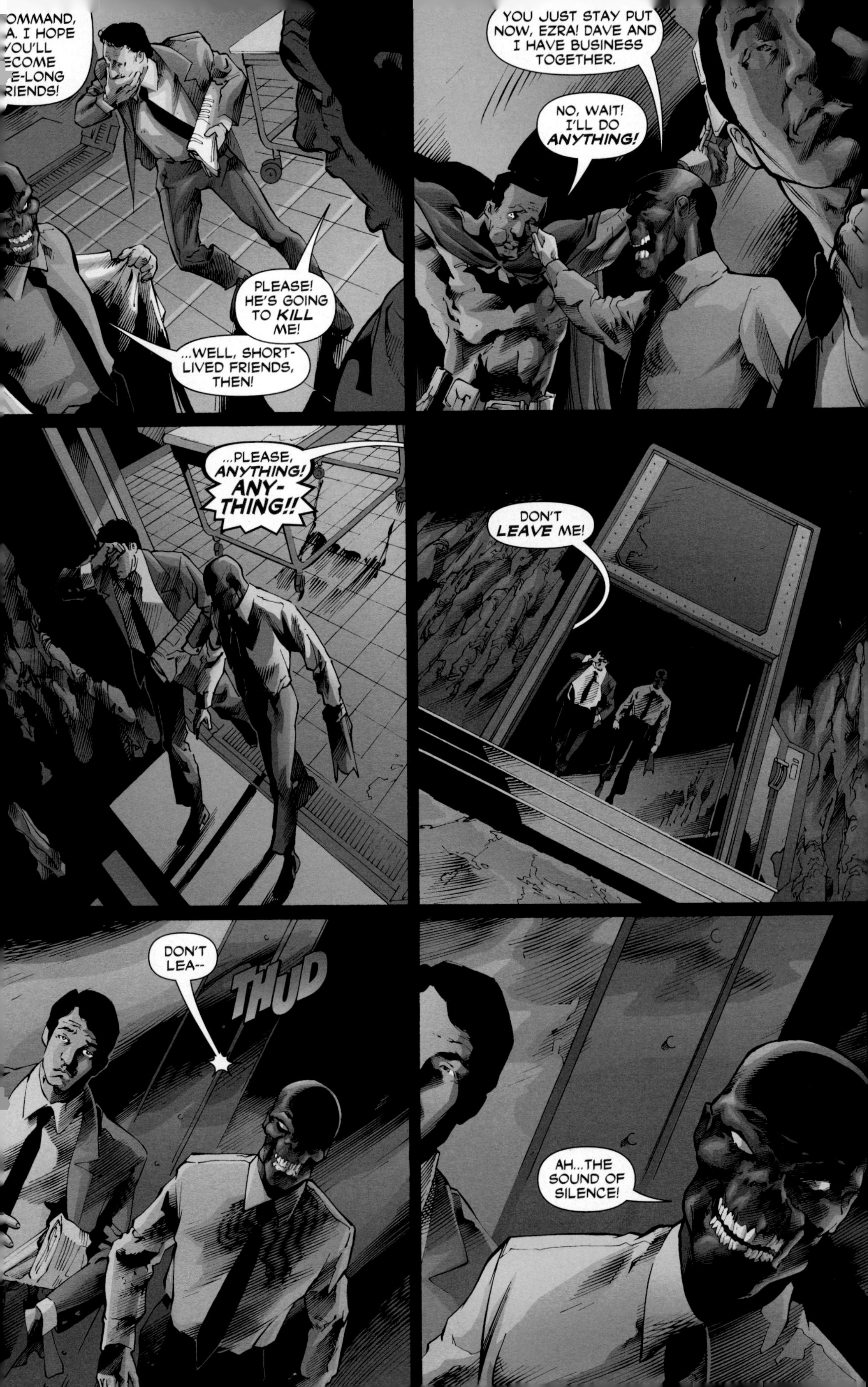
OMMAND, A. I HOPE YOU'LL ECOME E-LONG RIENDS!
PLEASE! HE'S GOING TO KILL ME!
...WELL, SHORT-LIVED FRIENDS, THEN!
YOU JUST STAY PUT NOW, EZRA! DAVE AND I HAVE BUSINESS TOGETHER.
NO, WAIT! I'LL DO ANYTHING!
...PLEASE, ANYTHING! ANY-THING!!
DON'T LEAVE ME!
DON'T LEA--
THUD
AH...THE SOUND OF SILENCE!

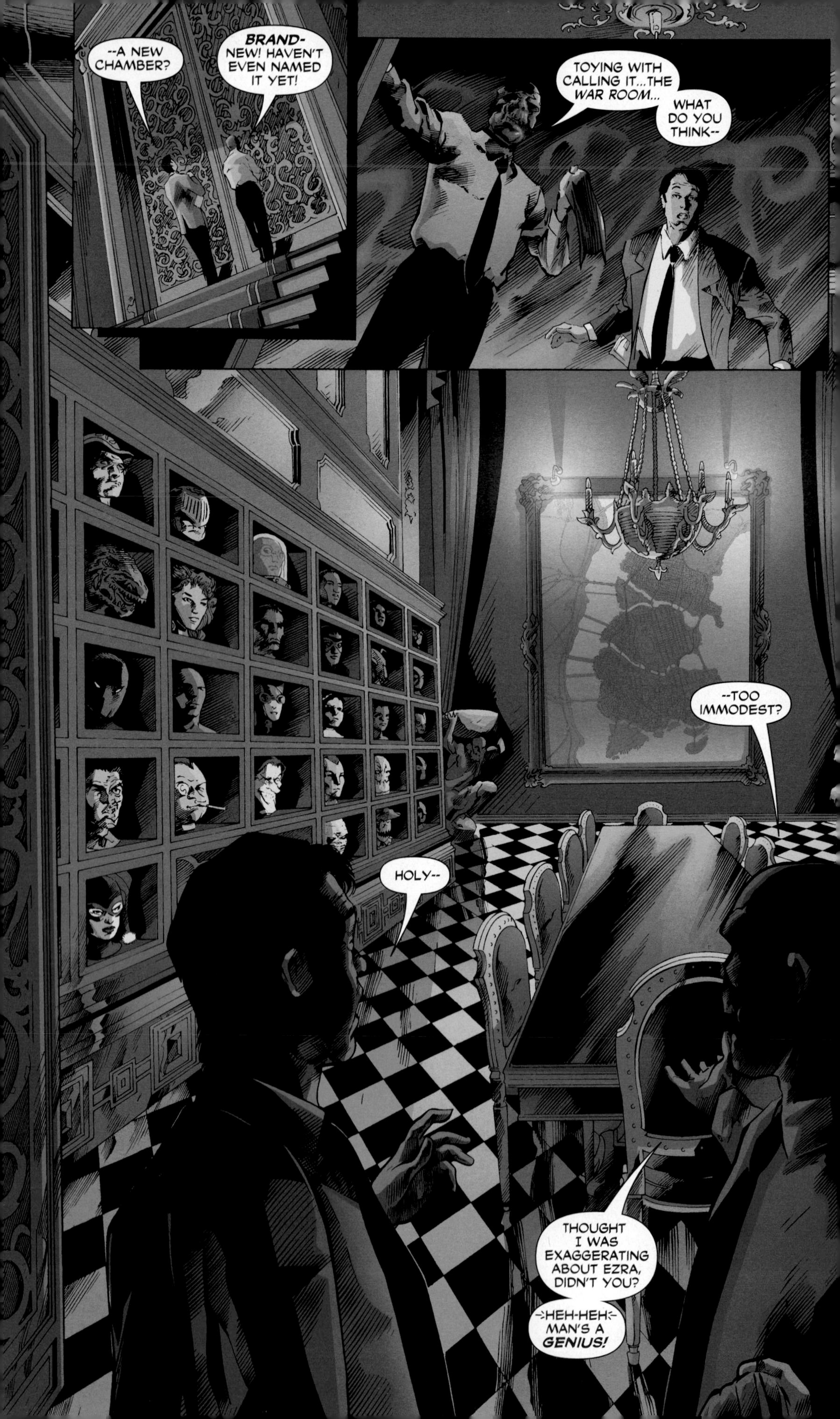
--A NEW CHAMBER?
BRAND- NEW! HAVEN'T EVEN NAMED IT YET!
TOYING WITH CALLING IT...THE *WAR ROOM*...
WHAT DO YOU THINK--
--TOO IMMODEST?
HOLY--
THOUGHT I WAS EXAGGERATING ABOUT EZRA, DIDN'T YOU?
HEH-HEH MAN'S A *GENIUS!*

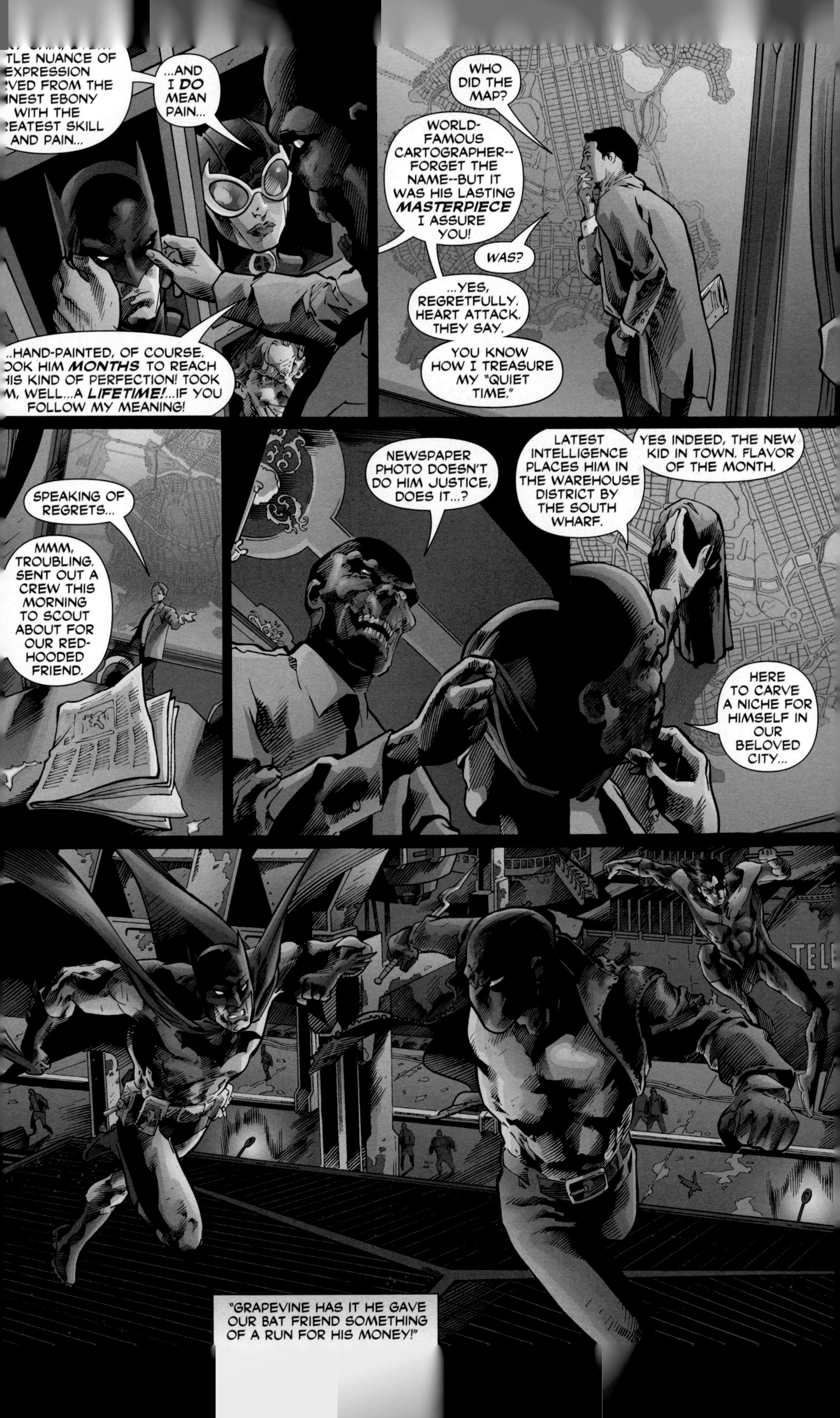
TLE NUANCE OF EXPRESSION VED FROM THE INEST EBONY WITH THE REATEST SKILL AND PAIN...
...AND I DO MEAN PAIN...
..HAND-PAINTED, OF COURSE. OOK HIM MONTHS TO REACH HIS KIND OF PERFECTION! TOOK M, WELL...A LIFETIME!...IF YOU FOLLOW MY MEANING!
WHO DID THE MAP?
WORLD-FAMOUS CARTOGRAPHER--FORGET THE NAME--BUT IT WAS HIS LASTING MASTERPIECE I ASSURE YOU!
WAS?
...YES, REGRETFULLY. HEART ATTACK, THEY SAY.
YOU KNOW HOW I TREASURE MY "QUIET TIME."
SPEAKING OF REGRETS...
MMM, TROUBLING. SENT OUT A CREW THIS MORNING TO SCOUT ABOUT FOR OUR RED-HOODED FRIEND.
NEWSPAPER PHOTO DOESN'T DO HIM JUSTICE, DOES IT...?
LATEST INTELLIGENCE PLACES HIM IN THE WAREHOUSE DISTRICT BY THE SOUTH WHARF.
YES INDEED, THE NEW KID IN TOWN. FLAVOR OF THE MONTH.
HERE TO CARVE A NICHE FOR HIMSELF IN OUR BELOVED CITY...
"GRAPEVINE HAS IT HE GAVE OUR BAT FRIEND SOMETHING OF A RUN FOR HIS MONEY!"

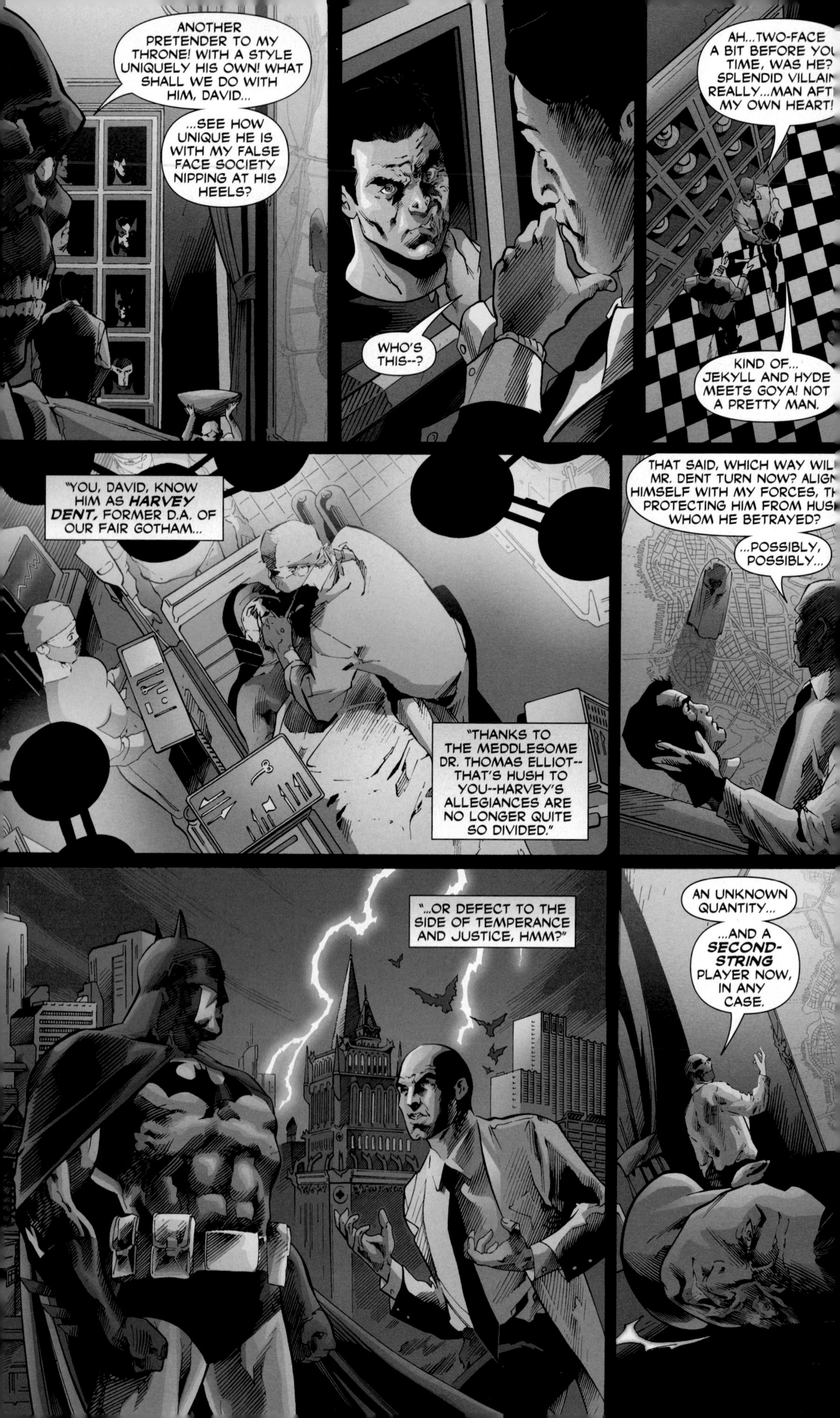
ANOTHER PRETENDER TO MY THRONE! WITH A STYLE UNIQUELY HIS OWN! WHAT SHALL WE DO WITH HIM, DAVID...
...SEE HOW UNIQUE HE IS WITH MY FALSE FACE SOCIETY NIPPING AT HIS HEELS?
WHO'S THIS--?
AH...TWO-FACE A BIT BEFORE YOU TIME, WAS HE? SPLENDID VILLAIN REALLY...MAN AFT MY OWN HEART!
KIND OF... JEKYLL AND HYDE MEETS GOYA! NOT A PRETTY MAN.
"YOU, DAVID, KNOW HIM AS HARVEY DENT, FORMER D.A. OF OUR FAIR GOTHAM...
"THANKS TO THE MEDDLESOME DR. THOMAS ELLIOT--THAT'S HUSH TO YOU--HARVEY'S ALLEGIANCES ARE NO LONGER QUITE SO DIVIDED."
THAT SAID, WHICH WAY WIL MR. DENT TURN NOW? ALIGN HIMSELF WITH MY FORCES, TH PROTECTING HIM FROM HUS WHOM HE BETRAYED?
...POSSIBLY, POSSIBLY...
"...OR DEFECT TO THE SIDE OF TEMPERANCE AND JUSTICE, HMM?"
AN UNKNOWN QUANTITY...
...AND A SECOND-STRING PLAYER NOW, IN ANY CASE.

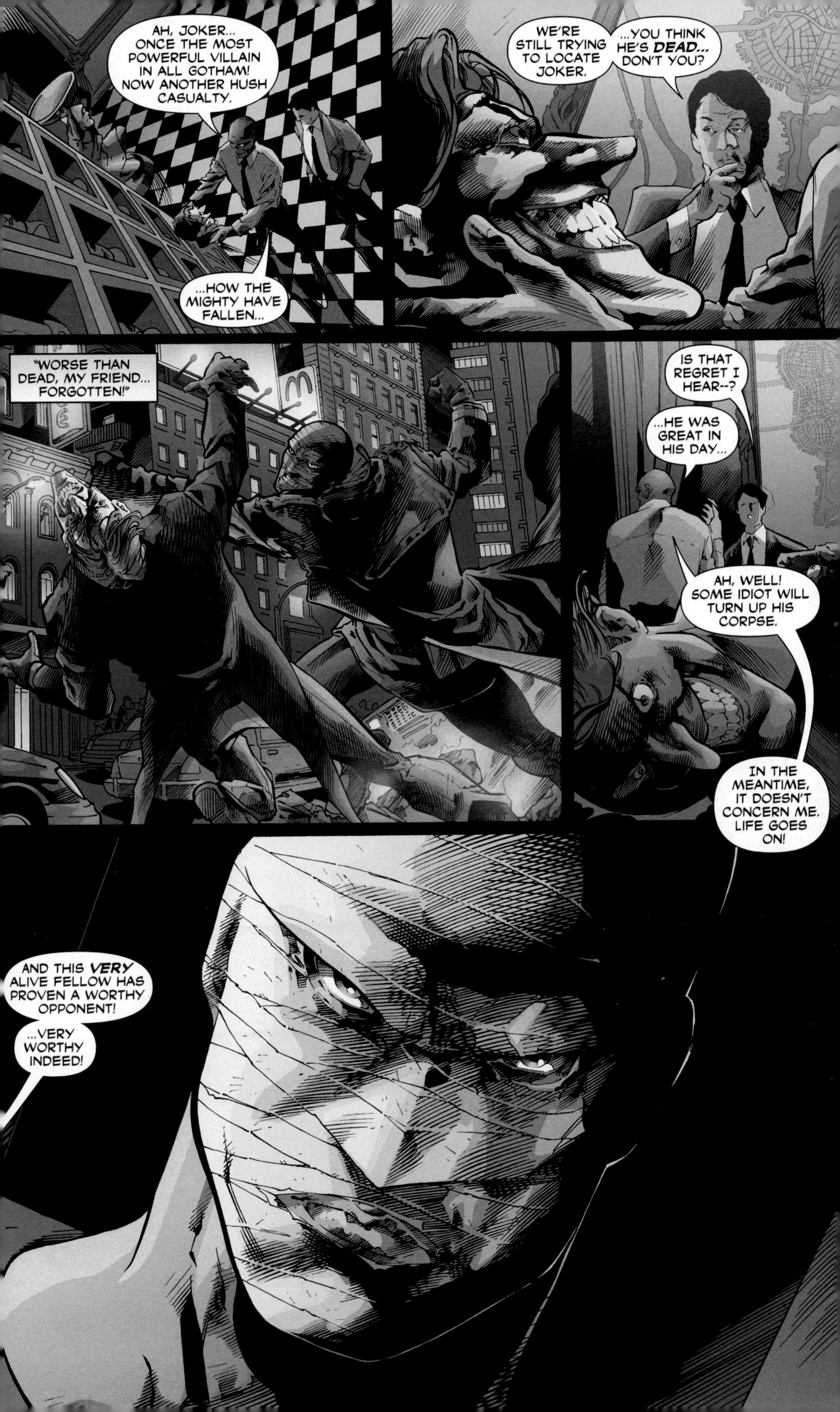
AH, JOKER... ONCE THE MOST POWERFUL VILLAIN IN ALL GOTHAM! NOW ANOTHER HUSH CASUALTY.
...HOW THE MIGHTY HAVE FALLEN...
WE'RE STILL TRYING TO LOCATE JOKER.
...YOU THINK HE'S **DEAD...** DON'T YOU?
"WORSE THAN DEAD, MY FRIEND... FORGOTTEN!"
IS THAT REGRET I HEAR--?
...HE WAS GREAT IN HIS DAY...
AH, WELL! SOME IDIOT WILL TURN UP HIS CORPSE.
IN THE MEANTIME, IT DOESN'T CONCERN ME. LIFE GOES ON!
AND THIS **VERY** ALIVE FELLOW HAS PROVEN A WORTHY OPPONENT!
...VERY WORTHY INDEED!

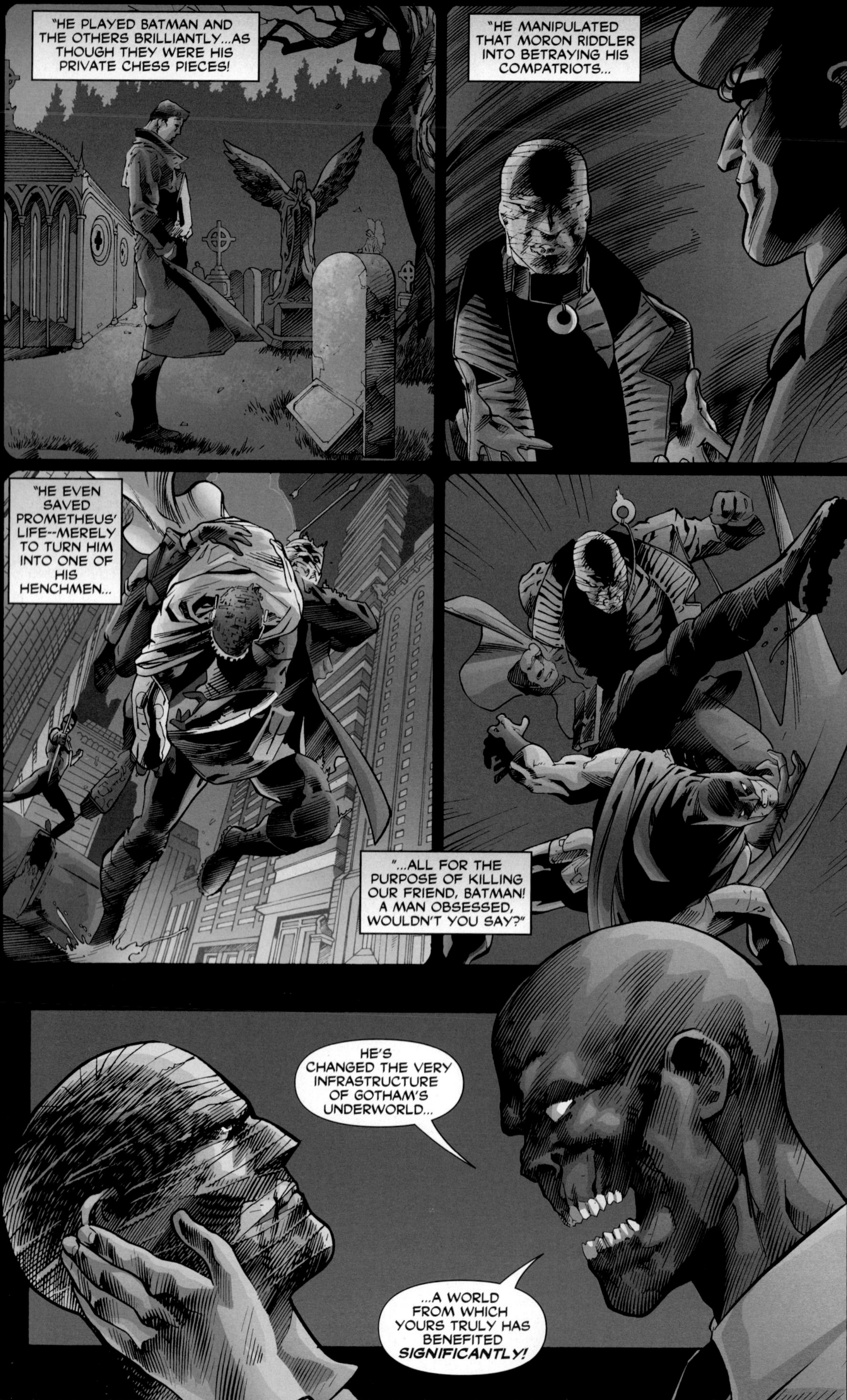
"HE PLAYED BATMAN AND THE OTHERS BRILLIANTLY...AS THOUGH THEY WERE HIS PRIVATE CHESS PIECES!
"HE MANIPULATED THAT MORON RIDDLER INTO BETRAYING HIS COMPATRIOTS...
"HE EVEN SAVED PROMETHEUS' LIFE--MERELY TO TURN HIM INTO ONE OF HIS HENCHMEN...
"...ALL FOR THE PURPOSE OF KILLING OUR FRIEND, BATMAN! A MAN OBSESSED, WOULDN'T YOU SAY?"
HE'S CHANGED THE VERY INFRASTRUCTURE OF GOTHAM'S UNDERWORLD...
...A WORLD FROM WHICH YOURS TRULY HAS BENEFITED SIGNIFICANTLY!

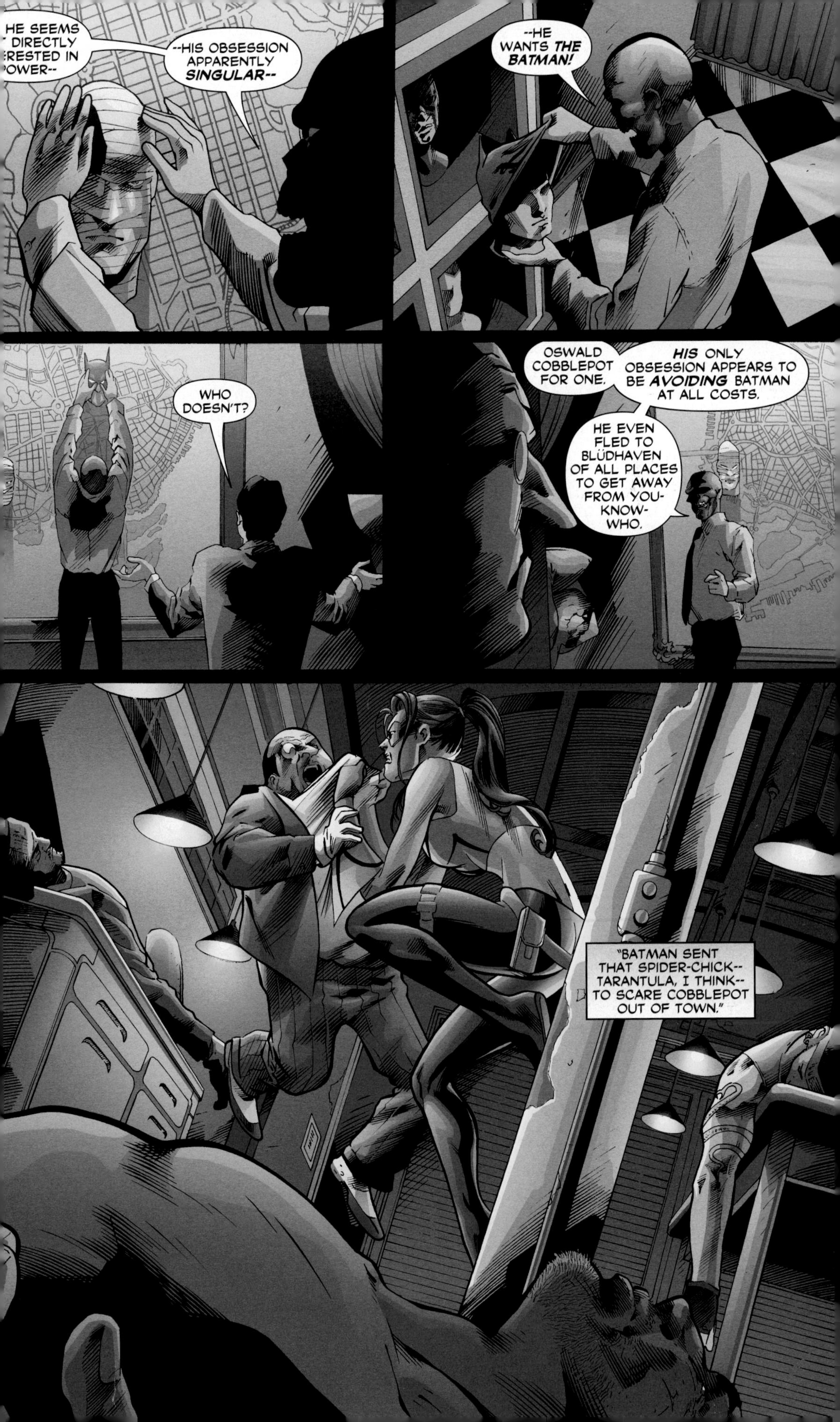
HE SEEMS
DIRECTLY
ERESTED IN
POWER--
--HIS OBSESSION APPARENTLY SINGULAR--
--HE WANTS THE BATMAN!
WHO DOESN'T?
OSWALD COBBLEPOT FOR ONE.
HIS ONLY OBSESSION APPEARS TO BE AVOIDING BATMAN AT ALL COSTS.
HE EVEN FLED TO BLÜDHAVEN OF ALL PLACES TO GET AWAY FROM YOU-KNOW-WHO.
"BATMAN SENT THAT SPIDER-CHICK--TARANTULA, I THINK--TO SCARE COBBLEPOT OUT OF TOWN."

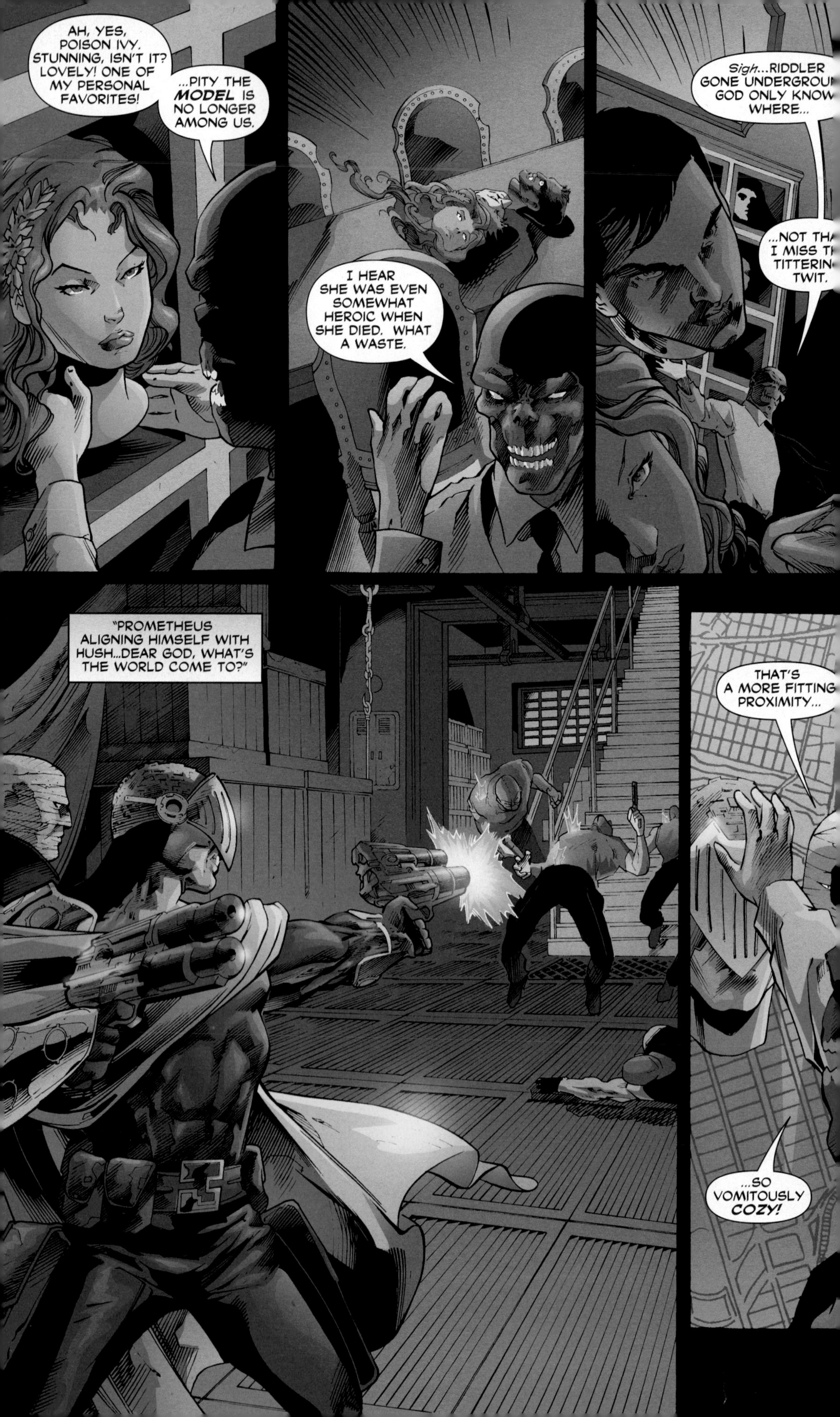
AH, YES, POISON IVY. STUNNING, ISN'T IT? LOVELY! ONE OF MY PERSONAL FAVORITES!
...PITY THE MODEL IS NO LONGER AMONG US.
I HEAR SHE WAS EVEN SOMEWHAT HEROIC WHEN SHE DIED. WHAT A WASTE.
Sigh...RIDDLER GONE UNDERGROU GOD ONLY KNOW WHERE...
...NOT THA I MISS T TITTERIN TWIT.
"PROMETHEUS ALIGNING HIMSELF WITH HUSH...DEAR GOD, WHAT'S THE WORLD COME TO?"
THAT'S A MORE FITTING PROXIMITY...
...SO VOMITOUSLY COZY!

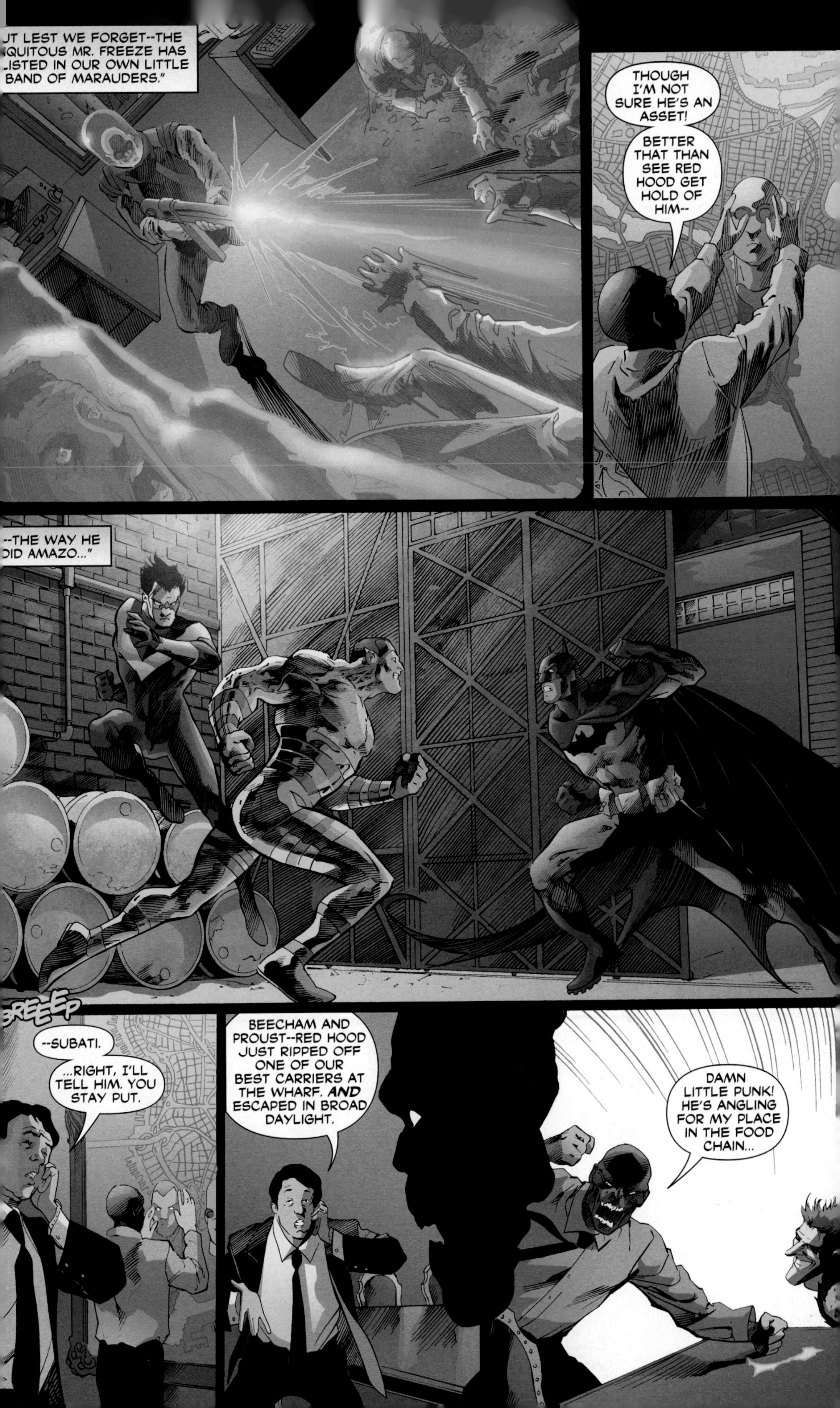
UT LEST WE FORGET--THE
IQUITOUS MR. FREEZE HAS
LISTED IN OUR OWN LITTLE
BAND OF MARAUDERS."
THOUGH I'M NOT SURE HE'S AN ASSET!
BETTER THAT THAN SEE RED HOOD GET HOLD OF HIM--
--THE WAY HE DID AMAZO..."
BREEEP
--SUBATI.
...RIGHT, I'LL TELL HIM. YOU STAY PUT.
BEECHAM AND PROUST--RED HOOD JUST RIPPED OFF ONE OF OUR BEST CARRIERS AT THE WHARF. AND ESCAPED IN BROAD DAYLIGHT.
DAMN LITTLE PUNK! HE'S ANGLING FOR MY PLACE IN THE FOOD CHAIN...

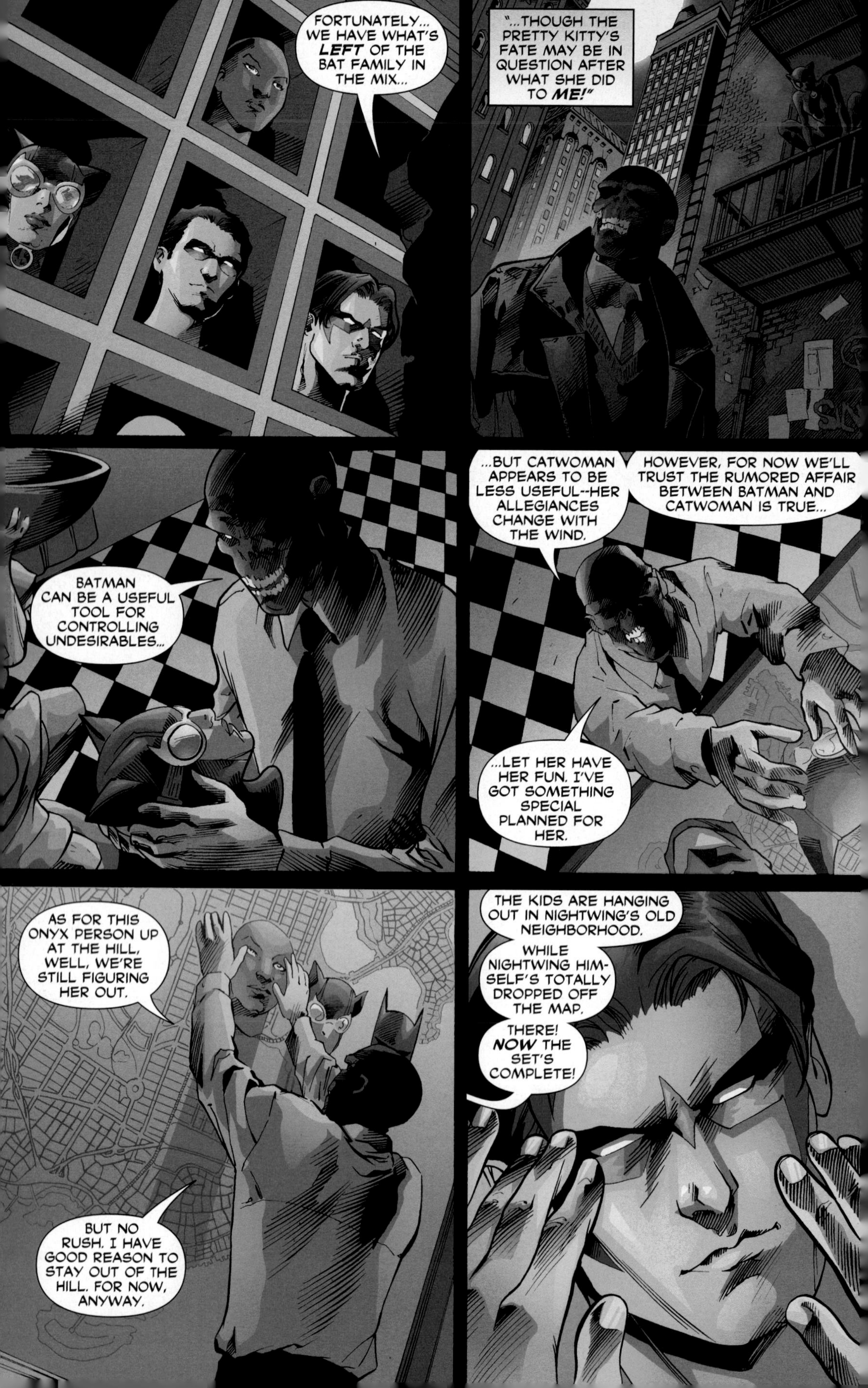
FORTUNATELY... WE HAVE WHAT'S LEFT OF THE BAT FAMILY IN THE MIX...
"...THOUGH THE PRETTY KITTY'S FATE MAY BE IN QUESTION AFTER WHAT SHE DID TO ME!"
BATMAN CAN BE A USEFUL TOOL FOR CONTROLLING UNDESIRABLES...
...BUT CATWOMAN APPEARS TO BE LESS USEFUL--HER ALLEGIANCES CHANGE WITH THE WIND.
HOWEVER, FOR NOW WE'LL TRUST THE RUMORED AFFAIR BETWEEN BATMAN AND CATWOMAN IS TRUE...
...LET HER HAVE HER FUN. I'VE GOT SOMETHING SPECIAL PLANNED FOR HER.
AS FOR THIS ONYX PERSON UP AT THE HILL, WELL, WE'RE STILL FIGURING HER OUT.
BUT NO RUSH. I HAVE GOOD REASON TO STAY OUT OF THE HILL. FOR NOW, ANYWAY.
THE KIDS ARE HANGING OUT IN NIGHTWING'S OLD NEIGHBORHOOD.
WHILE NIGHTWING HIMSELF'S TOTALLY DROPPED OFF THE MAP.
THERE! NOW THE SET'S COMPLETE!

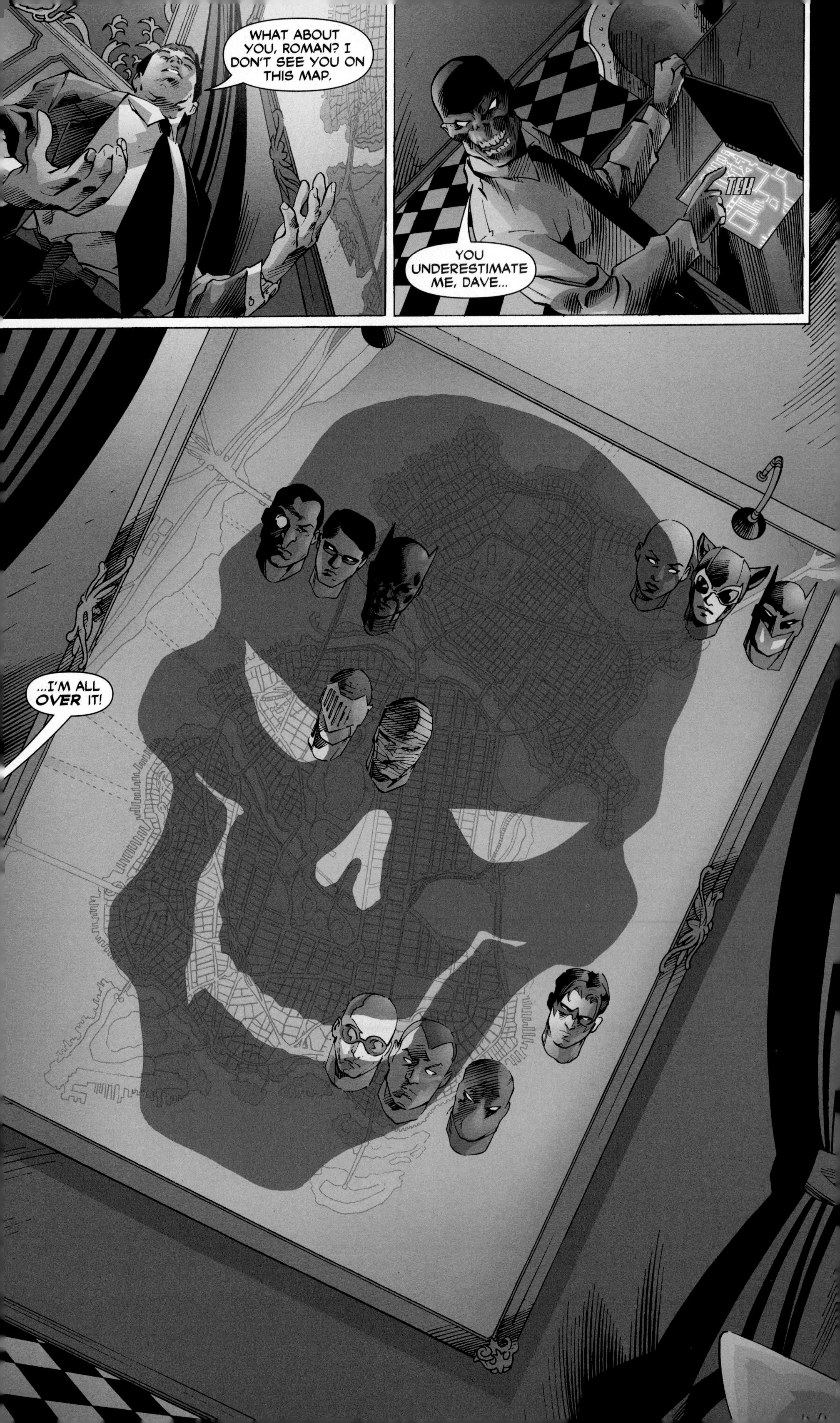
WHAT ABOUT YOU, ROMAN? I DON'T SEE YOU ON THIS MAP.
TEK
YOU UNDERESTIMATE ME, DAVE...
...I'M ALL OVER IT!

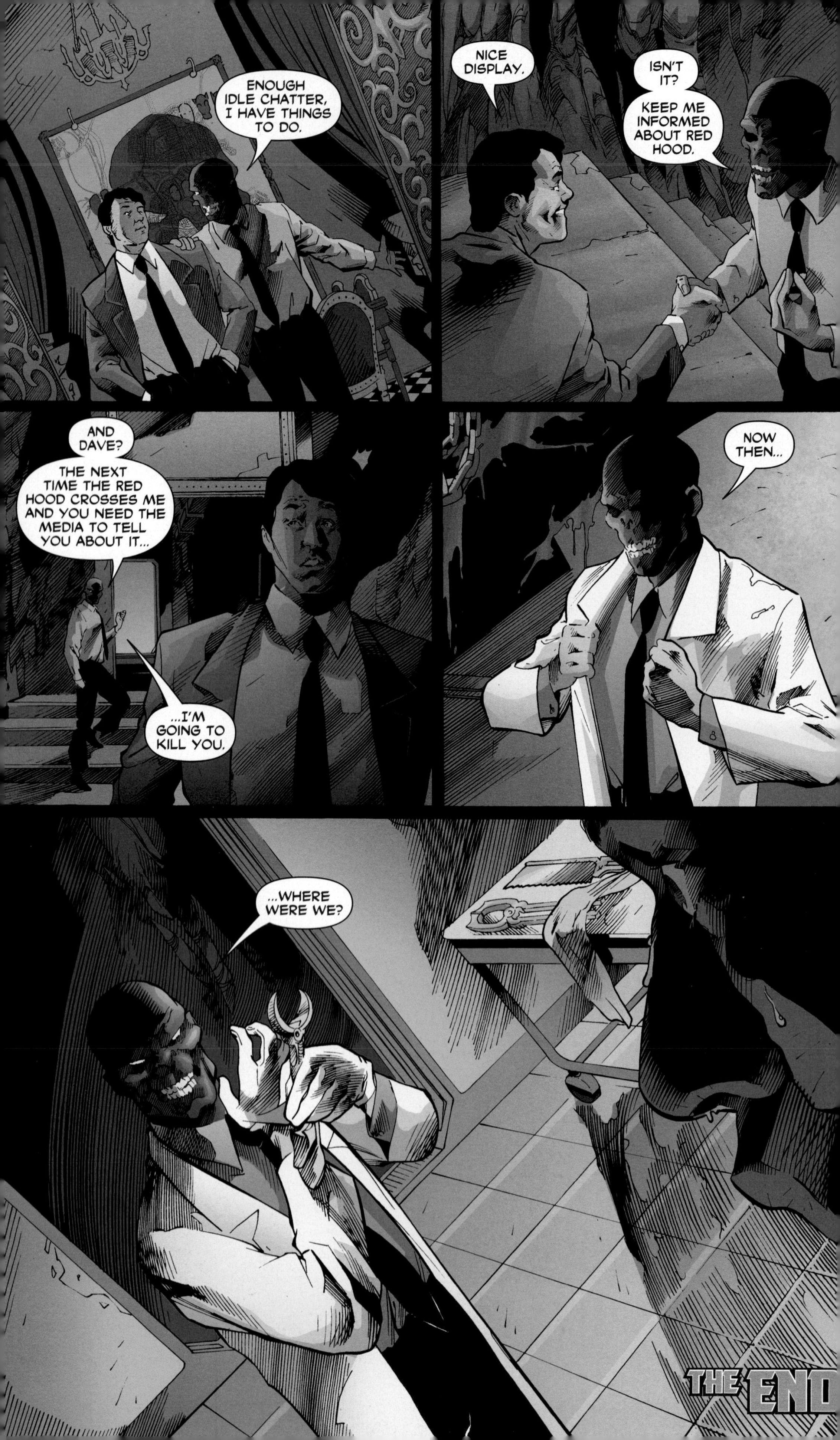
ENOUGH IDLE CHATTER, I HAVE THINGS TO DO.
NICE DISPLAY.
ISN'T IT?
KEEP ME INFORMED ABOUT RED HOOD.
AND DAVE?
THE NEXT TIME THE RED HOOD CROSSES ME AND YOU NEED THE MEDIA TO TELL YOU ABOUT IT...
...I'M GOING TO KILL YOU.
NOW THEN...
...WHERE WERE WE?
THE END

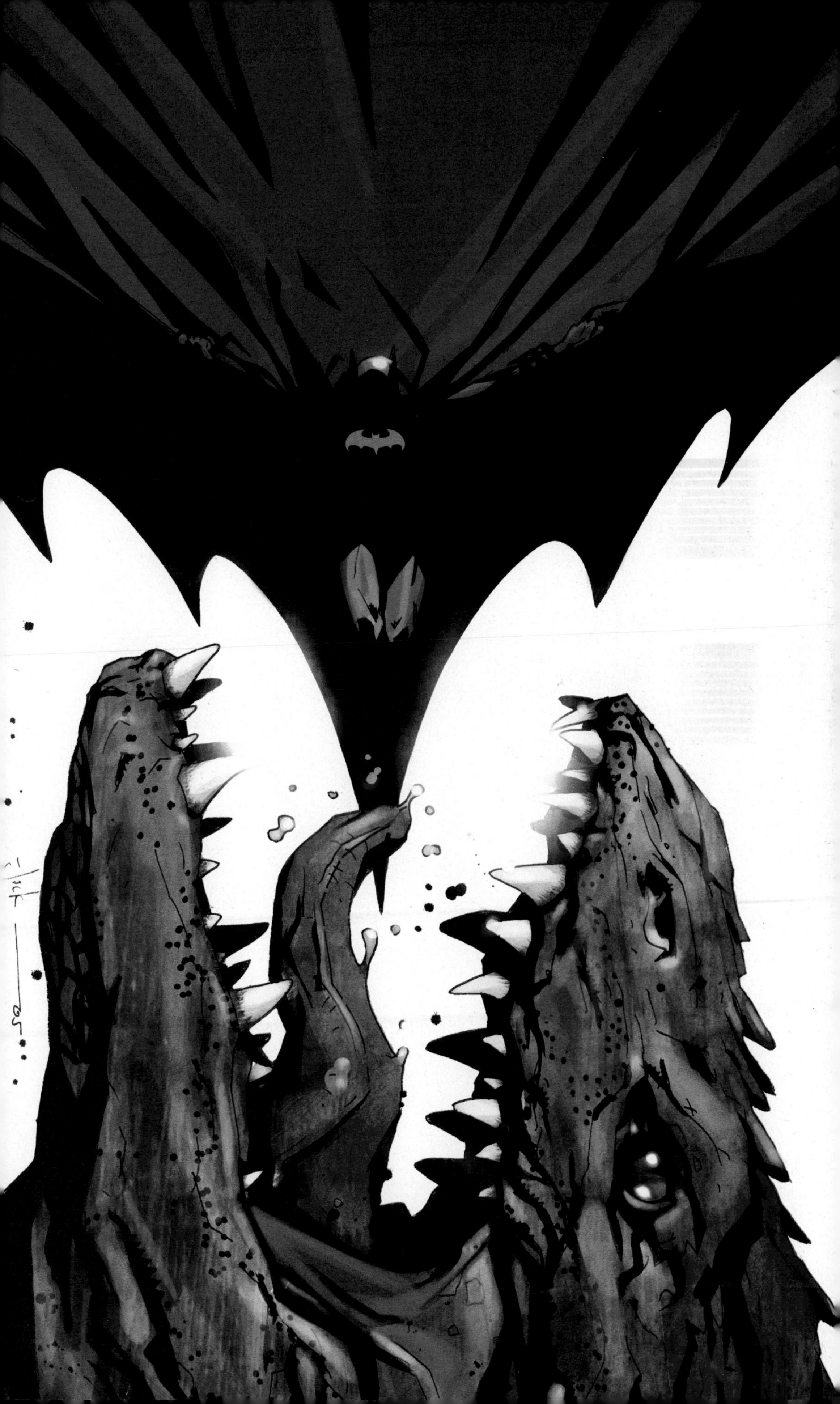

COVER ART BY
MATT WAGNER

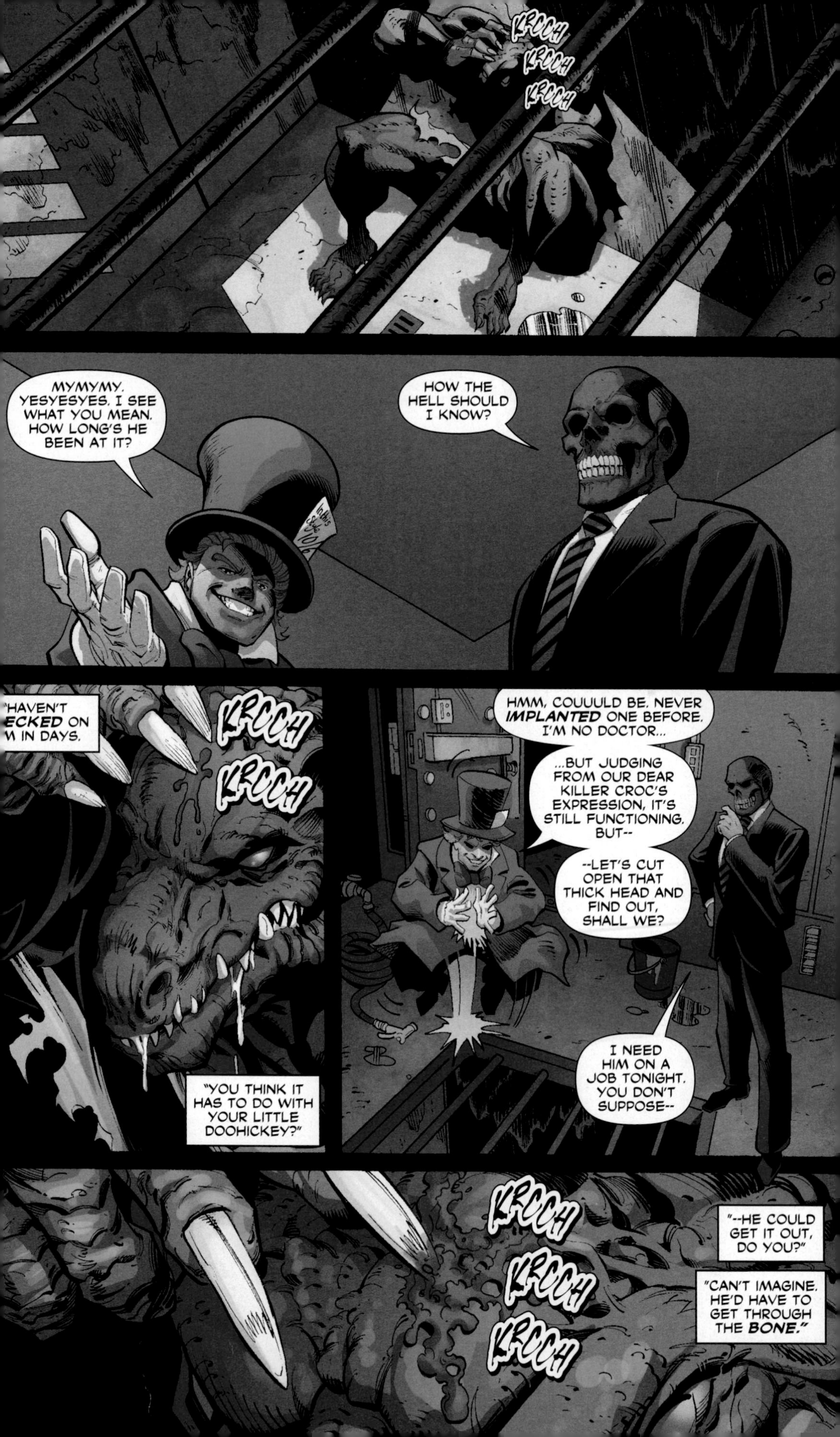
KROOCH
KROOCH
KROOCH
MYMYMY. YESYESYES. I SEE WHAT YOU MEAN. HOW LONG'S HE BEEN AT IT?
HOW THE HELL SHOULD I KNOW?
'HAVEN'T ECKED ON M IN DAYS.
KROOCH
KROOCH
"YOU THINK IT HAS TO DO WITH YOUR LITTLE DOOHICKEY?"
HMM, COUUULD BE. NEVER *IMPLANTED* ONE BEFORE. I'M NO DOCTOR...
...BUT JUDGING FROM OUR DEAR KILLER CROC'S EXPRESSION, IT'S STILL FUNCTIONING. BUT--
--LET'S CUT OPEN THAT THICK HEAD AND FIND OUT, SHALL WE?
I NEED HIM ON A JOB TONIGHT. YOU DON'T SUPPOSE--
KROOCH
KROOCH
KROOCH
"--HE COULD GET IT OUT, DO YOU?"
"CAN'T IMAGINE. HE'D HAVE TO GET THROUGH THE *BONE.*"

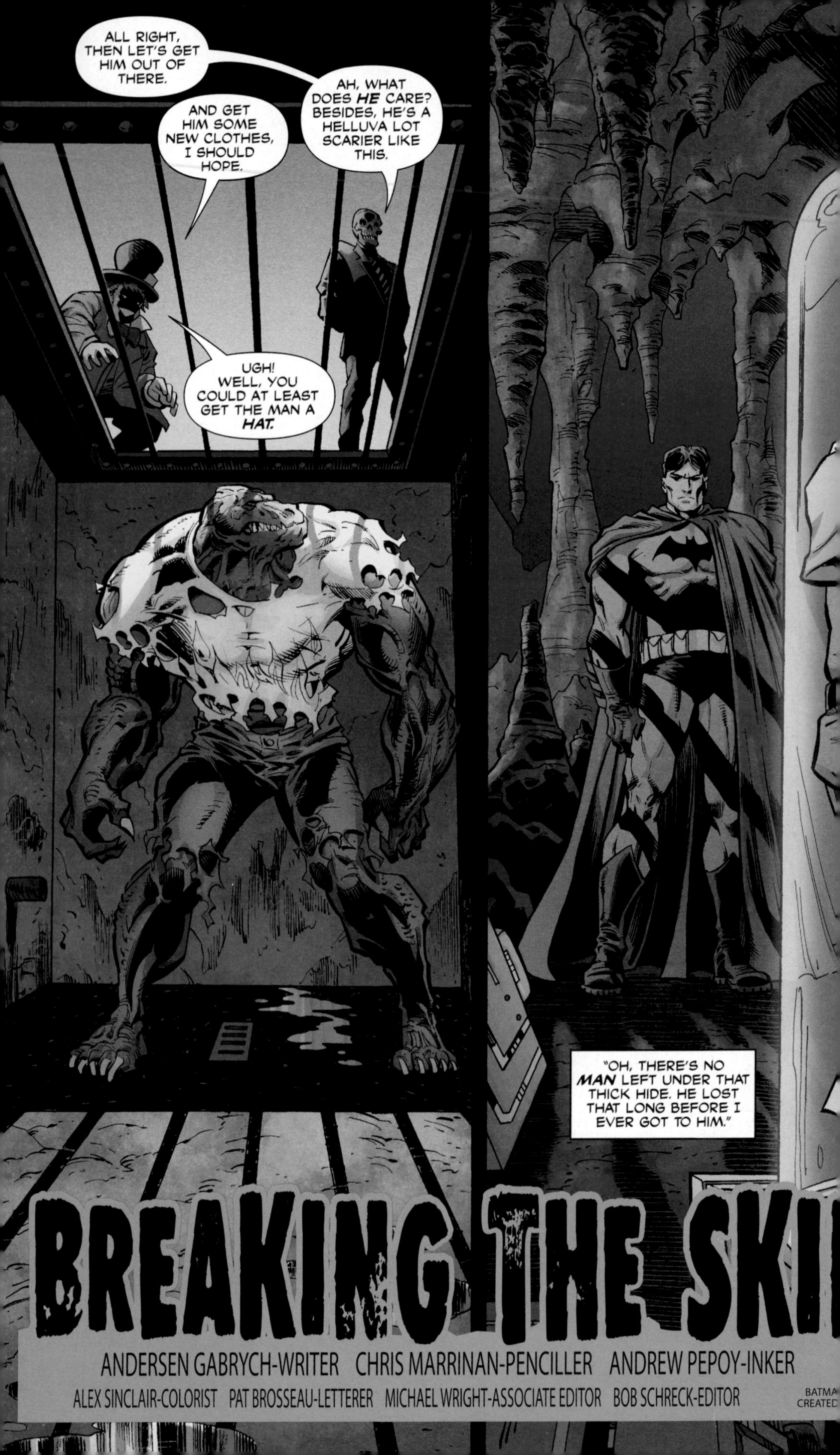
ALL RIGHT, THEN LET'S GET HIM OUT OF THERE.
AND GET HIM SOME NEW CLOTHES, I SHOULD HOPE.
AH, WHAT DOES HE CARE? BESIDES, HE'S A HELLUVA LOT SCARIER LIKE THIS.
UGH! WELL, YOU COULD AT LEAST GET THE MAN A HAT.
"OH, THERE'S NO MAN LEFT UNDER THAT THICK HIDE. HE LOST THAT LONG BEFORE I EVER GOT TO HIM."
BREAKING THE SKI
ANDERSEN GABRYCH-WRITER CHRIS MARRINAN-PENCILLER ANDREW PEPOY-INKER
ALEX SINCLAIR-COLORIST PAT BROSSEAU-LETTERER MICHAEL WRIGHT-ASSOCIATE EDITOR BOB SCHRECK-EDITOR

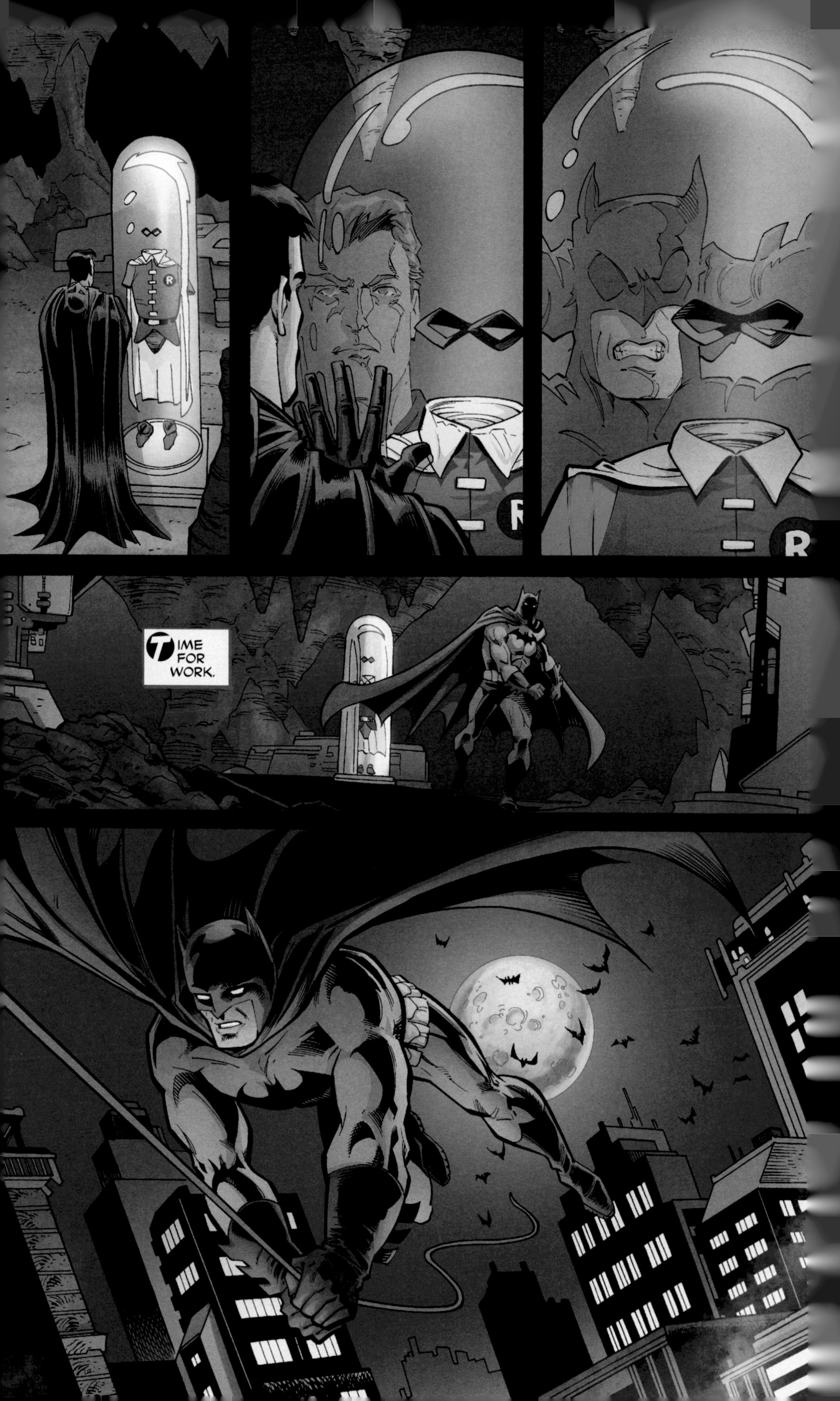
TIME FOR WORK.

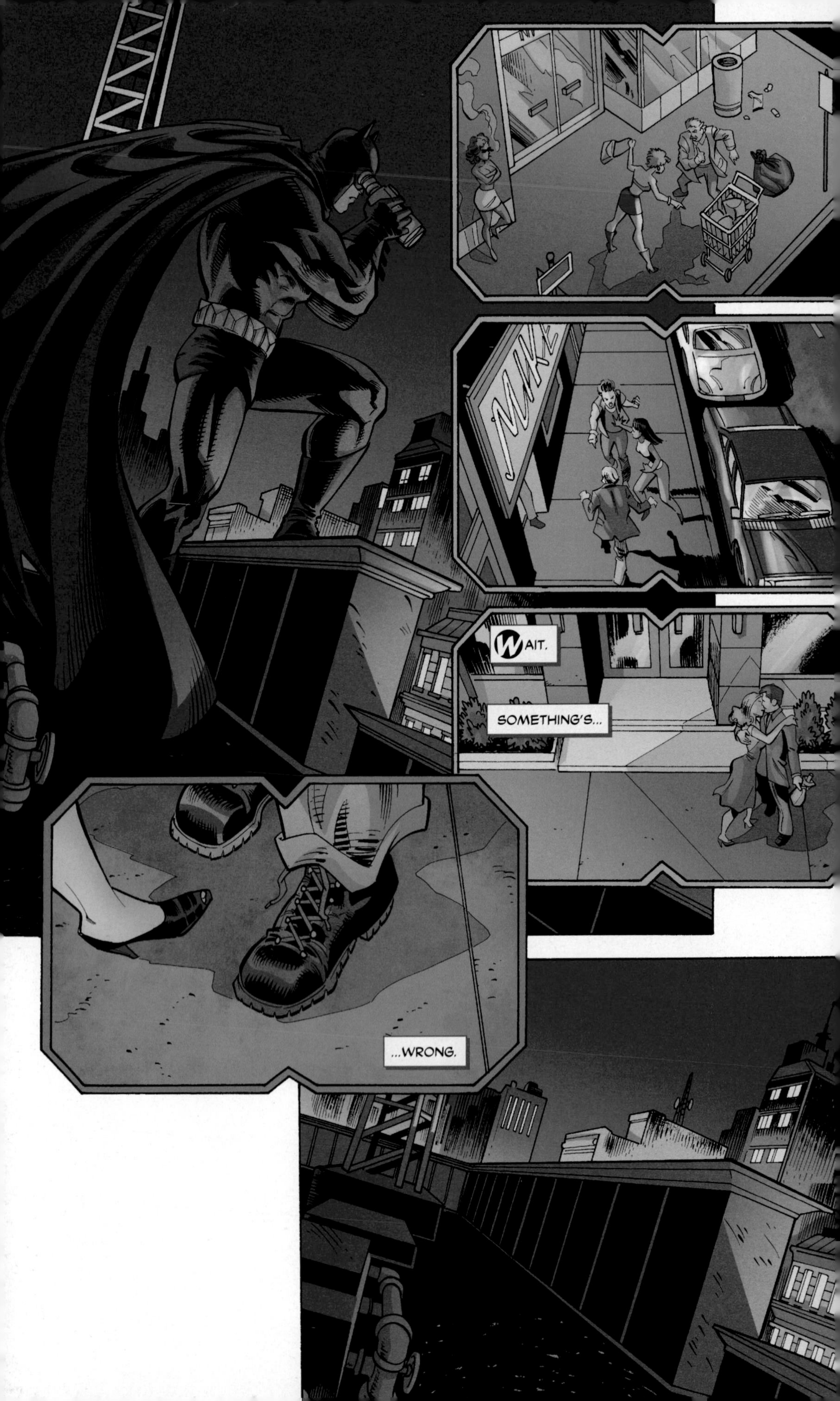
WAIT.
SOMETHING'S...
...WRONG.

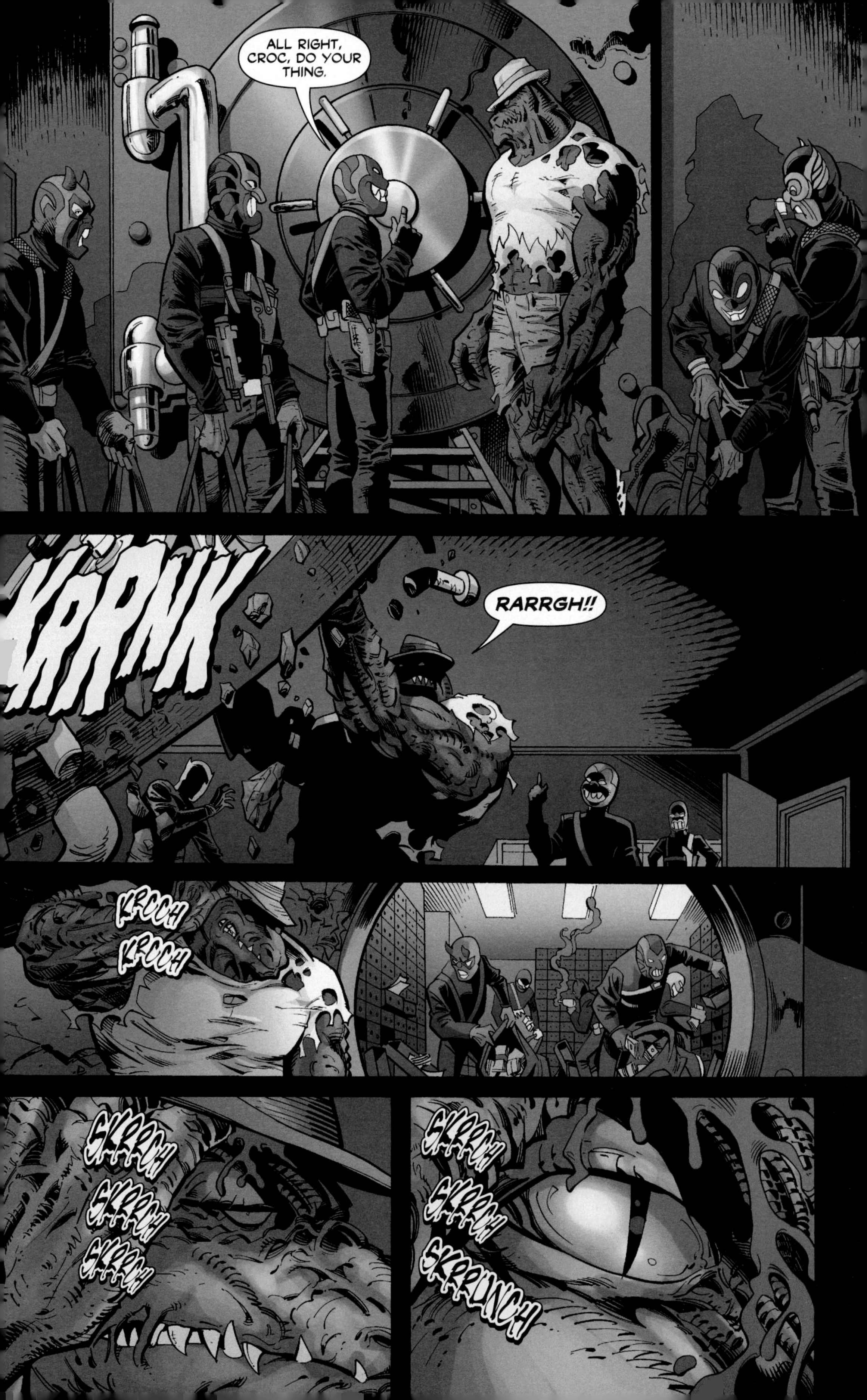
ALL RIGHT, CROC, DO YOUR THING.
KRRNK
RARRGH!!
KRCCH
KRCCH
SKRRCH
SKRRCH
SKRRCH
SKRRCH
SKRRCH
SKRRUNCH

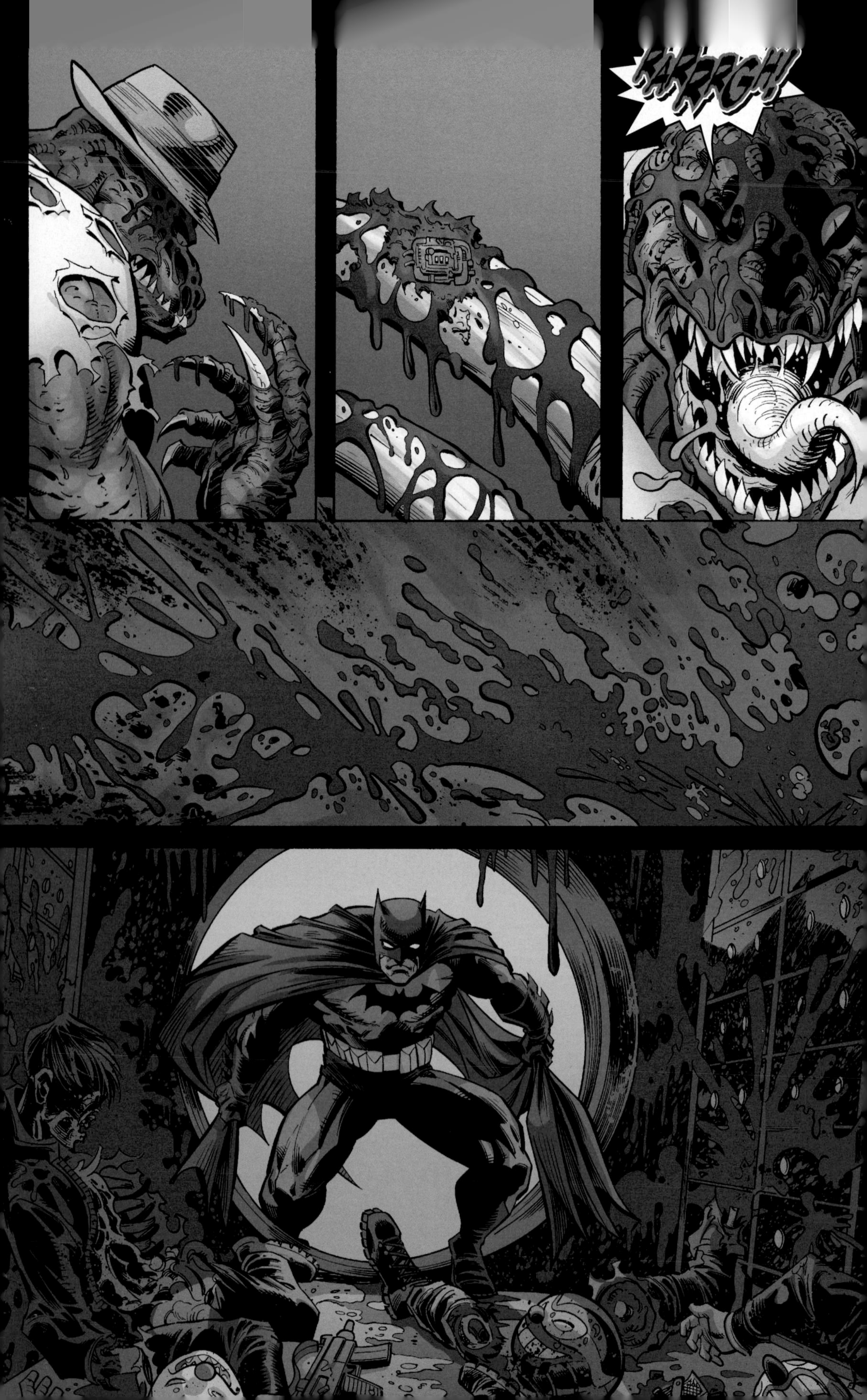
KAKRRGH!

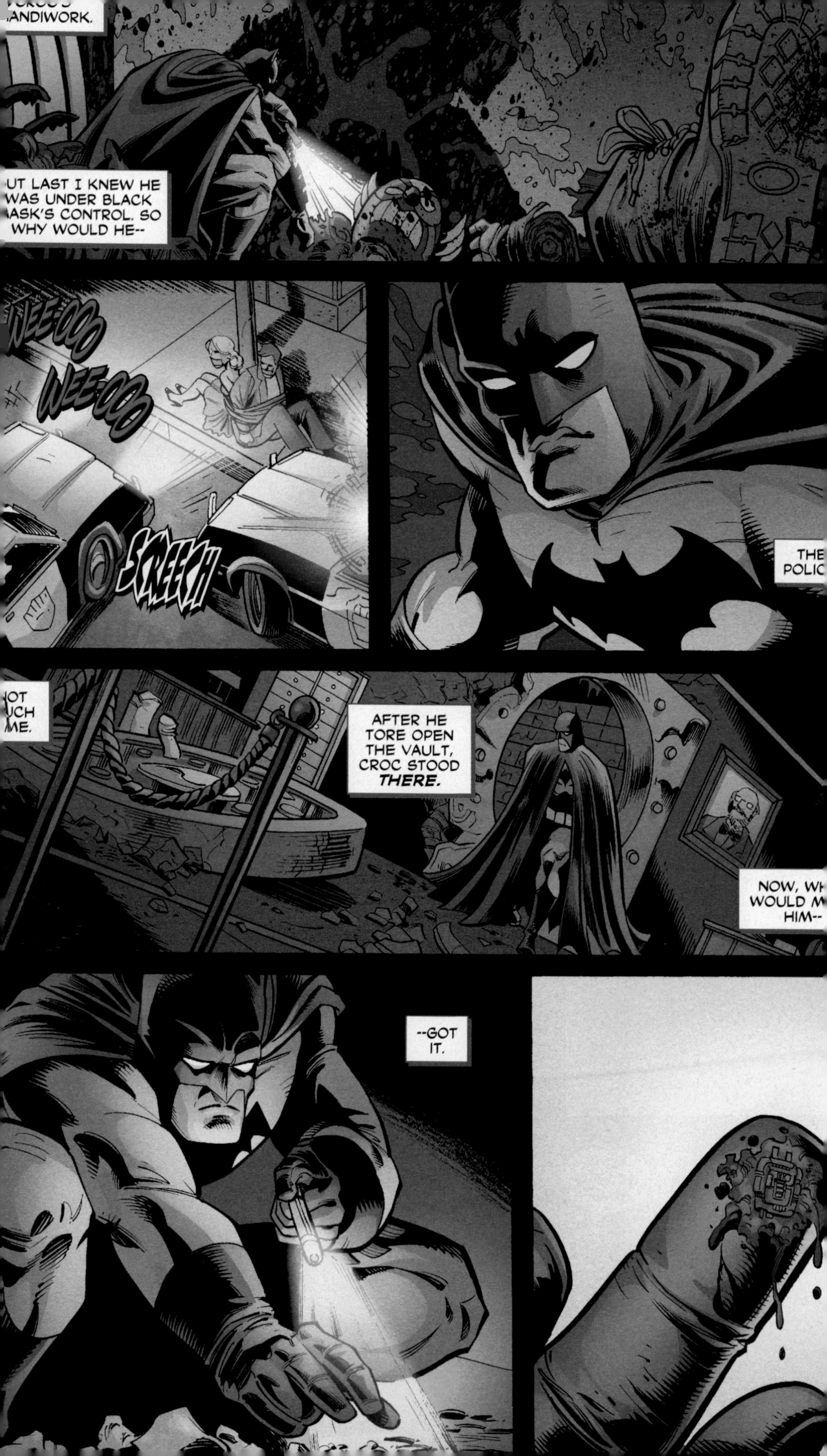

HANDIWORK.
UT LAST I KNEW HE WAS UNDER BLACK ASK'S CONTROL. SO WHY WOULD HE--
WEE-OOO
WEE-OOO
SCREECH
THE POLIC
NOT UCH ME.
AFTER HE TORE OPEN THE VAULT, CROC STOOD THERE.
NOW, WH WOULD M HIM--
--GOT IT.

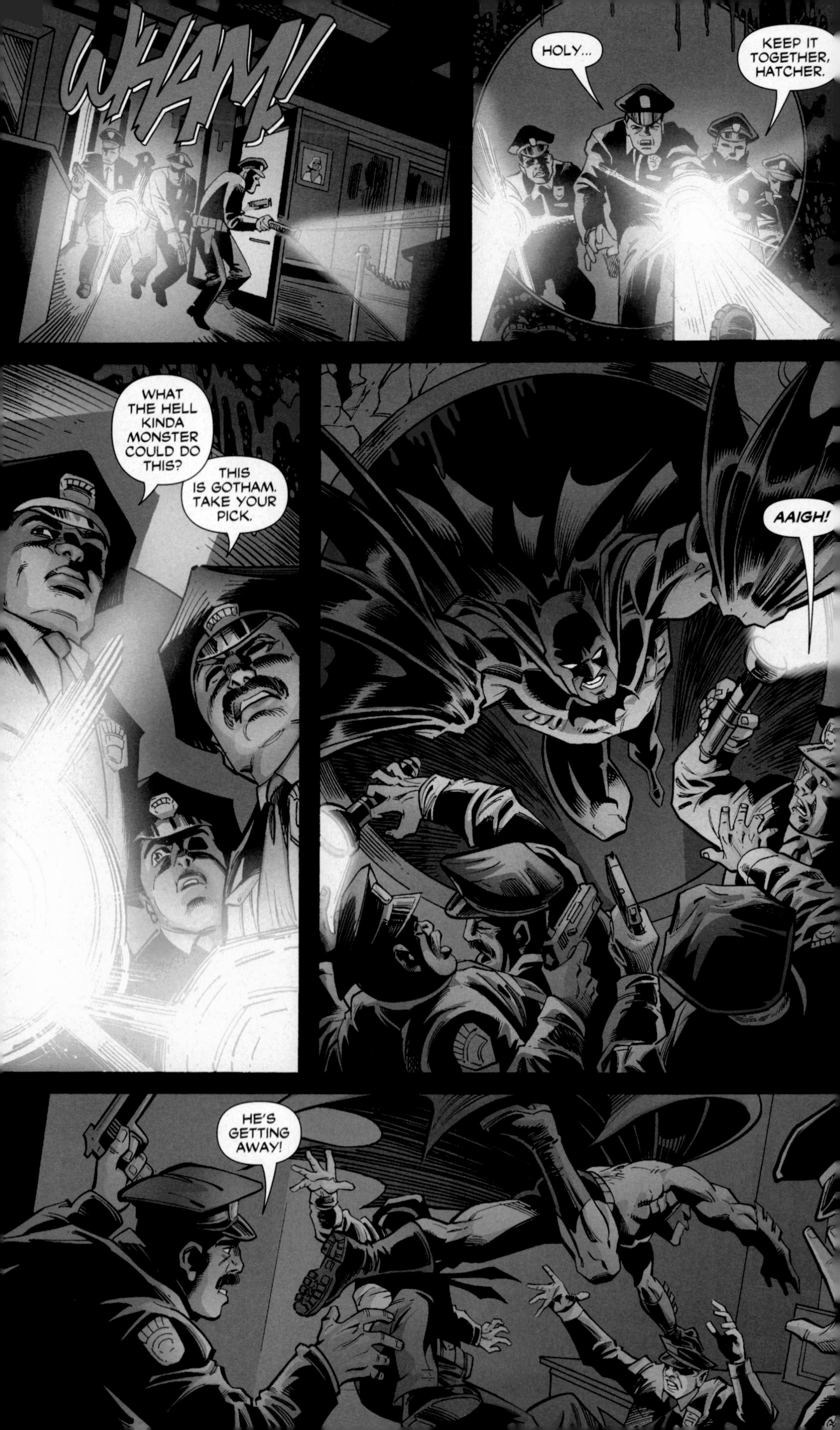
WHAM!
HOLY...
KEEP IT TOGETHER, HATCHER.
WHAT THE HELL KINDA MONSTER COULD DO THIS?
THIS IS GOTHAM. TAKE YOUR PICK.
AAIGH!
HE'S GETTING AWAY!

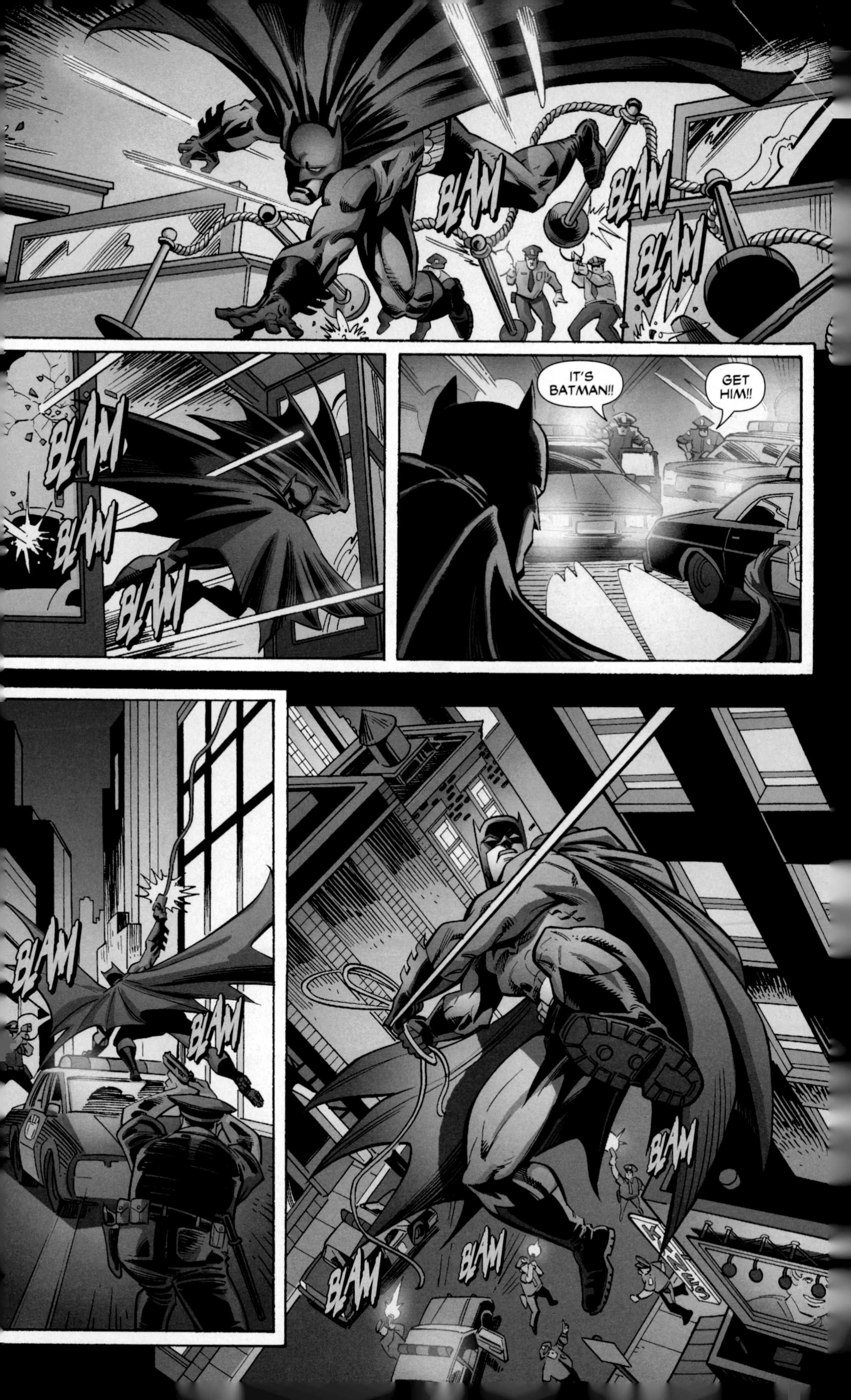
BLAM
BLAM
BLAM
BLAM
BLAM
BLAM
IT'S BATMAN!!
GET HIM!!
BLAM
BLAM
BLAM
BLAM
BLAM

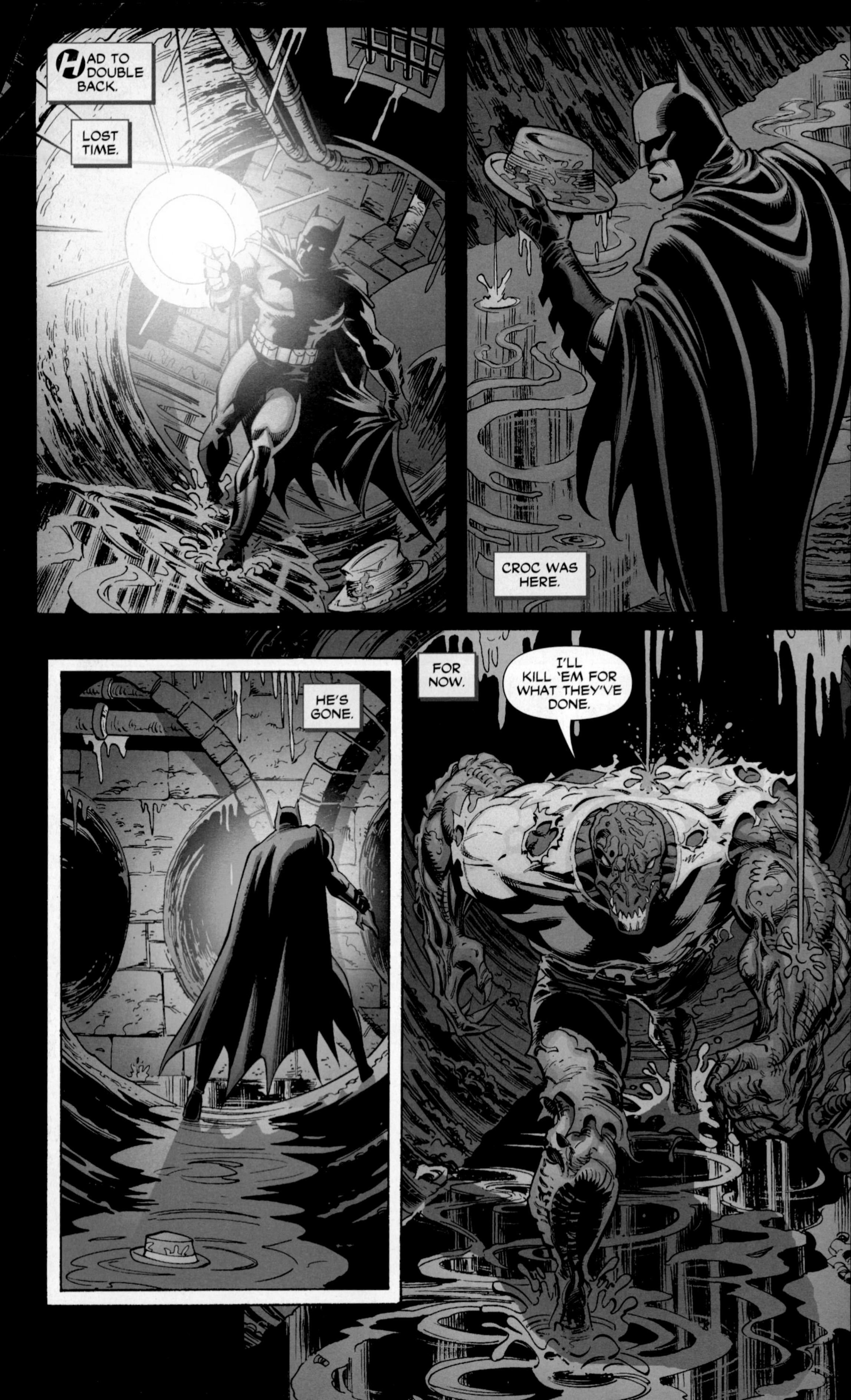
HAD TO DOUBLE BACK.
LOST TIME.
CROC WAS HERE.
HE'S GONE.
FOR NOW.
I'LL KILL 'EM FOR WHAT THEY'VE DONE.

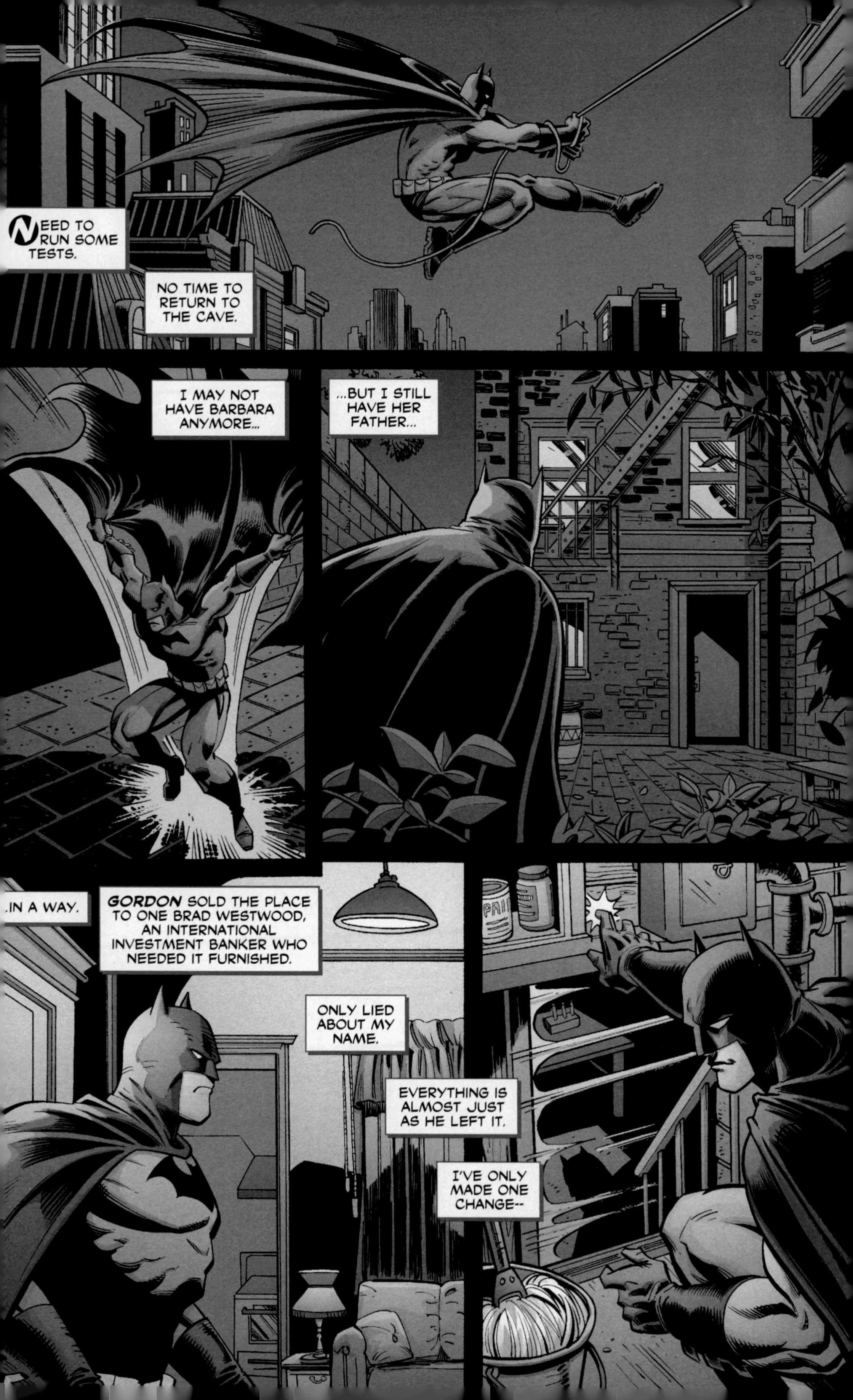
NEED TO RUN SOME TESTS.
NO TIME TO RETURN TO THE CAVE.
I MAY NOT HAVE BARBARA ANYMORE...
...BUT I STILL HAVE HER FATHER...
..IN A WAY.
GORDON SOLD THE PLACE TO ONE BRAD WESTWOOD, AN INTERNATIONAL INVESTMENT BANKER WHO NEEDED IT FURNISHED.
ONLY LIED ABOUT MY NAME.
EVERYTHING IS ALMOST JUST AS HE LEFT IT.
I'VE ONLY MADE ONE CHANGE--

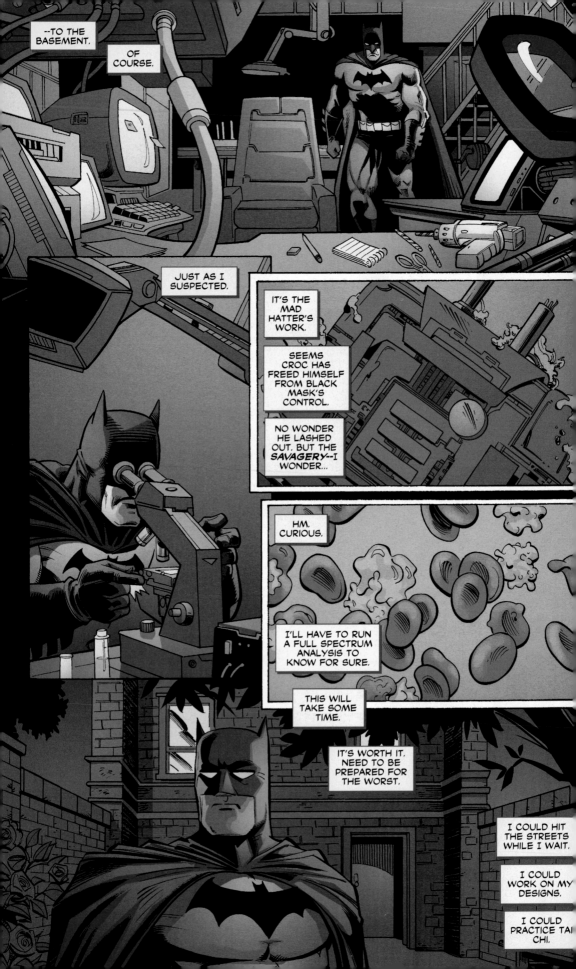

--TO THE BASEMENT.

OF COURSE.

JUST AS I SUSPECTED.

IT'S THE MAD HATTER'S WORK.

SEEMS CROC HAS FREED HIMSELF FROM BLACK MASK'S CONTROL.

NO WONDER HE LASHED OUT. BUT THE *SAVAGERY*--I WONDER...

HM. CURIOUS.

I'LL HAVE TO RUN A FULL SPECTRUM ANALYSIS TO KNOW FOR SURE.

THIS WILL TAKE SOME TIME.

IT'S WORTH IT. NEED TO BE PREPARED FOR THE WORST.

I COULD HIT THE STREETS WHILE I WAIT.

I COULD WORK ON MY DESIGNS.

I COULD PRACTICE TAI CHI.

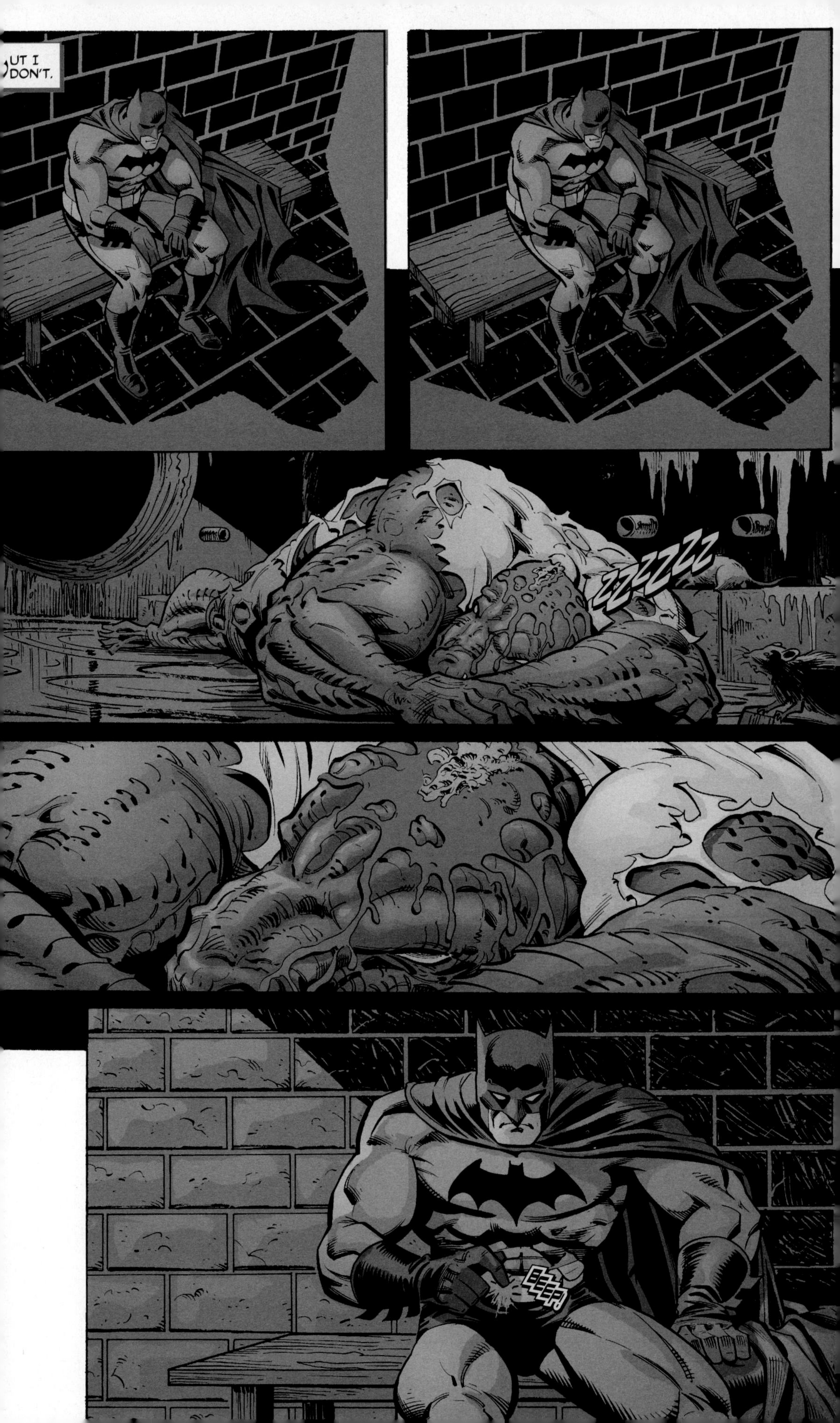
UT I DON'T.
ZZZZZZZ
BEEP!

DAMMIT.

THIS DOESN'T BODE WELL FOR CROC.

AND BY PROXY THE...

HATTER.

CROC IS A CARNIVORE.

HE'LL WORK HIS WAY UP THE FOOD CHAIN.

ENDING WITH BLACK MASK.

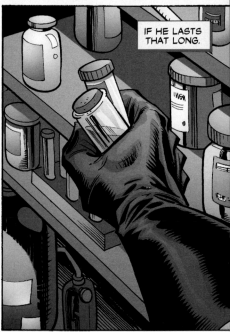

IF HE LASTS THAT LONG.

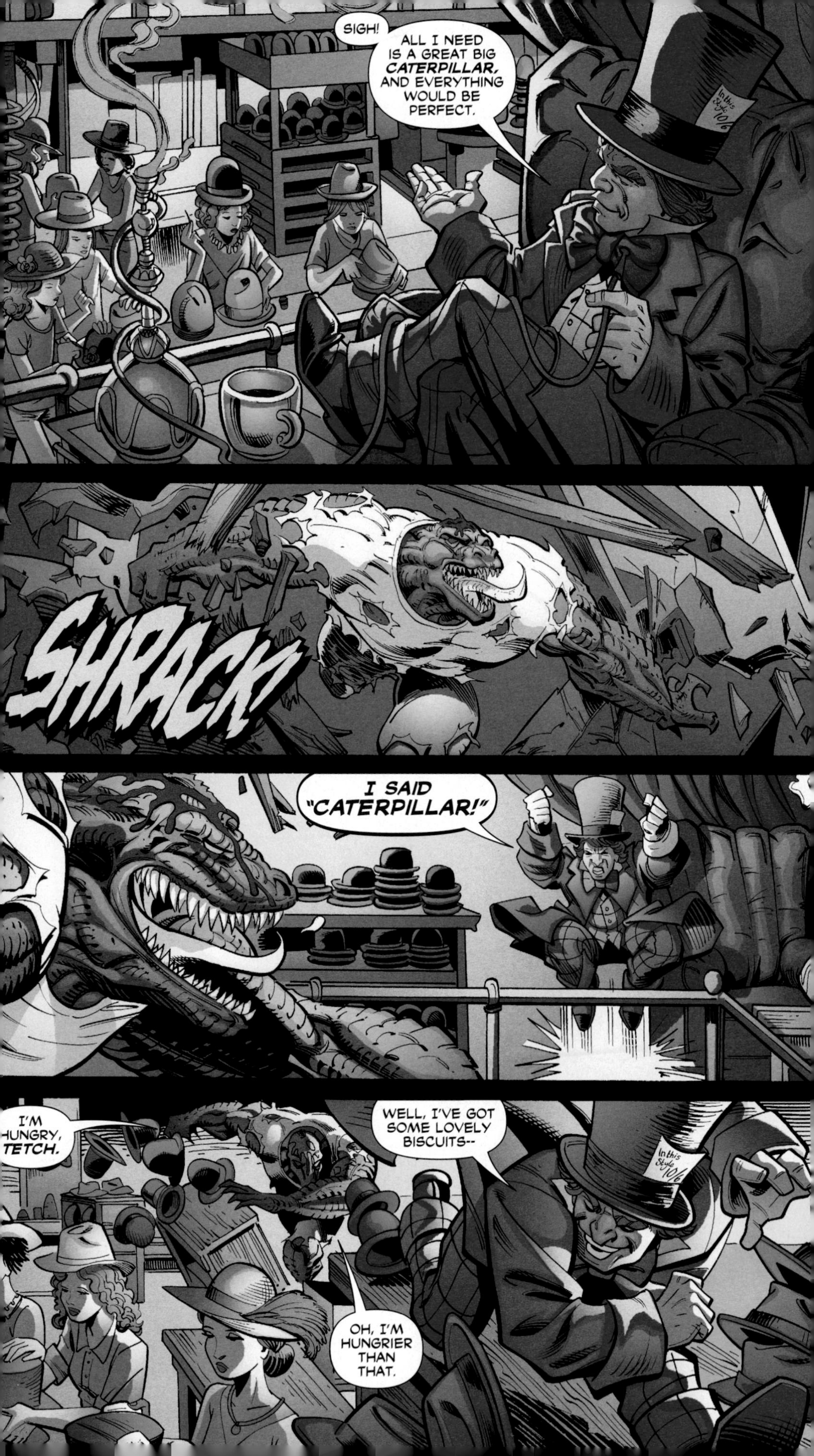
SIGH!
ALL I NEED IS A GREAT BIG CATERPILLAR, AND EVERYTHING WOULD BE PERFECT.
In this Style 10/6
SHRACK!
I SAID "CATERPILLAR!"
I'M HUNGRY, TETCH.
WELL, I'VE GOT SOME LOVELY BISCUITS--
In this Style 10/6
OH, I'M HUNGRIER THAN THAT.

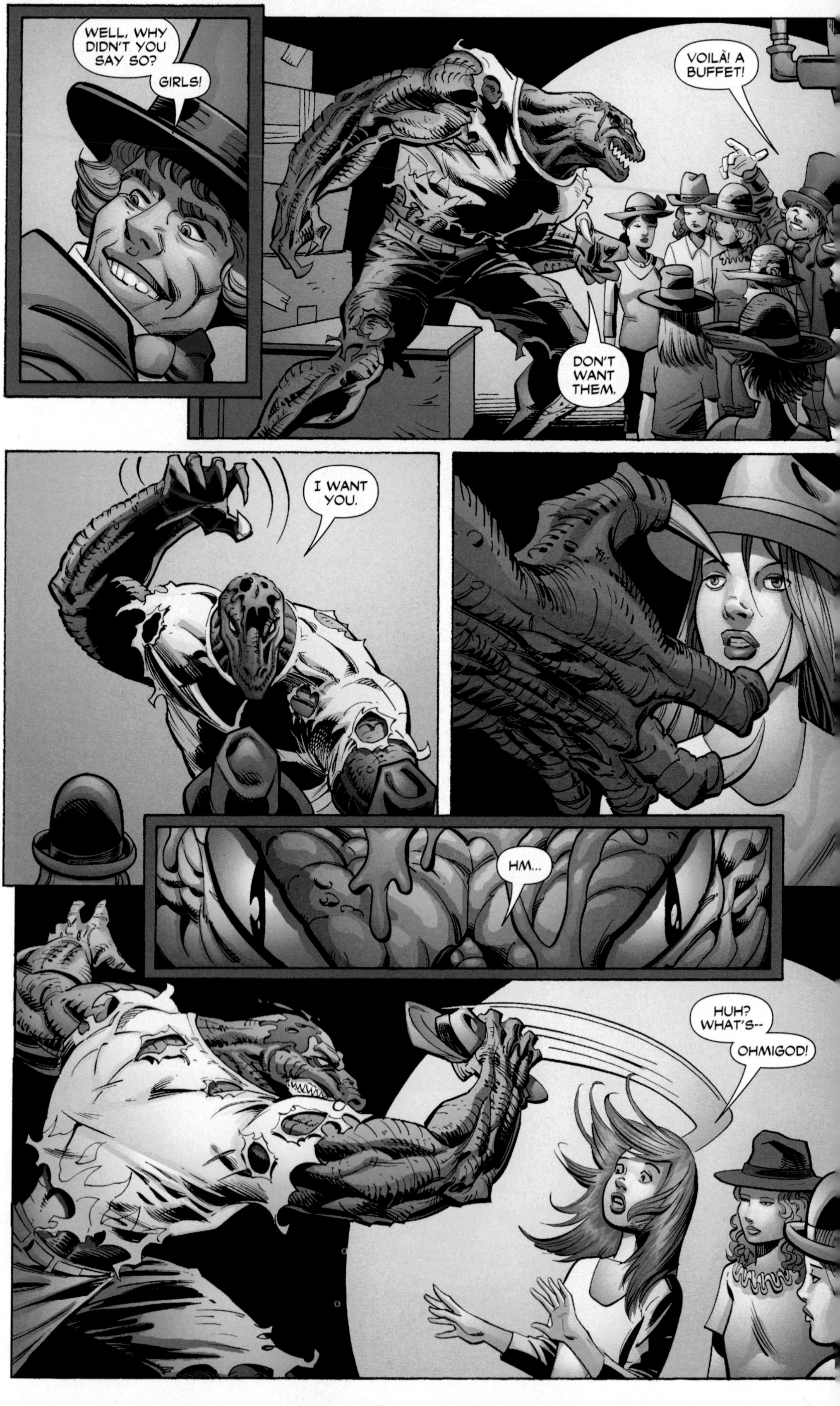
WELL, WHY DIDN'T YOU SAY SO?
GIRLS!
VOILÀ! A BUFFET!
DON'T WANT THEM.
I WANT YOU.
HM...
HUH? WHAT'S--
OHMIGOD!

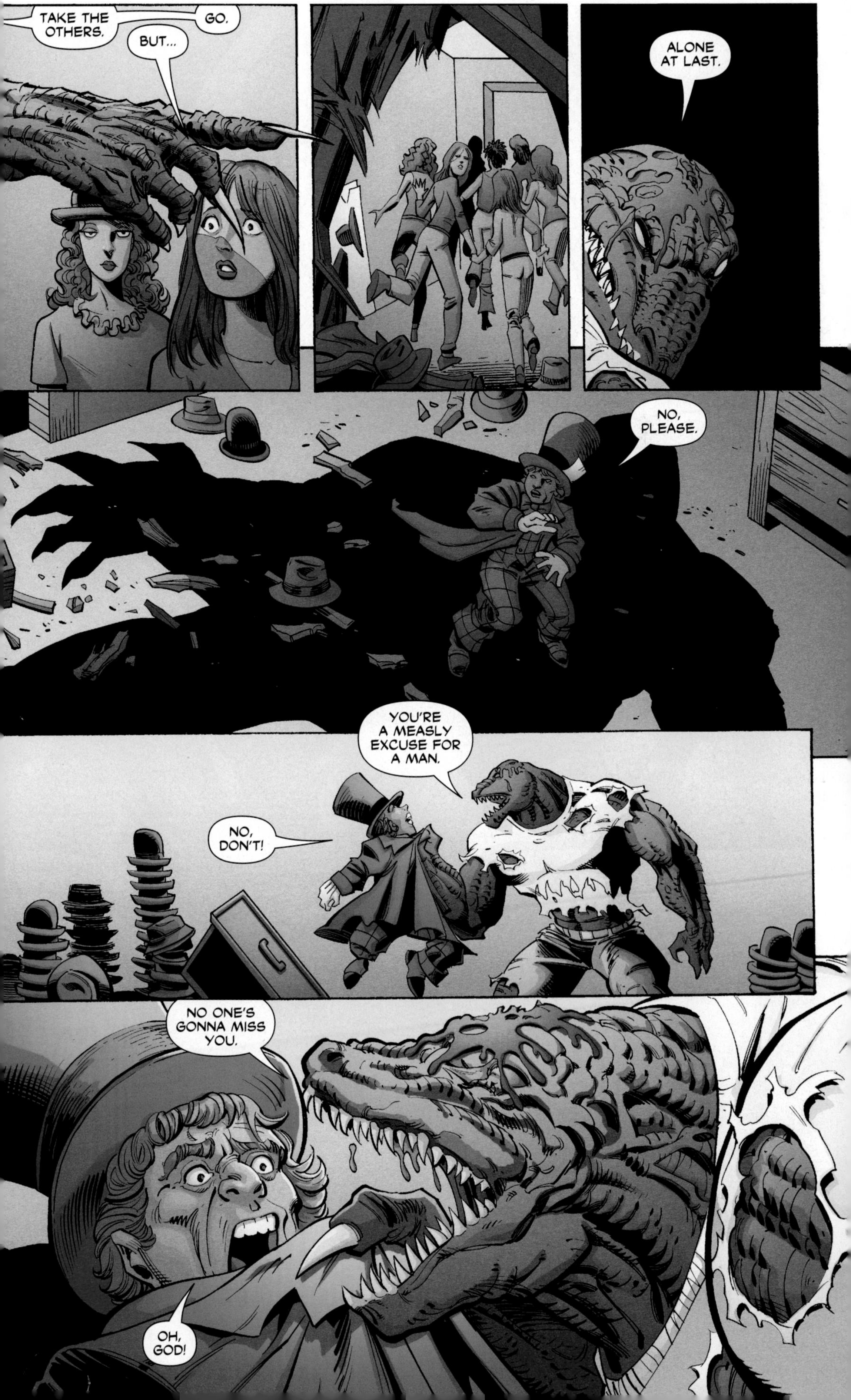
TAKE THE OTHERS.
GO.
BUT...
ALONE AT LAST.
NO, PLEASE.
YOU'RE A MEASLY EXCUSE FOR A MAN.
NO, DON'T!
NO ONE'S GONNA MISS YOU.
OH, GOD!

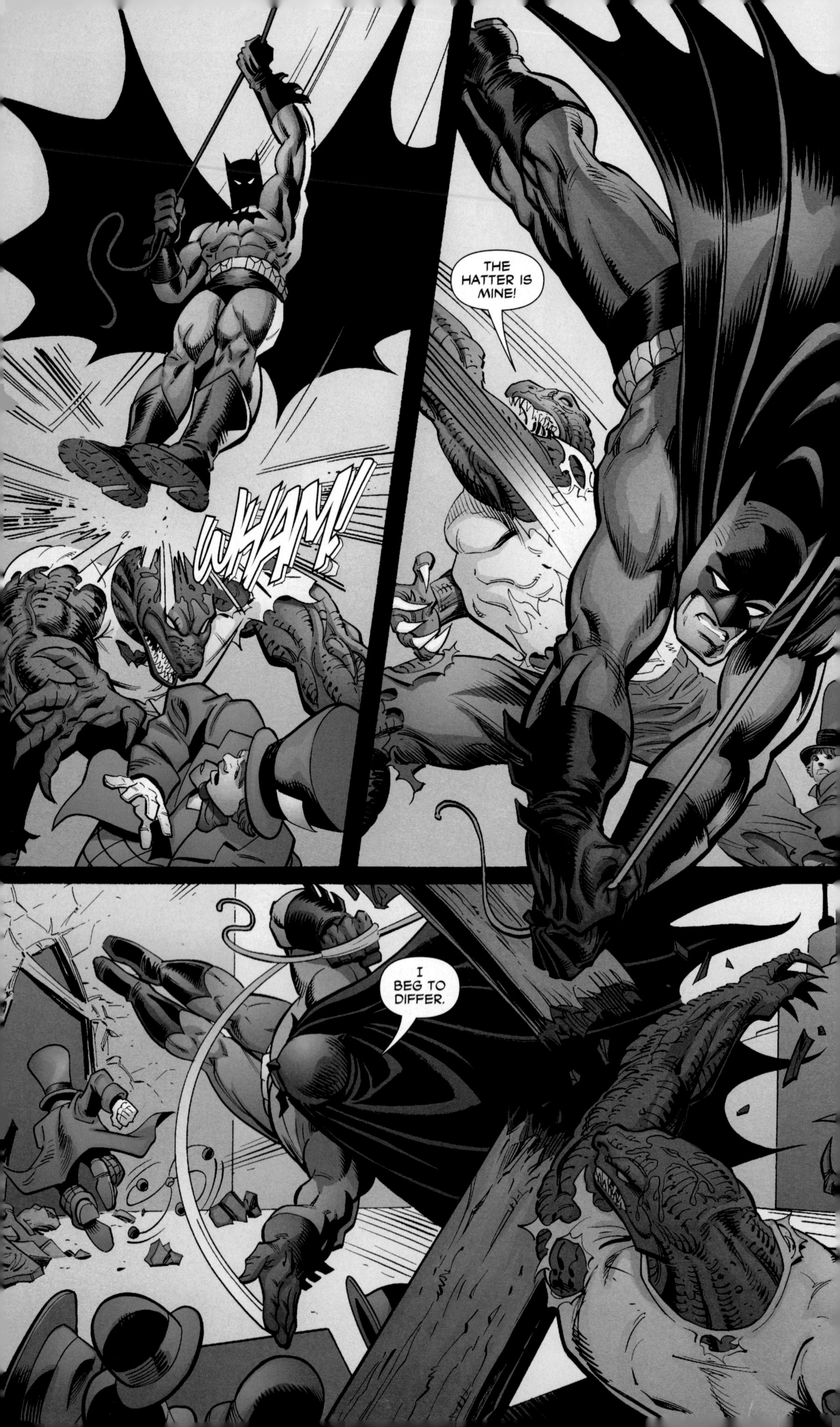
WHAM!
THE HATTER IS MINE!
I BEG TO DIFFER.

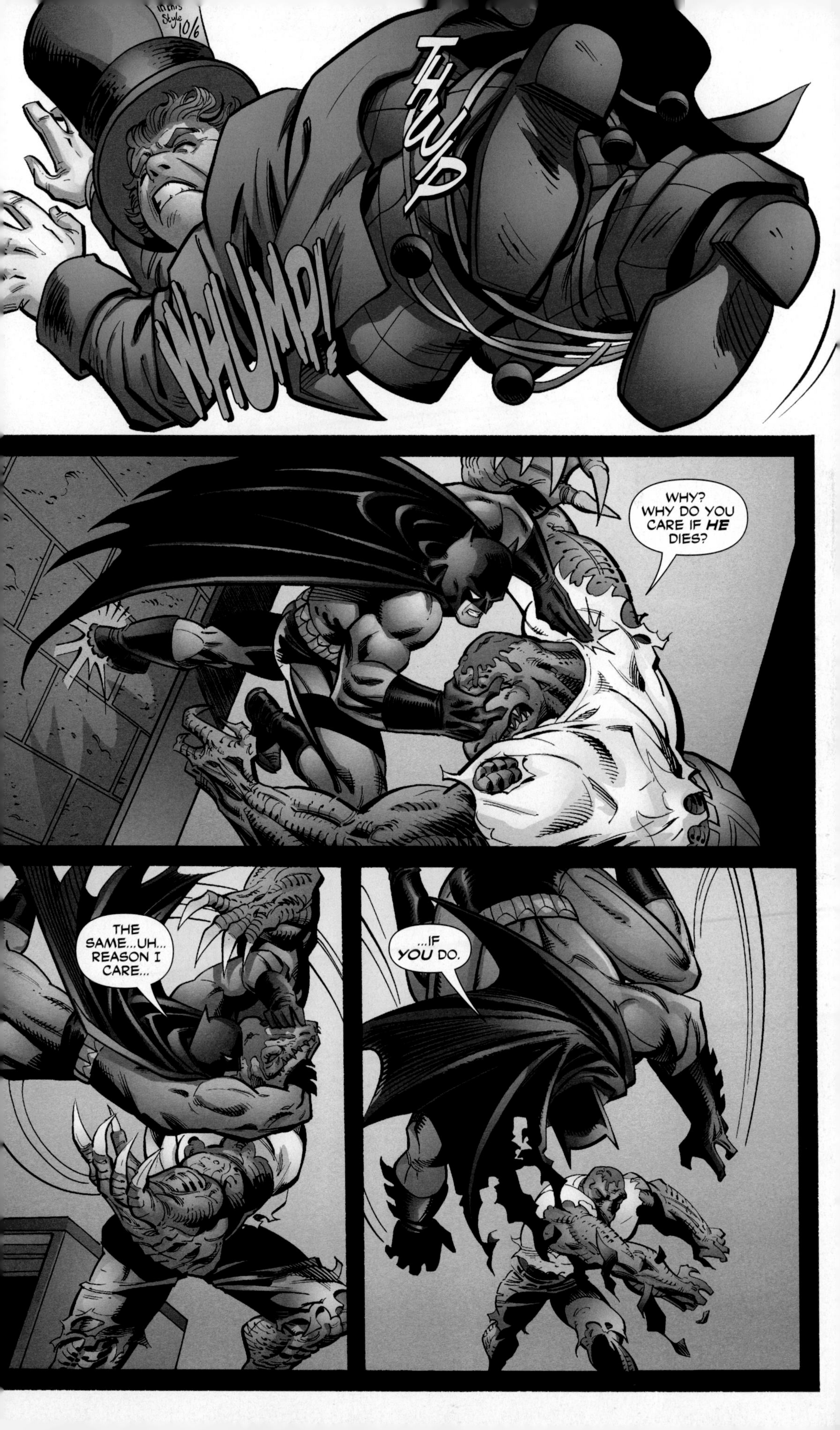

In this Style 10/6
THWIP
WHUMP!
WHY? WHY DO YOU CARE IF HE DIES?
THE SAME...UH... REASON I CARE...
...IF YOU DO.

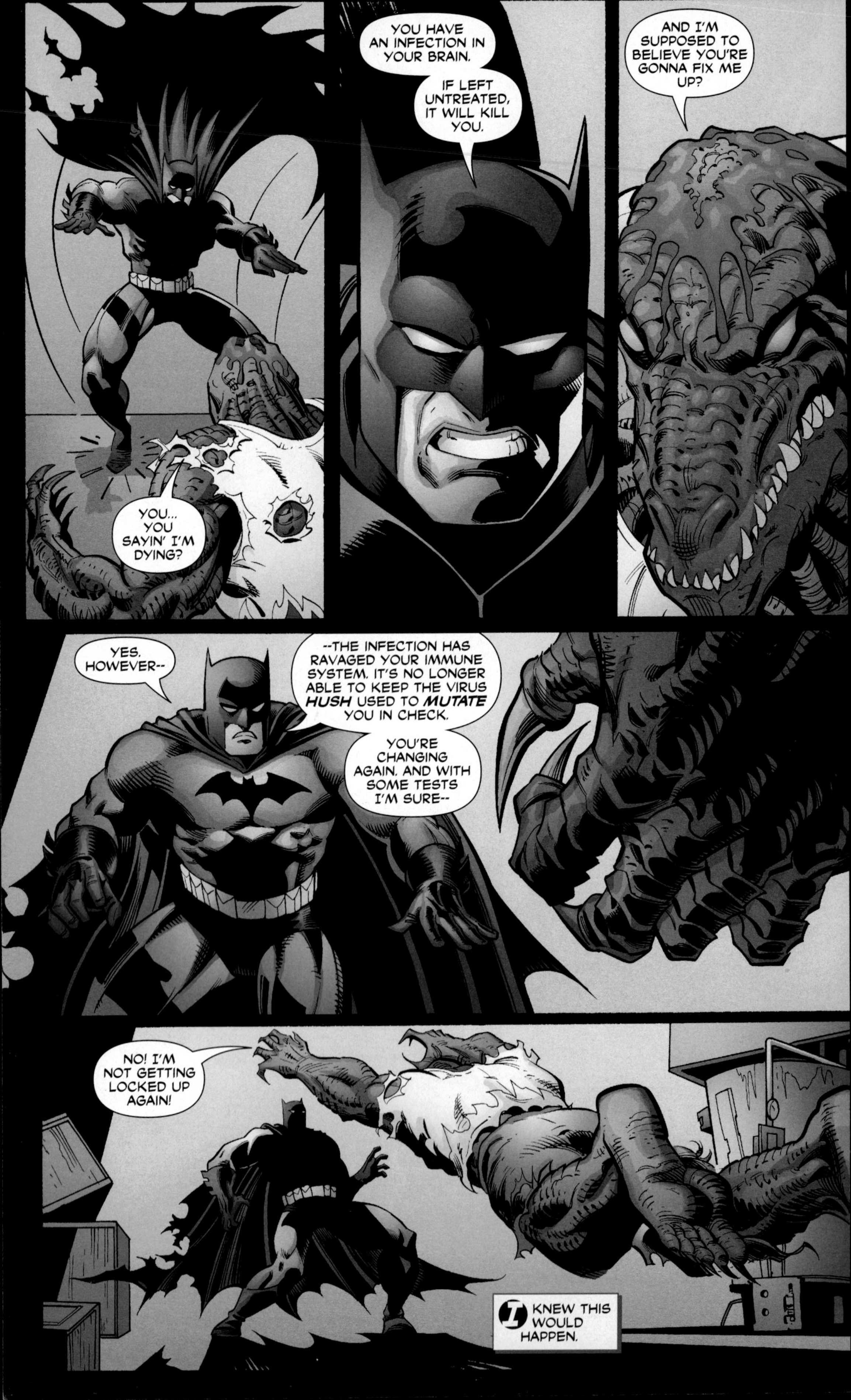

YOU... YOU SAYIN' I'M DYING?
YOU HAVE AN INFECTION IN YOUR BRAIN.
IF LEFT UNTREATED, IT WILL KILL YOU.
AND I'M SUPPOSED TO BELIEVE YOU'RE GONNA FIX ME UP?
YES. HOWEVER--
--THE INFECTION HAS RAVAGED YOUR IMMUNE SYSTEM. IT'S NO LONGER ABLE TO KEEP THE VIRUS *HUSH* USED TO *MUTATE* YOU IN CHECK.
YOU'RE CHANGING AGAIN. AND WITH SOME TESTS I'M SURE--
NO! I'M NOT GETTING LOCKED UP AGAIN!
I KNEW THIS WOULD HAPPEN.

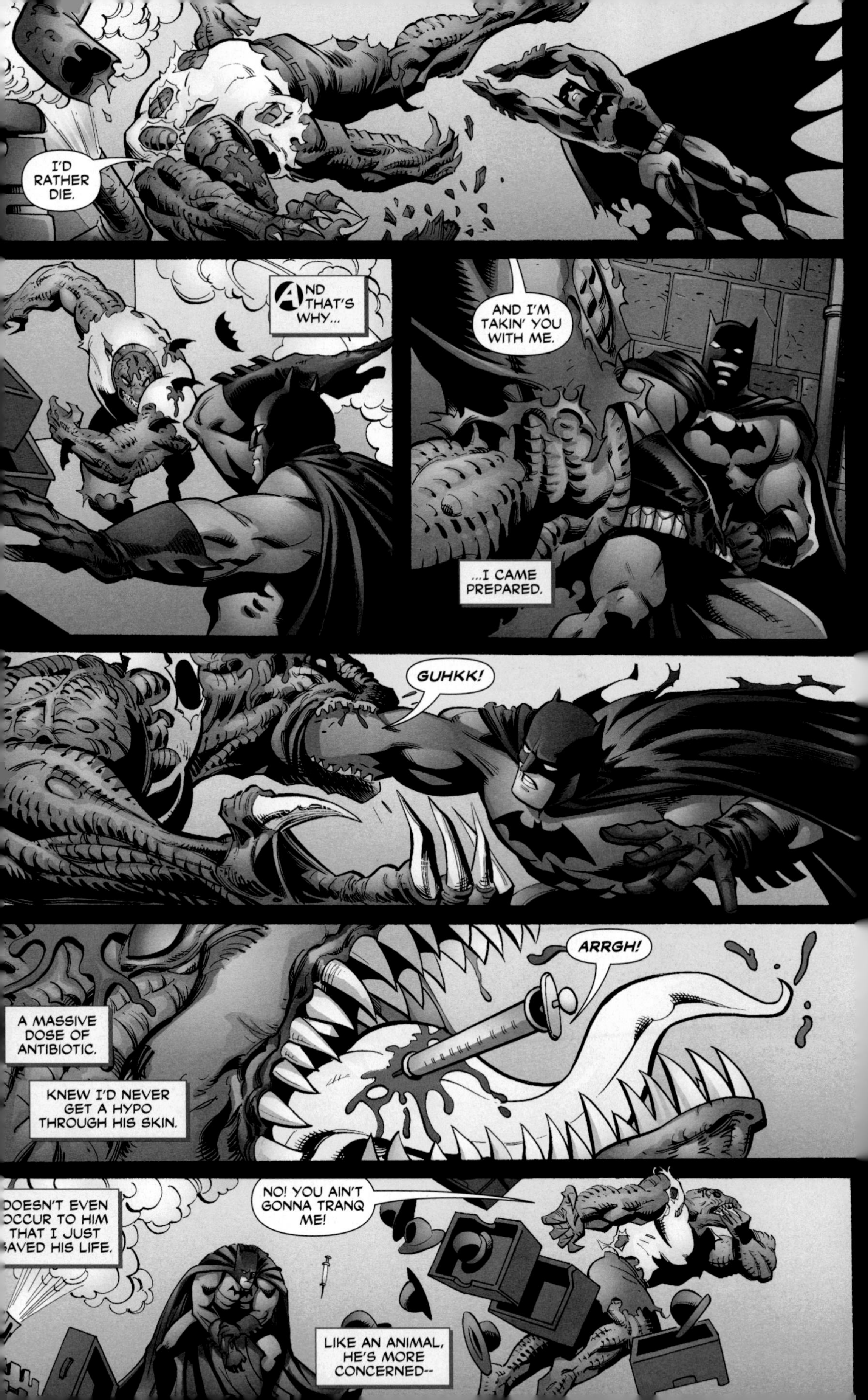
I'D RATHER DIE.
AND THAT'S WHY...
AND I'M TAKIN' YOU WITH ME.
...I CAME PREPARED.
GUHKK!
ARRGH!
A MASSIVE DOSE OF ANTIBIOTIC.
KNEW I'D NEVER GET A HYPO THROUGH HIS SKIN.
DOESN'T EVEN OCCUR TO HIM THAT I JUST SAVED HIS LIFE.
NO! YOU AIN'T GONNA TRANQ ME!
LIKE AN ANIMAL, HE'S MORE CONCERNED--

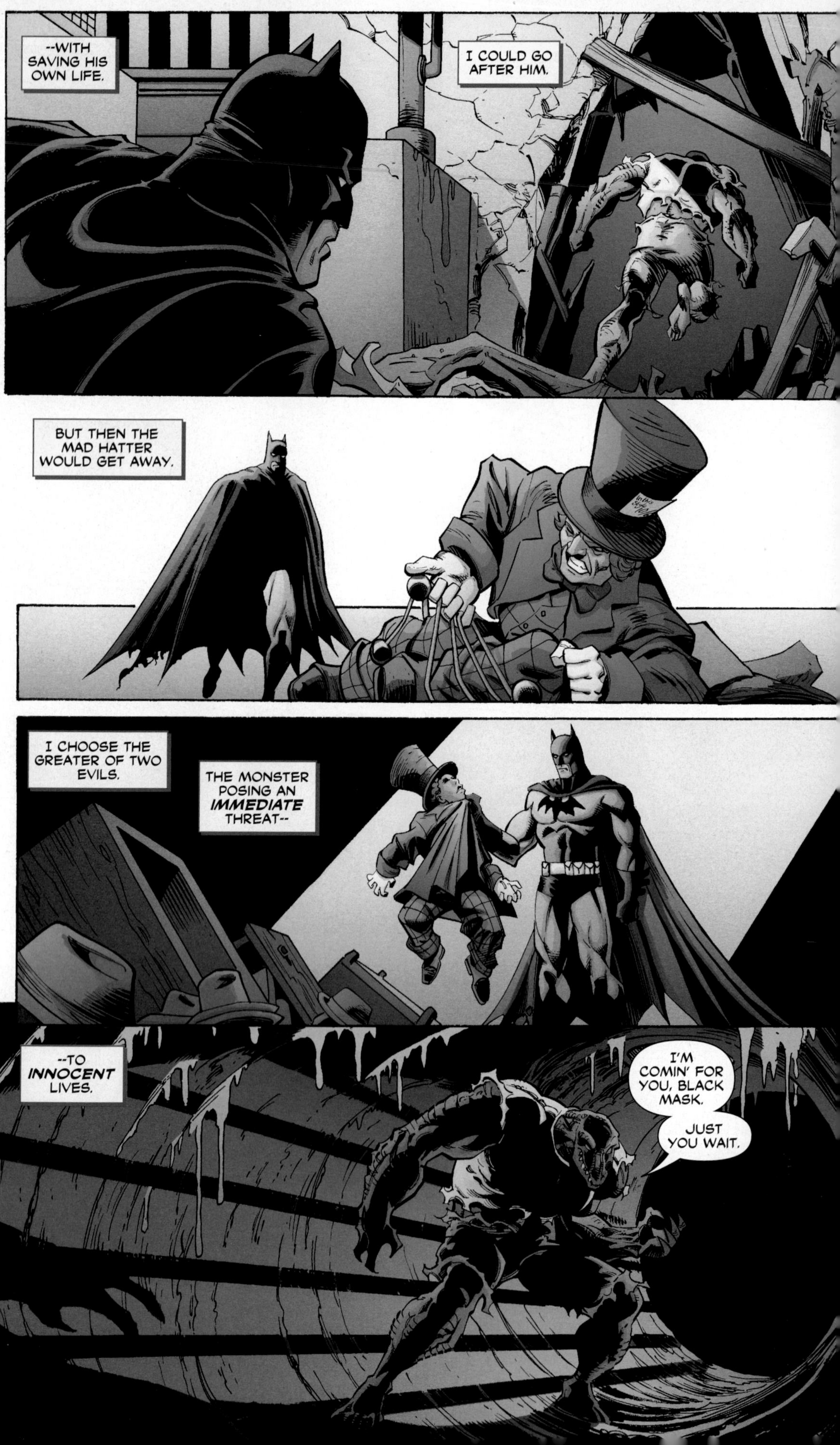
--WITH SAVING HIS OWN LIFE.
I COULD GO AFTER HIM.
BUT THEN THE MAD HATTER WOULD GET AWAY.
I CHOOSE THE GREATER OF TWO EVILS.
THE MONSTER POSING AN *IMMEDIATE* THREAT--
--TO *INNOCENT* LIVES.
I'M COMIN' FOR YOU, BLACK MASK.
JUST YOU WAIT.

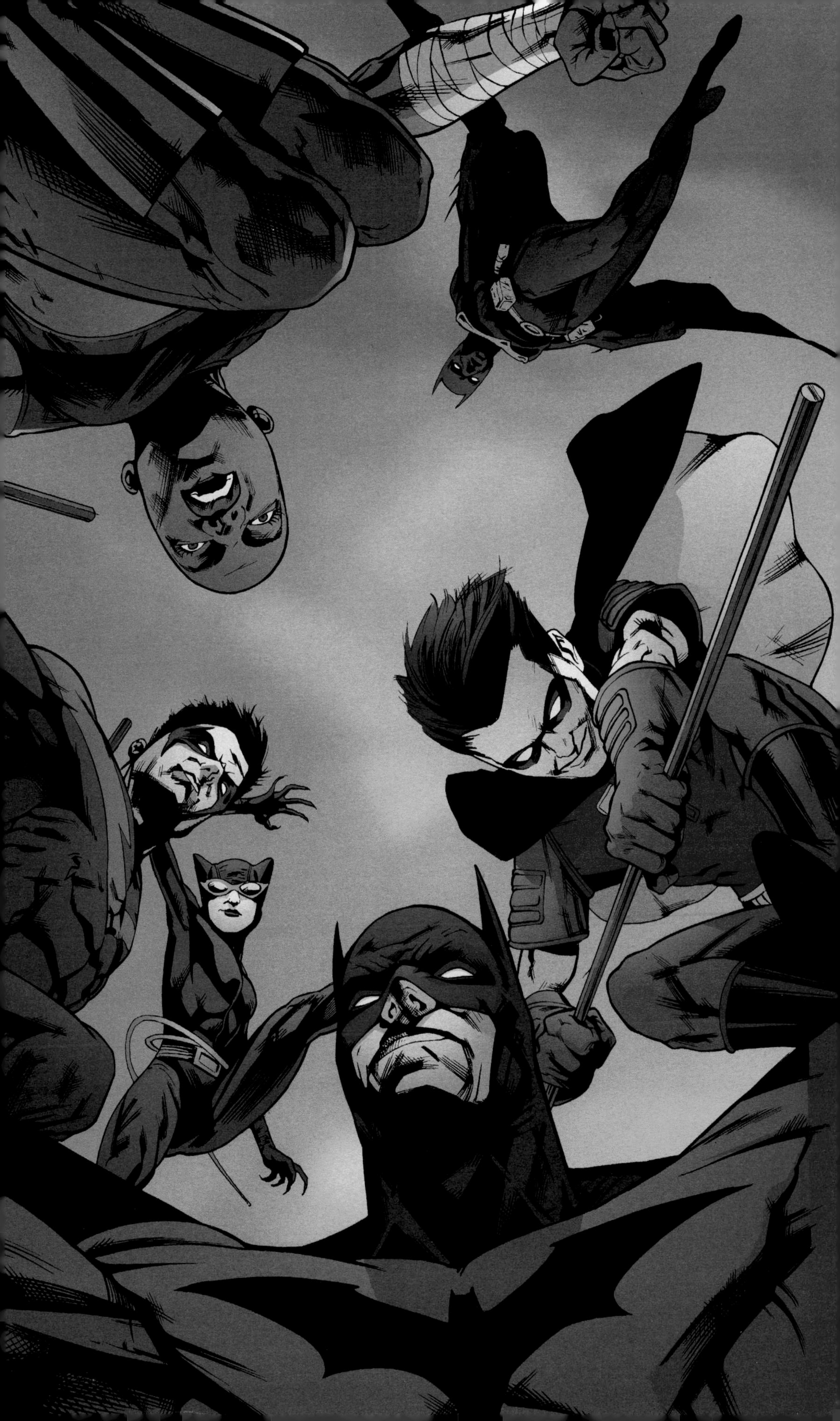

COVER ART BY
AL BARRIONUEVO,
BIT,
& GUY MAJOR

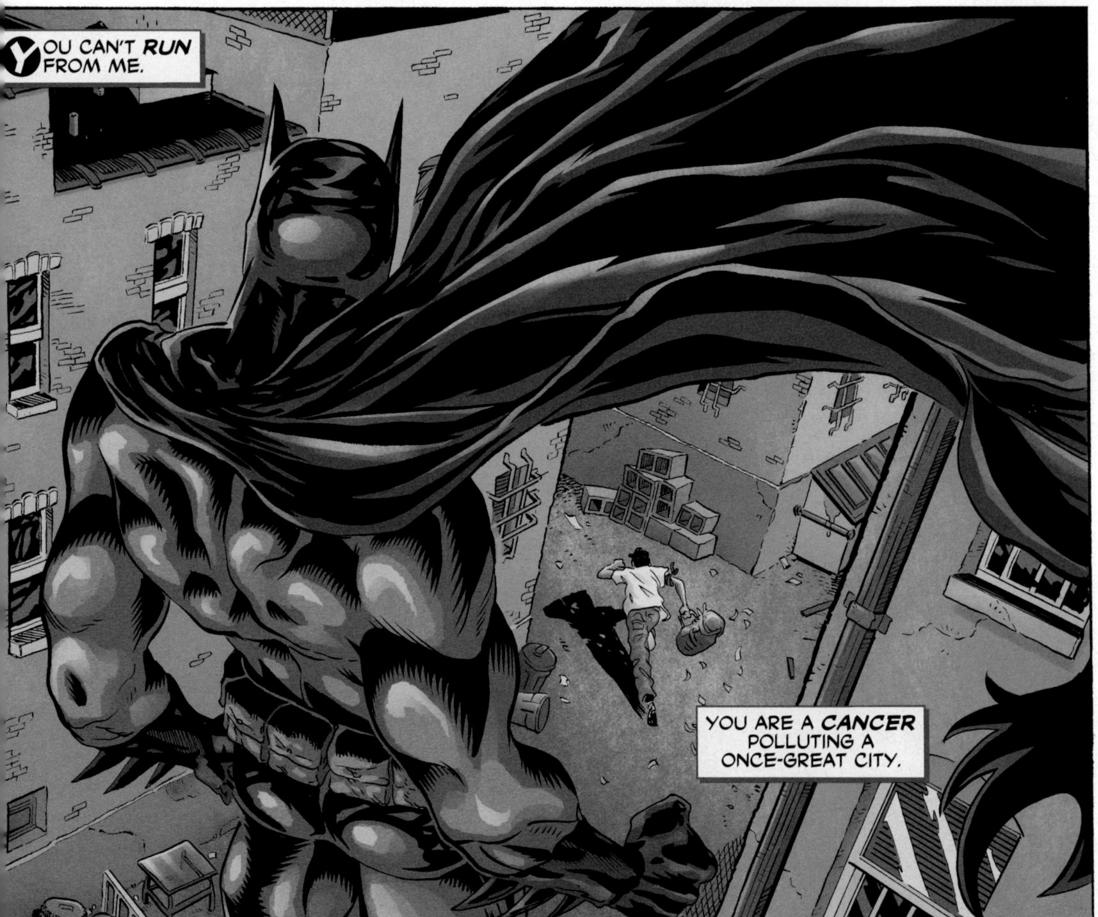
YOU CAN'T RUN FROM ME.
YOU ARE A CANCER POLLUTING A ONCE-GREAT CITY.
YOU ARE IRREDEEMABLE.

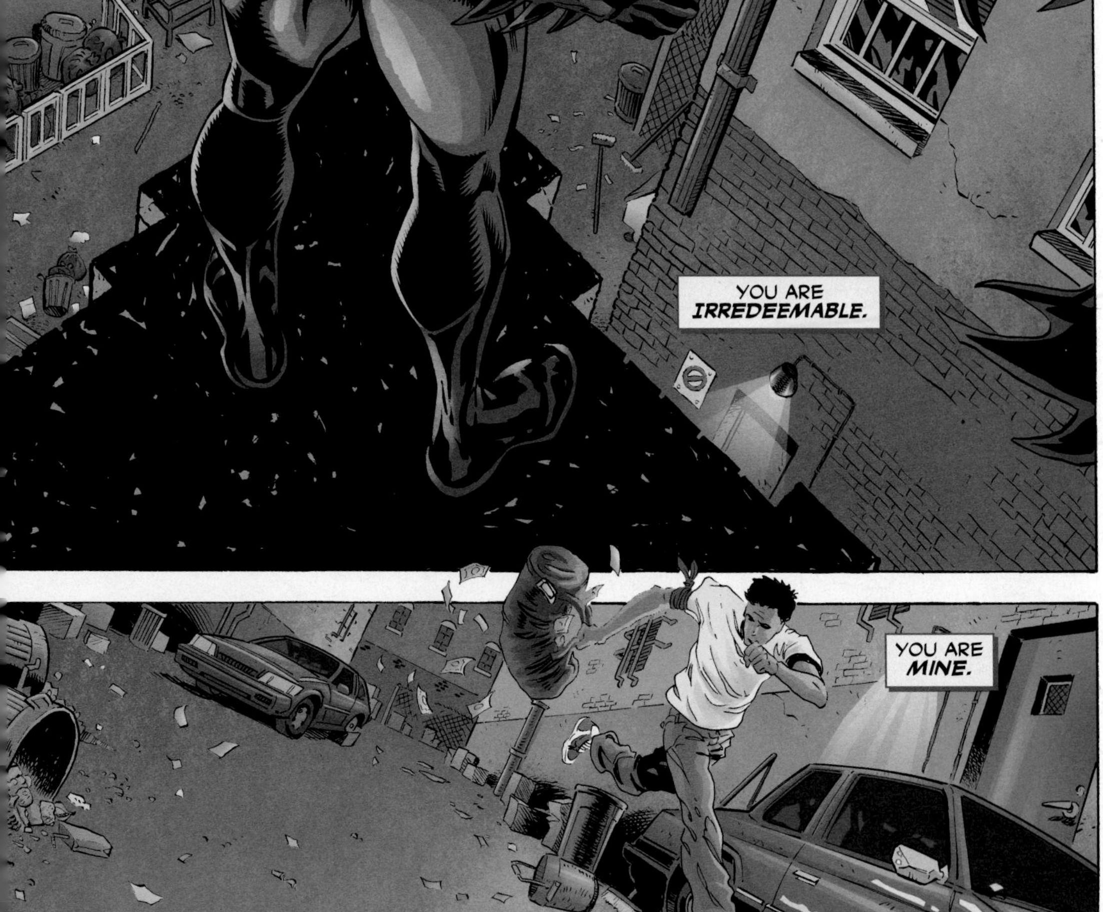
YOU ARE MINE.

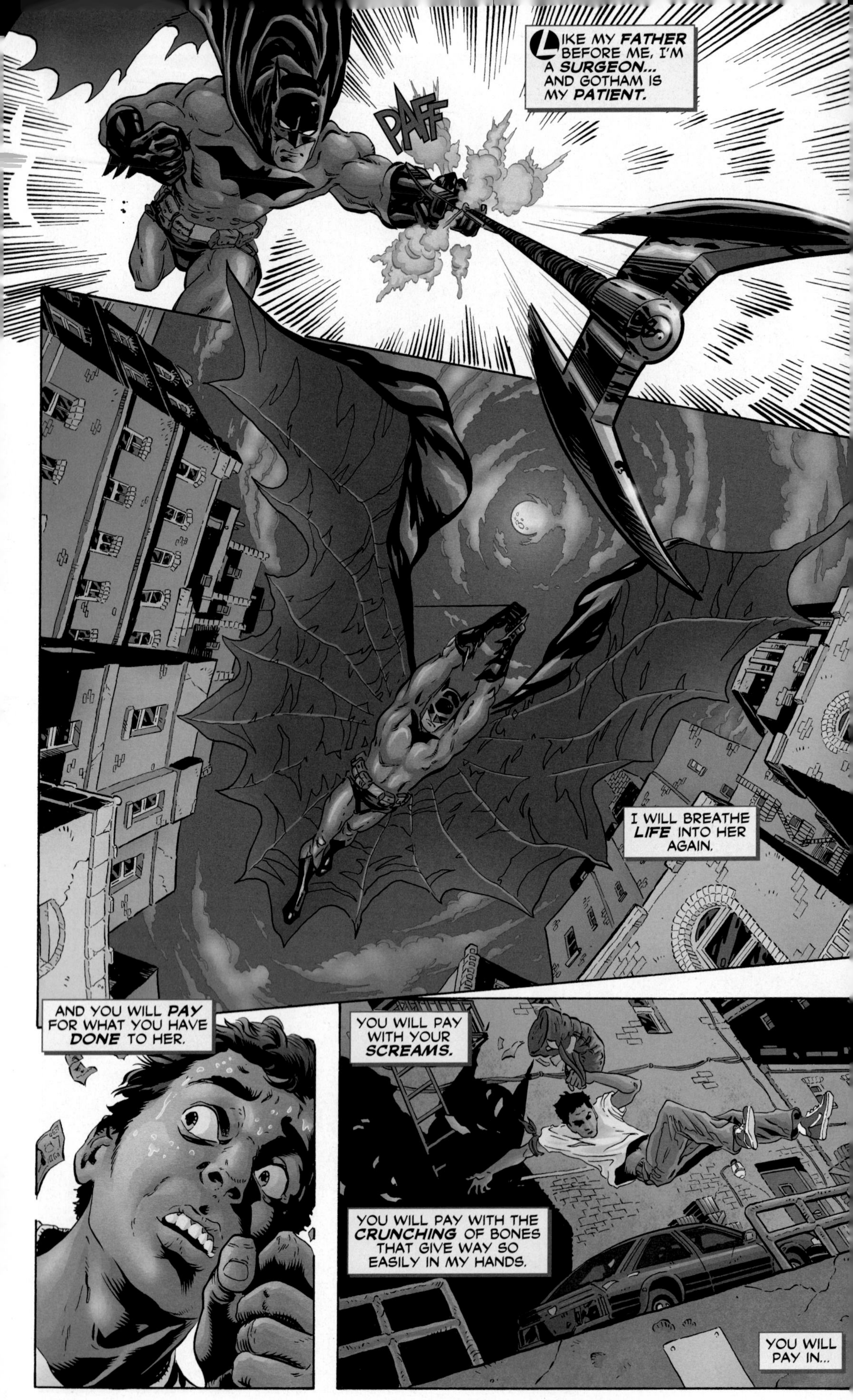
LIKE MY FATHER BEFORE ME, I'M A SURGEON... AND GOTHAM IS MY PATIENT.
PAFF
I WILL BREATHE LIFE INTO HER AGAIN.
AND YOU WILL PAY FOR WHAT YOU HAVE DONE TO HER.
YOU WILL PAY WITH YOUR SCREAMS.
YOU WILL PAY WITH THE CRUNCHING OF BONES THAT GIVE WAY SO EASILY IN MY HANDS.
YOU WILL PAY IN...

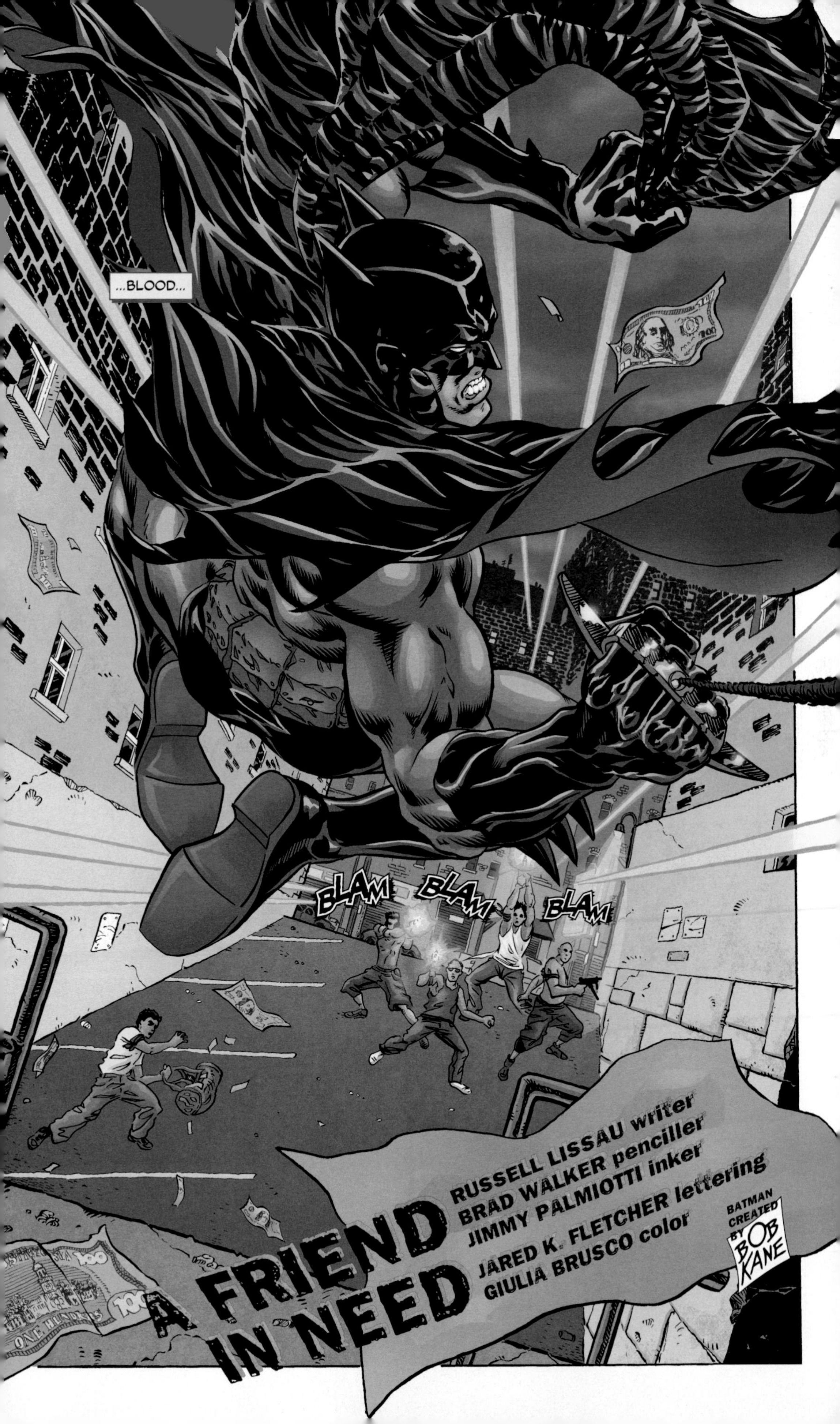
...BLOOD...
BLAM
BLAM
BLAM
A FRIEND IN NEED
RUSSELL LISSAU writer
BRAD WALKER penciller
JIMMY PALMIOTTI inker
JARED K. FLETCHER lettering
GIULIA BRUSCO color
BATMAN CREATED BY BOB KANE

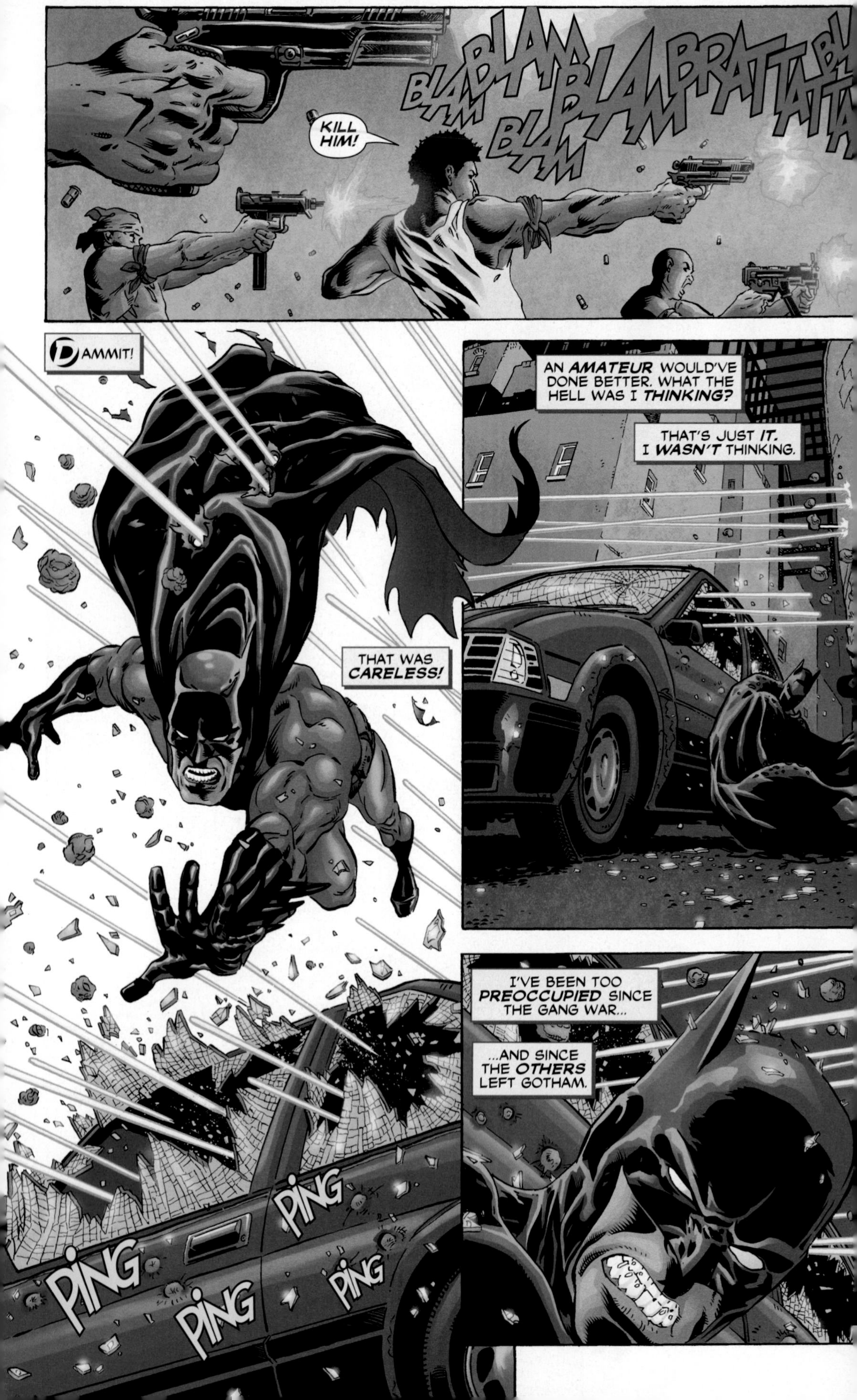
BLAM BLAM BLAM BLAM BLAM BLAM BRATTATATTA
KILL HIM!
DAMMIT!
THAT WAS CARELESS!
AN AMATEUR WOULD'VE DONE BETTER. WHAT THE HELL WAS I THINKING?
THAT'S JUST IT. I WASN'T THINKING.
I'VE BEEN TOO PREOCCUPIED SINCE THE GANG WAR...
...AND SINCE THE OTHERS LEFT GOTHAM.
PING
PING
PING
PING

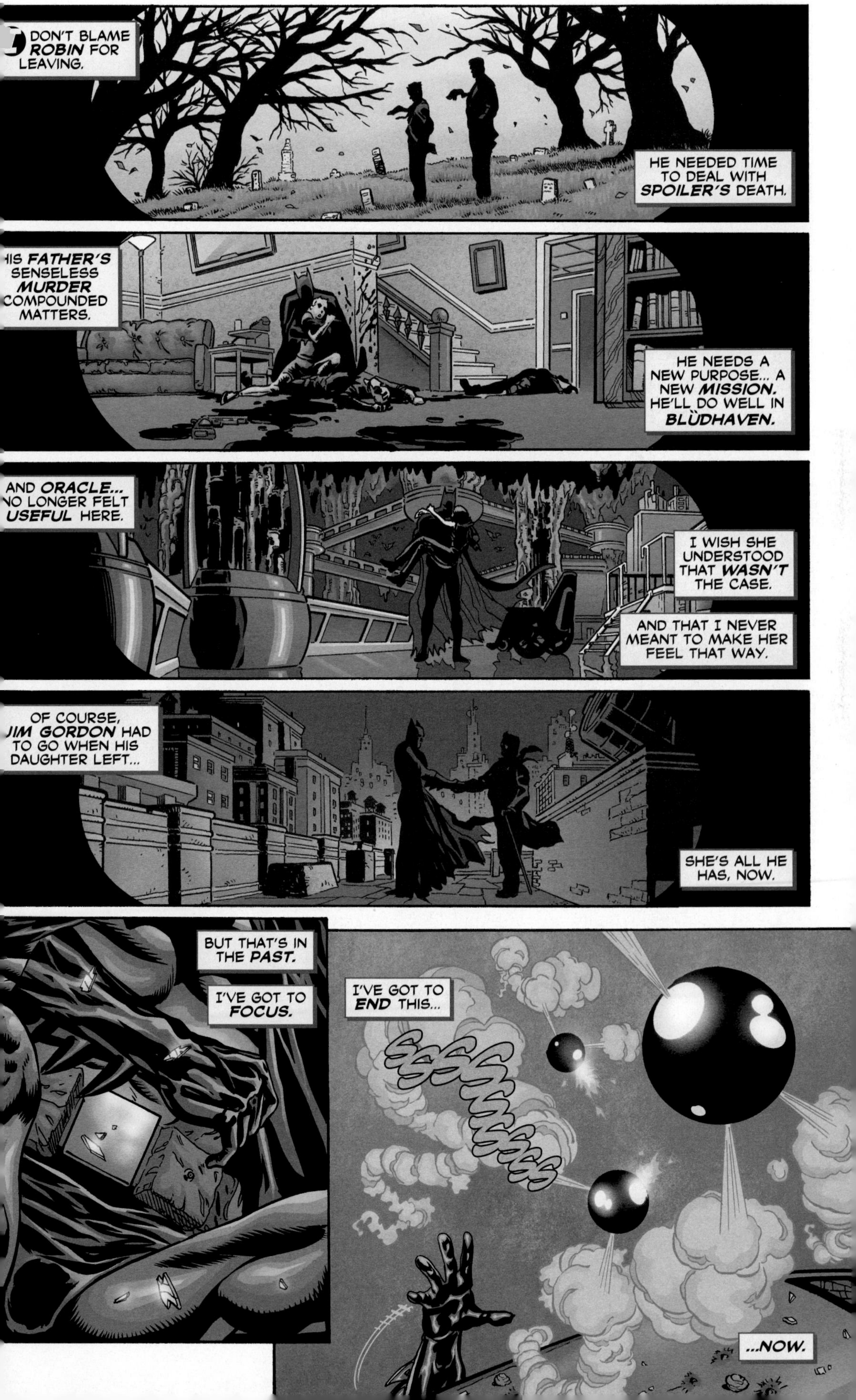
I DON'T BLAME ROBIN FOR LEAVING.
HE NEEDED TIME TO DEAL WITH SPOILER'S DEATH.
HIS FATHER'S SENSELESS MURDER COMPOUNDED MATTERS.
HE NEEDS A NEW PURPOSE... A NEW MISSION. HE'LL DO WELL IN BLÜDHAVEN.
AND ORACLE... NO LONGER FELT USEFUL HERE.
I WISH SHE UNDERSTOOD THAT WASN'T THE CASE.
AND THAT I NEVER MEANT TO MAKE HER FEEL THAT WAY.
OF COURSE, JIM GORDON HAD TO GO WHEN HIS DAUGHTER LEFT...
SHE'S ALL HE HAS, NOW.
BUT THAT'S IN THE PAST.
I'VE GOT TO FOCUS.
I'VE GOT TO END THIS...
SSSSSSSSSS
...NOW.

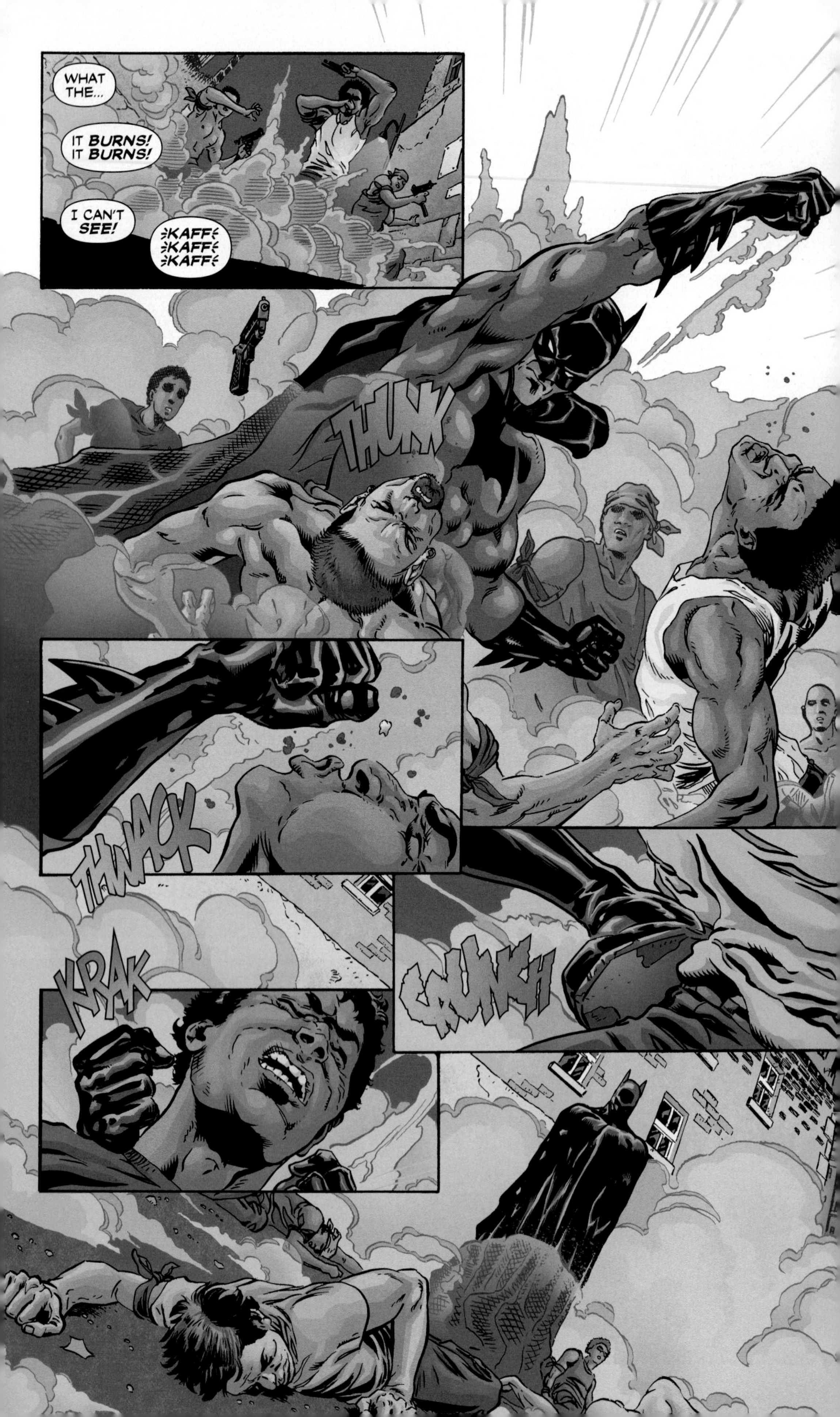
WHAT THE...
IT BURNS! IT BURNS!
I CAN'T SEE!
KAFF KAFF KAFF
THUNK
THWACK
KRAK
CRUNCH

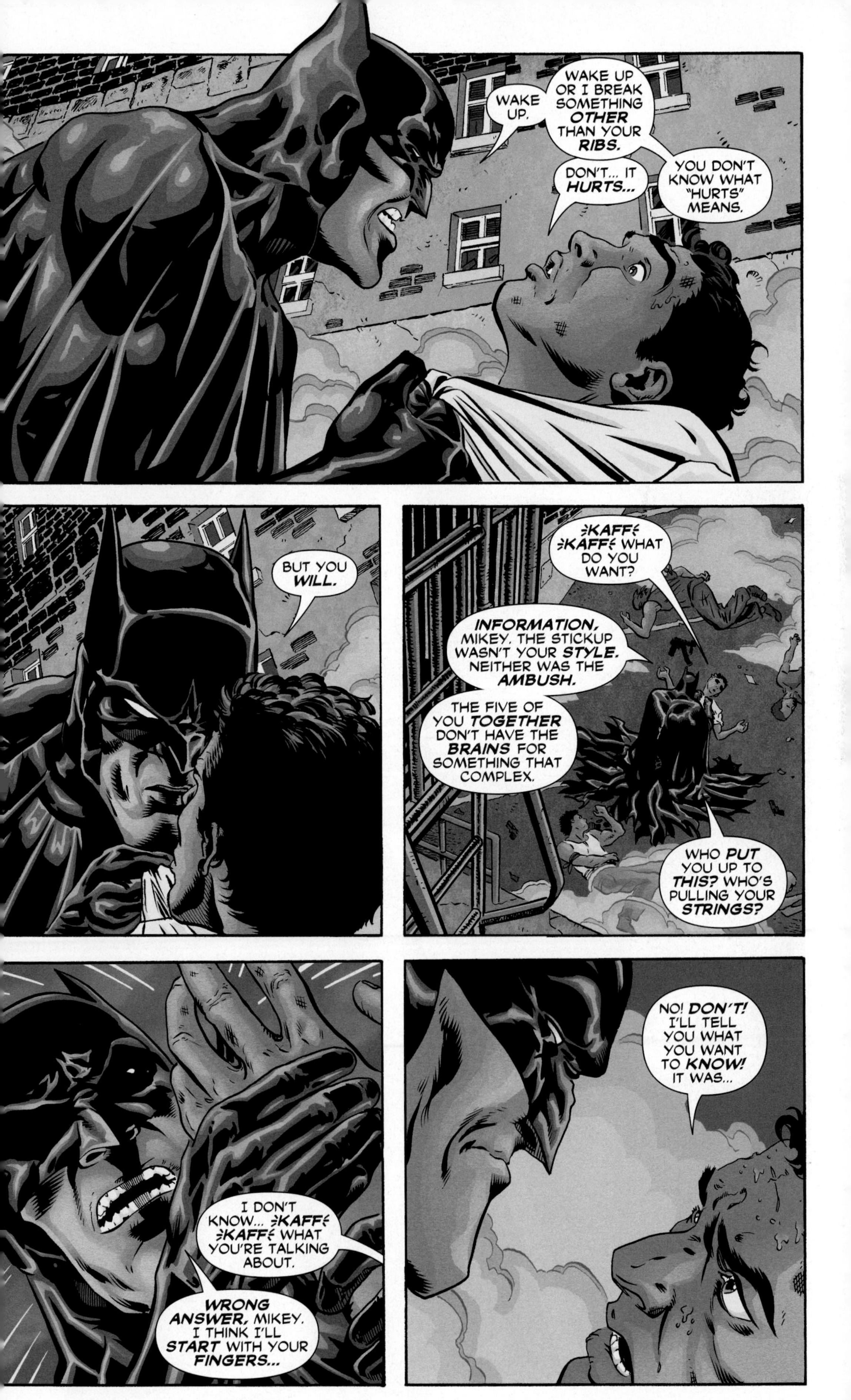

WAKE UP.
WAKE UP OR I BREAK SOMETHING OTHER THAN YOUR RIBS.
DON'T... IT HURTS...
YOU DON'T KNOW WHAT "HURTS" MEANS.
BUT YOU WILL.
KAFF KAFF WHAT DO YOU WANT?
INFORMATION, MIKEY. THE STICKUP WASN'T YOUR STYLE. NEITHER WAS THE AMBUSH.
THE FIVE OF YOU TOGETHER DON'T HAVE THE BRAINS FOR SOMETHING THAT COMPLEX.
WHO PUT YOU UP TO THIS? WHO'S PULLING YOUR STRINGS?
I DON'T KNOW... KAFF KAFF WHAT YOU'RE TALKING ABOUT.
WRONG ANSWER, MIKEY. I THINK I'LL START WITH YOUR FINGERS...
NO! DON'T! I'LL TELL YOU WHAT YOU WANT TO KNOW! IT WAS...

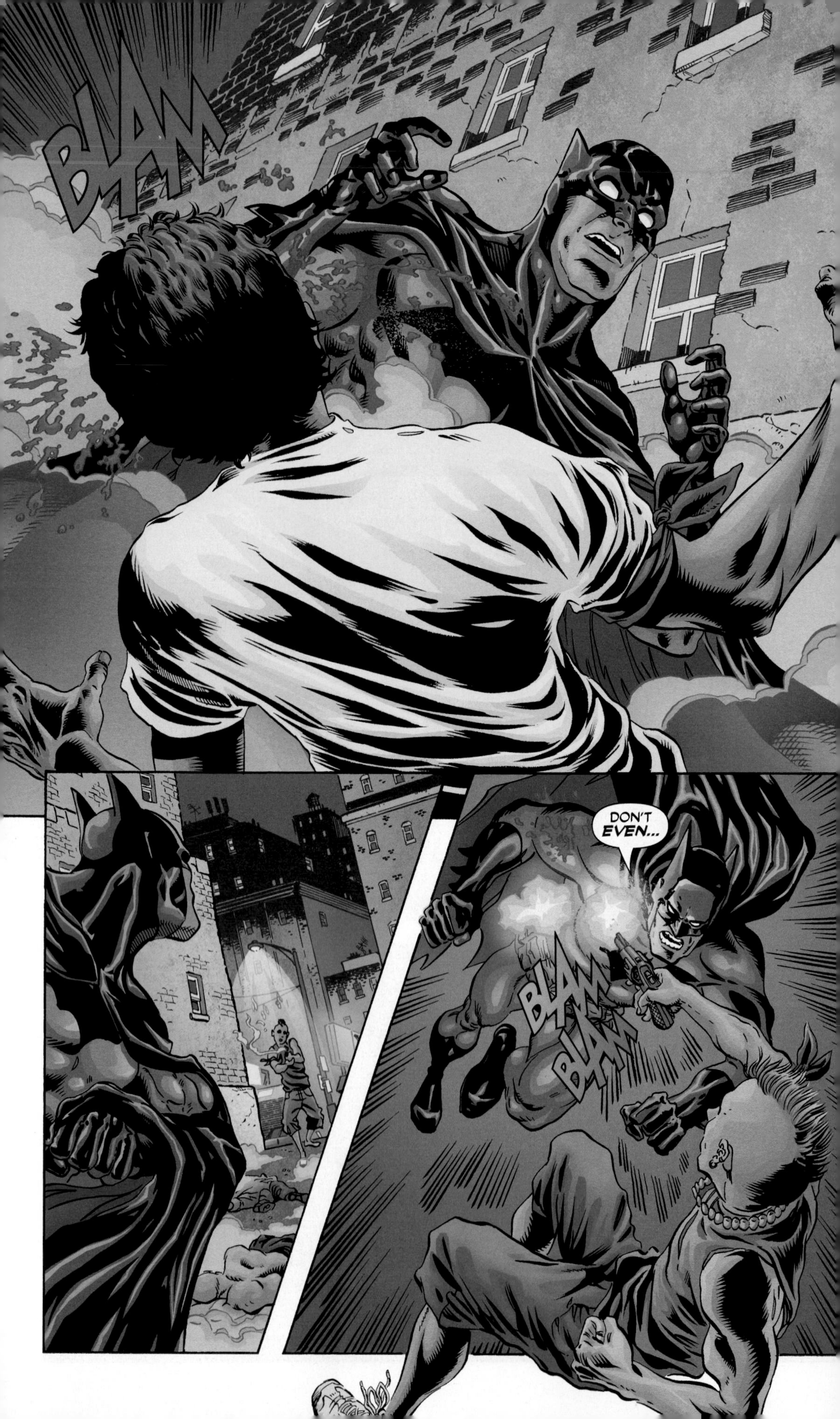
BLAM
DON'T EVEN...
BLAM
BLAM

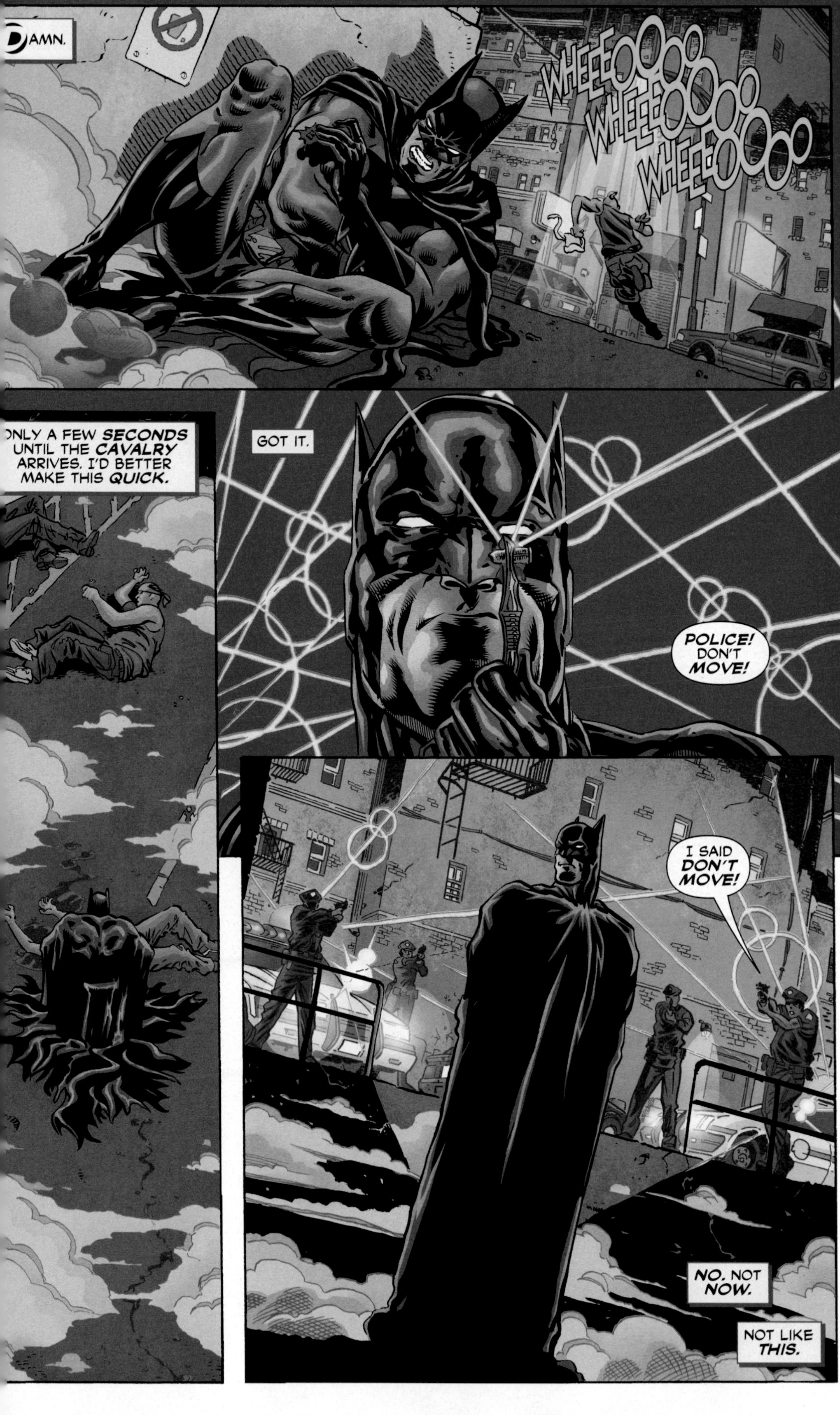
DAMN.
WHEEEOOOOO WHEEEOOOOO WHEEEOOOOO
ONLY A FEW SECONDS UNTIL THE CAVALRY ARRIVES. I'D BETTER MAKE THIS QUICK.
GOT IT.
POLICE! DON'T MOVE!
I SAID DON'T MOVE!
NO. NOT NOW.
NOT LIKE THIS.

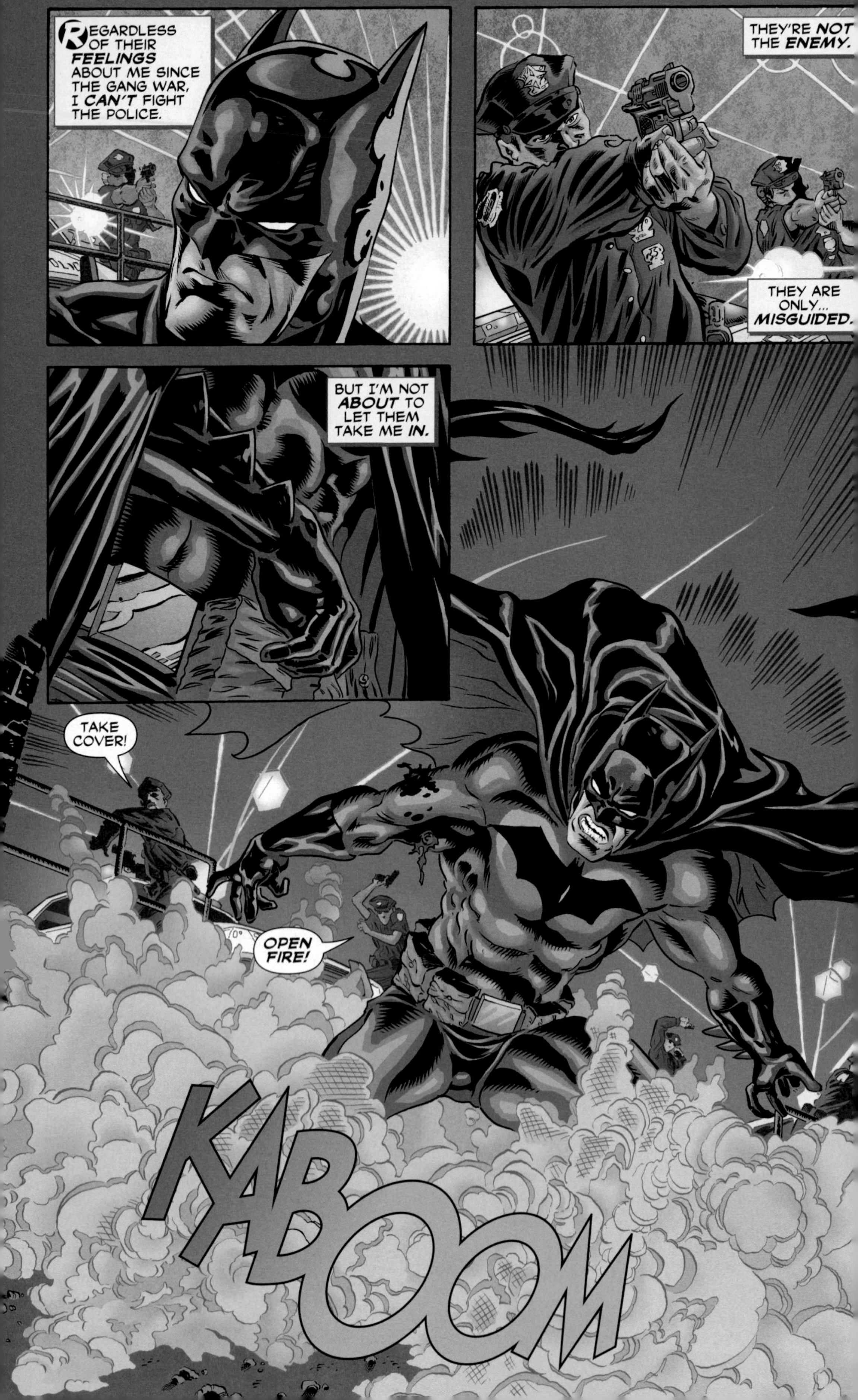
REGARDLESS OF THEIR FEELINGS ABOUT ME SINCE THE GANG WAR, I CAN'T FIGHT THE POLICE.
THEY'RE NOT THE ENEMY.
THEY ARE ONLY... MISGUIDED.
BUT I'M NOT ABOUT TO LET THEM TAKE ME IN.
TAKE COVER!
OPEN FIRE!
KABOOM

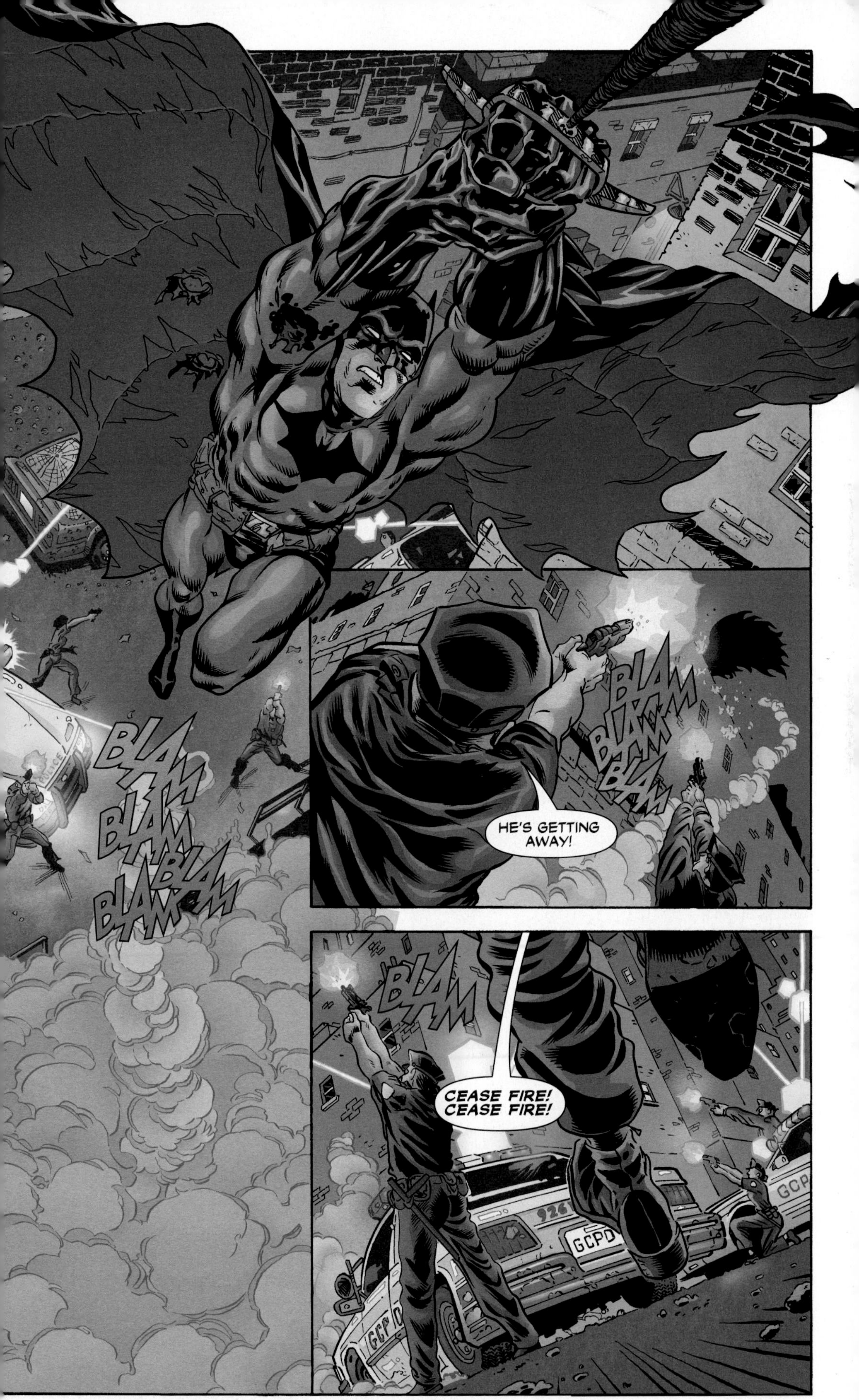
BLAM
BLAM
BLAM
BLAM
BLAM
BLAM
BLAM
BLAM
HE'S GETTING AWAY!
BLAM
CEASE FIRE! CEASE FIRE!

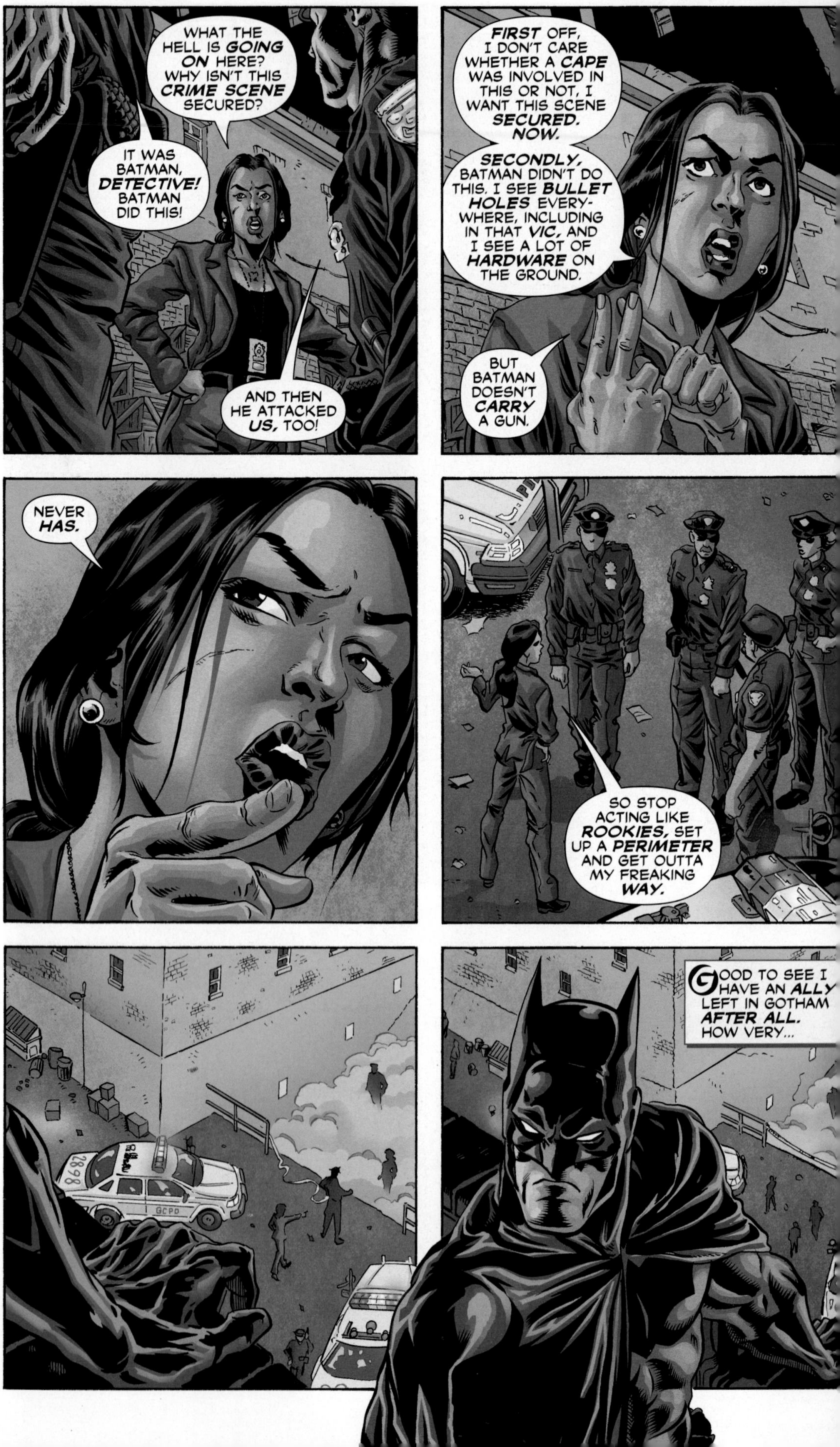
WHAT THE HELL IS GOING ON HERE? WHY ISN'T THIS CRIME SCENE SECURED?
IT WAS BATMAN, DETECTIVE! BATMAN DID THIS!
AND THEN HE ATTACKED US, TOO!
FIRST OFF, I DON'T CARE WHETHER A CAPE WAS INVOLVED IN THIS OR NOT, I WANT THIS SCENE SECURED. NOW.
SECONDLY, BATMAN DIDN'T DO THIS. I SEE BULLET HOLES EVERY-WHERE, INCLUDING IN THAT VIC, AND I SEE A LOT OF HARDWARE ON THE GROUND.
BUT BATMAN DOESN'T CARRY A GUN.
NEVER HAS.
SO STOP ACTING LIKE ROOKIES, SET UP A PERIMETER AND GET OUTTA MY FREAKING WAY.
GCPD
GOOD TO SEE I HAVE AN ALLY LEFT IN GOTHAM AFTER ALL. HOW VERY...

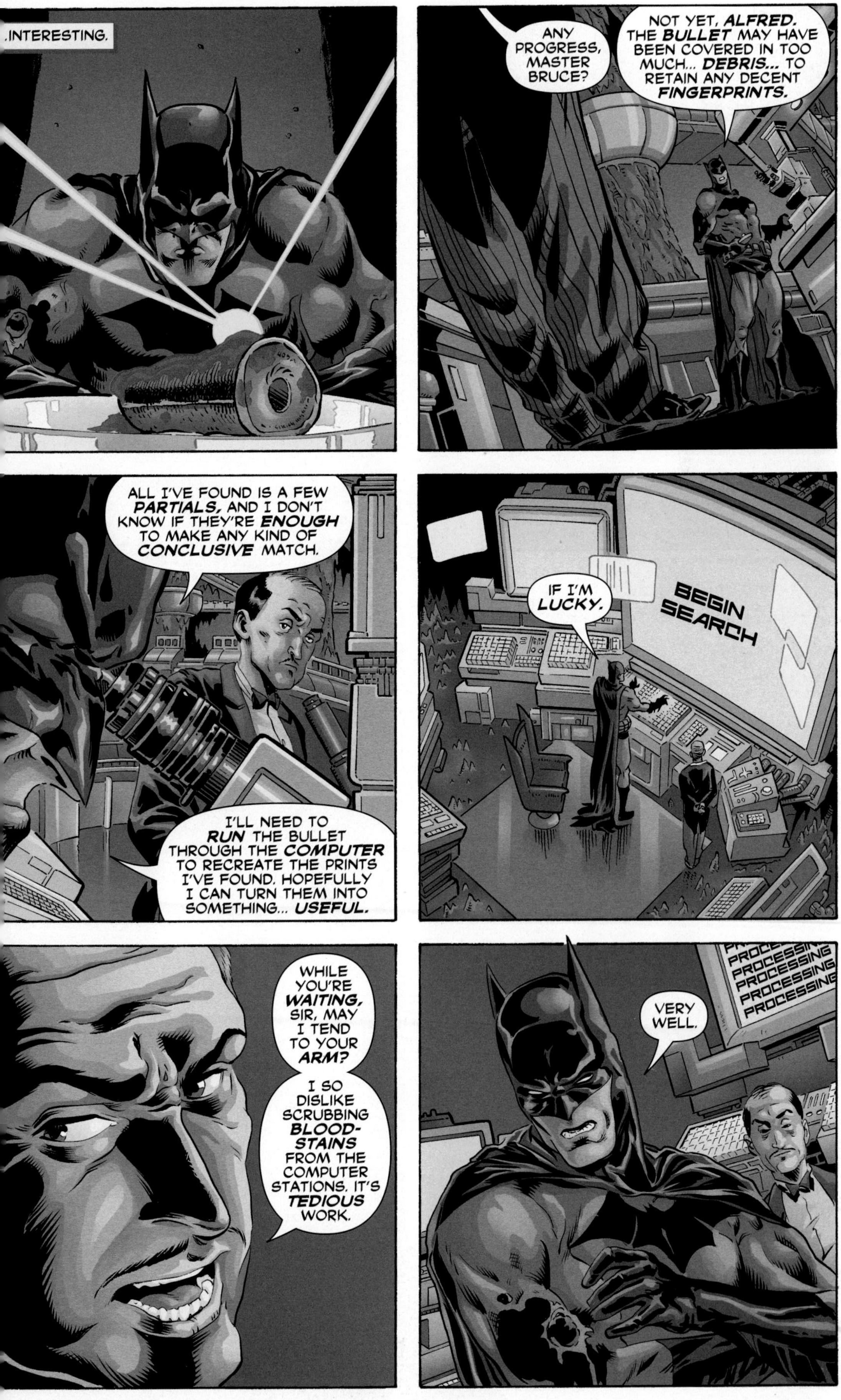
.INTERESTING.
ANY PROGRESS, MASTER BRUCE?
NOT YET, ALFRED. THE BULLET MAY HAVE BEEN COVERED IN TOO MUCH... DEBRIS... TO RETAIN ANY DECENT FINGERPRINTS.
ALL I'VE FOUND IS A FEW PARTIALS, AND I DON'T KNOW IF THEY'RE ENOUGH TO MAKE ANY KIND OF CONCLUSIVE MATCH.
I'LL NEED TO RUN THE BULLET THROUGH THE COMPUTER TO RECREATE THE PRINTS I'VE FOUND. HOPEFULLY I CAN TURN THEM INTO SOMETHING... USEFUL.
IF I'M LUCKY.
BEGIN SEARCH
WHILE YOU'RE WAITING, SIR, MAY I TEND TO YOUR ARM?
I SO DISLIKE SCRUBBING BLOOD-STAINS FROM THE COMPUTER STATIONS. IT'S TEDIOUS WORK.
PROCESSING
PROCESSING
PROCESSING
PROCESSING
VERY WELL.

JUST A *FEW* MORE *STITCHES*, MASTER BRUCE.

THANK YOU, ALFRED. GOOD *WORK*, AS EVER.

I LIVE TO *PLEASE*, SIR.

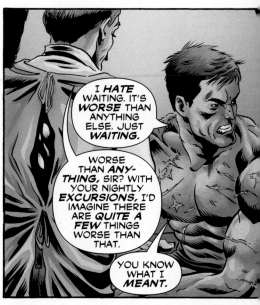

I *HATE* WAITING. IT'S *WORSE* THAN ANYTHING ELSE. JUST *WAITING*.

WORSE THAN *ANYTHING*, SIR? WITH YOUR NIGHTLY *EXCURSIONS*, I'D IMAGINE THERE ARE *QUITE A FEW* THINGS WORSE THAN THAT.

YOU KNOW WHAT I *MEANT*.

I HAVE THE BEST *COMPUTERS* MONEY CAN *BUY* OR SCIENCE CAN *DEVISE*, BUT STILL THEY WORK AT A *SNAIL'S PACE*.

REMIND ME TO DUMP MY *WAYNE-TECH* STOCK, SIR.

BEEP BEEP BEEP

HRM. IT SEEMS THE COMPUTERS *HEARD* YOU.

JACK HUNTER

GCPD CASE #97110

JACK HUNT

GCPD C #97

IF I MAY *ASK,* SIR: WHAT *NOW?*

WHAT DO YOU *MEAN?*

AFTER RECENT *EVENTS,* YOUR *RELATIONSHIP* WITH THE *GOTHAM CONSTABULARY* IS... PRECARIOUS, AT BEST.

I'D SAY IT'S NONEXISTENT.

BE THAT AS IT MAY, I ASSUME YOU PLAN TO *APPREHEND* THIS MISCREANT. WHAT DO YOU THEN PLAN TO *DO* WITH HIM?

IT'S NOT AS IF YOU CAN SIMPLY *WALK* INTO THE STATION HOUSE AND HAND HIM OVER. THEY'D JUST AS SOON LOCK *YOU* UP.

THAT'S A GOOD *POINT.*

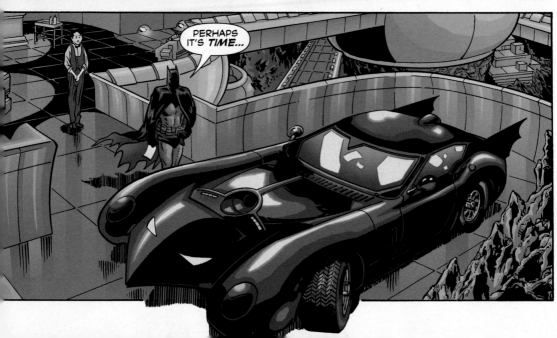

PERHAPS IT'S *TIME...*

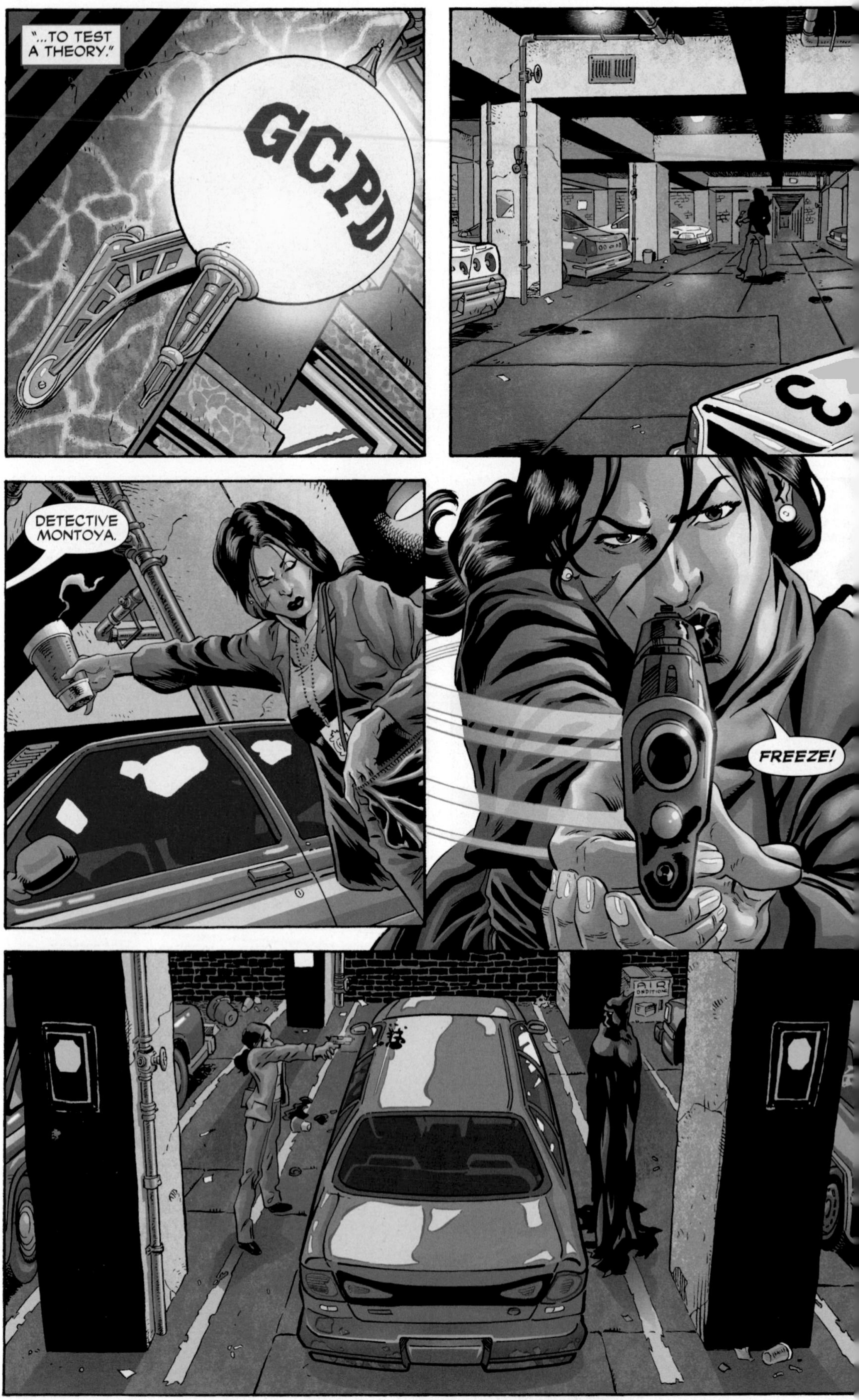
"...TO TEST
A THEORY."
GCPD
DETECTIVE
MONTOYA.
FREEZE!

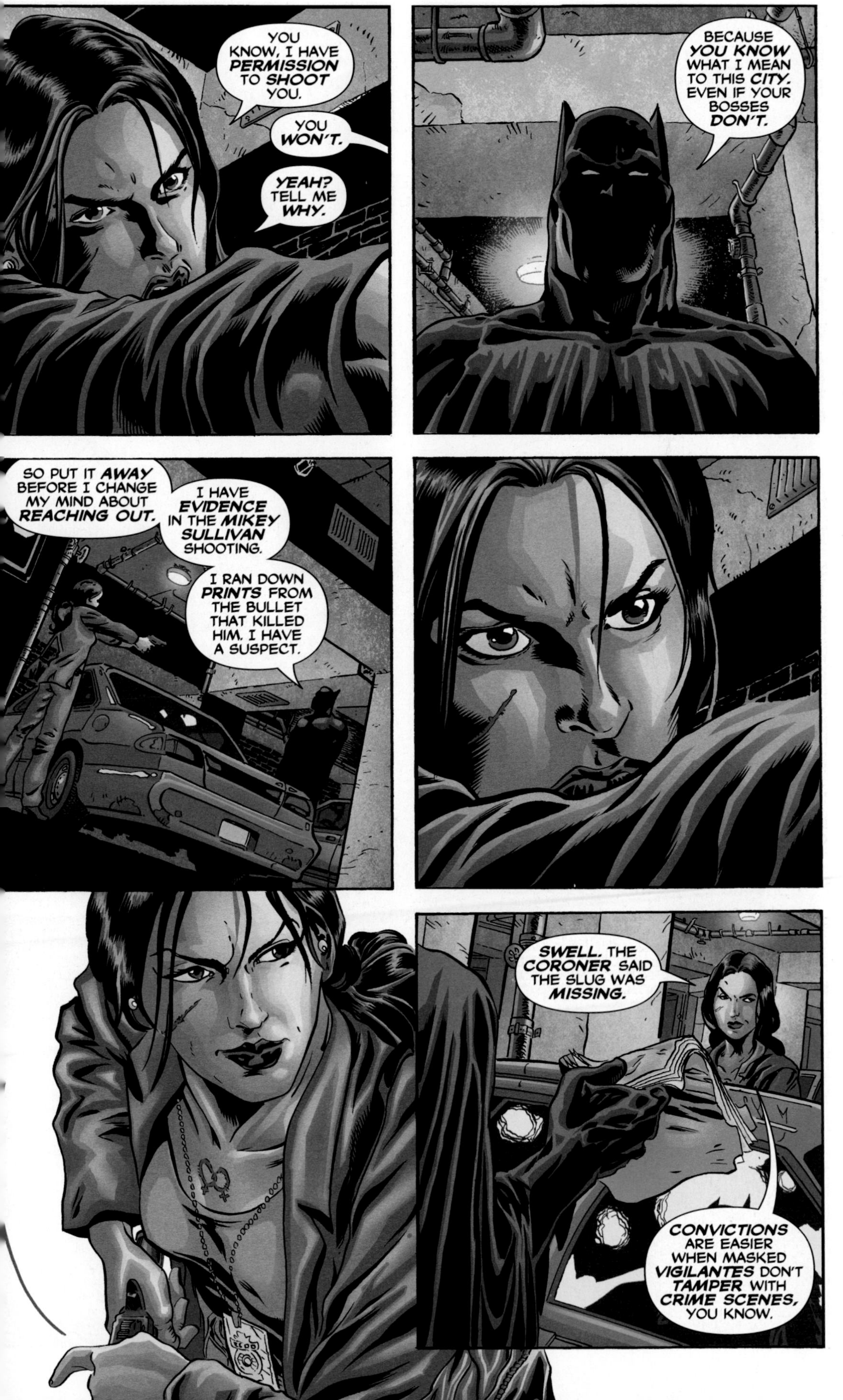

YOU KNOW, I HAVE PERMISSION TO SHOOT YOU.
YOU WON'T.
YEAH? TELL ME WHY.
BECAUSE YOU KNOW WHAT I MEAN TO THIS CITY. EVEN IF YOUR BOSSES DON'T.
SO PUT IT AWAY BEFORE I CHANGE MY MIND ABOUT REACHING OUT.
I HAVE EVIDENCE IN THE MIKEY SULLIVAN SHOOTING.
I RAN DOWN PRINTS FROM THE BULLET THAT KILLED HIM. I HAVE A SUSPECT.
SWELL. THE CORONER SAID THE SLUG WAS MISSING.
CONVICTIONS ARE EASIER WHEN MASKED VIGILANTES DON'T TAMPER WITH CRIME SCENES, YOU KNOW.

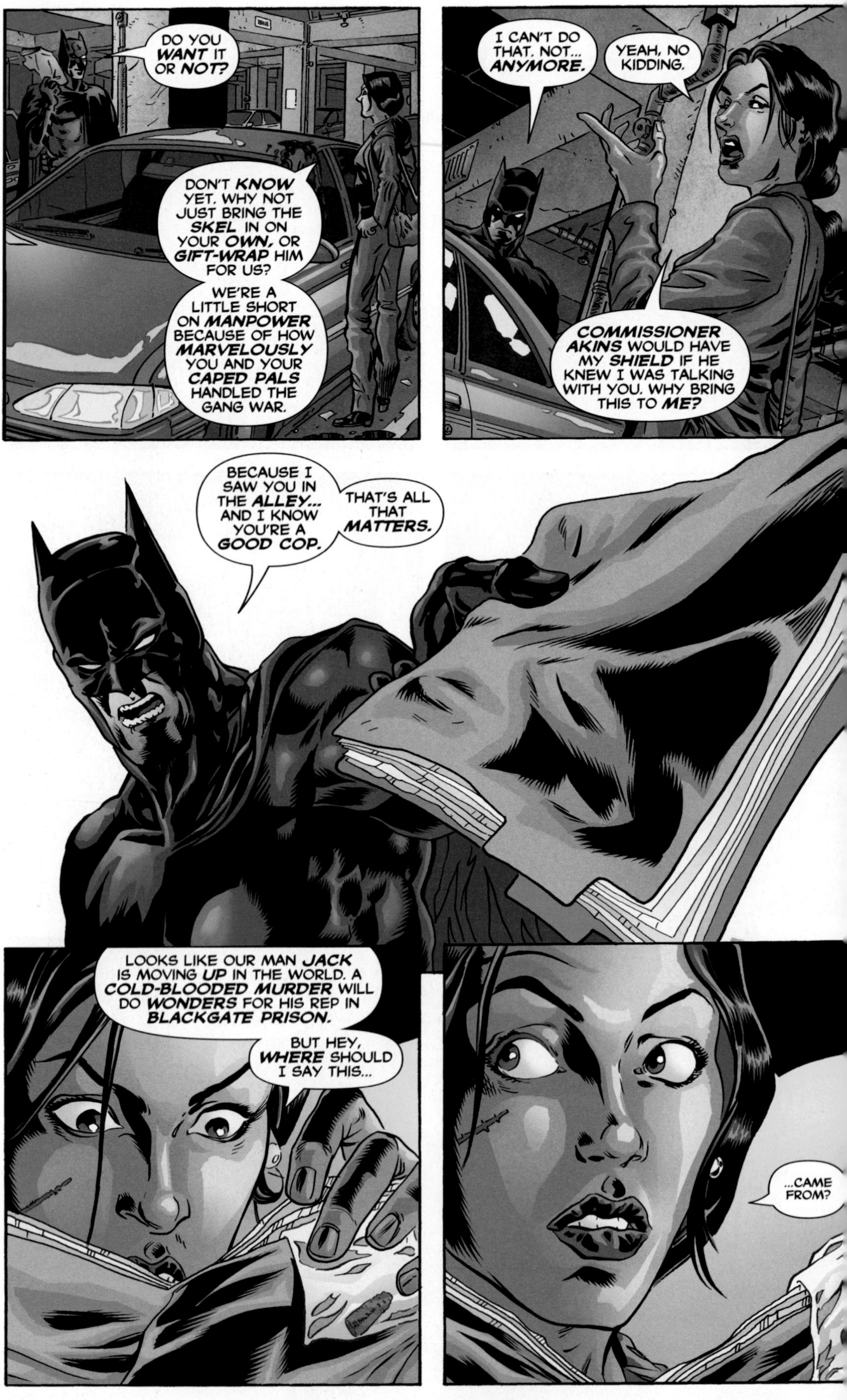
DO YOU WANT IT OR NOT?
DON'T KNOW YET. WHY NOT JUST BRING THE SKEL IN ON YOUR OWN, OR GIFT-WRAP HIM FOR US?
WE'RE A LITTLE SHORT ON MANPOWER BECAUSE OF HOW MARVELOUSLY YOU AND YOUR CAPED PALS HANDLED THE GANG WAR.
I CAN'T DO THAT. NOT... ANYMORE.
YEAH, NO KIDDING.
COMMISSIONER AKINS WOULD HAVE MY SHIELD IF HE KNEW I WAS TALKING WITH YOU. WHY BRING THIS TO ME?
BECAUSE I SAW YOU IN THE ALLEY... AND I KNOW YOU'RE A GOOD COP.
THAT'S ALL THAT MATTERS.
LOOKS LIKE OUR MAN JACK IS MOVING UP IN THE WORLD. A COLD-BLOODED MURDER WILL DO WONDERS FOR HIS REP IN BLACKGATE PRISON.
BUT HEY, WHERE SHOULD I SAY THIS...
...CAME FROM?

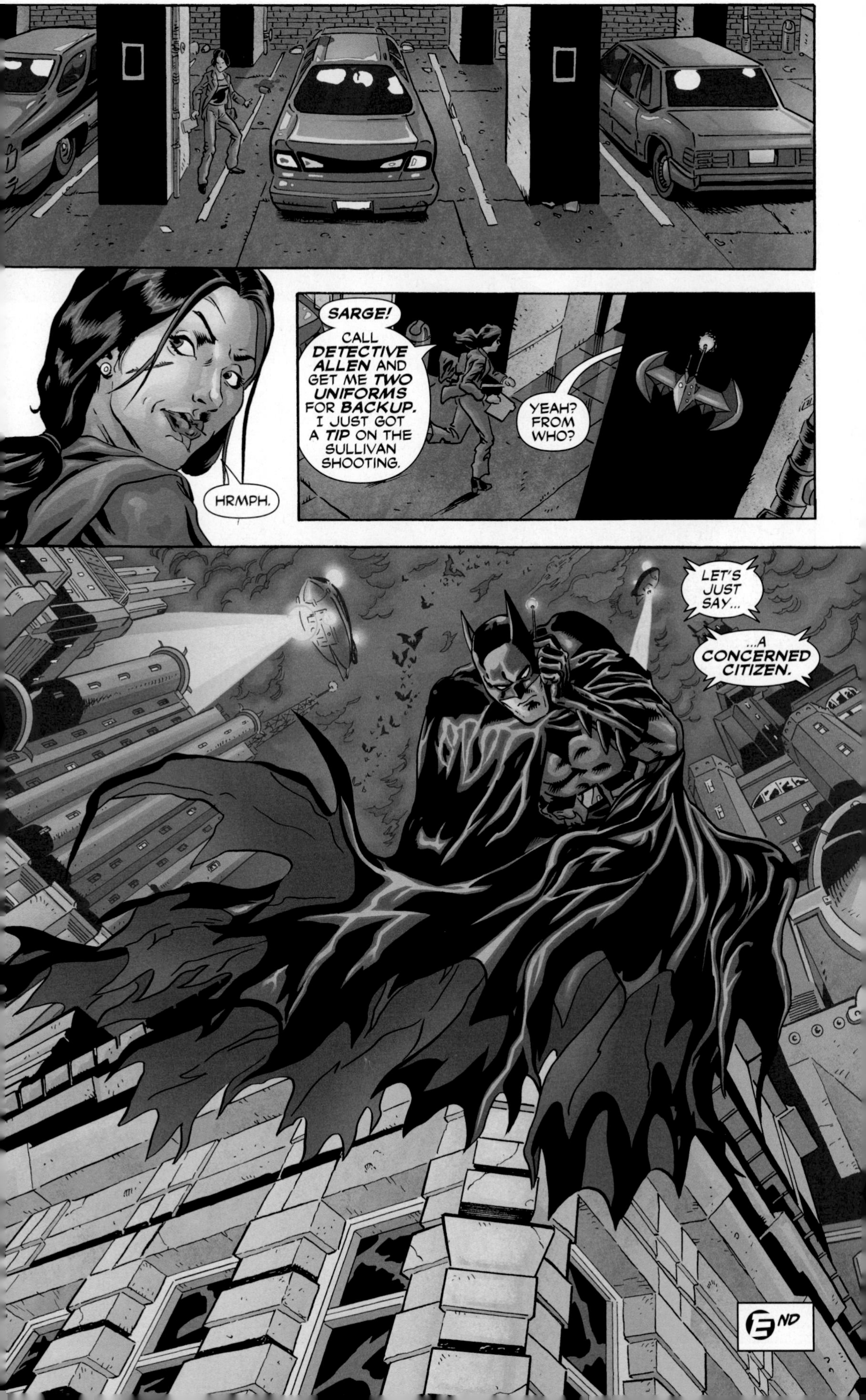
HRMPH.
SARGE!
CALL DETECTIVE ALLEN AND GET ME TWO UNIFORMS FOR BACKUP. I JUST GOT A TIP ON THE SULLIVAN SHOOTING.
YEAH? FROM WHO?
LET'S JUST SAY...
...A CONCERNED CITIZEN.
END

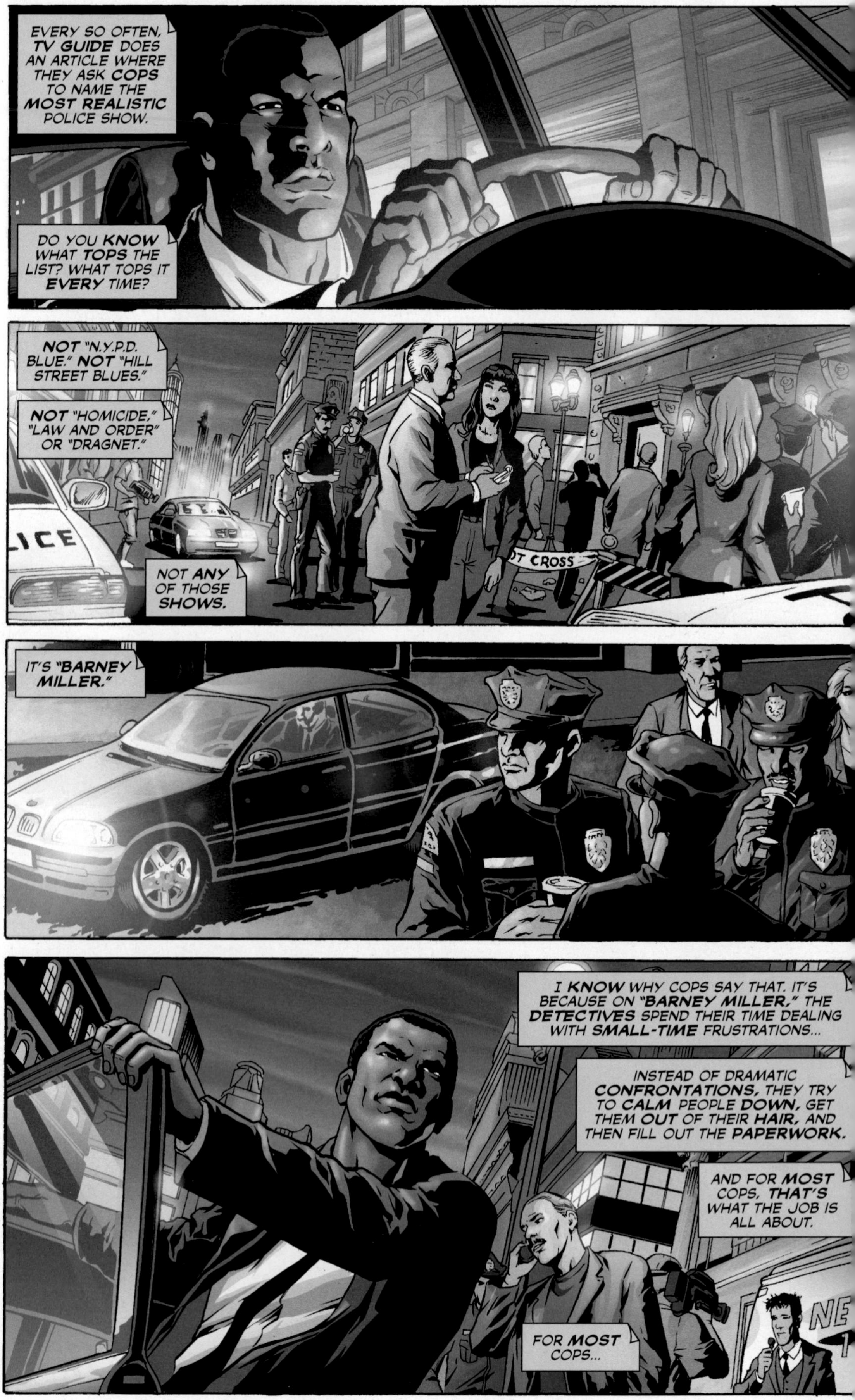
EVERY SO OFTEN, TV GUIDE DOES AN ARTICLE WHERE THEY ASK COPS TO NAME THE MOST REALISTIC POLICE SHOW.
DO YOU KNOW WHAT TOPS THE LIST? WHAT TOPS IT EVERY TIME?
NOT "N.Y.P.D. BLUE." NOT "HILL STREET BLUES."
NOT "HOMICIDE," "LAW AND ORDER" OR "DRAGNET."
NOT ANY OF THOSE SHOWS.
IT'S "BARNEY MILLER."
I KNOW WHY COPS SAY THAT. IT'S BECAUSE ON "BARNEY MILLER," THE DETECTIVES SPEND THEIR TIME DEALING WITH SMALL-TIME FRUSTRATIONS...
INSTEAD OF DRAMATIC CONFRONTATIONS, THEY TRY TO CALM PEOPLE DOWN, GET THEM OUT OF THEIR HAIR, AND THEN FILL OUT THE PAPERWORK.
AND FOR MOST COPS, THAT'S WHAT THE JOB IS ALL ABOUT.
FOR MOST COPS...

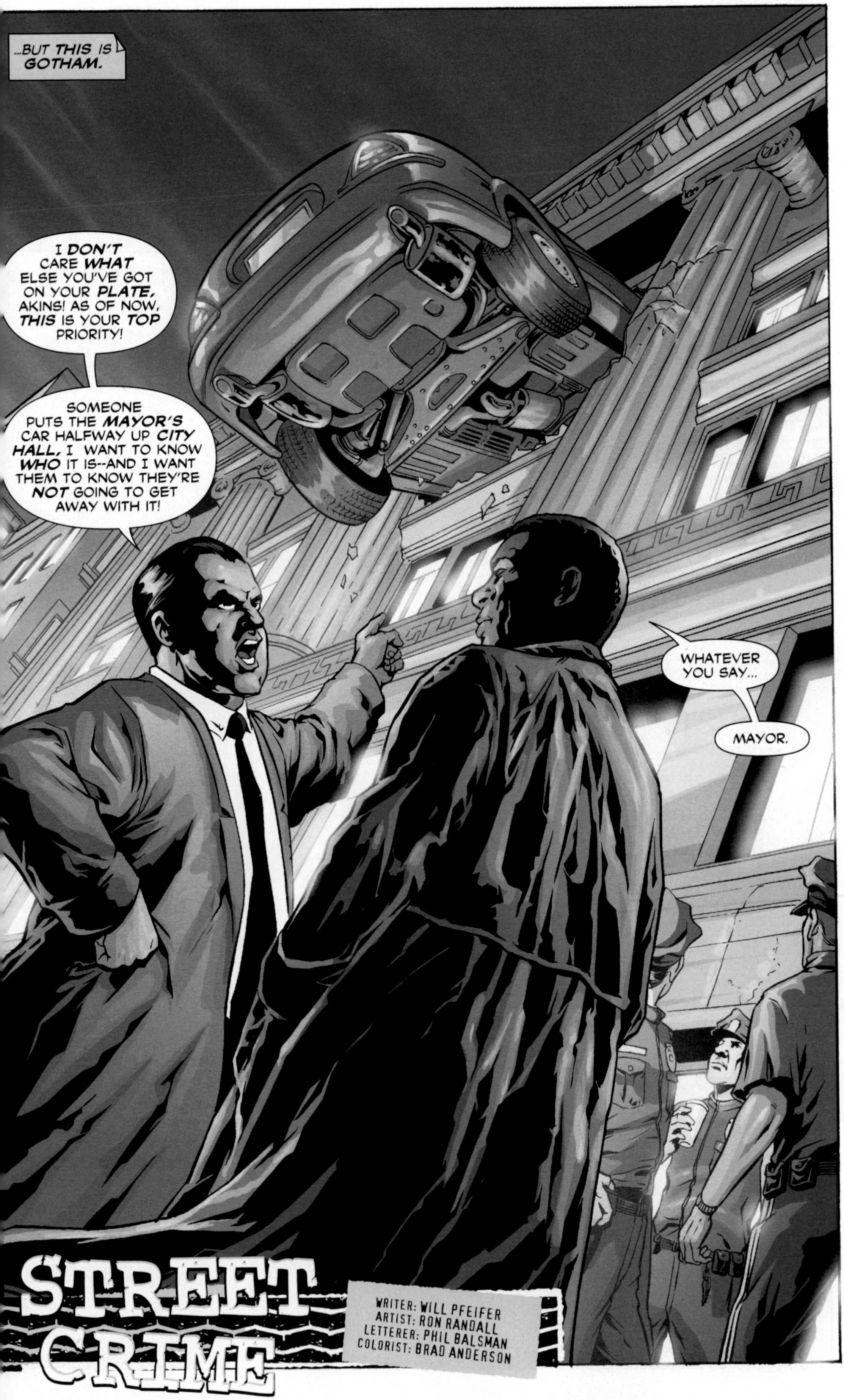
...BUT THIS IS GOTHAM.
I DON'T CARE WHAT ELSE YOU'VE GOT ON YOUR PLATE, AKINS! AS OF NOW, THIS IS YOUR TOP PRIORITY!
SOMEONE PUTS THE MAYOR'S CAR HALFWAY UP CITY HALL, I WANT TO KNOW WHO IT IS--AND I WANT THEM TO KNOW THEY'RE NOT GOING TO GET AWAY WITH IT!
WHATEVER YOU SAY...
MAYOR.
STREET CRIME
WRITER: WILL PFEIFER
ARTIST: RON RANDALL
LETTERER: PHIL BALSMAN
COLORIST: BRAD ANDERSON

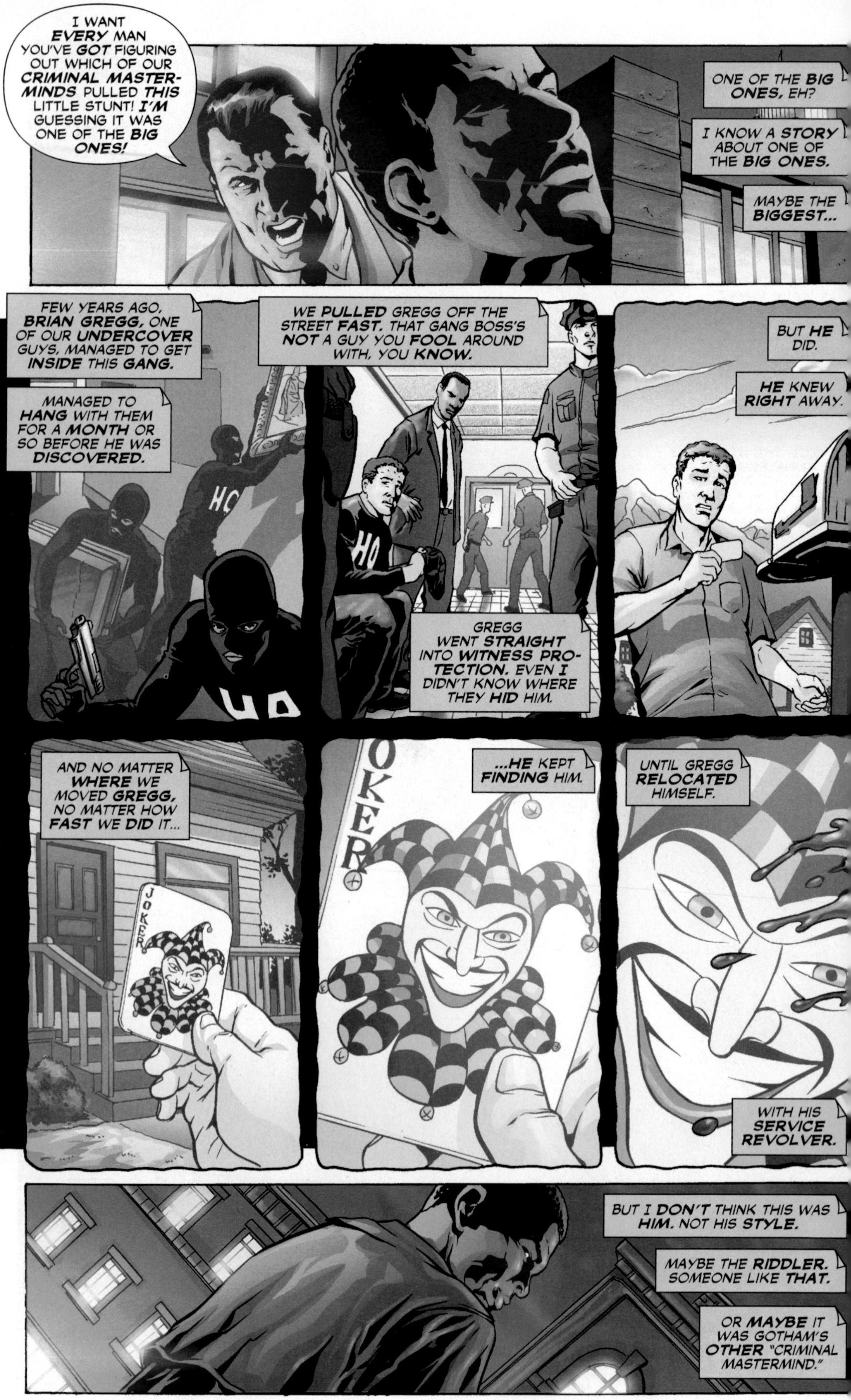

I WANT EVERY MAN YOU'VE GOT FIGURING OUT WHICH OF OUR CRIMINAL MASTER-MINDS PULLED THIS LITTLE STUNT! I'M GUESSING IT WAS ONE OF THE BIG ONES!
ONE OF THE BIG ONES, EH?
I KNOW A STORY ABOUT ONE OF THE BIG ONES.
MAYBE THE BIGGEST...
FEW YEARS AGO, BRIAN GREGG, ONE OF OUR UNDERCOVER GUYS, MANAGED TO GET INSIDE THIS GANG.
MANAGED TO HANG WITH THEM FOR A MONTH OR SO BEFORE HE WAS DISCOVERED.
HQ
WE PULLED GREGG OFF THE STREET FAST. THAT GANG BOSS'S NOT A GUY YOU FOOL AROUND WITH, YOU KNOW.
GREGG WENT STRAIGHT INTO WITNESS PRO-TECTION. EVEN I DIDN'T KNOW WHERE THEY HID HIM.
BUT HE DID.
HE KNEW RIGHT AWAY.
AND NO MATTER WHERE WE MOVED GREGG, NO MATTER HOW FAST WE DID IT...
JOKER
...HE KEPT FINDING HIM.
UNTIL GREGG RELOCATED HIMSELF.
WITH HIS SERVICE REVOLVER.
BUT I DON'T THINK THIS WAS HIM. NOT HIS STYLE.
MAYBE THE RIDDLER. SOMEONE LIKE THAT.
OR MAYBE IT WAS GOTHAM'S OTHER "CRIMINAL MASTERMIND."

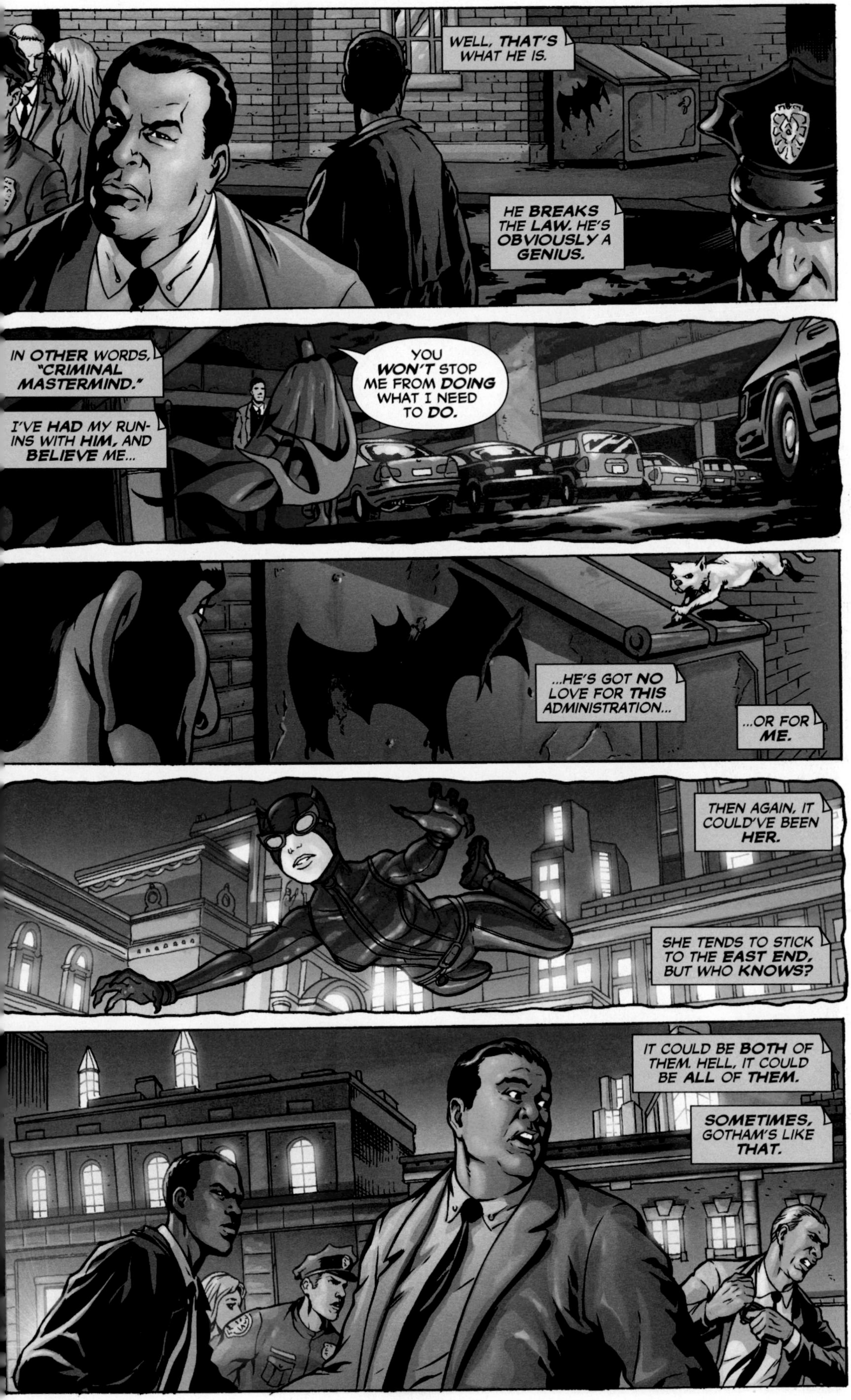

WELL, THAT'S WHAT HE IS.
HE BREAKS THE LAW. HE'S OBVIOUSLY A GENIUS.
IN OTHER WORDS, "CRIMINAL MASTERMIND."
YOU WON'T STOP ME FROM DOING WHAT I NEED TO DO.
I'VE HAD MY RUN-INS WITH HIM, AND BELIEVE ME...
...HE'S GOT NO LOVE FOR THIS ADMINISTRATION...
...OR FOR ME.
THEN AGAIN, IT COULD'VE BEEN HER.
SHE TENDS TO STICK TO THE EAST END, BUT WHO KNOWS?
IT COULD BE BOTH OF THEM. HELL, IT COULD BE ALL OF THEM.
SOMETIMES, GOTHAM'S LIKE THAT.

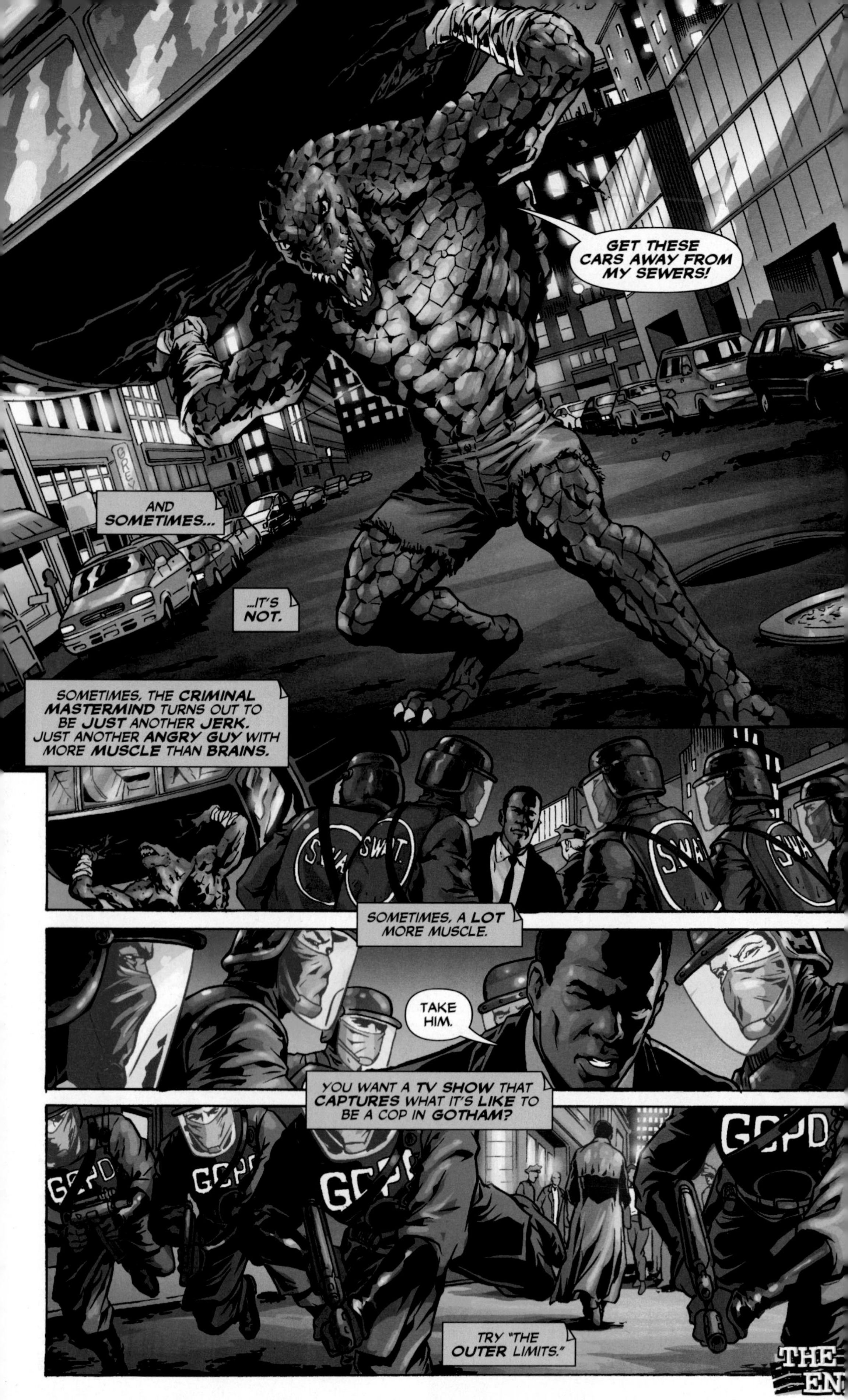
GET THESE CARS AWAY FROM MY SEWERS!
AND SOMETIMES...
...IT'S NOT.
SOMETIMES, THE CRIMINAL MASTERMIND TURNS OUT TO BE JUST ANOTHER JERK. JUST ANOTHER ANGRY GUY WITH MORE MUSCLE THAN BRAINS.
S.W.A.T.
SOMETIMES, A LOT MORE MUSCLE.
TAKE HIM.
YOU WANT A TV SHOW THAT CAPTURES WHAT IT'S LIKE TO BE A COP IN GOTHAM?
GCPD
TRY "THE OUTER LIMITS."
THE EN

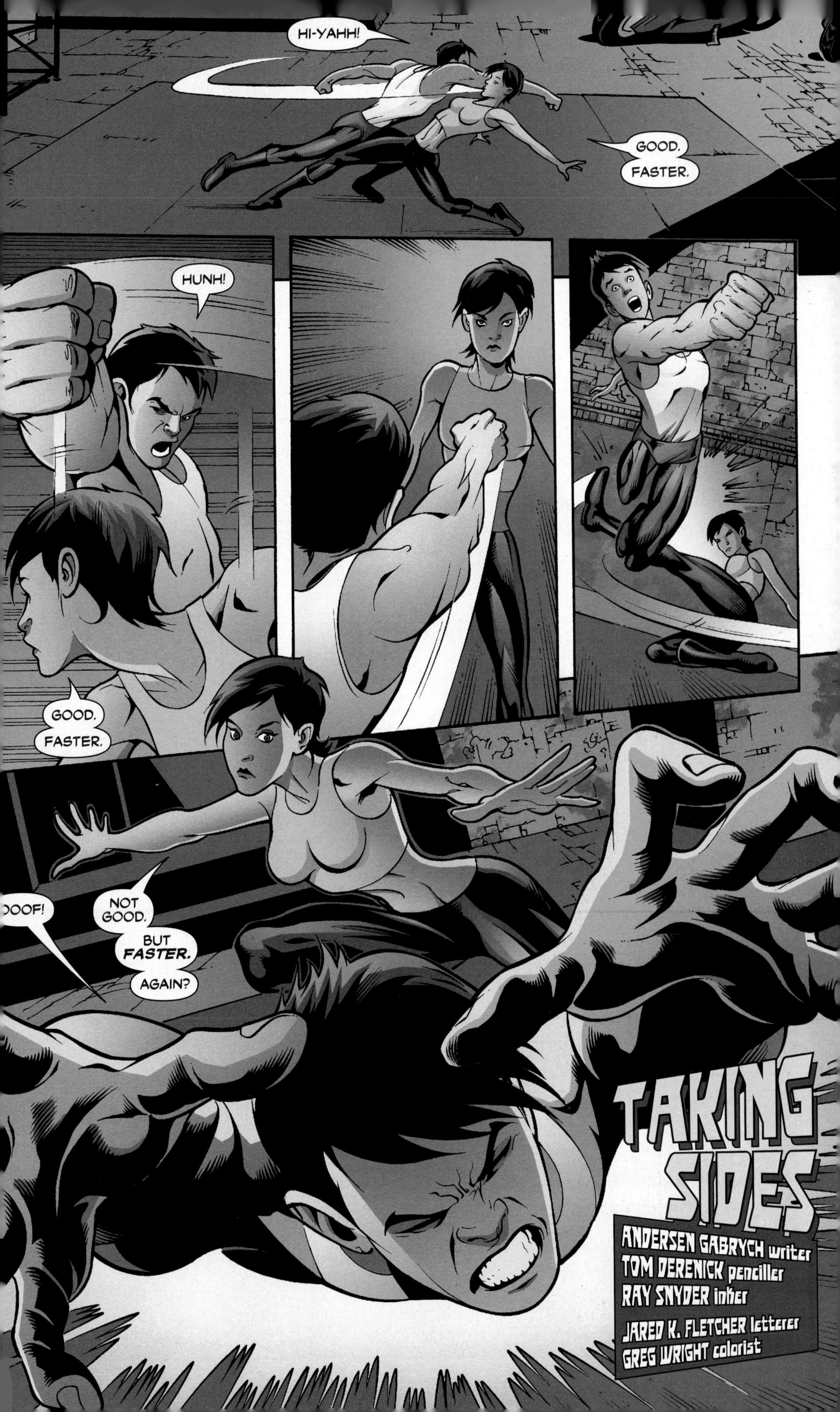
HI-YAHH!
GOOD. FASTER.
HUNH!
GOOD. FASTER.
OOOF!
NOT GOOD. BUT FASTER. AGAIN?
TAKING SIDES
ANDERSEN GABRYCH writer
TOM DERENICK penciller
RAY SNYDER inker
JARED K. FLETCHER letterer
GREG WRIGHT colorist

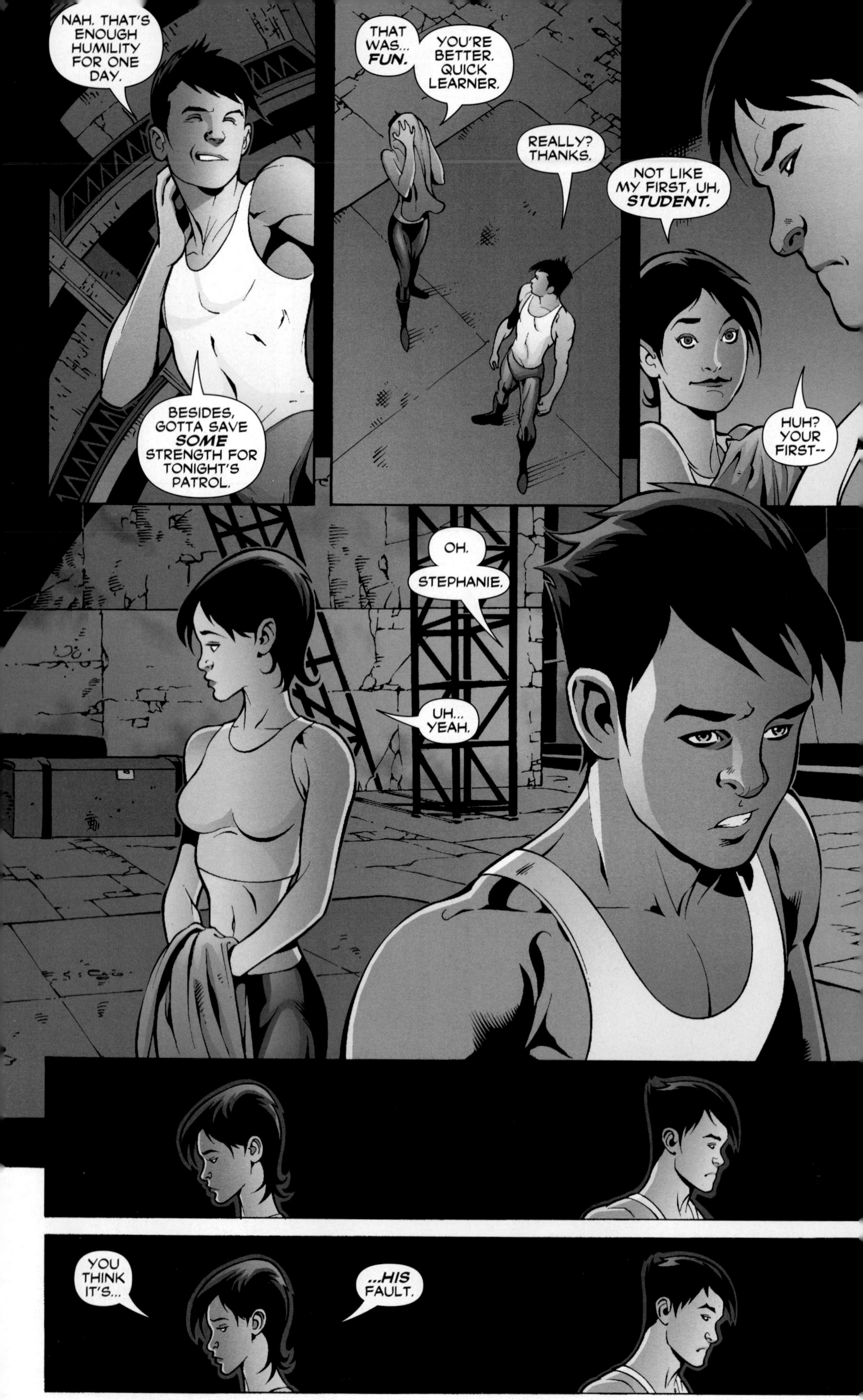
NAH. THAT'S ENOUGH HUMILITY FOR ONE DAY.
BESIDES, GOTTA SAVE SOME STRENGTH FOR TONIGHT'S PATROL.
THAT WAS... FUN.
YOU'RE BETTER. QUICK LEARNER.
REALLY? THANKS.
NOT LIKE MY FIRST, UH, STUDENT.
HUH? YOUR FIRST--
OH.
STEPHANIE.
UH... YEAH.
YOU THINK IT'S...
...HIS FAULT.

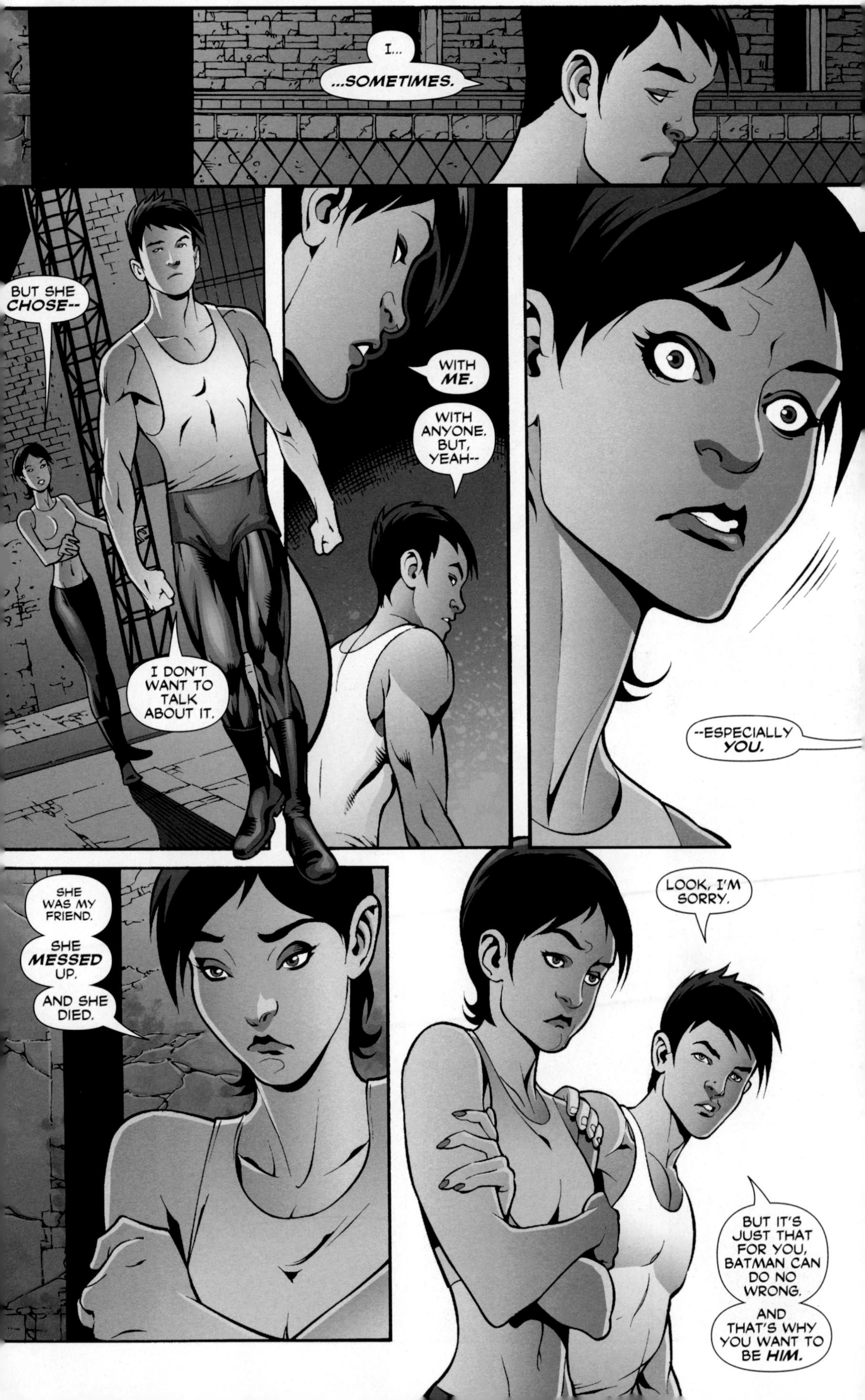

I...
...SOMETIMES.
BUT SHE CHOSE--
I DON'T WANT TO TALK ABOUT IT.
WITH ME.
WITH ANYONE. BUT, YEAH--
--ESPECIALLY YOU.
SHE WAS MY FRIEND.
SHE MESSED UP.
AND SHE DIED.
LOOK, I'M SORRY.
BUT IT'S JUST THAT FOR YOU, BATMAN CAN DO NO WRONG.
AND THAT'S WHY YOU WANT TO BE HIM.

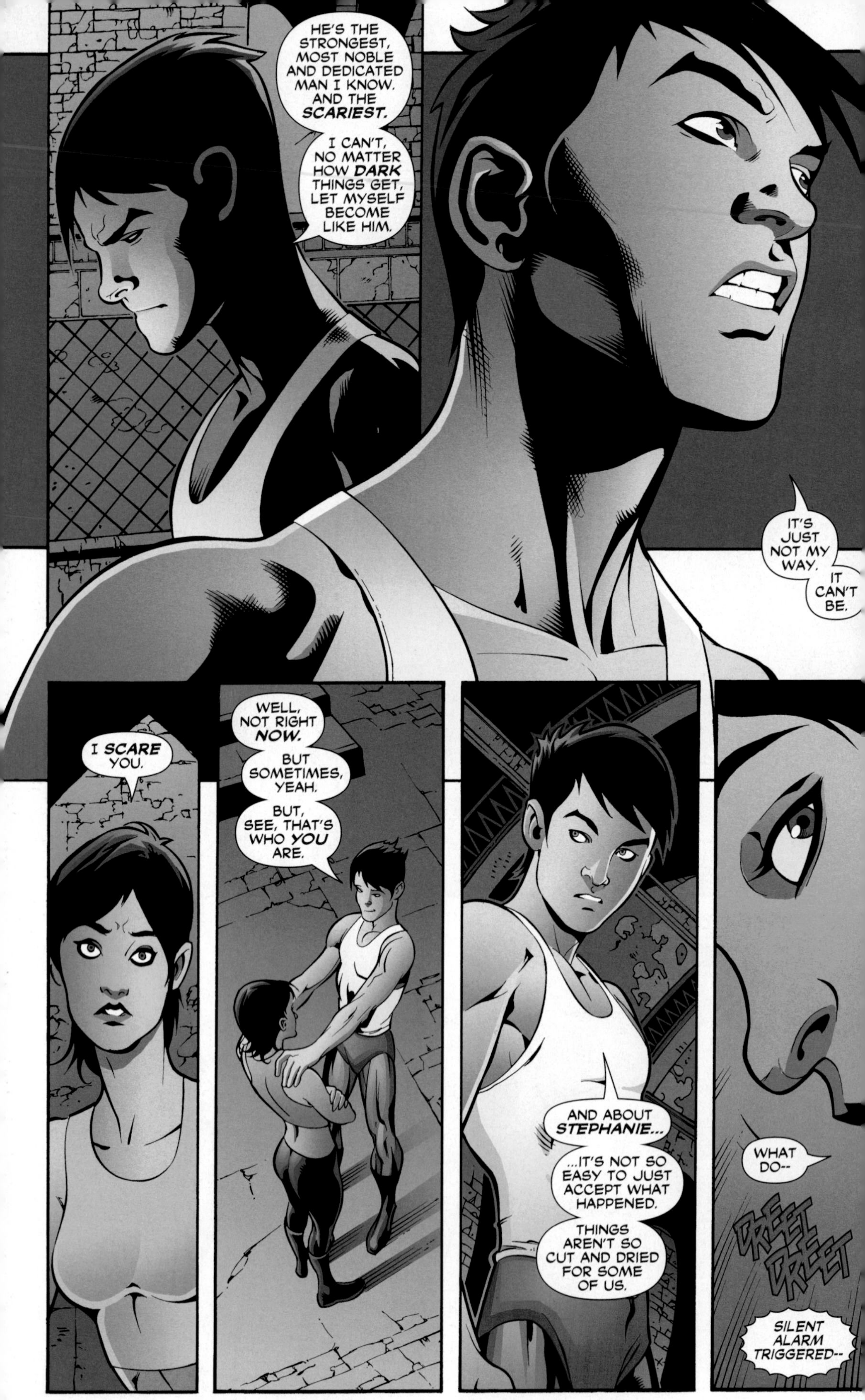

HE'S THE STRONGEST, MOST NOBLE AND DEDICATED MAN I KNOW. AND THE SCARIEST.
I CAN'T, NO MATTER HOW DARK THINGS GET, LET MYSELF BECOME LIKE HIM.
IT'S JUST NOT MY WAY.
IT CAN'T BE.
I SCARE YOU.
WELL, NOT RIGHT NOW.
BUT SOMETIMES, YEAH.
BUT, SEE, THAT'S WHO YOU ARE.
AND ABOUT STEPHANIE...
...IT'S NOT SO EASY TO JUST ACCEPT WHAT HAPPENED.
THINGS AREN'T SO CUT AND DRIED FOR SOME OF US.
WHAT DO--
DREET DREET
SILENT ALARM TRIGGERED--

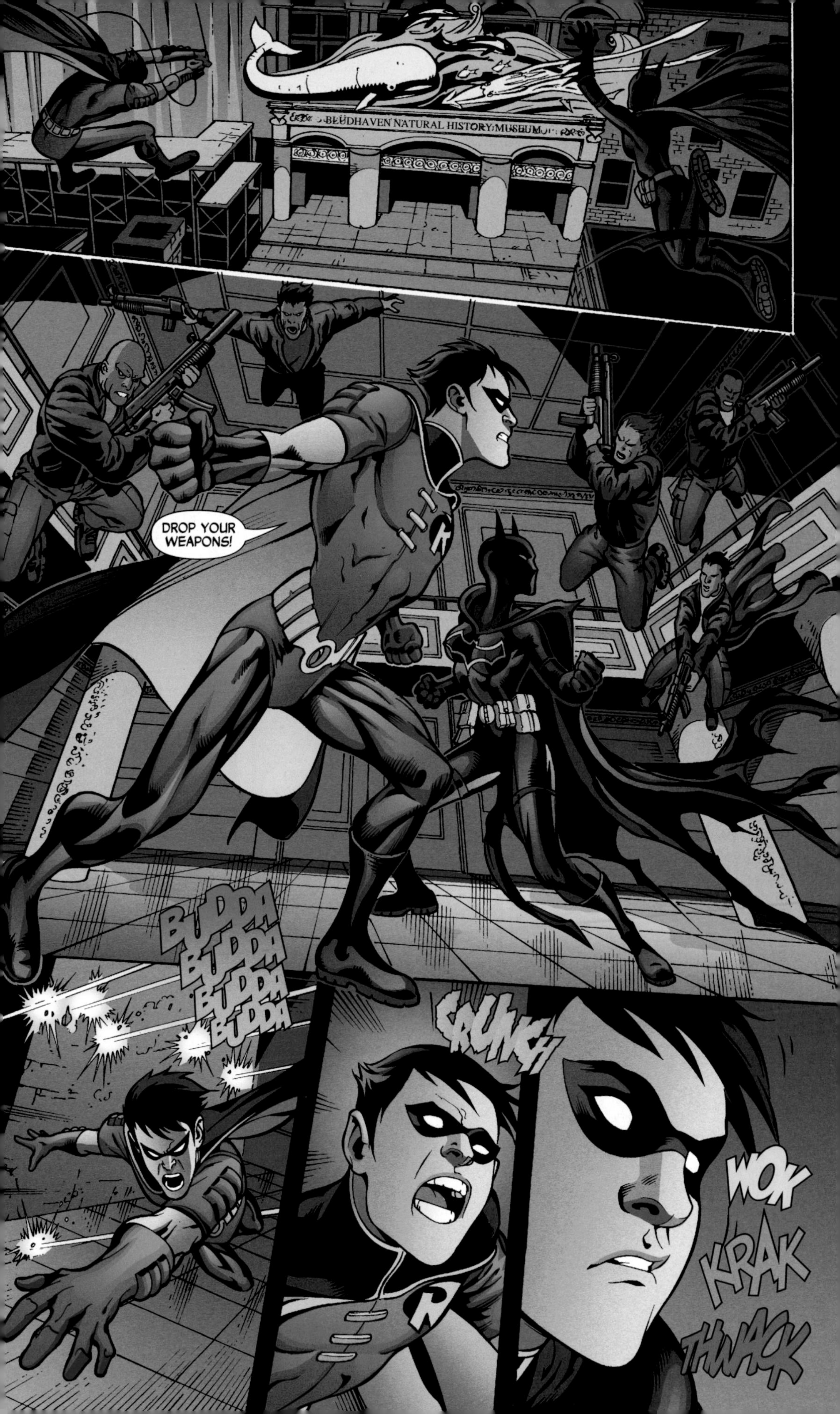
BLÜDHAVEN NATURAL HISTORY MUSEUM
DROP YOUR WEAPONS!
BUDDA BUDDA BUDDA BUDDA
CRUNCH
WOK
KRAK
THWACK

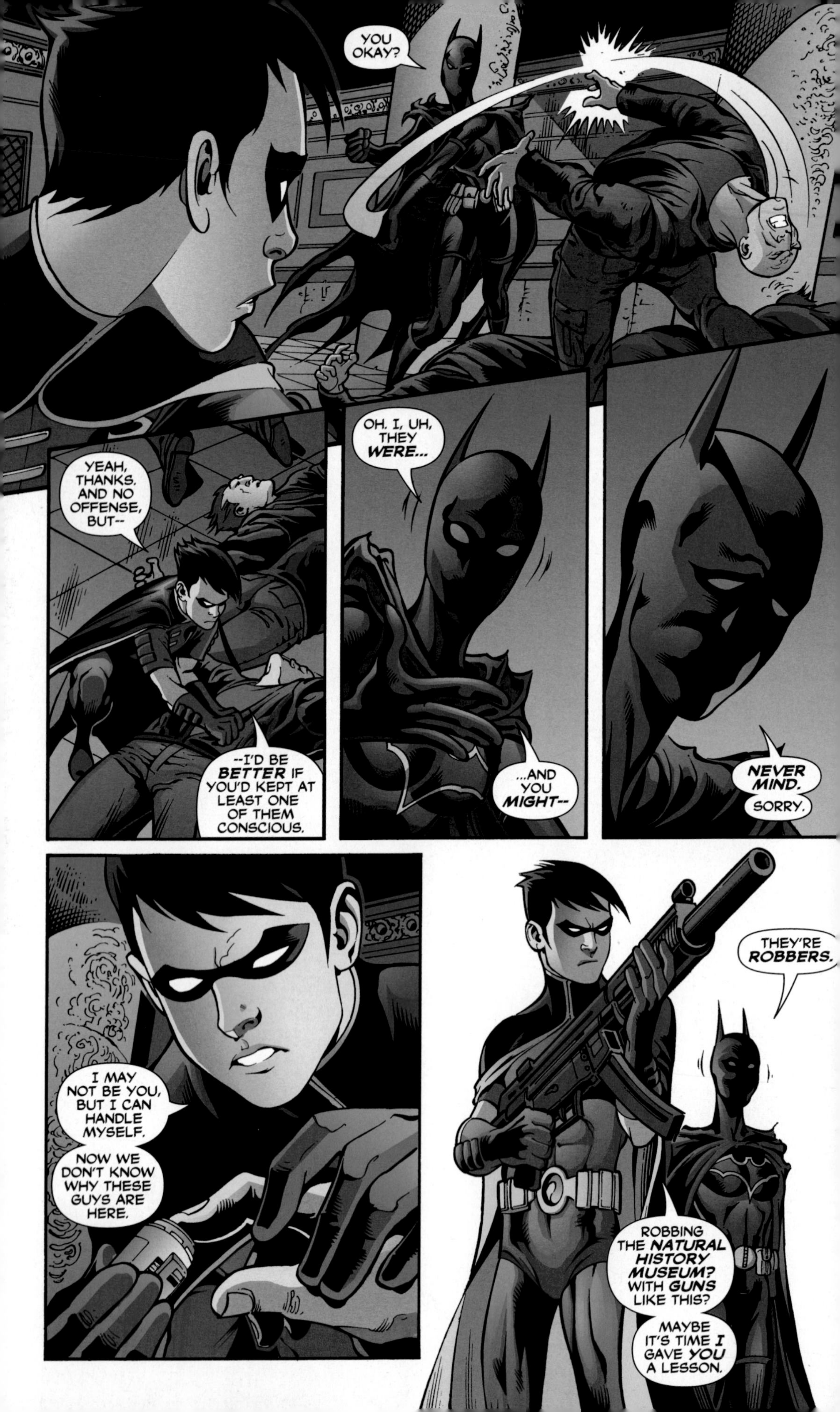

YOU OKAY?
YEAH, THANKS, AND NO OFFENSE, BUT--
--I'D BE BETTER IF YOU'D KEPT AT LEAST ONE OF THEM CONSCIOUS.
OH, I, UH, THEY WERE...
...AND YOU MIGHT--
NEVER MIND.
SORRY.
I MAY NOT BE YOU, BUT I CAN HANDLE MYSELF.
NOW WE DON'T KNOW WHY THESE GUYS ARE HERE.
THEY'RE ROBBERS.
ROBBING THE NATURAL HISTORY MUSEUM? WITH GUNS LIKE THIS?
MAYBE IT'S TIME I GAVE YOU A LESSON.

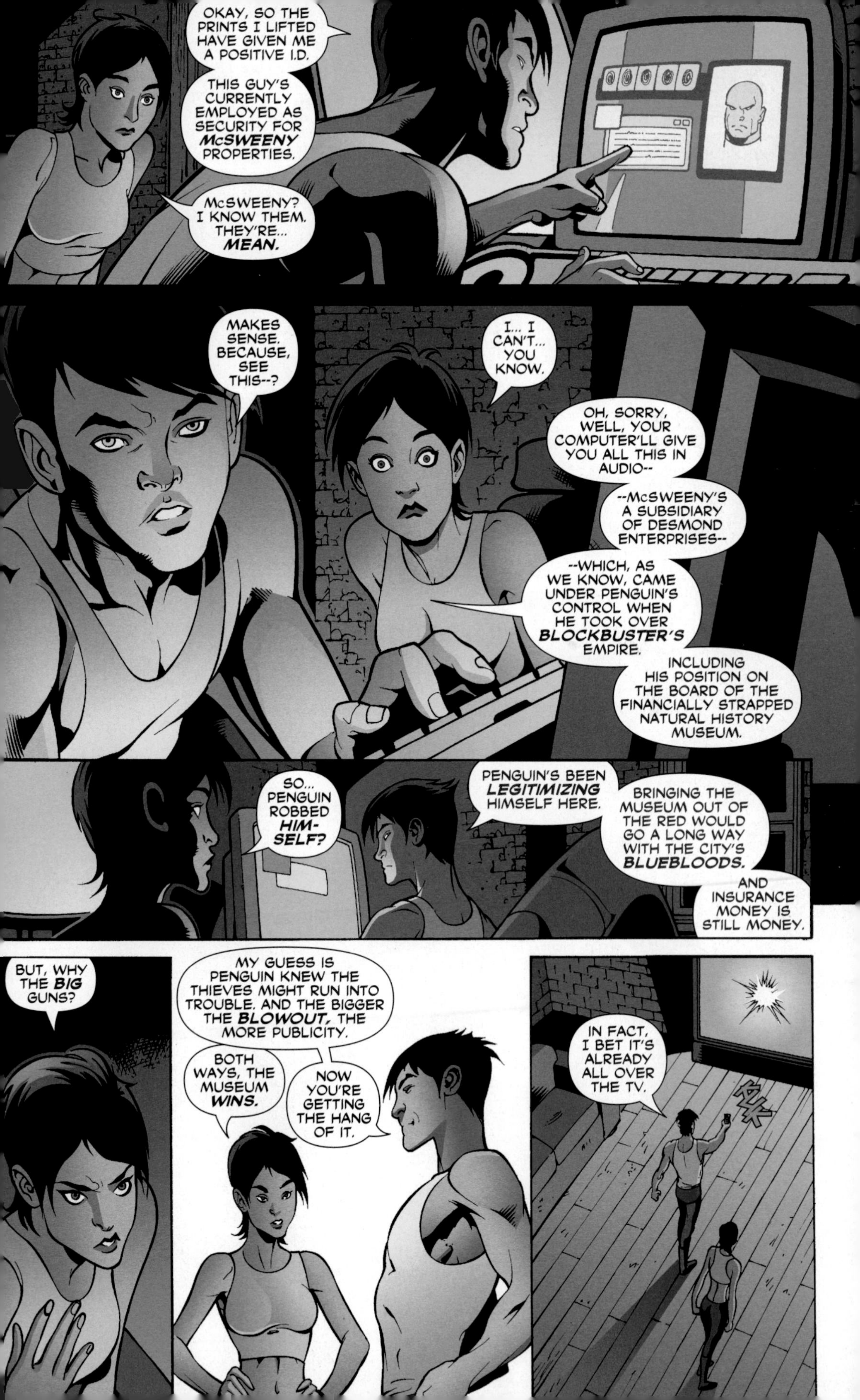
OKAY, SO THE PRINTS I LIFTED HAVE GIVEN ME A POSITIVE I.D.
THIS GUY'S CURRENTLY EMPLOYED AS SECURITY FOR McSWEENY PROPERTIES.
McSWEENY? I KNOW THEM. THEY'RE... MEAN.
MAKES SENSE. BECAUSE, SEE THIS--?
I... I CAN'T... YOU KNOW.
OH, SORRY, WELL, YOUR COMPUTER'LL GIVE YOU ALL THIS IN AUDIO--
--McSWEENY'S A SUBSIDIARY OF DESMOND ENTERPRISES--
--WHICH, AS WE KNOW, CAME UNDER PENGUIN'S CONTROL WHEN HE TOOK OVER BLOCKBUSTER'S EMPIRE.
INCLUDING HIS POSITION ON THE BOARD OF THE FINANCIALLY STRAPPED NATURAL HISTORY MUSEUM.
SO... PENGUIN ROBBED HIM-SELF?
PENGUIN'S BEEN LEGITIMIZING HIMSELF HERE.
BRINGING THE MUSEUM OUT OF THE RED WOULD GO A LONG WAY WITH THE CITY'S BLUEBLOODS.
AND INSURANCE MONEY IS STILL MONEY.
BUT, WHY THE BIG GUNS?
MY GUESS IS PENGUIN KNEW THE THIEVES MIGHT RUN INTO TROUBLE. AND THE BIGGER THE BLOWOUT, THE MORE PUBLICITY.
BOTH WAYS, THE MUSEUM WINS.
NOW YOU'RE GETTING THE HANG OF IT.
IN FACT, I BET IT'S ALREADY ALL OVER THE TV.
KLIK

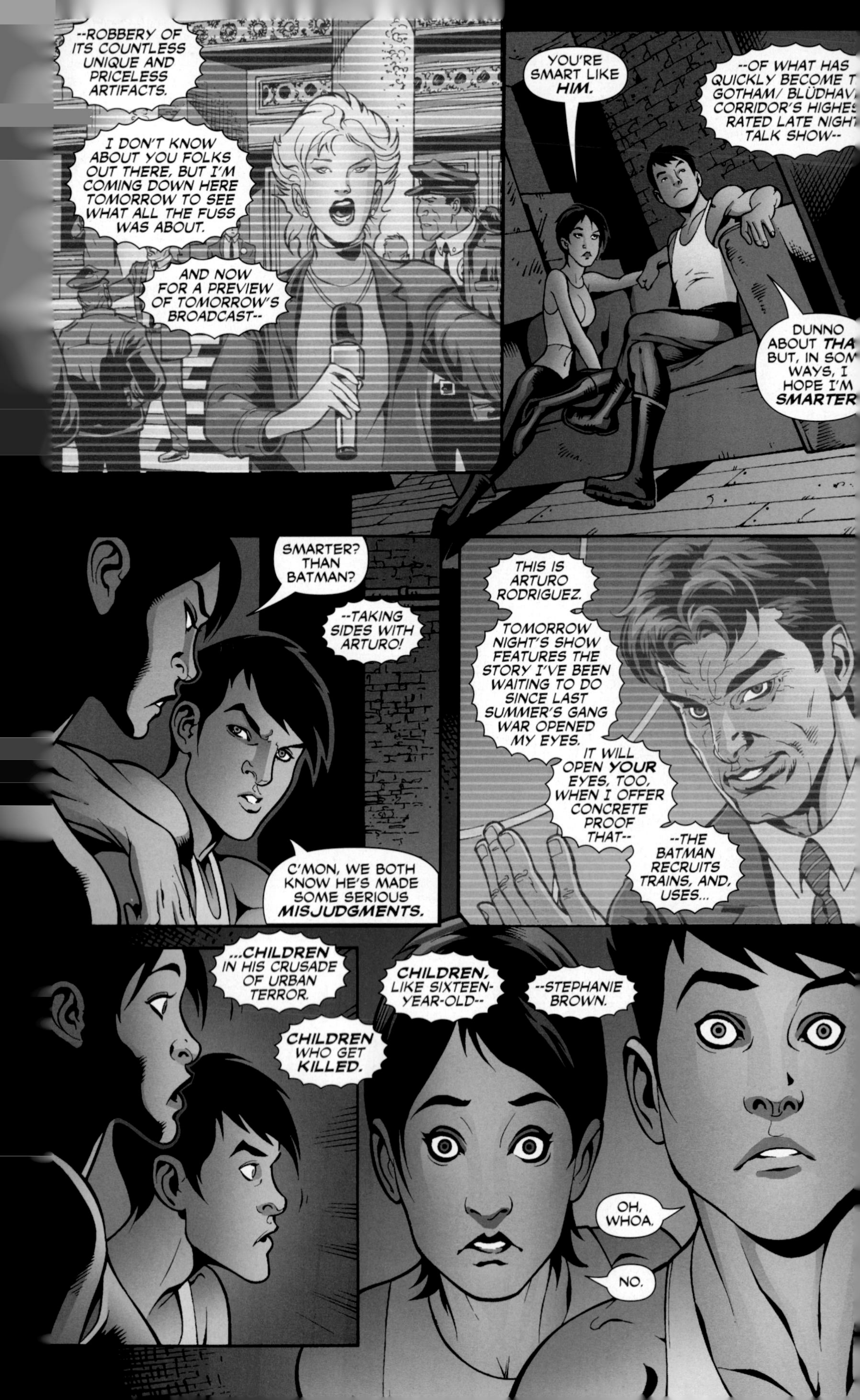
--ROBBERY OF ITS COUNTLESS UNIQUE AND PRICELESS ARTIFACTS.
I DON'T KNOW ABOUT YOU FOLKS OUT THERE, BUT I'M COMING DOWN HERE TOMORROW TO SEE WHAT ALL THE FUSS WAS ABOUT.
AND NOW FOR A PREVIEW OF TOMORROW'S BROADCAST--
YOU'RE SMART LIKE HIM.
--OF WHAT HAS QUICKLY BECOME T
GOTHAM/ BLÜDHAV
CORRIDOR'S HIGHES
RATED LATE NIGHT TALK SHOW--
DUNNO ABOUT THA
BUT, IN SOM
WAYS, I HOPE I'M SMARTER
SMARTER? THAN BATMAN?
--TAKING SIDES WITH ARTURO!
C'MON, WE BOTH KNOW HE'S MADE SOME SERIOUS MISJUDGMENTS.
THIS IS ARTURO RODRIGUEZ.
TOMORROW NIGHT'S SHOW FEATURES THE STORY I'VE BEEN WAITING TO DO SINCE LAST SUMMER'S GANG WAR OPENED MY EYES.
IT WILL OPEN YOUR EYES, TOO, WHEN I OFFER CONCRETE PROOF THAT--
--THE BATMAN RECRUITS TRAINS, AND, USES...
...CHILDREN IN HIS CRUSADE OF URBAN TERROR.
CHILDREN WHO GET KILLED.
CHILDREN, LIKE SIXTEEN-YEAR-OLD--
--STEPHANIE BROWN.
OH, WHOA.
NO.

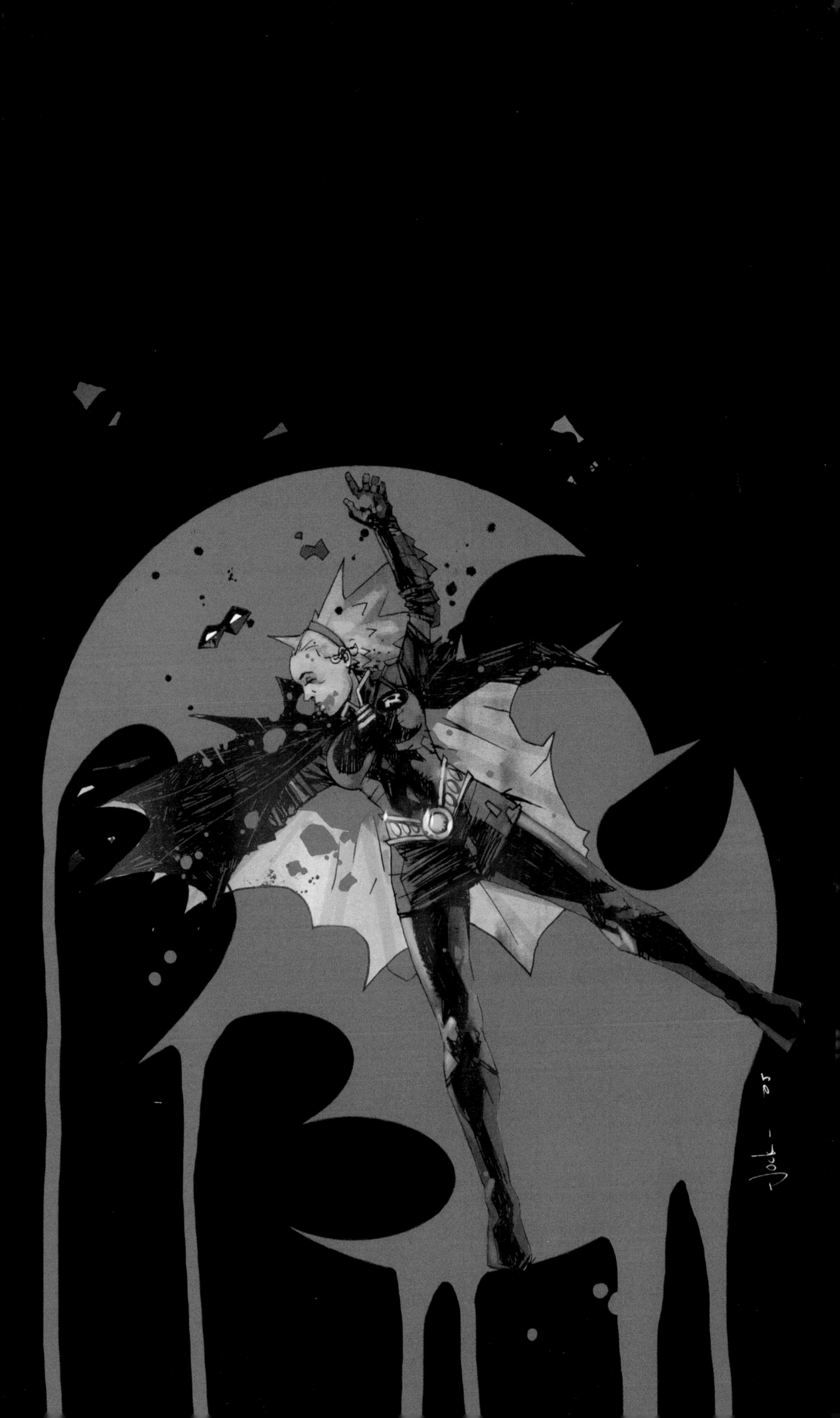

COVER ART BY
JOCK

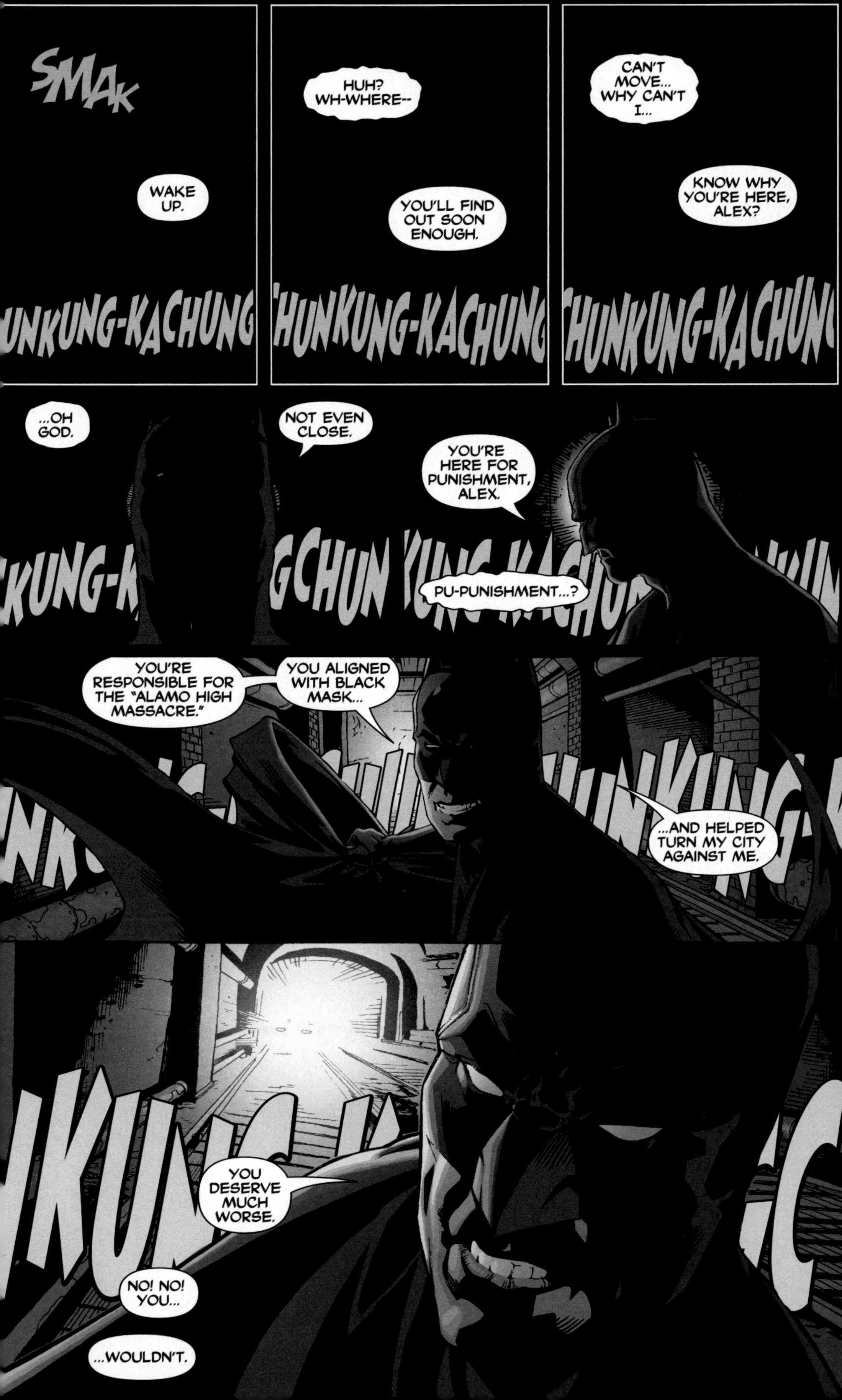
SMAK
WAKE UP.
CHUNKUNG-KACHUNG
HUH? WH-WHERE--
YOU'LL FIND OUT SOON ENOUGH.
CHUNKUNG-KACHUNG
CAN'T MOVE... WHY CAN'T I...
KNOW WHY YOU'RE HERE, ALEX?
CHUNKUNG-KACHUNG
...OH GOD.
NOT EVEN CLOSE.
YOU'RE HERE FOR PUNISHMENT, ALEX.
PU-PUNISHMENT...?
YOU'RE RESPONSIBLE FOR THE "ALAMO HIGH MASSACRE."
YOU ALIGNED WITH BLACK MASK...
...AND HELPED TURN MY CITY AGAINST ME.
YOU DESERVE MUCH WORSE.
NO! NO! YOU...
...WOULDN'T.

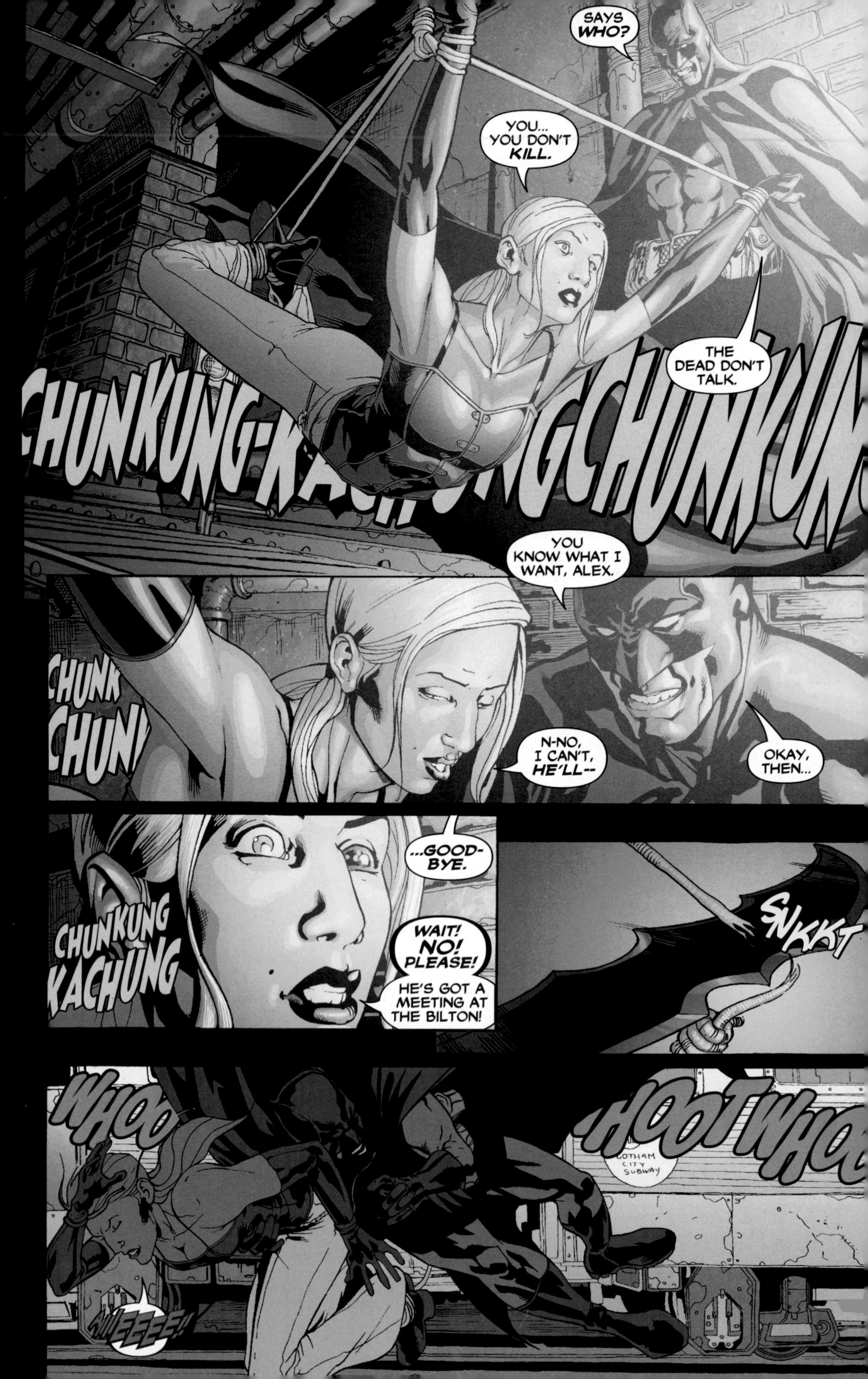
SAYS WHO?
YOU... YOU DON'T KILL.
THE DEAD DON'T TALK.
CHUNKUNG-KACHUNGCHUNKUN
YOU KNOW WHAT I WANT, ALEX.
CHUNK CHUN
N-NO, I CAN'T, HE'LL--
OKAY, THEN...
...GOOD-BYE.
CHUNKUNG KACHUNG
WAIT! NO! PLEASE!
HE'S GOT A MEETING AT THE BILTON!
SNKKT
WHOO
HOOTWHOO
GOTHAM CITY SUBWAY
WIIEEEE!!

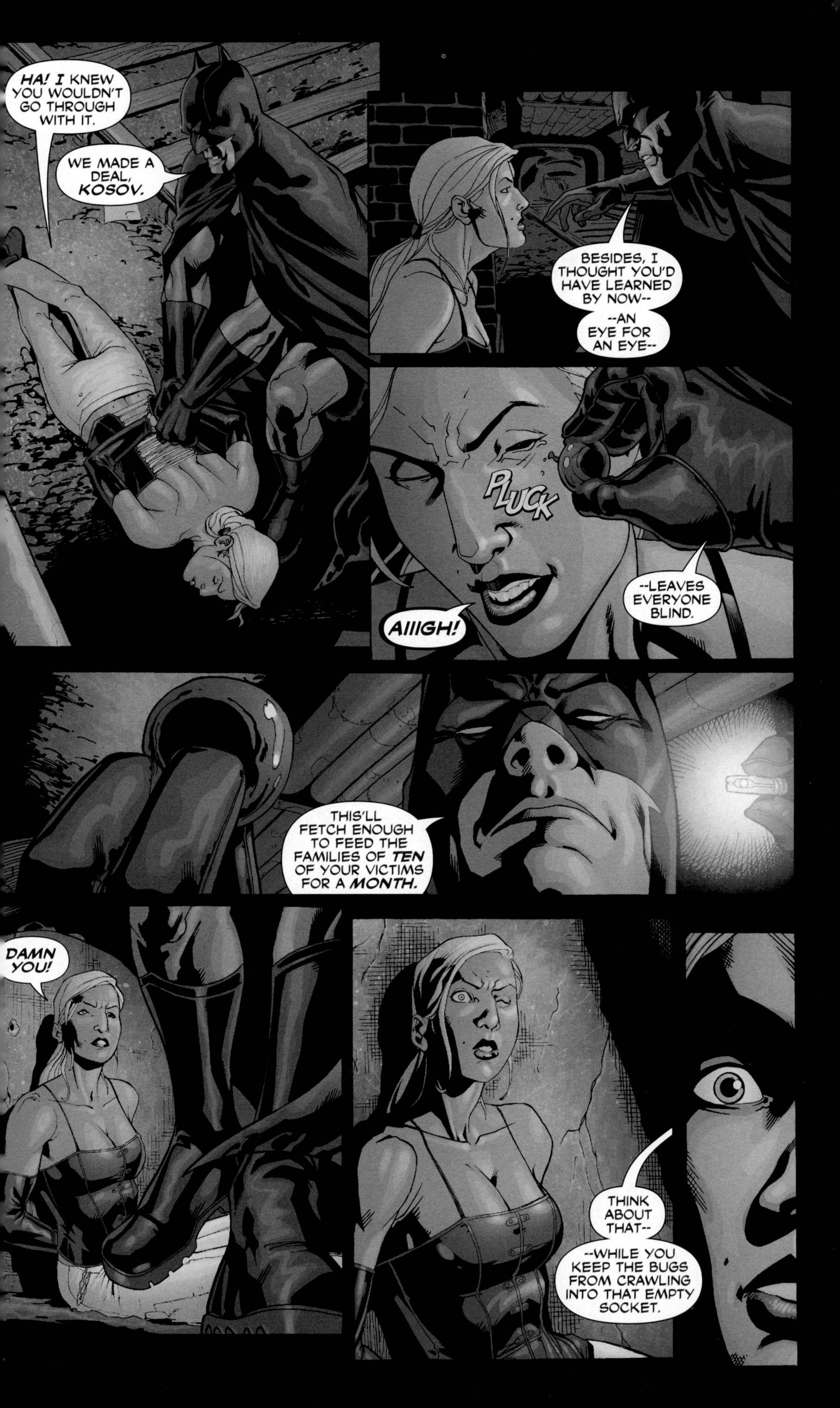
HA! I KNEW YOU WOULDN'T GO THROUGH WITH IT.
WE MADE A DEAL, KOSOV.
BESIDES, I THOUGHT YOU'D HAVE LEARNED BY NOW--
--AN EYE FOR AN EYE--
PLUCK
AIIIGH!
--LEAVES EVERYONE BLIND.
THIS'LL FETCH ENOUGH TO FEED THE FAMILIES OF TEN OF YOUR VICTIMS FOR A MONTH.
DAMN YOU!
THINK ABOUT THAT--
--WHILE YOU KEEP THE BUGS FROM CRAWLING INTO THAT EMPTY SOCKET.

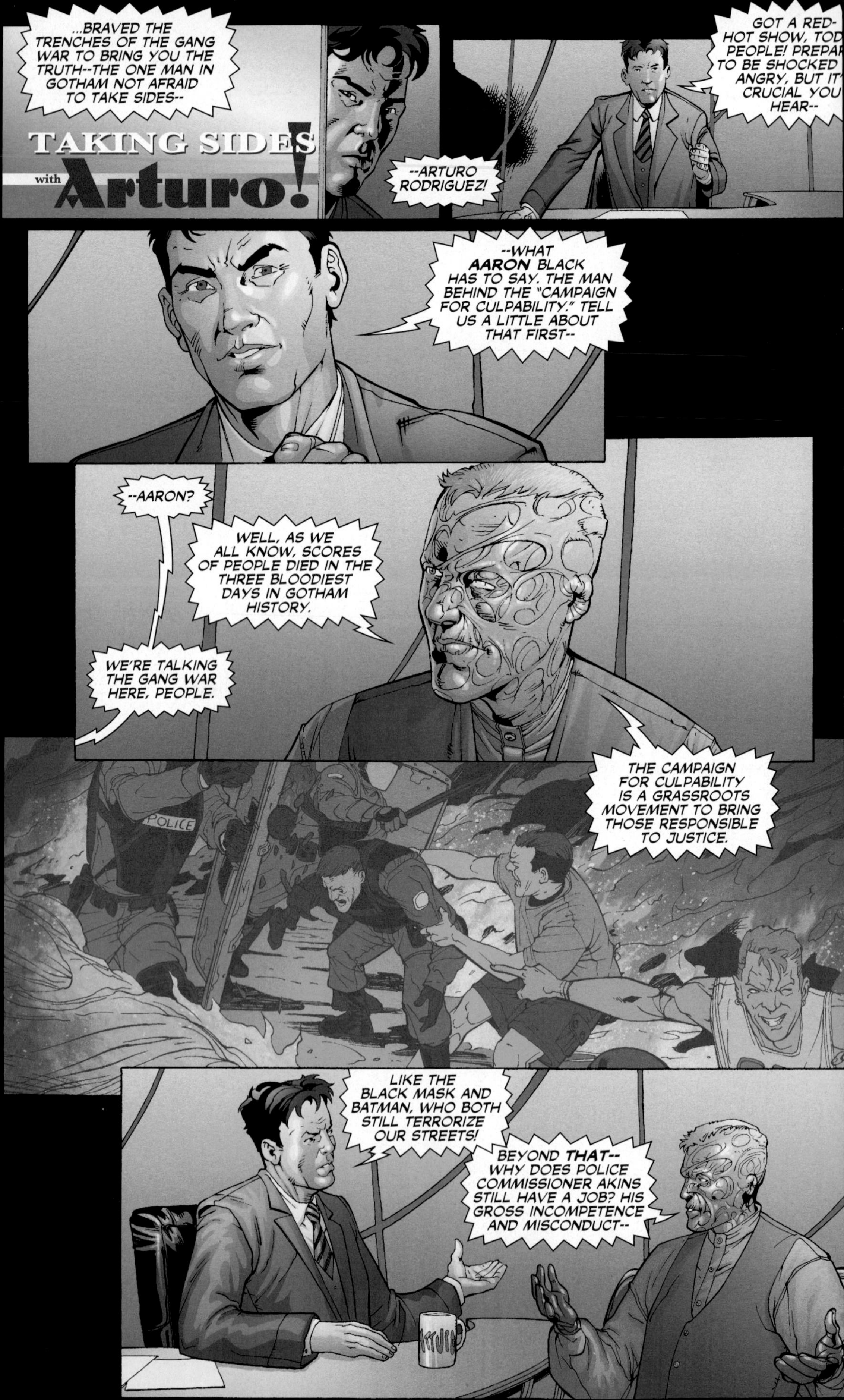
...BRAVED THE TRENCHES OF THE GANG WAR TO BRING YOU THE TRUTH--THE ONE MAN IN GOTHAM NOT AFRAID TO TAKE SIDES--
TAKING SIDES with Arturo!
--ARTURO RODRIGUEZ!
GOT A RED-HOT SHOW, TOD PEOPLE! PREPAR TO BE SHOCKED ANGRY, BUT IT' CRUCIAL YOU HEAR--
--WHAT AARON BLACK HAS TO SAY. THE MAN BEHIND THE "CAMPAIGN FOR CULPABILITY." TELL US A LITTLE ABOUT THAT FIRST--
--AARON?
WE'RE TALKING THE GANG WAR HERE, PEOPLE.
WELL, AS WE ALL KNOW, SCORES OF PEOPLE DIED IN THE THREE BLOODIEST DAYS IN GOTHAM HISTORY.
THE CAMPAIGN FOR CULPABILITY IS A GRASSROOTS MOVEMENT TO BRING THOSE RESPONSIBLE TO JUSTICE.
POLICE
LIKE THE BLACK MASK AND BATMAN, WHO BOTH STILL TERRORIZE OUR STREETS!
BEYOND THAT-- WHY DOES POLICE COMMISSIONER AKINS STILL HAVE A JOB? HIS GROSS INCOMPETENCE AND MISCONDUCT--
ARTURO

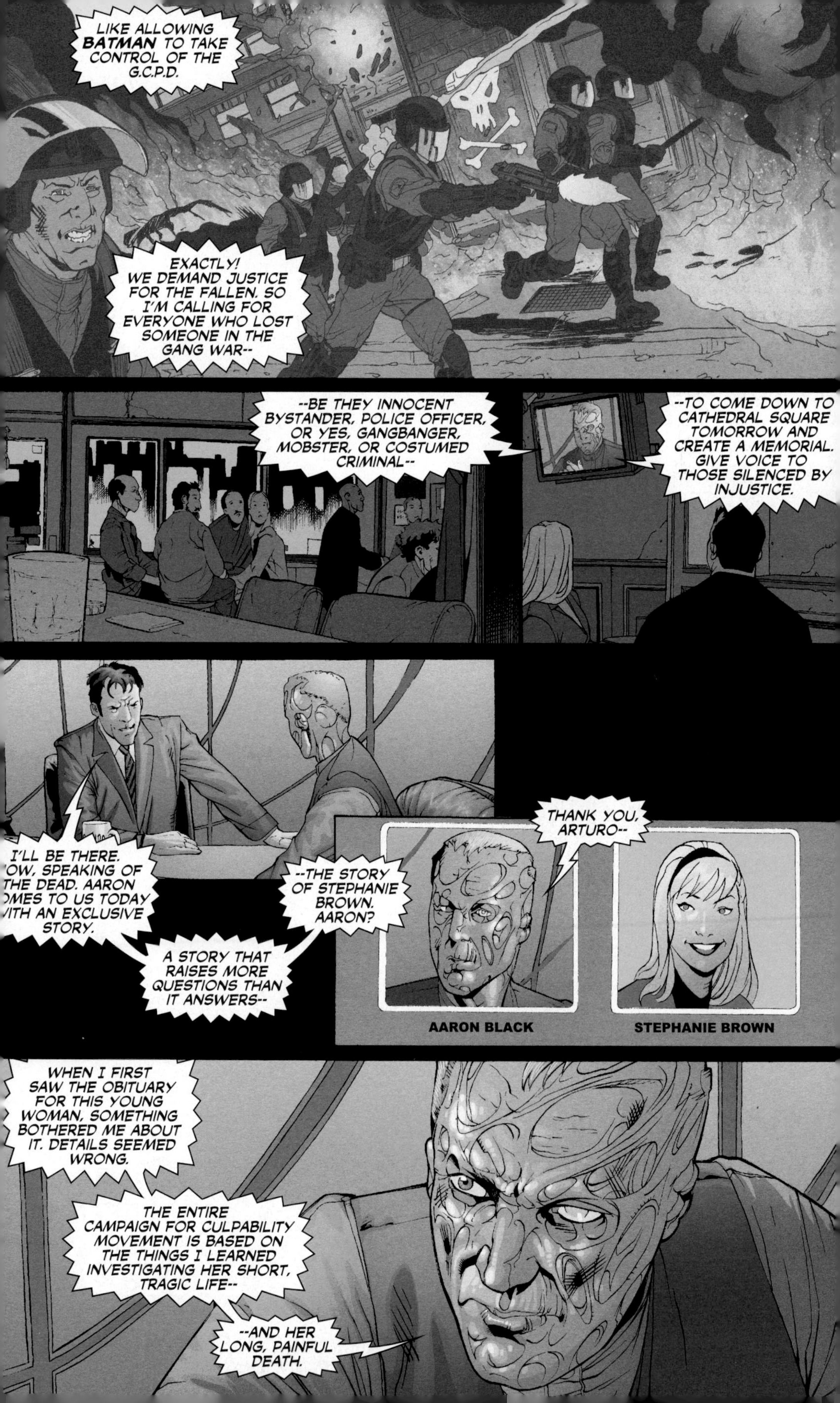
LIKE ALLOWING BATMAN TO TAKE CONTROL OF THE G.C.P.D.
EXACTLY! WE DEMAND JUSTICE FOR THE FALLEN. SO I'M CALLING FOR EVERYONE WHO LOST SOMEONE IN THE GANG WAR--
--BE THEY INNOCENT BYSTANDER, POLICE OFFICER, OR YES, GANGBANGER, MOBSTER, OR COSTUMED CRIMINAL--
--TO COME DOWN TO CATHEDRAL SQUARE TOMORROW AND CREATE A MEMORIAL. GIVE VOICE TO THOSE SILENCED BY INJUSTICE.
I'LL BE THERE. OW, SPEAKING OF THE DEAD. AARON OMES TO US TODAY ITH AN EXCLUSIVE STORY.
A STORY THAT RAISES MORE QUESTIONS THAN IT ANSWERS--
--THE STORY OF STEPHANIE BROWN. AARON?
THANK YOU, ARTURO--
AARON BLACK
STEPHANIE BROWN
WHEN I FIRST SAW THE OBITUARY FOR THIS YOUNG WOMAN, SOMETHING BOTHERED ME ABOUT IT. DETAILS SEEMED WRONG.
THE ENTIRE CAMPAIGN FOR CULPABILITY MOVEMENT IS BASED ON THE THINGS I LEARNED INVESTIGATING HER SHORT, TRAGIC LIFE--
--AND HER LONG, PAINFUL DEATH.

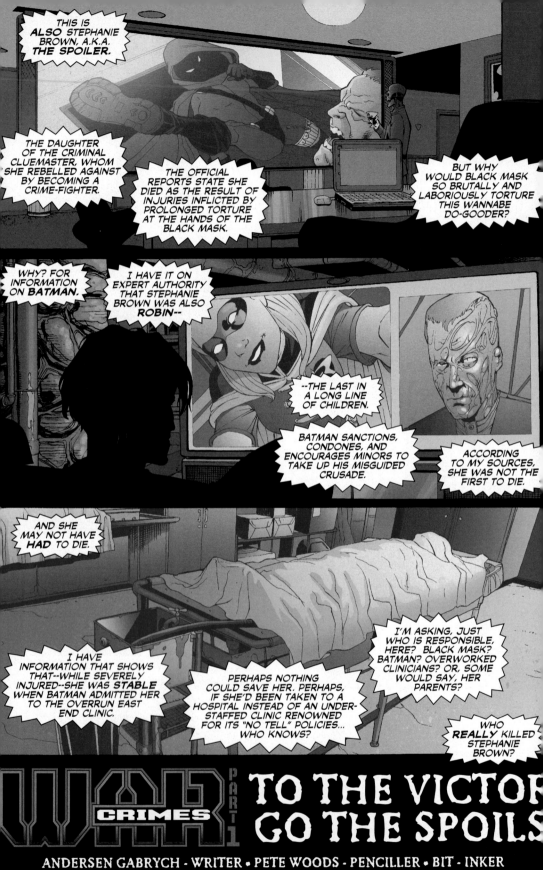

THIS IS **ALSO** STEPHANIE BROWN, A.K.A. **THE SPOILER.**

THE DAUGHTER OF THE CRIMINAL **CLUEMASTER,** WHOM SHE REBELLED AGAINST BY BECOMING A CRIME-FIGHTER.

THE OFFICIAL REPORTS STATE SHE DIED AS THE RESULT OF INJURIES INFLICTED BY PROLONGED TORTURE AT THE HANDS OF THE **BLACK MASK.**

BUT WHY WOULD BLACK MASK SO BRUTALLY AND LABORIOUSLY TORTURE THIS WANNABE DO-GOODER?

WHY? FOR INFORMATION ON **BATMAN.**

I HAVE IT ON EXPERT AUTHORITY THAT STEPHANIE BROWN WAS ALSO **ROBIN--**

--THE LAST IN A LONG LINE OF CHILDREN.

BATMAN SANCTIONS, CONDONES, AND ENCOURAGES MINORS TO TAKE UP HIS MISGUIDED CRUSADE.

ACCORDING TO MY SOURCES, SHE WAS NOT THE FIRST TO DIE.

AND SHE MAY NOT HAVE **HAD** TO DIE.

I HAVE INFORMATION THAT SHOWS THAT--WHILE SEVERELY INJURED--SHE WAS **STABLE** WHEN BATMAN ADMITTED HER TO THE OVERRUN EAST END CLINIC.

PERHAPS NOTHING COULD SAVE HER. PERHAPS, IF SHE'D BEEN TAKEN TO A HOSPITAL INSTEAD OF AN UNDER-STAFFED CLINIC RENOWNED FOR ITS "NO TELL" POLICIES... WHO KNOWS?

I'M ASKING, JUST WHO IS RESPONSIBLE, HERE? BLACK MASK? BATMAN? OVERWORKED CLINICIANS? OR, SOME WOULD SAY, HER PARENTS?

WHO **REALLY** KILLED STEPHANIE BROWN?

WAR CRIMES PART 1
TO THE VICTOR GO THE SPOILS

ANDERSEN GABRYCH - WRITER • PETE WOODS - PENCILLER • BIT - INKER

ROB LEIGH - LETTERER • JASON WRIGHT - COLORIST
NACHIE CASTRO - ASSOCIATE EDITOR • MATT IDELSON - EDITOR

BATMAN CREATED BY BOB KANE

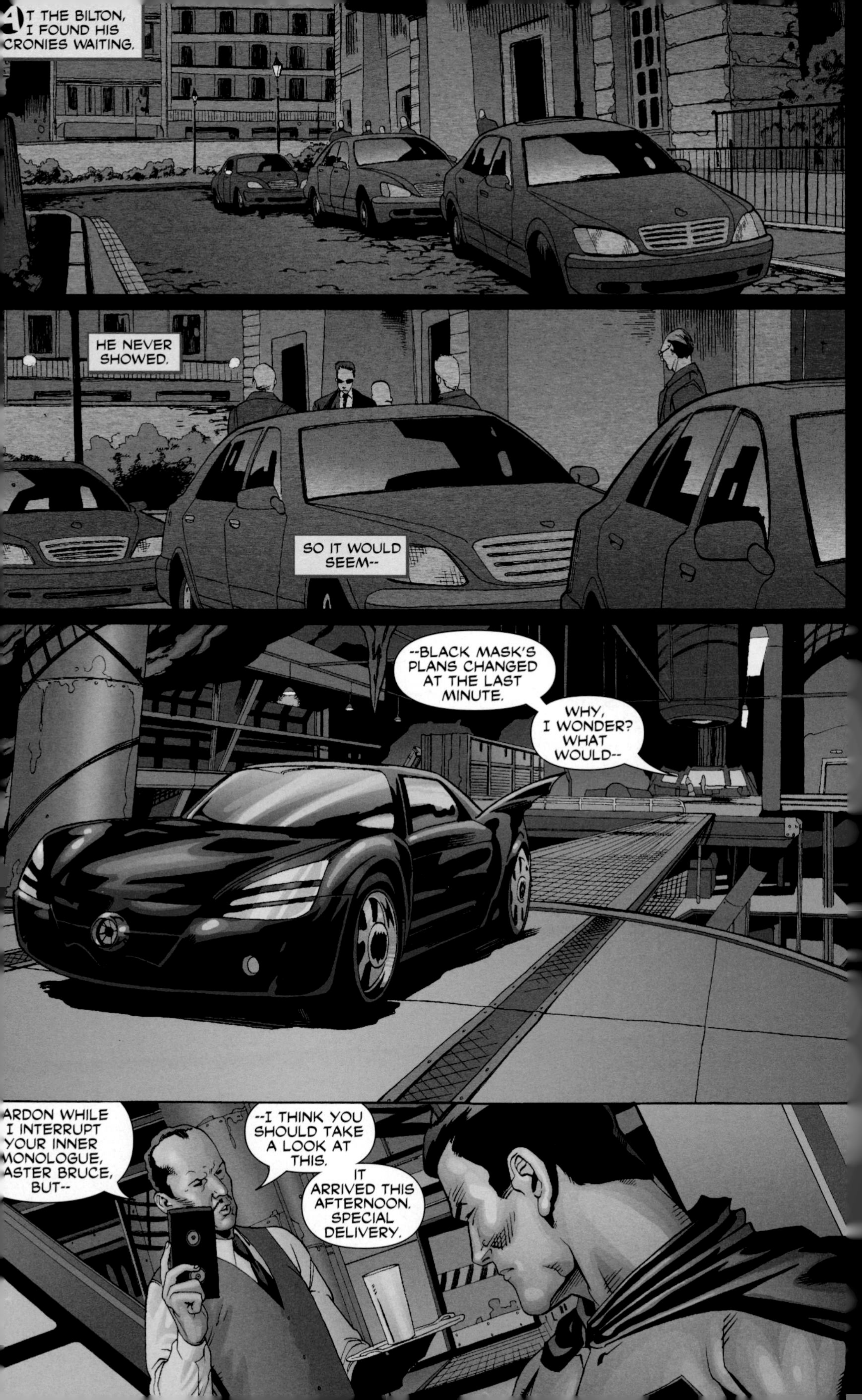
AT THE BILTON, I FOUND HIS CRONIES WAITING.
HE NEVER SHOWED.
SO IT WOULD SEEM--
--BLACK MASK'S PLANS CHANGED AT THE LAST MINUTE.
WHY, I WONDER? WHAT WOULD--
ARDON WHILE I INTERRUPT YOUR INNER MONOLOGUE, ASTER BRUCE, BUT--
--I THINK YOU SHOULD TAKE A LOOK AT THIS.
IT ARRIVED THIS AFTERNOON, SPECIAL DELIVERY.

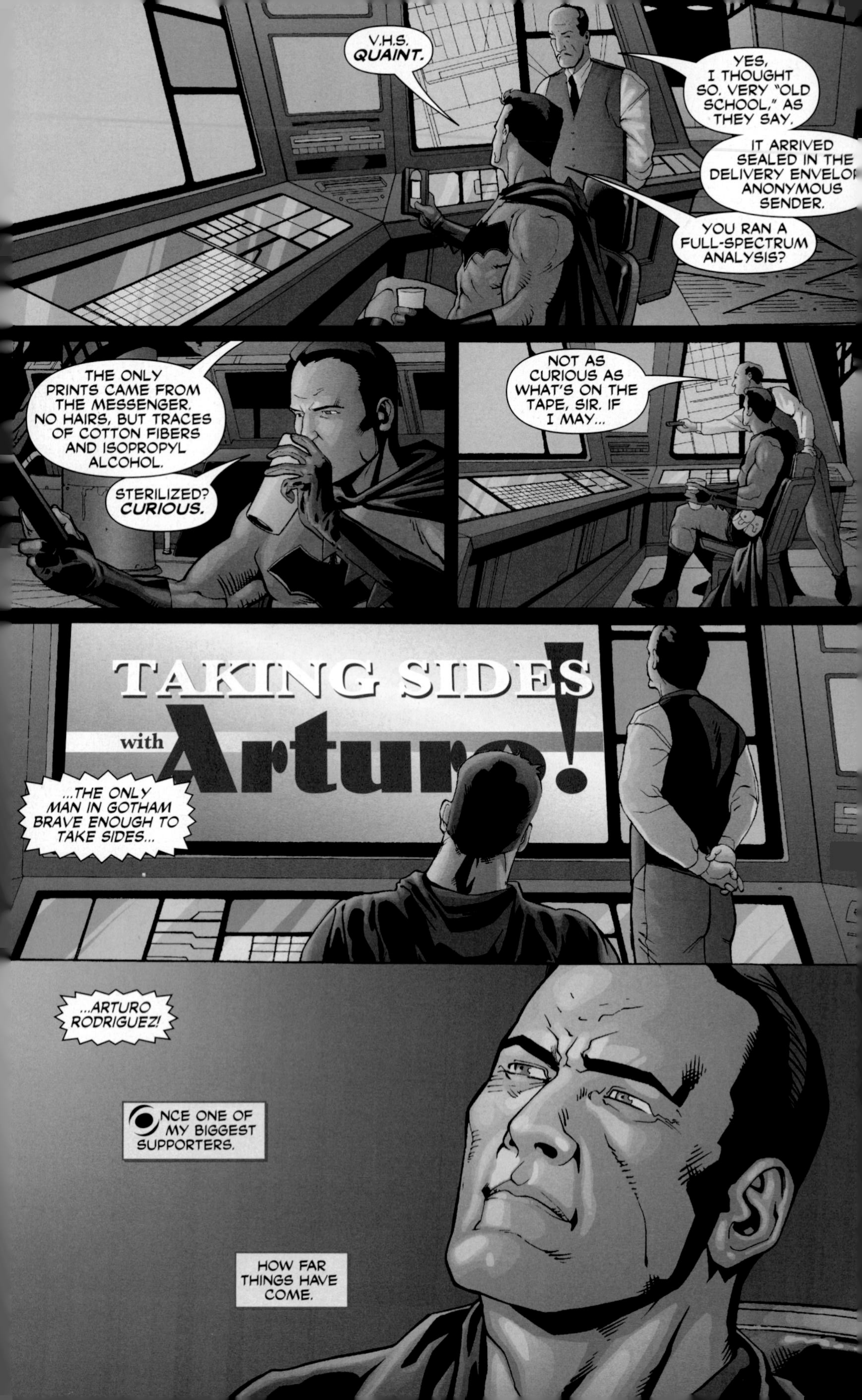
V.H.S. QUAINT.
YES, I THOUGHT SO. VERY "OLD SCHOOL," AS THEY SAY.
IT ARRIVED SEALED IN THE DELIVERY ENVELOP ANONYMOUS SENDER.
YOU RAN A FULL-SPECTRUM ANALYSIS?
THE ONLY PRINTS CAME FROM THE MESSENGER. NO HAIRS, BUT TRACES OF COTTON FIBERS AND ISOPROPYL ALCOHOL.
STERILIZED? CURIOUS.
NOT AS CURIOUS AS WHAT'S ON THE TAPE, SIR. IF I MAY...
TAKING SIDES with Arturo!
...THE ONLY MAN IN GOTHAM BRAVE ENOUGH TO TAKE SIDES...
...ARTURO RODRIGUEZ!
ONCE ONE OF MY BIGGEST SUPPORTERS.
HOW FAR THINGS HAVE COME.

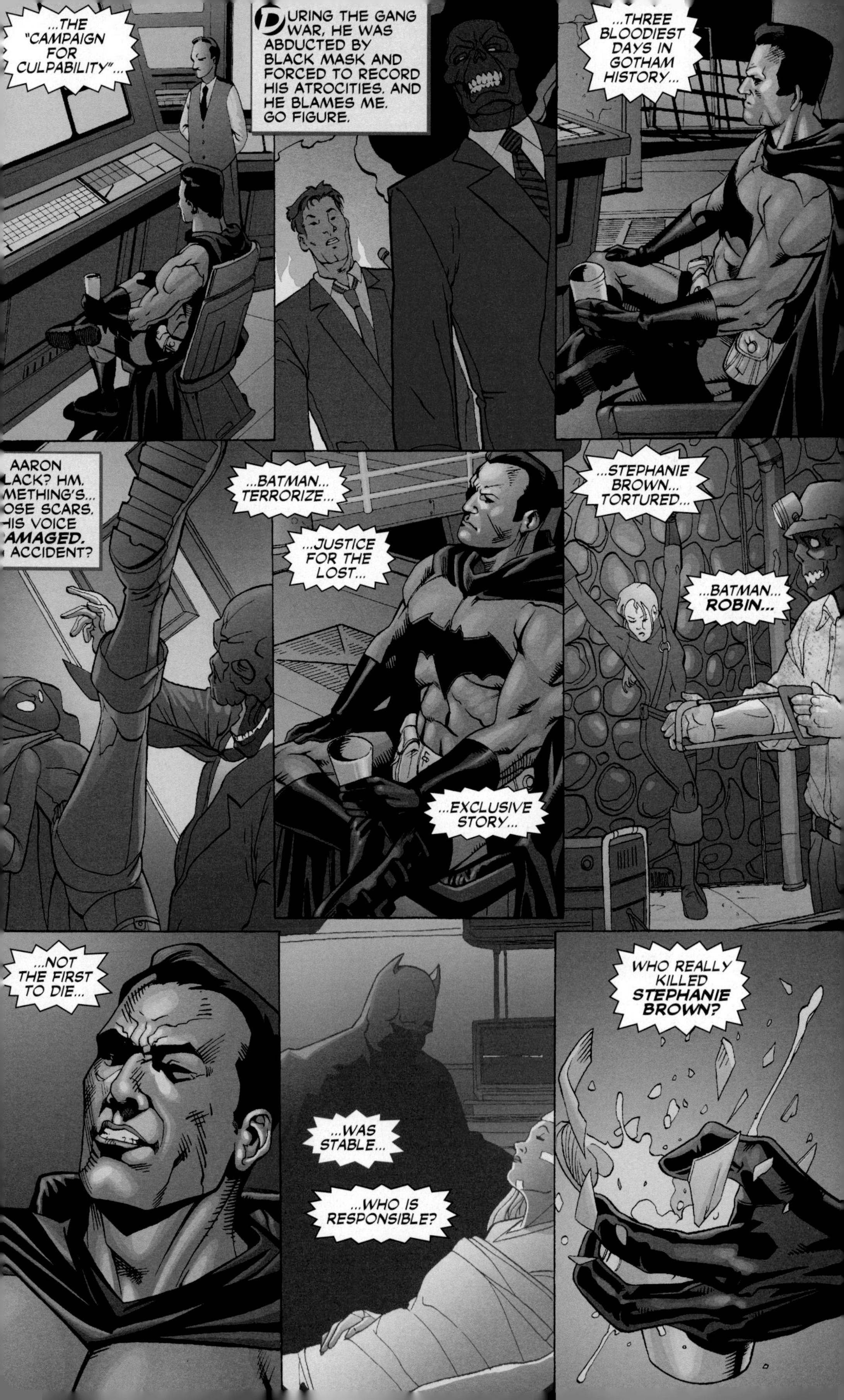
...THE "CAMPAIGN FOR CULPABILITY"...
DURING THE GANG WAR, HE WAS ABDUCTED BY BLACK MASK AND FORCED TO RECORD HIS ATROCITIES. AND HE BLAMES ME. GO FIGURE.
...THREE BLOODIEST DAYS IN GOTHAM HISTORY...
AARON LACK? HM. METHING'S... OSE SCARS. HIS VOICE AMAGED. ACCIDENT?
...BATMAN... TERRORIZE...
...JUSTICE FOR THE LOST...
...EXCLUSIVE STORY...
...STEPHANIE BROWN... TORTURED...
...BATMAN... ROBIN...
...NOT THE FIRST TO DIE...
...WAS STABLE...
...WHO IS RESPONSIBLE?
WHO REALLY KILLED STEPHANIE BROWN?

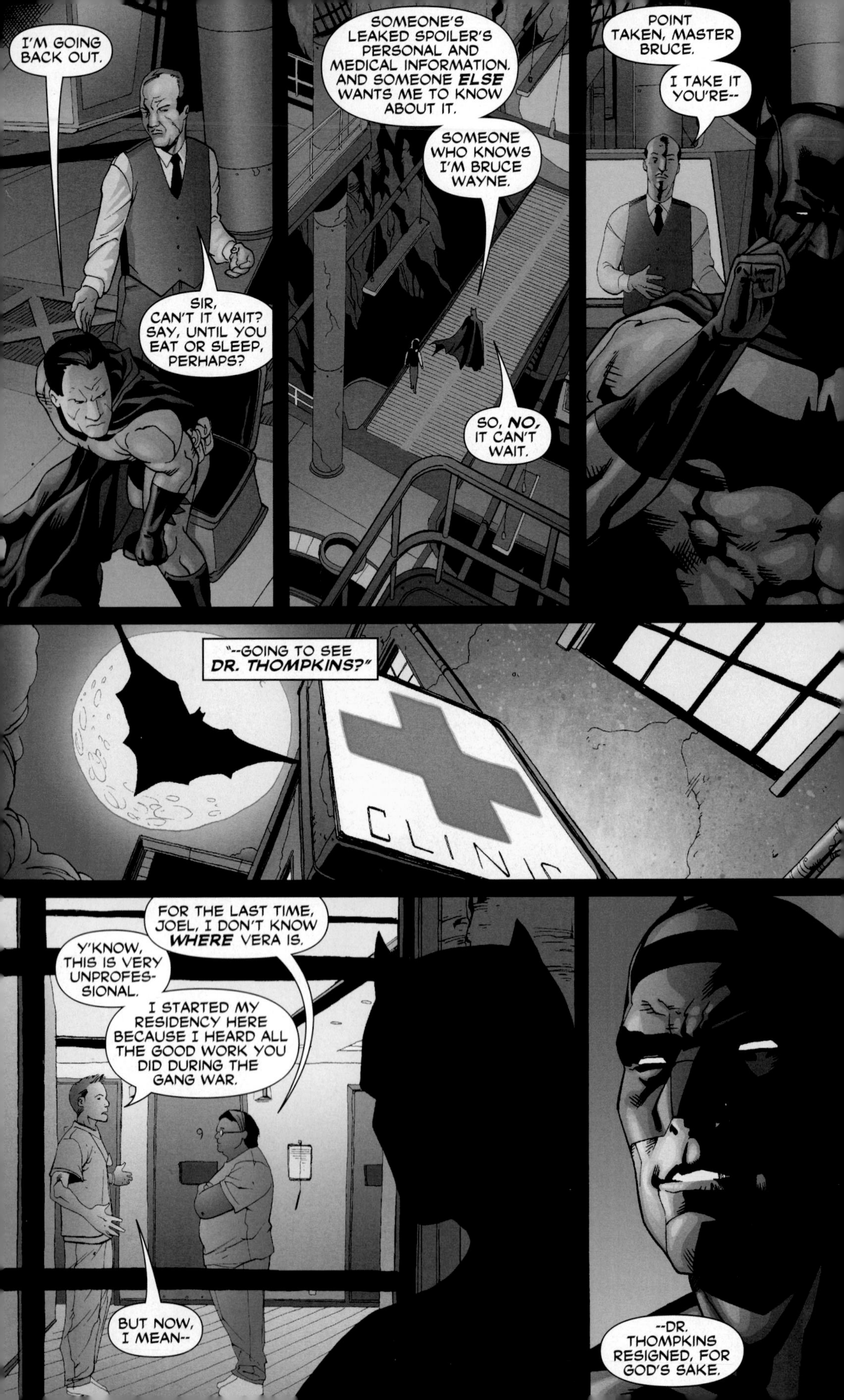

I'M GOING BACK OUT.
SIR, CAN'T IT WAIT? SAY, UNTIL YOU EAT OR SLEEP, PERHAPS?
SOMEONE'S LEAKED SPOILER'S PERSONAL AND MEDICAL INFORMATION. AND SOMEONE ELSE WANTS ME TO KNOW ABOUT IT.
SOMEONE WHO KNOWS I'M BRUCE WAYNE.
SO, NO, IT CAN'T WAIT.
POINT TAKEN, MASTER BRUCE.
I TAKE IT YOU'RE--
"--GOING TO SEE DR. THOMPKINS?"
CLINIC
FOR THE LAST TIME, JOEL, I DON'T KNOW WHERE VERA IS.
Y'KNOW, THIS IS VERY UNPROFES-SIONAL.
I STARTED MY RESIDENCY HERE BECAUSE I HEARD ALL THE GOOD WORK YOU DID DURING THE GANG WAR.
BUT NOW, I MEAN--
--DR. THOMPKINS RESIGNED, FOR GOD'S SAKE.

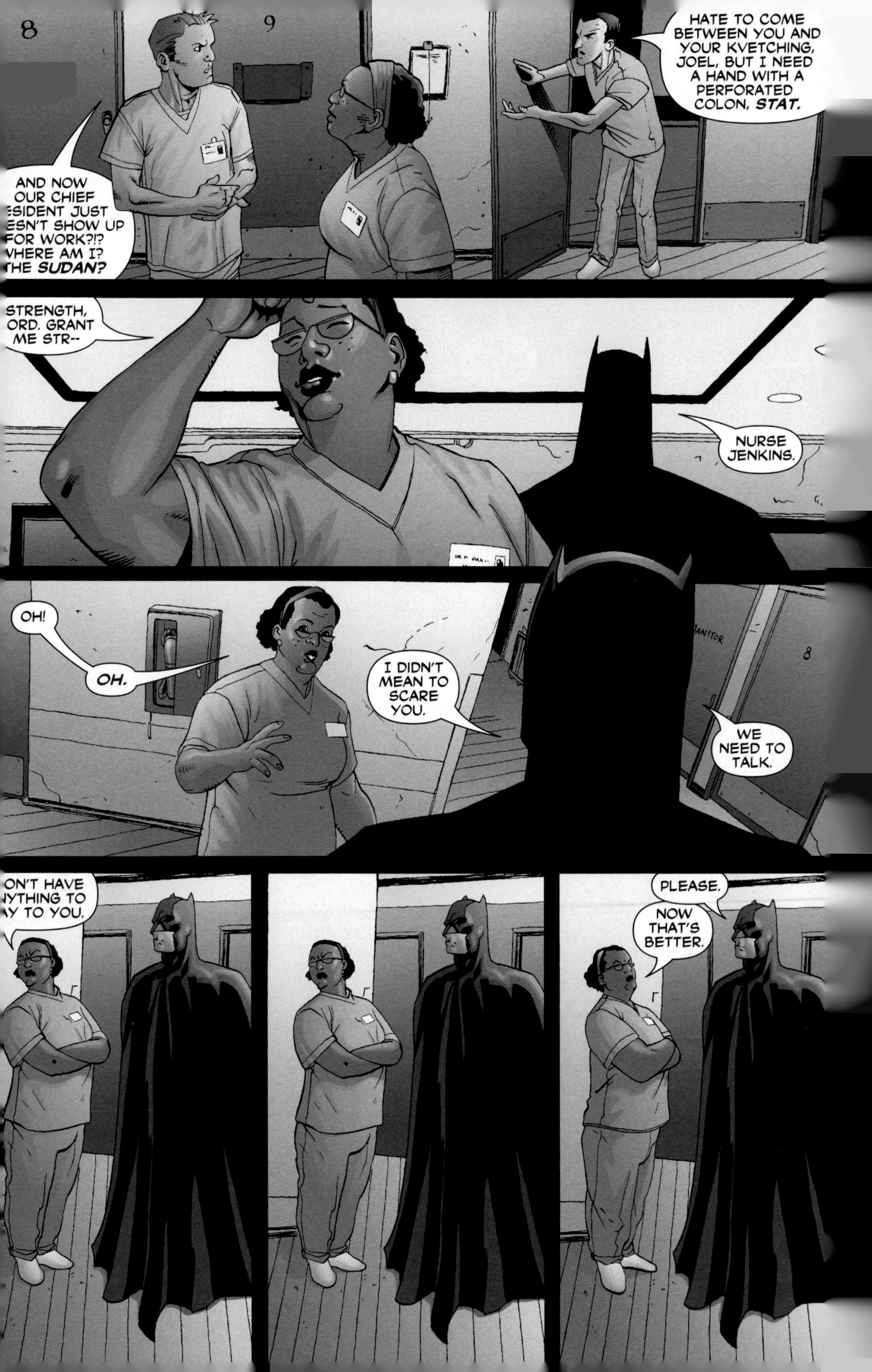

8
9
AND NOW OUR CHIEF ESIDENT JUST ESN'T SHOW UP FOR WORK?!? VHERE AM I? THE *SUDAN?*
HATE TO COME BETWEEN YOU AND YOUR KVETCHING, JOEL, BUT I NEED A HAND WITH A PERFORATED COLON, *STAT.*
STRENGTH, ORD. GRANT ME STR--
NURSE JENKINS.
OH!
OH.
I DIDN'T MEAN TO SCARE YOU.
JANITOR
8
WE NEED TO TALK.
ON'T HAVE YTHING TO Y TO YOU.
PLEASE.
NOW THAT'S BETTER.

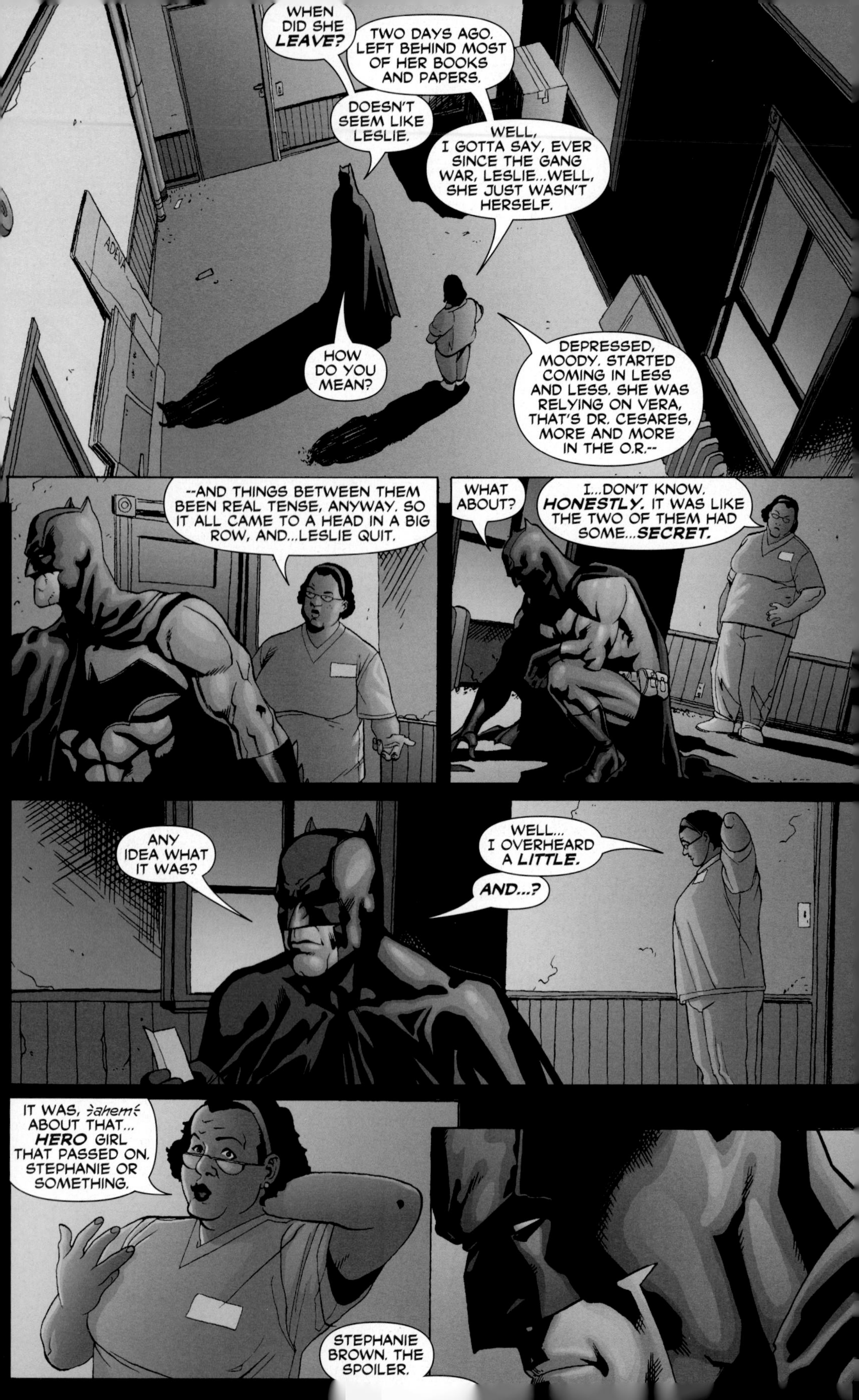
WHEN DID SHE LEAVE?
TWO DAYS AGO. LEFT BEHIND MOST OF HER BOOKS AND PAPERS.
DOESN'T SEEM LIKE LESLIE.
WELL, I GOTTA SAY, EVER SINCE THE GANG WAR, LESLIE...WELL, SHE JUST WASN'T HERSELF.
HOW DO YOU MEAN?
DEPRESSED, MOODY. STARTED COMING IN LESS AND LESS. SHE WAS RELYING ON VERA, THAT'S DR. CESARES, MORE AND MORE IN THE O.R.--
--AND THINGS BETWEEN THEM BEEN REAL TENSE, ANYWAY. SO IT ALL CAME TO A HEAD IN A BIG ROW, AND...LESLIE QUIT.
WHAT ABOUT?
I...DON'T KNOW. HONESTLY. IT WAS LIKE THE TWO OF THEM HAD SOME...SECRET.
ANY IDEA WHAT IT WAS?
WELL... I OVERHEARD A LITTLE.
AND...?
IT WAS, ahem ABOUT THAT... HERO GIRL THAT PASSED ON, STEPHANIE OR SOMETHING.
STEPHANIE BROWN. THE SPOILER.

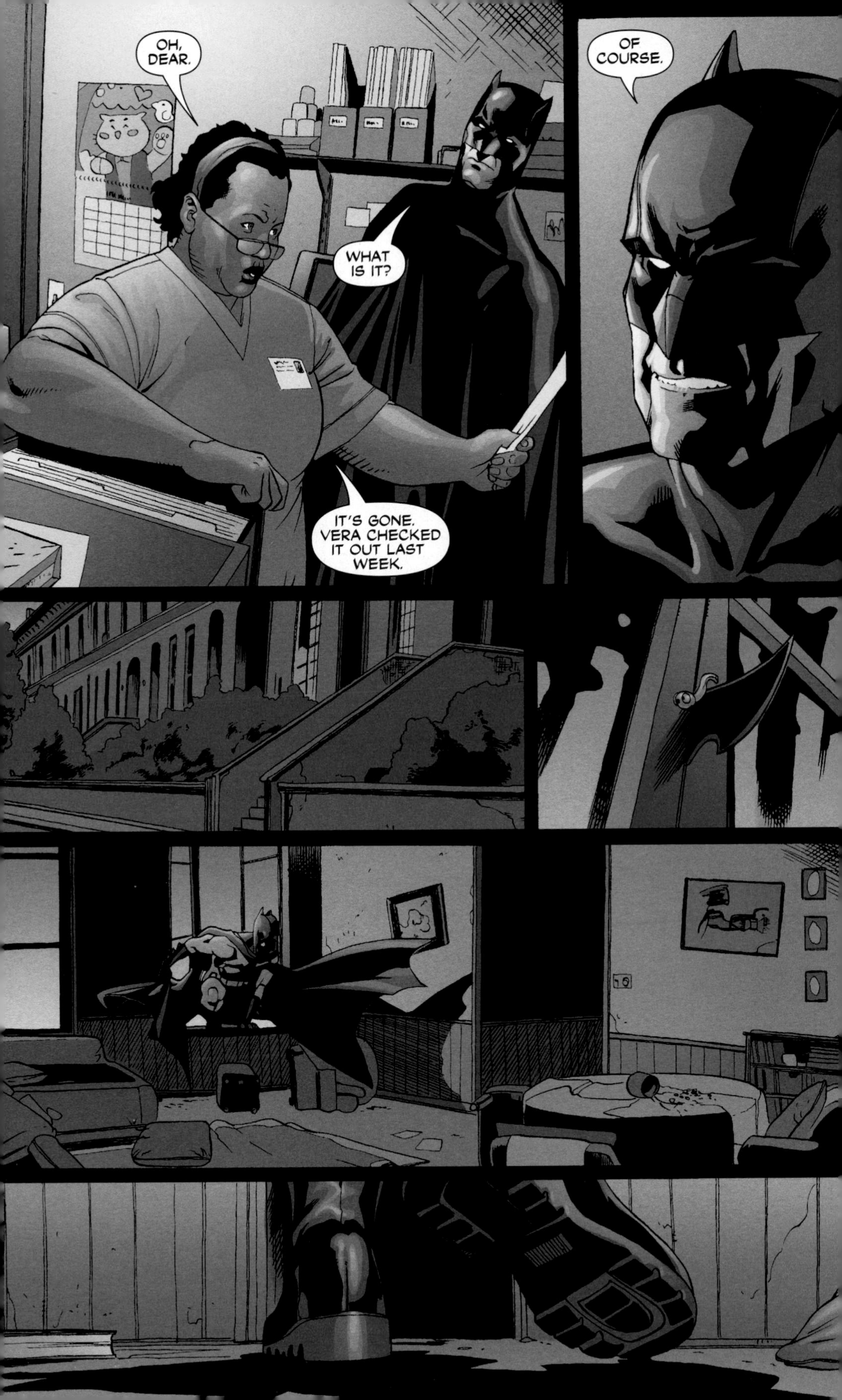
OH, DEAR.
WHAT IS IT?
IT'S GONE. VERA CHECKED IT OUT LAST WEEK.
OF COURSE.

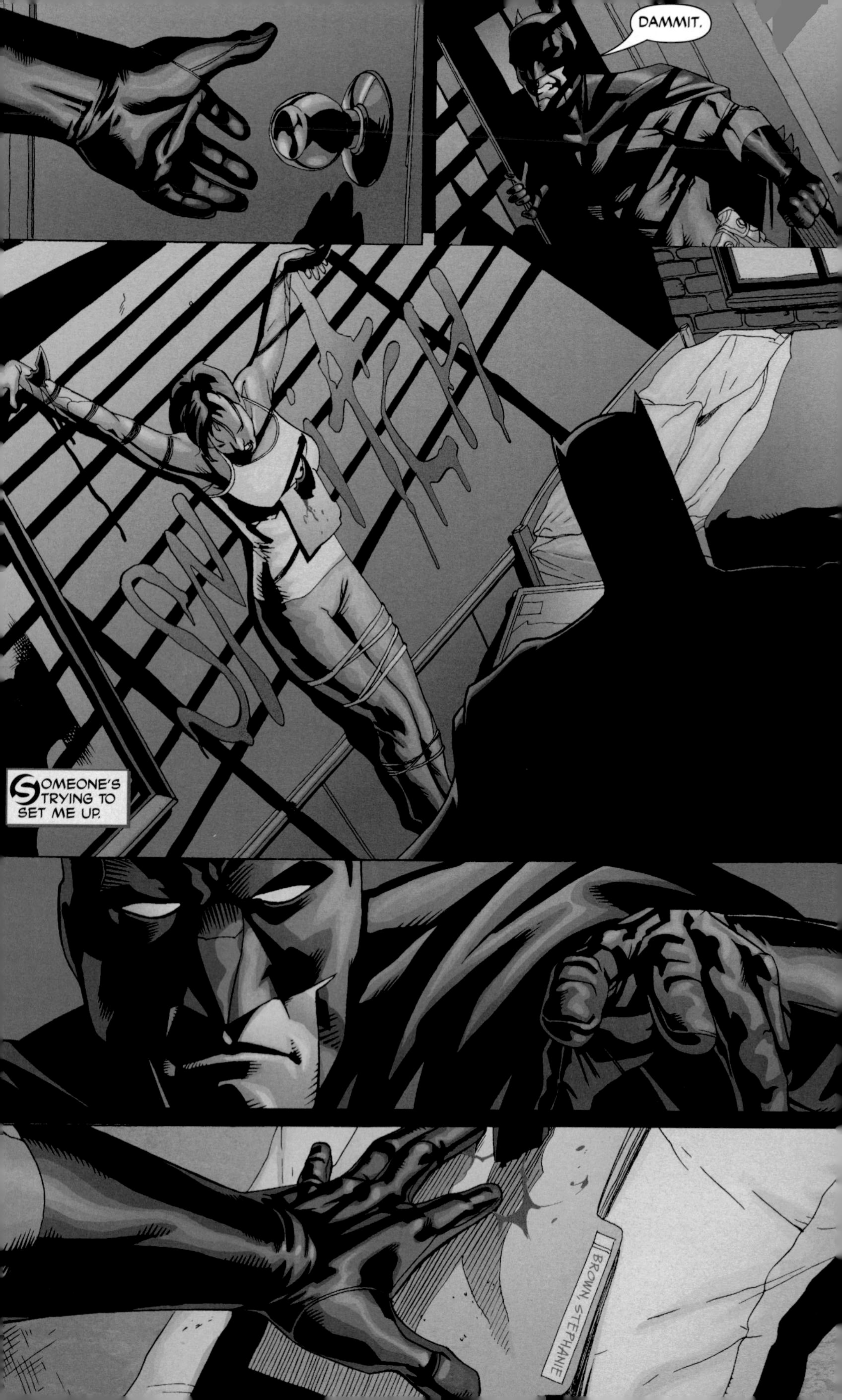
DAMMIT.
SOMEONE'S TRYING TO SET ME UP.
BROWN, STEPHANIE

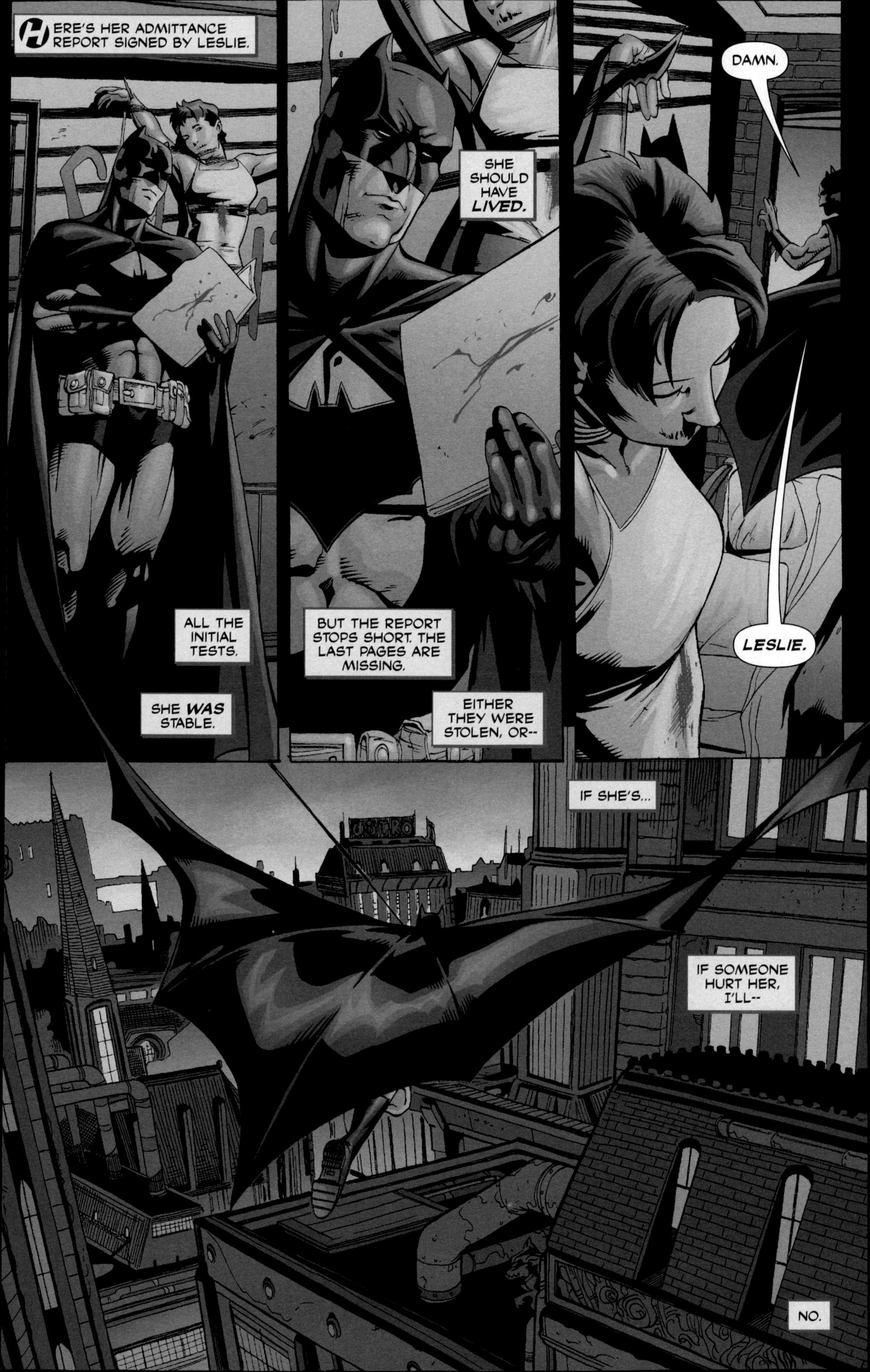
HERE'S HER ADMITTANCE REPORT SIGNED BY LESLIE.
ALL THE INITIAL TESTS.
SHE WAS STABLE.
SHE SHOULD HAVE LIVED.
BUT THE REPORT STOPS SHORT. THE LAST PAGES ARE MISSING.
EITHER THEY WERE STOLEN, OR--
DAMN.
LESLIE.
IF SHE'S...
IF SOMEONE HURT HER, I'LL--
NO.

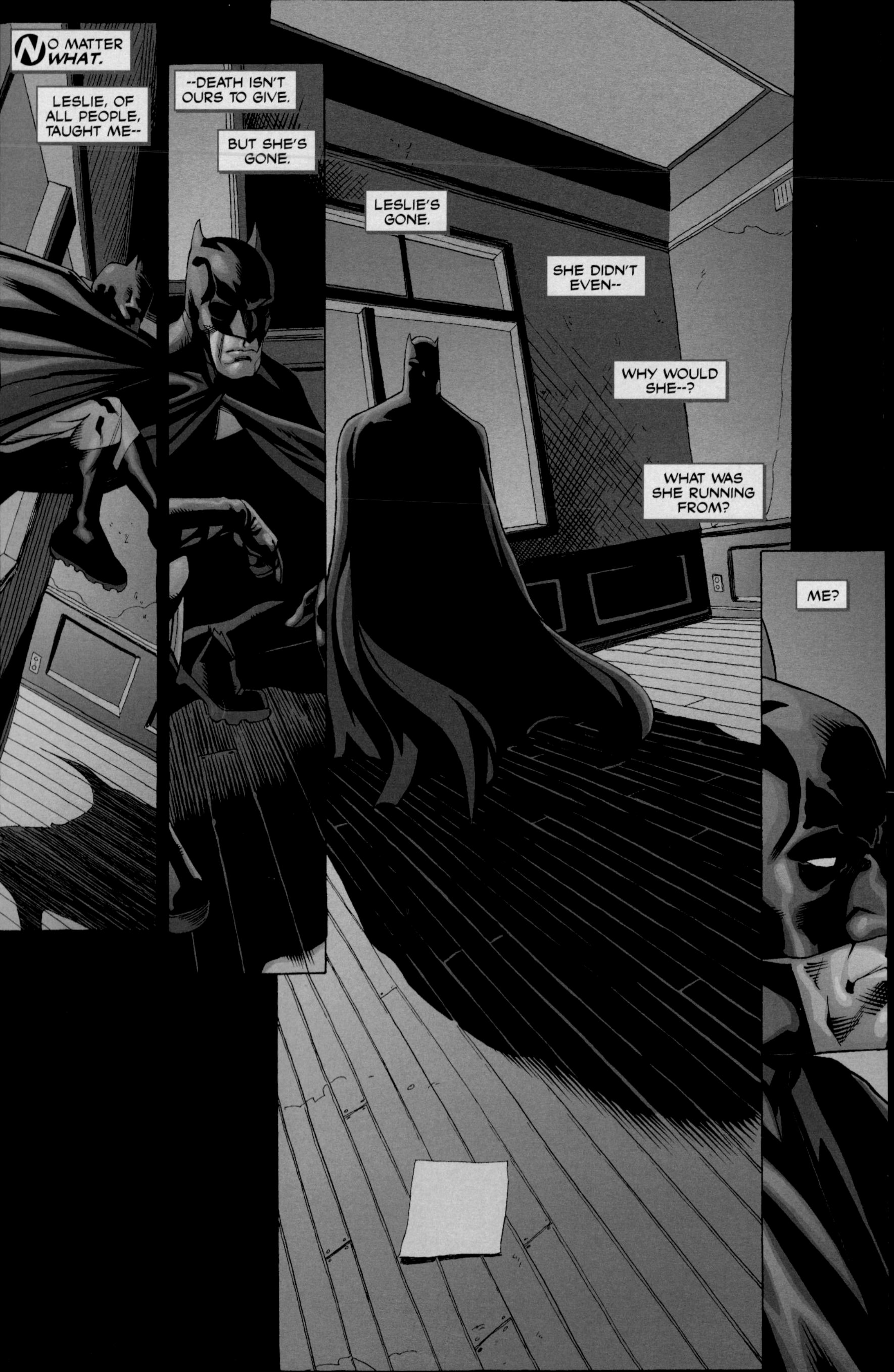
NO MATTER WHAT.
LESLIE, OF ALL PEOPLE, TAUGHT ME--
--DEATH ISN'T OURS TO GIVE.
BUT SHE'S GONE.
LESLIE'S GONE.
SHE DIDN'T EVEN--
WHY WOULD SHE--?
WHAT WAS SHE RUNNING FROM?
ME?

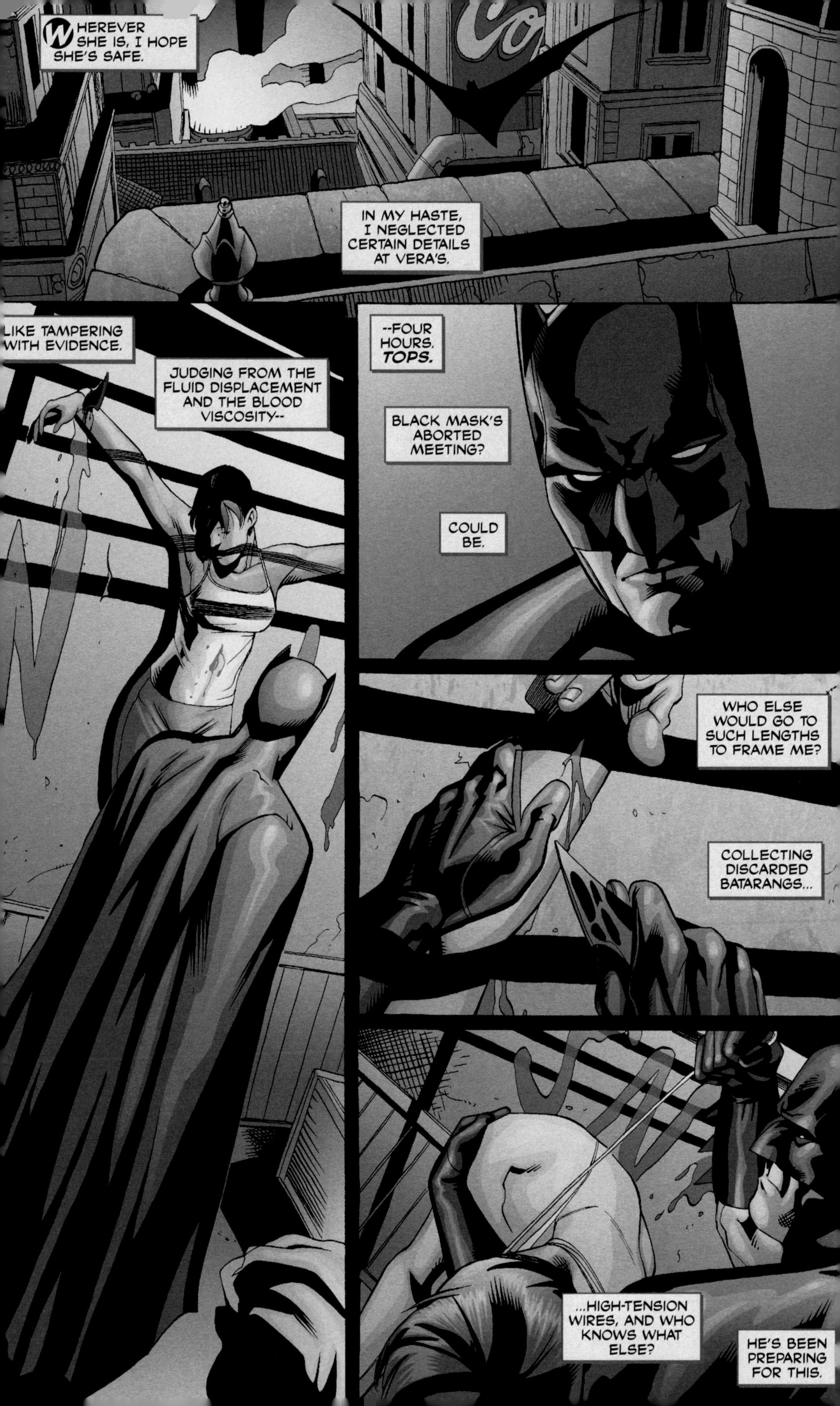
WHEREVER SHE IS, I HOPE SHE'S SAFE.
IN MY HASTE, I NEGLECTED CERTAIN DETAILS AT VERA'S.
LIKE TAMPERING WITH EVIDENCE.
JUDGING FROM THE FLUID DISPLACEMENT AND THE BLOOD VISCOSITY--
--FOUR HOURS. TOPS.
BLACK MASK'S ABORTED MEETING?
COULD BE.
WHO ELSE WOULD GO TO SUCH LENGTHS TO FRAME ME?
COLLECTING DISCARDED BATARANGS...
...HIGH-TENSION WIRES, AND WHO KNOWS WHAT ELSE?
HE'S BEEN PREPARING FOR THIS.

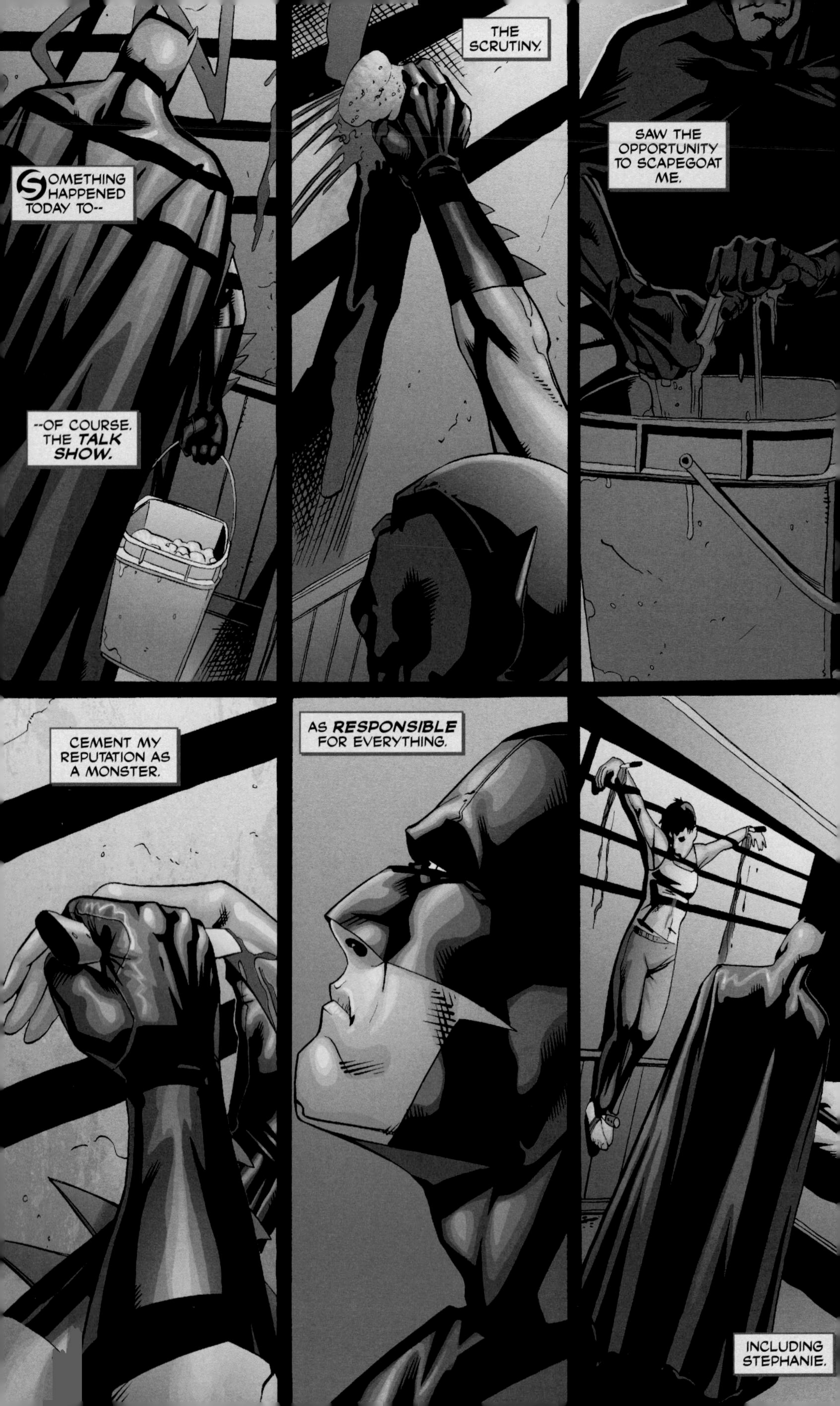
SOMETHING HAPPENED TODAY TO--
--OF COURSE. THE TALK SHOW.
THE SCRUTINY.
SAW THE OPPORTUNITY TO SCAPEGOAT ME.
CEMENT MY REPUTATION AS A MONSTER.
AS RESPONSIBLE FOR EVERYTHING.
INCLUDING STEPHANIE.

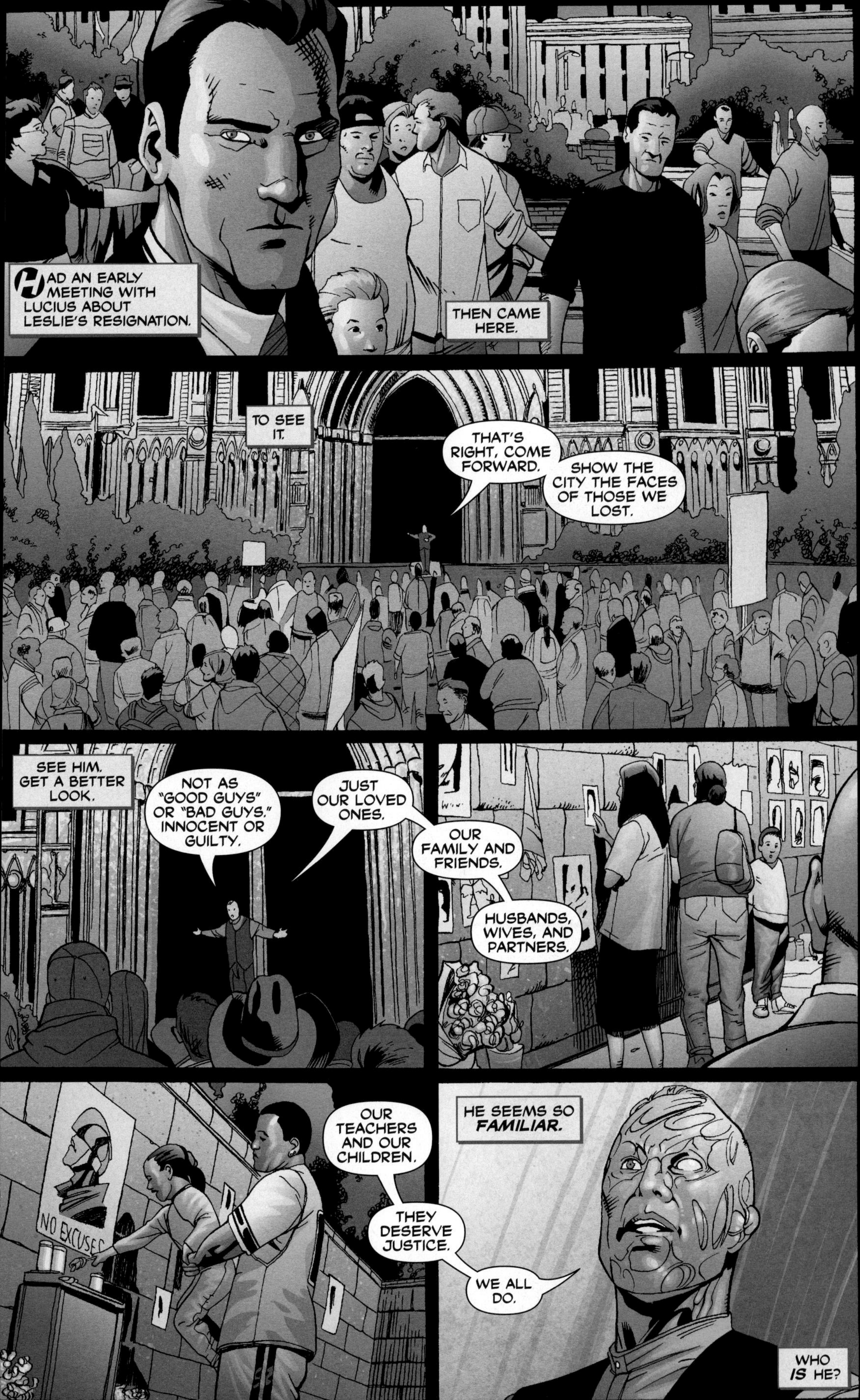
HAD AN EARLY MEETING WITH LUCIUS ABOUT LESLIE'S RESIGNATION.
THEN CAME HERE.
TO SEE IT.
THAT'S RIGHT, COME FORWARD.
SHOW THE CITY THE FACES OF THOSE WE LOST.
SEE HIM. GET A BETTER LOOK.
NOT AS "GOOD GUYS" OR "BAD GUYS," INNOCENT OR GUILTY.
JUST OUR LOVED ONES.
OUR FAMILY AND FRIENDS.
HUSBANDS, WIVES, AND PARTNERS.
NO EXCUSES
OUR TEACHERS AND OUR CHILDREN.
THEY DESERVE JUSTICE.
WE ALL DO.
HE SEEMS SO FAMILIAR.
WHO IS HE?

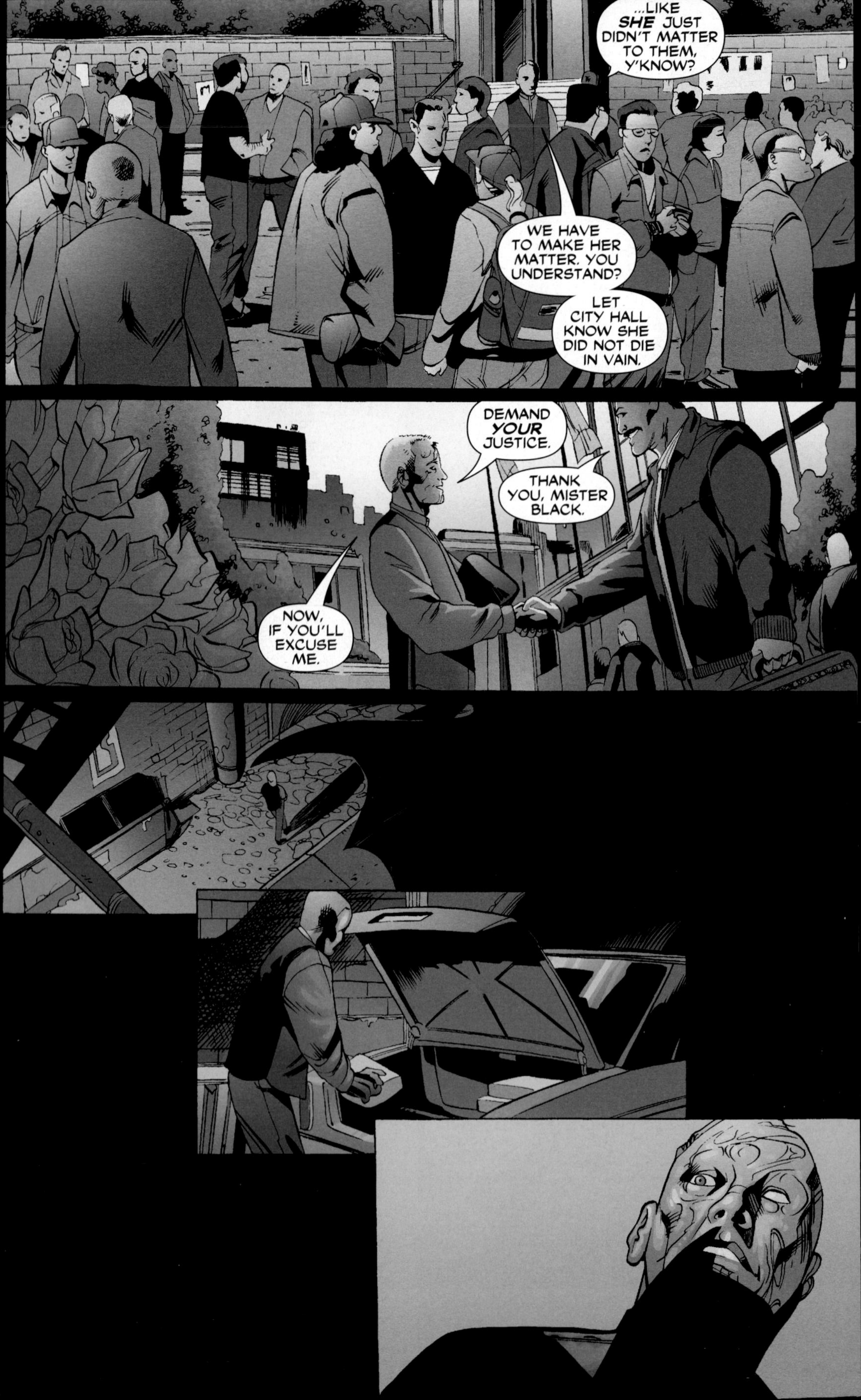
...LIKE SHE JUST DIDN'T MATTER TO THEM, Y'KNOW?
WE HAVE TO MAKE HER MATTER. YOU UNDERSTAND?
LET CITY HALL KNOW SHE DID NOT DIE IN VAIN.
DEMAND YOUR JUSTICE.
THANK YOU, MISTER BLACK.
NOW, IF YOU'LL EXCUSE ME.

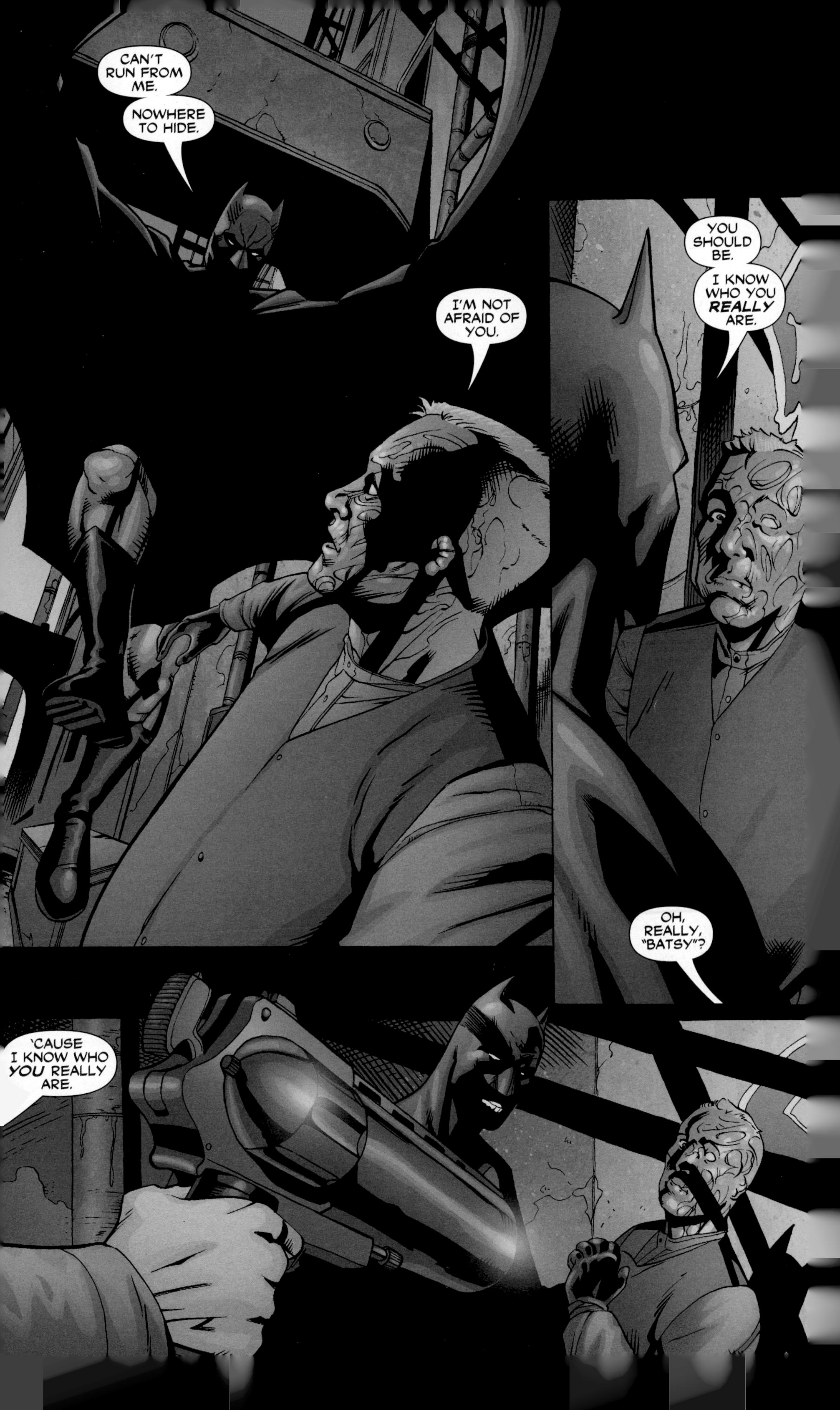
CAN'T RUN FROM ME.
NOWHERE TO HIDE.
I'M NOT AFRAID OF YOU.
YOU SHOULD BE.
I KNOW WHO YOU ***REALLY*** ARE.
OH, REALLY, "BATSY"?
'CAUSE I KNOW WHO ***YOU*** REALLY ARE.

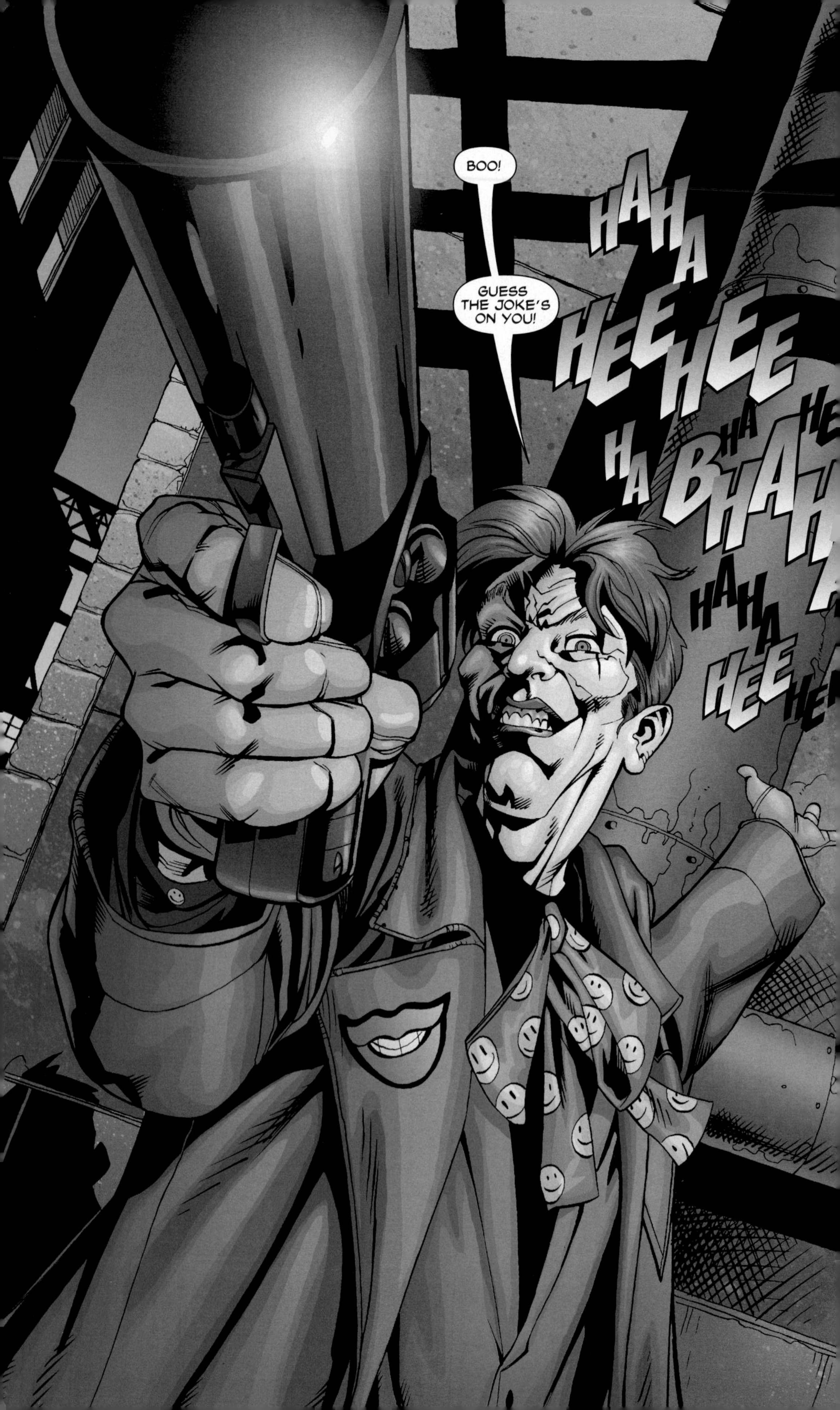
BOO!
GUESS THE JOKE'S ON YOU!
HAHAHA
HEEHEEHEE
HA HA BHAHAHA HE
HAHAHA
HEEHEE

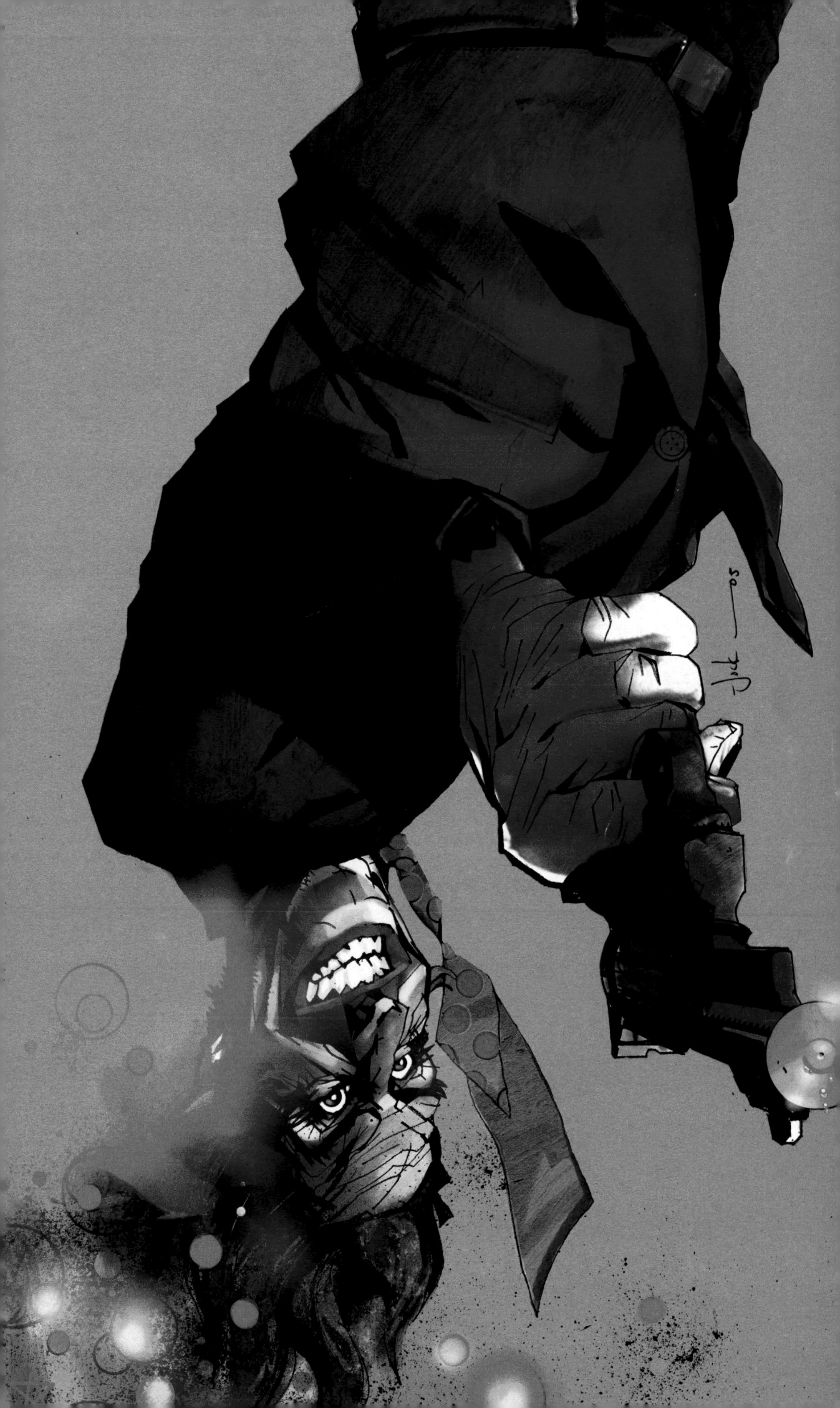
Jock 05

COVER ART BY
JOCK

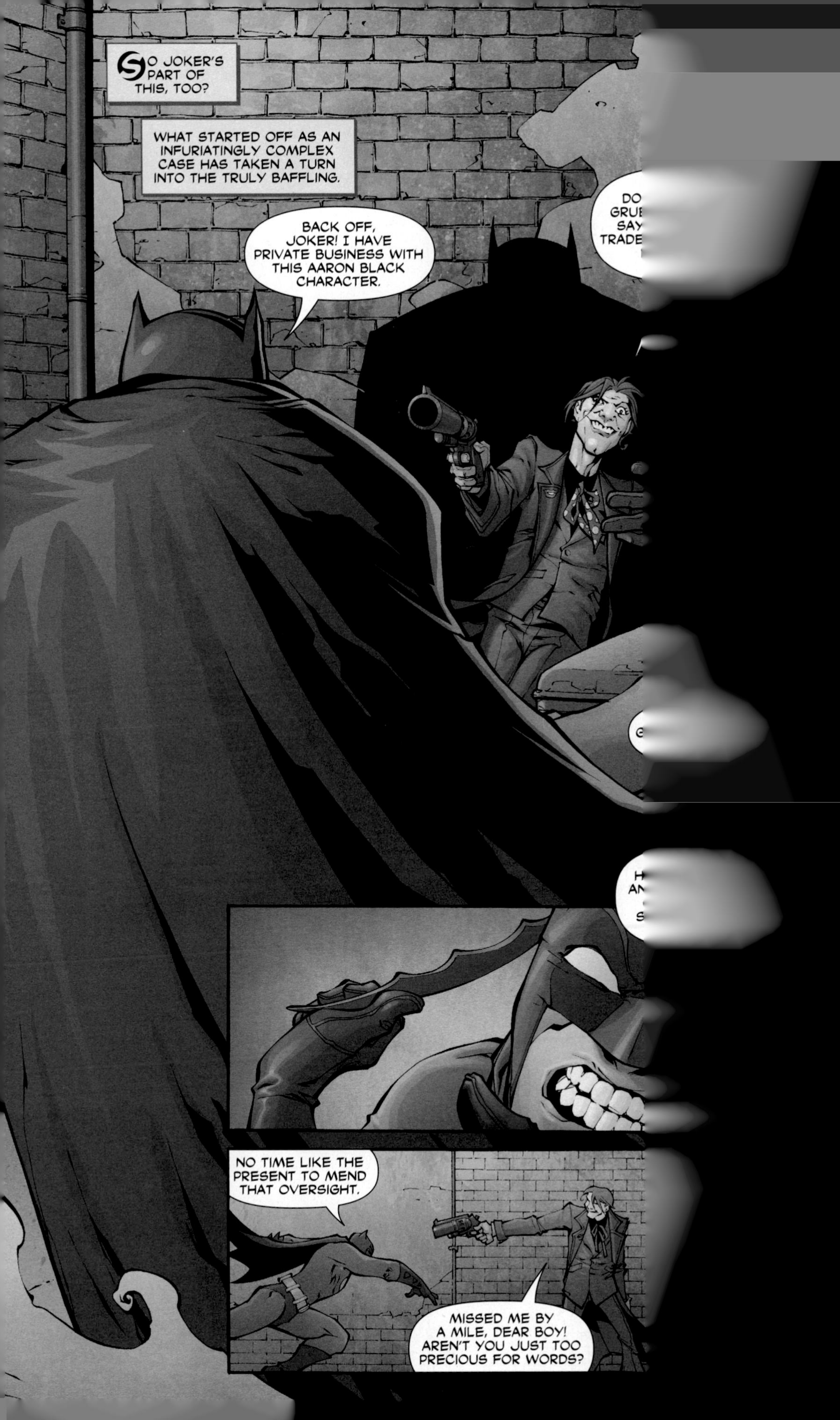
SO JOKER'S PART OF THIS, TOO?
WHAT STARTED OFF AS AN INFURIATINGLY COMPLEX CASE HAS TAKEN A TURN INTO THE TRULY BAFFLING.
BACK OFF, JOKER! I HAVE PRIVATE BUSINESS WITH THIS AARON BLACK CHARACTER.
NO TIME LIKE THE PRESENT TO MEND THAT OVERSIGHT.
MISSED ME BY A MILE, DEAR BOY! AREN'T YOU JUST TOO PRECIOUS FOR WORDS?

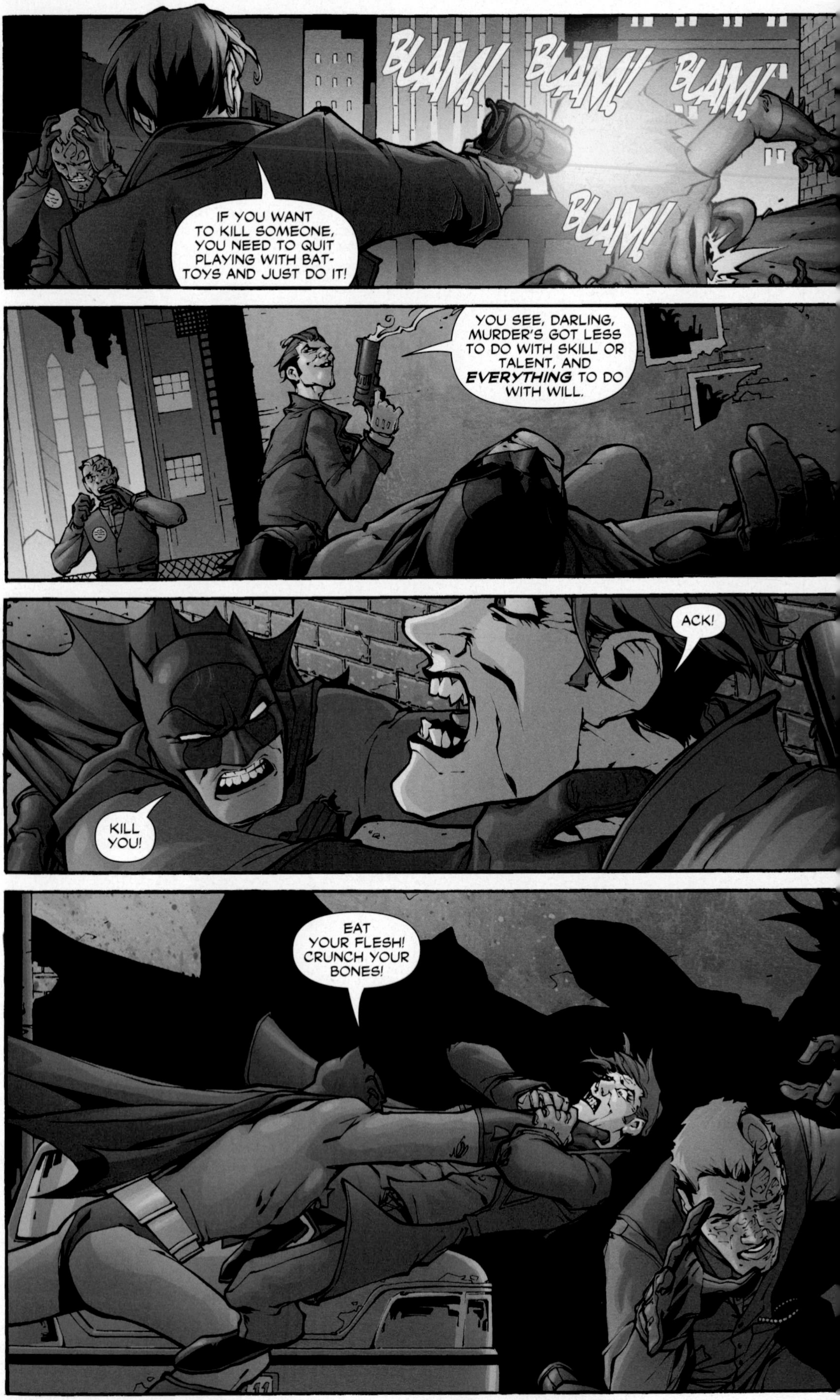
BLAM! BLAM! BLAM!
BLAM!
IF YOU WANT TO KILL SOMEONE, YOU NEED TO QUIT PLAYING WITH BAT-TOYS AND JUST DO IT!
YOU SEE, DARLING, MURDER'S GOT LESS TO DO WITH SKILL OR TALENT, AND EVERYTHING TO DO WITH WILL.
ACK!
KILL YOU!
EAT YOUR FLESH! CRUNCH YOUR BONES!

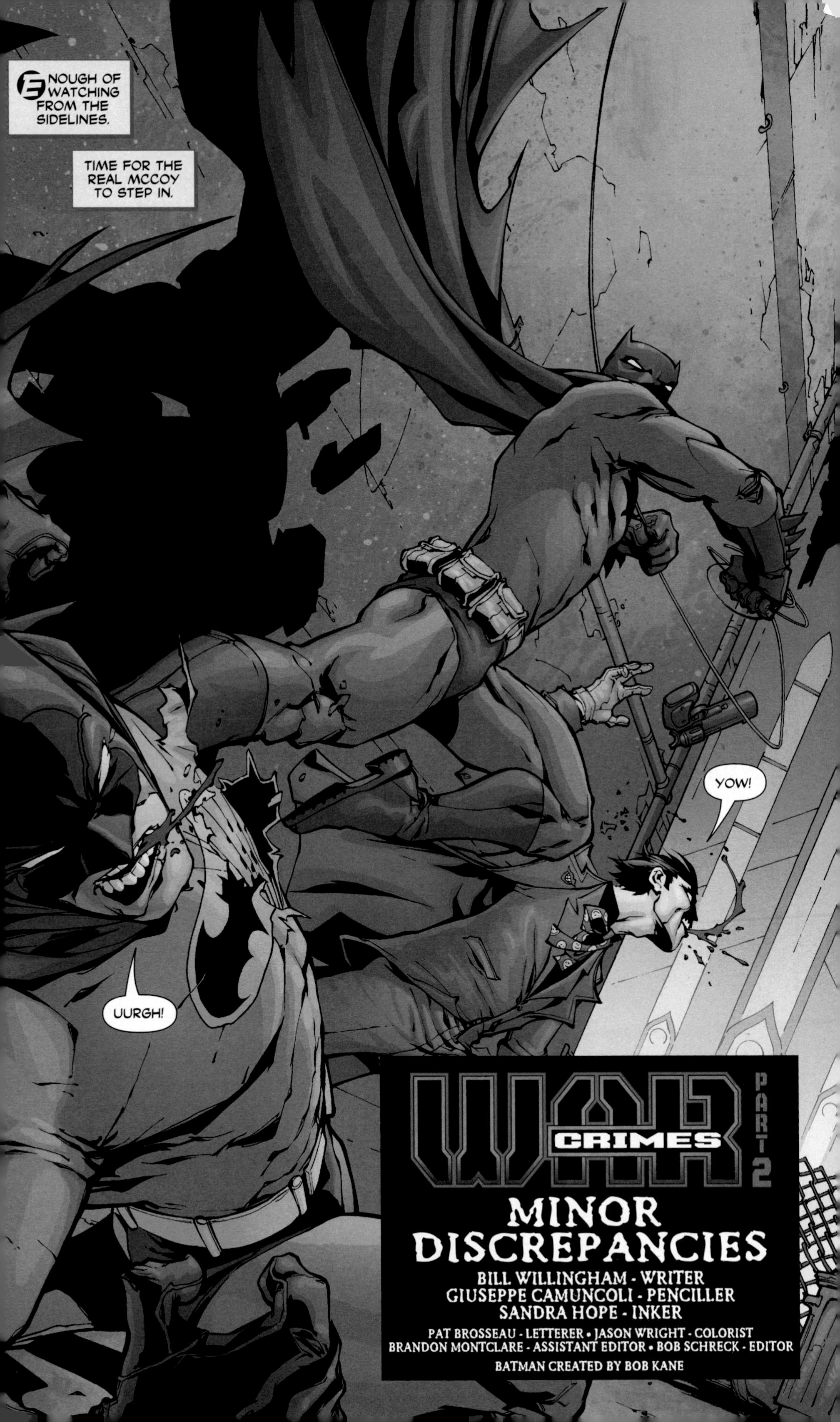
ENOUGH OF WATCHING FROM THE SIDELINES.
TIME FOR THE REAL MCCOY TO STEP IN.
YOW!
UURGH!
WAR CRIMES PART 2
MINOR DISCREPANCIES
BILL WILLINGHAM - WRITER
GIUSEPPE CAMUNCOLI - PENCILLER
SANDRA HOPE - INKER
PAT BROSSEAU - LETTERER • JASON WRIGHT - COLORIST
BRANDON MONTCLARE - ASSISTANT EDITOR • BOB SCHRECK - EDITOR
BATMAN CREATED BY BOB KANE

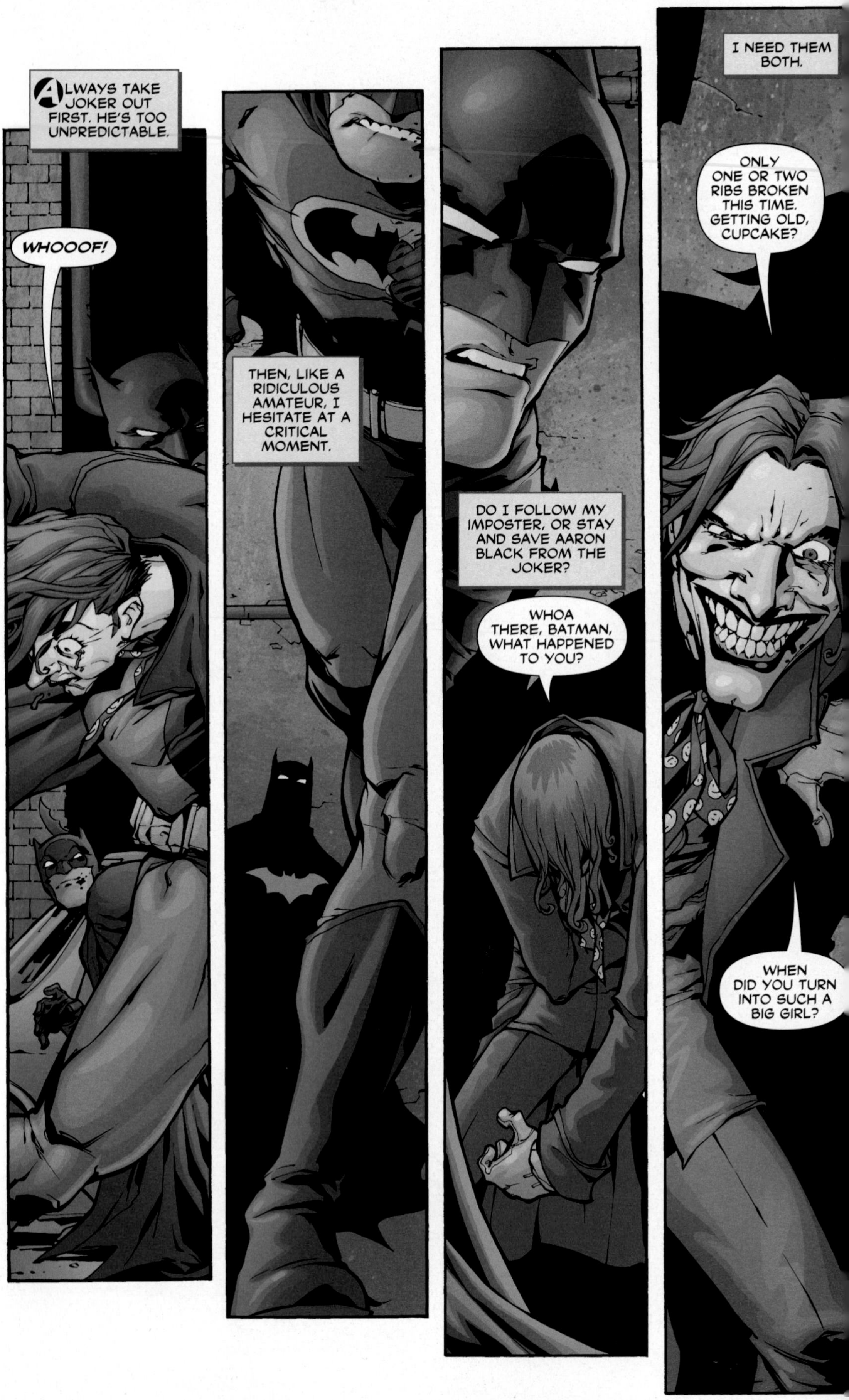

ALWAYS TAKE JOKER OUT FIRST. HE'S TOO UNPREDICTABLE.
WHOOOF!
THEN, LIKE A RIDICULOUS AMATEUR, I HESITATE AT A CRITICAL MOMENT.
DO I FOLLOW MY IMPOSTER, OR STAY AND SAVE AARON BLACK FROM THE JOKER?
WHOA THERE, BATMAN, WHAT HAPPENED TO YOU?
I NEED THEM BOTH.
ONLY ONE OR TWO RIBS BROKEN THIS TIME. GETTING OLD, CUPCAKE?
WHEN DID YOU TURN INTO SUCH A BIG GIRL?

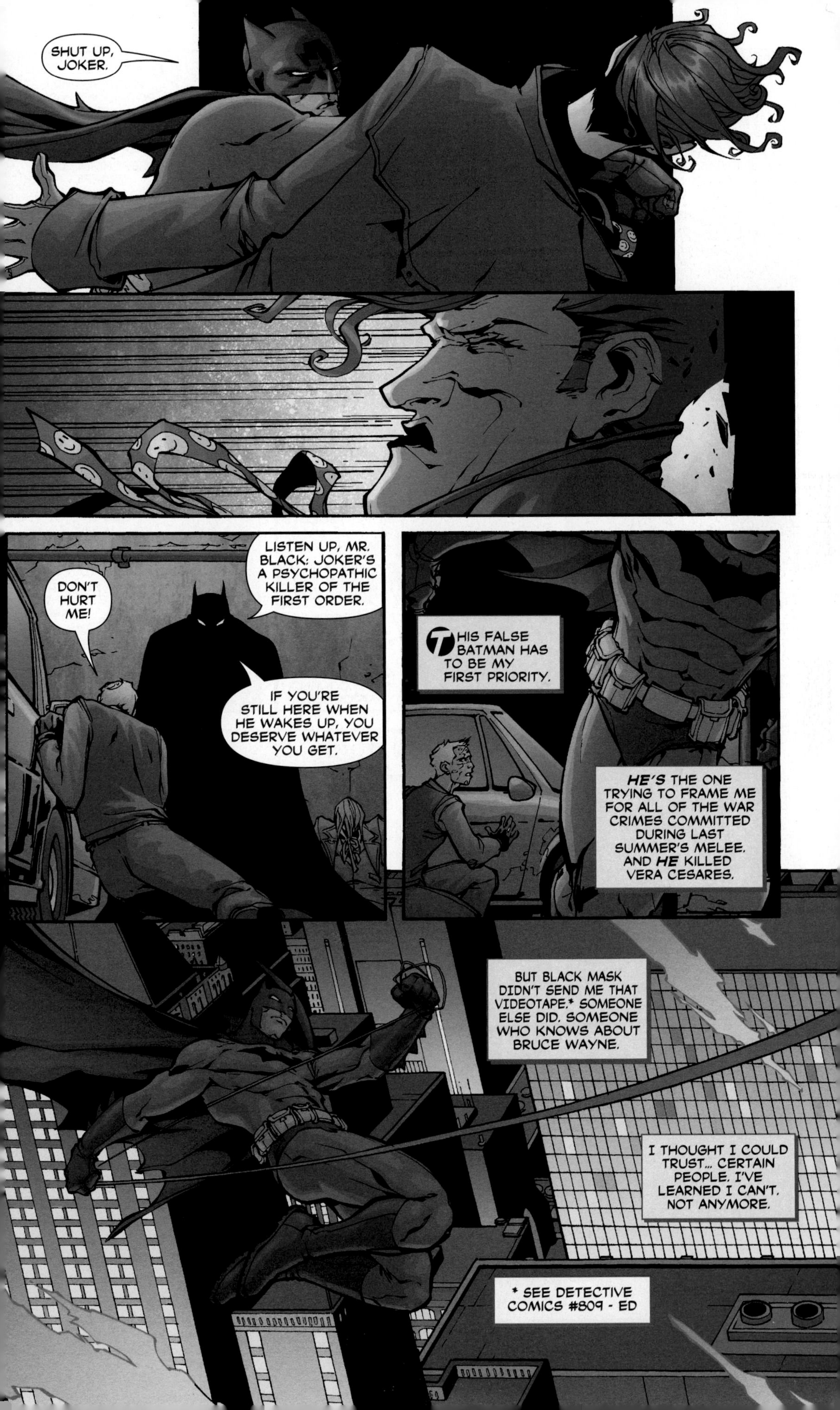

SHUT UP, JOKER.
DON'T HURT ME!
LISTEN UP, MR. BLACK; JOKER'S A PSYCHOPATHIC KILLER OF THE FIRST ORDER.
IF YOU'RE STILL HERE WHEN HE WAKES UP, YOU DESERVE WHATEVER YOU GET.
THIS FALSE BATMAN HAS TO BE MY FIRST PRIORITY.
HE'S THE ONE TRYING TO FRAME ME FOR ALL OF THE WAR CRIMES COMMITTED DURING LAST SUMMER'S MELEE. AND HE KILLED VERA CESARES.
BUT BLACK MASK DIDN'T SEND ME THAT VIDEOTAPE.* SOMEONE ELSE DID. SOMEONE WHO KNOWS ABOUT BRUCE WAYNE.
I THOUGHT I COULD TRUST... CERTAIN PEOPLE. I'VE LEARNED I CAN'T. NOT ANYMORE.
* SEE DETECTIVE COMICS #809 - ED

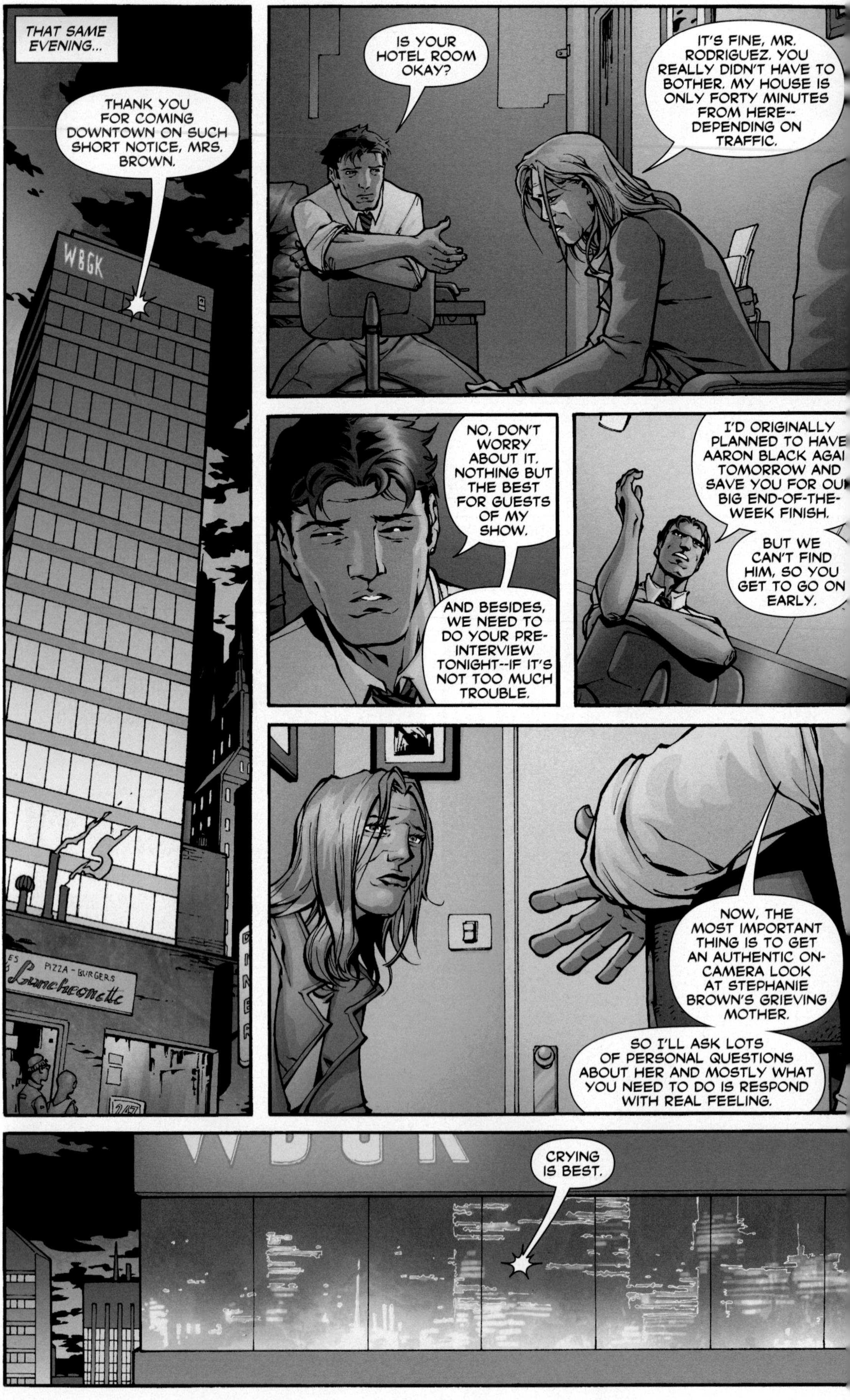
THAT SAME EVENING...
THANK YOU FOR COMING DOWNTOWN ON SUCH SHORT NOTICE, MRS. BROWN.
WBGK
PIZZA - BURGERS
Luncheonette
IS YOUR HOTEL ROOM OKAY?
IT'S FINE, MR. RODRIGUEZ. YOU REALLY DIDN'T HAVE TO BOTHER. MY HOUSE IS ONLY FORTY MINUTES FROM HERE-- DEPENDING ON TRAFFIC.
NO, DON'T WORRY ABOUT IT. NOTHING BUT THE BEST FOR GUESTS OF MY SHOW.
AND BESIDES, WE NEED TO DO YOUR PRE-INTERVIEW TONIGHT--IF IT'S NOT TOO MUCH TROUBLE.
I'D ORIGINALLY PLANNED TO HAVE AARON BLACK AGAI TOMORROW AND SAVE YOU FOR OU BIG END-OF-THE-WEEK FINISH.
BUT WE CAN'T FIND HIM, SO YOU GET TO GO ON EARLY.
NOW, THE MOST IMPORTANT THING IS TO GET AN AUTHENTIC ON-CAMERA LOOK AT STEPHANIE BROWN'S GRIEVING MOTHER.
SO I'LL ASK LOTS OF PERSONAL QUESTIONS ABOUT HER AND MOSTLY WHAT YOU NEED TO DO IS RESPOND WITH REAL FEELING.
CRYING IS BEST.

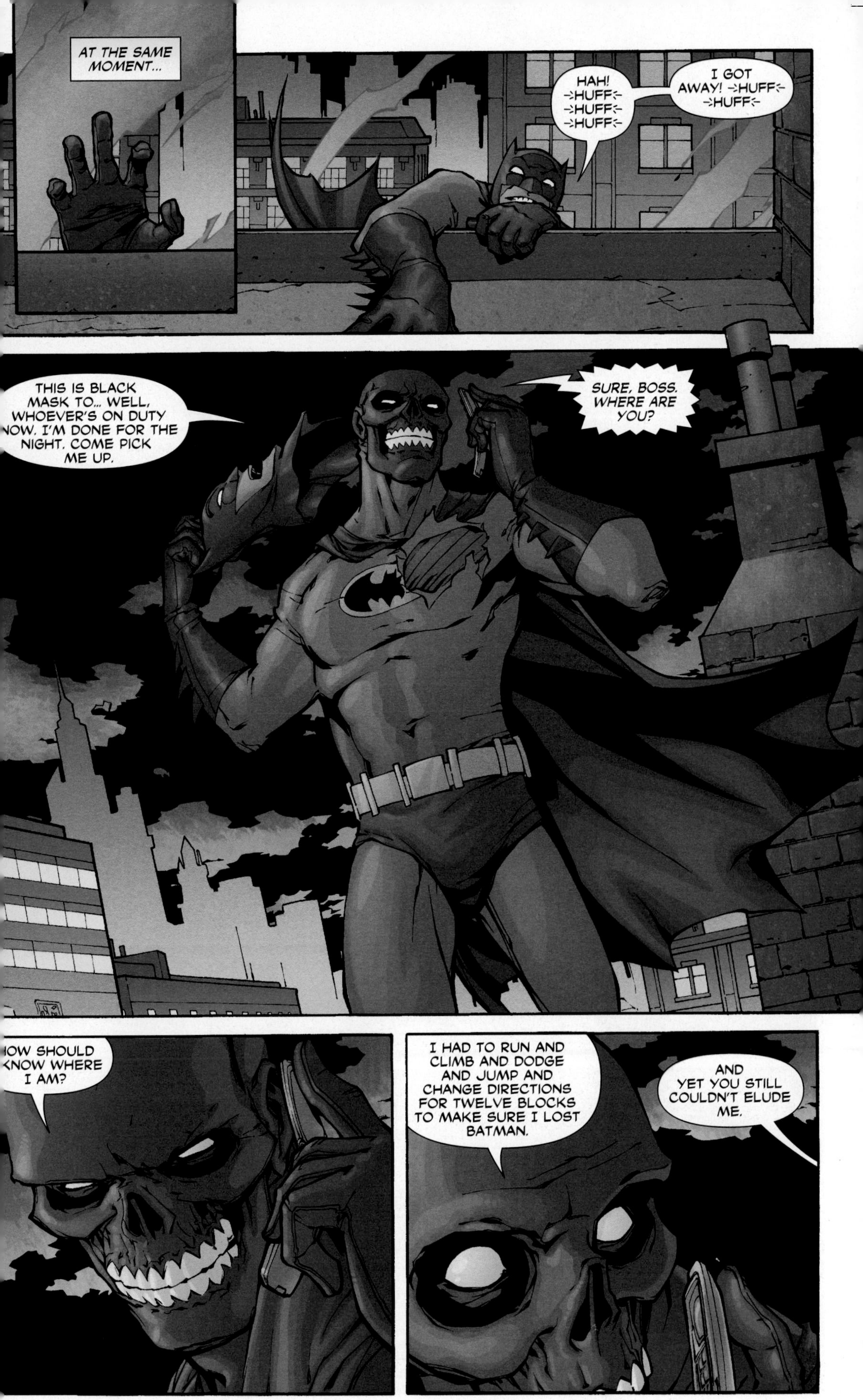
AT THE SAME MOMENT...
HAH! -HUFF- -HUFF- -HUFF-
I GOT AWAY! -HUFF- -HUFF-
THIS IS BLACK MASK TO... WELL, WHOEVER'S ON DUTY NOW. I'M DONE FOR THE NIGHT. COME PICK ME UP.
SURE, BOSS. WHERE ARE YOU?
HOW SHOULD I KNOW WHERE I AM?
I HAD TO RUN AND CLIMB AND DODGE AND JUMP AND CHANGE DIRECTIONS FOR TWELVE BLOCKS TO MAKE SURE I LOST BATMAN.
AND YET YOU STILL COULDN'T ELUDE ME.

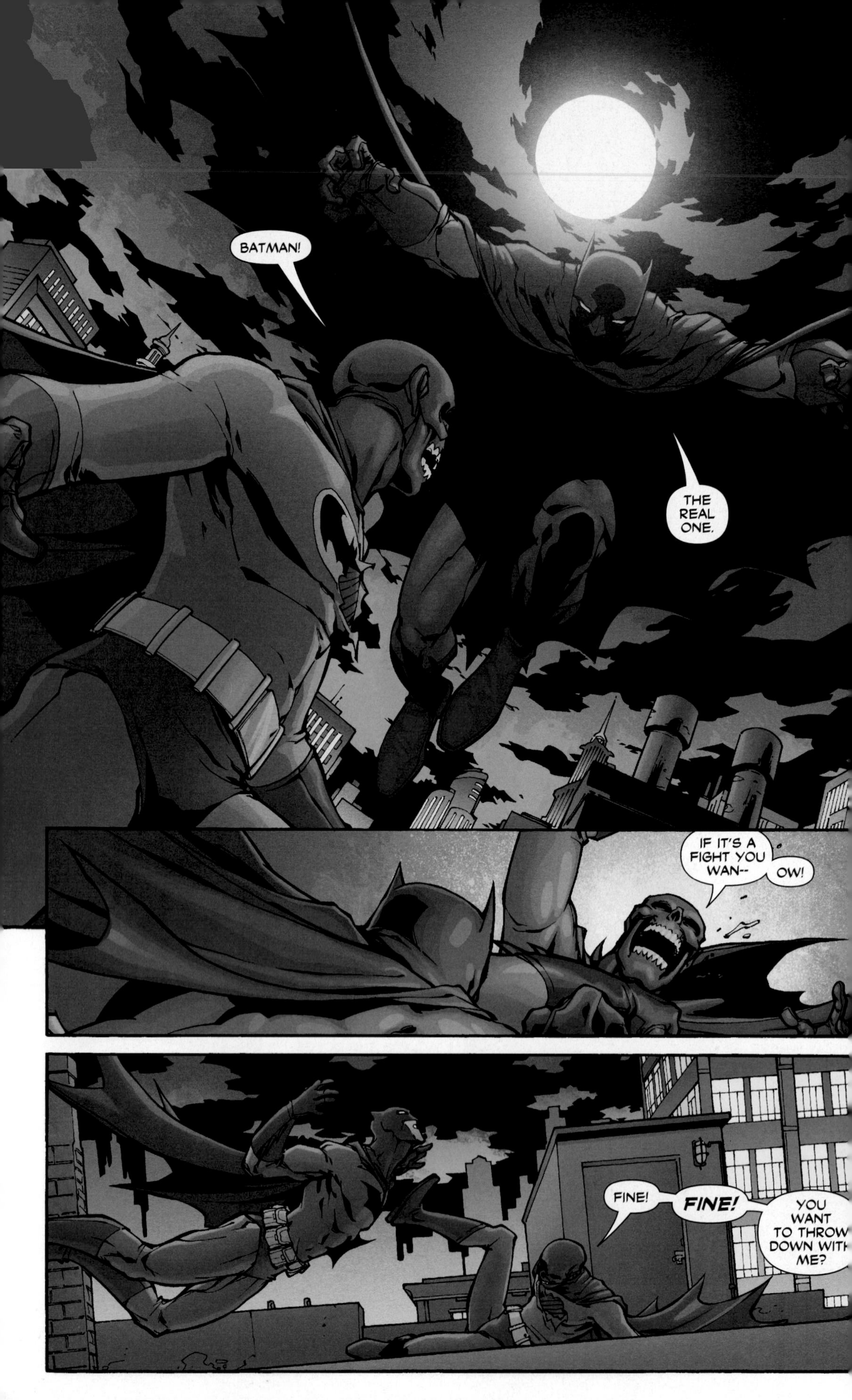
BATMAN!
THE REAL ONE.
IF IT'S A FIGHT YOU WAN--
OW!
FINE!
FINE!
YOU WANT TO THROW DOWN WITH ME?

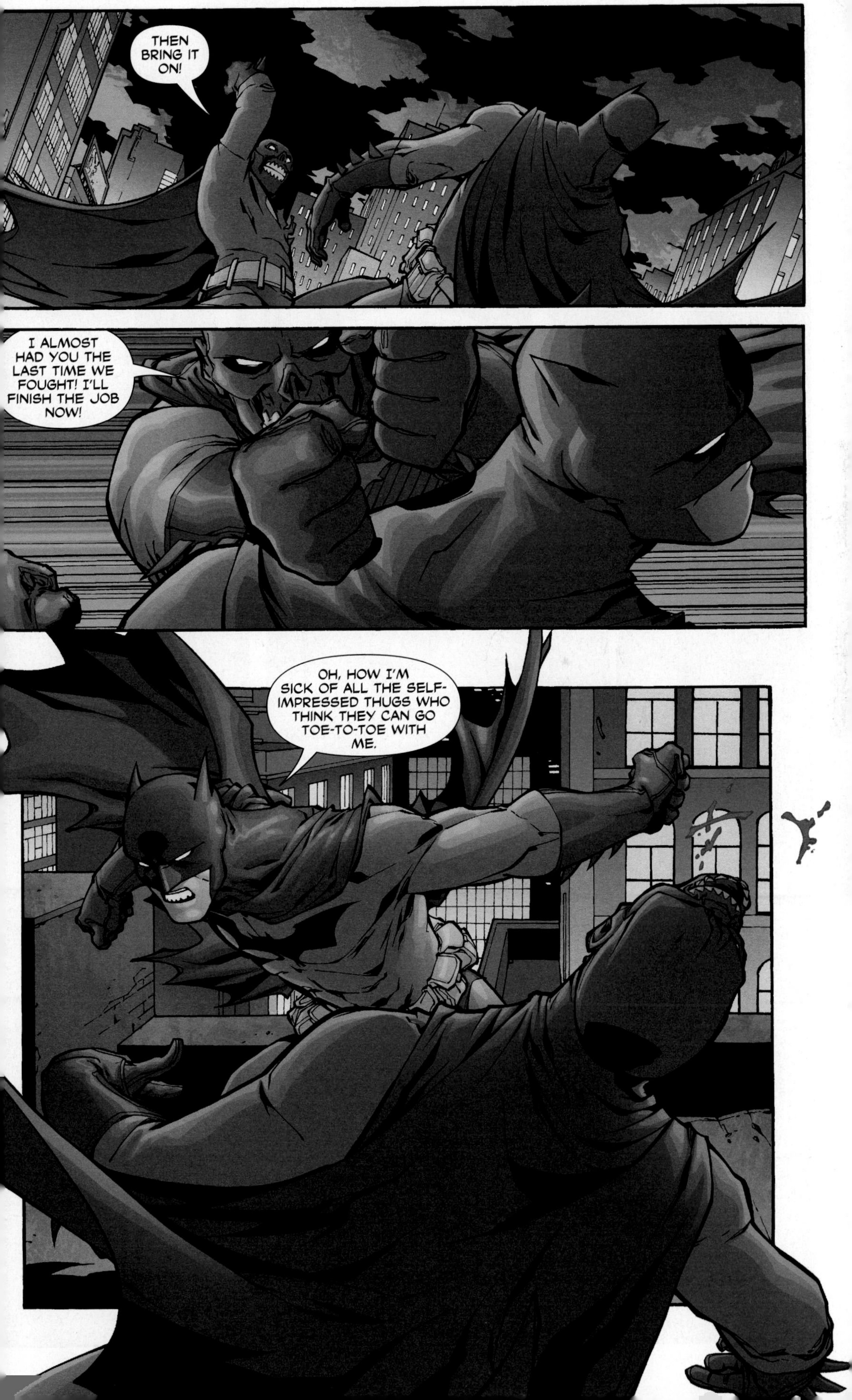
THEN BRING IT ON!
I ALMOST HAD YOU THE LAST TIME WE FOUGHT! I'LL FINISH THE JOB NOW!
OH, HOW I'M SICK OF ALL THE SELF-IMPRESSED THUGS WHO THINK THEY CAN GO TOE-TO-TOE WITH ME.

THE LAST TIME WE FOUGHT I WAS WOUNDED AND NEARLY EXHAUSTED FROM THREE DAYS OF NON-STOP FIGHTING.
AND EVEN WITH ALL THOSE ADVANTAGES, THE BEST YOU COULD DO WAS BARELY HOLD YOUR OWN.
PATHETIC.

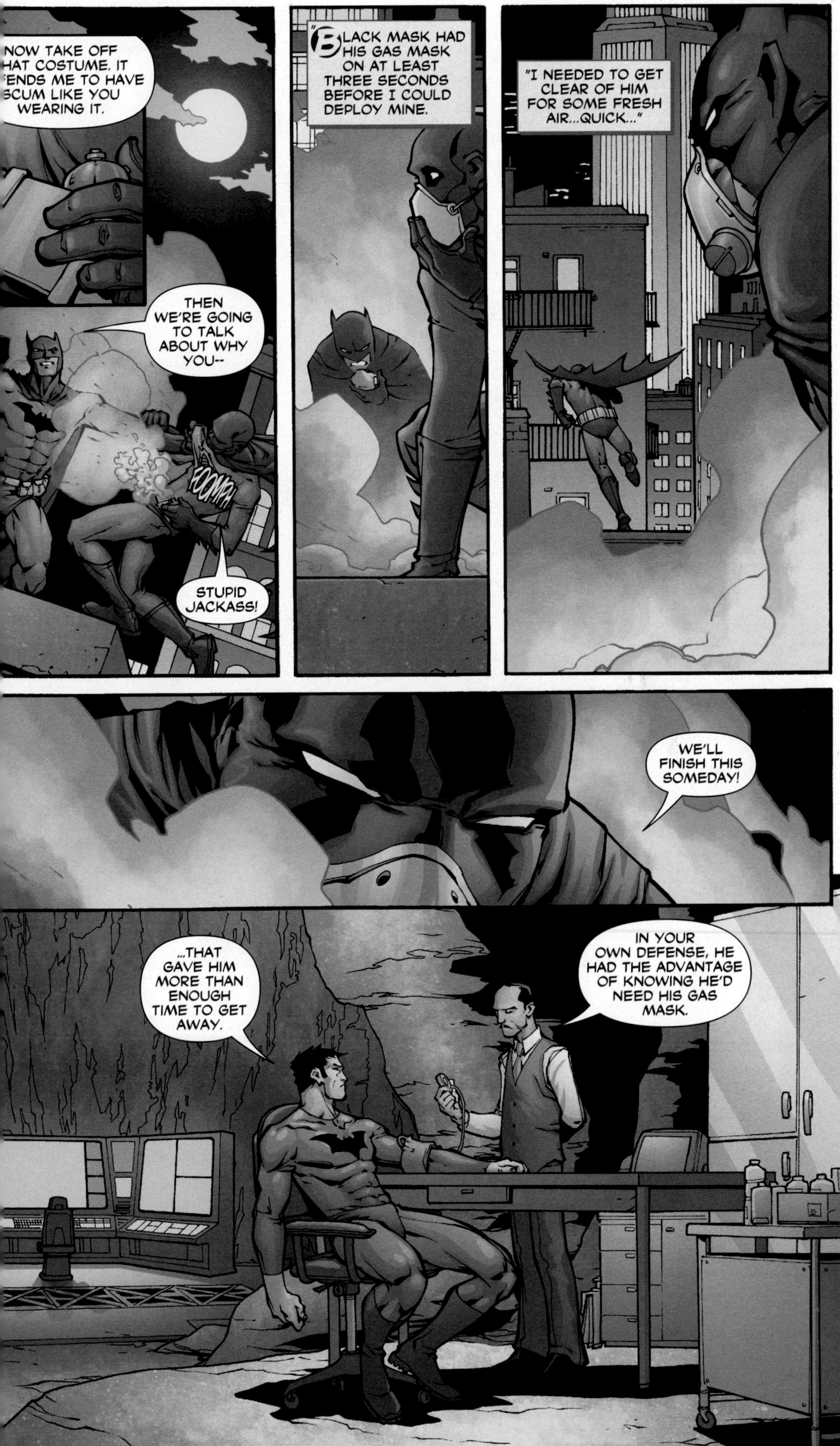
NOW TAKE OFF
HAT COSTUME. IT
FENDS ME TO HAVE
SCUM LIKE YOU
WEARING IT.
THEN WE'RE GOING TO TALK ABOUT WHY YOU--
FOOMPH
STUPID JACKASS!
"BLACK MASK HAD HIS GAS MASK ON AT LEAST THREE SECONDS BEFORE I COULD DEPLOY MINE.
"I NEEDED TO GET CLEAR OF HIM FOR SOME FRESH AIR...QUICK..."
WE'LL FINISH THIS SOMEDAY!
...THAT GAVE HIM MORE THAN ENOUGH TIME TO GET AWAY.
IN YOUR OWN DEFENSE, HE HAD THE ADVANTAGE OF KNOWING HE'D NEED HIS GAS MASK.

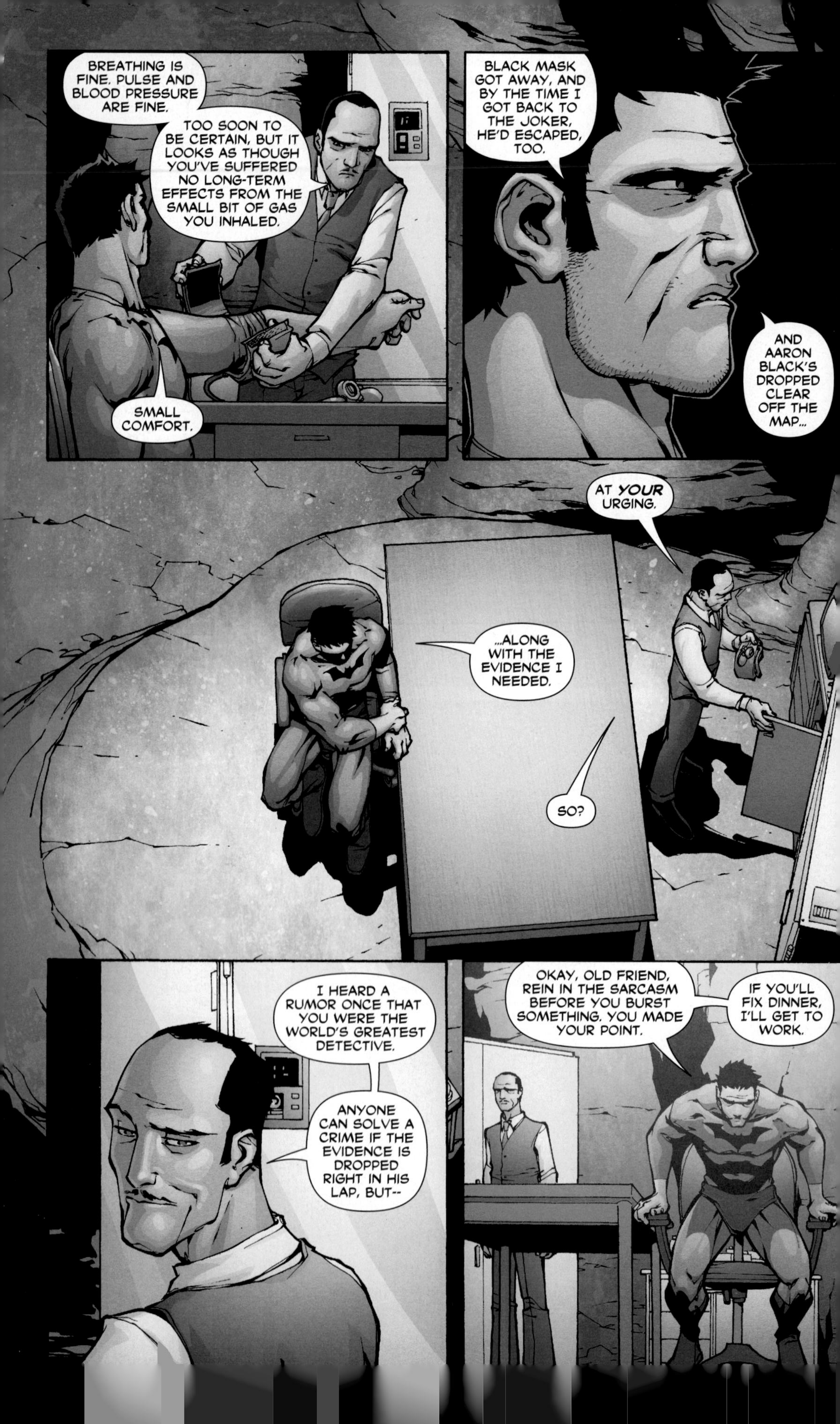
BREATHING IS FINE. PULSE AND BLOOD PRESSURE ARE FINE.
TOO SOON TO BE CERTAIN, BUT IT LOOKS AS THOUGH YOU'VE SUFFERED NO LONG-TERM EFFECTS FROM THE SMALL BIT OF GAS YOU INHALED.
SMALL COMFORT.
BLACK MASK GOT AWAY, AND BY THE TIME I GOT BACK TO THE JOKER, HE'D ESCAPED, TOO.
AND AARON BLACK'S DROPPED CLEAR OFF THE MAP...
AT *YOUR* URGING.
...ALONG WITH THE EVIDENCE I NEEDED.
SO?
I HEARD A RUMOR ONCE THAT YOU WERE THE WORLD'S GREATEST DETECTIVE.
ANYONE CAN SOLVE A CRIME IF THE EVIDENCE IS DROPPED RIGHT IN HIS LAP, BUT--
OKAY, OLD FRIEND, REIN IN THE SARCASM BEFORE YOU BURST SOMETHING. YOU MADE YOUR POINT.
IF YOU'LL FIX DINNER, I'LL GET TO WORK.

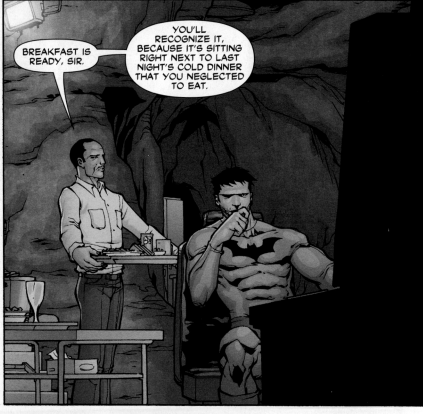

BREAKFAST IS READY, SIR.

YOU'LL RECOGNIZE IT, BECAUSE IT'S SITTING RIGHT NEXT TO LAST NIGHT'S COLD DINNER THAT YOU NEGLECTED TO EAT.

I PRESUME YOU'VE MADE PROGRESS?

SOME.

I'VE BEEN COMPARING VARIOUS OFFICIAL RECORDS RELATING TO THE GANG WAR AND THERE ARE IN- CONSISTENCIES.

LOOK AT THESE AFTER- ACTION RECORDS SUBMITTED BY LESLIE'S CLINIC.

THE TIMES AND QUANTITIES OF MEDICATIONS ADMINISTERED DON'T JIBE WITH THEIR NEXT RESTOCKING OF INVENTORY.

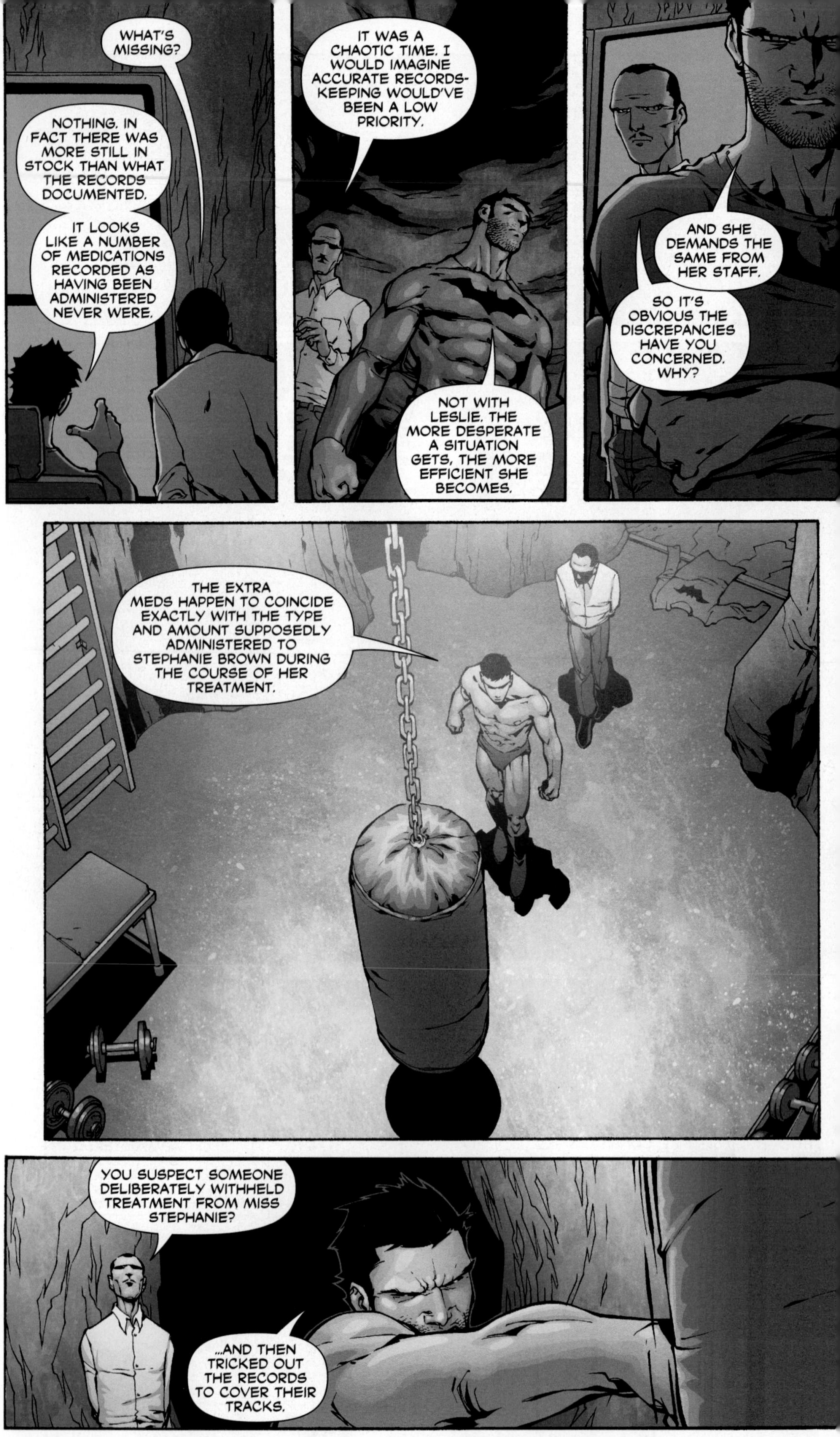
WHAT'S MISSING?
NOTHING. IN FACT THERE WAS MORE STILL IN STOCK THAN WHAT THE RECORDS DOCUMENTED.
IT LOOKS LIKE A NUMBER OF MEDICATIONS RECORDED AS HAVING BEEN ADMINISTERED NEVER WERE.
IT WAS A CHAOTIC TIME. I WOULD IMAGINE ACCURATE RECORDS-KEEPING WOULD'VE BEEN A LOW PRIORITY.
NOT WITH LESLIE. THE MORE DESPERATE A SITUATION GETS, THE MORE EFFICIENT SHE BECOMES.
AND SHE DEMANDS THE SAME FROM HER STAFF.
SO IT'S OBVIOUS THE DISCREPANCIES HAVE YOU CONCERNED. WHY?
THE EXTRA MEDS HAPPEN TO COINCIDE EXACTLY WITH THE TYPE AND AMOUNT SUPPOSEDLY ADMINISTERED TO STEPHANIE BROWN DURING THE COURSE OF HER TREATMENT.
YOU SUSPECT SOMEONE DELIBERATELY WITHHELD TREATMENT FROM MISS STEPHANIE?
...AND THEN TRICKED OUT THE RECORDS TO COVER THEIR TRACKS.

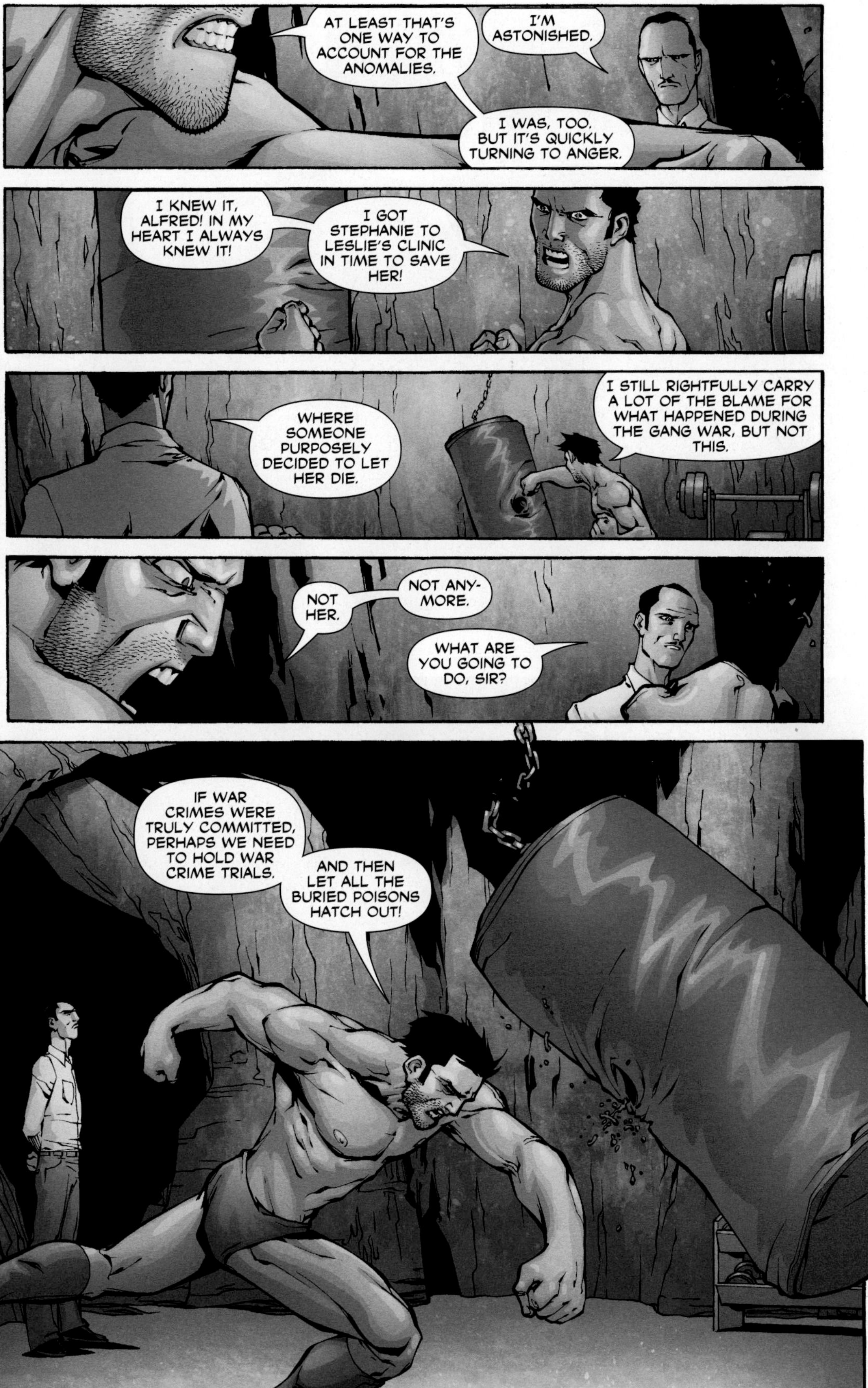
AT LEAST THAT'S ONE WAY TO ACCOUNT FOR THE ANOMALIES.
I'M ASTONISHED.
I WAS, TOO. BUT IT'S QUICKLY TURNING TO ANGER.
I KNEW IT, ALFRED! IN MY HEART I ALWAYS KNEW IT!
I GOT STEPHANIE TO LESLIE'S CLINIC IN TIME TO SAVE HER!
WHERE SOMEONE PURPOSELY DECIDED TO LET HER DIE.
I STILL RIGHTFULLY CARRY A LOT OF THE BLAME FOR WHAT HAPPENED DURING THE GANG WAR, BUT NOT THIS.
NOT HER.
NOT ANY-MORE.
WHAT ARE YOU GOING TO DO, SIR?
IF WAR CRIMES WERE TRULY COMMITTED, PERHAPS WE NEED TO HOLD WAR CRIME TRIALS.
AND THEN LET ALL THE BURIED POISONS HATCH OUT!

WELCOME BACK TO "GOOD MORNING GOTHAM!" NOW, BEFORE WE GO TO SUSAN SASH AND THE WEATHER, WE WANT TO REMIND YOU NOT TO MISS TODAY'S SIZZLING EDITION OF "TAKING SIDES WITH ARTURO!"

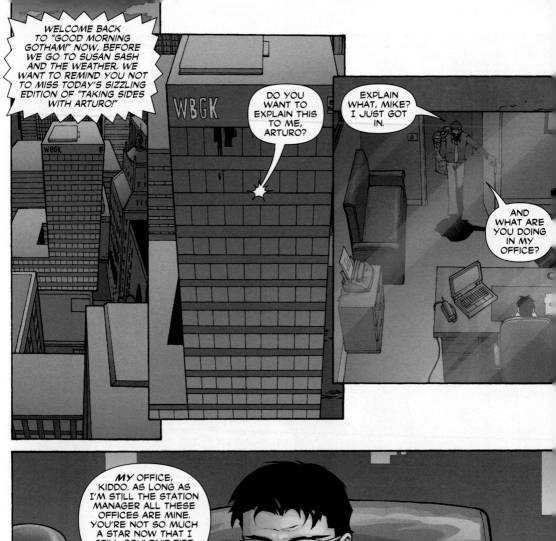

DO YOU WANT TO EXPLAIN THIS TO ME, ARTURO?

EXPLAIN WHAT, MIKE? I JUST GOT IN.

AND WHAT ARE YOU DOING IN MY OFFICE?

MY OFFICE, KIDDO. AS LONG AS I'M STILL THE STATION MANAGER ALL THESE OFFICES ARE MINE. YOU'RE NOT SO MUCH A STAR NOW THAT I STILL COULDN'T FIRE YOU IN A GOTHAM SECOND.

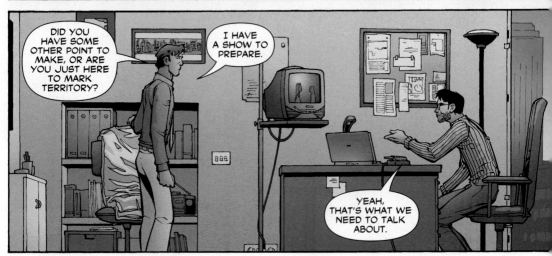

DID YOU HAVE SOME OTHER POINT TO MAKE, OR ARE YOU JUST HERE TO MARK TERRITORY?

I HAVE A SHOW TO PREPARE.

YEAH, THAT'S WHAT WE NEED TO TALK ABOUT.

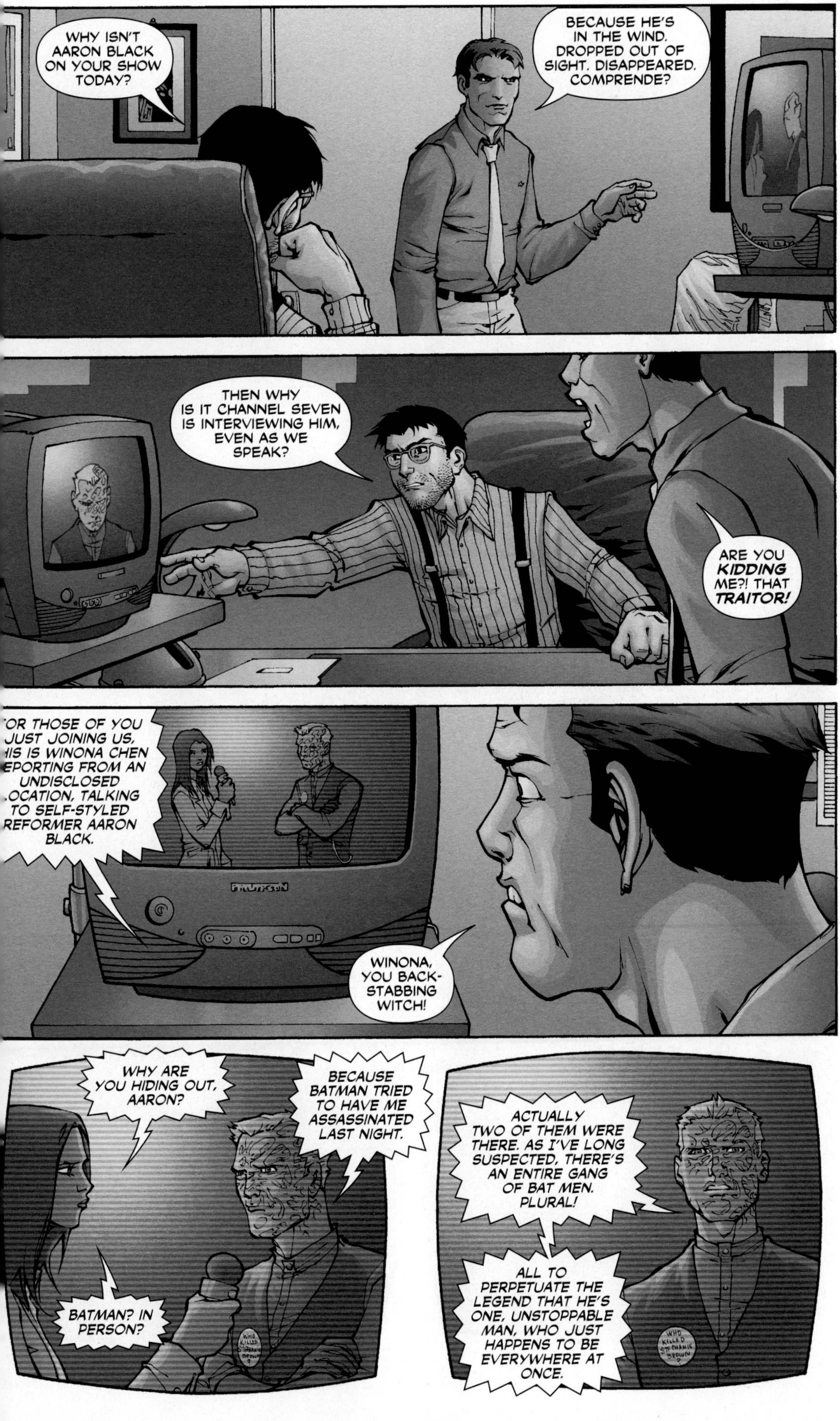
WHY ISN'T AARON BLACK ON YOUR SHOW TODAY?
BECAUSE HE'S IN THE WIND. DROPPED OUT OF SIGHT. DISAPPEARED. COMPRENDE?
THEN WHY IS IT CHANNEL SEVEN IS INTERVIEWING HIM, EVEN AS WE SPEAK?
ARE YOU *KIDDING* ME?! THAT *TRAITOR!*
OR THOSE OF YOU JUST JOINING US, HIS IS WINONA CHEN EPORTING FROM AN UNDISCLOSED OCATION, TALKING TO SELF-STYLED REFORMER AARON BLACK.
WINONA, YOU BACK-STABBING WITCH!
WHY ARE YOU HIDING OUT, AARON?
BECAUSE BATMAN TRIED TO HAVE ME ASSASSINATED LAST NIGHT.
BATMAN? IN PERSON?
ACTUALLY TWO OF THEM WERE THERE. AS I'VE LONG SUSPECTED, THERE'S AN ENTIRE GANG OF BAT MEN. PLURAL!
ALL TO PERPETUATE THE LEGEND THAT HE'S ONE, UNSTOPPABLE MAN, WHO JUST HAPPENS TO BE EVERYWHERE AT ONCE.

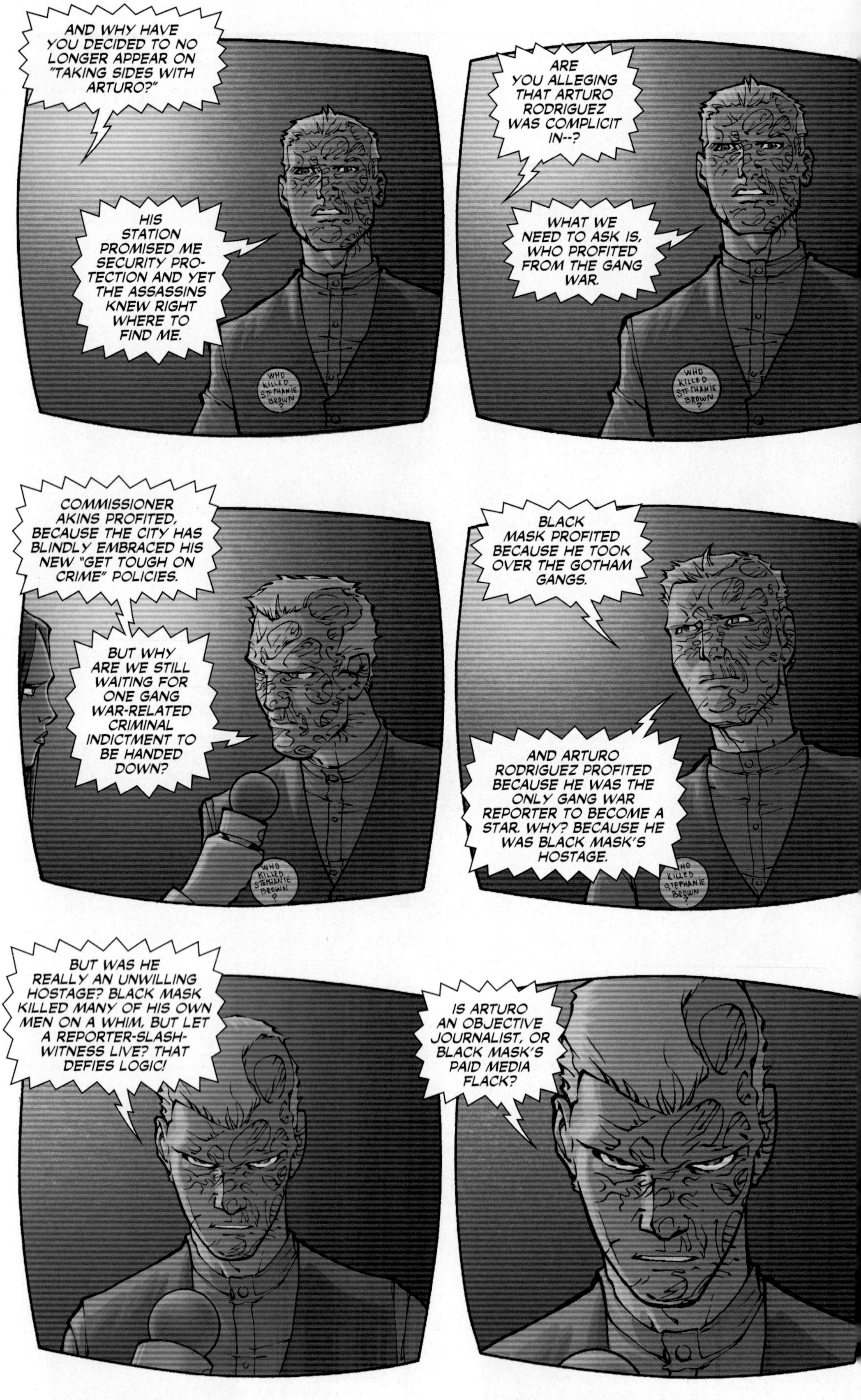
AND WHY HAVE YOU DECIDED TO NO LONGER APPEAR ON "TAKING SIDES WITH ARTURO?"
HIS STATION PROMISED ME SECURITY PROTECTION AND YET THE ASSASSINS KNEW RIGHT WHERE TO FIND ME.
WHO KILLED STEPHANIE BROWN?
ARE YOU ALLEGING THAT ARTURO RODRIGUEZ WAS COMPLICIT IN--?
WHAT WE NEED TO ASK IS, WHO PROFITED FROM THE GANG WAR.
WHO KILLED STEPHANIE BROWN?
COMMISSIONER AKINS PROFITED, BECAUSE THE CITY HAS BLINDLY EMBRACED HIS NEW "GET TOUGH ON CRIME" POLICIES.
BUT WHY ARE WE STILL WAITING FOR ONE GANG WAR-RELATED CRIMINAL INDICTMENT TO BE HANDED DOWN?
WHO KILLED STEPHANIE BROWN?
BLACK MASK PROFITED BECAUSE HE TOOK OVER THE GOTHAM GANGS.
AND ARTURO RODRIGUEZ PROFITED BECAUSE HE WAS THE ONLY GANG WAR REPORTER TO BECOME A STAR. WHY? BECAUSE HE WAS BLACK MASK'S HOSTAGE.
WHO KILLED STEPHANIE BROWN?
BUT WAS HE REALLY AN UNWILLING HOSTAGE? BLACK MASK KILLED MANY OF HIS OWN MEN ON A WHIM, BUT LET A REPORTER-SLASH-WITNESS LIVE? THAT DEFIES LOGIC!
IS ARTURO AN OBJECTIVE JOURNALIST, OR BLACK MASK'S PAID MEDIA FLACK?

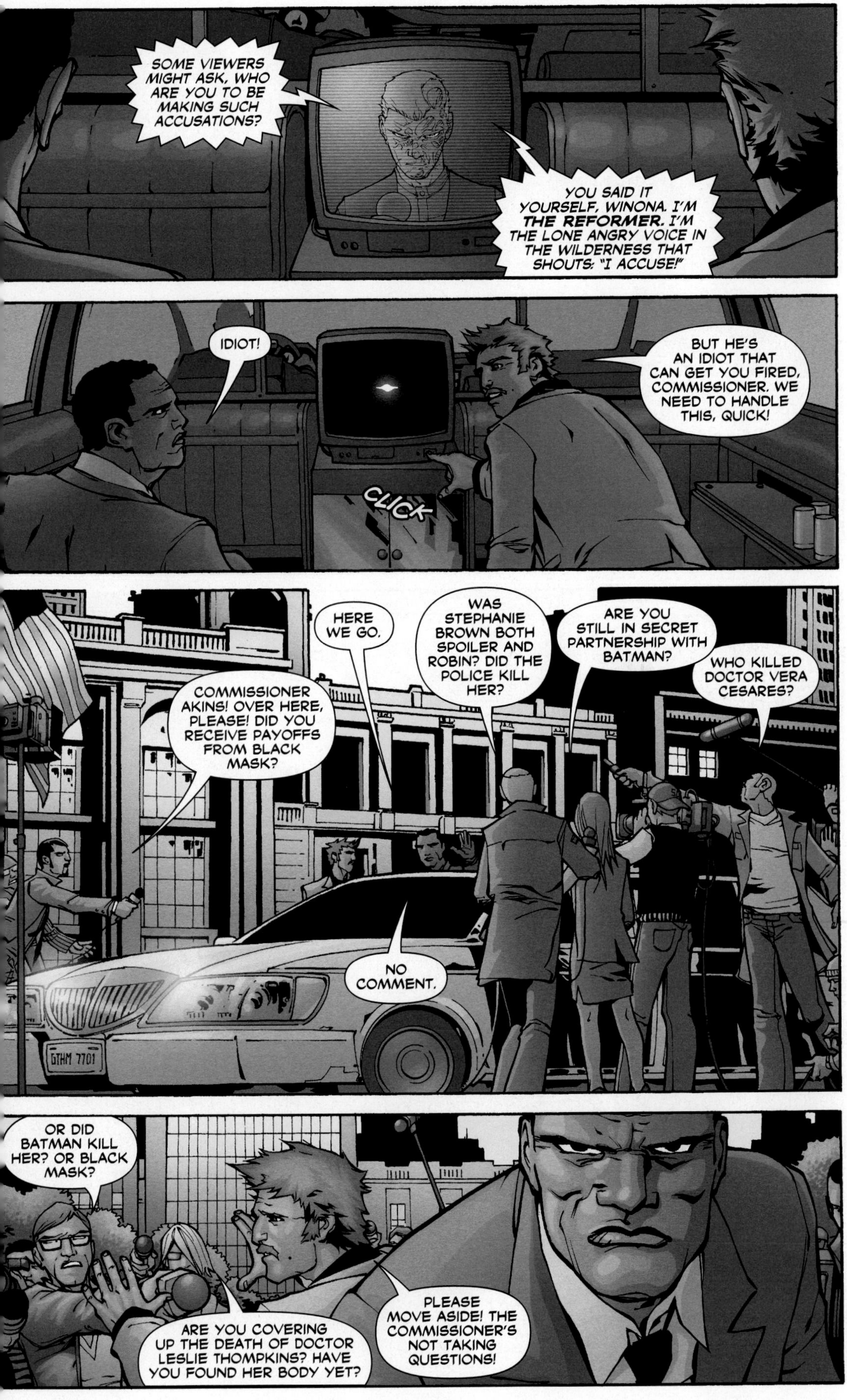

SOME VIEWERS MIGHT ASK, WHO ARE YOU TO BE MAKING SUCH ACCUSATIONS?
YOU SAID IT YOURSELF, WINONA. I'M THE REFORMER. I'M THE LONE ANGRY VOICE IN THE WILDERNESS THAT SHOUTS: "I ACCUSE!"
IDIOT!
BUT HE'S AN IDIOT THAT CAN GET YOU FIRED, COMMISSIONER. WE NEED TO HANDLE THIS, QUICK!
CLICK
COMMISSIONER AKINS! OVER HERE, PLEASE! DID YOU RECEIVE PAYOFFS FROM BLACK MASK?
HERE WE GO.
WAS STEPHANIE BROWN BOTH SPOILER AND ROBIN? DID THE POLICE KILL HER?
ARE YOU STILL IN SECRET PARTNERSHIP WITH BATMAN?
WHO KILLED DOCTOR VERA CESARES?
NO COMMENT.
GTHM 7701
OR DID BATMAN KILL HER? OR BLACK MASK?
ARE YOU COVERING UP THE DEATH OF DOCTOR LESLIE THOMPKINS? HAVE YOU FOUND HER BODY YET?
PLEASE MOVE ASIDE! THE COMMISSIONER'S NOT TAKING QUESTIONS!

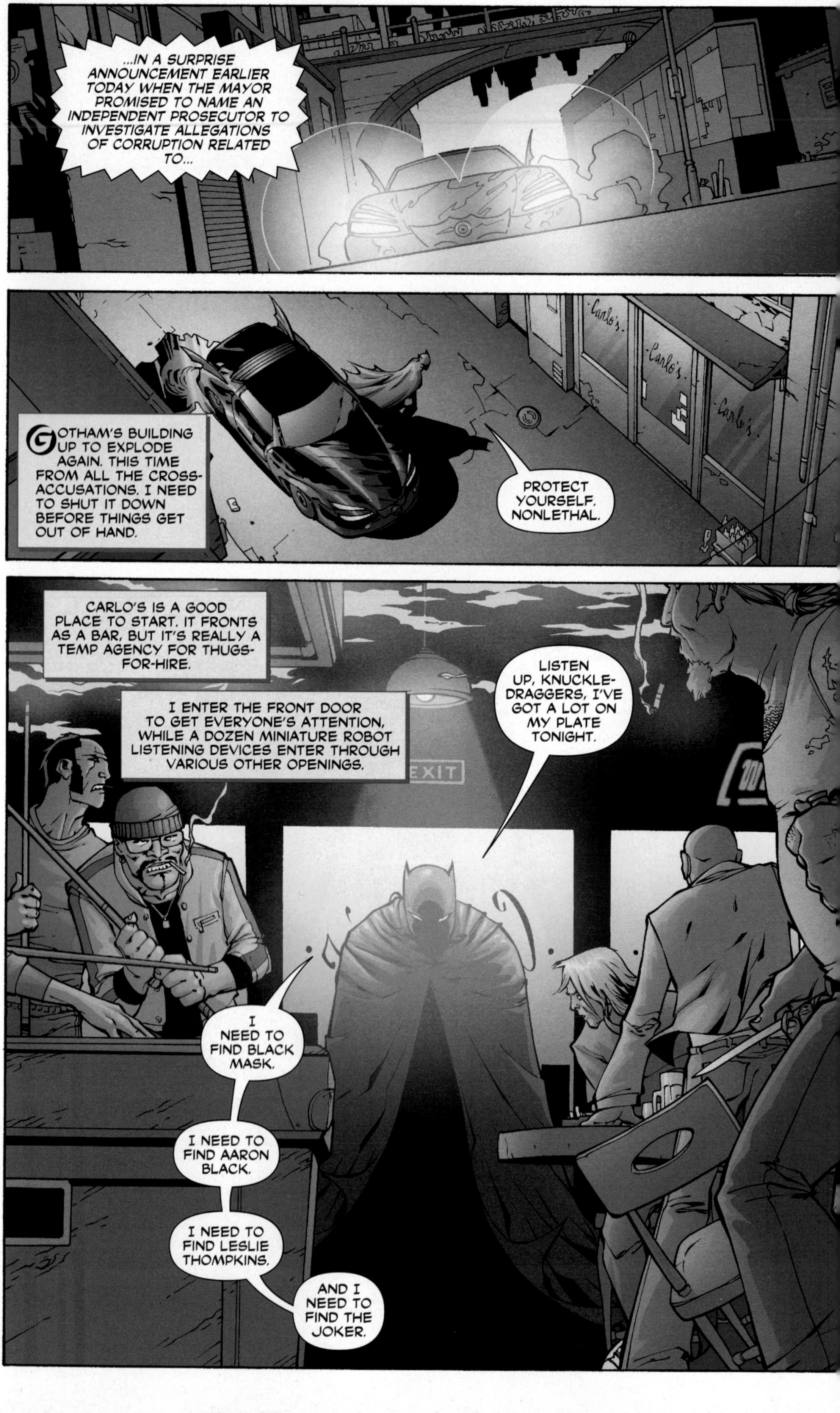
...IN A SURPRISE ANNOUNCEMENT EARLIER TODAY WHEN THE MAYOR PROMISED TO NAME AN INDEPENDENT PROSECUTOR TO INVESTIGATE ALLEGATIONS OF CORRUPTION RELATED TO...
GOTHAM'S BUILDING UP TO EXPLODE AGAIN. THIS TIME FROM ALL THE CROSS-ACCUSATIONS. I NEED TO SHUT IT DOWN BEFORE THINGS GET OUT OF HAND.
Carlo's
PROTECT YOURSELF. NONLETHAL.
CARLO'S IS A GOOD PLACE TO START. IT FRONTS AS A BAR, BUT IT'S REALLY A TEMP AGENCY FOR THUGS-FOR-HIRE.
I ENTER THE FRONT DOOR TO GET EVERYONE'S ATTENTION, WHILE A DOZEN MINIATURE ROBOT LISTENING DEVICES ENTER THROUGH VARIOUS OTHER OPENINGS.
EXIT
LISTEN UP, KNUCKLE-DRAGGERS, I'VE GOT A LOT ON MY PLATE TONIGHT.
I NEED TO FIND BLACK MASK.
I NEED TO FIND AARON BLACK.
I NEED TO FIND LESLIE THOMPKINS.
AND I NEED TO FIND THE JOKER.

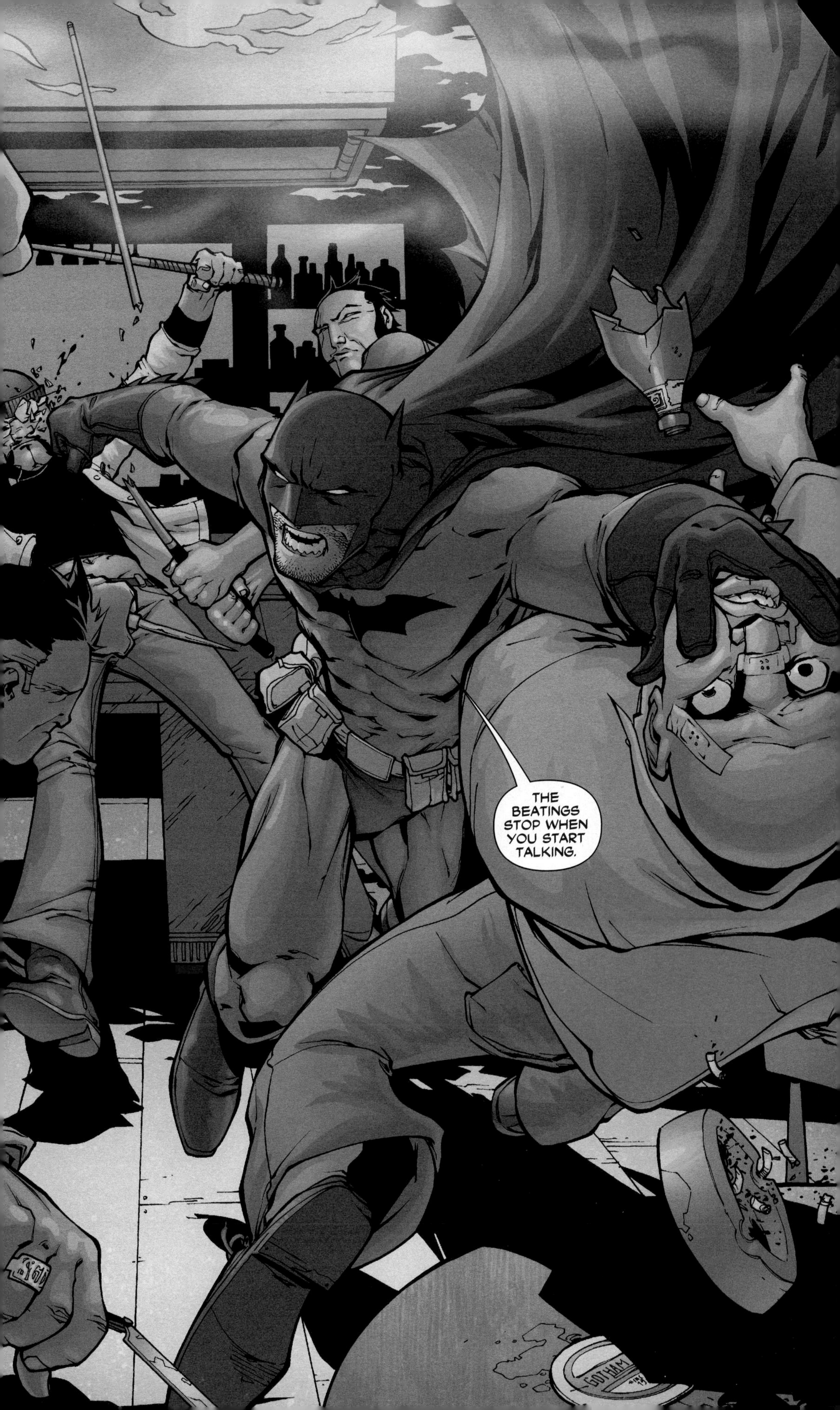
THE BEATINGS STOP WHEN YOU START TALKING.

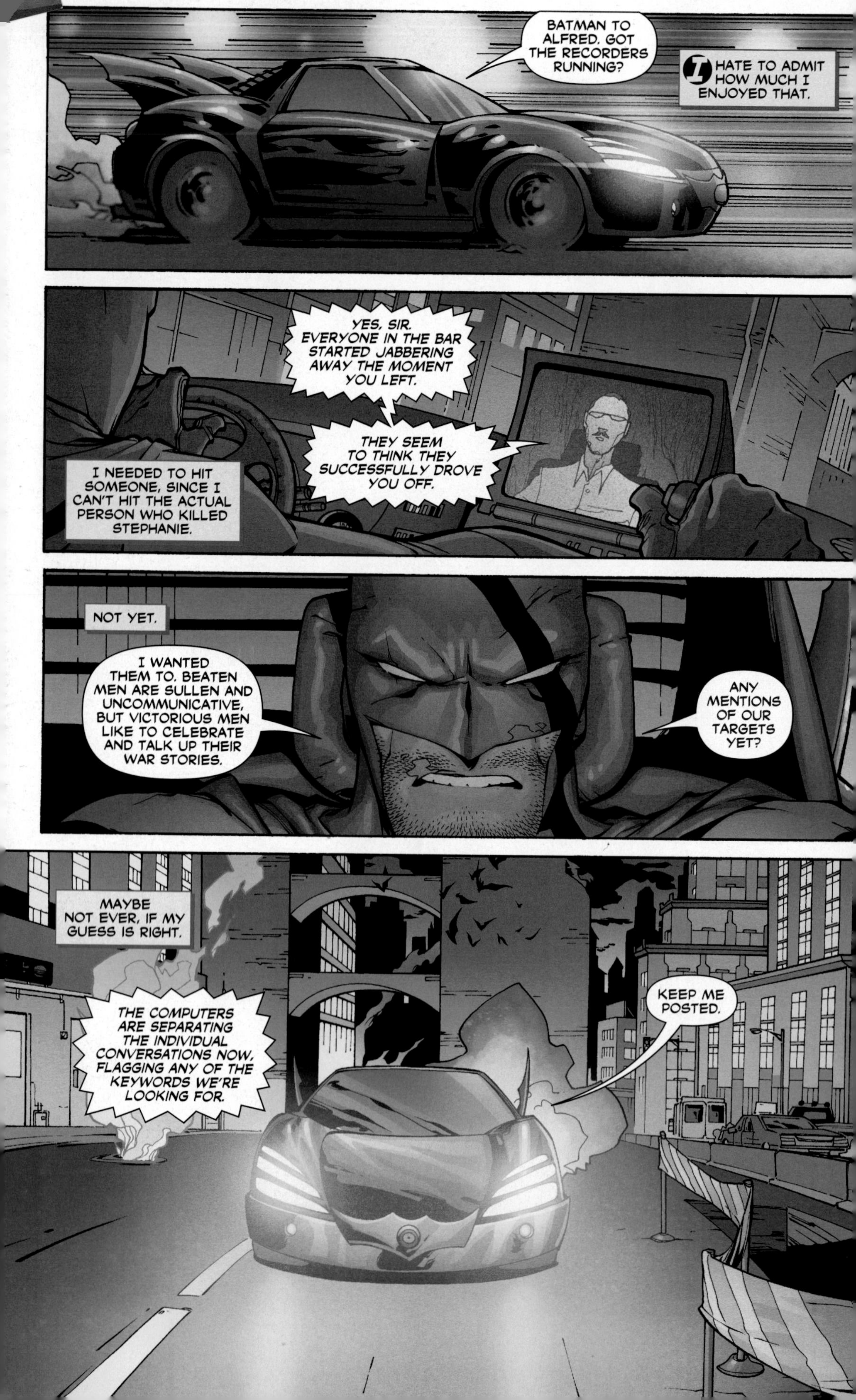
BATMAN TO ALFRED. GOT THE RECORDERS RUNNING?
I HATE TO ADMIT HOW MUCH I ENJOYED THAT.
YES, SIR. EVERYONE IN THE BAR STARTED JABBERING AWAY THE MOMENT YOU LEFT.
THEY SEEM TO THINK THEY SUCCESSFULLY DROVE YOU OFF.
I NEEDED TO HIT SOMEONE, SINCE I CAN'T HIT THE ACTUAL PERSON WHO KILLED STEPHANIE.
NOT YET.
I WANTED THEM TO. BEATEN MEN ARE SULLEN AND UNCOMMUNICATIVE, BUT VICTORIOUS MEN LIKE TO CELEBRATE AND TALK UP THEIR WAR STORIES.
ANY MENTIONS OF OUR TARGETS YET?
MAYBE NOT EVER, IF MY GUESS IS RIGHT.
THE COMPUTERS ARE SEPARATING THE INDIVIDUAL CONVERSATIONS NOW, FLAGGING ANY OF THE KEYWORDS WE'RE LOOKING FOR.
KEEP ME POSTED.

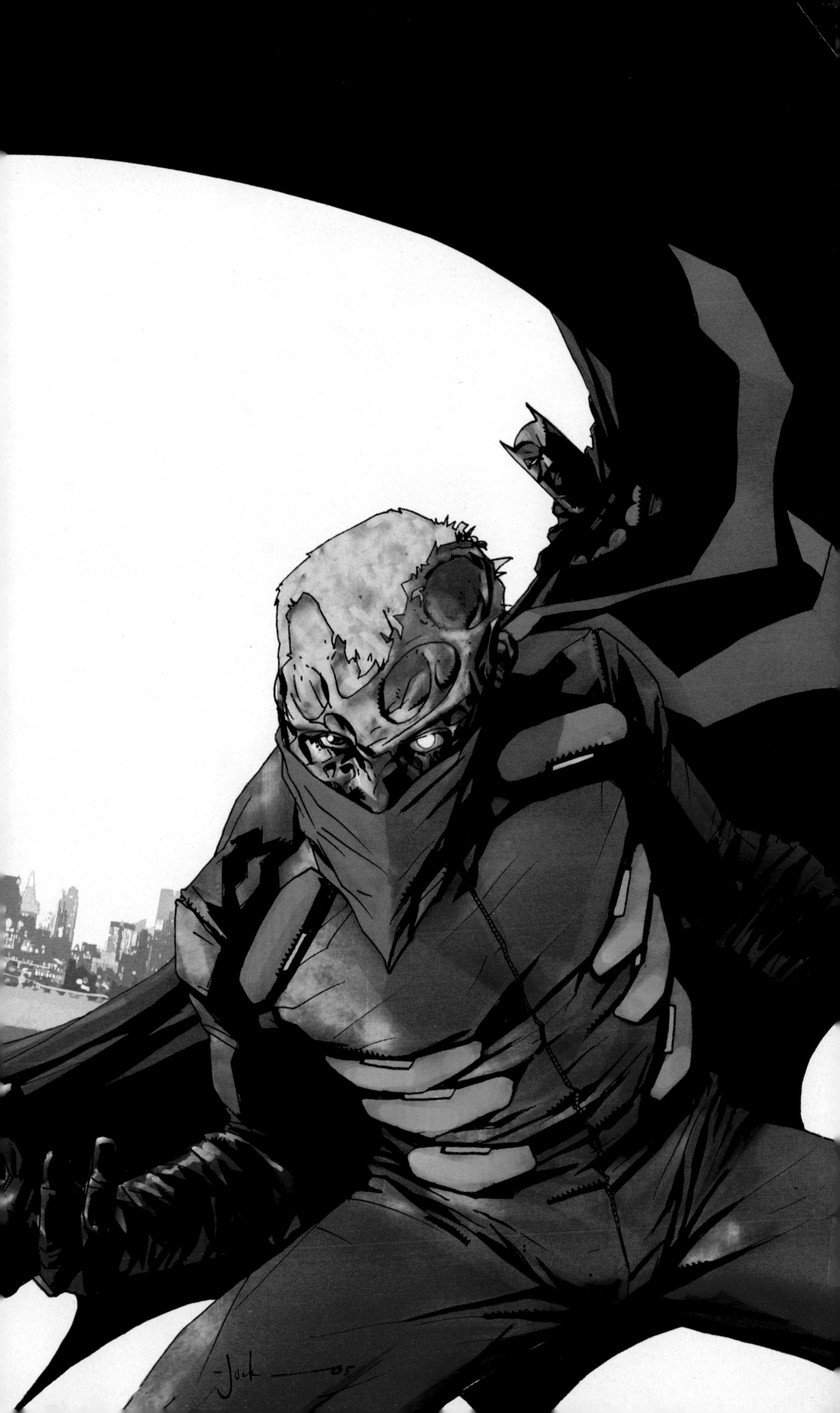

COVER ART BY
JOCK

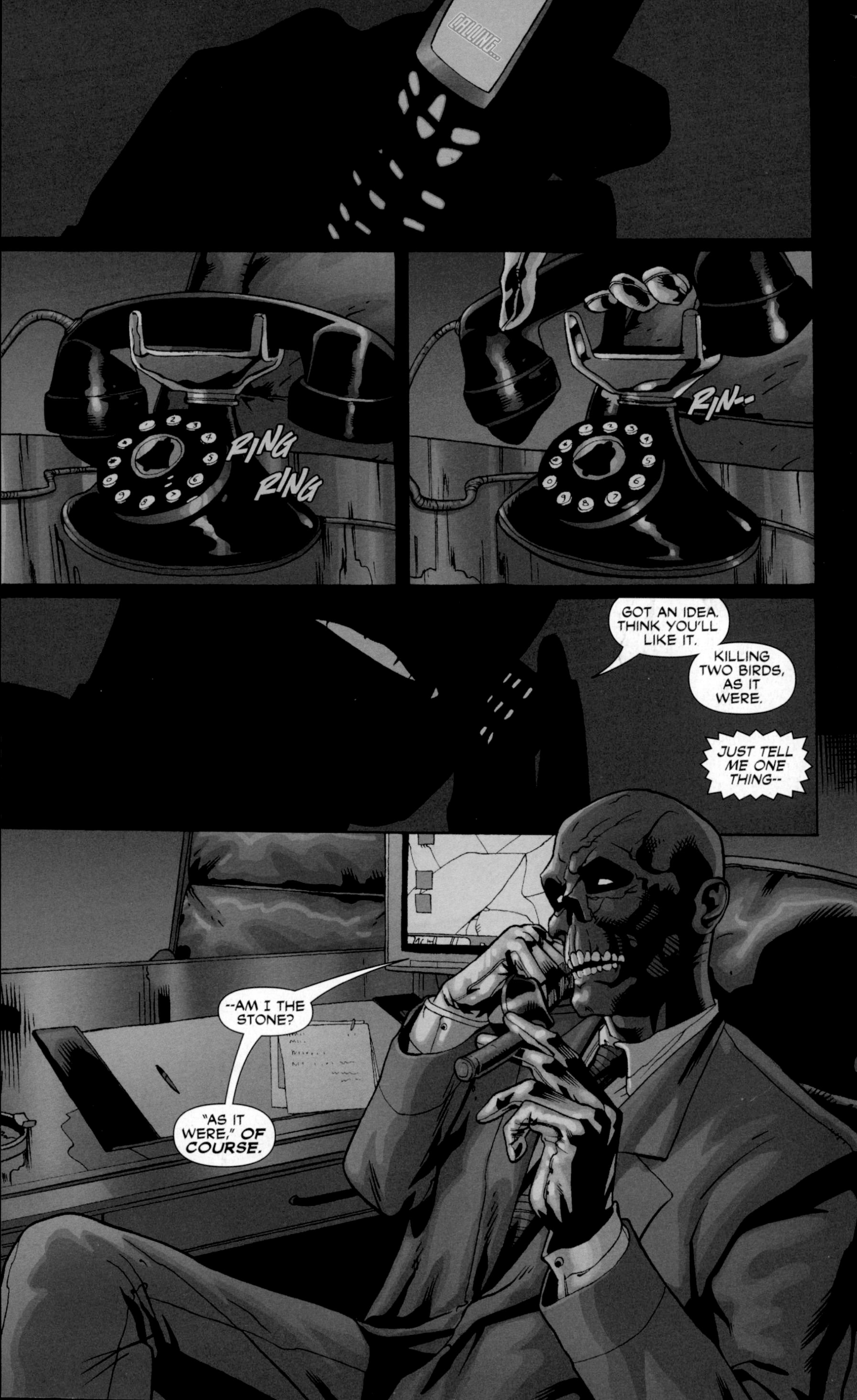
CALLING...
RING
RING
RIN--
GOT AN IDEA. THINK YOU'LL LIKE IT.
KILLING TWO BIRDS, AS IT WERE.
JUST TELL ME ONE THING--
--AM I THE STONE?
"AS IT WERE," OF COURSE.

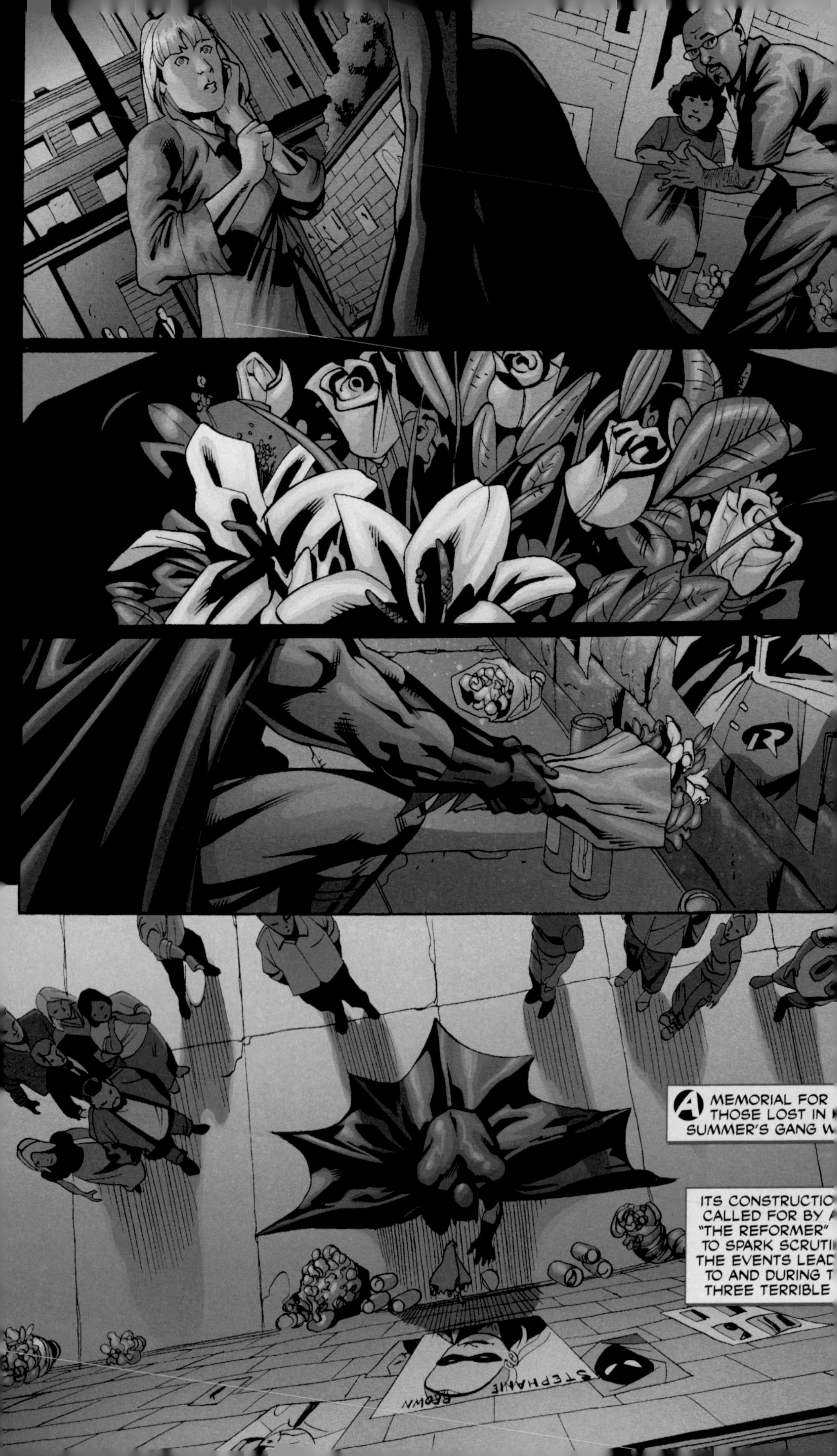
MEMORIAL FOR
THOSE LOST IN
SUMMER'S GANG W
ITS CONSTRUCTIO
CALLED FOR BY
"THE REFORMER"
TO SPARK SCRUTI
THE EVENTS LEAD
TO AND DURING T
THREE TERRIBLE
STEPHANIE
BROWN

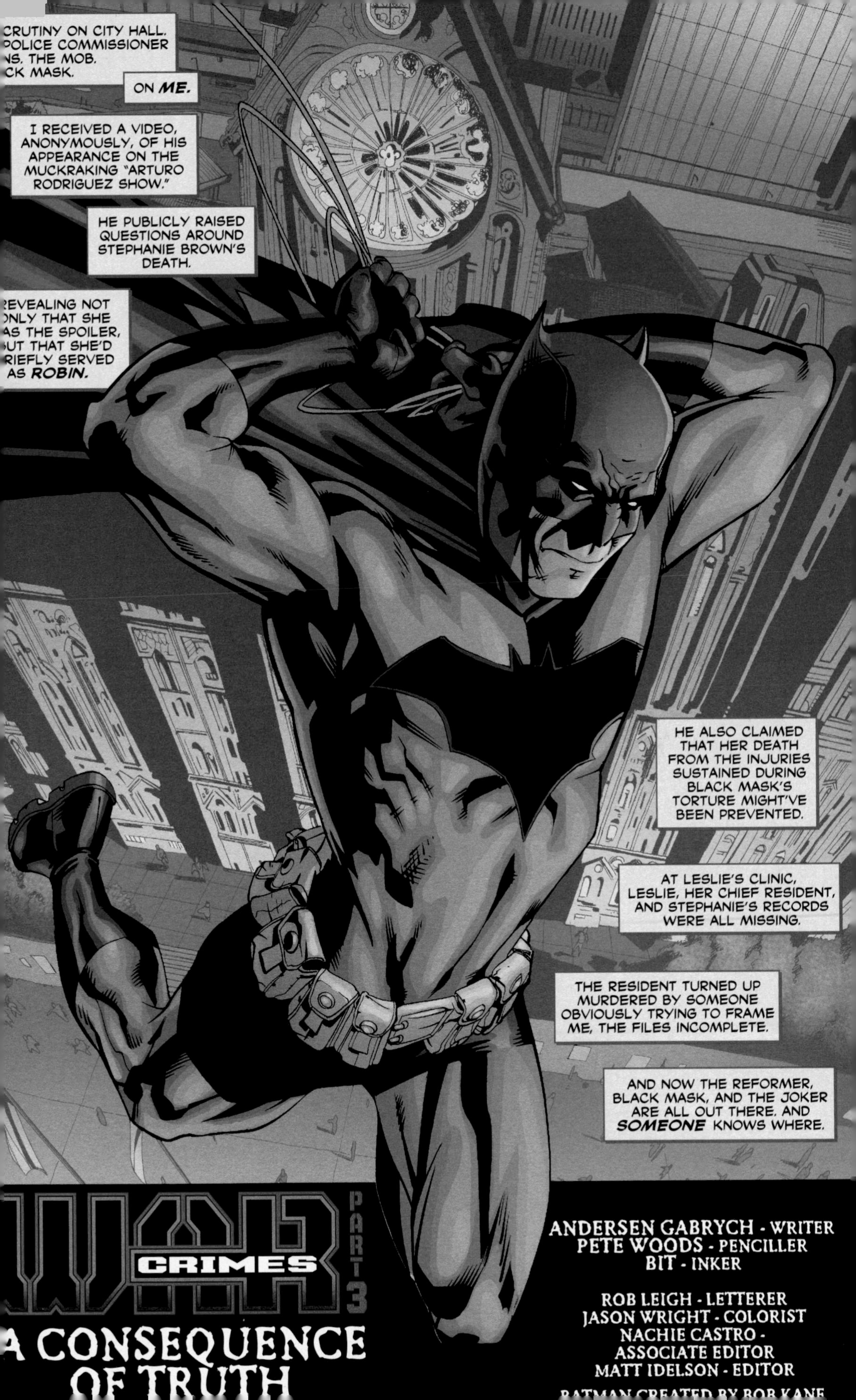

CRUTINY ON CITY HALL.
POLICE COMMISSIONER
NS. THE MOB.
CK MASK.
ON ME.
I RECEIVED A VIDEO, ANONYMOUSLY, OF HIS APPEARANCE ON THE MUCKRAKING "ARTURO RODRIGUEZ SHOW."
HE PUBLICLY RAISED QUESTIONS AROUND STEPHANIE BROWN'S DEATH.
EVEALING NOT
NLY THAT SHE
AS THE SPOILER,
UT THAT SHE'D
RIEFLY SERVED
AS ROBIN.
HE ALSO CLAIMED THAT HER DEATH FROM THE INJURIES SUSTAINED DURING BLACK MASK'S TORTURE MIGHT'VE BEEN PREVENTED.
AT LESLIE'S CLINIC, LESLIE, HER CHIEF RESIDENT, AND STEPHANIE'S RECORDS WERE ALL MISSING.
THE RESIDENT TURNED UP MURDERED BY SOMEONE OBVIOUSLY TRYING TO FRAME ME, THE FILES INCOMPLETE.
AND NOW THE REFORMER, BLACK MASK, AND THE JOKER ARE ALL OUT THERE. AND SOMEONE KNOWS WHERE.
WAR CRIMES PART 3
A CONSEQUENCE OF TRUTH
ANDERSEN GABRYCH - WRITER
PETE WOODS - PENCILLER
BIT - INKER
ROB LEIGH - LETTERER
JASON WRIGHT - COLORIST
NACHIE CASTRO - ASSOCIATE EDITOR
MATT IDELSON - EDITOR
BATMAN CREATED BY BOB KANE

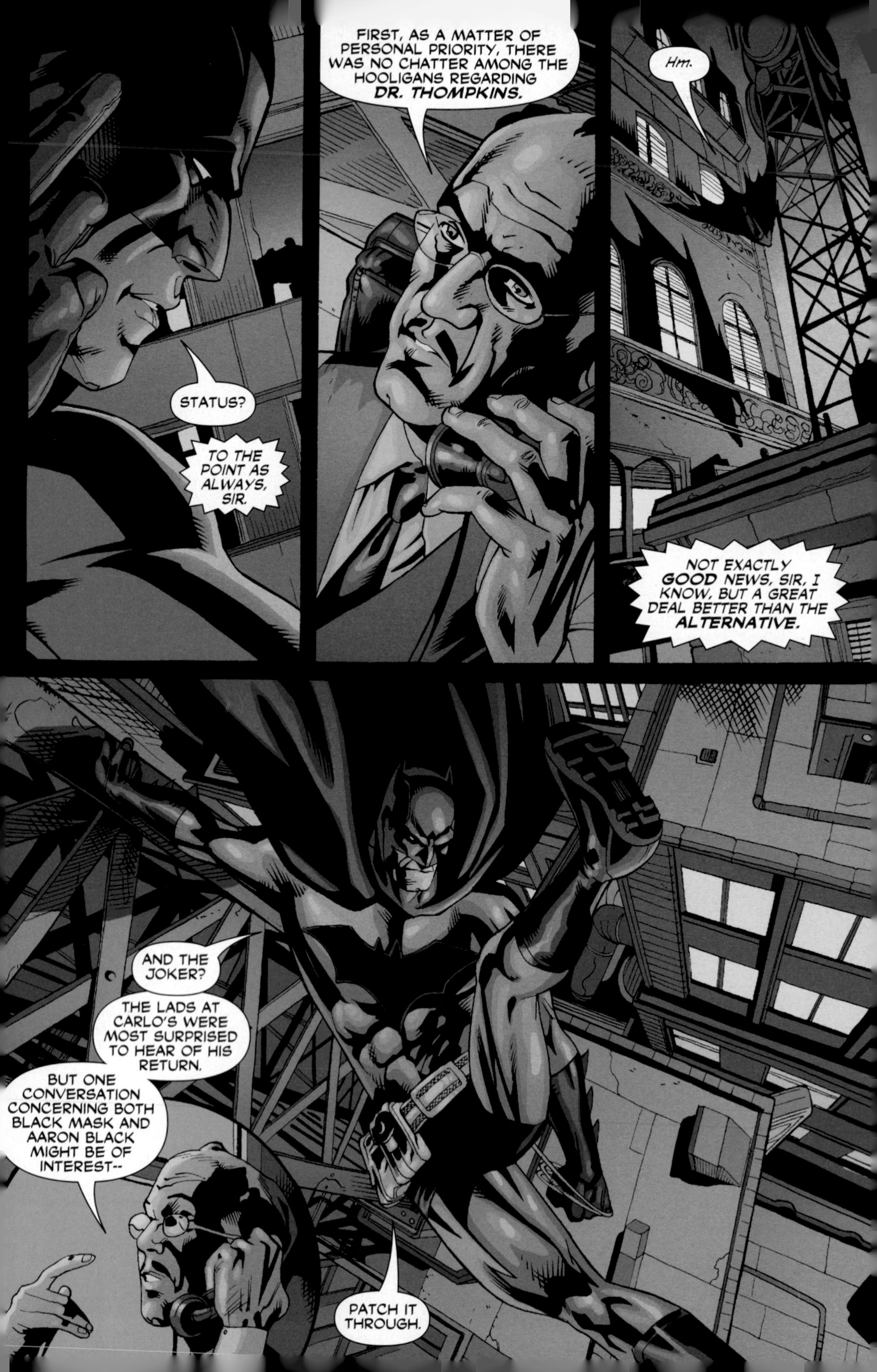

STATUS?
TO THE POINT AS ALWAYS, SIR.
FIRST, AS A MATTER OF PERSONAL PRIORITY, THERE WAS NO CHATTER AMONG THE HOOLIGANS REGARDING DR. THOMPKINS.
Hm.
NOT EXACTLY GOOD NEWS, SIR, I KNOW, BUT A GREAT DEAL BETTER THAN THE ALTERNATIVE.
AND THE JOKER?
THE LADS AT CARLO'S WERE MOST SURPRISED TO HEAR OF HIS RETURN.
BUT ONE CONVERSATION CONCERNING BOTH BLACK MASK AND AARON BLACK MIGHT BE OF INTEREST--
PATCH IT THROUGH.

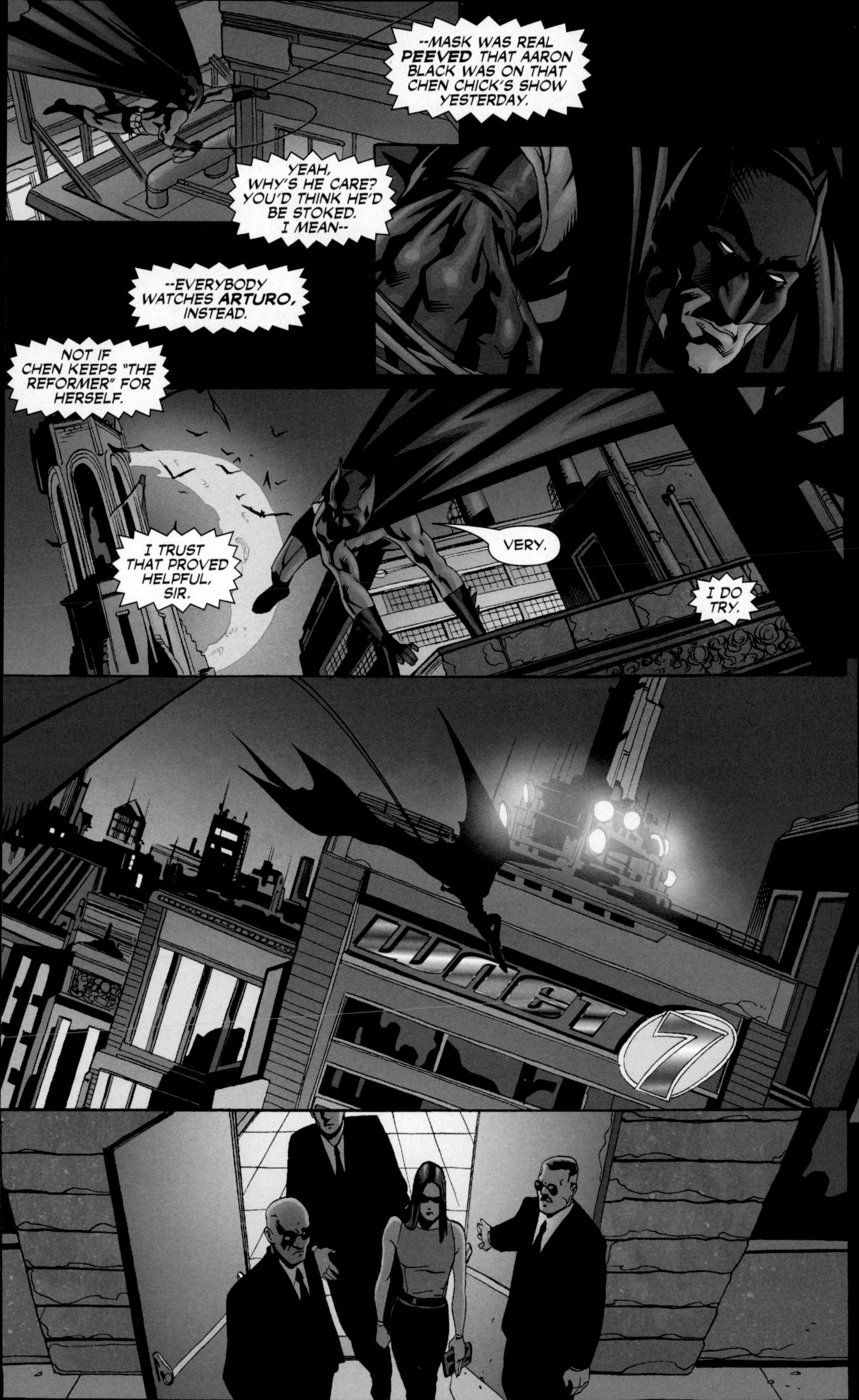
--MASK WAS REAL PEEVED THAT AARON BLACK WAS ON THAT CHEN CHICK'S SHOW YESTERDAY.
YEAH, WHY'S HE CARE? YOU'D THINK HE'D BE STOKED. I MEAN--
--EVERYBODY WATCHES ARTURO, INSTEAD.
NOT IF CHEN KEEPS "THE REFORMER" FOR HERSELF.
I TRUST THAT PROVED HELPFUL, SIR.
VERY.
I DO TRY.
WNCT 7

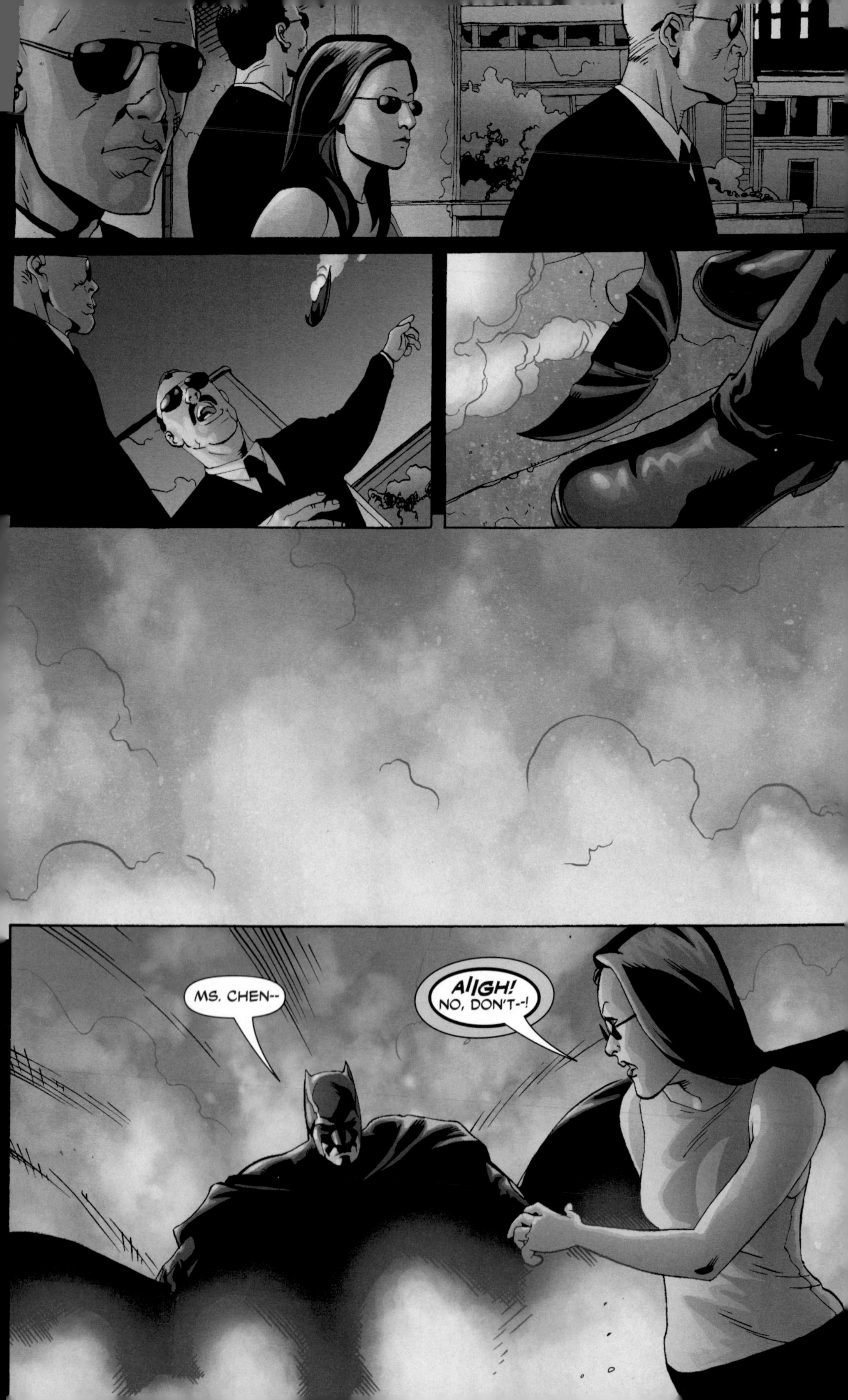
MS. CHEN--
AIIGH!
NO, DON'T--!

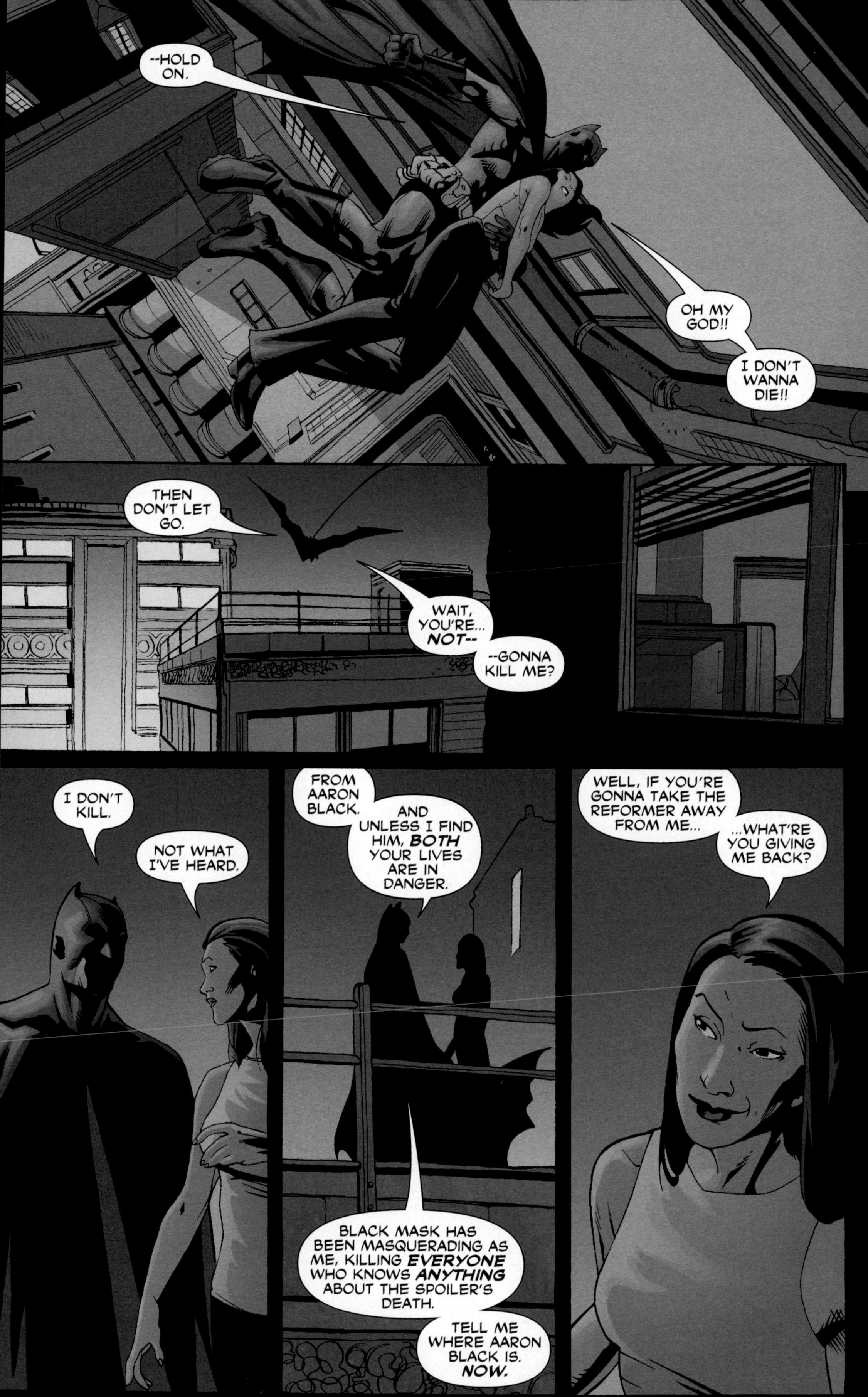
--HOLD ON.
OH MY GOD!!
I DON'T WANNA DIE!!
THEN DON'T LET GO.
WAIT, YOU'RE... NOT--
--GONNA KILL ME?
I DON'T KILL.
NOT WHAT I'VE HEARD.
FROM AARON BLACK.
AND UNLESS I FIND HIM, BOTH YOUR LIVES ARE IN DANGER.
BLACK MASK HAS BEEN MASQUERADING AS ME, KILLING EVERYONE WHO KNOWS ANYTHING ABOUT THE SPOILER'S DEATH.
TELL ME WHERE AARON BLACK IS. NOW.
WELL, IF YOU'RE GONNA TAKE THE REFORMER AWAY FROM ME...
...WHAT'RE YOU GIVING ME BACK?

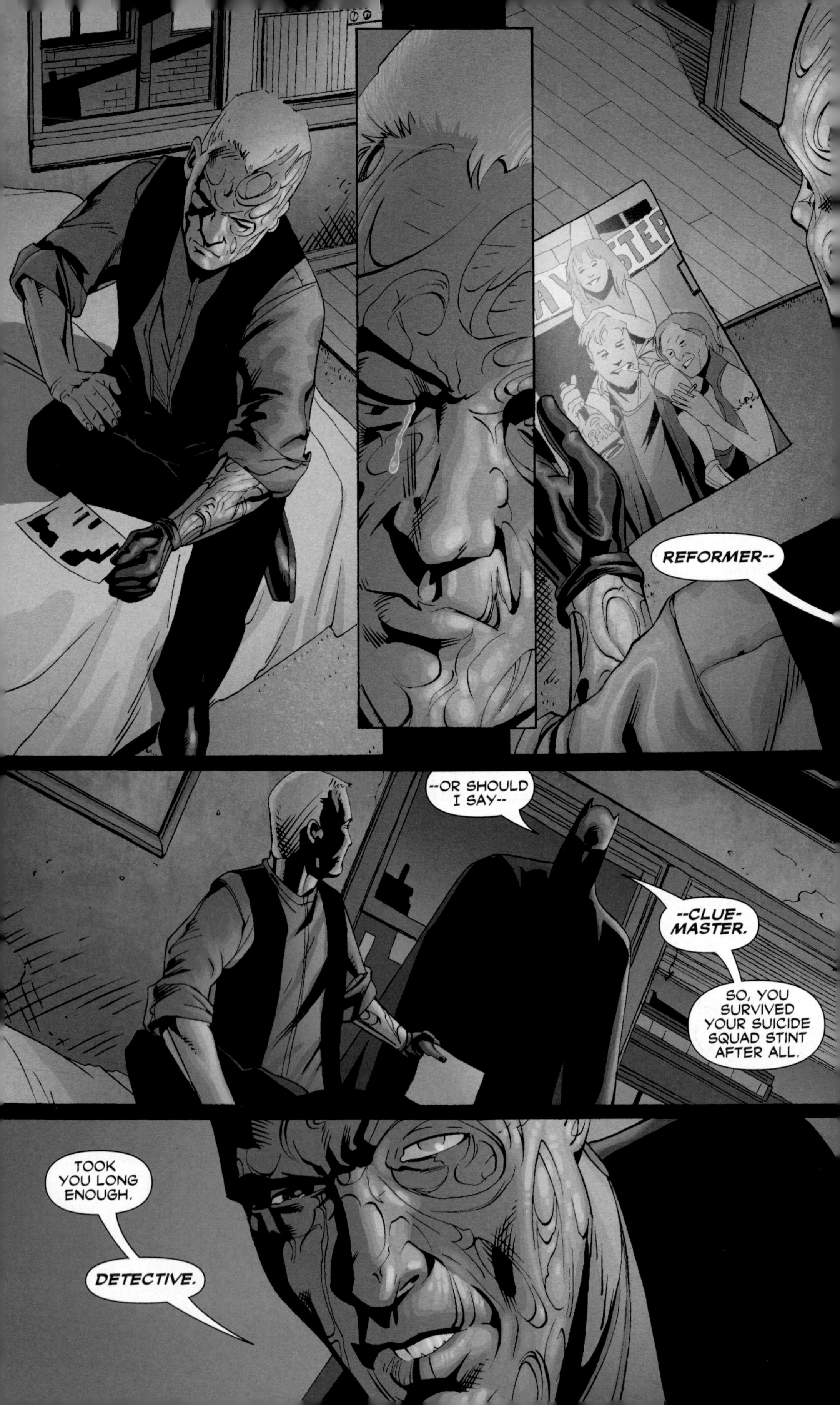
REFORMER--
--OR SHOULD I SAY--
--CLUE-MASTER.
SO, YOU SURVIVED YOUR SUICIDE SQUAD STINT AFTER ALL.
TOOK YOU LONG ENOUGH.
DETECTIVE.

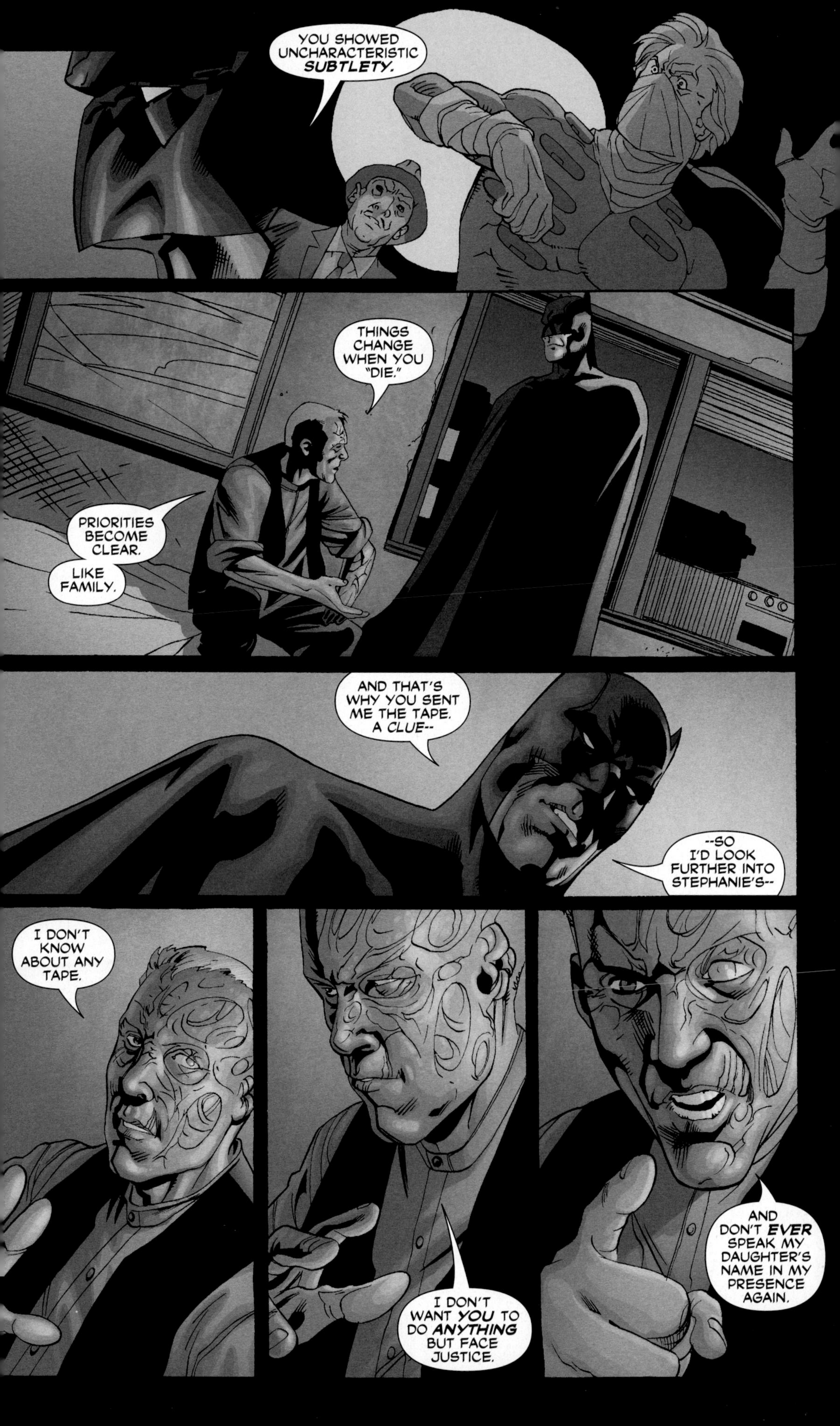
YOU SHOWED UNCHARACTERISTIC SUBTLETY.
THINGS CHANGE WHEN YOU "DIE."
PRIORITIES BECOME CLEAR.
LIKE FAMILY.
AND THAT'S WHY YOU SENT ME THE TAPE. A CLUE--
--SO I'D LOOK FURTHER INTO STEPHANIE'S--
I DON'T KNOW ABOUT ANY TAPE.
I DON'T WANT YOU TO DO ANYTHING BUT FACE JUSTICE.
AND DON'T EVER SPEAK MY DAUGHTER'S NAME IN MY PRESENCE AGAIN.

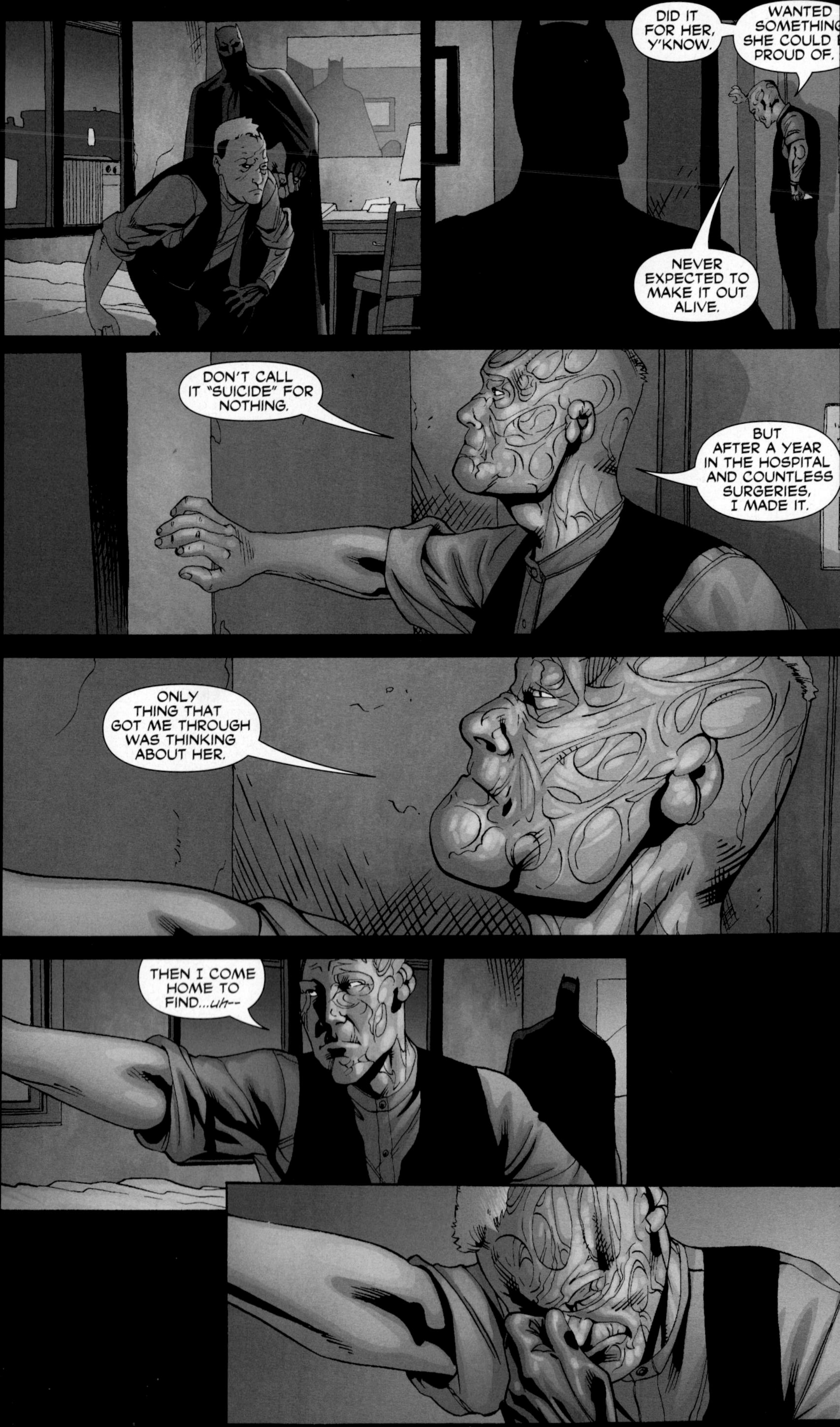

DID IT FOR HER, Y'KNOW.
WANTED SOMETHING SHE COULD BE PROUD OF.
NEVER EXPECTED TO MAKE IT OUT ALIVE.
DON'T CALL IT "SUICIDE" FOR NOTHING.
BUT AFTER A YEAR IN THE HOSPITAL AND COUNTLESS SURGERIES, I MADE IT.
ONLY THING THAT GOT ME THROUGH WAS THINKING ABOUT HER.
THEN I COME HOME TO FIND...*uh*--

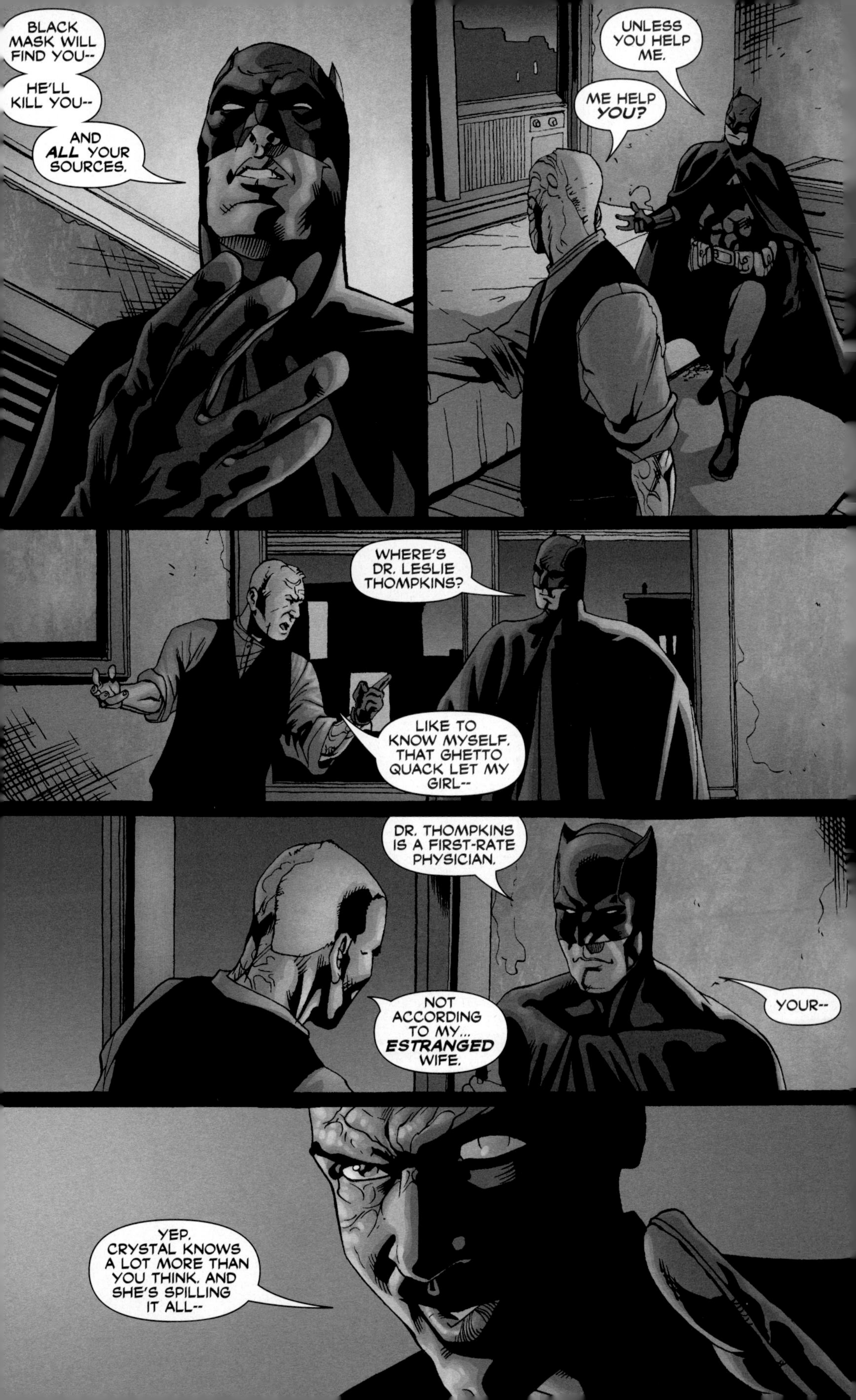
BLACK MASK WILL FIND YOU--
HE'LL KILL YOU--
AND ALL YOUR SOURCES.
UNLESS YOU HELP ME.
ME HELP YOU?
WHERE'S DR. LESLIE THOMPKINS?
LIKE TO KNOW MYSELF. THAT GHETTO QUACK LET MY GIRL--
DR. THOMPKINS IS A FIRST-RATE PHYSICIAN.
NOT ACCORDING TO MY... ESTRANGED WIFE.
YOUR--
YEP. CRYSTAL KNOWS A LOT MORE THAN YOU THINK. AND SHE'S SPILLING IT ALL--

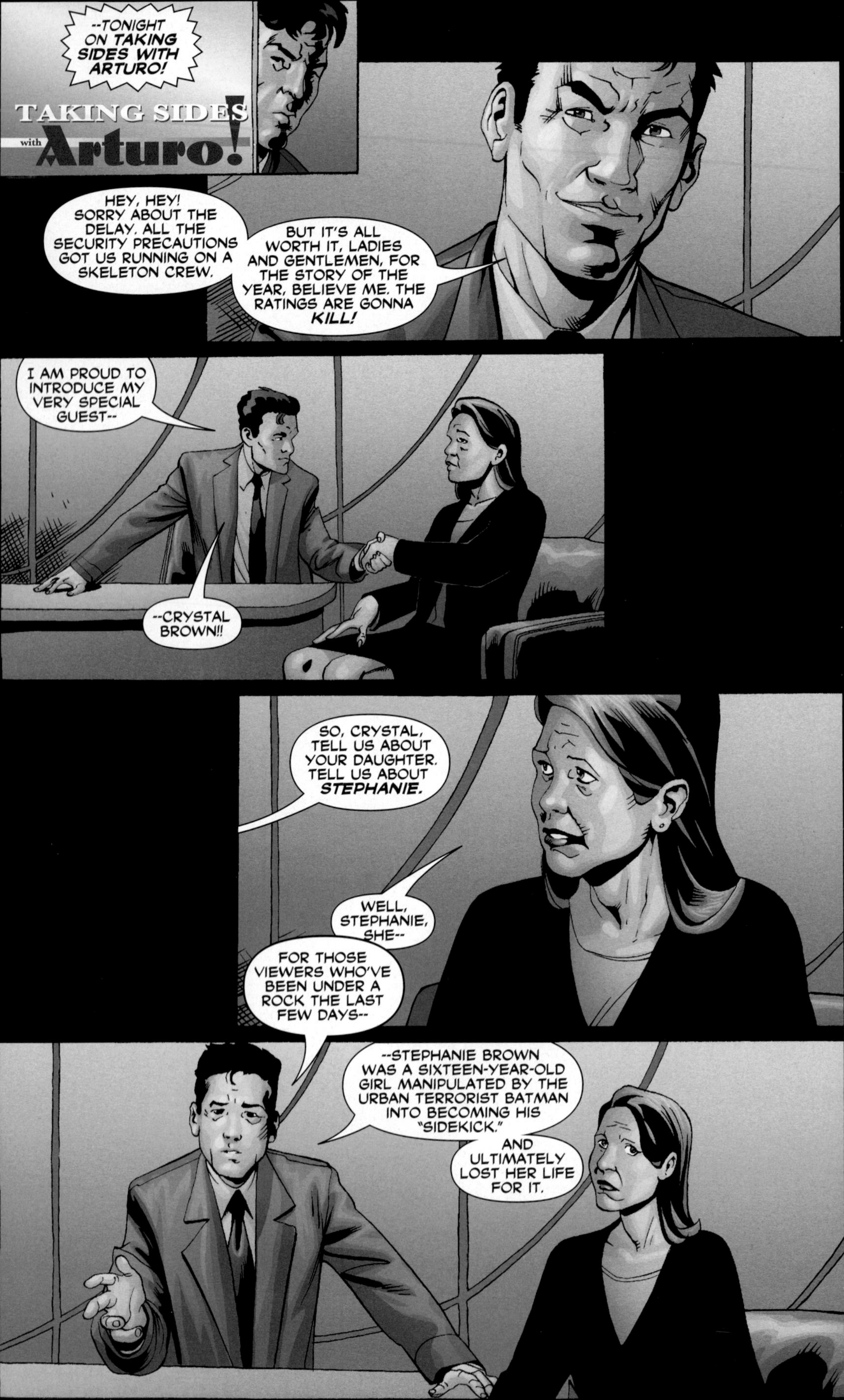
--TONIGHT ON TAKING SIDES WITH ARTURO!
TAKING SIDES with Arturo!
HEY, HEY! SORRY ABOUT THE DELAY. ALL THE SECURITY PRECAUTIONS GOT US RUNNING ON A SKELETON CREW.
BUT IT'S ALL WORTH IT, LADIES AND GENTLEMEN, FOR THE STORY OF THE YEAR, BELIEVE ME. THE RATINGS ARE GONNA KILL!
I AM PROUD TO INTRODUCE MY VERY SPECIAL GUEST--
--CRYSTAL BROWN!!
SO, CRYSTAL, TELL US ABOUT YOUR DAUGHTER. TELL US ABOUT STEPHANIE.
WELL, STEPHANIE, SHE--
FOR THOSE VIEWERS WHO'VE BEEN UNDER A ROCK THE LAST FEW DAYS--
--STEPHANIE BROWN WAS A SIXTEEN-YEAR-OLD GIRL MANIPULATED BY THE URBAN TERRORIST BATMAN INTO BECOMING HIS "SIDEKICK."
AND ULTIMATELY LOST HER LIFE FOR IT.

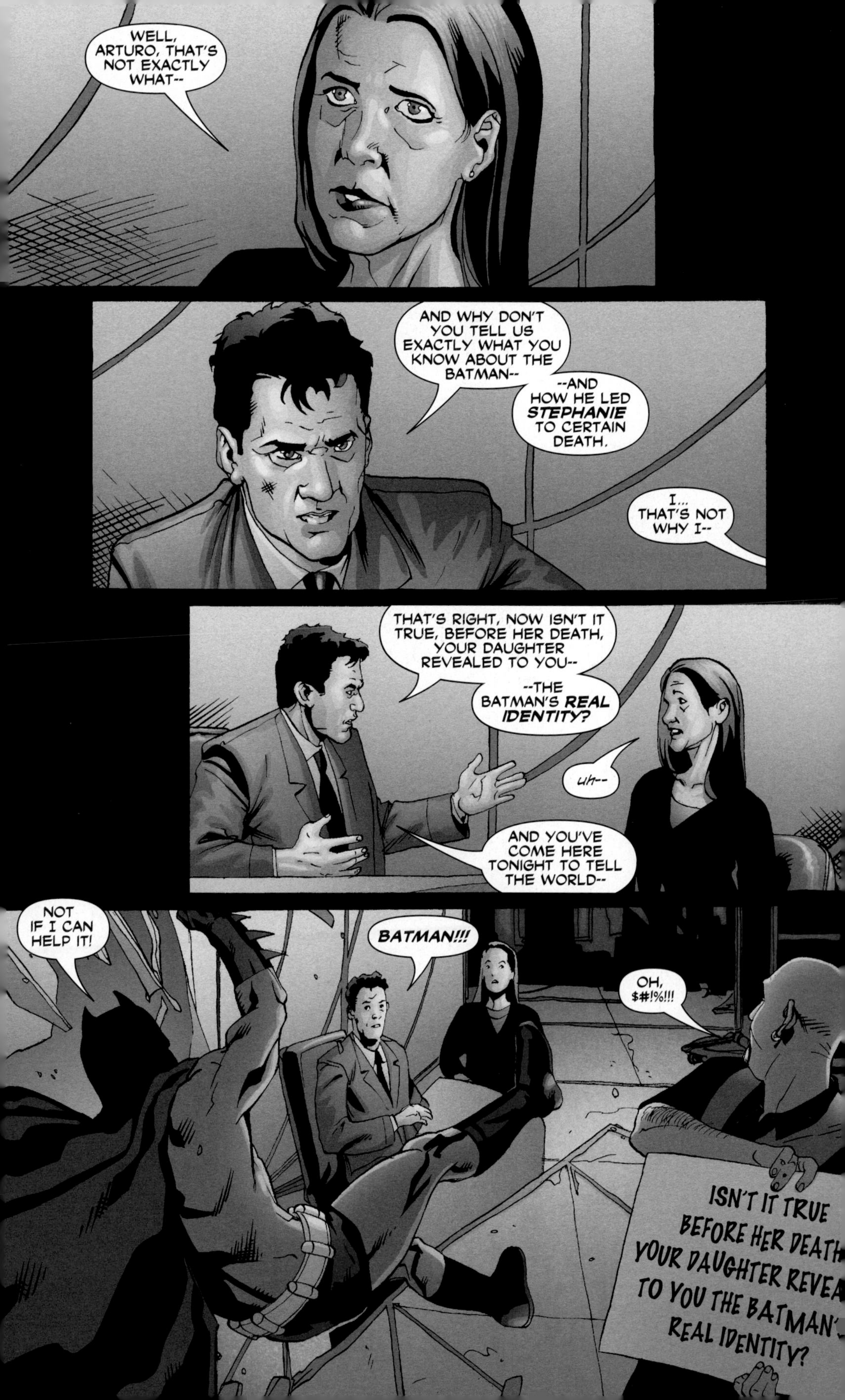
WELL, ARTURO, THAT'S NOT EXACTLY WHAT--
AND WHY DON'T YOU TELL US EXACTLY WHAT YOU KNOW ABOUT THE BATMAN--
--AND HOW HE LED STEPHANIE TO CERTAIN DEATH.
I... THAT'S NOT WHY I--
THAT'S RIGHT, NOW ISN'T IT TRUE, BEFORE HER DEATH, YOUR DAUGHTER REVEALED TO YOU--
--THE BATMAN'S REAL IDENTITY?
uh--
AND YOU'VE COME HERE TONIGHT TO TELL THE WORLD--
NOT IF I CAN HELP IT!
BATMAN!!!
OH, $#!%!!!
ISN'T IT TRUE BEFORE HER DEATH YOUR DAUGHTER REVEA TO YOU THE BATMAN' REAL IDENTITY?

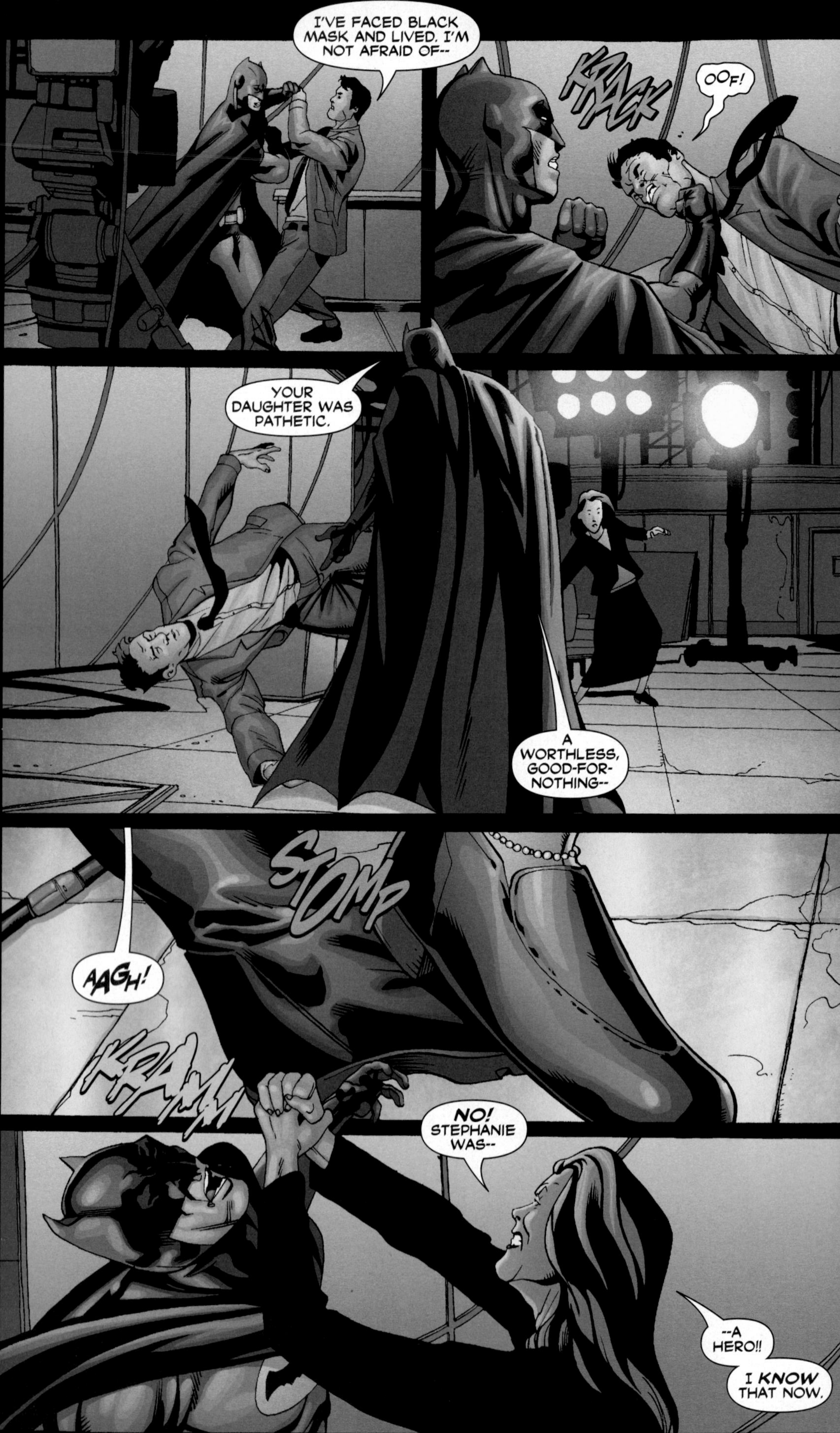
I'VE FACED BLACK MASK AND LIVED. I'M NOT AFRAID OF--
KRACK
OOF!
YOUR DAUGHTER WAS PATHETIC.
A WORTHLESS, GOOD-FOR-NOTHING--
STOMP
AAGH!
KRAMM
NO! STEPHANIE WAS--
--A HERO!!
I KNOW THAT NOW.

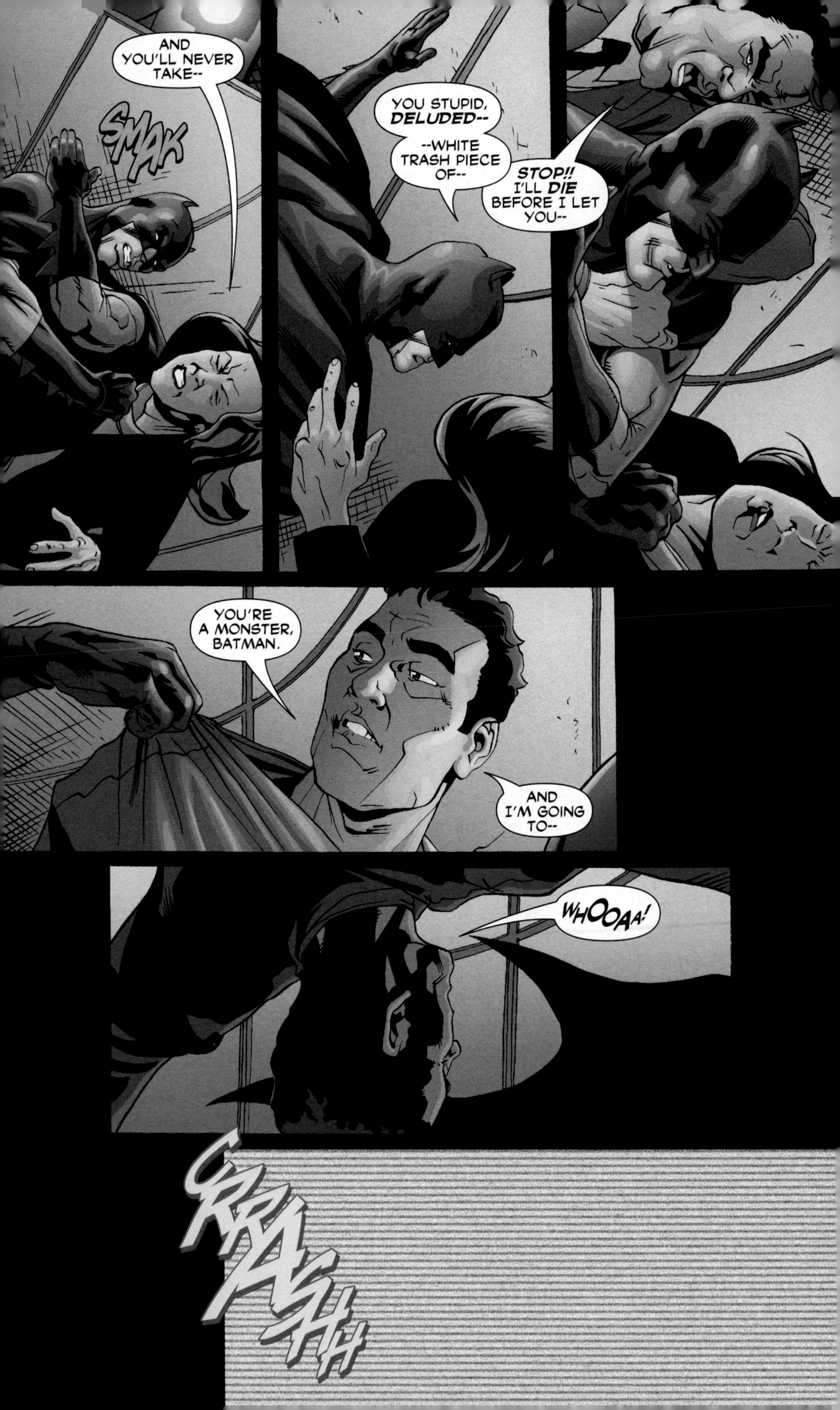
AND YOU'LL NEVER TAKE--
SMAK
YOU STUPID, DELUDED--
--WHITE TRASH PIECE OF--
STOP!! I'LL DIE BEFORE I LET YOU--
YOU'RE A MONSTER, BATMAN.
AND I'M GOING TO--
WHOOAA!
CRASHH

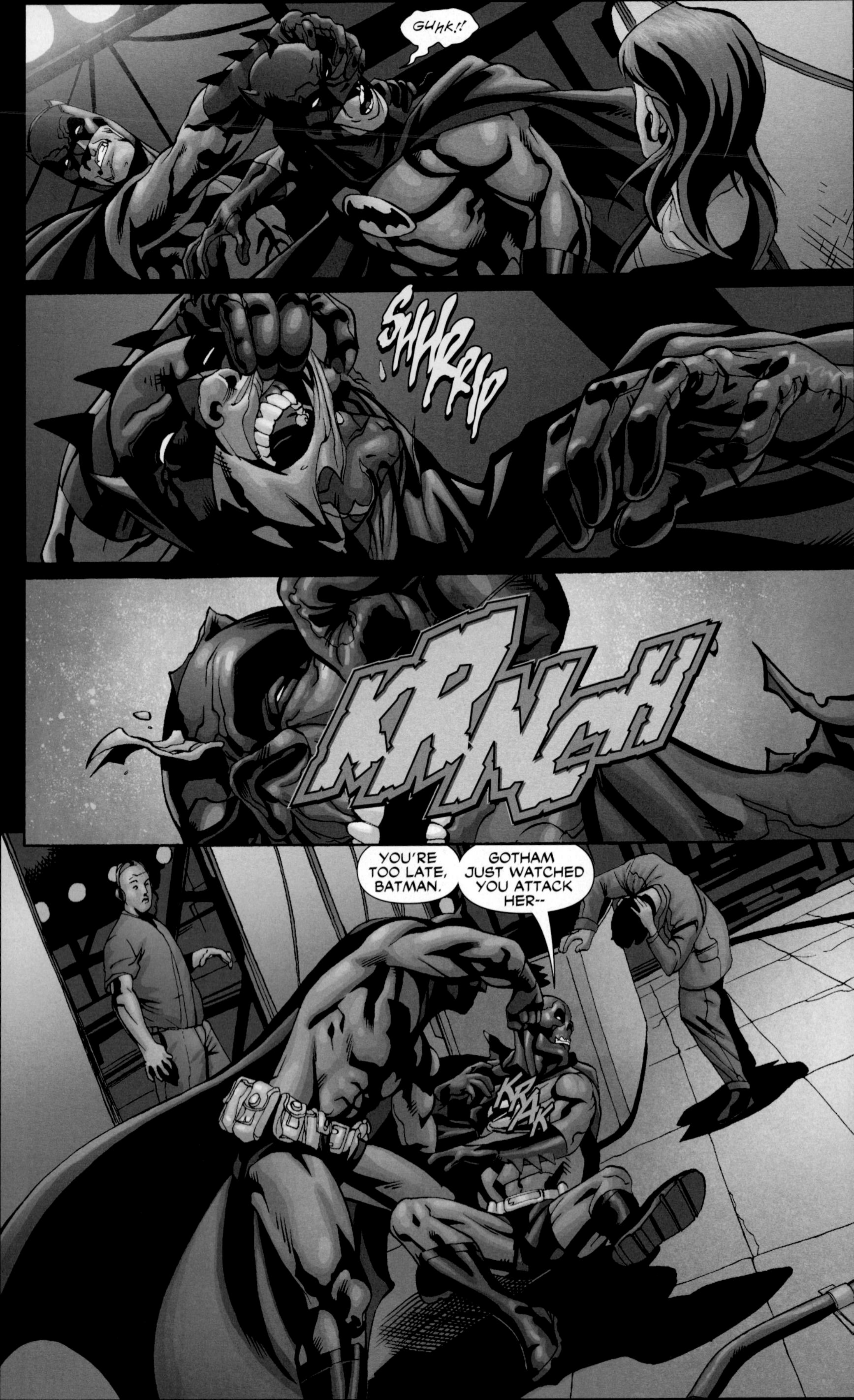
GUNK!!
SHHRRIP
KRNCH
YOU'RE TOO LATE, BATMAN.
GOTHAM JUST WATCHED YOU ATTACK HER--
KRAK

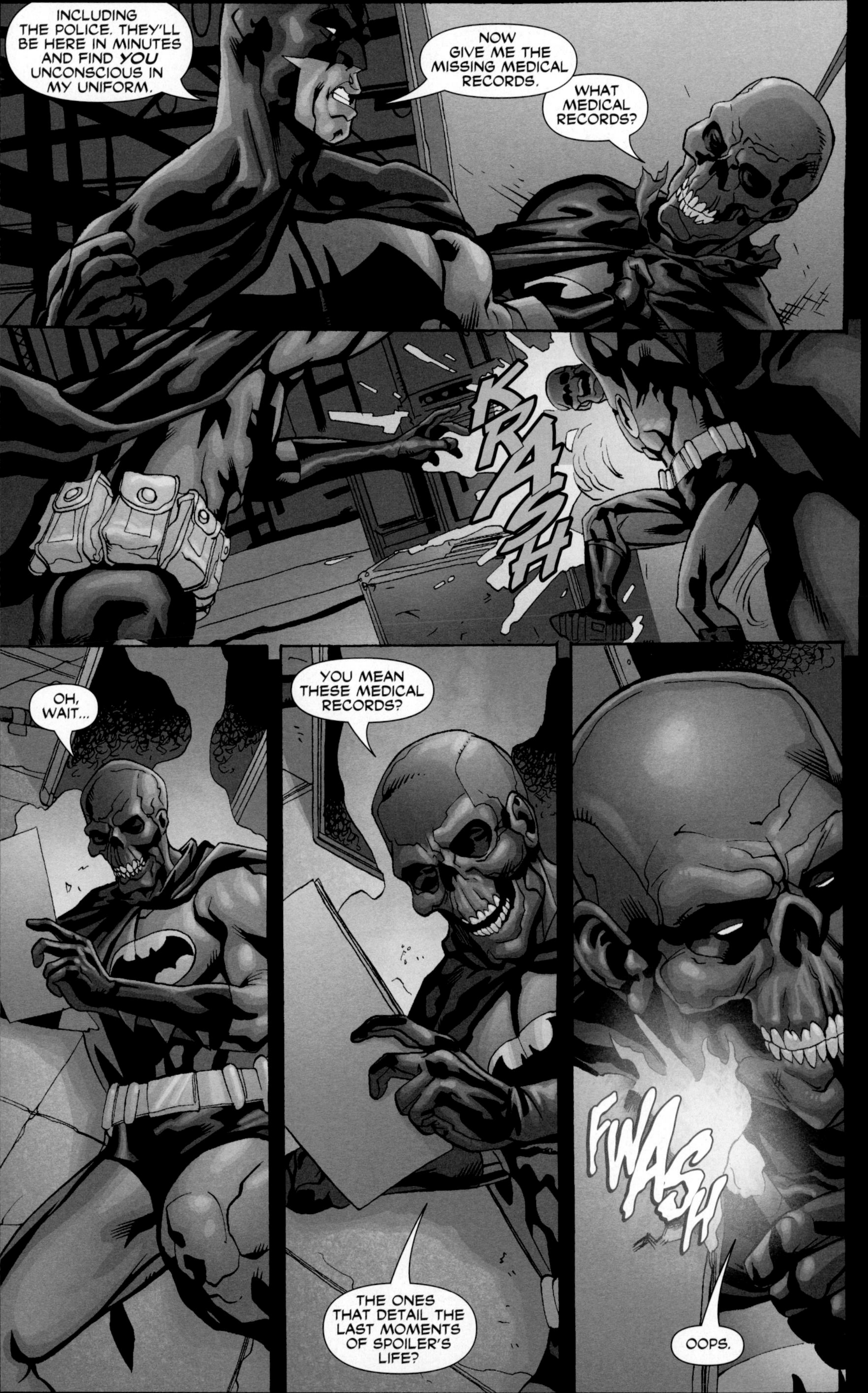
INCLUDING THE POLICE. THEY'LL BE HERE IN MINUTES AND FIND *YOU* UNCONSCIOUS IN MY UNIFORM.
NOW GIVE ME THE MISSING MEDICAL RECORDS.
WHAT MEDICAL RECORDS?
KRASH
OH, WAIT...
YOU MEAN THESE MEDICAL RECORDS?
THE ONES THAT DETAIL THE LAST MOMENTS OF SPOILER'S LIFE?
FWASH
OOPS.

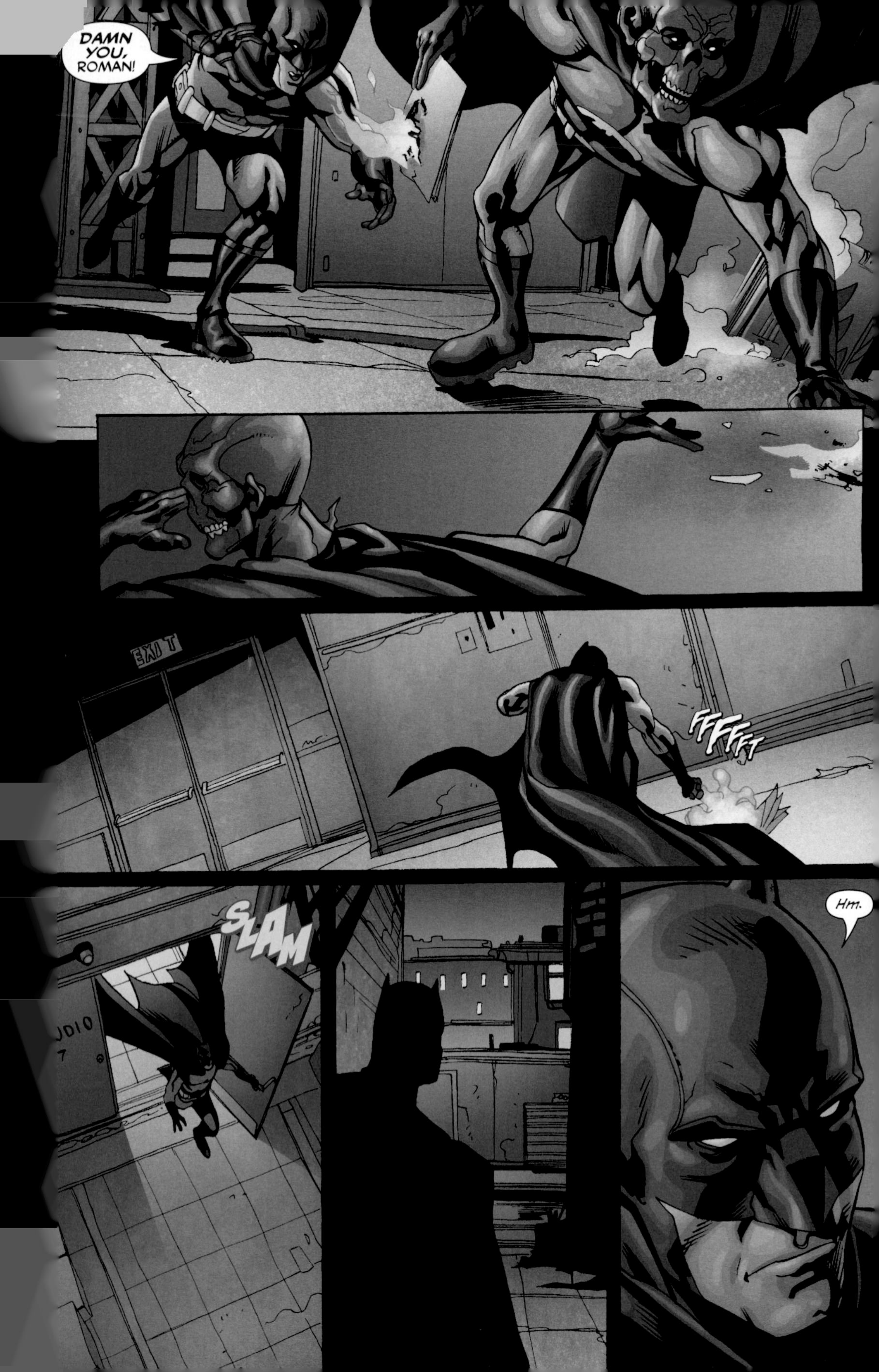
DAMN YOU, ROMAN!
EXIT
FFFFFT
SLAM
Hm.

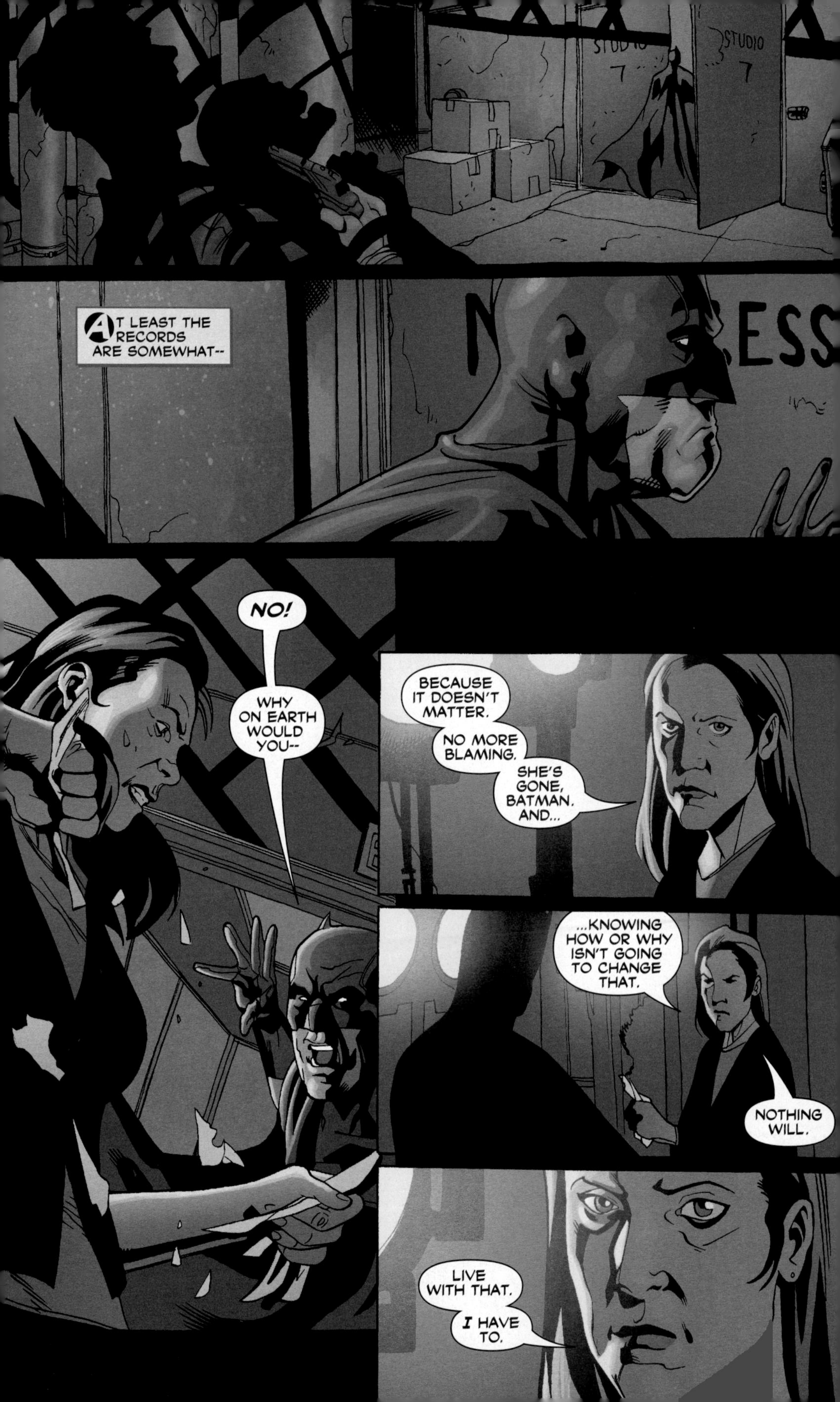
STUDIO 7
STUDIO 7
AT LEAST THE RECORDS ARE SOMEWHAT--
NO!
WHY ON EARTH WOULD YOU--
BECAUSE IT DOESN'T MATTER.
NO MORE BLAMING.
SHE'S GONE, BATMAN. AND...
...KNOWING HOW OR WHY ISN'T GOING TO CHANGE THAT.
NOTHING WILL.
LIVE WITH THAT.
I HAVE TO.

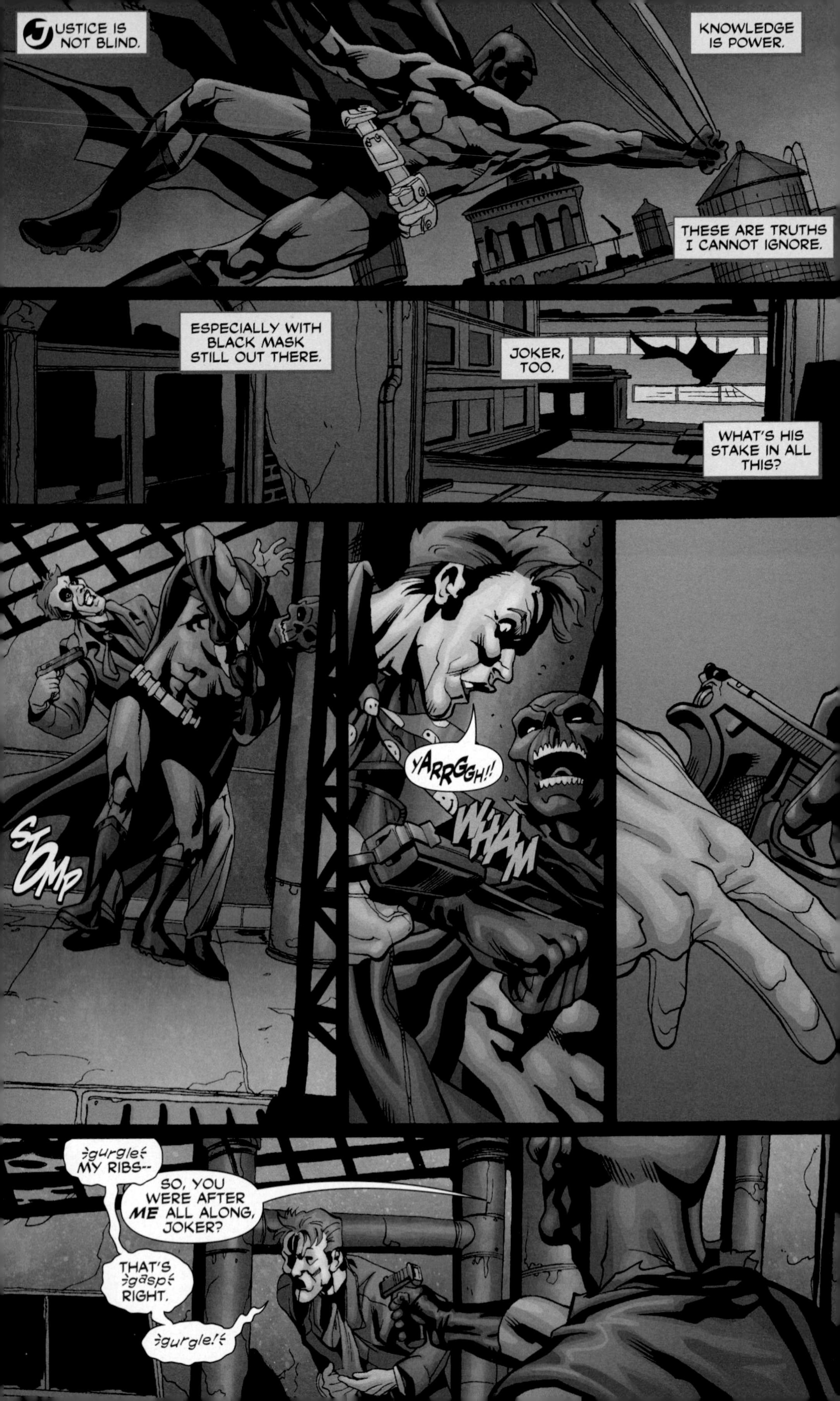
JUSTICE IS NOT BLIND.
KNOWLEDGE IS POWER.
THESE ARE TRUTHS I CANNOT IGNORE.
ESPECIALLY WITH BLACK MASK STILL OUT THERE.
JOKER, TOO.
WHAT'S HIS STAKE IN ALL THIS?
STOMP
YARRGGH!!
WHAM
>gurgle< MY RIBS--
SO, YOU WERE AFTER ME ALL ALONG, JOKER?
THAT'S >gasp< RIGHT.
>gurgle!<

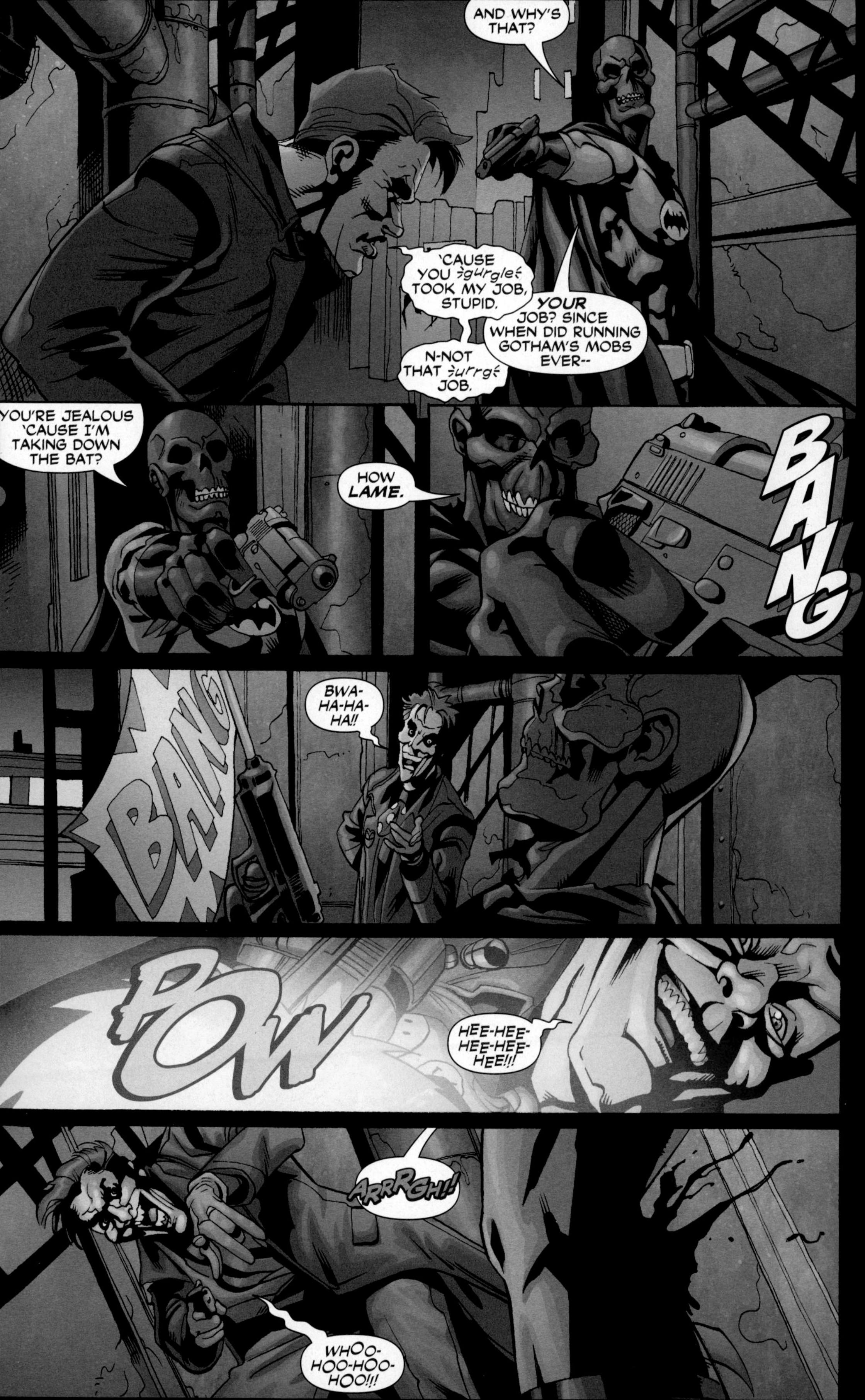
AND WHY'S THAT?
'CAUSE YOU ⦃gurgle⦄ TOOK MY JOB, STUPID.
YOUR JOB? SINCE WHEN DID RUNNING GOTHAM'S MOBS EVER--
N-NOT THAT ⦃urrg⦄ JOB.
YOU'RE JEALOUS 'CAUSE I'M TAKING DOWN THE BAT?
HOW LAME.
BANG
BANG
BWA-HA-HA-HA!!
POW
HEE-HEE-HEE-HEE-HEE!!!
ARRRGH!!
WHOO-HOO-HOO-HOO!!!

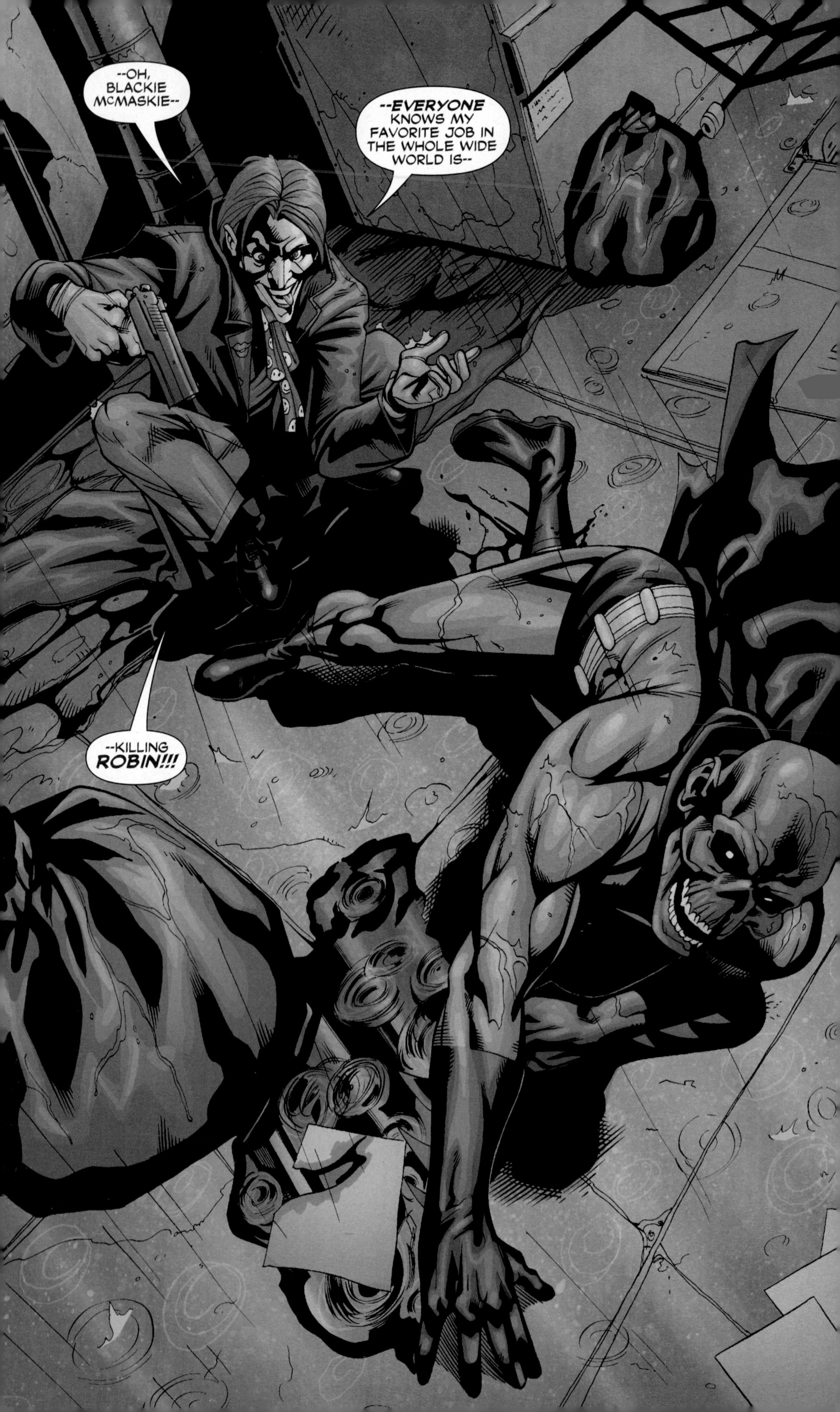
--OH, BLACKIE McMASKIE--
--EVERYONE KNOWS MY FAVORITE JOB IN THE WHOLE WIDE WORLD IS--
--KILLING ROBIN!!!

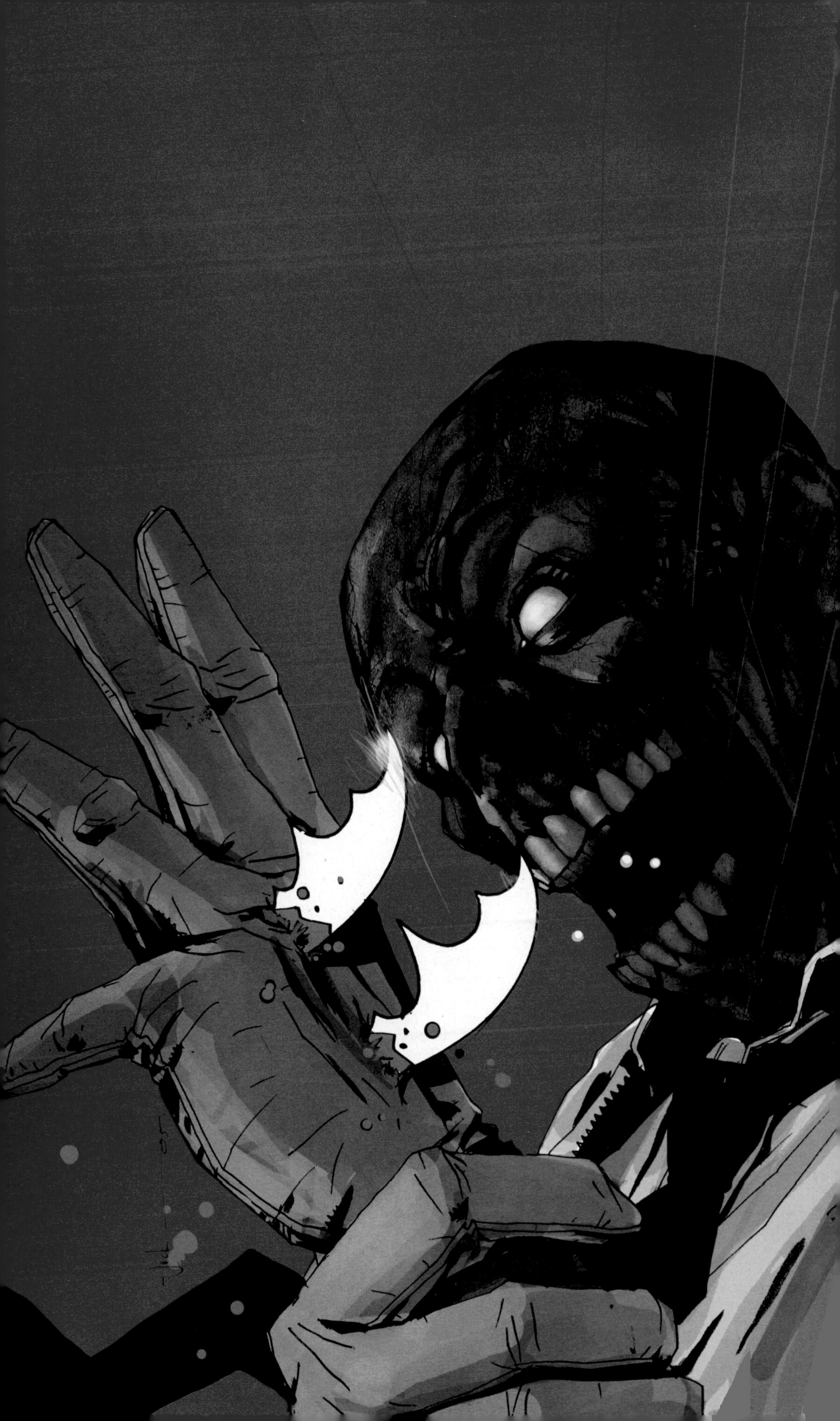

COVER ART BY
JOCK

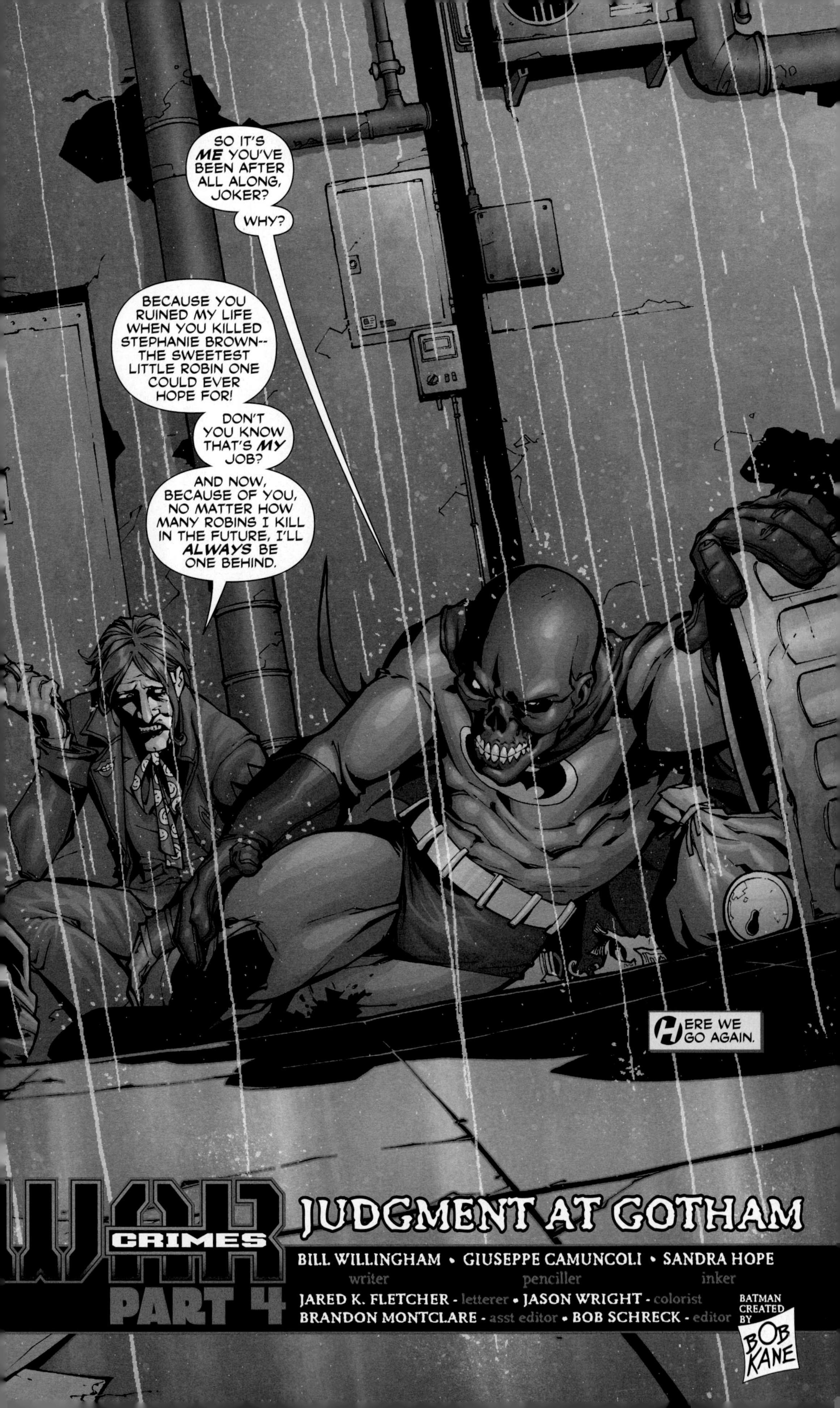

SO IT'S *ME* YOU'VE BEEN AFTER ALL ALONG, JOKER?
WHY?
BECAUSE YOU RUINED MY LIFE WHEN YOU KILLED STEPHANIE BROWN-- THE SWEETEST LITTLE ROBIN ONE COULD EVER HOPE FOR!
DON'T YOU KNOW THAT'S *MY* JOB?
AND NOW, BECAUSE OF YOU, NO MATTER HOW MANY ROBINS I KILL IN THE FUTURE, I'LL *ALWAYS* BE ONE BEHIND.
HERE WE GO AGAIN.
WAR CRIMES PART 4
JUDGMENT AT GOTHAM
BILL WILLINGHAM • GIUSEPPE CAMUNCOLI • SANDRA HOPE
writer penciller inker
JARED K. FLETCHER - letterer • JASON WRIGHT - colorist
BRANDON MONTCLARE - asst editor • BOB SCHRECK - editor
BATMAN CREATED BY BOB KANE

JOKER AND BLACK MASK ARE DETERMINED TO KILL EACH OTHER.

SAY GOODNIGHT, GRACIE.

AND I'M HONESTLY TEMPTED TO LET THEM.

THINK I'M BEATEN? NEVER!

BUT, AS MUCH AS THAT WOULD SOLVE SO MANY PROBLEMS, I CAN'T.

I'M BLACK MASK!

DO YOU IMAGINE I WOUL EVER LET MYSE BE BEATEN BY SC DERANGED ESCAP FROM THE NUT HOUSE?

ENOUGH!

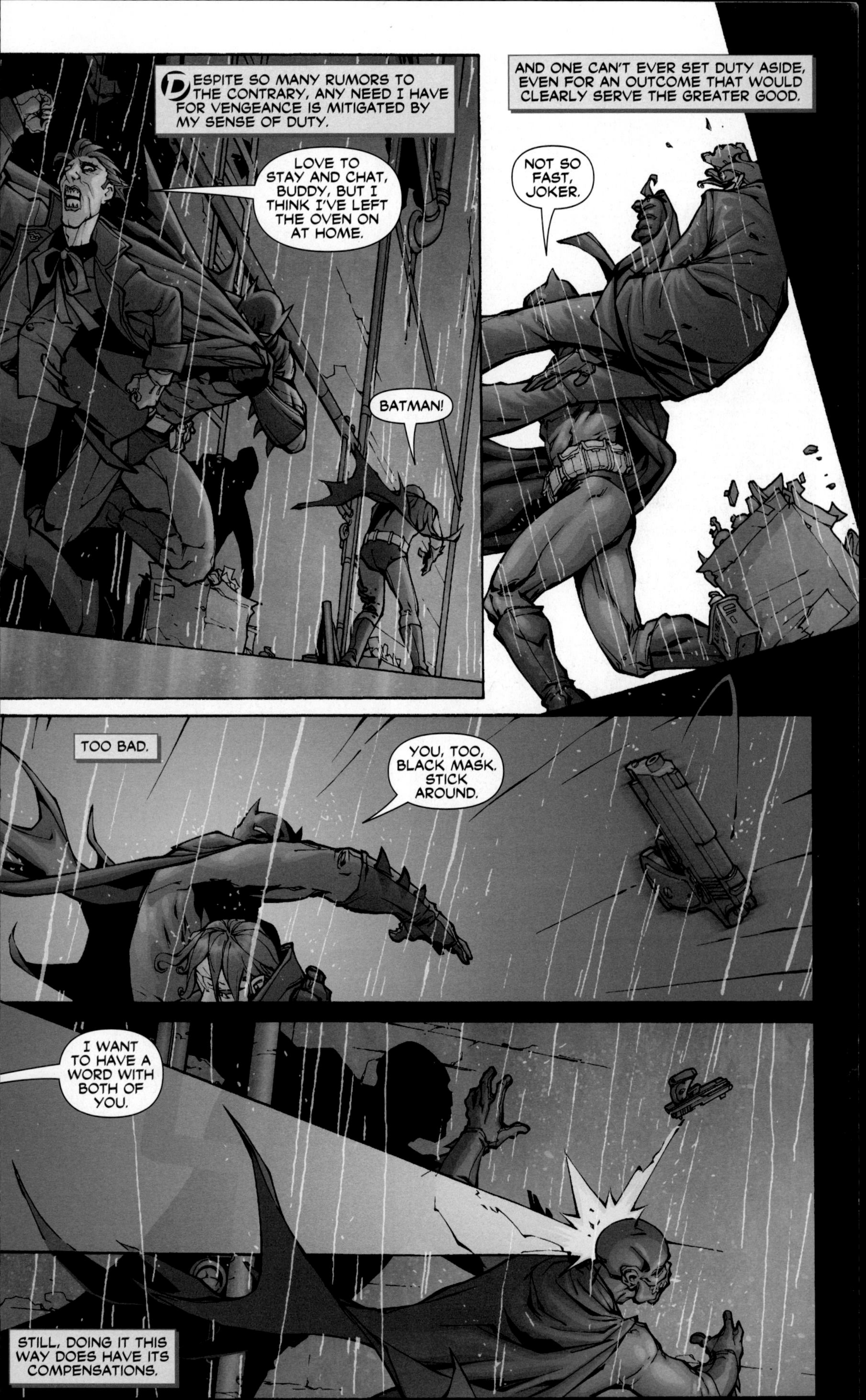
DESPITE SO MANY RUMORS TO THE CONTRARY, ANY NEED I HAVE FOR VENGEANCE IS MITIGATED BY MY SENSE OF DUTY.
LOVE TO STAY AND CHAT, BUDDY, BUT I THINK I'VE LEFT THE OVEN ON AT HOME.
BATMAN!
AND ONE CAN'T EVER SET DUTY ASIDE, EVEN FOR AN OUTCOME THAT WOULD CLEARLY SERVE THE GREATER GOOD.
NOT SO FAST, JOKER.
TOO BAD.
YOU, TOO, BLACK MASK. STICK AROUND.
I WANT TO HAVE A WORD WITH BOTH OF YOU.
STILL, DOING IT THIS WAY DOES HAVE ITS COMPENSATIONS.

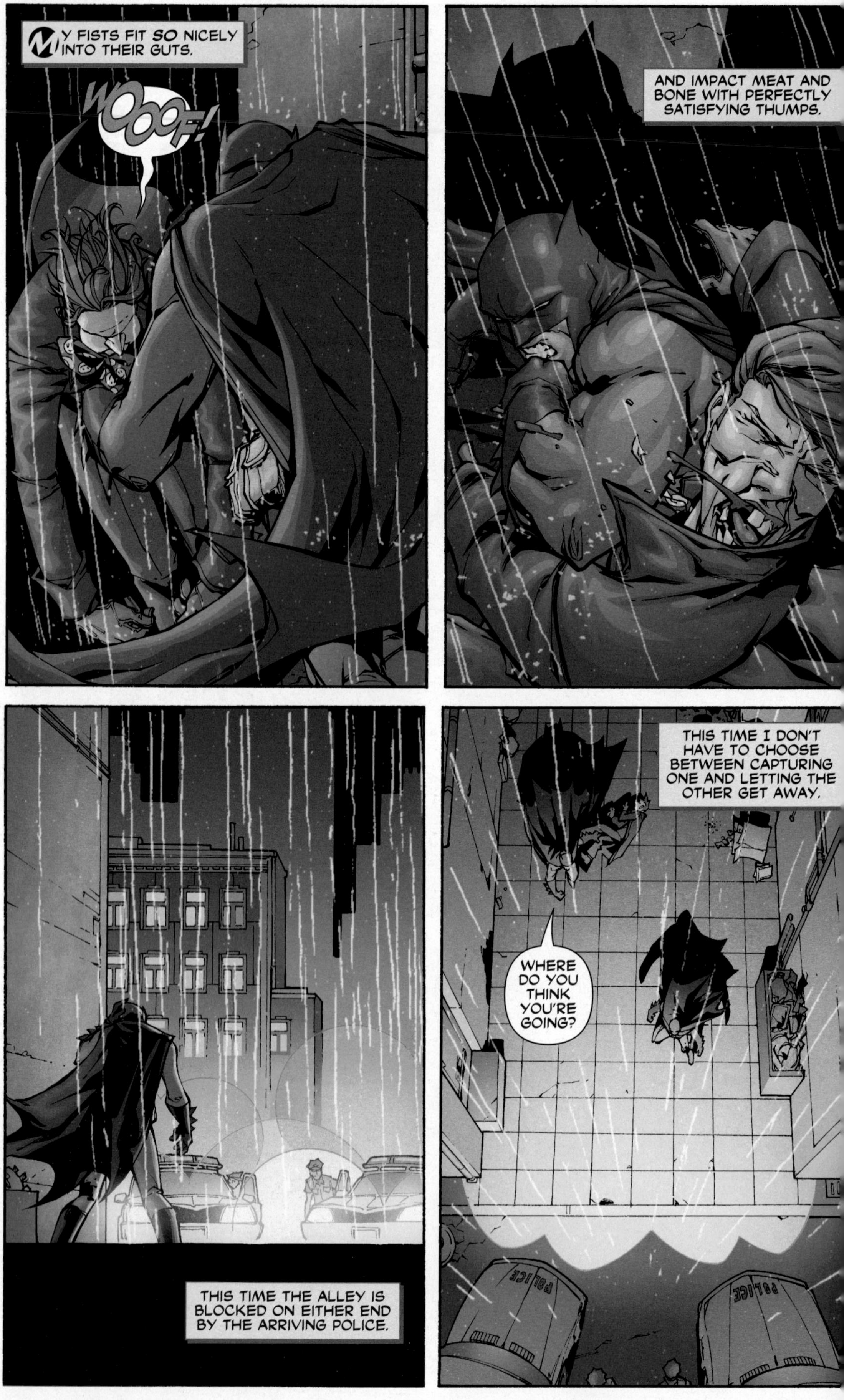
MY FISTS FIT SO NICELY INTO THEIR GUTS.
WOOOF!
AND IMPACT MEAT AND BONE WITH PERFECTLY SATISFYING THUMPS.
THIS TIME THE ALLEY IS BLOCKED ON EITHER END BY THE ARRIVING POLICE.
THIS TIME I DON'T HAVE TO CHOOSE BETWEEN CAPTURING ONE AND LETTING THE OTHER GET AWAY.
WHERE DO YOU THINK YOU'RE GOING?
POLICE
POLICE

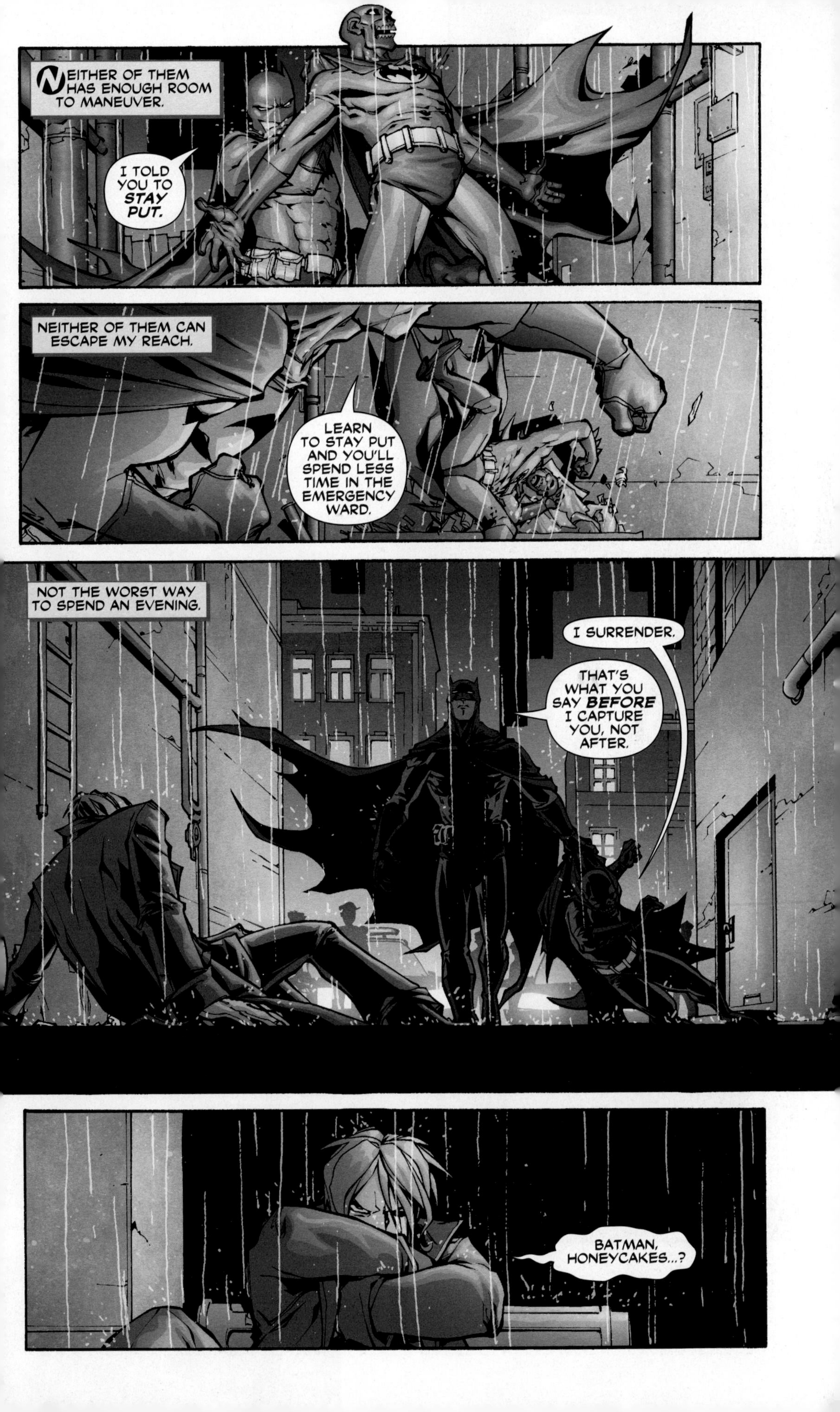
NEITHER OF THEM HAS ENOUGH ROOM TO MANEUVER.
I TOLD YOU TO STAY PUT.
NEITHER OF THEM CAN ESCAPE MY REACH.
LEARN TO STAY PUT AND YOU'LL SPEND LESS TIME IN THE EMERGENCY WARD.
NOT THE WORST WAY TO SPEND AN EVENING.
I SURRENDER.
THAT'S WHAT YOU SAY BEFORE I CAPTURE YOU, NOT AFTER.
BATMAN, HONEYCAKES...?

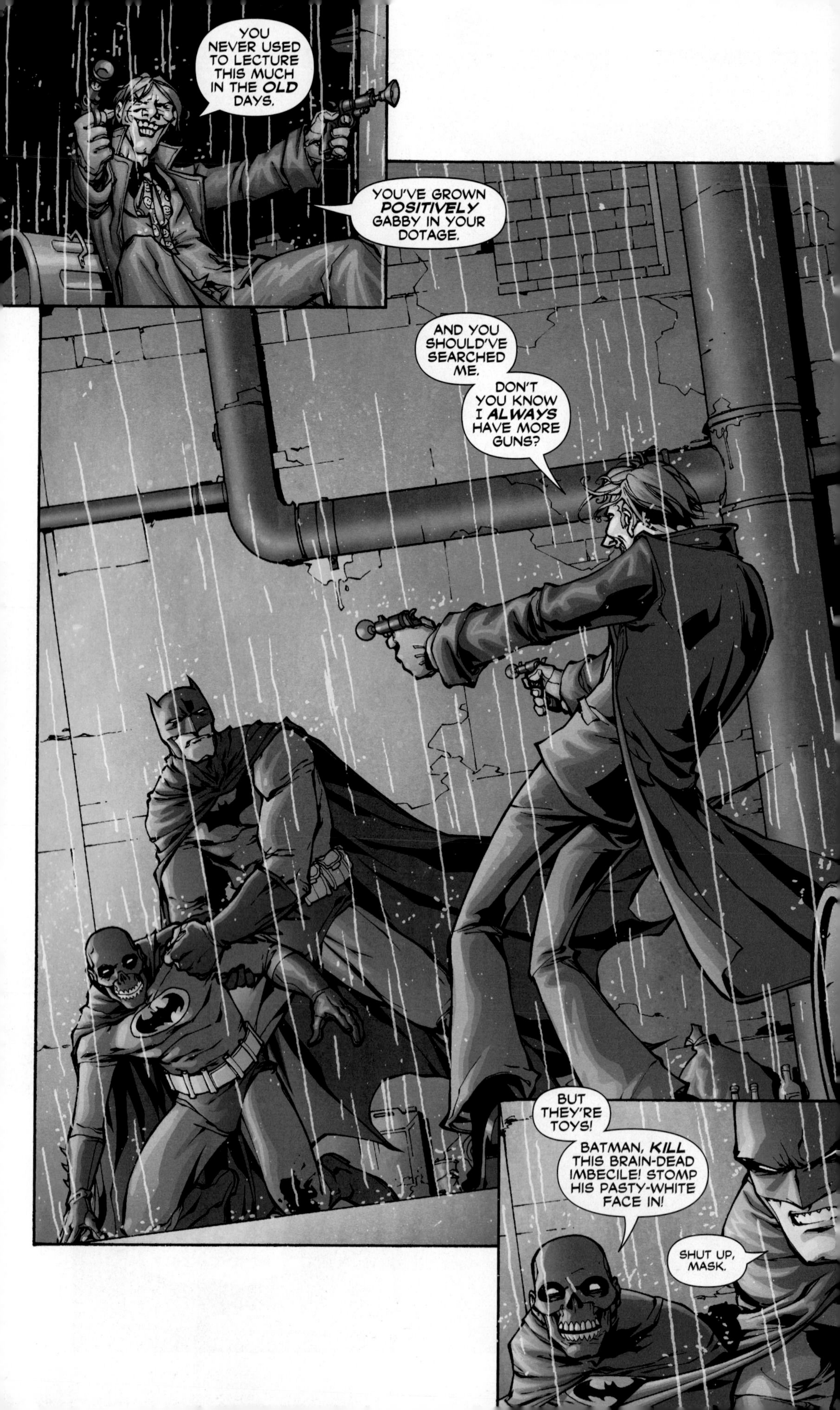
YOU NEVER USED TO LECTURE THIS MUCH IN THE OLD DAYS.
YOU'VE GROWN POSITIVELY GABBY IN YOUR DOTAGE.
AND YOU SHOULD'VE SEARCHED ME.
DON'T YOU KNOW I ALWAYS HAVE MORE GUNS?
BUT THEY'RE TOYS!
BATMAN, KILL THIS BRAIN-DEAD IMBECILE! STOMP HIS PASTY-WHITE FACE IN!
SHUT UP, MASK.

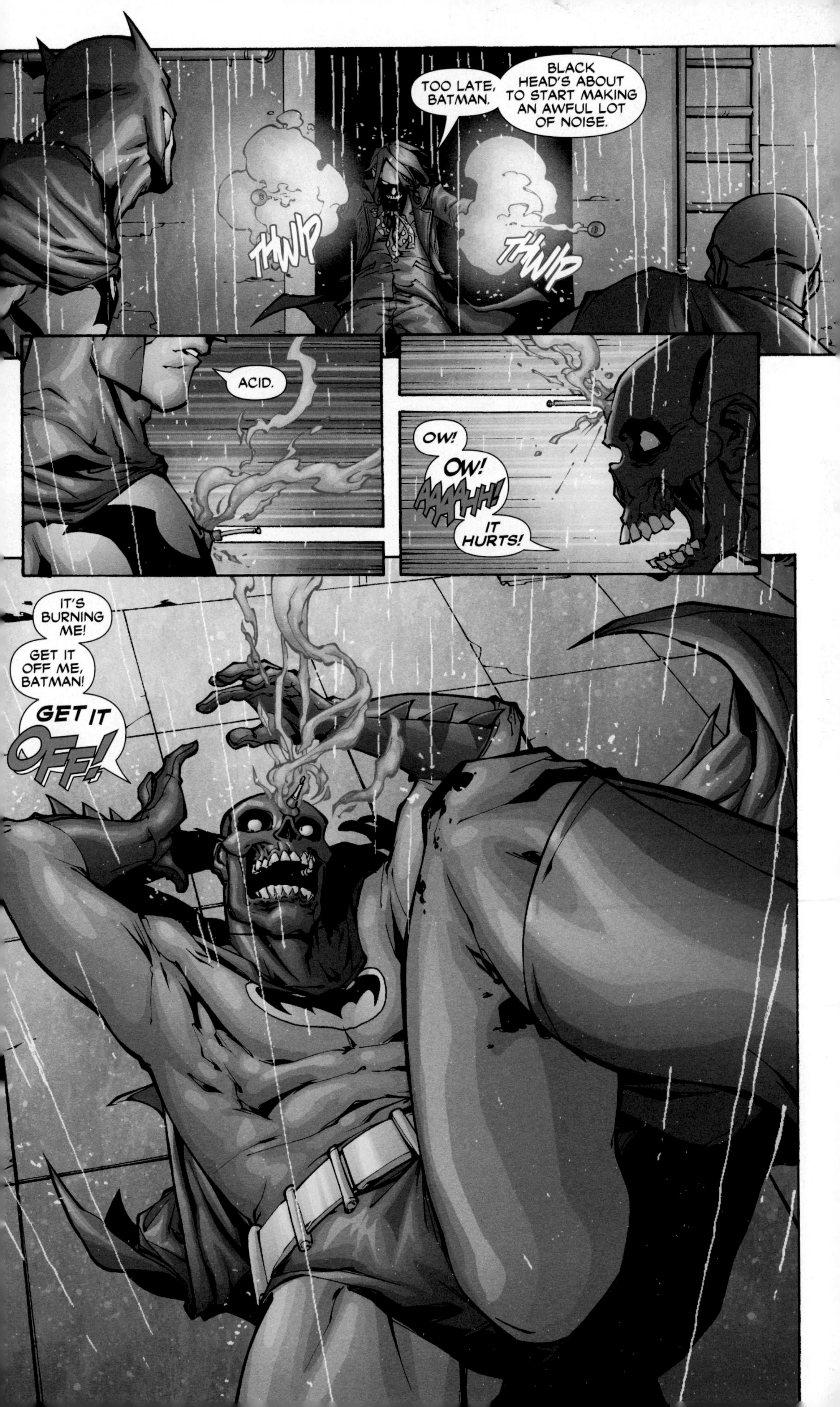
TOO LATE, BATMAN.
BLACK HEAD'S ABOUT TO START MAKING AN AWFUL LOT OF NOISE.
THWIP
THWIP
ACID.
OW!
OW!
AAAAHH!
IT HURTS!
IT'S BURNING ME!
GET IT OFF ME, BATMAN!
GET IT OFF!

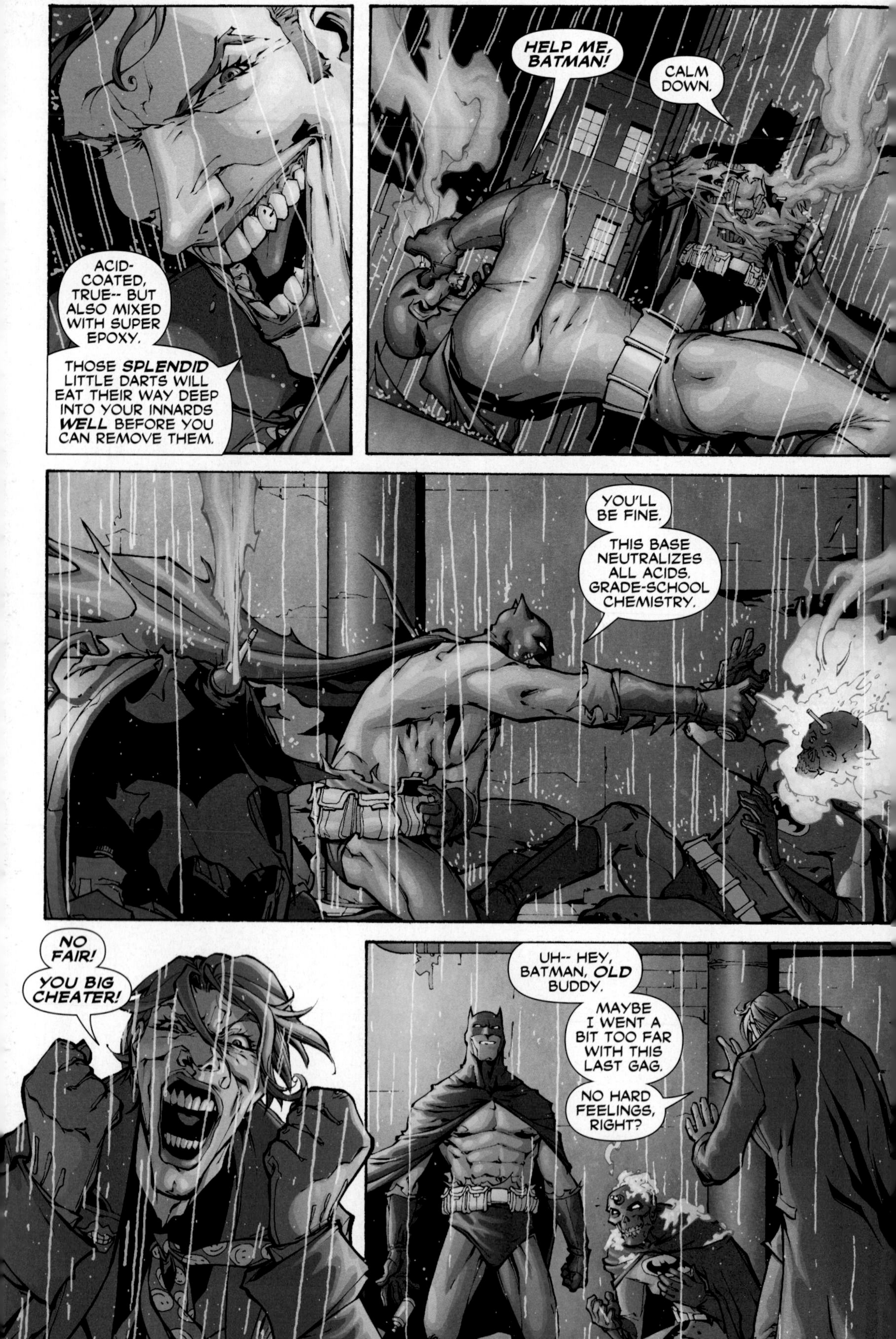
ACID-COATED, TRUE-- BUT ALSO MIXED WITH SUPER EPOXY.
THOSE SPLENDID LITTLE DARTS WILL EAT THEIR WAY DEEP INTO YOUR INNARDS WELL BEFORE YOU CAN REMOVE THEM.
HELP ME, BATMAN!
CALM DOWN.
YOU'LL BE FINE.
THIS BASE NEUTRALIZES ALL ACIDS. GRADE-SCHOOL CHEMISTRY.
NO FAIR!
YOU BIG CHEATER!
UH-- HEY, BATMAN, OLD BUDDY.
MAYBE I WENT A BIT TOO FAR WITH THIS LAST GAG.
NO HARD FEELINGS, RIGHT?

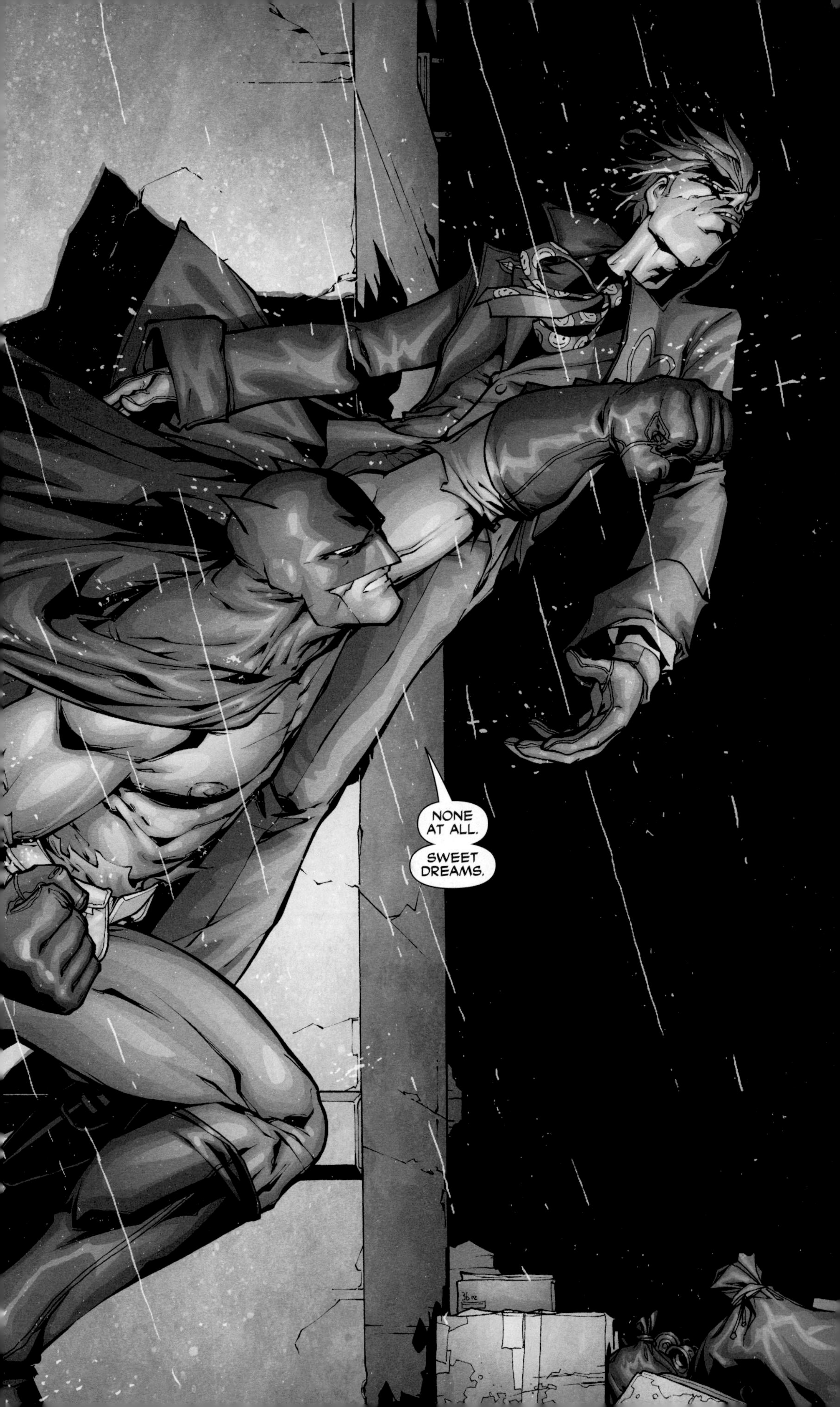
NONE AT ALL.
SWEET DREAMS.

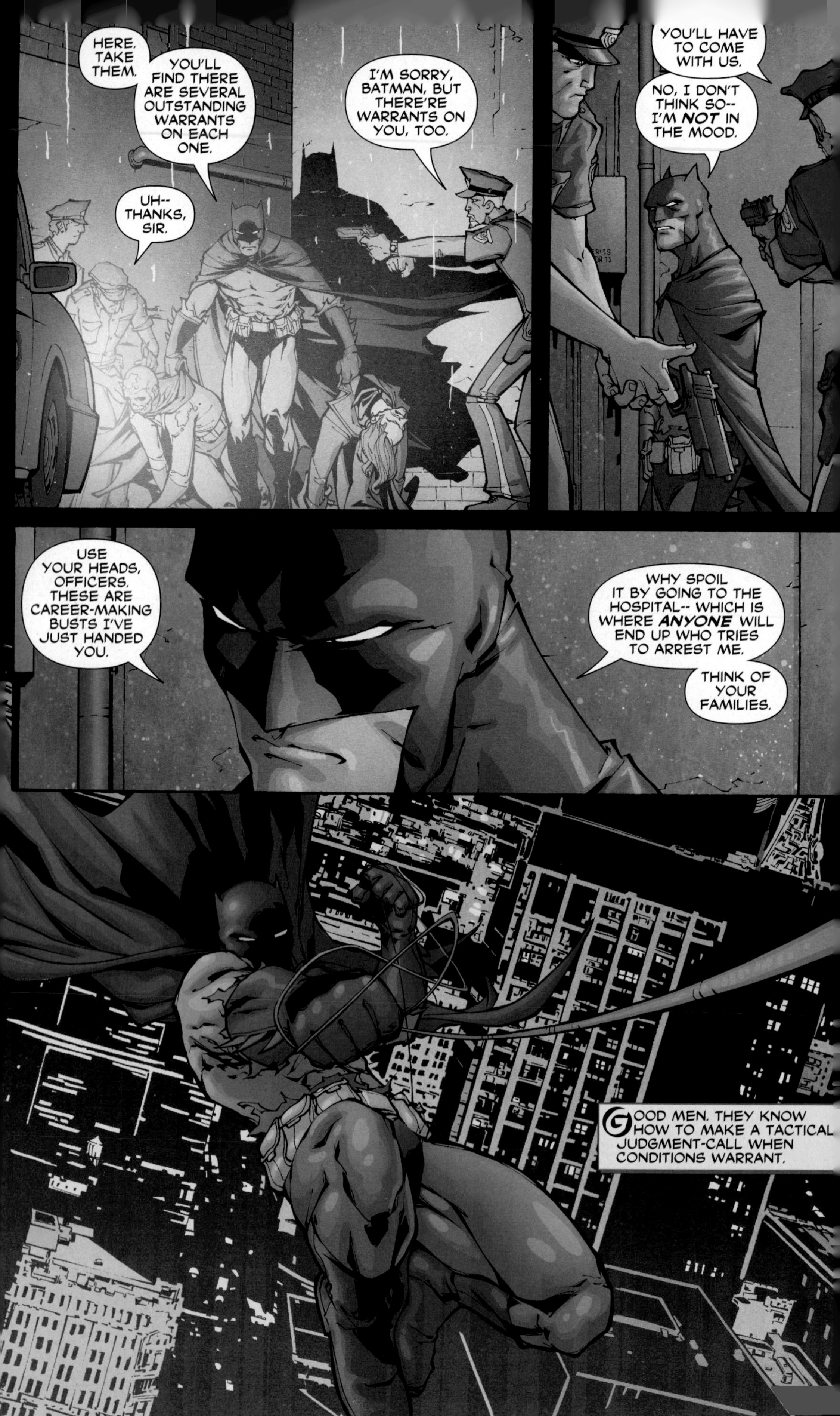

HERE. TAKE THEM.
YOU'LL FIND THERE ARE SEVERAL OUTSTANDING WARRANTS ON EACH ONE.
UH-- THANKS, SIR.
I'M SORRY, BATMAN, BUT THERE'RE WARRANTS ON YOU, TOO.
YOU'LL HAVE TO COME WITH US.
NO, I DON'T THINK SO-- I'M NOT IN THE MOOD.
USE YOUR HEADS, OFFICERS. THESE ARE CAREER-MAKING BUSTS I'VE JUST HANDED YOU.
WHY SPOIL IT BY GOING TO THE HOSPITAL-- WHICH IS WHERE ANYONE WILL END UP WHO TRIES TO ARREST ME.
THINK OF YOUR FAMILIES.
GOOD MEN. THEY KNOW HOW TO MAKE A TACTICAL JUDGMENT-CALL WHEN CONDITIONS WARRANT.

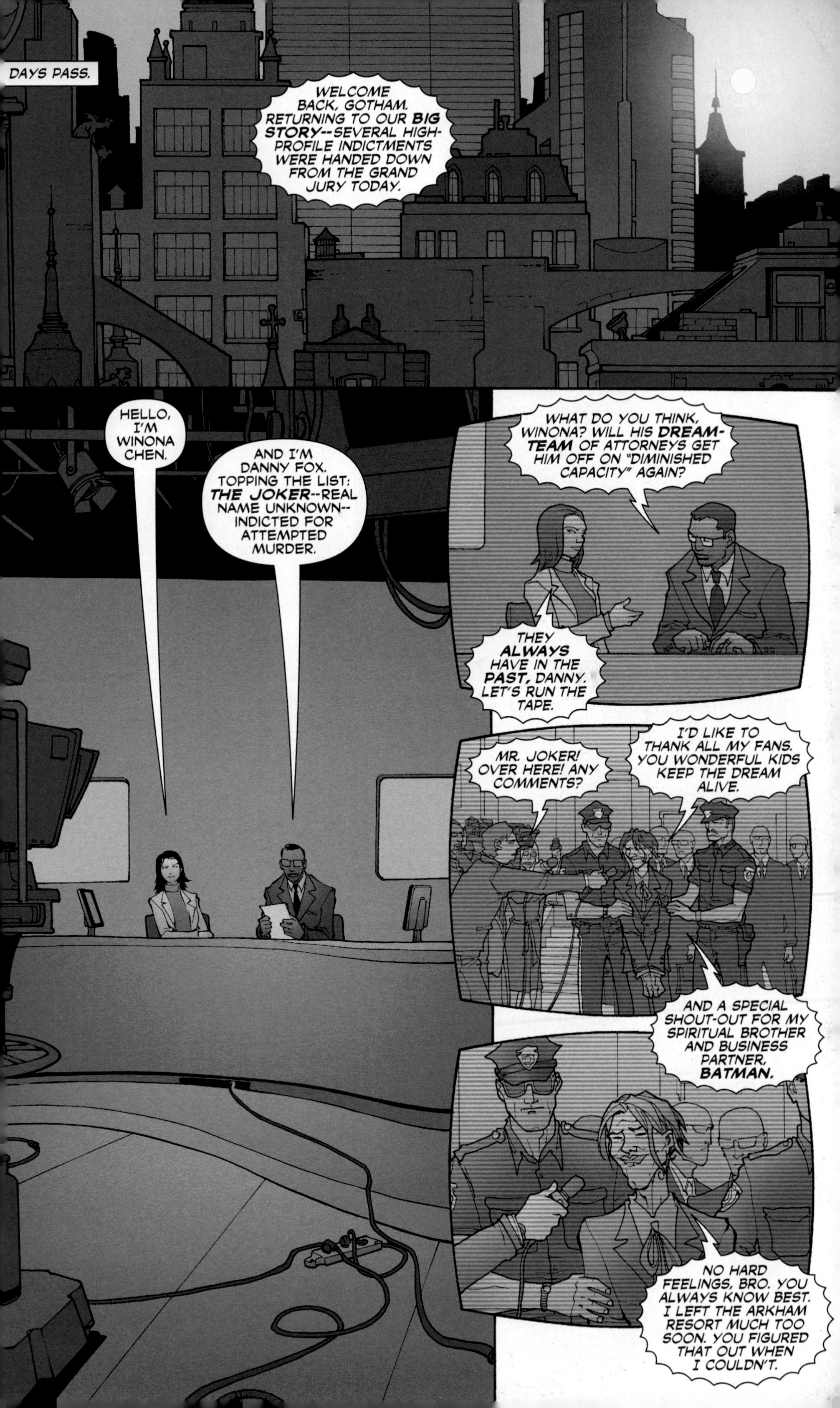
DAYS PASS.
WELCOME BACK, GOTHAM. RETURNING TO OUR BIG STORY--SEVERAL HIGH-PROFILE INDICTMENTS WERE HANDED DOWN FROM THE GRAND JURY TODAY.
HELLO, I'M WINONA CHEN.
AND I'M DANNY FOX, TOPPING THE LIST: THE JOKER--REAL NAME UNKNOWN--INDICTED FOR ATTEMPTED MURDER.
WHAT DO YOU THINK, WINONA? WILL HIS DREAM-TEAM OF ATTORNEYS GET HIM OFF ON "DIMINISHED CAPACITY" AGAIN?
THEY ALWAYS HAVE IN THE PAST, DANNY. LET'S RUN THE TAPE.
MR. JOKER! OVER HERE! ANY COMMENTS?
I'D LIKE TO THANK ALL MY FANS. YOU WONDERFUL KIDS KEEP THE DREAM ALIVE.
AND A SPECIAL SHOUT-OUT FOR MY SPIRITUAL BROTHER AND BUSINESS PARTNER, BATMAN.
NO HARD FEELINGS, BRO. YOU ALWAYS KNOW BEST. I LEFT THE ARKHAM RESORT MUCH TOO SOON. YOU FIGURED THAT OUT WHEN I COULDN'T.

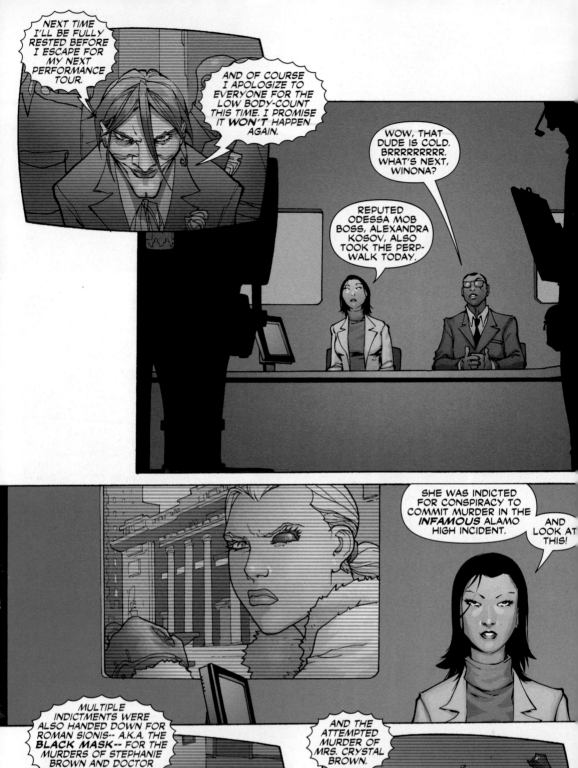

NEXT TIME I'LL BE FULLY RESTED BEFORE I ESCAPE FOR MY NEXT PERFORMANCE TOUR.

AND OF COURSE I APOLOGIZE TO EVERYONE FOR THE LOW BODY-COUNT THIS TIME. I PROMISE IT *WON'T* HAPPEN AGAIN.

WOW, THAT DUDE IS COLD. BRRRRRRRR. WHAT'S NEXT, WINONA?

REPUTED ODESSA MOB BOSS, ALEXANDRA KOSOV, ALSO TOOK THE PERP-WALK TODAY.

SHE WAS INDICTED FOR CONSPIRACY TO COMMIT MURDER IN THE *INFAMOUS* ALAMO HIGH INCIDENT.

AND LOOK AT THIS!

MULTIPLE INDICTMENTS WERE ALSO HANDED DOWN FOR ROMAN SIONIS-- A.K.A. THE *BLACK MASK*-- FOR THE MURDERS OF STEPHANIE BROWN AND DOCTOR VERA CESARES.

AND THE ATTEMPTED MURDER OF MRS. CRYSTAL BROWN.

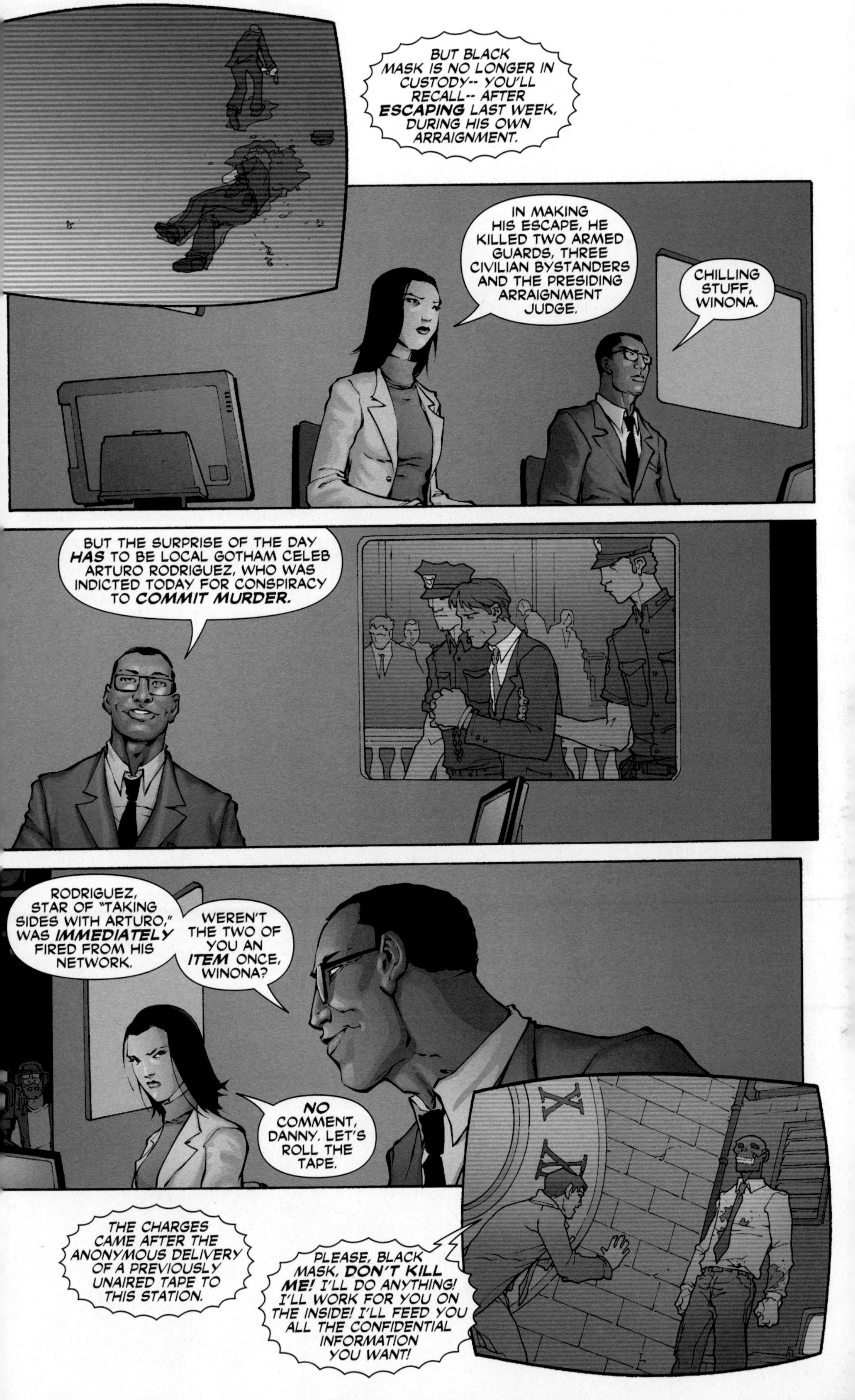
BUT BLACK MASK IS NO LONGER IN CUSTODY-- YOU'LL RECALL-- AFTER **ESCAPING** LAST WEEK, DURING HIS OWN ARRAIGNMENT.
IN MAKING HIS ESCAPE, HE KILLED TWO ARMED GUARDS, THREE CIVILIAN BYSTANDERS AND THE PRESIDING ARRAIGNMENT JUDGE.
CHILLING STUFF, WINONA.
BUT THE SURPRISE OF THE DAY **HAS** TO BE LOCAL GOTHAM CELEB ARTURO RODRIGUEZ, WHO WAS INDICTED TODAY FOR CONSPIRACY TO **COMMIT MURDER.**
RODRIGUEZ, STAR OF "TAKING SIDES WITH ARTURO," WAS **IMMEDIATELY** FIRED FROM HIS NETWORK.
WEREN'T THE TWO OF YOU AN **ITEM** ONCE, WINONA?
NO COMMENT, DANNY. LET'S ROLL THE TAPE.
THE CHARGES CAME AFTER THE ANONYMOUS DELIVERY OF A PREVIOUSLY UNAIRED TAPE TO THIS STATION.
PLEASE, BLACK MASK, **DON'T KILL ME!** I'LL DO ANYTHING! I'LL WORK FOR YOU ON THE INSIDE! I'LL FEED YOU ALL THE CONFIDENTIAL INFORMATION YOU WANT!

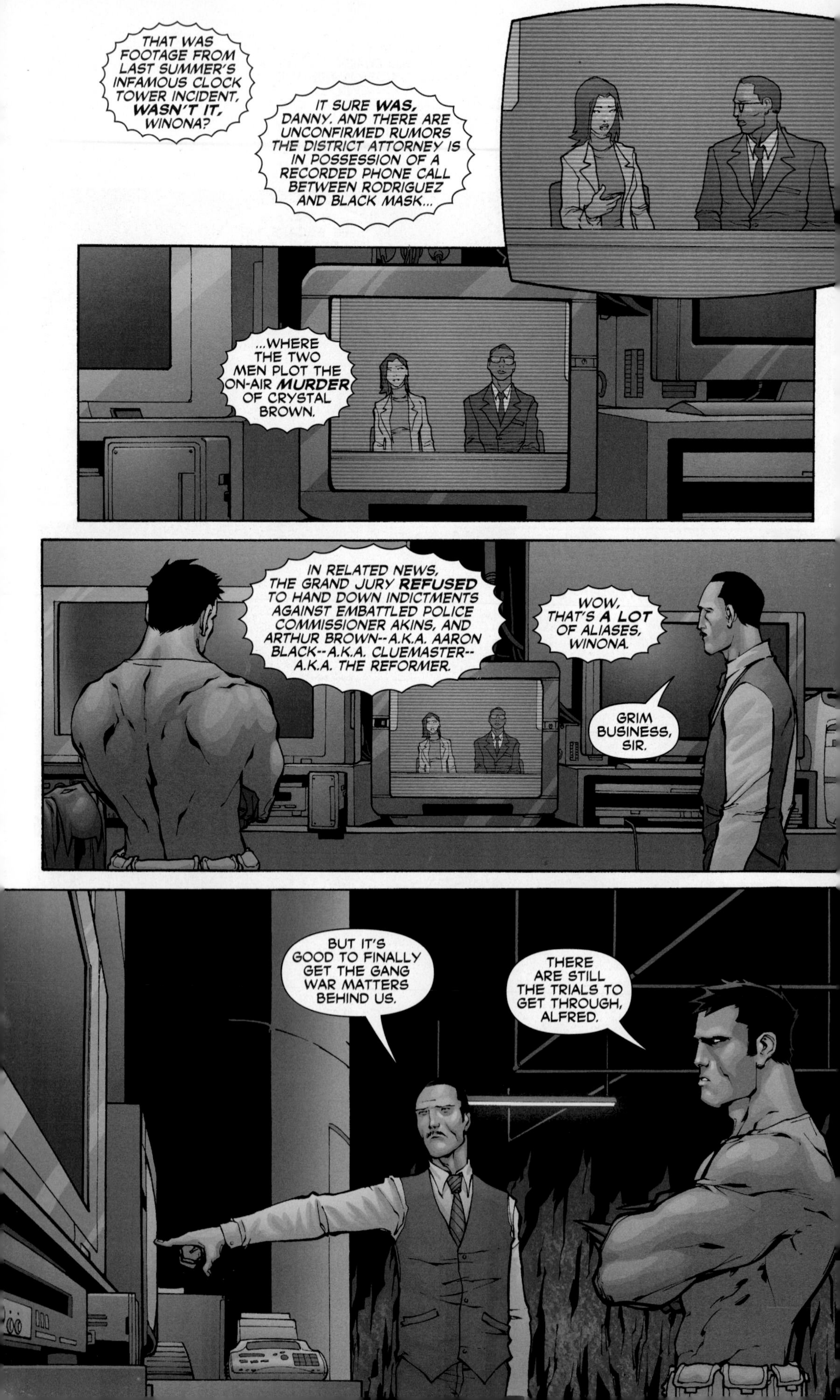
THAT WAS FOOTAGE FROM LAST SUMMER'S INFAMOUS CLOCK TOWER INCIDENT, **WASN'T IT,** WINONA?
IT SURE **WAS,** DANNY. AND THERE ARE UNCONFIRMED RUMORS THE DISTRICT ATTORNEY IS IN POSSESSION OF A RECORDED PHONE CALL BETWEEN RODRIGUEZ AND BLACK MASK...
...WHERE THE TWO MEN PLOT THE ON-AIR **MURDER** OF CRYSTAL BROWN.
IN RELATED NEWS, THE GRAND JURY **REFUSED** TO HAND DOWN INDICTMENTS AGAINST EMBATTLED POLICE COMMISSIONER AKINS, AND ARTHUR BROWN--A.K.A. AARON BLACK--A.K.A. CLUEMASTER--A.K.A. THE REFORMER.
WOW, THAT'S **A LOT** OF ALIASES, WINONA.
GRIM BUSINESS, SIR.
BUT IT'S GOOD TO FINALLY GET THE GANG WAR MATTERS BEHIND US.
THERE ARE STILL THE TRIALS TO GET THROUGH, ALFRED.

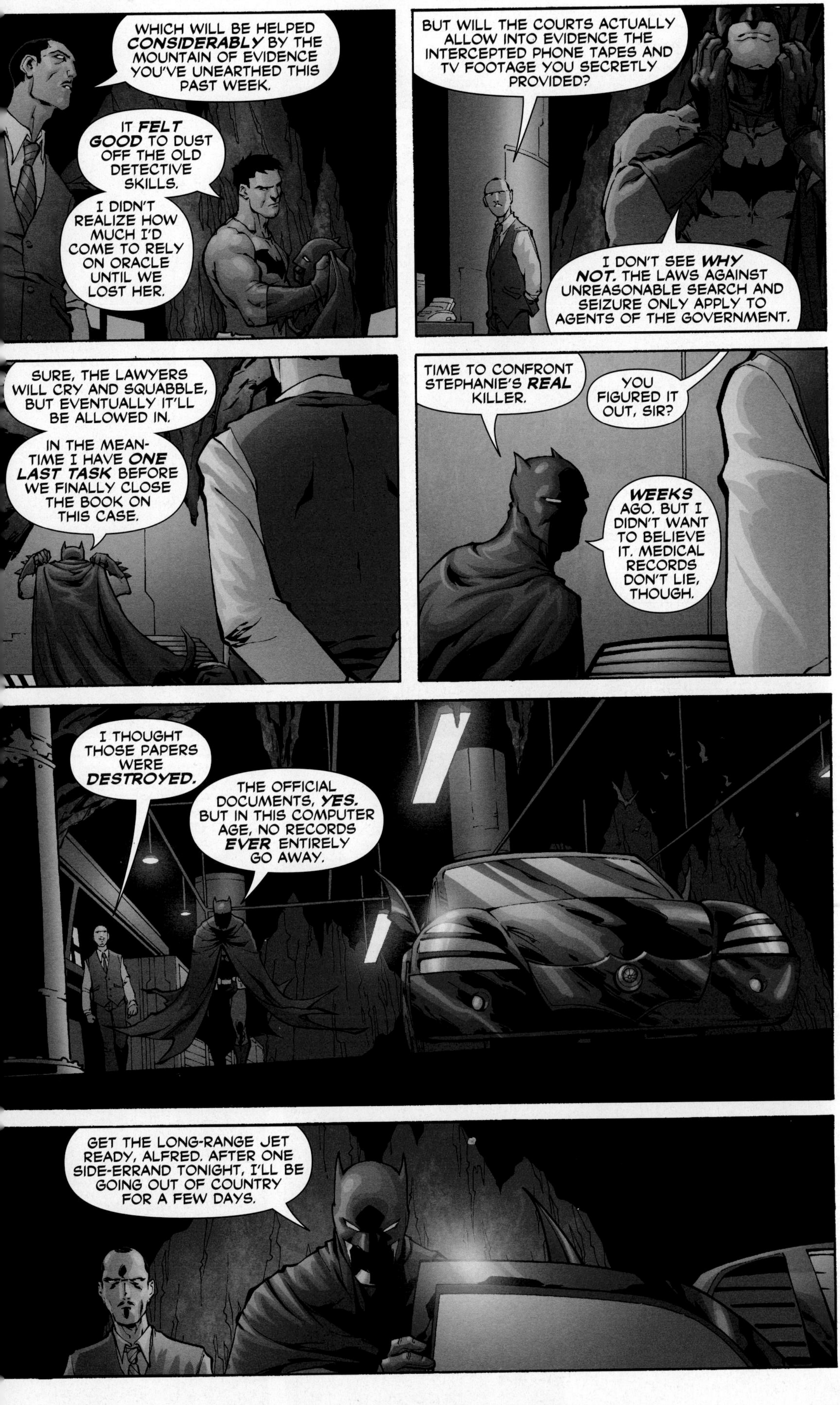

WHICH WILL BE HELPED CONSIDERABLY BY THE MOUNTAIN OF EVIDENCE YOU'VE UNEARTHED THIS PAST WEEK.
IT FELT GOOD TO DUST OFF THE OLD DETECTIVE SKILLS.
I DIDN'T REALIZE HOW MUCH I'D COME TO RELY ON ORACLE UNTIL WE LOST HER.
BUT WILL THE COURTS ACTUALLY ALLOW INTO EVIDENCE THE INTERCEPTED PHONE TAPES AND TV FOOTAGE YOU SECRETLY PROVIDED?
I DON'T SEE WHY NOT. THE LAWS AGAINST UNREASONABLE SEARCH AND SEIZURE ONLY APPLY TO AGENTS OF THE GOVERNMENT.
SURE, THE LAWYERS WILL CRY AND SQUABBLE, BUT EVENTUALLY IT'LL BE ALLOWED IN.
IN THE MEAN-TIME I HAVE ONE LAST TASK BEFORE WE FINALLY CLOSE THE BOOK ON THIS CASE.
TIME TO CONFRONT STEPHANIE'S REAL KILLER.
YOU FIGURED IT OUT, SIR?
WEEKS AGO. BUT I DIDN'T WANT TO BELIEVE IT. MEDICAL RECORDS DON'T LIE, THOUGH.
I THOUGHT THOSE PAPERS WERE DESTROYED.
THE OFFICIAL DOCUMENTS, YES. BUT IN THIS COMPUTER AGE, NO RECORDS EVER ENTIRELY GO AWAY.
GET THE LONG-RANGE JET READY, ALFRED. AFTER ONE SIDE-ERRAND TONIGHT, I'LL BE GOING OUT OF COUNTRY FOR A FEW DAYS.

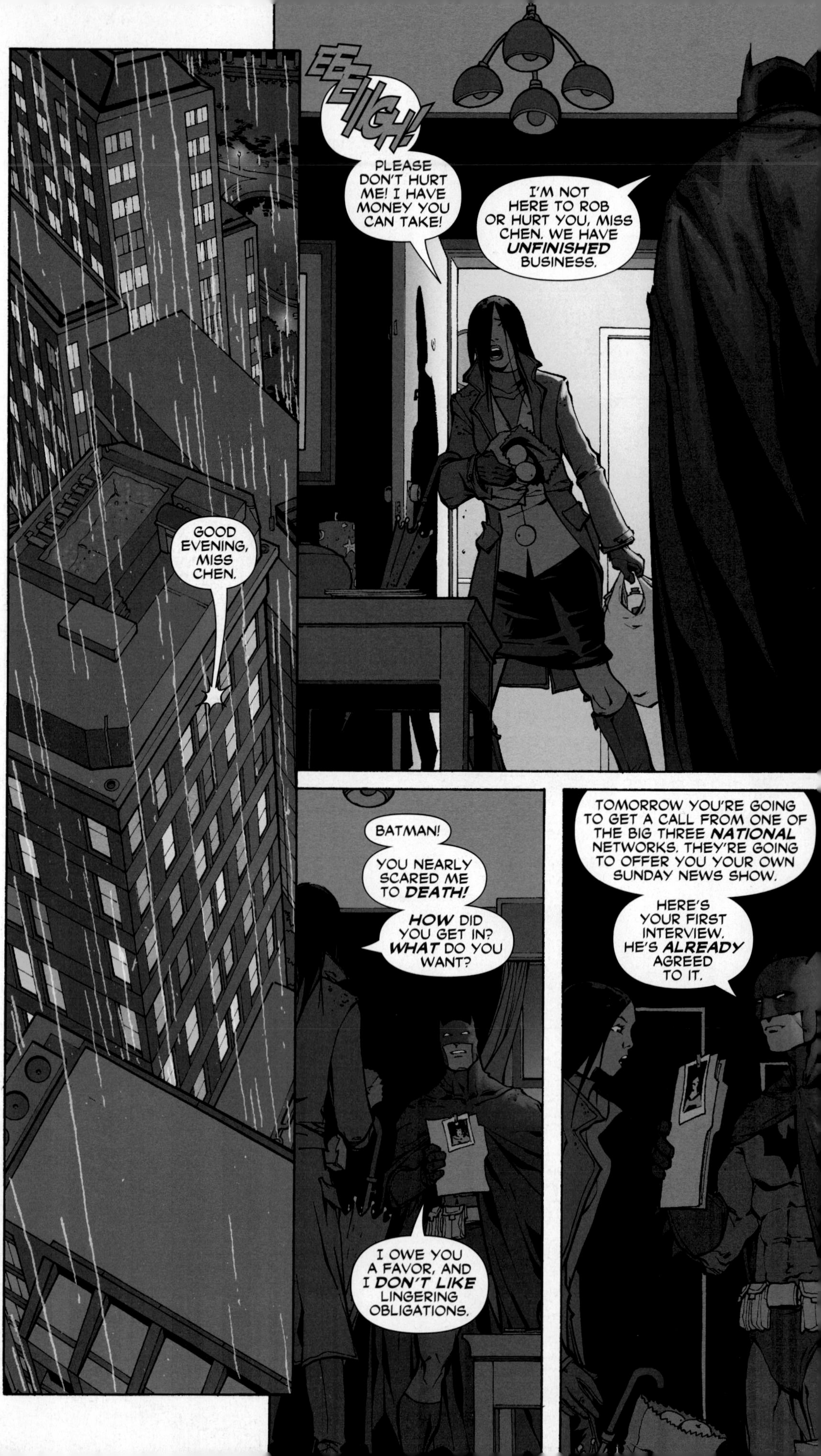
GOOD EVENING, MISS CHEN.
EEEIIIGH!
PLEASE DON'T HURT ME! I HAVE MONEY YOU CAN TAKE!
I'M NOT HERE TO ROB OR HURT YOU, MISS CHEN. WE HAVE UNFINISHED BUSINESS.
BATMAN!
YOU NEARLY SCARED ME TO DEATH!
HOW DID YOU GET IN? WHAT DO YOU WANT?
I OWE YOU A FAVOR, AND I DON'T LIKE LINGERING OBLIGATIONS.
TOMORROW YOU'RE GOING TO GET A CALL FROM ONE OF THE BIG THREE NATIONAL NETWORKS. THEY'RE GOING TO OFFER YOU YOUR OWN SUNDAY NEWS SHOW.
HERE'S YOUR FIRST INTERVIEW. HE'S ALREADY AGREED TO IT.

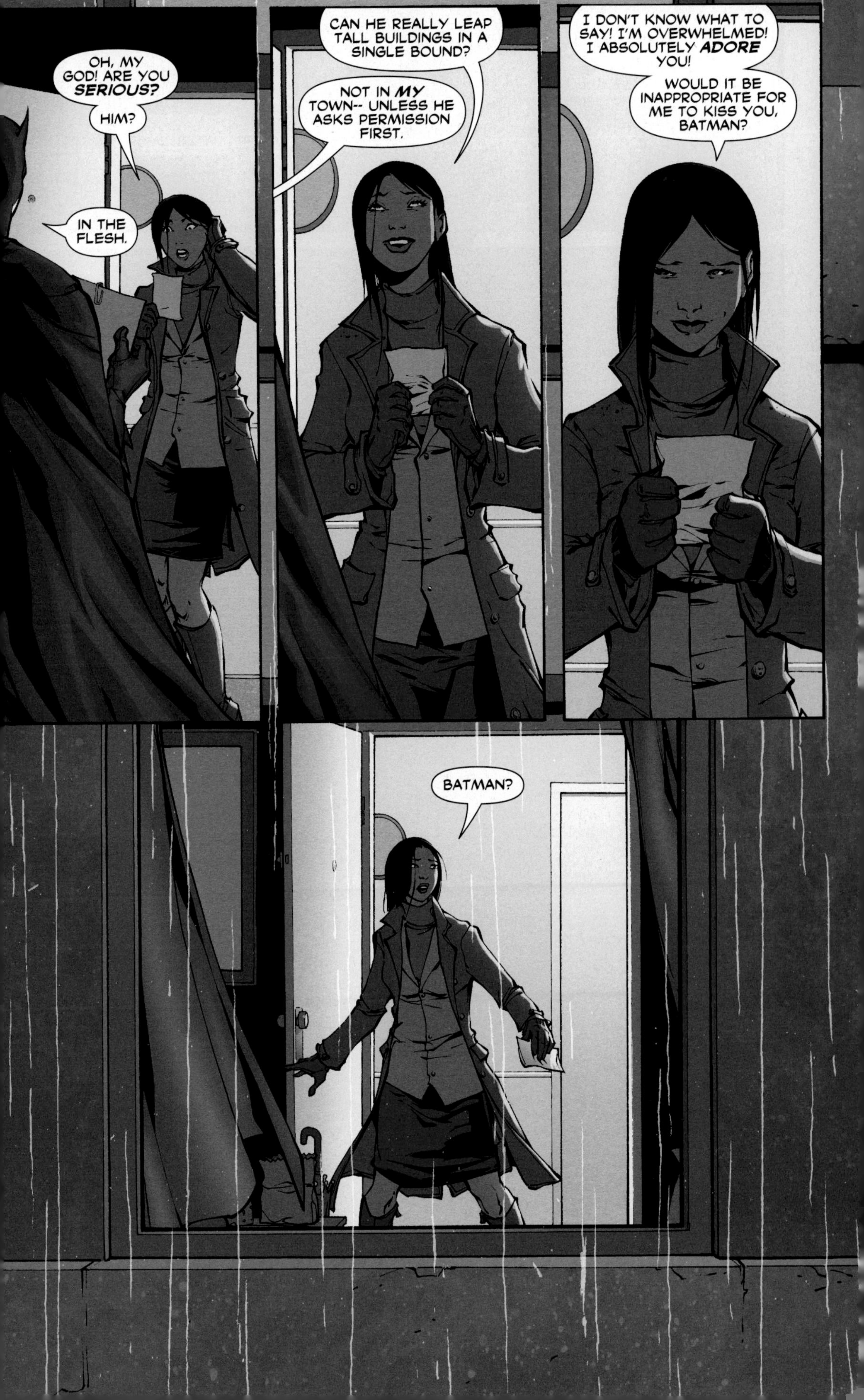
OH, MY GOD! ARE YOU SERIOUS?
HIM?
IN THE FLESH.
CAN HE REALLY LEAP TALL BUILDINGS IN A SINGLE BOUND?
NOT IN MY TOWN-- UNLESS HE ASKS PERMISSION FIRST.
I DON'T KNOW WHAT TO SAY! I'M OVERWHELMED! I ABSOLUTELY ADORE YOU!
WOULD IT BE INAPPROPRIATE FOR ME TO KISS YOU, BATMAN?
BATMAN?

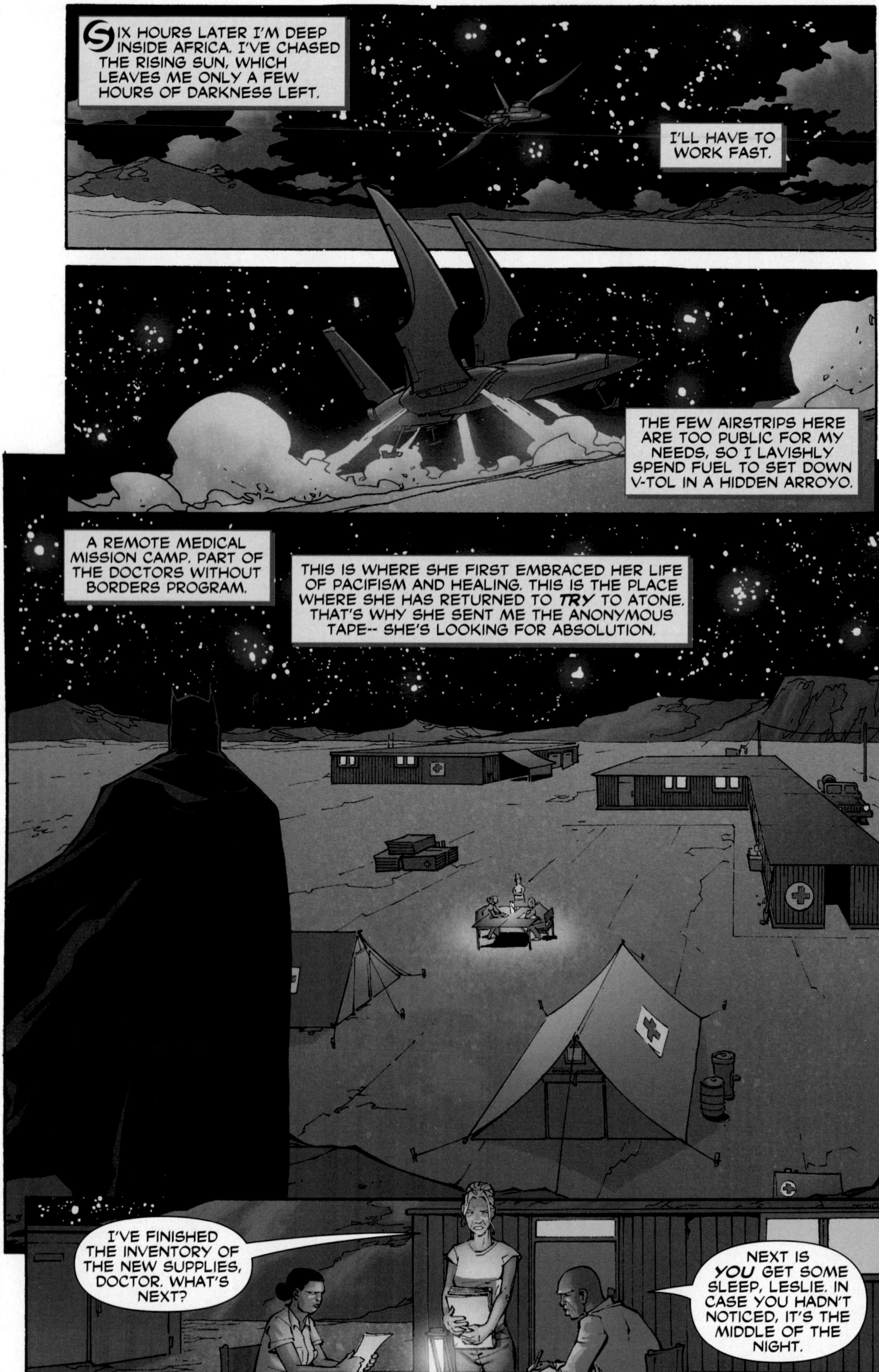
SIX HOURS LATER I'M DEEP INSIDE AFRICA. I'VE CHASED THE RISING SUN, WHICH LEAVES ME ONLY A FEW HOURS OF DARKNESS LEFT.
I'LL HAVE TO WORK FAST.
THE FEW AIRSTRIPS HERE ARE TOO PUBLIC FOR MY NEEDS, SO I LAVISHLY SPEND FUEL TO SET DOWN V-TOL IN A HIDDEN ARROYO.
A REMOTE MEDICAL MISSION CAMP. PART OF THE DOCTORS WITHOUT BORDERS PROGRAM.
THIS IS WHERE SHE FIRST EMBRACED HER LIFE OF PACIFISM AND HEALING. THIS IS THE PLACE WHERE SHE HAS RETURNED TO TRY TO ATONE. THAT'S WHY SHE SENT ME THE ANONYMOUS TAPE-- SHE'S LOOKING FOR ABSOLUTION.
I'VE FINISHED THE INVENTORY OF THE NEW SUPPLIES, DOCTOR. WHAT'S NEXT?
NEXT IS YOU GET SOME SLEEP, LESLIE. IN CASE YOU HADN'T NOTICED, IT'S THE MIDDLE OF THE NIGHT.

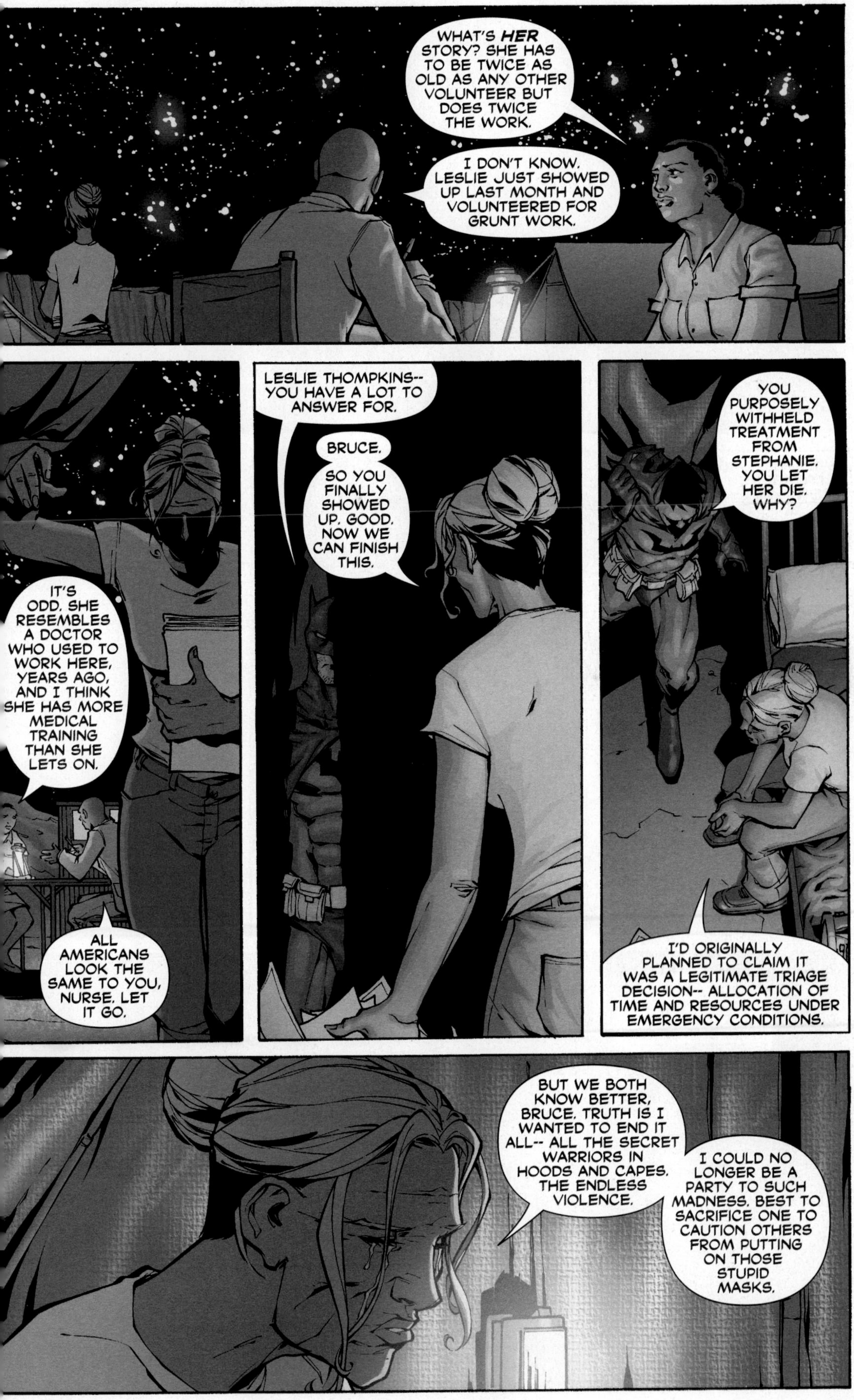
WHAT'S **HER** STORY? SHE HAS TO BE TWICE AS OLD AS ANY OTHER VOLUNTEER BUT DOES TWICE THE WORK.
I DON'T KNOW. LESLIE JUST SHOWED UP LAST MONTH AND VOLUNTEERED FOR GRUNT WORK.
IT'S ODD. SHE RESEMBLES A DOCTOR WHO USED TO WORK HERE, YEARS AGO, AND I THINK SHE HAS MORE MEDICAL TRAINING THAN SHE LETS ON.
ALL AMERICANS LOOK THE SAME TO YOU, NURSE. LET IT GO.
LESLIE THOMPKINS-- YOU HAVE A LOT TO ANSWER FOR.
BRUCE.
SO YOU FINALLY SHOWED UP. GOOD. NOW WE CAN FINISH THIS.
YOU PURPOSELY WITHHELD TREATMENT FROM STEPHANIE. YOU LET HER DIE. WHY?
I'D ORIGINALLY PLANNED TO CLAIM IT WAS A LEGITIMATE TRIAGE DECISION-- ALLOCATION OF TIME AND RESOURCES UNDER EMERGENCY CONDITIONS.
BUT WE BOTH KNOW BETTER, BRUCE. TRUTH IS I WANTED TO END IT ALL-- ALL THE SECRET WARRIORS IN HOODS AND CAPES. THE ENDLESS VIOLENCE.
I COULD NO LONGER BE A PARTY TO SUCH MADNESS. BEST TO SACRIFICE ONE TO CAUTION OTHERS FROM PUTTING ON THOSE STUPID MASKS.

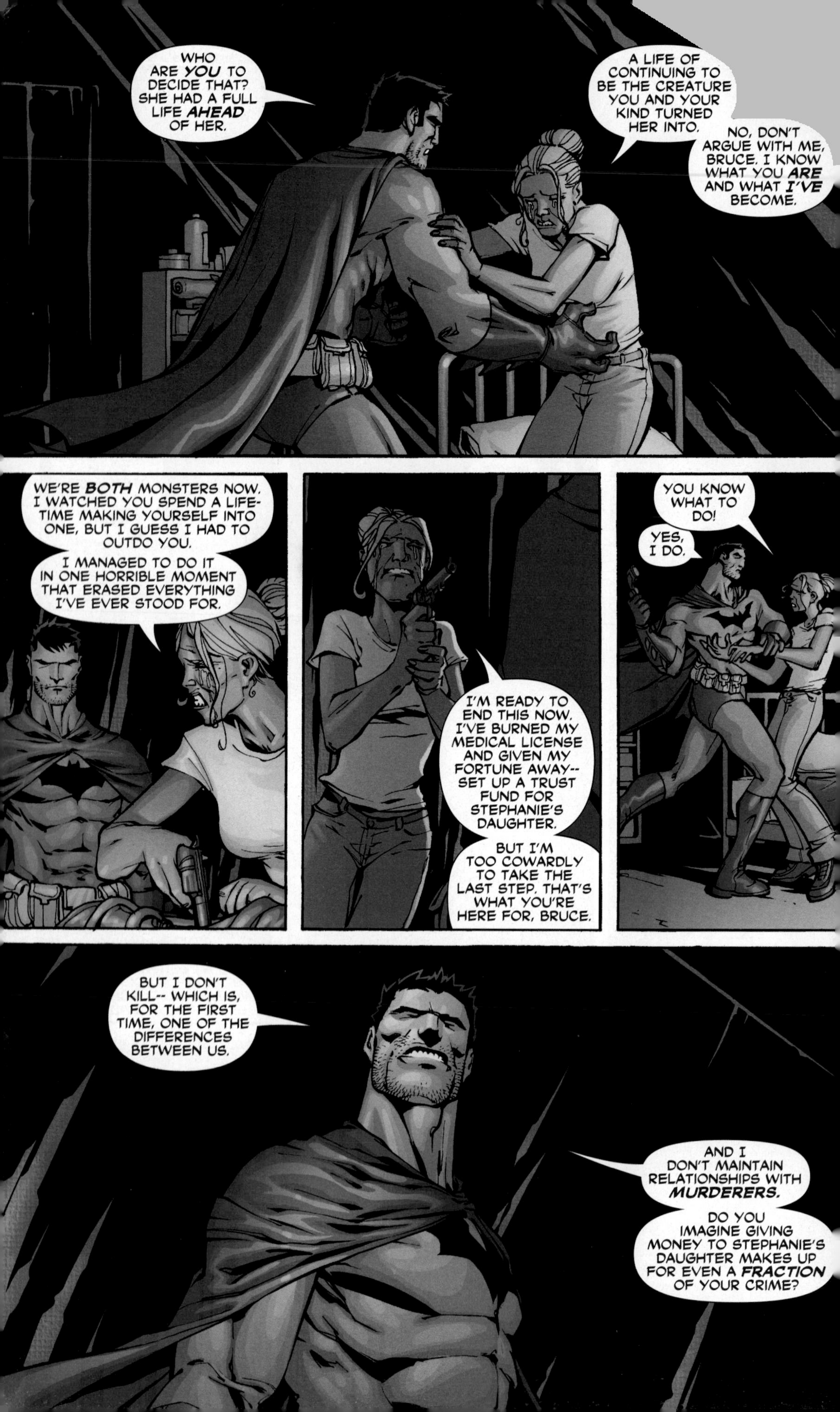
WHO ARE YOU TO DECIDE THAT? SHE HAD A FULL LIFE AHEAD OF HER.
A LIFE OF CONTINUING TO BE THE CREATURE YOU AND YOUR KIND TURNED HER INTO.
NO, DON'T ARGUE WITH ME, BRUCE. I KNOW WHAT YOU ARE AND WHAT I'VE BECOME.
WE'RE BOTH MONSTERS NOW. I WATCHED YOU SPEND A LIFETIME MAKING YOURSELF INTO ONE, BUT I GUESS I HAD TO OUTDO YOU.
I MANAGED TO DO IT IN ONE HORRIBLE MOMENT THAT ERASED EVERYTHING I'VE EVER STOOD FOR.
I'M READY TO END THIS NOW. I'VE BURNED MY MEDICAL LICENSE AND GIVEN MY FORTUNE AWAY-- SET UP A TRUST FUND FOR STEPHANIE'S DAUGHTER.
BUT I'M TOO COWARDLY TO TAKE THE LAST STEP. THAT'S WHAT YOU'RE HERE FOR, BRUCE.
YOU KNOW WHAT TO DO!
YES, I DO.
BUT I DON'T KILL-- WHICH IS, FOR THE FIRST TIME, ONE OF THE DIFFERENCES BETWEEN US.
AND I DON'T MAINTAIN RELATIONSHIPS WITH MURDERERS.
DO YOU IMAGINE GIVING MONEY TO STEPHANIE'S DAUGHTER MAKES UP FOR EVEN A FRACTION OF YOUR CRIME?

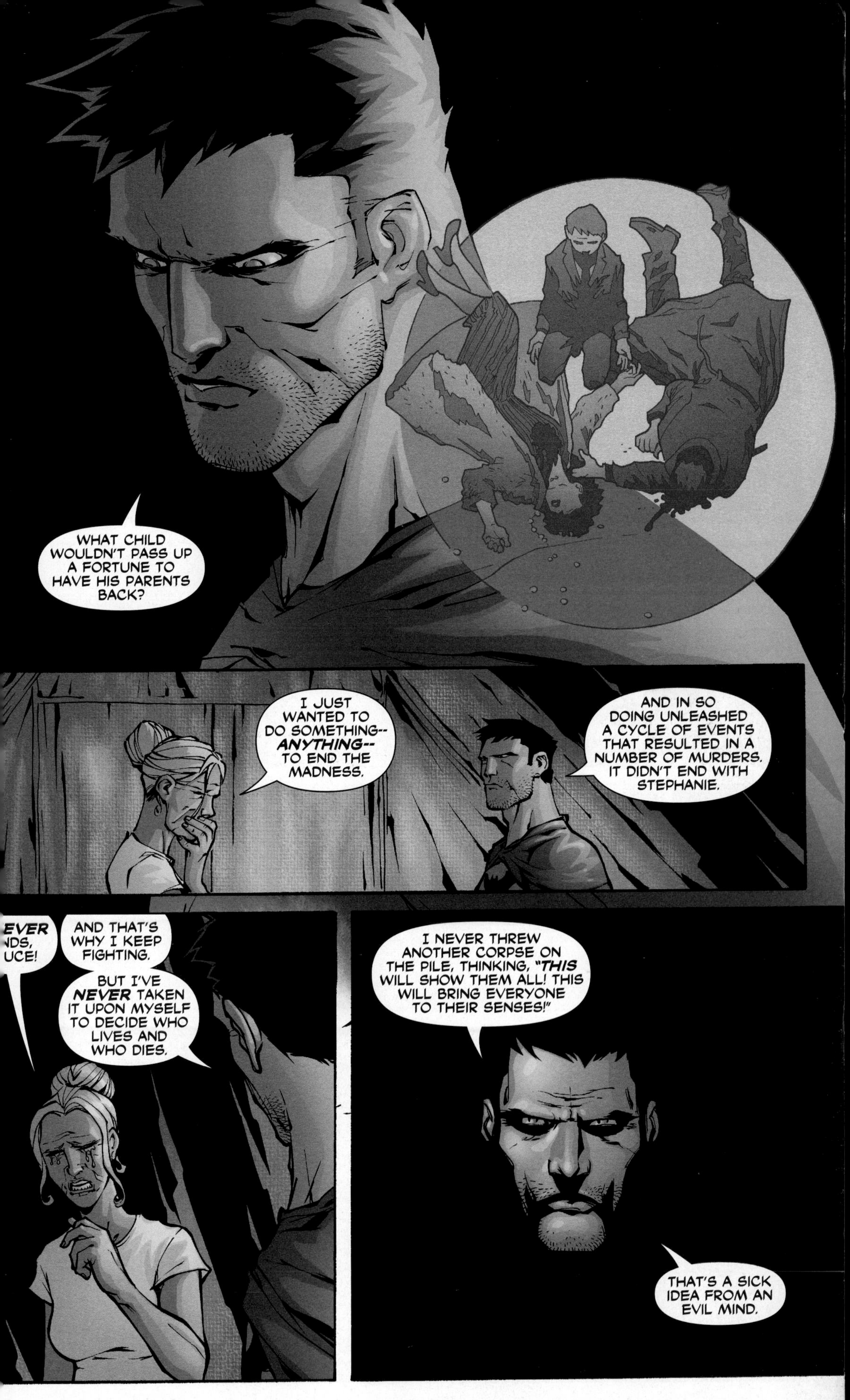

WHAT CHILD WOULDN'T PASS UP A FORTUNE TO HAVE HIS PARENTS BACK?
I JUST WANTED TO DO SOMETHING-- ANYTHING-- TO END THE MADNESS.
AND IN SO DOING UNLEASHED A CYCLE OF EVENTS THAT RESULTED IN A NUMBER OF MURDERS. IT DIDN'T END WITH STEPHANIE.
EVER NDS, UCE!
AND THAT'S WHY I KEEP FIGHTING.
BUT I'VE NEVER TAKEN IT UPON MYSELF TO DECIDE WHO LIVES AND WHO DIES.
I NEVER THREW ANOTHER CORPSE ON THE PILE, THINKING, "THIS WILL SHOW THEM ALL! THIS WILL BRING EVERYONE TO THEIR SENSES!"
THAT'S A SICK IDEA FROM AN EVIL MIND.

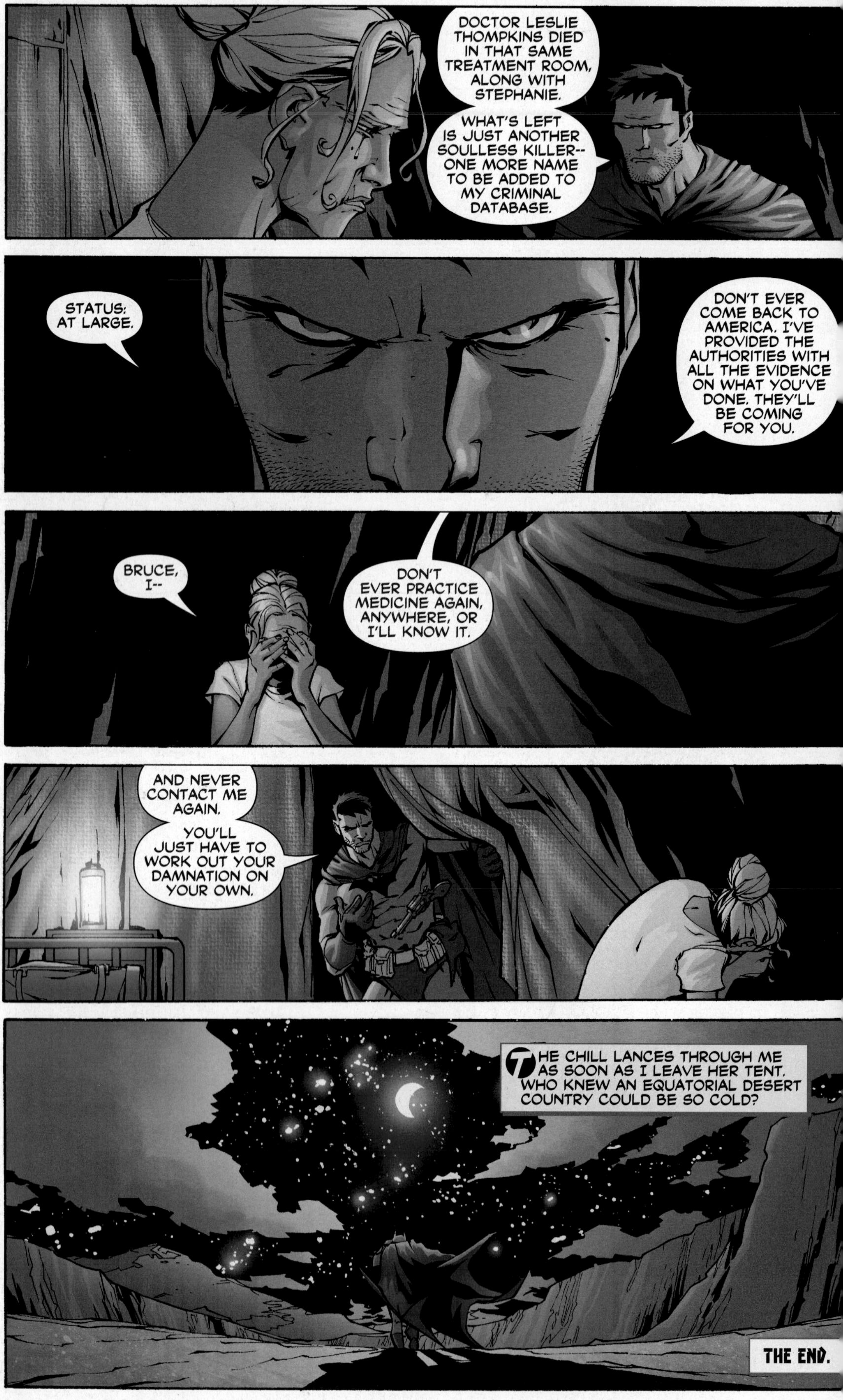
DOCTOR LESLIE THOMPKINS DIED IN THAT SAME TREATMENT ROOM, ALONG WITH STEPHANIE.
WHAT'S LEFT IS JUST ANOTHER SOULLESS KILLER-- ONE MORE NAME TO BE ADDED TO MY CRIMINAL DATABASE.
STATUS: AT LARGE.
DON'T EVER COME BACK TO AMERICA. I'VE PROVIDED THE AUTHORITIES WITH ALL THE EVIDENCE ON WHAT YOU'VE DONE. THEY'LL BE COMING FOR YOU.
BRUCE, I--
DON'T EVER PRACTICE MEDICINE AGAIN, ANYWHERE, OR I'LL KNOW IT.
AND NEVER CONTACT ME AGAIN.
YOU'LL JUST HAVE TO WORK OUT YOUR DAMNATION ON YOUR OWN.
THE CHILL LANCES THROUGH ME AS SOON AS I LEAVE HER TENT. WHO KNEW AN EQUATORIAL DESERT COUNTRY COULD BE SO COLD?
THE END.

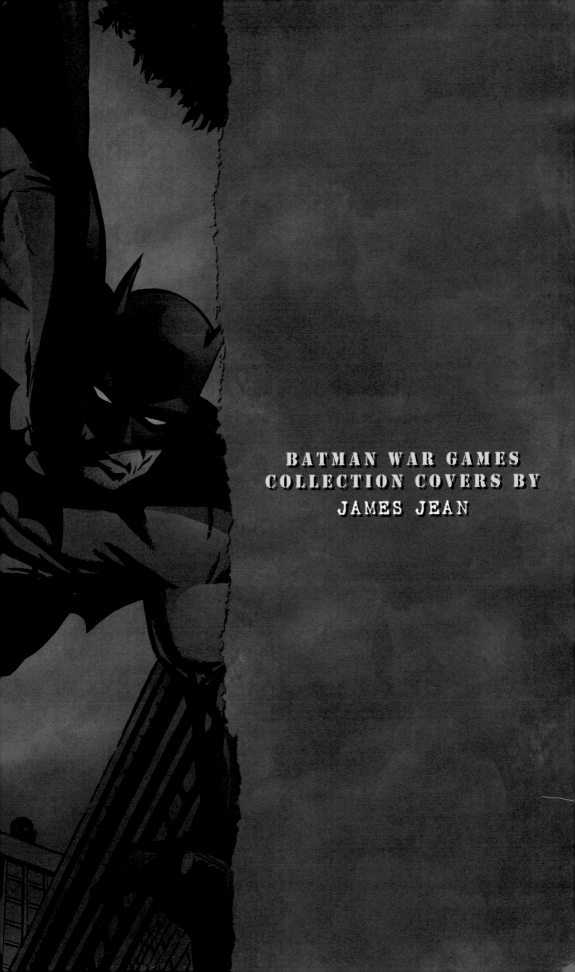

BATMAN WAR GAMES
COLLECTION COVERS BY
JAMES JEAN

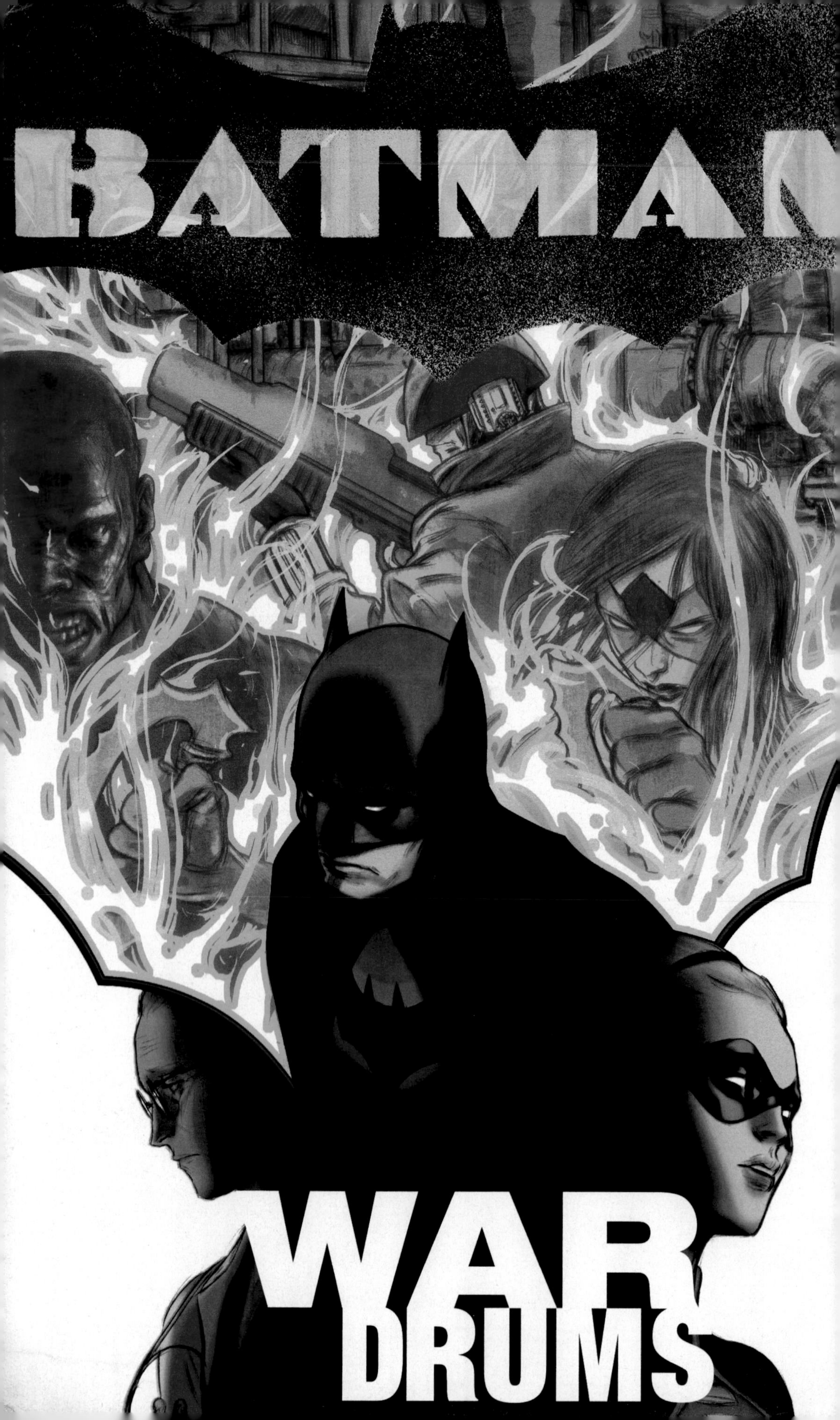
BATMAN
WAR
DRUMS

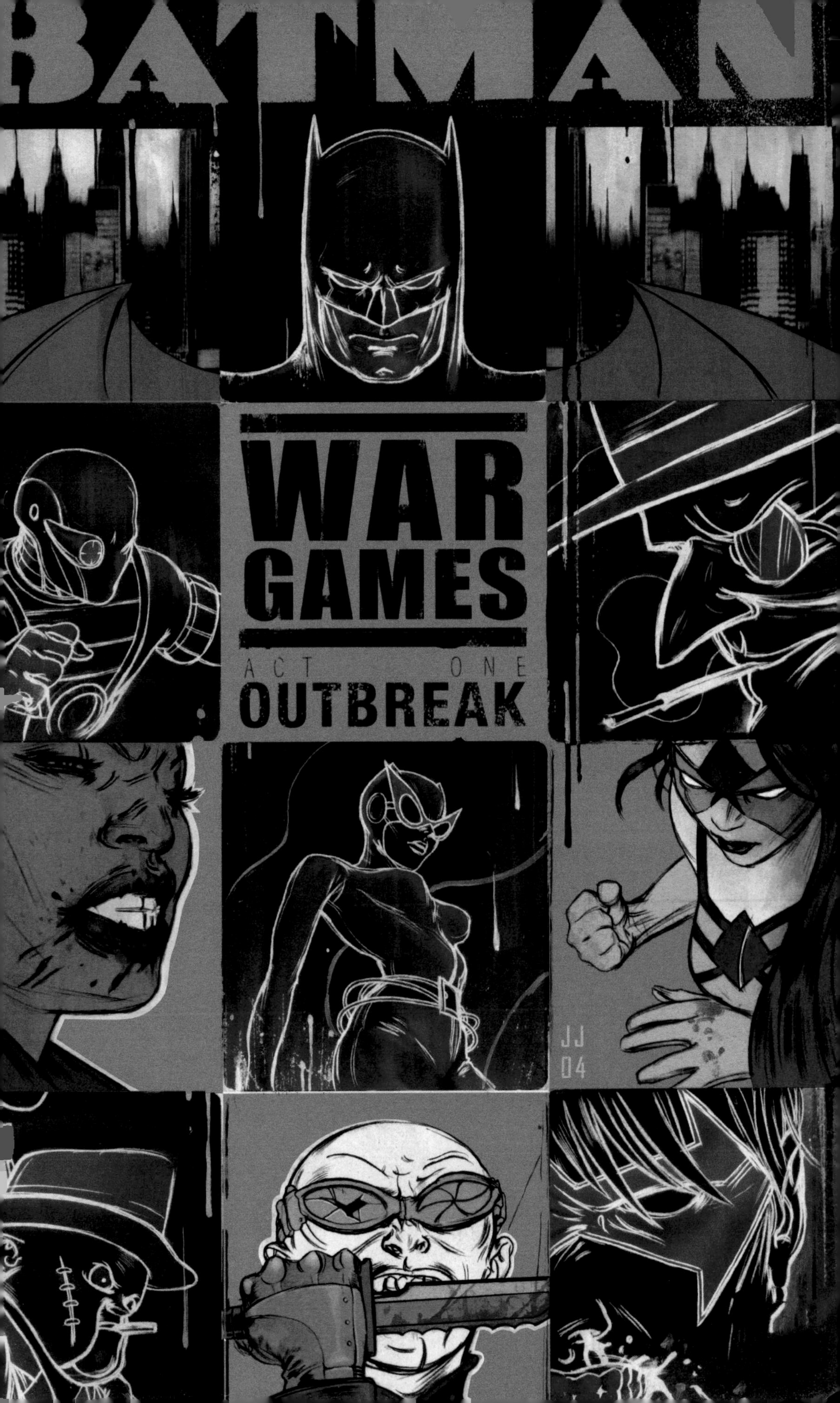
BATMAN
WAR GAMES
ACT ONE
OUTBREAK
JJ 04

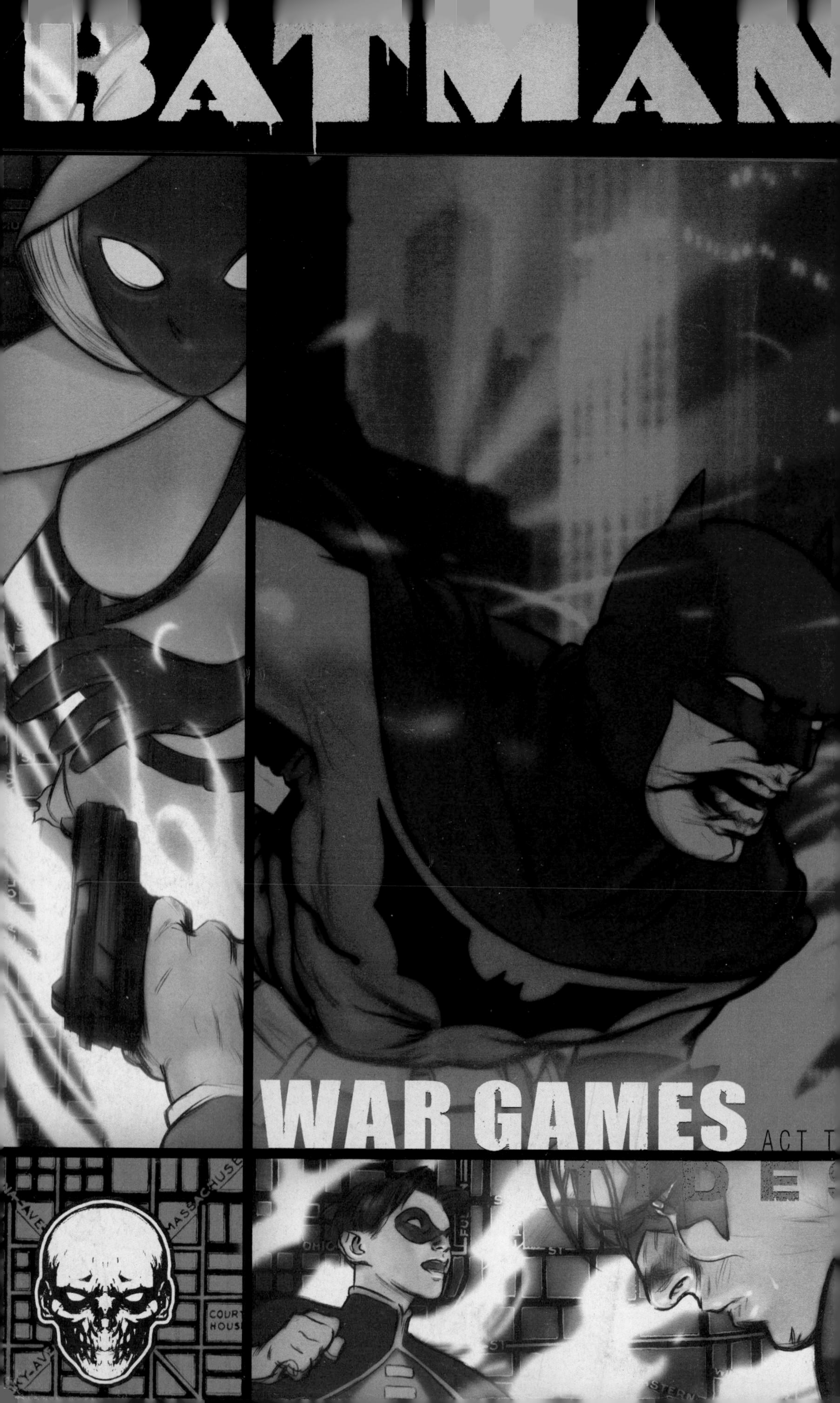
BATMAN
WAR GAMES
ACT
COURT HOUSE

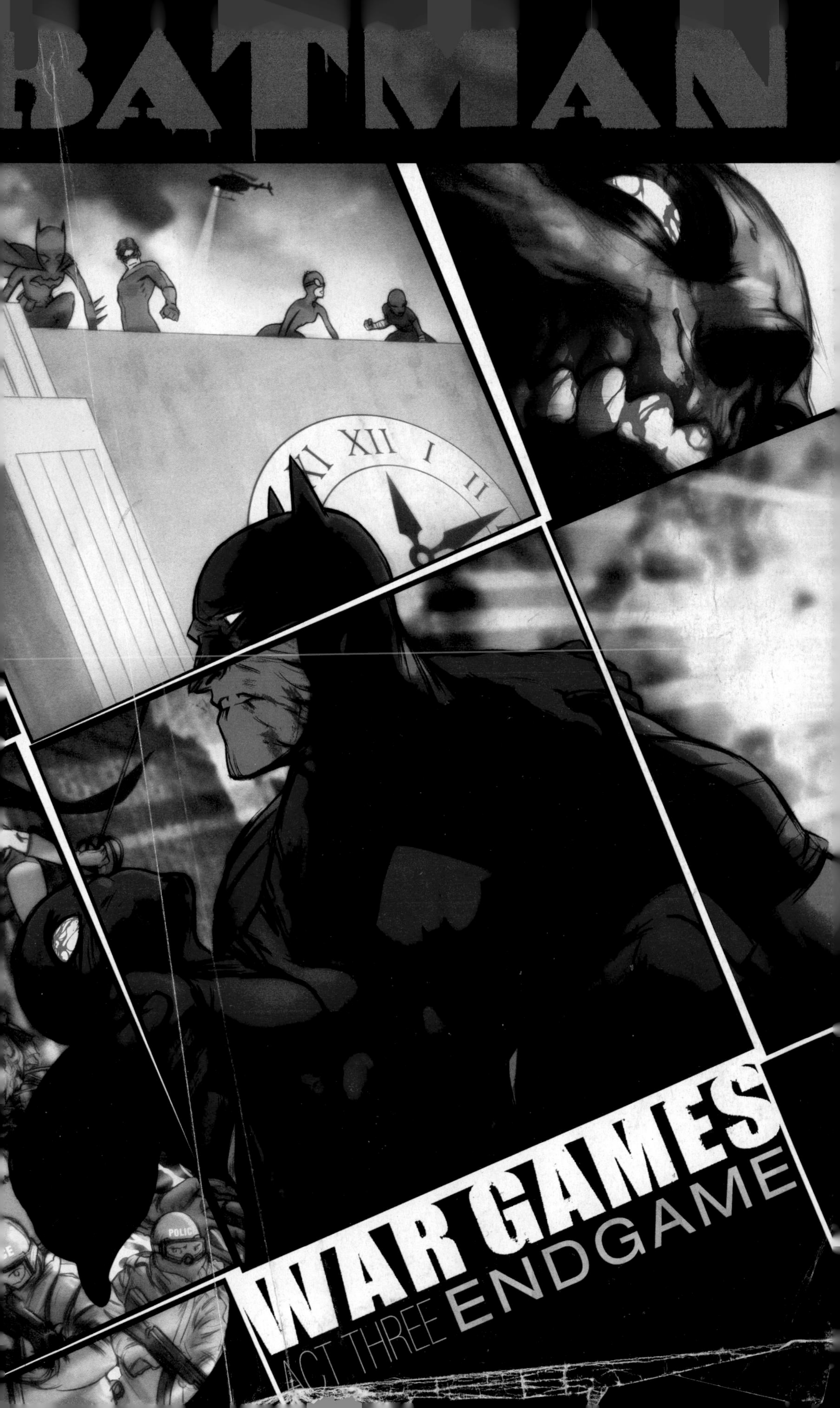
BATMAN
WAR GAMES
ACT THREE
ENDGAME
POLIC

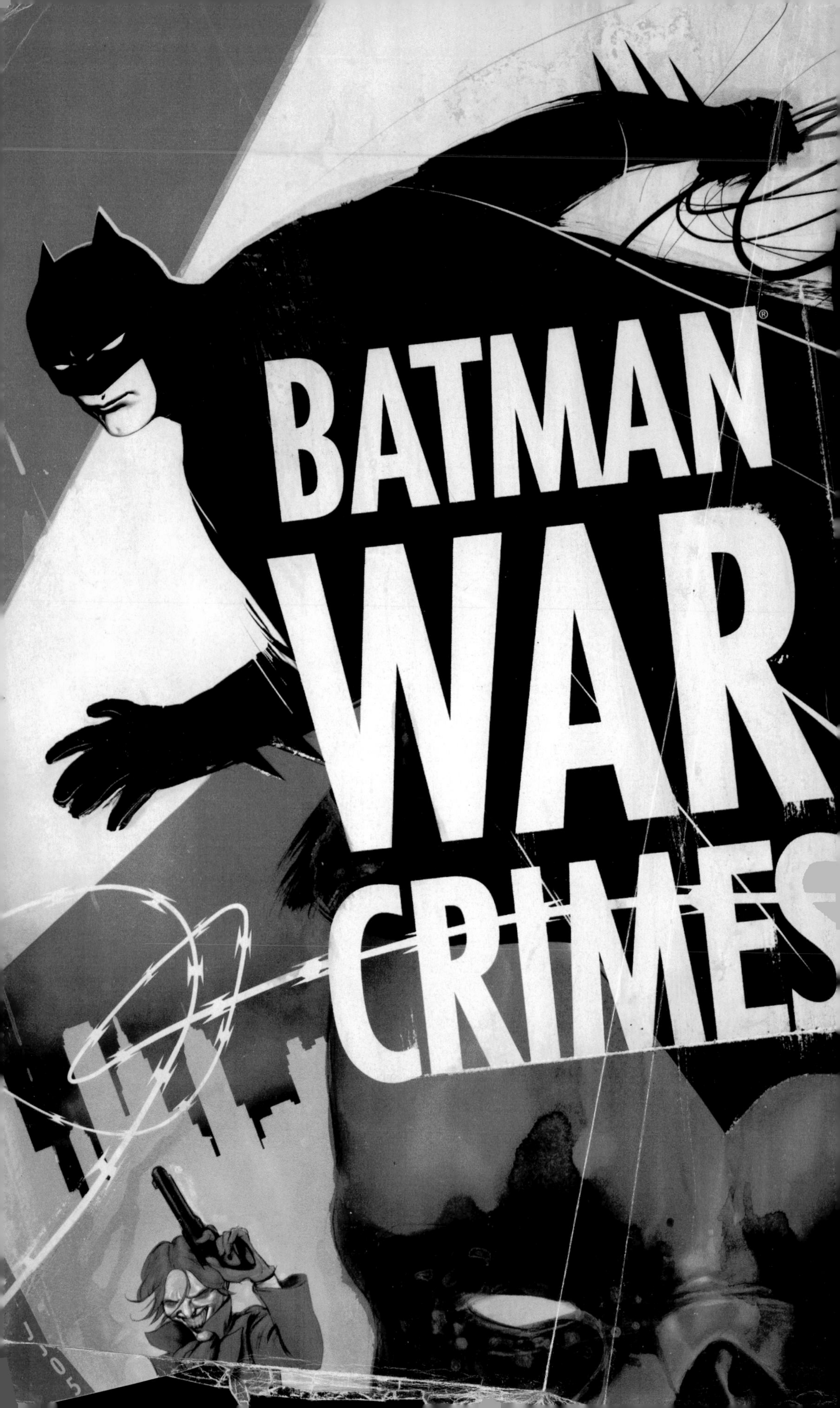
BATMAN®
WAR
CRIMES